THE A-Z OF
GARDEN PLANTS

THE **A-Z** OF
GARDEN PLANTS

bay books

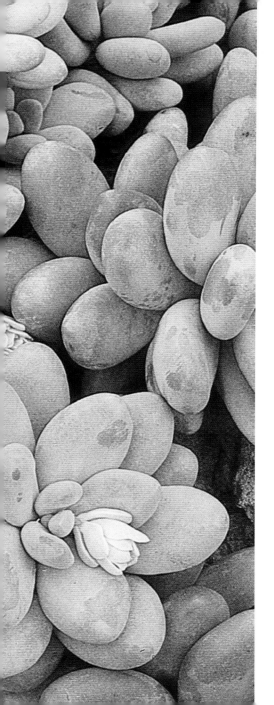

CONTENTS

A 6

B 104

C 162

D 308

E 346

F 388

G 408

H 444

IJ 480

K 502

L 516

M 570

N 620

O 640

P 658

QR 758

S 796

TU 870

V 914

W 932

XYZ 942

INDEX 954

Climate map 1008

A

Abelia to Azara

Abelia (fam. Caprifoliaceae)

Native to India, the Himalayas, Japan and China, these showy, low-branching evergreen shrubs bear fragrant pink or white flowers, with long-lasting reddish sepals. An orange marking may appear in the throat of the flowers. Advanced *Abelia* grows densely and works well as foundation or border planting.

CULTIVATION Plant *Abelia* in rich, well-drained soil in full sun or partial shade. They thrive when well watered. Propagate in summer and fall from semi-hardwood cuttings, 15–18 cm (6–7 in) long. These strike easily in the open if they have some shade or if well protected from strong sun and wind. In winter strike from hardwood cuttings, 20–25 cm (8–10 in) long. In spring each year prune lightly to the desired shape and remove some of the old canes at ground level.

CLIMATE Zones 6 and 7 and above.

SPECIES *A*. x *grandiflora* is often referred to as glossy abelia. It is a dense, bushy shrub, with

BELOW Tolerant of a wide range of conditions, *Abelia* x *grandiflora* is an easy-care shrub useful for informal hedging or screening.

oval, glossy, bronze-green leaves and smallish bell-shaped flowers in pink, tinged with white, between summer and fall in most areas. Cultivar 'Variegata', also known as 'Francis Mason' or golden abelia, has a similar growth and flowering to *A*. x *grandiflora*, but has rich yellow variegations. To achieve the golden color, plant in full sun. *A. schumannii* from China is a slender, arching shrub with dull leaves and rosy pink flowers from summer to fall. *A. uniflora*, from China, is dense and bushy, with dark green leaves. It produces single pinkish white flowers with an orange throat, from summer to fall.

Abeliophyllum (fam. Oleaceae)

Originating from Korea, *Abeliophyllum* was introduced into western gardens in the 1920s and became popular for ornamental gardens as it grows easily to about 1 m (3 ft) and is quite hardy. The leaves of this shrub are similar to those of abelia. Related to *Fontanesia*, it is a deciduous shrub, with long, narrow, heart-shaped leaves and white, four-petalled, fragrant flowers, with small, orange centers, like those of *Forsythia*. It blooms in early spring.

BELOW The pretty, scented flowers of *Abeliophyllum distichum* are thickly clustered on woody stems in spring before the leaves emerge.

CULTIVATION Plant in a well-drained loamy soil in a sheltered sunny position and protect from frost during flowering. Prune when flowering has finished because the flowers bloom on the previous year's shoots. Propagate under glass from cuttings of half-ripe wood in late summer or fall, or from seed or by layering.

CLIMATE *Abeliophyllum* is suitable for zone 6 and above.

SPECIES *A. distichum* is the only species. It grows to a height and spread of about 1.5 m (5 ft).

Abies (fam. Pinaceae)
Fir

The name of this genus of 50 species, which occurs naturally only in the northern hemisphere, derives from the Latin *abeo*, 'I rise', as some grow to majestic heights. Like the majority of conifers, the firs are evergreen. The short, stiff needles of most species are usually flat, clothing the twigs evenly, but on the outer branches on the lower part of the tree they part and twist upward. The needles of some species are radially arranged, perfectly, on all twigs, while others form two separate, flat rows on either side of the twig. Generally, the needles have two silver bands on the undersurface. Most *Abies* species are worth growing in large, cool climate gardens for their extraordinary symmetry and beautiful foliage, color and texture. Heights given for the various species are for trees grown in conditions that mirror their habitat. In other regions they will usually be much shorter.

CULTIVATION Firs grow well throughout the cooler and cold regions of the US but do not like hot summers and are not drought-resistant. They can be grown quite successfully in tubs in warmer coastal areas if they are placed in a cool spot. Plant in deep soil of medium to high fertility, and make sure that the subsoil is kept moist throughout the year. Propagate from seed. Germination usually takes

ABOVE *Abies pinsapo*, Spanish fir, develops a looser, less formal shape as it ages. Its cones are purple-brown when young.

place easily a short time after sowing which is best done in early spring. Grafting is only used for propagating prized selections and cultivars. The scion must be taken from the tip of an erect leading shoot, otherwise the resulting plant will have the horizontal growth of a side-branch.

CLIMATE Zones 3 to 7 depending on the species.

SPECIES *A. alba*, European silver fir, zone 5, grows to 30 m (100 ft) or more in height, becoming pyramid-like and broad-tipped with age. The dark green leaves are 2–3 cm (about 1 in) long and they grow in two rows. *A. balsamea*, balsam fir or balm of Gilead, zone 3, grows 10–20 m (33–65 ft) high and forms a narrow pyramidal shape. The dark green, 2–3 cm (about 1 in) long leaves are either blunt or notched and also grow in two rows. The dwarf Hudsonia Group is better known. *A. cephalonica*, Grecian fir, zone 6, grows to 30 m (100 ft) in a pyramidal shape. The stiff, sharp, shiny green leaves are 2–3 cm (about 1 in) long and blueish gray underneath. *A. firma*, Japanese fir, zone 6, grows to 30 m (100 ft) or more in a pyramidal shape, becoming broader at the top with age. The shiny green leaves are 2.5 cm (1 in) long, acute or sometimes forked at the apex, and they grow in two rows. A fast-growing species, *A. grandis*, or giant fir, zone 6, grows to 20–30 m (65–100 ft) in height and forms a pyramidal shape. The leaves are colored shiny dark green, 3–6 cm (1–2½ in) in length, with notched apexes, and growing in two horizontal rows. *A. homolepis*, Nikko fir, zone 5, grows 20–30 m (65–100 ft) in height to a pyramidal shape. The dark green leaves are 2 cm (1 in) long and either acute or notched. *A. lasiocarpa*, alpine fir, zone 3, grows 15–25 m (50–80 ft) in height and forms a pyramidal shape with an irregular outline. The sharp-pointed, pale grayish green leaves are 2–3 cm (about 1 in) long. Cultivar 'Compacta' grows to about 1 m (3 ft) forming a compact pyramidal shape. It has blueish green foliage. *A. magnifica*, Californian red fir, zone 6, grows 15–25 m (50–80 ft) in height in a column-like shape and has downward sweeping branches and crowded leaves. The shiny dark green leaves are 2–3 cm (about 1 in) long, with notched apexes. *A. pinsapo*, Spanish fir, zone 7, grows 15–25 m (50–80 ft) in height, forming a broad pyramidal shape, with a rounded crown and downward sweeping branches. The dark green leaves are 1–2 cm (about 1 in) long, rigid and sharp-pointed. They are arranged radially on the twigs. Cultivar 'Glauca' is widely grown because of its blueish gray foliage. *A. spectabilis*, Himalayan fir, zone 6, grows to 30 m (100 ft) or more to a broad pyramid-like shape. Leaves are 3–6 cm (1–2½ in) long, shiny dark green, and blunt or notched.

Abutilon (fam. Malvaceae)
Chinese lantern, flowering maple

The beautiful, lantern-shaped flowers and shapely, maple-like leaves make these evergreen shrubs a popular choice. The leaves of some are variegated and the pendulous flowers come in a range of colors from purple, bright red and pink to yellow, orange and white.

CULTIVATION The abutilons, being tender, are mostly grown under glass but *A. megapotamicum*, is hardy in mild climates.

CLIMATE Zones 9 and 10.

SPECIES *A.* x *hybridum* grows densely when regularly pruned, with maple-like green leaves and abundant flowers in various colors from spring to fall. There are many cultivars of *A.* x *hybridum* but they may not all be available in all areas. They include 'Boule de Neige', pure white, to 1.2 m (4 ft); 'Carmine', carmine pink, to 1.8 m (6 ft); 'Eclipse', orange, to 1.8 m (6 ft); 'Emperor', crimson, to 1.2 m (4 ft); 'Jubilee', rose pink, to 1.8 m (6 ft); 'Kuller's Surprise', red with yellow center, to 1.8 m (6 ft); 'Souvenir de Bonn', orange-striped flowers and also attractive green and cream variegated leaves, to 2.4 m (8 ft); 'Sydney Belle', pure yellow, to 1.2 m (4 ft); 'Tunisia', salmon pink, to 1.8 m (6 ft); 'Yellow Gem', soft yellow flowers, to 1.8 m (6 ft). *A. megapotamicum*,

BELOW *Abutilon megapotamicum*, most often seen in its variegated form, is long flowering. It makes a great filler or groundcover.

which is commonly known as Brazilian bell or lantern flower, originates from South America. It is a sprawling plant with long, drooping branches and small, arrow-shaped leaves. From spring to fall, the small pendulous flowers have slender yellow petals and red calyces with prominent stamens. Cultivar 'Variegatum' has prettily variegated leaves which light up a shaded area.

Acacia (fam. Mimosaceae)
Wattle

The botanical name 'acacia' came from the Greek akakia meaning 'a thorn' and many of the African species are known as thorn trees. However, many species, over 750, ranging from shrubs to tall trees, are native to Australia. It is believed the common name 'wattle' originated from the Aboriginal name for the plant, wattah. Geographical descriptions have been adopted in Australia to describe certain species–*Acacia baileyana* is often referred to as Cootamundra wattle. Members of this family are found in several other parts of the world where they are generally known as 'mimosas'. Wattle has been used in Australia for many purposes, both by the Aboriginals and the first settlers. The Aboriginal peoples tapped the roots of certain desert species for water, and the pioneers learned that wattle could be plastered with mud or clay to produce building materials. Wattle and daub houses were common in the early years of settlement because wattles were generally available, growing profusely in almost all areas. They grow quickly and flower early. Some are short-lived, lasting for only eight to ten years, while others live longer. Wattles in full flower are exquisite. The blossom varies in color from golden yellow, which is the most familiar, to orange and white. The flowers are either ball-shaped or bar-shaped and the foliage is extremely variable. All species have bipinnate (feathery) leaves when young, although the leaves of many Australian species mature into a variety of different shapes. In fact, many Australian wattles do not have true 'leaves' but leaf-like parts known as phyllodes which are

ABOVE *Acacia baileyana*, Cootamundra wattle, is the most frequently cultivated of all wattles. Its bright yellow flowers light up the winter months.

modified leaf stems or petioles. The seeds of the wattle have a hard waxy coat. For this reason, and because the seeds germinate through heat, they are usually the first plants to appear following a bushfire. As different species of wattle flower in different seasons, it is possible to plant a garden of wattles so that at least one is flowering at any time of the year, provided the climate is suitable for them of course. Plant tall species for shade, low-growing species in rockeries and pots, and interesting cultivars for the color contrast of their blossoms and leaves.

CULTIVATION In frost-prone climates, wattles are grown under glass, either in pots of well-drained soil-based potting compost, or in a soil border. They make fine plants for a large cool conservatory or greenhouse. Generally wattles can be easily propagated from seed at most

ABOVE *Acacia podalyriifolia*, valued for its winter and spring flowers, may be attacked by a leaf miner which causes blisters on its leaves.

RIGHT *Acacia binervia*, coastal myall, is long-lived and forms a fine tree if planted in the open. It also makes a good hedge or screen.

times of the year. First pour boiling water over the seeds and allow them to stand for 12 hours. Discard any seeds that remain floating. Plant seeds in a free-draining mix, cover lightly and water in gently. It will take one to four weeks for the seeds to germinate under glass. It is interesting to watch the small, feathery leaves develop into the more mature forms. Both are sometimes visible on the seedling. Young plants should be kept moist. In frost-free climates, they will grow in almost any type of well-drained soil, with an open aspect, provided they are protected from heavy winds. Most can endure very dry conditions. Don't grow other plants around their roots or under their branches. Trim immediately after flowering to improve bloom production and to prolong their life.

CLIMATE Suitable for zones 8 to 10.

SPECIES As it is impossible to list all species, a selection of wattles have been chosen for their horticultural merit. Not all of the following species are available outside of Australia but nevertheless there is a good representative selection available in the US, where many are grown in California and Arizona. *A. baileyana*, Cootamundra wattle, is the best known of the New South Wales species. It has blueish silver leaves and clusters of golden-yellow flowers during winter and spring. It grows quickly to 5–8 m (16–26 ft) and is useful as a windbreak and for shade and shelter. New purple, red and yellow-leaved forms are being cultivated. *A. beckleri*, from South Australia, is a drought-resistant shrub, with dense, leathery, gray-green foliage and large, sweetly perfumed flowers, 2 cm (1 in) in diameter, in winter. The flowers are the largest of all the species. It grows 2–4 m (6–12 ft) in height. *A. binervia* grows 8–12 m (26–40 ft) tall and is ideal for coastal planting. It has grayish foliage. *A. browniana*, a dense Western Australian shrub, is attractive and grows well in sandy soils to 1–2 m (3–6 ft). It has small, dark green, fern-like foliage and deep yellow globe-shaped blossoms which appear from winter to spring. *A. cardiophylla*'s fine, soft, drooping foliage makes it a favorite with gardeners. Commonly known as Wyalong wattle, it grows to a height of 2–3 m (6–10 ft), with golden blossoms from winter and spring. *A. decora*, showy wattle, is a bushy wattle which grows to a height and width of 2 m (6 ft). In spring, masses of golden ball-shaped flowers appear among blueish green curved leaves. Useful in dry areas, it adapts to most soils. *A. drummondii*,

Drummond wattle, from Western Australia, has dark, ferny leaves and rod-shaped golden flowers between winter and spring. It grows to about 1.5 m (5 ft). A few good cultivars have been produced. *A. ericifolia*, from Western Australia, has superb gray-green foliage and masses of beautiful bright yellow flowers at the ends of its branches from winter and spring. It reaches a height of about 1 m (3 ft), with a rather flat top, and is an attractive shrub all year round. *A. iteaphylla*, Flinders Range wattle, from South Australia, grows to 3–4 m by 3–5 m (10–13 ft by 10–16 ft) and is resistant to drought and frost. It has beautiful, rather pendulous foliage, with purple new growth which complements bright yellow globe-shaped flowers that bloom in winter. *A. longifolia*, Sydney golden wattle or Sally wattle, flowers in spring. A rapid-growing species to 4.5 m (14 ft), it does well in pure sand in seaside gardens. It can also be useful as a nurse tree. *A. melanoxylon*, zone 8, is generally too tall for all but rural areas, growing to 30 m (100 ft) in gullies. Blackwood, as it is commonly known, is prized by cabinet-makers for its timber. *A. myrtifolia*, myrtle wattle, is a small, neat wattle which grows to 2 m (6 ft). Suitable for container cultivation, it has red-green foliage and cream flowers which bloom in winter. It does well in moist, well-drained conditions. *A. podalyriifolia*, Queensland silver wattle, is a useful, fast-growing wattle with gray foliage and beautiful, large gold ball-shaped flowers in spring. It grows to 6 m (20 ft) high. *A. pravissima*, Ovens wattle, has small, triangular-shaped gray leaves, powdery yellow blooms in late winter and spring and weeping branches. It tolerates wet and cold conditions and grows to 2 m (6 ft). The prostrate form is a variety which is especially suitable as groundcover or soil-binder. *A. pubescens*, downy wattle, from the central and southern tablelands of New South Wales, was one of the first Australian plants grown in early colonial gardens. It is a pretty shrub, with soft downy foliage and golden flowers in summer. It grows to 5 m (16 ft). *A. pycnantha*, broad-leafed golden wattle, comes from the dry inland of Victoria and New South Wales. It makes a good sand-binder for shallow soils. Its large, perfumed golden-yellow flowers bloom in spring. *A. ulicifolia* 'Brownii', Brown's wattle, is a semi-prostrate species, with sharply pointed leaves and lemon flowers in winter and spring. It reaches only 20 cm (8 in).

BELOW In frost-prone climates, Acacia melanoxylon, blackwood, can be grown in a pot or soil border in a cool greenhouse or conservatory.

Acalypha (fam. Euphorbiaceae)

Copper leaf

These gaudy shrubs, with variegated foliage and small tassel-like flowers, are very tender and in frost-prone climates are grown in warm humid greenhouses, conservatories, or as house plants. They can be used for summer bedding.

ABOVE This collection of *Acalypha* hybrids shows some of the great range of leaf colors and patterns available.

CULTIVATION Under glass, grow in pots of well-drained soilless potting compost. Outdoors, especially when used for bedding, plant in well-drained light soil, in a warm spot in the garden, with protection from winds which damage the leaves. A southerly aspect is suitable. Although suited to coastal districts, they should be sheltered from strong salt-laden wind. Water during summer and prune lightly in late winter. Propagate from hardwood cuttings in winter and protect young plants from the cold.

CLIMATE Subtropical to tropical.

SPECIES *A. wilkesiana* comes from Fiji and the nearby South Pacific islands. It grows into a dense, leafy bush if regularly pruned and well fertilized. It has attractive, shining, ovate leaves, to 20 cm (8 in), bronze-green with rosy red margins to 6 mm (¼ in) wide. The cultivar *laciniata* 'Variegata' has shiny, deep green, lance-shaped leaves, 15 cm (6 in) long, with a 3–6 mm (⅛–¼ in) toothed cream margin. Foliage texture is fine and somewhat lacy. 'Marginata', the best known variety, has oval-shaped reddish brown and bronze-green leaves,

15 cm (6 in) long and 13 cm (5 in) wide, with a rosy red 6 mm (¼ in) margin and a notched apex. 'Metallica' has shiny purple oval leaves to 15 cm (6 in) long, marked red on top and bronze-green below. The leaves do not have the usual margin. 'Triumphans', the largest of these varieties, has pinkish oval leaves, marked with bronze-green. The leaves are about 23 cm (9 in) long and crimped at the apex. These acalyphas are very striking and although susceptible to wind damage they are valuable for imparting a tropical touch to the garden as temporary summer bedding plants.

Acanthopanax (fam. Araliaceae)

This genus includes about 20 species of hardy deciduous trees and shrubs, most originating from the Himalayas and central Asia. Their thick, prickly branches have earned them their

BELOW Grown for its decorative foliage effect, *Acanthopanax sieboldianus* has been classified in the genus *Eleutherococcus* by some botanists.

name which comes from the Greek akanthos, a spine or thorn. Their small green flowers are quite unimpressive, but their long, handsome leaves, usually divided into leaflets, and clusters of black or purplish berries make them attractive outdoor plants.

CULTIVATION This plant does well in a well-drained loamy soil in a sunny position, with some shade from larger plants. The most effective propagation method is by seed, though germination may take up to two years. Sow seed in spring. Try suckers, root cuttings or ripened shoots in fall.

CLIMATE Zone 6 and above.

SPECIES The three species mentioned can be grown throughout a large part of the US. *A. henryi*, a shrub, grows to 3 m (10 ft). It has spiny shoots, long tapered leaves and green flowers that are densely packed. *A sieboldianus* the most commonly grown, has attractive foliage, slender arching branches and greenish white flowers which appear in clusters on slender stalks, 5–10 cm (2–4 in) long. It grows to 3 m (10 ft). *A. simonii* grows to 3 m (10 ft) and has yellow shoots, dark green leaves and clusters of green flowers.

Acanthus (fam. Acanthaceae)
Bear's breech, oyster plant

From southern Europe and North Africa, this intriguing perennial has handsome leaves, often up to 1 m (3 ft) long, and curious purplish and white flowers densely arranged on tall, erect spikes. The stunning leaves are found as a motif on capitals of Greek Corinthian columns.

CULTIVATION Plant in rich soil in a sunny or partly shaded position and water well to ensure rapid growth. Prune spent flowers and dead leaves. It is usually grown from seed or by division in spring. The seedlings should be potted when they are large enough to handle. Divide by lifting an established clump and

ABOVE *Acanthus mollis*, grown mainly for its foliage, is self-supporting although tall when in flower.

detaching the strong side shoots. Make sure the shoots have fibrous roots and a sound crown. Remove the leaves and water well until re-established.

CLIMATE Zone 6 and above.

SPECIES *A. mollis*, from the Mediterranean, makes a beautiful feature plant. It is a robust, leafy clump up to 1 m (3 ft) wide and 1 m (3 ft) tall. The large, dark green leaves are deeply serrated and veined. The purple and white flowers appear in late summer. *A. spinosus*, ranging from Italy to Turkey, can grow to 1.5 m (5 ft). The spiny-edged, dark green leaves are deeply incised almost to the midrib. Flowers are white with purple bracts, appearing from late spring to midsummer.

Acer (fam. Aceraceae)

Maple

Widely grown in the US, particularly in the cooler and cold northern states where some are native plants, these deciduous trees and shrubs are loved for their magnificent foliage which colors beautifully in fall. They have distinctive, hand-shaped leaves, insignificant flowers and winged seeds, known as samaras, joined in pairs.

CULTIVATION For planting, a deep, sandy loam is best; add leaf mould or other organic matter to the soil to ensure moisture retention as the leaf tips of most varieties burn easily if the soil becomes dry. Propagate species by seed and sow as soon as it is ripe. All varieties and cultivars should be budded or grafted. Pruning is unnecessary except in order to trim excessive growth or to correct wayward branches. It may be necessary to thin the new growth after pruning.

CLIMATE Many species are suited to zone 6.

ABOVE 'Atropurpureum', a burgundy-foliaged cultivar of the Japanese maple, provides excellent contrast with green-leaved trees or shrubs.

BELOW Acer palmatum, Japanese maple, has been widely hybridized to produce many fine and cut leaf forms.

SPECIES *A. buergerianum* (syn. *A. trifidum*), from China and Japan, is a slender tree which grows quickly to 6 m (20 ft) and can be recognized by its triangular-lobed leaves which turn red and yellow in the fall. *A. campestre*, English or hedge maple, from Europe and western Asia, grows 6 m (20 ft) in height and colors yellow in fall. *A. cappadocicum*, from western Asia, grows to 15 m (50 ft) and has large leaves. 'Aureum' has yellow leaves on opening and in fall while 'Rubrum' has red leaves on opening and yellow in fall. *A. carpinifolium*, hornbeam maple, from Japan, grows to 9 m (30 ft) and has plain, oval, fine-toothed leaves with parallel veins. The leaves measure 8–10 cm (3–4 in). *A. davidii*, from China, is grown for its glossy, white-striped bark. It has large, heart-shaped leaves and can grow to 9 m (30 ft). *A. ginnala*, the Amur maple, from China and Japan, is a bushy shrub which grows to about 6 m (20 ft). The three-lobed leaves turn red in fall. The bark of *A. griseum*, paperbark maple, from central China, peels attractively, and the three-lobed leaves change to red and orange in fall. It grows to about 12 m (40 ft). *A. hookeri*, from the Himalayas, grows to 6 m (20 ft) and has long heart-shaped leaves, bronze-colored in early spring, red in fall. *A. monspessulanum*, the Montpellier maple from southern Europe, grows to 6 m (20 ft) and has small, broad three-lobed leaves with reddish winged seeds. *A. negundo*, box elder, zone 3, from North America, is a quick grower to about 12 m (40 ft). It has become rather invasive in some districts, producing a great quantity of seed which disperses and germinates readily. 'Elegans' has yellow-margined leaves and grows to around 6 m (20 ft). 'Variegatum' has broken white margins on its leaves and reaches a height of around 6 m (20 ft). *A. palmatum*, the Japanese maple, is a shapely, bushy tree with small, five-pointed leaves which turn red, gold and purple in fall. It grows to 5 m (16 ft). There are an extremely large number of varieties of this popular maple, including the well-known 'Atropurpureum', with deep purple foliage which later turns red. *A. pensylvanicum*, the striped maple from North America, zone 3, grows to 6 m (20 ft). It has large, three-lobed leaves and white-striped bark. *A. saccharinum*, silver maple, zone 3, grows 25–40 m (80–130 ft), with pinkish flowers and bright green five-lobed leaves, silvery beneath, which color yellow and then red in the fall. *A. saccharum*, the sugar maple of North America, zone 3, grows upwards of 15 m (50 ft) and produces flaming fall colors. *A. saccharum* subsp. *nigrum*, the black maple from North America, zone 3, reaches a mature height of 15–30 m (50–100 ft).

Achillea (fam. Asteraceae)
Yarrow, milfoil

Native to Europe, North America and Asia, this hardy, pungently aromatic perennial has fern-like foliage and rounded, flat heads of tiny, tightly packed blooms ranging in color from bright yellow to white, pink, salmon and cerise. Achilleas are useful for borders and rockeries, and make good cut flowers.

CULTIVATION Achilleas will grow in any soil, but do best in sunny, well-drained positions in temperate climates. Although they are sun loving, they will flower quite well in semi-shade. Divide plants in fall or early spring. Cut back old growth in winter to encourage fresh young spring growth.

CLIMATE Zone 6 and above.

SPECIES *A. ageratifolia* has tufted, silvery gray foliage and white flowers. Growing to 15–20 cm (6–8 in) high, it is ideal for rockeries. *A. chrysocoma* has mats of green leaves and heads of densely packed yellow flowers. *A. filipendulina*, fern-leaf yarrow, has impressive plate-like, golden yellow flower heads, 7–10 cm (3–4 in) in diameter, on long, stiff stems. If cut in early summer and hung head down in a cool, dry place, the flowers will retain their bright

color and can therefore be used for dried floral arrangements. They grow to 1.5 m (5 ft). *A. millefolium*, common yarrow, with round flat heads of white flowers, is classed as a weed in the US. Many pretty cultivars are available. These cultivars are not as invasive as the species. *A. ptarmica*, with white flowers and light foliage, grows to 60 cm (24 in). Cultivar 'The Pearl' has double flowers. *A. tomentosa* has finely serrated mat-like foliage, yellow flowers, and grows to 24 cm (10 in). 'Aurea' has woolly, fern-like foliage and flat heads of darker yellow flowers. It grows to 15 cm (6 in).

Achimenes (fam. Gesneriaceae)

These perennials of South America and the West Indies have delicate, brilliantly colored flowers. They are ideal pot plants for the warm greenhouse or conservatory and they make attractive house plants. They are effective, too, when used in hanging baskets or pots.

CULTIVATION Although best raised from tubers planted in late winter to early spring, they can

BELOW Colorful *Achimenes* belong to the Gesneriad family which includes popular plants such as African violet, gloxinia and Cape primrose.

BELOW *Achillea filipendulina* is an excellent cut flower for fresh or dried arrangements. Cultivars such as 'Gold Plate' and 'Coronation Gold' are worth seeking out.

also be easily propagated from seed. Use a light fibrous compost, with a good scattering of sand. Place pieces of crock or charcoal in the bottom of the container as these plants require good drainage. The pots or baskets can be dried out in winter and the tubers stored until spring.

CLIMATE Subtropical to tropical.

SPECIES Although there are some 26 species of *Achimenes*, those most commonly grown are the cultivars of *A. longiflora*. These plants are herbaceous, dying back completely during the winter and spring. New growth appears from late spring to early summer, and they flower through midsummer to fall. They rarely grow more than 30 cm (12 in) in height. The tubular or funnel-shaped flowers come in a range of colors including white, blue, hot pink, purple and deep red. The attractive foliage is red on the underside.

Acmena (fam. Myrtaceae)

Acmena is a genus of evergreen shrubs and trees native to the eastern coast of Australia. Usually found along rivers or in rainforests, they have grayish brown scaly bark and lustrous green aromatic foliage. In warm areas, the smaller species make lovely hedges and garden ornamentals. In frost-prone areas it is advisable to grow them instead in pots in a cool greenhouse or in a conservatory.

CULTIVATION Under glass in pots of well-drained, soil-based potting compost. Outdoors, although they prefer rich, moist, well-drained soils, with ample water, they will grow in cool, semi-shaded spots. Propagate from seed which germinates rather slowly, ripening in fall and winter. Sow in a mix of sharp sand and peat or vermiculite at the rate of 3:1. *Acmena* can also be grown from shoot cuttings taken in the fall. Carefully remove the leaves from the lower two-thirds of the cutting. Dust with hormone rooting powder and place in the same sand and peat mix that was recommended for seeds.

ABOVE *Acmena smithii* has pinky bronze new growth, a lovely feature of many rainforest species.

Acmena is susceptible to scale insects, but it is possible to control these pests with the use of white oil spray.

CLIMATE Zone 10 and above.

SPECIES Not all species are available in all areas. *A. australis* is a tall tree which grows to 25 m (80 ft). Small, pinkish white flowers in terminal sprays are followed by red fruits, 2–3 cm (about 1 in) in diameter. *A. hemilampra*, a smaller species which grows naturally as far north as New Guinea, to a height of 10 m (33 ft), has larger glossy dark leaves, white flowers and round white fruits. *A. smithii*, the most widely grown species, better known as lilly pilly, is a bushy shrub or small tree with dark green foliage. It has shiny leaves, bronze-tipped when young, and greenish white fluffy flowers in terminal sprays and round, shiny, pinkish-purplish fruits. Lilly pilly grows to 6 m (20 ft) tall and makes a fine hedge plant. It withstands pruning and can be frost-sensitive.

Acokanthera (fam. Apocynaceae)
Bushman's poison, winter sweet

A dense shrub, Acokanthera has thick, leathery leaves and pleasant, sweet-smelling white flowers fol-lowed by small, oval, blackish purple fruit. In frost-free climates these plants can be used effectively in shrub borders among finer textured foliage, but in colder climates grow in pots or beds in a cool greenhouse or conservatory. All parts of the plant are poisonous if they are eaten.

CULTIVATION When growing in pots under glass use a well-drained soil-based potting compost. Plant in a warm, frost-free position, with

BELOW *Acokanthera oblongifolia* is a fine fragrant shrub for the cool greenhouse or conservatory.

protection from cold winds. Prune into shape after flowering. Propagate from seed sown in early spring.

CLIMATE Zone 10 and above.

SPECIES *A. oblongifolia*, a native of South Africa, has large green leaves which turn purplish in winter, sweetly perfumed white flowers from winter to spring and blackish fruit. It grows to 4 m (13 ft).

Aconitum (fam. Ranunculaceae)
Monkshood

In mid to late summer these herbaceous perennials produce tall, slender spires of helmet-shaped flowers in shades of blue, purple, white and yellow. Being tall, aconitums are useful in the garden, particularly for planting at the back of a border. All parts of this plant are poisonous if eaten so it should not be accessible to young children.

CULTIVATION Aconitums require cool temperate climates. Grow in rich soil in partial shade, water regularly and fertilize in spring. The best

BELOW Aconitums are best planted in groups where they can remain undisturbed for many years. They do well under deciduous trees.

flowering may not occur until two or three years after they are planted. Propagate either by seed or by root division. Staking is generally needed only when the position is very exposed.

CLIMATE Moist, cool to cold areas.

SPECIES *A. lycoctonum*, wolfsbane, zone 3, has purple-lilac flowers. *A. napellus*, monkshood, zone 6, grows to over 1 m (3 ft) high, bearing deep blue spires of flowers in summer. There are a number of named cultivars of *Aconitum* in existence, most of them with flowers in various shades of lilac and blue. There is a good choice of species available in the US. Some species and cultivars that are less often grown have yellow or white flowers.

Acorus (fam. Araceae)

This hardy, herbaceous, grass-like perennial has tough, sword-like leaves and small cream flowers. It works well as an edging for shallow ornamental ponds and lakes. It is known for its aromatic and medicinal properties.

BELOW The texture and shape of low-growing *Acorus gramineus* makes it ideal for mass planting in borders or as edging.

CULTIVATION Plant *Acorus* in late winter to spring. Propagate by dividing established clumps in fall or spring as they are vigorous growers.

CLIMATE Suitable for cool and cold areas to the subtropics.

SPECIES *A. calamus*, sweet flag, zone 3, has small, pale yellow-green flowers and tangerine-scented leaves. When crushed, the roots also release a pleasant fragrance. An iris-like plant, it grows to about 1 m (3 ft) tall. Although too invasive for small garden pools, it is a useful border plant for large ponds and artificial lakes. Cultivar 'Variegatus' can be used in a medium-sized pool or grown in a shady position in moist soil. With its yellow-striped leaves, it resembles a small variegated flax. *A. gramineus*, zone 5, grows to 45 cm (18 in) high, making it suitable for small garden ponds and moist areas around pools. Cultivar 'Pusillus', a miniature from Japan, is useful for planting in aquariums as it grows to only 8 cm (3 in).

Acradenia (fam. Rutaceae)
Whitey wood

Native to Australia, this shrub or small tree has been introduced to other parts of the world but is seldom grown outside its country of origin. Yet it is attractive and frost-hardy shrub or small tree and is well worth garden space. In very cold climates it can be grown in pots in a cool conservatory.

CULTIVATION *Acradenia* can be propagated from semi-ripe cuttings rooted in a mix of equal parts coarse sand and peat or peat substitute. It can also be raised from seed if available. It requires a moist, fertile soil, partial shade and shelter from cold winds.

CLIMATE Cool, moist climate; zone 8.

SPECIES *A. frankliniae*, one of the two species, occurs naturally along river banks on the edges

ABOVE Starry white flowers and handsome aromatic foliage are features of spring-flowering *Acradenia frankliniae.*

of rainforests on Tasmania's west coast. It is an upright grower to about 3 m (10 ft) in height. In late spring a profusion of pretty white flowers in terminal clusters appear. When crushed, the long, narrow, bright green leaves give out a pleasant fragrance.

Actinidia (fam. Actinidiaceae)

Originally from East Asia, these decorative climbers have open, usually white, blossoms and berry fruits which can be edible or poisonous, depending on the species. The genus includes the edible kiwi fruit, *A. chinensis.*

CULTIVATION Grow in sun or semi-shade and propagate from seed sown in spring, by cutting or by layering in early spring. Plant vines of

ABOVE *Actinidia kolomikta* has beautiful foliage, splashed with pink and white. In cool areas, grow against a wall for winter protection.

both sexes close together if fruits are required. One male vine is usually enough to pollinate six to eight female vines.

CLIMATE Suitable for zones 5 to 8 depending on species.

SPECIES *A. arguta*, zone 5, grows vigorously, reaching the tops of tall trees. It has large, shiny green leaves and white flowers tinged with green in midsummer. The fruit of this species is edible, with a pleasant, though somewhat acid taste. *A. deliciosa*, Chinese gooseberry or kiwi fruit, zone 8, comes from the Yangtze Valley in China. It grows less vigorously but is more decorative, with large, heart-shaped leaves and creamy white flowers. The egg-shaped fruits, covered with reddish hairs, are edible, quite delicious and now grown in warm areas around the world. *A. kolomikta*, zone 5, is grown mainly for its decorative foliage which is bright metallic green in spring, developing pink and white markings later in the season. The midsummer white blossoms are fragrant. *A. polygama*, silver vine, zone 6, has very pale decorative leaves and white flowers. The fruit is considered a delicacy in Japan where it is eaten salted.

Actinodium (fam. Myrtaceae)
Swamp daisy, Albany daisy

This decorative shrub, related to Eucalyptus, is native to Western Australia but is not freely available outside its home country. There are two species, neither of which is very hardy, and in cool or cold climates, they are best grown in pots in a cool conservatory.

CULTIVATION Under glass, grow in pots of well-drained, acid, soil-based potting compost. Outdoors, swamp daisies grow best in mild climates, expecially in coastal areas, and in acid soil. They like full sun and plenty of water in summer. Propagate from seed if available. The flowers are attractive dried.

BELOW An excellent cut flower, *Actinodium cunninghamii* produces shrubby growth but is generally not long lived in the garden.

CLIMATE Can be grown in zone 9.

SPECIES *A. cunninghamii* grows to about 1 m (3 ft) in height. It has thin stems topped with white daisy-like, papery flowers with pink or orange centers. The narrow, but thick, leaves are quite tiny and close to the stem.

Actinostrobus (fam. Cupressaceae)

From the southern coast of Western Australia, this genus of only two species of native conifers is closely related to *Callitris* (the Australian cypress pine). They are of interest mainly to Australian gardeners as they are one of that country's few genera of conifers.

CULTIVATION As they are frost-tender conifers they can be grown in gardens only in zone 10 and above. In their natural habitat most rainfall is in winter followed by very hot, dry summers. These conifers do not adapt well to cultivation. In cold climates cultivation should be attempted only in pots or tubs under glass. Propagation is by seed, which germinates readily.

CLIMATE Zone 10 and above.

BELOW The neat cylindrical cones of *Actinostrobus pyramidalis* are a decorative feature of this unusual conifer.

SPECIES *A. pyramidalis* has very coarse green foliage, sometimes quite dense. The cones are shiny gray-brown and grow 1.5 cm (½ in) long and as broad at the base. This shrub or small tree makes a good formal feature plant or tub specimen. It can grow between 1 and 4 m (3–13 ft) tall.

Actinotus (fam. Apiaceae)
Flannel flower

Native to Australia and New Zealand, this small genus of annual and biennial herbs grows wild in woodland, sandstone and alpine areas. Both the daisy-like flowers, which appear in spring and summer, and the foliage have a whitish, woolly, flannel-like appearance and texture. The woolly hairs and flannel-like appearance are an adaptation to heat and dryness in the coastal species and to extreme conditions in the alpine species. Their gray, finely divided foliage provides good landscape contrast and color, and some alpine species have potential as rockery plants. They are not well known outside their native countries and in fact even there they are a bit of a challenge to grow. It would be best to grow them as pot plants in a cool greenhouse or conservatory or as half-hardy annuals. Their flowers are excellent for cutting for use in floral arrangements.

CULTIVATION These plants need an acidic sandy soil with added humus, good drainage and moisture. Propagate from seed, although germination is often poor. Outdoors in suitable climates seed can be sown in seed beds in spring and the young plants planted out in fall. In frost-prone climates treat them as half-hardy annuals: raise under glass in spring and plant out when frosts are over. Grow pot plants in well-drained, soil-based potting compost.

CLIMATE Mild and subtropical climates, including coastal.

SPECIES There are various species but only the following are in general cultivation.

ABOVE *Actinotus helianthi* provides long-lasting cut flowers, decorative alone or mixed with other native species.

A. helianthi, flannel flower, is the best known. A robust plant, found in heathland or forest, it grows to a height of 60 cm (24 in) with velvety, greenish white foliage and large white or pale green flowers with flannel appearance and texture. *A. minor*, miniature flannel flower, has tiny white flowers.

Adansonia (fam. Bombaceae)
Baobab

Native to the tropics, these extraordinary deciduous trees have huge bloated trunks, up to 9 m (30 ft) in diameter, with a rather small mass of twisted branches and twigs at the top. They grow to 15 m (50 ft).

CULTIVATION Baobabs are grown as specimen trees in the tropics but in colder climates can be grown in pots or tubs in a warm glasshouse or conservatory.

CLIMATE Suitable for zone 10 and above.

SPECIES *A. digitata*, monkey-bread tree or baobab, from tropical Africa, produces drooping fragrant white flowers and also fibrous hairy fruit 30 cm (12 in) long. The bark

ABOVE The heavy, swollen trunk of this baobab, *Adansonia digitata*, is partly concealed behind a protective fence.

of the baobab is sometimes used for fiber. *A. gregorii*, native to the Northern Territory and northern areas of Western Australia, is grown in tropical parts of Australia.

Adenandra (fam. Rutaceae)

Originating from South Africa, this attractive evergreen shrub has small leaves, with glandular dots, and single flowers produced on several short twigs, giving the appearance of a cluster.

CULTIVATION All of the species below thrive in frost-free or virtually frost-free climates and are rarely cultivated outside their country of origin. If necessary protect plants from frost in winter and spring. Any well-drained soil is suitable. Propagate from seed in spring or from semi-ripe cuttings in fall under glass.

ABOVE Single, white flowers and tiny, aromatic leaves are features of this pretty South African shrub, *Adenandra uniflora*, known as enamel flower

CLIMATE Wide moisture and temperature range, excluding extremes of dry inland and cold high areas; zone 10.

SPECIES *A. amoena* has slender downy shoots and single white flowers with a purple streak at the base of the petals. It grows 30–60 cm (12–24 in). *A. coriacea* is a small shrub with tapered leaves and pinkish white flowers. *A. fragrans* grows well in most conditions, rarely exceeding 90 cm (36 in) in height and spread. It has long, narrow serrated leaves and densely clustered rose pink flowers. Sweet smelling and long lasting, they are suitable for cut flower arrangements. *A. uniflora* has small pointed leaves and single white flowers, streaked with deep rose or crimson, in spring. It will also flourish in most conditions, and reaches 60–90 cm (24–36 in).

Adenanthos (fam. Proteaceae)
Basket flower

Related to *Banksia*, *Grevillea* and *Hakea*, this genus of 16 named species of varying sizes grows naturally in coastal and near coastal areas of Western Australia. The leaves of most species are covered with short gray hairs and are most attractive. Because of its appeal, the foliage is sought by florists. The often abundant flowers are tubular-shaped and vary in color from light amber to red. These shrubs are well suited to seaside gardens.

CULTIVATION In their natural habitat these shrubs grow in very deep sandy soils, sometimes with clay or rock subsoil providing root anchorage. All species are sensitive to frost, although *A. pungens* can withstand light frost, and all require good drainage and some shelter when young. Growth is moderate. Propagate from cuttings taken in fall. Root in a sharp sand and peat or vermiculite mix of 3:1 in non-humid conditions. Seed is difficult to collect and also difficult to germinate.

CLIMATE Zone 9 and above.

SPECIES *A. argyreus* is a prostrate species, having red flowers and small, silky, grayish-colored leaves. *A. barbigerus*, hairy jugflower or gland

BELOW *Adenanthos barbigerus*, the hairy jugflower, one of the better-known species, is a small shrub up to 1 m (3 ft).

flower, grows to about 1 m (3 ft). It has hairy gray-green foliage and bright red flowers. *A. cuneatus* has flattish, silvery gray leaves and red flowers. *A. cunninghamii* is a small shrub with narrow divided leaves and reddish brown flowers. *A. flavidiflorus*, to 1.2 m (4 ft), is an open, spreading shrub, with very pleasing silky gray-green foliage and reddish flowers which bloom for most of the year. There is also a yellow form. *A. meisneri* grows to 1.2 m (4 ft) high and 2 m (6 ft) wide. A leafy, spreading shrub, with divided mid-green leaves, it produces numerous tubular-shaped flowers in purple and cream. *A. obovatus* is a small, spreading shrub, with almost oval-shaped leaves and bright red flowers in leafy sprays between late winter and spring. It grows to 1 m (3 ft). *A. pungens* has sharp-tipped, divided leaves. The prostrate form grows in the shape of a dome to a height of 35 cm (14 in) and a spread of 3 m (10 ft). The showy, tubular-shaped, light pink or red flowers cover the plant in spring. It makes a beautiful groundcover. *A. sericeus*, woolly bush, is a taller shrub, growing erect to 2–3 m (6–10 ft), with silky, grayish leaves and red-brown flowers. It does very well in sandy soil and is useful for seaside planting as it is salt-resistant. It can also make a very good windbreak. Few species are likely to be found outside their country of origin.

Adenium (fam. Apocynaceae)
Desert rose

Native to the Middle East and tropical and subtropical Africa, this tall succulent shrub has a bloated trunk, woody base and thick branches arranged in spirals. The funnel-like flowers are pink. The desert rose is not widely cultivated in the US.

CULTIVATION Generally grown in pots in a warm greenhouse. Use well-drained cactus compost. Provide maximum light. Water well in summer, keep almost dry in winter. Propagate from fresh seed.

CLIMATE Suitable for cultivation in zone 9 and above. Must be frost free.

ABOVE The flush of bright pink flowers on *Adenium obesum* transforms the squat, grayish stems of this drought-tolerant plant.

ABOVE This well-tended cultivar of *Adiantum aethiopicum* is shown to perfection in a hanging basket.

BELOW *Adiantum capillus-veneris* is more cold-tolerant than many other species of maidenhair fern.

SPECIES *A. obesum* has a thick base, short branches, clusters of shiny, green, leathery leaves and large pink flowers. It grows to 2 m (6 ft). *A. obesum* subsp. *oleifolium* has a very large, round, tuberous base, erect branches, clusters of long, narrow leaves and pink flowers.

Adiantum (fam. Adiantaceae)
Maidenhair fern

The delicate appearance of this popular genus of ferns belies the vigorous growth it can achieve under appropriate conditions. Comprising over 200 species worldwide, there are hardy maidenhair ferns suitable for growing in the garden as well as more tender kinds for growing as pot plants in the warm greenhouse or conservatory. This plant has a creeping rhizome, which differs with the species, dark glossy stems, and both upright and pendent fronds.

CULTIVATION These ferns are not difficult to grow provided they have shade, moisture and protection from wind. Most species need additional water during the summer. They are good container plants and also grow well in gardens where there is filtered sunlight. They like a potting mix with a high peat content. Fertilize the soil with a weak solution of soluble fertilizer. Take care to avoid the foliage.

ABOVE *Adiantum hispidulum* can be grown as a ground-cover or container plant. The foliage is more leathery than that of many other maidenhairs.

BELOW Some cultivars of *Adiantum raddianum* are suitable for the garden, others for the conservatory.

CLIMATE Warm humid conditions for most; zone 10 for the majority of species.

SPECIES *A. aethiopicum*, zone 9, southern maidenhair, is native to Africa and Australia. The extensive, wiry rhizome has many branches and the numerous fronds, growing to 30 cm (12 in) long or more, have wedge-shaped leaflets with tiny serrations on their edges. *A. capillus veneris*, common maidenhair or Venus' hair, zone 8, is found worldwide, in tropical and temperate regions. The rhizome is short. The fronds, up to 50 cm (20 in) long, have very dark, polished stems and serrated leaflets that vary in size and shape. *A. formosum*, blackstem or giant maidenhair, zone 9, is found in Australia's New South Wales, Queensland and Victoria and also New Zealand. The extensive rhizome has many branches and many erect, forked fronds, up to 120 cm (48 in) long, with dark green, roughly diamond-shaped leaflets, 20 mm (1 in) in length. *A. hispidulum*, zone 9, is from New South Wales, Queensland, Victoria, the Northern Territory and New Zealand. It has a short, branched, wiry rhizome and erect fronds, up to 35 cm (14 in) long, with pale to dark green leaflets to 12 mm (½ in) in diameter. It adapts to hot, dry conditions by curling its fronds. The new fronds are pale pink in color. An extensive range of cultivars of maidenhair ferns can be obtained from specialist growers.

Aechmea (fam. Bromeliaceae)

Native to Central and South America, the *Aechmea* species are among the showiest of the bromeliads. Although these plants are large and the leaves are usually spiny, they are often used as house plants. The leaves may grow to 1 m (3 ft) in length, at times much less, and form a central vase which should be kept filled with water. They are sometimes marked with unusual bars, stripes or margins. The inflorescences rise on a single central stem, sometimes combining several colors, and are followed by long-lasting berries. *Aechmea*

ABOVE The yellow flowers of *Aechmea pineliana* are surrounded by striking pink to scarlet bracts, an outstanding decorative feature.

ABOVE There is a great range of floral forms in the *Aechmea* genus. The inflorescence of this one resembles that of the waratah, Telopea.

flowers, bracts and berries can retain their color on the plant for several months.

CULTIVATION The species develop root-feeding systems when grown in soil. Use a very open compost of fibrous soil and old leaf mould. They can also be grown epiphytically by attaching them securely to trees or pieces of driftwood. Regardless of the method of culture, light, warmth and humidity are the main requirements. Reduce moisture during the cooler months. A weak liquid fertilizer can be applied in summer. Propagate from the sucker-like offshoots known as pups. Take them from the side of the plant, pot in a tray, using a sandy peat mixture, and later put them into 15 cm (6 in) pots. They require a minimum temperature in winter of 18°C (64°F).

CLIMATE Warm to hot, moist to tropical.

SPECIES *A. caudata* 'Variegata', a variegated type, differs from the others, with a compact branching inflorescence of golden flowers. *A. chantinii* has pretty, silver-barred leaves, with yellow-white flowers and long orange bracts. *A. fasciata* is an exceptional flowering species with silver banding on the leaves, dusty blue flowers and pink bracts. Var. *purpurea* has purple leaves. *A.* Foster's Favorite Group has shiny purple-red leaves with a drooping inflorescence of purple flowers followed by red berries. *A. lueddemanniana* is a large plant with rosy flowers followed by purple berries. *A. orlandiana* has orange flowers and zig-zag markings on attractive leaves. *A. racinae*, a beautiful small bromeliad, with yellow flowers and red berries, grows well in baskets. *A. tillandsioides* produces an unusual inflorescence of red flowers, white bracts and berries colored blue.

Aeonium (fam. Crassulaceae)

Native to the Canary Islands, North Africa and the Mediterranean, these sometimes short-lived succulents range in size from 60 cm (24 in) in diameter to small rosettes, which are just 3 cm (about 1 in) in diameter. The leaves are arranged in terminal rosettes. They are occasionally stemless, and they also vary considerably in both texture and thickness. Attractive, star-shaped flowers in yellow, red or cream emerge from the rosette center in the spring. In some species the flowering head dies after setting seed or producing offsets. Some of the species are self-fertile.

CULTIVATION Grow as pot plants in a cool greenhouse or conservatory in frost-prone climates. Outdoors, these plants like full sun or partial shade, light and well-drained soil. While most species are easy to grow, some of the more tender species, such as *A. tabuliforme*, need protection in winter from excessive rain. Propagate from seed or cuttings in spring and summer.

CLIMATE Zone 9 and above.

SPECIES *A. arboreum* has erect stems, branching mostly from the base, green rosettes and golden yellow flowers. It grows to 1 m (3 ft). 'Atropurpureum' has plain green leaves in winter, turning purplish brown in summer. *A. canariense* has very large, almost stemless, green rosettes growing to 50 cm (20 in) in diameter. The leaves are soft and velvety and the flowers are pale green. *A. haworthii* is a bushy plant which grows to 60 cm (24 in). It has thin stems, dense rosettes, blueish green leaves, with red margins, and white flowers. *A. lindleyi* is a small dense bush, with thin, gnarled branches, sticky leaves covered in minute hairs and small dark green rosettes which close into tight balls during the resting period. The flowers are golden yellow. *A. lindleyi* var. *viscatum* has soft, hairy, sticky rosettes and yellow flowers on curved stems. The young branches are furry, becoming sticky and black as they mature. It is quite a tall plant. *A. tabuliforme* is a remarkable species which also has a crested form. It has a stemless, flat rosette, the center of which rises to a cone from which the flowering stem emerges to become a pyramid of flowers colored sulphur yellow. *A. tortuosum* is the smallest of the species, the loose rosettes forming 15 cm (6 in) high cushions. The leaves are light green, soft and hairy and the flowers are golden yellow.

Aerides (fam. Orchidaceae)

It is possible that this orchid's name means 'children of the air' and that it was adopted because of the epiphytic nature of the plant. Found throughout tropical Asia, this genus comprises around 50 species, few of which have been cultivated. The plants have upright stems but the sprays of flowers are usually pendulous. Most are pleasantly scented. Thick roots appear along the stems and these roots should not be forced into pots. The leaves are strap-shaped or tapering.

CULTIVATION Outside tropical regions aerides are grown in an intermediate to warm greenhouse or conservatory with high humidity and good, filtered light. Grow in a compost formulated

ABOVE A variegated *Aeonium arboreum* has foliage resembling a flower. As a single rosette before branching, it makes an elegant potted plant.

ABOVE The unusual shape and texture of the flowers of *Aerides odorata* makes this a favorite with orchid enthusiasts.

for epiphytic orchids, in hanging orchid baskets, or mount the plants on pieces of bark. Water sparingly in winter, freely in the growing season. Relatively easy to grow in tropical regions, they do best in an orchid house tied to a piece of hardwood. They need plenty of light and air. When all roots are exposed to the air, frequent misting several times a day is advisable. Full morning sun or late afternoon sun is desirable, with some shading during the heat of the day in summer. However, these plants can be hardened to withstand full sun all day. Healthy plants will have brown or green root tips, 2 cm (1 in) or more in length, which may turn gray around the end of fall, heralding the arrival of a resting season when extra watering and fertilizing should cease until the roots begin to grow again. Propagate from tip cuttings, 30–60 cm (12 –24 in) long. Cut the stem about

10 cm (4 in) under a pair of roots. Place the cuttings in the shade and water frequently, with a fine mist, until new root growth begins. Then pot or tie to boards. The remaining part of the plant will generally throw a side shoot which can be grown on without disturbance.

CLIMATE Warm and humid. Grown under glass except in the tropics.

SPECIES *A. crassifolia* has a short stem which bears up to ten mauve flowers. *A. crispa* has long, drooping, white flowers, with rose lips. *A. flabellata*, a handsome species from northern Thailand, does well in glasshouses. Compared with the other species, it is quite short, with closely spaced leaves about 15 cm (6 in) long. The inflorescence is about 25 cm (10 in) long, with 10 to 15 flowers. The petals and sepals are yellowish with brown blotches. The tip is fringed with purple markings on a white background, and the throat is yellow. *A. odorata* is grown in many countries in Southeast Asia. Owing to its variable appearance, this species has been given different names. Generally, it has long stems to 1.5 m (5 ft), with 25 cm (10 in) long leaves. The inflorescences are 40 cm (16 in) long and

ABOVE In warm weather, clusters of tubular scarlet to orange flowers adorn the twining stems of *Aeschynanthus speciosus*.

drooping, and bear up to 30 perfumed flowers. The sepals and petals are white, marked with lavender, and the mid-lobe dark purple.

Aeschynanthus (fam. Gesneriaceae)
Lipstick plant or vine

Native to India, Asia and New Guinea, this genus comprises over 100 species of epiphytic subshrubs or vines. The showy, funnel-shaped flowers come in shades of red, orange and creamish green. The fleshy, mostly elliptical-shaped leaves are sometimes leathery to the touch and generally appear in whorls of three or four.

CULTIVATION Grow these tropical plants in hanging baskets of soilless compost in a warm greenhouse or conservatory, or as house plants. High humidity is needed together with shade from direct sun. Propagate by stem or root cutting or by division. The plant can also be grown from seed.

CLIMATE This genus is native to subtropical forests.

SPECIES *A. bracteatus*, from India and the Himalayas, has clusters of red flowers. *A. ellipticus* is from New Guinea. The leaves are dark green, the stems are densely covered in red hairs and the flowers are salmon pink, covered with darker pink hairs. *A. lobbianus*, from Indonesia, has trailing dark green leaves and bright red flowers with purple calyces. *A. pulcher*, red bugle vine or lipstick plant, from Java, has purplish-edged leaves and bright red flowers. *A. speciosus*, from Borneo and Malaysia, has clusters of large orange-red flowers at the ends of the branches.

Aesculus (fam. Hippocastanaceae)
Horse chestnut, buckeye

This genus of about 15 species of hardy, deciduous trees and shrubs are native to south-eastern Europe, north-eastern Asia and North America. Generally quite large, some reaching

ABOVE *Aesculus* x *carnea* is one of the world's most spectacular deciduous trees. The flowers sit like candles on top of the branches.

30 m (100 ft), they are useful for large gardens, avenues and parks. While lasting only from late spring to early fall, their beautiful foliage provides excellent shade and decoration. The attractive flowers are white, yellow or red, and sometimes variegated. This is one of the most handsome of all deciduous trees.

CULTIVATION Horse chestnuts flourish in temperate to cool and moist climates. Most are easily grown in deep, well-drained soil, with some protection from strong winds. Propagate by seed in fall, although this tree frequently sows its own seeds. It can also be increased by side grafting, budding or root cutting.

CLIMATE Most species are hardy in zone 5.

SPECIES *A.* x *carnea*, red horse chestnut, zone 4, is exceptionally beautiful, with large clusters of soft rose-colored flowers. It grows to a height of about 15 m (50 ft). It will thrive if protected from hot summer winds. *A.* x *carnea* 'Briotii' has larger clusters of deeper red flowers. *A. hippocastanum*, the common horse chestnut, has a large, spreading, rounded head and clusters of white flowers with red patches. It grows well only in truly cool climates where it can reach heights of 30 m (100 ft). Parts of this plant, including the nuts and nectar, are very poisonous if eaten. *A. indica*, Indian or Himalayan horse chestnut, zone 7, grows to 18 m (60 ft). Although similar to the common horse chestnut, the sprays of white flowers are marked with yellow and red and are much longer. *A. pavia*, red buckeye, is a small North American shrub with red flowers that grows to 4 m (13 ft).

Aethionema (fam. Brassicaceae)
Stone-cress

This genus of about 60 species originates from the Mediterranean. Mostly perennials, they grow well in cooler American gardens where they are useful for rock gardens and borders. They have trailing stems, fleshy leaves, and flowers in various shades of red, pink and purple from early summer onwards.

CULTIVATION Aethionemas prefer a light limy soil with good drainage and a dry, sunny position. They will survive for many years without replanting. Propagate the perennial types from cuttings taken in summer or by division or seed in spring. The annuals and biennials can only be propagated from seed.

CLIMATE This genus is suitable for zone 7 and above.

SPECIES *A. coridifolium* and the very similar *A. grandiflorum* are attractive perennials, growing 15–25 cm (6–10 in) high. They have rosy pink flowers and intense grayish blue leaves, and make pretty, decorative border plants. 'Warley Rose', neat and shrub-like, with a profusion of deeper pink flowers, is the cultivar most commonly grown.

Agapanthus (fam. Liliaceae)
African lily

Native to southern Africa, agapanthus are very popular with gardeners in mild climates because of their handsome foliage and beautiful lily-like flowers. The glossy, dark green leaves are strap-shaped, arching gracefully outwards, and blue or white flower heads are borne on long, erect stems to 1 m (3 ft) tall.

CULTIVATION African lilies are easy to cultivate and will thrive even if neglected. Almost any soil will suit, provided it is not waterlogged. To flower, they need full sun; for an attractive foliage border, they should be planted in fairly

ABOVE A massed planting of *Aethionema grandiflorum* provides a carpet of color through late spring to early summer.

ABOVE Massed agapanthus in bloom make a striking display, flowering throughout summer in the northern hemisphere.

ABOVE This lovely head of white agapanthus shows masses of buds still to open.

dense shade. Set new plants 60 cm (24 in) apart and water well during the first six months. Remove spent flower stems and any dead leaves. Fertilize in spring with a complete fertilizer. African lilies do well in tubs: one large plant is enough for a 30–40 cm (12–16 in) tub. Good soil and drainage is essential. Water well in spring and summer when necessary, when the flowers are being formed. Propagate by dividing the clumps during late winter or early spring. Dig up the clump and pull it apart, making sure that each plant has a sound crown and some good roots. Prune the fleshy roots and cut back the leaves if necessary.

CLIMATE Zones 7 to 9 depending on the species.

SPECIES *A. africanus* and *A. praecox* subsp. *orientalis*, both zone 9, are quite distinct. The latter and its cultivars are used more widely in American gardens. Many agapanthus hybrids have been produced which are hardy in zone 7 and above and these are more suited to gardens in cooler climates. Their flowers come in many shades of blue and also white. They are offered under cultivar names.

Agapetes (fam. Ericaceae)

From the higher parts of central Asia, these woody, evergreen shrubs have alternate leaves and five-lobed flowers which vary greatly in color. They are grown in a cool greenhouse or conservatory in frost-prone areas.

CULTIVATION This plant can be grown outdoors in frost-free climates. It also grows well in pots or other containers and is suitable for the greenhouse. Acid soil or compost is needed. Strike cuttings in a warm place in the summer. Repot as the shrubs increase in size–up to the size of a 15 cm (6 in) pot. Prune after flowering if a small, dense shape is required.

CLIMATE These shrubs are suitable for zone 9 and above.

SPECIES Not all may be available in all parts of the US. *A. serpens*, an arching climber and the usual one grown, has bright red tubular flowers with darker, V-shaped markings.

BELOW Scarlet bell-like flowers weigh down the fine stems of *Agapetes serpens.* These plants are related to rhododendrons and heathers.

Agastache (fam. Lamiaceae)

These perennials, which last about three to four years, are a good choice for borders, shrubberies or garden beds because they flower profusely for a long period. The leaves are pleasantly aromatic. One species is very attractive to bees and is also used in herbal teas.

CULTIVATION Propagate from seed or by division of the existing clumps. Pot or plant out young plants in mid-spring. If planted in rich soil, they will thrive. *A. mexicana* is hardy but requires shelter from harsh winter conditions, and may require staking because the stems are pliable.

CLIMATE Most of these perennials can be grown in zone 8 and above.

SPECIES *A. foeniculum*, anise hyssop, a perennial native to central North America, grows to 60–120 cm (24–48 in) and produces attractive spikes of purple flowers from late summer to fall. The aniseed-flavored leaves are used as a seasoning in foods and herbal teas. *A. mexicana*, Mexican bergamot or giant hyssop, zone 9, is a well-known species. Its

ABOVE Giant hyssop and Mexican bergamot are two common names applied to *Agastache mexicana* with its deep rose-colored flowers.

long spikes of salvia-like flowers in rose-pink to crimson appear between mid and late summer. It grows to 60 cm (24 in). *A. rugosa*, Korean mint, is also a perennial. It resembles anise hyssop, but its rather minty flavor is quite different. It is also used in teas and as a flavoring.

Agathis (fam. Araucariaceae)
Kauri, kauri pine

This genus of around 13 species of evergreen conifers is native to the South Pacific region, with only three or four species cultivated. These tall, erect, slow-growing trees, most with huge, column-shaped trunks, produce timber that is relatively straight and free of knots. The leaves of the kauris differ from those of nearly all other conifers in that they are large, flat and leathery. The cones, too, are different, and look rather like a small pineapple. The pattern on the cones has inspired the name of the genus which derives from the Greek word for 'a ball of string'.

CULTIVATION Agathis are grown in pots under glass in areas prone to frost. They do well outdoors in warm frost-free climates. Both species described below can be propagated from seed.

CLIMATE Grow in frost-free areas; zones 9 to 10 and above depending on species.

SPECIES *A. australis*, New Zealand kauri, is highly valued around the world for its timber and gum. While it grows beautifully in the wild in the North Island of New Zealand, in cultivation it is not particularly easy to establish. Although slow growing, it can reach heights of 50 m (160 ft). It has a compact, conical shape, with a trunk of around 8 m (26 ft) in perimeter. Its narrow, mid-green leaves, about 5 cm (2 in) long, turn coppery brown in cold weather. A humid climate and deep soil are essential for its cultivation. *A. robusta*, Queensland kauri, is prized for its knot-free timber. This tall, frost-hardy

ABOVE *Agathis robusta*, the Queensland kauri, is a slow-growing conifer that can be grown in pots or tubs under glass.

evergreen, zone 9, grows to 45 m (150 ft), and has a much more open and erect growth pattern than the New Zealand species. Its straight trunk is 3–4 m (10–13 ft) in diameter and its deep green leaves are 5–10 cm (2–4 in) long. It occurs naturally in widely separated areas of Queensland and can therefore be cultivated in quite different climates. If cultivated in warmer coastal areas it is able to adapt to a variety of soil types and grows quickly. However, it can also be grown successfully in cooler coastal regions.

Agave (fam. Agavaceae)

Century plant

Native to South and Central America, this genus includes around 300 species, many of which have been cultivated commercially for the fibers in their leaves and 'pulque', the main ingredient for local alcoholic beverages in Mexico. Widely distributed in their native habitat, some species have also become naturalized in various parts of the world. They come in various sizes, from giant rosettes of 2–3 m (6–10 ft) in diameter to tiny ones as small as 2 cm (1 in). The common name was adopted because it was originally believed that the plants flowered only every 100 years. It is now known that some flower after five years, while others flower only when they reach 30–50 years of age. All species have succulent leaves and flowering stems which emerge from the center of the plant as a mast-like stalk, which grows extremely fast and tall. From this, some species produce branched inflorescences with numerous flowers which are self fertile. Some species also produce little bulbs in the axils of the flowering stem, which facilitate propagation.

CULTIVATION In frost-prone areas these plants are grown in a cool glasshouse or conservatory.

ABOVE The unusual bird-attracting flowers of *Agave americana* are carried on a tall, sturdy branched stem high above the foliage.

ABOVE Spineless foliage of *Agave attenuata* makes this an attractive choice for either garden or container growing.

ABOVE *Agave attenuata* makes a good foil for the large, dark green lobed leaves of elephant ears, an Alocasia species.

They can be stood outside for the summer or used in summer bedding displays. They like very well-drained, gritty soil or compost. Under glass provide really bright light but shade from very strong sun as it may burn the foliage. Outdoors provide a position in full sun.

CLIMATE Grow in frost-free areas; zone 9 and above.

SPECIES *A. americana*, which is grown outdoors in the south-west US region, grows to 3 m (10 ft) tall and quite wide. A stemless rosette, it has thick, fleshy, strap-shaped leaves, blueish in color, with marginal teeth and a sharp point. Offsets are produced freely. The flowering stem, which appears after about 30 years, is 5–8 m (16– 26 ft) tall. All of the cultivars have shorter leaves than the species itself and various markings. 'Marginata' has yellow margins on its leaves; 'Medio-picta' has a central yellow stripe; 'Striata' has thin, rather random, longitudinal yellow stripes. *A. attenuata* branches from the base to form a large clump. It is a softer, dense rosette of pale green leaves with neither spines nor teeth. The tall stem grows to about 3 m (10 ft), curving over to form a floral arch. The flowers continue to bloom for several months. *A. parviflora* grows to only about 15 cm (6 in) in diameter. It has hard, stiff, narrow leaves, marked with white lines, a terminal spine and white threads hanging from the margins of the leaves. *A. sisalana*, sisal hemp, a very large species from Mexico, is cultivated for fiber in various parts of the world. *A. victoriae-reginae*, a very striking species from Central America, grows symmetrically to about 60 cm (24 in) in diameter. A dense rosette, it has dark green, narrow, keeled leaves, marked and edged with white. After 20 years creamy yellow flowers appear in spring and summer.

Ageratum (fam. Asteraceae)
Floss flower

Some plants of this genus of around 40 species of annuals, perennials and shrubs native to the tropical Americas have become naturalized and highly invasive in tropical and warm zones. The only species commonly cultivated as a half-hardy annual is *A. houstonianum*, the annual floss flower or rather its many cultivars which are used for summer bedding.

ABOVE A massed display of soft pink and mauve ageratum in a summer bedding scheme. It flowers all summer.

CULTIVATION *Ageratum* prefers full sun but will tolerate some shade. It will grow in poor soil if it receives lots of water in dry weather. It is raised from seed sown in a heated propagating case in a warm greenhouse during early spring. This will produce young plants for setting out in bedding schemes and patio containers in late spring or early summer, when the frosts are over. It is easily raised and seed germinates freely in the right conditions.

CLIMATE Frost-free conditions are needed for Ageratum.

SPECIES *A. houstonianum*, which is native to tropical Mexico, has dull, hairy, heart-shaped leaves and fluffy flower heads in lavender, blue, pinkish mauve or white. It grows to about 45 cm (18 in) in height. Many cultivars have been produced for summer bedding, with flowers in shades of blue, from light to dark, shades of pink and mauve, and also white.

Aglaonema (fam. Araceae)

Aglaonemas are tropical perennials which are mainly cultivated as pot plants in warm greenhouses and conservatories, or as house plants. Some have extremely beautiful ornamental leaves. The exotic lily-like flowers are usually in shades of gold or green. They will tolerate medium to poor light. Most are native to Malaysia, Indonesia and the Philippines.

CULTIVATION Aglaonemas require rich soil, good drainage, warmth, moderate light, humidity and shelter. They do not like direct sun. Keep the soil damp, but not wet, and decrease water during winter. Use a liquid fertilizer while the plant is in active growth. Propagation may be difficult and is usually successful only in a glasshouse from tip cuttings or by division.

CLIMATE Warm subtropics to tropics; elsewhere as an indoor plant.

SPECIES *A. commutatum* and its numerous cultivars are most commonly grown. The foliage may be striped, blotched or splashed with white, cream or silver. Popular cultivars include 'Pseudobracteatum' and 'Treubii'. All grow to about 25–30 cm (10–12 in) high. *A. costatum*, a spotted evergreen, is a suckering type which reaches about 20 cm (8 in). There are many shades of green and white on the leaves.

ABOVE *Aglaonema commutatum* is a tough plant that survives in low light much better than most indoor plants.

Agonis (fam. Myrtaceae)

This small genus of Western Australian evergreen trees and shrubs has graceful foliage and flowers. The white, sometimes pink, flowers appear in masses along the branches in spring and summer. The trees grow rapidly and are adaptable. They are suitable for ornamental planting and in frost-prone climates can be grown in a cool glasshouse.

CULTIVATION In frost-prone climates grow in pots of well-drained potting compost in a cool glasshouse or conservatory. Outdoors these trees and shrubs require a warm, well-drained spot. Once established, they are able to survive without much water, but need to be kept fairly moist when young. Prune only if necessary to improve their shape. Propagate from ripened seed in spring and sow in a sharp sand and peat mix of 3:1. Seeds germinate easily.

CLIMATE Agonis are suited to growing in zone 10.

SPECIES Not all are readily available outside their country of origin. *A. flexuosa*, willow myrtle, is the best known species. It has rough, dark gray bark, weeping foliage, aromatic green leaves and tiny white flowers which bloom in summer. The fruit is red when ripe, with small black seeds, from which the plant propagates itself. It is a robust tree, reaching 7 m (23 ft) in height. 'Variegata' is shrubby and grows to a height of 3 m (10 ft), with very attractive foliage marked in pink and cream. It seldom flowers. *A. juniperina*, juniper myrtle, is an upright tree, with rich green narrow leaves, which are highly perfumed, and masses of white flowers. It is very attractive and grows to a height of 7 m (23 ft). *A. linearifolia*, an upright shrub with dense foliage and white summer flowers, grows to 3 m (10 ft). *A. marginata* is a small tree with small, soft, oval leaves, with silky hairs, and white flowers with pink centers. *A. parviceps* has very small, dense, narrow leaves and clusters of small white flowers. It grows upright to 2 m (6 ft).

ABOVE Dainty white flowers stud the arching branches of *Agonis flexuosa* in spring. The foliage is highly aromatic.

Ailanthus (fam. Simaroubaceae)

This tree, 'tall enough to reach the skies', is native to Asia and the Pacific region. However, it has become naturalized in many parts of the world, and is highly invasive in some areas. It has pinnate leaves which change color in the

ABOVE The fast-growing, deciduous *Ailanthus altissima*, known as the tree of heaven, is very hardy and fairly widely planted in the US.

fall. Fast growing, it reaches heights of 20–30 m (65–100 ft) and often forms a thicket of suckers.

CULTIVATION These trees do well in any soil and, once established, their growth is vigorous. They can tolerate high levels of atmospheric pollution and are fairly widely planted in the US. Propagate from either seed or suckers.

CLIMATE Cold and temperate climates; zone 4 and above.

SPECIES *A. altissima*, tree of heaven, is a striking deciduous tree which grows quickly up to 20–30 m (65–100 ft). It has long leaves, small greenish-colored flowers and orange-red winged fruit. The male flowers have an unpleasant smell. *A. vilmoriniana* grows to 6–15 m (20–50 ft). It is cultivated in China to provide food for silkworms.

Aiphanes (fam. Arecaceae)

This genus comprises 30–40 species of palms native to tropical America, but is not widely grown outside countries of origin.

BELOW Tropical *Aiphanes caryotifolia* has leaflets shaped like those of the fish-tail palm. It is uncommon in cultivation.

CULTIVATION In frost-prone areas grow in a large container, filled with rich potting compost, in a heated glasshouse or conservatory. It will take a few years to outgrow the tub. Outdoors plant in a partially shaded, sheltered spot. Propagation is by seed only, but this is not readily available.

CLIMATE Can be grown outside only in zone 10 and above.

SPECIES *A. caryotifolia*'s most striking feature is the long, blackish, needle-like spines which arm the trunk, leaf-stalks and leaflets. The ornamental leaves, or fronds, grow up to 2 m (6 ft) long and the large, fresh green leaflets are shaped like a fish tail, with frilled or ruffled ends.

Ajuga (fam. Lamiaceae)
Bugleweed

Mostly originating from Europe, this genus of about 40 species has been widely used for healing wounds in times past. Most species have running stems and make excellent groundcover. They are often found in moist, shady places in woodland gardens, and have become naturalized garden escapes in some parts of North America. The leaves are green, purplish or variegated. These plants are decorative and also useful in preventing soil erosion.

CULTIVATION Ajuga needs shade and cool, light, moist, rich soil. Dress well with organic matter at planting time and enrich with complete fertilizer (45 g per square metre; 1½ oz per square yard) in early spring. Propagation is very easy as these plants root from every node, whether in contact with the ground or not. The leafy nodes usually have many roots below their leaves. When detached, these divisions grow rapidly. Before potting, shorten the leaves by half to reduce moisture loss. If planting out, place about 20–30 cm (8–12 in) apart. Pruning is unnecessary as excess plants can simply be dug up to thin the growth or restrain their spread.

ABOVE *Akebia quinata* has pretty foliage and unusual bell-like flowers. This is a light climber which does not need heavy support.

ABOVE *Ajuga reptans* is ideal for edging garden beds and as dense groundcover in light shade.

CLIMATE Ajuga is suitable for zone 6 and above.

SPECIES *A. reptans* is an excellent low-growing perennial with height to 15 cm (6 in). Its dark green leaves have a metallic bronze sheen and are attractively crinkled. The bright blue flower spikes bloom freely in spring and early summer. The many cultivars have different-colored leaves: 'Multicolor' has colorful variegated leaves in green, pink and cream; and the well-known 'Atropurpurea' has deep bronze-purple foliage.

Akebia (fam. Lardizabalaceae)

Native to China and Japan, these two species of hardy, twining climbers are grown for their pretty perfumed flowers and distinctive leaves. Useful for pillars and pergolas, they grow quickly to around 9 m (30 ft).

CULTIVATION Plant in well-drained soil in a sunny position and cut back every three or four years. Propagate from seed or from cuttings taken in summer.

CLIMATE Akebias are suitable for zone 5 and above.

SPECIES *A. quinata*, from China and Japan, is the best known of the species. It has attractive clusters of semi-evergreen leaves, divided into five-stalked leaflets, and purplish flowers in spring. The flowers have an unusual chocolate scent. Interestingly, both male and female appear on the one stem and the female flower is two or three times larger than the male. In mild climates, this plant sometimes produces cylindrical-shaped. edible fruit. *A. trifoliata* is a deciduous climber. The three-lobed leaves open bronze before becoming green. Sprays of purple flowers appear in spring.

Alberta (fam. Rubiaceae)

There are only three to five species of this South African genus of ornamental shrubs or trees.

CULTIVATION In frost-prone climates alberta can be grown in pots or in a soil bed in a cool

ABOVE The scarlet tubular flowers of *Alberta magna* are displayed to perfection against its dark glossy foliage.

greenhouse or conservatory. Propagation is from cuttings but these may present a challenge.

CLIMATE Zone 10 and above. Thrives in warm coastal areas.

SPECIES *A. magna*, an evergreen shrub or small tree, is not freely available. It is seen in botanic gardens mostly, where it grows to between 2 and 5 m (6–16 ft), although it can reach up to 9 m (30 ft) in its native habitat. It is grown for its glossy, dark green leaves and its attractive, erect spikes of tubular orange-red flowers in winter and spring.

Albizia (fam. Mimosaceae)

Silk tree

Native to tropical and subtropical areas of Asia, Africa and Australia, this genus comprises over 150 species which are closely related to the wattles. Some species are grown for their timber, especially in Southeast Asia. The ferny, wattle-like leaves fold up at night and the clustered bundles of stamens have a silky appearance. Albizias are grown for the beauty of their flowers and foliage. In areas prone to frost, tender species are grown under glass. Outdoors they are suitable for shade and for quick-growing shelter. They are sometimes used as shade trees in tea and coffee plantations. They also make attractive street trees as they can withstand pruning on a regular basis.

CULTIVATION Tender species can be grown in pots of well-drained soil-based compost in a cool greenhouse or conservatory. Outdoors, these trees enjoy a light, well-drained soil. The pea-shaped seed pods provide abundant seeds for ease of propagation. Seed sown in spring can produce plants of 2.5 m (8 ft) by winter.

CLIMATE Depends on species; some thrive in zone 7, others in zone 9.

SPECIES *A. julibrissin*, pink silk tree, zone 7, is native to central Asia. A hardy, deciduous tree, it reaches 6–9 m (20–30 ft) in height. It has deep green fern-like foliage and rounded brushes of translucent pink stamens, which look like silky tassels. Its appearance changes at night as the leaves fold up. *A. lebbeck*, Siris

BELOW *Albizia julibrissin*'s flowers sit on top of the branches, which become more horizontal as the tree matures.

tree, zone 9, from tropical parts of Asia, is an excellent deciduous shade and street tree. It grows 12–14 m (40–45 ft) tall. It is sensitive to frost but can withstand heat and drought. It has pretty sprays of creamy pink flowers. *A. lophantha*, cape or crested wattle, zone 9, is native to Western Australia, and now naturalized on the east coast of Australia. It is valued for its rapid growth, its salt tolerance and its suitability for seaside plantings. The dense cylindrical spikes of greenish yellow flowers have a strange smell, so planting albizias close to the house should be avoided.

Alcea (fam. Malvaceae)

Hollyhock

This is a large genus of short-lived biennial and perennial herbs from Europe and central Asia.

CULTIVATION Hollyhocks like a well-dug soil, with added organic material, and a sunny position sheltered from strong wind. Propagate from seed sown in seed beds in late spring or early summer. Plant out the seedlings when they are about six to eight weeks old. Care must be taken not to let snails and slugs attack them at this stage. Apply a balanced fertilizer a few weeks later and water regularly to ensure healthy, well-grown plants. Spray with a fungicide in humid weather to help control rust.

CLIMATE Zone 7 and above.

SPECIES *A. rosea* is a perennial flowering in summer. It has for long been very popular with English gardeners for their cottage and country gardens. With the cottage-garden style becoming popular in other parts of the world, including the US, this delightful old-fashioned plant should become more widely grown. It was susceptible to rust disease, and so suffered a period of neglect. However, hybrids bred for annual cultivation with greater resistance are now available and hollyhocks are once more becoming popular. This species has tall, spire-like stems, to 2.5 m (8 ft) or more, and

ABOVE Hollyhocks, *Alcea* cultivars, once the mainstay of cottage gardens, are again being grown to provide height and accent to low plantings.

roundish, rough-textured leaves with lobed margins. The axillary flowers are either single or double and come in white or shades of pink, red or mauve.

Alchemilla (fam. Rosaceae)

Lady's mantle

There are over 250 species of this genus in Europe and in the northern temperate zones and tropical mountains of Africa. One hardy, herbaceous, low-growing species, *A. mollis*, is often grown in cool areas. Its leaves are covered with silvery hairs. Masses of small, greenish yellow flowers appear in summer. These plants form dense clumps and are used in rockeries or borders.

CULTIVATION Alchemilla does best in temperate climates and alpine regions. The main

ABOVE The sharp citrus-colored flowers of *Alchemilla mollis* can be used effectively for contrast with other flowers or plants with dark foliage.

requirement is good drainage. Any reasonable soil is suitable. It seeds freely so propagation is simple. Place a small plastic bag over the spent flower heads, collect seed and sow in spring.

CLIMATE Alchemilla thrives in zone 6 and above.

SPECIES *A. mollis*, lady's mantle, is a well-loved perennial, growing to around 30 cm (12 in); it works well as a groundcover. Its decorative, wavy-edged leaves are quite soft and furry. Masses of greenish yellow flowers appear in summer. Both *A. mollis* and *A. xanthochlora* (which is less commonly cultivated) have a long history of use in herbal medicine. *A. alpina* is similar but is a smaller, mat-forming species.

Alectryon (fam. Sapindaceae)
Soap berry

There are about 18 species of these evergreen trees valued for their hardwood. Oil is also derived from the fleshy fruit of some of the species. Native to Australia, New Zealand, Malaysia and the Pacific Islands, several species can be found in the rainforests of north-eastern Queensland and New South Wales. Most of the species have pinnate leaves and red four-lobed fruits.

CULTIVATION These trees can be grown from seed or cuttings. In frost-prone areas, grow tender species under glass. Outdoors, they grow best in deep, rich soils, in semi-shade when young. All species like a reliable water supply in dry conditions.

CLIMATE Zone 10 for most species.

SPECIES It is unlikely that all species are available in the US. *A. coriaceus* grows to 4–8 m (13–26 ft) in height, with dense bushy growth, and is thus suitable for shelter belts or hedges. The greenish spring flowers are followed by pretty red fruits which contain the shiny black seeds. *A. excelsus*, titoki or New Zealand ash, zone 8, grows to 10–15 m (33–50 ft) high. It has large compound leaves and dull red flowers, followed by scarlet fruits with shiny black seeds. *A. forsythii* is a small tree, often with a twisted form, that grows to 6–8 m (20–26 ft). The dark red flowers from late

BELOW *Alectryon subcinereus* has unusual fruits which split when ripe to expose dark seeds in bright red pulp.

spring to early summer are followed by fruits similar to the other species. *A. subcinereus*, smooth rambutan, is usually 4–6 m (13–20 ft) high and 2–4 m (6–13 ft) wide, with either a single trunk or as a multi-branched shrub. Tolerant of some coastal exposure and some frost, and a good sand binder, it is a useful plant. The fruits which follow the summer flowers are quite leathery. *A. tomentosus*, red jacket or woolly rambutan, is much larger than the other species, reaching 10–18 m (33–60 ft) under good conditions. The foliage gets its woolly description from the masses of rust hairs appearing on the young shoots. The flowers are borne from winter to spring, followed by fruits ripening during fall and early winter. It is a good shade tree and tolerates some frost, but size restricts its use to large gardens or parks.

Aleurites (fam. Euphorbiaceae)

Native to Asia and the Hawaiian and Pacific Islands, this genus of tropical trees is grown mainly for its seeds which, although poisonous, produce oils used for dying and waterproofing fabrics. With their spring flowers, these trees do make excellent shade trees. In frost-prone climates grow in a cool greenhouse or conservatory.

CULTIVATION Aleurites need to be grown in acid soil or potting compost. Outdoors, plant in a sunny spot. Fertilize each spring and water well in dry weather.

CLIMATE Suitable for zone 10.

SPECIES Unfortunately, these are not freely available outside their countries of origin. *A. cordata*, Japan wood-oil tree, has toothed leaves and warty fruits which contain the valuable seeds. It grows to 9 m (30 ft). *A. moluccana*, candle nut, varnish tree or Indian walnut, is larger, growing to 20 m (65 ft). It has a frosty appearance from a distance. The leaves are slightly hairy and the flowers white.

BELOW The seed kernels of *Aleurites moluccana* have a heavy oil content and are used as candles by Polynesian peoples, giving rise to the name candle nut.

Allamanda (fam. Apocynaceae)

Of these 12 species of evergreen climbers and shrubs from the tropical Americas, the most commonly grown is a vigorous climber that produces an abundance of distinctive, golden, trumpet-shaped flowers, 7–10 cm (3–4 in) across.

BELOW Allamandas need strong support and plenty of room to spread.

ABOVE *Allamanda cathartica* grows vigorously so needs plenty of space when grown under glass.

CULTIVATION In frost-prone areas grow in a warm humid greenhouse or conservatory. In the tropics, grow outdoors in full sun or partial shade in a humus-rich soil. Water well during the growing period. To achieve a bushy form, cut back the canes in late winter and pinch out new growth. Climbing plants need strong support and tying in until they are established. Propagate in spring and summer from greenwood cuttings and root them in heat.

CLIMATE Zone 10 and above.

SPECIES *A. cathartica* is the most popularly cultivated species in the US. With lance-shaped leaves and yellow flowers in summer, it provides a dense cover for walls. Cultivar 'Hendersonii' has yellow flowers with a white-spotted throat; 'Nobilis' has strongly perfumed bright yellow flowers; 'Williamsii' has yellow flowers with a reddish brown throat; *A. schottii* has bright yellow stripes at the base of golden flowers and a more bushy growth habit than *A. cathartica*.

Allium (fam. Alliaceae)

This large genus of hardy bulbous herbs comprises more than 700 species that grow in temperate climates around the world. Relatives of the common onion, they mostly have a strong oniony smell. The leaves are either broad and flat or narrow and hollow, and the flowers bloom in spring and summer. Pretty ornamental varieties look attractive in pots, borders or rockeries. The spent flower heads make an unusual and softening addition to dried flower arrangements.

CULTIVATION Alliums like well-drained soil and full sun. They can adapt to temperate, cool and subtropical climates. Plant bulbs in fall at a depth equal to twice their diameter. Propagate by seed or by separating young bulbs in summer or fall when dormant.

CLIMATE Alliums can be grown in zones 5 to 9 depending on species.

ABOVE The large, round flower heads of *Allium christophii* dry well for use in dried floral arrangements.

SPECIES Most of these are suitable for zone 8. *A. aflatunense* is almost 1 m (3 ft) high, with purple-lilac flowers. *A. cyaneum* has blue, bell-shaped flowers growing to 30 cm (12 in) high. *A. macleanii* has deep violet flowers and grows to 1 m (3 ft) high. *A. moly*, zone 7, is an easily grown species with bright yellow flowers to a height of 15 cm (6 in). *A. narcissiflorum* has bright rose pink, bell-shaped flowers and grows to 30 cm (12 in). *A. neapolitanum* produces large, attractive white flowers suitable for cutting. *A. senescens* with starry rose to whitish flowers, grows 30 cm (12 in) high.

Allocasuarina (fam. Casuarinaceae)
She-oak

The 60 species in this Australian genus were formerly included in *Casuarina* which now has fewer than 20 species. These evergreen trees and shrubs mostly have drooping foliage, with the true leaves reduced to very small scales where the needle-like branchlets join. Male and female flowers are borne on separate trees and wind-pollinated. After flowering, woody cones of various shapes and sizes are produced. In suitable climates, many are fast growers and are used for windbreaks, shade and shelter.

CULTIVATION In frost-prone climates, grow in pots of soil-based potting compost in a cool conservatory or greenhouse. These trees and shrubs are best grown in full sun. Most prefer good quality soil and ample summer moisture.

CLIMATE This genus is suitable for zone 9 and above.

SPECIES *A. decaisneana*, desert oak, grows to 6–12 m (20–40 ft), with a straight trunk, graceful gray-green weeping foliage and large, cylindrical woody cones. This is an ideal tree for harsh, hot, arid conditions. *A. littoralis*, black she-oak, is a coastal species tolerant of poor soils and exposed conditions. It is fast-growing, reaching 9 m (30 ft) and, although adaptable to a range of conditions, is best grown in warmer areas. *A. verticillata* (syn.

ABOVE Laden with flowers about to shed their pollen, this she-oak takes on a rusty appearance. Some species tolerate drought.

A. stricta), drooping she-oak, is a graceful small tree reaching 7–10 m (23–33 ft), although much smaller in exposed windy or seaside situations. Once established, it is tolerant of light frosts and drought.

Alloxylon (formerly *Oreocallis*, fam. Proteaceae)
Tree waratah

This small genus of evergreen subtropical trees is native to Australia and South America. Their decorative foliage and brilliant scarlet flowers make them attractive trees to cultivate.

CULTIVATION In frost-prone climates, grow in a cool greenhouse or conservatory. Use well-drained soil-based compost. Outdoors, plant in rich, well-drained soil in a warm spot sheltered from strong wind. Ample summer water is needed, at least until the trees are well established. Propagate from fresh seed or from semi-ripe cuttings taken in summer or early fall.

CLIMATE Zone 9 and above.

ABOVE The brilliant, rich red flowers of *Alloxylon flammeum* last for many weeks but may not be as prolific as this under glass.

SPECIES *A. flammeum* (syn. *Oreocallis wickhamii*), tree waratah or red silky oak, grows to 25 m (80 ft) in its habitat but is more usually 6–15 m (20–50 ft) in cultivation. The glossy lobed leaves are variable in shape and the scarlet flowers are crowded on the ends of the branches. In sheltered situations the spring flowers last for many weeks. *A. pinnatum* (syn. *Oreocallis pinnata*), Queensland waratah tree, reaches 18–20 m (60–65 ft) in tropical rainforest situations but very much less in cultivation. The bright scarlet flowers on 4 cm (1½ in) stalks appear on the tips of the branches in spring. Not all are available outside their countries of origin.

Allspice (*Pimenta dioica*, fam. Myrtaceae)

Allspice belongs to a small genus of aromatic trees, native to tropical America and the West Indies. This tree grows to about 12 m (40 ft) and has prominently veined 15 cm (6 in) long leaves and small white flowers in late

ABOVE This prolific crop of tiny fruits on allspice will be harvested, dried and powdered for culinary use.

spring. Allspice, used for flavoring foods and liqueurs, is obtained from the dried unripened fruit.

CULTIVATION Generally grown in a warm greenhouse or conservatory. In frost-free climates, plant outdoors in a well-drained, peaty soil in a sunny position. Propagate by layers in spring or by taking softwood shoots in summer.

CLIMATE Zone 10 and above.

Almond

(*Prunus dulcis*, syn. *P. amygdalus*, fam. Rosaceae)

A deciduous tree from south-west Asia, it is grown for the edible kernel within the stone. It reaches 8–10 m (26–33 ft). The sweet, pink-blossomed almond is valued for the bland oil obtained from the nut. This is used in fine cookery and confectionery, while the remaining 'cake' is used in the production of soap and cosmetics.

CULTIVATION This plant prefers a warm, dry, inland climate, with most of the rainfall occurring in winter or early spring. Mediterranean conditions are perfect. In areas

ABOVE The downy peach-like fruit of almond, *Prunus dulcis*, splits at maturity to reveal the familiar woody nut.

experiencing late frosts the flowers and subsequent yield will be damaged. Humid coastal areas will generally experience problems with fungal disease. A moderately rich soil, well drained and textured, is essential for encouraging deep root penetration. Phosphate and nitrogen based fertilizers encourage fruit formation and stimulate growth. Organic matter should also be added. It is best to prune the tree into a vase shape, with an open center. Clean out the dead wood and branches and keep the tree to a managable size. The almond bears fruit on the previous year's wood and from the spurs of older wood. Through judicious pruning, both old and new wood will remain productive. Harvest in summer. The fruit from the center of the tree is the last to ripen, so use this as a guide for harvesting. Shake the trees by hand and collect the fruit on a groundsheet spread out below. Some cultivars are self-fertile, others need a pollinator.

CLIMATE Zone 7 and above.

Alnus (fam. Betulaceae)
Alder

Native to the cold and cooler areas of the northern hemisphere, alders are slender upright trees which belong to the birch family.

ABOVE *Alnus jorullenis* is a pretty tree, best planted in open areas away from buildings to prevent the roots causing damage.

They are deciduous. Catkins appear in spring before the leaves. Alders are useful for protecting streams and river banks and as shelter trees against coastal winds. In the past, they were used extensively in shipbuilding. The timber of some species was also used for musical instruments and clogs, and for harbor and estuary piles. They are often found on riverbanks and some will even grow in swampy, salty soils.

CULTIVATION Alders enjoy moist, cool soils. Propagate from seed dried in fall and sown in spring. Alternatively, propagate from hardwood cuttings taken in winter and rooted in a garden frame. Large specimens will withstand heavy pruning and can be transplanted during the dormant winter period.

CLIMATE Zones 2 to 9 depending on the species.

SPECIES *A. cordata*, Italian alder, zone 6, is a pyramid-shaped tree which grows to 9 m (30 ft).

ABOVE Woody female cones and slender male catkins are decorative features of the common alder, *Alnus glutinosa*, which enjoys moist soils.

Alocasia (fam. Araceae)

Originating from tropical Asia, the name was adapted from colocasia, or taro, the well-known tropical food. Alocasias have spectacular arrow-shaped foliage, sometimes silvery in color, with prominent green veins. They make superb indoor plants. The sap may cause problems for people with sensitive skin. They are known by various common names, including elephant's ears.

CULTIVATION Outside the tropics, alocasias are grown in a warm humid greenhouse or conservatory. Grow them in pots of humus-rich compost and provide medium light levels. Outdoors grow in a shady spot in humus-rich but well-drained soil. Propagate by division in spring.

CLIMATE Warm subtropics to tropics.

SPECIES *A.* x *argyraea* has dark green leaves with a silver sheen and shiny reddish brown

BELOW *Alocasia plumbea* is variable in habit with either dark olive green (as here) or purple-flushed leaves. It is a tall plant, 4–5 m (13–16 ft) in height.

Its shiny, heart-shaped leaves are like those of the silver birch, and the seed pods are like small pine cones. *A. glutinosa*, common or black alder, zone 3, can reach a height of 20 m (65 ft). Young growth is sticky and resistant to cold. The male catkins are yellow and the female ones are tiny and upright. The timber of this European species was traditionally used to make clogs and to bind river banks. Cultivars with different leaf colors and shapes can be obtained. *A. incana*, gray alder, zone 2, grows to 15 m (50 ft) and is suitable for very wet conditions. The leaves are green on top and grayish on the underside. 'Aurea', golden alder, has pretty yellow shoots and leaves. In the winter the bare stems are an orange-yellow color. *A. rubra*, the American red alder, zone 5, is a fast grower and reaches a height of 22 m (70 ft). In the spring it produces reddish pendulous catkins. The bark is gray-white. It is a good specimen for coastal planting and it is adaptable to both infertile and moist soils. *A. tenuifolia*, mountain alder, suitable for zone 2, is a native of North America. It has oval-shaped leaves and grows to 9 m (30 ft).

undersides. It grows to 60 cm (24 in). *A. cuprea*, giant caladium, has 45 cm (18 in) long leaves which are purple on the underneath and dark green on top. *A. macrorrhiza*, giant taro, is cultivated in many tropical countries for its edible rhizome and shoots. It can grow to over 4 m (13 ft) tall in tropical zones. It has a wide natural distribution from India, through Malaysia, and across to Papua New Guinea and northern Australia. *A. odora*, sweet alocasia, has fragrant flowers, similar to a greenish calla lily, and large, deep green, arrow-shaped leaves. It grows to a height of 1 m (3 ft). *A. zebrina* grows to over 1 m (3 ft), with 20–30 cm (8–12 in) leaves on long stalks and zebra-like markings in pale green and black.

Aloe (fam. Aloaceae)

This genus of succulents is native to Africa. Some species have also become naturalized in other parts of the world such as the Mediterranean and eastern India. Many of the species have been used medicinally for over 2000 years. Today, several species are still used in medicines and also in cosmetics. There are

BELOW *Aloe vera* is easily grown in the ground or in containers. It has been used medicinally for centuries in the Mediterranean and Arabia.

ABOVE *Aloe arborescens* displays tapering, torch-like flowers above gray-green rosettes of spiny foliage.

about 300 known species, as well as many natural hybrids and cultivars. They range widely in habit from large trees down to creepers and tiny stemless plants. The leaves are usually arranged in rosettes and are mostly very fleshy. They contain a clear, thick, bitter sap. Attractive cylindrical flowers in pink, yellow and shades of red appear in summer or fall in long-stemmed sprays. Most are self-sterile.

CULTIVATION In frost-prone climates, aloes are grown in a cool greenhouse or conservatory, or as house plants, but they can be placed outdoors for the summer if desired. They are grown outdoors in relatively frost-free regions such as southern California. In pots under glass, plants need a well-drained, gritty potting compost and full light. Give very little water when plants are dormant. Outdoors, plant in a well-drained, sandy, moderately rich soil in a place that receives the morning sun and some shade. Propagate from offsets or seed in spring or summer.

CLIMATE Zone 9 and above.

SPECIES Most of the species described below are from South Africa, unless otherwise mentioned.

A. arborescens, a well-known, popular species, has become naturalized in many countries. It has a shrubby habit, dense rosettes of fleshy, toothed leaves and red flowers. This species is both salt- and drought-resistant. *A. aristata* is a small, stemless rosette of dark green leaves, with bands of white tubercles across both surfaces, serrated margins and spikes at the tips. It produces orange-red flowers and offsets from the base. *A. distans*, a sprawling plant, which branches from the base, has small, triangular, sharp-pointed leaves, with warty spines and yellow teeth along the margins, and red flowers. *A. ferox* is rather striking. The dense rosette is comprised of toothed, lance-shaped leaves, irregularly spined in reddish brown on both surfaces. The vivid scarlet-orange blooms appear in summer on erect, closely packed spikes. *A. polyphylla* is quite a rare species and highly sought after. Almost stemless, the rosettes comprise numerous leaves arranged in ascending, spiralling rows. Under cultivation, the plant generally loses its spirals and grows flat. The flowers are green with purple tips. *A. saponaria* forms a stemless rosette. The leaves are marked with white and toothed in brownish yellow on the margins. Pinkish coral flowers appear on tall, branched stems. *A. variegata*, partridge breast, is a stemless, thicket-forming species, with terminal clusters of flesh pink blooms. The green leaves are heavily marked with white. It offsets from the base. *A. vera* (syn. *A. barbadensis*) from the Mediterranean is widely cultivated, especially in the Caribbean, for the juice from its leaves which is used extensively in cosmetics. The juice also has possible medical applications. *A. vera* grows 30–50 cm (12–20 in) and has yellow flowers.

Alonsoa (fam. Scrophulariaceae)
Mask flower

This genus of about 12 species of evergreen shrubs, subshrubs and perennials, native to Peru, is gradually becoming more widely grown. They have small leaves on erect stems and trumpet-like flowers in the summer and

ABOVE The scarlet flowers of *Alonsoa warscewiczii* appear over a long period in summer and fall. There is a pretty salmon pink cultivar too.

fall. The flowers are quite curious, for the trumpet appears to be twisted upside down. In frost-prone climates alonsoas are mainly used as annuals for summer bedding.

CULTIVATION For summer bedding plants, sow seed in spring in heat under glass and plant out when frosts are over. Provide a position in full sun.

CLIMATE Grow in frost-free areas; zone 10.

SPECIES *A. warscewiczii* is a multi-branched upright perennial, which grows to 30–90 cm (12–36 in). The flowers are in shades of orange through to red and bloom from summer to fall.

Alphitonia (fam. Rhamnaceae)
Red ash

Native to the east coast rainforests of Australia, as well as to the Philippines and Malaysia, this genus comprises five or six species, one of which is occasionally grown.

ABOVE The shining green leaves of the red ash, *Alphitonia excelsa*, are gray on their undersides. Pale green berries turn black at maturity.

ABOVE Easy to cultivate, *Alpinia purpurata* has brilliant red bracts which provide long-lasting color in warm-climate gardens or under glass.

CULTIVATION Red ash must be grown under glass in frost-prone climates. In the right climate it is easily grown, requiring only a well-drained soil. It is drought-resistant.

CLIMATE Can be grown in frost-free areas. Suitable for zones 9 and 10.

SPECIES *A. excelsa*, an evergreen, has smooth, broad, oval, olive-green leaves, with a silvery undersurface, forming a fairly dense crown. It produces small, cream-colored, perfumed flowers and dull, blue-black berries. It grows to a maximum height of 15 m (50 ft).

Alpinia (fam. Zingiberaceae)
Ginger lily

This is a genus of about 250 species native to warm humid areas of Southeast Asia, China, India and Australia. All are evergreen perennials growing from rhizomes with a light ginger scent. These plants need room to spread as many are fairly vigorous. Upright cane-like stems vary with species, but may be up to 3 m (10 ft). Broad, lance-shaped leaves are carried up the stems.

CULTIVATION In frost-prone climates grow these plants in a warm greenhouse or conservatory with high humidity and bright light, in a soil-based potting compost. Outdoors grow in a warm sheltered area in well-drained soil, heavily enriched with organic matter. They need ample water during the warmer months. Clumps can be lifted and divided in late winter to early spring.

CLIMATE These plants are suitable for zone 10 and above.

SPECIES *A. calcarata*, Indian ginger, grows over 1 m (3 ft) high. The lower petals of the yellow flowers are attractively marked with deep red or magenta. They bloom during summer. *A. purpurata*, red ginger blossom, is a vigorous grower to 3 m (10 ft) or so. The true flowers are white but these are totally overshadowed by the showy, bright red bracts.

Alstroemeria (fam. Alstroemeriaceae)
Peruvian lily

This genus of large, showy perennials originates from South America, mostly from

ABOVE A bright scarlet Alstroemeria makes a vivid splash of color in the garden and a delightful cut flower.

BELOW Pink Alstroemeria is very popular as a long-lasting cut flower.

Chile. They come in colors of red, yellow and purple and have thick, fibrous rootstocks. Peruvian lilies have been extensively selected and hybridized by commercial flower growers.

CULTIVATION These plants do well in mild gardens in a sunny, moist, but well-drained spot, provided they are protected from frost during their first winter. Once established, they will thrive for years. Peruvian lilies are best bought as established pot-plants because they

do not like their roots being disturbed. They can be propagated from seed sown in situ or by carefully breaking the seed pods to avoid damage to the brittle roots. Plant 12 cm (5 in) deep in rich soil. Clumps can be divided, with care, in fall or spring. These attractive lilies make wonderful cut flowers.

CLIMATE Plants can be grown in zones 8 or 9 depending on species.

SPECIES *A. aurea* is the most common and hardiest of the species, growing to 1 m (3 ft). The leaves are twisted, narrow and lance-shaped and the flowers are yellow, red to bright orange, or spotted brown. Cultivars are available. The herb lily, *A. haemantha*, zone 9, has reddish yellow, green-tipped flowers, spotted with purple. *A. ligtu*, from Chile and Argentina, produces flowers from white through lavender to pink and red. Hybrids of this species are amongst the most popular.

Alternanthera (fam. Amaranthaceae)

Copperleaf

There are about 200 species in this genus of annuals and perennials, mainly native to tropical and warm regions of the Americas. Some species are considered weeds, some are edible and some are grown ornamentally for their colorful foliage. The flowers of many species are insignificant. The ornamental species are used in summer bedding schemes and as edging plants. Several of the perennial species are grown as annuals in cooler climates for seasonal summer color.

CULTIVATION Grow all species in full sun in well-drained soil enriched with organic matter. Plant out after frost. Water regularly to establish and give deep soakings during hot, dry periods. If growing these plants on poor soils, apply blood and bone or pelletted poultry manure in spring to encourage more vigorous growth. Low-growing types used as edging plants can be clipped over if they become leggy or straggly. This maintains tight, compact growth.

ABOVE This small-leaved *Alternanthera* has bronze and pinky red foliage. It can be used as a border for annuals or for carpet bedding.

ABOVE *Althaea officinalis*, the marsh mallow, is now regaining some of its former popularity and is recommended for cottage and English-style gardens.

CLIMATE Zone 10 and above.

SPECIES *A. dentata* 'Rubiginosa' is a shrubby plant, growing between 30 and 60 cm (12–24 in) high. It is valued for its striking, dark reddish purple, almost black, foliage and is most often used in bedding schemes or for strong foliage contrast. It was popular in Victorian bedding schemes and is creating interest again today. *A. ficoidea* is a small-leaved perennial that grows 20–30 cm (8–12 in) high if it is left unclipped. The foliage is mid-green and the various cultivars are patterned in combinations of red, orange, yellow and purple colors. 'Amoena' is a dwarf form, which is rarely more than 5–8 cm (2–3 in) in height. *A. philoxeroides*, which is known as alligator weed, is a very serious weed of waterways, especially in warm regions where its spread is extremely rapid.

Althaea (fam. Malvaceae)
Marsh mallow

The name derives from the Greek, meaning 'to cure', as the roots, leaves and flowers were once used as medicines. Native to Europe, the marsh mallow has spread to many parts of the world. Once considered rather old-fashioned, the marsh mallow is now enjoying renewed popularity with the increasing interest in cottage-style gardening. However, plants are susceptible to rust disease and also damage from flea beetles.

CULTIVATION This plant likes a deep, well-manured garden bed, plenty of water and a sunny position. Drainage must be excellent. Stake plants firmly or grow them against a wall for protection from wind. Cut stems to within 10 cm (4 in) of the ground after flowering. Sow seed in summer in an outdoor nursery bed and transplant seedlings in fall into their flowering positions. Place crowns 4–5 cm (1½–2 in) below the soil level, and plant in groups to achieve maximum effect.

CLIMATE Extremely hardy; can be grown in zone 3 and above.

SPECIES *A. officinalis*, the marsh mallow, a native of the European marshes, produces pink flowers in summer. Cultivars with double or single flowers are available.

Alyogyne (fam. Malvaceae)

This is a small group of shrubs which originate from the warmer parts of Western Australia, South Australia and the Northern Territory. Often found in hot, sandy, coastal regions, they have soft, lobed leaves and single, hibiscus-like flowers in white, yellow, pink, mauve or purple, sometimes with red centers. They bloom abundantly from spring to summer.

CULTIVATION In frost-prone climates grow in pots of soil-based potting compost in a cool greenhouse or conservatory. Plants can be stood outside for the summer. Although adaptable, alyogyne prefers a semi-shaded position and moist, well-drained soil. All species like slow-release fertilizers. Propagate from seed if available, or from cuttings of firm shoots. Plant seed or cuttings in a mix of coarse sand and peat or vermiculite in a ratio of 3:1. *A. huegelii* can be espaliered successfully and responds well to light pruning.

CLIMATE Suitable for growing outside in zone 10 and above.

SPECIES *A. hakeifolia* grows to 3 m (10 ft) in height and has mauve or yellow-cream flowers.

A. huegelii (syn. *Hibiscus huegelii*), lilac hibiscus, is a native of Western Australia. This semi-deciduous, desert shrub grows to a height of 2–3 m (6–10 ft) and flowers in summer. The largish, single blooms are a beautiful shade of lilac or pink, with dark red centers, and the soft, lobed leaves are mid-green, with irregularly toothed margins. Good purple-flowering forms are also available. It is seen to best advantage when mass planted or used as a hedge.

Amaranthus (fam. Amaranthaceae)
Molten torch

There are 60 species of *Amaranthus*, all annuals, occurring in both tropical and temperate regions. Some are grown for their beautiful colors, unusual flowers and adaptability to hot conditions. In frost-prone climates they are used for summer bedding, or grown as pot plants in a cool to warm greenhouse or conservatory. These showy plants look superb as the centerpiece of circular garden beds.

CULTIVATION Sow seed under glass in spring, in a warm propagating case, and plant out young

ABOVE In frost-prone climates, *Alyogyne huegelii* is an ideal shrub for the cool greenhouse or conservatory.

ABOVE *Amaranthus caudatus* is a tall-growing, summer-flowering annual.

plants when danger of frost is over, spacing them 50 cm (20 in) apart each way. They like a fertile, well-drained soil rich in humus. Water plants regularly during dry periods in summer. Mulch during hot weather. A liquid manure can be used later to ensure an attractive display. Tall varieties may need protection from wind.

CLIMATE Can be grown outside all year round in zone 10 and above.

SPECIES *A. caudatus*, love-lies-bleeding or tassel flower, is a tall, branching annual growing 1 m (3 ft) or more. It has pale green, oval leaves and drooping, tail-like, dark red flowers. *A. hypochondriachus* 'Erythrostachys', Prince's feather, resembles *A. caudatus*, but it tends to grow taller and the erect flowers are a deeper dull crimson. *A. tricolor*, Joseph's coat, is another tall species, with brilliantly variegated leaves in purple, red, green and yellow. Cultivar 'Splendens', fountain plant, also grows to 1 m (3 ft) or more. The leaves are generally dark purplish red, with a crown of lighter rosy red upper leaves.

BELOW The colorful foliage of *Amaranthus tricolor* needs no flowers to put on a dazzling show.

Amaryllis (fam. Amaryllidaceae)
Belladonna lily

This genus was named for Amaryllis, a shepherdess in Greek mythology. *A. belladonna*, literally 'beautiful lady', is the only true *Amaryllis*.

CULTIVATION These bulbs are generally planted in late summer, although early spring planting is also acceptable. Place in a sunny position in well-drained soil, with the tops of the bulbs just above the surface of the soil. Water well during the growth period. Once established, the bulbs can be divided during spring when the plant is dormant. However, do not divide too often as bulbs that are rather crowded tend to flower better.

CLIMATE Zone 8 and above.

SPECIES *A. belladonna*, native to South Africa, is not just beautiful but also easy to grow. It has glorious, trumpet-shaped, rose-pink, perfumed flowers in fall and grows up to 45 cm (18 in) in height. The strap-like leaves appear after the flowers. There are various other color forms, ranging from white to purple, which are hybrids or selected forms.

BELOW The lovely flowers of *Amaryllis belladonna* can be cut for indoor decoration but give better value left in the garden.

Amelanchier (fam. Rosaceae)

Shadbush, juneberry

The species in this genus are native to North America, Europe and Asia and are almost essential garden plants. Small, very hardy, deciduous trees or shrubs, amelanchiers have a short flowering period, followed by edible roundish blue-black berries, and the most superb fall foliage. They can withstand very cold and dry conditions.

CULTIVATION Amelanchiers thrive in lime-free (acid), fertile, moisture-retentive soil and will take full sun or partial shade. They can be propagated from seed sown as soon as ripe in an outdoor seed bed, or from semi-ripe cuttings in summer.

CLIMATE Amelanchiers prefer a cool, moist climate.

SPECIES *A. canadensis*, shad bush, service berry or June berry, zone 4, is a neat, erect tree which grows to 8 m (26 ft). In spring the foliage is a downy bronze and in fall it is a rich orange-yellow. Drooping sprays of lacy white flowers cover the whole tree in spring. *A. x grandiflora*, zone 4, is a spreading tree to about 8 m (26 ft) high. It has several notable cultivars, all showing either superior fall color or abundant spring blossom. *A. laevis*, zone 5, is similar to *A. canadensis* but it has larger flowers. The new foliage is pinkish and the fall leaves are a deep, rich red color. *A. lamarckii*, zone 4, grows to less than 10 m (33 ft). This species has become naturalized in parts of Europe.

Amherstia (fam. Caesalpinaceae)

Pride of Burma, orchid tree

A monotypic genus, that is with only one species, this magnificent tree is native to Burma, though it is becoming very rare in its natural habitat of tropical forest.

CULTIVATION Outside the tropics this tree can be grown in a pot or tub of soil-based potting compost in a warm greenhouse with high humidity and bright light. In such conditions it rarely flowers. Outdoors it needs well-drained, deep, fertile soil and an abundant supply of water throughout the growing season. Mulching with organic matter is also beneficial. It is usually propagated from semi-ripe cuttings, with bottom heat and misting, or alternatively by layering. The seed is not always fertile, but this would be the simplest method if it was possible to obtain good seed.

ABOVE Those who have seen this tree, *Amherstia nobilis*, in flower describe it as one of the world's loveliest. Flowers hang in graceful clusters.

ABOVE Vivid red fall color is a feature of *Amelanchier* species, small decorative trees native to North America.

CLIMATE Can be grown outdoors only in warm humid to hot tropical climates; elsewhere Amherstia should be grown under glass.

SPECIES *A. nobilis*, pride of Burma or orchid tree, is a fast-growing evergreen, to 12 m (40 ft) or more in humid tropical climates. The leaves are very long and consist of numerous small leaflets, giving a lacy, graceful effect. The unusual flowers are bright red, shaded with pink. Thought to resemble orchids, these hang in long clusters.

Ammobium (fam. Asteraceae)
White paper daisy, winged everlasting

Belonging to the paper daisy clan, *Ammobium* is native to the tablelands of south-eastern Australia. This hardy perennial, usually grown as an annual, forms quite a large clump. The flowers are like paper daisies, smallish and white, with yellow centers, and the leaves are a silvery gray.

CULTIVATION This plant is suitable for both pots and garden, but looks best sown in informal drifts. Plant in a light garden soil in a sunny position. Raise plants from seed sown in spring in situ. Alternatively sow seed in trays under glass in well-drained seed compost, prick out seedlings into further trays and plant out in late spring or early summer, when frosts are over.

CLIMATE Zone 9 and above.

SPECIES *A. alatum* grows to a height of 1 m (3 ft). The foliage forms a basal rosette of soft, grayish, woolly leaves and the shining white and yellow flowers, up to 2 cm (1 in) in diameter, bloom abundantly in summer. The flowers are suitable for dried arrangements as they retain their true color if cut before the bracts are fully open and hung in bunches upside down in a shady, airy spot to dry.

Ampelopsis (fam. Vitaceae)

Many species from this genus are now classified with *Parthenocissus* or *Vitis*. These two species of climbing plants have deciduous, grape-like, lobed leaves, often coloring beautifully in fall. The small, insignificant flowers are followed by bunches of small, round berries.

CULTIVATION *Ampelopsis* makes a pretty, delicate covering for arches, lattice, wrought iron and small houses. It prefers a well-mulched light soil, containing plenty of well-

BELOW The small purplish berries of *Ampelopsis brevipedunculata* will mature in time to a clear blue.

ABOVE One of many species known as paper or everlasting daisies, *Ammobium alatum* is a low-growing perennial with silvery leaves.

rotted organic matter, and filtered sunlight. Protection from drying winds is essential. Propagate from hardwood cuttings in fall or winter or from seed if available. It also layers easily.

CLIMATE Zone 5 and above.

SPECIES *A. aconitifolia*, comes from Mongolia and is far less common in cultivation. Its small greenish flowers are succeeded by orange berries. *A. brevipedunculata* originates from Asia. It has twisting tendrils, pink new growth and lobed green leaves. The foliage colors well in fall and the berries change to a bright blue color when ripe.

Anchusa (fam. Boraginaceae)
Bugloss, alkanet

Found naturally in Europe, western Asia and northern and southern Africa, this genus comprises both annuals and perennials which make very pretty borders and container plants. Most species have gray-green hairy leaves and small blue flowers.

CULTIVATION Plant in well-drained garden soil in full sun. Anchusas are often self-seeding, but can also be propagated by division or root cuttings if true types are required.

CLIMATE Very hardy; suitable for zone 3 and above.

SPECIES *A. azurea* is a hardy perennial with large, coarse, hairy leaves and hundreds of small, round, brilliant blue flowers during the early summer. It grows to 1 m (3 ft). Cultivars, such as 'Loddon Royalist' and 'Morning Glory' produce flowers in various shades of blue, from pale to a very rich deep blue.

Androsace (fam. Primulaceae)
Rock jasmine

There are over 100 species of these small plants native to temperate areas of the northern hemisphere. These delicate, evergreen perennials are suitable only for cool regions. Commonly grown in rock gardens, they have tiny primula-like flowers. Many rock jasmines form mounds or cushions of growth.

CULTIVATION Plant in a well-drained, gritty soil, or scree, in full sun. In winter, the soil can be allowed to dry out before watering and the foliage must be kept dry. Propagate from cuttings taken in spring or by dividing the clumps.

BELOW Few perennials provide a better display of clear blue flowers during early summer than the bugloss, *Anchusa azurea.*

BELOW Ideal for edging or ground covering, *Androsace lanuginosa* spills over onto paving from its garden bed.

CLIMATE Very hardy; suited to zones 3 to 6.

SPECIES *A. lanuginosa*, zone 6, native to the Himalayas, is a low trailing plant, with rosettes of silvery gray leaves and tight heads of pale pink flowers in mid to late summer. It grows to about 15 cm (6 in) high. *A. pubescens*, zone 5, from the Pyrenees, is a cushion-forming, small species rarely growing more than 6–8 cm (2½–3 in) high. White flowers with a green or yellow eye appear in late spring to early summer. *A. sarmentosa*, zone 3, forms mats of hairy rosettes, with heads of pale pink flowers on short stems. It grows to about 8 cm (3 in) high, with a spread of some 25 cm (10 in).

Anemone (fam. Ranunculaceae)

Of the 120 species in this genus, quite a wide range is grown in American gardens. Many are native to Europe and western Asia, but there are species native to Japan, the Americas and most areas of the northern temperate zone. This genus contains herbaceous perennials as well as tuberous types.

CULTIVATION Spring-flowering anemones should be planted out in late summer to early fall, the tuberous types with their pointed ends down. Plant where they are to grow as they do not transplant well. Woodland anemones will grow in shade, but *A. coronaria* should be given plenty of sun and shelter from wind. *A. hupehensis* prefers partial shade and shelter from strong winds. It can be transplanted in late winter or early spring. All anemones prefer well-drained soil containing plenty of organic matter. Overly wet or poorly drained soil will rot the roots or tubers. Once vigorous growth is established, water regularly and apply fertilizer as the buds begin to form.

CLIMATE Anemones can be grown in zones 5 to 8.

SPECIES Best known to gardeners is probably the spring-flowering *A. coronaria*, zone 8. It is also widely grown for the cut flower market. Flower colors include white, red, pink, blue and

ABOVE The rich colors of double forms of *Anemone coronaria* give equal pleasure in the garden and the vase.

purple. The most popular strains are the De Caen Group with single flowers, and St Brigid Group with double flowers. The woodland anemones, *A. blanda* and *A. nemorosa*, grow in cooler zones, often becoming naturalized under trees which suits their woodland origin. They are also spring flowering. The Japanese windflower, *A. hupehensis*, is a tall-growing

BELOW A pale pink form of the fall-flowering *Anemone hupehensis*, a reliable flowerer year after year.

perennial, often reaching more than 1 m (3 ft) in height. This flowers in fall, with single- or double-flowered forms in white, pink and lavender pink. Although deemed to be invasive by some growers, it is easily controlled. Numerous other species are grown in American gardens, and are worth looking out for.

Angelica

(*Angelica archangelica*, fam. Apiaceae)

There are about 50 species of angelica, few of which are commonly cultivated. These perennial herbs provide bold contrast when grown in a mixed border, but are mostly grown for commercial use. Aromatic oil from the roots and leaves is used for flavoring liqueurs and the young shoots are candied for decorating confectionery. Fresh leaves are also used in salads. *Angelica archangelica* has large, deeply divided, bright green leaves and clusters of green-yellow flowers in summer. It grows to around 1.5 m (5 ft) in height.

CULTIVATION Angelica will thrive in any well-drained, manured garden soil, providing there is plenty of moisture and morning sun. Propagate from seed in late summer. These plants can also be increased by division.

ABOVE Angelica is grown for its ornamental foliage and imposing inflorescence, as well as for its culinary use.

CLIMATE Angelica can be grown in zone 4 and above.

Angiopteris (fam. Marattiaceae)
Giant fern, king fern

This genus of very large tropical ferns appears to be quite ancient as fossil remains of similar fronds date as far back as the Palaeozoic era. One of the many species of this genus, *A. evecta*, is native to Australia's tropical Queensland, tropical Asia and the western Pacific. All species have fleshy stalks and coarse, thick fronds.

CULTIVATION Outside the tropics or subtropics Angiopteris should be grown in a tropical greenhouse. This handsome fern makes a very good specimen plant. It is usually quite easily grown from the dormant buds contained in the fleshy scales which are found at the base of the fronds. Pot the buds in a mix of sand and peat. Growth should be visible within 12 months. In terms of feeding, the soil must contain plenty of decayed organic matter so

ABOVE Needing plenty of room to spread, *Angiopteris evecta* is an imposing fern to feature in a warm, humid greenhouse.

that it can retain some moisture at all times.

CLIMATE Suitable for gardens in zone 10 and above.

SPECIES *A. evecta*, giant or king fern, is huge, with a thick, woody trunk up to 1 m (3 ft) in diameter in very old specimens and arching fronds up to 5 m (16 ft) in length. The bipinnate fronds are glossy green and the upright stipes are swollen at the base. This is a very attractive feature plant when care is taken to make sure it is well grown.

Angophora (fam. Myrtaceae)
Apple myrtle

There are around 13 species of angophoras, all native to the sandstone areas along the east coast of Australia. While angophoras appear similar to eucalypts, they are distinguishable by differences in their growth patterns and in the color and texture of their bark. In addition, eucalypts mostly have smooth fruit capsules, while the fruit capsules of the angophora are ridged. The flowers are similar, except that the eucalypt bud has a cap or operculum. When young, the differences are scarcely visible. With their lovely, spreading foliage, angophoras are useful shade trees for the

ABOVE The massed heads of creamy flowers of *Angophora hispida* appear in the summer.

ABOVE Pinky gray contorted branches are one of the most outstanding features of the Sydney red gum, *Angophora costata*.

garden. They may also attract lots of birds when they are grown outdoors.

CULTIVATION In frost-prone climates angophoras can be grown in a cool greenhouse in full light. Grow them in pots or tubs of well-drained, soil-based potting compost. Outdoors, these plants are adaptable and do best in light, well-drained soils. The seeds ripen in the capsules in fall and are prone to insect damage while they are on the tree. Collect seeds before they fall. They will germinate readily in a damp mix of sharp sand and peat at the rate of 3:1. Young plants should be kept moist.

CLIMATE Grow outdoors in zones 9 and 10.

SPECIES *A. bakeri* has a spreading, sometimes gnarled, growth pattern. The bark is quite rough, the leaves are narrow, the cream flowers bloom profusely and the fruit capsules are rounded in shape. It grows 8 m (26 ft) in height. *A. costata*, smooth-barked apple, is an elegant tree, with a superb pinkish white trunk, clusters of small, cream-colored flowers in spring and summer, and bell-shaped fruit capsules. It grows to 10–25 m (33–80 ft). Also commonly known as Sydney red gum, it is the dominant species in much of the sandstone areas of greater Sydney and further afield. *A. floribunda*, roughbarked apple, has bright green foliage, white-cream flowers with tiny petals and oval fruit capsules. It, too, has a spreading, gnarled growth pattern and reaches a height of 10 m (33 ft). *A. hispida*, a quite shrubby dwarf species, has a maximum height of around 3 m (10 ft). It has relatively large, heart-shaped leaves with wavy edges. The young growth is clothed in red bristles and the summer flowers are large and creamy white. *A. subvelutina* (syn. *A. intermedia*) grows to a height of 7 m (23 ft). It has broad leaves, two-lobed at the base, clusters of white flowers and velvety, ridged fruit capsules. The young growth is bristly.

Angraecum (fam. Orchidaceae)

This genus comprises about 200 known species, many of which are indigenous to Madagascar. Some of these have very small flowers and are not of great horticultural significance. The remainder are native to tropical Africa and the Seychelles.

CULTIVATION *Angraecum* requires warm glasshouse conditions, heated in winter to at least 15°C (59°F), preferably slightly higher. These plants need high humidity, shade, plenty of water and open compost, with large pieces of charcoal, broken pots and fir bark, to allow water to drain away and to provide good aeration to the roots. The plants should be disturbed as little as possible. The climbing types can be fixed to a tree fern into which the roots will enter. As the upper roots feed the plant, it is necessary to apply liquid fertilizer to

ABOVE Long, pale green spurs or sepals are a special feature of the lovely *Angraecum eburneum* (syn. *A. superbum*), a collector's item.

them. However, the accumulation of fertilizer salts in the tree fern fiber will kill orchids, so thoroughly wash out any excess salts before adding more fertilizer. The species of *Angraecum* usually produce small plants at the base of the stem. These can be grown on, producing specimen plants, or they can be removed when roots have developed and planted out to increase stock.

CLIMATE Angraecum is native to wet tropical climates.

SPECIES *A. eburneum* (syn. *A. superbum*) is a very popular species which can grow to 1.8 m (6 ft) in height. It has greenish white flowers which are 7–10 cm (3–4 in) across, with a spur of about the same length. The lip is white. *A. eichlerianum*, a climbing species, has yellowish green or brownish green flowers, around 7 cm (3 in) across, during spring and summer. The spur measures about 12 cm (5 in) in length. *A. infundibulare* is very similar to *A. eichlerianum*, but the flowers appear during fall and winter. *A. sesquipedale* is a slow-growing species to around 90 cm (36 in). To obtain maximum growth, ensure that there is plenty of light, particularly during the growing period. It is important to encourage leaf growth as the number of flower shoots produced is the same as the number of leaves grown each spring or summer. This orchid has strap-like leaves, white, waxy, star-shaped, winter flowers 12 cm (5 in) across, and a very long spur.

Anigozanthos (fam. Haemodoraceae)
Kangaroo paw

All species of this fascinating plant come from south-west Western Australia. In fact, the striking *A. manglesii* is the floral emblem of Western Australia. A number of species are available in the US, such as *A. manglesii*, *A. flavidus* and some others of the many hybrids that have been produced. Their curious, woolly, paw-shaped flowers bloom over a long period at various times of the year and come in an outstanding range of colors from orange, pink and yellow to various shades of green and red. In the garden, they may attract wildlife. All of the species can be grown as border plants, or as pot plants under glass.

CULTIVATION In frost-prone climates kangaroo paws are grown in pots in a frost-free greenhouse or conservatory. They are best in a compost of loam, leaf mould and coarse sand,

ABOVE The floral emblem of Western Australia, Anigozanthos manglesii, with its tubular flowers opening. The flowers are rich in nectar.

ABOVE Modern hybrids of kangaroo paw make better garden subjects for a wide range of climates than the true species.

and in full light. Outdoors they look their best in groups, among rocks or combined with attractive native grasses. As all species are prone to attack by slugs and snails, use a snail-killing bait regularly. Blackening of the foliage, or ink disease, may be a problem, so do not overwater in warm humid weather or during the summer months. Hybrids that have some resistance to ink disease are now available. Propagate either by seed or by root division in fall, which is more reliable. If using seed, sow in a well-drained, sandy mixture and cover lightly with soil. Germination is generally rapid. If dividing, it is best to pot new divisions until they are re-established. Divide clumped plants at least once every three years. Anigozanthos are well suited to pots or tubs, with good drainage, and can be used for long seasonal display on balconies and patios.

CLIMATE Suitable for growing outdoors in zone 10 and above.

SPECIES *A. bicolor* has greenish yellow spring flowers, with red stems to 45 cm (18 in), and narrow strap-shaped leaves to 30 cm (12 in) long. It can tolerate wet conditions. If the plants are not robust, the foliage will die down in summer. The most commonly cultivated species is *A. flavidus* and extensive hybridization is being carried out, mostly using this hardy species as one parent. It has strappy, 60 cm (24 in) long leaves which form a spreading clump to 1 m (3 ft) across and greenish yellow to reddish flowers that are very attractive to birds. It is a vigorous grower. Cultivar 'Pink Joey' has smaller pink and red flowers and foliage. *A. humilis*, catspaw, is a smaller species which grows to a height of 25 cm (10 in). It has light green foliage and dense terminal clusters of flowers during winter and spring. Colors vary from orange, orange-red and brown-red to various shades of pink and yellow. Colors often combine. This species can become a herbaceous perennial, dying down in summer, and rejuvenating in fall. *A. manglesii*, red and green kangaroo paw, is quite a regal plant, with bright green and red flowers on long stems to 1.5 m (5 ft) and grayish green strap-like leaves which form clumps. The flowers bloom in spring. *A. preissii* has beautiful orange-red flowers in spring and narrow, dark green leaves which die down after flowering. *A. viridis*, green kangaroo paw, has bright, almost iridescent, forest green flowers and narrow leaves to 30 cm (12 in) long. This species can tolerate dampness more than most kangaroo paws. It has a dormant period in summer.

ABOVE Anise or aniseed can be grown in a container. The rounded leaves with serrated margins are quite decorative.

Aniseed (*Pimpinella anisum*, fam. Umbelliferae)

A highly aromatic annual, aniseed has a long history of use as a medicinal herb as well as a culinary and flavoring herb. It was known to the ancient Greeks and Romans who used it as a food additive for its aromatic and digestive qualities. It is also mentioned in the Bible. Aniseed is still used today in medicines, confectionery and for flavoring liqueurs. It is only one species in a genus of about 140 which occur naturally in parts of Africa, Europe and Asia. It generally grows to about 50 cm (20 in) high, with masses of small white flowers.

CULTIVATION Plant in well-drained soil in a warm position. Propagate from seed, sown in early to mid-spring where the plants are to grow.

CLIMATE Most conditions except tropics. Fully hardy.

Anomatheca (fam. Iridaceae)

Of these four species of cormous plants from tropical and South Africa, only one species is cultivated widely. Their growth resembles that of the freesia.

ABOVE Rewarding and trouble-free, *Anomatheca laxa* tolerates a wide range of growing conditions. Unwanted seedlings are easily removed.

CULTIVATION In very cold areas grow in pots in a cool glasshouse. These plants will grow in full sun or partial shade and can tolerate a wide range of soil types. They self-seed, or the corms can be lifted and divided in fall.

CLIMATE Warm zones as far as the subtropics and cool temperate zones. Hardy in cool climates if protected in winter.

SPECIES *A. laxa* (syn. *Lapeirousia laxa*), which is sometimes called scarlet freesia or painted petals, grows to 20 cm (8 in) in height and produces coral red flowers which have darker markings, in the spring. This species has a tendency to self-seed. The white form, 'Alba', is not very vigorous.

Anopterus (fam. Escalloniaceae)

These attractive evergreen Australian shrubs are native to the forests of Tasmania and mountainous areas of New South Wales and Queensland. Both species are good garden ornamentals. The smooth, thick, shiny leaves, narrow at both ends have a leathery appearance. The flowers begin as pink bud clusters, opening to terminal sprays of heavy-textured, cup-shaped, whitish pink flowers to 2 cm (1 in) across.

ABOVE The heavy-textured, white, bell-shaped flowers of *Anopterus glandulosus* are outstanding against the dark leathery leaves.

CULTIVATION Grow in a cool glasshouse in very cold climates. Needs lime-free compost or soil. Provide full light but shade from direct sun. Outdoors grow in cool, moist woodland conditions with partial shade. Propagate from semi-ripe cuttings in the summer. They may be slow to root.

CLIMATE Can be grown outside in zone 8 and above.

SPECIES *A. glandulosus*, Tasmanian laurel, is a large, leafy, sometimes straggly, shrub which grows to 5 m (16 ft) in height. Its dark green, glossy leaves are generally narrow, elliptical and toothed and its waxy, pinkish white, cup-shaped flowers appear in terminal sprays in spring. It needs a shady position and a peaty soil. *A. macleayanus*, a smaller, neat species, has attractive, red-veined foliage and terminal sprays of white flowers.

Anthemis (fam. Asteraceae)

This genus comprises about 100 species native to Europe, the Mediterranean and western Asia. These small, herb-like, perennial plants provide a dazzling display in rockeries and

ABOVE Mass planting of an *Anthemis* cultivar with white flowers. Most varieties have yellow flowers.

borders. They have strongly scented, feathery leaves and single, daisy-like flowers that last well when cut. If they are not allowed to flower, they can also be used to cover dry banks. Some are very vigorous.

CULTIVATION These plants are extremely easy to grow in ordinary, well-drained garden soil if positioned in full sun. Propagate from short tip cuttings at almost any time of the year. Plants can be divided in late winter.

CLIMATE Zone 6 and above.

SPECIES *A. cretica* subsp. *cretica* is a greenish gray cushion of foliage to 25 cm (10 in) high, with white daisy-like flowers 4 cm (1½ in) in diameter. *A. marschalliana* has neat cushions of finely cut silvery leaves to 20 cm (8 in) high and 3 cm (1¼ in) bright yellow flowers on delicate stems. *A. tinctoria*, dyer's chamomile, grows to 50 cm (20 in) in mound-like clumps. Masses of golden flowers appear on stiff stems above the crinkled, fern-like foliage during spring. Cultivars, such as 'Wargrave', provide blooms in varying shades of yellow.

Anthurium (fam. Araceae)

These perennials from tropical America have leaves of various shapes, from elliptical to heart-shaped, and brilliantly colored, glossy, lily-like flowers. They are usually grown indoors, but can be grown outdoors in warmer climates. Anthuriums make superb cut flowers. There are over 700 species of *Anthurium*, both ground growers and epiphytes, though few are in general cultivation.

CULTIVATION Except in warm climates, grow in a warm humid greenhouse with good light but shade from strong sun. Anthurium is best grown in a compost of loam, leaf mould and coarse sand. Water well, making sure that the soil does not become soggy, although the plants should be allowed to dry out somewhat between waterings in winter. Propagate by division in late winter.

ABOVE Anthuriums have brightly colored flowers that look almost artificial. Most are in shades of red or pink.

CLIMATE Grow outdoors in zone 10 and above.

SPECIES *A. andraeanum*, flamingo lily, has deep green leaves, variably heart-shaped, on long stalks. The flowers are unusual, resembling broad, lacquered leaves. From the center, yellow spadices emerge. This species grows to 1 m (3 ft). Cultivar 'Rubrum' is a brilliant red; others are pink, white and orange-red. *A. crystallinum*, crystal anthurium or strap flower, has splendid velvety green foliage with silvery veins and grows 60 cm (24 in) in height. *A. scherzerianum*, flamingo flower or pigtail anthurium, grows to 40 cm (16 in) or more. It has red flowers, spiralled spadices in orange or yellow, and elliptical or narrow leaves.

Antigonon (fam. Polygonaceae)
Coral vine

These fast-growing climbers are excellent for pergolas, trellises or lattice, and also look pretty cascading from the tops of walls. They have simple leaves and long sprays of delicate flowers with heart-shaped petals. The flowers last well when cut.

ABOVE *Antigonon leptopus* will scramble over a large area in one growing season. Hot pink flowers make a great show.

ABOVE *Antirrhinum majus*, or snapdragons, both tall and dwarf forms, have been great favorites for annual displays for many years.

CULTIVATION In cool and cold climates grow in a cool greenhouse or conservatory, in a pot or tub of soil-based compost. Provide full light. Outdoors this plant does best in a sunny, sheltered position. Any soil is suitable, but they do require good drainage and heavy mulching. Water well in spring and summer. Remove spent flower heads and cut out old growth in spring. Propagate from seed or from soft tip cuttings.

CLIMATE Zone 10 and above.

SPECIES *A. leptopus* is a slender, deciduous creeper, the long sprays of bright pink flowers ending in coiling tendrils by which it climbs. It grows to 6 m (20 ft). Although it dies back in winter, it is useful for covering unsightly sheds or fences. Cultivar 'Album' has white flowers.

Antirrhinum (fam. Scrophulariaceae)
Snapdragon

Originating from Europe and North America, these showy annuals and perennials have unusual two-lipped flowers, which give the plants their common name, and narrow leaves. They come in a variety of types: erect, prostrate, tall or dwarf. Snapdragons look their best in massed plantings or borders and make excellent cut flowers.

CULTIVATION They prefer a fertile, well-drained soil and a sunny position. Continuous cutting of the flowers will ensure further crops. Propagate from seed. Single-colored or multi-colored seed selections are available. Some are very susceptible to rust, a fungal disease. Look for varieties which have some resistance.

CLIMATE In frost-prone climates, grown as half-hardy annuals.

SPECIES *A. majus*, snapdragon, forms dense bushes of many upright stems, with long green leaves and the familiar frilly, two-lipped flowers. Hybrids are available in all sizes and colors, and combinations of colors, except true blue.

Aphelandra (fam. Acanthaceae)

Aphelandra comprises around 170 species of shrubs from tropical America, grown mainly for their striking foliage. They have terminal spikes of densely packed flowers surrounded by brightly colored bracts and large, opposite,

ABOVE With its boldly striped leaves, zebra plant (*Aphelandra squarrosa*) is worth growing for the effect of its foliage alone.

often showy, leaves. Some of the species are very popular indoor plants.

CULTIVATION Whether grown as a house plant or in a greenhouse, *Aphelandra* requires warm, humid conditions and a soil-based compost containing leaf mould. Provide full light but shade from strong sun. Give lots of water in the warmer months, but water less in the winter. It is best when grown in a smallish pot as it appears to prefer to be rather pot-bound. Propagate from half-green cuttings from the side shoots.

CLIMATE Grow outdoors only in zone 10 and above.

SPECIES *A. squarrosa*, zebra plant, is a native of South America. It grows upright to 1 m (3 ft), sometimes more. It has large, glossy, dark green leaves, heavily veined in white and pink, and flower spikes of bright golden yellow in spring.

Apple (*Malus domestica*, fam. Rosaceae)

Apples are the most widely cultivated fruit of temperate regions. They are also very ornamental trees for the garden, being lovely in blos-

som, providing shade in summer, bearing delicious, decorative fruit and changing to delightful colors in fall. Apples have been cultivated for at least 3000 years, having been bred and improved from wild crab apples. The earliest domesticated apples were probably introduced to Britain by the Romans who were skilled in grafting and pruning and able to produce superior fruit. The wild crab apples had their origins in Europe and Asia. Over the centuries, a huge range of seedlings were raised, and the best were selected and propagated but generally not recorded. From about the 17th century, varieties were given names which identified the particular fruit with certainty. As America, Australia and New Zealand were settled, new seedlings were raised and the best of these were returned to Britain. There are today over 2000 varieties of apple grown in the Apple Collection of the Brogdale Horticultural Trust in Kent, England, not far from the East Malling Research Station where research on apple rootstocks has led to the widespread use of dwarfing rootstocks all over the world. Apples were popular before refrigeration as they stored well. They were often the only fruit available in winter. They are valued as fresh fruit, and for desserts and jellies, cider-making and unfermented fruit juice.

CULTIVATION Apples for the home garden are usually propagated by budding or grafting on to dwarfing rootstocks such as 'Northern Spy', 'MM 106' and 'M 9'. The 'M' numbers have their origins in East Malling. Without the research conducted there, seedling apples and many varieties would otherwise be too large both for the home garden and the commercial grower who needs trees of manageable size. Apples require cross-pollination for reliable cropping so more than one variety should be planted. Crab apples will often cross-pollinate edible apple varieties too. Plant trees less than 10 m (33 ft) apart to ensure adequate pollination. Trees on 'Northern Spy' or 'MM 106' should be planted only 3–4 m (10–13 ft) apart and those on 'M 9' only 2 m (6 ft) apart. Plant labels should give information on the rootstock

ABOVE An apple tree is an asset in the garden, being both attractive and productive. Fruit should be picked only when fully ripe.

used. Shelter from strong wind helps provide protection for pollinating insects, as well as protecting the blossom from premature shedding and the developing fruits from damage. Trees should be planted in deep, well-drained soil, enriched with manure or compost. Avoid low ground which may be a frost pocket or susceptible to late spring frosts which could ruin the blossom and therefore fruit set. Bare-rooted trees should be planted in late fall or winter, while container-grown trees can be planted out at any time of year. Water trees in well after planting if the soil is dry but do not apply fertilizer at this time. The first fertilizer should be applied in spring following planting. Mulching with well-decayed compost or manure is beneficial at any time. Give trees deep regular watering through the flowering and fruit setting period.

PRUNING AND TRAINING Training and pruning is done in summer and winter and there may be a good deal of this to do in the early years. Older trees may need the removal of some of the oldest wood each year to make way for younger, more fruitful growth. The main pruning season for apples is winter. Most fruits are formed on wood that is two years old or older. Fruit buds are the very plump, round buds rather than the more slender leaf buds. Young trees, however, may have terminal buds on short shoots.

Formerly apples were pruned in a vase shape, but nowadays the central leader system, which produces a pyramidal-shaped tree, is preferred, as this results in a tree with a strong structure and encourages early fruiting. In the long term, there is actually less pruning, though a good deal must be done in the formative years. Trees that are multi-budded, which means they have several varieties on the one stock, must still be vase pruned. The aim of central leader pruning is to develop a tree with three or four layers of branches growing from the central stem or trunk outwards and upwards at an angle of about 30–40 degrees from horizontal. Ideally there should be about four branches in each layer, with a space of about 50 cm (20 in) between layers. This is a simple method of training and pruning. If in doubt, consult a specialist fruit-growing nursery, publications from your Department of Agriculture, or books or brochures written by experts in your area.

Apples should begin cropping by their third season and should continue producing good fruit for about 40 years, and often considerably longer in cool to cold climates. Hand-thinning when the fruit is about marble to cherry size helps in producing regular, reliable crops. Apples should not be harvested all at once as they ripen over several weeks. Fruit picked too early will taste poor and shrivel; fruit picked when too mature will keep poorly. Fully mature fruit can be picked with a slight lift and twist, and should come away from the tree with the stalk intact.

PESTS AND DISEASES Unfortunately, apples are susceptible to attack from a number of insect pests and diseases. Scab and mildew are the two most common diseases, while a condition known as bitter pit is common in some types and during some seasons. Insect pests include apple maggot, the codling moth, fruit fly, woolly apple aphid, scale insects, mites and various moths. Semi-dwarfing rootstocks have some resistance to woolly aphid. In many regions much time and effort is put into the control of these pests and diseases.

CLIMATE Apples grow best in areas with mild summers and cool to cold winters. If the winters are too mild, there will be less blossom and the fruiting will be poor. If the summers are too hot, the fruit may be burnt by the sun and the quality will suffer. Apples are happiest in zones 6 to 8.

VARIETIES It is important to choose cultivars of apple that are suited to your climate. Bear in mind that apples need cool to cold winters so that they can become dormant. Therefore in regions with mild winters they do not take a proper rest as they are not subjected to sufficient winter cold, and consequently they do not perform well. It is best to consult your local nursery or specialist fruit grower for advice on the best cultivars for your area. Among good apple cultivars, 'Delicious', which came to prominence in 1893 as a prize-winning, high quality red apple, is now the world's most widely cultivated apple, especially in warmer regions. It can be cross-pollinated by several varieties including 'Golden Delicious', 'Spartan' and 'Granny Smith'. 'Golden Delicious', a heavy cropper, was introduced in 1916; 'Granny Smith', grown in all the warmer fruit-growing regions, was a chance seedling that first fruited in 1868 in Ryde, New South Wales, Australia, and is used for pollinating many varieties. 'Cox's Orange Pippin', raised in the United Kingdom in 1825, has a rich, sweet flavor. It is the main apple variety grown in England, although it went out of favor for many years because of disease problems. 'McIntosh' was first selected in Canada in 1811 and has been distributed from the 1870s onwards. 'McIntosh' has numerous cultivars and is a very popular variety for cool to cold regions. 'Gravenstein', which is claimed to have

ABOVE This is the popular 'Granny Smith' apple. Pretty white apple blossom will be followed by fruit set

arisen as a seedling in Europe in the 1600s, is widely grown in the US and particularly good for California's north coast. Some good modern dessert cultivars include 'Idared', an apple which is very suited to storage; 'Suntan', another late cultivar, which resembles 'Cox's Orange Pippin'; and the early-maturing 'Discovery' with fairly frost-tolerant blossom and crisp, sweet fruits.

Apricot (*Prunus armeniaca*, fam. Rosaceae)

The genus *Prunus* comprises around 400 species, *P. armeniaca* being the one we know as apricot. A small, perennial, deciduous tree, it is native to temperate Asia and from the plum branch of the rose family. The skin of this oval, orange-colored stone fruit is slightly downy. Apricots ripen in summer, the exact time according to variety.

CULTIVATION Apricot trees like a well-drained, reasonably fertile soil. If planting a number of trees, place 6–7.5 m (20–24 ft) apart in each direction. For lighter soils the apricot can be budded on the seedling of an apricot or peach,

ABOVE Ripening apricots, *Prunus armeniaca*, gradually develop pinkish tones before assuming their rich orange color at maturity.

and for heavier soils it can be budded on the Myrobalan plum. The tree bears fruit on the previous year's wood, as well as on spurs two years and older, so that only light pruning is needed to keep the tree in bounds and to bring on new fruiting wood. Prune in winter to a vase shape to encourage strong leaders, to facilitate picking of the fruit, and to allow in light and air which will help to combat disease. This also allows good development and ripening of fruit on inner branches.

CLIMATE Apricots can be grown in zones 6 to 8 but best results are obtained in zone 9. Widely grown in the California area.

VARIETIES Because there are a number of varieties, it is possible to select several which are suitable for a fairly wide range of areas. Planting different varieties will also guarantee long fruiting seasons. Well-known and widely grown cultivars include 'Alfred' which ripens in mid to late summer but tends to have a biennial cropping habit; the heavy cropping 'Bredase' is a late summer to early fall cultivar; 'Early Moorpark' is another heavy cropper which ripens in midsummer; 'Farmingdale' ripens in midsummer, is heavy cropping and reasonably disease-resistant; 'Hemskirke', ripens in late summer; and the very popular, regular cropping

cultivar 'Moorpark' ripens in late summer. Other good modern cultivars, especially for the north, are 'Earliril', 'Goldcot', 'Moongold', 'Sungold' and 'Veecot'.

Aptenia (fam. Aizoaceae)

This genus of dwarf succulents originating from South Africa produces free-branching sprawlers. The flowers are borne terminally on short stalks in summer and come in white or a pinkish color, through to purple.

CULTIVATION In frosty climates they are bedded out for the summer or planted on rock gardens, and overwintered in a cool greenhouse. Plant in a well-drained, sandy soil in full sun. Propagate from seed or from cuttings.

CLIMATE Suitable for growing outside all year in zones 9 and 10.

SPECIES *A. cordifolia* is a low-growing, mat-forming species to 5 cm (2 in) with shiny, almost heart-shaped, pale leaves and purplish red flowers. *A. c.* 'Variegata' has white markings on the leaves. *A. lancifolia* grows similarly to the others, but has narrow, blunt leaves and pink to white flowers.

BELOW Succulent-leaved *Aptenia cordifolia* adapts well to basket culture and can tolerate some drought without dying.

Aquilegia (fam. Ranunculaceae)
Columbine

The common name for these graceful perennials comes from the Latin for 'dove'. Native to Europe and Asia, they have fern-like foliage and beautiful star-shaped, spurred flowers in interesting colors.

CULTIVATION Columbine likes a well-drained, loose soil and filtered sun. It seeds freely in the garden, but seedling plants may not come true to the parent. If true stock is required, propagate from fresh selected seed and isolate from other varieties. Strong plants may be divided in spring. First year flowers may disappoint in cool areas, but should improve in the next year.

CLIMATE Many thrive in zone 4 and above, including *A. vulgaris*.

SPECIES *A. vulgaris*, granny's bonnets or columbine, is the species from which most garden plants derive. It has lacy, fern-like, blueish green leaves and star-shaped flowers with spurs of varying lengths. From this species has come a great range of hybrids,

ABOVE Modern long-spurred hybrids of *Aquilegia vulgaris* are available in an extensive color range.

including bi-colored, double-centered and long-spurred flowers. There are now columbines in various shades of blue, pink and copper, as well as red and cream. Dwarf forms are also available, flowering in spring or early summer. Many other species and hybrids are grown in cool climates.

Arabis (fam. Brassicaceae)
Rock cress

Native to Europe and Asia, these hardy, low-growing perennials and some annuals are suitable for rock gardens, wall crevices, borders and pebble gardens. They are vigorous growers in cool, moist conditions but easily removed if invasive. They have narrow leaves and profusely blooming small, round flowers.

CULTIVATION Rock cress requires a cool to warm climate. Plant in a well-drained soil in full sun and propagate from offsets from the parent plant in warm weather or from cuttings in early summer.

CLIMATE Some species, including *A. alpina*, are extremely hardy and will tolerate zone 4.

ABOVE This double-flowered aquilegia hybrid has the appearance of an old-fashioned granny's bonnet.

ABOVE *Aralia elata* is cultivated for its fine, decorative foliage. The flowers age to a dull pink before the berries form.

ABOVE The double white form of rock cress resembles its relative, the stock. Flowers have a light scent.

SPECIES *A. alpina* subsp. *caucasica* (syn. *A. albida*) forms a low, spreading mat of oval, gray-green leaves and masses of round white or pink flowers. It grows to 15 cm (6 in). Cultivar 'Flore Pleno' produces double flowers. 'Variegata' grows to 15 cm (6 in), and produces silver variegated leaves.

Aralia (fam. Araliaceae)

This variable genus of deciduous shrubs and small trees originates from Asia and North America. As it belongs to the ivy family, some of the species have a suckering habit. They have attractive, large, compound leaves and terminal clusters of greenish white flowers.

CULTIVATION Aralias do best in warm or cool climates in an enriched soil with lots of mulch to protect the roots. It is important to provide shelter from hot, drying winds. Propagate from seed, with bottom heat, or from root cuttings in winter; this is especially so for variegated cultivars.

CLIMATE *A. elata* is very hardy and can be grown in zone 4.

SPECIES *A. elata*, Japanese angelica, is usually a shrub with horizontal branching but can grow to a medium-sized tree of 8–10 m (26–33 ft). It is generally prickly, with large compound leaves and decorative clusters of tiny white flowers followed by small, round fruits that ripen to black. 'Variegata' is a highly individual specimen tree with leaves which are edged and marked in white.

Araucaria (fam. Araucariaceae)

This remarkable genus of 19 species of evergreen conifers grows naturally only in the southern hemisphere, mostly in New Caledonia, but also in Australia, New Guinea, Norfolk Island and South America. It is from South America that the genus gets its name: from the Araucan Indians of southern Chile, home of the fascinating monkey puzzle tree (*A. araucana*). Most araucarias have a single straight, tall trunk, only occasionally forked, with many small side branches. The leaves of some species curve inward and overlap; in others, they are larger, flatter and spreading. All are sharp-pointed, especially when young. The seed cones vary in size, from 5–6 cm (2–2½ in) to around 25 cm (10 in). Although araucarias are large for home gardens, most make handsome street trees in warm climates.

ABOVE The Norfolk Island pine is grown as a pot plant where the climate is unsuitable for garden cultivation.

CULTIVATION Araucarias prefer deep, moist, well-drained, reasonably fertile soil, and a sunny position, but will grow in a range of soil types. Propagate from seed sown in spring.

CLIMATE There are species suited to various climate zones.

SPECIES *A. araucana*, monkey puzzle, zone 7, is an extraordinary tree, its crowded branches like a tangle of thick, dark green ropes, draped in regular curves. Its common name, in fact, came from the remark that 'it would puzzle a monkey to climb it'. It has stiff, sharp-pointed, overlapping leaves, each up to 5 cm (2 in) long and 2.5 cm (1 in) wide. Cultivated specimens seldom reach more than 20 m (65 ft). It does well in a cool, misty climate, but will not tolerate winter temperatures lower than about –20°C (–4°F). It is the hardiest species and is suitable for cultivation in many parts of the US, where it will eventually grow into a large, stately specimen, dominating the skyline. *A. bidwillii*, bunya-bunya pine, zone 9, is native to the warm-temperate rainforests of Australia's southern Queensland. This species appears to tolerate cooler and drier conditions than the other Australasian species, and it can be grown outside successfully in Mediterranean climates. Long, straight branches extend outwards from the straight trunk, carrying bunches of quite large, dark green, prickly leaves only at the extremities. The bunya-bunya develops into a perfect umbrella shape at the apex, with huge cones resembling a pineapple. *A. columnaris*, New Caledonian pine, zone 10, is similar to *A. heterophylla*, but has shorter, more crowded branches, longest near the top of the tree. The trunk is usually slightly curved. It is rarely planted these days, probably because of the scarcity of seed, although trees between 50 and 100 years old can often be seen in Australia. *A. cunninghamii*, hoop pine, zone 10, is native to New Guinea and the subtropical rainforests of Australia where it is also grown for its timber. Its natural habitats

BELOW Monkey puzzle, *Araucaria araucana*, native to cloud forests of the Chilean Andes and Argentina, is a long-lived tree for cool climates.

range from deep coastal sands to craggy ridge-tops with almost no soil. The hoop pine grows relatively quickly to heights of 30 m (100 ft) or more. It has a straight trunk and upward-pointing branches. The bunches of thick, sombre green foliage are scattered over the crown, producing an unmistakable silhouette. The small, pointed leaves curve inwards, while the younger ones are longer and prickly. The common name refers to the ridges that encircle the trunk as the tree matures. *A. heterophylla*, Norfolk Island pine, zone 10, is a familiar sight on the Australian coast, although mostly known as a pot plant in other parts of the world. It is easily distinguishable from the other species by its pyramidal shape and its whorls of symmetrical branches. It has triangular, scale-like, deep green leaves. Both *A. heterophylla* and *A. bidwillii* are susceptible to attack by the yellow-banded mealy bug. *A. hunsteinii*, klinki pine, zone 10, grows naturally in the New Guinea highlands and shows promise as a quick-growing ornamental in suitable climates. Its foliage is like that of *A. bidwillii*.

ABOVE *Arbutus unedo* is at its prettiest when the bell-shaped flowers appear with the ripe fruits from the previous season.

BELOW Ideal for small gardens, *Arbutus unedo* provides year-round interest with its attractive foliage, flowers, fruit and bark.

Arbutus (fam. Ericaceae)
Strawberry tree

Comprising around 20 species of spreading, evergreen trees, this genus was named for its fruit, which are the size and color of small strawberries. It has attractive, reddish, peeling bark, thick-textured, alternate leaves and white flowers which precede the rather tasteless fruit.

CULTIVATION Arbutus likes reasonably fertile, well-drained soil, but can adapt to a wide range of soils. Plant in a sunny, open position with shelter from coastal winds. Prune only to develop the shape. Propagate from seed sown in spring.

CLIMATE Suitable for zones 7 or 8 and above, depending on species.

SPECIES *A.* x *andrachnoides*, zone 8, from south-eastern Europe and western Asia, is a

small tree which may be spreading or upright, growing to about 8 m (26 ft) high and wide. It has very attractive reddish peeling bark and sprays of white or pink-tinged flowers. It rarely sets fruit. *A. menziesii*, or madrone, zone 7, from the west coast of the United States, grows 15–20 m (50–65 ft) or more in its habitat but is much smaller cultivated. It has white urn-shaped flowers in spring, followed by orange or red fruits. *A. unedo*, zone 8, from southern Europe and Ireland, is a dome-shaped tree with attractive reddish bark used for tanning. In fall the waxy white flowers and orange fruit look very pretty against dark green foliage.

Archidendron (fam. Fabaceae)

Native to coastal eastern Australia, as well as parts of Southeast Asia, these trees are suited to warm, coastal gardens and rarely grown outside their native countries.

CULTIVATION *Archidendron* does well in humid coastal conditions, with some shade. Use a well-composted soil. Cutting back of these trees, particularly mature specimens, is recommended. This is best done in late winter. Propagate from seed collected from the split pods.

CLIMATE Suited to outdoor cultivation in zones 9 and 10.

ABOVE The colorful spiral seed pods of *Archidendron grandiflorum* twist as they mature and split open to reveal shiny seeds.

SPECIES *A. grandiflorum*, laceflower tree, has large, compound leaves, large spring flowers, tipped with crimson, and flattened, spiral seed pods containing shiny black seeds. The flowers are beautiful with a delicious honeysuckle fragrance. This lovely tree grows to 5–9 m (16–30 ft) tall. *A. sapindoides* (syn. *Pithecellobium pruinosum*), snow wood or stink wood, also has large, compound leaves, but its flowers are balls of creamy white tassels and its seed pods orange-red in color. Its common name, stink wood, refers to the offensive smell of its freshly cut wood. This species grows to 6 m (20 ft) in height and in width.

Archontophoenix (fam. Palmae)

This small genus of subtropical palms, native to eastern Australia, grows to about 20 m (65 ft) with smooth, solitary trunks up to 15 cm (6 in) in diameter. The fronds arch gracefully from a smooth green 'crownshaft'. Large sprays of tiny, perfumed flowers are followed by masses of grape-sized red fruit.

CULTIVATION In frost-prone climates, grow under glass. Young plants make good tub plants. These species germinate and develop more quickly than most other palms. They can be grown in most fertile soils, though they require plenty of moisture. Grow in semi-shade until around 5 m (16 ft) tall. Propagate from seed. CLIMATE Suitable for zone 10.

SPECIES *A. alexandrae*, Alexandra palm, is a tropical lowland species occurring naturally in swampy areas of the Queensland coast, north of Rockhampton. This palm can be distinguished by the glistening, silvery hairs on the underside of the fronds and the spreading sprays of cream flowers. *A. cunninghamiana*, Bangalow or piccabeen palm, is found on the subtropical east coast, south of Rockhampton. It grows rapidly when young to heights of 4–5 m (13–16 ft) and ultimately to 20 m (65 ft). It requires shade during the early stages of growth if it is to remain vigorous. It enjoys a cooler climate and can tolerate light frosts. The

ABOVE Bangalow palm, *Archontophoenix cunninghamiana*, bears a cascade of pink to pale violet flowers at the base of the crownshaft.

fronds of the Bangalow palm are green on the undersides and the long sprays of pale violet flowers hang quite vertically.

Arctotis (fam. Asteraceae)

These colorful perennials and annuals come originally from southern Africa and make an excellent groundcover or border plant. The gray foliage is deeply cut and the daisy-like flowers bloom profusely in spring and summer. The colors range from creamy yellow to deep orange to shades of pink, claret and cyclamen. The flowers often feature centers with contrasting shades.

CULTIVATION In frost-prone climates, these plants can be grown as annuals for summer bedding. Plant perennials in a warm, sunny

ABOVE Arctotis does well in hot sunny spots on banks or at the edges of garden beds where it can spread..

position. The annuals grow well in pots in a rich potting mixture, with added sand. Water regularly, decreasing the amount given in winter. Propagate from seed sown in fall for spring flowers and in spring for summer flowering.

CLIMATE These plants are suitable for zone 9 and above.

SPECIES *A. acaulis* is a perennial with orange-red flowers. It can grow to a height of 15 cm (6 in). Hybrid annuals, 30–60 cm (12–24 in) tall, are also available in white and a range of reds. The range which is grouped as *A. x hybrida* is the type most commonly grown.

Ardisia (fam. Myrsinaceae)
Coral berry

This genus of around 250 species is native to tropical and warm areas, including Malaysia and China. These pretty trees and shrubs are often found in Japanese gardens, but are also successful indoors. They have glossy, leathery leaves, small, white or dark pink fragrant flowers and showy, berry-like fruits which sometimes survive for over a year.

ABOVE *Ardisia crenata*, equally at home in the ground and in containers, has handsome foliage and persistent red berries.

CULTIVATION *Ardisia* requires partial shade and a well-drained, humus-rich soil. It does best in a warm, humid climate or in a well-lit room if grown indoors. Collect seed from the plants and sow in spring, or propagate from semi-ripe cuttings in summer.

CLIMATE Zone 10.

SPECIES *A. crenata* comes in single-stemmed forms for potting and multi-stemmed forms for the garden. The wavy-edged, shiny green leaves form layered circles and the fragrant white or deep brownish pink flowers are followed by long-lasting rich red berries. It grows to 1 m (3 ft). This species, often confused with *A. crispa*, is also fairly well known and invariably grown in greenhouses or homes. There is also a white-flowered cultivar named 'Alba'.

Areca (fam. Palmae)

This genus of about 50 species of palms originates from the regions of Malaysia and Melanesia. Many of the species have now been reclassified under other genera, though all are feather-type palms and all have the distinctive 'crownshaft'. The fronds grow to no more than 2 m (6 ft) in length. Smallish sprays of flowers bear egg-shaped fruits in either orange or red.

CULTIVATION In frosty climates, grow as pot plants under warm glass in soilless compost. Outdoors, grow in well-drained soil, heavily enriched with organic matter. Provide shelter from strong wind and water well, especially during spring and summer. Propagate from fresh seed which should germinate within three months with bottom heat.

CLIMATE Zone 10 and above.

SPECIES *A. catechu*, betel palm, is uncommon outside the tropics, although it has become well known for its fruit, the betel nut, widely used for its narcotic properties. This slender, single-stemmed palm grows to 10–15 cm (4–6 in), with relatively few fronds, large, crowded leaflets and orange fruit, about 5 cm (2 in) long. *A. triandra* has green ringed stems, 1.5 m (5 ft) long fronds, with broad leaflets, scarlet fruit, and is a popular ornamental species throughout the tropics.

ABOVE Betel nuts are the fruits of the ornamental palm *Areca catechu* which is native to tropical Asia.

Arenga (fam. Palmae)

This genus is native to Southeast Asia and the islands of the western Pacific, with one species found in northern Queensland. It is closely related to the genus *Caryota*, or fishtail palm. Like *Caryota*, it produces a three-seeded fruit, which is rare among palms. They also flower similarly, producing an inflorescence among the top fronds, followed successively by inflorescences at lower points along the stem. The whole stem then dies. Some *Arenga* species are single-stemmed, which means that the whole plant dies, but most form clumps, with suckers from the base, and these take over, each in turn maturing, flowering and dying.

CULTIVATION In frosty climates, grow as pot plants under warm glass in soilless compost.

ABOVE Ideal as an understorey plant beneath taller trees, *Arenga engleri* produces dense masses of decorative fronds.

Outdoors, grow in well-drained soil containing plenty of organic matter. For best appearance of the fronds, they should be grown with shelter from strong wind. With bottom heat some seeds may germinate within two months, while others may take one year.

CLIMATE Zone 10 and above.

SPECIES *A. australasica*, the Australian native species, has only been cultivated quite recently. It has several stems and long, erect fronds. This species grows very slowly in the initial stages to about 10 m (33 ft) tall and is suitable only for frost-free climates. *A. engleri*, Formosan sugar palm, is a compact, clumping palm which grows to about 2.5 m (8 ft) tall. The hardiest of the species, it has been cultivated as an ornamental. It has fronds of crowded, deep, dull green leaflets and sprays of orange flowers, hidden among the leaves. The flowers have a very strong, sweet, spicy smell and are followed by masses of deep red fruits, the flesh of which is irritating to the skin. *A. pinnata*, sugar palm or gomuti palm, will grow as far south as 35°, provided there is no frost. It acquired its common name, sugar palm, from the sugary syrup that flows from the young inflorescences when cut. It is a huge single-stemmed palm with gigantic fronds, up to almost 10 m (33 ft) long. The trunk is covered in very coarse, stiff, blackish fibers. *A. tremula*, a native of the Philippines, will not tolerate cool conditions as *A. engleri* will. Grown well, it is a handsome palm.

Argyranthemum (fam. Asteraceae)
Marguerite daisy

This shrub is easy to grow, producing daisy-like flowers for long periods if dead flowers are removed regularly. The flowers last well after cutting. Picking them encourages the plant to produce new shoots.

CULTIVATION In frost-prone climates, grow as a summer bedding or patio-tub plant. Plant in any ordinary garden soil in full sun. They will

ABOVE Marguerite daisies are perennial favorites, flowering so profusely that their foliage is all but obscured.

ABOVE Dark purple and white stripes are a characteristic of the hooded flowers of *Arisaema amurense*.

tolerate a little shade, but may become leggy. Propagate from cuttings of the unflowered shoots, 5–8 cm (2–3 in) long, which generally root easily in any season except winter. Prune after flowering if the flowers have not been picked regularly. In warm climates these plants quickly become woody so are best pruned regularly and repropagated every two to three years.

CLIMATE Zones 9 and 10.

SPECIES *A. frutescens* is a bushy, evergreen subshrub, with deeply cut leaves and daisy-like flowers up to 5 cm (2 in) across. It grows to around 1 m (3 ft). Many hybrids have been produced, and they come in a range of colors and forms: white, pink or yellow, single, double or anemone-centered.

Arisaema (fam. Araceae)

These tuberous-rooted perennials from Asia, Africa and eastern North America are unusual woodland plants not grown as widely as they deserve to be. They have interesting hooded flowers, similar to the arum lily, and are often boldly striped.

CULTIVATION Most species will grow in moist, shady areas, but may require a glasshouse in cool zones. Outdoors they should be planted in an average, moist soil. Fertilize occasionally in summer. The glasshouse varieties should be potted in spring in a mixture of peat, leaf mould, loam and sand. Water freely in summer, but cease watering in late fall and keep dry until spring. Propagate from seed sown in spring or by division of the tuberous roots.

CLIMATE Zone 6 for species below, but zone 8 for *A. speciosum*.

SPECIES *A. amurense* produces green hoods in summer and grows to 15 cm (6 in). *A. dracontium* has finely etched leaves, green hoods and a purple-mottled stem. It grows to 60 cm (24 in). *A. speciosum* is greenish purple, with violet flowers in spring, and grows to 30–60 cm (12–24 in).

Aristolochia (fam. Aristolochiaceae)

Dutchman's pipe

These perennial, mostly climbing, shrubs are rapid growers and are useful plants for screens, trellises and pergolas. They have round or heart-shaped leaves and flowers which are unusual more than beautiful. Some species are tender in cool and cold parts of the US and should be grown in a cool or warm greenhouse or conservatory, depending on where they originate.

CULTIVATION Under glass, grow in tubs of soilless compost and in bright light; shade from strong sun. Outdoors, plant in ordinary garden soil. Propagate from seed in spring or semi-ripe cuttings in summer.

CLIMATE Depends on species.

SPECIES *A. macrophyllya* (syn. *A. durior*), zone 6, is a dense, woody twiner, with glossy dark green leaves, either round or kidney-shaped. The purplish or yellow-green flowers have a curious shape, like an old-fashioned tobacco pipe. *A. littoralis* (syn. *A. elegans*), calico flower, zone 9, is also quite widely grown in the US. It has fleshy, heart-shaped leaves and maroon flowers with white markings.

ABOVE With their sombre coloring, *Aristolochia* flowers have a slightly sinister appearance.

Aristotelia (fam. Elaeocarpaceae)

Named for Aristotle, the Greek philosopher, this small genus of evergreen trees and shrubs is, with the exception of one species, native to New Zealand.

CULTIVATION *Aristotelia* needs sheltered conditions, rich soil and a temperate to cool climate. Propagate from cuttings of ripe wood in the fall.

CLIMATE Aristotelia is suitable for zone 8 and above.

SPECIES *A. serrata* (syn. *A. racemosa*), New Zealand wineberry, has simple leaves, rose-colored flowers and edible, dark red berry fruit. It grows to about 5 m (16 ft). It is a good hedging plant and does well in coastal gardens.

ABOVE Generally evergreen, *Aristotelia serrata* may be deciduous in cold climates. Fast-growing, its new foliage is pink.

Armeria (fam. Plumbaginaceae)

Thrift, sea pink

Native to northern temperate regions, these small perennials occur naturally on exposed cliffs, mountains and coastal fringes. They grow well in seaside gardens and are also useful as edging plants.

CULTIVATION Good air circulation and free drainage are essential, otherwise basal rot will occur. Plant in a sandy soil and propagate from seed in fall or semi-ripe cuttings in the summer.
CLIMATE Zone 4 and above for *A. maritima*.

SPECIES *A. maritima*, native to the Mediterranean, is a very old cottage garden plant. The narrow, grayish green leaves form a neat, ball-like mass, and rounded heads of white to deep pink flowers appear on erect stems to 30 cm (12 in) tall. There are numerous cultivars with variously colored flowers.

ABOVE Massed bright pink flowers held on slender stems belie the tough nature of *Armeria maritima*. It thrives in exposed situations.

Arnica (fam. Asteraceae)

Rarely cultivated outside specialized herb gardens, these herbaceous, hardy perennials are from North America, Europe and the East.

CULTIVATION These plants like a sunny location, with an average soil. *A. montana* will not tolerate lime. Propagate by division of the roots in spring. Plant out either in fall or spring.

CLIMATE Very hardy; zones depend on species.

SPECIES *A. angustifolia* subsp. *alpina*, zone 2, grows to 35 cm (14 in) and has bright yellow-orange flowers in summer. *A. chamissonis*, zone 2, has yellow flowers in late summer and grows to 60 cm (24 in). *A. montana*, mountain tobacco, zone 6, grows to 30 cm (12 in), with showy yellow flowers in early summer. There is a long history of use of this species for medicinal purposes.

ABOVE Both the roots and the flowering heads of *Arnica montana* have long been used in preparations of herbal medicines.

Aronia (fam. Rosaceae)

Chokeberry

Because of their brilliant color in fall, these deciduous shrubs from North America make good specimens. They have toothed leaves,

ABOVE Pretty red berries resembling cherries appear on *Aronia arbutifolia* in fall, adding interest to garden displays.

white or pink flowers and masses of glossy red or black berries in late summer and fall.

CULTIVATION Aronia will grow well in part shade, but cool climates and full sun are the conditions which will produce the best fall color and more abundant fruit. They are reasonably adaptable, provided they are planted in light soils with lots of summer mulch. Propagate from seed or sucker.

CLIMATE These shrubs are suitable for zone 6 and above.

SPECIES *A. arbutifolia* has glossy green elliptical leaves, grayish and downy on the undersides, turning deep red in fall. The attractive white flowers are followed by brilliant red berries. This shrub may be too invasive for small gardens as its suckering habit can lead to formation of clumps of 4 m (13 ft) wide or more. It grows to 2–3 m (6–10 ft).

Artemisia (fam. Asteraceae)
Wormwood

From the arid regions of Europe, North America and Asia, these small shrubs and perennials are grown for their attractive, aromatic, silvery foliage. They are useful for borders or large rockeries, and are well suited to coastal gardens. They have feathery leaves and dense clusters of small flowers. Some of the species have medicinal properties, and others are used as herbs in salads and other dishes.

CULTIVATION *Artemisia* is generally easy to grow, but likes light, well-drained soil and a sunny position. It should be pruned by one-third each year to maintain its shape. Propagate from cuttings during the warm weather.

CLIMATE Wide range of conditions.

SPECIES *A. absinthium*, common wormwood, zone 4, has silvery gray dissected leaves and dense yellow flower heads in summer. It grows to 1 m (3 ft). *A. dracunculus*, tarragon, zone 3, grows 50 cm (20 in), with green leaves and greenish white flowers. Pick frequently to maintain a bushy plant. Tarragon is used for flavoring vinegar, meat dishes and salads. *A. lactiflora*, white mugwort, zone 4, is an attractive species from China, with downy, fern-like, aromatic gray leaves, silver on the undersides, and clusters of tiny white flowers in the summer. It grows to 2 m (6 ft) tall. *A. ludoviciana*, white sage, zone 5, grows to 1 m (3 ft), with narrow silvery foliage and white

BELOW The woolly gray-green foliage of *Artemisia pontica* forms a billowing shrub.

ABOVE The highly aromatic foliage of southernwood, *Artemisia abrotanum*, is used in insect repellents as well as for flavoring foods.

flowers. Cultivars of *Artemisia* which make fine garden plants include 'Powis Castle', zone 8, and *A. absinthium* 'Lambrook Silver', zone 4.

Arthropodium (fam. Liliaceae)
New Zealand rock lily

This genus of about 10 species of tufted, herbaceous plants is native to Australia, New Zealand and New Caledonia. They have fibrous, fleshy roots, grass-like leaves and sprays of white or purplish flowers during summer.

CULTIVATION *Arthropodium* likes a warm, temperate climate and does best in a sandy loam in a protected position. Propagate by division, or by seed or suckers in spring.

CLIMATE Zones 8 and 9.

SPECIES *A. candidum*, from New Zealand, has narrow, linear leaves, 15 cm (6 in) long, and white flowers. It grows to about 35 cm (14 in). *A. cirrhatum*, rengarenga or New Zealand rock lily, zone 9, is the species commonly grown. It is larger and stouter than *A. candidum* and is especially suitable for rock gardens. It has fleshy leaves of 60 cm (24 in) long, and branched sprays of white flowers, about 30 cm (12 in) long, in late spring or early summer. It grows to about 1 m (3 ft).

Artichoke, globe

(*Cynara scolymus*, fam. Asteraceae)

In times past this plant from the Mediterranean was thought to be an aphrodisiac. It is, in fact, the true artichoke. A tall perennial, related to the thistle, it has delicate gray-green leaves and immature flower

ABOVE Mass plantings of *Arthropodium cirrhatum* make a decorative display in a mixed border or when used to define a path.

ABOVE The rounded flower buds of this globe artichoke, *Cynara scolymus*, are ready for harvest while they are young and tender.

heads. It will crop year after year in summer and is enjoyed as a vegetable throughout much of the US. It is also a very decorative plant.

CULTIVATION Artichokes like a light, rich sandy loam and a sunny position protected from heavy frost. Some wind protection is also desirable. Water well during the growing season and use a complete fertilizer with plenty of potash. Weed control is a must. Seed should be sown in beds during spring and the seedlings should then be transplanted into a permanent bed at about 60 cm (24 in) apart. Artichokes can also be propagated from the suckers of older plants that have provided good yields. Plant suckers 90 cm (36 in) apart in early spring. By planting suckers every two or three years, continuity of production is ensured.

CLIMATE Zone 6 and above.

Artichoke, Jerusalem

(*Helianthus tuberosus*, fam. Asteraceae)

Related to the sunflower, this plant has nothing to do with Jerusalem! It comes, in fact, from North America where it was first cultivated by the native Americans in the 18th century. It then spread to Europe, acquiring the label 'Jerusalem' from an English interpretation of the Italian name for the plant, girasole, meaning 'turn towards the sun'. It is not an artichoke, but its potato-like tuber has a similar taste. The tubers can be baked, roasted, boiled, or simply grated.

CULTIVATION Jerusalem artichokes do well in a normal garden soil but about half a cup of potash-enriched, complete fertilizer should be applied to the soil around each plant. The soil must be dug deeply. They can grow in sun or shade, but need plenty of water during the growing season. As with the globe artichoke, remove all weeds. The tubers should be harvested four to five weeks after flowering, or when the top wilts. Tubers can be planted in the fall or the spring, to a depth of 10–15 cm (4–6 in) and between 30 and 75 cm (12–30 in) apart.

CLIMATE Very hardy; Jerusalem artichokes grow in zone 4 and above.

Arum (fam. Araceae)

Native to Europe and the Middle East, these perennial, often herbaceous, plants are suitable for moist, shady places such as woodland gardens and shrub borders. They have tuberous root systems and large, showy leaves. The colored spathes and spadix form rather unusual hooded flowers which are often used for floral decoration.

CULTIVATION Plant in a humus-rich soil in a shaded spot or in a position receiving only filtered sunlight. Propagate in fall by division of the tubers or by offsets. It does best in a warm to cool climate.

CLIMATE Zone 6 and above is suitable for most.

SPECIES *A. italicum* is a tuberous perennial with arrow-shaped leaves, growing to about 45 cm

ABOVE Jerusalem artichokes look like sunflowers. From planting to harvesting tubers takes around five months.

ABOVE Cuckoo pint and lords-and-ladies are two names given to *Arum maculatum* in its native Britain. It is very vigorous.

ABOVE Like most perennials, *Aruncus dioicus* looks its best when mass planted. Here, it is a feature of a bog garden.

(18 in) high. The leaves are mid to dark green, with white markings. The summer flower is a green to white spathe. This is an ideal plant for shady gardens, although it can become invasive in warm climates. *A. maculatum*, known also in its native Britain as cuckoo pint and lords-and-ladies, is a very vigorous grower. *A. palaestinum*, black calla, zone 9, has long-stemmed green leaves and large, velvety, bell-shaped, purplish black flowers which turn pale green inside in spring. This species grows to 1 m (3 ft) in height.

Aruncus (fam. Rosaceae)
Goat's beard

This small genus comprises two or three perennial plants, one of which is commonly grown in cool climates. The fern-like foliage and tall, arching flower sprays make them a handsome addition to the garden.

CULTIVATION Plant in a semi-shaded position in moist, rich soil. Propagate by seed sown in spring or summer. *Aruncus* does well in woodland conditions, or beside a pool or creek.

CLIMATE Cool to cold, suitable for zone 7 and above.

SPECIES *A. dioicus*, goat's beard, produces a mass of rich green foliage and gracefully arching plumes of small white flowers in summer. 'Kneiffii' is similar, but smaller, with finely dissected foliage.

Arundinaria (fam. Poaceae)
Bamboo

This group of running bamboos is native to Asia, Japan and North America. Climatically they are suitable for planting in many parts of the US, although they can be very invasive as sprouts can come up some distance away from the original plants. Care should be taken to confine them.

CULTIVATION Propagate this type of bamboo by cutting off the top of a young shoot, leaving several lower nodes. For the large species, take a length of 1.5 m (5 ft). Plant in rich, moist soil to about 25 cm (10 in). Healthy rhizomes, about 35 cm (14 in) long, can also be used. They should be yellowish, with good buds and lots of small fibrous roots. Plant about 20 cm (8 in) deep.

ABOVE An American bamboo, the impressive *Arundinaria gigantea* is known as canebrake or southern bamboo in the United States.

ABOVE With its attractive evergreen growth, *Asarum caudatum* makes a dense groundcover.

CLIMATE Zones 6 to 8 according to species.

SPECIES Although many species are cultivated, especially in Japan and China, few species are grown by American gardeners. *A. gigantea* zone 6, is the species sometimes grown in gardens. It reaches 4–5 m (13–16 ft) high. *A. pygmaea* (now correctly *Pleioblastus pygmaeus*), dwarf bamboo, zone 8, grows to only about 30 cm (12 in) and is ideal for both tub culture and bonsai. The foliage is bright green and the stems are attractively marked in purple. Both species are vigorous growers.

Asarum (fam. Aristolochiaceae)

These small, rhizomatous perennials are native mainly to North America but also eastern Asia and Europe. They make excellent groundcover in woodland gardens, shrub borders and the like, but they are not as widely grown in gardens as they deserve to be. The flowers that they produce are pitcher-shaped but they are often hidden by the dense foliage.

CULTIVATION These woodland plants would be difficult to grow in warm or tropical regions. They need a moist, rich soil and are propagated by division of the rhizome.

CLIMATE Cool. Suitable for zone 7 and above but *A. europaeum* can grow in zone 5.

SPECIES *A. canadense*, wild ginger, has kidney-shaped leaves, brownish purple flowers in spring and a pungent rootstock. It grows to about 30 cm (12 in) tall. *A. caudatum* grows to the same height, and produces heart-shaped leaves on long stalks and brownish red flowers in the summer. *A. europaeum* produces drooping greenish purple or brown flowers and shiny green leaves. This species grows to a height of about 25–30 cm (10–12 in).

Asparagus (fam. Asparagaceae)
Asparagus fern

This large genus includes perennial herbs, shrubs and woody vines, either erect or climbing. Many species are grown for their decorative qualities, either to accompany cut flowers or as indoor pot plants. The leaves are usually needle-like, or in the form of fine phyllodes, and the flowers are small and inconspicuous. They are mostly tender and grown in a cool or intermediate greenhouse or conservatory or as house plants.

CULTIVATION A normal potting mix suits asparagus plants grown in containers, provided the mix is kept moist. They grow well indoors if given sufficient light and occasional liquid fertilizer or plant pills. *A. setaceus* (syn. *A. plumosus*) does well outside in zone 9 in a sheltered, semi-shaded position and *A. densiflorus* Sprengeri Group will also survive in zone 9 in a sunny position but needs some protection.

CLIMATE Frost-free climates for most.
SPECIES *A. densiflorus* 'Myersii' (syn. *A. meyeri*) has erect or spreading stems up to 60 cm (24 in), forming long, narrow plumes of rich green foliage. *A. densiflorus* and its cultivars have fine feather-like foliage on upright or trailing stems. Best known is the *A. densiflorus* Sprengeri Group which is very tough and can be grown outdoors in zone 9. It has light green, needle-like foliage and prickles on trailing stems. The tiny white flowers are not very conspicuous and are followed by red berries. Both of the above species make very attractive indoor plants. *A. officinalis*, the edible asparagus, has erect, herbaceous stems, to about 1.5 m (5 ft), and branched, feathery leaves. The greenish white flowers are small and the females produce red berries (see Asparagus, *A. officinalis*). *A. setaceus* (syn. *A. plumosus*), the common asparagus fern, is a vigorous climber with sharp prickles and dark green feathery leaves. It has very small white flowers and black berries.

Asparagus

(*Asparagus officinalis*, fam. Asparagaceae)

This perennial, herbaceous garden vegetable, which has been around for many centuries,

ABOVE The asparagus fern, *Asparagus densiflorus* Sprengeri Group, is widely grown as a house or greenhouse plant and can be grown outside in zone 9.

can continue producing for 15 years or more. Native to the coasts of Asia and Europe, it is grown only for its tender, edible, early spring shoots, or spears, which grow upwards every spring from underground rhizomes.

CULTIVATION Asparagus requires a reasonably fertile, well-drained soil, with a regular water supply. A soil reaction of about pH 6 is the most suitable. Before planting, it is important to dig the soil well. Weed control is also essential. Animal manures, composted materials and inorganic fertilizers, will all assist in continual production. Asparagus can be established in two ways. First, seed can be sown in early spring in warmer areas, and later in colder regions. Sow about 2.5–3 cm (about 1 in) deep. The first harvest will occur in the third year. Second, the plant can be established

ABOVE The ferny foliage of edible asparagus is allowed to grow tall once harvesting of the spears is over.

by planting one- or two-year-old roots, sold as 'crowns'. The older the roots, the shorter the time before the crop is ready for harvest. A dozen plants is sufficient for the average family's needs. Generally it takes about three years for a bed to produce. With good care it can be kept in production for 15 years. The first cutting of spears should be limited to between four and six weeks; as the plants mature, the period for cutting can be increased gradually until a maximum of 12 weeks of harvesting has been reached. In late fall or winter, at the end of the growing season, cut back the yellowing tops to ground level.

CLIMATE Wide range, from zone 4 to 9; needs cool winters.

VARIETIES Cultivars include the popular 'Martha Washington' and the all-male 'Jersey Giant'. If purchasing crowns, find out whether they are male or female plants. The males produce more spears and start earlier each season; the female plants have slightly larger spears. If sowing seed, select male plants in the second season.

Asperula (fam. Rubiaceae)
Woodruff

This genus of mostly herbaceous perennials includes many species native to the Mediterranean, Europe and Turkey. They grow well in alpine rock gardens.

CULTIVATION These plants need moist, but well-drained, soil. Propagation is generally by seed, although the perennial types can be divided. All species do well in cool regions if planted in a shady spot.

CLIMATE Wide moisture and temperature range, but best in areas with cold winters.

SPECIES *A. orientalis*, an annual with rough leaves and strongly perfumed blue flowers in summer, grows to 30 cm (12 in). *A. tinctoria* is a prostrate type with white flowers, also in summer. Its roots are the source of a red dye.

ABOVE Ground-covering *Asperula orientalis* forms a dense mat of foliage topped with blue or white flowers.

Asphodelus (fam. Asphodelaceae)
Asphodel

Easily grown in the open, these herbaceous perennials have impressive spikes of funnel-shaped flowers which bloom during spring and summer. The species most often grown are native to the Mediterranean and western Asia.

ABOVE The sword-like foliage of Asphodelus cerasiferus is topped with graceful spires of white flowers emerging from pink buds.

ABOVE Variegated *Aspidistra elatior* needs more light than the plain green form to retain its color.

CULTIVATION The hardy asphodel is easy to grow. Plant in an open, semi-shaded position or in a border. Propagate by division of the roots in fall or winter.

CLIMATE Zones 6 to 8 for most.

SPECIES *A. acaulis*, zone 9, grows to around 25 cm (10 in) and bears pink flowers in spring. *A. albus* has white flowers, also in spring, and reaches 60 cm (24 in). The silver rod, *A. cerasiferus*, to 1.3 m (4 ft), bears large silvery white flowers throughout summer.

Aspidistra (fam. Convallariaceae)
Cast-iron plant

One of the toughest house plants, Aspidistra became very popular during Victorian times. Originally from China, Japan and the Himalayas, it has long, stiff, shiny, dark green leaves which grow from a clump at the base. While excellent for the house, it is also a suitable specimen for shaded verandahs and patios, and for growing in shaded areas under trees.

CULTIVATION When grown in pots as house or greenhouse plants, use a soil-based potting compost and provide bright light but at the same time shade from strong sun. Be careful with watering, that is, moderately in summer and very little in winter. Do not overfeed. Propagate by division in spring.

CLIMATE Zone 9 and above.

SPECIES *A. elatior* grows to 1 m (3 ft). It has long, leathery dark green leaves on stiff stems, while the leaves of cultivar 'Variegata' are striped green and white. The small cream to dark purple flowers grow close to the soil. However, those grown indoors seldom flower.

Asplenium (fam. Aspleniaceae)
Spleenwort

Found naturally in rainforests throughout the world, this genus of ferns comprises over 650 species. All of the species have creeping rhizomes and simple, pinnate or bipinnate fronds.

CULTIVATION Most species come from warm climates and are grown in cool to warm greenhouses or conservatories, although a few are hardy. Under glass, grow in pots of compost consisting of loam, leaf mould and coarse sand. They need bright light but shade from strong sun, and moderate atmospheric humidity. Although requiring plenty of water during the warmer months, most species are tolerant of dry periods. The bird's nest ferns, particularly, tolerate dry conditions well. *A. bulbiferum* is propagated from the tiny plantlets growing from the little bulbs at the ends of the fronds, while *A. flabellifolium* reproduces from the plantlets at the tips of the fronds. Other species grow from spores or from division of the rhizome.

CLIMATE Most are tender and grown under glass.

SPECIES They may not all be available outside their countries of origin. *A. australasicum* and the closely related *A. nidus*, known as bird's nest ferns, are probably the most commonly cultivated species. Widespread in rainforests and more open forests, where they grow on rocks or trees, they are also ideal for shaded areas or under trees where they enjoy dappled sunlight. The long, wavy-edged, undivided fronds grow to between 50 cm (20 in) and 2 m (6 ft). The central 'nest' catches falling leaf litter which breaks down into humus and helps to nourish the plant. *A. bulbiferum*, mother spleenwort or hen and chickens, is a native of Australia and is widely cultivated. The robust rhizome is covered in scales and the attractive, tripinnate, erect fronds gently arch to 1.2 m (4 ft) long. The stems are green on the upper side and dark beneath, and the fine leaflets are dark green. This plant is distinguishable from other species by the small plantlets produced at the tips of the stems. *A. flabellifolium*, necklace fern, is a

ABOVE These mature specimens of bird's nest ferns exhibit lines of brown spore cases on the undersides of the fronds

BELOW The 'nest' of Asplenium australasicum catches falling leaves which gradually decay, providing food for the plant.

native of Australia and New Zealand. It has a short rhizome, narrow, often prostrate, fronds up to 30 cm (12 in) long and wedgeshaped leaflets. *A. flaccidum*, weeping spleenwort, is found in all of Australia's eastern mainland states and Tasmania. It has a short, scaly rhizome, drooping bipinnate fronds and thick, narrow, bright green leaflets which are 1 cm (⅓ in) long. *A. lyalli*, from New Zealand, has

1 m (3 ft) long pinnate fronds, with grayish, scaled stems and leathery, oval-shaped leaflets, 15 cm (6 in) long.

Astartea (fam. Myrtaceae)

False baeckea

These pretty flowering shrubs, native to Western Australia, are similar to their tea-tree relatives (*Leptospermum* species). Rarely grown outside their native country, they make excellent garden ornamentals in frost-free climates as they bloom profusely for most of the year, and also work well as an informal hedge or low windbreak, if trimmed and watered well to encourage bushiness. These plants can reach 1 m (3 ft) in height and a spread of 1.3 m (4 ft). The long, arched branches, laden with fresh sprays of the delicate flowers, look very pretty in a vase. The open, five-petalled flowers come in white or pink – often with a deeper pink at the base. In spring and fall, these shrubs are absolutely covered in blooms.

CULTIVATION Grow in pots under glass in frost-prone climates. Outdoors they are easily cultivated and are resistant to drought and wind, although a warm, sheltered position

ABOVE Pretty, white flowers and small, neat leaves make *Astartea heterantha* a desirable garden shrub.

improves flowering. Plant in any lime-free garden soil in either an open or shaded location and water well during hot weather. Prune regularly. Propagate from semi-ripe cuttings in fall. Root them in sharp sand and peat or vermiculite at a rate of 3:1. They can also be propagated from seed.

CLIMATE Warm temperate, frost-free, including coastal gardens.

SPECIES *A. fascicularis* produces dense sprays of starry, long-lasting, whitish pink flowers almost all year round. This species grows at a medium rate to 1 m (3 ft) and flowers when young. Prune to encourage a bushy shape. *A. heterantha*, a low-growing, compact shrub, has masses of small, starry, pinkish white flowers, which display their blooms most profusely in spring and fall.

Aster (fam. Asteraceae)

Perennial aster, Michaelmas daisy

Native to the northern hemisphere, this large genus comprises over 250 species of mostly herbaceous perennials. The Greek aster meaning 'a star', refers to the shape of the flower. The annual aster is *Callistephus chinensis*, or China aster, and botanically is not an aster at all. Most true asters have leafy clumps at ground level from which emerge flower stems up to 1.5 m (5 ft) high. Clusters of showy, daisy-like flowers are produced from late summer to fall in colors of blue, violet, purple, mauve, pink, red or white, with a central disc of yellow or black. Asters make excellent cut flowers and will last well if the water is changed frequently.

CULTIVATION Plant in an open, sunny position in well-drained soil, enriched with organic fertilizer, and dressed with complete fertilizer at 40 g per square metre (1½ oz per square yard). Animal manure or compost should be applied generously to the beds as a mulch. Set new plants, with their crowns at soil level, about 45 cm (18 in) apart (20 cm or 8 in for

ABOVE *Aster amellus* is a neat, clump-forming perennial for a late summer show.

ABOVE *Aster novi-belgii* and its cultivars are reliable, easy-care perennials, available in a great color range.

the dwarf hybrids) in clumps of five to seven of each variety. Water well in spring and summer, adding 40 g (1½ oz) of complete fertilizer per plant in late spring and summer to ensure healthy growth and large flowers. When the flowers have faded on the plant, cut back the long stems to ground level and tidy the clumps. Sometimes flowers will be produced in smaller numbers in late fall. A generous mulch around the old clump in late winter helps these plants to conserve moisture. Propagate by division of the established clumps in late winter or early spring. A single, well-grown crown can produce at least 15 new plants, with sound crowns and roots, in one year.

CLIMATE The following species will grow in zone 2, except for *A. amellus* which requires zone 5.

SPECIES *A. amellus*, Italian aster, is a compact plant growing to 60 cm (24 in). It has large flowers in a range of colors from pale pink to shades of blue, with a distinctive golden disc in the center. There are several named varieties. All flower during late summer and fall. *A. novae-angliae*, New England aster, is from eastern North America. This species has downy stems and narrow, gray-green, stem-clasping leaves, and grows to 2 m (6 ft). The large flowers come in pink, red or blue. There are

several modern cultivars. All flower in late summer and fall. *A. novi-belgii*, also from eastern North America, is the most commonly grown. Many cultivars are available, mainly from perennial plant specialists. They grow to between 50 cm (20 in) and 1.5 m (5 ft). The slender stems branch near the top, the leaves are narrow, smooth and stem-clasping, and the flowers appear in clusters of 20 to 30 in white, pink, mauve, blue, purple or red, with golden yellow or reddish discs. All flower profusely from late summer and fall. The dwarf hybrids are very pretty, with a similar color range to that of *A. novi-belgii*. The flowers bloom from late summer and fall. The dwarfs grow to 15–30 cm (6–12 in) in height and suit front row or rock garden planting. There are numerous cultivars of dwarf aster and all of them are worth growing in gardens. Garden centers specializing in perennials should have a good range of cultivars of varying heights and colors.

Astilbe (fam. Saxifragaceae)

These herbaceous perennials form clumps, the foliage growing about 30 cm (12 in) high. They have attractive, fern-like foliage and large, branched clusters of showy, feathery flowers in white, pink or red. In some varieties the young

ABOVE Feathery pale pink flowers on astilbes add a light touch to a perennial planting scheme.

ABOVE *Astilbe* 'Jo Ophorst' flowers have upright side branches which give this cultivar a stiff look, unusual in this genus.

foliage is a beautiful coppery red. The flower stems grow vertically to 1 m (3 ft) or more.

CULTIVATION Generally these plants need a cool, moist position in partial shade, but in cool zones they can also be planted in the open, provided the soil is rich and retains moisture. A soil pH value of around 6–7 is recommended, and the soil should contain a large amount of organic matter. For best effect, space plants 30 cm (12 in) apart, with the crown at soil level, in clumps of five or more. Astilbes require frequent watering during dry times from spring onwards during growth and flowering. Mulch each plant to conserve moisture and apply 25 g (1 oz) of fertilizer per plant during late spring and summer to encourage rapid growth and abundant flowers. After flowering, cut spent stems to ground level and remove dead leaves. In severe climates, a mulch of loose, open compost over the clumps helps to protect the crowns from frost. To propagate, divide the clumps in late winter, ensuring that each new plant has a sound crown and roots.

CLIMATE Zone 6 and above.

SPECIES The modern astilbes are generally hybrids of *A. chinensis*, *A. japonica* and *A. grandis*. All flower in summer in colors ranging from white, salmon and pink to dark crimson. Most widely grown are cultivars of *Astilbe* x *arendsii*, many of which were bred in Europe, where they are widely grown and among the most popular plants for moist places. They are generally dwarf or low-growing, compact plants and come in a wide range of colors–all shades of pink, plus red shades and white.

Astrantia (fam. Apiaceae)

Masterwort

These herbaceous perennials are favorites for open spots in gardens of the northern hemisphere. The unusual heads of bristly, star-like flowers are surrounded by bracts resembling parchment and the decorative leaves are deeply divided. They look very pretty in a vase and last well.

CULTIVATION *Astrantia* grows well in any ordinary, reasonably rich soil in an open position, providing the site is not too hot or dry.

ABOVE *Astrantia major rosea* should be planted where the intricate flowers can be viewed at close quarters.

Regular watering is essential. Propagate from seed or division in spring.

CLIMATE Moist and cool areas; zone 6 and above.

SPECIES *A. major* is the most widely grown species. It grows to 1 m (3 ft) and can be planted in damp or boggy ground. The flowers are in white or various shades of pink. *A. maxima* has bright green leaves and pretty pink flowers. It grows to 60 cm (24 in). *A. minor* grows to only 25 cm (10 in). This small species has pale purplish flowers flushed with green.

Astroloma (fam. Epacridaceae)
Heath

Native to Australia, these small, densely foliaged shrubs make attractive ornamentals and are also suitable as undershrubs and as rockery plants. However, few are available or grown outside their country of origin. They have interesting bell-shaped spring flowers, sometimes with different colored tips, resembling little cigars. The edible berries have a sweet apple taste.

CULTIVATION Because these shrubs have deep, penetrating root systems, they require deep, sandy, well-drained soil. They also need full sun or partial shade. Most of the species come from dry areas, so seed should be sown in almost pure sand. With the Western Australian species, seed is difficult to collect and germinate. *Astroloma* will also propagate from fall cuttings, though these can be slow to strike. Root in a sharp sand and peat or vermiculite mix at the rate of 3:1. Some species may be available from specialist shrub nurseries.

CLIMATE Most will thrive in zone 8 and above.

SPECIES *A. ciliatum* is a prostrate, slow-growing shrub, with a deep root system, which forms a dense, leafy mound. It has masses of dark green, pungent leaves and tubular, deep purplish red flowers with yellow styles. They bloom profusely in winter and early spring. *A. compactum* is a prostrate, densely foliaged shrub with rigid, pungent, light green leaves and masses of bright red flowers along the ends of its branches from winter to spring. It is resistant to light frosts. *A. conostephioides*, flame heath, is a stiff, dwarf shrub with grayish

ABOVE *Astroloma conostephioides* is seen here growing in the sandy desert conditions of its natural habitat.

green pungent foliage and scarlet tubular flowers. *A. humifusum*, native cranberry, has grayish foliage and red, curved, bell-shaped flowers. It is a mat-forming, prostrate shrub. *A. pallidum*, from Western Australia, is a small shrub with creamy pink flowers. *A. pinifolium*, a low, spreading shrub, has mossy, pine-like foliage and diffuse deep yellow or pink flowers, often green-tipped.

Astrophytum (fam. Cactaceae)
Star cactus, bishop's cap

These popular cactuses, originally from Mexico, vary in size and form, from globular to elongated to star-shaped. They are hard-skinned and divided into prominent ribs, and are covered with tufts of short hair which appear as small white spots. The spines, when present, are strong or papery and the yellow, diurnal, summer flowers are quite short.

CULTIVATION Except in favorable climates, they are grown in pots in a cool greenhouse, using a proprietary cactus compost. Provide bright light but shade from strongest sun. Keep dry in the dormant season. Outdoors, they need full sunlight, lots of water in spring and summer, and protection from rain in winter. Otherwise, they are easy to grow and frost-resistant.

CLIMATE Zone 9 and above.

SPECIES *A. asterias*, sea urchin cactus, does resemble a sea urchin. This highly valued species has a globular body divided into broad, vertical ribs, each with a row of small white areoles. It has no spines. The body is grayish green and the flowers are large and yellow with a red center. It prefers half-shade and less water than the others. *A. capricorne* is a larger plant with high, rounded ribs, flat, twisted spines which grow to 70 mm (3 in) long, and large yellow flowers with red centers. The white tufts are sometimes almost absent and at other times quite dense. *A. myriostigma*, bishop's cap, the most common of the species, is quite unusual looking. It has a globular body, with

ABOVE *Astrophytum myriostigma* is an almost spineless cactus, its bare body finely speckled with white scales.

five to eight ribs and very dense tufts. It, too, is spineless. The glossy yellow summer blooms are smaller than those of the other species. *A. ornatum* is a larger plant, with eight sharp ribs and sometimes bands of tufts. This species has straight, sharp, amber spines and pure yellow flowers.

Athrotaxis (fam. Taxodiaceae)

The three species of this genus of conifers from Tasmania in Australia are occasionally grown where the climate is suitable, particularly in mild or frost-free areas with a cool growing season such as the Pacific Coast. They are very slow-growing but have interesting foliage and a rather compact, asymmetrical habit, generally not reaching tree size until 20 to 30 years old.

CULTIVATION *Athrotaxis* prefers a moist, cool-temperate climate, rich, well-drained, slightly acid soil, and full sun or partial shade. Cultivation is not difficult under these conditions. Propagate from seed or cuttings which strike quite easily.

CLIMATE Will thrive in zones 8 and 9.

SPECIES *A. cupressoides*, a small, open, irregularly shaped tree, grows to a height of around 10 m (33 ft). The pale green leaves are closely pressed to thick, fleshy branchlets.

ABOVE King Billy pine, *Athrotaxis selaginoides*, growing in a rugged gully in its Tasmanian habitat.

ABOVE A pretty selection of the lady fern, *Athyrium filix-femina*, is the Plumosum Group, well named for its feathery fronds.

A. laxifolia grows to about 10 m (33 ft). It has longer leaves, not as closely pressed as those of *A. cupressoides*. *A. selaginoides*, King William (or Billy) pine, one of Tasmania's most famous timber trees, can reach heights of 30 m (100 ft) or more in its native habitat. It has a straight trunk, with irregular side branches and very small, narrow, dark green leaves, pointed at the tips. It is not an especially attractive tree, but it can live to a great age and size.

Athyrium (fam. Woodsiaceae)

This large group of ferns is widely distributed in many parts of the world, but is represented by the greatest number of species in eastern and south-eastern Asia.

CULTIVATION Some of these ferns are hardy and make good garden plants in moist positions with partial or full shade. The soil should have a good supply of humus to help it retain moisture. Plant in spring or fall. These are ideal ferns for shrub borders, woodland gardens and shady courtyards.

CLIMATE Very hardy; will grow in zone 2 and above.

SPECIES *A. filix-femina*, lady fern, is probably the most widely cultivated of the species. It is native to many parts of the northern hemisphere and can survive quite cold climates, being totally deciduous in winter. There is a huge range of cultivars which are well represented in the US. Some have extremely feathery fronds. *A. nipponicum* 'Pictum', the painted fern from Japan, suited to zone 4, is a small fern with silvery streaks in the center of each leaflet.

Atriplex (fam. Chenopodiaceae)
Saltbush

In their native environment, these shrubs are generally found in coastal and inland salt marsh and lake areas. The leaves are leathery and often toothed and the flower segments are deciduous. When they fall, two bracts enlarge to enclose the fruit. With their unusual grayish white foliage, they have potential as landscape contrast plants. They can adapt to alkaline soils and can withstand hot, dry conditions. Because of their sand-binding qualities, they are useful plants for seaside gardens.

ABOVE The interesting structure of a saltbush, *Atriplex species*, is shown here. Saltbush can survive very hostile growing conditions.

CULTIVATION Saltbush thrives in a sunny, well-drained situation. Propagation is mostly by tip cuttings taken in summer or fall. These root easily in a sharp sand and peat or vermiculite mix at the rate of 3:1. These shrubs can also be propagated from the ripened seeds, which should be scarified before planting. Layering is also possible.

CLIMATE Drier temperate and high areas; zone 8.

SPECIES Most of these are not readily available in the US. *A. cinerea*, a coastal silvery gray shrub with spongy fruit, grows to 1 m (3 ft) tall. *A. halimoides*, from Western Australia, is a dwarf shrub with gray-white foliage. *A. holocarpa* has small, silvery, blueish white leaves, inconspicuous flowers and small, round, creamy pink fruit. It grows to 1 m (3 ft), forming a spreading mound. *A. muelleri* is a sprawling gray shrub with cut-off leaves and round fruit bracts. *A. nummularia*, old man saltbush, is the largest species, growing to 2.5 m (8 ft). It has gray-green foliage and flattish bracts. *A. paludosa*'s natural habitat is the salt marsh. It is a spreading bush to 1 m (3 ft), with heart-shaped fruit. *A. prostrata*, creeping saltbush, from Western Australia has tiny white leaves and flat fruit bracts. *A. semibaccata*, berry saltbush, grows well in coastal areas. It is a spreading, prostrate, silvery green shrub with diamond-shaped red fruit bracts. *A. spinibractea*, spiny saltbush, is from inland Australia. A trailing, prostrate species with scattered silvery foliage, its fruit bracts have tiny curved spines. *A. spongiosa*, pop saltbush, also from Western Australia, is a small shrub with clusters of large inflated bracts and gray-white foliage.

Aubrieta (fam. Brassicaceae)
Rock cress

Mostly native to southern Europe, these low-growing, trailing perennials, to around 15 cm (6 in), are among the most popular rockery plants. They are also suitable for planting on sunny banks or stone walls, particularly in exposed or coastal areas where other plants may fail. They form dense mats of gray-green leaves and produce an abundance of pink, lilac and purple starry flowers in spring.

CULTIVATION Aubrietas thrive in light, sandy soil in a sunny, protected position. Very acid soils should be limed before planting. Do not overwater when the plant is not in flower. They flower best the second year after planting. Grow from seed, or from cuttings taken in fall.

ABOVE One of the many lovely hybrids of *Aubrieta deltoidea* forms a mound of lilac-pink flowers.

CLIMATE Zone 7.

SPECIES *A. deltoidea* is the true species, but the best results are obtained from the many cultivated varieties that have been developed. Some of these have semi-double, brightly colored flowers which bloom profusely in spring. Cultivars 'Argenteovariegata' and 'Aureovariegata' have variegated foliage. Excellent cultivars often grown have flowers in the crimson, pink, mauve and violet color range.

Aucuba (fam. Aucubaceae)
Japanese laurel

With this genus, flowers of the two sexes occur on different plants so that both male and female plants need to be grown to obtain the pretty berries. While they grow well outdoors, they can also be potted for indoor use.

CULTIVATION These shrubs thrive in most moist, well-drained soils. The variegated types, in particular, need shade, otherwise the leaves will burn. *Aucuba* grows vigorously, particularly if it is kept moist, so regular pruning will be required to maintain the shape and to constrain it. Propagate from half-ripe tip cuttings in summer.

ABOVE Gold dust plant, *Aucuba japonica* 'Variegata', is an evergreen shrub with large, shiny leaves which are generously spotted with gold.

CLIMATE Zone 8 and above.

SPECIES *A. japonica* is the most widely cultivated species. It has thick, soft, shiny deep green leaves and small maroon flowers. If pollinated, the female plant bears drooping clusters of long red berries. Cultivar 'Variegata', spotted laurel or golddust plant, has large, shiny leaves, generously spotted with gold; 'Crotonifolia' has large green leaves, with white and gold spots; 'Serratifolia' has long, dark green leaves with deeply cut edges; 'Picturata' has impressive mottled foliage, with a yellow blotch at the center of each leaf.

Aurinia (fam. Brassicaceae)
Golden tuft, gold dust

This small genus of biennials and perennials is native to Europe and western Asia. Forming rosettes of slightly hairy, mainly lance-shaped leaves, they have four-petalled yellow or white flowers. They are useful for rock gardens and sloping banks, or as garden edging.

CULTIVATION These plants are best grown in well-drained soil enrich-ed with organic matter. Regular watering is needed in dry spring or summer weather. Shear over plants after flowering to ensure compact growth. Propagate from seed or tip cuttings taken in late spring through summer.

ABOVE Golden yellow flowers of *Aurinia saxatilis* cascade from a low wall beside an Italian lavender.

CLIMATE Zone 3.

SPECIES *Aurinia saxatilis* (syn. *Alyssum saxatile*) is the only species common in cultivation. It forms a low mound, 10–30 cm (4–6 in) high, spreading to around 40 cm (16 in). Clear yellow flowers appear in great profusion in mid to late spring. There are cultivars with flowers in white, cream, lemon and rich gold. The foliage of cultivar 'Variegata' has creamy margins.

Austromyrtus (fam. Myrtaceae)
Ironwood

This genus, unlikely to be available in the the US, comprises over 30 species of the myrtle family native to Australia, their natural habitat being the tropical and subtropical, occasionally temperate, rainforest- and scrublands of the east coast. They have the typical small, broad leaves, white flowers and berry-like fruit of the myrtles. These ironwoods, as they are commonly known, produce very hard, durable timber.

CULTIVATION These tender plants require an average soil and a sunny position. Propagate from cuttings or from the abundant seed.

CLIMATE Warm and subtropical climates.

ABOVE The pretty white flowers of *Austromyrtus tenuifolia* strongly resemble myrtle. This species is a good understorey plant.

SPECIES *A. acmenioides*, white myrtle, thrives in scrublands from the south coast of New South Wales through to Queensland. It has smooth bark and produces extremely hard timber. *A. dulcis* is a low-growing, spreading species suitable for groundcover or for spilling over walls. The foliage has pinky red tones in cold weather and the white flowers sometimes appear in abundance. *A. tenuifolia* grows 2–3 m (6–10 ft) and produces blue-green berries in fall. It is well suited to shaded sites.

Avocado (*Persea americana*, fam. Lauraceae)

Thought to be from the West Indies and Central America, the avocado can now be found in warm climates throughout the world, even in places with occasional light frosts. This evergreen tree comes in erect-growing types, which reach up to 12 m (40 ft), as well as spreading types. It has shiny dark green leaves and very small spring flowers. Its round or pear-shaped fruits have a hard green or purple skin with creamish green pulpy flesh which is very nutritious. It is a high energy food, low in carbohydrate and high in vitamins and minerals. Avocado is used in salads and soups, and also as an accompaniment to seafood, chicken, pasta, and many other foods. Grafted trees start bearing lightly in three to five years, but the fruits will not ripen unless taken from the tree. Seedling trees can take much longer to produce.

CULTIVATION In frost-prone climates, grow in pots in a cool greenhouse as a foliage plant only. In areas where avocados are grown for their fruits, cuttings can be taken from good-bearing trees and grafted onto the seedling rootstock of suitable trees, especially those with resistance to the fungal root rot, phytophthora. Otherwise, plants can be bought from a nursery. Planting times are not crucial, except that the small plants should be given time to establish before the hot weather sets in. They should be planted about 5 m (16 ft) apart in a reasonably fertile soil, with good surface and subsurface drainage, as these plants

ABOVE Avocados must be picked before they will ripen fully. Thickened yellow stalks indicate maturity.

cannot tolerate 'wet feet'. Poor drainage contributes to phytophthora. These trees respond well to NPK fertilizers and to calcium and magnesium from dolomite. This treatment will create a suitable, slightly acid pH of 6.5–7. A generous amount of organic matter from animal manure or mulch, for example, helps to reduce the risk of phytophthora by keeping up the activity of soil micro-organisms.

CLIMATE Zone 10 and above.

VARIETIES Where avocados are grown outdoors as a crop, availability of cultivars will vary according to area. Cultivars are generally classified as belonging to a particular area such as West Indian, Guatemalan or Mexican. Better crops can be achieved through cross-pollination, but avocados are self-fertile and capable of cropping alone. Cultivars like 'Hass', 'Duke' and 'Fuerte' are the most popular, with 'Fuerte' accounting for about 50 per cent of all varieties planted. Small-growing trees like 'Wurtz' and 'Rincon' may be better for the home garden. They grow to about 4 m (13 ft).

Azalea (see Rhododendron)

Azara (fam. Flacourtiaceae)

These temperate South American shrubs and small trees have small, glossy, dark green leaves and rather insignificant cream to yellow flowers which cluster close to the younger growth. Almost all the species have a distinctive vanilla-like perfume.

CULTIVATION Azaras do well in moist, slightly acid soils in full sun. The root systems form fibrous mats, so they should not be positioned near other plants. Propagate from cuttings in summer.

CLIMATE Azaras are suitable for zones 8 and 9.

SPECIES *A. integrifolia* is a small tree, growing to about 8 m (26 ft), with sprays of creamy yellow flowers. *A. lanceolata* has a sweet fragrance, different from the usual vanilla-like perfume of this genus. It has showy flowers, consisting mainly of stamens, followed by pale mauve berries. This graceful tree grows to around 6 m (20 ft) and prefers cool soil and plenty of sun from above. *A. microphylla*, box leaf azara, is a vigorous evergreen from Chile. It has rather fine foliage, resembling that of Buxus, though with a more open appearance. It grows to about 7 m (23 ft) and is ideal for planting against walls.

ABOVE The neat, glossy foliage of *Azara microphylla* has given rise to the common name of box leaf azara.

B

Babiana to Buxus

Babiana (fam. Iridaceae)

Baboon flower

Native to South Africa, these lovely plants grow from corms. The pretty, cup-shaped flowers, rather like freesias, come in lilac, blue, yellow, pink and red, and the slender, stiff leaves are ribbed or slightly pleated and quite hairy.

CULTIVATION Grow in the open in mild areas and in pots in a cool greenhouse in cold climates. Outdoors they need an open, sunny position with well-drained soil. Good for rock gardens and borders. In pots, grow in well-drained, soil-based potting compost in good light but shade from strong sun. Plant corms in fall, about 8 cm (3 in) deep and 3–5 cm (1–2 in) apart. They flower in spring.

CLIMATE Zone 9.

SPECIES *B. plicata* has fragrant spring flowers, from lilac through to red, and grows 20 cm (8 in) in height. *B. rubrocyanea* has scarlet or bright blue flowers and grows to a height of 15 cm (6 in). *B. stricta* is the most commonly grown species, with flowers in various shades of blue, lilac or white. Var. *sulphurea* grows to 20 cm (8 in) and has pale yellow to white flowers.

Backhousia (fam. Myrtaceae)

This small genus of evergreen flowering shrubs and trees is native to Australia and New Guinea. They are grown for their attractive, aromatic foliage and small, cup-shaped flowers, with long stamens, and do well in cool subtropical and tropical climates. They make excellent garden specimens and shade trees. Planted outdoors in southern Florida, elsewhere under glass.

CULTIVATION In frost-prone areas, grow in pots of soil-based potting compost in a cool greenhouse. Provide good light but shade from strong sun. Outdoors they enjoy rich, moist soil. Propagate from cuttings of half-ripened wood taken in fall. Dust cuttings with rooting hormone and place in a coarse sand and peat or vermiculite mix of 3:1. Cuttings strike easily.

CLIMATE Zone 10.

SPECIES Not all are available in the US. *B. anisata*, aniseed tree, grows to 20 m (65 ft) in its natural rainforest habitat. When crushed, the foliage has an aniseed smell. It has glossy leaves, 10 cm (4 in) long, and abundant clusters

ABOVE Magenta and royal blue flowers on separate plants of *Babiana stricta* exemplify some of the colour range.

ABOVE Fluffy cream flowers are borne in profusion on the tops of branches of the aromatic *Backhousia citriodora*.

of fragrant whitish pink flowers in spring. *B. citriodora*, lemon-scented myrtle or sweet verbena, is a dense, ornamental small tree, between 7 and 10 m (23–33 ft) tall in cultivation. The shiny leaves are velvety beneath, and the showy clusters of cream flowers bloom in late spring and summer. This species has a strong lemon-camphor fragrance and a commercial oil, over 90 per cent citral, is obtained from the leaves. It is slightly frost-sensitive. *B. myrtifolia*, scrub myrtle, is a bushy shrub or small tree, growing to 6 m (20 ft) in height. Both the glossy leaves and the clusters of whitish yellow flowers are perfumed. The young growth is softly hairy, as too are the undersides of the leaves. This species is frost-hardy. *B. sciadophora*, known as shatter wood, is a bushy shrub or small tree, with blunt, glossy leaves and creamy flower umbels. It grows to a height of about 5 m (16 ft).

Baeckea (fam. Myrtaceae)

Many of these evergreen shrubs grow naturally all over Australia. At least 70 species are found in Australia, with a few occurring in other countries, such as New Caledonia. They have neat, wiry foliage and tiny leaves. Pretty white, pink or mauve flowers, resembling those of the tea-tree, are produced in spring and summer, and make very attractive cut flowers. Some of the species are useful for rock gardens or as potted plants. They come from a wide range of habitats and climatic zones.

CULTIVATION In frost-prone areas, grow in a cool greenhouse in pots of acid, soil-based potting compost, in good light but with shade from strong sun. Outdoors, these plants prefer partial shade, but will tolerate full sun. Moist, well-drained soil is ideal, though they can withstand some drought, frost and poor soil conditions. *B. linifolia* and *B. virgata* can even tolerate moderately bad drainage. Prune bushes lightly after flowering. Like many Australian plants, they do not like their roots being disturbed, so it is wise not to transplant once they have reached an advanced level.

ABOVE *Baeckea imbricata* has tiny stem-clasping leaves and flowers like *Leptospermum*, tea tree, to which it is related.

CLIMATE Zone 9.

SPECIES Not all are available in the US. *B. behrii* grows to a height of 2 m (6 ft). It has fine foliage, with small white flowers in summer. *B. crenatifolia*, fern-leaf heath myrtle, is a small, spreading shrub, with dense, fern-like leaves and white flowers during summer. *B. linifolia*, flax-leaf heath myrtle, is a native of eastern Australia. This beautiful, pendulous shrub has narrow, thread-like foliage and masses of starry white flowers in early spring. It will grow to 2 m (6 ft). *B. preissiana* is easy to grow and produces delicate sprays of white blooms in spring which make excellent cut flowers. *B. ramosissima*, rosy heath myrtle, is a dainty groundcover or low shrub to 30 cm (12 in) high. It has delightful pink flowers in spring and summer. *B. virgata*, twiggy heath myrtle, is the most common species. It is a bushy, erect shrub which grows to 2.5 m (8 ft). Useful as a screen, it produces an abundance of pretty white flowers in summer.

Ballota (fam. Lamiaceae)

These hardy, herbaceous perennials, with attractive gray-white foliage, are useful as groundcover and border plants. The apple

ABOVE Previously used in folk medicine, *Ballota nigra* is now not often cultivated because of its rampant growth habit.

ABOVE The yellow-gold canes of *Bambusa vulgaris* 'Striata' are randomly striped in green. An established clump is a great feature for large gardens.

green leaves gradually turn silver, while the top leaves are velvety white. The inconspicuous mauvish red flowers can be dried, the leaves retaining their silvery tones.

CULTIVATION Cuttings taken with a heel strike easily in the spring or the fall.

CLIMATE Suitable for zone 8.

SPECIES *B. nigra*, black horehound, has ovate leaves and grows to 1 m (3 ft). A nasty-smelling herb, it spreads rapidly and can be invasive.

Bambusa

(see also *Arundinaria*, fam. Poaceae)

Bamboo

Bamboo has had enormous influence throughout the world. It is used for food and shelter, furniture and utensils, bridges and scaffolding. A Taoist saying warns, 'No man can live without a bamboo tree near his house, but he can live without meat'. Chinese calligraphy runs down the page, instead of across it, because bamboo was their first medium for writing and the ribbed stems allowed for easy downward markings. It is said that bamboo can actually be seen and heard growing. On quiet days in swampy parts of Asia and tropical United States, strong crackling sounds can be heard–like something being torn or ripped. This is the sound the bamboo shoot makes as it tears away from its protective sheath. Bamboo can live for up to 150 years or more, depending on the species and conditions. It is said that once a bamboo flowers it dies and, indeed, it is rarely seen in flower in general cultivation. The common name derives from the Indian word for bamboo–bambos. In China, bamboo is so highly regarded that there are six different names for it. All species of *Bambusa* are large, grassy, clump-forming plants, with graceful stems and ribbed leaves. Some make elegant pot plants for indoors, balcony gardens or small, paved courtyards.

CULTIVATION Plant in a rich, loamy soil which retains moisture. Bamboo likes water and thrives along watercourses in its natural habitat. Do not prune. Propagate by division of the clumps at the end of winter. Bamboos are often slow to adapt in the first year but, once established, they grow fast.

CLIMATE Suitable for zone 9 but zone 10 for *B. vulgaris*.

SPECIES *B. multiplex* (syn. *B. glaucescens*) is a perennial from China. It grows to a height of 4–10 m (13–33 ft). It has flat, mid-green leaves, 12 cm (5 in) long. Some varieties have yellow stems and gray-blue leaves; others have variegated yellow and green stems, with mottled rose and green leaves. *B. ventricosa*, Buddha's belly, is vigorous, growing to 5–25 m (16–80 ft) high, depending on conditions. It can be dwarfed by growing it in a container. If it is stressed by poor conditions, the internodes on the stems become short and swollen giving rise to its common name. *B. vulgaris*, feathery bamboo, has banded yellow stems and 20 cm (8 in) long leaves. Native to Southeast Asia, it can grow to more than 20 m (65 ft). Cultivars of this species with striped canes are very attractive. This particular species is also cultivated for its new shoots which are used as food. The pointed shoots emerging from the ground are harvested and eaten, especially in China, Japan and Korea. Various species are grown for edible shoots but this is the main one.

Banana (*Musa species*, fam. Musaceae)

Native to tropical Asia, where many varieties are grown, this large, herbaceous perennial is rather like a palm. It has exotic red or orange-yellow flowers, long, broad leaves and bunches of the fruit we know so well. Some varieties are

ABOVE This lady-finger banana carries a small bunch of very green fruit suspended on a stout stalk amongst the large leaves.

grown for fiber, some as ornamentals, some for cooking and some for eating fresh. The fruit is a staple food as it is high in carbohydrate.

CULTIVATION In frost-prone climates, grow in large pots or tubs or in a soil border in a cool or intermediate greenhouse. Grow in soil-based potting compost and provide bright light but shade from strong sun. They can be stood outside for the summer. Outdoors, a warm sheltered hillside site, facing south, with plentiful rainfall, is perfect. The soil should be moist, deep, fertile and well drained. Weed control is essential, especially the containment of grasses like couch and kikuyu. Propagate from the suckers. A single stalk bears a single bunch, then dies. However suckers grow alongside the trunk from the rhizome below the ground. To ensure continuing production, select one vigorous sucker and destroy the others. The new plant will bear fruit in about one year.

CLIMATE Zone 10.

SPECIES *M. acuminata*, Cavendish group, is a popular variety in parts of the tropical world. *M. x paradisiaca*, sugar banana or lady's finger, grows to around 5 m (16 ft) and is well suited to the home garden.

Banksia (fam. Proteaceae)

Banksia was named after the English botanist, Sir Joseph Banks, who collected the first specimen, *B. serrata*, at Botany Bay in 1770. All 70 species are native to Australia, many to the south-west corner of Western Australia. Banksias are grown for their foliage and their striking flower spikes which look superb in a vase with other natives and last for a long time. Hundreds of flowers are clustered into the cone-like spike, some shaped like huge acorns, some like candles, others like spheres. They range in size up to 35 cm (14 in). They come in reds, oranges, gold, yellow, rust, lime and silver-blue. Some are multi-colored. The foliage varies from fine and deep green to large, deeply serrated and silvery gray, but is always stiff. Banksias are suitable for drying and the seed cones are also favorites for dried arrangements. Banksia flowers, especially from Western Australia, are becoming a valuable export for Australia.

CULTIVATION In frost-prone areas grow in pots of well-drained, soil-based potting compost in a cool greenhouse or conservatory, in bright light but with shade from strong sun. Outdoors, the banksias of eastern Australia need slightly acidic, well-drained soil. The effect of using an over-rich soil is evident from a lightening of the green of the leaves. The Western Australian species require good drainage but appear to be able to utilize lime-enriched soil far more effectively than the eastern species. Banksias are usually grown from seed from the cones. Heat the cones in a hot oven to release the seeds, place the cones in cold water for 24 hours, then dry. The seed should drop out easily.

ABOVE *Banksia spinulosa* 'Stumpy Gold' has a horizontal growth habit, making it ideal groundcover.

BELOW 'Burgundy' is an unusually colored cultivar of the heath banksia, *Banksia ericifolia*.

CLIMATE Grows in relatively frost-free areas. Zones 9 and 10.

SPECIES It is unlikely that all of these are available outside their native Australia. *B. asplenifolia*, rock banksia, is a very hardy species from Queensland and New South Wales. It grows to 3 m (10 ft). It has thick, dark green, serrated leaves and lemon-green flower spikes to 15 cm (6 in) long in fall and winter. *B. baueri*, possum or koala banksia, from Western Australia, grows to 3 m (10 ft) tall,

ABOVE *Banksia prionotes* is sometimes given the name acorn banksia for the form and color of its flower spikes.

with very large grayish yellow flowers, 30 cm (12 in) long and 25 cm (10 in) wide, and serrated foliage. *B. baxteri*, Baxter banksia, from Western Australia, grows to 3 m (10 ft) tall and does well in sandy soils. With its dome-shaped yellow flowers and deeply lobed foliage, it is excellent for cut flowers. *B. caleyi*, also from Western Australia, has dark green serrated foliage and deep yellow or red pendulous flowers in spring and summer. It grows to 2 m (6 ft) tall. *B. canei*, mountain banksia, from New South Wales and Victoria, is a flat-topped, hardy species which grows to 3 m (10 ft) tall. Its blue-gray buds open to lemon spikes, 10 cm (4 in) long. *B. dryandroides*, from Western Australia, is one of the most decorative of the genus, with saw-toothed foliage and amber flowers. A spreading shrub in its natural environment, it grows to 1 m (3 ft). *B. ericifolia*, heath banksia, from New South Wales, is one of the most popular of the species. A robust, healthy plant, with reddish flowers and bright green linear leaves, it grows quickly to a height of 4 m (13 ft). *B. integrifolia*, coast banksia, from Queensland, New South Wales and Victoria, has green leaves, silvery underneath, and lemon-yellow flowers. It is a fast-growing species, reaching heights of around 10 m (33 ft). *B. marginata*, silvery banksia, from New South Wales, Victoria and South

Australia, is suitable for coastal areas. While it is hardy, it can become dwarfed and shrubby if it is planted in poor soil. Its lime to gold spikes flower for a long period. It grows to 5 m (16 ft). *B. media*, from Western Australia, grows 4 m (13 ft) and produces large yellow to brownish yellow flowers and wedge-shaped, olive green leaves. *B. petiolaris*, from Western Australia, has thick, prostrate, creeping stems with 30 cm (12 in) long serrated leaves and erect yellow flowers. *B. praemorsa*, cut-leaf banksia, is a coastal species from Western Australia, which grows up to 3 m (10 ft) tall. It has wedge-shaped leaves and reddish purple flowers up to 30 cm (12 in) long. *B. prionotes*, orange banksia, from Western Australia, grows to 7 m (23 ft) tall. It is eagerly sought by florists because of its striking, pinkish orange and gray flowers. *B. robur*, large-leaf banksia, is often found in swamp country. A hardy species from Queensland and New South Wales, it grows to 2 m (6 ft), and has huge leaves and greenish yellow flowers. *B. serrata*, saw banksia, from Queensland, New South Wales and Victoria, grows to 8 m (26 ft) tall and produces grayish

BELOW *Banksia serrata* often develops interesting forms, with its gnarled trunks and branches.

yellow flowers. Also very hardy, it can tolerate wet soils. *B. spinulosa*, hairpin banksia, is a variable, hardy species from Queensland, New South Wales and Victoria. Its red to gold spikes flower for long periods. It grows to 3 m (10 ft) tall.

Baptisia (fam. Papilionaceae)
False indigo, wild indigo

Native to the drier regions of North America, these hardy, herbaceous perennials are quite similar to lupins. They are very useful plants as they provide masses of color for the garden. Being legumes, they can enrich the soil.

CULTIVATION Baptisia should be planted in a sandy loam, enriched with compost, in a sunny, well-drained position amongst other herbaceous plants. Propagate from seed sown in winter or spring, or by division in early spring. Little fertilizer is needed for leguminous plants but a complete plant food may be applied lightly in spring.

CLIMATE Zone 6 and above.

SPECIES *B. australis* is a bushy plant, with deep sage green leaves and indigo blue early summer flowers. It grows to 1.5 m (5 ft). *B. bracteata* grows to 40 cm (16 in) and has

ABOVE Rich blue flowers and blue-green foliage make *Baptisia australis* a worthwhile addition to the perennial border.

cream summer flowers. *B. leucantha* has white summer flowers and grows to 1 m (3 ft). *B. perfoliata* has yellow flowers in fall and also grows to 1 m (3 ft). *B. tinctoria* has yellow flowers in summer and can be used as a dye plant as a substitute for the true indigo, *Indigofera tinctoria*. It grows to 1 m (3 ft).

Barbarea (fam. Brassicaceae)
Winter cress

This small genus of biennial and perennial herbs originates from Asia and Europe. They have an upright, branching habit, sprays of small yellow flowers, feather-shaped leaves sometimes used in salads, and spreading pods. Some of the species have become a nuisance, having developed into weeds.

CULTIVATION Plant in any normal garden soil and water well in summer to avoid drying out. Propagation can be either from cuttings or by division of the roots.

ABOVE *Barbarea vulgaris* is eaten raw in salads or lightly boiled as a vegetable.

CLIMATE Zone 6 and above.

SPECIES *B. rupicola*, a perennial herb from the Mediterranean, is often used as an ornamental. It grows to 30 cm (12 in) and has flowers relatively large for the genus. *B. verna*, early cress or Belle Isle cress, is one of the species used as a vegetable, particularly in Britain and Europe. *A biennial*, with fairly large, early spring flowers, it grows to 60 cm (24 in). *B. vulgaris*, yellow rocket, has become naturalized in North America. It has smallish, bright yellow flowers, glossy deep green leaves, and grows to 30–75 cm (12–30 in). This is the species most often used in cooking. It can become invasive.

Barklya (fam. Fabaceae)

Native to small areas of Australian coastal rainforest from central Queensland to northern New South Wales, this handsome evergreen tree grows to about 8 m (26 ft). It has striking golden-orange flower spikes in early summer and glossy, heart-shaped leaves. It is unlikely to be available in the US.

CULTIVATION *Barklya* needs fertile, well-drained soil, full sun and adequate water in summer.

ABOVE An ideal tree for warm climate gardens, *Barklya syringifolia* has a dense canopy, striking flowers and moderate proportions.

Pruning is recommended to encourage a good shape. Propagate from seed or semi-ripe cuttings in fall. It would need glass protection in frost-prone climates.

CLIMATE Thrives in the subtropics and tropics.

SPECIES *B. syringifolia*, gold blossom tree, is the only species of this genus. The stiff, bright gold flower spikes are shown to perfection against the dark green foliage.

Barleria (fam. Acanthaceae)

Originating from tropical India, Asia and Africa, this large genus of fast-growing, evergreen shrubs is not widely grown in the US.

CULTIVATION Grow in an intermediate greenhouse in cool and cold climates, in pots of acid, soil-based compost. Shade from strong sun. In warm climates plant outdoors in acid soil, enriched with manure and compost. These shrubs need heat and humidity in

ABOVE *Barleria obtusa*, from South Africa, is less often grown than B. cristata, but is just as pretty.

summer and dry winters. Propagate from cuttings under glass.

CLIMATE Zone 10.

SPECIES *B. cristata*, Philippine violet, is not a violet and actually comes from India and Burma! It has narrow, pointed, bright green leaves and white or mauve tubular flowers, with spiny margins. This shrub looks very pretty in summer when in full bloom. *B. obtusa* is slightly smaller and is usually around 60 cm (24 in). It has small, oval leaves and clusters of short, blueish mauve winter and spring flowers with five distinct lobes. The flowers of this species do not have spines.

Barringtonia (fam. Lecythidaceae)

These medium-sized mainly evergreen trees are mostly from tropical Asia and the Pacific with some from East Africa. The large leaves cluster at the ends of the branches and the fascinating flowers are formed of short petals and masses of long stamens. Usually in white or a reddish color, they bloom profusely on pendulous stems.

ABOVE *Barringtonia acutangula* is rarely seen in cultivation despite its spectacular display of delicate red flowers.

CULTIVATION In zone 10 it makes a good seaside plant. In cooler zones you can grow it in pots, in a warm greenhouse providing bright light. Propagate from seed.

CLIMATE Zone 10.

SPECIES Not all are available in the US. *B. asiatica*, the fish poison tree, occurs mainly in seaside areas around the Indian and Pacific Oceans. It is a small tree, growing to about 5 m (16 ft), with long, shiny leaves and striking white flowers with long stamens. A four-sided fruit develops after flowering. This fruit is extremely buoyant and capable of floating long distances. Fishermen use them as floats for nets. While few other species of *Barringtonia* are cultivated, they should be more widely grown as the foliage is very attractive, turning brilliant red before falling, mainly in spring. New growth commences almost at once.

Basil, sweet

(*Ocimum basilicum*, fam. Lamiaceae)

One of the most widely loved of the herbs, particularly in the Mediterranean, this tender annual has light green, oval leaves and small, white flowers at the ends of the stems. The delightfully fragrant leaves have traditionally been used, fresh or dried, in tomato dishes, but they also add a delicious flavor to soups and stews, meat and vegetables, particularly eggplant and spinach, and even some of the popular Asian dishes.

CULTIVATION Basil likes a light, rich soil and a warm, sunny position. In cool or cold climates, harvest the leaves before the end of fall as frost or sudden cold changes may kill the plant. In hot areas, basil will grow all year round as the seeds self-sow. Propagate from seed, sown in mid-spring, and thin the seedlings to a distance of 25 cm (10 in) between each plant. Once the plant is established, nip out the center growth to encourage a good shape. This can be used in the kitchen. Once the plant has flowered, cut it

ABOVE In warm weather, basil grows rapidly. It can be grown in pots near the kitchen door for ready access to the fresh leaves.

ABOVE *Bauera rubioides* 'Ruby Glow' has much more vividly colored flowers than the species.

right back and hang the leaves to dry in a shady, airy spot.

CLIMATE Can be grown outdoors all year round in zone 10.

VARIETIES Sweet basil grows to a height of 75 cm (30 in) and its soft leaves, when rubbed, have a warm, spicy, clove-like aroma. The tiny white flowers bloom in fall. Cultivars include 'Citriodorum', with lemon-scented leaves, and 'Purpurascens', a decorative type with dark purple leaves. 'Dark Opal' has attractive, deep purple-bronze leaves.

Bauera (fam. Cunoniaceae)

This Australian genus comprises four species of small, evergreen shrubs with attractive, heath-like, divided foliage. It is grown for its pretty, six-petalled flowers, similar to those of *Boronia*, which range from white to deep pink. Sometimes straggly in the wild, they can under cultivation become quite beautiful shrubs. *B. rubioides* is the one usually grown in the US.

CULTIVATION In very frosty climates, grow in pots of compost consisting of loam, leaf mould

and sand, in a cool greenhouse or conservatory. Ensure good light but shade from strong sun. Outdoors, they do best in open, sandy, peaty soil in a cool part of the garden, though they will grow in full sunlight. Provide a plentiful supply of moisture, particularly in summer, as they must not dry out. Prune after flowering and propagate from semi-hardwood cuttings in spring. Place under a clear cover in a light, sandy soil, with a supporting frame. Water regularly. They should take root within four to six weeks. They can also be raised from seed.

CLIMATE Zone 9 and above.

SPECIES *B. capitata* is a small, roundish bush, which grows well in heath-like areas, generally to only 30 cm (12 in). It has distinctive three-lobed leaflets and terminal clusters of dark pink flowers. *B. rubioides*, river rose or dog rose, from New South Wales, is commonly found growing on moist, shady creek banks. This pretty, spreading shrub bears delicate pink or white flowers, which look like small button-shaped roses, throughout most of the year. It grows to around 1 m (3 ft). Var. *alba*, the white form, is native to southern Australia and Tasmania. *B. sessiliflora*, showy *Bauera*, is restricted to Victoria where it is found, in particular, along the rivers and creeks of the

Grampians. It grows to around 1.2 m (4 ft). Clusters of rosy purple or magenta open-petalled flowers bloom freely in spring. This species needs a semi-shaded position and moist soil at all times. Too much sun causes yellowing of the dark green, stalkless foliage.

Bauhinia (fam. Papilionaceae)
Butterfly tree

Native to South America, South Africa, Asia and Australia, this genus comprises about 300 species of showy evergreen trees, shrubs and climbers. Bauhinias are grown for their unusual, beautiful flowers, often resembling a butterfly. They are popular in Hawaii and California. Their leaves are divided into two equal lobes which are said to represent the two brothers Bauhin after whom this genus is named.

CULTIVATION In very frosty areas, grow in an intermediate greenhouse, in pots of soil-based potting compost. Provide bright light but shade from strong sun. Outdoors, protect young plants from frost for the first two winters. Plants raised from seed show color

BELOW *Bauhinia variegata* is a good choice for small gardens or for street planting.

ABOVE Flowers of most species of *Bauhinia* resemble orchids in color and shape.

BELOW *Bauhinia galpinii* makes an excellent screen or windbreak plant.

variation from mauve to purple, sometimes to pure white. Seed from white forms usually comes true, and a white form can be identified by the paler green wood of the stems. The best forms are raised from semi-hardwood cuttings in fall. Bauhinias prefer a light, fertile, well-drained soil and full sun.

CLIMATE Zone 9 and above.

SPECIES Not all are available outside their native countries. *B.* x *blakeana* is known as the Hong Kong orchid tree and is the floral emblem of Hong Kong. This fine species has long sprays of large, reddish purple blooms which last for an extensive period. When young, this species is sensitive to frost. It grows to 2.5 m (8 ft). *B. carronii*, Queensland ebony, is an Australian native, with white flowers, edged with purple, produced in summer. It grows 6–10 m (20–33 ft) and is able to tolerate hot, dry conditions. *B. corymbosa* (syn. *B. scandens*) is a beautiful climber with masses of delicate pink flowers, 5 cm (2 in) across, in the spring and summer. It grows to 3 m (10 ft). *B. galpinii*, from South Africa, is a spectacular, low-growing species good for hedges, with sweetly perfumed, salmon red flowers and round, pale green, veined leaves. It grows to 2.5 m (8 ft) and flowers all summer. *B. hookeri*, an Australian native, grows to 12 m (40 ft), with large white flowers, edged in red. It is suitable for hot, wet coastal gardens. *B. variegata*, also called the orchid tree, originates from India and China. It grows to 2.5 m (8 ft), spreading to the same width. The leathery, dull green leaves grow to 20 cm (8 in) long and the fragrant, orchid-like, rosy purple flowers are 4–5 cm (1½–2 in) across. They bloom throughout spring and summer, and even in fall if there have been good summer rains. This species is semi-deciduous in colder areas. Var. alba grows 6–12 m (20–40 ft) tall and is the popular white-flowered form.

Bay tree (*Laurus nobilis*, fam. Lauraceae)

This tree has been in cultivation around the Mediterranean since the time of the earliest civilizations. The ancient Greeks made the leaves into laurel wreaths which were awarded for achievement in sport or war, while the baccalaureate was given for excellence in learning and the arts. This tradition also gave rise to the phrase 'resting on your laurels', which is still applied to those who refrain from further effort after winning an accolade. The dark, leathery leaves, with their pungent aroma, have many culinary uses, both fresh and dried. They are an essential part of a bouquet garni, the other herbs being parsley, marjoram and thyme. Tied in a bunch, this is added to soups, stews and casseroles and removed after cooking. Bay leaves are also used to flavor fish, meat, poultry and marinades. To dry, pick the leaves off the stalks and spread on

ABOVE Although mainly grown as a culinary herb, the bay makes a lovely ornamental if formally trained as a standard.

wire racks or hang them in bunches in a dry, airy place. Bay trees can be grown in the ground or in tubs. In the ground, they may grow into trees of 10–12 m (33–40 ft) high in suitable climates, but are more likely to be multi-stemmed or single-trunked and shrubby growing, from 6 to 8 m (20–26 ft) tall. Bay trees grown in pots are trimmed into formal shapes or grown as standards.

CULTIVATION Propagate from semi-hardwood cuttings taken from midsummer to late fall. They should be grown in full sun in well-drained soil. Apply slow-release fertilizer in spring if soil is poor and feed pot-grown plants regularly. Pruning is not generally needed unless the trees are to be trained into a formal shape. Scale insects of various species can be a pest. Small infestations can be wiped off with a damp cloth, while larger numbers may need spraying with white oil.

CLIMATE Best in regions with hot, dry summers and cool to cold, wet winters; zones 8 and 9.

Bean, broad (*Vicia faba*, fam. Leguminosae)

This upright-growing annual reaches over 1.5 m (5 ft) in good conditions and is used both for human and animal food. It is a spring and summer crop for cool areas, where it can be sown in the spring. Alternatively it is sown in fall for overwintering and producing earlier crops the following year. This bean will not produce good results under hot, dry conditions. The fresh pods are usually boiled or steamed until tender and served with a white or butter sauce. Alternatively, the seeds can be dried. Both the seeds and the pods are rich in protein.

CULTIVATION Plant these beans in a reasonably fertile, well-limed soil, with good drainage. They also like a sunny position and ample water during the growing season. Sow seed at a depth of 5 cm (2 in), then thin seedlings to a distance of 15 cm (6 in). As the plants mature, apply complete fertilizer in bands about 30 cm (12 in) from each side of the plants. However, too much nitrogen in the fertilizer will delay flowering. Mulching with animal manure or composted material will encourage the development of healthy plants. The beans are ready to pick in about 20 weeks. Tall varieties may need support. Stakes can be placed around a group of plants with twine stretched between the stakes to support the plants.

BELOW Broad beans close to maturity are tall and heavy, needing support to keep the plants upright.

CLIMATE Grow broad beans as an annual in cool climates.

VARIETIES There are numerous varieties, both short and tall growers.

Bean, common

(*Phaseolus* species, fam. Leguminosae)

Generally, the varieties derive from about three species, but fall into two groups–green beans, including scarlet runner and snap or French beans, which are produced for the fresh market, and dry types, including pinto, Barlotto, red kidney, white kidney, red Mexican and cannelino, the seeds of which are often used to produce canned products such as baked beans. Stringless beans are often preferred for practical purposes and because they produce less fibrous material in the pod itself, resulting in a tastier flavor and a shorter cooking time.

CULTIVATION Sow seed in spring in an ordinary garden soil to a depth of 2–5 cm (1–2 in). Some varieties require overnight soaking in water to expedite germination, which normally takes about two weeks, and climbing beans require a trellis or wire on which to climb. It is a good idea to create raised rows, with side furrows to catch the water. Space plants and rows at about 10–12 cm (4–5 in). Once the seedlings have

BELOW Dwarf beans are easy to cultivate and manage, but may not crop as heavily as some of the climbing varieties.

emerged, shallow cultivation will assist in controlling weeds. Apply fertilizer and water well at this stage. Once the beans have cropped, pick continuously to prolong the life of the plant and to increase production.

CLIMATE Beans are frost-tender so grow as summer annuals.

VARIETIES There are many varieties, especially of scarlet runner and snap or French beans, but buy whatever is offered locally. There are climbing and dwarf varieties of both scarlet runner and snap or French beans. The dwarf kinds are convenient for growing in containers or in situations where it is not convenient to provide supports, but climbing beans produce the heavier crops and they should be grown in preference to dwarfs where quantity is required.

Bean, Lima

(*Phaseolus lunatus*, fam. Leguminosae)

Although a perennial, this bean is grown as an annual. However, it is not as widely grown as scarlet runner and snap or French beans. It comes in both dwarf and climbing types, the earlier maturing dwarfs being the most reliable. Because the climbers grow slowly, the beans ripen late and are often killed by frost.

ABOVE The butter bean or Lima bean has become more popular in recent years and seed is readily available.

Lima beans contain more fat than other beans. There are numerous varieties of Lima bean (also known as butter bean).

CULTIVATION These plants like long warm periods and very mild weather at flowering time. If grown in other climates, they will usually not produce maximum quality and yield.

CLIMATE The Lima bean is frost-tender so grow as a summer annual.

Beaucarnea (syn. Nolina)
Pony tail

Now correctly called Nolina and native to Mexico, these succulent trees have large, swollen trunks, clusters of long, thin, linear leaves at the tips of the branches and sprays of whitish flowers. Rarely considered beautiful, these plants always attract interest.

CULTIVATION These frost-tender plants are generally grown as pot plants indoors or in a cool greenhouse. They need a well-drained, soil-based potting compost and maximum light. Water sparingly in winter. In frost-free climates, they make good specimen plants outdoors in a sunny, well-drained position. Propagation is from seed sown under glass.

CLIMATE Suitable for outdoor cultivation in zone 10.

SPECIES *B. recurvata*, the most commonly cultivated species, is capable of reaching 8 m (26 ft), although it generally grows to a much smaller height. The branching stems have long, flat leaves sprouting from the top. Mature plants produce a tall, branching flower spike of creamy yellow blooms. *B. stricta* grows to about 6 m (20 ft) and has blue-green foliage with rough, yellowish margins.

Beaufortia (fam. Myrtaceae)

Related to *Melaleuca*, this genus of 17 evergreen shrubs is native to Western Australia.

Those occurring naturally in the dry, sandy inland areas of that state do not adapt easily to garden conditions. When well grown, they make pretty ornamentals and are useful for attracting birds to the garden. All are lovely shrubs, with delicate, unusually patterned foliage. The brushes appear at the ends of the branches in summer and come in a range of colors from yellow, orange, red and crimson to mauve and purple.

CULTIVATION In frosty climates, grow in pots in a cool greenhouse, using well-drained, soil-based, lime-free or acid compost, and provide maximum light. Outdoors, except for *B. sparsa*, these shrubs do best in a well-drained, sunny position, with a dry, acidic, sandy soil. Propagate from semi-ripe cuttings or from seed. Humid conditions may kill or stunt seedlings, causing them to take years to mature, and in colder climates it is preferable to strike the cuttings under glass.

CLIMATE *Beaufortia* can be grown outdoors in zone 9.

SPECIES *B. decussata* has thick branches, stiff, oval-shaped leaves, and produces spiky scarlet brushes in fall. It grows to 2.5 m (8 ft). *B. orbifolia*, heath bottlebrush, produces superb red and green brushes at the end of the stems in summer and fall. It reaches about 1.5 m (5 ft) in height. *B. purpurea* is a smaller species, growing to 1 m (3 ft). It has short, stiff, grayish blue foliage and small, rounded brushes of mauve flowers, with purple stamens, in the spring and summer. *B. sparsa*, gravel bottlebrush, is the best known of the species. It grows to 2 m (6 ft) and has small, oval, light green leaves and large clusters of soft orange-red flowers. It prefers a semi-shaded position and a temperate climate, and will tolerate damp. *B. squarrosa*, sand heath bottlebrush, is difficult to cultivate. It grows to 3 m (10 ft) and produces orange-red or buff flowers from spring to fall.

Beaumontia (fam. Apocynaceae)

Herald's trumpet, trumpet flower

From Indonesia, Malaysia and India, these evergreen vines are grown in subtropical areas

BELOW *Beaufortia orbifolia* is a decorative species that may have potential for the cut flower market.

ABOVE This venerable specimen of *Beaucarnea recurvata* has a wide, flaring trunk and bears a prolific show of flowers.

for their handsome, deep green leaves, clusters of large, showy, trumpet-shaped, white flowers and their sweet fragrance. In cold climates, they are valued as lovely specimens for the greenhouse.

CULTIVATION In frost-prone climates, grow in an intermediate or warm greenhouse, in pots of soil-based compost or in a soil border, and ensure maximum light. Water very sparingly during the winter, at which time cooler conditions should be provided. Propagate from seed in spring or from semi-ripe cuttings in summer.

CLIMATE Suitable for growing outdoors in zone 10.

SPECIES *B. grandiflora*, Nepal trumpet flower from India, is the only species cultivated. This beautiful climber, which grows to 3 m (10 ft), needs solid support for its thick stems. It would be suitable for the medium-sized to large conservatory or greenhouse.

Beet (*Beta vulgaris*, fam. Chenopodiaceae)

This annual has been cultivated for over 2000 years. A true root crop, it is fairly easy to grow under reasonable conditions. Beet is delicious as a salad vegetable, as an accompaniment to hot dishes, and even deep fried in a light batter. Beet soup, or borsch, is also very appetizing.

CULTIVATION Well-drained soil and a sunny position are the main requirements. Sow seed directly into the soil where the plants are to grow as transplanting sets back time to maturity and they may not thrive. Soak the seed in water overnight, then sow thinly in rows, 40 cm (16 in) apart, at a depth of 2 cm (1 in). If it is necessary to thin the plants, the tops of the very young beet can be eaten as a green vegetable. Once established, apply half a cup of agricultural lime per square metre (yard), and then continue with a soaking of half-strength soluble fertilizer every two weeks. Weed

ABOVE Beetroot must be kept growing rapidly to ensure tender tasty roots. Leaves will be sweeter too.

carefully. Beet will mature in 10 to 12 weeks. Avoid growing during extreme summer heat.

CLIMATE Zone 5 and above.

VARIETIES A good seed catalogue will list many varieties. Most popular are the small globe-shaped varieties, but there are also long-rooted beetroots available.

Begonia (fam. Begoniaceae)

Native to tropical and subtropical regions, this genus comprises over 900 species. Many thousands of cultivars have also been produced and it is now possible to enjoy begonias throughout the year in many different climates, either indoors or out. Begonias can be divided into three main groups: fibrous-rooted and tuberous plants, which are both valued for their flowers, and rhizomatous begonias, mostly grown for their foliage. Begonias can be enjoyed as house plants, garden plants in suitable climates, or for seasonal bedding.

CULTIVATION *Tuberous begonias* can be raised from seed, tubers or cuttings from new shoots on tubers. Seedlings require sterile soil, with a

ABOVE The exquisite yellow flower edged in scarlet makes this tuberous begonia a triumph for the grower.

drainage layer in the bottom of the container, followed by a mixture of finely sieved loam, sand and peat in equal quantities. Sow the seed thinly over the surface and press very lightly into the soil. Water by standing the container in a tray of water until the moisture creeps to the surface. Cover the container with a sheet of glass or plastic and keep in a shaded, sheltered place. Don't cover the glass with paper or anything at all as begonias are one of the few plants that need some light to germinate their seed. Seedlings should start to appear within two to four weeks. At this stage, prop up the glass with a wedge to allow some air to circulate. Don't remove the cover altogether until most seedlings have appeared and are growing well. Make sure that adequate shade and shelter are maintained. The seedlings should be pricked out into small pots or nursery beds as soon as possible. If raising the begonias from tubers, the dormant tubers can be started in early spring by placing them, hollow end up, in trays of moist peat until the shoots appear. When the third leaf appears, transfer the tubers to individual 13 cm (5 in) pots filled with potting mix containing some peat. Keep the pots moist in a shady position, protected from frost and strong wind. Alternatively, cuttings can be taken from newly sprouted tubers. Keep the strongest shoot which will become the main stem of the plant and cut out the lesser shoots as soon as established. Make a clean cut in the tuber just below the basal ring. Crowd the cuttings into a pot filled with propagating mix and keep them shaded and moist. When new growth is vigorous, transfer them to larger pots and eventually plant out in the garden in a suitable climate or use them as indoor decoration. The display of potted begonias will be showier if the two small female flowers on each side of the more spectacular male flower are removed when small to direct energy into the larger bloom. Do not do this, however, if you wish to harvest seed. Plant tubers or small plants in a well-drained garden bed in a semi-shaded position. They like a rich soil with plenty of humus. The crowns of the tubers should be no more than 12 mm (½ in) below the surface. Water well, but do not overwater in humid coastal areas. Do not feed tubers until they have formed roots, otherwise they will rot. Begonias should be fed only with organic plant food. Protect from the hot summer sun. Ideally, they should receive full sun until about 11 a.m., with about 70 per cent shade thereafter. Tuberous begonias should be lifted and stored during the winter but regular watering and feeding should continue into early fall as the tubers must store food for the following season. If in a frost-prone area, transfer bedding begonias to pots and keep them in a warm, sheltered position until mid-fall. Then reduce watering and allow the plants to dry off and die down. The stems can then be easily removed. Lift the tubers from the soil and clean them carefully, brushing away soil and taking care to remove any remaining stem which might cause them to rot. Dry on a rack out of the direct sun for several days until the tubers feel firm and hard. Store during winter on racks in a dry, airy spot or in pots filled with clean dry sand or peat.

Fibrous-rooted begonias are grown for summer bedding. They are raised from seed sown in early spring. They prefer temperate to warm conditions, damp soil and protection from excessively hot sun. They will be killed by frost so do not plant out until all danger of frost is over.

Rhizomatous begonias grow rapidly from rhizome cuttings, but a more popular method

ABOVE *Begonia scharffii* forms a rounded shrub about 1 m (3 ft) high, the dark red undersides of its leaves complementing the flowers.

of propagation is by leaf cutting. Propagate in spring and summer, choosing leaves with strong stems. Make a clean cut to the stem with a knife. Place the stem in an open mix of sand, peat and vermiculite, and keep in a warm, humid environment. Roots should develop within three weeks. Tufts of new leaves will appear where the stem joins the leaf on rex begonias, and at the end of the stem for other species. Another method is to cut some leaves into small pieces, scatter them on trays of peaty soil and keep in a humid environment. Adventitious buds will soon develop. Alternatively, cut a leaf into triangular slices, with a main vein running through the point of each slice. Plant the slices with the points about 5 mm (¼ in) deep in a propagating mix of, for example, two parts sand and one part peat. Rex begonias prefer a light, but rich, soil with plenty of humus. Perfect drainage is essential as they are very prone to root rot. Overwatering must be avoided. Keep soil moist but not soggy. If they dry out, they should revive quite quickly if the pot is soaked in water up to its rim until the whole root ball is soaked. Water early in the morning so that the leaves have a chance to dry during the day. If fungal diseases appear, remove and destroy the infected leaves and spray with a fungicide. Keep rex begonias in warm, draught-free spots out of direct sunlight. Old specimens can be repotted or top dressed in spring or summer, but be careful not to bury the rhizome too deeply. It should rest just on top of the soil. During winter, most rhizomatous begonias, including the rex varieties, go through a dormant phase when the leaves may look shabby and wilted, but they will recover in spring. Keep the soil fairly dry during this period and do not apply fertilizer.

CLIMATE Begonias are frost-tender and can be grown outdoors all year round only in zone 10 and above.

SPECIES *Tuberous begonias* are loved for their superb double flowers which bloom profusely in dazzling colors ranging through pink, rose, red, cerise, vermilion, salmon-orange, bronze, yellow, cream, white, and a combination of these shades. The modern, summer-flowering tuberous begonias, those known as *B.* x *tuberhybrida*, have very large flowers–some growing to 30 cm (12 in) in diameter–and strong stems, and are resistant to disease. Some have frilled or ruffled petals; others have petals which are similar to those of hollyhocks, roses, camellias, carnations, and even daffodils.

Fibrous-rooted begonias, both summer-flowering varieties from *B. semperflorens* and winter-flowering varieties from *B. socotrana*, look pretty in garden beds and conservatories respectively. In addition to their brilliantly colored flowers, they have attractive glossy foliage. Some are known by the name of wax-leaf begonias. Sometimes spotted or speckled, they come in shades of deep green, bronze, dark red or yellow. The popular name 'angel wing' refers to the graceful leaf shape of some of the varieties. *B. acutifolia* has white flowers in spring. *B. foliosa* has white or rose flowers in summer. Var. *miniata* bears scarlet flowers in winter. *B. incarnata* has rose flowers in winter. *B. scharffii*'s pale pink flowers bloom in winter.

ABOVE A *Begonia coccinea* hybrid with cane-like stems. These begonias make superb house plants.

B. semperflorens cultivars produce pink, red or white flowers in summer. *B. socotrana* has produced many cultivars such as 'Gloire de Lorraine'. Tree begonias, also fibrous-rooted, make elegant pot plants and feature plants in the garden. Long-flowering shrubs with bamboo-like canes and handsome foliage, they do well in shady positions providing they receive ample moisture. Because they are shallow rooted, they can be grown successfully where there is not much soil. Plants that are recommended include *B. coccinea* and its cultivars.

Begonias grown for their foliage are usually cultivars of *B. rex* and are remarkable for the immense variety in their beautifully colored and patterned leaves. Other species grown for their ornamental leaves include *B. bowerae*. The delicate green leaves are stitched with black at the edges. *B.* 'Cleopatra' has golden-green star points on chocolate brown. *B. heracleifolia* has deeply lobed leaves. *B. maculata* has spotted white leaves. *B. masoniana*, iron cross, has a dark purplish cross on each bright green leaf. The foliage of *B. metallica* has a metallic lustre, while *B. sanguinea*'s is bright green on top, blood red underneath.

Belamcanda (fam. Iridaceae)
Leopard lily

The main species grown is a herbaceous lily-like plant originating in China, Japan, eastern Russia and northern India. It grows from a fleshy rhizome, having attractive, sword-shaped leaves and spotted, star-shaped flowers, generally in shades of orange, red or yellow, depending on the variety. The flowers are followed by clusters of shiny, ornamental seeds which extend the decorative display. Leopard lilies are a lovely addition to the mixed border.

CULTIVATION Easily grown, these plants are adaptable to a range of climates and conditions. However, they should be grown in full sun in well-drained soil enriched with organic matter. They can be grown from seed or by division of the rhizomes in late winter to early spring. They are also suitable for container growing where several should be crowded in for a good effect.

CLIMATE Suited to zone 8.

SPECIES *B. chinensis* may grow over 1 m (3 ft) high in good conditions. It has decorative,

ABOVE An easy-care member of the iris family, *Belamcanda chinensis* bears its spotted flowers in succession through the season.

sword-shaped foliage and spotted flowers in shades of red, orange or yellow. These are produced in spring or summer, depending on the district. Shiny, black, ornamental seeds follow the floral display.

Bellis (fam. Asteraceae)
Common daisy

The name of this genus derives from the Latin bellus, meaning 'pretty', and these perennials are certainly very attractive but considered a lawn weed in many cool-climate gardens. The original common name was 'day's eye', as the plant opens and closes its flowers according to the intensity of the light. These daisies have been cultivated for centuries and were often found alongside buttercups in English gardens. Today, they are popular rockery, edging and spring bedding plants. Although perennial, they are generally grown as biennials.

CULTIVATION Common daisies are suited to cool and cold climates and look wonderful among other colorful spring flowers and bulbs. They can be planted in almost any type of well-drained soil and in full sun or partial shade. Raise plants from seed sown in an outdoor seed bed in early summer. Plant out in flowering positions in fall.

CLIMATE Zone 4 and above.

SPECIES *B. perennis*, the common daisy, is often found growing in lawns. It grows to 10 cm (4 in) and produces white flowers from early spring onwards. Although a weed, this species is the parent of many cultivars developed for the garden. There are many cultivars, with fully double or pompon-like flowers, in shades of red, pink and white.

Berberidopsis (fam. Flacourtiaceae)

This exquisite evergreen semi-climbing shrub from Chile has leathery, dark green leaves and pendulous clusters of deep crimson flowers in summer.

CULTIVATION This shrub needs a warm spot and good drainage. It generally enjoys woodland conditions of dappled sunlight and shelter. If planting near a wall, make sure that the plant is positioned a little away from the wall to avoid dryness in summer and waterlogging in winter. In mild areas, plant in a shady spot in

ABOVE *Bellis perennis* can be massed in containers or grown as garden edging.

ABOVE The bright crimson flowers of the coral plant, *Berberidopsis corallina*, are suspended on fine stalks like cherries.

light, peaty soil with plenty of organic matter. It does not like lime. Propagate from semi-ripe cuttings taken in late summer or by layering young stems in the spring.

CLIMATE This plant can be grown in zone 8.

SPECIES *B. corallina* has clusters of small, crimson flowers during summer to early fall. If growing conditions are suitable, the floral display will be brilliant.

Berberis (fam. Berberidaceae)

Barberry

Native to Asia, Europe and the Americas, this genus comprises more than 450 species of attractive evergreen and deciduous shrubs. They are often used as hedges or as specimens because they grow densely and produce clusters of delightful yellow or orange flowers, as well as berries in various colors. Some of the smaller species work well in rockeries.

CULTIVATION All of the species do best in cool to warm temperate climates, and are widely grown in in gardens in the US, though many evergreens are not hardy in northern states. They prefer moist yet well-drained soils and much prefer alkaline or limy conditions. Acid soils can be limed well ahead of planting time. Propagate from hardwood or semi-hardwood cuttings of about 12 cm (5 in) in length taken in mid to late winter. Remove the lower thorns and insert into a light mix. Make sure that the mix is not allowed to dry out. Berberis are relatively trouble-free but may be attacked by aphids or powdery mildew from time to time. Some species of Berberis are an alternative host for wheat rust so these are not grown in wheat-growing areas.

CLIMATE There are species suited to various climatic zones.

SPECIES *B. darwinii*, zone 7, an evergreen from Chile, has small, shiny, holly-like leaves of deep green, golden flowers and small blue-black berries. It grows 2–3 m (6–10 ft) and is an excellent hedging plant. *B. linearifolia*, zone 6, another evergreen from Chile, reaches 3 m (10 ft) with apricot flowers and oval, blue-black berries. *B. x rubrostilla*, zone 6, produces yellow flowers and large, red, pear-shaped berries along the stems. This deciduous shrub grows to 1.2 m (5 ft). The leaves color a rich red in fall. *B. thunbergii f. atropurpurea*, zone 4, a round-headed deciduous shrub, is chiefly grown for its purple-red to coppery foliage which turns crimson in fall in cool areas. The pale yellow spring flowers are followed in colder climates by small red berries. It grows 1–2 m (3–6 ft) high. There are other cultivars of this species, including 'Aurea', with yellow foliage, and 'Atropurpurea Nana', a dwarf form, rarely growing more than

ABOVE Bright yellow flowers contrast well with the darker foliage of *Berberis* species and cultivars.

ABOVE A closely clipped hedge of *Berberis* forms a living fence. Barberry will tolerate quite harsh conditions.

50 cm (20 in) high. *B. wilsoniae*, zone 6, is a spreading, semi-evergreen shrub growing to 1 m (3 ft) high and 2 m (6 ft) across. The small, rounded leaves color in fall, and clusters of yellow flowers are followed by pretty, reddish pink berries.

Bergamot (*Monarda didyma*, fam. Lamiaceae)
Bee balm, Oswego tea

The tea drunk by the North American colonists at the Boston Tea Party in 1773 after they had refused to buy tea from Britain was made from the leaves of bergamot. Bergamot is still used today as a tea, but is also used to flavor salads and pork and veal dishes. The whole plant has a delicious fragrance and the flowers are rich in nectar. Bees are attracted to them, hence the common name, bee balm. The flowers and leaves dry well and are used in potpourri. Oil of bergamot, popular in aromatherapy, does not come from this plant but from *Citrus bergamia*.

CULTIVATION Bergamot likes a rich, moist soil and full sun or partial shade. In spring, apply a dressing of well-rotted poultry manure. It dies right back in fall and should be cut to the

ABOVE Bergamot grows rapidly in warm weather, blending easily into the ornamental garden as well as the herb garden.

ground at this time. Give plenty of water in dry weather or it will completely die out. It is easily propagated from runners or, alternatively, from seed or by division.

CLIMATE Zone 4 and above.

VARIETIES *M. didyma* has rough, hairy leaves and showy red flowers, similar to those of honeysuckle, in summer. It grows to 1 m (3 ft). Apart from being cultivated for its culinary and drying uses, bergamot is also grown in perennial borders. Several cultivars have been produced, with pink, mauve and scarlet flowers. Cultivars 'Cambridge Scarlet' and 'Croftway Pink' are probably the most popular.

Bergenia (fam. Saxifragaceae)

These easily grown perennials have large, mainly evergreen leaves and thick rhizomatous rootstocks. In some countries they are known as elephant ears. The foliage is rich green and the flowers come in a variety of shades of pink, mauve, crimson, purple or white. The plants flower in late winter in warm areas, but mainly in spring in cool zones, and are often grown as edging plants or in rock gardens. Some leaves turn red or are streaked with red in cold weather and may die back completely in some districts.

ABOVE Often flowering in late winter, *Bergenia* x *schmidtii* provides a long-lasting display of pink flowers set against lustrous, deep green foliage.

CULTIVATION Bergenia is easy to grow in most soil types. It is best in shade or semi-shade in warm areas but can be grown in sun in cool zones. It needs regular thorough watering in hot weather. It is easily propagated by dividing and replanting sections of the rhizome.

CLIMATE There are species to suit various climatic zones.

SPECIES *B. ciliata*, zone 7, native to the Himalayas, has drooping white, rose or purple flowers and grows to 30 cm (12 in). *B. cordifolia*, zone 3, from Siberia, has large, glossy, roundish leaves and clusters of delicate pinkish flowers on erect stems in spring. It looks attractive in plant borders and is useful for cutting. *B. crassifolia*, zone 3, has smooth leaves and pink, lilac or purple flowers in winter and spring. It grows to 50 cm (20 in). *B. purpurascens*, zone 4, from India, has purple flowers and small green leaves turning purple in winter. *B.* x *schmidtii*, zone 5, has pinky mauve flowers growing to 30–45 cm (12–18 in). This species is widely grown. There is an increasing range of lovely cultivars of these plants now coming onto the market.

Beschorneria (fam. Agavaceae)

Originally from Mexico, these evergreen succulents have large, fleshy leaves forming into clumps to about 1 m (3 ft) high. Dramatic red stalks produce an interesting raceme of funnel-shaped green flowers surrounded by red bracts. The flowers are edible and the leaves have been used as a soap substitute.

CULTIVATION While they are not at all difficult to cultivate, these succulents prefer a warm climate and a well-drained, sandy compost of mortar rubble and loam. They propagate easily from offshoots potted in sandy soil at almost any time of the year.

CLIMATE Can be grown in zone 9 and above.

SPECIES *B. tubiflora* grows to over 1 m (3 ft)

ABOVE Stiff gray-green leaves and a dramatic flowering spike make *Beschorneria yuccoides* a good focal plant for the garden

high, with a compact basal rosette of gray-green foliage. The flower stems, which are generally taller than the foliage, have red-purple bracts holding reddish green flowers in spring. *B. yuccoides*, Mexican lily, is quite spectacular, with long, sword-shaped, fleshy, gray-green leaves, and brilliant apple green flowers and red bracts. It grows to a height of 2 m (6 ft).

Betula (fam. Betulaceae)
Birch

There are about 60 species of birch, all of which are deciduous trees or shrubs native to the northern hemisphere. Birches play a rich role in the folklore of the northern Europeans and the indigenous peoples of North America, although many beautiful species are also native to China and the Himalayas. Many species have a long history of usage, some of which continues today. Mostly slender and graceful, the birch is one of the most popular ornamental trees. They have small, heart-shaped, vivid green leaves, with fine stalks. Some of the species are grown for the quality and color of their bark, which may take several years to develop, and for their golden fall leaves. Quick-growing in the early stages, they reach heights of 7–18 m (23–60 ft), but are still suitable for smallish gardens because they do not spread too widely. However, birches look their best when planted in groups.

CULTIVATION Birches are generally adaptable to a wide range of conditions, although they prefer light soil and an open situation. Most varieties will thrive provided they have abundant summer moisture. Birches benefit from mulching to keep their roots cool. The species can be grown from seed collected in late summer and stored in the refrigerator until early spring. Sow seed on a moist soil and lightly cover. Cultivars must be budded or grafted onto seedling trees. Birches are prone to aphids and, in the Pacific Northwest, some species are attacked by bronze birch borer.

CLIMATE There are species to suit various climatic zones.

SPECIES *B. nigra*, river birch, grows in a pyramid shape to 15 m (50 ft) and is suitable for zone 4. It does well on the banks of rivers and lakes, its natural habitat in North America. The mature trunk is rugged and blackish, while the young trunk is much lighter in color. *B. papyrifera*, canoe birch or paper birch, zone 1, also from North America, reaches a height of 15 m (50 ft) and has white papery bark which peels off to reveal pale orange-brown bark. *B. pendula*, European or silver birch, zone 2, is the most commonly grown species and one of the most elegant. It has attractive silvery white bark and small, bright green leaves which turn gold in fall. *B. pendula* cultivar 'Dalecarlica', cut-leaf birch, from Sweden, reaches a height of 10 m (33 ft) and has unusual deeply lobed

ABOVE The effect of planting birches in groups is well illustrated in this garden.

leaves. Cultivar 'Fastigiata', upright silver birch, is column-shaped. Cultivar 'Purpurea', purple birch, is tall and slender with pretty purple leaves. Cultivar 'Youngii', weeping birch, is a small tree which will grow to a height of 4 m (13 ft) if the trunk is supported by a sturdy stake. Its beautiful branches weep to the ground, making it a good lawn specimen. It grows well in cold areas. *B. populifolia*, gray birch, zone 4, from North America, is similar to silver birch and grows to 10 m (33 ft). It has smooth, pale gray bark and long, narrow leaves.

Bignonia (fam. Bignoniaceae)
Cross vine

This beautiful evergreen climber will cover a large area very quickly with its long, narrow, glossy leaves and striking clusters of orange trumpet-shaped flowers. Its long, terminal tendrils cling to surfaces by means of tiny discs. There were previously many climbing plants included in this genus but this is now the only species.

CULTIVATION Best grown in a cool greenhouse or conservatory in very frosty climates. Outdoors, this plant will need a trellis or wire for support. It is best grown in full sun, with shelter from cold winds. The soil should be well drained and heavily enriched with organic matter. Water regularly throughout spring and summer, but much less often in cooler weather. Propagate from semi-hardwood cuttings taken in late summer to early fall or from ripe seed if available.

CLIMATE Zone 9 and above.

SPECIES B. capreolata, cross vine, blooms in late spring or summer. The flowers are orange-red and are produced in abundance.

Billardiera (fam. Pittosporaceae)

This genus consists of some 30 species, mainly twining plants, all native to Australia. These delicate climbers are grown for their beautiful bell-shaped or starry flowers and showy, succulent berries, once a favorite of the Aboriginals. When in flower and fruit, they attract birds to the garden. Because they are not invasive, they are useful plants, and are equally at home in the garden or in pots, or can even be used as a groundcover.

CULTIVATION These climbers are ideal for a cool greenhouse or conservatory in frost-prone climates. They need lime-free compost or soil and bright light. Outdoors, these plants prefer moist, improved soils, although B. scandens will grow in most soils, even clay, and B. cymosa can tolerate limy soils. However they like morning sun or filtered sunlight and can adapt well to semi-shade. Propagate from the ripened seeds of the fleshy fruits, and sow in a coarse sand and peat mix. With the exception of B. scandens, the seeds may not germinate easily, some taking up to twelve months. Cuttings are more reliable. Take 10–15 cm (4–6 in) cuttings of semi-ripened wood in summer or fall, with lower leaves removed.

CLIMATE Suitable for outdoors in zone 9. B. longiflora will take zone 8.

SPECIES Not all are available outside their native Australia. B. bicolor, painted Billardiera, is a shrubby twiner from Western Australia suitable for a small trellis. It has lance-shaped, wavy-edged leaves which are blue-gray and very showy, open-petalled flowers in white, cream or yellow, striped with violet. Small purple berries follow the flowers. B. cymosa, sweet appleberry, grows naturally in the dry inland of Australia. A slender, shrubby twiner, it has lance-shaped, shiny leaves, open starry flowers in colors ranging from cream and greenish white to red, purple and pinkish violet. The oblong red berries have a pleasant acidic taste. New color forms produce bright green flowers and delicate blue flowers. B. erubescens, from Western Australia, is a fine, moderately vigorous climber with shiny, dark green, oval leaves and clusters of large,

ABOVE Bignonia capreolata is a fine climber for the cool greenhouse or conservatory, or for gardens in relatively frost-free climates.

ABOVE *Billardieria ringens*, from Australia, bears orange flowers intermittently from winter to fall.

bright red, tubular flowers over a long period in summer. With support, this species can reach 3–5 m (10–16 ft). *B. longiflora* is native to the cool, moist forests of New South Wales, Victoria and Tasmania. This species has shiny, narrow, dark green leaves and pendent tubular flowers in bright greenish yellow, sometimes with purplish color along the edges of the petals. The shiny, purple or red, oblong berries grow to 2 cm (1 in) in length. This is the purple appleberry which is favored for its fruit. *B. ringens*, Chapman creeper, is native to Western Australia. This fine climber or creeper, with longish, dark green leaves, grows to 5 m (16 ft). The orange flowers in dense clusters of up to twenty flowers turn deep red. As the youngest opens from the middle, a superb color effect is created. The flowers from winter to fall are followed by small, dry fruits. *B. scandens*, common appleberry, is a non-vigorous twiner. The most common of the eastern species, it has narrow, wavy-edged leaves and bell-shaped, pendulous flowers in greenish yellow, often tinged with purple stripes. The oblong yellow-green berries have a sweet acidic taste. The flowers and fruits develop on the plant over a long period.

Billbergia (fam. Bromeliaceae)
Vase plant

These tubular or vase-shaped plants are among the most strikingly beautiful of the bromeliads.

ABOVE *Billbergia nutans* is easy to grow and always delights with its many-colored flowers.

In their natural habitat of tropical South America they can be found suspended on trees, in ground colonies or on rocks. However they are easy to cultivate. With their exotic flowers and foliage, they make superb indoor plants, although the flowering heads do not last well. If allowed to multiply, each upright tube will bear an inflorescence in several colors at once.

CULTIVATION In frost-free areas billbergias can be grown outdoors as groundcover in shady places. In frost-prone climates grow in an intermediate greenhouse or conservatory, or as house plants, either as epiphytes by mounting them on pieces of driftwood or bark, or in pots of soilless compost which contains plenty of peat or chipped bark. They like maximum light but not direct sun. The plants' vases should be kept filled with water, which should be changed frequently. Water well during the growing season and provide adequate humidity. Propagate from offsets in the spring.

CLIMATE Zone 10 and above.

SPECIES *B. horrida* has stiff, banded leaves and an erect inflorescence with green flowers. It is a medium-sized species. *B. leptopoda*, permanent wave plant, has remarkable gray-green leaves, spotted with silver, and a red, blue and yellow inflorescence. It grows to about 30 cm (12 in). *B. nutans*, Queen's tears or friendship plant, is smaller and quite easy to grow. Often found growing on windowsills, it has a uniquely colored inflorescence in pale green, navy blue and pink. *B. porteana* is a large species with dramatic, spotted leaves, green flowers and eye-catching rosy bracts. *B. pyramidalis*, foolproof plant, forms a rosette of plain green leaves from which appears an erect, thistle head inflorescence in brilliant red. *B. zebrina* has long leaves, banded in silver, and a pendulous yellow inflorescence, surrounded by large pink bracts.

Bismarckia (fam. Arecaceae)

Bismarck palm

This genus comprises only one species of palm native to Madagascar where it grows on the drier side of the island. The fronds have been used as roofing thatch and for weaving baskets. A type of sago comes from the trunk.

CULTIVATION In frost-prone climates, grow in pots of soil-based potting compost in an intermediate to warm greenhouse or conservatory. Provide bright light but not direct sun. Outdoors, soils should be well drained and improved by the addition of decayed organic matter. Water regularly when the plants are young; mature palms are fairly tolerant of long dry spells.

CLIMATE Zone 10 and above.

SPECIES *B. nobilis*, Bismarck palm, is fast growing in good conditions where it can reach a height of 20 m (65 ft). It is a fan palm with heavy blue-green fan leaves which can grow to 3 m (10 ft) across. The leaf stalks are also blue-

ABOVE Beautiful blue-gray fans of *Bismarckia nobilis*, a palm best grown in tropical regions.

green and the self-cleaning trunk is fairly broad and sturdy.

Bitter melon

(*Momordica charantia*, fam. Cucurbitaceae)

Bitter cucumber, bitter gourd

This fruit is shaped like a cucumber but is pale green in color and has a lumpy, warty surface. It grows to around 20–25 cm (8–10 in) long.

ABOVE The strange, warty-skinned fruit of bitter melon or bitter cucumber is widely used for culinary purposes in Asian countries.

Bitter melon is an integral part of the diet of several Asian countries. In India and Sri Lanka, it is a popular addition to curries. The fruit is eaten when very young and extremely bitter, though the pulp becomes sweet on ripening. The juice has some medicinal value. This slender, annual climber is mostly grown on a trellis to keep the fruits off the ground. It grows 3–4 m (10–13 ft) high.

CULTIVATION Bitter melon needs very warm conditions. Grow in well-drained soil enriched with organic matter. Given regular water and fertilizer, it grows vigorously. Seed should be sown in spring once the soil has warmed.

CLIMATE Grow as a summer annual.

Bixa (fam. Bixaceae)
Lipstick tree

This evergreen tree, native to tropical America, is a good subject for a warm greenhouse or conservatory. In frost-free climates it is often grown as a hedge or screen plant.

CULTIVATION Under glass, grow in pots of soil-based potting compost. Provide maximum light. If growing outdoors, plant in full sun in well-drained soil which is heavily enriched with organic matter. This tree requires plenty of water in the summer.

ABOVE Rich red fruits of *Bixa orellana* give rise to the common name of lipstick tree.

CLIMATE Zone 10 and above.

SPECIES *B. orellana*, lipstick tree, is the only species, growing to about 10 m (33 ft). It has long, slightly glossy leaves and sprays of flowers that may be deep rose pink to white. The flowers are followed by bristly reddish fruits containing dark red seeds. The dye obtained from the fruits was originally used by indigenous Americans as body paint. It was also used as a dye for cloth. This dye is almost tasteless and is used nowadays as a food and cosmetic coloring. It is not often grown in the US but is planted in southern Florida.

Blackberry (Rubus species)

The blackberry is one of the most popular cane fruits grown. It is also found growing wild and can become a weed in gardens, especially if neglected. Cultivated blackberries–cultivars–are the ones to grow; there are both thornless and thorny versions. In the US there are cultivars suited to various climates, so it is important to select blackberries suited to your area. A local nursery will be able to supply appropriate cultivars. The fruits of all cultivars ripen in summer or fall.

CULTIVATION Blackberries are not difficult to grow provided you have chosen cultivars that are suited to your climate. They should be planted in full sun for optimum growth and fruit production and the plants should be sheltered from strong winds. Like other berry fruits, they should be bought dormant and bare-rooted, in winter, and planted out as soon as possible at about 3 m (10 ft) intervals. A trellis, or wires between posts, will be needed for training and support. The soil should be well prepared by digging in animal manure or compost a month or more before planting. As new growth commences, apply a light dressing of blood, fish and bone or other slow release fertilizer. Mulching around the plants conserves moisture and improves growing conditions. Most trailing berries produce fruit on the canes produced in the previous year. Pruning of blackberries

ABOVE Ripe, succulent blackberries can be eaten fresh or cooked. Thornless varieties are the best choice for cultivation in home gardens.

ABOVE The flowers of Christmas bells, *Blandfordia nobilis*, are heavy textured, almost waxy.

consists of cutting out completely all canes which have produced fruits. This is best done in late winter. The new, unfruited canes are then trained into their supports. The most commonly used method of training canes is the fan system, where stems are trained into the shape of a fan. The new canes are tied into the center of the fan as they grow and after pruning are spaced out into the fan shape.

CLIMATE In general, zones 6-8, but it is more important to choose cultivars suited to your climate.

Blandfordia (fam. Blandfordiaceae)
Christmas bells

The flowers are produced in summer and in their native Australia are used as Christmas decoration, hence the common name. In their native country they are also grown commercially as cut flowers.

CULTIVATION In frost-prone climates they are grown in pots in a cool greenhouse or conservatory. The rhizomes can be potted in fall, using acid, soilless potting compost. Ensure maximum light when in growth. Dry off during winter when the plants are dormant. In the garden, plant in a position in full sun, in well-drained, lime-free soil.

CLIMATE Zone 9 and above.

SPECIES *B. grandiflora*, large Christmas bell, from New South Wales, has showy flowers, varying from deep red with yellow tips to pure yellow. *B. nobilis*, Christmas bell, is also native to New South Wales. It grows to 1 m (3 ft), with brownish red flowers, tipped with yellow. *B. punicea*, Tasmanian Christmas bell, is found only in Tasmania. It has tall, coarse, rush-like leaves and grows in sandy soil. All species are protected in the wild.

Blechnum (fam. Blechnaceae)
Hard fern, water fern

Widely distributed in temperate to tropical climates throughout the world, this genus consists of some 200 terrestrial and epiphytic ferns which grow from rhizomes. The largest number occurs in the southern hemisphere, and these are invariably tender in the northern hemisphere, in which case they are grown under glass. However, in the US a few hardy blechnums are commonly grown, especially in woodland gardens. The majority occur in damp or swampy places. Some species have firm, thick, dark green fronds, while others

ABOVE The new growth of *Blechnum nudum* or fishbone water fern is pinky red. It is a native of Australia.

have softer fronds which are lighter in color. The rhizomes are covered with glossy brown scales and range from short-creeping to long-creeping.

CULTIVATION These ferns require ample moisture, as well as shade and protection from wind. The soil should be the normal peaty mix suitable for ferns. There should be ample organic matter for moisture retention, but the soil should also drain freely. Feed monthly during the warmer months with quarter-strength soluble fertilizer. They can be grown in the garden or greenhouse according to species, although some are more easily cultivated than others.

CLIMATE The species below are suited to zone 9 and above unless otherwise indicated.

SPECIES *B. camfieldii* grows naturally near saltwater inlets and creeks or in swampy, low-lying areas of Australia's northern New South Wales and southern Queensland. With age, it grows a small trunk about 1 m (3 ft) tall and the upright fronds turn dark green. The young fronds are bronze-pink. *B. cartilagineum*, gristle fern, comes from the drier areas of the eastern states of Australia and northern Tasmania. It has a short-creeping rhizome, covered in black scales, and the fronds are erect or semi-erect, changing in color from pink to pale green as they mature. *B. chambersii*, lance water fern, is found growing in well-shaded, moist areas of southern Australia and New Zealand. It has drooping, dark green fronds, up to 60 cm (24 in) long. *B. minus*, soft water fern, has pinkish fronds when young and glossy, erect, bright green fronds as it matures. It also forms a trunk with age. Its natural habitat is wet gullies in much of Australia and New Zealand. It is able to tolerate full sun, provided it receives adequate moisture and it will increase easily from offsets. *B. nudum*, fishbone water fern, grows naturally in cool, moist, protected areas of the eastern states of Australia, Tasmania and South Australia, where it often forms dense colonies. The upright fronds form a spreading rosette. *B. patersonii*, strap water fern, has an erect rhizome and dark green fronds, soft pink when young. They grow up to 40 cm (16 in) long and can vary in shape, from undivided to segmented. Strap water fern requires good soil and a well-protected, damp, shady position if it is to thrive. *B. penna-marina*, zone 8, is a very small species found in Australasia and southern South America. It is common in gardens in the US. Its narrow, wiry, branching rhizome is long-creeping and short, dark green fronds grow only to 20 cm (8 in) long. *B. wattsii*, hard water fern, is a vigorous grower. In its native range, which is moist mountainous areas of all Australian states except Western Australia, it spreads by underground stolons to form tangled groundcover. It can be grown easily in a large pot or in a protected spot in the garden.

Blueberry (*Vaccinium species*, fam. Ericaceae)

The blueberry originates from the eastern United States and in earlier times was a popular fruit with the indigenous Americans. It is still

ABOVE Blueberries starting to ripen show a flush of purple-blue color. Ripening fruit needs protection from birds.

popular today and is grown in home gardens as well as commercially. A fast-growing deciduous shrub, it has good fall leaf color, small white flowers and shiny black berries.

CULTIVATION Blueberries do best in moist acidic soils with a pH of about 5. If the soil is not naturally acidic, use a chemical fertilizer to increase the acid content. Propagate by division of the clumps or rootstock, by layering or by cuttings. Seeds are not reliable and do not come true. In the home garden, allow about 2.5 m (8 ft) between the plants and the rows to allow for a 2.5 m (8 ft) growth across. Plant in a hole or trench about 30 cm (12 in) deep. These shrubs will produce fruit in three to four years or less and, if given proper care, should be productive for many more.

CLIMATE Blueberries are very hardy, surviving in zone 2.

SPECIES *V. angustifolium* is a low-growing species, popularly known as the low-bush blueberry, which has been improved by selection and breeding but not widely cultivated. It grows to about 20 cm (8 in). The tall blueberry, *V. corymbosum*, more popularly known as the high-bush blueberry, is the most improved species, with many cultivars available, and is also the most widely cultivated. The cultivars grown for fruit are female. They are self-fertile, producing crops with their own pollen, but heavier crops of fruits are produced when two or more cultivars are grown together. Related species include the cranberry, the whortleberry or bilberry, and the huckleberry.

Bok choy

(*Brassica rapa*, Chinensis Group, fam. Brassicaceae)

Pak-choi, Chinese white cabbage

Bok choy belongs to the family which covers the most important and varied groups of Asian vegetables in cultivation. It is in fact a non-heading type of Chinese cabbage, also known as pak-choi and Chinese white cabbage. Grown in China since the fifth century, bok choy has smooth, green leaves and thick, white, crisp mid-veins and stalks. A good source of vitamin C and dietary fiber, it is widely used in Chinese and Vietnamese cooking. Some varieties of this fast-growing vegetable do well in warm, humid conditions but most are best grown in the cooler conditions of spring or fall. If growing this vegetable in warm districts, select varieties resistant to bolting.

ABOVE Ideal for home gardens, bok choy matures rapidly in well-prepared ground. Plant small amounts in succession to suit household needs.

CULTIVATION To ensure good drainage, grow bok choy in a raised bed. Dig in plenty of organic matter four to six weeks before planting and give the soil a light dressing of lime just prior to planting. Space plants 20–30 cm (8–12 in) apart and keep them growing rapidly by maintaining constant soil moisture. Weed control is essential. In ideal conditions, plants can be ready for harvest in as little as six weeks.

CLIMATE Grown as a summer or fall vegetable.

Boltonia (fam. Asteraceae)

These hardy, herbaceous perennials are native to North America and Asia. The flowers are like the Michaelmas daisy (Aster), usually white, purple or violet, and the leaves are alternate.

CULTIVATION Suitable for borders or groups, they will take to almost any type of soil and do well both in sun and shade. Plant in fall for late summer flowers. Propagate by seed or by division of the roots in spring.

CLIMATE Suitable for zone 6.

ABOVE Easily grown *Boltonia* flowers in later summer and fall and, like its relations, the perennial asters, makes a good cut flower.

SPECIES *B. asteroides*, false chamomile, a North American species, grows 1.2–2 m (4–6 ft) tall, with lance-shaped leaves which are up to 12 cm (5 in) long. The long, stalkless flowers resemble those of the Michaelmas daisy and are white, violet or purple. Var. *latisquama* produces sprays of blueish violet flowers. This showy plant grows up to 1.2–1.5 m (4–5 ft). 'Nana', with pinkish rays, grows to 1 m (3 ft).

Bombax (fam. Bombacaceae)
Silk cotton tree

These large deciduous trees occur naturally in the tropical forests of Asia, Africa and Australia, and grow well only in hot climate gardens. All are softwoods and all flower during spring with a showy display of scarlet or white. Some have spiny trunks or branches.

CULTIVATION In frost-prone climates, grow as foliage plants in pots in a warm greenhouse or conservatory. It is unlikely they will flower under glass. Use soil-based potting compost and provide maximum light.

ABOVE Occurring naturally in tropical Asia, *Bombax* is widely cultivated in the warm subtropics and tropics.

CLIMATE Zone 10 and above.

SPECIES *B. ceiba*, red silk cotton tree, can grow to 35 m (115 ft) high. It has a spiny trunk and branches and palmate leaves. The striking, fleshy red flowers, laden with honey, last about three weeks, providing a startling contrast to the bare branches. When the blooms fall, they form an attractive carpet under the tree. After flowering, large seed pods form, the seeds encased in thick silky hairs which have been used for kapok.

Borage (*Borago officinalis*, fam. Boraginaceae)

Originally from the Mediterranean, this decorative, annual herb is grown for the faint, cucumber-like flavor of its leaves which are used to flavor salads and cool drinks. Borage leaves can also be cooked lightly and eaten like spinach. The flowers, too, are used in salads and are sometimes crystallized using sugar and water solution for use in cake decoration. Borago officinalis has leaves shaped oblong to ovate and lovely, star-shaped, blue or white flowers. It grows to 60 cm (24 in). Borage has a tendency to self-seed in the garden.

CULTIVATION This hardy herb grows well even in poor soil and is self-sowing. Alternatively, propagate from seed, cuttings or division of the rootstock in spring.

CLIMATE Borage is suitable for growing in zone 7 and above.

ABOVE Seen here with spring onions, blue borage flowers add a touch of color to herb or vegetable gardens.

Boronia (fam. Rutaceae)

This genus comprises around 100 species prized for their sweet flowers and delightful fragrance. Most of the species have aromatic leaves, and in some the flowers are also highly perfumed. All Australian natives, they have simple or compound leaves and purple, pink, white, brown or yellow flowers.

CULTIVATION Boronias need acid or neutral soil. In very frosty climates, grow in pots or soil borders in a cool greenhouse or conservatory. Use acid soil-based potting compost and provide maximum light. Outdoors, boronias prefer a cool position, protected from hot winds, and a deep, cool, sandy loam, with a gritty texture. Very good drainage is essential. Boronias should not be allowed to dry out. To create bushy specimens, tip prune the plants after flowering. Propagate from short soft-tip cuttings in spring or early summer. Strike in pots in a mixture of coarse sand and peat. A frame is advisable. Boronias do not last well if grown in the house.

CLIMATE Zone 9 and above.

ABOVE *Boronia pinnata*, with its bright pink flowers, can be cut for indoor decoration.

ABOVE 'Jack Maguire's Red' is an unusual red form of the well-loved brown boronia, *Boronia megastigma*.

ABOVE The broad yellow petals of *Bossiaea heterophylla* resemble bright moths. The flowers are produced in fall.

SPECIES Not all boronias are available outside their native Australia. *B. heterophylla*, Kalgan boronia, is a frost-hardy species, with feathery leaves and masses of pink, cup-shaped, fragrant flowers in spring. It grows to 2 m (6 ft). *B. ledifolia*, Sydney boronia, is a rounded evergreen that grows to 1 m (3 ft) tall. It has rosy pink, starry flowers in winter and spring. The flowers of this species are pleasantly perfumed but the leaves are not. *B. megastigma*, brown boronia, is a fragrant, slender bush which prefers a semi-shaded position. It grows to 1 m (3 ft) tall. Its flowers are purplish brown outside and dull yellow inside. The blooms make excellent cut flowers. *B. pinnata*, feather-leaf boronia, is an open, slender bush, to 2 m (6 ft) tall, which can be grown in most areas. Its pink, highly perfumed flowers usually form in clusters of three. *B. serrulata*, native rose, has small, bright green, serrated leaves and clusters of bright rose, cup-shaped, spring flowers. Both the leaves and the flowers are perfumed.

Bossiaea (fam. Papilionaceae)

Found in all Australian states, this genus comprises around 50 species of small or prostrate, decorative shrubs. These tough, hardy plants are easy to grow and in very frosty climates make good subjects for a cool greenhouse or conservatory. They have small, simple leaves, sometimes absent, and mostly yellow and red, pea-shaped flowers.

CULTIVATION The seeds of this plant are held within the flattened pod. The hard coat of the seeds needs treatment before sowing. Carefully nick the seed coat or, alternatively, pour boiling water over the seeds and allow them to stand for 12 hours. Swollen seeds will germinate more easily. Sow in a mixture of coarse sand and peat at a rate of 3:1. Plant in a well-drained, sunny position. Under glass, grow in pots of soil-based potting compost in bright light.

CLIMATE Zone 9 is suitable.

SPECIES Bossiaeas are not usually available outside their native Australia. *B. heterophylla* is a small, erect, open shrub which produces large yellow and brown flowers in fall. *B. linophylla* has a rounded habit, with linear leaves, erect stems and yellow flowers in late winter and spring. It is also available in a bronze-foliaged form.

Bougainvillea (fam. Nyctaginaceae)

While these vigorous, evergreen climbers originate from tropical and subtropical South America, its cultivars in many colors have now

ABOVE This showy bougainvillea has been given strong support and trained to grow in tree form.

been developed in many other parts of the world. Most have quite vicious, hooked thorns and are able to climb over other plants or supports. Bougainvillea has alternate, mostly ovate leaves, which grow to 15 cm (6 in) long, and produces cream flowers which are insignificant. However, the persistent, brilliantly colored bracts surrounding the flowers are very beautiful.

CULTIVATION Although bougainvilleas are frost-tender they are able to survive light frosts and are widely grown in gardens in the far south and California. In the north they make excellent plants for cool conservatories and greenhouses. Under glass, grow in a soil border or in pots or tubs of soil-based potting compost and provide maximum light. Water well in the growing season and less in winter. Outdoors grow in a sunny spot with well-drained soil.

Bougainvilleas do best in a light, sandy loam, requiring additional food and water during spring and summer. Prune immediately after flowering by cutting back the stems to within 6 cm (2 in) of the older wood. This will encourage the growth of new wood and abundant flowers in the following season. From time to time, remove the older stems at the base of the plant. Propagate from hardwood cuttings taken in spring or summer. Some species root more reliably than others. To grow as standards, set a thick stake, such as 80 mm (3 in) galvanized iron piping or 80 x 80 mm (3 x 3 in) hardwood, in a concrete block. The stake should be about 2 m (6 ft) high from ground level. Remove all but the main stem from a small or semi-advanced plant and tie it to the stake. Rub the side buds off as they appear. When the plant reaches the top of the stake, allow the top growth to spread, and continue to remove the side buds along the main trunk. Trim the head to a globular shape. Bougainvilleas can also be grown as hedges. They often become very dense, producing a blaze of color throughout spring and summer. Some of the newer hybrids flower almost continuously. They can be trained to a low groundcover growth with wooden frames, and the more vigorous will quickly climb trees and walls. If trained on trellises, they need strong support. Do not plant them on old fences.

CLIMATE Zone 9 and above.

SPECIES Not all of the following cultivars will be available in all areas but there are many more of equal merit to choose from. *B.* x *buttiana* is a hybrid from which many stunning cultivars have been produced. 'Golden Glow', formerly known as 'Hawaiian Gold', has large clusters of golden yellow bracts that turn apricot with age and grows to about 4 m (13 ft). 'Louis Wathen', from India, is a lively tango color and 'Mrs Butt' (called 'Crimson Lake' in the United States) has large sprays of crimson heart-shaped bracts which deepen to different tones of magenta. The true flowers have a star-like shape. 'Mrs McClean' has star-shaped flowers

ABOVE Bougainvillea 'Louis Wathen' is an unusual shade between old gold and rich apricot

and orange bracts and 'Scarlet Queen' is a rich crimson like 'Mrs Butt', but the true flowers are not star-shaped. 'Barbara Karst' has a bushy habit, producing masses of brilliant red flowers almost continuously. It will flower at an early age, even in quite small containers. The even bushier 'Temple Fire' grows to only 90 cm (36 in) and is very suitable for containers. Its cerise or rosy violet bracts change to a terracotta-pink with age. *B. glabra* is a vigorous scrambler with smooth, bright green leaves, weak thorns and purplish pink bracts, smaller than those of many of the cultivars. Cultivar 'Sanderiana', paper flower, produces an abundance of papery, vivid rose bracts. This thorny climber can grow to 6 m (20 ft). 'Magnifica Traillii', previously known as 'Magnifica', has splendid, bright purple bracts. From the Seychelles, it grows to 8 m (26 ft) and is tolerant of frost down to–7°C (19°F). *B. spectabilis* is a striking species, with an interesting woolly covering on its leaves, short spines and rich purple bracts to 5 cm (2 in) long. The following cultivars have been developed from this species: 'Lateritia', an extremely vigorous, spreading rambler, with terracotta red bracts which age to a bronze-gold, and the very beautiful and prolific 'Scarlet O'Hara' whose deep burnt orange bracts age to orange-scarlet, then to crimson. The parentage of some of the new cultivars mentioned below is unknown. Most of these new cultivars are less vigorous than the older types and are suitable for container planting. 'Easter Parade' grows to 4 m (13 ft), with rather pointed, soft pale pink bracts. 'Killie Campbell' grows strongly to 6 m (20 ft) and its deep red bracts change from coppery red to ruby red, and sometimes to cyclamen. 'Orange King', also a strong grower, has large bundles of coppery bronze flowers, ageing to apricot and flesh pink. 'Snow Cap' is a very new development with intriguing variable bracts: some varieties have both white and purple bracts, while others have just white or purple. All of the varieties are worth planting. 'Surprise' (sometimes known as 'Mary Palmer'), with pure white bracts and magenta bracts on the one plant, is one of the most beautiful of all the bougainvilleas. At times the colors are on separate branches, at others they are on the one stem. Highly sought-after double-flowered cultivars have also been developed and these are often extremely striking. 'Klong Fire', to around 2.5 m (8 ft), has beautiful double carmine bracts, 'Thai Gold' has double golden yellow bracts, while 'Pagoda Pink' is in the most delightful pink, tinged with lavender. 'Bridal Bouquet', also known as 'Limberlost Beauty', has double white bracts, edged with bright pink. When grown in semi-shade, the bracts of this cultivar take on a green shade, resulting in a very pretty and unusual floral display.

Bouvardia (fam. Boweniaceae)

These evergreen, perennial shrubs mostly originate from Mexico and Central America. They are valued for their very beautiful, fragrant flowers, which are often used in posies and for table decoration. The terminal cymes of tubular, four-lobed flowers come in red, yellow or white and the leaves are opposite or whorled. Bouvardias were very popular in Victorian times and earlier this century but few are now regularly grown.

CULTIVATION These shrubs are generally grown under glass, except in frost-free areas. They need a cool greenhouse or conservatory and maximum light. Grow in pots of soil-based potting compost. Outdoors, grow in a warm,

ABOVE A bright pink cultivar of *Bouvardia ternifolia* makes a lovely garden shrub. Flowers cut well but last longer on the plant.

ABOVE *Bowenia serrulata* occurs naturally as an under-storey plant in dappled shade. It adapts well to cultivation in containers or the ground.

sunny position in rich, well-drained soil. Water well and feed regularly during the growing period. In late summer, cut back the shoots of the previous year's growth to within 25 mm (1 in) of their base. Propagate from cuttings of the young shoots taken in early fall.

CLIMATE Zone 9 and above.

SPECIES *B. jasminiflora* produces fragrant white flowers and grows to 60 cm (24 in) in height. *B. leiantha* has ovate leaves, downy on the undersides, in whorls of three to five, and smooth, deep red flowers. *B. longiflora* has opposite, ovate or lance-shaped leaves and solitary, fragrant, snow-white flowers. This pretty bush grows to 1.5 m (5 ft). *B. ternifolia* has lance-shaped to ovate leaves in whorls of three or four, and scarlet flowers, downy on the outside.

Bowenia (fam. Boweniaceae)

This genus of cycads from Australia comprises only two species, with a very restricted distribution, found quite rarely in their native Queensland, Australia. These cycads are characterized by their bipinnate leaves, unlike the other cycad genera which all have pinnate leaves. They have tuberous underground stems, 50 cm (20 in) long arching fronds and spiny, dark green leaflets. The cones are borne close to the ground, the female bearing the seeds which are surrounded by blueish gray flesh.

CULTIVATION These slow-growing plants usually produce only one new frond each year. However, they are fairly easy to grow. They make good house plants or they can be grown in a warm greenhouse or conservatory, in pots of compost consisting of leaf mould, chipped bark and coarse sand or grit in equal parts. Provide bright light but shade from direct sun. In frost-free climates, they can be planted in the garden; grow in partial shade and humus-rich soil.

CLIMATE Zone 10.

SPECIES *B. serrulata*, Byfield fern, is found in a very small area in the north-eastern part of Australia. It is distinguishable by its leaflets which are sharply serrated. The species that is most often grown is *B. spectabilis* which has very decorative foliage.

Boysenberry

(*Rubus ursinus* var. *loganobaccus*, fam. Rosaceae)

It is thought that the boysenberry is an offshoot of the loganberry group, which grows naturally in California, though the exact parentage is not known. It produces large, dark wine-red, almost black, berries around 4 cm (1½ in) long and 3 cm (1 in) thick. These tart, soft, juicy berries are used for making jams and drinks.

CULTIVATION Boysenberries do well in a reasonably fertile, well-dug soil, enriched with a good supply of well-rotted manure. As they are trailing plants, space them about 1.8 m (6 ft) apart and support them with a trellis or wire netting. Weed control is essential and plenty of water should be given during the growing season. Prune the plant each year to encourage the growth of the new, vigorous canes which will bear the next year's fruit.

CLIMATE This fruit grows in zone 6.

ABOVE Well-established plantings of boysenberry, *Rubus ursinus var. loganobaccus*, will continue cropping for many years if pruned.

Brachychiton (fam. Sterculiaceae)

Flame tree, bottle tree, lacebark

These striking Australian natives are mostly found in subtropical New South Wales and

ABOVE Massed waxy, scarlet bells of the Illawarra flame tree, *Brachychiton acerifolius*, are produced on bare branches.

BELOW Kurrajong, *Brachychiton populneus*, has variably shaped leaves and a sturdy, tapering trunk.

Queensland. In frost-prone climates, they are grown in pots or tubs under glass. The brachychitons have beautiful flowers and foliage, but may not bloom under glass.

CULTIVATION Grow in an intermediate or warm greenhouse in pots of soil-based potting compost. Provide maximum light. Water

ABOVE The hugely swollen trunk of *Brachychiton rupestre* is seen as a novelty, but this feature enables it to store water to survive long droughts.

Queensland lacebark tree, is a lovely, shapely tree which grows to a height of 20 m (65 ft). Its deep pink, bell-shaped flowers appear when the tree is leafless. At other times it is densely clad in bright green foliage. Its trunk is covered in deeply ribbed, greenish bark. *B. populneus*, kurrajong, is a popular shade, street or fodder tree because it can withstand drought. The abundant creamy white flowers are produced among the foliage and are followed by seed pods. The hairy seeds, if they are handled, can irritate the skin. *B. rupestre*, Queensland bottle tree, is from the warm areas of northern Australia and grows to a height of 20 m (65 ft). Curiously shaped, its fat, bottle-shaped trunk can reach 2 m (6 ft) in diameter. It has cream flowers which are blotched with red internally, and its leaves are narrow and dark green.

Brachyglottis (fam. Asteraceae)

This genus of about 30 species native to New Zealand and Tasmania comprises evergreen trees and shrubs, herbaceous perennials and climbers. It includes plants with a very attractive range of foliage types. All have daisy-type flowers. Most can be grown in exposed coastal regions where some species are used as hedges.

sparingly in winter, normally in summer. Outdoors, the plants are slow growing and may take several years to flower. They may need pruning. They need good soil and it must be well drained. Propagate from seed in early spring. Germination is usually good.

CLIMATE Zone 9 or 10.

SPECIES *B. acerifolius*, Illawarra flame tree, is a magnificent tree, arguably one of the world's best. It reaches heights of 20 m (65 ft) in ideal conditions. The handsome, maple-like leaves are shed annually and the tree produces its beautiful, bright red, bell-shaped flowers on the bare branches. The seed pods that follow contain a number of hairy seeds. Flowering is erratic. For example, flowers may cover one tree fully at six or seven years of age, while trees from the same batch of seed may reach 15 years of age without flowering, or flower on only part of the tree, while the rest of the tree remains foliaged. For this reason, it is preferable to grow flame trees from grafts of good, reliable flowerers, even though this may be more expensive. Plant in a sunny position to achieve the best from the color. *B. discolor*,

ABOVE To maintain its attractive form and foliage, *Brachyglottis repanda* is best cut back hard at the end of winter.

CULTIVATION All species need well-drained soil and a full-sun position. They are best propagated from semi-hardwood cuttings taken in late summer to early fall.

CLIMATE There are species suited to various climatic zones.

SPECIES *B. bidwillii*, zone 9, is a dense shrub to 1 m (3 ft) or more, with leathery leaves, dark green above and gray-white below. It produces small, white, summer flowers. *B. Dunedin* hybrids, zone 7, cover a range of attractive cultivars with bright yellow flowers. Most grow between 1.5 and 2 m (5–6 ft) high. *B. elaeagnifolia*, zone 9, grows to about 3 m (10 ft). It has very decorative glossy foliage and the cream to yellow flowers appear in summer. *B. repanda*, zone 10, is a spreading shrub, 3 m by 3 m (10 ft by 10 ft). The wavy-edged leaves are dark green above and furry white beneath. Creamy white, scented flowers appear in summer.

Brachyscome (fam. Asteraceae)

These low-growing Australian annuals and perennials make pretty border, edging or bedding plants and are also useful as groundcover. They have simple or branching stems, finely divided foliage and masses of pretty daisy-like flowers in white, blue or lilac, sometimes solitary, at other times loosely clustered. Of over 60 species, there are few in general cultivation.

CULTIVATION Brachyscome species are generally grown as half-hardy annuals, sown in the spring under glass and planted out when danger of frost is over. They like a sandy soil and dry, sunny conditions.

CLIMATE Zone 9 and above.

SPECIES *B. iberidifolia*, Swan River daisy, is a branching, fast-growing annual to about 30 cm (12 in), with lacy green foliage and rose or white daisy-like summer flowers. There are

ABOVE A *Brachyscome multifida* cultivar with a profusion of small starry flowers and attractive, soft, feathery foliage.

numerous cultivars in various colors including blue, purple, pink and white. *B. multifida* is a neat species, with soft, divided foliage and pinkish mauve flowers.

Brachysema (fam. Papilionaceae)

Brachysema is a small genus of low or prostrate shrubs, found mostly in Western Australia, most of which adapt well to a range of conditions. The foliage is variable, from attractive, oval green leaves, silvery and velvety on the undersides, to leafless stems. All species, except one, have bright red pea flowers. The spreading species make very good ground-covers or trailing plants. The species are frost-tender and are therefore generally grown under glass, or outdoors only where there is little risk of frost.

CULTIVATION Grow in pots in a cool greenhouse or conservatory with maximum light. Use a soilless potting compost. Outdoors, grow in a free-draining soil, well mulched with manure or compost. Propagate from the hard-coated seeds contained within the fruit. Nick the seed coat with a knife or cover the seeds with boiling water and stand for 12 hours. Those which are fertile swell and will germinate first. Sow in a coarse sand and peat mix of 3:1. Alternatively, propagate from 10 cm (4 in)

ABOVE The deep crimson flowers of *Brachysema celsianum* contrast well with the gray-green foliage.

cuttings taken in fall. Remove the lower leaves, dust with hormone powder and place in the same sand and peat mix.

CLIMATE Zones 9 or 10.

SPECIES Not often available outside their native country. *B. aphyllum* is an unusual, spreading, prostrate plant, with thick, gray-green, leafless stems and large, erect, bright red flowers. This species is sensitive to frost. *B. celsianum*, Swan River pea, is the most common species and provides excellent groundcover. This dense, leafy plant grows to 1 m (3 ft) high and spreads to about 2.5 m (8 ft), and will tolerate quite heavy, damp soil as long as it has protection from very hot sun. It has gray-green foliage and the red flowers are sometimes hidden. *B. praemorsum* is a leafy, prostrate shrub, spreading to over 1 m (3 ft), which makes a good groundcover. It has almost triangular

leaves and erect red-purple flowers which bloom over a long period.

Bracteantha

(formerly *Helichrysum*, fam. Asteraceae)

Everlasting daisy

This particular genus of Australian everlasting or paper daisies was formerly classified with Helichrysum. One of the species is the most commonly cultivated of all the everlasting daisies.

CULTIVATION The species below is grown as a half-hardy annual, although it is strictly a short-lived perennial. It is used for bedding out in the summer. Sow seed under glass in spring and germinate in warmth. Plant out when danger of frost is over. In warmer areas sow in flowering position in late spring. This plant likes well-drained soil and an open, sunny position. Although it is tolerant of drought, better results will be achieved by regular watering during dry weather. Flowers for drying, for indoor decoration, should be picked when they are only half open.

CLIMATE Zone 9 and above, but grown as a summer annual.

SPECIES *B. bracteata* is a strong-growing

BELOW Some modern cultivars of *Bracteantha* include flame shades. The papery flowers look almost artificial in the garden or in the vase.

perennial, up to 1 m (3 ft), often best grown as an annual. The foliage is a dull mid-green but the daisy-type flowers are bright golden yellow with a glossy sheen. Of the several good cultivars available, 'Dargan Hill Monarch' is one of the best. This species provides good cut and dried flowers.

Brahea (fam. Arecaceae)
Hesper palm

Native to southern California, Mexico and Central America, these fan palms are grown quite widely in California in streets and gardens, but but in cooler and cold climates they are generally grown as pot plants indoors or in cool or intermediate conservatories. Although slow-growing, they are worth planting for their attractive foliage, compact size, and tolerance of strong sun and dry atmospheres. They have solitary, thick trunks and neat, compact crowns of generally pale-colored leaves, divided to around half their depth into many narrow segments.

ABOVE Blue hesper palm, *Brahea armata*, is a spectacular sight in full bloom as the long, flowering stems arch out from the crown.

CULTIVATION Except in frost-free areas, grow in pots or tubs under glass or indoors, in a well-drained, soil-based potting compost. Provide maximum light but shade from direct sun. Outdoors, grow in a sunny position in any soil that has good drainage. Propagate from seed sown in spring in a temperature of 27°C (81°F).

CLIMATE Zone 9 or 10.

SPECIES *B. armata*, blue hesper palm, is a very handsome species, with its stiff, pale blue-gray leaves and long, slender, arching inflorescences radiating from the crown. From the ends of the dozen or so drooping inflorescences hang clusters of tiny grayish white flowers. Under cultivation, the blue hesper palm grows only to about 6 m (20 ft) and its clean, elegant, gray trunk to about 40 cm (16 in) in diameter. After the flowers have died off, a sprinkling of small, yellowish fruits appear. This species is native to southern California. *B. brandegeei*, San Jose hesper palm, also from southern California, is taller and faster growing than *B. armata*, with a more slender trunk clad in a thatch of persistent, dead leaves. *B. dulcis*, whose natural habitat is from western Mexico to Guatemala, has narrowly segmented leaves, green above, glaucous below, which are shorter than the inflorescences. The trunk grows 3–6 m (10–20 ft) tall and 15–20 cm (6–8 in) in diameter. *B. edulis*, Guadelupe palm, native to Guadelupe Island, off western Mexico, is slow growing. Its stout trunk grows 50 cm (20 in) in diameter and to 10 m (33 ft) in height. The large leaves have many finely tapering segments, pale green on both sides and the inflorescences are shorter than the leaves. The large, black fruits have sweet flesh.

Brassavola (fam. Orchidaceae)

There are around 17 species of these beautiful epiphytic orchids from tropical America. Most have long, thin pseudobulbs producing a single, cylindrical leaf. The white or greenish, long-lasting flowers are often pendulous and are very fragrant at night.

ABOVE Growing happily on a tree trunk, *Brassavola nodosa* is a true epiphyte. It has no pseudobulbs to store moisture.

CULTIVATION These orchids are grown in an intermediate greenhouse or conservatory. They take lower temperatures than many other orchids and like maximum light, without shade, and a moist atmosphere. The plants should be watered liberally during the summer but kept dry in the winter when they are resting. They are best grown in orchid baskets, using a special orchid compost (one formulated for epiphytes). As an alternative, plants can be mounted on slabs of bark.

CLIMATE Zone 10 and above.

SPECIES *B. cucullata* has very small pseudobulbs which terminate in leaf stalks concealed in white sheaths. The leaves grow to 20 cm (8 in). The flowers are white, shaded to green at the tips, and the hooded lip has inward-curving margins and a long, pointed tip. The solitary flowers, about 5 cm (2 in) across, are produced in fall. *B. nodosa* has no pseudobulbs. The erect or pendulous, gray-green leaves are rather thick and about 20 cm (8 in) long. The flowers, produced abundantly several times a year, are highly scented at night. They are white to greenish white, with a prominent, rounded white lip.

Breadfruit (*Artocarpus altilis*, fam. Moraceae)

This tropical fruit is widely cultivated in the Pacific Islands as a staple food, generally eaten baked or boiled. Ripe fruits are sweet and can be mashed to a paste and eaten as a dessert. The leaves are large and deeply lobed, with a very handsome appearance. The foliage has a wide range of uses, including thatching for roofs, clothing and as a wrap for baking foods. These trees can grow to over 15 m (50 ft) tall.

CULTIVATION If grown at all in the US it is just for novelty value under glass, although young specimens make attractive foliage plants. It needs a warm greenhouse and should be grown in a tub of soil-based potting compost.

CLIMATE Breadfruit is grown outside only in the tropics.

ABOVE The starchy breadfruit is a staple food in many areas of the Pacific Islands. The trees have very ornamental foliage too.

Breynia (fam. Euphorbiaceae)

Can only be grown outdoors in the warmest areas, with wind protection and well-drained soil. Elsewhere grow in a warm greenhouse or conservatory or as houseplants. They are also useful for warm seaside gardens, though they

ABOVE *Breynia nivosa* (syn. *B. disticha*) is a slender, ever-green shrub, with an attractive pink and white cultivar.

must be protected from strong winds. *Breynia* has small, oval leaves and single, inconspicuous flowers.

CULTIVATION In Europe, *Breynia* is grown in a warm greenhouse or conservatory, or as a house plant. They are best in pots of soil-based potting compost and in maximum light, but with shade from direct sun. Plants will need pruning to keep them to a manageable size.

CLIMATE Subtropics and tropics.

SPECIES *B. nivosa* (syn. *B. disticha*), known as the snow bush, is the most commonly grown species. The cultivar 'Rosea Picta' is even more desirable as its oval leaves are mottled pink and white. The flowers are insignificant. It grows 1 m (3 ft) or more high and would make a pretty addition to the conservatory or windowsill indoors.

Broccoli, sprouting

(*Brassica oleracea*, Italica Group)

A cool-climate garden vegetable, broccoli is related to the cauliflower. The immature flower heads of sprouting broccoli, really clusters of buds, are the parts we eat. Generally, broccoli has been steamed and served hot as a vegetable. These days, it is also used in pasta sauces, salads and stir-fries.

CULTIVATION Sprouting broccoli is a long-term crop. Sow seed in an outdoor seed bed in spring and transplant young plants to their cropping positions in early to middle of summer. Space plants 60 cm (24 in) apart each way. The plants will be ready for harvesting in the following late winter and spring. Sprouting broccoli needs very fertile soil and plants may need staking in windy locations.

CLIMATE Suited to zone 8.

VARIETIES There are both purple-sprouting and white-sprouting cultivars. The former are the hardier and are also more productive.

Brodiaea (fam. Alliaceae)

This genus of 15 species of hardy corms grows in a range of habitats in western North America. Slender stemmed, with grass-like leaves, they produce pretty clusters of

ABOVE Sprouting broccoli is a long-term but very produc-tive vegetable crop, suited to cool climates. The immature flower heads are the parts we eat.

bell-shaped blooms during spring and summer. The flowers are mainly in shades of violet and blue, but may also be pink. Many species of this genus have been reclassified under *Dichelostemma* and *Triteleia*.

CULTIVATION *Brodiaea* can be grown in containers, as a border plant, or in a rock garden. They will tolerate very light shade. The soil should be well drained, but contain enough organic matter to retain some moisture. Bulbs should be planted 5–7 cm (2–3 in) deep in early to mid-fall. These plants need ample moisture during spring and early summer, but should be kept fairly dry in late summer and fall. In areas with cold winters protect corms from frost with a mulch. Propagate from seed sown in early spring or from offsets of bulbs in fall.

CLIMATE Zones 8 and 9.

SPECIES *B. californica* grows to 45 cm (18 in), with blue to purple flowers to about 4 cm (1½ in) long. *B. coronaria* grows to around the same height and has violet or purple flowers.

B. elegans has deep mauve blooms and its flower stems grow to 50 cm (20 in). *B. minor* is smaller, to 30 cm (12 in), with pink or violet flowers. *B. stellaris* is a miniature variety, to 15 cm (6 in), with tiny purple blooms.

Bromelia (fam. Bromeliaceae)

This genus of plants belongs to the bromeliad family of the West Indies and tropical America. The stiff leaves are edged with sharp, mostly hooked, spines and form basal rosettes from which the dense sprays of fleshy, three-petalled flowers arise. The bracts are usually bright red and the fruit is a yellow to orange colored berry. A number of cultivars with variegated foliage have been developed.

CULTIVATION Except in the warmest areas bromelias need to be grown in a warm greenhouse or conservatory. Alternatively, they make good house plants. A humid atmosphere is needed for healthy growth. Grow in pots of soilless potting compost (a special bromeliad compost may be available). Grow plants in the smallest possible containers as they dislike

ABOVE *Brodiaea*, with flowers often blue or purple, is an attractive cormous subject for mixed and herbaceous borders.

ABOVE The unusual inflorescence of *Bromelia balansae* is surrounded by stiff, scarlet bracts. Spined leaves deter predators.

over-potting. Water well in the growing season but keep drier in winter. Provide bright light but shade the plants from direct sun.

CLIMATE Only grown outdoors in the subtropics and tropics.

SPECIES *B. balansae* has very sharp spines on its stiff, gray-green leaves, which grow to 1.4 m (5 ft) in length. Some of these leaves in the center of the plant turn red during flowering. A spike of violet flowers is produced in summer. *B. pinguin* has narrow, light green leaves about 2 m (6 ft) long. White, pink or reddish colored flowers are borne in a short, mealy panicle. The fruit of the species is edible. *B. serra* has grayish-green leaves to 1.4 m (5 ft) long which turn pink, and a spike of blue-purple flowers and bright red bracts.

Browallia (fam. Solanaceae)

Native to South America, these annuals or perennials have pretty blue, violet or white tubular, five-lobed flowers and generally simple leaves. They are tender plants which are grown as pot plants to decorate greenhouses or conservatories (intermediate conditions are required for these plants).

CULTIVATION Sow seed in early spring to produce plants for flowering during the summer.

ABOVE For a long flowering period through the warm months, it is hard to surpass the blue-flowered Browallia speciosa.

Germinate the seed at 18°C (64°F). Seedlings are best potted into soil-based compost. Provide bright light but shade from strong sun. If winter or spring flowering is required, sow seed in late summer.

CLIMATE Generally grown outdoors only in tropical climates.

SPECIES *B. americana* is a glabrous annual, with oval leaves to 7 cm (2¾ in) long and blue or violet flowers. It grows to 60 cm (24 in). The cultivar 'Caerulea' has pale blue flowers and 'Nana' is a dwarf plant in the same color as the parent. *B. speciosa* grows to 1.5 m (5 ft) tall and is shrubby at the base. Usually grown as an annual, it has oval leaves and blue, violet or white flowers. There are several cultivars of both species.

Brugmansia (fam. Solanaceae)

Angel's trumpet

These large shrubs or small trees originate from South America, many from the Andes. All have narcotic alkaloid properties but are widely grown as ornamentals in warm regions. They have simple leaves and large, pendulous, trumpet-shaped flowers with flaring mouths which are very striking.

CULTIVATION In areas subject to regular hard frosts, brugmansias are grown in a cool greenhouse or conservatory. Use large pots or tubs and a soil-based potting compost. Provide maximum light. Keep only just moist in winter. Plants can be placed outside for the summer. For outdoor cultivation, grow in any moderately fertile, well-drained soil in full sun or partial shade, with shelter from very strong winds.

CLIMATE Zone 9 and above.

SPECIES *B. arborea* occurs from Ecuador to northern Chile. It grows 2–4 m (6–12 ft), with pure white trumpet flowers. *B. x candida*, widely grown in South America, has mostly

ABOVE Elegant, white, trumpet flowers with fluted margins are a feature of the lovely *Brugmansia suaveolens.*

white flowers, occasionally yellow or pink. It grows 3–6 m (10–20 ft). *B. sanguinea*, 10–12 m (33–40 ft), has red flowers, ageing to yellow. *B. suaveolens*, 2–4 m (6–12 ft), is a commonly grown species and has white trumpet flowers which are fragrant at night.

Brunfelsia (fam. Solanaceae)

Morning, noon and night; yesterday, today and tomorrow

These attractive, free-flowering shrubs and trees are natives of South America and the West Indies. Mainly evergreen, they have pretty, fragrant flowers, either in terminal clusters or solitary, and simple, alternate, entire leaves. Many flower in late winter to spring.

CULTIVATION In frost-prone climates, grow in an intermediate greenhouse or conservatory, in pots or tubs of soil-based potting compost. Provide good light but shade from direct sun. Outdoors, plant in a rich, well-drained soil in a sunny spot which is shaded during the hottest part of the day. Lightly prune established plants before new growth starts. Propagate from softwood cuttings in spring or early summer.

CLIMATE Zone 10.

SPECIES *B. americana*, lady-of-the-night, has oblong to oval leaves, white flowers, fading to yellow in midsummer, and yellow berries. It grows to 2 m (6 ft). *B. australis* is an erect or spreading shrub which grows to only 60 cm (24 in). It has oval to oblong leaves, dark green on top with lighter green below, and dark purple summer flowers which fade quickly to nearly white. *B. latifolia*, almost a dwarf shrub, has oval leaves and whitish to lavender flowers, with purple or lighter centers. Sometimes the flowers are solitary, sometimes they form small clusters. *B. pauciflora* is similar to *B. australis* but with much larger blooms, generally of a richer purple color, fading to pale blue, then to white. This is a spring-flowering species.

ABOVE *Brunfelsia latifolia* shows its pretty flowers at several stages of maturity.

Brunnera (fam. Boraginaceae)

From Siberia and the Mediterranean, these perennials are generally grown only in cool climates. They have hairy stems, oval leaves and broad clusters of small blue flowers. They are often grown as groundcover or as border plants.

CULTIVATION *Brunnera* will grow successfully in ordinary, moist, well-drained garden soil in semi-shade. Propagate by root cuttings during the winter.

CLIMATE This plant is very hardy and will thrive in zone 3.

SPECIES *B. macrophylla* grows to 45 cm (18 in), with slender stems, basal leaves and blue summer flowers, about 6 mm (¼ in) across. There are several cultivars of this species, including 'Dawson's White' which has leaves with wide, creamy white margins.

BELOW With clear forget-me-not blue flowers, *Brunnera macrophylla* is a lovely perennial for cool climate gardens.

Brunonia (fam. Brunoniaceae)

Native to inland Australia, this single-species genus has tufted rosettes of foliage and blue cushion-like flowers. The leaves are covered in long, silky hairs. The plant is unlikely to be available outside its native Australia.

ABOVE The unusual flowers of *Brunonia australis* can be appreciated only at close quarters.

CULTIVATION Propagate from seed contained in the small, nut-like fruit which falls from the plant when ripe. The seed will germinate easily in moist, well-drained sand if placed in a sunny, warm position or in seedboxes. Plant out in early spring.

CLIMATE Suitable for zone 9.

SPECIES *B. australis*, blue pincushion, is a very pretty perennial, with tall stems, to 40 cm (16 in), bright cornflower blue flower heads, up to 4 cm (1½ in) across, with yellow stamens slightly longer than the flowers. From late spring to fall, these plants make a very striking display, either in the garden, as pot plants, or as groundcover in rockeries.

Brunsvigia (fam. Amaryllidaceae)

These tender, bulbous plants are originally from South Africa. In summer and fall, a dazzling display of large, funnel-shaped, red or pink flowers radiate from the tops of the tall, bare stems.

CULTIVATION The bulbs, which grow as large as 25 cm (10 in) across, like a rich, well-drained soil and full sun when planted in the garden. Water only when growth begins and continue

ABOVE Also known as candelabra lily, *Brunsvigia josephinae* bears its rose pink flowers on sturdy stems before the leaves appear.

until the leaves turn yellow, then cease altogether. In climates prone to hard frosts, grow in a cool greenhouse or conservatory, in pots of soil-based potting compost. Plant in fall. The neck of the bulb should be above compost level. Ensure maximum light and water normally when in growth but very little when dormant.

CLIMATE Suitable for outdoor cultivation in zone 9.

SPECIES *B. josephinae*, Josephine lily, produces bright red flowers, 6 cm (2½ in) long. The ribbed leaves, to 1 m (3 ft) long and 4 cm (1½ in) wide, appear after flowering. This species grows to 45 cm (18 in).

Brussels sprouts

(*Brassica oleracea* Gemmifera Group, fam. Brassicaceae)

This annual develops small, green, compact buds in the leaf axils along the stem. These buds are what we eat. Brussels sprouts are boiled or steamed and eaten in winter. They have been cultivated in Europe for about 400 years.

CULTIVATION Brussels sprouts are sown in spring, from early to late in the season depending on

ABOVE The small, round buds of Brussels sprouts can be seen developing in the axils of the leaf bases.

whether you want to harvest the crop in late fall, in the middle of winter or in early spring. Varieties for early cropping are not so hardy as those bred to withstand the winter. Seed can be sown in seed trays or cell trays under glass, especially early sowings, or in an outdoor seed bed. Plant out when they are large enough, 45–60 cm (18–24 in) apart each way depending on height of the variety (dwarfs need less space than tall ones).

CLIMATE Zone 8 and above.

VARIETIES There are varieties available to produce fall, winter and spring cropping. Brussels sprouts do not like long, excessively hot summers. Where this may be a problem choose heat-tolerant cultivars.

Buckinghamia (fam. Proteaceae)

Ivory curl flower

This Australian genus was previously known to contain only one species. Another has now been added. Both species are native to forests of the coastal ranges of Queensland where they grow in well-drained soils of volcanic origin. It is unlikely that this genus is available outside its country of origin.

CULTIVATION In frost-prone climates, grow ivory curl flower in a warm greenhouse or conservatory in pots of soil-based potting

ABOVE Massed curly, cream flowers of *Buckinghamia celsissima* attract insects and many types of birds.

compost and provide maximum light. In warm, sunny, coastal areas, these relatively pest-free trees grow best in soil which is well-drained and rich in organic matter, provided they are exposed to plenty of moisture. They are best left unpruned, although some gardeners like to cut off the lower branches.

CLIMATE Zone 10.

SPECIES *B. celsissima*, ivory curl flower, is quite a beautiful tree, with attractive foliage that may extend from the top of the tree to ground level, and long, cream flower spikes, similar to grevillea. The flowers grow to 20 cm (8 in) in length and appear from mid to late summer from the time the tree is about three years old. It grows to heights of about 10 m (33 ft), although in its wild state it may reach 25 m (80 ft) or more. *B. ferruginiflora* grows to about 30 m (100 ft) tall in its native habitat but as it has not been grown in gardens for very many years its ultimate height under cultivation is unknown. The flowers of this plant are perfumed and creamy in color, but are covered with rusty brown hairs. The leaves tend to be lobed during some stages of growth but are simply shaped when they are more mature.

Buckwheat

(*Polygonum fagopyrum* syn. *Fagopyrum esculentum*, fam. Polygonaceae)

This annual plant has been cultivated for at least 1500 years in China and was introduced to Europe in the 15th century. It may have originated in northern India. Often found naturalized, it is nevertheless grown as a crop. Its good-quality flour is used for baking cakes, bread and crumpets, and in Japan for making dough noodles and dumplings. Beer is sometimes brewed from the grain. It also has a long history of use in herbal medicines. It has small, triangular leaves and clusters of fragrant, white flowers near the top of the plant, which grows to about 60 cm (24 in) high.

CULTIVATION Buckwheat grows well on poor soils and has a relatively short growing season. Seed should be planted in spring and the crop harvested in fall.

CLIMATE Grow as a seasonal annual during warmer months.

ABOVE Although grown mainly as a source of high protein flour, buckwheat is an attractive plant with pretty white flowers.

Buddleja (fam. Buddlejaceae)
Butterfly bush

Mostly native to eastern Asia, but with some species from Africa and the Americas, these evergreen or deciduous shrubs are generally hardy and easy to grow. Most have pointed, lance-shaped, opposite leaves but the flowers vary, sometimes appearing as spikes or globes, at other times, in clusters or whorls. The fragrance of the flowers attracts butterflies, hence the common name. Buddleja grows rapidly but may be relatively short lived.

CULTIVATION These shrubs thrive in rich, well-drained soil in a sunny position, though they will grow in most soil types. Propagate from semi-ripe cuttings taken in summer, hardwood cuttings in fall or winter, or soft tip cuttings in spring. *B. davidii* cultivars should be pruned back hard in early spring to control size and to maintain vigorous growth and good flowering.

CLIMATE There are species for various climates.

SPECIES *B. alternifolia*, zone 5, has long, arching branches, clusters of small, lilac, fragrant flowers and alternate gray leaves, hairy on the undersides, to 10 cm (4 in) long. A deciduous, weeping shrub, it grows to 3 m (10 ft). *B. davidii*, zone 5, the best known of the species, is a hardy, deciduous shrub growing vigorously to a height and spread of about 3 m (10 ft). It becomes very dense when

ABOVE Cones of densely packed, tiny flowers of this white *Buddleja* provide nectar for butterflies.

regularly pruned. The fragrant flowers in lilac with orange eyes grow in long spikes to 25 cm (10 in) and the dark green, lance-shaped leaves are grayish underneath. Cultivar 'Ile de France' has rich purple-blue flowers; 'Nanho Blue' is a dwarf variety to 2 m (6 ft), with heliotrope-mauve flowers; 'Magnifica', with rose-purple flowers, also grows to 2 m (6 ft). Cultivar 'Pink Pearl' has soft mauve-pink flowers. 'Variegata' has large spikes of lavender flowers and cream and green foliage; veitchiana is similar to 'Variegata', but does not have variegated foliage. Cultivar 'Black Knight' has flowers in the deepest purple; 'Charming' has lavender-pink flowers; 'Dubonnet' has deep purple flowers. *B. farreri*, zone 9, has small, rose-mauve flowers and variable, heart-shaped leaves, white-felted below and 10–20 cm (4–8 in) long. It is a semi-deciduous species to 3 m (10 ft) tall. *B. officinalis*, zone 9, has sprays of fragrant, lilac flowers with orange markings in winter and spring and narrow, gray, heart-shaped leaves, woolly white or yellow beneath. This evergreen grows to 3 m (10 ft). *B. salvifolia*, zone 9, another evergreen, grows vigorously and densely to 2.5 m (8 ft). It produces terminal clusters of pretty, sweetly perfumed, pale lilac flowers, with orange throats, in late fall and early winter. The long, heart-shaped leaves are gray-green on top and whitish below.

Bulbine (fam. Asphodelaceae)

This group of clump-forming succulent and non-succulent plants from South and East Africa, and also Australia, are very variable. They may be bulbous, tuberous perennials or even annuals. The long, narrow leaves are sometimes grooved on the top or rounded, and mostly form rosettes. Small, starry flowers colored yellow, white or a rich orange are borne in dense, terminal racemes.

CULTIVATION A cool greenhouse or conservatory will be needed in areas prone to hard frosts. Grow in pots of very well drained, soil-based potting compost, with maximum light and

ABOVE Starry yellow flowers stud the grassy foliage of *Bulbine bulbosa*, in mid to late spring.

plenty of ventilation. Water normally in growing season but do not water in winter. In the garden, grow in a sunny spot in any well-drained soil. Propagate from seed or by division of clumps in spring.

CLIMATE Zone 9 is suitable for *Bulbine*. Most tolerate light frosts.

SPECIES *B. alooides*, from South Africa, forms clumps with age. The rosettes are quite large, about 25 cm (10 in) in diameter, and the flat, tapering, light green leaves are very fleshy. Sprays of yellow, self-fertile flowers are borne on tall stems. Sometimes several stems are produced by the one plant. *B. bulbosa*, bulbine lily, from eastern Australia, has a bulbous stem base from which grow linear, onion-like leaves, 15–30 cm (6–12 in) long. The leaves are grooved on the upper side, blunt-tipped and fleshy. The yellow flowers are about 25 mm (1 in) across. *B. frutescens* is a branching plant, up to 60 cm (24 in) tall, with fibrous roots. The bright green leaves are 22 cm (9 in) long and 4–8 mm (⅙–⅓ in) wide. This species produces many bright yellow, white or rich orange flowers in its racemes. *B. semibar-*

bata (which is now known as Bulbinopsis semibarbata), is a perennial with fibrous roots, native to Australia. The leaves form a dense rosette, with 30 cm (12 in) stems topped with a raceme of yellow flowers.

Bulbinella (fam. Asphodelaceae)
Golden wand lily

Native to South Africa and New Zealand, this small genus of hardy, herbaceous perennials is related to Bulbine. It has fleshy, tuberous rhizomes, shiny, succulent, grass-like leaves and terminal racemes of yellow, orange or white flowers on bare stems. They make very pretty border plants for warm climates. Depending on the species and district, they may flower from late winter through to summer.

CULTIVATION In areas of hard frosts, grow in a cool greenhouse or conservatory in pots of well-drained, soil-based potting compost. Outdoors, these plants like a sunny or partially shady spot and rich, light, acid to neutral soil,

ABOVE Clear yellow flowers of *Bulbinella floribunda* light up the garden for several weeks in late winter and spring.

mulched with well-rotted manure in spring. *B. hookeri* thrives in somewhat dry conditions. Propagate from seed or by division in spring. They flower best when clumps are not disturbed for some years.

CLIMATE Zone 9.

SPECIES *B. floribunda*, from South Africa, has 15 cm (6 in) long racemes of bright yellow flowers. It grows to 75 cm (30 in). *B. hookeri*, from New Zealand, grows to a little under a metre (3 ft) tall; its bright orange-yellow flowers form racemes to 25 cm (10 in) long. These bloom in spring or summer. *B. rossii*, a sturdy New Zealand species, grows over 1 m (3 ft) high and has bright yellow flowers in spring.

Bulbophyllum (fam. Orchidaceae)

This very large genus of 1000 to 1200 orchids is distributed widely, mostly in the tropics. Many species are found in New Guinea. It is possible to select only a few species here to give a general idea of the genus. This plant usually has a conspicuous pseudobulb and a single leaf, sometimes two, growing from the top of the pseudobulb, but in some cases it has a long rhizome which bears a number of well-spaced pseudobulbs. These are hard to contain

BELOW Fine, feathery, cream flowers on this *Bulbophyllum* are best appreciated at close quarters.

in a pot so may be better grown in a basket. The leaves vary greatly in size between the species.

CULTIVATION Grow bulbophyllums in a cool to intermediate greenhouse or conservatory. They are best grown in orchid baskets or shallow, hanging pots, in special compost formulated for epiphytic orchids, which includes coarse bark and charcoal. You should be able to buy this from an orchid nursery. Alternatively, plants can be mounted on slabs of bark which can then be hung up in the greenhouse. During the summer, plants need high humidity and shade from direct sun. Water normally and freely at this time but do not water in winter, when the compost must be dry. Mist spray the plants with tepid water several times a day in summer. No shading is needed in winter. New pseudobulbs can be encouraged to grow by placing a layer of sphagnum moss on top of the compost or on the surface of the bark slab. These orchids grow fairly slowly but this is not an excuse for excessive feeding. Apply a very weak liquid fertilizer solution every week or two during the growing season.

CLIMATE Grown outdoors only in tropical and subtropical climates.

SPECIES *B. globuliforme* is probably one of the smallest orchids of any type, with pseudobulbs about 2 mm ($\frac{1}{12}$ in) in diameter; the leaf is 1.5 mm ($\frac{1}{16}$ in) long and the flower parts vary from 1 to 3 mm ($\frac{1}{25}$–$\frac{1}{8}$ in). Native to Australia's northern New South Wales and southern Queensland, this plant is rarely seen because it grows on the upper branches of the hoop pine, *Araucaria cunninghamii*. *B. lobbii* is an exceptional orchid from Indonesia, Borneo and Malaysia. This species is difficult to plant in a pot as the pseudobulbs appear at up to 8 cm (3 in) intervals along the rhizome. However the roots of the new pseudobulbs will adhere to the outside of the pot. The rhizome can actually be trained across a number of pots. The leaves of this plant can reach 25 cm (10 in) in length and 7 cm (2¾ in) in width. The single, erect, yellow-brown inflorescence measuring 7–10 cm (2¾–4 in) across, is produced from any node on the rhizome. It flowers in summer. Although it grows in the wild at an altitude of 1200 m (40 000 ft), it needs to be housed under glass outside the subtropics. *B. longiflorum* occurs naturally in Southeast Asia and Papua New Guinea and in Cape York in northern Australia. The pseudobulb is 2–3 cm (1 in) high and produces a single leaf to 15 cm (6 in) long. The erect raceme of six or seven flowers, arranged in a half-circle, arises from the base of the pseudobulb. The greenish cream flowers, with purple dots or blotches, are spectacular. This species does reasonably well outdoors in frost-free areas but may need extra warmth to flower. In areas which experience frost, it will need to be grown under shelter.

Burchellia (fam. Rubiaceae)
Buffalo-wood, wild pomegranate

This genus consists of only one species–an evergreen shrub, native to South Africa.

CULTIVATION In climates prone to hard frosts, grow in a cool greenhouse in pots of soil-based potting compost and in maximum light. Outdoors, the buffalo-wood needs to be grown in a warm, sheltered position in free-draining soil enriched with compost or manure. It does not usually need to be pruned. Propagate from semi-hardwood cuttings taken in late summer or fall.

CLIMATE Zone 9.

SPECIES *B. bubalina* is the sole species of the genus. It has glossy, wavy leaves, to 10 cm (4 in), and clusters of swollen, tube-like, bright red flowers, about 2.5 cm (1 in) long, during spring or summer.

Burnet (*Sanguisorba minor*, fam. Rosaceae)

This perennial herb has pretty, fern-like leaves and clusters of green-white, thimble-shaped flowers in summer. It grows to around 30 cm (12 in) in height and can be used as ground-cover, provided the flower stalks are cut off, as they scatter seeds freely. The leaves have a pleasant, cucumber-like flavor and can be used in salads and in fruit drinks or punches.

CULTIVATION Burnet is quite hardy and will do well in most climates. Plant in well-drained, moderately rich soil in a sunny position and give plenty of water in dry weather. Fertilize in

ABOVE Easy-care shrub *Burchellia bubalina* grows 2–3 m (6–10 ft) high, with dark, glossy foliage and red or orange, tubular flowers in spring to summer.

ABOVE Salad burnet does not need to be confined to the herb garden as its pretty foliage and flowers team well with ornamentals.

spring if soil is very poor. Propagate from seed or by division in fall or spring. Once established, burnet will self-sow.

CLIMATE Zone 5 and above.

Bursaria (fam. Pittosporaceae)
Sweet bursaria, prickly box

Native to Australia, these shrubs or trees make lovely ornamental plants and are also useful as hedges. Most are rather spiny. Height is also variable: in alpine areas they are prostrate; in coastal river valleys they grow up to 10 m (33 ft) tall. Masses of fragrant, cream or white flowers appear in summer, followed by branched clusters of unusual, brown, heart-shaped seed pods.

CULTIVATION These plants will adapt to most garden situations and soils. Propagate from the seeds contained in the papery pods or from 10 cm (4 in) long tip cuttings in fall. Remove the leaves from the cuttings and dust with hormone powder. Both seeds and cuttings should be placed in a coarse sand and peat mix at the rate of 3:1.

CLIMATE Zone 8.

SPECIES *B. longisepala* has crowded short leaves, with many slender spines, clusters of white, starry flowers and brown seed capsules.

This species is shrub-like. *B. spinosa*, sweet bursaria or native box, is found throughout Australia as either a thorny shrub or small tree, depending on its habitat. The leaves vary from small to 3–4 cm (1–1½ in) long, from leafy to leafless, from lightly spined to heavily spined. The dense panicles of highly perfumed, tiny, cream or white starry flowers look very pretty in summer. This is a useful and easily grown hedging plant.

Butia (fam. Arecaceae)

Originating from South America, only one of the eight species of this palm is common in cultivation elsewhere in the world. Because the foliage color provides good contrast, it is an interesting addition to mixed palm plantings and makes a good specimen tree as well.

CULTIVATION In areas prone to frosts, grow this palm in a cool greenhouse or conservatory. As a young plant it makes a fine specimen. Grow in a pot of soil-based potting compost and do not subject the plant to direct sun, but provide good light. Outdoors, this palm tolerates full sun from a young age. Adaptable to both dry inland and exposed coastal conditions, it is also tolerant of a wide range of soil types. It does, however, need good drainage. This palm does best if given regular water and fertilizer during the growing season.

ABOVE Clouds of nectar-rich, scented flowers cover the prickly *Bursaria spinosa* throughout summer. It provides both food and shelter for small birds.

ABOVE Adaptable to a range of climates and conditions, *Butia capitata* provides foliage contrast with its arching gray-green fronds.

CLIMATE Warmest parts of zone 9 or zone 10.

SPECIES *B. capitata*, wine palm or jelly palm, is so called because of its edible fruits which can be boiled and strained to make jelly or fermented into wine. Rarely growing more than 6–8 m (20–26 ft) high, it can be fairly slow. It has a sturdy, clean trunk and gray-green arching fronds which make it very distinctive. It is an excellent feature palm or contrast when planted with other palms. There are some distinct named varieties of this palm. *B. yatay*, Yatay palm, a native of Argentina, may grow 10–12 m (33–30 ft) with its trunk covered in old leaf bases. The fronds are a silvery green.

Buxus (fam. Buxaceae)

Box, boxwood

These evergreen trees and shrubs are mainly cultivated as hedges, screens or edging plants, and also as formally shaped container plants. The very hard wood is used in a variety of timber products. The small leaves are stiff and shiny, and the cream flowers are small and insignificant. There are about 70 species of box, native to Europe, the Mediterranean, South Africa, eastern Asia and the West Indies.

CULTIVATION Box does best in partial shade but it will tolerate full sun provided the soil remains moist. It can tolerate a range of soils, but the soil must be free draining. For hedging, the soil

BELOW This box hedge has been trained and shaped to enclose and echo the form of the garden seat.

ABOVE Dwarf edging box, *Buxus sempervirens* 'Suffruticosa' can be tightly clipped for formal edging.

must be well dug and heavily enriched with organic matter to ensure that the plants will thrive. Space plants 30–50 cm (12–20 in) apart, except for the dwarf forms which should be planted 15 cm (6 in) apart. Pruning and shaping may need to be done several times during the growing season. Propagate from semi-ripe cuttings taken from early summer through to fall. The species may also be grown from seed.

CLIMATE There are species for various climatic zones.

SPECIES *B. balearica*, zone 8, from the western Mediterranean, is capable of growing to 8 m (26 ft) or more and is best suited to warm climates. *B. microphylla*, zone 6, and especially the form var. *japonica*, Japanese box, grows between 1 and 2.5 m (3–8 ft) high. There are numerous cultivars of *B. microphylla* which are much preferred to the species and they are commonly planted. The leaves are rounder and a paler green than those of English box. It grows well in cool zones and also suits warm areas better than *B. sempervirens*. *B. sempervirens*, common or English box, zone 5, grows 2–9 m (6–30 ft). Numerous cultivars are available, including 'Suffruticosa', a dwarf variety used for edging garden beds. These are the species most commonly grown but others are regularly grown in their country of origin.

C

Cabbage to Cytisus

Cabbage

(*Brassica oleracea*, Capitata Group, fam. Brassicaceae)

Native to southern Europe, this leafy vegetable has been cultivated for many centuries and is believed to be a descendant of the coastal European sea or wild cabbage. Although a biennial, it is treated as an annual when cultivated in the garden. The mature head of this familiar vegetable is used extensively in salads, as a vegetable accompaniment to main meals, such as corned beef, or for pickling. It provides Vitamins A, B and C, as well as minerals, calcium and iron, and was thought by the Greeks to be a cure for hangovers!

CULTIVATION Although reasonably easy to grow, it is very important to sow and plant cabbages at the correct time, according to type. Spring cabbages, those for harvesting during the spring, are sown in late summer through to early fall. They are planted out 23 cm (9 in) apart in rows spaced 30 cm (12 in) apart. Cabbages for cropping in early summer are sown in late winter through to early spring. The young plants are planted out 38 cm (15 in) apart each way. Summer cabbages, grown for the main summer crop, are sown in early to mid-spring. They are also planted 38 cm (15 in) apart each way. Cabbages for fall cropping should be sown in late spring or early summer.

ABOVE A planting of healthy cabbages close to harvest. Sowing seed over several weeks extends the cropping time.

Their spacing is 38 cm (15 in). Winter cabbages, which are the hardiest, are sown in the period late spring to early summer. They need more space and therefore young plants are set out 45 cm (18 in) apart each way. In warm climates cabbages are often grown as a winter or spring crop during the cool season.Seed of all cabbages can be sown in cell trays under glass, or into an outdoor seed bed. The seedlings should be planted out when they are about 8 cm (3 in) high. Cabbages like an alkaline soil and this also helps to protect the plants from clubroot disease. Therefore lime the site for cabbages after winter digging if the soil is acid. Apply a balanced general-purpose fertilizer before planting. Cabbages should be kept well watered as necessary in spring and summer. Unfortunately cabbages are prone to several serious pests and diseases such as root maggots and club-root disease, so to help prevent a build up of these in the soil it is necessary to grow cabbages in rotation with other crops, never growing them on the same piece of ground more than once in every three years. Do not delay harvesting for too long or the heads may split open and generally deteriorate.

CLIMATE Cabbages are not very hardy and are suited to Zones 8 and 9. They are grown as seasonal annuals or biennials. In cold climates, summer and fall cabbages are the best ones to attempt.

VARIETIES Spring cabbages (early cabbages) have small, pointed or rounded heads. They may also be loose-leaved and harvested as 'spring greens'. The summer cabbages (mid-season cabbages) have large, rounded heads, as do the fall cabbages (late cabbages). The latter include red cabbages, which are often used for pickling and salads. Winter cabbages (late cabbages) also have large, rounded heads. There are two types: those that are used fresh are known as Savoys and have wrinkled leaves, while the smooth, white-leaved cultivars are grown for storage. There are many cultivars of all of these types and seed catalogues should list a good selection.

Caesalpinia (fam. Caesalpiniaceae)

From the tropical regions of Asia, America and parts of Africa, these deciduous or evergreen trees, shrubs or climbers are grown for their exquisite red or yellow flowers which bloom all year in the right climate. Often prickly, they have mostly fern-like foliage, and the flat seed pods are quite a feature. There are at least 70 species of *Caesalpinia*, many cultivated for their timber in their native areas. Some are purely ornamental, but others are grown for dyes, tannins or medicines.

CULTIVATION In frost-prone climates, grow in a cool greenhouse or conservatory. Use soil-based potting compost and provide maximum light. Outdoors, Caesalpinia does well in a reasonably rich garden soil in a temperate climate, with full sun and plenty of water. Prune in winter to create an attractive shape. Propagate from seed in fall or spring or from tip cuttings. Sow or plant in sand or vermiculite.

CLIMATE Zone 10 and above, but *C. pulcherrima* can grow in zone 9.

ABOVE Shrubby *Caesalpinia gilliesii* is an evergreen, carrying its unusual flowers throughout summer.

SPECIES *C. coriaria*, divi-divi, is a South American tree which grows to 10 m (33 ft). It has beautiful yellow flowers and reddish-colored seed pods. *C. echinata* is often known as Brazilian redwood and peachwood. The heartwood of these trees is used for making violin bows and the tree is also a source of red dye. *C. ferrea*, leopard tree or Brazilian ironwood, is a deciduous tree, growing 10–12 m (33–40 ft) high. It has a rather vase-shaped open crown and the mottled bark of the trunk is very decorative. The foliage is red at first, becoming green as it matures. Yellow flowers bloom in spring, followed by flat pods which may be up to 10 cm (4 in) in length. It makes a good street tree and is an excellent small tree for home gardens. *C. gilliesii*, bird of paradise, is also from South America. This rather prickly shrub produces striking, bird-like, yellow flowers, with long, silky, prominent, red stamens. *C. pulcherrima*, Barbados pride or dwarf poinciana, is probably the species seen most often and is similar to *C. gilliesii*. This shrub grows rapidly to 5 m (16 ft) and bears bright orange-yellow flowers with prominent, red stamens. *C. spinosa*, or tara, is from Cuba and South America. A prickly-limbed small tree, it produces dense sprays of fragrant, yellow flowers.

Cajanus (fam. Papilionaceae)

These shrubby, leguminous perennials, thought to be natives of tropical Africa, have soft, hairy, pointed leaves, to 10 cm (4 in) long, and sprays of yellow or orange flowers, followed by hairy seed pods. They are frequently grown in the tropics for their edible seeds. They are not often grown in the US.

CULTIVATION In frost-prone climates, these would have to be grown in an intermediate greenhouse or conservatory. Use pots, and fill with soil-based potting compost. Propagate from seed or cuttings.

CLIMATE Zone 10.

ABOVE Grown throughout the tropics as a staple food and also as a fodder crop, pigeon pea, *Cajunus cajan*, is a legume that improves the soil too.

SPECIES *C. cajan*, pigeon pea, grows to 3 m (10 ft) and has yellow flowers marked with mahogany.

Caladium (fam. Araceae)

Originally from tropical America, these deciduous perennials have tuberous rhizomes and large, spear-shaped or ovate leaves, attractively patterned in red, pink, white and green. They flourish in tropical areas where they hybridize amongst themselves to produce

ABOVE Rich foliage color in two or more tones is a feature of all caladiums.

a myriad of different leaf colorings. The bloom resembles that of an arum lily but is much smaller. Caladiums are grown for their handsome foliage, not their flowers.

CULTIVATION Caladiums can only be grown permanently in the garden in tropical or subtropical climates. They need shade. Elsewhere grow as summer bedding plants in shade, or as pot plants in a warm greenhouse or conservatory. They also make good houseplants. Grow them in a soilless potting compost and provide high humidity and shade from direct sun, although good light is recommended. The tubers are potted in spring and started into growth. Water plants well in summer but gradually withhold water in fall until the compost dries out. The tubers are dormant over winter, when they should be kept warm and barely moist.

CLIMATE Zone 10 and above.

SPECIES Most fancy-leaved caladiums are hybrids grouped under *C.* x *bicolor*. Heights vary from about 25 cm to 45 cm (10–18 in).

Calamintha (fam. Lamiaceae)

From Asia and Europe, these perennial herbs have woody-based stems, simple, opposite leaves, and broad, flat-topped clusters of tubular flowers. The foliage is strongly aromatic and resembles catmint (*Nepeta* species) to which this genus is related.

CULTIVATION *Calamintha* can be planted in any well-drained soil, provided it has a sunny position. Propagate from cuttings of the young shoots in summer or by division in early spring.

CLIMATE Will thrive in zone 6.

SPECIES *C. grandiflora* has toothed, ovate leaves and pink summer flowers. It grows to 45 cm (18 in). *C. nepeta*, the most commonly grown species, grows up to 60 cm (24 in). It

ABOVE *Calamintha* species make good groundcover or filler plants for seasonally dry areas. Excess rain in summer sets them back.

has a creeping rootstock and gray-green toothed leaves, and produces mauve or pink flowers in summer. *C. sylvatica* has hairy, creeping stems, roundish to oval green leaves and pink or lilac flowers, spotted white on the lower lip. It grows to about 80 cm (32 in).

Calandrinia (fam. Portulacaceae)

Rock purslane

Native to South America, California and Australia, these low-growing, half-hardy annual and perennial succulents are useful for

ABOVE Flowering after rain in desert regions, this *Calandrinia* species is a delight with its pale-centered, rose-magenta flowers.

planting in sunny rock gardens and borders. They produce fleshy leaves and short-lived, brilliantly colored flowers, in various shades of magenta through to rose, over long periods. The flowers are sometimes borne in sprays, and are followed by capsule-shaped fruits.

CULTIVATION In climates prone to frost, they are grown as annuals for summer display in the garden, or in pots under glass. Outdoors, these succulents like a light, rich, crumbly soil. Propagate from seed sown under glass in early spring. Perennials can be increased from stem cuttings in summer.

CLIMATE Zones 9 or 10.

SPECIES : Not all species are freely available. *C. balonensis*, parakeelya, is found in the wild in the arid areas of Australia. An annual, it spreads to over 1 m (3 ft) in diameter and bears masses of pink flowers up to 2.5 cm (1 in) across. *C. burridgei* comes from South America and grows to 30 cm (12 in). It has rose or dazzling coppery-red flowers. *C. ciliata*, from Peru and Ecuador, is a hairy-leafed annual, with purple through to white flowers. It grows to 30 cm (12 in). Var. menziesi grows to double this size, with rose-red or crimson flowers. *C. grandiflora*, from Chile, has paddle-shaped leaves to 20 cm (8 in) and light purple flowers. It grows to 1 m (3 ft). *C. umbellata*, from Peru, is a dwarf, trailing perennial to 15 cm (6 in), with crimson blooms. It is the hardiest of the species.

Calanthe (fam. Orchidaceae)

Calanthe orchids are distributed widely in the tropical and temperate areas of Asia, Polynesia and Madagascar. There is also one species in Australia. Many hybrids and cultivars have been produced. These plants may be terrestrial or epiphytic, deciduous or evergreen. The broad, ribbed leaves grow to 1 m (3 ft) long. Drooping sprays of spurred blooms appear on long, upright stems in winter, spring or summer in colors ranging from lavender

ABOVE The pure white flowers of *Calanthe triplicata* appear on a bold spike in winter. This is a long-leaved, evergreen species.

through to rose and white.

CULTIVATION These orchids are grown in a cool or warm greenhouse or conservatory depending on their origins. Use a special orchid compost, obtainable from orchid growers. They like maximum light and high humidity. Water normally and freely in summer. The evergreens are kept only slightly moist in winter but the deciduous species are kept dry when they are dormant. Plants are potted on annually in spring and can be propagated by separating the older pseudobulbs from the main plant.

CLIMATE Zone 10.

SPECIES *C. triplicata*, the Australian species, has evergreen, broad, ribbed leaves to 90 cm (36 in) and tall spikes of pure white flowers in winter. *C. veitchii* grows to 1 m (3 ft), with pink flowers produced during winter. There are numerous cultivars of this hybrid. *C. vestita*, a deciduous species, has white flowers with a red or orange eye.

Calathea (fam. Marantaceae)

The name of this genus derives from the Greek kalathos, a basket, and refers to its use in weaving by the native American peoples. Calatheas are grown for their splendid foliage. Variously patterned on top in green, brown, purple, pink and maroon feathery markings, generally with purple undersides, the leaves emerge from the base of the plant on long, slender, upright stems. The strength of the coloring on the leaves is often affected by the environment. The insignificant yellow or white flowers are borne in small sprays.

CULTIVATION Calatheas will grow well under fernery-type conditions, with shade, in subtropical and tropical zones. Otherwise, they should be grown in a warm glasshouse or conservatory. They also make good house plants. Humid conditions, with open shade, produce the best foliage. If planting in pots, place crock or charcoal in the pots to give good drainage, along with a mix of loam, peat, leaf mould and sand, or a good quality mix high in organic matter. Propagate by division.

CLIMATE Calatheas will grow in zone 10 and above.

SPECIES *C. argyraea*, whose origin is uncertain, has deep green leaves, banded with silvery-gray

ABOVE Peacock plant, *Calathea makoyana*, has handsomely patterned and colored foliage.

above. *C. louisae*, from Central and South America, has dark green leaves, with white feathering down the center, and grows to 2 m (6 ft). *C. makoyana*, the peacock plant from Brazil, is thought by many to be one of the most magnificent foliage plants and is the ideal choice for growing as a house plant. The light green leaves have deep green blotches on top and deep green edges. *C. majestica* 'Roseolineata', to 90 cm (36 in), is from Guyana, Colombia and Ecuador. Its green leaves are marked with slender, parallel lines in rich pink fading to white. *C. mediopicta*, from Brazil, has green leaves marked with silver feathering. It grows to 60 cm (24 in). *C. picturata* 'Argentea' from Brazil, has shiny glaucous leaves leaves, with white feathering. It grows to 40 cm (16 in). *C. veitchiana* grows to 1.2 m (4 ft) tall. From tropical South America, it has dark green leaves, blotched with yellow along the midribs and light green bands. The dark green areas on the top of the leaves are colored purple on the reverse. *C. zebrina*, zebra plant, from Brazil, has broad, velvety, deep green leaves, with yellowish green midribs, veins and edges. It grows to 1 m (3 ft).

Calceolaria (fam. Scrophulariaceae)
Slipper flower, pouch flower

Deriving from the Latin calceolus, a slipper or small shoe, the name of this genus refers to the curious, pouch-like flowers which come in vivid red through to yellow, pink and mauve, with contrasting blotchings and markings. The large, crinkled, spreading leaves are also attractive. Hybridization has resulted in many improved blooms and many magnificent colors.

CULTIVATION The large-flowered hybrid calceolarias are mainly grown as annuals or biennials in cool greenhouses or conservatories. They require a rich, free-draining potting mix and bright light without direct sun, and regular watering. However, do not allow the compost to become excessively wet.

ABOVE Bright yellow and red are just two of the colors available amongst the hybrids of *Calceolaria* species.

The *C. Herbeohybrida* Group cultivars are raised from seed sown either in spring or in late summer. Do not cover the seeds with compost. Germinate at 18°C (64°F).

CLIMATE Zone 9 and above.

SPECIES Although the genus is large and comprises annuals, biennials, perennials and shrubby plants, the main one that is cultivated is the *C. Herbeohybrida* Group of cultivars which are biennials. They make excellent pot plants and the pouched flowers come in brilliant colors including red, yellow and orange, often with brightly contrasting spots.

Calendula (fam. Asteraceae)
Pot marigold

Named for calendula's habit of flowering throughout the year in its native habitat in the Mediterranean, only one of the 20 known species is widely grown, although hybridization has produced many stunning colors and types. Easily grown, they are perfect edging and border plants and provide good cut flowers.

CULTIVATION Calendulas will grow in full sun in any garden soil. They develop quickly, often

ABOVE Massed calendulas in warm tones of yellow, orange and tan make an attractive garden display.

ABOVE In shallow water at the edge of a pool and in full sun *Calla palustris* will form large colonies and produce white spathes in summer.

flowering eight to ten weeks after sowing, although flowering generally takes longer in cool zones. Propagate from seed sown directly into the ground where plants are to flower. Sow in spring for summer flowers or in fall for spring flowers.

CLIMATE Zone 6 and above.

SPECIES *C. officinalis*, pot marigold, is a hardy annual flowering in spring and summer and growing to 60 cm (24 in). Its many-petalled, daisy-like flowers, to 10 cm (4 in) across, come in cream through to apricot and orange. The soft, hairy foliage is pale green. This plant has a long history of usage as a medicinal, cosmetic and culinary herb. There are many cultivars available in shades of orange, yellow and cream. Good seed catalogues will list a large selection.

Calla (fam. Araceae)
Bog arum

This hardy aquatic or marginal perennial grows in the wild on the edges of streams, ponds and lakes in temperate parts of the

world. The ovate to heart-shaped leaves grow from the base of the plant, and the wide, white spathes are followed by clusters of red berries. In favorable climates, callas tend to spread and often become escapees from the garden. In fact, it is the only plant known to be fertilized by water snails. Calla should not be confused with the calla lily which is the common name for plants belonging to another genus (see *Zantedeschia*).

CULTIVATION Callas are usually planted in the shallow water at pool edges. Plants need a position in full sun if they are to flower well. Propagate by division of the rhizomes in spring.

CLIMATE Zone 4 and above.

SPECIES *C. palustris* is the only species and grows to a height of 20 cm (8 in).

Calliandra (fam. Mimosaceae)
Powder puff tree

This genus is native to tropical and subtropical America, India, Africa and Madagascar. The common name has been adopted for the brush-like flowers which are typical of this genus of low-growing trees and shrubs. The flowers come in shades of purple, red and white and followed by seed pods. Foliage consists of soft, double pinnate leaves. They provide colorful accents amongst other shrubs or when planted in small groups. In subtropical and tropical areas they are often used as informal hedges or screens. In frost-prone climates they are grown in an intermediate greenhouse or conservatory.

CULTIVATION Under glass, grow in pots of soil-based compost in maximum light. Outdoors, grow in fertile soil in a sunny position. Propagate by seed or semi-ripe cuttings.

CLIMATE Zone 10 and above.

SPECIES *C. haematocephala*, a shrub or small spreading tree growing to 4 m (13 ft), has fine, feathery leaves and an abundance of flowers composed of pinky red stamens. *C. selloi* is a strongly branched shrub which grows to 3 m (10 ft) or more. Its flowers appear in terminal heads as clusters of pinkish purple stamens up to 4 cm (1½ in) long. *C. tweedii*, red tassel flower, grows to about 3 m (10 ft), with bright red staminate flowers through spring and summer. *C. haematocephala* and *C. tweedii* are the most commonly cultivated species.

Callicarpa (fam. Verbenaceae)

Callicarpas are neat, small to large deciduous shrubs occurring in mainly subtropical and tropical regions of the world, including China and North and South America. They bear clusters of colorful berries that persist through the entire winter. In climates prone to frost, they will grow in an intermediate greenhouse or conservatory.

CULTIVATION The hardier species make good garden plants in cool climates. More tender ones must be grown under glass in areas prone to frost. Outside, grow in any fertile, well-drained soil in full sun or partial shade. Under glass, grow in tubs of soil-based potting compost in maximum light. Prune into shape during late winter if necessary. Propagate by semi-ripe cuttings in summer or by layering in spring.

CLIMATE Depends on origin of species chosen.

SPECIES *C. americana*, beauty berry, zone 6, grows to 2 m (6 ft) and has blue-mauve flowers in late spring to early summer. Deep violet berries, formed in fall, persist over a long period. *C. bodinieri*, zone 6, from China, has dense cymes of small pink flowers, followed by violet fruit. It grows to 3 m (10 ft). Considered to be the best garden species, var. *giraldii* has

ABOVE *Calliandra* species are fairly quick-growing, easy-care shrubs with a long flowering period.

ABOVE The colorful berries that follow flowering give *Callicarpa* species many months of decorative effect.

brilliant violet berries. Its foliage changes color in fall. *C. dichotoma*, zone 6, a native of China, has purplish leaves, small pink flowers and lilac-colored fruit, and grows 2 m (6 ft). *C. japonica*, zone 8, from Japan, is a compact species, growing to 1.5 m (5 ft). Its pink or white flowers are followed by violet berries.

Callicoma (fam. Cunoniaceae)

Black wattle

This eastern Australian genus comprises only one species, an evergreen tree growing to 15 m (50 ft) in its native forest habitat, although much less in cultivation.

CULTIVATION In frost-prone climates, grow in a cool greenhouse. Outdoors, *Callicoma* likes rich soil and plenty of moisture, with some protection from wind and heat. Propagation from seed and tip cuttings is quite easy.

CLIMATE Zone 9.

SPECIES *C. serratifolia*, a small to medium tree, 6–12 m (20–40 ft) under cultivation, has elliptical to lance-shaped, shiny, toothed leaves, woolly white on the undersides. The small, creamy yellow flowers, resembling

BELOW Known as black wattle, *Callicoma serratifolia* has fluffy, cream flowers and pink new growth. It is unrelated to wattle.

wattles, have no petals, and appear in dense, round heads to 3 cm (1 in) in diameter. The seeds are borne in small capsules.

Callisia (fam. Commelinaceae)

Inch plant

This genus comprises about 20 species of sprawling, creeping or semi-erect perennials, some of which have fragrant flowers. They are native to tropical America, Mexico and the south-east USA. In frost-prone parts of Europe, they are grown in an intermediate greenhouse or conservatory.

CULTIVATION Under glass, grow in pots of very well drained, soil-based potting compost and ensure maximum light. Propagate in spring from tip cuttings.

CLIMATE Zone 10 and above.

SPECIES *C. elegans*, striped inch plant, is a climber from southern Mexico. It has dark green, rounded, spear-shaped leaves, striped in silvery white, and white flowers. The leaves grow to 7.5 cm (3 in) long and the stems to 60 cm (24 in). The whole plant is clothed with minute soft hairs. *C. fragrans* has loosely branched, fleshy stems to 1 m (3 ft), rounded,

BELOW *Callisia fragrans* forms dense, groundcovering expanses of semi-succulent foliage. The masses of tiny flowers are scented.

spear-shaped leaves up to 25 cm (10 in) long and fragrant white flowers. This species is popular for basket cultivation. Cultivar 'Melnickoff' has pale yellow or white, irregularly striped leaves.

Callistemon (fam. Myrtaceae)
Bottlebrush

Although native to Australia, so many callistemons are grown in California that many Americans think they are native to their country. They are, in fact, the true bottle-brushes. Callistemons are showy shrubs and trees, grown now in many parts of the world as ornamentals and street trees, and as greenhouse plants in frosty areas. They are easily cultivated, and are favored by nectar- and pollen-feeding birds. Most species flower twice a year, in spring to early summer and more lightly in fall. Numerous species are available in the US and among the most popular are *C. citrinus* and its cultivars, *C. linearis*, *C. rigidus*, *C. salignus* and *C. viminalis* and its cultivars.

CULTIVATION In areas prone to frosts, grow the tender and half-hardy species in a cool greenhouse or conservatory, in pots of soil-based potting compost. Provide light and airy conditions. Outdoors, grow in acid to neutral soil. Although callistemons are adaptable, they prefer a moist, well-drained position. Mature trees should never be transplanted. Propagate from seed contained in the woody capsules borne along the stems. Place capsules on a tray or in a paper bag in a warm place to release the fine seed. Sow on light, sandy soil, and barely cover. Callistemons can also be propagated from tip cuttings taken in spring or, more easily, in fall. Place in a 3:1 sharp sand and peat mix and keep moist. Most callistemons are free from garden pests. After flowering, prune back most of the spent blossoms to discourage woodiness and to ensure vigorous new flowering in the following season.

CLIMATE Zone 9 for most.

ABOVE A superb red cultivar of *Callistemon citrinus*, one of the hardier species.

BELOW *Callistemon viminalis* has a pronounced weeping habit that resembles that of willows.

SPECIES *C. acuminatus* is a windresistant plant, with crimson brushes, suitable for coastal gardens. It grows to 3 m (10 ft). *C. brachyandrus* can tolerate dry conditions and grows to 2.5 m (8 ft). It has needle-like

ABOVE The sharp pink flowers of *Callistemon citrinus* 'Reeves Pink' make this a most striking shrub for the garden.

BELOW The bright gold tips of the stamens on the squat flowers of *Callistemon macropunctatus* are very prominent and distinctive.

foliage and red brushes with yellow tips. *C. citrinus*, zone 8, a hardy, vigorous species, with red brushes, was one of the first callistemons to be cultivated. Despite its name, the foliage has more of a eucalyptus oil fragrance than a citrus aroma. There are a number of cultivars including 'Burgundy', with deep red, summer brushes; 'Mauve Mist', with mauve brushes; 'Candy Pink', with deep pink, summer brushes; 'Endeavour', with large red brushes; 'Reeves Pink', a small, 2 m (6 ft) shrub with soft pink brushes; and 'Red Clusters', which grows to only 1 m (3 ft), with clusters of late summer, red brushes (a white form is also available). *C. linearis*, zone 8, has masses of fine, bronze-red flower spikes and stiff, narrow leaves. It grows to about 3 m (10 ft). *C. macropunctatus* has scarlet, gold-tipped flowers and grows to 3 m (10 ft). A deep red form is also available. *C. pallidus*, from New South Wales, Victoria, Tasmania and South Australia, grows well in cold areas. *C. paludosus* has creamy to pale pinkish flowers and grows 3 m (10 ft). *C. phoeniceus*, fiery bottlebrush, from Western Australia, has dazzling scarlet brushes and thick, rather glossy leaves. It grows to 3 m (10 ft). *C. pinifolius*, a native of the Sydney region, grows to 2 m (6 ft), with fine foliage and red flowers. *C. salignus*, zone 8, is tree-like, growing 8–12 m (26–40 ft), and can withstand very wet conditions. The new foliage growth is flushed with pink, while the mature brushes are creamy white. It flowers in spring. There is also a red form. *C. shiressii* grows to 4 m (13 ft), with cream brushes in spring. *C. sieberi*, zone 7, native to alpine areas of Australia, has pale yellow brushes and fine foliage. A late flowering shrub, with lovely pink bud bracts, it grows 2 m (6 ft). *C. speciosus*, showy bottlebrush from Western Australia, has the largest, deep red brushes of the species and grows 2–3 m (6–10 ft). *C. viminalis* is a very hardy species from coastal Queensland and northern New South Wales, with graceful weeping foliage and red brushes. It grows to 8 m (26 ft). Cultivar 'Captain Cook' is a very good form, growing to 2 m (6 ft) and flowering profusely over a long

ABOVE Masses of cream to lemon flowers appear on *Callistemon salignus* in spring, with a smaller flush in fall.

period. It has red brushes. 'Hannah Ray', with scarlet brushes, grows to 4 m (13 ft). *C. viridiflorus* has yellowish green brushes in summer and grows to 2 m (6 ft).

Callistephus (fam. Asteraceae)
China aster

Native to China, this genus comprises only one species which was introduced into European gardens by Jesuit missionaries during the 18th century. It is a flower that has been cultivated by the Chinese for 2000 years. Many hybrids have since been developed and they come in a range of sizes and colors, including almost every shade of blue and red, and white, and in single, semi-double or double forms. Some have also been bred for wilt resistance and early blooming. The China aster is now a garden favorite and an excellent cut flower.

CULTIVATION Propagate from seed sown in early spring under glass or in late spring where the plants are to flower. Plant out when frosts are over, 15–45 cm (6–18 in) apart, according to the expected size of the mature plant. To encourage the development of beautiful flowers, protect from strong wind and too much direct sun until established, keep moist but not wet and feed with weak liquid manure when the buds appear.

ABOVE China asters make a great massed display in the summer garden. A few white flowers highlight the harmonious pinks and purples.

CLIMATE Zone 10, but Callistephus can be grown as a summer annual in cooler climates.

CULTIVARS The cultivars are derived from *Callistephus chinensis*, the only species, and there are many of them. They are all bushy annuals which flower in summer and fall. The flowers may be single, like daisies, or fully double, some resembling chrysanthemums. Some cultivars have attractive quilled petals. There are both dwarf and tall cultivars and they come in shades of red, pink, purple, blue and white. The tall kinds make excellent cut flowers. There are cultivars available which are resistant to the disease aster wilt. A good seed catalogue will list a large selection of China asters.

Callitris (fam. Cupressaceae)
Cypress-pine

Callitris is very similar to the true cypresses (*Cupressus*) of the northern hemisphere. Like the true cypresses, their cones are almost round and bear many seeds. Their foliage is also very similar, differing only in density and the arrangement of the minute scale leaves. The cones of some of the species do not

ABOVE Staggered rows of *Callitris* species will form an effective windbreak when fully mature.

ABOVE A *young Callitris* rhomboidea has dense, slightly weeping foliage down to the ground.

automatically open when the seed matures. Instead, the seeds are retained, often becoming larger and woodier with age. These old cones are found in dense clusters close to the main trunk and open and release their seeds only when the tree finally dies or is damaged or killed by fire. However, species such as *C. columellaris* shed their seeds each year. Fourteen species of this genus of conifers are found growing in the wild almost everywhere in Australia. Cypress-pines make good ornamentals and are useful as screens or windbreaks, though only a few species have been widely cultivated. The columnar species are particularly suitable where a plant with a narrow base is needed. If a less formal effect is required, *Callitris* may be a better choice than *Cupressus* as the foliage of this cypress-pine is usually greener and less dense. Growth is reasonably fast. However, bear in mind that these are quite tender plants and in frost-prone areas should be grown in a cool conservatory.

CULTIVATION Under cultivation, cypress-pines appear to prefer a well-drained clay or deep sandy soil and a full sun position. Although most are not recommended for seaside gardens, they can tolerate wind but dislike disturbance of the soil around their roots. Propagation is by seed. With species that retain their seed, cut off some of the old woody cones and leave them in a warm, dry place. They will open up and release plenty of seed fairly quickly and will also germinate quite rapidly if planted shallowly in a fine sandy soil. The seedlings, too, grow rapidly. Cuttings are very difficult to strike.

CLIMATE Zone 9 if relatively frost-free and zone 10.

SPECIES *C. columellaris* comes in three forms: white cypress-pine, Bribie Island or coast cypress-pine, and tropical cypress-pine. All three have very fine foliage. The cones are smallish and rounded on the outside, with fairly thin scales. They release their seed each year. *C. endlicheri*, black cypress-pine, a native of temperate regions of eastern Australia, generally grows into a narrow, pyramid-shaped tree, 10–20 m (33–65 ft) tall, with sharply pointed crown and dark green, fairly coarse foliage. It adapts reasonably well to cultivation, but is slower growing and less ornamental than some of the other species.

C. oblonga, Tasmanian cypress-pine, is like *C. rhomboidea*, but it grows more stiffly and has coarser foliage. It has elongated cones, rather than the usual roundish ones. Generally thought of as only a Tasmanian native, it can be found growing naturally on the east edge of the dividing range in New South Wales and southern Queensland. It is most suitable for cool climates. *C. preissii*, slender cypress pine, has three subspecies, including the well-known scrub cypress-pine or mallee pine. These small trees, which often branch at ground level, grow widely across the southern half of Australia. The cones look rather like those of *C. columellaris* but are a bit larger. *C. rhomboidea*, Port Jackson pine, is the most commonly cultivated species in south-eastern Australia. Its columnar form, dense, grayish green foliage and typical nodding 'brush' at the apex make it quite a handsome specimen. Under the right conditions, it grows quite rapidly to 8–10 m (26–33 ft), and reaches 4–5 m (13–16 ft) within five years of planting. It occurs naturally over a large area of rocky country from eastern central Queensland to the Grampian Ranges of western Victoria, and Tasmania.

Calluna (fam. Ericaceae)

Heather, ling

Although this is the famous plant of the Scottish moors, it can also be found in England, Europe and north-west America (where it was probably introduced). Comprising only the one species, this hardy, evergreen shrub ranges, throughout its varieties, from 15 to 90 cm (6 to 36 in) in height. Masses of small, purple flowers cover *C. vulgaris* in the late summer, although other colors can be obtained in the named varieties.

CULTIVATION Heather does best in moist, cool conditions, in lime-free, peaty soil. Trim off the old flower heads in early spring to encourage bushiness. Propagate from 2.5 cm (1 in) long non-flowering shoots, planted in a mixture of sand and peat in mid to late summer.

ABOVE Massed heathers, *Calluna* species, make good groundcovers for exposed areas in cool regions.

CLIMATE Zone 4.

VARIETIES 'Alba' cultivars have white flowers, double in 'Alba Plena', 'Aurea' has yellow-gold leaves and 'Cuprea' is noted for its copper-colored foliage. The many cultivars including 'Blazeaway', 'Golden Feather', 'Red Haze', 'Robert Chapman' and 'Searlei Aurea', provide both a range of flower colors and a range of foliage colors that in winter often change to deeper tones.

Calocedrus

(syn. *Libocedrus*, fam. Cupressaceae)

Incense cedar

The name of this genus of conifers means 'beautiful cedar' and the name is apt. It comprises only three species, one from the western areas of the United States, the other two from eastern Asia. This distribution is typical of some other genera within the family, *Cupressaceae*, including *Thuja* and *Thujopsis* and is thought to point to areas into which such plants retreated during the ice ages. *Calocedrus* has flattened sprays of flattened branchlets and four rows of scale leaves.

CULTIVATION To achieve maximum growth, these conifers need a cool climate, high rainfall

ABOVE One of the most attractive conifers, *Calocedrus decurrens* has soft foliage and develops a very good form.

and deep, reasonably fertile soil, although beautiful smaller specimens can be produced in warmer coastal areas if a suitably cool microclimate is present. *C. formosana* is the species most likely to adapt to warmer areas. Propagate from seed as cuttings are difficult to strike and do not generally produce reliable plants or good tree forms.

CLIMATE There are species suited to various climatic zones.

SPECIES *C. decurrens* (syn. *Libocedrus decurrens*), California incense cedar, zone 6, is the North American species. It forms either a broad or narrow column shape, depending on its position and the climate in which it grows. A superb tree, with deep glossy green foliage, it mostly reaches 10 m (33 ft) under cultivation, although growing to 35 m (115 ft) in the wild. The soft, aromatic timber is used in cabinet-making. The beautiful *C. formosana*, zone 9, from Taiwan, and *C. macrolepis*, zone 9, a native of Burma and south-western China, are little known outside Southeast Asia.

Calocephalus (fam. Asteraceae)
Cushion bush

Native to Australia, these annuals, perennials and low shrubs grow to 30–90 cm (12–36 in) and are well suited for borders and as groundcovers. The ball-like flowers appear in clusters at the ends of the stems.

CULTIVATION In frost-prone areas, grow in a cool, light and airy greenhouse. Outdoors, *Calocephalus* likes an open, sunny position and sandy loam. To propagate, take cuttings 5 cm (2 in) long and remove the white fluff from the lower part. Plant in a mixture of sand and peat in late summer.

CLIMATE Zone 9.

SPECIES *C. brownii* has grayish branches and tiny, thin, silvery white leaves which form a silvery clump to about 45 cm (18 in), decorated with white, ball-like flowers in summer. As it is salt- and wind-resistant, it is especially suitable for seaside gardens.

BELOW In the right climate, *Calocephalus brownii* makes an excellent groundcover, acting as a soil or sand binder.

Calochortus (fam. Liliaceae)
Mariposa lily, globe tulip, star tulip

Native to western North America and Mexico, these bulbous herbs produce exquisite flowers, usually in yellow, white or mauve, often with intriguingly patterned petals. They bloom in spring and summer, either singly or in clusters.

ABOVE A single row of petals forms a cup to frame the richly patterned center of this species of *Calochortus*.

CULTIVATION Plant bulbs in fall to a depth of 10–15 cm (4–6 in) in very well drained soil and full sun. In wet climates, *Calochortus* are best grown in pots of soil-based potting compost in an unheated greenhouse as they dislike extremely wet conditions. The bulbs should be kept dry once the leaves have died down. Propagation is from seed, offsets or from bulbils produced in the leaf axils of some species.

CLIMATE Best in dry climates; zone 9.

SPECIES *C. amabilis*, golden globe tulip, has golden yellow, pendulous flowers. It grows to 45 cm (18 in). *C. luteus* produces yellow to orange flowers, streaked with red or brown, and grows to 60 cm (24 in). *C. macrocarpus*, green-banded mariposa lily, has lavender flowers, with a green band down the middle of the petals. It grows to 60 cm (24 in). *C. nitidus* grows to 50 cm (20 in). It has white, lilac or purple flowers, flawlessly marked on each petal with a deep purple spot. *C. uniflorus* has much longer, lilac flowers, with crimson veins. It grows to 25 cm (10 in). *C. venustus*, white mariposa lily, grows to 25 cm (10 in), with pale lilac flowers, spotted reddish brown. Varieties of *C. venustus* sometimes grow taller than the species and have creamy yellow, crimson or white flowers, with purple or rose-colored markings.

Calodendrum (fam. Rutaceae)
Cape chestnut

This evergreen tree from South Africa should be more widely cultivated for its floral display. The beautiful, large, massed heads of pink flowers appear at the ends of the branches in late spring and early summer. It has oval, deep or grayish green leaves, dotted with oil glands that produce a noticeable aroma. Calodendrum makes an excellent street tree, provided it is not under power lines. *Calodendrum* is suitable for cultivation in California and Florida.

CULTIVATION This beautiful tree needs a rich soil, regular water and warm, sunny or subtropical conditions. They grow slowly when they are young and mature to variable heights, shapes and flowering ability. Propagate by cuttings of young wood in warm conditions.

CLIMATE Warmest parts of zone 9 and zone 10.

SPECIES *C. capense* is the only species cultivated. It has shiny, oval leaves to 13 cm

ABOVE In full bloom, Cape chestnut, *Calodendrum capense*, is one of the loveliest of all flowering trees.

ABOVE The orchid-like flowers of Cape chestnut shown in exquisite detail.

(5 in) long and flesh pink flowers marked with purple dots. The trees have a fairly broad-domed crown and grow to 10–15 m (33–50 ft) tall.

Calostemma (fam. Amaryllidaceae)

Garland lily

An Australian native from the plains of Queensland, New South Wales, Victoria and South Australia, this single-species genus of bulbous plants produces terminal clusters of trumpet-shaped, lily-like flowers on upright stems. It has narrow, strap-shaped, fleshy leaves similar to those of the snowdrop. The foliage dies down every year and appears again when flowering is complete. It is not often grown in the US.

CULTIVATION In climates prone to hard frosts, grow in pots in a cool greenhouse, using a well-drained, soil-based potting compost. Outdoors, *Calostemma* likes moist conditions but also does well on rock gardens. Propagate from the fleshy seeds contained in the capsular fruits. Even established plants can be transplanted easily, or they can be divided in early spring.

CLIMATE Zone 9.

SPECIES *C. purpureum*, garland lily, is a very striking species, with its mass of small, trumpet-shaped, reddish purple to pink flowers balancing on its sturdy, erect stems 80 cm (32 in) in length. It has dark green, fleshy, strap-like leaves to 30 cm (12 in), which appear after flowering.

Calothamnus (fam. Myrtaceae)

Net bush, one-sided bottlebrush

Related to *Callistemon*, the 25 species are found mainly in the south-west area of Western Australia. Usually called by their common name, one-sided bottlebrush, because their flowers are borne on only one side of the stem, they are widely used as specimens or hedges. They have soft, pine-like foliage and flowers in various shades of red or cream in spring and summer.

CULTIVATION In areas prone to hard frosts, grow in a light, airy, cool greenhouse or conservatory in pots of soil-based potting compost. Outdoors, *Calothamnus* is a very drought-resistant genus. Although tolerant of some frost, it needs protection from heavy frosts. It does best in warm to hot conditions. Prune

ABOVE Flowering in summer to fall, *Calostemma purpureum* mostly has pink to purple flowers although yellow forms are recorded in the wild.

ABOVE Opening flowers of *Calothamnus quadrifidus* show yellow pollen tipping the feathery flower tops.

ABOVE Flowering early in spring, *Caltha palustris* thrives in permanently boggy soil.

after flowering, otherwise it will become rather untidy and leggy.

CLIMATE Zone 9.

SPECIES *G. gilesii*, Giles net bush, is a good choice as a hedge plant and will tolerate exposed positions. It has stiff, pointed leaves and bright crimson flowers, and grows to 2 m (6 ft). *C. quadrifidus*, crimson cluster net bush, is the most widely grown species. It has slender stems, deep green foliage and feathery bundles of rich crimson stamens. It grows 2–3 m (6–10 ft). *C. sanguineus*, blood red net bush, has silky foliage and red tassel-like flowers. Short-branching, it grows to 2.5 m (8 ft). *C. villosus*, woolly net bush, is possibly the most attractive of the species, with masses of showy, silvery, pine-like leaves and deep, rich red flowers. It grows to 2 m (6 ft).

Caltha (fam. Ranunculaceae)
Marsh marigold

These plants are found growing in bogs and marshes, and on banks of lakes and streams, in Europe, North America, Mexico and parts of Asia. They generally have heart-shaped, plain leaves and yellow or white flowers. Marsh marigolds are pretty planted around garden ponds.

CULTIVATION Caltha likes an open, sunny position and wet soil. The water supply should not be stagnant. To propagate, lift and divide the roots in spring after flowering.

CLIMATE Zone 3.

SPECIES *C. leptosepala* has leaves 10 cm (4 in) long and small, silvery white flowers. It grows to 30 cm (12 in). *C. palustris*, marsh marigold or kingcup, is a very hardy, deciduous or semi-evergreen perennial which grows 30–60 cm (12–24 in). It has dark green, rounded leaves and beautiful, bright yellow flowers, 5 cm (2 in) across, which provide excellent color in spring. The cultivar 'Flore Pleno' is stunning, with double, brilliant yellow flowers and is the most popular marsh marigold.

Calycanthus (fam. Calycanthaceae)
Allspice

The most conspicuous feature of these hardy, deciduous shrubs from North America is their

ABOVE All parts of the Carolina allspice, *Calycanthus floridus*, are highly aromatic. Plant this near a path so its fragrance can be enjoyed.

highly aromatic wood, leaves, bark and flowers. *Calycanthus* has oval leaves, rough on the surface, and unusual summer flowers, resembling tiny magnolias in shape, in various shades of red or reddish brown. Grow these shrubs in shrub or mixed borders.

CULTIVATION Plant in late winter or early spring in full sun or partial shade, and in moist, fertile soil that contains plenty of organic matter. Propagate from seed sown in fall, by layering in spring, or by removing suckers in spring.

CLIMATE Zone 5 for *C. floridus*, zone 8 for *C. occidentalis*.

SPECIES *C. floridus*, Carolina allspice, has broad, oval, glossy, pale green leaves to 12 cm (5 in) and reddish brown flowers. It grows 2–3 m (6–10 ft). This species has a straggling growth pattern and is therefore very suitable for planting near a trellis, fence or wall. *C. occidentalis*, Californian allspice, is the

species most suited to warmer climates. Highly aromatic, it has larger, coarser and more pointed leaves than *C. floridus* and light brown flowers. It grows to 3.5 m (11 ft).

Calytrix (fam. Myrtaceae)

Of the 70 or so species of this genus, most occur naturally in Western Australia. Few of the eastern species are generally cultivated. The small leaves are pungently aromatic when crushed and the starry flowers, with a number of fine stamens, are quite unusual. They bloom in masses of white, yellow, pink, rose or violet from spring through to summer.

CULTIVATION In frost-prone climates, they are grown in a light, airy, cool greenhouse or conservatory, in pots of acid, soil-based potting compost. Outdoors, grow in full sun or semi-shade and in very well drained, acid to neutral soil. Propagate from semi-ripe cuttings during summer.

BELOW *Calytrix microphylla* has bright pink flowers and tiny leaves.

CLIMATE Zone 9.

SPECIES *C. alpestris*, snow myrtle, is an erect or spreading shrub growing to 1.5 m (5 ft). It has fine, dark foliage and pink buds opening to white, star-like flowers in spring. *C. tetragona*, common fringe myrtle, grows in many parts of Australia. It has narrow, heath-like leaves which are sometimes hairy, and star-shaped, pink or white flowers. It grows between 90 cm and 1.2 m (36–48 in) high. This is the species most often grown in gardens.

Camassia (fam. Hyacinthaceae)
Camass

In their native habitat of North America, these hardy bulbs are generally found in woods, while in the garden they are pretty as border plants. They make good cut flowers in early summer. Their leaves are long and the showy flower spikes range from purple to blue to white.

CULTIVATION Plant these bulbs 10 cm (4 in) deep and 7–10 cm (3–4 in) apart in a moist, loamy soil in a sunny or semi-shaded position in early fall. Water well after planting but don't water

ABOVE The subtle blue of the flowers on *Camassia cusickii* develops best when grown in partial shade.

again until leaves appear unless conditions are exceptionally dry. The bulbs can be lifted and divided every three years. If they produce seed, sow in a warm position in spring.

CLIMATE Zone 5, or zone 3 for *C. leichtlinii*.

SPECIES *C. cusickii* is easy to grow and produces large bulbs. Masses of 2 cm (1 in) long, star-shaped lavender flowers appear on each erect stem. They grow to 60–90 cm (24–36 in). *C. leichtlinii* grows to the same height, and has cream-white flowers, or blue to violet flowers in its subspecies. *C. quamash* also produces large bulbs which were used for food by the indigenous North American peoples in times past. The flower spikes range from dark blue to nearly white and are carried on 60 cm (24 in) stems.

Camellia (fam. Theaceae)

The original camellias came from various parts of China and other parts of Southeast Asia but they have been widely hybridized to produce an enormous number of cultivars. Camellias are among the most loved and popular shrubs of all, the plant from which we get tea, *C. sinensis*, being no doubt the best known form. Their glossy green foliage and showy flowers are a great asset to the garden, particularly as the various species can bloom from fall

ABOVE The dainty, cream flowers of *Camellia lutchuensis* have a sweet fragrance. This lovely species may be grown in the ground or in a container.

ABOVE This rosy pink *Camellia* japonica has a lovely cupped form as its many layers of petals unfold.

ABOVE There are numerous cultivars of *Camellia vernalis* and they are among the hardiest camellias.

through to spring. The flowers come in white, pink, deep rose or deep red, with many combinations of these colors. These evergreen shrubs range from 1 m (3 ft) to 5 or 6 m (16–20 ft) high, depending on the variety; in their native habitats some grow into trees 8–10 m (26–33 ft) tall. Most flower after two or three years and they reach maturity after 10 to 20 years. They are very long lived and make ideal garden plants. They can be used as hedges, espaliers, lawn specimens or in pots or mixed shrub borders. It is best to select camellias when they are in flower to ensure that the right one is chosen. Specialist camellia nurseries and other large nurseries display flowers during the main flowering season.

CULTIVATION Camellias need a slightly acid, well-aerated soil, rich in decayed organic matter. Heavy, badly drained soils can cause root rot and frequently death of the plants. They also need protection from cold, drying winds and early morning sun. Most grow well in filtered sun, although some varieties can tolerate full sun. Sasanquas can take more sun than most other camellias and reticulatas need full sun for some part of the day. Some cultivars of *C. japonica*, such as 'The Czar', 'Great Eastern', 'Moshio' and 'Emperor of Russia', like full sun. Regular, deep watering is needed in warmer months to ensure a steady level of moisture in the soil. Well-mulched, established plants need a deep soaking only once a week, but in warm, dry weather younger plants need watering twice a week. A slow-release, general-purpose fertilizer should be applied in early spring. Plants should be mulched well in early spring with rotted cow manure, compost or leaf mould, taking care not to allow the mulch to pack up around the plant stems. Little pruning is required; cutting blooms for the vase is usually enough to keep camellia plants compact. However, any thin, spindly, unproductive growth can be cut from the center of the shrub at almost any time. Old, overgrown camellias can be rejuvenated by quite heavy pruning as long as cuts are made directly above a leaf or leaf bud. If severe pruning is needed, do it in stages rather than shocking the plant by removing all its foliage at once. Propagate from semi-ripe cuttings taken in late summer, though they may be slow to root. Make sure that moisture is maintained in the cutting compost and that warm humid conditions are provided for rooting. Some varieties are hard to grow on their own roots and these can be grafted onto understocks of *C. sasanqua*.

CLIMATE Zone 8 for most.

VARIETIES There are four main camellia types in cultivation: *C. sasanqua*, *C. japonica*, *C. reticulata* and *C. x williamsii*. Of these, *C. japonica* is the species most people think of when camellias are mentioned. There is a staggering number of varieties to choose from in colors of white through palest to darkest pink to deep reds and combinations of these colors. They are usually classified by flower type: single, semi-double, formal double, paeony form and anemone form. Some of the darker flowered camellias are tolerant of quite sunny conditions, but the whites and pale pinks should not be planted where they

receive early morning sun. *C. japonica* works well as a specimen or in a border as a background plant. Some varieties are also suitable for tubs. If different varieties are chosen, it is possible to have flowers from late fall until spring. *C. reticulata* has the largest, most spectacular blooms of all the camellias but the shrubs themselves are more sparse and open in foliage. Many of the more recently developed hybrids are crosses between *C. japonica* and *C. reticulata* which gives the shrubs denser leaf cover and longer flowering, coupled with very large, showy flowers. Generally, *C. reticulata* needs lighter soils, with better drainage and more direct sun, than the other camellias. This species and its varieties make ideal specimens and container plants. *C. sasanqua* has fragile flowers which make a wonderful show in the garden from fall until the middle of winter, depending on the variety. They come in single, semi-double or double, in white, palest pink, rose pink, cerise or scarlet, and are also available in various sizes and forms, from the low, spreading 'Shishigashira' to the tall, vigorous shrubs 'Plantation Pink' and 'Jennifer Susan' which grow to 5 m (16 ft) or more. Sasanquas are excellent hedging plants and some cultivars with pendulous growth can be trained as espaliers. The smaller, more compact types make good container plants. Sasanquas are tolerant of a wider range of conditions than the other types. Most grow in sun or shade, although they do not grow successfully in full sun in hot, dry areas. *C. x williamsii* is a very fine group of camellias bred by crossing *C. japonica* and *C. saluensis*. The original crosses were made in Cornwall, England by J. C. Williams who gave them their name. Flowers come in the same color range as the other camellias but most are semi-double in

TOP LEFT *Camellia sasanqua* 'Shishigashira' has been stiffly espaliered onto a masonry wall in a courtyard.

LEFT Cultivars of *C. reticulata* typically have wavy pink or red petals. The blooms are large–about 10 cm (4 in) across.

form. Some of the most popular cultivars are 'Donation', 'Elsie Jury', 'E. G. Waterhouse' and 'Water Lily'. Bear in mind that there are many hundreds of cultivars of camellias and that not all of those mentioned may be available in all areas.

Campanula (fam. Campanulaceae)
Bellflower

The Latin word campanula means 'small bell' and refers to the delicate, bell-shaped flowers of this large genus of about 300 species of annuals, biennials and perennials from North America, Europe and Asia. They look extremely pretty in borders, rockeries and hanging baskets. One of the species, *C. rapunculus*, has edible roots and leaves and is sometimes used as a salad vegetable.

ABOVE 'Alba', the white form of *Campanula persicifolia*, lights up darker foliage in partly shaded garden areas.

CULTIVATION Depending on the species, bellflowers can be cultivated in borders and rock gardens and as container plants. Plant in spring or fall in a rich soil in a sunny or semi-shaded position. Support may need to be given to the tall species. Propagate from seed, by division of old clumps in spring, or by cuttings taken after the flowers are finished. Sow seed in the spring in a fine compost and leave in a shaded position until the seedlings appear. Border species with creeping roots can be propagated by division in fall. With the rock garden species, plant in a well-drained, gritty soil in an open, sunny position. *C. isophylla*, popularly known as falling stars, is one of the tender species and because it has a trailing habit is grown in hanging baskets in a cool greenhouse or conservatory. It also makes a good house plant provided the room is cool.

CLIMATE There are campanulas available for various climatic zones.

TALL SPECIES *C. glomerata*, zone 2, is an erect perennial growing to 45 cm (18 in). It has hairy, ovate leaves and terminal, deep violet-blue flowers, measuring around 7.5 cm (3 in) across. *C. latifolia*, zone 3, grows to 1 m (3 ft), with pendulous, purplish blue flowers. *C. medium*, Canterbury bells, zone 8, is quite stunning, with its spires of bell-shaped flowers in violet, blue, pink or white. An upright, branching, hairy plant, with crowded basal leaves, it is an annual or biennial. Cultivar 'Calycanthema', cup and saucer, has an enlarged calyx matching the color of the petals. *C. persicifolia*, zone 3, is a popular species and also a very attractive one. It has a branched, creeping rootstock, leathery, lance-shaped, bright green leaves and delightful, large, blue bell flowers. It grows 30–100 cm (12–40 in). Cultivar 'Alba' grows to 1 m (3 ft), with single, pure white flowers; 'Moerheimii' grows to 1 m (3 ft), with large, semi-double, white flowers on slim stems; 'Blue Gardenia' grows to 60 cm (24 in), with large, double, bright blue flowers; 'Telham Beauty' reaches to 1 m (3 ft) and has large, single, china blue

ABOVE *Campanula isophylla* is a popular hanging basket plant for the cool greenhouse.

blooms. *C. rotundifolia*, zone 3, Scotch hare bell or blue bell, is a perennial which grows to 45 cm (18 in). It is many-stemmed, with dainty, drooping, blue bell flowers.

TRAILING AND DWARF SPECIES *C. cochleariifolia*, zone 6, fairy's thimble, is a perennial, with underground runners and lovely, pendulous, pale blue bell-shaped flowers, which grows to 10 cm (4 in). Cultivar 'Alba' is an excellent rockery or wall plant, growing to only 10 cm (4 in). It produces masses of pretty white bells borne on fine stems. *C. x haylodgensis*, cultivar 'Warley White', zone 5, is a sprawling, tufted perennial, with double, white flowers. It grows 22 cm (9 in) in height. *C. isophylla*, zone 9, is an evergreen, trailing perennial, native to the mountainous areas of northern Italy, which grows to 10 cm (4 in). It has ovate leaves and star-shaped, blue, summer flowers. Cultivar 'Alba', with white flowers, looks very pretty in baskets. It grows to 10 cm (4 in). *C. portenschlagiana*, zone 4, from the mountains of southern Europe, is a trailing species, to 15 cm (6 in), and suitable for rock gardens. It has deep purple bellflowers and masses of small, ivy-like leaves. *C. poscharskyana*, zone 3, is a hardy tufted perennial to 20–30 cm (12 in). Suitable for growing on banks or walls, it flourishes in either sun or shade. It has long sprays of starry, lavender-blue flowers.

Campsis (fam. Bignoniaceae)
Trumpet-creeper

Originally from China and North America, these deciduous, woody climbers produce very showy, orange-red, trumpet-shaped flowers in late summer. Attractive and hardy, they are suitable for growing near walls or fences.

CULTIVATION *Campsis* is best grown against a warm, sunny wall. Any well-drained, yet moisture-retentive soil is suitable. Campsis need regular pruning in late winter. Side shoots are cut back to within three or four buds of the main woody framework. Plants cling to walls by means of aerial roots but they may need additional support, especially when young. Propagate from root cuttings in winter or by layering in the spring.

CLIMATE Zone 4 for most, but zone 7 for *C. grandiflora*.

SPECIES *C. grandiflora*, Chinese trumpet-creeper, is the most popular species, with gaudy, dark orange flowers up to 8 cm (3 in) across. It usually grows to a height of 6 m (20 ft) but in subtropical areas it can grow to 15 m (50 ft). The most vigorous of the species, it can become invasive. *C. radicans*, trumpet-vine, is similar, but it has slightly smaller flowers. *C. x tagliabuana* is a hybrid

ABOVE The large, orange-red trumpets of this *Campsis* hybrid appear over a long period.

group of the two major species described above. The most popular cultivar of this hybrid is 'Madame Galen' which is very vigorous and has dark apricot-colored flowers and deep green, pinnate foliage.

Canavalia (fam. Papilionaceae)

This plant group is fairly widely spread through the tropics, and especially the American tropics. Several species have been grown variously for green manure crops, for stock feed or for their edible beans. May not be readily available in the US.

CULTIVATION Grow under glass in climates which are prone to frosts. Outdoors, canavalias should be grown in well-drained soil in an open, sunny position. Propagate from seed which has been soaked overnight before sowing.

CLIMATE Zone 10.

SPECIES *C. ensiformis*, Jack bean, sword bean or sabre bean, is an annual which came originally from tropical America. It grows from 1.5 to 2 m (5–6 ft) high and has pink to purple flowers. The immature seeds contain alkaloids and are poisonous if eaten. The mature pods and seeds are said to be edible. *C. rosea* (syn. *C. maritima*), beach bean, is native to a number of parts of the world. It is a trailing or

scrambling plant which makes a good sand-binder, because of its habit of forming large mats. The flowers are rosy pink to mauve and appear in summer. The seeds are toxic if eaten raw but can be treated to make them edible.

Canna (fam. Cannaceae)

Originally from tropical America, these robust perennials are very well suited to warm temperate and subtropical areas. In frost-prone climates, cannas are used for summer display in gardens and overwintered in the dormant state under glass. In their natural habitat, cannas grow from 75 cm (30 in) to 3 m (10 ft) tall. With their terminal clusters of showy, colorful flowers and striking foliage, they are very useful for planting in large garden beds.

CULTIVATION Cannas grow from thick rhizomes. In frost-prone climates, these are started into growth in a warm greenhouse in early spring. Put them in pots of soilless potting compost. Plant out when danger of frost is over, in early summer. Lift in fall when frosts have started, cut down stems and foliage, and store rhizomes for the winter in slightly moist peat

ABOVE The brilliant splash of color of massed cannas makes a bold statement in a large garden.

ABOVE *Canavalia rosea* (syn. *C. maritima*), beach bean, produces rosy pink to mauve flowers in summer.

ABOVE Red-speckled yellow flowers of a showy Canna hybrid.

in frost-free conditions. In frost-free climates, plants can be left in the ground all year round. Water regularly and well in summer during dry weather and feed with a liquid fertilizer. Large clumps can be divided in the spring when potting or planting.

CLIMATE Zone 10.

SPECIES There are many cultivars of cannas and these are generally preferred to the species. They are available in a range of heights and colors, from dwarf to tall, and in shades of red, pink, salmon, yellow, orange and white. There are also cultivars with bicolored flowers. Among many other good cannas are *C. flaccida* which grows to 1.5 m with 60 cm long leaves and yellow flowers. This species is the prime parent of over 200 modern varieties. A very well-known canna is *C. indica*, popularly called Indian shot, which grows to around 1 m in height and produces 45 cm long leaves. The flowers are bright red. This species from tropical America has become naturalised in various warm and tropical areas including the far south of North America.

Cantua (fam. Polemoniaceae)

These South American evergreen shrubs produce pendulous clusters of attractive, satiny red, white or violet flowers, similar to fuchsias, from late winter to summer.

CULTIVATION In frosty areas, grow in a cool greenhouse or conservatory in pots of soil-based potting compost. Outdoors, grow against a warm wall or in a border, in full sun and with well-drained soil. Propagate from semi-ripe cuttings in summer.

CLIMATE Zone 9.

SPECIES *C. bicolor*, yellow-tube cantua, grows to about 1.25 m (4 ft), with yellow and red flowers. *C. buxifolia*, sacred flower of the Incas, has very beautiful, rose-colored flowers, 7.5 cm (3 in) long. However, this species is rather straggly unless it is staked or trained against a wall or fence. It grows to about 2 m (6 ft) or more in warmer climates.

ABOVE The long, tubular flowers of *Cantua buxifolia* have a silky sheen and the color is iridescent when it is seen in bright light.

Cape gooseberry

(*Physalis peruviana*, fam. Solanaceae)

Native to Peru, this plant is not a true gooseberry. A perennial cultivated as an annual, it can live for three years in frost-free climates but should be cut down after each crop. It grows to around 90 cm (36 in) tall and to a width of 1.5 m (5 ft), and produces a rounded yellow berry, surrounded by a papery covering. The fruit is used in jams, eaten fresh or stewed.

CULTIVATION The Cape gooseberry is generally grown as a summer annual in a cool greenhouse. Seeds are sown during spring in seed trays or pots and germinated in warmth. The seedlings are potted up into small pots and then eventually planted 75 cm (30 in) apart in a soil border, or put into 25 cm (10 in) pots. Pinch out young plants to create bushy specimens. Provide canes for support. Feed during the summer with a tomato fertilizer and carry out moderate watering. Where summers are very warm or hot grow in a sunny spot in the garden.

CLIMATE Zone 10, but grown as a summer annual in all climates.

VARIETIES There are several varieties; check the seed catalogues.

ABOVE The berries of Cape gooseberry are enclosed in a papery calyx which splits open as the fruit ripens.

Capparis (fam. Capparaceae)

Caper bush

These evergreen shrubs and trees are found in most tropical, subtropical and dry inland areas. There are about 250 species in this genus. They produce yellow or white flowers, ovate leaves and edible fruits. Only one species, *C. spinosa*, is commonly grown.

CULTIVATION This plant needs a frost-free situation and good drainage. Propagate from semi-hardwood cuttings in late summer.

CLIMATE Zone 10 for most.

SPECIES *C. mitchellii*, tree caper, native orange or native pomegranate, is a thorny species native to inland eastern Australia and useful as a shade tree in hot, dry areas. It grows 3–9 m (10–30 ft) tall, with large, cream flowers and hairy berries which are 5 cm (2 in) across. *C. spinosa*, caper bush, zone 9, is a tangled, thorny shrub from the dry, rocky areas of the Mediterranean. Not particularly attractive, it is grown for its flower buds which have been pickled and used as condiments for many centuries. It grows from about 90 cm (36 in) to 1.5 m (5 ft) in height and produces large white flowers with long stamens. Var. *inermis* is thornless and has white flowers flushed with red.

ABOVE Masses of long stamens are a feature of the pink-flushed, white flowers of *Capparis spinosa*, cultivated for its immature flower buds.

Capsicum

(*Capsicum annuum*, fam. Solanaceae)

Sweet pepper, red pepper, chilli pepper

These peppers from tropical South America are very different from the black and white peppers (*Piper* species) used as spices. They are mostly grown as annuals and are cultivated in a similar way to tomatoes and eggplant. Capsicums are grown for their fruit which comes in many shapes, sizes and degrees of pungency, ranging from the sweet or mild flavored to the very hot. Mild capsicums are used as vegetables and in salads, and today are very popular roasted. They are also used in stuffings, seasonings, sauces and pickles. Chilli peppers are used frequently in Mexican and Asian cooking. Paprika, the Hungarian name for red pepper, is obtained from the less pungent, pointed variety and cayenne pepper, or red pepper, is the grounds of the small, pungent varieties. Several species of this genus of perennials can be grown as ornamental annuals in pots or in garden borders.

CULTIVATION The edible peppers are grown as summer annuals, either in an intermediate greenhouse if summers are cool, or outdoors in areas with warm or hot summers, planting out when danger of frost is over. Sow seeds in mid-spring in seed trays or pots and germinate them in a temperature of 20°C (68°F). Pot seedlings

ABOVE A basket of colorful capsicums ready to add flavor and color to a variety of dishes.

individually into small pots and eventually plant 45–60 cm (18–24 in) apart in a soil border, or pot into 25 cm (10 in) pots. Pinch out young plants to encourage bushiness. Tall varieties may need staking. Water moderately, and in summer feed with tomato fertilizer once every two weeks. Provide a humid atmosphere under glass. The fruits can be picked green, or left to ripen and change color. The ornamental capsicums are raised in the same way and potted on until they are in 12.5 cm (5 in) pots. They can be grown in an intermediate greenhouse and make good house plants.

CLIMATE Zone 10, but grown in all climates as summer annuals.

VARIETIES Seed catalogues list a range of both culinary and ornamental varieties. Culinary peppers are derived from *Capsicum annuum*, an annual or short-lived perennial; the ornamentals are from this species and also *C. frutescens*.

Caraway (*Carum carvi*, fam. Apiaceae)

Caraway has been used since Biblical times, both as a flavoring and as a medicine. Originally from northern and central Europe

ABOVE Ornamental capsicums are generally grown as pot plants under glass; they also make good house plants.

ABOVE Upright clusters of immature fruits on caraway, Carum carvi, will ripen and split to shed their aromatic seeds.

and Asia, it later became naturalized in North America. It is a thick-rooted biennial, with feathery leaves, rather like parsley, and clusters of white, summer flowers. It grows to 60 cm (24 in). When ripe, the fruit of the caraway plant splits into two small, dark brown, crescent-shaped, aromatic seeds. Most parts of the plant are edible. Caraway seeds have a pleasant, spicy taste and are used in cakes, breads and cheeses, as well as in curries, pickles, and meat and fish dishes. The aromatic oil contained in the seed aids digestion and is still sometimes used as a breath sweetener. It is also used as a flavoring in liqueurs. The roots can be boiled and served with white sauce or butter, and the young leaves can be used in green salads and to garnish vegetables, such as marrow, zucchini and spinach.

CULTIVATION Any well-drained, ordinary garden soil will suit this plant, but it does need a sheltered, sunny position. Sow seed direct into shallow holes 15 cm (6 in) apart, with 20 cm (8 in) between rows. Sow in spring to reap seed the following summer. To encourage continuous growth, give plenty of water during dry periods and apply a complete fertilizer alongside the plants. Weed control is important. Before the seeds drop from the flowering heads, cut off all the heads and dry them in a shady place. When the seeds begin to fall away easily from the heads, shake out the seeds, separate them from the debris and store in an air-tight container well away from the light.

CLIMATE Zone 3.

Cardamine (fam. Brassicaceae)
Bitter cress, lady's smock

These hardy annual, biennial or perennial herbs were once used as sedatives in medicine. Native to Europe and much of the northern hemisphere, some species have become weeds.

CULTIVATION Cardamine does well in moist, rather boggy gardens. Propagate from seed sown in the spring or by division of the rootstock in fall.

CLIMATE Zone 4.

SPECIES *C. pratensis*, a perennial widely distributed in Europe, has small, pale mauve or lilac flowers in spring and summer and lance-shaped to oblong leaves. It adapts well to rock gardens or cool, moist to boggy borders. Propagation is usually by offsets, although it can also be started from seed. It is used as cress in some parts of Europe.

ABOVE *Cardamine pratensis* does well in damp ground and is generally not invasive.

Cardamom

(*Elettaria cardamomum*, fam. Zingiberaceae)

This is a rhizomatous perennial, to 3 m (10 ft), with a tall, leafy stem and shorter flowering stems. After flowering, it produces small, irregularly shaped seed capsules, of a light greenish gray, each containing several brown seeds. It is widely cultivated in Asian countries and has been imported into European countries since the time of the Romans. The seeds of the cardamom plant are mostly used as a spice in cooking, particularly in Asian and Indian curries. They are also used in cakes, pastries and breads, and often in coffee in the Middle East. The essential oil from its seeds is used in perfumes.

CULTIVATION The cardamom is a native of India and other tropical countries and is grown for its seeds only in tropical climates. In frost-prone climates, it makes a pleasing foliage plant in a warm greenhouse or conservatory. Grow in pots of soil-based potting compost with added chipped bark. Shade from direct sun and provide a humid atmosphere. Water well in the growing season but far less in winter. Propagation is by division of the rhizomes in spring.

CLIMATE Zone 10 and above.

ABOVE In cool and cold climates, the cardamom, *Elettaria cardamomum*, makes a pleasing foliage plant in a warm greenhouse or conservatory.

Cardiocrinum (fam. Liliaceae)

These giant lilies from eastern Asia and the Himalayas were formerly included in the genus Lilium.

CULTIVATION Most species are fairly rare and are difficult to grow unless the climatic conditions are right. Plant the bulbs in fall just below the surface, with plenty of space between the bulbs to achieve the best effect. They like partial shade and cool soil. Seed should be freshly gathered and sown in fall. They may take up to five years to flower. The main bulb dies after flowering and setting seed, but the plant continues to survive through offset bulbs produced around the main bulb.

CLIMATE Zone 7.

SPECIES *C. giganteum* grows with towering majesty to 2–3 m (6–10 ft) in height. The large, funnel-shaped, white, fragrant flowers are borne almost horizontally. The trumpet-shaped flowers have deep pink stripes inside.

ABOVE Strictly for cool climate gardens, *Cardiocrinum giganteum* is certainly eye-catching.

Carex (fam. Cyperaceae)

Sedge

Many species of Carex are native to New Zealand and are somewhat tender in the north. They are found mainly in wet or moist habitats. Sedges differ from grasses and rushes in that they have solid stems and sheathing leaf bases. The leaves are flat and grass-like, and the tiny brown or green flowers, sometimes just like 'seeds', form clusters or spikes, which are suitable for dried flower arrangements. Carex is suitable for rock, pebble or water gardens, or around ponds. Some species can be invasive but most are attractive grassy plants which make good garden features.

CULTIVATION Sedges require moist conditions and humus-rich soil, and sun or partial shade. Propagate by division in spring.

CLIMATE Zone 9 for most species.

SPECIES Among the most suitable hardy species for American gardens are *C. comans*, with clumps of very fine leaves, bronze-colored in some forms; the yellow-leaved *C. elata* 'Aurea'; and white and green striped

ABOVE Massed *Carex* species provide interesting foliage and shape contrast with other shrubby plants.

C. morrowii 'Variegata'. All are suited to zone 7. *C. secta*, common along the waterways of New Zealand, forms thick tussocks and is very useful for stabilizing bank erosion. It has light gray-green leaves and sometimes grows to 1 m (3 ft) in height. It is also suited to zone 7.

Carissa (fam. Apocynaceae)

Cultivated widely in tropical areas throughout the world, *Carissa* is grown in cool greenhouses or conservatories in most parts of North America. In suitable climates, it can be grown in shrub or mixed borders or it can equally well be used for hedging.

ABOVE Although often used purely as a hedge, *Carissa macrocarpa* produces large fruits sold in markets in its native South Africa.

CULTIVATION Grow in pots of soil-based potting compost under glass and provide maximum light but shade from direct sun. Prune back to restrict size after flowering if necessary. Outdoors, hedges are trimmed when flowering is over. Propagate from semi-ripe cuttings in summer.

CLIMATE Zone 10 and above.

SPECIES *C. bispinosa*, hedge thorn, has white flowers in spring and red berries. This species grows to 2 m (6 ft). *C. macrocarpa*, Natal plum, grows to around 5 m (16 ft) high. Cultivated as a hedge plant, especially in its native South Africa, the fruit is popular for use in making jams and preserves.

Carmichaelia (fam. Papilionaceae)

A native of New Zealand, this genus of shrubs has a range of forms. Some species are prostrate, others erect; most have flattened or cylindrical green stems which perform the same functions as the leaves which fall very quickly, leaving the twigs bare. The leaves are either simple or pinnate, the small, fragrant, pea-shaped flowers are borne in lateral sprays and the fruit is a small, leathery pod. These attractive shrubs are particularly well suited for sheltered borders.

CULTIVATION Tender species should be grown in a cool greenhouse in areas which are prone to frosts. Outdoors, *Carmichaelia* does best in mild climates and will grow in many types of soil, but not clay. Plant in spring or fall and provide protection from frost during the first winter. Prune only if it is necessary to improve the shape of the plant. Propagate from cuttings of half ripe wood. Place the cuttings in a polythene container and keep in a cool place.

ABOVE Giant-flowered broom from New Zealand, *Carmichaelia williamsii* has curiously shaped stems and cream or pale yellow flowers.

CLIMATE Zone 9 for most species.

SPECIES *C. flagelliformis*, zone 8, is a much-branched shrub, with sprays of very tiny flowers. It grows to around 2 m (6 ft). *C. odorata* is a spreading species, to 2 m (6 ft) or so, with drooping branches. The fragrant, purple-veined white flowers bloom from late spring through to midsummer. *C. williamsii*, zone 8, is also much branched, with large, cream or pale yellow flowers, 25 mm (1 in) long, either solitary or in sprays of two or six. It grows to 3.5 m (11 ft) or more and needs a mild, coastal climate.

Carnegiea (fam. Cactaceae)

Saguaro

Found growing naturally in Mexico, Arizona and southern California, this familiar, tree-like cactus is huge, sometimes growing to 15–20 m (50–65 ft) in height in its natural habitat. It is the largest of all the cactuses.

CULTIVATION Except in the south and California this cactus is generally grown in an intermediate greenhouse, in pots of well-drained, alkaline cactus compost. It needs maximum light and airy conditions.

CLIMATE Zone 9.

ABOVE Creamy white flowers of the saguaro cactus emerge straight out of the thick branches.

SPECIES *C. gigantea*, the only species, is very slow growing. It takes a long time to come to flowering, but the large, sweetly perfumed, white flowers, which bloom at night, are most attractive.

Carpentaria (fam. Arecaceae)

This palm genus comprises only one species which occurs primarily around Darwin in northern Australia and on the nearby northern coast and islands. A fast-growing, feather-leafed palm, with a crownshaft, it is distinguished from related genera, such as *Archontophoenix*, *Normanbya* and *Ptychosperma*, by its fruits.

CULTIVATION In frost-prone climates, grow this palm as a young plant in a warm greenhouse or conservatory, or as a house plant. Use a soil-based potting compost and provide maximum light but shade from direct sun, and high humidity. Propagate from seed sown in spring. Germinate at 27°C (81°F).

CLIMATE Zone 10 and above.

ABOVE The crownshaft of *Carpentaria acuminata* are red fruits and multi-branched, flowering stems.

SPECIES *C. acuminata* is a tall, single-stemmed palm, fairly similar to the bangalow (*Archontophoenix cunninghamiana*) in stature and general form. The inflorescences are a notable characteristic as they appear in continuous succession at the base of the crownshaft and bear lots of small, greenish yellow flowers. Masses of bright scarlet, cherry-sized fruits are borne in panicles mainly during late spring and summer.

Carpenteria (fam. Hydrangeaceae)
Tree anemone

This evergreen shrub from California, with its deep green leaves and fragrant, pure white flowers, can be extremely beautiful if the plant is growing under the right conditions. The summer flowers resemble single roses or anemones.

CULTIVATION Though it is not widely known to the average gardener, the tree anemone is ideally suited to both warm and cooler climates. Plant in the spring or the fall in well-drained garden soil, which is slightly sandy, in a sunny position. Give regular, deep waterings, though do not water too often during the growing season. Apply a general purpose, slow-release fertilizer in the spring. Prune back any overlong shoots after the plants have finished flowering. Propagate from semi-ripe cuttings in the summer.

ABOVE The pure white flowers of *Carpenteria californica* are a delight in the garden.

CLIMATE Zone 7.

SPECIES *C. californica* is the only species. It has narrow, soft, deep green leaves, grayish-green on the undersides, and fragrant, white flowers, with gold centers, borne in clusters of five or six.

Carpinus (fam. Corylaceae)
Hornbeam

These small to medium trees and shrubs have smoothly fluted gray bark, alternate, toothed leaves, catkins of tiny, unisexual flowers and clusters of dry, winged fruits. They produce hard, fine-grained wood, which is very good for tools and joinery, and are also planted as hedges and specimens.

CULTIVATION Hornbeams like a cooler climate and do well in most soils. Propagate the species from seed sown in fall, although this does not usually germinate until spring. Cultivars must be grafted or budded onto seedling stocks of *C. betulus*.

ABOVE Hornbeam, *Carpinus betulus*, adapts well to formal training and clipping. Here it forms a broad, pyramidal dome.

CLIMATE Zone 5.

SPECIES *C. betulus*, common or European hornbeam, is a tree 10–15 m (33–50 ft) tall, but often pollarded, with beech-like buds and leaves, and a fluted, rough trunk. The leaves turn golden brown in fall and remain through the winter, making it very attractive as a hedge. It does well in chalky soils. 'Columnaris' grows in a slender, pyramidal shape; 'Fastigiata' also with a pyramidal form, though broader than 'Columnaris', is useful for street planting; 'Incisa' has narrow, deeply tooth-edged leaves; 'Pendula' has drooping branches; and 'Purpurea' has purple young leaves. *C. caroliniana*, American hornbeam or blue beech, grows slowly to under 12 m (40 ft). It has ovate, blue-green leaves which turn yellow in fall.

Carpobrotus (fam. Aizoaceae)
Hottentot fig

This genus of around 30 species of succulents is native to South Africa, Australia and North and South America. All of the species are prostrate plants forming large mats of three-sided, fleshy leaves, which makes them very useful as sand-binding plants. They are also grown for their edible fruit and abundant large, brightly colored spring and summer flowers. Mostly purplish, the flowers can also be bright pink and occasionally yellow.

BELOW An ideal seaside groundcover, *Carpobrotus glaucescens* has pinkish mauve flowers mainly in spring.

CULTIVATION In areas prone to frost, grow in pots in a cool greenhouse, or use outdoors as summer display or bedding plants. Outdoors, these succulents grow almost anywhere in poor, sandy soils. They need full sun to open their flowers. Propagate from stem cuttings in summer.

CLIMATE Zone 9.

SPECIES *C. acinaciformis*, native to South Africa's Natal and Cape Province, has large, grayish green, sabre-shaped leaves and huge, crimson-purple flowers, 12 cm (5 in) across. This species has become naturalized in various warm coastal areas of the world and is splendid in full bloom. *C. edulis*, also from Cape Province and Natal, has become naturalized in California and parts of Australia. This spreading species makes an excellent sand-binder. It has dull green foliage and large, yellow flowers, turning pinkish. This species has edible fruit. *C. glaucescens*, native to eastern Australia and Norfolk Island, is also a spreading plant, with reddish stems, blueish leaves and light purple flowers.

Carrot

(*Daucus carota* subsp. *sativus*, fam. Apiaceae)

First domesticated in Afghanistan, the carrot has been cultivated for around 2000 years. It is an herbaceous biennial but is grown as an annual. This popular root vegetable is delicious both raw and cooked, and is also very nutritious as it contains sugar, mineral salts, vitamins and carotene.

CULTIVATION Carrots like a sunny position and prefer light or sandy soils which are nevertheless reasonably fertile but with a low nitrogen content. Do not grow in freshly manured soil as it causes deformed roots. The soil pH should ideally be 6–6.5. Successive sowings can be made for a long supply of roots. Carrots take from nine to twelve weeks to mature, but immature roots can be pulled for

ABOVE The feathery foliage of carrots adds a decorative touch to the vegetable garden.

use as 'baby carrots'. Always sow in cropping positions as carrots dislike being transplanted. Start sowing in spring but wait until the soil temperature exceeds 7°C (19°F). Early in the season, carrots can be sown under cloches, which help to warm the soil. Sow seeds 1 cm (⅓ in) deep in rows 15 cm (6 in) apart. Thin out to 4–8 cm (1½–3 in), depending on size. Carrot fly maggots can be a serious problem. To overcome this, surround the crop with a 90 cm (36 in) high screen of very fine mesh or plastic sheeting. Alternatively, sow seeds during early summer, at which time the flies' activities have ceased. If possible choose resistant varieties. Keep carrots well watered during dry weather. Maincrop and late varieties can be stored in moist sand in a cool dry place for use during the winter.

CLIMATE Carrots are grown in all climates as a spring and summer annual, but in areas with severe winters do not leave roots in the ground over winter – lift and store in fall.

VARIETIES Refer to seed catalogues for varieties available in your area. They are grouped according to time of maturity and shape and size of root. Early carrots have small, cylindrical roots; mid-season varieties are medium-sized with longer, cylindrical roots; maincrop carrots have medium-sized, broadly conical roots; and late varieties have very large, cylindrical roots. The last two are the best ones for storing.

Carya (fam. Juglandaceae)
Hickory

The name of this genus derives from the Greek karya, meaning 'walnut tree'. They are mostly found in North America and Asia and are cultivated for their hard timber and their ornamental value, although some species are also produced for their edible nuts. Caryas are large, deciduous trees with attractive, pinnate leaves which color yellow, orange or gold in fall. The tiny male flowers are borne in catkins at the base of the new growth and the female flowers appear in clusters at its tip. The nut is housed in a thick, green, fleshy covering, similar to that of a walnut.

CULTIVATION Caryas like an ordinary garden soil. They are fairly slow growers and are not easily transplanted. Propagate from stratified seed, sown in spring, or by root sprouts. The edible varieties are propagated by grafting.

ABOVE The pecan nut tree, *Carya illinoinensis*, is both decorative and productive.

ABOVE Pecan nuts are large and slow to ripen. The kernels are edible, with a pleasant, sweet taste.

CLIMATE There are species suited to various climatic zones.

SPECIES *C. aquatica*, bitter pecan, zone 7, has lance-shaped leaves, yellow-downy when young, and a reddish brown, egg-shaped, angled nut. It grows to over 20 m (65 ft). *C. cordiformis*, bitternut, zone 5, also grows to around 27 m (88 ft). The fruit is generally borne in pairs of threes and contains the bitter kernels; the bright yellow, winter buds are quite distinctive. *C. glabra*, pignut, zone 5, is a medium-sized tree which grows to around 15 m (50 ft). The small, ridged nut is enclosed in a thin skin and contains a dry-tasting kernel. *C. illinoinensis*, pecan nut, zone 6, is a deciduous tree which grows to around 10 m (33 ft) tall and 6–7 m (20–23 ft) wide. It has yellow-downy winter buds and smooth, oblong, light brown nuts, with a dark stripe. The kernels are edible, with a pleasant, sweet taste. There are numerous cultivars which should be chosen according to climate.

Caryopteris (fam. Verbenaceae)
Blue spiraea, bluebeard

These low-growing, rather spreading, deciduous shrubs and perennials from eastern Asia have opposite, toothed, aromatic leaves and generally blue flowers which bloom in late summer and fall. They are commonly grown in mixed and shrub borders and are valued for their late flowers: massed planting gives the best effect.

ABOVE *Caryopteris incana* has distinctly veined leaves and whorls of rich violet flowers spaced at intervals up the stem.

CULTIVATION These plants like sun and a free-draining soil that is not too heavy. Plant in spring and protect from frost for the first winter. They are frost-hardy once established. Prune reasonably severely in spring, cutting back the old growth to within two buds from the base. After pruning, feed generously to encourage growth and abundant flowers. Propagate species from seed sown in fall and germinated in a cold frame, and species and cultivars from softwood cuttings in spring, rooted in a greenhouse. In early summer, greenwood cuttings can be taken and these are slightly easier to root, again under cover.

CLIMATE Zone 6 for *C. incana*, zone 7 for *C. clandonesis*.

SPECIES *C. incana*, bluebeard, is a shrub, often treated as a perennial. It grows to 1.5 m (5 ft) with ovate leaves, grayish-downy on the undersides, and blue to violet, fall flowers. 'Candida' has white flowers. *C. x clandonensis*, a hybrid of *C. incana* x *C. mongholica*, has vigorous gray-green foliage and lavender blue flowers. This bushy plant grows to 1 m (3 ft). Various attractive cultivars are available.

Caryota (fam. Arecaceae)
Fishtail palm

Comprising around 12 species of palms, this genus is native to the tropics of Asia and Malaysia, and the Cape York Peninsula of Australia. Unlike other genera of palms, it has bipinnate leaves, and the leaf segments have a distinctive, roughly triangular shape, hence the common name, fishtail palm. The fruits produce quite an irritant juice and should not be eaten. Fishtail palms are valued as ornamentals, particularly in the tropics, and also make attractive indoor plants. Under the right conditions they can grow very fast. For example, if grown in the tropics, the single-stemmed species can occasionally pass through their whole life cycle in only 15 to 20 years.

CULTIVATION In most parts of North America, fishtail palms are grown in intermediate to warm greenhouses or conservatories, or as

ABOVE Large clusters of tassel-like flowering stems appear on all species of *Caryota*.

house plants in warm rooms. Grow them in pots or tubs of soil-based potting compost and while they need maximum light they should not be subjected to direct sun. Fishtail palms can be propagated from seed, which germinates fairly easily if fresh, needing a temperature of 27°C (81°F). *C. urens* clumps can be divided, but the divisions can be slow to re-establish.

CLIMATE Zone 10 and above.

SPECIES *C. mitis*, clustered fishtail palm, originates from Southeast Asia and the Philippines. The most cold-tolerant of the species generally cultivated, it has 2 m (6 ft) long, graceful leaves, with reasonably widely spaced, asymmetrical leaflets. It is clump-forming, with masses of densely packed stems, spreading to around 1.5 m (5 ft) in diameter at the base. The stems vary greatly in height, the tallest reaching 6–8 m (20–26 ft). *C. rumphiana* grows widely in Malaysia and also extends into northern Queensland. A solitary-stemmed palm, with huge leaves, it grows to heights of 20 m (65 ft) or more, although it is not cultivated as often as the other species listed. *C. urens*, jaggery palm, is a native of India and parts of Southeast Asia. Also solitary-stemmed, this species is widely grown in the tropics for its ornamental value, as well as for sugar and alcohol production in its native habitat. It has a smooth, stout trunk, rarely more than 10 m (33 ft) in height, and a large, rather heavy-looking crown owing to the densely packed, semi-pendulous leaf segments. Mature palms produce huge inflorescences, comprising a spectacular drape of green, flower-bearing branches, sometimes up to 5 m (16 ft) long. The inflorescences are produced successively further down the trunk until the tree dies.

Cashew

(*Anacardium occidentale*, fam. Anacardiaceae)

Native to tropical America, this evergreen, spreading tree is grown in the tropics around

ABOVE The edible nut of the cashew is enclosed in a larger casing. Shelling and roasting is a tedious process.

the world for its delicious nuts. It can be grown in zone 10 but in this zone does not fruit very freely. The tree grows best in semi-arid, hot climates. The nuts are enclosed in a double-shelled, kidney-shaped, orange fruit which is about 2 cm (1 in) in length. After being roasted to destroy the acid juice, the nuts are sweet, oily and nutritious, and are either eaten raw or used in cooking. The nut also yields an oil, similar to olive oil, which in some countries is used to flavor wine, especially madeira. The fleshy, pear-shaped stalk known as 'cashew apple', is juicy, slightly acid, and eaten by native peoples or fermented to make wine. The tree produces a white, acrid juice or gum used to make varnish for woodwork.

CULTIVATION The cashew is not often cultivated in North America and plants are not readily available. If attempted, it should be grown in a pot or tub in a warm greenhouse or conservatory as a novelty foliage plant. Grow it in well-drained, soil-based potting compost. Propagate from seed.

CLIMATE Cashew grows in zone 10 but does best in higher zones.

Cassava

(*Manihot esculenta,* syn. *M. utilissima,* fam. Euphorbiaceae)

Tapioca, manioc, mandioca

A shrubby plant growing to about 3 m (10 ft), cassava has woody stems, palmate leaves and swollen tuberous roots, which are the parts that are eaten. It is one of the most important food crops of the wet tropics. Cassava is known as tapioca in some Asian countries, while in most western countries tapioca is the name applied to the manufactured product made from the roots. Cassava meal and tapioca are served alone, boiled or mashed, or used in soups and puddings. Cassava is also fermented to make an alcoholic drink, while other byproducts are derived from the juices extracted from the plant. The numerous cultivars are classed as either bitter or sweet, depending on the amount of cyanide present in the root. The roots must be carefully prepared before use as they are extremely poisonous to both people and animals if eaten raw. These plants are almost immune from insect attack because of the presence of this substance.

CULTIVATION Cassava is not often cultivated in North America and in most areas would need to be grown in a warm greenhouse or conservatory, where it would have mainly novelty value. It is grown from the tuberous roots or stem cuttings in spring. Plant in humus-rich soil and water well in the growing season.

CLIMATE Tropical regions only.

Cassia (fam. Caesalpiniaceae)

This genus of annuals, sub-shrubs, shrubs and trees is now divided into several groups. In fact a great many species of familiar cassias have now been placed in the genus *Senna*. Natives of tropical and temperate regions around the world, including North and South America, some are deciduous, some are evergreen. Generally they have pinnate leaves and showy clusters of flowers. The seed pods are mostly flattened or cylindrical, and sometimes winged.

ABOVE Cassava is grown only in the tropics where it is one of the most important food crops.

ABOVE Even from a distance, *Cassia fistula* makes an impact on the landscape. Trees can grow very large in the right climate.

ABOVE Sprays of clear yellow flowers of *Cassia fistula* are borne profusely on trees grown in the true tropics.

CULTIVATION In frost-prone climates, grow in an intermediate or warm greenhouse or conservatory, in pots of soil-based potting compost. Maximum light is needed. Outdoors, most species prefer a moderately well drained soil containing plenty of organic matter. Some will tolerate a little shade. Propagate from seed sown in spring. Hard seeds may need a light abrading with sandpaper before soaking overnight in cold water. Prune back after flowering to encourage bushy growth or to avoid seed setting. The tree-like species will be too tall to prune.

CLIMATE Zone 10 and above for the following species.

SPECIES *C. brewsteri*, cigar cassia, is found growing in the rainforests of Australia. This tree reaches around 9 m (30 ft), with long sprays of yellow and red flowers. The pod, up to 30 cm (12 in) long, is shaped like a large cigar. *C. fistula*, golden shower, is a slender tree which grows to 9 m (30 ft). It has fragrant, pale yellow flowers in sprays 30–45 cm (12–18 in) long and cylindrical pods, which are often as

long as 60 cm (24 in). *C. grandis*, pink shower, has lateral sprays of large, rose-colored flowers and rather flattened pods, 60 cm (24 in) long. The tree grows to 15 m (50 ft). *C. javanica*, Java shower, is a wide-spreading tree which can grow to 10 m (33 ft) tall under cultivation. It has showy sprays of rose-pink flowers above the leaves, and cylindrical pods which can be 60 cm (24 in) long.

Cassinia (fam. Asteraceae)

Native to Australia, New Zealand and South Africa, these evergreen shrubs belong to the large daisy family. They have heath-like foliage which is often quite untidy looking. The leaves are generally very small and the massed heads of small, yellow or white flowers are borne at the ends of the stems. Most species have aromatic foliage and some are suitable for drying.

CULTIVATION Grow in full sun in reasonably fertile, well-drained soil which contains plenty of humus. Prune in spring by cutting back the old flowered shoots to within about 2.5 cm (1 in) of the old wood. Propagate from semi-ripe cuttings in summer under glass, or take hardwood cuttings in winter, again rooting them under glass.

CLIMATE Zone 9 for most.

ABOVE *Cassinia fulvida*, popularly known as golden heath, is one of the hardier species and has an overall golden glow.

SPECIES Few of these are grown in the US. *C. aculeata*, common cassinia, is an Australian native. It grows to around 3 m (10 ft), with small, hairy, sticky leaves and small, dense clusters of mainly off-white or cream flowers with papery bracts in summer. *C. arcuata* grows to around 2 m (6 ft). This Australian native has tiny, aromatic leaves and pendulous heads of fawn-colored flowers. It is often known as biddy bush or Chinese scrub. *C. denticulata*, from New South Wales, is an erect-growing shrub up to 2–3 m (6–10 ft), dwarfed in alpine areas. It has stiff, lance-shaped, light green leaves and cream flowers. *C. fulvida* (syn. *C. leptophylla* subsp. *fulvida*), golden heath, zone 8, is from New Zealand and grows to 2 m (6 ft). The dark green leaves are yellowish underneath and the tiny, yellowish flowers appear in clusters. *C. quinquefaria* is an open, rounded Australian shrub, 2–3 m (6–10 ft) tall, with linear leaves on sticky branchlets and feathery clusters of glossy white or pale brown bell-shaped flowers during summer. *C. uncata*, also native to Australia, is a stiff, upright shrub which grows to 2 m (6 ft). Its curved leaves are thread-like and rather rough, and its shining, light yellow to brownish flower heads bloom nearly all year.

Cassiope (fam. Ericaceae)

These hardy, low-growing, evergreen shrubs are found growing in arctic and mountainous regions. Related to the heathers, they have scale-like or linear leaves and single, small, nodding white or pinkish flowers followed by capsule-shaped fruit.

CULTIVATION Cassiopes do well in a cool, moist, lime-free soil in a semi-shaded situation. Propagate from semi-ripe cuttings in summer. If a mist-propagation unit is available, this provides the best conditions in which to root them. Alternatively, layer stems in the spring.

CLIMATE Zone 3 for many species; zone 5 for *C. mertensiana*.

ABOVE Low-growing *Cassiope mertensiana* has white, bell-like flowers that have distinctive red calyces.

SPECIES *C. lycopodioides* is a prostrate species, the small, thread-like branchlets forming a dense mat. It has white, bell-shaped flowers. *C. mertensiana* is a semi-erect plant to 15–25 cm (6–10 in). The shoots are loosely clad with leaves in four rows and the flowers are a creamy white color. *C. tetragona* has erect shoots, deep green, needle-like, overlapping leaves, crowded around the stems, and single, white flowers. It grows to around 30 cm (12 in).

Castanospermum (fam. Papilionaceae)

This genus of only one species originates from the rainforests of north-eastern Australia. It is grown for its handsome timber and its attractive, evergreen foliage which makes it a useful shade tree. Grown in the warmer regions of the US.

CULTIVATION In climates where hard frosts occur, grow as a pot plant in an intermediate greenhouse or conservatory where it makes a pleasing foliage specimen. Use a soil-based potting compost. Provide maximum light but shade from direct sun. Outdoors, plant in a light soil in a sunny position.

CLIMATE Zone 9 and above.

TOP A young black bean tree, *Castanospermum australe*, has a perfect, dome-shaped crown.

ABOVE The showy red and yellow flowers of the black bean tree are often almost hidden by the foliage.

SPECIES *C. australe*, Moreton Bay chestnut or black bean tree, grows to 18 m (60 ft) and has large, glossy, pinnate leaves, sprays of striking yellow to orange-red pea-flowers with long stamens, and large, bean-like seed pods. The fruit of this tree is poisonous if eaten raw, though it is the subject of much research as it has potential for use in drugs for the treatment of AIDS.

Casuarina (fam. Casuarinaceae)
She-oak

This genus now comprises only 12 species, the remainder having been transferred to the genus *Allocasuarina*. Many are native to Australia, though some are found in the South Pacific and the islands to the north of Australia. These evergreen trees have weeping, needle-like branchlets, the true leaves being the tiny scale-like formations at the junctions of the branchlets. The flowers are inconspicuous and are followed by woody cones of variable shape and size. Fast-growing, they are useful as windbreaks, and as shade and amenity trees, and some make excellent soil binders. Different species are useful for different soil and climatic conditions, including coastal headlands, swamps and river banks.

CULTIVATION In areas subject to frosts, grow as young plants in pots or tubs in a cool greenhouse or conservatory, using soil-based potting compost, and provide maximum light. Outdoors, casuarinas prefer an open, sunny position. All species, except *C. glauca*, which thrives in swampy ground, like quite well drained soil. Propagation is from seed sown in spring.

CLIMATE Zones 9 and 10 are suitable.

ABOVE Sparsely foliaged trees of *Casuarina* species survive in a harsh arid region.

ABOVE Graceful, needle-like foliage of river oak, *Casuarina cunninghamiana*, and a cluster of buds about to open.

SPECIES Widely planted in warm regions including California and Florida. *C. cristata*, belah, to 12 m (40 ft), is drought-resistant and makes an ideal windbreak or decorative tree for arid areas. It has gray-green foliage. *C. cunninghamiana*, river oak, is the largest of the species and grows to 20–30 m (65–100 ft) in favorable conditions. Fast-growing, it is useful as a shade and shelter tree, but is particularly useful for stabilizing soils on river banks. It must have ample summer water but is tolerant of several degrees of frost. *C. equisetifolia*, horsetail tree, can grow to 5–10 m (16–33 ft), depending on the conditions prevalent. It can tolerate strong, salty winds and poor soils, although on exposed sites its growth can be stunted. It has no tolerance for frost. This species has been widely planted in coastal areas of China where its timber is used in a variety of ways. *C. glauca*, swamp oak, occurs naturally along tidal estuaries in eastern Australia. It has a very

upright growth habit, to 15–20 m (50–65 ft), and under sheltered conditions can spread as wide as 5 or 6 m (16–20 ft). It does best in deep, good quality soil, with ample water.

Catalpa (fam. Bignoniaceae)

Native to East Asia and North America these deciduous trees are fast-growing and useful as shade and ornamental trees as they are very attractive when in bloom. They have a round head, large, simple, long-stalked leaves, terminal sprays of bell-shaped flowers mainly in white or pink tones marked with purple and yellow, and long, narrow, bean-like fruit.

CULTIVATION Catalpas can be planted in any moderately rich, well-drained soil but will do best in a light, friable soil if well watered in summer. Because of the large leaves, some protection from wind is necessary. Propagate from seed sown in fall in a garden frame, from softwood cuttings in spring or early summer, or from root cuttings in winter. Cultivars can also be grafted in winter or budded in summer.

CLIMATE Zone 5 for most species.

ABOVE A young tree of *Catalpa fargesii*, from western China (zone 6), has been planted as a lawn specimen.

SPECIES *C. bignonioides*, common catalpa or Indian bean, has large, ovate leaves, downy on the undersides, and sprays of white flowers, similar to foxgloves, which are striped yellow and spotted purplish brown on the inside. It is a wide, spreading tree, 12–15 m (40–50 ft) tall. 'Aurea' rarely grows more than 10 m (33 ft). The attractive golden foliage lasts throughout the growing year and colors a deeper gold during fall. 'Nana' is a dwarf variety, rarely more than 2 m (6 ft) high, and frequently grafted onto upright understocks to form standards with umbrella-like, dense heads.

Catananche (fam. Asteraceae)
Cupid's dart

Derived from the Greek katanangke, the name of this genus of annuals and perennials refers to the use of this plant as a spell in love potions in times of antiquity. The narrow leaves are borne near the base of the stem and the long-stalked, blue or yellow flower heads are surrounded by papery, silvery colored bracts. *C. caerulea* is the only species which is generally cultivated. This plant looks very pretty in borders and the blooms make excellent cut or dried flowers. The dried flowers make a pretty winter decoration.

CULTIVATION *Catananche* does best in an average, well-drained garden soil in an open, sunny position. The commonly grown *C. caerulea*, however, although a perennial, can be short-lived, especially if the soil is clay, and it is often grown as an annual or biennial. Propagate from seed which is sown in the early spring in a garden frame, or alternatively, sown in its flowering position later in the season.

CLIMATE *Catananche* will thrive in zone 7.

SPECIES *C. caerulea*, which is a short-lived perennial, is similar to the cornflower in growth and habit. It grows to 60 cm (24 in). 'Alba' has white rays; 'Bicolor' is white with a deep blue center.

Catharanthus (fam. Apocynaceae)
Madagascar periwinkle

This is a genus of about eight evergreen annual or perennial plants mostly from Madagascar; only one species is commonly cultivated.

CULTIVATION Grown as a seasonal annual in cool climates, this plant is often cultivated for massed display or for long-lasting potted color. It needs well-drained soil, with some added

ABOVE The pretty flowers of *Catananche caerulea* are blue or lilac-blue and have darker centers.

ABOVE *Catharanthus roseus* is best mass planted to give a long-lasting display of color.

humus, plenty of water during the warmer months and occasional applications of fertilizer. Water sparingly in winter and propagate from seed or cutting.

CLIMATE Zone 10, but grown as a summer annual in cool climates.

SPECIES *C. roseus*, Madagascar periwinkle, is a slightly succulent, evergreen perennial which grows 30–50 cm (12–20 in) high. Flattish flowers, typically in rose pink, red, white or mauve, are produced over many months, during spring and summer. There are several cultivars. All parts of the plant will cause severe burning and irritation if they are ingested. However, this plant also contains numerous alkaloids which have been used in the manufacture of drugs to treat leukaemia in children. These alkaloids can also cause reactions.

Cattleya (fam. Orchidaceae)

Native to Central and South America, this genus comprises over 40 species of mostly epiphytic orchids, as well as countless hybrids, making it one of the most widely grown of the orchid groups. The genus divides to two main groups, the unifoliates (with one leaf at the top of the pseudobulb) and the bifoliates (with two leaves). Both types are widely grown and in the US are cultivated in a cool or intermediate greenhouse or conservatory, or as house plants on windowsills. Most flower between fall and spring, few in summer. *Cattleya* is related to *Laelia*, *Sophronitis*, *Epidendrum* and *Brassavola* and hybrids are available in many colors from cross-breeding with these genera, sometimes three or four genera parenting a single plant.

CULTIVATION Under glass or indoors, these orchids are grown in pots or in slatted orchid baskets. Use a compost formulated for epiphytic orchids, containing chipped bark and charcoal, which should be available from specialist orchid growers. They like bright light

TOP This large, showy bloom is typical of popular hybrids of *Cattleya*.

ABOVE The pure white simplicity of this *Cattleya* is very appealing.

but should be shaded from direct sun. High humidity, coupled with plenty of ventilation, will ensure the right growing conditions. Water normally as required in summer but considerably reduce watering in winter. Liquid feed weekly in the summer. Propagation is by division of congested plants when repotting them in spring.

CLIMATE Zone 10 and above.

ABOVE A cross between *Laelia* and *Cattleya* produced this complex and unusual flower.

SPECIES *C. amethystoglossa*, a bifoliate from Brazil, is splendid when in flower, bearing up to 12 flowers, each about 8 cm (3 in) across. The amethyst sepals and petals are spotted and blotched in a deeper shade and the lip is colored rich purple. *C. bowringiana*, a bifoliate from Central America, is very popular as it is grows quickly and flowers profusely. The stems grow up to 50 cm (20 in) high and produce five to ten terminal flowers in rosy lilac, the lip in a deeper shade, and the yellow throat marked with purple streaks. The broad, tongue-shaped lip has frilled margins. *C. labiata*, from Brazil, is a superb species and the parent of many, many hybrids. A unifoliate type, it produces between two and five flowers, each being about 15 cm (6 in) across. It has broad, frilled, rose-lavender petals, with a large lip in the same color, a rich crimson front and a yellow throat. Few species are grown, except by collectors. Most growers prefer the showier hybrids.

Cauliflower

(*Brassica oleracea*, Botrytis Group fam. Brassicaceae)

Although a biennial, cauliflower is mainly grown as an annual. It is easiest to grow in cool climates, being more difficult in regions with hot dry summers or very cold winters. It is the edible, immature flower head of this popular vegetable that we enjoy eating as a cooked vegetable with white sauce, or in salads. The condensed flowers and flower stems form the swollen head or curd. There are varieties of cauliflower suitable for harvesting in summer, fall and winter.

CULTIVATION Cauliflowers do best in a well-manured, deeply dug, loamy soil, with a pH of 6–7. They also need good drainage and plenty of sun. Prepare the soil about three weeks before planting the seedlings by adding old manure or compost and about 100 g (3 oz) of complete fertilizer per square metre (square yard). Keep weeds down and water liberally. The seeds germinated in pots or trays should be transplanted when about 10–15 cm (4–6 in) high. Space smaller varieties about 50 cm (20 in) apart within rows and between rows, and the larger at 60–75 cm (24–30 in). Sowings must be made at the correct time. Varieties for early summer cutting are sown in fall in a garden frame or in midwinter in a heated greenhouse, and are planted out in mid-spring. Varieties for harvesting in summer and fall are sown in spring in a greenhouse or in late spring outdoors. They are transplanted in early summer. Winter cauliflowers are sown outdoors in early summer and transplanted in midsummer. The ideal temperature for germination is 21°C (70°F). They need a generous soaking of water once a week, to

ABOVE A perfectly formed head of cauliflower ready for harvest.

encourage the roots to move downwards in the soil. Watch for attack by insect pests and diseases. In addition, a deficiency of the trace element molybdenum sometimes occurs and this can cause a condition called 'whiptail', which prevents flower set. Adding lime to the soil before planting will reduce acidity which prevents molybdenum being released to the plant. As a preventative measure where soils are very acid, spray the plants with sodium molybdenate at the rate of 7 grams (¼ ounce) to 11 litres (20 pints) of water. As the curds mature, tie the outer leaves over them to prevent discoloration and to keep them tender. Harvest the heads before they open up, while still firm.

CLIMATE Zone 8.

VARIETIES These vary according to location. Good seed catalogues will list a range of summer, fall and winter cauliflowers.

Ceanothus (fam. Rhamnaceae)

Californian lilac

These pretty, decorative, evergreen shrubs originate mostly from California and other parts of western North America where they are much grown. They grow quickly, but may be short lived in some climates. A few species are deciduous and many flower both in spring and fall. Many hybrids and cultivars have also been developed, particularly in France and England.

CULTIVATION Ceanothus need a well-drained soil and full sun, generally doing best in an open situation, though they may require staking. They can be trained against a sunny wall in cool regions. Prune after flowering to retain shape and stability. Propagate from cuttings of firm, heeled sideshoots, taken in fall. Strike in a light sandy loam, without heat, and pot as soon as they strike. Ceanothus dislike root disturbance, and transplanting of advanced plants is not advisable.

CLIMATE Prefers a cool climate or areas with

ABOVE A profuse show of jacaranda blue flowers on this lovely *Ceanothus* almost obscures the foliage.

hot, dry summers and cold, wet winters.

SPECIES *C. cyaneus* grows 2 m (6 ft) tall and produces cornflower blue flowers. *C. dentatus*, with deep blue flowers, is one of the hardiest, most frost-resistant species. It grows to 3 m (10 ft). *C. impressus*, zone 7, is a low-growing or prostrate plant, with a dense, spreading habit. Clusters of pretty, deep blue flowers bloom profusely during the spring. *C. thyrsiflorus* is a very hardy species, with bright blue early flowers, which grows to 4 m (13 ft). The cultivars and hybrids include 'A. T. Johnson', to 4 m (13 ft), with rich blue flowers in spring and fall; 'Burkwoodii' with bright blue flowers; 'Marie Simon', to 2 m (6 ft), with large clusters of pink flowers; *C. x veitchianus*, a very hardy hybrid, to 4 m (13 ft), with deep, bright blue flowers. New low-growing cultivars have been developed in California, including 'Emily Brown', with violet flowers; 'Joyce Coulter', with dark blue flowers; 'Julia Phelps', with cobalt blue flowers; and 'Yankee Point', a very hardy, wide-spreading plant, with bright blue flowers. All are suitable for growing on banks.

Cedrela (syn. Toona)

There are six species in this genus, now correctly known as Toona, which is native to

ABOVE Woody capsules on *Cedrela odorata* hold the winged seeds. The long, compound leaves are made up of numerous, slender leaflets.

ABOVE The aromatic leaves of *Cedronella canariensis* are sometimes used in potpourri or herbal teas.

tropical America and Asia. They may be deciduous or evergreen. Although not true cedars, their reddish, aromatic heartwood resembles cedar.

CULTIVATION These trees are normally grown in the tropics, although the hardy *C. sinensis* is grown in the US as a specimen tree. Grow in well-drained soil and full sun.

CLIMATE Most of these species need a tropical climate.

SPECIES In the US, the deciduous *C. sinensis*, zone 6, is the species usually grown. *C. odorata*, cigar box cedar, from the West Indies, grows between 15 and 25 m (50–80 ft) tall and produces an aromatic timber which is used to make mothproof chests and cigar boxes.

Cedronella (fam. Lamiaceae)
Balm of Gilead

There is only one species in this genus from the Canary Islands.

CULTIVATION In areas prone to frost, grow in a cool conservatory or outdoors as a summer annual. Sow seed in early spring under glass. Outdoors, grow in full sun.

CLIMATE Zone 9.

SPECIES *C. canariensis*, a bushy shrubby perennial, has nettle-shaped, aromatic leaves and, in summer, lilac, pink or white flowers. It grows to 1.2 m (4 ft).

Cedrus (fam. Pinaceae)
Cedar

Native to North Africa, the Mediterranean and the western Himalayas, three of the four closely related species of this genus are among the best known of the large, evergreen ornamentals. Typical of the genus are the needle-like leaves, which are densely clustered on short shoots except on the leading shoots of branches; the solitary, erect, almost smooth seed cones, covered with broad, flat, tightly packed conescales; and the large pollen cones, about 10 cm (4 in) long, which are borne singly on the short branchlets. The winged seeds are released through disintegration of the cone. With their symmetry, color, texture, hardiness, and relative freedom from pests and diseases, cedars are a real asset to the garden. As most are often more tolerant of warmer climates and are faster growing than many other large conifers, they are more frequently seen in these areas.

CULTIVATION Cedars like a deep, well-drained, highly organic soil. They are best planted in an open position in full sun, away from other plants. The species are best cultivated from seed, which germinates easily, and the cultivars by grafting. The foliage color variants can be grown from seed, and seedlings of the color required can be selected at a well-developed growth stage. These handsome trees require little further care.

CLIMATE There are species for various climatic zones.

SPECIES *C. atlantica*, Atlas cedar, zone 6, is still found growing in the Atlas Mountains of Morocco, Algeria and Tunisia where it originated. Under cultivation it is a rather broad-headed tree to 25 m (80 ft) under the right conditions in cooler areas, though much smaller in warmer coastal regions. It has stiff, ascending branches, short leaves, 1.5–2.5 cm (½–1 in) long, and barrel-shaped seed cones which are 7 cm (3 in) in length. Of the foliage color variants, Glauca Group with steel blue foliage, and 'Aurea', with yellowish green foliage, are the most widely grown. *C. deodara*, deodar cedar, zone 7, from the western Himalayas, is the fastest growing species and the best for warmer coastal conditions, although well suited to colder areas too. It has larger needles and cones than the other species and the tips of the branches and leading shoots are rather pendulous. As a younger tree, the deodar grows symetrically, with the spreading, lower branches sweeping the ground but tapering upward to a long, slender, nodding leading shoot. With age, however, these trees are often broad-headed and more horizontally branched. Cultivar 'Aurea', with yellow-tipped branches, grows as vigorously as *C. deodara* and is very popular. *C. libani*, cedar of Lebanon, zone 5, grows wild in the mountains of Lebanon, Syria and northern Turkey. The leaves of this species are similar in size to the Atlas cedar, the cones slightly longer. It develops a broad, flat-topped shape, with huge lower limbs. Not as widely grown as other species, specimens are mainly seen in large, old gardens.

Celastrus (fam. Celastraceae)
Staff vine, bittersweet

These hardy, deciduous, vine-like climbers are grown for their brilliantly colored, red and gold fruits which are retained through winter. They need plenty of room to climb as they reach at least 6m (20 ft).

CULTIVATION *Celastrus* will grow in any ordinary garden soil. Propagate by shoots layered in fall, by seed sown in spring or from root cuttings in fall. Root semi-ripe cuttings during summer. Plant out in their dormant winter period. No pruning is necessary. Male and female plants must be grown together to obtain fruits.

ABOVE The stiff, steely blue foliage of the *Cedrus atlantica* Glauca Group is held on almost horizontal branches.

ABOVE Planted for the autumnal effects of its golden foliage and fruits, *Celastrus orbiculatus* may spread into unwanted areas as birds love the berries.

CLIMATE There are species for various climatic zones.

SPECIES *C. angulatus*, zone 5, from China, has 20 cm (8 in) long leaves, which turn yellow in fall, and orange or red fruits. *C. orbiculatus*, oriental bittersweet, zone 4, from Asia, grows 10–12 m (33–40 ft). Its leaves also turn yellow in fall and the fruits are orange or red. *C. scandens*, American bittersweet, zone 4, from North America, grows to 8 m (26 ft) or more.

Celeriac

(*Apium graveolens* var. *rapaceum*, fam. Apiaceae)

Celery root, knob celery, root celery, turnip-rooted celery

This celery relative is grown as an annual under cultivation for its thickened, turnip-like, edible root. Used in salads, soups and stews, it can also be boiled and served mashed with oxtail, lamb chops or braised beef. A popular vegetable in Europe, it is known to have been cultivated by the ancient Egyptians.

ABOVE The celery-like stems of celeriac are bitter and generally not eaten. The strangely swollen root has a celery flavor.

CULTIVATION Celeriac is grown in the same way as celery, in soil heavily enriched with aged manure or compost. Sow in cell trays or ordinary seed trays in early spring under glass. Germinate at 15°C (59°F). Plant out when frost is over, 30 cm (12 in) apart each way. Celeriac needs a long growing season. Harvest in fall and protect from hardest frost with straw.

CLIMATE Zone 8, but grown as a seasonal crop.

Celery

(*Apium graveolens* var. *dulce*, fam. Apiaceae)

This biennial is treated as an annual in garden cultivation and is grown for its stalk. Native to the Mediterranean, celery was used medicinally by the ancient Egyptians, Greeks and Romans. Today, this crisp vegetable is mostly eaten raw or used in the stockpot or in stews.

CULTIVATION Celery is not easy to grow and seed can be difficult to germinate. It requires a climate with a long season of warm days and cool nights, good quality soil with plenty of organic matter added to ensure a balance

ABOVE Terracotta drainage pipe is used here to exclude light from maturing celery so that the stems will be blanched.

between water-holding capacity and good drainage, and a pH of 5.5–6.7. If the soil has a pH of less than 5.5, liming is necessary, preferably with dolomite, as this contains magnesium. Celery also needs an abundance of water. Sow seeds and plant out as for celeriac (see above). Celery does not transplant well so care should be taken not to disturb the roots too much. Transplant on a cool day or late in the day when less water loss from the plant will help prevent dehydration. Space plants 30 cm (12 in) apart within rows and about 50 cm (20 in) between rows. Protect from frost. Weed control is essential as celery is a shallow-rooted crop. Water well during dry periods and apply a side dressing of animal manures and a weekly banding of complete liquid fertilizer. Poultry manure is very suitable but as it is 'hot', one light application is sufficient. Blanching, the exclusion of light from the plant, is recommended as this reduces the green color. This can be achieved by close planting so that the leaves shield out the light: by placing a cardboard cylinder around each plant or by putting strips of plastic, stiff paper, boards or even sheet iron on each side of the plant. After one or two weeks of blanching, the plants can be harvested by cutting stalks at soil level.

CLIMATE Warm to cool zones.

VARIETIES There are two groups: self-blanching varieties which are blanched by close planting, and trench celery where individual plants need to be blanched.

Celmisia (fam. Asteraceae)
New Zealand daisy

Mostly native to New Zealand, these evergreen perennials and subshrubs can be grown in cool climates on rock gardens where they make fine and unusual foliage plants. The leaves are often silvery and the plants produce daisy-like flowers in summer.

CULTIVATION These daisies must have a moist, well-drained, sandy acid soil in a position enjoying full sun or partial shade, preferably in a climate with cold winters. Large numbers of seeds are released from the flattened, dry seeds of the plant when ripe, usually in mid to late summer. The seed germinates and grows quite slowly. Tufts of well-established plants can be divided in spring or cuttings can be taken from the perennial, creeping rootstocks of some species.

CLIMATE Zone 7.

ABOVE *Celmisia* species, New Zealand daisies, have small, star-like, daisy flowers.

SPECIES *C. argentea*, from the alpine regions of New Zealand, has narrow, needle-like foliage and large white flowers. *C. coriacea* produces longish, silvery, rather stiff and leathery leaves and a flowering stem that sometimes reaches 1 m (3 ft), with very large, white summer flowers to 8 cm (3 in) in diameter. Many varieties have been produced in New Zealand. *C. gracilenta*, from New Zealand, has narrow, silvery, straplike leaves and soft, white, daisy flowers in summer. It grows to about 40 cm (16 in). *C. lyallii* is a New Zealand alpine species, with narrow, linear leaves resembling grasses and small to largish, white daisy flowers in summer. It grows to about 45 cm (18 in). *C. sessiliflora*, from New Zealand, is a low, tufting plant to 10 cm (4 in), with large, white, gazania-like flowers. The most commonly grown of the New Zealand alpine species is probably *C. spectabilis*. It has brownish white foliage and white, summer flowers, and grows to 20 cm (8 in).

Celosia (fam. Amaranthaceae)

Native to tropical Asia, these annuals produce plume-like flowers similar to grasses or crested cockscombs. They provide attractive summer garden displays, and the long-lasting blooms make excellent cut flowers. They are also grown as summer pot plants in intermediate conservatories or greenhouses.

CULTIVATION Sow seed in spring and germinate at 18°C (64°F). Plant out when danger of frost is over. Outdoors, grow in full sun and well-drained moist soil.

CLIMATE Zone 10, but grown as a summer annual.

SPECIES The species is *C. argentea* var. *cristata*, but it is split into two groups. The Cristata or Cockscomb Group has tightly packed flowers, creating a crested or coral-like flower head. There are many cultivars in a range of colors including reds and yellows. Cultivars in the Plumosa Group, popularly known as Prince of

ABOVE Bright gold and rich red flowering plumes are a feature of the annual *Celosia*.

Wales' feathers, have feathery, pyramid-shaped flower heads and are generally the most popular for use as pot plants and summer bedding. Again there is a wide range of bright colors including reds and yellows.

Celtis (fam. Ulmaceae)

Hackberry, nettle tree, sugar berry

This genus comprises about 100 species of evergreen or deciduous trees and shrubs from tropical and temperate regions of Europe, Asia and America. Several species of these fast-growing trees are used as street and shade trees in public places. They color well in fall in cool areas. The ripe berries are edible and attractive to birds which transport the seed into areas where it is not wanted, producing a weed problem in some regions.

CULTIVATION Plant in an ordinary, well-drained soil in full sun. Prune during winter, only when young, to encourage a good shape. The best method of propagation is from seed sown in a garden frame or in an outdoor seed bed in the fall. Germination is variable.

CLIMATE There are species for various climatic zones.

SPECIES *C. australis*, nettle tree, zone 6, from the Mediterranean and the Middle East, grows to 20 m (65 ft) and has deep green leaves which become yellow in fall before they fall. *C. occidentalis*, hackberry, zone 4, is native to North America, growing to 25 m (80 ft). It has rough-notched, corky bark, 12 cm (5 in) long leaves and orange-red to dark purple berries when full grown. *C. sinensis*, Japanese hackberry, zone 7, is a native of China, Japan and Korea. It grows to 20 m (65 ft) and has 10 cm (4 in) long leaves and dark orange fruits.

ABOVE Foliage of the North American *Celtis occidentalis* turns pale gold during fall in cold winter regions.

Centaurea (fam. Asteraceae)

These plants have been grown for many centuries and are said to have healed a wound on the foot of Chiron, one of the centaurs of Greek mythology. Mostly of European origin, but now grown worldwide, these annuals and perennials make useful bedding and border plants, pot plants and background texture plants. In form the flowers are rather like thistles. Some species have become serious weeds.

CULTIVATION These plants like a rich soil and at least half a day's sun. Effective drainage and good air circulation are vital as *Centaurea* is susceptible to mildew. Propagate annuals from seed sown in spring where they are to flower. Perennials are propagated by division of established clumps in early spring. They do not require much care apart from weeding and perhaps staking for some of the taller kinds.

CLIMATE There are species for various climatic zones.

SPECIES *C. cyanus*, cornflower, zone 6, is an annual, 40–50 cm (16–20 in) tall, which provides very good cut flowers. It has narrow, cottony leaves and the flower heads range in color from white to blue to rose. *C. dealbata*, zone 3, grows to 1 m (3 ft), with pinkish purple flowers and silvery white, lobed leaves. *C. macrocephala*, zone 3, to 1.5 m (5 ft), makes a good border plant. It has large, yellow, thistle-like flowers, to 10 cm (4 in) in diameter, in summer. *C. montana*, zone 3, is among the easiest to grow. It produces deep blue flowers in late spring and summer, and grows to about 50 cm (20 in). Var. *alba* has white flowers; rosea has pink flowers. *C. moschata*, (now

ABOVE The flower color of *Centaurea cyanus* varies from bright, deep blue through paler tones to white.

known as *Amberboa moschata*), sweet sultan, zone 8, is a bushy annual, with smooth, lobed leaves and fragrant, white, yellow or purple flowers.

Centella (fam. Apiaceae)

This genus of small, evergreen plants is mostly native to South Africa, with one species extending throughout the tropical and subtropical regions of the world.

CULTIVATION Not very widely grown, this genus needs a cool greenhouse in frost-prone climates. Propagate from cuttings or stem divisions, with roots attached. It requires ample water during warm months and at least half a day's sun.

CLIMATE These plants grow in zone 9 if relatively frost-free.

SPECIES *C. asiatica* (syn. *Hydrocotyle asiatica*, *C. cordifolia*) is found in many parts of the world and is said to lessen the effects of arthritis. It also has many applications in folk medicine, being used as a healing agent. A prostrate, spreading plant, to 1–2 m (3–6 ft), with round or kidney-shaped leaves, it inhabits the margins of swamps and other wet spots. Though it is somewhat invasive, its preferences make it a useful groundcover for boggy places and poolsides in either shady or open positions.

ABOVE *Centella asiatica* grows naturally in damp or swampy ground but is not widely cultivated in America.

Cephalocereus (fam. Cactaceae)
Old man cactus

Native to Mexico, this cactus genus contains three species, of which one is commonly grown. It is most often grown as a curiosity in pots or other containers.

CULTIVATION Grow in an intermediate greenhouse in pots of well-drained cactus compost and in maximum light. Water regularly in the growing period but keep dry in winter.

CLIMATE Zone 10.

SPECIES *C. senilis* is covered in long, white hair and develops a flowering point on one side near the apex of the stem, from which cream, nocturnal flowers are produced. It grows to 45 cm (18 in).

ABOVE Old man cactus, *Cephalocereus senilis*, often grown as a curiosity, can be kept in a container for many years.

Cephalotaxus (fam. Cephalotaxaceae)
Plum-yew

All of these species of yew-like conifers are native to eastern Asia. Mostly shrubs, though occasionally small trees, their branches spread

ABOVE This mature specimen of *Cephalotaxus fortunei* is carrying a heavy crop of fruits. The finely divided foliage is also visible.

horizontally to ground level and their dark green leaves are similar to those of the yew. They are dioecious, with pollen sacs on the male plant and seed-bearing scales on the female. Following pollination, the large seeds develop to around the size and shape of olives, and are green or brown depending on the species. They tolerate warmer climates better than the yews and are quite tough and usually free from disease.

CULTIVATION The main requirements are a moist soil and a sunny location. However, where summers are very hot grow in partial shade. Trimming is only necessary if a more formal effect is required. Propagate by seed if obtainable or by cuttings which strike easily. *C. harringtonia* cultivar 'Fastigiata' can be propagated only from cuttings.

CLIMATE Zone 7.

SPECIES *C. fortunei*, Chinese plum-yew, is originally from China. This tall, handsome shrub or small tree has irregular, spreading branches, sometimes reaching 10 m (33 ft) in height with age. The gently curved leaves,

around 5–8 cm (2–3 in), are the longest of all the species. The oval fruits are shiny brown when ripe. *C. harringtonia*, Japanese plum-yew, from China, Korea and Japan, is a bushy shrub or tree which grows to around 6m (20 ft). It has long, horizontal branches, crowded branchlets, upward-pointing leaves, 2–3 cm (about 1 in) long, and brown seeds when ripe. Best known and most interesting of all in cultivation is cultivar 'Fastigiata'. It is different from the species as it has densely crowded, vertical branches and rarely grows taller than 5 m (16 ft) and wider than 2 m (6 ft). The small leaves are radially arranged in densely clustered whorls. It is usually sterile.

Cerastium (fam. Caryophyllaceae)

Native to Europe and America, these tufted or mat-forming plants, with gray leaves and white flowers, are suitable for rockeries or banks, particularly those which need binding to prevent erosion. Most species require cutting back each year as they can become invasive. A few species like *C. glomeratum*, mouse-eared chickweed, are common garden weeds.

CULTIVATION *Cerastium* must be grown in an open position in full sun. The soil must be well drained, but need not be rich. Propagate by seed, by small divisions or from cuttings which strike very easily. Plant in early spring.

BELOW *Cerastium tomentosum* forms dense, decorative groundcover in this formal circular bed.

CLIMATE Zone 4.

SPECIES *C. alpinum*, to 12 cm (5 in), is suitable for rock gardens, but needs good drainage. This perennial has tufts of silvery leaves and white, spring flowers. Var. *lanatum* is very woolly with white foliage. *C. tomentosum*, snow-in-summer, the most commonly cultivated of the species, is a vigorous grower, with a prostrate, creeping habit. It has tiny, gray leaves and a profusion of starry, white flowers in late spring and summer. There are several varieties and cultivars which may sometimes be available, but the species itself is commonly grown.

Ceratonia (fam. Caesalpiniaceae)
Carob, St John's bread, locust tree

This genus of only one species comes from the Mediterranean where it grows up to 15 m (50 ft) in height. The seed pods contain a sweet, edible pulp, known as carob, which has become popular as a chocolate substitute in recent years. The pods have also been used as emergency animal fodder. The edible but very hard seeds are reputed to have been the carat weight of gem traders.

ABOVE A cluster of ripe and unripe pods on a mature *Ceratonia siliqua.*

CULTIVATION The carob will grow on any well-drained soil, but likes the same moderate climate as the citrus tree. Propagate from seed soaked overnight before sowing 2 cm (¾ in) deep in light soil. Harden off the seedlings and transplant in spring. Cuttings can be taken in fall.

CLIMATE Zone 9.

SPECIES *C. siliqua* has pinnate leaves, composed of rounded, shiny leaflets, and sprays of red flowers, followed by flattened, leathery seed pods to 25 cm (10 in). It grows 10–12 m (33–40 ft) high under general cultivation.

Ceratopetalum (fam. Cunoniaceae)

This genus is not widely grown in the US but in its native Australia some species, including coachwood, are cultivated for their fine, fragrant timber. Grow outdoors in the south, under glass elsewhere.

CULTIVATION These do well in a free-draining soil in a relatively frost-free area. Shelter from strong winds is necessary. Propagate from fresh seed or from cuttings taken in fall and rooted

ABOVE *Ceratopetalum gummiferum* makes a fine show in frost-free gardens when adorned with its pinky red flower calyces.

under glass. Plant in spring. Choose a good color type, although color may be improved by sprinkling a small handful of sulphate of iron around the roots in early spring and by watering generously.

CLIMATE Zone 10.

SPECIES These may not be easy to obtain in the US. *C. apetalum*, coachwood, is a large tree which needs rich soil and plentiful summer water. It has large leaves and scented wood, and grows to 20 m (65 ft). The light, aromatic timber is used in veneers and furniture-making. *C. gummiferum*, New South Wales Christmas bush, is a large shrub or small tree, with dark green leaves and a profusion of pretty, small, cream flowers in spring. When the flowers die, the calyces behind the petals turn red and enlarge, giving the impression of red flowers. It needs plenty of moisture but good drainage.

Ceratostigma (fam. Plumbaginaceae)

This small genus of attractive perennial herbs or shrubs is native to Africa, India and China.

CULTIVATION *Ceratostigma* does best in lighter soils, though it will grow in almost any type of soil. Plant in a sunny position in spring.

ABOVE *Ceratostigma willmottianum* is a decorative filler plant that is also tough and easy care.

Propagate by detached suckers in spring or fall. Some species may be cut back by severe frost, but will shoot again from the base in spring. Do not cut dead shoots away until spring, as they serve to protect the new growth.

CLIMATE There are species suited to various climatic zones.

SPECIES *C. plumbaginoides*, zone 5, is an herbaceous perennial from China. Its oval, mid-green leaves color orange and red in fall and its deep blue flowers bloom in late summer. *C. willmottianum*, zone 7, is a hardy, deciduous, spreading shrub, to 1 m (3 ft), mostly with mid-green leaves that turn purple or red in fall and sky blue flowers from summer to fall. It is a useful filler plant, being both decorative and hardy.

Cercidiphyllum (fam. Cercidiphyllaceae)

Comprising only one species and native to China and Japan, this hardy, deciduous tree is grown for its beautiful foliage. It is generally cultivated as a specimen tree.

CULTIVATION *Cercidiphyllum* likes rich, moist soil and an open position, and will tolerate lime, but best fall color is in acid or neutral

ABOVE Although cultivated mainly as an ornamental, *Cercidiphyllum japonicum* is grown in its native Japan for its strong timber.

soil. It grows best in a cool to temperate climate. Fertilize every three or four years. Propagate by seed sown in spring.

CLIMATE Zone 5.

SPECIES *C. japonicum*, katsura tree, grows quickly to about 12 m (40 ft) under cultivation, though in its native habitat it can reach heights of 40 m (130 ft). The trees have upward-sweeping branches and handsome foliage in fall. The leaves change from bronze-purplecrimson in early spring to light green and finally to brilliant gold and scarlet in fall.

Cercis (fam. Caesalpiniaceae)

From southern Europe, western North America and Asia, these hardy, deciduous trees, 5–15 m (16–50 ft) tall, produce an abundance of pea-shaped flowers in shades of purple, pink or rose, and sometimes white. Usually the flowers appear in clusters or sprays along the bare branches before the leaves, followed by beautiful pods which remain on the tree for a long time. The leaves on most species are similar to those of *Bauhinia*, but more heart-shaped. The species are reliable bloomers in dry situations.

CULTIVATION The species like a deep, well-drained loam, but will grow in most soils. Prune lightly and propagate by cuttings, layering or seed. Cuttings of dormant hardwood are reliable but may be slow to root.

CLIMATE There are species suited to various climatic zones.

SPECIES *C. canadensis*, zone 4, Eastern redbud, is a splendid tree when in flower. It grows |7–12 m (23–40 ft), with rosy flowers 1 cm (⅓ in) long. 'Alba' has single white flowers and 'Plena' produces double flowers. *C. chinensis* (syn. *C. japonica*), Chinese redbud, zone 6, grows 15–17 m (50–56 ft) and has purple-pink flowers, 2 cm (¾ in) in length, and 12 cm (5 in) long seed pods. *C. occidentalis*, western

ABOVE An unusually large specimen of *Cercis siliquastrum* is stunning in full bloom.

redbud, zone 7, has a shrubby habit, growing to around 5 m (16 ft). It produces red flowers, 2 cm (¾ in) long, and 6 cm (2½ in) long seed pods. *C. siliquastrum*, Judas tree, zone 6, to 12 m (40 ft), makes a lovely garden subject, with its profuse clusters of rosy purple to pink flowers and 10 cm (4 in) long pods. The foliage colors in fall. This species prefers hot, dry summers and frosty winters. *C. f. albida* has white flowers.

Cereus (fam. Cactaceae)

This genus of tall, night-flowering cactuses, found throughout South America, comprises 25 species.

CULTIVATION These cactuses are generally grown in pots of well-drained cactus compost in an intermediate greenhouse or in a conservatory. Provide maximum light. Water regularly in spring and summer but keep dry in winter. Can be grown outdoors in relatively frost-free regions.

CLIMATE Zone 10.

ABOVE *Cereus peruvianus* (syn. *C. uruguayanus*) is a striking feature plant. Silver torch cactus is growing behind it.

ABOVE Prettily marked, heart-shaped leaves are the ornamental feature of *Ceropegia linearis* subsp. *woodii*. The small, tubular flowers are fairly insignificant.

SPECIES *C. peruvianus* is a popular cactus which grows erect to around 5 m (16 ft). It has deep green-blue, ribbed stems and downy, brown areoles with yellow spines. The fragrant, nocturnal, white and brown-green summer flowers are followed by red, globe-shaped fruit. This species may also be sold as *C. uruguayanus*.

Ceropegia (fam. Asclepiadaceae)

This large genus of succulents is found throughout much of the tropics, including the Canary Islands, tropical Africa, Madagascar, tropical Asia, New Guinea and northern Australia. Most are climbing plants, though there are a few shrublets, often with thickened roots. The leaves are generally opposite, and mostly deciduous, but some species have heart-shaped, linear or elliptical leaves. The flowers come in shades of purple, green or brown. All have a long tube, usually swollen at the base, and some have a stalk arising from the base of a leaf.

CULTIVATION In frost-prone climates, these plants are grown in a warm greenhouse or conservatory, or as house plants. Grow in pots (or hanging baskets for trailing species) of well-drained cactus compost. Provide maximum light but shade from direct sun. Water regularly in the growing season but keep dry in winter. Propagate from seed in spring or stem cuttings in summer.

CLIMATE Zone 10.

SPECIES Not all these are available. *C. dichotoma*, from the Canary Islands, is an upright-growing species, with thick, green-gray stems forming wide clumps up to 1 m (3 ft). Sparse, narrow leaves occur only on the new stems. The very slender, pale yellow flowers are borne in clusters, the expanded lobes uniting at the tips and separating as the flower dies. This species must be kept quite dry in winter. *C. haygarthii*, native to southern Africa, has stout, twining stems and very fleshy, veined, opposite leaves in pairs. The flower has a swollen base above which the purple-spotted tube curves sharply, gradually expanding to a funnel shape, with the five lobes bending over to form a five-part purple cover. *C. sandersonii*, parachute plant, from Mozambique, is another vigorous species, with pairs of heart-shaped leaves on twining stems and distinctive flowers which look like mottled green parachutes. *C. linearis* subsp. *woodii*, chain of hearts, from Zimbabwe and Cape Province, has many heart-shaped, silver and purple leaves and small, purple flowers. The thin, twining stems grow out of a tuberous caudex, and these tubers also form at the nodes of the stems.

Cestrum (fam. Solanaceae)

These heat-loving evergreen shrubs from tropical and subtropical America produce delightfully showy flowers, comprising pendulous clusters of long tubes, mostly in red, orange or yellow, followed by purple, red or white berries. The simple, narrow leaves are deciduous in some of the least commonly cultivated species, and they are believed to be poisonous to stock. Some of the species have quite an overpowering fragrance.

CULTIVATION In frost-prone areas, grow in pots or soil border in a cool to intermediate

ABOVE *Cestrum parqui* is one of the hardier species and very vigorous in habit.

greenhouse or conservatory. Ensure maximum light. Outdoors, grow in a sunny sheltered spot in well-drained soil. Propagate by cuttings in spring or summer.

CLIMATE Zone 10 for most.

SPECIES *C. elegans* is an attractive species with red flowers and red berries. Var. *smithii* produces rose red blooms over a long period. *C. fasciculatum*, zone 9, grows to 3 m (10 ft) and has purplish red flowers. Var. *coccineum* bears scarlet flowers. *C.* 'Newellii', zone 9, produces an abundance of crimson flowers. *C. nocturnum*, night scented jasmine, grows to 4 m (13 ft) and has shiny, glabrous leaves to 20 cm (8 in) long. The profuse clusters of small, greenish white tube-like flowers open at night to release an intense perfume. *C. parqui*, zone 9, willow jasmine, has blueish green leaves to 15 cm (6 in), fragrant, greenish yellow flowers and purple berries. It has become a noxious weed in many areas and is poisonous to farm stock.

Chaenomeles (fam. Rosaceae)
Flowering quince

Native to China and Japan, these hardy, deciduous, spreading shrubs are rather spiky. They make attractive ornamentals, particularly in winter and spring when the bare branches are covered with an abundance of flowers in shades from red through to white, and are also useful as a decorative, informal hedge.

CULTIVATION These quinces prefer cooler areas but they can be grown in fairly warm districts. Plant in any fairly well-drained soil in a sunny position. Once established, these shrubs will tolerate dryness and wind. Very old stems can be cut out at the base. Propagate from semi-ripe cuttings in summer or by layering in spring.

CLIMATE Zone 5.

SPECIES *C. japonica*, Japanese quince, produces profuse orange-red flowers, followed by small fruit which is made into jelly and is

ABOVE Colorful blossom on the bare branches of *Chaenomeles* species signals the end of winter.

delicious served with ricotta cheese. It grows to 1 m (3 ft), sometimes more. *C. speciosa*, from China, is grown more for its beautiful, bright scarlet blooms which make excellent cut flowers than for its fruit, though this too can be made into jelly. This species has produced many cultivars including 'Alba', with single, white flowers tinged with pink; 'Cardinalis', which has single or semi-double, bright red flowers; 'Moerloosei', with single, white flowers striped in rose-pink; 'Nivalis', with single, pure white flowers suitable for cutting; 'Rosea Plena', with semi-double, pink flowers; 'Rubra Grandiflora', with large, single, deep crimson flowers; and 'Simonii', which has a spreading growth habit and large, double, rich crimson flowers. *C.* x *superba*, a hybrid of *C. japonica* and *C. speciosa*, is a spiny, branching type which grows 1.2–1.5 m (4–5 ft) and produces white, pink, orange or red flowers. It has many cultivars but the best known is 'Crimson and Gold' whose large, deep red flowers have a cluster of deep yellow anthers in the center.

Chamaecyparis (fam. Cupressaceae)
False cypress

This genus from North America and eastern Asia includes only seven wild species of these tall forest trees, although it has produced a greater number of ornamental cultivars than any other conifer group. The false cypresses are very useful garden subjects owing to the great diversity of form and color their many cultivars provide, and include many of the dwarf conifers favored for rock gardens and tubs, or as bonsai specimens. The tall-growing wild forms are not grown as often as the cultivars, with the exception perhaps of *C. lawsoniana*. However, if provided with sufficient space and appropriate conditions, they will all make very handsome trees.

CULTIVATION The species are fairly easy to grow, needing only light and well-drained, reasonably deep soil. Most of the colored foliage cultivars need a lot of sun so that the color can develop to its true intensity. Nearly all can be shaped as required by judicious pruning or pinching out of the shoots, but they will not normally regenerate from the cut stumps if the larger branches are pruned off. If intensive pruning is necessary, make sure that the stumps are covered by the surrounding foliage. It is possible to propagate both the species and the cultivars from cuttings, although some are difficult to strike. Root semi-ripe cuttings in late summer in a garden frame. They should have a portion of brown or ripe wood at the base to ensure rooting. Species can be raised from seed sown in spring in an outdoor seed bed. Some dwarf cultivars are propagated commercially by grafting in late winter but this is not an easy technique for the home gardener.

CLIMATE Zone 6 for the majority of the species.

SPECIES *C. lawsoniana*, Lawson cypress, is found growing naturally in the humid, coastal forests of north-western North America. This majestic forest tree has been known to attain

ABOVE Lawson cypress, *Chamaecyparis lawsoniana*, has a strong, pyramidal form with dense foliage to the gound.

heights of 60 m (200 ft) in the wild and can reach 30 m (100 ft) in cultivation, given the appropriate soil and climatic conditions. It matures to a narrow, pyramidal form, with a dense curtain of gray-green foliage. A myriad of cultivars is now available in a multitude of forms, among them dwarf, juvenile-foliaged, golden, variegated and blue-gray. Cultivar 'Allumii' develops a narrow, pyramidal shape, with deep blue-gray foliage in erect, crowded, flattened sprays. It grows 2–5 m (6–16 ft) tall. 'Ellwoodii' is a dense, compact, columnar or oval form to about 3 m (10 ft), with deep blue-green juvenile foliage. 'Erecta' is normally 2–3 m (6–10 ft) tall but can reach 6 m (20 ft) or more with age. It has a pyramidal shape, with very thick, green foliage. 'Erecta Aurea' is similar to 'Erecta' but smaller and slower growing, with golden yellow foliage on the outside and green in the center. 'Fletcheri' grows to a pyramidal shape, 2–5 m (6–10 ft) tall, with blueish green, semi-juvenile foliage. 'Minima' is a dwarf, globular form, growing to a height of 30–50 cm (12–20 in) with densely packed, fan-like, plain green branchlet sprays. 'Minima Aurea' and 'Minima Glauca' have respectively golden yellow and blue-green foliage. 'Nana' is similar to 'Minima' but with a more central stem and a more upright habit; it also has a slightly pointed top. 'Silver Queen' is a broadly pyramidal type, with an extended apex, which reaches a height of 3–6 m (10–20 ft). The foliage is borne in large, flat sprays and the very pale green, almost white, younger branchlets change to a deeper green in the center of the plant. 'Wisselii' attains a pyramidal, open shape, has a height of 2–5 m (6–16 ft) and has many outward-pointing or erect narrow spires of blue-gray foliage. *C. obtusa*, hinoki cypress, grows to a fine, tall tree, valued for its timber in its native Japan and Taiwan. It has flattened branchlet-sprays. The leaves on the undersides of the sprays are distinctively edged in bright, blueish white. This species is almost unknown in cultivation, but many cultivars are available, of which the following is a selection. 'Crippsii' is very popular and grows well in exposed coastal areas and in poor, sandy soils. Broadly based, it grows in a pyramidal shape to 6–8 m (20–26 ft) with age. It is covered in crowded, out-curving, bright golden yellow foliage which contrasts with the

BELOW Lutea', a golden form of *Chamaecyparis lawsoniana*, is planted in rows to line a drive.

green of the interior. 'Fernspray Gold' is slow growing to 1–2 m (3–6 ft) tall. It has long, plume-like branches nodding at the tips and fresh green, fern-like foliage. The short, lateral branchlets are not flattened as in most of the species and cultivars. *C. pisifera*, sawara cypress, from Japan, also grows to a very tall tree in its native habitat. It is identifiable by the long, sharp points of its adult leaves, which give the foliage a prickly feel. The many cultivars make excellent garden plants as they are more tolerant of strong sun and dry soil conditions. 'Boulevard', a semi-dwarf, columnar form, to 2 m (6 ft), is one of the most appealing blue-foliaged cultivars in the genus. It has juvenile foliage, with short, crowded branchlets and needle-like leaves, dull blue-green above and brilliant, blueish white beneath. 'Filifera Aurea' has a spreading habit, with pendulous side-branches which droop down below the stem base. It grows 1.5–3 m (5–10 ft) tall and is very suitable for rockeries and tubs. The foliage is tipped with gold in spring and summer and pale lemon yellow in fall and winter. 'Plumosa Compressa' rarely grows to more than 20 cm (8 in) tall. It has a dense globe of prickly, juvenile, yellowish green foliage and densely packed branchlets. 'Squarrosa' has been known in Japan since the end of the 18th century. Broadly columnar to conical in habit, it reaches 8–10 m (26–33 ft) in height as it ages. The juvenile, pale blue-gray foliage in quite loose, feathery sprays develops pinkish tones in winter. *C. thyoides*, swamp white cedar, zone 5, is a native of North America where it usually occurs as a rather scrubby tree in poor, swampy ground. Under cultivation, however, this species can grow to a columnar tree of 7–15 m (23–50 ft). The fine branchlets are grouped into many tiny, flattened sprays which appear at different angles, giving an irregular appearance to the dull green foliage. Cultivars include 'Andelyensis', a columnar, compact form, which grows to 3 m (10 ft), with blue-gray foliage; and 'Ericoides' growing to 1–2 m (3–6 ft), with a habit which can be upright oval to pyramidal. The juvenile bronze-green foliage turns to a dull bronze-purple color in the winter.

Chamaedorea (fam. Arecaceae)

Bamboo palm, parlour palm

One of the largest genera of palms, *Chamaedorea* is possibly the most widely cultivated too. Most of the species are rainforest plants which grow as understorey plants, and are characterized by their small size and slender stems. Many are native to Mexico and Central America, and some to the northern parts of South America. There is a great range in stem and leaf size. Some are single-stemmed; others form clumps, sometimes comprising hundreds of stems. In most the stems are attractively ringed like bamboo, with the intervals between rings smooth and dark green. In a few species the leaves are undivided, with only a V-shaped notch at the leaf apex. The flowers are dioecious and are borne on stalked inflorescences with relatively few, short,

BELOW *Chamaedorea seifrizii*, a clustering parlour palm, does well indoors or out.

ABOVE *Chamaedorea costaricana* has spectacular, coral red flowering stems.

flower-bearing branches. On female plants, the small, fleshy, yellow flowers are sometimes followed by smooth black or red fruits. Inflorescence branches generally become fleshy and brightly colored (yellow-orange or red) as the fruits form. Nearly all of the species make excellent indoor or outdoor subjects. They adapt well to indoor conditions and blend happily with ferns and other foliage plants outdoors in frost-free locations. Some of the larger, clumping species can tolerate sun and are perfect for massed effects in landscaping.

CULTIVATION These palms are easy to grow as indoor plants and can thrive for years in the one container if the conditions are appropriate, as they are not worried by being root bound. The clump-forming species will generally require larger containers. Keep out of direct sunlight as this will cause burning or yellowing of the leaves. If planted outdoors they need shade, a well-drained, friable, acid soil and a cool root run. Plants of both sexes are needed if fruit production is required and it is recommended that the female flowers be hand pollinated, using a small watercolor brush, though this is not essential. Propagate

from seed which will germinate in six to eight weeks under warm conditions. The seedlings of most species grow rapidly. The clump-forming species can be propagated by division. Use largish divisions with plenty of roots, otherwise re-establishment may be slow.

CLIMATE Zone 10.

SPECIES *C. costaricana*, bamboo palm, from Costa Rica, has a densely clumping habit and grows 2.5–4 m (8–13 ft) tall. The stems have a diameter of 1.5–2.5 cm ($\frac{2}{3}$–1 in) and the generally rather pale green leaves are 60–80 cm (24–32 in) long with up to 40 segments of medium width. The inflorescences emerge from sheaths of pendent leaves and grow to 80 cm (32 in) long. They have relatively long, flowering branches which turn deep coral-red when fruiting. The shiny, round fruits ripen to black. This species can tolerate a small amount of direct sun without harm to its appearance. *C. elegans*, parlour palm, from Mexico and Guatemala, is the most popular species, many being sold as indoor plants. It grows generally 30–100 cm (12–36 in) tall, but can reach 2 m (6 ft) with age. The closely ringed single stems are 1–2 cm ($\frac{1}{3}$–$\frac{3}{4}$ in) in diameter. The somewhat crowded leaves grow 20–40 cm (8–16 in) long, with 12 to 16 narrow, deep green segments either side of the midrib. The inflorescences produce small, round, orange-red fruits which ripen to black. *C. erumpens*, bamboo palm, from Guetemala and Honduras, is similar to *C. costaricana* but has shorter leaves with very few leaflets, often with a very broad pair of fused terminal leaflets. The much shorter inflorescences tend to burst through the leaf sheaths. *C. microspadix*, bamboo palm, is an undemanding clustering palm which can be grown indoors or in a shady part of the garden. It rarely exceeds 3 m (10 ft) in height, with its bamboo-like ringed stems topped with dark green foliage. It is very attractive in fruit which is borne in great quantities. The bright orange fruit ripens to deep red. It is quick to germinate and easy to grow.

Chamaerops (fam. Arecaceae)

European fan palm

Occurring along the Mediterannean coast, this is the only palm native to Europe, though it also occurs in north-western Africa. These palms can be single- or multiple-trunked; they have smallish, fan-shaped leaves, deeply divided into narrow, stiff, gray-green segments, with slender stalks, edged with spines. The sheathing leaf-bases quickly break down, leaving a mass of gray fibers, which densely clothe the stems even after the leaves have fallen. These palms are unisexual. The male flowers are not readily seen, while the female flowers are borne on very short, stiff, many-branched inflorescences, reminiscent of those of many other palms. The round, glossy orange-brown fruits are about 2 cm (¾ in) in diameter, each containing only one seed. *Chamaerops* is a very attractive, compact palm useful for growing in open, sunny positions among other tall, slender types.

ABOVE *Chamaerops humilis* takes many years to form such an impressive clump.

CULTIVATION Often grown as a pot plant indoors or in a cool greenhouse or conservatory. Best in soil-based potting compost and bright light, but shaded from sun. Outdoors, this palm grows in a wide range of conditions but will not tolerate poor drainage. It prefers a warm, sunny position, but can be grown successfully in partial shade. It is hardy and can tolerate both moderate frosts and hot, dry conditions. *Chamaerops* is quite slowgrowing and a good-sized clump may take up to 50 years to develop. Large plants transplant easily, though heavy equipment would be necessary, and are perfect specimens for use in landscaping. Propagate from seed which germinates fairly readily.

CLIMATE Zone 9.

SPECIES *C. humilis*, the only species, is most commonly a clump of several stems of various heights, the tallest around 4–5 m (13–16 ft), each with quite a round crown comprised of numerous leaves. Its growth form is very variable.

Chamelaucium (fam. Myrtaceae)

Geraldton wax

Only one of the 20 species of this shrubby plant from Western Australia is widely cultivated. The pretty Geraldton wax is ideal for growing on sunny banks with dry soil, or in other dry parts of the garden. It also makes a good pot plant for the cool greenhouse or conservatory. The flowers are excellent for cutting.

CULTIVATION In areas prone to frost, grow under glass in pots of lime-free, soilless potting compost and provide light, airy conditions. Outdoors, grow Geraldton wax in neutral to acid soil with good drainage. A poor or moderately fertile, sandy or gravelly soil gives good results. Plants must have a sunny position. Prune after flowering to encourage a compact shape and to avoid ugly, old wood developing. Cutting back into old hardwood

ABOVE The pale, waxy flowers of *Chamelaucium uncinatum* 'Blond' open from dark crimson buds.

may kill this shrub. Propagate from semi-ripe cuttings taken in late summer. Seed can be tried in spring under glass but germination can be difficult. Do not cover seed with compost. Germinate seed at 18°C (64°F).

CLIMATE Zone 10.

SPECIES *C. uncinatum*, Geraldton wax, grows to 3 m (10 ft). The leaves are slender and needle-like, and masses of lovely, waxy, white, pink or rose flowers appear in winter and spring. A number of cultivars have been produced. These include various color forms, as well as those with extra large or tiny flowers.

Chamomile

(*Matricaria recutita*, fam. Asteraceae)

The common name refers to two herbs which, although very similar, have different uses. Roman or lawn chamomile (*Chamaemelum nobile*, syn. *Anthemis nobilis*) is used as a groundcover or as a lawn. But it is *Matricaria recutita*, known as wild chamomile, that is the one we know so well, the flower heads of which are dried and used as herbal teas. Apart from the soothing tea they produce, they have been used for centuries as inhalations and compresses because of their anti-inflammatory properties. They are also used in potpourri.

ABOVE The wild chamomile, *Matricaria recutita*, is a sweetly fragrant annual which is native to Europe and Asia.

CULTIVATION Wild chamomile likes a rich soil and is generally grown in rows to increase the number of flower heads produced. Propagate from seed which germinates readily. Pick the flowers carefully, dry them in the oven and store in a dark place until used.

CLIMATE Suitable for zone 9.

SPECIES *Matricaria recutita*, sweet, false or wild chamomile, differs mainly from *Chamaemelum nobile* in the amount of oil available from the flower head. It blooms from late spring through summer.

Chasmanthe (fam. Iridaceae)

Native to South Africa, this genus comprises about three species of corms, similar to gladiolus, except that the flower stem ends in a spike of long, hooded tubes with spreading lobes. They can be found in colors from yellow through to red and have sword-shaped leaves. Chasmanthe can flower in the spring or summer.

ABOVE *Chasmanthe floribunda* is very adaptable in its growing requirements and is generally not as invasive as the related *Crocosmia* species.

CULTIVATION These plants tolerate most soils as long as they are well drained. They can be grown in full sun or part shade. Cut off any old foliage as fresh growth begins in spring. Propagate by division of clumps in spring.

CLIMATE Zone 9.

SPECIES *C. aethiopica* generally grows to less than 1 m (3 ft), with slender, red-yellow, tube-like flowers with maroon throats. *C. floribunda*, the most popular garden species, has broader leaves and produces similar, but more abundant, flowers in orange-red or yellow. It can grow to 1.5 m (5 ft) in good conditions.

Cheilanthes (fam. Adiantaceae)

This large genus of around 180 species of ferns is found around the world, often in rocky or desert conditions. They are mostly evergreen and tolerate drought very well. They grow from rhizomes, which may be upright or horizontal, and have pinnate fronds on black stems. They are ideal ferns for rock gardens or for planting in walls in dry climates. Tender species are grown in a cool greenhouse or conservatory.

CULTIVATION *Cheilanthes* need well-drained soil enriched with plenty of organic matter, and full sun. Under glass, grow in pots of very well drained, soil-based potting compost, with maximum light and plenty of ventilation. Keep the humidity low.

CLIMATE There are species suited to various climatic zones.

SPECIES These may not be readily available in the US. *C. distans*, bristly oak fern, zone 10, is found in many parts of Australia and New Zealand. While it prefers dry conditions, it is often found on damp parts of sandstone ridges. It is a small, bristly, rather hairy fern, to about 12 cm (5 in), with a short, creeping, branched rhizome, erect fronds and widely spaced leaflets. *C. tenuifolia*, rock fern, zone 10, is also widely distributed throughout Australia and New Zealand and is found growing in both damp and dry situations, although always in a position where it receives a reasonable amount

BELOW *Cheilanthes tenuifolia* needs to be grown under glass in frost-prone climates but it makes an attractive pot plant.

of sun. It, too, has a short, creeping, branched rootstock. The stems are black, as with most ferns in this family, the fronds are erect, varying from 12 to 70 cm (5–28 in) in height depending on where they are growing, and the leaflets are shiny, blunt and mostly triangular in shape.

Cheiranthus

(now correctly *Erysimum*, fam. Brassicaceae)

Wallflower

Wallflowers are native to Europe and, although strictly perennial, are grown as biennials for spring bedding. They are particularly favored in cottage gardens. They bloom in the spring and have sweetly fragrant flowers. The true wallflower is *Cheiranthus cheiri* (syn. *Erysimum cheiri*), and there are many cultivars available in a wide range of colors. They are frequently grown with tulips in bedding schemes.

CULTIVATION Plants are raised annually from seed sown in an outdoor seed bed in early summer. The seedlings are transplanted to a nursery bed to grow on and then planted in their flowering positions in the fall. They need a very well drained soil as cold, wet conditions in winter can lead to death. They favor an alkaline soil. Ensure shelter from cold, drying winds and for best flowering, provide a sunny position. Discard plants after they have flowered.

CLIMATE Zone 7.

SPECIES *C. cheiri* (syn. *Erysimum cheiri*), English wallflower, is an upright, branching plant, growing to 20–40 cm (8–16 in) or more, with yellow or yellowish brown flowers. Parent to a number of fragrant hybrids, it is grown as a late winter-spring flowering biennial in most places.

Chelone (fam. Scrophulariaceae)

Shell flower, turtlehead

The genus name derives from the Greek kelone, a tortoise, referring to the hooded, gaping flowers which also gave rise to the common name, turtlehead. Most of these gaudy, North American perennials have ovate, toothed, shiny leaves.

CULTIVATION These plants like a rich soil, sun or partial shade, and regular water. Propagate by seed or by division in early spring.

BELOW *Chelone obliqua* is useful in garden borders as it flowers in late summer to fall when color may be scarce.

BELOW The warm, rich colors of biennial wallflowers are decorative in late winter or spring.

CLIMATE There are species suited to various climates.

SPECIES *C. glabra*, zone 3, has lance-shaped leaves, to 15 cm (6 in), and white or pinkish flowers, bearded on the lower lip. It grows to 1 m (3 ft). *C. lyonii*, zone 8, has ovate leaves and rosy purple flowers, and grows to 1 m (3 ft). *C. obliqua*, zone 6, grows to 60 cm (24 in). It has rose-colored flowers, the lower lip bearded and pale yellow.

Chenopodium (fam. Chenopodiaceae)

One species in this genus is an edible perennial, sometimes grown for its shoots and leaves which are used as vegetables, blanched and served with butter or hollandaise sauce. Other species have been used in folk medicine and as culinary herbs. The genus is part of the same botanical family of which beetroot and spinach are members.

CULTIVATION Plant in a free-draining, light soil in a sunny position. Sow seed in spring and thin the seedlings in two stages to a distance of 45 cm (18 in) apart. If the shoots are to be cut,

BELOW Good King Henry, *Chenopodium bonus-henricus*, has been used for centuries as a spinach substitute. The leaves were also used medicinally in former times.

topdress the plants with about 12 cm (5 in) of good compost or leaf mould at the end of the season. Cut the shoots just under soil level, the same as for asparagus. Pick leaves during spring, taking only a few at a time so that growth is not discouraged.

CLIMATE Wide moisture and temperature range. Zone 5.

SPECIES *C. bonus-henricus*, Good King Henry, is a hardy perennial, suitable for temperate through to cold regions. The leaves are said to taste like spinach and the young shoots are similar to asparagus.

Cherimoya

(*Annona cherimola*, fam. Annonaceae)

This small, evergreen tree grows naturally in the Andes of Peru and Ecuador and is widely cultivated for its fruit. The flesh of the fruit is soft, white and delicately flavored, containing hard, black, bean-like seeds. A good-sized cherimoya weighs nearly 500 grams (1 lb). The flavor is generally regarded as more delicious than that of the custard apple. The cherimoya makes an attractive ornamental, with its

BELOW A close relative of the custard apple, cherimoya is said by some to taste like pineapple. This tree is cropping well.

velvety green leaves, fragrant, pale yellow flowers and pale green fruit. This tree is cultivated in California but is not suited to the Florida climate.

CULTIVATION As the cherimoya is a native of the mountainous areas of the tropics, it requires mild, frost-free conditions. It may be grown from seed but the cultivars are far superior. If available, these will be grafted plants. Plant trees 7–9 m (23–30 ft) apart. They should bear fruit in three to four years. A poor crop may mean poor pollination.

CLIMATE Zone 10. Not suited to lowland tropical climates. Needs a relatively dry climate..

ABOVE Cherries are delicious to eat and decorative too. Ripening fruit is attractive to birds.

Cherry

(*Prunus avium*, *P. cerasus*, fam. Rosaceae)

Of the hundreds of varieties of cherry cultivated, most are parented by two very old species, *P. avium* (sweet cherry) and *P. cerasus* (sour cherry). All are small, deciduous trees, very pretty when in bloom with their lovely blossoms gracing their bare branches, and the cherry is one of the most commonly home-grown orchard fruits. The sweet cherry is delicious raw and cooked in pies, while the small, bitter, wild cherry is used in liqueur.

CULTIVATION Sweet cherries are vigorous trees but these days are normally bought on dwarfing rootstocks and grown mainly as fan-trained trees on walls, as this is the least space-consuming method for small gardens. They can also be grown as standard or bush trees. Sweet cherries need a deep, fertile, well-drained soil and a sheltered site in full sun. Fan-trained trees and bush trees on dwarfing rootstocks are spaced 4.5 m (15 ft) apart. Trees on more vigorous rootstocks need correspondingly more space. Fan-trained trees will need regular summer pruning by cutting back the side shoots to within six leaves of the main framework branches. Some cultivars of sweet cherry are self-fertile so one tree should be sufficient, but this is not always the case and two varieties may be needed which flower at the same time and pollinate each other. Obtain advice on cultivars when buying trees from a specialist fruit nursery. Sour or acid cherries are not as vigorous as sweet cherries and therefore are better for small gardens. The Morello is the most widely grown of the acid cherries and as it is self-fertile, it can be grown alone. Acid cherries need the same conditions and are grown in the same way as sweet cherries but they can be planted closer. Trees on dwarfing rootstocks can be planted 3.6 m (11 ft) apart. Pruning of fan-trained trees is different as fruits are produced on the previous year's side shoots, so these are cut out after fruiting, leaving the new side shoots to fruit the following year. All cherries benefit from the application of a general-purpose fertilizer in late winter each year. You may need to protect the fruits from birds. Fan-trained trees can have fine netting hung in front of them.

CLIMATE Cherries are best in zones 6 to 8. They need cool or cold winters, but not excessively cold. Conversely very warm or hot climates are not suitable. The sour cherry is much more adaptable climatically than the sweet cherry.

VARIETIES There are many varieties of cherries, especially sweet cherries, but these vary from one region to another. It is best to request a catalogue from a specialist fruit nursery to see what is available in your area. Such catalogues also usually offer much useful advice on choosing suitable varieties. You need to make sure the variety chosen is self-fertile or whether it needs another variety to pollinate it. Obviously it is sensible to choose the heaviest cropping varieties, as cropping capacity does vary. Cherries ripen in the summer, exact timing depending on variety.

Chervil (*Anthriscus cerefolium*, fam. Apiaceae)

Thought to be from south-eastern Europe and western Asia, this annual herb has been used since ancient times for both medicinal and culinary purposes. An important ingredient in French cooking, the leaves are used as flavoring in salads, soups and stuffings, and in fish, poultry and egg dishes. In cultivation, *A. cerefolium* is treated as a summer crop. It has waxy, deeply cut, bright green leaves and flat clusters of small white flowers borne terminally on the flower stems in summer. It grows to around 45 cm (18 in).

ABOVE Chervil foliage is decorative as well as useful in the kitchen. It can be happily incorporated into the ornamental garden.

CULTIVATION Plant chervil at the back of a herb border as it is quite tall. Sow seed direct into shallow drills in spring. Thin to 10 cm (4 in) apart within the rows, with 20 cm (8 in) between rows. Encourage vigorous growth by pinching off the flower buds as they appear. Cut the first leaves six to eight weeks after sowing, then pick at any time of the year starting with the outside ones first as this allows the inner ones to continue growing. If self-sown plants or seed is required, leave some of the plants to go to seed. Dry the leaves by spreading them over a wire mesh in a cool, dark, airy place. When the leaves are dry and brittle, crumple them up, discard the midribs and store them in airtight containers. Seeds can also be kept in this way.

CLIMATE Zone 7.

Chestnut (*Castanea sativa*, fam. Fagaceae)

Chestnuts roasting is a fairly common sight in the streets of many European countries during winter. These sweet, edible nuts, about 25 mm (1 in) across, have a thin, brown shell and are enclosed in very prickly husks. *C. sativa*, Spanish or European chestnut, is a native of southern Europe, northern Africa and western Asia. It is a handsome tree with toothed leaves, valued both for timber and nuts. It reaches a

ABOVE Edible chestnuts, *Castanea sativa*, are enclosed in a prickly, green casing.

height of 30 m (100 ft). In suitable climates, it is very long lived.

CULTIVATION Chestnuts like a deep, well-drained, light, acid soil and full sun or partial shade. It is advisable to plant two or more trees of cultivars grown for their fruits to ensure that cross-pollination takes place.

CLIMATE Zone 6.

Chilli (*Capsicum annuum*, fam. Solanaceae)

Most hot chillies are pungent varieties of *Capsicum annuum*. Tropical American in origin, they grow on small, shrubby, annual plants that produce white flowers in the leaf axils. The flowers are followed by the fruits which come in a great variety of sizes and shapes. Most have red flesh at maturity. Cayenne pepper is made from the powdered dried fruits. The long, red cayenne types are slender, growing to around 12 cm (5 in) in length, while the very hot, small, red cayenne grows to only 6 cm (2½ in) on a much smaller plant. There are other varieties and the mature fruits of some are very hot indeed. Hot weather produces hotter chillies that become even hotter and sweeter as they ripen, the seeds being hotter than the flesh. *Capsicum frutescens*, tabasco, originates from tropical South America but today it is widely cultivated throughout much of India and Southeast Asia. It is a perennial but is normally grown as an annual. The name 'tabasco' comes from a southern Mexican town and this species is best known as the manufactured tabasco sauce made from matured chillies. The plant is very similar to that of *C. annuum* but the fruits are held on upward-pointing stalks. Cultivation is the same as for other *Capsicum* species.

CULTIVATION Chillies are grown as summer annuals, either in an intermediate greenhouse if summers are cool, or outdoors in areas with warm or hot summers, planting out when danger of frost is over. Sow seeds in mid-spring in seed trays or pots and germinate them in a

ABOVE This chilli cultivar is still a long way off maturity. Fruits will be bright red when they are ready to be harvested.

temperature of 20°C (68°F). Pot seedlings individually into small pots and eventually plant them 45-60 cm (18–24 in) apart in a soil border, or pot into 25 cm (10 in) pots. Pinch out young plants to encourage bushiness. Tall varieties may need staking. Water moderately, and in summer feed with tomato fertilizer once every two weeks. Provide a humid atmosphere under glass. The fruit is picked when fully colored, either for fresh use or for drying.

CLIMATE Zone 10, but it is possible to grow chillies in all climates as summer annuals.

Chimonanthus (fam. Calycanthaceae)
Winter sweet

Of this small genus of flowering shrubs from China and Japan, only one species is generally cultivated.

CULTIVATION Winter sweet likes a cool climate, rich soil, a sunny, sheltered position and plenty of water in dry weather. Plant in spring or fall. Regular pruning is not needed. Propagate by layering in spring or from softwood cuttings in spring, rooted under glass.

CLIMATE Zone 7.

ABOVE Tolerant of severe cold, this *Chimonanthus praecox* growing in partial shade has a rather open form.

SPECIES *C. praecox* is a richly perfumed, deciduous shrub growing to 3 m (10 ft). The yellow and red flowers are borne on its bare branches during winter. Dried flowers can be used like lavender to scent linen closets.

Chionanthus (fam. Oleaceae)

Comprising about 100 species of evergreen and deciduous trees and shrubs native to tropical and subtropical parts of eastern Asia and temperate parts of the eastern states of the United States, this genus occurs in a variety of habitats, from forest and woodland to open scrub and beside streams. Several species are cultivated as ornamentals.

CULTIVATION *Chionanthus* prefers a cool to cold climate and moist, fertile soil. It is best sheltered from very strong wind, but needs full sun exposure. Propagate by seed, layering, or grafting and budding.

CLIMATE There are species suited to various climatic zones.

SPECIES *C. retusus*, fringe tree, zone 6, from China, grows to 3 m (10 ft), with blunt, elliptical leaves, up to 10 cm (4 in), topped with a canopy of small, white flowers in summer. *C. virginicus*, old man's beard or white fringe tree, zone 4, from America, produces pendulous sprays of white flowers among its leaves, which are larger than on *C. retusus*. It grows to around 3 m (10 ft).

Chionodoxa (fam. Hyacinthaceae)
Glory of the snow

Native to Crete, Turkey and Cyprus, the dainty, star-like flowers of this small genus of dwarf bulbs appear in early spring. The flowers are mainly blue and white, but also come in pink

BELOW A cloud of creamy white flowers obscures the framework of *Chionanthus retusus*.

BELOW This delightful little bulbous plant, *Chionodoxa luciliae*, is suitable for cool climates only where it will flower in early spring.

or white. Ideal for rock gardens or for massing in shrub borders.

CULTIVATION Plant the bulbs about 8 cm (3 in) deep in fall, in any soil that has good drainage. Best flowering is in full sun. Propagate from offsets at planting time, or from seed sown in spring. These bulbs often self-sow freely.

CLIMATE Zone 4.

SPECIES *C. luciliae* produces clusters of blue and white flowers. It grows to about 15 cm (6 in) in height. *C. nana* (syn. *C. cretica*) produces several delicate, blue and white flowers to a stem. It grows to 15 cm (6 in). The delightful *C. sardensis*, from western Turkey, has large clusters of drooping, deep blue flowers. Height is up to 20 cm (8 in) but often much less.

Chives (*Allium schoenoprasum*, fam. Alliaceae)

These hardy perennials belong to the same family as the onion, garlic, shallot and leek. As they do not contain the same amount of sulphur as onion, their flavor is milder and they are more digestible. Chives are a real asset to the kitchen: they can be used to garnish almost any dish, and they add an onion-like taste to omelettes, salads, potatoes and soups. *A. schoenoprasum* grows from tiny bulbs in clumps of long, round, hollow stems to about 30 cm (12 in) tall. It produces pretty, mauve, clover-like blossoms in spring and summer. Chives make an attractive border plant.

CULTIVATION Chives do well in a rich, well-drained soil in a sunny, open position. They usually die right down during winter, particularly in cold climates. They should be covered with straw in areas of heavy frost. When they start shooting again in spring, and the stems reach 5 cm (2 in), divide the clumps and plant 15 cm (6 in) apart. This is important as they can die if overcrowded, for large clumps take a lot of nutrients from the soil. For this reason, too, it is a good idea to mulch

ABOVE Chives grow and flower rapidly in spring once soil warms. Grow them in a container for convenient picking.

them with well-rotted organic matter such as manure or compost. Pick both the flowers and the stems as this improves the plant. Cut the outside stems of each bunch with scissors, to just above soil level.

CLIMATE Suitable for zone 5 and above.

Chlidanthus (fam. Amaryllidaceae)

Only one species of this small genus of bulbs from South America is cultivated. It has strap-like leaves and rather pendulous inflorescences.

CULTIVATION These tender bulbs are grown in a cool greenhouse in frost-prone climates. Plant shallowly in spring in pots of soil-based potting compost. Keep dry in winter. Outdoors grow in a sunny, sheltered position with well drained, humus-rich soil.

CLIMATE Zone 9.

SPECIES *C. fragrans*, native to the Peruvian Andes, produces fragrant yellow flowers with a tube, to 8 cm (3 in) long, ending in star-like

ABOVE The clear yellow flowers of the frost-tender *Chlidanthus fragrans* appear in summer and have a strong scent.

ABOVE Variegated *Chlorophytum comosum* makes a lovely edging for a path in dappled sunlight.

lobes. They appear in summer before the leaves. This species grows to about 30 cm (12 in) high.

CLIMATE Zone 10.

SPECIES *C. capense* has plain green leaves to 60 cm (24 in) and small, white flowers. This species does not form plantlets. *C. comosum*, popularly known as the spider plant, is the species most often grown, especially its cultivar 'Variegatum', with green and white-striped leaves. It produces an abundance of plantlets which follow the white flowers.

Chlorophytum (fam. Anthericaceae)

Native to Africa, these widely grown tropical plants, with an abundance of narrow, grass-like leaves, are grown as pot plants in frost-prone climates. They make very good house plants. They also make very good summer bedding plants, associating well with colorful flowering plants. They produce plantlets on long arching stems which take root easily when set in soil.

CULTIVATION Grow in pots of soil-based potting compost in a cool or intermediate greenhouse or conservatory, in maximum light, but shade from direct sun. They take a lot of watering in summer, less in winter. Outdoors, they can be grown in sun or partial shade. Propagate from plantlets or by division.

Chocho (*Sechium edule*, fam. Cucurbitaceae)
Chayote, vegetable pear

Very popular in its native South America, this perennial fruit grows on a strong vine and can be planted to hide unsightly structures in the garden. It produces abundant pear-shaped, pale green fruit which is generally served boiled or baked as a vegetable, although it is quite delicious stewed and made into pies. The larger root tubers are eaten like potatoes in some tropical countries.

CULTIVATION Chochos have a long growing season. They need reasonably fertile soil, improved with rotted manure, and a sunny location. Weed control is essential and this can be assisted by shallow cultivation. Provide

ABOVE Growth of chocho vines is dense and vigorous in warm conditions.

ABOVE *Choisya ternata* in full bloom delights with its good looks and fragrance.

protection against snails, slugs and slaters. Grow from the sprouted fruit, spaced 2.5–3.5 m (8–11 ft) apart, with the sprouted, narrow part sitting above the soil. Chochos planted in spring bear in late summer and fall. In frosty areas, they will be killed out at this stage. When vines die down, prune them away and new vines will appear in spring. One plant is sufficient for an average family.

CLIMATE Zone 10.

Choisya (fam. Rutaceae)
Mexican orange blossom

These hardy, evergreen shrubs from Mexico look very pretty with their masses of sweetly scented, starry flowers against the glossy, dark green leaves. Only one of the species is commonly grown.

CULTIVATION *Choisya* will grow in any reasonably fertile soil. It will tolerate seaside conditions, but not direct exposure to salt-laden winds. Prune into shape after flowering. Propagate from semi-ripe cuttings in summer.

CLIMATE Zone 7.

SPECIES *C. ternata* grows into a rounded bush, to 3 m (10 ft), with fragrant leaves and white flowers, resembling orange blossom, for several months of the year. Cultivar 'Sundance' has golden yellow foliage when grown in full sun.

Chorisia (fam. Bombaceae)

Native to South America, these exceptionally beautiful, tropical trees have very spiky trunks, large, hibiscus-like flowers, alternate, compound leaves and pear-shaped capsular fruits.

CULTIVATION In climates which are prone to frost, grow in a warm greenhouse or conservatory in pots containing soil-based potting compost. Provide maximum light but shade from direct sun. Water well in summer and moderately during the rest of the year. Outdoors, they need a sunny spot and well-drained, acid or neutral soil well supplied with organic matter. Propagate from seed sown in warmth in spring.

CLIMATE Zone 10.

SPECIES *C. insignis*, from Peru and Argentina, has white or white- and yellow-streaked flowers in fall and winter. It grows 15 m (50 ft) or so tall. *C. speciosa*, floss silk tree, from

ABOVE *Chorisia speciosa*, the floss silk tree, is fast growing in mild climates. Trees flower from a young age too.

Brazil, grows very tall in its native habitat, but only to around 20 m (65 ft) when cultivated elsewhere. It produces single flowers in pink, violet, cream or yellow spotted with brown at the base, and never produces two trees exactly alike. The orchid-like flowers appear in fall. The floss silk tree has the advantage of producing its flowers at a young age. The seeds are embedded in silky fibers inside the fruits.

Chorizema (fam. Papilionaceae)

This genus of some 18 species of decorative shrubs, mostly native to Western Australia, are hardy and quite easy to grow in the right climate and conditions. They have simple, alternate leaves and produce abundant sprays of orange and red pea flowers.

CULTIVATION They are grown in a cool greenhouse or conservatory in areas where hard frosts are likely. Grow in pots of acid, soil-based or soilless compost, in good light with shade from direct sun, and with ample ventilation. Outdoors, grow in well-drained, acid or neutral, humus-rich soil, in full sun. Propagate from seed after soaking in hot water.

ABOVE Flame pea, *Chorizema cordatum*, has vibrantly colored flowers which make an impressive show.

CLIMATE Zone 9.

SPECIES *C. cordatum*, Western Australian flame pea, is the most widely cultivated of the species. It has thin, weak branches and prolific, loose sprays of yellow, orange, red and cerise flowers in late winter and spring. It grows to 1.5 m (5 ft).

Choy sum

(*Brassica parachinensis*, fam. Brassicaceae)

False pak-choi, Chinese tsai shim

The whole of this plant is edible, including the yellow flowers. It may be eaten boiled, steamed or fried, and is a rich source of calcium, dietary fiber and vitamin A, also supplying a little potassium. It is an upright grower and has elliptical, mid-green leaves, with green stems and veins. Choy sum is a fast growing plant, flowering when it has seven or eight leaves. These are harvested just as the first flower buds begin to open.

ABOVE A closely planted commercial crop of Chinese tsai shim is being harvested. Leaves are bundled before packing for market.

CULTIVATION Soil should be well drained and contain plenty of organic matter. Dig in manure or compost four to six weeks before planting. Unless soils are known to be alkaline, apply a light dressing of lime to the planting area prior to sowing the seed. Space plants about 20 cm (8 in) apart. Keep them growing actively by regular watering and keep the area free of weeds. Plants are ready for harvest about seven to eight weeks after sowing.

CLIMATE Best in cool conditions. Grow as a summer or fall annual in all climates.

Chrysalidocarpus (fam. Arecaceae)

Only three species of this genus of palms, native to Madagascar and its neighbor the Comoros Islands, are known to be cultivated, two being quite uncommon. *C. lutescens* is the most widely grown in the tropics, often used in landscaping because of its elegant, multi-stemmed habit, the color of its foliage and stem, and its rapid growth and ease of culture. It also makes a fine indoor or glasshouse specimen in cooler regions if enough space, warmth and light are available.

CULTIVATION In frost-prone climates, grow in pots or tubs in an intermediate or warm greenhouse or conservatory, or as house plants. Use soil-based potting compost. Provide bright light but not direct sun. Outdoors *C. lutescens* needs a rich, well-drained yet moisture-retentive soil and a position in full sun. It will also take partial shade and is tolerant of wind, although this can cause slight burning of the leaf tips. Propagate by seed sown in spring and germinate in a temperature of 26°C (79°F). Propagation may also be possible from suckers.

CLIMATE Zone 10.

SPECIES *C. lutescens*, golden cane palm or butterfly palm, from Madagascar, is a multi-stemmed species, older plants sometimes comprising around 50 densely crowded stems to 6–8 m (20–26 ft) tall and 8–12 cm (3–5 in) in diameter. The stems increase in number by suckers branching off the bases of previous stems, mostly at or just above ground level, and growing almost vertically upward. Characteristics include the yellowish green color of the sheaths and leaf stalks. The leaves are also yellow-green in color, about 2 m (6 ft) long,

BELOW This cluster of ringed canes of *Chrysalidocarpus lutescens* has a mass of new growth emerging from its base.

arching very gently, then curving upward; the narrow leaflets are regularly spaced and upward-pointing. Small yellow flowers are crowded on the stiff, fleshy branches of the inflorescence and the pale greenish yellow fruits, about 2 cm (¾ in) long, ripen to purple. *C. madagascariensis* another species from Madagascar, is also multi-stemmed, to 10 m (33 ft) tall, with thicker stems than *C. lutescens*. It is not often grown.

Chrysanthemum (fam. Asteraceae)

The chrysanthemum probably originated in China, but was also introduced into Japan a very long time ago. It features widely in the art of both countries, and some of the single, yellow, daisy types seen in old Chinese illustrations are undoubtedly the ancestors of the magnificent flowers we know today. The garden or florists' chrysanthemum (*C.* x *morifolium*) is the feature of fall garden displays (its natural flowering being in fall) and is now available year round as a potted plant in bloom. It is also valued as a long-lasting cut flower and in many parts of the Western world is regarded as a symbol of Mother's Day. Chrysanthemums are 'short day plants' and will not bloom if exposed to too many hours of light. Professional growers manipulate the growing conditions and especially the hours of light to which the plants are exposed.

CULTIVATION Florists' chrysanthemums need to be grown in full sun, with protection from strong wind. The soil must be well drained but heavily enriched with manure or compost before planting. These plants are fairly shallow-rooted so benefit from mulching with organic matter. Water heavily at least once a week, more often in sandy soils, through the growing season, tapering off as plants begin to die back in winter. Feed about once a month with complete plant food through the growing period. Tall growers need staking. As flower buds form, leave them as they are or remove smaller side buds if you wish to produce fewer, larger blooms. For garden display, most growers tend to leave all or most of the buds. After flowering, cut plants 10–15 cm (4–6 in) above soil level and remove all old foliage and rubbish. Propagate in spring by lifting and dividing the clumps, using the newest suckers to start fresh plantings, or from cuttings of new growth. Potted plants that have finished blooming can be cut back and planted out into the garden where they should flower at the normal time of year, though the blooms will never be as choice as when the plant was first

BELOW LEFT Quilled petals are characteristic of the open, 'spider' chrysanthemums. Color shading is attractive.

BELOW Large trusses of russet pink chrysanthemums add traditional fall tones to the garden.

ABOVE A spectacular, white spider chrysanthemum with conspicuous, pale green center. This type of chrysanthemum needs weather protection when coming into bloom.

purchased. Depending on ultimate size, space plants 40–50 cm (16–20 in) apart. Plants are susceptible to fungal diseases such as leaf spots, powdery mildew, rust and white rust, and also attack from aphids and occasionally the chrysanthemum leaf miner. *C. carinatum* needs full sun and well-drained soil. In warm areas, sow seed in fall; in cool areas, sow in spring once the soil has warmed. Space plants 30–40 cm (12–16 in) apart.

CLIMATE Cool to warm temperate climates; zone 5 for the hardiest.

SPECIES *C. carinatum*, painted daisy, is an annual species which grows to about 60 cm (24 in). Blooming in spring or summer, the showy, daisy-like flowers feature concentric bands of strongly contrasting colors in white, red, yellow or purple. *Chrysanthemum x morifolium* is known once again by its familiar name. These plants have dull green, very aromatic foliage and may grow between 20 cm (8 in) and 2 m (6 ft) high, depending on the variety. Numerous flower types have been classified by specialist societies. Some of the types are known as decorative, anemone-centered, spider, pompon, quill, exhibition and incurved. This range of forms is further varied by the colors which cover white, cream, yellow, pink, lilac, burgundy, apricot and mahogany in an amazing range of shades. Many of the singles grown for the cut flower trade have contrasting, lime green centers. Chrysanthemums are long-lasting cut flowers, provided all the foliage below the water line is removed and the water is changed frequently.

Chrysocoma (fam. Asteraceae)

Related to the aster, these South African shrubs grow 60 cm (24 in) or less. They have small, straight, alternate leaves and short-stalked, round, yellow flower heads.

CULTIVATION Chrysocoma does best in areas where the minimum winter temperature does not fall below 7°C (45°F), so in frost-prone areas, grow in a cool greenhouse or conservatory. It likes soil which is well drained and a sunny, sheltered position. In pots, use a compost of equal parts of peat, sand and loam. Water well in spring and summer but only moderately at other times of the year. Propagate from cuttings taken in the spring.

BELOW *Chrysocoma coma-aurea* can be grown in a container or in the ground. Prune after flowering to maintain compact growth.

CLIMATE Zone 10.

SPECIES *C. coma-aurea* is a small, evergreen shrub, to 45 cm (18 in), with yellow flowers, straight stems and smooth, flat, entire leaves.

Chrysophyllum (fam. Sapotaceae)

This genus consists of around 80 species of evergreen, tropical trees mainly from the Americas, although some species also occur in West Africa and Australia. Many have edible fruit, while some are grown for their fine timber.

CULTIVATION In frost-prone climates, grow as pot plants in a warm greenhouse. These trees prefer fertile, deep soil, with plenty of organic matter. Water regularly throughout the warmest months of the year. Propagate from seed or from cuttings if bottom heat is available.

CLIMATE Warmest parts of zone 10.

SPECIES *C. cainito*, star apple or cainito, grows 12–15 m (40–50 ft) in good conditions. This handsome tree has glossy foliage and smooth, purple to pale green fruits, with white, edible flesh. The star shape is evident when the fruits are cut transversely. *C. oliviforme*, known as damson plum in Jamaica, is native to tropical America. It grows to 10 m (33 ft) and has small, purplish fruit.

Cimicifuga (fam. Ranunculaceae)
Bugbane

Allegedly used in Europe to eradicate bed bugs, these hardy, herbaceous, northern hemisphere perennials usually grow 1–2 m (3–6 ft) in height and work well at the back of a border. They have large, compound leaves and spikes of small white flowers. They are thought to be an effective insect repellent.

CULTIVATION These plants need a lot of moisture. Propagate from seeds sown 6 mm (¼ in) deep in boxes in fall or by division of the roots in spring.

CLIMATE Zone 5 for most species.

SPECIES *C. americana* grows 1–1.5 m (3–5 ft) tall and produces creamy white flowers in

ABOVE *Chrysophyllum imperiale* is a large, imposing tree that produces heavy shade with its dense clusters of whorled foliage.

ABOVE Grown today as an ornamental, *Cimicifuga racemosa* has a long history of medicinal use by the native Americans. The dark, knotted roots were the part used.

summer. *C. racemosa*, black cohosh or black snakeroot, grows 2–3 m (6–10 ft), with broad spikes of white flowers. *C. rubifolia* has large, heart-shaped leaves at the base and grows to 2 m (6 ft). *C. simplex*, from Russia, China and Japan, is a clump-forming perennial which grows to over 1 m (3 ft). Spikes of white flowers are borne in early to mid-fall. Cultivars include 'Brunette' which has dark, purple-brown foliage.

Cineraria

(see *Pericallis* x *hybrida*, fam. Asteraceae)

Cinnamomum (fam. Lauraceae)

Camphor tree

These aromatic trees and shrubs have considerable commercial value: *C. camphora* yields camphor oil and the bark of *C. zeylanicum* is used to make cinnamon, commonly used in curries and cakes. Mostly shapely evergreens, they have dense, leathery foliage, sprays of small bisexual or unisexual flowers, and blue-black berries.

CULTIVATION In frost-prone climates, grow in an intermediate greenhouse or conservatory as foliage plants. Use soil-based potting compost. Outdoors, in the right climate, these trees are easy to grow. Propagate from seed sown in spring in warmth or from semi-ripe cuttings in summer.

CLIMATE Zone 10 and above.

SPECIES *C. camphora*, camphor tree, originating in tropical Asia, is the most widely grown species. It has 12 cm (5 in) long leaves, whitish on the undersides, and yellow flowers. It can grow as tall as 30 m (100 ft). The fine timber is used in cabinetwork as it carves well. *C. zeylanicum*, cinnamon tree, a native of India and Sri Lanka, grows to 9 m (30 ft), with yellowish white flowers. The well-known spice is derived from the ground bark of the tree and is used in both sweet and savory dishes.

ABOVE Camphor tree, *Cinnamomum camphora*, is a broad, dome-shaped tree, but in frosty climates it makes a good foliage plant under glass.

Cissus (fam. Vitaceae)

This large genus comprises around 350 species. Mainly climbers and vines, they are native to tropical and warm areas throughout the world. Many of the tropical species have edible leaves and berries, with a history of use in folk medicine. Grown principally for their handsome foliage, several species are used indoors as potted plants or in hanging baskets. Some are used as groundcover in mild climates.

CULTIVATION All species of *Cissus* are frost-sensitive, and in cool and cold climates should be grown in pots in a cool to intermediate greenhouse or conservatory, or as house plants. They grow best in soil-based potting compost and are suitable plants for shade or subdued light, although they will be equally happy in bright light, but they should be shaded from direct sun. They can be grown in hanging baskets. Most species can be propagated easily enough from semi-ripe cuttings which are taken in summer and rooted with bottom heat.

CLIMATE This genus is suitable for zone 10 and above.

SPECIES *C. antarctica*, kangaroo vine, from Australia's Queensland and New South Wales, is one of the most commonly cultivated species. A climber often used as a groundcover, it has almost oval, bright green leaves with toothed margins, insignificant flowers and round, blackish purple fruits measuring about 1 cm (⅓ in) in diameter. *C. discolor*, begonia treevine, from Indonesia, is generally grown indoors for its attractive foliage. The large, velvety leaves are metallic green, with white, purple and pink markings on the top and deep crimson below. This species is very cold-sensitive and needs winter warmth and humidity. *C. hypoglauca*, water vine, is a vigorous, woody vine, native to parts of eastern Australia. It produces a canopy of blueish gray leaves, each consisting of five leaflets. The young leaves and shoots are rusty green and small, the yellow flowers measure 4 mm (⅙ in) across, and the large, purplish black fruits are edible, but sour. *C. quadrangularis*, from eastern Africa, southern Asia and Malaysia, is a tendril climber. It has succulent, four-angled stems, arranged in segments, with sparse, heart-shaped, deciduous leaves, small green flowers and clusters of blackberry-like fruit. *C. rhombifolia*, grape ivy, is the species most used indoors. Numerous cultivars, including 'Ellen Danica', are widely grown.

Cistus (fam. Cistaceae)
Rock rose

These delightful Mediterranean shrubs have simple, opposite leaves and papery, flattish, white, pink or purple flowers with a yellow splash at the base of the petals. They are well suited to coastal areas but are also frost-hardy, and the smaller species make excellent rock garden plants. They are often short-lived.

CULTIVATION *Cistus* is easy to grow but thrives in a light, well-drained soil in a reasonably sheltered spot. No pruning is necessary apart from the removal of seed-heads. Propagate from semi-ripe cuttings in summer or fall.

CLIMATE Zone 8 for most of the species and hybrids.

BELOW *Cistus* x *purpureus*, with its bright, cerise pink flowers, is one of the earliest developed hybrids in this group.

BELOW Often seen indoors, *Cissus rhombifolia* looks lovely trained over a white pergola.

SPECIES *C.* x *cyprius*, gum cistus, has narrow, fragrant leaves and large, long-stalked clusters of white flowers, marked with red inside. It grows to 2 m (6 ft). 'Albiflorus' produces plain, white flowers. *C. incanus*, Mediterranean rose, grows to 1 m (3 ft), with rosy purple flowers and broad, blunt leaves. There are many cultivars of cistus. 'Doris Hibberson' grows to 1 m and has gray-green leaves and crinkled, pure pink flowers; 'Peggy Sammons' has light purple-pink blooms, height 1 m (3 ft); and 'Silver Pink' produces silvery pink blooms, height 75 cm (30 in). *C. ladanifer*, laudanum, produces a resin used in perfumery. The pure white flowers have a deep red blotch at the base of each petal.

Citharexylum (fam. Verbenaceae)
Fiddlewood

Commonly known as fiddlewood because the timber is used to make musical instruments (the kithara was an ancient Grecian stringed instrument), these trees and shrubs are evergreen in their native tropical America, but semi-deciduous in cooler climates. The foliage of the species listed turns deep orange before falling. The leaves are simple, opposite, more or less elliptical and generally entire, although sometimes coarsely toothed. The spiky sprays of small, yellow or white flowers are delightfully fragrant.

CULTIVATION In cool, frosty climates, grow in a cool greenhouse or conservatory. Outdoors, fiddlewoods do best in a reasonably rich soil in a warm spot in the garden. They quickly grow into a bushy tree or large shrub, but do not reach the heights they achieve in their native habitat. Prune if they require it in the late winter or early spring, before new growth starts. Propagate from cuttings.

CLIMATE Zone 9.

SPECIES *C. fruticosum*, from the West Indies, grows into a tree of about 9 m (30 ft) tall. It has entire leaves 10–15 cm (4–6 in) long and sprays

ABOVE The leaves of *Citharexylum spinosum*, fiddlewood, change color before they fall.

of white flowers, 10–12 cm (4–5 in) long, which appear at any time through the year. *C. spinosum* is a larger tree, also from the West Indies, where it reaches 15 m (50 ft). It has deep green, oval, toothed leaves, to 20 cm (8 in), and 30 cm (12 in) long sprays of white flowers at any time between winter and early summer.

Clarkia (fam. Onagraceae)
Satin flower

Native to western North America, these colorful annuals make very attractive cut flowers, but the leaves should be removed as they have an unpleasant odor when they are placed in water.

BELOW A selection of *Clarkia amoena* hybrids are crowded together to make this lovely display of cut flowers.

CULTIVATION Clarkia thrives in a light soil in a sunny position. Sow seeds in fall or early spring where they are to grow, as they do not transplant easily, and thin to about 30–40 cm (12–16 in) apart when they reach 5–8 cm (2–3 in) high.

CLIMATE Zone 8.

SPECIES *C. amoena*, the most commonly cultivated species, is a pretty annual with lance-shaped, mid-green, alternate leaves. The flowers are borne either singly or in sprays. Numerous strains in mixed colors are offered in the US, the colors including shades of red, pink, orange, scarlet and purple. Heights vary from 45 to 75 cm (18–30 in). They flower in late spring if sown in fall and produce flowers in summer from spring sowings.

Cleistocactus (fam. Cactaceae)
Silver torch cactus

These cactuses from South America are mainly columnar in habit and densely spiny. They

BELOW The upright columnar shape of *Cleistocactus strausii* is silhouetted by low sunlight. Tubular flowers emerge sideways from the column.

produce tubular flowers. In frost-prone climates, grow in an intermediate greenhouse or conservatory, or in warmer climates, in an outdoor cactus garden.

CULTIVATION Under glass, grow in pots of well-drained cactus compost and provide maximum light. Water regularly in the growing season but keep dry in winter. Outdoors plant in full sun with well-drained, sandy soil.

CLIMATE Zone 9 or 10.

SPECIES *C. strausii*, from Bolivia, is the species most commonly grown. When mature, it produces an abundance of red flowers late in summer. In its native habitat, it is pollinated by hummingbirds.

Clematis (fam. Ranunculaceae)
Traveller's joy, virgin's bower

There are at least 200 species and countless hybrids of clematis, mostly from the northern hemisphere, with a few native to the southern hemisphere, including Australia and the Pacific region. Clematis often climb high into trees from which their flowers tumble out over the canopy so are useful for covering free-standing arches or walls. If planted under the right conditions and well cared for, clematis are reasonably fast growing and long lived. Most clematis plants produce blooms within the first couple of years after planting. Some flower in spring only, and others flower either throughout spring and summer or during summer and early fall. The large-flowered, deciduous forms known as Jackmanii hybrids have been developed from several species and have some of the most spectacular flowers imaginable. They come in a great range of brilliant, single colors–white, blue, purple, crimson and cerise–as well as bicolors.

CULTIVATION All clematis like a well-drained soil enriched with decayed organic matter. Often described as needing a 'cool root run', they

ABOVE Traveller's joy, *Clematis aristata*, is a mass of delicate, starry flowers in spring or early summer.

need soil that remains cool and moist at all times. It is important to give regular, deep watering during spring and summer. *C. aristata* and *C. pubescens* prefer dappled sunlight; most others prefer full sun but will tolerate semi-shade in cool climates. Feed in spring, as growth starts, with complete plant food and a dressing of well-rotted manure. These twining climbers are happy with any sort of support, for example a tree, pergola or lattice. The timing and method of pruning depends on the species or cultivar grown. Some pruning may be needed to train these climbers to their structures or supports. Many of the *Jackmanii* hybrids should be pruned in late winter, just before new growth commences. However, sometimes it is best to leave them until they have filled their allotted space. Some should be pruned only very lightly. Ask the local nursery, or refer to the plant label, if in doubt. *C. montana* flowers on the previous season's growth, so pruning should be confined to the removal of spent flowers and directional cutting to restrict size if necessary. Very old vines may require the removal of old canes at ground level to make way for younger, more vigorous growth. Propagate species from seed and cultivars from softwood cuttings in spring, rooting them under glass. All can be grown from stems layered to the ground in spring ready for cutting and lifting at the end of the following winter. Some hybrids can be grafted, though suitable species understocks must be used. This is usually not an option for home gardeners.

CLIMATE A great many clematis, including the large-flowered hybrids, are suited to zone 6.

SPECIES *C. alpina*, zone 5, native to Europe and Asia, grows vigorously to 2 m (6 ft) and produces small, violet-blue, lantern-like flowers in the spring. Cultivars include 'Columbine', with pale blue flowers; 'Pamela Jackman', with deep blue flowers; and 'White Moth', with white flowers. *C. aristata*, old man's beard or goat's beard, zone 7, is an Australian species found growing in moist, sheltered areas where it loves to clamber up into trees or over old stumps where its fragrant, white, starry flowers are best displayed. The spring and summer flowers are followed by fluffy white seed heads,

ABOVE *Clematis montana* var. *rubens* is shown to advantage tumbling over an archway.

which persist for several months, becoming fluffier as they mature. The species is variable, and there are many forms. *C. armandii*, from China, grows to 5 m (16 ft), with evergreen foliage and small, fragrant, whitish flowers. *C. flammula* grows 2–5 m (6–16 ft), with fragrant, white flowers late in the season. *C. foetida*, zone 8, from New Zealand, produces an abundance of fragrant, greenish yellow flowers in long sprays from spring to early summer. 'Jackmanii' and other large-flowered hybrids sometimes reach 3 m (10 ft) in height and produce by far the largest flowers of all the cultivated clematis. 'Barbara Jackman' has blue-mauve flowers; 'Comtesse de Bouchaud' has mauve-pink flowers; 'Gipsy Queen' has purple flowers; 'Lady Betty Balfour' has blue-purple flowers; 'Jackmani Superba' has purple flowers; 'Lincoln Star' has raspberry pink flowers; 'Nellie Moser' has mauve and carmine flowers; and 'Perle d'Azur' has light blue flowers. Many others are also available. *C. macropetala*, zone 5, from Asia, reaches 3 m (10 ft) high and has small, lantern-like, double violet flowers in spring. Cultivars of this species are available. *C. montana*, one of the best known species, is a vigorous, decid-uous vine from the Himalayas, with small, white flowers. Var. *rubens* is also widely grown. *C. recta*, zone 3, from Europe, is a herbaceous plant, to 2 m (6 ft), which bears profuse, fragrant white flowers. 'Purpurea' has purple leaves. *C. rehderiana*, from China, grows to 6 m (20 ft) in height, with fragrant, straw yellow flowers. *C. stans*, zone 4, from Japan, is a late-flowering, herbaceous type, to 2 m (6 ft), with blue flowers. *C. tangutica*, from Asia, bears bright yellow, bell-shaped flowers late in the season and grows to 3 m (10 ft).

Cleome (fam. Capparidaceae)
Spider plant

A genus of annuals and perennials mostly native to tropical America, one species blooms for a long time in summer and is often grown to add height and color to borders. One annual species is common in cultivation. They have

ABOVE Tall-growing *Cleome hassleriana* has a very long flowering period through summer.

simple or compound palmate leaves and pretty flowers, in a variety of colors, with narrow petals and long, protruding stamens. The flowers are produced either singly or in sprays.

CULTIVATION These plants prefer a mild climate with plenty of sun and some shelter from wind. In frost-prone climates, grow under glass. Sow in spring, just under the surface in light, rich soil. Water sparingly.

CLIMATE Not critical; grown as a seasonal annual.

SPECIES *C. hassleriana*, spider flower, grows upright to 1.5 m (5 ft). It has strongly scented glands, compound palmate leaves, spiny stems and solitary, dark pink flowers which fade to white during the day. Several cultivars are available in pure white and various shades of pink. *C. lutea* grows to 1.5 m (5 ft), with yellow-orange flowers.

Clerodendrum (fam. Verbenaceae)
Glory bower

This is a large genus of trees, shrubs and climbers from tropical and warm regions of the world. Many of the species have their origins in China and Japan or tropical Africa. These beautiful, deciduous or evergreen shrubs, with their abundance of brilliantly colored flowers, are the showpiece of many gardens. They have opposite or whorled, simple leaves up to 30 cm (12 in) long, and terminal sprays of white, violet or red flowers.

CULTIVATION Tender species are grown in a warm greenhouse or conservatory in frost-prone climates. Outdoors, *Clerodendrum* likes a well-enriched soil, a warm, sunny climate and plenty of water in summer. Plant in fall. Propagate from seed sown in spring or from semi-ripe cuttings in summer, and provide bottom heat for both.

CLIMATE Zone 10 for many species.

SPECIES *C. bungei*, glory flower, zone 8, grows to 2 m (6 ft), with long, coarsely toothed, ovate leaves and long clusters of deep pink flowers. This species is sweetly perfumed. *C. speciosissimum* produces crimson and scarlet blooms in summer. *C. splendens* is a bushy plant, with felt-like leaves and scarlet summer flowers. *C. thomsoniae*, bleeding heart, flourishes in the tropics and can be grown outdoors in a warm location in many other regions. This climber can also be grown as a glasshouse or indoor plant in cooler areas. Clusters of red flowers with white calyces appear in summer. *C. ugandense*, blue butterfly bush, grows to 2.5 m (8 ft) and produces delicate, light blue flowers with long stamens over an extended period in the summer.

Clethra (fam. Clethraceae)
White alder

Native to North America, Europe and eastern Asia, these evergreen or deciduous trees and shrubs, with handsome oval leaves, bear long sprays of small, sweetly perfumed flowers in summer.

CULTIVATION *Clethra* likes a well-drained, lime-free soil and plenty of water. An equable climate, free from drying winds, is essential. These are ideal plants for a woodland garden.

ABOVE *Clethra arborea* is a small, neat shrub, very fragrant in flower.

BELOW Clear blue flowers are produced by *Clerodendrum ugandense* in summer and fall.

Plant in spring. Propagate from seed sown in fall or spring, from semi-ripe cuttings in summer, or by layering in spring.

CLIMATE There are species for various climatic zones.

SPECIES *C. alnifolia*, sweet pepper bush, zone 3, from North America, grows to 2.5 m (8 ft), with long spikes of delicate, spicily fragrant, white flowers and small leaves which color yellow in fall. 'Rosea' produces buds and flowers tinged with pink. *C. arborea*, lily of the valley tree zone 9, from Madeira, needs to be grown in a cool greenhouse in frost-prone climates. It has narrow, elliptical leaves and many, fragrant, white flowers, similar to lily of the valley. *C. barbinervis*, zone 5, from Japan, is a deciduous tree or shrub, 6–9 m (20–30 ft) tall, with white flowers.

Clianthus (fam. Papilionaceae)
Glory pea, parrot's beak

Known by a number of common names, this exceptionally beautiful flowering shrub is a native of New Zealand. While suitable for a range of conditions, it is not very widely grown. It is low to medium growing, with a

BELOW The lovely, curved flowers of *Clianthus puniceus* vary in color. This pinky red form is particularly pretty.

spreading habit, and has soft, rather succulent, fern-like foliage. Its striking flowers bloom profusely during summer. The genus formerly included Sturt's desert pea (*Clianthus formosus*), now known as *Swainsona formosa*.

CULTIVATION *C. puniceus* comes true from seed, which is the usual method of propagation. Because the seeds have a hard, waxy coat, it is necessary to first nick them carefully on the outside edge, opposite the embryonic shoot, or to carefully abrade them with sandpaper. Then soak for 24 hours in cold water, not boiling water. Plant seedlings in a mixture of sharp sand and peat. Selected color forms can sometimes be increased by soft cuttings raised under glass; new plants should be started every three or four years. These plants grow naturally in areas where soils are rich in minerals, so in cultivation, fertilizer should be added during the growing season. Use either a slow-release type or a diluted liquid type. Once established, this species is drought resistant. In climates with hard frosts, grow in a cool conservatory or greenhouse.

CLIMATE Zone 8 or 9.

SPECIES *C. puniceus*, glory pea, is a spreading, rather short-lived shrub from New Zealand, which grows 1.5–2 m (5–6 ft) tall. The pendulous flower stalks bear varying numbers of scarlet, beak-shaped blooms, each 5 cm (2 in) long. The keel of the flowers is laden with honey which attracts birds to the garden. Now almost extinct in its native New Zealand, where it was first cultivated by the Maoris, it has been made available by horticulturists in a number of interesting color forms.

Clitoria (fam. Papilionaceae)
Butterfly pea, pigeon wings

This genus of delightful shrubs and perennials, native to tropical regions, generally has a climbing habit. In cool and cold climates prone to frost, they are grown in a warm greenhouse or conservatory. The showy

ABOVE *Clitoria ternatea* carries rich purple-blue flowers through the warmer months.

ABOVE *Clivia nobilis*, with its narrow tubular flowers, is less often cultivated than *C. miniata*.

flowers are characteristic of the pea family. The small, alternate, pinnate leaves are mid-green on top and gray or paler green on the undersides.

CULTIVATION Under glass, grow in pots of soil-based potting compost and provide maximum light. Climbing plants will need some support. Outdoors grow in full sun with moist yet well-drained soil.Propagate from seed sown in warmth as soon as available.

CLIMATE Zone 10 and above.

SPECIES *C. cajanifolia* (syn. *C. laurifolia*), a herb to about 60 cm (24 in), is sometimes grown in tropical regions as a cover crop. It has oblong leaves, notched at the apex and pale and softly hairy on the undersides, and lilac-violet flowers. *C. ternatea*, the most commonly cultivated, is a lovely twining species to 4.5 m (15 ft). It has oblong-ovate leaves, beautiful, bright blue flowers, with greenish yellow centers, and flat, pea-like pods. It is also found in white and double-flowered forms.

Clivia (fam. Amaryllidaceae)
Kaffir lily

Suitable for growing in a shady corner or under a tree in frost-free gardens, or in an intermediate greenhouse or conservatory where frosts occur, these brightly colored South African natives produce clusters of tubular flowers in the winter, spring or summer. They grow from fleshy, bulb-like roots and have attractive, evergreen, strap-shaped leaves.

CULTIVATION Under glass, grow in pots of soil-based potting compost and allow plants to become pot bound as this increases their flowering. They like bright light. Water regularly in summer but considerably reduce watering in winter. Propagate by division in the spring.

CLIMATE Zone 10.

SPECIES *C. miniata*, to 45 cm (18 in), can be grown indoors and flowers best when it is pot bound. However, it is most useful as an understorey plant under trees where soil is often dry and filled with roots. Once established, it spreads despite the tough conditions. It produces orange-red flowers in umbels of twelve to twenty. Some clear yellow forms are now appearing in nurseries. *C. nobilis*, Cape clivia, grows to 45 cm (18 in), with longer, rather pendulous, late spring umbels, the tubular flowers colored orange and tipped with green. It is less often cultivated than *C. miniata*.

Clove (*Syzygium aromaticum*, fam. Myrtaceae)

The common name derives from the Latin clavus, a nail, and refers to the shape of the clove. The spice that gives such a distinctive flavor to apples, cakes, puddings and meats comes from the dried flower buds of the clove tree. Originally from the Moluccas, Zanzibar, Madagascar and the West Indies, it is an evergreen, to 9 m (30 ft), with bright yellow flowers. An orange studded with cloves emits a very pleasant, long-lasting fragrance and is thought to repel insects, and oil of cloves is one of the oldest remedies for toothache. The oil is simply rubbed onto the tooth or gum.

CULTIVATION The clove is not often grown in North America although it would succeed in the warmest parts of the south. In other regions grow in a warm greenhouse in a large pot or tub of soil-based potting compost.

BELOW Cloves are used whole or powdered in a range of dishes. Oil of cloves is distilled from the buds, stalks and leaves.

Provide maximum light but shade from direct sun. Pick the buds when light red and dry in the sun until they turn red-brown.

CLIMATE Zone 10 and above.

Clytostoma (fam. Bignoniaceae)
Love charm, Argentine trumpet vine

Previously included in the genus *Bignonia*, these attractive South American plants, with evergreen leaves and showy trumpet flowers, climb by means of coiled tendrils. Outside the subtropics, these plants may be deciduous.

CULTIVATION Grow in a warm greenhouse or conservatory in frost-prone climates. Use large pots or tubs filled with soil-based potting compost. Ensure maximum light, shade from direct sun and a humid atmosphere. Support of some kind will be needed for the stems. Thin out some of the oldest growth at the end of the flowering season. In frost-free climates grow outdoors in a sunny spot with well-drained, fertile soil. Propagate from semi-ripe cuttings in summer, or from seed in spring. Provide bottom heat for both.

CLIMATE Zone 10 and above.

BELOW below The vigorous growth of *Clytostoma callistegioides* will cover a large area in one growing season.

SPECIES *C. callistegioides* grows quickly and densely, producing a profusion of pale violet flowers, with darker striping in the throats, in summer. It will grow 10 m (33 ft) in a season in warm conditions.

Cobaea (fam. Cobaeaceae)
Cup and saucer vine

Only one species of this small genus of perennial climbing plants, native to Mexico, is cultivated, often as an annual. When the flower is turned upside down, the large green calyx forms a saucer for the cup-shaped bloom, hence the common name. These vines are used for covering pergolas and other garden structures and bear late summer flowers.

CULTIVATION In climates prone to frost, grow as a summer annual outdoors, or in a cool greenhouse or conservatory. Outdoors, grow in a soil enriched with compost or manure and water regularly, particularly when the plant is young. This vine prefers a sunny position. Pinch back the growing tips to produce a bushier plant. By early winter it generally looks unsightly. It is often easier to remove it rather than prune it. As propagation is easy, a new plant can be started for the next season. Grow from seed, which has been notched before sowing, and plant just under the surface of the soil.

ABOVE Newly opened flowers on *Cobaea scandens* will age to mauve or lilac.

CLIMATE Zone 9.

SPECIES *C. scandens*, a fast-growing, rampant vine, is the species most commonly grown. It produces striking flowers, 5 cm (2 in) in diameter, in creamish green, turning to lilac and purple. The form *alba* has white flowers. This species grows to at least 10 m (33 ft) in height and clings by means of tendrils.

Coccoloba (fam. Polygonaceae)

This large genus of evergreen trees and shrubs originates from tropical and subtropical America. They are not often grown outside their native country.

CULTIVATION In frost-prone climates, grow in a warm greenhouse or conservatory in pots of soil-based potting compost. Outdoors, they grow best in a fertile, sandy soil in full sun. Propagate from seed, semi-ripe cuttings or by layering.

CLIMATE Zone 10.

SPECIES *C. diversifolia*, pigeon plum, is a tall shrub, to 3 m (10 ft), with shiny, bright green leaves and spikes of pale, yellowish green flowers in summer, followed by reddish purple fruits. *C. uvifera*, sea grape, is also a small tree, but it grows taller, to about 6 m (20 ft). It has

ABOVE Sea grape, *Coccoloba uvifera*, carries long strands of small berries that will continue ripening to a deep purple or red.

heartshaped, shiny, leathery leaves and long sprays of fragrant, white flowers, followed by bunches of reddish purple, edible fruits resembling grapes. It is resistant to salt spray and wind.

Cochlospermum (fam. Bixaceae)

This genus comprises around 12 species of tropical trees and shrubs, most of which are xerophytes, plants which have adapted to extremely dry conditions. Many have underground storage tubers which enable them to survive harsh conditions; these also become deciduous through their normal dry season. Many flower when they are leafless in the dry season. They are not often grown outside their native country.

CULTIVATION In climates which are prone to frosts, grow in a warm greenhouse or conservatory as a foliage plant. Use very well drained, soil-based potting compost and provide maximum light, very little humidity, and keep dryish in the winter. If grown outdoors, they need full sun and well-drained, moderately rich soil.

ABOVE *Cochlospermum gillivraei* with bright, yellow flowers, is rare in cultivation. The flowers are similar to those of *C. religiosum.*

CLIMATE Zone 10 and above.

SPECIES *C. religiosum* (syn. *C. gossypium*), silk cotton tree, is native to Burma and India, growing 7–10 m (23–33 ft) high. It is cultivated in those countries both as a source of a commercially used gum and for the silky hairs of the fruits which are used to stuff pillows. It is also grown in several tropical countries, especially outside temples in India, as an ornamental. The bright yellow flowers generally appear on the leafless tree in the dry season.

Coconut (*Cocos nucifera,* fam. Arecaceae)

The coconut palm has become naturalized, and is cultivated, throughout tropical areas of the world. It is economically one of the world's most important plants, whole cultures depending on it for its myriad uses: housing and shelter, clothing, baskets, mats, ropes and, of course, its edible flesh, milk, oil and sugar. It is grown in plantations but does especially well in coastal areas where its tolerance for exposure to strong, salty winds is legendary. *Cocos nucifera* is a solitary trunked palm which can exceed 20 m (65 ft) in height in the tropics. The trunk is often slightly curved and topped with feather fronds. There are a

BELOW A cluster of colorful coconuts high in a palm. All parts of the coconut palm and its fruit are put to practical use.

ABOVE A dense grove of coconut palms, *Cocos nucifera*, flourishes in a tropical garden.

number of varieties selected for heavy bearing or resistance to disease. A disease known as lethal yellows is very serious as there is no control for it to date. It is not present in all parts of the world as yet.

CULTIVATION In frost-prone climates, the coconut palm is grown as a small, potted specimen in a warm greenhouse or conservatory, or used as a house plant. Grow in soil-based compost, and provide bright light (but shade from direct sun) and moderate humidity. Outdoors, grow in well-drained, humus-rich soil in full sun. Propagate from seed, which is the coconut itself. Germinate at 30°C (86°F). It may take several months to germinate.

CLIMATE Zone 10 and above.

Codiaeum (fam. Euphorbiaceae)
Croton

Native to Malaysia and Polynesia, crotons are grown for their decorative foliage. They do well outdoors in tropical and subtropical regions, as well as indoors and in glasshouses in cooler areas. Their glossy, leathery leaves are immensely variable in shape, and mostly highly colored and variegated and are good subjects for pot plants. Their flowers are quite insignificant.

CULTIVATION IIn North America, except perhaps for the extreme south, codiaeums are grown in a warm greenhouse or conservatory, or used as house plants. Grow in pots of soil-based potting compost. Provide bright light (but shade from direct sun) and high atmospheric humidity. If plants become too tall they can be cut back and will re-shoot from the older stems. Propagation is from summer cuttings or air-layering. All pruning or propagation wounds should be dusted with powdered charcoal to stop them oozing sap.

CLIMATE Zone 10 and above.

SPECIES *C. variegatum* var. *pictum*, the only species cultivated, has produced many cultivars in a myriad of colors and patterns.

BELOW A bed of mixed croton cultivars, *Codiaeum variegatum* var. *pictum*, is just as colorful as a bed of flowers.

The leaves may have combinations of red, yellow, bronze and green, and they come in different shapes and sizes, some being narrow, others broad and lobed. It is not always easy to buy named cultivars. Usually plants are bought as unnamed pot plants from garden centers and florists.

Coelogyne (fam. Orchidaceae)

Comprising around 100 species, this genus of spectacular epiphytic orchids is found growing in Southeast Asia, India and New Guinea. Most of the species produce long, dense flower sprays, either pendulous or erect, in cream, yellow or green, with brown markings. The species most commonly known in cultivation has scented, white flowers.

CULTIVATION *C. cristata* makes a good house plant. The others are best grown in an intermediate greenhouse or conservatory. The best containers are slatted wooden orchid baskets. Grow the plants in an orchid compost formulated for epiphytic orchids, which should be available from orchid nurseries. The plants need bright light but shade from direct sun, and a humid atmosphere in summer, when they should be watered regularly. Feed weekly. Keep plants dry in winter. Species from tropical climates like *C. massangeana* and *C. pandurata* need a warm greenhouse and should be kept moist all year round.

CLIMATE Zone 10 and above.

SPECIES *C. cristata*, angel orchid, the most commonly cultivated of the species, bears drooping sprays of large, pure white, fragrant flowers from winter through to spring. It is advisable to elevate the pots to enhance the superb display of flowers. *C. flaccida* also flowers from winter through to spring, with smaller blooms in rich cream or white. *C. massangeana*, a native of Thailand, Java and Borneo, has long sprays of fragrant, yellow flowers, 5 cm (2 in) in diameter, in yellow with brown shadings on the lip. *C. pandurata*, black orchid, from Borneo, produces arching sprays of fragrant, green flowers, the lip heavily veined in black.

Coffea (fam. Rubiaceae)
Coffee

This is a genus of about 40 species of trees and shrubs native to tropical Africa and the Mascarene Islands. These pretty evergreens have cream or white, scented flowers and small, two-seeded, red berries. While *C. arabica* and *C. liberica* are cultivated on a mass scale for their seeds, or coffee 'beans', gardeners generally grow them only as ornamental plants.

CULTIVATION In frost-prone climates, coffee plants are grown as foliage pot plants in an intermediate to warm greenhouse or conservatory. They are easily grown in soil-based potting compost and they relish high

BELOW The scented, white flowers of *Coelogyne cristata* are best enjoyed in raised pots, which allow the flowers to cascade.

ABOVE *Coffea arabica* makes an attractive ornamental shrub, especially in full bloom.

humidity. Propagate from seed sown in spring, or from semi-ripe cuttings in summer. Provide bottom heat for both.

CLIMATE Zone 10.

SPECIES *C. arabica*, Arabian coffee, is the main source of quality coffee. It is also a decorative garden plant. This shrub grows to 4.5 m (15 ft), with shiny, oval, dark green leaves, red fruit and fragrant, white flowers in late summer. *C. canephora*, robusta coffee, is used in the manufacture of instant coffee. *C. liberica*, Liberian coffee, produces a rather inferior coffee with a bitter flavor. It has a shrubby growth habit, to 6m (20 ft), and produces white, summer flowers and black fruit.

Colchicum (fam. Colchicaceae)

Fall crocus

This genus, mostly from Europe and Asia, is not related to the crocus, despite its common name, though the flowers are rather similar. These hardy, bulbous plants, to 30 cm (12 in) in height, produce flowers in shades of pink, lilac and purple from late summer through to fall, before the foliage appears in spring. They are often found in rock gardens and borders in cool climate gardens and also make good container plants.

CULTIVATION Fall crocus needs a well-drained, loamy soil and plenty of sun, and will flower as soon as the weather cools down. Plant the corms 7 cm (3 in) deep and about 15 cm (6 in) apart during summer. Water abundantly in dry weather once growth starts and feed in early spring. Allow foliage to mature and die off in the summer, no matter how untidy it appears.

CLIMATE There are species suited to various climatic zones.

SPECIES *C. agrippinum*, zone 5, produces lilac flowers with a distinctive checked pattern of purplish maroon. *C. autumnale*, zone 5, meadow saffron, produces masses of lavender pink flowers. 'Album' has pure white flowers. *C. byzantinum*, zone 6, comes in rose pink or purple. *C. speciosum*, zone 6, has lilacpurple flowers. A number of very good, named cultivars of various species are available, including 'Waterlily', 'The Giant' and 'Autumn Queen'.

BELOW *Colchicum* flowers appear in masses in fall, although the leaves wait until spring to emerge.

Coleonema (fam. Rutaceae)

Widely grown in mild areas, this small genus of eight evergreen, flowering shrubs originates from South Africa. The foliage is small and heath-like and the flowers have a heather-like fragrance. They make good hedges and borders, although they require clipping, and can also be grown in pots or tubs.

CULTIVATION In climates prone to regular hard frosts, grow in a cool greenhouse or conservatory. An acid potting compost is needed, together with maximum light and good ventilation. To grow outdoors, plant in well-drained, acid or neutral soil in a sunny spot. Tip prune plants regularly from their earliest stages of growth, otherwise they will become thin and straggly, but do not cut back hard as this can kill them. Prune lightly after they have flowered, around late spring, and pinch the young tips several times during summer.

CLIMATE Zone 9.

SPECIES *C. album* (syn. *Diosma alba*) is a very compact shrub growing to 1 m (3 ft). It has masses of small branches, with very small, narrow leaves and tiny, white, starry flowers, usually in spring, though they may appear at any time in the year. *C. pulchrum* is a more upright shrub growing to 1.5 m (5 ft), with much-branched, long, slender shoots and masses of tiny, pink flowers in spring and summer. A red-flowering type is available, and a dwarf form, 'Sunset Gold', has golden foliage when grown in full sun.

Coleus

(now correctly *Solenostemon*, fam. Lamiaceae)

Flame nettle, painted nettle

Of the 60 shrubby, sometimes succulent, perennials in this genus from Asia and tropical Africa, only a few are widely cultivated. *Coleus blumei* (now correctly *Solenostemon scutellarioides*) is the best known and is a popular pot plant grown for its colorful foliage. It has scores of cultivars, often with multicolored leaves. They are generally grown as annuals and are also planted out for the summer in bedding schemes.

CULTIVATION Grow in an intermediate greenhouse or conservatory or in a warm room indoors. Alternatively, plant out for the summer. Sow seeds in early spring on the

BELOW Quick-growing and easy-care *Coleus* produces a range of leaf colors to rival any flower.

BELOW *Coleonema pulchrum* makes a good hedge in the right climate, provided it is clipped little and often. In frosty areas, grow under glass.

surface of the compost and germinate at 24°C (75°F). Alternatively, propagate from softwood cuttings in spring. Under glass, grow in pots of soil-based potting compost. Provide bright light, but shade from direct sun. Plant out, if required, when frosts are over, in a sheltered position with full sun or partial shade.

CLIMATE Zone 10.

SPECIES *C. blumei*, (syn. *Solenostemon scutellarioides*) from Southeast Asia and Malaysia, has produced many cultivars, including seed-raised bedding types, in colors ranging from yellow and red to rust shades, pink, gold and purple. Often the leaves are multicolored, although there are named cultivars in single colors which are propagated from cuttings.

Coltsfoot (*Tussilago farfara*, fam. Asteraceae)

This hardy perennial is generally cultivated only by herb specialists. It is used in herbal tobacco and is reputed to relieve coughs, bronchitis and asthma. The flowers are used as an eye bath for complaints like conjunctivitis, and the leaves are rich in Vitamin C. *Tussilago farfara* has a thick, white, creeping rhizome. The yellow, spring flowers precede the leaves and are followed by a ball of down from which seeds are dispersed. The fragrant, leathery leaves are covered with down on the undersides. Often found growing wild in eastern North America, flowers are picked in early spring, leaves in summer. Gardeners generally consider coltsfoot a weed.

CULTIVATION This hardy plant will grow in any average soil but likes a cool climate.

CLIMATE Zone 5.

Columnea (fam. Gesneriaceae)

From tropical America and the West Indies, these splendid, tropical, trailing shrubs are suitable for warm climates or glasshouses.

ABOVE The name coltsfoot derives from the leaf shape. Growing wild in Europe, western Asia and North Africa, it is no longer commonly cultivated.

BELOW 'Early Bird' is an outstanding cultivar of *Columnea scandens*. Growth is compact and it has a long flowering period.

Epiphytic in nature, they are best grown in hanging baskets so that the trails of showy, tubular flowers can be displayed to advantage. The small, neat leaves have a velvety texture. In their natural habitat they are pollinated by hummingbirds.

CULTIVATION Grow in a warm greenhouse or conservatory, or in a warm room indoors. Plant in hanging baskets or pots in soilless potting compost. Provide good light (but shade from direct sun) and a humid atmosphere. Avoid overwatering. Propagate from stem tip cuttings in spring, in warm, humid conditions.

CLIMATE Zone 10 and above.

SPECIES *C. gloriosa*, column flower, grows to over 1 m (3 ft). The dense leaves are covered in purple or red hairs on top and purplish red hairs underneath. Two-lipped scarlet flowers with bright yellow throats appear in spring. *C. hirta*, growing to 1 m (3 ft), has reddish, hairy stems, very hairy leaves and reddish orange flowers. *C. microphylla*, to 1 m (3 ft), has reddish brown, hairy stems and small, round leaves clothed in green or reddish hairs. The yellow and scarlet flowers appear in spring and summer.

Colutea (fam. Papilionaceae)

Bladder senna

Mostly from southern Europe, these deciduous, flowering shrubs or small trees develop large, inflated, bladder-type pods. They have attractive, pea-like flowers and pinnate leaves. They should do well in mild and warm climates, and will tolerate coastal exposure, dry soils and pollution.

CULTIVATION Plant in an average well-drained soil in a sunny position. Propagate from seed sown in spring in a garden frame, or from semi-ripe cuttings in summer.

CLIMATE Zone 6.

ABOVE The inflated seed pods of *Colutea* x *media* make bladder senna an apt common name. The leaves are sometimes used to adulterate true senna preparations.

SPECIES *C. arborescens* grows to 4.5 m (15 ft) with bright yellow flowers over a long time in summer. *C.* x *media* grows 3 m (10 ft) in height and width, with rust-colored flowers in the summer. Pods of both become translucent as they age.

Colvillea (fam. Caesalpiniaceae)

A single-species genus, native to Madagascar, this evergreen tree is sometimes grown as a specimen in tropical areas to display its showy flowers.

BELOW Large, showy trusses of orange-red to old gold flowers deck the crown of *Colvillea racemosa* in fall or early winter.

CULTIVATION In frost-prone climates, grow in an intermediate greenhouse or conservatory. It needs bright light and shade from direct sun, and a moderately humid atmosphere. Outdoors, grow in full sun in humus-rich soil which drains freely. Water regularly throughout the growing season, with only very occasional waterings during winter.

CLIMATE Warmest parts of zone 10.

SPECIES *C. racemosa* is an upright-growing tree, 8–15 m (26–50 ft) tall, with feathery foliage on its wide-spreading branches. It has orange-scarlet flowers in long sprays through late fall to winter.

Combretum (fam. Combretaceae)

Of this extremely varied genus of tropical evergreen trees and shrubs, many are climbers. The flowers are unusual, opening from spikes of clustered, round buds to brush-type blooms, somewhat similar to those of the bottlebrush (*Callistemon* spp). The medium-sized leaves are oval in shape and can be very decorative in themselves.

CULTIVATION Grow in a warm conservatory or greenhouse in frost-prone climates, in a tub or large pot of soilless compost. These plants need

BELOW The flowers of *Combretum* species open from tight rows of buds to form flares of brush-like stamens.

bright light and a moderately humid atmosphere. After they have flowered, cut back the side shoots to three or four buds. Provide supports for the stems.

CLIMATE Zone 10.

SPECIES *C. erythrophyllum*, bush willow, is a shapely tree to 12 m (40 ft). The leaves turn red or orange in fall and winter and the flowers are a greenish white color. *C. loeflengi* is a shrubby climber to 1.5 m (5 ft) with orange and green flowers. *C. paniculatum* is a tall, prickly vine with large sprays of coral red flowers, often borne before the leaves, and pink or orange fruit, around 4 cm (1½ in) in diameter.

Comfrey

(*Symphytum officinale*, fam. Boraginaceae)

Comfrey has long been well regarded by herbalists as a medicinal herb. Since the Middle Ages, when it was called knitbone and bone-set, comfrey has been used to aid the repair of fractures and broken bones and as a poultice for swellings, bruises and sprains. Its root has been shown to contain choline and

BELOW Mostly grown as an ornamental today, comfrey was long used in herbal medicine. The leaves accelerate the making of compost.

allantoin which appear to assist the healthy proliferation of red blood cells and generally improve circulation. Today it is used externally only as most internal use has proved to be dangerous to health. Originating from the Caucasus, *Symphytum officinale* is a perennial, to 1 m (3 ft), with coarse, hairy leaves and strong stalks. Pretty, bell-shaped flowers in pendulous clusters bloom in late spring through summer in a range of colors, from cream to pink, purple, lavender and blue. Comfrey is useful to gardeners as it breaks down rapidly and helps accelerate decomposition of other plant material.

CULTIVATION This hardy plant prefers a damp, shady place. Grow from seed or propagate by root division in fall. Allow plenty of room for root growth. Comfrey tends to spread through the garden so establish a soil barrier if this proves to be a problem.

CLIMATE Zone 5 and above.

Congea (fam. Verbenaceae)

This small genus of climbing plants, native to Southeast Asia, is rarely seen in cultivation outside the tropics. One species is occasionally grown in large greenhouses, but this is mainly restricted to conservatories on large estates or botanic gardens.

CULTIVATION Grow in a warm greenhouse or conservatory in frost-prone climates. Use a soil-based potting compost. Provide maximum light but shade from direct sun. Provide supports for the stems. Prune after flowering to contain the plant. Outdoors, grow in moisture-retentive, fertile soil in full sun. Propagate from seed or semi-ripe cuttings and provide bottom heat for both.

CLIMATE Zone 10.

SPECIES *C. tomentosa*, or shower orchid, is an evergreen climber from Burma and Thailand, not related to orchids at all. From late winter

ABOVE Pink to lilac bracts of *Congea tomentosa* remain after the flowers have fallen. This spectacular vine smothers the crown of a large tree.

to spring it produces sprays of white flowers backed by violet-purple to white bracts. The stems, leaves and bracts are covered with fine, downy hairs. This vine can grow 3–5 m (10–16 ft) in cultivation but more in its native state.

Conophytum (fam. Aizoaceae)
Cone plant

There are over 80 species of these dwarf, very succulent perennials, known as 'mimicry

BELOW Quaint-looking *Conophytum bilobum* produces its yellow, daisy-like blooms in summer, the flowers appearing between the two lobes.

plants', all native to South Africa. Their small, fleshy bodies come in a variety of shapes–conical, globose, egg, heart or subcylindrical–and consist of two joined, very fat leaves. The top surface of the leaves is variable and may be convex, concave, flat and fissured, or double-lobed. The short-stalked late summer or fall flowers come in white, cream, yellow, copper, pink, orange or violet, and vary in size from 8 to 30 mm (⅓–1 in) in diameter. Some of the species flower in the evening with fragrant, white or cream blooms. New bodies are formed within the old which dry up to a papery, protective sheath for the duration of the resting period.

CULTIVATION Grow in an intermediate greenhouse or conservatory in shallow pots of well-drained, soil-based potting or cactus compost, containing plenty of grit and sand. Plants need maximum light and a dry atmosphere and must be kept completely dry from the end of spring until the middle of summer. At other times, water only moderately. Propagate from seed sown in spring or by separating and rooting the plant bodies in late summer.

CLIMATE Zone 10.

SPECIES *C. bilobum*, a two-lobed species with a slightly flattened body, branches with age, growing up to 5 cm (2 in) tall and about 2 cm (¾ in) thick. The lobes are rounded and grayish green in color, with a red edge. The yellow flowers are up to 3 cm (1 in) across. *C. calculus* has a small, round body, a flattened, chalky, grayish green surface and a small, round fissure from which arise the 12 mm (½ in) flowers, in yellow, tipped with brown. This species becomes mat-forming with age. *C. fenestratum* also forms a mat with age. Its body has a deep fissure which divides each dark olive green to brown body into two sections, joined only near the base. The top surface is glossy, flattened and marked with translucent spots, and the flowers are a pinkish purple color. *C. pictum* is reddish in color,

with a green flattened top, covered in reddish brown spots and vein-like lines. The creamy flowers bloom at night.

Conospermum (fam. Proteaceae)
Smoke bush

This genus comprises around 40 species of flowering shrubs, mostly from Western Australia. When in flower in spring, these shrubs, with their masses of pale lavender, ash gray, blue or white flowers, resemble clouds of smoke, hence their common name. They have potential for gardeners, but are not easy to cultivate. The sprays of soft, woolly, dense flowers, with their intricately branched heads, are ideal both for dried arrangements and as cut flowers. The shrubs themselves provide landscape contrast and can also be trimmed into an informal hedge. Some low-growing species make good rockery plants. As their natural habitat is mostly the sandy, coastal regions of Western Australia, they are perfect for coastal gardens as they are salt-tolerant and wind-resistant. In frost-prone climates, these shrubs are best grown in a cool greenhouse or conservatory.

CULTIVATION Under glass, grow in pots of soil-based potting compost in bright light and airy conditions. In the garden, plant in a well-

BELOW The smoke bush *Conospermum stoechadis* in its native habitat, showing its flower plumes from which the common name is derived.

drained sunny spot. Most of the species will not tolerate humid climates. Propagate from fresh seeds, which ripen in summer, and sow in a 3:1 mixture of coarse sand and peat. Alternatively, propagate from 10 cm (4 in) long tip cuttings, taken in early spring or fall. These can be slow to strike. An application of fungicide before planting is recommended to avoid damping off or wilting. Do not water too much during the summer months.

CLIMATE Zone 9.

SPECIES Few of these are available outside their native country. *C. brownii* is a very pretty shrub, with its almost oval leaves and neat umbels of white flowers with sapphire blue centers. It grows to only about 30 cm (12 in). *C. ephedroides*, another small shrub, has reed-like foliage, slender stems and clusters of bright blue flowers which are excellent when cut. *C. mitchellii*, Victorian smoke bush, grows to 3 m (10 ft), with creamy white flowers in spring. *C. triplinervium*, tree smoke bush, is reasonably easy to grow and forms a tall shrub or small tree, to 3–4 m (10–13 ft). The upright plumes of soft grayish white blooms make good cut flowers in early spring.

Conostylis (fam. Haemodoraceae)

Native to Western Australia, these mostly perennial, tufted herbs are closely related to the kangaroo paw (*Anigozanthos*) and in growth habit are similar to the Japanese iris. They have dense, terminal heads of starry flowers and narrow, flat, strappy leaves, which form thick clumps when mature. They do well in sunny, well-drained rockeries and make excellent pot plants. They are not often grown outside their native Australia.

CULTIVATION In frost-prone climates, *Conostylis* should be grown in a cool greenhouse or conservatory. To propagate, divide the spreading clumps in early fall. Grow the new plants in pots until established, then plant out in an open, well-drained, sunny spot in the

ABOVE A mound of *Conostylis setigera* viewed from above shows its starry, yellow flowers.

garden. Some of the species, particularly *C. stylidioides*, are very tolerant of salty soils. This species is propagated from its aerial roots, which are an adaptation to the sand plain and salt pan habitats in which it is sometimes found.

CLIMATE Zone 9 if the area is relatively frost-free.

SPECIES *C. aculeata* has woolly, grayish, slightly spiny leaves and dense heads of yellow flowers in spring and summer. It grows 10–30 cm (4–12 in) and makes a useful rockery plant. *C. bealiana*, a low-growing shrub to 5–15 cm (2–6 in) tall, has narrow, linear leaves and deep yellow to orange flowers in late winter. *C. setigera*, bristly cottonheads, has tough, linear leaves, with rough margins, and profuse, creamy yellow flower heads in spring. It grows 15–30 cm (6–12 in). *C. stylidioides*, mat cottonheads, is different from the other species, forming mats and spreading by its aerial roots. It grows 5–10 cm (2–4 in), producing masses of yellow, star-like, spring flowers, 10–12 mm (about ½ in) long.

Consolida (fam. Ranunculaceae)
Larkspur

This genus of 40 species of annuals from the Mediterranean east to central Asia, was at one

ABOVE Larkspurs, *Consolida* species, make lovely garden plants or cut flowers.

time grouped with *Delphinium*, but botanic variations distinguish them. One species is widely grown for garden ornament and as a cut flower.

CULTIVATION Sow directly where plants are to grow, in fall in mild areas for spring flowering, and in spring in cool zones for summer flowering. Plant in full sun with protection from strong wind. The soil should be well drained and enriched with organic matter. Give ample water once plants are growing strongly.

CLIMATE Zone 7.

SPECIES *C. ajacis* and *C. orientalis* are the parents of the many strains of garden larkspur available today. They are upright growers to over 60 cm (24 in) tall. The foliage is finely divided and decorative. The flowers may be blue, white or shades of pink through to almost red, and many are doubles. They make excellent cut flowers.

Convallaria (fam. Convallariaceae)

Lily-of-the-valley

Lily-of-the-valley is renowned for its lovely, bell-shaped flowers and delicate, haunting fragrance which is an important ingredient in the making of perfumes. It is difficult to grow in areas where the winters are not sufficiently cold. It grows to 15 cm (6 in) and produces broad, blade-like leaves.

CULTIVATION *Convallaria* does best in woodland conditions, with rich soil, semi-shade and ample moisture. Plant out the bulbs or 'pips' in early winter and top dress every year with peat or leaf mould. Under suitable conditions, these plants multiply rapidly. Indoors, lily-of-the-valley can be grown from pips gently forced into early flower. Plant the pips, with just the tips showing, in sphagnum moss. Keep in a dark, moist place for a week and water regularly. Gradually expose them to more light, then place in normal light, but not direct sun, about two weeks after planting. They will start flowering about a week later. Propagate by seed or by division of the existing clumps in spring or fall.

CLIMATE Zone 3.

SPECIES *C. majalis*, the most widely cultivated species, has tiny, pendent, white flowers. The

ABOVE The dainty, bell-like flowers of *Convallaria majalis* peep out from amongst the broad green leaves.

red berries which follow the flowers are poisonous, and quite dangerous as they are sweet enough to be tempting, especially to children. Cultivar 'Fortin's Giant' produces larger flowers; *rosea* produces pink flowers.

Convolvulus (fam. Convolvulaceae)

This large genus of twining or trailing, annual or perennial herbs sometimes have a shrubby habit. Many varieties can be as invasive as morning glory (*Ipomoea*) which it resembles, though *Convolvulus* is more delicate in appearance, the bell-shaped flowers do not open as wide and the leaves are simpler and smaller. Several species with long-flowering periods are widely grown as groundcovers.

CULTIVATION *Convolvulus* enjoys a light, well-drained soil and full or part sun. The trailing species need support or a high position from which the stems can fall. Trim back in winter to avoid it becoming invasive. Sow seed in spring. Propagate perennials and shrubs by cuttings in spring or summer.

CLIMATE Depends on species; generally, warm to cool temperate; some are frost-tender, others hardy.

BELOW *Convolvulus sabatius* (syn. *C. mauritanicus*) flowers for many months, making it an excellent groundcover or spillover plant.

SPECIES *C. cneorum*, silverbush, zone 8, is a spreading groundcover, with silky, silver gray leaves and either white or pink flowers. *C. incanus* zone 4, is a trailing perennial, growing to 15 cm (6 in), with silvery leaves and blueish white, summer flowers. *C. sabatius* (syn. *C. mauritanicus*), zone 9, is a useful, easy-care groundcover, with gray green leaves and lavender blue flowers in spring and summer. *C. tricolor*, dwarf morning glory, zone 8, is an annual, growing to 30 cm (12 in). It has rich blue flowers with white feathering and a yellow center.

Coprosma (fam. Rubiaceae)
Mirror plant

Mostly grown for their attractive glossy foliage, these evergreen shrubs or small trees are native to Southeast Asia, Australia and New Zealand. Their oval leaves are very shiny, and often variegated, the flowers are insignificant and the small, colorful fruits are pretty. Many species grow to 3 m (10 ft), less in cool temperate regions.

CULTIVATION In frost-prone climates, grow in pots of soil-based potting compost in a cool,

BELOW *Coprosma* x *kirkii* is an ideal groundcover for nature strips or courtyards as it tolerates harsh conditions.

airy greenhouse with maximum light. Coprosmas are tolerant of strong, salt-laden winds, making them perfect for coastal gardens. They do well in any type of soil, including sand. Water well in summer and prune back every year to encourage branching. Propagate from cuttings taken in spring. Strike in a sandy compost.

CLIMATE Zone 9 if the area is relatively frost-free.

SPECIES *C.* x *kirkii* is a low maintenance groundcover which may grow 30–50 cm (12–20 in) high, though often less, and spreads horizontally over a large area. Small, shiny, green leaves grow densely on stiffish stems. There is also a form with cream and green leaves. *C. repens* has glossy, rich green leaves, small white flowers and clusters of berries which change in color from green to orange. This shrub, which grows to 3 m (10 ft), makes an excellent hedge plant which can be clipped to shape. Cultivar 'Argentea' has silver-variegated leaves; 'Marble Queen's' leaves are marbled with yellow and lime green; 'Picturata' has a central yellow blotch on its leaves; 'Variegata' has a broad, yellow margin around its leaves.

Cordyline (fam. Agavaceae)
Cabbage tree

This genus comprises about 15 species which are spread throughout Australia, New Zealand and the Pacific, with one species found in tropical America. They have stiff, palm-like leaves, sometimes variegated, and panicles of mostly white flowers, though they can be lilac, blue, yellow or a reddish color. In frost-prone climates, they are grown as pot plants in a cool to warm conservatory or greenhouse, or as house plants. *C. australis* is often used in summer bedding schemes.

CULTIVATION Under glass, grow in pots of soil-based or soilless potting compost. Variegated or colored-leaved plants are best in bright light

ABOVE A deep burgundy cultivar of *Cordyline fruticosa* (syn. *C. terminalis*). It makes a good pot plant.

though shaded from direct sun, but plain green plants need maximum light. Outdoors, plants need a rich, well-drained soil and a position in partial shade or full sun. Propagate from seed sown in spring under glass, or by detaching and potting rooted suckers in spring.

CLIMATE Zone 10.

SPECIES *C. australis*, New Zealand cabbage palm, is the hardiest species and will thrive outdoors in zone 9. It is often used in summer bedding schemes in climates prone to regular hard frosts. In former times, the pith and inner root were dried and steamed, and made into a sweet porridge, and the leaves were woven into baskets by the Maoris. An attractive plant, particularly when young, it forms a rosette of leaves, up to 90 cm (36 in), and will grow to 3–4 m (10–13 ft) under appropriate conditions, branching into many heads. Sprays of creamy white flowers appear in summer, followed by blueish white berries. 'Veitchii' has bright crimson midribs and leaf bases. *C. stricta*, Australian cabbage tree, grows to 3 m (10 ft) and has long sprays of white, blue or lilac flowers. *C. fruticosa* (syn. *C. terminalis*), known as ti, from eastern Asia, grows up to 3 m (10 ft), with white, yellow or reddish flowers. However, it is mostly grown for its richly colored foliage. Many named forms are available. It is a very popular pot plant and makes a good house plant.

Coreopsis (fam. Asteraceae)

Tickseed

These hardy annuals and perennials are grown for their showy, daisy-like flowers. They do well in hot, dry spots in the garden and make excellent border plants, often growing under conditions other annuals and perennials find intolerable.

CULTIVATION These plants like full sun, but must be watered only periodically. Propagate annuals from seed sown in spring and early summer and the perennials from seed sown in spring outdoors, or in late winter under glass. Simply scatter the seed into spare corners of the garden after the soil has been dug over. If kept moist, the seed will germinate freely. Thin at seedling stage to about 20 cm (8 in) apart. The perennials can also be propagated by stem cuttings in spring or early summer, or by division of the clumps in fall.

CLIMATE There are species suited to various climatic zones.

SPECIES *C. gigantea*, zone 8, is the only succulent species. It has a tall, thick, fleshy stem to 2 m (6 ft) high, fern-like leaves, crowded at the apex, and flat-topped clusters of bright yellow flowers in summer. *C. grandiflora*, zone 7, is a clump-forming perennial which grows 50–90 cm (20–36 in) high. It flowers from spring to late summer with disc florets much darker than the surrounding rays, or petals, especially in cultivars like 'Early Sunrise'. *C. lanceolata*, zone 3, is a perennial, to around 50 cm (20 in), with bright yellow flowers in summer and fall. This species has become naturalized in many parts of the world and is often seen on roadsides and along railway lines. *C. tinctoria*, zone 3, has also become naturalized in some places. This annual produces yellow or crimson flowers, and a number of cultivars offer a range of colors from yellow and bronze through to crimson and maroon. *C. verticillata*, zone 6, has fine, feathery foliage and early summer flowers. It grows 50–80 cm (20–32 in) high.

Coriander

(*Coriandrum sativum*, fam. Apiaceae)

This pungent herb has been around for many, many centuries and is believed to be indigenous to southern Europe, though it tends to grow wild in countries where it has been introduced. It is grown both for the seed and for the leaves, both of which are used extensively in Asian and Indian curries and other meat, fish and potato dishes. Coriander has become a very popular cooking ingredient and garnish in the last decade or so. It is claimed to be an aphrodisiac and to have

BELOW *Coreopsis tinctoria*, with contrasting disc flowers at its center, is less often cultivated than other species.

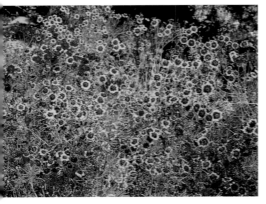

ABOVE In addition to its culinary value, flowering coriander is a decorative addition to the herb garden.

medicinal properties. Coriander has one of the most beautiful aromas of all the spices and yet the young fruit and leaves have a very offensive odor. The parsley-like leaves are bright green in color and the small seeds are oval and ridged. Terminal heads of pinkish white flowers appear from early to late summer. The plant grows to between 40 and 90 cm (16–36 in) high.

CULTIVATION Coriander grows quickly if planted in rich, well-drained soil in full sun and given plenty of water. Sow seed direct in drills in fall or spring and thin to 40 cm (16 in) between plants and between rows. Weed control is essential, especially when seedlings are very young. Seeds should be allowed to ripen on the plant before harvesting and, before removing, should be thoroughly dried. The seeds can be sun dried, but not the leaves. Store seeds in airtight containers. Some strains of coriander rapidly run to seed in warm climates.

CLIMATE Zone 7.

Cornus (fam. Cornaceae)
Dogwood

These hardy, deciduous shrubs and trees originate from temperate parts of the northern hemisphere, especially North America. American forest dogwoods are a distinctive feature in spring when in bloom, and again in fall with their foliage. Over the centuries nearly every part of these plants has been used in some way: the bark and twigs as medicine and tooth powder; the bark, with sulphate, to make ink; the wood for making tools; the roots for red dye; and the fruit as a substitute for olives.

CULTIVATION Dogwoods grow naturally in woodland environments so they prefer cool roots. They should be heavily mulched or cultivated among slow-growing shrubs or with groundcover at their base. Propagate from seed or cuttings, or by division for spreading species. Some varieties are budded or grafted on seedling stocks to ensure gold or silver variegations or particular fruit coloration. All species can be transplanted, even when quite large, except for the evergreen C. *capitata*, which cannot be successfully transplanted beyond 1.5 m (5 ft) in height. All benefit from pruning, especially those with colored stems which should be cut hard at the end of winter or in very early spring.

CLIMATE There are species suited to various climatic zones.

SPECIES C. *alba*, Tartarian dogwood, zone 3, has a wide spreading habit and grows to 3 m (10 ft) tall. The attractive, deep red winter shoots and the red, twiggy branches are the main features of this striking species. The leaves are oval in shape and the small flowers are yellowish white. C. *capitata*, zone 8, from the Himalayas, is an evergreen tree, to 16 m (52 ft), with creamy white bracts followed by large, red fruit. C. *florida*, zone 5, flowering dogwood, is a most beautiful tree in all seasons, with an abundance of large, white

ABOVE In cool climates, flowering dogwood, *Cornus species*, is a highlight of spring.

bracts (the flowers) in spring, attractive fall foliage, and red fruits in summer. It has a wide, spreading habit and grows to 12 m (40 ft) tall in its habitat, but about 6–8 m (20–26 ft) in cultivation. Var. *pluribracteata* has double pink flowers; rubra has red flowers. *C. kousa*, Japanese flowering dogwood, zone 5, grows to 6m (20 ft), with dense, deep green foliage, showy, white bracts in early summer and strawberry-like fruits, 2 cm (¾ in) in diameter. *C. mas*, cornelian cherry, zone 5, is a European tree growing to 6 m (20 ft) in height. The small, yellow flowers, borne in spring on

BELOW Pretty pink bracts surround the small flowers of pink dogwood, *Cornus florida* f. *rubra*.

bare branches, are followed by edible, red fruit. *C. nuttallii*, Pacific dogwood, zone 7, is a lovely, slender tree growing to heights of 20 m (65 ft) in its habitat, though in cultivation it is generally a tall shrub. It has cream flowers which turn pink, red or orange fruit, and red and gold fall foliage. This species can flower both in spring and fall.

Corokia (fam. Escalloniaceae)

Native to New Zealand, these hardy, evergreen shrubs have clusters of small, star-shaped, sweetly perfumed, yellow flowers, followed by yellow or red berries. Tolerant of exposed conditions and severe cold, they are mostly grown as coastal hedge plants and low groundcovers, although they also make attractive garden shrubs.

CULTIVATION These shrubs will put up with almost any conditions, including heavy shade, but are slow growing. Propagate from cuttings or from the abundant seed.

CLIMATE Zone 8.

SPECIES *C.* x *virgata* 'Cheesemanii', from species *C. buddlejoides* and *C. cotoneaster*,

ABOVE *Corokia cotoneaster* is a crowded mass of fine, tangled stems topped with yellow flowers. This has been used as a bonsai subject.

grows to 3 m (10 ft) and is an excellent seaside shrub. It has terminal clusters of yellow, starry flowers and oval, red fruits in fall. *C.* x *virgata* 'Red Wonder' has attractive, red berries in winter while 'Yellow Wonder' has yellow berries. *C. cotoneaster*, wire netting bush, to 2.5 m (8 ft), is a rounded, sparsely foliaged shrub, with twiggy branches. The bright yellow, starry flowers are borne in clusters and followed by orange or red berries. This extremely hardy shrub is salt- and frost-resistant, and can be clipped into a hedge. *C. macrocarpa*, to 6 m (20 ft), has whitish branches and leaves, yellow flowers and red berries in winter.

Coronilla (fam. Papilionaceae)
Crown vetch

Native to Europe, the Mediterranean and Asia, these dense, hardy shrubs are useful as groundcover or for controlling erosion. The perfumed, pea-shaped flowers are borne in umbels and the small leaflets are soft and feathery.

CULTIVATION *Coronilla* does well in any well-drained, sunny position. Propagate from seed sown in spring, or in fall in mild areas, or by cuttings taken in late fall. Cuttings strike quite

BELOW European crown vetch, *Coronilla varia*, is one of the prettiest of the species. It has naturalized in parts of the United States.

easily in sandy loam. These plants can be cut back hard in late winter to early spring.

CLIMATE There are species suited to various climatic zones.

SPECIES *C. emerus*, scorpion senna, zone 6, is the most popular of the species. The common name is derived from the slim, jointed seed pod which resembles a scorpion's tail. This deciduous shrub grows to 2.5 m (8 ft) and has fern-like leaves and yellow flowers, marked in red. *C. valentina*, zone 9, also quite popular, grows 1.5 m (5 ft), with blueish gray foliage and bright yellow flowers in late winter and early spring.

Correa (fam. Rutaceae)
Australian fuchsia

These dense, evergreen shrubs, mostly from the south-east of Australia, are very attractive to birds as their bell-shaped flowers are rich in honey. Many new forms are available, with lovely red and green bells flowering for an extended time.

CULTIVATION In climates prone to frosts, grow in pots in a cool, airy conservatory or green-house. They need a lime-free (acid) potting compost and maximum light. Outdoors, grow in acid to neutral, well-drained yet moisture-retentive soil, in full sun or partial shade. Propagate from semi-ripe cuttings in summer. Provide bottom heat.

CLIMATE Suitable for zone 9 if relatively frost-free.

SPECIES *C. alba* is a good sand binder and suitable for exposed, coastal conditions. This low, compact shrub grows to 1.5 m (5 ft), with white, starry, summer and fall flowers and rounded, downy leaves. *C. backhousiana*, growing to 1 m (3 ft), has dark green foliage and creamish green winter bells. *C. glabra* is a rounded shrub to 2 m (6 ft), with green winter bells and smooth, rounded leaves.

ABOVE Small, tubular, red bells appear on *Correa reflexa* over many months.

C. pulchella is a small, dainty shrub to 60 cm (24 in). Under inland conditions, it grows into an erect shrub, while on the coast it forms a spreading groundcover. It has small, bright pink to red bells in winter. *C. reflexa* grows to 2 m (6 ft), with red bells, tipped with yellow, in winter, and has produced a number of forms, including a green-flowered type and one suitable for growing in pots.

Corydalis (fam. Papaveraceae)
Fumitory

Originally from the temperate regions of the northern hemisphere, this very large group of plants comprises both annuals and perennials, most with tuberous roots. The foliage is soft and fern-like and the spurred, tubular flowers may be yellow, blue, purple or shades of pink. The intense blue forms are highly prized amongst cool-climate gardeners. They look very pretty in rockeries or borders. Some species tend to self-seed when conditions are favorable.

CULTIVATION These plants are easy to grow in any ordinary, well-drained garden soil in a sunny or partly shaded position. Propagate the annuals from seed sown directly into the garden in spring and the perennials by division of the clumps or tuber offsets in late winter to very early spring.

CLIMATE Many of the species listed below are suited to zone 6.

SPECIES *C. cava*, fumewort, is a tuberous perennial, to 20 cm (8 in), with deep rose to purple flowers. *C. lutea* is a perennial with yellow flowers over a long period. It grows to 45 cm (18 in). *C. nobilis*, a tuberous perennial, to 60 cm (24 in), produces sprays of pale yellow flowers, with darker yellow tips, and spotted with purple. *C. ochroleuca*, zone 5, is a perennial, to about 35 cm (14 in), with yellowish white flowers. *C. sempervirens*, Roman wormwood, is an annual, growing to 50 cm (20 in), with pink to purple flowers, tipped in yellow. Cultivar 'Rosea' has red flowers.

BELOW *Corydalis ochroleuca* has cream-colored flowers marked with yellow, and delightful ferny foliage.

Corylopsis (fam. Hamamelidaceae)
Winter hazel

Native to China and Japan, these hardy, deciduous shrubs bear their bell-shaped, fragrant, yellow flowers in trails along the previous season's shoots. The blunt-toothed leaves appear after the flowers in spring.

CULTIVATION *Corylopsis* needs an acid soil so it is best planted in conditions that suit rhododendrons and magnolias. Propagation is generally by layering or from seed, though cuttings taken in late spring through summer can succeed. Advanced shrubs will transplant easily during their dormant season.

CLIMATE Suited to zone 6.

SPECIES *C. glabrescens*, from Japan, is a large shrub, to 6 m (20 ft), with hairy leaves and small lemon yellow flowers in spring. *C. pauciflora*, buttercup winter hazel, is a branching shrub, to 2 m (6 ft), with early spring flowers. *C. sinensis*, from China, grows to 5 m (16 ft), with ribbed, oval, hairy leaves and lemon yellow flowers. *C. spicata*, spike winter hazel, from Japan, is one of the best garden forms. This low-growing, bushy shrub,

generally less than 2 m (6 ft) tall, has heart-shaped, grayish leaves and fragrant, pendent flowers enclosed in greenish bracts.

Corylus (fam. Corylaceae)
Hazelnut, filbert

While mostly grown for their nuts, these hardy, deciduous trees and shrubs from temperate regions of the northern hemisphere also work well as ornamentals, screens and windbreaks. Catkins produced by the male flowers and twisted branches of some species are used in floral art. Contorted hazels also make interesting bonsai specimens.

CULTIVATION Two trees are necessary for pollination and the production of nuts. Hazelnut trees are wind-pollinated so trees should be planted in blocks. Planting several different cultivars should ensure heavier cropping. Propagate by planting nut seeds, or by layers, suckers or cuttings. Layering is considered the easiest method.

CLIMATE There are species suited to various climatic zones.

SPECIES *C. avellana*, common hazel, zone 4, grows to 5 m (16 ft). Cultivar 'Aurea' has

ABOVE Cascades of yellow flowers appear on *Corylopsis sinensis* before the leaves appear, making this a choice specimen tree for cool gardens.

ABOVE Winter is the season to enjoy *Corylus avellana* 'Contorta', when its gnarled and twisted branches are not hidden by foliage.

golden leaves; 'Contorta' (syn. 'Harry Lauder's Walking Stick' or 'Crazy Filbert') has incredibly twisted branches. *C. chinensis*, Chinese hazel tree, zone 6, reaches heights of 40 m (130 ft). *C. colurna*, Turkish hazel tree, zone 4, grows to 25 m (80 ft). *C. maxima*, giant filbert tree, zone 5, is the species grown commercially, mostly in the United States. It grows to about 5 m (16 ft). Cultivar 'Purpurea' is one of the few shrubs which will grow in heavy clay and dense shade. Reaching 3–4 m in height, it has handsome, heavily veined, dark purple leaves.

Corymbia (fam. Myrtaceae)

Bloodwoods, ghost gums

Of the 113 species of Australian trees in this genus, many were formerly included in *Eucalyptus* and 33 are new species. The genus includes trees known as bloodwoods which are a major component of the flora of northern Australia and a significant component of woodland and forest floras in some more southern parts of that continent. The bloodwood group of trees is distinguished from some other eucalypts by its compound inflorescences, comprising numerous individual flowers in a dome-shaped group. The fruits (woody capsules or 'gumnuts') are generally urn-shaped, and sometimes rather large, and the bark peels off the trees in small, polygonal scales giving a tessellated appearance where it persists. The species described below are just a few of the more commonly cultivated members of this genus.

CULTIVATION. These trees are usually grown from seed, although some are now being successfully raised from cuttings taken from the lignotuber, a storage organ just below ground level. Soil type and climatic requirements vary greatly between species, but there should be a species to suit every situation and district. Numerous species are grown in California and Arizona where they are a very common sight. In climatic zones below 9–10 grow as young foliage plants in pots or tubs in a cool, airy greenhouse or conservatory.

ABOVE Extensively cultivated for its beautiful branch structure and white trunk, *Corymbia citriodora* has a light, open canopy.

CLIMATE Zone 9–10.

SPECIES Not all of these are readily available outside their native Australia. *C. calophylla* (syn. *Eucalyptus calophylla*), the marri or red gum from Western Australia, is a variable tree from 12 to 25 m (40–80 ft), with a dense canopy. It generally flowers profusely in late summer and fall with conspicuous flowers that are usually white or cream but occasionally pink. It is very attractive to birds and bees when in flower so is useful for honey production. The red gum is used for large gardens, parks and shelter belts in its native state. *C. citriodora* (syn. *E. citriodora*), lemon-scented gum, is one of the most frequently grown Australian trees. It reaches heights of 15–30 m (50–100 ft). Tall, straight, gray-white trunks and spreading, but not dense, canopies are characteristics of this tree. It is native to areas of far North Queensland but is adaptable to cultivation in a very wide range of soils and climates. The foliage is very strong smelling as it contains the essential oil citronella which is produced commercially. *C. ficifolia* (syn. *E. ficifolia*), the red flowering gum from Western Australia, is generally seen as a fairly small tree of around 7–8 m (23–26 ft) outside its habitat where it grows from 6 to 15 m (20–50 ft). Good specimens flower profusely in summer in various shades of red, orange, pink or white, but it is almost impossible to predict flower color at an immature stage. However, seed saved from strong-colored flowers will often come true to type. It does very well in areas of low humidity and low or absent summer rainfall. It makes a delightful small tree for home gardens or for street plantings. *C. maculata* (syn. *E. maculata*) is native to Queensland, New South Wales and Victoria. It is a tall tree, 20–30 m (65–100 ft) high, with a lovely trunk mottled with cream, blue and gray. Generally too large for home gardens, it is ideal for large parks or acreages. The canopy is often quite light allowing understorey plants to be grown successfully beneath it. If planted in very open situations, the crown becomes much wider and also shadier. The timber is hard and heavy with a range of commercial applications. *C. papuana* (syn. *E. papuana*), ghost gum, is native to vast areas of tropical Australia. It is well known in Central Australia where its extremely white trunk makes a startling contrast to its surrounds. Height ranges from 10 m (33 ft) to more than 15 m (50 ft). In its variety of habitats it may be associated with rocky ridges or even flat, sometimes marshy, ground. In the dry season it may be totally deciduous. This tree does not adapt to cultivation in temperate or coastal regions. The range of habitats is so diverse that seed should be collected from trees in the local area where it is to grow to ensure suitability. *C. ptychocarpa* (syn. *E. ptychocarpa*), swamp bloodwood, from Western Australia and the Northern Territory, may grow to anywhere between 8 and 15 m (26–50 ft) tall, or even more. Although the tree shape may be straggly, the floral display is outstanding. Groups of flowers may be 30 or 40 cm (12–16 in) across, often weighing down the branches. The flowers may be pink, red or white, but all are attractive to honey-eating birds. The ribbed fruit which follow the flowers are also very attractive. The leaves of this species are very large.

Corynocarpus (fam. Corynocarpaceae)

The species of this genus are native to New Guinea, north-eastern Australia and New Caledonia. The trees were probably introduced to New Zealand from Vanuata or New Caledonia. In times past, the nut-like kernels of some of the species were used as food by the Maoris and the trunks were used for building canoes.

CULTIVATION In frost-prone climates, use a warm greenhouse or conservatory. Slower-growing

ABOVE A popular form of the evergreen *Corynocarpus laevigatus* is the variegated 'Albovariegatus'. This is good for container growing under glass.

forms are suitable. Propagate from seed in spring and germinate with bottom heat. Outdoors grow in sun or partial shade.

CLIMATE This genus requires at least zone 10.

SPECIES *C. laevigatus*, karaka, is the New Zealand evergreen tree which grows to about 10 m (33 ft). It has shiny, oval leaves; long, stiff sprays of white flowers from late winter to early summer; and fleshy, plum-like, orange fruits, about 2 cm (¾ in) in diameter, in fall. Cultivar 'Albovariegatus' is a silver-variegated form. These slow-growing forms rarely grow taller than 2 m (6 ft) and are suited to container growing.

Cosmos (fam. Asteraceae)

From Mexico and Central America, these tender annuals and perennials have delicate, fern-like foliage and broad, daisy-like flowers in single or double forms. There are about 12 species in the genus. As some species are quite tall, they make excellent background plants for borders, and also provide cut flowers in a range of interesting colors. Choose freshly opened flowers, scald the bottoms of the stems in boiling water for 15 seconds, then plunge into cold water.

CULTIVATION In frost-prone climates, sow seed under glass in mid-spring, germinate with bottom heat, and plant out when frosts are over. Alternatively, sow where the plants are to flower in late spring. *Cosmos* likes a well-drained, yet moisture-retentive soil that is not too rich, and a position in full sun. It is important to remove the dead flower heads regularly as this encourages more flowers to follow. In frost-prone areas, the tubers of *C. atrosanguineus* should be lifted in fall and stored in slightly moist peat in a frost-free greenhouse over winter. Propagate from basal cuttings in spring.

CLIMATE Zone 9 for most species.

SPECIES *C. atrosanguineus*, black cosmos, is a clump-forming perennial, growing to 1 m (3 ft), with a bushy habit, dark, brownish red, summer flowers and a distinctive, chocolate aroma. *C. bipinnatus* is an erect, bushy annual, to 1 m (3 ft), producing white, rose or purple flowers in late summer. Popular cultivars of this species include 'Candystripe', 'Sea Shells' and the Sensation Series. *C. sulphureus*, yellow cosmos, grows 1 m (3 ft), with pale yellow flowers. There are several cultivars available with flowers in various shades of orange, red or yellow. Some cultivars have semi-double flowers. These all make a dazzling summer display.

Costmary

(*Tanacetum balsamita*, syn. *Chrysanthemum balsamita*, fam. Asteraceae)

Alecost

Cultivated in herb gardens throughout Europe since antiquity, this aromatic herb has balsam-scented leaves. In former times, costmary was added to ale to impart a tang, hence the adoption of the common name, alecost. The highly fragrant leaves can be used as a tea or

ABOVE Cosmos will give many months of color in the garden if spent flowers are regularly removed.

ABOVE Costmary has been grown in Europe for centuries. Today it is cultivated as an ornamental, although it is still used in folk remedies.

when roasting beef or chicken: when brewed or cooked, the mintish smelling leaves give a lemony flavor. Costmary is also used in potpourris as it enhances the perfume of other ingredients. *Tanacetum balsamita* is a perennial, with a creeping rootstock, which grows to around 1 m (3 ft). It has long, slender leaves and white ray flowers with vivid yellow centers that open only in bright sunlight. The yellow disc florets are all that most people notice.

CULTIVATION Costmary can be grown in most soils, but likes a sunny, dry location. Water in dry weather and feed in spring. Propagate by root division in spring.

CLIMATE This species can be grown in zone 6.

Cotinus (fam. Anacardiaceae)
Smoke tree

This genus comprises two or three species of deciduous shrubs or trees, with yellow wood and milky sap, grown mostly for their handsome fall color. The loose sprays of yellow flowers age to a soft gray, giving the effect of smoke plumes.

CULTIVATION Species are propagated from seed. Cultivars such as the purple-leaved forms are propagated by layering in spring. If the long stems are cut every 100 mm (4 in), and bent round in a semi-circular trench, a new plant will usually shoot from the sections. Advanced plants can be transplanted in the winter, and established plants should be pruned back in the dormant season to ensure an abundance of spring foliage.

CLIMATE Zone 5.

SPECIES *C. coggygria*, smoke bush, is a bushy, spreading shrub, growing 3–5 m (10–16 ft). The branched, hairy sprays of pale pink, late summer flowers turn smoky purple as they mature. The Purpureus Group has green leaves which take on brilliant fall color, and purple 'smoke'; 'Royal Purple' is clothed with very deep purple leaves; and 'Velvet Cloak' produces rich purple foliage which turns red-purple in fall. *C. obovatus*, American smoke tree, is among the finest of the fall foliage trees. The oval leaves change to orange, scarlet, yellow and purple, remaining on the tree for some time if protected from wind. It grows to about 10 m (33 ft) high.

BELOW The dark reddish purple foliage of a *Cotinus coggygria* cultivar will turn bright scarlet in fall.

Cotoneaster (fam. Rosaceae)

This genus comprises around 200 species of deciduous and evergreen shrubs and trees from temperate regions of the northern hemisphere. In their various forms, they make useful garden specimens, rock garden and embankment plantings, and hedges and espaliers. They have rather pretty flowers, mostly in white, and brightly colored fruit through fall into winter.

CULTIVATION Species are raised from seed sown outside in fall, but cultivars and hybrids are propagated from semi-ripe cuttings in summer. All are easily grown in most well-drained soils and are suited to full sun or partial shade. Some of the deciduous species may be semi-evergreen in mild climates.

CLIMATE There are species suited to various climatic zones.

SPECIES *C. conspicuus*, zone 6, is a twiggy, evergreen shrub, 1–2 m (3–6 ft) tall, with arched, spreading branches. It produces white flowers with red anthers and masses of brilliant red fruits from late summer through to fall. *C. franchettii*, zone 6, is a pretty, evergreen shrub, to 3 m (10 ft), with silvery gray leaves. It produces white to pink flowers in early summer and brilliant orange-red fruits which last into winter. *C. frigidus*, Himalayan tree cotoneaster, zone 7, is a very beautiful, deciduous or semi-evergreen tree to 6–8 m (20–26 ft), with abundant sprays of red fruit. *C. glaucophyllus*, zone 7, is a low-branching, evergreen shrub, to 3 m (10 ft) or more, with orange fruits. *C. horizontalis*, zone 4, a deciduous shrub, to 1 m (3 ft), is useful for covering walls where little support is available. Its branches have a distinctive, herringbone pattern, its fine foliage turns a range of fall colors and its berries are colored red. *C. lacteus*, zone 6, a tall, evergreen shrub, growing to around 4 m (13 ft), has large leaves and large bunches of red fruits late in the season. Another choice for the tops of walls and embankments is *C. microphyllus*, zone 7. An evergreen which grows to 1 m (3 ft) tall and spreads to 3 m (10 ft) wide, it produces red fruits from the late summer through to winter. *C. pannosus*, zone 7, an evergreen or semi-evergreen growing to 3 m (10 ft), has tangled, wiry branches and dull red fruits, which turn to a deeper red. *C. salicifolius*, zone 6, an evergreen or semi-evergreen species, to 4 m (13 ft), makes an attractive hedge plant and can be trimmed to shape. It has masses of bright red fruits that last well into winter.

ABOVE *Cotoneaster horizontalis* can be seen at its best trailing over a bank or a wall.

Cotyledon (fam. Crassulaceae)

Native to Africa, this disparate genus of succulents, comprising mostly shrublets, form clumps with age. Crowded, spiralling branches, thick, fleshy foliage and terminal inflorescences characterize this genus. The leaves are arranged in pairs, and the flowers are mostly bell-shaped, with reflexed petals and yellowish, orange or red, or occasionally violet. The foliage is sometimes deciduous in what is the dormant season for that species.

ABOVE *Cotyledon orbiculata*, with its silvery gray leaves, should have protection from rain.

CULTIVATION In frost-prone climates, cotyledons are grown in pots in an intermediate greenhouse or conservatory, or as house plants. Grow in well-drained cactus compost, available from garden centers, and provide maximum light but shade from direct sun. Do not wet the foliage and keep the plants dry in winter. Propagate from seed or from stem cuttings.

CLIMATE Zone 10.

SPECIES *C. buchholziana*, from Cape Province, a low-growing species, has grayish green stems and red scales on the younger twigs. The deciduous leaves are linear, thickened and grooved and the flowers are a reddish brown on the outside. *C. macrantha* grows 30–80 cm (12–32 in). It is a robust, branching plant, with large, thick, almost round, glossy green leaves with red margins. Pendulous, bell-shaped, bright red flowers appear in abundance in summer and fall, lasting for about a week. *C. orbiculata*, growing to 80 cm (32 in), has

leaves that are thickly coated with a white, waxy bloom. Var. *oblonga* has thick, wavy-edged leaves, frosted white; oophylla, a lovely miniature, has thick, egg-shaped, downy leaves.

Couroupita (fam. Lecythidaceae)
Cannon-ball tree

Most of the species of this small genus of trees native to tropical America are rarely grown outside their countries of origin. One species from Guyana is cultivated, though mainly in botanic gardens and parks.

CULTIVATION The canon-ball tree is rarely grown in North America, but it is sometimes planted in the warmest parts of Florida. Where it can be grown outdoors, it does best in well-drained soil, heavily enriched with organic matter, in full sun or partial shade. Propagate from seed.

CLIMATE Warmest parts of zone 10.

ABOVE The cannon-ball tree, *Couroupita guianensis*, is an extraordinary sight with its burden of heavy, round, velvety fruits.

SPECIES *C. guianensis*, the cannonball tree, is at least partly deciduous and may grow to over 35 m (115 ft). An extraordinary sight in flower, the tree trunk is decked with orange-scarlet to pink flowers with prominent and unusual, skewed stamens. The flowers exude a strong fragrance. The large brown fruits, the cannon balls, which follow the blooms, are arrayed up and down the tree trunk, too. The fruits are rather evil-smelling and represent a real hazard for passers-by as they can fall without warning when they have ripened.

Craspedia (fam. Asteraceae)
Billy buttons

Native to Australia and New Zealand, these annual and perennial herbs, with their round, yellow flower heads, look very pretty growing en masse in the garden. They also make unusual pot plants. The white, woolly foliage of the alpine species provides an attractive landscape feature. The alpine species can be quite demanding in their requirements.

CULTIVATION Most species like a moist but well-drained, sunny position in the garden. They produce an abundance of seed which can be sown under glass with bottom heat in spring. Perennial species can be divided in spring.

ABOVE Billy buttons, *Craspedia uniflora*, is a cheerful little plant to brighten the garden. The plant flowers profusely in summer.

CLIMATE Zone 8 for most species.

SPECIES These are not always easy to obtain in the US. *C. chrysantha*, golden billy buttons, has white foliage and round, velvety, yellow flower heads, with brownish bracts. *C. globosa*, drumsticks, is a bushy perennial, with silvery gray foliage and round, yellow flower heads. *C. uniflora* is a perennial found both in Australia and New Zealand. It has woolly, greenish white foliage and single, button-like flowers in summer, ranging in color from white in alpine areas of New Zealand to yellow and orange.

Crassula (fam. Crassulaceae)

This large genus of succulents comprises around 300 species, mostly from tropical and South Africa, though some are found in tropical America and Madagascar. They range in size from tiny succulents to large shrubs. The leaves are mostly stemless, and often joined at the base; sometimes they clasp and surround the stem. Usually very small, the flowers are borne in a terminal, flat cluster, and range in color from white and pink to yellow, greenish and bright red. Some species have tuberous roots.

ABOVE The pale pink flowers of *Crassula arborescens* look delicate against the large, fleshy leaves.

CULTIVATION In frost-prone climates, these succulents are grown in an intermediate greenhouse or conservatory, or as house plants. Grow them in pots of well-drained cactus compost in maximum light with a dry atmosphere. Keep the compost only slightly moist in winter. Water normally at other times. Propagate from seed, stem or leaf cuttings in the spring.

CLIMATE Zone 10.

SPECIES *C. arborescens*, silver jade plant, makes a good pot plant. It grows to 3 m (10 ft) tall, with flat, fleshy, rounded, grayish green leaves with red margins. The starry flowers are pale pink but do not last for long. *C. ovata* is similar to *C. arborescens*, but smaller, and it has shiny, dark green, rather oblique leaves and whitish pink flowers. *C. schmidtii* is a small, hairy, mat-forming species, with rosettes of linear, fleshy green leaves which are spotted in red. The leaves are red on the undersides and the flowers are a deep pinkish red.

Crataegus (fam. Rosaceae)
Hawthorn

Native to temperate areas of Europe, Asia and North America, this large genus comprises about 200 species of smallish, deciduous trees or shrubs, usually with clusters of pretty, white blossoms, red fruits and brightly colored fall foliage. Most of the species have long, sharp thorns. They are popular ornamentals and street trees and are very attractive to birds. Traditionally they were used as hedges and living fences, tolerating very exposed sites.

CULTIVATION Hawthorns are very hardy trees, best suited to cool climates and open, sunny situations. Propagate from seed which may take 18 months to germinate. Ripe fruits or seeds should be stratified in sand outdoors, and allowed to weather. The seeds should be cleaned of flesh and skin, then sown normally. Cultivars must be grafted or budded on to seedling stocks. Fairly large specimens can be

ABOVE 'Paul's Scarlet', a cultivar of *Crataegus laevigata*, flowers in mid to late spring..

transplanted in winter. Crataegus are particularly suitable for shallow chalky soils, although they will flourish in any soil, provided it is well drained.

CLIMATE All of the species listed here are suited to zone 5.

SPECIES *C. crus-galli*, cockspur thorn, is a very hardy, small, flat-topped tree to 10 m (33 ft). It has long, curving thorns and red fruits that persist well after the leaves turn red in fall. *C.* x *lavallei*, French hawthorn, is grown for its beautiful fall color. It has 5 cm (2 in) long thorns, glossy green leaves, partly serrated around the edges, and white flowers with red stamens. It grows to 6 m (20 ft). *C. laevigata*, English hawthorn, is a small shrubby tree, native to Europe, which grows to 8 m (26 ft). It has produced many cultivars, including 'Paul's Scarlet' with double, crimson flowers. 'Plena' has double, white flowers; 'Rosea Flore Pleno' has double, pink flowers. *C. phaenopyrum*, Washington thorn, is a striking tree, to 10 m (33 ft), with sharp thorns, maple-like leaves which turn scarlet and orange in fall, small, crimson, persistent fruit and clusters of fragrant, white, midsummer flowers.

Cress (fam. Brassicaceae)

There are various types of cress, all of which are grown for their edible leaves and used in salads, sandwiches, soups and stews. Some have a peppery or spicy flavor.

CULTIVATION *Barbarea verna* is propagated from seed sown direct in early spring and fall. The tufts of leaves should be harvested four or five weeks later. If left, the plant will sprout again in the following year. For *Lepidium sativum*, sow seed direct in drills at any time of year, except in cool areas, where it should be grown outdoors only in the warmer months. Dig in a complete fertilizer prior to sowing. Space plants 30 cm (12 in) apart in semi-shade. Water well during dry periods and harvest when the plants are a few centimetres high. If planting with mustard, sow the cress a few days earlier to allow for the longer growing time. *Nasturtium officinale* seed should be sown in troughs in spring or fall, or in trenches

ABOVE More familiar at seedling stage, garden cress (*Lepidium sativum*), if uncut, will grow 25–40 cm (10–16 in) high.

filled with rich potting mix or humus-rich soil. Water cress requires a semi-shaded position. Soak well before planting and water heavily as needed. Never allow the water to become stagnant. Alternatively, water cress can be propagated by root division. Cut leaves as required; the more the leaves are cut, the more the plant branches out.

CLIMATE Zone 6.

SPECIES *Barbarea verna*, land cress or winter cress, is sometimes mistaken for water cress. A biennial that is mostly treated as an annual in cultivation, it is grown for its edible leaves and stems which have a hot, spicy flavor. *Lepidium sativum*, known as garden cress, originates from northern Africa and western Asia but has become naturalized in North America. It is a fast-growing, hardy annual with an upright growth habit. The edible, parsley-like leaves are rich in iron and vitamins, and are used in salads, sandwiches, soups and stews. It grows to 30 cm (12 in). *Nasturtium officinale*, water cress, is a perennial herbaceous plant found growing along the banks of shallow, slow-moving, fresh water streams. Its leaves have a peppery flavor, adding a tang to stuffings, soups and stews.

Crinodendron (fam. Elaeocarpaceae)
Chilean lantern tree

From temperate parts of South America, this small genus of attractive, evergreen trees and shrubs need sheltered woodland conditions to thrive. They have glossy, dark green leaves and striking, urn-shaped, flowers which may be red or white.

CULTIVATION These trees do best in a cool climate in a slightly acid soil. They can be grown in sun or partial shade. Crinodendrons grow well in conditions that suit azaleas and rhododendrons. As they like cool roots, the roots should be shaded by other plants or heavily mulched. Propagate by cuttings taken in late summer or fall, or from seed.

ABOVE Looking rather like a Christmas tree, the stiff branches of *Crinodendron hookerianum* are decked with pretty, lantern-like, red flowers.

CLIMATE Zone 8.

SPECIES *C. hookerianum*, Chilean lantern tree, is a tall shrub or small tree growing to about 8 m (26 ft). It has narrow, shiny, dark green, lance-shaped leaves, toothed and veined, and small, pendulous bells of rich crimson flowers. In cool climates, these should be carried from late spring through summer. *C. patagua*, to 14 m (46 ft), is easy to grow and can tolerate drier conditions. It has narrow, ovate leaves and white, cup-shaped flowers.

Crinum (fam. Amaryllidaceae)

Native to tropical and warm climates around the world, these bulbous plants are similar to *Amaryllis* and *Hippeastrum*. While known as lilies, they do not belong to the lily family. These clump-forming plants are very easy to grow and their pretty flowers come in white, pink or red.

CULTIVATION Crinums like rich soil and moisture during their growing period, but require no

ABOVE *Crinum x powellii*, most often seen in its pink form, has scented flowers that last well when cut.

water during their semi-dormant, winter period. Bulbs must be planted with at least two-thirds of the bulb above soil level. In climates prone to hard frosts, grow in pots in a cool greenhouse or conservatory. Propagate by offsets from bulbs or by division of the clumps.

CLIMATE Zone 9 for most species.

SPECIES *C. asiaticum* var. *sinica*, from China, has thick, strappy leaves and flowers comprised of a green tube and white segments. It grows to 1 m (3 ft). *C. bulbispermum*, a South African species, has narrow, glossy leaves and white or pink, funnel-shaped flowers in summer. *C. moorei*, a popular species, is larger than *C. bulbispermum* and has pink or white flowers. Var. *album* has white flowers. *C. x powellii*, zone 7, a hybrid, grows to 60 cm (24 in) in height, with pink to rose flowers. It blooms from the late summer into the fall.

Crocosmia (fam. Iridaceae)

This genus of cormous plants from South Africa has tall, grassy, arching or upright leaves and, in summer, spikes of usually brilliantly colored flowers. They are popular for mixed borders and they also make good cut flowers.

CULTIVATION All of the species are hardy, the montbretias especially so. Plant corms in the early spring, 8 cm (3 in) apart and 6 cm (2½ in) deep, in a well-drained, sandy loam in a sunny position. They can be left to form clumps but it is best to divide them about every three years. *Crocosmia* can also be propagated from seed, though montbretia seed, which does not come true, is used in the main for the production of new varieties.

CLIMATE All of the following species are suited to zone 7.

SPECIES *C. aurea*, coppertip, which grows to 1.2 m (4 ft), has sword-shaped leaves and yellow flowers which turn a reddish color. *C. x crocosmiiflora*, montbretia, grows to 1 m (3 ft) or more, and has large, bright orange-red to yellow flower spikes. However, it has become a weed in many areas (particularly so in warm, temperate climates) and must be controlled where it may cause problems. Cultivar 'Emily McKenzie' has large, orange-red flowers with brown markings; 'Jackanapes' is a popular cultivar having bicolored flowers in orange-red and yellow; 'Golden Fleece' (syn. 'Gerbe d'Or') has lemon-yellow flowers; vigorous 'Lucifer' grows to over 1 m (3 ft) high and produces rich tomato red flowers; and 'Rheingold' (syn. 'Golden Glory') has pure yellow flowers. Some of these cultivars may not be available. Consult a good mail-order bulb or perennials catalogue. *C. masoniorum*, growing to a height of 1 m (3 ft), produces tangerine flowers.

Crocus (fam. Iridaceae)

These pretty corms bloom either in fall, winter or spring in a large range of colors including white, yellow or lilac. The flowers are shaped like goblets and the leaves are grass-like, with a single, white stripe down the center. Many garden hybrids have also been developed, these being mostly of Dutch origin. Commercial saffron used for color and flavoring, particularly in Indian dishes, comes from the dried red-yellow-orange stigmas of *Crocus sativus*. Saffron is the most costly spice in the world; 75,000 flowers are required to make 30 grams (1 oz) of pure saffron.

BELOW Fall-flowering *Crocus serotinus* subsp. *salzmannii*, a Spanish species, is worth trying in warmer areas.

ABOVE Scarlet-orange flowers on a *Crocosmia* hybrid give a long display on a trouble-free plant.

CULTIVATION Crocuses thrive in a light, rich, well-drained soil in full sun, but they will also grow in most soils and in partial shade. They are suitable for planting amongst grasses, in rockeries or in pots. Plant the corms about 8 cm (3 in) deep, with a similar distance between plants, in the late summer for fall-flowering kinds, and in the fall for the winter- and spring-flowering crocuses. Leave undisturbed unless they become congested. Corms can be lifted when the foliage dies down. They can be grown from seed sown in fall, but they will generally take two to three years to produce flowers.

CLIMATE There are crocuses suited to various climatic zones.

SPECIES (flowering in fall) *C. kotschyanus*, zone 5, to 8 cm (3 in), has rosy purple flowers. *C. serotinus* subsp. *salzmannii*, zone 6, to 6 cm (2½ in), has silvery lilac flowers. *C. sativus*, saffron, zone 6, to 12 cm (5 in), produces purple-based, lilac flowers with long, brightly colored stigmas. It is worth trying in warmer areas. *C. speciosus*, zone 4, grows to 12 cm (5 in), with bright lilac flowers, feathered with purple. Cultivar 'Albus' produces white flowers and scarlet stigmas; 'Cassiope' has blue flowers, with yellow at the petal base; and 'Oxonian' has deep violet-blue flowers.

SPECIES (late winter-flowering) *C. biflorus*, Scotch crocus, zone 4, grows to 10 cm (4 in), with white to lilac flowers. In some areas this particular species flowers in the spring. *C. chrysanthus*, zone 4, growing 5–8 cm (2–3 in), generally produces yellow flowers, but they can vary from white to lilac. Numerous choice cultivars are available, including 'E. A. Bowles', with rich yellow flowers; 'Snow Bunting', with white flowers; 'Blue Pearl' and 'Cream Beauty'. *C. imperati*, zone 7, grows to 8 cm (3 in). Its flowers are colored purple on the inside and fawn on the outside, with purple feathering. *C. tommasinianus*, zone 5, one of the more easily cultivated species, grows

6–8 cm (2½–3 in). Its flowers are lavender on the inside and pale gray on the outside. Cultivars include 'Barr's Purple' and 'Ruby Giant'.

SPECIES (flowering in spring) *C. vernus*, Dutch crocus, zone 4, is a variable species, growing to 8 cm (3 in), bearing white to purple flowers which are sometimes feathered. It does particularly well in rock gardens or under deciduous trees. Cultivars of the large Dutch crocuses will grow to 12 cm (5 in) and they flower early in the season. The cultivars include 'Jeanne d'Arc', with white flowers, purple at the base; 'Little Dorrit', with silvery blue flowers; 'Pickwick', with silvery blue flowers which are striped in deep lilac; 'Queen of the Blues', with lavender flowers which are purple at the base; and the cultivar 'Remembrance' which produces violet flowers.

Crossandra (fam. Acanthaceae)

The leaves of this tropical genus are either opposite or whorled and the large, tubular, red or yellow flowers are borne profusely in bracted spikes. In cool and cold climates, grow in pots or tubs in a warm greenhouse or conservatory.

ABOVE The pale apricot to orange flowers on *Crossandra infundibuliformis* are very appealing. Once popular as a potted plant, it is less often seen now.

CULTIVATION Under glass, grow in pots of soil-based or soilless potting compost. Provide maximum light but shade from strong sun. Ensure a humid atmosphere. Propagate from semi-ripe cuttings in summer. Pinch out growing tips of young plants to ensure bushy specimens.

CLIMATE At least zone 10.

SPECIES *C. infundibuliformis* is a shrubby plant growing to 1 m (3 ft), with spikes of fan-shaped, orange or orange-pink flowers which may appear at any time during the year.

Crotalaria (fam. Papilionaceae)

Rattle-box, bird flower

The common name given to this genus of plants derives from the Greek crotalum, a castanet or rattle, and refers to the rattling of the seeds when the inflated pods are shaken. Mostly from tropical regions, this large genus

ABOVE *Crotalaria agatiflora* is known as the canary bird bush in some parts of the world.

consists of annuals, perennials and shrubs from Africa and Madagascar, but extending to many other parts of the world. They have simple or pinnate leaves and pea-shaped flowers, generally in racemes, the flowers often resembling birds perched on twigs. Their long flowering period and unusual blooms make them a very popular choice for the greenhouse or conservatory.

CULTIVATION In frost-prone climates, grow plants in pots in an airy, intermediate greenhouse or conservatory. Use soil-based potting compost, and provide maximum light but shade from direct sun. Prune back lightly after flowering to restrict size and maintain a good shape. Propagate from seed sown in spring, or from semi-ripe cuttings in summer, both with bottom heat.

CLIMATE At least zone 10.

SPECIES Not all these species are available in the US. *C. agatiflora*, a popular species, is an open, evergreen shrub, 2–3 m (6–10 ft) high, with terminal sprays of greenish yellow flowers, tipped in brownish purple, in summer. *C. cunninghamii*, parrot plant, an Australian native shrub, grows to 90 cm (36 in), with grayish, hairy leaves and bird-like green flowers. *C. laburnifolia*, Queensland bird flower, grows to 3 m (10 ft). The yellowish green flowers, borne in terminal sprays, look like birds attached to the stems by their beaks. *C. spectabilis* is an annual, growing to around 1 m (3 ft) high. It has thick branches, entire leaves and terminal sprays of profuse purplish flowers. This species is cultivated as a fodder plant in some countries.

Crowea (fam. Rutaceae)

This genus comprises three species of compact, evergreen shrubs, all native to Australia, which will often spot flower throughout much of the year, although more profusely in their major flowering period, usually throughout summer to fall.

ABOVE Some hybrid croweas like this strong pink-flowered form have more upright growth than the species.

CULTIVATION In frost-prone climates, grow in pots in a cool, airy conservatory or greenhouse. Use soil-based potting compost. Provide maximum light but shade from direct sun. After flowering cut back the old-flowered shoots fairly hard. Outdoors plants need good drainage and full sun or, in hot areas, partial shade. Propagate from semi-ripe cuttings in summer, or from seed in spring, providing bottom heat for both.

CLIMATE Zone 10.

SPECIES *C. exalata*, to 30–60 cm (12–24 in), has starry, pink flowers along the stems, through summer and fall, and lance-shaped leaves. *C. saligna*, which grows to 30–60 cm (12–24 in), has deeper pink flowers with yellow anthers. This species has the largest flowers. Foliage of all species is aromatic.

Cryptanthus (fam. Bromeliaceae)
Earth star

These dwarf plants from South America, mostly Brazil, are grown for their attractive rosettes of stiff, spiny-edged leaves which come in a variety of remarkable stripes and bandings. The insignificant white flowers are borne in a small cluster deep in the center of the rosette.

CULTIVATION *Cryptanthus* is an excellent genus of terrestrial bromeliads for the warm greenhouse or conservatory, or for an indoor terrarium. They like warm, humid conditions with bright light, but shaded from direct sun, and grow well in an open, free-draining soilless potting compost. Propagate from rooted offsets in summer. Pot them up into small pots.

CLIMATE At least zone 10.

SPECIES *C. acaulis* has wavy-edged leaves in various shades of green. 'Ruber' has reddish leaves. *C. fosterianus* has green, red and gray leaves, banded in brown. *C. zonatus*, zebra plant, is so named because its foliage looks similar to the skin of a zebra. The greenish gray leaves are banded horizontally in ivory and brown. Leaves of the cultivar 'Zebrinus' are deep gray-green, banded transversely with white.

BELOW Earth stars, *Cryptanthus* species, are best viewed from above to appreciate their subtle coloring.

Cryptomeria (fam. Taxodiaceae)

Japanese cedar

This genus of conifers, comprised of only one species native to China and Japan, is best known by its numerous cultivars. The juvenile and dwarf cultivars are among the most attractive and reliable conifers for general garden use. The species is a tall, straight-trunked tree, with brown, fibrous bark, inward-curving leaves arranged spirally on the branchlets and small, roundish cones, about 2 cm (¾ in) in diameter. It is rarely grown outside its native area where it is cultivated for its timber.

CULTIVATION Cryptomerias are best suited to cool, moist climates and they do not grow well in areas of low rainfall or exposed coastal conditions. They like a sheltered position in partial shade or full sun. They do well in any reasonable garden soil, even appearing to tolerate slightly poor drainage. The taller forms

ABOVE Although its cultivars are more commonly grown, the species *Cryptomeria japonica* is an attractive and adaptable conifer.

often exhibit tufts of dead brown foliage, which should not be cause for alarm. Propagate the species from seed and the cultivars from cuttings, which seem to take root fairly easily.

CLIMATE Cryptomerias are suitable for zone 6.

SPECIES *C. japonica*, Japanese cedar, may reach over 40 m (130 ft) in height after very many years in its native Japan. It rarely exceeds 20 m (65 ft) in cultivation, forming a broad-based, pyramidal tree, which tapers into a long, narrow crown. The foliage of young trees is often quite dense but this becomes more open as the tree matures. It is dark green to olive in color. Popular cultivars include the very dwarf 'Compressa' which occasionally grows to 1 m (3 ft) with age. It is roundish in shape, generally with a short trunk visible at the base. The branchlets are very short and dense, and the leaves are short and prickly. In cooler areas, it colors a deep reddish bronze in winter. 'Elegans', the oldest and best known cultivar, may grow 4–5 m (13–16 ft) in 10 years and may eventually reach 8–10 m (26–33 ft). It has a broad, columnar or slightly conical growth habit. The foliage is of the juvenile type, but very different from the spiky, juvenile foliage of some of the dwarf cultivars. In spring and summer, it is a dull, slightly bronzy green, but in winter it changes to a deep plum color, most pronounced in cooler climates. This cultivar is prone to storm damage as its branches are weak and brittle, so it is best grown among other trees or large shrubs. Derived from 'Elegans' are the cultivars 'Elegans Aurea', with a more compact habit and yellow-green foliage, which does not change color in winter, and 'Elegans Compacta', which grows to about 3 m (10 ft) tall and turns a bronze-brown in winter. 'Globosa Nana', the popular dwarf conifer, forms a dense, billowing mound of plain green, adult-type foliage which does not change color. Although it generally reaches about 1 m (3 ft) or less in height, it may reach 2 m (6 ft) or more with age.

Ctenanthe (fam. Marantaceae)

These evergreen, mainly Brazilian plants are grown for their foliage effects. The leaves may be patterned in silver, yellow, gray or creamy pink. They have a compact growth habit and, as they are frost-tender, are grown in a warm greenhouse or conservatory in frost-prone climates, where they are also popular as house plants.

CULTIVATION These plants grow well in pots of soilless potting compost. Provide maximum light but shade from direct sun. High humidity is recommended for best growth; in the growing season plants can be mist sprayed daily with plain water. Outdoors, they make good groundcover in a moist spot which is in partial shade. Propagate by division in spring.

CLIMATE These plants require at least zone 10.

SPECIES *C. lubbersiana*, which grows to 60 cm (24 in), is the most commonly grown of the species. It has slender, forking stems and lance-shaped, long-stalked, green leaves, variegated in yellow above and mottled with pale green below. *C. oppenheimiana*, to 1 m (3 ft), is a vigorous, clump-forming species. It produces broad leaves, light green above and purple beneath. The cultivar 'Tricolor' is variegated with cream and both light and dark shades of green.

Cucumber

(*Cucumis sativus*, fam. Cucurbitaceae)

Originally native to India, these succulent fruits are produced in a number of sizes and shapes on an annual tendril vine. They are very popular in salads and as an accompaniment with bananas and yoghurt to curries and other hot dishes. They are also popular for pickling with dill and other spices. Although some people customarily peel the skin, it is better for it not to be removed before eating, because an enzyme that aids digestion is present in this covering which helps to counter indigestion.

CULTIVATION This plant needs plenty of space in order to achieve its full potential. Cucumbers like a reasonably fertile soil, dug deeply with organic matter. Add some complete plant food

ABOVE Some cultivars of cucumber bear prolific crops of small, smooth, apple-shaped fruits.

ABOVE *Ctenanthe oppenheimiana* has broad, silver stripes on its dark green leaves.

at the same time. Make some small mounds about 1 m (3 ft) apart. Plant four to six seeds around the top of each mound. When the seeds germinate, thin out to the best three plants. Seed should be sown in spring once the soil has started to warm. As the vines grow, provide ample water and keep the weeds down. Because the plant has separate male and female flowers, crop failure can be caused by poor pollination, and to counter this problem hand pollinating may help. This is best done in the morning. Pinch off the ends of runners to encourage flowering and fruit setting. In frost-prone climates, plants can be raised in pots under glass in spring and planted out when danger of frost is over. Sow one seed per small pot. Plants are also frequently grown under glass as a summer crop in frost-prone climates. They can either be planted in a soil border or in large pots or growing bags. Plants, under glass or outside, will require some means of support–they are trained vertically. The best temperature range for cucumbers is 18°–30°C (64°–86°F). The temperature should not drop below 10°C (50°F). Seeds need a temperature of 20°C (68°F) in order to germinate.

CLIMATE Cucumber is suited to zone 10, but is grown as a summer crop in all climates.

VARIETIES *Cucumis sativus* has produced many cultivars. Some have been bred to resist mildew and other diseases. Cultivars specially bred for growing under glass (known as English greenhouse cucumbers) generally bear all-female flowers on the main stem, so the side shoots are stopped at two leaves. The hardier ridge cucumbers are suitable for growing outdoors or in garden frames in cool climates. Some cucumber cultivars have apple-shaped fruits.

Cucumber, African horned

(*Cucumis metuliferus*, fam. Cucurbitaceae)

Cucumis metuliferus has three-lobed, roughly heart-shaped leaves, with toothed margins, and

ABOVE Kiwano or African horned cucumber may be bright orange when fully ripe. The flesh is watery, with a fairly bland flavor.

spiny, oblong fruit, 7–10 cm (3–4 in) long, which turn golden yellow when they are ripe. The stems are covered with bristly hairs. This edible fruit is native to tropical and South Africa and is not widely grown in the US. It is usually eaten with a spoon straight from the shell.

CULTIVATION African horned cucumbers can be grown in the same way as ordinary cucumbers (see above). They need warm growing conditions and they will not tolerate frost. As the plants carry both male and female flowers, pollination must be carried out by hand if natural pollinators such as bees are not present. The swollen base of the female flower develops into fruit once it is fertilized.

CLIMATE Zone 10, but grown as a summer crop in all climates.

Cumquat (see Kumquat)

Cunninghamia (fam. Taxodiaceae)

China fir

Comprising two species of fir-like conifers, one from China, the other from Taiwan, *Cunninghamia* is closely related to *Cryptomeria*, but it has longer, broader, curved leaves, which taper to a sharp point. The seed cones are similar to those of *Cryptomeria*.

ABOVE Much rarer in cultivation than *Cunninghamia lanceolata*, *C. konishii*, from Taiwan, is a distinctive conifer to feature in cool gardens.

Mostly planted in parks and large gardens, these unusual trees should be more widely grown.

CULTIVATION Cunninghamias prefer deep, moisture-retentive soil with good drainage. They grow in full sun or partial shade but need shelter from hot or cold drying winds. They are good for moist climates. Propagate from seed in spring or from semi-ripe cuttings in summer, in a garden frame.

CLIMATE Cunninghamias will grow in zone 7.

SPECIES *C. lanceolata*, originating in central China, is slow growing until it reaches about 1.5 m (5 ft), and it eventually attains a height of between 10 and 20 m (33–65 ft), though in its natural habitat it grows much taller. The glossy green or brownish green foliage is very decorative. Cones containing fertile seed are sometimes produced during the juvenile phase. This species makes an imposing specimen tree. It is cultivated as a timber tree in China and Taiwan.

Cunonia (fam. Cunoniaceae)
Red alder, butter knife bush

Originally from New Caledonia and South Africa, these evergreen shrubs or trees have opposite or whorled leaves, either entire or pinnate, small flowers with four to five sepals and petals, and capsule-shaped fruit.

CULTIVATION In areas prone to frosts, grow in an intermediate greenhouse or conservatory as a foliage specimen. Best in pots of soil-based potting compost, with maximum light but shaded from direct sun. May need to prune lightly in spring to restrict size. Outdoors grow in a sunny, well-drained position. Propagate from seed in spring or semi-ripe cuttings in summer, both with basal warmth.

CLIMATE Zone 10.

SPECIES *C. capensis*, butter knife bush, from South Africa, is the only species in general cultivation. It is often only a small tree or shrub, to 4 m (13 ft), but can be tree-like and grow 12–15 m (40–50 ft) in ideal conditions. It

BELOW The dark, leathery foliage of *Cunonia capensis* is attractive in itself, even without the spikes of white, autumnal flowers.

produces 15 cm (6 in) long, white flower spikes in late fall. The long, flattish flower buds on long stalks resemble butter knives, hence the common name. Its timber is used commercially.

Cuphea (fam. Lythraceae)

Mostly from Mexico and tropical America, these frost-tender subshrubs and perennials are grown for their profuse, showy flowers and they make excellent pot plants for intermediate greenhouses and conservatories. Sometimes they are grown as annuals and bedded out for summer.

CULTIVATION Under glass, grow in pots of soil-based potting compost. Plants need bright light but shade from direct sun and a moderately humid atmosphere. Outdoors, plant in full sun or partial shade. Propagate from seed in early spring or from softwood cuttings in late spring. Both need bottom heat.

CLIMATE Zone 10.

SPECIES *C. hyssopifolia*, which grows to 60 cm (24 in), has crowded, narrow leaves and axillary flowers, with a green calyx and six purple, pink or white petals. *C. ignea*, cigar

BELOW In frost-prone climates, cupheas can be bedded out for the summer. This *Cuphea hyssopifolia* has been used to edge a formal garden.

flower, growing to 1 m (3 ft), is the most commonly cultivated species. It has a shrubby growth habit, thickening with regular pruning. The leaves are lance-shaped and the numerous, solitary flowers have a slender, bright red calyx, with a white mouth and dark ring at the end. They bloom almost all year round, but are most profuse in summer and fall.

x Cupressocyparis (fam. Cupressaceae)
Leyland cypress

The parents of this intergeneric hybrid are generally thought to be *Chamaecyparis nootkatensis* (nootka cypress) and *Cupressus macrocarpa* (Monterey cypress). Originating in Great Britain, it is widely grown there as a screen or tall hedge, and has also been grown for timber production because of its extremely vigorous growth. It combines the strong, leading shoots of the Monterey cypress with the flattened, branchlet sprays of the *Chamaecyparis*.

CULTIVATION The combination of parent species suggests that Leyland cypress thrives best in cool, humid, maritime climates. It prefers a deep, well-drained, reasonably fertile soil. It may need protection from wind when very young, but will tolerate exposed windy sites once established. Water regularly and deeply through the first two or three summers. Propagation is from semi-ripe cuttings taken in late summer and rooted in a garden frame.

CLIMATE Zone 7. They do best in cool, moist, conditions.

SPECIES Numerous cultivars of *x C. leylandii*, Leyland cypress, have been named, varying in growth habit and foliage color. All are tall trees, reaching heights of over 30 m (100 ft). However, in some regions where *x C. leylandii* has been grown for a number of years, heights rarely exceed 10 m (33 ft) or so. For a conifer, it grows fast. Cultivars include 'Castlewellan', with yellow foliage and a broad, columnar shape, widely used as

ABOVE This hedge of Leyland cypress has had an opening cut into it to include a gate.

hedging when kept to about 4 m (13 ft); 'Leighton Green', with a columnar shape and the flattened fern-like sprays typical of *Chamaecyparis*; and 'Naylor's Blue', with a narrow, columnar shape and a blue-gray tone to its foliage.

Cupressus (fam. Cupressaceae)

Cypress

This genus of around 20 species of conifers occurs in the warm temperate regions of the northern hemisphere, with the greatest number in the south-west of North America. Some species are found in the Himalayas, while *C. sempervirens* is a native of the Mediterranean and western Asia. Generally very isolated from one another geographically, they are very close in character. The cypresses are striking trees, noted for their rapid growth and robust appearance under such adverse conditions as hot, dry climates, hard soil and exposure to strong wind. They come in a variety of shapes, colors and foliage textures. Unlike the closely related *Chamaecyparis*, they have provided few, if any, dwarf cultivars.

CULTIVATION The cypresses are remarkably hardy and adaptable, so it is difficult to generalize about soil preferences. As with most conifers, they do not do well in very shallow, nutrient-deficient soils. The soil should be improved by the addition of organic matter and applied fertilizer. Most species prefer a climate with cold winters and hot summers, and a relatively dry atmosphere. They grow into very shapely trees when planted out in the open. Cypresses also thrive on exposure to wind (though for most species not salt-laden wind) and generally do not require staking if planted out when small. Pruning is not normally necessary, though cypresses can be clipped into topiary or arches. They can be easily propagated from seed; the seedlings grow extremely quickly and should be planted out when young. They will also grow from cuttings, this method being necessary for named cultivars or where a particular growth form is required. They do not strike easily from cuttings, so the use of a hormone rooting powder and a glass or plastic cover to retain humidity is recommended.

CLIMATE There are species suited to various climatic zones.

SPECIES *C. cashmeriana*, Kashmir cypress, zone 9, is one of the most beautiful of all the conifers. It is a pyramidal-shaped tree, to 30 m (100 ft), with lacy, pendulous, blue-gray foliage. This species can tolerate only very light frost and prefers a sheltered position. *C. glabra* (syn. *C. arizonica* var. *glabra*), Arizona cypress, zone 7, is a dense, column-shaped tree, to about 15 m (50 ft), broadening with age. Its most outstanding characteristic is the blue-gray color of the foliage. It has crowded, cord-like branchlets, which grow quite thickly, closely arranged leaves and reddish, flaking bark. This frost-hardy species does very well in dry regions, but can also tolerate coastal conditions. *C. funebris*, Chinese weeping cypress or mourning cypress, zone 8, a native of China, is an attractive, trouble-free tree which generally grows to

ABOVE Tightly pruned *Cupressus macrocarpa* gives complete privacy and shelter from wind.

about 15 m (50 ft) tall, with a rather short trunk and a broadly pyramidal crown. The lower limbs spread close to the ground, the small branchlets arranged in pendulous sprays. The mature tree bears an abundance of small, brown cones. *C. lusitanica*, Portuguese or Mexican cypress, zone 9, was introduced to Europe in the 16th century. Although quite variable, it can grow into a broad-headed tree up to 20 m (65 ft) tall, with gray-green foliage and slightly pendulous branch tips. The short, fine branchlets, sharp-tipped leaves and smallish, globular cones are characteristic of this attractive tree. It is a fairly fast grower and can tolerate warm conditions. Cultivar 'Glauca Pendula', a smaller tree of irregular, spreading habit, with large, weeping branches, is quite popular. *C. macrocarpa*, Monterey cypress, zone 8, is almost extinct in its native habitat around Monterey on the Californian coast, but in cultivation is known for its vigor and size, up to 25 m (80 ft). It thrives as a windbreak or shelter plant in mild to warm regions, although it can be prone to insect attack and disease in some areas. The foliage is dull green and emits a characteristic smell when it is crushed, and the shiny brown cones also vary in length. Sometimes this tree forms a straight, central trunk, with a central leader; at other

times it branches low into many large limbs, which ascend at an angle, their leading shoots eventually dominating the crown of the tree and giving it a characteristic, spiky outline. There are several golden-foliage cultivars of *C. macrocarpa* and these are more popular than the species. The best known is 'Goldcrest', which forms a narrow cone shape decked in dense, bright golden foliage. It grows to about 5 m (16 ft) in height and makes an eye-catching specimen plant in the garden. Other good golden cultivars include 'Donard Gold', with a tall, conical habit of growth; 'Golden Pillar' which also forms a narrow cone shape; 'Horizontalis Aurea', a small grower with a broad, flat habit; and 'Lutea' which forms a broad column up to 28 m (90 ft) in height, whose young foliage is yellow. *C. sempervirens*, Italian cypress or pencil pine, zone 8, is an outstanding feature of Mediterranean landscapes, having grown there since ancient times. It reaches up to 30 m (100 ft) tall, even in cultivation, and can be distinguished by its very large, pale brown cones (which appear even on young trees), its dense, dark gray-green foliage, its fine branchlets arranged in small, flattened sprays, and its dense, small, blunt-tipped leaves. It has a columnar shape, the very slender column changing with maturity to a broader outline, while *C. sempervirens* 'Stricta' is a narrow, columnar form, with dense, dark green foliage. *C. sempervirens* has given rise to few cultivars however, though 'Swanes Gold' has become popular in home gardens. It forms a narrow, tapering, dense column of light yellow or green-yellow. Though it is smaller and slower growing than the species, it can reach to heights of 6–8 m (20–26 ft). *C. torulosa*, Bhutan cypress, zone 8, originating from the Himalayas, is a variable species, especially in growth habit. It can be recognized by its bright green foliage, its long, thin, slightly curved branchlets, its crowded, overlapping scale leaves and its smallish cones, similar to those of *C. lusitanica*. The most highly valued form of this species is a densely foliaged tree, about 15 m (50 ft) tall, with a broadly based crown, often touching the ground, but narrowing higher up and tapering into a long, cone-shaped apex. Not as fast growing as some other cypresses, it is often seen in cool areas where it is long lived.

Currant (*Ribes species*, fam. Grossulariaceae)

Although originally from the temperate northern hemisphere, currants are now cultivated in most cool temperate regions of the world. The tart, edible fruit or berries of these deciduous, frost-tolerant bushes or shrubs, to about 1.5 m (5 ft), are delicious eaten fresh with cream, or made into puddings, jams and jellies.

CULTIVATION Both black currants and red currants need a rich, deep, well-drained soil, well worked before planting. They also require shelter from hot or strong winds and sufficient water during dry spells. Weed control is essential. Propagate from hardwood cuttings, planted in fall or winter. Space plants in rows 1.2 m (4 ft) apart. An alternative method of propagation is mound layering. Prune out the oldest stems each year in winter to leave plenty of young, fruit-bearing wood and to remove any dead, weak or diseased wood. Apply a complete fertilizer as new growth starts and compost or manure to increase the water-holding capacity of the soil. These plants are host to white pine blister rust, so in certain forest areas they are not allowed to be grown. Check with a nursery or county agent. Well fed, watered and protected from insect pests, they will crop well for 15 to 20 years.

CLIMATE Currants give best results in zones 6 to 8.

SPECIES All are summer fruiting. The black currant is *Ribes nigrum*, and many cultivars have been produced, particularly in Europe, classed according to time of ripening as early, mid-season and late. In the US cultivars resisant to white pine blister rust have been bred. Red and white currants are derived from *R. rubrum* and cultivars of the former are grouped under mid or late season.

Curry leaf (*Murraya koenigii*, fam. Rutaceae)

Native to India and Sri Lanka, this pungent and highly aromatic leaf is always used in

ABOVE Black currant, *Ribes nigrum*, is a plant with attractive lobed leaves, though the flowers are small. Many Ribes species are most ornamental.

ABOVE Curry leaf, *Murraya koenigii*, has attractive, highly aromatic foliage and can be grown as a pot plant under glass.

curries in regions from which it originates. Murraya koenigii forms a small tree or tall shrub, with compound leaves, clusters of small white flowers and small blackberry-like fruits. It is not commonly cultivated, except in some tropical regions.

CULTIVATION In frost-prone climates, grow as a pot plant in an intermediate greenhouse or conservatory, using soil-based potting compost. Outdoors plant in a sunny, well-drained spot. Propagate from seed sown in spring and germinated in a heated propagating case.

CLIMATE At least zone 10.

Cussonia (fam. Araliaceae)
South African cabbage tree

Valued chiefly for their handsome, lobed, pinnate leaves, this genus of evergreen shrubs and small trees originates from tropical and South Africa and the Mascarene Islands. A large cluster of greenish flower spikes protrudes above the canopy of this tree.

CULTIVATION In frost-prone climates, grow as a pot or tub plant for its foliage, in an intermediate to warm greenhouse or conservatory. Outdoors, in the right climate, cussonias like a moist, loamy soil.

CLIMATE Zone 10 at least.

SPECIES *C. paniculata*, cabbage tree, to 3–4.5 m (10–15 ft), has large, attractive, blueish green leaves, composed of up to 12 leaflets, each 30 cm (12 in) long. The long panicles of yellow flowers appear in late summer. *C. spicata*, spiked cabbage tree, is the most widely cultivated species. It grows to 6 m (20 ft), with fewer, shorter leaflets and greenish yellow flower spikes in fall. Both of these species are available in the US.

Custard apple

(*Annona reticulata, Annona squamosa* x *cherimola*, fam. Annonaceae)

These semi-deciduous trees from tropical America have large, simple leaves, attractive fleshy flowers and delicious, edible fruit. They can grow to more than 5 m (16 ft) in height. The fruits may be irregularly heart-shaped or round and warty, sometimes weighing up to 2 kg (4½ lb). The rich, custard-like flesh, containing numerous, large, brown or black seeds, is a favorite food in the tropics.

CULTIVATION In frost-prone climates *Annona* species are grown as foliage plants in an intermediate greenhouse, in large pots or tubs of soil-based potting compost. The following information applies to outdoor cultivation in mild, frost-free climates. Custard apple trees need deep, rich, alluvial, well-drained soil. They prefer a sheltered, warm aspect in areas with good rainfall. They are sensitive to cold, frost and extreme heat, which can damage

ABOVE In frost-prone climates, *Cussonia spicata* can be grown as a foliage pot plant under glass.

ABOVE The flowers of custard apple, *Annona reticulata*, are enclosed in fleshy sepals. Grafted trees bear fruit after three to seven years, depending on the variety.

new growth. Warm weather in spring and summer and cool winters are required for pollination and fruit set from mid-spring to late summer. Weed control is essential around young trees. Prune after the buds start to swell to build up a good framework. After about three years, only light pruning is necessary to encourage new fruiting wood and improve the shape of the trees. They are propagated by grafting onto rootstocks of *A. cherimola*, which is resistant to *Phytophthora* soil fungus. Plant trees 4 m (13 ft) apart within the row, with 4–6 m (13–20 ft) between rows. By running the rows from north to south the plants will receive the maximum light; if planted on undulating ground they should be planted on the contour. The fruit takes about six months to mature. Clip off the fruit, retaining a small stem on the fruit, when the skin turns a greenish cream color. It will take only a few days to ripen, ready for eating. Custard apple trees are long lived, and can produce fruit till over 30 years of age.

CLIMATE Zone 10. A dry, rather than humid, climate is preferred.

SPECIES *Annona reticulata*, sugar apple or bullock's heart, is the common custard apple of tropical gardens. It has a reddish yellow to brownish red skin and each segment of the flesh contains one brown seed. The flesh is sweet, but grainy. *Annona squamosa* x *cherimola*, Queensland custard apple, is sometimes known as 'African Pride'. This hybrid bears fruit in its third year, in fall to early winter, and is slightly more tolerant of cool weather than some other types. Considered by many to be the best of the custard apples, it has fewer seeds and delicious flesh, free from the grainy texture of some of the other varieties. Cultivar 'Pink's Mammoth' does not bear fruit until about six years old, but it does produce larger, better quality fruit which continue into midwinter.

Cyathea (Cyatheaceae)
Tree fern

There are over 600 species in this genus of handsome tree ferns, found growing naturally in cool, moist gullies in tropical and subtropical regions around the world. Some species are native to cool montane regions with frequent fog or mist and semi-permanent cloud cover. Others occur naturally in warmer regions, but often at high altitude. The trunk varies from thick to slender, depending on the

BELOW It is a delight to be able to view from above the crown of lovely fronds of *Cyathea cooperi*.

species, but is always erect. The large fronds spread and curve, and are variably divided. They all bear scales, but of varying types. The fertile fronds have round spore cases, along the leaflets on either side of the mid-veins. Stems of these tree ferns bear the scars of old fronds.

CULTIVATION In areas prone to frost, grow in a cool to warm greenhouse or conservatory. They will need a large pot or tub containing soil-based compost with added leaf mould. They need good light but shade from direct sun, and a humid atmosphere. Spray trunk and foliage with plain water in growing season. Outside, these ferns are cultivated in a similar way to other tree ferns, but individual species may have specific requirements. Generally, they like a mild to warm climate, plenty of moisture, and protection from hot sun and strong wind. Propagate from spores.

CLIMATE Zone 9, provided it is relatively frost-free.

SPECIES C. *australis,* rough tree fern, has a narrow, tall, rough trunk, which turns black with age. Both the trunk and the stems are covered in shiny brown scales. The large, light green fronds become darker when exposed to increased sunlight. When planting or transplanting this species, the roots must be kept intact. The hole into which the tree fern is to be planted should be reasonably large and the soil enriched with leaf mould. It can tolerate sun, provided its roots are kept moist. C. *cooperi,* Cooper's tree fern, from north-east and eastern areas of Australia, has a large trunk, which frequently reaches 9 m (30 ft) in maturity, with oval scars from the old stems. The fronds are large and quick growing and the stems are covered in cream scales, edged with reddish brown 'thorns'. C. *cunninghamii,* slender tree fern, is found growing naturally in the cooler southern parts of Australia. It has a slender trunk, to 6 m (20 ft), fine, tall, scaly stems, and upward-curving leaflets. This soft tree fern needs protection from frost, wind and intense sun, but will do well in cool, moist gullies.

C. *dealbata,* ponga or silver fern, is New Zealand's national emblem. The trunk, to 10 m (33 ft) tall, bears a mass of spreading fronds, colored silver-gray on the undersides. The fine stems are covered in long, brown, shiny scales. This handsome species can produce offshoots from the base. C. *medullaris,* mamakee or black tree fern, from New Zealand, is a tall species, which reaches 10 m (33 ft). The trunk is marked with the characteristic scar pattern and the fronds are large and spreading.

Cycas (fam. Cycadaceae)
Sago cycad

This important genus of cycads is widely distributed throughout tropical Australia, Africa and Asia, as well as the islands off the coast of India and in the western Pacific. Common names given to these cycads often include the word 'palm', but they are in no way related to palms. Of the 20 or so species,

BELOW A handsome specimen of *Cycas revoluta* has a male cone maturing in its center.

only *C. revoluta* is widely cultivated, with *C. media* sometimes available too. In climates which are prone to frost, they are grown as pot plants in an intermediate greenhouse or conservatory, and they also make good house plants.

CULTIVATION Under glass, grow in pots of well-drained, soil-based potting compost, with added chipped bark, in bright light but with shade from sun, and a moderately humid atmosphere. Outside, plants will thrive in well-drained but moisture-retentive soil in a position providing full sun. Propagate from offsets in spring, or from seed sown in a heated propagating case.

CLIMATE Zone 10. Warmest parts of zone 9 for *C. revoluta*

SPECIES *C. media*, a native of Australia, is generally a single-stemmed plant, 1.5–3 m (5–10 ft) tall. The stem is topped by a circle of long-stalked leaves, each about 1.5 m (5 ft) long, and the thin, flat leaflets are up to 20 cm (8 in) long and about 1 cm (⅓ in) wide. *C. revoluta*, Japanese sago palm, from southern Japan and China, is a popular ornamental and is also widely used as a bonsai subject in Japan where it has been cultivated for centuries. Although known to reach 8 m (26 ft) tall, cultivated plants are seldom taller than 2.5 m (8 ft). This fairly cold-hardy species sometimes has a branched stem, either at ground level or higher up, and densely crowded, narrow leaflets, giving the straight, upward-pointing, shiny, brownish green leaves a solid appearance.

Cyclamen (fam. Primulaceae)

Cyclamen are an enchanting group of plants, admired for their attractive, mostly marbled foliage and distinctive flowers with swept back, slightly twisted petals. Some, such as the florists' cyclamen, have large showy flowers, while many of the species have small flowers, growing only 8–10 cm (3–4 in) high. Some

ABOVE Compact forms of cyclamen can be planted as seasonal features in sheltered parts of the garden.

cyclamen flower in fall or winter, others in late winter and spring. Native to parts of Europe and countries around the Mediterranean, all share a need to be kept rather dry during their dormant period. The smaller varieties make a great show when planted in masses or drifts. The floral display is quite long-lasting and even out of flower the marbled leaves make a good ground-cover for many months of the year. Cyclamen are perfect for a lightly shaded spot under a tree, and for rock gardens and containers. In cool climates, they can be grown in more sunny areas than in warmer zones. Cyclamen blooms do not cut well. For indoor color, use potted plants of the florists' cyclamen.

CULTIVATION Cyclamen like a well-drained soil, with a high organic content, and do best beneath deciduous trees where there is some winter sun but dappled sunlight for the rest of the year. If the soil is poor, sprinkle with blood and bone or complete plant food when they begin to grow. Fertilizer can also be applied after flowering. Water well in windy or very dry weather, but check to see if the soil is dry on the surface only as overwatering will rapidly rot the tubers. Plant tubers very shallowly. The florists' cyclamen are grown in pots in a cool greenhouse or conservatory. They are usually raised from seed sown in late summer and planted so that the tops of the tubers are showing above the compost surface. Use well-drained, soil-based compost.

CLIMATE There are species suited to various climatic zones.

SPECIES *C. coum*, zone 6, flowers from late winter into spring and has largish, deep pink flowers on short stems. A white form of this species is available. Fall-flowering *C. hederifolium*, zone 6, has beautifully marbled foliage of 8–10 cm (3–4 in) length. The small, clear pink flowers protrude above the leaves. This species also has a white form. *C. persicum*, zone 9, has handsomely marbled foliage and spectacular flowers, with swept back petals, in every shade of pink and red, purple, cerise and white, as well as in bicolors. Some have a light perfume. This is the florists' cyclamen grown as a pot plant under glass or in the home. It flowers throughout the fall and winter period. *C. repandum*, zone 7, is a spring-flowering species. The foliage is a reddish color on the underside.

Cymbalaria (fam. Scrophulariaceae)

From western Europe, these creeping, herbaceous perennials can be grown as groundcover but are invariably short lived. Sometimes they are grown as potted indoor plants. They have small, lobed leaves and spurred flowers in summer.

CULTIVATION Plant in a shady spot and provide plentiful moisture. Sow seed in a normal potting mix in spring and fertilize every three months during the growth period. Good drainage is essential. Whether grown outdoors or in a pot, *Cymbalaria* is best suited to a temperate climate. Spray foliage of indoor plants with water during the growing season. *C. muralis* often appears as a volunteer, especially in cracks of walls or paving.

ABOVE This dainty, little scrambling plant, *Cymbalaria muralis*, looks pretty in hanging baskets. It may also be used as groundcover.

CLIMATE There are species suited to various climatic zones.

SPECIES *C. hepaticifolia*, a trailing species to 2.5 cm (1 in), produces purplish lilac flowers in summer. *C. muralis*, variously known as Aaron's beard, Kenilworth ivy, pennywort, ivy-leafed toadflax, mother of thousands and climbing sailor, zone 3, grows to 1 m (3 ft) and, depending on the variety, produces lilac, pink, white or blue summer flowers. It is a pretty plant but considered a weed by some.

Cymbidium (fam. Orchidaceae)

Cymbidiums are among the most widely hybridized of all orchids, with thousands of cultivars. They are widely distributed from Southeast Asia and China to the lower Himalayas and Australia. They are either terrestrial or epiphytic, and range from the large flowered, cool-growing species, to smaller flowered, warmer growing species and miniatures. The species have tufts of narrow, green leaves, with thick pseudobulbs or elongated stems, and racemes of gorgeous flowers, seldom more than 3 cm (1 in) across, in many colors, ranging from white to many shades of cream, yellow, pink, red, brown and

ABOVE This large, white cymbidium hybrid is the type often favored for wedding bouquets.

RIGHT Gold, russet and crimson are some of the stronger colors available in cymbidium hybrids.

green, or combinations of these tones. The cup-shaped petals are almost of equal size. With some species, the roots tend to penetrate into the bark or the decayed wood of hollow branches and often can grow very long. Hybrids, which are those most commonly cultivated, have long, sword-shaped leaves and large, showy blooms in a huge range of colors.

CULTIVATION Cymbidiums are grown as pot plants under glass in frost-prone climates and they also make good house plants, particularly the miniature hybrids. These orchids flower mainly during the winter and spring. Cymbidiums are mainly cool-growing orchids and can therefore be grown in a cool to intermediate greenhouse or conservatory. Indoors, they are best grown on a light windowsill in a cool room. Plants are grown in pots of orchid compost, which should be available from specialist orchid nurseries. Terrestrial or epiphytic compost is suitable. Make sure it contains some lumps of charcoal. Do not use too large a pot and ensure the compost is firmed well. During summer, the plants need maximum light but shade from direct sun, which can cause scorching of the foliage. The greenhouse or room should be well ventilated. The plants need moderate watering in summer plus feeding with a liquid fertilizer at approximately weekly or ten-day intervals. Mist spray with plain water daily or twice daily. During winter, ensure maximum light and cut down on the watering, keeping the compost only slightly moist. When the plants outgrow their pots (allow them to become pot-bound), pot on in early or mid-spring. At this time, large plants can be divided if you want to increase them. Another method of propagation is to remove the old, leafless backbulbs in spring and pot them up individually. In Mediterranean climates, cymbidium orchids are often grown in a shade house, such as a lath structure. Some growers place their plants outdoors for the summer if the weather is warm, in the dappled shade of a tree. It is important to watch out for pests, as these orchids are prone to attacks by several kinds, including red spider mites, mealybugs, whitefly and aphids.

CLIMATE Zone 9 or 10.

SPECIES *C. canaliculatum*, from northern Australia and parts of northern New South Wales, is a variable species with several recognized varieties. It has hard pseudobulbs, rough, grooved, pointed leaves and fragrant flowers which range in color from greenish yellow to reddish purple and are often spotted. Perfect drainage and good light are essential, and care should be taken not to overwater this species, especially in the winter. *C. finlaysonianum*, grown widely in Thailand, is an epiphytic type which does well in warm conditions. It produces many flowers on a drooping stalk, up to 60 cm (24 in) long, in brownish yellow, flushed with purple. *C. lowianum*, a native of Burma and northern Thailand, is one of the larger flowered, cool-growing species. It is a terrestrial type, with long, large leaves and an arching inflorescence comprised of numerous flowers in greenish yellow, streaked with brown. The lip is white with a maroon patch. *C. madidum*, from northern New South Wales and Queensland, has large pseudobulbs, thin, soft leaves and long racemes of small flowers, greenish yellow on the inside and brown outside. This species works well in pots. *C. pumilum*, from China, has produced many miniature hybrid *Cymbidium* cultivars. *C. suave*, from the coastal areas of New South Wales and Queensland, has a thick, rough stem, long, slender leaves and fragrant annual flowers, ranging from greenish yellow to greenish brown with a purple labellum.

Cynoglossum (fam. Boraginaceae)
Hound's tongue

From temperate zones, these rough-stemmed biennials and short-lived perennials have alternate, simple leaves and terminal, one-sided sprays of small blue, purple or white flowers. The foliage and stems are hairy and the fruits containing the seeds form a prickly burr which can stick to clothing or animal fur.

CULTIVATION *Cynoglossum* likes good drainage and sun, though it will tolerate poor quality

ABOVE Hound's tongue, *Cynoglossum amabile*, brings a patch of clear blue to the late summer garden.

soil. Propagate from seed, sown in fall in a garden frame for perennials, in spring in flowering positions for annuals and biennials. Perennials can also be divided in spring.

CLIMATE There are species suited to various climatic zones.

SPECIES *C. amabile*, Chinese forget-me-not, zone 7, is a biennial which grows to 60 cm (24 in), with lance-shaped or oblong leaves and small sprays of pink, blue or white flowers. Clear sky blue flowers are the most often seen. *C. nervosum*, zone 5, a perennial to 1 m (3 ft), has lance-shaped or oblong leaves and bright blue flowers.

Cyperus (fam. Cyperaceae)

One of this family of ornamental, rush-like, semi-aquatic plants was used by the ancient Egyptians to make paper. This genus comprises around 600 species of annuals and perennials, the perennials being the most commonly cultivated. They form rosettes of grass-like leaves, with terminal sprays of bisexual flowers borne in spikes, which make interesting cut

ABOVE Graceful stems of papyrus (*Cyperus papyrus*) arch out over a shallow pool. The tufted flower head is light and airy.

flowers. They do well as indoor plants or in pots in a sunny pond.

CULTIVATION In frost-prone climates, tender species are grown in an intermediate greenhouse or conservatory. Stand the pots in trays of water to keep the compost steadily moist. Outdoors, grow in the moist soil at the edges of a pool. Propagate by division in the spring.

CLIMATE Zone 10.

SPECIES *C. involucratus* (syn. *C. alternifolius*), umbrella plant, forms a rosette of grass-like leaves, crowned by a whorl of shorter leaves which look like the ribs of an umbrella. The green flower spikes appear in summer. This species requires ample moisture at the roots. *C. papyrus* is the papyrus or paper plant of ancient Egypt and may be the bulrush of the Bible. The stems of this elegant plant, which is suitable for shallow ponds, grow to 2.5 m (8 ft) and its leaves take the form of sheaths.

Cypripedium (fam. Orchidaceae)
Lady's slipper, moccasin flower

A genus of about 40 species of terrestrial orchids native to northern temperate regions, many are now rare and endangered in the wild. They grow from a slender rhizome, and have pleated leaves and flowers which are quite prominently pouched. The flowers, which are borne singly or in racemes, are usually red, pink, white or yellow, with the pouched lip in contrasting yellow, purple, pink or white. Hybrids are being actively developed from both the Asian and the North American species.

CULTIVATION These orchids need a sheltered position in dappled shade, woodland conditions and a humus-rich soil which drains well but retains a little moisture at all times. Water regularly during warm, dry weather. They can be divided with care in spring but the divisions must be replanted at once in order to avoid desiccation.

ABOVE The grossly inflated lip of this *Cypripedium* hybrid gives the flower a bizarre appearance. These orchids are popular with collectors.

CLIMATE Depends on the species grown; some are quite frost-hardy.

SPECIES *C. calceolus*, lady's slipper, zone 5, has oval, mid-green leaves and summer flowers of purple-brown with a pouched yellow lip. It may grow to about 40 cm (16 in) high and wide. *C. reginae*, zone 4, showy lady's slipper, may grow to over 70 cm (28 in) high. Its flowers which are white with a bright rose pink pouched lip, also appear in the summer.

Cyrtanthus (fam. Amaryllidaceae)

This South African genus of around 50 species of bulbous herbs produces beautiful, tubular, fragrant blooms on tall stems. The flowers are borne in drooping umbels in spring and summer in colors of red, white, salmon or pale yellow. These bulbs do well in pots and the blooms are used for long-lasting cut flowers.

CULTIVATION In frost-prone climates, *Cyrtanthus* are grown in pots in a cool to intermediate greenhouse or conservatory. Pot the bulbs when dormant, using soil-based potting compost. The neck of the bulb should be above compost level. Provide maximum light but shade from direct sun. Keep the plants barely moist when dormant, but water well in the growing period. Outdoors plant in a sunny spot with well-drained soil rich in humus. Planting depth equals twice the depth of the bulb.

CLIMATE Zone 10.

SPECIES A fairly well-known species that deserves to be more widely grown is *C. brachyscyphus*, which has 30 cm (12 in) long, bright green leaves, and clusters of tubular, red flowers in spring and summer on stems up to 30 cm (12 in) high. It is one of the hardier species and could be grown outside in a Mediterranean climate. *C. elatus* (formerly *Vallota speciosa*), Scarborough lily, has broad, strappy leaves, to 50 cm (20 in), and large, bright red, trumpet-shaped flowers in late summer to fall. 'Alba', a white-flowering form, is not often seen in cultivation. *C. mackenii*, ifafa lily, is a delightful species, well worth growing. It has 30 cm (12 in) long leaves and bears umbels of pure white flowers on stalks around 30 cm (12 in) tall. Var. *cooperi* produces umbels of five to ten yellow or cream flowers. *C. speciosa* has broad leaves, up to 60 cm (24 in) long, and produces scarlet trumpet-shaped flowers, often borne in groups of eight to ten on one 30 cm (12 in) long stem. Cultivar 'Alba' has white flowers, while 'Delicata' has salmon-pink blooms.

Cyrtomium (fam. Dryopteridaceae)

This genus of 20 species of terrestrial ferns is found from eastern Asia through to South Africa, and in Central and South America. One species in particular has become naturalized in many areas and is widely cultivated. These ferns generally have a heavily scaled, thick crown and pinnate, firm, dark green fronds, glossy on top, varying from erect to pendulous.

CULTIVATION These hardy ferns can be grown under almost any conditions. Although they prefer shade, they can tolerate some sun, unlike many other ferns. Although frost-hardy, exposed fronds can be burnt. If this occurs, cut them back for they will grow again when the weather is warmer.

BELOW Scarborough lily, *Cyrtanthus*, has several bright scarlet flowers on each stem.

ABOVE Holly fern, *Cyrtomium falcatum*, is evergreen with rather hard, dark green leaflets. It is the most popular species grown.

CLIMATE This genus is suited to growing in zone 9.

SPECIES *C. falcatum*, holly fern, is the species most commonly grown in the US. It has a short, creeping rhizome, oblong or lance-shaped fronds and glossy, dark green leaflets, paler in color on the undersides, with a spiky, holly-like appearance. The stem is smothered with large, brown scales. Both of the available cultivars, 'Butterfieldii' and 'Rochfordianum', have more intricate leaflets than the species.

Cytisus (fam. Papilionaceae)
Broom

Native to the Mediterranean and islands of the Atlantic, a number of species of this large genus of flowering, evergreen or deciduous shrubs are common in cultivation. Hardy and fast-growing, though generally short-lived, they are suitable for shrub borders and rock gardens. Their adaptability even in poor ground led to their being used in the Middle Ages as an emblem of good fortune. They have a heath-like appearance, with simple or compound leaves and terminal sprays of pretty, pea-type flowers which bloom profusely from early spring to summer, depending on species and growing conditions.
CULTIVATION These shrubs prefer a slightly acid, well-drained soil, a sunny position and a temperate climate. Provide ample water in summer if necessary. Propagate from seed sown in spring or fall in a garden frame, or from semi-ripe cuttings in mid to late summer.

CLIMATE There are species suited to various climatic zones.

SPECIES *C. multiflorus*, white Spanish broom, zone 6, grows to 3 m (10 ft), with white, axillary flowers in spring. *C.* x *praecox*, zone 5, is a semi-weeping, deciduous type, to 1.2 m (4 ft), with numerous, creamy yellow flowers along its branches in spring and has very small, silky, gray-green leaves. 'Albus' is a small variety, with rather drooping branches and white flowers. *C. scoparius*, common broom, zone 5, has been declared a noxious weed in some regions. Growing to 2 m (6 ft), it has an arching, branched habit, producing solitary, yellow flowers or axillary flowers in pairs. Many hybrids are available in a number of shades of pink, red and orange. The form andreanus has yellow and red flowers. This species and *C. multiflorus* have produced numerous cultivars, including 'Burkwoodii', 'Cornish Cream', 'Pomona', 'Lord Lambourne' and 'Lilac Time'.

BELOW In spring, this *Cytisus* species is almost smothered in bright yellow flowers.

D

Daboecia to Dysoxium

Daboecia (fam. Ericaceae)

Named after an Irish saint, these small, upright or prostrate evergreen shrubs are popular for rock gardens or the margins of pathways in cooler areas. The pretty, urn-shaped flowers may bloom for most of the year, but mainly through the summer into the fall.

CULTIVATION These shrubs like a lime-free, peaty soil and full sun. Prune to remove spent flower heads. Propagate by seed, or by cuttings of half-ripe wood.

CLIMATE Best in cool to warm temperate climates.

SPECIES *D. azorica*, zone 8, to 20 cm (8 in), produces spikes of bright rose red flowers in the summer. *D. cantabrica*, St Dabeoc's heath, zone 6, has an upright, spreading habit and grows to 60 cm (24 in). The green leaves are white on the undersides and the purplish red flowers are borne on spikes around 10 cm (4 in) long. The form alba has white flowers; 'Atropurpurea' produces deep purple-pink blooms; 'Bicolor' has purple and white blooms; and 'Praegerae' is pink.

BELOW *Daboecia* species are close relatives of heaths and heathers. Cerise pink *D. cantabrica* 'Atropurpurea' is a choice variety.

Dacrydium (fam. Podocarpaceae)

Endemic to the southern hemisphere, these conifers are mostly found in New Zealand, one is native to Australia's Tasmania and a few to Southeast Asia and the Pacific Islands. The young leaves are soft and awl-shaped, while the mature leaves are scale-like and densely crowded. In the tall species, the outer branchlets droop, producing a graceful silhouette. Male and female flowers are borne on separate trees, the males appearing as short spikes in the axils of the upper leaves and the females near the branchlet tips. Each seed is set in a cup-shaped, fleshy, mostly scarlet, base.

CULTIVATION These trees need a cool temperate climate, rich, deep soil and adequate moisture. The Huon pine tolerates some frost and light snow. Propagate from seed or from cuttings taken in fall. If growing from self-sown seedlings, make sure they are no more than 15 cm (6 in) tall when transplanting as they can be difficult to re-establish.

CLIMATE Suited to cool to warm temperate climates.

SPECIES *D. cupressinum*, New Zealand rimu, zone 9, has attractive, dark bronze-green foliage. It is slow growing, but can reach

BELOW The delicate, weeping foliage of *Dacrydium cupressinum* is an asset in any garden.

heights of 60 m (200 ft) in the wild, though seldom more than 10 m (33 ft) in cultivation. As a young tree it is very beautiful as its weeping habit is more pronounced. The timber is used in building and cabinet-making. *D. franklinii*, Huon pine, the Tasmanian species, zone 8, is a very striking tree, though not as tall as the rimu, with pendulous branches and dark green, scale-like leaves. Now quite scarce, the timber from the Huon pine is extremely beautiful and valuable, being straight-grained, soft, smooth and uncommonly durable. In the past it was used extensively for boat building and joinery, many pieces of Tasmanian antique furniture being made from this superb timber. This species is now reclassified as *Lagarostrobus franklinii*.

Dahlia (fam. Asteraceae)

This genus was discovered in the mountains of Mexico by a Spanish physician in the 17th century. In the 20th century many flower forms were developed and cultivars produced. Today it is possible to choose from decorative, cactus, pompon, paeony-flowered, waterlily, single and collarette dahlias. Dahlias therefore come in many different flower forms and in every imaginable color. Flower sizes range from tiny pompons at less than 5 cm (2 in) across, to very large blooms, 30 cm (12 in) or more wide, and they may be single, double or semi-double. Dahlia plants grow from 30 cm (12 in) to nearly 2 m (6 ft) high, while the tree dahlia can reach 5 m (16 ft) in height. Shrubby dahlias have a very long flowering period from early summer until late fall and make first-class cut flowers. Tree dahlias flower from middle to late fall.

CULTIVATION Dahlias like rich, well-drained soil, heavily enriched with manure or compost, as they are heavy feeders. They need full sun all day, with protection from strong wind. Plant dormant tubers in mid-spring, 10–15 cm (4–6 in) deep, with the neck containing the dormant buds pointing up. Spacing between plants depends on the variety. Small growers should be set 30 cm (12 in) apart, while very large

TOP Bedding dahlias grown as annuals provide many weeks of color from summer into fall.

ABOVE A fine example of the collarette dahlia with its central ring of short florets – the collar.

growers should be 75–100 cm (30–40 in) apart. Stakes and labels should be put in at planting time to avoid damaging the tubers later. Water well after planting the tubers, but further watering is usually unnecessary until after growth begins. An alternative technique is to start dormant dahlia tubers into growth in early spring in a heated greenhouse, in boxes of moist peat, and to take basal cuttings when the shoots are about 5 cm (2 in) high. Root them with bottom heat, pot up rooted cuttings individually, and plant out the young plants when frosts are over. Bedding dahlias are raised from seed sown in early spring under glass. Again they are planted out when frosts are over. Once flowering has begun, feed dahlias monthly with blood, fish and bone, or with complete plant food. A mulch of decayed animal manure will provide extra nutrients for the plants and will also help to retain soil moisture. During growing and flowering, give deep, weekly waterings. Cut flowers or dead-head regularly to prolong blooming. Tree dahlias are unsuitable for cutting. Snails love dahlia foliage and flowers so take care to control them. In frost-prone climates, fall frosts will kill off the top growth. At this stage, lift the tubers, dry them off and store in a cool, frost-free place for the winter. Bedding dahlias are discarded at the end of the season.

CLIMATE Zone 10.

VARIETIES A wide range of varieties is available from specialist growers whose details are in gardening magazines. Most garden centers carry a small range in spring.

Dais (fam. Thymelaeaceae)

Native to South Africa and Madagascar, this genus contains only two species, one of which is cultivated in the garden.

CULTIVATION Plant in a sunny, well-drained spot, with shelter from wind. Propagate from cuttings taken in midsummer.

BELOW *Dais cotinifolia* is a medium to tall shrub suitable for warm gardens.

CLIMATE Zone 9, provided the area is relatively frost-free.

SPECIES *D. cotinifolia* is an upright, partly deciduous tree, which in very warm areas may be evergreen. It grows rapidly to 5 m (16 ft), and has oval leaves and umbrella-shaped heads of mauve-pink summer flowers. It is not frost-hardy but tolerates fairly low temperatures.

Dampiera (fam. Goodeniaceae)

Named after explorer William Dampier, this genus comprises around 70 species of plants and shrubs, including many good rockery plants, most of which are native to Western Australia. The abundant fan-shaped, five-petalled flowers make a pretty display in spring and summer. The flowers range in color from light blue to purple and the attractive light green to silvery gray foliage varies in shape and size.

CULTIVATION In frost-prone climates, grow in an intermediate greenhouse or conservatory. Use soil-based potting compost and provide maximum light but shade from direct sun. Outdoors, the plants need well-drained, acid or neutral soil in sun. Propagate perennials by division in spring and shrubs by semi-ripe cuttings in summer, both under glass.

CLIMATE Zone 10.

SPECIES Few are available outside their native Australia. *D. diversifolia*, from Western Australia, is a prostrate, perennial creeper or groundcover, with dense, short, leafy branches and masses of small, purplish blue flowers in spring and summer. This species is hardy and frost-resistant, and suckers readily. *D. linearis* is a low-growing, suckering species, to 15 cm (6 in), with blueish purple flowers which bloom from winter through to summer. *D. purpurea*, from eastern Australia, is an upright, hairy shrub, to 1 m (3 ft), with purple flowers, mostly borne at the top. *D. rosmarinifolia*, mostly found in the mallee areas of South Australia, Victoria and New South Wales, forms spreading

ABOVE *Dampiera diversifolia* is the species most likely to be available. It is a good groundcover in the right climate.

ABOVE The familiar dandelion is reputed to be one of the 'bitter herbs' of the Passover mentioned in the Bible.

clumps and produces a brilliant display of bright blue flowers in spring. *D. stricta*, a native of eastern Australia, is a prostrate, perennial species, with stems to 1 m (3 ft) long and a height of 30 cm (12 in). The pale blue flowers can be sparse and not as showy as those of many other species. *D. wellsiana*, from Western Australia, is a very attractive, low-growing, spreading perennial, with spoon-shaped leaves and an abundance of mid-blue flowers, with yellow throats, in spring to early summer.

Dandelion

(*Taraxacum officinale*, fam. Asteraceae)

Known in Europe for many centuries where it is highly regarded for its nutritional and medicinal value, it is thought of by many as a common, invasive lawn and garden weed. Dandelions, however, can be controlled by lawn weed killer. Rich in vitamins, fats, proteins and other nutrients, dandelion is reputed to be useful for loss of appetite, kidney, liver and gall bladder complaints, and arthritis and rheumatism. The leaves taste like endive and can be used in salads and soups or as a vegetable. The leaves of the dandelion are deeply toothed and the bright yellow flowers, containing many seeds, are borne on straight stems, to 20 cm

(8 in), in the spring, summer and fall. When mature, the flower becomes a head of light, fluffy fruits that are blown away by wind.

CULTIVATION For best results, make sure the soil is rich and moist. Propagate from root cuttings in winter or from seed in spring, but flower heads should be removed before seeds set to keep the plants from spreading.

CLIMATE Zone 5.

Daphne (fam. Thymelaeaceae)

These deliciously fragrant, deciduous and ever-green shrubs, named for the nymph of Greek mythology, are grown throughout the world, except in the tropics. The pretty, waxy, winter or spring flowers are borne in short terminal heads above either narrow or oblong leaves. Some species are upright and shrubby, others low and semi-prostrate. All parts of these plants are highly toxic if eaten.

CULTIVATION Daphnes need a well-drained soil, rich in humus, and cool roots. Plant in a semi-shaded position, or in full sun in cool climates. Do not overwater, especially in winter. Being shallow-rooted, daphne is sensitive to root disturbance, so keep the root zone well mulched. Propagate from cuttings or from seed. The flower sprays can be cut without harming the

ABOVE In winter *Daphne odora* carries tight, posy-like clusters of pale flowers with a haunting perfume.

plant. Cutting sprigs of flowers for the house is usually all the pruning needed.

CLIMATE There are species suited to various climatic zones.

SPECIES *D.* x *burkwoodii*, zone 5, is a hardy, semi-evergreen or deciduous upright-growing shrub, to 1 m (3 ft), with dense clusters of pale pinkish white flowers. There are a number of named cultivars of this species, several of which have variegated cream or gold foliage. *D. cneorum*, zone 4, an evergreen growing to 30 cm (12 in), has a slow, spreading growth habit and an abundance of pink flowers. *D. genkwa*, zone 5, is a deciduous species, to 1 m (3 ft), with erect, slender branches and clusters of delicately scented, lilac-blue flowers. It is suitable for planting in cold climates. *D. odora*, zone 7, a native of China and the most widely grown species in mild areas, is an evergreen, to 1.5 m (5 ft), with a bushy, spreading habit. Its reddish

pink buds open to pinkish white, intensely perfumed flowers. The form alba has pure white flowers while 'Auriomarginata' has leaves edged with yellow.

Darwinia (fam. Myrtaceae)
Scent myrtle

Named after Charles Darwin's grandfather, this genus comprises 60 species of flowering shrubs, mostly from Western Australia. They are characterized by stiff foliage and unique blooms formed of clusters of tiny, mostly reddish, perfumed flowers, frequently enclosed by large and colorful, bell-shaped bracts. These beautiful shrubs flower over a long period and are also useful for attracting birds to the garden.

CULTIVATION In frost-prone climates, grow in an airy, cool greenhouse or conservatory, in pots of soilless potting compost, with maximum light but shade from direct sun. In the garden, grow in a sunny, sheltered spot with sandy, well-drained soil. Propagate from semi-ripe cuttings under glass in summer, or by layering in spring.

CLIMATE Needs to be frost-free; at least zone 9.

SPECIES Few if any of these species are available outside their native Australia. *D. citriodora*, lemon-scented myrtle, from Western Australia,

BELOW *Darwinia rhadinophylla* may be difficult to cultivate. Low and spreading, it rarely exceeds 20–30 cm (8–12 in) in height.

grows to 1 m (3 ft) and has reddish flowers and grayish green foliage. *D. fascicularis*, a native of New South Wales, has dense, softer foliage than many other species and grows to 1 m (3 ft). Clusters of red and green button-like flowers bloom in spring. *D. leiostyla*, to 1 m (3 ft), has deep pink to scarlet bells in spring. *D. macrostegia*, Mondurup bell, to 2 m (6 ft), has a weeping habit, narrow foliage, and produces yellow and red bell-shaped flowers. *D. meeboldii*, Cranbrook bell, from Western Australia, has densely crowded leaves and bells with greenish white petals and red bracts.

Date *(Phoenix dactylifera, fam. Arecaceae)*

Generally thought to be a native of the Arabian Peninsula and northern Africa, the date palm is one of the oldest cultivated plants, and has been grown for commercial purposes since about 4000 BC. Some of the countries bordering the Mediterranean have established an export market for dates and date palm products worldwide, and palm groves have been established in California and Mexico. The date palm has many uses. The annual edible fruit has been a staple food in many desert and tropical regions since ancient times, a fermented drink and sugar are produced from the sap, and the seeds are roasted and used as a substitute for coffee, or pressed for the oil they yield. The trunk is used for building and the fronds for thatching roofs. The date palm is also grown as an ornamental. It is an evergreen, dioecious tree, reaching heights of 30 m (100 ft) and producing annual, large clusters of reddish brown or yellowish green fruit, of cylindrical or oblong shape. The fruit is 2–8 cm (¾–3 in) long and the clusters can weigh as much as 90 kg (200 lb).

CULTIVATION In cool and cold climates, the date palm is grown as a small, potted, ornamental foliage plant in a warm greenhouse or conservatory, or as a house plant. Best in soil-based potting compost, with maximum light but shade from direct sun. Propagate from seed germinated in a temperature of 24°C (75°F). The following information is for outdoor cultiva-

ABOVE A mature date palm can set very heavy crops. Commercial varieties are selected for large fruit.

tion in suitable climates. The date palm can be grown in a variety of climates, but to achieve fruit production it needs a free-draining sandy loam, high temperatures night and day and sufficient water. Humidity at ripening time or rain at blossom time may ruin the crop. Propagate from suckers found near the base of the plant. When the roots have struck, plant out cuttings about 9 m (30 ft) apart in early spring. Keep moist while the root system is being established. Trees grown from suckers should begin to bear fruit in five to six years; once they blossom, fruit will set in about seven months. One male plant is able to pollinate about 25 females but this is not without difficulty, and sometimes pollination by hand will be required. If the dates ripen unevenly, it may be necessary to pick them every few days.

CLIMATE Warmest parts of zone 9, and zone 10.

Daucus (fam. Apiaceae)

Of this genus of more than 25 species of herbs from Europe, western Asia and northern Africa, only one is of horticultural importance. It has finely dissected foliage and compound umbels of small, white flowers, surrounded by bracts.

CULTIVATION Sow seed outdoors in spring in well-drained soil.

CLIMATE Grow Daucus as a biennial in all climates.

SPECIES *D. carota*, wild carrot or Queen Anne's lace, is a biennial with thick roots, and grows to 1 m (3 ft). It has attractive, lacy umbels of white flowers in summer and can be included in a mixed border or wild garden. The subspecies sativus has produced many cultivars. These are the carrots commonly grown in vegetable gardens.

ABOVE Dainty flower heads of Queen Anne's lace add an airy touch to the garden and are lovely in posies too.

Davallia (fam. Davalliaceae)
Hare's foot fern

This genus of ferns comprises some 40 species, mostly from Southeast Asia, with a few in Australia and New Zealand. Mostly epiphytes, they are found growing in elevated positions in rainforests and other very moist situations. They have long, creeping, solid rhizomes covered with scales in gray, brown, silver or black. The fronds are usually large and triangular-shaped, while the leaflets vary from very fine to coarse and broad. These exceptionally beautiful ferns are perfect for hanging baskets.

CULTIVATION Davallias are grown in an intermediate greenhouse or in a conservatory, or as house plants in frost-prone climates. They can be grown in hanging baskets in a mix of peat or peat substitute, coarse sand and well-rotted bark chips, with a touch of dolomitic limestone and some charcoal lumps. They like bright light, but shade from direct sun, and a humid atmosphere. Mist spray the leaves daily in summer with plain water. The rhizomes can be divided in spring to propagate a plant. Each piece of rhizome must have some roots attached.

CLIMATE Zone 10.

SPECIES *D. denticulata*, toothed davallia, one of the few ground specimens, is from Asia, but is also found in north-eastern Queensland. The rhizome has brown scales and the fronds are finely divided. *D. fejeensis*, from Fiji and other tropical regions, is possibly the most beautiful

ABOVE *Davallia pyxidata* colonizes the ground with its creeping rhizomes topped with lacy fronds.

of the species. It is very delicate, with fine, feathery leaflets, and needs protection from frost and cold in winter. *D. pyxidata*, a native of eastern Australia, is one of the most commonly grown species. The rhizome is covered with brown scales and the long, coarse, feathery fronds are a glossy, dark green.

Davidia (fam. Davidiaceae)
Dove tree, handkerchief tree

Dove tree, one common name for this single-species genus from western China, derives from the unusual, bird-like white bracts surrounding its flowers. This tree should be given pride of place in the garden as an outstanding specimen tree.

CULTIVATION Davidia thrives in woodland conditions, with moist yet well-drained soil, partial shade or sun, and shelter from cold winds. Propagate from seed sown in a garden frame in fall.

ABOVE A large specimen of *Davidia involucrata* in full bloom is an unforgettable sight. The white floral bracts are distinctive even from a distance.

CLIMATE Zone 6. Prefers a cool, moist climate.

SPECIES *D. involucrata* is a hardy, deciduous tree, to 15 m (50 ft), with broad, ovate leaves, downy underneath, insignificant reddish brown flowers and the characteristic large, leafy bracts. Var. *vilmoriniana* is similar, but the undersides of the leaves are hairless.

Daviesia (fam. Papilionaceae)
Bitter pea, bacon and eggs

These shrubs are native to all states of Australia, most originating from Western Australia. They are one of the plants commonly referred to as 'bacon and eggs'. While not many species are cultivated, they make interesting specimens either for the shrub border or cool conservatory. Characteristic of the over 100 species are their one-seeded triangular pods. Some are leafless, others prickly, but all produce pea flowers during summer.

CULTIVATION Where frosts are likely, grow in a cool greenhouse or conservatory. Outdoors, Daviesia requires light, open, sandy soil and plenty of sun. Propagate by seed.

CLIMATE Zone 9.

SPECIES These are unlikely to be available outside their native Australia. *D. brevifolia*, to 1 m

ABOVE *Daviesia ulicifolia* is a species suited to areas of very low rainfall.

(3 ft), has leafless, zig-zag stems, small prickles and rich, red flowers. *D. cordata*, to 1 m (3 ft), has large, heart-shaped leaves and clusters of yellow and red flowers. *D. horrida* produces clusters of small, yellow and brown flowers and reaches up to 2 m (6 ft). *D. mimosoides* is an open, often pendulous shrub, which grows to 1.5 m (5 ft), with lance-shaped leaves and clusters of numerous, small, yellow flowers.

Delonix (fam. Caesalpiniaceae)
Poinciana, flamboyant tree

This magnificent tree, native to Madagascar, is one of the most beautiful flowering trees in the world. Only one species is cultivated. Used as a street tree in the tropics, it makes an outstanding specimen tree for home gardens or parks.

CULTIVATION In frost-prone climates, poinciana is grown in an intermediate greenhouse or conservatory but only as a foliage plant as it does not flower in pots or tubs. Use a soil-based potting compost, and provide maximum light. In gardens in the right climate, Delonix needs a sheltered position in full sun and well-drained soil. Propagate from seed sown in spring. Germinate in a temperature of 21°C (70°F).

CLIMATE At least zone 10.

BELOW Poinciana has spectacular flowers, but does not produce them if pot-grown.

SPECIES *D. regia* is a partly deciduous tree growing to only around 12 m (40 ft) high, but at times its umbrella-like canopy is as wide, or even wider across. It is the most stunning tree when the masses of superb, showy, scarlet-orange flowers bloom in summer amongst the beautiful, feathery foliage. The flowers are followed by flat, woody pods about 50 cm (20 in) long.

Delphinium (fam. Ranunculaceae)

Mostly from the northern hemisphere, these hardy annuals, biennials and perennials are attractive plants, with tall spires of showy flowers. They are extremely popular in Europe and the United Kingdom as they do best in colder climates. In warm climates, few species are grown and it is preferable to treat them as annuals. In cool regions, they flower freely and last longer and are better treated as perennials. Delphiniums are known mostly by their beautiful, blue color, though today many hybrids are available in red, pink, white and yellow. In the US, the Elatum Group is the most popular of the perennial delphiniums, with thick flower

BELOW Spires of rich purple-blue flowers of delphinium highlight cool gardens in summer.

D

ABOVE Palest lilac is amongst the range of colors now available in Delphinium hybrids.

spikes in early summer to midsummer. There are tall, medium and small cultivars in this group. Delphiniums are useful for borders, providing excellent cut flowers.

CULTIVATION Delphiniums require a rich soil, with added lime, and very good drainage. Propagate the Elatum Group delphiniums from sturdy basal cuttings in the spring. They are best rooted under glass with bottom heat. Seeds of annual delphiniums can be sown under glass in early spring and planted out in late spring. Space the tall hybrid varieties 50 cm (20 in) apart, with 50 cm (20 in) between rows, and the smaller types 30 cm (12 in) apart, with 40 cm (16 in) between rows. Once established, give regular applications of liquid fertilizer as they are heavy feeders and, during the flowering season, a heavy dressing of complete fertilizer. In the warm summer months, it is advisable to mulch the surface soil so that the roots are kept cool. Most of the taller types need individual stakes to protect them from wind damage. The new shoots are susceptible to attack by snails and slugs which should be removed.

CLIMATE Zone 3.

SPECIES *D. elatum* grows to 2 m (6 ft), with spikes of flowers in many colors, lasting from late spring through to fall. Most garden delphiniums and many cultivars have arisen from this species. *D. grandiflorum*, butterfly delphinium, is an annual or perennial, to 45 cm (18 in), with white or blueish violet, early summer flowers. Specialist growers feature dozens of choice cultivars of delphinium.

Dendrobium (fam. Orchidaceae)

This genus comprises over 900 species of orchids which grow profusely throughout the southern hemisphere, particularly in India, New Guinea and Australia. They are extremely disparate in size and flower form and, with the

BELOW The lovely Cooktown orchid, *Dendrobium bigibbum*, is the floral emblem of Queensland.

many hybrids that have been raised, in color as well. Colors range from near white through yellow to mauve and dark purple. Some come in pure colors but most are bicolored or variegated.

CULTIVATION These frost-tender orchids are grown in an intermediate greenhouse or conservatory in frost-prone climates. Many are epiphytic and the usual way to grow them is on slabs of bark hung up in the greenhouse, surrounding the roots with sphagnum moss. Alternatively, they can be grown in pots of compost formulated for epiphytic orchids, which should be available from specialist orchid nurseries. Instead of pots they can be grown in slatted wooden orchid baskets hung up in the greenhouse. They need small containers if they are to flower freely. In spring and summer the plants like a humid atmosphere and partial shade, plus ample watering. Mist spray the plants every day and liquid feed about once a week. In fall and winter the plants need maximum light, when they should be kept dry. Propagate from division in spring when the plant has outgrown its container.

CLIMATE At least zone 10.

SPECIES *D. falcorostrum*, *D. kingianum* and *D. speciosum* are all native to Australia. These

ABOVE Unusual in both color and form, this *Dendrobium* cultivar would bring delight to any grower.

species, especially *D. kingianum*, have been extensively hybridized to produce some lovely and unusual cultivars. *D. bigibbum*, the Cooktown orchid, is popular in cultivation for its mainly rich pink to purple blooms. *D. speciosum* reaches 1 m (3 ft) or more in diameter when mature. However, *D. nobile* and its numerous cultivars is probably the soft-cane dendrobium most often grown. This species has white flowers, marked with rosy pink and magenta, with a dark purple throat. The cultivars provide an enormous color range. In all, 52 species are native to Australia. Three extremely colorful species of *Dendrobium* are well worth growing: *D. chrysotoxum*, *D. densiflorum* and *D. fimbriatum*, all from the lower Himalayas or Burma. A good orchid nursery should be able to supply many species and hybrids of Dendrobium.

Dendrocalamus (fam. Poaceae)
Giant bamboo

Suitable for tropical and subtropical climates, in frost-prone areas these bamboos are grown in pots or tubs in a warm greenhouse or conservatory. This genus includes the largest bamboos in the world. They are clump-forming, with new shoots coming from the parent plant itself. The stem and rhizome are one. The upper part of the short rhizome produces buds, one of which grows upwards to make a new plant. Many of these bamboos have economic uses in their native countries, being used for construction, raft building and buckets, as well as for their edible shoots.

CULTIVATION To propagate clump-forming bamboos, dig up a 50 cm (20 in) length of a one-year-old branchless stem, cutting it off as near as possible to the parent plant and retaining two or three nodes. Bury in the ground in a horizontal position 20 cm (8 in) deep. Alternatively, bury diagonally, two-thirds below the ground, one-third above.

CLIMATE At least zone 10.

ABOVE The robust canes of *Dendrocalamus giganteus* form an impenetrable barrier. This is a source of paper pulp in Southeast Asia.

ABOVE Rotenone extracted from the vine *Derris elliptica* is widely used in insecticides, as well as being a fish poison.

SPECIES *D. giganteus*, worra, from India, is the world's largest bamboo, growing to 35 m (115 ft) tall, with thick stems up to 25 cm (10 in) in diameter. *D. strictus*, male bamboo or Calcutta bamboo, grows to 20 m (65 ft), with thick stem walls and curved upper branches. It is the best known of the Indian bamboos and cultivated there for paper pulp.

Derris (fam. Papilionaceae)
Jewel vine, flame tree

Native to Southeast Asia and northern Queensland, some of these woody climbers and trees are cultivated, mainly in Malaysia and Indonesia, for the production of rotenone (derris), a low-toxicity insecticide safe for humans and animals, though fish are affected by it. In fact, the Australian Aborigines have long used the roots of some *Derris* species for poisoning fish.

CULTIVATION Grown in a warm greenhouse in frost-prone climates, but not often cultivated in the US.

CLIMATE Zone 10.

SPECIES *D. elliptica*, derris or tuba root, from Malaysia and Indonesia, is the main source of commercial rotenone. It is a large climber, with divided leaflets, brownish and silky on the undersides, and white, flushed with pink-lilac, pea-shaped flowers. *D. microphylla*, native to Malaysia and India, is a tree, to 5 m (16 ft) or more, with sprays of pea-shaped flowers colored red through to purple. The leaflets are whitish underneath. *D. robusta*, from India and Ceylon, is a tree, to 12 m (40 ft), with grayish foliage and sprays of white flowers. *D. scandens*, Malay jewel vine, is found in both tropical Asia and Queensland. This climber produces abundant sprays of rose pink flowers.

Deutzia (fam. Hydrangeaceae)

These free-flowering, hardy, deciduous shrubs are mostly native to Japan, China, temperate

ABOVE *Deutzia gracilis*, sometimes called wedding bells, bears a mass of cascading white blossom.

Central America and the Philippines. The leaves are dull green, pointed and slightly rough. The bark of mature species is brown and peeling. White to pink, starry flowers are produced in spring or early summer. Many are fragrant. Hybrids adaptable to various situations have been raised.

CULTIVATION *Deutzia* species can be grown in most soils and can tolerate partial shade and severe cold. Propagate from cuttings taken in fall or winter. These shrubs transplant easily as they are dormant in winter, though the tops may need to be trimmed. Prune annually after flowering by cutting back old flowered shoots to new shoots lower down. Remove some of the oldest wood completely.

CLIMATE There are species suited to various climatic zones.

SPECIES *D. gracilis*, Japanese snowflower, zone 4, is one of the most popular species, growing to about 1 m (3 ft). Tight clusters of pure white, papery flowers cover the entire plant when in bloom. *D. longifolia* 'Veitchii', zone 6, grows to 2 m (6 ft), with pointed leaves, whitish on the undersides, and purplish rose buds, opening to pink flowers. *D. x magnifica*, zone 5, a hybrid growing to 2 m (6 ft), has pure white, double flowers. *D. scabra*, zone 5, has an erect growth habit to 3 m (10 ft) and pinkish white flowers. Cultivars include 'Candidissima', with double, white flowers and 'Pride of Rochester', with double, white flowers, the outside petals flushed with rosy purple.

Dianella (fam. Phormiaceae)

Flax lily

These long-lived perennials are found in Australia, New Zealand, the Pacific Islands, tropical Asia and East Africa. They are clump-forming, rhizomatous plants, with tufts of long, fibrous, strap-like leaves on thick stalks. Dianellas have a long flowering period, beginning in spring and followed by blue berries. They add texture to mixed borders and are also suitable for rockeries or as edging plants.

CULTIVATION Propagate from ripe seed or by offsets struck in light soil in a moist, shady spot in the cooler months of the year. Most species like plenty of moisture when young. Once established, they are drought- and frost-resistant.

CLIMATE Zone 9.

ABOVE *Dianella revoluta* is a species of flax lily tolerant of quite cool conditions.

SPECIES *D. caerulea*, from eastern Australia and New Guinea, grows to 1 m (3 ft), with small, blue flowers, then blue berries. *D. ensifolia*, umbrella dracaena, is a tropical species to 2 m (6 ft). It has whitish to blue flowers with yellow anthers. *D. intermedia*, a native of New Zealand, has a creeping rhizome and small, greenish white to purplish white flowers with yellow anthers. It grows to 1 m (3 ft). *D. laevis*, which occurs in most states of Australia, was used by the Aborigines for weaving baskets. It has bright green, strap-like leaves and blue flowers with yellow anthers, followed by blue berries. It grows to 1 m (3 ft). *D. revoluta*, a native of New South Wales and Tasmania, grows to 1 m (3 ft), with strap-like leaves, small, deep blue flowers, with yellow or brown anthers, and blue berries.

Dianthus (fam. Caryophyllaceae)

Carnation, pinks

This large genus of annual, biennial or perennial plants is mostly native to Europe and the Mediterranean. In antiquity, Dianthus was considered the divine flower, the flower of Jupiter or Zeus. It has been cultivated for many centuries, especially as a source of oil for use in soaps and perfumes. Many of the species are fragrant and are attractive to butterflies. These are often referred to as clove-scented. They are easy to grow, being hardy in most climates. Carnations are some of the best cut flowers of the genus. In fact, they are believed to be the most popular cut flower in world trade. Alpine species are suited to rockeries.

CULTIVATION Most *Dianthus* species like a slightly alkaline soil and sharp drainage, though some of the alpine species can tolerate acidic soils. All do well in sandy loam. Propagate the annual and biennial species from seed sown in spring, the perennials from cuttings taken in summer immediately after flowering. Root them in sharp sand.

CLIMATE There are *Dianthus* suited to various climatic zones.

ABOVE Annual *Dianthus chinensis* cultivars add dazzling color to summer bedding and are useful for filling patio containers.

SPECIES *D. alpinus*, zone 3, is a perennial, to 8 cm (3 in), suitable for growing in rockeries. It has long-petalled flowers, trimmed with reddish purple and speckled with white. *D. barbatus*, sweet William, zone 4, is a short-lived annual, biennial or perennial, to 60 cm (24 in), sometimes with double flowers, mostly in red, pink or purple, in late spring and early summer. It is a popular garden flower. Many cultivars are available. *D. caryophyllus*, carnation or clove pink, zone 8, is a short-lived, upright plant, to 1 m (3 ft), with silvery gray lance-shaped leaves and often double, large, fragrant flowers in white, pink, red, purple, yellow, apricot-orange and white, spotted with red. *D. chinensis*, Indian pink (often simply called dianthus), zone 7, from China, is mainly grown as an annual, with heights ranging from 15 to 70 cm (6–28 in). It has rose-lilac flowers with purple eyes. Cultivars are available in single or mixed colors. *D. deltoides*, maiden pink, zone 3, is a dwarf, mat-forming perennial. Its deep pink, single, fringed flowers bloom in spring and early summer. *D. gratianopolitanus*, Cheddar pink, zone 3, is a mat-forming perennial, to

ABOVE Cottage pinks, *Dianthus plumarius* varieties, are grown for their special fragrance as much as for their appearance.

15 cm (6 in), with very fragrant, rose pink flowers. *D. plumarius*, cottage pink or grass pink, zone 3, is a loosely tufted, evergreen perennial, to 40 cm (16 in), with narrow leaves and often fringed flowers in rose, purple, white or multicolors. *D. subacaulis*, zone 5, an alpine perennial to 5 cm (2 in), has a dense growth habit, a woody base and deep pink flowers.

Dicentra (fam. Fumariaceae)
Bleeding heart, Dutchman's breeches

These annuals and perennials from the colder parts of North America and northern Asia are mostly woodland plants, often originating in cool mountain areas. They have fibrous, rhizomatous or tuberous roots and pretty, lantern-like, pendulous flowers, borne on arching stems, from spring through summer.

CULTIVATION If tried in warmer areas, *Dicentra* must be positioned in a shady spot; in cooler areas, it will grow in either light shade or full sun provided the soil does not dry out at the roots. These plants should be well mulched to help them retain moisture. They prefer a rich loam soil, with some protection from wind. Propagate by seed or by careful division of the brittle roots in spring. To encourage good blooms, apply a light, liquid fertilizer prior to flowering.

ABOVE The bright pink, heart-shaped flowers of *Dicentra spectabilis* resemble tiny lockets.

CLIMATE There are species suited to various climatic zones.

SPECIES *D. cucullaria*, Dutchman's breeches, zone 5, is a tuberous species, to 25 cm (10 in), with white, yellow-tipped, pendulous, spurred flowers. *D. formosa*, wild bleeding heart, zone 6, grows to 45 cm (18 in). It has a fleshy rhizome and dainty, spurred, rose-purple flowers. *D. spectabilis*, Western bleeding heart, from Japan, has long been a favorite. It grows to 1 m (3 ft), with delicate rose red flowers. 'Alba' has white flowers.

Dichorisandra (fam. Commelinaceae)

Few species of this genus of about 25 evergreen perennials from tropical America are cultivated, though they should be more widely known as they are ideal for warm conservatories. They grow from fleshy roots, producing soft, cane-like growth, large, glossy leaves and showy flower spikes.

CULTIVATION As these are tropical plants they are grown in a warm greenhouse or conservatory in cool and cold climates. Use a soil-based potting compost, and grow the plants in good light but shaded from direct sun. They like a humid atmosphere. In the winter, keep the compost only slightly moist but water abundantly in summer. Propagation is by division in spring or from cuttings at any time of year.

CLIMATE Must be grown in frost-free conditions in warm areas.

SPECIES *D. thyrsiflora* grows 1.5 m (5 ft) or more high. The foliage is deep, glossy green and the rich, royal blue to purple flowers appear through midsummer to fall. *Dichorisandra* is an excellent perennial for growing under tall trees.

ABOVE With its royal blue flowers, *Dichorisandra thyrsiflora* is an outstanding understorey plant for warm gardens.

Dicksonia (fam. Dicksoniaceae)

From tropical and subtropical regions, including Australia, New Zealand and the South Pacific, this genus of evergreen to semi-evergreen tree ferns comprises around 25 species. The trunks can be either large or small, the large, spreading fronds are finely divided, and the hairy stems thicken towards the base. The spore cases on fertile fronds are protected by a

ABOVE *Dicksonia antarctica*, the soft tree fern, is the hardiest species and can be grown in many parts of the US.

pouch-shaped cup which breaks when ripe and releases the spores. These tree ferns make fine specimen plants, but if space permits, groupings of several create a much better effect.

CULTIVATION Grow in acid soil in partial or full shade. Give plenty of water to the base and trunk and a fine spray over the crown to keep the foliage healthy. Rotted leaf mould and aged cow manure are good soil conditioners. Propagate from spores. If transplanting these tree ferns, lift as much of the root structure as possible to avoid retarding growth, or cut off the trunk, making sure that the trunk is planted about 30 cm (12 in) deep in the new position. All of the fronds, except those at the central growing point, need to be removed if the trunk is severed from its roots. They should be moved only in summer during the growth period.

CLIMATE Wide moisture and temperature range, depending on the species grown.

SPECIES *D. antarctica*, soft tree fern, zone 8, is distributed throughout mountainous areas of eastern Australia and New Zealand. Hardy and adaptable, it is a popular garden species, needing some overhead protection. It has a solid trunk which can grow to 10 m (33 ft) high, a profusion of large, spreading fronds, providing a beautiful display, and stems which are covered in masses of reddish brown hairs. *D. fibrosa*, wheki-punga, zone 9, is a native of New Zealand. Its trunk grows to about 7 m (23 ft) tall and is a reddish brown color because of the masses of aerial rootlets. The dark green fronds grow profusely, and the stalks are covered with brown hairs when young, darkening with age. *D. squarrosa*, wheki, zone 9, also from New Zealand, has a black, slender, often branched trunk as young plants form at intervals up the trunk. The masses of glossy, green fronds, which are lighter on the undersides, form a rather flat top, unique to this handsome tree fern.

Dictamnus (fam. Rutaceae)
Burning bush, dittany, gas plant

Native to southern Europe and extending to northern China, this herbaceous perennial produces an inflammable oil, hence the adoption of its common names. It is grown for its fragrant, rose or white flowers produced in terminal sprays in early summer. The leaves also are fragrant, giving off a balsam or lemon scent when rubbed.

ABOVE A plant known for its very unusual and curious properties, *Dictamnus albus* has pretty, pale pink flowers like butterflies.

CULTIVATION *Dictamnus* prefers a light, well-drained soil and a sunny position, and is easily propagated from seed.

CLIMATE Zone 3.

SPECIES *D. albus*, the only species, grows to around 45 cm (18 in). Var. *purpureus* is widely grown and has light purplish flowers. The flower stems and the unripe fruits contain a volatile oil which can actually ignite in very hot weather. Surprisingly, this does not appear to harm the plant.

Dictyosperma (fam. Arecaceae)
Princess palm, hurricane palm

Now rarely found in its natural habitat of Mauritius and the Mascarene Islands, this palm genus comprises only one species and is found

ABOVE *Dictyosperma album* makes a good pot plant when young but needs a warm greenhouse in frosty climates.

in tropical and subtropical gardens. Can be grown outdoors in southern Florida but in the rest of the US it is grown in a warm greenhouse or conservatory.

CULTIVATION This palm makes a good pot or tub plant under glass when young. Grow in soil-based potting compost. Provide maximum light (but shade from direct sun), and a humid atmosphere. Outdoors, it needs shelter from wind and sun or partial shade. It can be raised from seed sown in spring. Provide a temperature of 30°C (86°F).

CLIMATE Zone 10.

SPECIES *D. album*, princess palm, is a graceful, slender palm which grows to 10 m (33 ft) or more. The pinnate leaves are 3–4 m (10–13 ft) long and the sharply pointed leaflets are evenly spaced along the midribs. The leaf bases form a crownshaft at the top of the slender, gray trunk which is closely marked with rings. The short-stalked inflorescences are enclosed by two deciduous bracts and the reddish yellow flowers, usually clustered in groups of three, are followed by small, egg-shaped fruits which ripen to purple-black.

Dieffenbachia (fam. Araceae)
Dumb cane

Originating from tropical America, these evergreen perennials, being valued for their decorative foliage, are grown as pot plants in frost-prone climates, in a warm greenhouse or conservatory, or as house plants. The large, oval leaves, radiating outwards and downwards from the central stem, are patterned in green, white, yellow or cream in a variety of streaks, splashes, spots and lines. All parts of the plants are poisonous, the sap causing swelling of the mouth and tongue.

CULTIVATION Provide a humid, moist environment, but water sparingly in winter. Propagate by stem cuttings taken in spring and fall, and struck in shade in a sharp sand mix. Trim off

ABOVE The foliage of *Dieffenbachia* cultivars is variously patterned in cream, yellow, white or silver.

leaves from cuttings to avoid moisture loss. Some species can also be easily propagated from basal suckers.

CLIMATE Zone 10.

SPECIES *D. amoena* is a robust species, to 2 m (6 ft) or more, with 1 m (3 ft) long leaves, marked with cream. *D. maculata* is very variable, but most commonly has 20 cm (8 in) long leaves with masses of cream markings. Cultivar 'Rudolph Roehrs' has pale yellowish green leaves with dark green midribs and margins and ivory veins. Many species, including *D. amoena* and *D. maculata*, now appear to be grouped with *D. seguine*. Few straight species are regularly offered for sale. Most gardeners grow one or more of the large range of cultivars readily available.

Dierama (fam. Iridaceae)
Wand flower, fairy fishing rod

Members of the Iris family, these mostly cold-tolerant plants from tropical and South Africa

ABOVE Silky flowers in two shades of pink hang from slender stems on *Dierama pulcherrimum.*

ABOVE The delicate flowers of *Dietes grandiflora* complement perfectly its sword-like foliage

have corms, long, sword-shaped leaves, and graceful, arching stems bearing tassels of pretty, funnel-shaped flowers. Most flower in summer, although in warmer areas they can be spring bloomers. Generally planted in moist soil at the edge of a pool.

CULTIVATION *Dierama* prefers rich, well-drained yet moist soil, with some protection from wind. Propagate from seed or from offsets of the corms produced in spring. Divide large, congested clumps in fall or late winter. Divisions will probably not flower the first season.

CLIMATE Mainly zone 9.

SPECIES *D. pendulum*, fairy fishing rod, zone 7, grows to 1 m (3 ft) or more, with long, nodding stems bearing flowers in pink through to lilac. *D. pulcherrimum*, to 1 m (3 ft), has drooping, pink flowers. Var. album, with white flowers, is one of several named varieties.

Dietes (fam. Iridaceae)

Of the six species of this genus of evergreen, rhizomatous perennials, five originate from tropical and South Africa, and one from Lord Howe Island, Australia. In warm weather, when in flower, they have very pretty, iris-like blooms. The stiff, sword-shaped foliage also makes them good landscaping subjects. In frosty climates, grow these perennials in a cool greenhouse.

CULTIVATION These drought-tolerant plants will grow in any well-drained, average soil in full sun. They can do well in partial shade, though flowering may be poorer. Once established, they self-seed, and clumps can be divided when overcrowded. Under glass, grow in soil-based potting compost with good light and ventilation.

CLIMATE At least zone 9.

SPECIES *D. bicolor* grows to 1 m (3 ft), with sword-like, mid-green foliage. Sprays of flattened, threepetalled, pale yellow flowers, with a conspicuous, brownish black, basal spot, appear in summer on wiry stems. Healthy plants will flower almost continuously. *D. grandiflora*, wild iris, to 1 m (3 ft), has similar foliage, but the flowers are larger, in white, marked with yellowish orange, brown and blue-mauve. *D. robinsoniana*, wedding iris, from Lord Howe Island, has richly fragrant, white flowers, 10 cm (4 in) across, with red and yellow spots near the base. The leaves and stems are up to 2 m (6 ft) tall.

Digitalis (fam. Scrophulariaceae)

Foxglove

These hardy biennial and perennial plants are mostly found in European woodlands, though some species are native to the Mediterranean and central Asia. They make excellent border or background plants. Digitalis is renowned for its medicinal properties, still being used today in the treatment of certain heart conditions. However, all plant parts can be poisonous if eaten and the sap may cause skin irritation.

CULTIVATION Foxgloves like a rich, moist soil, with some protection from wind, and look very attractive planted in drifts. They are self-seeding. All species are propagated by seed sown on the surface of compost in seed trays in the spring. Germinate in a garden frame.

CLIMATE Zone 8.

SPECIES *D. ferruginea*, rusty foxglove, is a biennial, to 1.2 m (4 ft), with rusty brown summer flowers. *D. grandiflora*, yellow foxglove, grows to 1 m (3 ft), with pale yellow flowers blotched brown. *D. lanata*, Grecian foxglove, is a biennial, growing to 1 m (3 ft), with creamy white flowers. *D. lutea*, a perennial to 1 m (3 ft), produces yellow to white flowers. *D. purpurea*, common foxglove, is a short-lived perennial, grown as a biennial. It reaches 1 m (3 ft) or more, with purple flowers, spotted in a deeper shade. Many good strains and varieties are available, including the Foxy Group strains and the Excelsior Group hybrids, with flowers in lovely soft colors, ranging from cream and yellow to pink and purple, that bloom all round the stems and do not droop. Flowers last surprisingly well when cut.

Dill (*Anethum graveolens*, fam. Apiaceae)

This fragrant annual from south-west Asia has long been known and enjoyed as a kitchen herb. It has finely cut, feathery, greenish blue leaves and umbels of flat, greenish yellow flowers in summer. It produces an abundance of small, flat seeds. The leaves, stems and seeds of the plant are all used for their aniseed flavor. The seeds are an important ingredient in dill pickles and the leaves are used in salads and for vegetable, fish, chicken, veal and lamb dishes. The leaf flavor is at its best just before the plant begins to flower. Dill adds a particularly delicious flavor to cucumber and fish. It also aids digestion and food assimilation.

BELOW Flowering spikes of tall foxgloves, *Digitalis purpurea* hybrids, blend with the purple heads of a Buddleja.

BELOW A prolific blooming of dill ensures that there will be plenty of seed to harvest in the coming weeks.

CULTIVATION Dill likes a warm spot, protected from wind. Sow seed in spring in shallow drills and thin later to 30 cm (12 in) between each plant. Water well in dry weather. Once established, these plants self-sow. The leaves should be picked when needed as they do not dry well. The seeds should be allowed to ripen on the plant. The plant turns a purplish red color when the seeds are ripe. Gather all seeds for drying and storing, as these plants can spread rapidly especially in warm areas.

CLIMATE Dill is a warm-season annual suited to temperate climates. Zone 8.

Dillwynia (fam. Papilionaceae)
Parrot-pea

The bright yellow, orange or red flowers of these Australian native shrubs add eye-catching color to gardens and greenhouses. In frost-prone climates, they are grown in a cool greenhouse or conservatory.

ABOVE The bright yellow and red, pea-type flowers of *Dillwynia glaberrima* are borne in spring.

CULTIVATION Outdoors, *Dillwynia* likes a sandy soil with good drainage and a partially shaded situation. Under glass, grow in pots of soil-based potting compost, in maximum light, with an airy atmosphere.

CLIMATE Zone 9.

SPECIES These are not easily available outside their native Australia. *D. glaberrima*, heath parrot-pea, is a spreading shrub, to 1 m (3 ft), with yellow flowers, purplish brown in the center. *D. hispida*, red parrot-pea, is a twiggy shrub, to 2 m (6 ft), with fine, needle-like foliage and clusters of yellow and brown flowers. *D. retorta*, eggs and bacon, is a rounded or upright shrub, to 1 m (3 ft), with twisted foliage and red-centered, yellow flowers. When in flower, it is extremely colorful. *D. sericea*, showy parrot-pea, grows to 1 m (3 ft), with small leaves and dense, terminal spikes of red and yellow flowers.

Dionaea (fam. Droseraceae)
Venus's fly trap

This fascinating plant from North America is probably one of the world's best known because of its carnivorous habit. The Venus's fly trap is immortalized in numerous books and horror movies.

BELOW Venus's fly trap, *Dionaea muscipula*, is a popular curiosity. A stone chip mulch over the surface keeps 'traps' from rotting on damp soil.

CULTIVATION *Dionaea* can be grown outdoors in mild climates but most people prefer to grow it in a shallow pot in a cool greenhouse or conservatory. It needs an acid compost consisting of equal parts peat and lime-free horticultural sand. Provide bright light, but shade the plant from direct sun. Stand the pot in a dish of water to keep the compost wet. In fall and winter the plant is dormant, and should be kept only barely moist. In the garden it likes full sun and very moist, acid soil.

CLIMATE At least zone 8.

SPECIES *D. muscipula*, Venus's fly trap, is the only species, growing to around 10–15 cm (4–6 in). It has a rosette of twin-lobed leaves, with sensitive sticky hairs on the upper surface and toothed edges, and spikes of very small, white flowers above the rosette in summer. But what it is renowned for is its ability to trap insects and digest them. Insects touch the leaves and are enfolded in the lobes.

Dioscorea (fam. Dioscoreaceae)

This tropical, tuberous genus has a large, thickened trunk, or tuber, sometimes above ground, covered in thick, corky bark, growing to 1 m (3 ft) in diameter, and sometimes up to 50 cm (20 in) tall. This fleshy caudex produces annual, twining shoots which become woody. The glossy, green, veined leaves are triangular to heart-shaped, and sometimes lobed. Flowers are inconspicuous. Some *Dioscorea* are grown in tropical regions as a staple food.

CULTIVATION In frost-prone climates, grow in an intermediate to warm conservatory or greenhouse, in pots of soil-based potting compost. Provide maximum light but shade from direct sun. The stems will need supports. When dormant, keep plant only barely moist, but water normally otherwise. Outdoors plant in deep, well-drained soil with full sun. Propagate from seed, germinated at 24°C (75°F).

CLIMATE Zone 10 for most species.

ABOVE Twining Australian native yam, *Dioscorea transversa*, bears unusual, three-winged, silver-brown fruits after flowering.

SPECIES *D. elephantipes* is the best known species in Europe. Others may not be available. *D. alata*, white yam or water yam, is grown as a staple food in its native Asia. It can produce huge tubers. *D. elephantipes*, Hottentot bread or elephant's foot, has a hemispherical trunk base, growing up to 1 m (3 ft) in diameter, and covered with bark divided into rough, symmetrically rounded segments, and glossy, heart-shaped leaves, with tessellated veins. *D. trifida*, cush-cush or yampee, from tropical America, produces several individual tubers.

Diospyros (fam. Ebenaceae)

This large genus is distributed through widely differing parts of the world. Various species are native to Asia, Africa, Madagascar and America. These deciduous or evergreen trees and shrubs contain several species which produce edible fruit, others which are grown for their ornamental value, and some, notably *D. ebenum* (ebony), which are cultivated for their timber.

ABOVE Fruits of *Diospyros virginiana* are very similar to those of persimmon, to which it is closely related.

The leaves are alternate, simple and entire, and the flowers are not particularly significant. Many of these trees and shrubs have spectacular fall foliage.

CULTIVATION Hardy species need a sheltered spot in full sun with well-drained, fertile soil. The persimmon can be grown as an espalier on a warm wall. Plant male and female plants for maximum fruit production, although lone females will produce some fruit. Tender species are grown in a cool to intermediate greenhouse in pots of soil-based potting compost.

CLIMATE There are species suited to various climatic zones.

SPECIES *D. digyna*, black sapote, zone 10, from Mexico and Central America, is a tropical evergreen which may grow 18–20 m (60–65 ft) in its habitat, but much smaller cultivated. The edible fruits, 8–10 cm (3–4 in) in diameter, almost black when ripe, contain soft brown flesh reputed to taste like chocolate pudding. *D. ebenum*, ebony, zone 10, produces the beautiful timber of the common name. It is a very large tree from India and Sri Lanka, but is rarely cultivated in the US outside botanical gardens.

New growth flushes on this evergreen are bright pink. *D. kaki*, persimmon, zone 8, from China, is a deciduous tree, 6–12 m (20–40 ft) tall, with glossy, green, oval leaves, downy on the undersides, to 20 cm (8 in) long, and yellowish white flowers. The orange-colored, smooth-skinned edible fruit is variable in shape, growing to 8 cm (3 in) in diameter, with soft, orange flesh and a persistent calyx. Many cultivars are available. *D. virginiana*, known as persimmon or possumwood in its native United States, zone 4, grows to about 20 m (65 ft) in its habitat, but when cultivated only to 10 m (33 ft). The edible fruit is yellow or orange when ripe and the timber is used commercially.

Diploglottis (fam. Sapindaceae)
Native tamarind

This native Australian evergreen may grow 25 m (80 ft) or more in its habitat, but only reaches 10–12 m (33–30 ft) under cultivation. It has soft, rust-colored shoots and buds, large

BELOW *Diploglottis australis* has handsome, compound leaves. The edible fruits may be eaten raw or used in jam.

sprays of abundant, white flowers and long, pinnate leaves. The fruit is edible, but rather acid. Other species in this genus are native to Australia, New Caledonia and Malaysia. However, they are unlikely to be available outside their native countries.

CULTIVATION *Diploglottis* is tender and in climates which are prone to frosts, should be grown in cool to intermediate greenhouses or conservatories, in pots of soil-based potting compost. Outdoors diploglottis likes a deep, fertile soil in a sunny spot and ample summer water. Propagate *Diploglottis* from seed germinated in a heated propagating case.

CLIMATE Zone 9.

SPECIES *D. australis* is found growing in coastal and nearby plateau areas of Queensland and New South Wales. It has shiny, slightly leathery, compound leaves. In its native habitat, it makes a good specimen or shade tree.

Diplolaena (fam. Rutaceae)
Western rose

The six species of this genus of small to medium-sized evergreen shrubs, with origins in Western Australia, make excellent garden ornamentals. They have soft, hairy leaves and pendulous flower heads, their stamens protruding from the surrounding green bracts. This genus is unlikely to be available outside its native Australia.

CULTIVATION In climates prone to regular frosts, grow in a cool greenhouse or conservatory in pots of soil-based potting compost. Outdoors, these shrubs do well in a well-drained limestone soil or sandy loam, in a warm, sunny spot. Propagate from seed or by cuttings in fall.

CLIMATE Zone 9.

SPECIES *D. angustifolia*, pineleaf western rose, grows to 1 m (3 ft). It has pendulous, red flower heads, encased in green, overlapping bracts,

ABOVE The pendent flowers of *Diplolaena grandiflora* are quite unusual. Prune after flowering to ensure plenty of new growth with flowering potential.

which appear from summer to fall. The narrow, linear leaves have a central groove and rolled edges. *D. grandiflora*, large western rose, is an upright shrub, to 2.5 m (8 ft), with egg-shaped, woolly leaves. The large, rose pink flowers, framed by green bracts, appear in winter and spring.

Disa (fam. Orchidaceae)

This genus of terrestrial orchids comprises about 100 species native to southern and tropical Africa, and Madagascar. Mostly grown by specialists in the past, they are now becoming more widely available. Although they supposedly originate from hot regions, these orchids do not like either extreme heat or cold.

CULTIVATION It is not easy to provide the conditions required by this genus. Disas should be grown in a mix of sphagnum moss, coir peat and bark. Keep them in a shady, cool to intermediate greenhouse with high humidity. Water well in summer but avoid overhead watering as the foliage is prone to rot. Keep the compost almost dry in winter.

ABOVE This very desirable *Disa* hybrid will have a long flowering period as a potted plant and also makes a good cut flower.

ABOVE As fall progresses, the lovely, textured foliage of *Disanthus cercidifolius* takes on warm, rich hues.

CLIMATE Zone 10 at least.

SPECIES *D. uniflora* is the most commonly cultivated species, producing between three and seven large flowers of bright scarlet with yellow veins, generally in midsummer.

Disanthus (fam. Hamamelidaceae)

This is a genus of one species of deciduous shrub from Japan, highly valued for its beautiful foliage.

CULTIVATION *Disanthus* can be grown in similar conditions to rhododendron and azaleas. It likes a cool, moist, peaty, acid soil and a sheltered position. These shrubs can be easily transplanted in winter during their dormant period. Propagate by layers or from seed sown in fall or spring.

CLIMATE Zone 8. Prefers cool and moist climates.

SPECIES *D. cercidifolius* reaches around 4 m (13 ft) in its native habitat. It has rather heart-shaped, blue-green leaves which color rich orange, scarlet or crimson in fall. Against light, the foliage takes on a luminous brilliance. Small, lightly scented, deep purple to red flowers appear in fall.

Dischidia (fam. Asclepiadeceae)

Endemic to southern India, Malaysia, the Philippines, New Guinea and Australia's northern Queensland, this genus of epiphytic, semi-succulent vines comprises about 80 species. They are unique plants as some of the leaves are transformed into large, fleshy, pear-shaped storage receptacles which catch the rain from which the aerial roots draw moisture and nutrients. These unusual vessels are also home to ants which it is thought help to pollinate the small, urn-shaped flowers. May not be readily available in the US.

CULTIVATION *Dischidia* needs warmth, humidity and branches of a tree on which to climb. It can

ABOVE The small, fleshy, coin-shaped leaves on *Dischidia nummularia* are spaced along the fine, string-like, pendulous stems.

be grown on timber logs or slabs, or in hanging baskets in very coarse bark. No soil is required. Outside the tropics glasshouse protection is necessary. Propagate from seeds or cuttings.

CLIMATE At least zone 10.

SPECIES *D. nummularia* is a beautiful foliage plant native to Queensland and Papua New Guinea where it is generally found growing on small trees. In its early growth stages it has small, round, fleshy leaves, some of which later develop into the characteristic pear shape. *D. rafflesiana*, a native of Malaysia, Papua New Guinea and northern Queensland, has oval leaves, some of which expand to the pear shape. The flowers are a creamy yellow.

Diuris (fam. Orchidaceae)
Donkey orchid, double tails

This genus of around 37 species of ground orchids is native to Australia. Unusually for orchids, many are native to open grassy areas. They form one or two underground tubers each year. Ranging in color from white to yellow, with orange, red, purple or brown markings, the flowers, borne on long stems, are unusual, with two upper petals shaped like ears and two lower petals like tails, hence the common name 'double tails'. The grass-like leaves die down after flowering.

CULTIVATION In frost-prone climates, grow in a cool greenhouse or conservatory in pots of terrestrial orchid compost with added leaf mould. Provide bright light but shade from direct sun. Outdoors, grow in fertile soil with added leaf mould and in full sun or light shade. Propagate by division.

CLIMATE Zone 9.

SPECIES *D. aurea*, growing to 60 cm (24 in), produces single, yellow flowers. *D. longifolia* has yellow and purplish brown flowers, with a flower stem to 40 cm (16 in) tall. *D. punctata* has white to purple, spotted flowers, also with stems to 40 cm (16 in).

ABOVE Flowering in late spring, *Diuris longifolia* is a lovely Australian terrestrial orchid.

Dodecatheon (fam. Primulaceae)

American cowslip, shooting star

These pretty, herbaceous perennials are mostly native to North America. Borne on leafless stems up to 30 cm (12 in) tall, the flowers, with reflexed petals, resemble cyclamen. The soft, strap-like leaves form a clump at the base.

CULTIVATION *Dodecatheon* prefers a light, loamy soil, rich in leaf mould, and a sheltered, partially shaded position. It should be kept moist but well drained. Propagate by seed, which is slow to germinate. Sow in fall and plant out in spring. Otherwise, divide two-year-old crowns in late fall or early winter in mild areas, and in early spring where it is cold.

CLIMATE Zone 6. *Dodecatheon* does best in cool climates.

SPECIES *D. alpinum*, to 12 cm (5 in), produces magenta, yellow and white flowers in late spring. *D. clevelandii*, to 30 cm (12 in), has violet-blue and yellow, or white, flowers in late spring. *D. hendersonii*, to 30 cm (12 in), has violet and yellow flowers in late spring. *D. meadia*, shooting star, zone 3, is one of the species generally

available, doing well in mountain gardens. It produces rose-purple flowers, with a white base and prominent yellow anthers, in early summer and grows 30–60 cm (12–24 in). *D. pulchellum*, to 20 cm (8 in), has pale lilac and yellow flowers in mid to late spring.

Dodonaea (fam. Sapindaceae)

Hop bush

Mostly native to Australia and New Zealand, some species of this genus were used as a hops substitute by early settlers, hence the common name. These woody shrubs are now generally grown for their decorative foliage and showy, attractively colored, three-angled fruits.

CULTIVATION Most of the species like well-drained soil and full sun or part shade. In climates where frosts are likely, grow in pots of soil-based compost in a cool greenhouse or conservatory. Propagate from lateral or tip cuttings 8–15 cm (3–6 in) long. Lightly prune to encourage a compact shape, possibly several times a year if these plants are being used for hedging. *Dodonaea* is prone to attack by scale insects which can be controlled by a white oil spray.

CLIMATE Zone 9.

BELOW This pretty American woodland plant, *Dodecatheon* species, with its rich cyclamen pink flowers, will readily colonize ground under deciduous trees.

BELOW In the right climate, *Dodonaea triquetra* is an easy-care shrub which is effective in mixed plantings.

SPECIES A good range of species is available in the US. *D. adenophora* is a hardy, erect, decorative shrub, to 2 m (6 ft), with sticky, dark green, fern-like foliage and red, winged fruits in fall and winter. *D. boroniifolia*, fern-leaf hop bush, is a bushy shrub, to 2 m (6 ft), which prefers a shady situation. It has fern-like, light green foliage and light green to purple fruits. *D. cuneata*, common hop bush, has wedge-shaped leaves and winged, red fruits. *D. lobulata*, lobed hop bush, is a very beautiful shrub, with fern-like leaves and red, winged fruits most of the year. It grows to 2 m (6 ft). *D. viscosa*, giant hop bush, is the most widely grown and makes a good hedging plant in a suitable climate. The leaves are shiny and sticky, and the summer fruits are not highly colored. Cultivar 'Purpurea', purple hop bush, from New Zealand, has beautiful, purple foliage, turning reddish in winter.

Dolichos (fam. Papilionaceae)

These evergreen or annual, climbing or twining plants are distributed through South Africa to India to eastern Asia and Australia. *Dolichos* is grown as a forage or green manure crop in some parts of the world. A rapid climber, it is useful for hiding unsightly fences or walls. The various species have now been transferred to other genera.

CULTIVATION In frosty climates, grow in a cool conservatory, or as summer annuals outdoors. These plants like light, loamy soil, and much water in summer. Let some pods mature and dry on the vine to save seed. Propagate by seed sown in early spring, or by spring cuttings.

CLIMATE Zone 9.

SPECIES *D. lablab*, now *Lablab purpureus*, is called by a variety of common names: hyacinth bean, lablab, bonavista bean, Indian bean, Egyptian bean and seim bean. It is a perennial, 30–60 cm (12–24 in) high, with rosy purple or white flowers through summer and wide, flat seed pods up to 8 cm (3 in) long. *D. lignosus*,

ABOVE *Dolichos lignosus* (ncw *Dipogon lignosus*), has a rampant growth habit and should be cut back before the flowers set seed.

now *Dipogon lignosus*, Australian pea, is a half-hardy perennial evergreen, to about 4.5 m (15 ft), useful for providing quick cover, particularly in dry, desert regions. It produces upright sprays of pea-like, pink to mauve flowers, marked with white. When hot enough, the long pods burst open and disperse seed over a wide area.

Dombeya (fam. Sterculiaceae)

This genus comprises over 200 species of ornamental, evergreen trees and shrubs, predominantly from Madagascar, though some originate from Africa. They come from a range of habitats, including forest margins and open scrub, and are cultivated for their lovely white, pink or red flowers.

CULTIVATION In frosty climates, grow in a warm greenhouse or conservatory, in pots of soil-based potting compost. Provide bright light but shade from direct sun. Prune lightly after flowering to restrict growth. Outdoors grow in full sun or partial shade in well drained yet moist soil.Propagate from seed sown in spring at 21°C (70°F), or from semi-ripe cuttings rooted in a heated propagating case.

ABOVE This very fine cultivar of *Dombeya* species has large, creamy pink flower heads that droop with their own weight.

CLIMATE Zone 10.

SPECIES *D. burgessiae*, mostly a shrub of 2–4 m (6–12 ft), has clusters of white, rose-tinted flowers, similar to hydrangeas, and pointed, three-lobed, slightly hairy leaves, grayish green in color. *D. tiliacea*, sometimes known as Cape wedding flower, is an attractive species, fast-growing and slender when young, reaching 8 m (26 ft) when mature. Pendulous clusters of two to four white flowers, tinged pink and finely veined, are borne at the ends of main and side branches between summer and fall.

Doodia (fam. Blechnaceae)
Rasp fern

These small ferns with creeping rhizomes and upright fronds come from a diverse range of habitats in Australasia and the Pacific.

CULTIVATION This is one of the easier ferns to raise. Propagate from spores. Carefully pot in a standard fern mixture and place in a sheltered and shaded spot. It is suitable for growing outdoors, particularly in rockeries. In frost-prone climates, tender species can be grown in a cool greenhouse.

ABOVE Pink-tipped new growth of *Doodia aspera* is very attractive.

CLIMATE Zone 9.

SPECIES *D. aspera*, prickly rasp fern, is prolific in open temperate to tropical forests in eastern Australia. It has a short, creeping rhizome with black scales, creamish colored stems, light green, upright fronds and serrated leaflets. *D. media*, common rasp fern, native to eastern Australia, New Zealand and Hawaii, is a small, hardy fern which thrives in crevices and rockeries. It has a short, creeping rhizome and coarse, upright fronds.

Doronicum (fam. Asteraceae)
Leopard's bane

Native to Europe and Asia, this genus comprises around 30 species of perennial herbs, with rich yellow, daisy-like flowers in spring or summer. They are excellent border plants and long-lasting cut flowers.

CULTIVATION Doronicums like a rich, moist soil and a sunny or partially shaded position. Propagate by division of the crowns every few years in spring. Alternatively, they can be propagated from seed sown from late spring to early summer.

CLIMATE There are species suited to various climatic zones.

ABOVE The ray-like florets of *Doronicum* species are fine and widely spaced..

SPECIES *D. austriacum*, zone 5, is a hairy plant, growing to 1 m (3 ft), and producing golden yellow flowers in the spring. *D. columnae* (syn. *D. cordatum*), spring beauty, zone 5, grows from fibrous rhizomes to a height of 60 cm (24 in) and it produces single, yellow flowers. *D. plantagineum*, to 80 cm (24 in), has deep yellow flowers in late spring. There are several named cultivars of this species, all well worth growing.

Dorotheanthus (fam. Aizoaceae)
Livingstone daisy

These succulent, prostrate annuals from Cape Province in South Africa produce an abundance of brightly colored flowers which close up when not exposed to full sunshine. Minute protuberances make their leaves glisten in the sun.

CULTIVATION Sow seed under glass in early spring, germinate at 19°C (66°F) and plant out young plants when danger of frost is over. Choose a site in full sun.

CLIMATE Zone 10 but grown as a summer annual in all climates.

SPECIES *D. bellidiformis*, Livingstone daisy, comes in white, pale pink, red, orange and

ABOVE Livingstone daisies, *Dorotheanthus bellidiformis*, provide a bright display of spring color.

white, tipped with red. Massed displays in rockeries, beds and planter boxes are very appealing.

Doryanthes (fam. Agavaceae)

This magnificent native Australian genus of two species has gained popularity recently. Most unusual and striking plants, they are half-lily, half-palm in appearance. Their stiff, sword-like foliage and rich red flower stems, 4–5 m (13–16 ft) high, make them wonderful accent plants.

CULTIVATION Doryanthes are grown in a cool greenhouse or conservatory in climates that are prone to frost. They could be stood outdoors for the summer, for instance, on a sunny patio. Grow them in pots or tubs of soil-based potting compost and provide maximum light. Water normally in the growing season but keep only slightly moist in winter. Propagate from seed sown in spring and germinate at 13°C (55°F). Alternatively, remove and pot up rooted suckers.

CLIMATE Zone 10.

SPECIES *D. excelsa*, Gymea lily, generally found in damp, coastal areas of Queensland and New

ABOVE The intricate beauty of the flowers on *Doryanthes excelsa* is often lost, when they are high up on their stems.

ABOVE The delicate, white flowers of *Doryphora sassafras* appear mainly in late winter to spring, but may spot bloom at other times.

South Wales, is an imposing plant, with broad, lance-shaped, light green leaves, up to 2 m (6 ft) long, and large heads of scarlet flowers borne on long, straight spikes, 4–5 m (13–16 ft) tall. *D. palmeri*, spear lily, is a native of Queensland, with red, funnel-shaped flowers on stems which tend to curve downwards. It grows to 5 m (16 ft) or more.

Doryphora (fam. Monimiaceae)
Sassafras

The two species of this genus are native to Australia–tall, handsome trees which do well in warm temperate areas. They have shiny, dark green, aromatic foliage and fragrant, white, star-shaped flowers. They are unlikely to be available outside their native Australia.

CULTIVATION In frost-prone areas, they would have to be grown in an intermediate to warm greenhouse or conservatory as young foliage plants. Grow them in pots or tubs of soil-based potting compost. They are slow growing. Propagate from the hairy, brown seeds. Sow them in a sandy seed compost and provide bottom heat.

CLIMATE Zone 10.

SPECIES *D. aromatica*, gray sassafras, from northern Queensland, reaches 35 m (115 ft) in its habitat, but is smaller in cultivation. This species forms a canopy of shiny, opposite leaves, with serrated margins. The trunk is gray, the white flowers are borne in clusters, and the fruit is club-shaped. The entire tree is strongly aromatic. *D. sassafras*, yellow sassafras, is a medium-sized to tall tree, to 30 m (100 ft), quite common along the eastern coast of Australia. The bark is gray, the foliage is bright, the flowers grow to 2 cm (1 in) in diameter and the fruit is oval in shape. This fine specimen tree is delightfully fragrant. The timber is also fragrant and because of its properties is a popular choice for furniture and insect-proof storage boxes.

Dracaena (fam. Agavaceae)

This genus comprises around 40 species of tropical, evergreen plants grown both indoors and outdoors for their foliage and often architectural form. They are quite variable: some are slender and spiky, while others are soft and shrubby. They are very popular as house plants as they do particularly well indoors, and they are also widely used for decorating conservatories. Their original habitats are also diverse as they may come from forest, scrub or open plain. In the main, they are native to tropical and West Africa, and also the Canary Islands.

CULTIVATION In frosty areas, grow in an intermediate to warm greenhouse or conservatory, in pots of soilless or soil-based potting compost. Plants, especially the variegated kinds, need good light but shade from direct sun. Provide a humid atmosphere. Propagate from stem sections without leaves, or from semi-ripe cuttings, in summer. They need basal heat to root.

CLIMATE Zone 10 at least.

BELOW *Dracaena marginata* provides a striking sculptural effect viewed against a terracotta-colored wall.

SPECIES *D. draco*, dragon tree, grows to 10 m (33 ft), with dull gray-green leaves to 60 cm (24 in) long. It is a very long-lived tree, becoming wide-crowned and umbrella-shaped as it ages, if grown in an open position. Mature trees produce white flowers followed by bright orange fruits. The resin from the stems is used in varnishes and photoengraving. *D. fragrans*, happy plant, to at least 4 m (13 ft), has long, pointed leaves. Many cultivars with many leaf variegations are available and popular, such as the Deremensis Group (syn. *D. deremensis*), with very diverse variegation, and 'Massangeana' which has very distinctive, yellow-striped leaves. *D. marginata* is a slender, robust plant to 5 m (16 ft) high, with narrow, sharp-pointed leaves to 60 cm (24 in) long. It grows well indoors in a dimly lit position. *D. surculosa* (syn. *D. godseffiana*), gold dust dracaena or spotted dracaena, is attractive, with green leaves irregularly spotted in white, pale gold or cream. It grows 1–1.5 m (3–5 ft).

Dracophyllum (fam. Epacridaceae)
Grass tree

Native to Australia and New Zealand, this genus consists of about 48 species of shrubs and trees, generally with sharply pointed, stem-clasping leaves and dense spikes of tubular flowers on one side of the stem.

BELOW Palest pink flowers emerge from spiky foliage on *Dracophyllum secundum*. It grows naturally on damp, sandstone ridges.

CULTIVATION *Dracophyllum* likes cool, shady conditions and moisture. Propagate from root cuttings in spring. Strike in sharp sand and repot with minimal disturbance. It tolerates pruning. In frosty climates, grow in a cool greenhouse.

CLIMATE Zones 9 and 10.

SPECIES *D. longifolium*, from New Zealand, is a large shrub or tree to 10 m (33 ft). It has dark green, leathery leaves, sometimes shaded with red, and sprays of white flowers. *D. paludosum*, to 2 m (6 ft), has spikes of white flowers in summer. *D. secundum*, necklace heath, from New South Wales, is a trailing plant, with spikes of white flowers.

Drimys (fam. Winteraceae)
Winter's bark

Only one species of this small genus of evergreen trees and shrubs, mainly native to South America, is common in cultivation.

CULTIVATION *Drimys* requires moist but well-drained conditions and shelter from strong winds. Propagate from seed, or from cuttings of half-ripe shoots taken in summer.

CLIMATE Zone 8.

ABOVE Tree-like in its habitat, fragrant *Drimys winteri* is often shrubby and multi-stemmed in cultivation.

SPECIES *D. winteri*, winter's bark, grows to 15 m (50 ft) in its habitat but is much smaller in cultivation. Its leaves and bark have a peppery aroma and its ivory-white flowers have a jasmine-like fragrance.

Drosera (fam. Droseraceae)
Sundew

This genus of insectivorous plants is quite widely distributed and includes many species native to south-western Australia. Small, sticky hairs on the tips of the leaves trap small insects. When an insect lands, the hairs fold inwards, snaring the creature. The sticky globules resemble dew drops, hence the use of the common name. Pretty little buttercup-like flowers appear in spring, mostly in white or pink.

CULTIVATION Sundews are generally grown in pots in a cool greenhouse, except in frost-free climates where they are grown in a bog garden. In the greenhouse, grow plants in a mix of peat and sand (equal parts), provide maximum light but shade from strong sun, and stand pots in dishes of water to keep the compost wet. Keep plants drier in winter.

CLIMATE Zone 9 for most species.

SPECIES *D. binata*, forked sundew, from New South Wales, Victoria, South Australia and

BELOW Sundews, *Drosera* species, have masses of small, sticky hairs on their foliage for trapping insects.

Tasmania, grows to 35 cm (14 in). It has forked leaves and large, creamish white, showy flowers from spring to early summer. *D. capensis*, from South Africa, is a delicate, striking species, to 15 cm (6 in), with purple flowers on leafless stems in the spring. *D. macrantha*, zone 8, from southwestern Western Australia, climbing sundew, produces white or pink flowers in spring. *D. petiolaris* and *D. spathulata* are two other Australian species cultivated. Both are small plants, with reddish leaves.

Dryandra (fam. Proteaceae)

All 65 species of shrubs in this genus are endemic to Western Australia. With showy flower domes and attractive, evergreen foliage, these bushy shrubs are related to *Banksia*. Their natural habitats include dry, rocky or sandy coastal areas and open scrub.

CULTIVATION In frost-prone climates, grow in a cool conservatory or greenhouse, in pots of acid, soil-based potting compost enriched with extra peat and sharp sand. Provide maximum light. Water sparingly in winter, normally in growing season. Outdoors, plants need a sunny spot with poor, acid to neutral, well-drained soil. They dislike root disturbance. Propagate from seed sown under glass in spring. Germinate at 18°C (64°F).

CLIMATE Zone 10.

SPECIES *D. floribunda*, hollyleaf dryandra, a more easily grown species, reaches up to 2.5 m (8 ft). Its flowers are a rich creamy color, with lighter colored bracts, and its stiff, holly-like foliage is toothed at the margins. Both the flowers and the foliage dry well. *D. formosa*, showy dryandra, is a beautiful, upright shrub, growing 3 m (10 ft), and grown for its rich orange, fragrant flowers, with lighter bracts, and its attractive, narrow, toothed foliage. *D. polycephala* has small, narrow, finely serrated leaves and a profusion of small, yellow flowers. It grows to 2–3 m (6–10 ft). *D. praemorsa*, cut-leaf dryandra, is a fine, bushy shrub, to 3 m (10 ft), with

ABOVE Dryandra flowers are yellow in the majority of species but can have orange or brown tones.

broad, prickly leaves and large, yellow flowers. *D. speciosa* is one of the most beautiful of the species and well suited to greenhouses as it grows to only 1.2 m (4 ft). Its silvery gray buds open to silky, salmon pink flowers, later turning a gold-brown color, surrounded by white bracts. This species provides excellent cut flowers.

Duranta (fam. Verbenaceae)
Sky flower

This genus of around 30 species of evergreen trees and shrubs, with long racemes or panicles of small flowers and very attractive fruits, is native mainly to South America and the Caribbean.

CULTIVATION In frost-prone climates, grow in an intermediate greenhouse or conservatory, or in pots of soil-based potting compost, with good light but shade from strong sun. Plants can be pruned in winter to contain growth. Outdoors, grow in full sun. Some species make good screens or hedges. Propagate from semi-ripe cuttings in summer, providing basal warmth.

CLIMATE Zone 10, but zone 9 for *D. erecta*.

ABOVE Ideal for screening, *Duranta erecta* is also very decorative when covered in lavender blue, summer flowers.

SPECIES *D. erecta* (syn. *D. repens*), golden dewdrop, pigeon berry or golden tears, is the most commonly grown of the species. This attractive, weeping, open shrub, with glossy, green, oval leaves, grows to 3 m (10 ft) high, and is often used as a screen plant. Abundant sprays of blue flowers appear through summer, followed by a profusion of bright yellow berries over a long period. All varieties of *D. erecta* do well in dry conditions once established. They make attractive hedges and can be trained as standards.

Durian (*Durio zibethinus*, fam. Bombacaceae)

Durian is extensively cultivated in the tropics for its remarkable fruits. The spiny green fruits are the size of a football and can weigh over 2 kg (4.5 lb). They are evil-smelling but have a creamy, edible pulp highly favored by people in Southeast Asian countries. The Chinese call it 'King of Fruits' and many thousands of tourists make a point of tasting it while visiting Malaysia, Thailand and nearby countries. The fast-growing evergreen tree producing these interesting fruits can reach heights of up to 20 m (65 ft). Rarely cultivated in the US except occasionally in Hawaii and botanical gardens.

ABOVE The heavy, spiny fruits of durian grow on very large trees with buttressed trunks. They fall when ripe.

CULTIVATION Durian is propagated from seed, although superior selections may be grafted onto seedling understocks.

CLIMATE This tree thrives only in true tropical conditions.

Dyckia (fam. Bromeliaceae)

These bromeliads from tropical South America have succulent, prominently toothed, barbed leaves and form the typical rosettes from which emerge tall, lateral stems of orange or yellow flowers. They are found in a variety of habitats, from the coast to quite high altitudes in the mountains.

CULTIVATION Very easy to grow, dyckias can be planted in the open garden in partial shade. If well drained, they will colonize in poor, rocky soils. They can tolerate light frost. Propagate from offsets or seed. They look best planted with other succulents. In areas prone to hard frosts, grow in an intermediate greenhouse or conservatory, in soilless potting compost. Provide maximum light. Keep compost almost dry in winter.

CLIMATE Zone 9. Tolerates light frost.

SPECIES *D. brevifolia*, from Brazil, has a dark green rosette of thorny, tapering leaves, up to

ABOVE Many species of *Dyckia* have heavily armed, silver-gray foliage. The tall, flowering spikes stand well clear of the leaves.

25 cm (10 in) long, with stripes on the under-side, and a profusion of yellow flowers. *D. fosteriana* is a very attractive species. The long, heavily armed, silvery, recurved leaves are tinged with red and the flowers are orange. *D. remotiflora* forms a dense rosette of arching, dark green leaves, with a slender stem of deep orange flowers appearing in late spring.

Dysoxylum (fam. Meliaceae)

Of these 80 species of trees, some are native to Australia and one to New Zealand. Occurring naturally in moist rainforests, they have large, shiny leaves. Sprays of white flowers are often borne on bare branches and are followed by large fruits, 3 cm (1 in) in diameter, containing large, bright red seeds. Often buttressed, they make good ornamental and shade trees in sub-tropical and tropical regions and are cultivated for their fine, reddish timber, used for decorative and cabinet work. These trees are not cultivated outside their native countries, except perhaps in botanical gardens.

CULTIVATION *Dysoxylum* likes a deep, moist soil and a subtropical climate. Propagate from ripened seed (the brilliant red seed covering is the outer skin of the true seed).

CLIMATE Zone 10.

SPECIES *D. fraserianum*, Australian mahogany or rosewood, grows to 40 m (130 ft) in its habitat, but is much smaller in cultivation. It has pinnate leaves, sprays of sweetly perfumed, white flowers, and round, leathery fruits, to 3 cm (1 in), containing the bright red seeds. The timber is rose-scented. *D. muelleri*, red bean, is a medium to large tree in its habitat, with dark yellow bark, divided leaves, sprays of small, white flowers and round fruits with scarlet seeds. The red timber is not fragrant. *D. oppositifolium* is a medium or small tree, with flaky, gray bark and pink wood. It produces sprays of white, bell-shaped flowers and oval, leathery fruits with red seeds. *D. spectabile*, kohekohe or New Zealand cedar, is considered one of New Zealand's most handsome trees, well suited as an ornamental. It is a medium-sized, very decorative tree, to 15 m (50 ft), with large, shiny leaves and white flowers similar to lily-of-the-valley. It has very large, leathery fruits, opening to brilliant, scarlet seeds.

BELOW *Dysoxylum muelleri* develops a dome shape when grown in the open but is taller and straighter in the forest.

E

Eccremocarpus to Exochorda

Eccremocarpus (fam. Bignoniaceae)

Chilean glory flower

Only one of these beautiful, evergreen climbers is commonly cultivated. They have opposite leaves with terminal, branched tendrils, and terminal sprays of tubular, yellow or orange flowers from spring to fall.

CULTIVATION In frost-prone areas, grow in a cool greenhouse or conservatory, or as a summer annual outdoors. In mild climates, eccremocarpus are grown as perennials, although they are short lived. Sow seeds in early spring under glass and germinate at 16°C (61°F). Under glass, grow in pots of soil-based potting compost and provide maximum light. Outdoors, grow in sun with well-drained soil. Supports will be needed for the stems.

CLIMATE Zone 9.

SPECIES *E. scaber*, Chilean glory flower, is a slender, woody climber, 3–4 m (10–13 ft) long, with dainty leaves, grown for its lopsided tubular flowers which come in either yellow, orange or scarlet. Fruit pods contain the winged seeds. The form aureus has golden yellow flowers, while the carmineus form has carmine red flowers.

ABOVE Scarlet-flowered *Eccremocarpus scaber* and one of its golden yellow varieties complement one another when grown together.

Echeveria (fam. Crassulaceae)

Predominantly native to Mexico and the central Americas, this popular genus comprises about 150 species of attractive, perennial succulents, all typically forming rosettes. Some species offset freely from the base to form large mats; others grow on tall stems. They have very succulent leaves, some smooth, some hairy, others powdery, and bell-shaped flowers. The stems bear either a few or many blooms and droop from the apex. Many very beautiful cultivars have been produced.

CULTIVATION In frost-prone climates, grow in an airy, intermediate greenhouse or conservatory, in pots of well-drained cactus compost, which can be bought from garden centers. Ensure maximum light. Water normally in growing period, but keep barely moist in winter. Potted plants can be stood outside for the summer. Some species are used for summer bedding. For permanent outdoor cultivation, choose a sunny spot with free-draining, poorish soil. Propagate from leaf cuttings or stem cuttings in summer, or from offsets in spring.

CLIMATE Zone 10.

SPECIES *E. agavoides*, from Mexico, has thick, almost triangular-shaped, pale green leaves,

BELOW The pale, silvery blue rosettes of *Echeveria elegans* multiply rapidly to make a lovely container or garden plant.

with hard, reddish brown tips, resembling spines. It produces numerous, small, dark pink flowers on long stems. *E. derenbergii*, a small, stemless rosette, about 6–8 cm (2½–3 in) across, from Mexico, has pale green leaves with red margins and sharp tips. The reddish yellow flowers appear on stems about 8 cm (3 in) tall. This easily grown species produces many offsets around the base. *E. elegans*, hen and chickens, forms mats of tight, basal rosettes, 10 cm (4 in) across, of ice-blue leaves, sometimes edged with red. The flowers are pink with yellow tips and appear on stalks 10–25 cm (4–10 in) long. *E. gibbiflora* is a quite large, loose rosette, to 40 cm (16 in) across, on a thick stem 10–20 cm (4–8 in) tall. Its red flowers are borne on a 60 cm (24 in) stem. *E. leucotricha* forms loose rosettes of quite thick, blunt leaves, covered with white felt and tipped with brown, felty hairs. The large, scarlet flowers are borne on tall stems. *E. pulvinata* has open rosettes of hairy, white, silky leaves, bright red in fall, borne on brown, downy stems. It produces reddish yellow flowers on 30 cm (12 in) stems from winter to spring. *E. secunda* is a stemless, saucer-like rosette, with wedge-shaped, blueish white leaves, sharply pointed at the tips, and red flowers with yellow tips. It offsets freely from the base.

Echinacea (fam. Asteraceae)
Coneflower

These showy perennials have large, daisy-like flowers from mid to late summer and are excellent for border planting. Their flowers are prominent, globe- or cone-shaped discs surrounded by slightly recurved ray florets. *E. purpurea* has a long history of use in herbal medicine. *E. angustifolia* also has potential. Research is continuing as these plants appear to increase the body's resistance to infection.

CULTIVATION *Echinacea* is easy to grow, but does best in a deep, rich loam and in a sunny position. While it thrives with regular summer watering, it can tolerate dry periods once established. It may require tying. Propagate from

ABOVE Clumps of the herbaceous purple coneflower, *Echinacea purpurea*, increase annually and need dividing every three to four years.

seed, by division in fall or early winter, or from root cuttings.

CLIMATE The following species thrive in zone 3.

SPECIES *E. angustifolia* has lance-shaped, entire leaves and rose-purple to white summer flowers. *E. purpurea*, purple coneflower, has broadly lance-shaped, toothed leaves and rose-purple flowers, with orange cone-shaped centers. It grows 1–2 m (3–6 ft). Cultivar 'Alba' has white ray flowers with greenish central discs. In suitable conditions the clumps multiply a good deal each season.

Echinocactus (fam. Cactaceae)

Native to North America and Mexico, these big, barrel-shaped, slow-growing cactuses have strong spines on acute ribs, flattened at the apex and woolly where the flowers appear. The short, funnel-shaped, sometimes self-fertile flowers open by day and close by nightfall. Tube, ovary and fruit are woolly and scaly.

CULTIVATION In frost-prone climates, grow in an airy, intermediate greenhouse or conservatory, in pots of cactus compost, obtainable from garden centers. Provide maximum light and do not water plants in winter. Outdoors, grow in a

ABOVE A well-grown golden barrel cactus, Echinocactus grusonii, is the focal point of this dry-climate garden.

sunny spot with well-drained soil. Propagate from seed in spring, in a warm propagating case.

CLIMATE Will grow in relatively frost-free areas. At least zone 9.

SPECIES *E. grusonii*, golden ball or golden barrel, from Mexico, is a huge, globe-shaped cactus, to 1 m (3 ft) tall and up to 80 cm (32 in) across. It has long, strong, golden spines, rather thin ribs and yellow flowers, up to 6 cm (2½ in) long, which grow in a circle from the woolly areoles at the plant's top. *E. platyacanthus* (syn. *E. ingens*) is a large, grayish green plant, to 1.5 m (5 ft) high and about 1 m (3 ft) across, with up to 50 high, rounded ribs and very sharp spines, 3–4 cm (about 1½ in) long. It has a woolly apex from which emerge yellow flowers, 20 mm (1 in) in diameter.

Echinocereus (fam. Cactaceae)
Hedgehog cactus

This very large genus of cactuses is from North America and Mexico. Ranging from tiny plants the size of a thimble to large clumps 1 m (3 ft) across, they are mostly tufted, soft and fleshy,

with notched or warty ribs. Spines vary from bristly and soft to sharp and stiff. Large, long-lasting, funnel-shaped flowers bloom from the stem sides in spring and summer. Brightly colored, most with vivid green stigma lobes, they open by day and close at nightfall. Fruit, tube and ovary are woolly and covered with masses of spines.

CULTIVATION In frost-prone climates, grow in an airy, intermediate greenhouse or conservatory, in pots of cactus compost, obtainable from garden centers. Provide maximum light and do not water plants in winter. Outdoors, grow in a sunny spot and in well-drained soil. Propagate from seed in spring, in a warm propagating case, or from stem cuttings in summer.

CLIMATE Will grow in relatively frost-free areas. At least zone 9.

SPECIES Most species are in cultivation, but only a few will be listed here. *E. chloranthus* produces greenish yellow flowers in spring. The stems grow to 25 cm (10 in) tall and 5 cm (2 in) or more thick. *E. enneacanthus*, strawberry cactus, bears purple-red flowers, followed by rounded, green or purple, edible fruits. The tufted stems grow 30 cm (12 in) tall and up to

BELOW A jewel-like, satiny flower emerges from the densely packed spines of a hedgehog cactus, Echinocereus species.

10 cm (4 in) thick. *E. knippelianus* is a small, soft, dark green cactus, with five ribs and only a few, short spines. The flowers are pale pink. *E. pectinatus* has bands of white to pink, comb-like spines and large, bright pink flowers. *E. reichenbachii*, lace cactus, grows to about 30 cm (12 in) tall and 8 cm (3 in) or so thick. The flowers are pink to purple. There are many forms of this species in cultivation, especially in its native United States. *E. triglochidiatus* is a squat form, growing to around 30 cm (12 in) tall and 20–25 cm (8–10 in) thick. It has persistent, white wool and bright scarlet or crimson flowers. Many varieties of this species are also in cultivation.

Echinops (fam. Asteraceae)
Globe thistle

These hardy, herbaceous perennials are widely distributed, from Europe and the Mediterranean, to tropical Africa and central Asia. Members of the daisy family, they are well suited to borders and also look attractive planted in drifts. The spiky, grayish green leaves form rosettes from which the globe-like, spiky flower heads emerge on tall stems. The individual flowers are either steel blue or white. They make excellent dried flowers,

BELOW Globe thistles, *Echinops species*, add contrast in form and color to a garden border.

particularly for winter arrangements, as the metallic sheen of the flower heads remains for some time after drying.

CULTIVATION *Echinops* does well in any garden soil in full sun. Propagate from seed sown in a sunny position, root cuttings or by division.

CLIMATE Zone 3 for the species below.

SPECIES *E. bannaticus*, from south-eastern Europe, grows to 1 m (3 ft) or more high. It has spiny, gray-green leaves and blue-gray flower heads in summer. Cultivar 'Blue Globe' has deep blue flowers. It will reflower if the stems are cut back after first bloom. 'Taplow Blue' has bright blue flower heads. *E. ritro*, small globe thistle, to 60 cm (24 in), has deeply cut, prickly leaves, glossy green above and downy below, and bright blue flower heads in summer. This species is suitable for drying. *E. sphaerocephalus*, great globe thistle, forms large clumps, to 2 m (6 ft), with silver-gray flower heads in summer and spiny, gray-green foliage.

Echinopsis (fam. Cactaceae)

The bright, glossy green cactuses from 50 to over 100 species making up this genus are all similar and native to South America. However, many hybrids have been developed from crossing *Echinopsis* and *Lobivia* and *Echinopsis* and *Chamaecereus*. These are available in many colors. These hybrids produce freely only from offsets. The bodies are mostly globe-shaped, at times cylindrical, and sharply ribbed, with ferocious spines. The large, mostly white, diurnal flowers are short-lived. Sometimes fragrant, they bloom in spring through to summer. All are self-sterile.

CULTIVATION In frost-prone climates, grow in an airy, intermediate greenhouse or conservatory, in cactus compost. Provide maximum light and do not water plants in winter. Outdoors, grow in a sunny spot with well-drained soil. Propagate from seed in spring, in a warm propagating case, or from offsets in spring.

ABOVE Plant forms in the *Echinopsis* genus range from globular to columnar or cylindrical, some producing dense colonies.

CLIMATE Will grow in relatively frost-free areas. At least zone 9.

SPECIES *E. backebergii* is a clump-forming, spherical, dark green cactus with notched ribs. The woolly areoles bear reddish spines which change to gray as they age. The spines may be curved or hooked. Summer flowers are diurnal and may be scarlet or violet. *E. chamaecereus*, a clumping or mat-forming cactus, has cylindrical stems and white or brownish spines. The bright orange to scarlet summer flowers are diurnal. *E. cinnabarina*, a clustering type, has a squat, rounded shape and bright scarlet flowers. *E. huascha* develops cylindrical stems and bears yellow or red flowers. *E. lageniformis* is tree-like, to about 2 m (6 ft) high, with columnar stems. The spines are rather fine and yellowish and the white flowers are nocturnal. *E. spachiana* is a more shrub-like cactus, with ribbed deep green stems branching from the base. It may grow 1–2 m (3–6 ft) high and spread 75 cm (30 in). The nocturnal, summer flowers are white with green outer petals.

Echium (fam. Boraginaceae)
Viper's bugloss

Native to the Mediterranean and the Canary Islands, these striking annuals and perennials

ABOVE The towering cones of rich purple-blue flowers on *Echium candicans* attract bees and other insects.

are grown for their tall spires of blue, purple, red, pink or white flowers massed in bracted, simple or forked heads. The leaves are gray-green and slightly wavy. Echium gives a lovely display but needs to be carefully sited as most grow quite large. Some species tolerate frost, others are quickly damaged by low temperatures.

CULTIVATION These plants do well in coastal conditions where they will tolerate poor, sandy soil, provided they have good drainage and full sun. Grow frost-tender species in a cool, airy greenhouse with maximum light, in pots of soil-based compost. Propagate from tip cuttings taken in summer. These are often difficult to strike. Alternatively, propagate from seed.

CLIMATE Zones 9 or 10; best in a Mediterranean climate of hot, dry summers and cold, wet winters.

SPECIES *E. candicans* (syn. *E. fastuosum*), pride of Madeira, is a frost-tender biennial, to 2.5 m (8 ft), with a wide-spreading habit. The hairy, grayish green, veined leaves form rosettes and the large spikes of rich blue flowers are borne on tall stalks in late spring or summer.

Edgeworthia (fam. Thymelaeceae)

This genus comprises two or three species of evergreen or deciduous flowering shrubs with papery bark from China and Japan. They have simple, alternate leaves crowded at the ends of branches. Dense heads of small, yellow, scented flowers are borne at the ends of the bare branches in spring.

CULTIVATION Edgeworthias dislike extremes, requiring mild conditions, good drainage and ample water in the growing season. Propagate from semi-ripe cuttings in summer, or from seed sown in fall and germinated in a garden frame.

CLIMATE Zone 8; provide a warm, sheltered position.

SPECIES *E. chrysantha* (syn. *E. papyrifera*), paper bush, is a deciduous shrub to 2 m (6 ft), with tough, supple shoots and oblong leaves. Large, terminal clusters of fragrant, rich yellow flowers appear in early spring before the leaves.

BELOW Known also as yellow daphne, fragrant *Edgeworthia chrysantha* can be cut for the house where its fragrance will fill the room.

This species has long been cultivated in Japan as a source of handcrafted paper.

Eggplant

(*Solanum melongena*, fam. Solanaceae)

Aubergine

Orginating in Asia, the eggplant or aubergine is grown for its fruit and is widely grown in the US. It is a popular vegetable in Europe, particularly in Mediterranean countries. The French use it as an ingredient in ratatouille, the Greeks use it as the basis of moussaka, and roasted eggplant can be bought from delicatessens and supermarkets everywhere. This tender annual is related to the potato and tomato, and produces a 30 cm (12 in) long, dark purple fruit. White or striped forms are available. Eggplant can be eaten at several stages of its growth.

CULTIVATION Requirements are similar to those for the tomato. In cool and cold climates, eggplants are best grown in a heated greenhouse, but in warmer climates, plants can be grown outside. They like a temperature of 25–30°C (77°–86°F) and moderate atmospheric humidity. They need a fertile soil, or can be grown in pots of soilless potting compost or in growing

BELOW A vigorous plant of eggplant or aubergine bears well. Flowers continue to appear while one crop of fruit is almost ripe.

bags. Sow seeds in spring under glass after soaking in warm water for a day, and germinate at 21°C (70°F). Pot seedlings individually into 9 cm (3½ in) pots. Plant out young plants when 10 cm (4 in) tall, outdoors only when there is no longer danger of frost. Choose a sunny, sheltered site. Plant 75 cm (30 in) apart. Under glass, pot young plants into 20–25 cm (8–10 in) pots.

CLIMATE Zone 10, but grown as a summer annual in all climates.

Elaeagnus (fam. Elaeagnaceae)

Originating from southern Europe, North America and Asia, these ornamental, evergreen or deciduous shrubs are grown for their attractive, often variegated foliage. They have alternate, simple leaves, covered with brown or silvery scales, inconspicuous flowers and occasionally small, red fruit. Many of the species have thorns. These shrubs are often grown as screens or hedges but also suit mixed borders.

CULTIVATION *Elaeagnus* does well in any dryish, ordinary garden soil, provided drainage is adequate. It prefers full sun, but can tolerate warm to cool conditions. Prune lightly in spring. Propagate from semi-ripe cuttings in summer or fall, from layers in spring, or from seed which may be very slow to germinate.

CLIMATE There are species suited to various climatic zones.

SPECIES *E. angustifolia*, oleaster, wild olive, Russian olive or silver berry, zone 2, is a spreading, deciduous tree, to 6 m (20 ft) with spiny branches, willow-like leaves and fragrant flowers. It is one of the species which bears fruit, which is large and silvery yellow in color. *E. pungens*, zone 7, the most commonly grown of the species, is an evergreen shrub, to 4.5 m (15 ft), which makes an excellent hedge. It has long, spiny branches and clusters of tiny, fragrant, cream flowers. The glossy, oval, green leaves have wavy edges, the undersides a silvery color, dotted with brown scales. Varieties include 'Maculata', an attractive, slow-growing shrub to 2–3 m (6–10 ft), with large, shiny leaves, splashed with yellow in the center, and 'Marginata', a good hedge or screen plant, with leaves edged in silver.

Elaeis (fam. Arecaceae)
Oil palm

This genus of palms comprises only two species, one from Africa, the other American, and is related to the coconut palm. Its fruit is reminiscent of the coconut as it has a hard, inner layer surrounding the seed, with three 'eyes' at the base. The flesh of the fruit yields an edible oil, also used in lubricants, and the African palm, in particular, has been widely cultivated for commercial purposes in the tropics. It also makes a handsome ornamental.

CULTIVATION In frost-prone climates, grow in a warm conservatory or greenhouse as young foliage plants, in pots or tubs of soil-based potting compost. Provide bright light but shade from strong sun. Propagate from seed after a week's soaking in water, and germinate at 24°C (75°F).

CLIMATE At least zone 10.

BELOW Tolerant of wind and a degree of pollution, cultivars of *Elaeagnus pungens* make good screening plants.

ABOVE The fruits of the oil palm, *Elaeis guineensis*, are congested and tucked into the base of the palm fronds.

SPECIES *E. guineensis*, African oil palm, is a single-stemmed palm growing to 20 m (65 ft) or more in maturity, though generally less in cultivation. It has a thick, straight, rough trunk, topped by a wide crown of large, plume-like leaves. The long, narrow leaflets are a glossy, deep green and the 3–4 cm (about 1½ in) long, blackish fruits are borne in short, dense clusters among the bases of the leaves. Oil is extracted from the seed kernel and the fruit pulp.

Elaeocarpus (fam. Elaeocarpaceae)

Native to the tropics and warm regions, this large genus comprises around 60 species of evergreen shrubs and trees, though only a few are commonly cultivated. They have alternate, simple leaves and axillary sprays of flowers. The ornamental species make attractive displays, having pretty flowers followed by decorative fruits. These are not readily available outside their country of origin.

CULTIVATION These excellent shade or specimen trees are suited for parks and large gardens. *E. cyaneus*, however, can be grown in the home garden. They do best in deep, well-drained, moderately fertile, acid to neutral soil, with added organic mulch. They need plenty of water in hot, dry weather. They are tolerant of only the lightest frost. In frost-prone climates, grow in a cool greenhouse or conservatory, in pots of soil-based potting compost and in maximum light.

CLIMATE Zone 9.

SPECIES *E. cyaneus*, blue-berry ash, grows 10–15 m (33–50 ft) tall, and is the species most often grown in home gardens, where it is often very much smaller. Native to coastal eastern Australia, it has pretty, fringed, white or pale pink flowers which are followed by deep blue fruits. *E. grandis*, quandong, is a large tree, to 35 m (100 ft), from the rainforests of eastern Australia. It produces greenish white flowers in winter, followed by large, blue berries. The common name, quandong, is applied in other areas to *Santalum* species. *E. kirtonii*, pigeon-berry ash or whitewood, is a large, round-headed tree from the coastal plains of New South Wales and Queensland which grows to 20 m (65 ft) in its habitat, but much less when cultivated. It has creamy white, summer flowers, followed by blue fruits.

ABOVE The dainty, fringed, bell flowers of *Elaeocarpus cyaneus* are followed by pretty, blue fruits.

Embothrium (fam. Proteaceae)

These slow-growing, evergreen trees from the central and southern Andes of South America look spectacular when in full bloom, though this can take around 10 years. Their flowers are similar to those of the tree waratah (*Alloxylon flammeum*).

CULTIVATION Best planted in a woodland garden or other sheltered area, in partial shade or full sun, in acid to neutral, humus-rich, moist soil. Propagate from semi-ripe cuttings in summer. Provide basal warmth.

CLIMATE Zone 8.

SPECIES *E. coccineum*, Chilean fire bush, grows 3–9 m (10–30 ft), with narrow, glossy, dark green leaves to 5 cm (2 in) long. The showy, bright scarlet flowers, to 5 cm (2 in) long, appear in mid-spring to early summer. Var. *lanceolatum* 'Norquinco' is an especially hardy form, grown for its graceful, arched branches and good blooming. The leaves are longer and narrower.

ABOVE Aptly named Chilean fire bush, *Embothrium coccineum* lights up the garden. The flowers attract nectar-feeding birds.

Emmenosperma (fam. Rhamnaceae)

Red ash, bonewood

This genus comprises three species of tall, handsome trees, two from Australia and one

ABOVE The succulent, yellow fruits of *Emmenosperma alphitonioides* often persist on the tree for many months.

from New Caledonia. They are unlikely to be available outside their country of origin.

CULTIVATION In frost-prone climates, these trees would have to be grown in a warm greenhouse or conservatory. As they grow quite slowly when young, they would seem to have potential as potted or tub-grown specimens. Outdoors in warm climates, these trees thrive in a rich, moist soil. Propagate from seed when ripe.

CLIMATE At least zone 10.

SPECIES *E. alphitonioides* is a tall, erect tree, with a slender trunk, found growing from the northern tip of Australia down the eastern coast to New South Wales. It has glossy, bright green leaves and dense, terminal clusters of small, creamy flowers, followed by attractive, bright yellow berries which remain on the tree through summer and fall. It reaches about 15 m (50 ft) in cultivation but may be slow-growing. This species yields a very fine timber.

Endive (*Cichorium endivia*, fam. Asteraceae)

This annual or biennial, thought to be a native of the Mediterranean, has produced some very good cultivars which are now widely grown. It

ABOVE The curly leaves of endive are extremely bitter if not harvested when young. Most growers prefer to blanch leaves.

is known to have been cultivated over many centuries and is believed to be one of the 'bitter herbs' of the Passover. Endive can be grown in slightly warmer areas than lettuce as it is tolerant of higher temperatures. Grown for its leaves, endive is slightly bitter and is delicious in salads with bacon and creamy or mustard dressing. It is grown as an fall and early winter crop in cool and cold climates.

CULTIVATION This crop performs at its best in a temperature range of 10°–20°C (50°–68°F). It will not be harmed by a light frost and the extra-hardy, broad-leaved cultivars will tolerate a temperature as low as -10°C (14°F). The curly-leaved cultivars are not so prone to running to seed in hot weather as the broad-leaved kinds. A fertile, moisture-retentive yet well-drained soil is best for endive, plus an open position in full sun. Sow seed in succession from late in spring to midsummer, outdoors in the site where they are to grow. Thin out seedlings to about 30 cm (12 in) apart each way. Harvesting can start within two to three months. Endive can be treated as a cut and come again crop. Broad-leaved cultivars especially are often blanched to remove the bitterness, but curly

leaved kinds can be blanched, too. Simply cover a plant with an inverted container, such as a bucket, for at least two weeks.

CLIMATE Zone 8.

Ensete (fam. Musaceae)
Abyssinian banana

Native to tropical Africa and Asia, these plants have large, banana-like leaves and drooping flower bracts. They make outstanding accent or feature plants in large gardens.

CULTIVATION In frost-prone climates, grow in pots or tubs in an intermediate greenhouse. Place or plunge outdoors for summer. Best grown in soil-based potting compost.

CLIMATE Zone 10.

SPECIES *E. ventricosum*, Abyssinian banana, makes an excellent garden specimen. It grows to 12 m (40 ft) in the wild, but much less in cultivation. The pseudostem is generally a pur-

ABOVE The lush foliage of *Ensete ventricosum* dominates a subtropical garden, while the stiff, gray-green Agave attenuata provides foliage contrast.

plish color and the leaves sometimes grow to 5 m (16 ft) long and 1.5 m (5 ft) wide, with a wide central midrib which is bright reddish pink underneath. The white flowers are concealed in reddish-bronze bracts. The inflorescence, which is produced in summer, may be over 1 m (3 ft) in length.

Entelea (fam. Tiliaceae)
Whau

This small, evergreen tree or shrub from New Zealand is available but not well known outside its native country. It has very light wood which is used by Maoris for fishing floats or building rafts.

CULTIVATION *Entelea* does best in mild, coastal areas. Drainage must be good and the soil should be enriched with compost or manure. Water freely in dry summer weather. In frost-prone climates, grow in a cool greenhouse or conservatory. Propagate from seed sown in spring or from cuttings in summer.

CLIMATE Zone 9.

SPECIES *E. arborescens* grows to 6 m (20 ft) and is recognized for its extremely light wood. The

BELOW *Entelea arborescens* has somehow earned the name of New Zealand mulberry. Flowers are much prettier than those of mulberry.

young, whitish foliage matures to jagged, hairy, 25 cm (10 in) long, mulberry-like leaves, with attractive veins. The white flowers, to 2.5 cm (1 in) across, have yellow stamens and are produced in pendulous clusters.

Epacris (fam. Epacridaceae)
Native heath

Native to eastern Australia and New Zealand, these evergreen, heath-like shrubs are suitable for shrub borders or, in frost-prone climates, for a cool conservatory or greenhouse. They have long, thin branches, tiny, prickly leaves and drooping clusters of tubular flowers on the stem ends. Some species flower almost continuously, but usually they bloom in spring and summer.

CULTIVATION Under glass, grow in pots of acid, soilless potting compost, and in maximum light but with shade from strong sun. Outdoors, these shrubs prefer a well-drained, fibrous, peaty soil, and can tolerate quite acidic conditions. Plant most species in a cool, moist, protected situation, but do not overwater in summer and avoid disturbing the soil where

ABOVE The long, tubular flowers of *Epacris longiflora* appear on the plant over many months.

possible. Apply a little blood and bone each spring. Prune annually after flowering. Propagate from cuttings in late spring through summer or from seed as soon as it is ripe.

CLIMATE Zone 9 if comparatively frost-free.

SPECIES *E. impressa*, common heath, is the floral emblem of Victoria. An erect shrub, to 1 m (3 ft), it has very narrow, prickly leaves and dense clusters of white, pink or red flowers, up to 20 mm (1 in) long, in spring and summer. This species is easy to grow and transplants well. *E. longiflora*, native fuchsia, is a straggly shrub, to 1 m (3 ft). A very good rockery plant, it produces rich crimson flowers, to 25 mm (1 in), tipped with white, from spring to summer. *E. microphylla*, coral heath, is an erect shrub to 1 m (3 ft). It has very tiny leaves and dense clusters of 6 mm (¼ in) long white bell flowers. A quite commonly grown species, it is suited to rock gardens.

Epidendrum (fam. Orchidaceae)
Crucifix orchid

Many species of this genus of epiphytic orchids are now classified in other genera.

BELOW A pinky red form of the crucifix orchid, *Epidendrum* species, will give a long display in the greenhouse.

Epidendrum now includes only the slender, reed-like orchids with the floral column completely united with the lip. Many excellent hybrids are available, though the white form is rare.

CULTIVATION : Throughout most of the US, these orchids are grown in a cool to intermediate greenhouse or conservatory, in pots of orchid compost, an epiphytic or terrestrial mix. Some plants may need their long stems supported. In the growing period, provide good light but shade from sun, ensure high atmospheric humidity, mist spray plants daily, water well and feed weekly. In winter, provide maximum light and keep compost only slightly moist, or completely dry for species with pseudobulbs. Propagate by division when plants have outgrown their pots.

CLIMATE At least zone 10.

SPECIES The most familiar of these orchids are the crucifix orchids. The bright orange form of *E. ibaguense* is most often seen. Others frequently cultivated have soft crimson or lilac flowers. Their long flowering period and easy care make them popular.

Epimedium (fam. Berberidaceae)

These low-growing, deciduous or evergreen perennials provide pretty groundcover for shaded, moist areas as under trees or in rock gardens. They have arrow or heart-shaped leaves, attractively marked in different colors through the year, and delicate flowers in early spring and summer. The flowers are pretty but fairly insignificant.

CULTIVATION *Epimedium* can be grown in any soil, but it prefers a sandy loam, with added leaf mould. Plant in fall or spring and prune just before the new growth begins in spring. Provide plentiful water in dry spring or summer weather. Epimedium helps to control weeds by blanketing the ground. Propagate by division of the rhizomes in fall or from seed.

ABOVE New growth on *Epimedium* species can be in tones of pink or bronze. Older leaves are plain green.

CLIMATE Cool, moist temperate and mild inland areas.

SPECIES *E. diphyllum*, to 20 cm (8 in), has small, white, pendulous flowers. *E. grandiflorum*, to 30 cm (12 in), produces white, pink, purple or yellow flowers. The foliage changes from deep green in summer to rich red and gold in fall, to pale pink and yellow tints in spring. *E. pinnatum*, zone 6, to 30 cm (12 in), has yellow and purple flowers. *E.* x *rubrum*, to 30 cm (12 in), has strikingly colored foliage and red and yellow flowers. *E.* x *versicolor* produces yellow flowers with rose-colored sepals. The young leaves are marked with red. *E.* x *youngianum*, to 30 cm (12 in), has drooping, white or pink flowers. 'Niveum' has pure white flowers; 'Roseum' has pinkish mauve flowers.

Epiphyllum (fam. Cactaceae)
Orchid cactus

From the rainforests of Mexico and South America, these epiphytic cactuses have broad, hanging, sometimes deeply lobed stems and large, white to cream, mostly scented flowers. Superb cultivars provide brightly colored, daytime flowers.

ABOVE The large, bright scarlet flowers on this *Epiphyllum* hybrid make a gorgeous show.

CULTIVATION These plants are sensitive to frost so except in tropical or subtropical climates are grown in a warm greenhouse or conservatory or as house plants, in pots or baskets in a soil-less cactus compost. They need bright light but shade from sun, and quite a humid atmosphere. Water normally in growing season and feed fortnightly; keep just moist in winter. Propagate in summer from stem sections.

CLIMATE Zone 10 at least.

SPECIES *E. crenatum* is an erect, much-branched plant, with cylindrical main stems, thick, flattened, notched branches and lovely creamy white, daytime flowers. This species is widely used in hybridizing. *E. hookeri* is a lovely, large plant, with narrow, flat, notched branches and white, nocturnal flowers with narrow petals. *E. oxypetalum* is tall, with pendulous, flat, slightly notched branches and cylindrical stems to 2 m (6 ft) long. Very large, white, nocturnal flowers bloom profusely in spring and summer.

Epipremnum (fam. Araceae)

This is a genus of eight species of tropical climbing vines from Southeast Asia and the western Pacific. Generally, they can be grown outdoors in the tropics only where they can be trained to climb up tree trunks. However, they make attractive indoor potted plants if their cultural requirements are met.

CULTIVATION Except in the tropics, grow in a warm greenhouse or conservatory, or as a house plant, in pots of soil-based or soilless potting compost. Plants need good light (but shade from direct strong sun), a humid atmosphere and supports for the stems unless they are to trail. A sphagnum moss-covered pole makes a good support. Propagate from stem-tip cuttings, or from leaf-bud cuttings, in summer, in a heated propagating case. Alternatively, layer a stem in spring or summer.

CLIMATE At least zone 10.

SPECIES *E. aureum*, golden pothos or devil's ivy, has slender stems and shiny, bright green, heart-shaped leaves, up to 30 cm (12 in) long, marbled in a golden cream color. Grown outdoors, it can reach 12 m (40 ft), however it is popular as an indoor plant and is often sold by its common names. Cultivar 'Marble Queen' has creamy white leaves, flecked with green, and green-striped stems; 'Tricolor' has green leaves, spotted and marked with colors gold, pale green and cream. *E. pictum* 'Argyraeum' is a slower grower, with matt, green, heart-shaped leaves, flecked in silver.

Episcia (fam. Gesneriaceae)
Flame violet

Grown mostly for their attractive ornamental leaves, these perennial creepers from tropical America and the West Indies also produce long-lasting colorful flowers if given the right conditions. The leaves are oval-shaped and downy, and delicately veined in shades of bronze, yellow and green. They are ideal glasshouse or hanging basket subjects, preferring high temperatures and a humid environment.

CULTIVATION Flame violets need a soilless potting compost, light shade and plentiful moisture in spring and summer. However, when watering, do not wet the leaves. Propagate from cuttings with several nodes, in a sand and peat mixture, in early summer.

BELOW Lipstick red flowers highlight the velvety, patterned leaves of *Episcia cupreata*. Many Episcia species are grown primarily for their foliage.

ABOVE *Epipremnum aureum*, devil's ivy, is a popular house plant. It has several cultivars, all heavily variegated.

CLIMATE At least zone 10.

SPECIES *E. cupreata*, flame violet, has handsome leaves, up to 12 cm (5 in) long and 7 cm (3 in) wide, veined with copper, red or silver. The flowers, 2.5 cm (1 in) long, are in red, marked with yellow. A number of named varieties are available, including 'Metallica', with pale green-veined leaves, edged with bright pink. *E. dianthiflora*, laceflower vine, produces small leaflets, 2.5 cm (1 in) long, often marked with red, as well as its normal leaves, and pure white, 5 cm (2 in) long, flowers, spotted with purple. *E. lilacina*'s leaves are green or greenish red on top and purple underneath. The leaves are 5 cm (2 in) long and the flowers, to 4 cm (1½ in), are lilac.

Eranthemum (fam. Acanthaceae)

This is a genus of about 30 species of mainly shrubby plants, native to tropical Asia. Few species are in cultivation but the one most commonly grown makes a good plant for a warm greenhouse or conservatory.

CULTIVATION Under glass, grow in pots of soil-based potting compost. Provide good light but shade from direct sun. Go easy on the watering: very little in winter and only moderate amounts in the growing season. Plants may need lightly cutting back after flowering to contain growth. Propagate from softwood cuttings in spring, in a heated propagating case.

CLIMATE At least zone 10.

SPECIES *E. pulchellum*, blue sage, originally from India, is a quick-growing shrub to a little over 1 m (3 ft). The dark green foliage is prominently veined and the clear blue flower spikes appear in late winter to early spring. This is a very easy-care plant in a suitable climate.

Eranthis (fam. Ranunculaceae)
Winter aconite

Native to Europe and Asia, these frost-hardy, tuberous plants produce yellow, cup-shaped flowers in early spring above a ruff of small, divided leaves. They are toxic to eat and the sap may cause skin irritation.

BELOW *Eranthis hyemalis* is a delightful plant for cool climate gardens. In woodland conditions, it forms large colonies.

ABOVE *Eranthemum pulchellum*, blue sage, makes a good pot plant for the warm greenhouse or conservatory and it flowers in winter.

CULTIVATION These plants can be allowed to naturalize under and around deciduous trees and shrubs to form carpets of flowers. Plant the tubers in the fall, 5 cm (2 in) deep, in moist soil which contains plenty of humus. A position in light or dappled shade or full sun would be suitable for these plants. Propagate in spring by dividing clumps, or raise from seed.

CLIMATE Zone 5. These plants are suited to cool climates only.

SPECIES *E. hyemalis*, with lemon-yellow flowers, is useful for growing under deciduous trees and around shrubs. It grows to 8–12 cm (3–5 in) high and is one of the first plants to flower in late winter or very early spring. *E. x tubergenii*, a hybrid coming from Holland, has larger, longer lasting yellow flowers. This species rapidly forms colonies if the conditions are suitable. Cultivar 'Guinea Gold' has deep yellow, fragrant flowers to 10 cm (4 in).

Eremocitrus (fam. Rutaceae)
Desert lime

This native Australian genus comprises only one species, a shrub or small, spiny tree, grown mainly as an ornamental, particularly in tubs.

BELOW Dense and spiny *Eremocitrus glauca* is suitable for arid regions with frosty nights. Heavy crops of fruit are borne in some seasons.

CULTIVATION Resistant to cold and drought, this desert plant can be grown outside in areas suited to other citrus trees and shrubs. It tolerates poor soil as long as it is well drained and it responds well to regular summer watering. It should be grown in full sun. Where hard frosts occur, grow in a cool greenhouse or conservatory.

CLIMATE Zone 9.

SPECIES *E. glauca* grows 1–3 m (3–10 ft) tall with alternate, simple, leathery leaves, small, white flowers, and fruit resembling tiny oranges. Although they have a rather bitter taste, the fruits are used for making jams and drinks, including liqueur. It can be used as an understock for other cultivated citrus.

Eremophila (fam. Myoporaceae)
Emu bush, poverty bush

This genus comprises over 200 species of evergreen shrubs found in arid areas of Australia, though mostly in Western Australia. The foliage varies greatly. Some species have smooth, green, slightly leathery leaves, while others have silvery gray, sticky foliage covered in fine, downy hairs. The pretty, bell-shaped flowers have recurved petals and many different colors, with red, pink, cream and purple being the most common. The prostrate forms of some species are most suitable as groundcover for dry, inland gardens.

CULTIVATION In areas prone to hard frosts, grow in an airy, cool greenhouse or conservatory, in pots of soil-based potting compost and with maximum light. *Eremophila* prefers a sharply drained alkaline soil and a sunny position. Propagate most species from cuttings taken in late spring. Seed is erratic in germination. Pruning after flowering helps keep plants vigorous.

CLIMATE Zone 9.

SPECIES Not all are available outside their native Australia. *E. alternifolia* is a rounded shrub,

ABOVE A very choice form of emu bush, *Eremophila maculata* has rich red flowers.

1–4 m (3–13 ft) tall, with tubular, pink flowers, spotted with red, from spring to fall. The leaves are small and narrow. *E. bignoniiflora* is a tall, weeping shrub, to 4 m (13 ft), with long, tapering, slightly sticky leaves and pendulous, cream flowers. It makes an excellent screen plant in dry areas. *E. longifolia*, a favorite food of the emu, is a large, rounded shrub, 3–7 m (10–23 ft) tall, with velvety, pink flowers, spotted inside, and long, narrow, pendulous leaves. *E. maculata*, spotted emu bush, is the most widely grown of the species. This beautiful shrub, 1–3 m (3–10 ft) tall, has red, orange, pink or white flowers, with spotted throats, for most of the year, though most abundantly in winter and spring. *E. oppositifolia* is a large, rounded shrub, often reaching 4 m, (13 ft) with pink, yellow or white flowers and beautiful, gray foliage. *E. scoparia* is an erect, slender shrub, to 1 m (3 ft), with violet, spring flowers and small, hooked leaves.

Eremurus (fam. Asphodelaceae)
Desert candle, foxtail lily

These splendid perennials from western and central Asia make a striking garden feature. The tall, straight stems rise from rosettes of strap-like leaves and each is crowned with a single flower spike comprising as many as 100 tiny, star-like flowers. The plants die back to the crown after flowering. Some species grow as tall as 3 m (10 ft) and all have fleshy, brittle roots.

CULTIVATION These plants are quite frost-hardy and can resist the coldest winters, remaining dormant from late summer to early spring. Plant in fall in a well-drained, sunny position, with protection from strong winds. Once planted they should not be disturbed for several years. *Eremurus* species can be grown from seed but may take up to three years to flower. Propagation is best by division, though this must be done very carefully as the roots break easily. If they do break when being lifted, clean the damaged roots and dust with sulphur before replanting 8–10 cm (4–5 in) deep.

CLIMATE Best in cool climates; plants need cold winters to flower.

SPECIES *E. olgae*, zone 6, grows to 1.5 m (5 ft) and produces sweetly fragrant, white flowers, tinged with pink. *E. robustus*, foxtail lily, zone 6, has pale pink, summer flowers and grows to

ABOVE Tall spires of white flowers on *Eremurus himalaicus* provide great impact in cool gardens during late spring or early summer.

3 m (10 ft). *E. spectabilis*, zone 6, grows to 1.5 m (5 ft) and has pale yellow flowers flushed with orange. *E. stenophyllus*, zone 5, grows to 1 m (3 ft), with narrow, linear leaves and yellow, summer flowers. Hybrids of this species and *E. olgae* have spectacular flowers, ranging from pure white through many shades of pink to orange-red.

Erica (fam. Ericaceae)

Heath

This spectacular genus of evergreen, flowering shrubs mostly originates from South Africa and Europe and comprises more than 700 species, though many beautiful types are still not cultivated. Careful choice of species can ensure year-round flowering. Heaths range in height from dwarf forms to those as tall as 4.5 m (15 ft). All bear clusters of small, bell-shaped or tubular flowers which remain on the plant for a long time. The most common colors are white, cream, pink, mauve and red. Very well suited to cool climates, they are popular in all their forms for use as groundcovers, mixed shrubs or specimens.

CULTIVATION Heaths are quite fussy plants. They need good drainage and full sun, and dislike lime and animal manure, preferring a fairly poor soil. Sometimes they are grown in a separate bed or 'heath garden' where their special requirements can be met if the natural conditions are not quite right. They should be disturbed as little as possible. Propagate from seed in spring, by layering or from semi-ripe cuttings, about 3–5 cm (1–2 in) long, taken with a heel.

CLIMATE There are heaths suited to various climatic zones.

SPECIES *E. arborea*, tree heath, zone 7, from Europe and northern Africa, bears masses of small, white, fragrant flowers, with black anthers, in spring. It grows 3–5 m (10–16 ft). The stems and roots of this plant are used to make briar pipes. *E. baccans*, berry heath, zone

ABOVE A cool-climate heath and heather garden features a spreading shrub of *Erica lusitanica*.

10, from South Africa, has salmon pink flowers during winter and spring, and an erect growth habit to 2.5 m (8 ft). The flowers make a rattling sound when shaken. *E. carnea*, winter heath, zone 5, from Europe, is well suited to cooler climate rockeries. It produces pink flowers in winter and spring. Recommended cultivars include 'Springwood Pink' and 'Springwood White'. *E. cinerea*, bell heath, zone 5, from Europe, is one of the loveliest species of all: from early summer it bears masses of purple bells. It is a smaller growing heath, to 60 cm (24 in), and is particularly suited to natural rock gardens. Many cultivars provide a large color range. *E.* x *darleyensis*, Darley Dale heath, zone 6, to 60 cm (24 in), is a valuable garden plant and one of the easiest to cultivate as it is hardy, adaptable and tolerant of some lime. In fall and winter, this shrub is covered with short spikes of cylindrical, rose pink flowers. Many cultivars are available. *E. erigena* (syn. *E. mediterranea*), Irish heath, zone 8, to 3 m (10 ft), is one of the best winter and spring flowerers, with a profusion of pink, black-eyed blooms. It can tolerate cold and some lime, and is fairly drought-resistant. Several varieties are available. *E. hiemalis*, winter heath, zone 9, with pink or white, winter flowers on tapering spikes, is suitable for growing in pots. *E. lusitanica*, Spanish or Portuguese heath, zone 8, is one of the most beautiful of the species. This hardy plant, 2–3 m (6–10 ft) tall, seeds freely, so is often found naturalized in suitable conditions. It produces pink buds which open to small, white, fragrant, bell flowers in late winter and spring.

Erigeron (fam. Asteraceae)
Fleabane

This large genus of perennial daisies originates predominantly from North America. They have thin, basal leaves and mostly erect stems, and produce masses of daisy-like flowers in varying colors with yellow centers. They differ from other daisies in having two or more rows of fine, thread-like petals. Fleabanes look very pretty in rockeries or at the front of borders where a splash of color is needed.

CULTIVATION All species like a moderately fertile, well-drained soil, shelter from strong winds and a sunny position, with the exception of *E. karvinskianus*, which tolerates semi-shade. They may need cutting back frequently as they spread rapidly, and the stems should be trimmed after flowering. Propagate from seed

BELOW Massed *Erigeron karvinskianus* outlines a bed of Italian lavender bordering a path.

in fall or by division of the clumps in fall or spring.

CLIMATE There are species suited to various climatic zones.

SPECIES *E. alpinus*, zone 5, is a hairy perennial, to 30 cm (12 in), with purple flowers, usually borne singly in summer and fall. *E. aureus*, zone 5, produces bright yellow flowers from the spring onwards. *E. glaucus*, beach aster or seaside daisy, zone 3, is a hardy, sprawling, rather succulent plant, to 15 cm (6 in), with hairy leaves and pink to purple, summer flowers. *E. x hybridus*, zone 6, has provided a range of attractive cultivars raised from crossing a number of species. They include 'Quakeress', 'Dignity', 'Pink Triumph', 'Vanity' and 'Wuppertal'. Most grow to about 30–45 cm (12–18 in) tall. *E. karvinskianus*, zone 7, is a popular rockery plant, also useful for paved areas as it self-seeds between cracks. It has trailing branches to 1 m (3 ft) long and tends to spread, requiring cutting back after summer and fall flowering. The flowers change in color from white through pink to purple and bloom abundantly throughout the year in mild climates. It grows up to 45 cm (18 in). This plant is becoming a noxious weed in some parts of the world. *E. speciosus*, zone 3, to 45 cm (18 in), has leafy stems and clusters of striking, violet flowers in summer and fall. This species provides excellent cut flowers.

Eriostemon (fam. Rutaceae)
Waxflower

Apart from one species from New Caledonia, this genus of highly ornamental, evergreen, flowering shrubs is native to Australia. They are frost-tender, low-growing, bushy shrubs, with a spreading habit, and small, mostly aromatic leaves. The five-petalled, waxy, star-like flowers bloom profusely over a long period.

CULTIVATION In frost-prone climates, grow in pots of acid, soil-based potting compost in a cool greenhouse or conservatory. Provide max-

ABOVE A good choice for the cool conservatory in frosty climates, *Eriostemon australasius* is smothered with starry, pink flowers over a long period.

imum light. Eriostemons like a loose, slightly acidic, well-drained soil and part shade. They respond to light pruning after flowering. Propagate from semi-ripe cuttings, taken during late summer or fall.

CLIMATE Zone 10.

SPECIES *E. australasius*, pink waxflower, is an elegant, erect shrub, 1–2 m (3–6 ft) tall, and very striking when in flower. The large, pink flowers are borne on pendulous branches from spring to fall and the foliage is a grayish green color. *E. buxifolius* is a rounded shrub, 1–2 m (3–6 ft) tall, with deep pink buds, changing to starry, white flowers, crowded at the end of branches. The leaves are scaly. *E. myoporoides*, long-leaf waxflower, is the species most often grown. It can grow to 2 m (6 ft) high and wide, but is often smaller. From fall through to spring the deep pink buds open to white flowers. The cultivar 'Clearview Pink' has pink-flushed flowers from red buds. *E. verrucosus*, fairy waxflower, has slender branches, with pink buds opening to white flowers in spring.

Erodium (fam. Geraniaceae)
Stork's bill

Comprising around 60 species of annuals, perennials and subshrubs native to Europe, including the Mediterranean, temperate Asia and Australia, and South America, these plants are useful additions to borders and rock gardens. They have small flowers and attractive foliage. The seed is ejected from the pod in a quite remarkable spiralling action, reversing when it reaches the ground. They are generally easy-care plants, and valued for their long flowering period.

CULTIVATION Plant in spring in neutral to alkaline, very well drained soil, in a sunny position. The small species appreciate protection from winter rains. Propagate from seed sown in fall in a garden frame, or by division in spring.

CLIMATE There are species suited to various climatic zones.

SPECIES *E. manescavii*, zone 6, a perennial from the Pyrenees, grows to 40 cm (16 in), with large, rosy purple flowers. *E. reichardii*, zone 7, a perennial from Europe, has white flowers, veined in pink, and grows to 7 cm (3 in). There

ABOVE Excellent for covering large expanses of ground, Erodium chamaedryoides 'Roseum' has pretty, lobed leaves and small, pink flowers.

are some forms with pink flowers and these are well worth buying if available. *E. trifolium*, zone 8, is a delicate perennial or biennial, to 30 cm (12 in), with soft, hairy foliage and masses of dainty white to pale pink flowers in spring and summer. Seed is freely produced and young seedlings will appear annually.

Eryngium (fam. Apiaceae)
Sea holly

This large genus of annuals, biennials and herbaceous or evergreen perennials originates mainly from Europe and South America. They are grown for their unusual, spiny flower heads which mostly have a blueish, metallic lustre. Dried, they keep their color and are used for winter arrangements. Sea holly has been used in folk medicine since antiquity. It has also been used as a vegetable and a flavoring agent.

CULTIVATION Eryngiums make good border plants, preferring a light, sandy soil, though they will grow in most soils provided they are well drained. They need full sun. *E. maritimum* is useful for seaside gardens but the soil must be deeply dug as it has long, thong-like roots. Propagate from seed in late spring or from root cuttings in winter. Seed should be sown where it is to grow as it does not transplant well.

CLIMATE There are species suited to various climatic zones.

SPECIES *E. agavifolium*, zone 7, from Argentina, is a tall, clump-forming perennial, to 1.5 m (5 ft), with narrow, spiny, green leaves and pale green-white flowers. The species *E. amethystinum*, zone 7, growing to 75 cm (30 in), has shiny, deep blue upper stems and deep blue flower heads in late summer. *E. maritimum*, zone 5, sea holly, from Europe, is a much-branched perennial, having silver-green, basal leaves and pale blue flowers from the summer through to the fall. It grows to 30 cm (12 in). *E. planum*, zone 4, grows to over 1 m (3 ft), with branching, blue stems and small, metallic blue flower heads.

Erysimum (fam. Brassicaceae)
Perennial wallflower

These hardy, annual, biennial and perennial plants are found in the wild only in the northern hemisphere. They look pretty in rockeries

ABOVE Mature flower heads of *Eryngium planum* are an unusual, steely blue.

ABOVE The perennial *Erysimum linifolium* has a long flowering period, from the middle of spring to the onset of

and borders, and are also well suited as edging and bank plantings. The leaves are mostly entire and the flowers come in various shades of yellow through to orange, pink and purple.

CULTIVATION *Erysimum* will grow in any garden soil, but requires a sunny spot. Clip over perennials lightly after flowering, to maintain a compact shape. Propagate all from seed sown in spring and perennials from softwood cuttings in summer.

CLIMATE Zone 6 for most species.

SPECIES *E. asperum*, zone 4, is a biennial or short-lived perennial with orange flowers in spring and early summer. *E. kotschyanum* is a perennial with bright yellow flowers, generally used as a groundcover as it grows to only 15 cm (6 in). *E. linifolium*, a perennial, to 45 cm (18 in), produces rosy lilac flowers from mid-spring to the early fall. Cultivars are usually more available than any of the species.

Erythrina (fam. Papilionaceae)
Coral tree

Grown for their brilliantly colored red or orange flowers, this genus of deciduous or semi-evergreen trees, shrubs and perennials, which sometimes grow to only 2 m (6 ft) and at other times to heights of 20 m (65 ft), is native to tropical and warm temperate parts of Asia, Africa and America, with two species from Australia. Used as an ornamental or shade tree, in some of its native environments the flowers are cooked and eaten, though some species are poisonous. In frost-prone climates, grow in a cool to intermediate greenhouse or conservatory. They flower in the summer and often through to fall.

CULTIVATION In the greenhouse, grow in pots of soil-based potting compost and provide maximum light. Outdoors grow in full sun and well-drained soil. Propagate from seed sown in spring. Germinate at 24°C (75°F). Take semi-ripe cuttings in summer.

ABOVE *Erythrina crista-galli*, the cock's comb or coral tree, carries its bright flowers in summer and fall.

CLIMATE Zone 10 for most species.

SPECIES *E. acanthocarpa*, tambookie thorn tree, from southern Africa, is one of the smaller species, growing up to 2.5 m (8 ft). The stiff branches and seed pods are very thorny, but the spectacular clusters of red and yellow flowers make it worth growing. This deciduous shrub does quite well in cooler gardens. *E. caffra*, South African coral tree, is a tall, semi-evergreen tree, to 18 m (60 ft). It has compound leaves, with three club-shaped leaflets, and clusters of brilliant scarlet flowers that bloom from winter through to spring. It is often seen as a shade tree in South Africa. *E. crista-galli*, cock's comb or coral tree, zone 9, from South America, is the best for warm temperate climates. In cool climates, it grows as a bushy perennial and the stems are cut down annually in early spring. It has spiny stems and leaves and dark red flowers in summer and fall. *E.* x *sykesii*, Indian coral tree, occurs naturally from eastern Africa to India. This deciduous tree grows 6–15 m (20–50 ft) and produces dense clusters of rich scarlet flowers on its spiny branches in winter. It has compound leaves with large, oval leaflets. *E. vespertilio*, bat's wing coral tree, is an Australian native from inland, open, subtropical forests, ranging in height from 6 m to 20 m (20–65 ft). It has a thick trunk, thorny branches and slender, stalked leaves, the triangular-shaped leaflets like open bat wings. Suitable for inland and coast, it has long, drooping clusters of red blooms.

Erythronium (fam. Liliaceae)
Dog's tooth violet, trout lily

Native to North America, Asia and Europe, these bulbous plants look very pretty growing in rockeries or woodland gardens. Each plant has two thin, basal, elliptical leaves, about 15 cm (6 in) long, and delicate, nodding flowers which may be solitary or several to a stem. They are spring bloomers, to 10–35 cm (4–14 in) in height.

CULTIVATION These bulbs will do very well under a tree in a soil rich in leaf mould, provided they are kept moist. Top-dress with compost or rotted manure yearly. They need partial or dappled shade. Plant corms in fall where they are to grow, 8 cm (3 in) deep and 10 cm (4 in) apart. Propagate by careful division of the corm after flowering. Seeds are very slow to germinate.

CLIMATE Moist cool to cold. Zone 5 for most species.

SPECIES *E. americanum*, trout lily, zone 3, has yellow flowers which are speckled with red, and mottled leaves. *E. dens-canis*, dog's tooth violet, zone 3, grows to 20 cm (8 in) and is the most widely grown of the species. It has attractive leaves, marbled in brown and green, and white, pink or lilac flowers. The common name refers to the small, tooth-shaped bulb. There are several outstanding cultivars of this species, including 'Pink Perfection', with clear pink flowers, 'Snowflake', with pure white flowers, and 'Purple King' which is burgundy-colored. *E. grandiflorum*, avalanche lily, has bright yellow flowers and grows best at a high altitude. *E. hendersonii* has intensely marbled leaves and pale lilac flowers with dark purple markings. *E. oregonum* has white to pink blooms, with yellow inside.

Escallonia (fam. Escalloniaceae)

This genus comprises some 50 species of hardy, evergreen shrubs and trees, most of which come from the Andes in South America. Many ornamental cultivars are also available. They are useful coastal plants and the shrubby types make good hedges, provided they are trimmed to encourage bushy growth. They have shiny, succulent, toothed leaves and dense sprays of white or pink flowers.

CULTIVATION Escallonias grow quickly, even in poor soils. Some species are quite hardy, but even the more tender kinds can take some frost if given the protection of a warm, sheltered wall. All require full sun. Propagate from semi-ripe cuttings in summer or fall. Prune

ABOVE Recurved petals on nodding flowers are a feature of *Erythronium species*. Its marbled foliage adds to its appeal.

ABOVE *Escallonia rubra* makes a dense windbreak or screen. In flower it is a very decorative asset to the garden.

lightly in mid-spring to prevent plants becoming straggly.

CLIMATE There are species suited to various climatic zones.

SPECIES *E. bifida*, zone 9, is an attractive shrub or small tree, to 5 m (16 ft), with oval, finely toothed, glossy leaves and dense clusters of white flowers in summer. It is long lived if grown in a suitably mild climate. *E.* x *exoniensis*, zone 8, is a popular hedge plant, generally growing to around 3 m (10 ft), with open, branching habit. It produces loose sprays of white flowers, tinged with pink, in summer. *E. iveyi*, a natural hybrid of *E.* x *exoniensis* and *E. bifida*, zone 8, is a strong, rounded shrub to 3 m (10 ft), with dense, terminal sprays of sweetly scented, white flowers, tinged with pink, from late summer to fall. *E. rubra* var. *macrantha*, zone 8, is a vigorous, dense shrub, to 3.5 m (11 ft), which makes an excellent hedge. It has glossy, deep green leaves and tight clusters of showy, rose-crimson flowers in late

spring and summer. Cultivar 'C. F. Ball', zone 7, is also a vigorous grower, to 2 m (6 ft), with open-branching habit and carmine red flowers. There are other fine escallonia cultivars derived from a range of species, including 'Apple Blossom', zone 8, a dwarf plant with large, soft pink, summer flowers; 'Donard Brilliance', zone 7, a graceful plant with large, rosy crimson flowers in summer; and 'Donard Seedling', zone 7, with pink buds and white flowers.

Eschscholzia (fam. Papaveraceae)
California poppy

These delightful, bright, spring to summer-flowering annuals are splendid massed in borders or in large drifts. They have soft, fern-like, blue-green foliage and tapering, four-petalled flowers in a saucer shape. The lovely flowers have a silky, papery texture.

CULTIVATION California poppies prefer a light, well-drained soil, though they will do well in most soils. However, they must have a full-sun situation, otherwise the flowers will close up. Propagate from seed sown in spring or early fall where they are to grow and thin the seedlings to 15 cm (6 in) apart. Once established, they

BELOW The bright orange-gold flowers of California poppy, *Eschscholzia californica*, are almost luminous in sunlight.

readily regenerate from seed. If self-sown plants are not required, cut off the faded flowers to prolong flowering.

CLIMATE Zone 6.

SPECIES *E. californica*, California's floral emblem, is the best known and most popular species. It grows 30–45 cm (12–18 in), producing many bright orange or cream flowers of 5 cm (2 in). The 'Ballerina' range contains double or semi-double flowers in red, pink, orange and yellow. Other good strains are the single-flowered Sunset Series and the semi-double Silk Series. There are also single-colored cultivars.

Etlingera (Zingiberaceae)
Torch ginger

A genus of about 60 species of rhizomatous perennials, these plants have cane-like stems and generally rather wide, long leaves. They bear their upright, torch-like flower spikes on top of leafless canes. The showy part of the flower is really a bract; the true flower is small and hidden inside the bract. The flowers of some species are used in curries and are popular ornamentals.

ABOVE Flowering spikes of *Etlingera elatior* create an impact in tropical gardens. The flowers may be used in curries too.

CULTIVATION Except in tropical climates, grow in a warm greenhouse or conservatory, in large pots or tubs of well-drained, soil-based potting compost. Shade from direct, strong sun. Provide a humid atmosphere. Water well in summer but keep plants fairly dry in winter. Propagate from seed or by division of the rhizomes.

CLIMATE Torch ginger is suitable for the tropics only.

SPECIES *E. elatior*, torch ginger or Philippine waxflower, can grow 5–6 m (16–20 ft) high in its habitat. Upright canes carry leaves often over 70 cm (28 in) long. These are dark green above and purplish beneath. The inflorescences grow to 30 cm (12 in) long, with deep pink bracts. The small red flowers with yellow or white margins are carried lower down amongst the smaller bracts. This plant has become naturalized in some tropical countries.

Eucalyptus (fam. Myrtaceae)
Eucalypt, gum tree

Eucalypts are far and away the dominant trees in Australia, with over 600 species, as well as many hybrids. Only a few of the species are found in the wild outside Australia, in the Philippines, New Guinea and islands nearby. The genus was first described scientifically in 1788, though the trees had been noted by William Dampier about a century earlier. It is believed Australia's Governor Phillip was first to record the common name, 'gum tree'.

Eucalypts are found in a wide range of habitats in their native Australia, from the cold, windy highlands of the snow country to the semi-arid interior and the fertile soils of the forests. They also vary extensively in habit from twisted shrubs to forest trees and dwarf types, or mallees, from the almost rainless inland, which produce a number of slender stems, 1–6 m (3–20 ft) tall, from woody rootstocks known as lignotubers found underground or at the base of the trunks. While most eucalypts have lignotubers, only the mallees develop such large rootstocks. In the more favorable conditions of the plains and open woodlands, the typical eucalypts–ironbarks and boxes–have short, straight trunks with rounded, spreading heads. In fertile, high rainfall areas, the eucalypt is very tall and straight, with a small head, at times reaching heights of 90 m (300 ft).

Many species have two distinct types of foliage, juvenile and adult, which differ in shape and color, the younger leaves being broader and often covered with a waxy bloom, giving them a blueish hue. In some species, the juvenile type of foliage prevails. Eucalypt flowers do not have sepals and petals: these are fused together into a cap, which covers the stamens and is shed as the flower opens. The flowers have numerous stamens in either white, yellow, pink or red, and in some cases, they are very large and showy. When the flower dies, the floral tube or receptacle containing the seeds continues to grow, then changes color, hardens and becomes a capsule, the 'gum-nut', which eventually opens to allow the seeds to disperse.

Eucalyptus species are extremely difficult to identify. The shape of the tree can alter markedly under different growing conditions. When attempting to identify a eucalypt, it is necessary to consider its leaves, both adult and juvenile, its bark, its flowers, particularly the shape of the cap, and its seed capsules. If it is not a cultivated specimen, but is growing naturally, its geographical location may also be of assistance.

The ironbarks have dark, deeply furrowed, persistent bark on the trunk and main branches. It is very hard and cannot easily be stripped off. Ironbark's durable, strong timber is used for bridges and wharfs.

The stringybarks have persistent bark but it is strong and fibrous, and not so hard. The peppermints also have fibrous, persistent bark, but the fibers are shorter and the bark paler. Their foliage is a rich source of fragrant oil which is used in perfumery and aromatherapy.

Similar to the peppermints in the appearance of their bark, but without the richness of their oil, are the boxes. The early settlers adopted the name 'boxes' because the timber was reminis-

TOP Flowers of *Eucalyptus sideroxylon* are often cream or white, but this bright rosy pink form is a favorite with gardeners.

ABOVE The rich color of the peeling bark of multi-stemmed *Eucalyptus curtisii* adds another dimension to this tree's appeal.

cent of the European box (*Buxus sempervirens*). The boxes provide some of the best hardwood for heavy construction work. Boxes and ironbarks hybridize freely with each other.

ABOVE In summer, the thin, reddish bark on *Eucalyptus mannifera* is shed to reveal the lovely, white trunk beneath.

ABOVE Flowers of *Eucalyptus sideroxylon* are often cream or white, but this bright rosy pink form is a favorite with gardeners.

Commercially, the eucalypts provide a wide variety of high quality hardwood. The foliage yields essential oils, and tannins are extracted from the bark. Flowering eucalypts provide large quantities of high grade honey. Many eucalypts assist in preventing erosion by wind and water. They make effective windbreaks and have been used to reclaim swampy ground. Eucalypts have been grown in many countries to such an extent that in some parts, such as California and Arizona, they are regarded as native trees. They have become invasive in South Africa.

The wide range of species available means that a tree may be selected to suit any soil or climate. However, it should be remembered before deciding to plant a eucalypt that many grow into trees too big for a suburban garden. They may not be deciduous but they drop leaves and twigs all year round. Some even drop occasional large branches. Many have spreading root systems, making them unsuitable for planting near houses. Seek professional advice if you are unsure which species to choose.

CULTIVATION Many species of *Eucalyptus* have adapted to the warmer regions of the US, particularly California and Arizona, and some can be grown outdoors in zone 8. In cooler areas they can be grown as young specimens in pots

The ash group comprises a small number of species, among them some of the tallest hardwoods in the world, such as *E. regnans* (mountain ash), with persistent, more or less fibrous bark on varying amounts of the trunk, sometimes extending to the branches.

The bloodwoods are so named because of the large amount of 'kino' in their veins and timber. However, they have now been separated from *Eucalyptus* and reclassified as *Corymbia*.

Last of the groups is the gum, which usually has a smooth trunk, with a covering of rough bark at the base. The bark is shed, creating a variety of patterns, at different times. However, the mahoganies, included in this group, are covered in rough, persistent bark.

of soil-based potting compost in a cool, airy greenhouse or conservatory. Provide maximum light. In the summer they can be placed outdoors. Inside or out they need a neutral to slightly acid soil. In the garden, provide a sunny site with wind protection. To grow *Eucalyptus* as shrubs, cut back the stems annually in early spring to within a few buds of the base (known as coppicing). Propagate from seed sown in spring. Germinate at 18°C (64°F).

CLIMATE Zone 10 unless otherwise specified below.

SPECIES. Not all are available outside their native Australia. *E. caesia*, zone 9, is a very decorative, mallee-type eucalypt from Western Australia. It is rare and endangered in the wild but is widely cultivated. The red-brown bark on the trunk peels in summer, exposing new green bark beneath. The branches are often pendulous and the leaves, buds and stems are covered with a gray-white bloom. The fairly large flowers are pink or crimson, with prominent gold anthers. Silver Princess or subsp. magna is the variety most often grown. This graceful, small tree grows 6–10 m (20–33 ft) high. *E. camaldulensis*, river red gum, zone 9, has the widest distribution of all eucalypts, occurring in patches through all states of Australia except Tasmania. It is adaptable to a wide range of climates and conditions and may grow between 15 and 50 m (50–160 ft) high, depending on those conditions. The timber is resistant to termite attack and highly sought after for construction and fine decorative work. The flowers provide copious amounts of nectar, making it a good honey and pollen tree. Too large for the home garden, it is ideal in many rural areas. *E. cinerea*, Argyle apple, grows 8–15 m (26–50 ft) tall and is noted for its silvery gray foliage, especially in its juvenile stage. This tree is often coppiced or hard pruned to maintain a supply of juvenile foliage. It is a good eucalypt for home gardens as it provides foliage contrast, with the foliage cover extending almost to the ground. This adaptable tree will tolerate quite a degree of frost. *E. cladocalyx*, sugar gum, zone

ABOVE The silvery bloom on the pendulous stems and caps of *Eucalyptus caesia* highlights the scarlet and gold fringe of flowers.

9, has been widely planted as a windbreak and shelter belt tree in many areas. The smaller form 'Nana' is ideal for this purpose. The species is variable ranging from 8 m (26 ft) to more than 30 m (100 ft) tall. This frost-tolerant tree is also drought-tolerant once established. *E. curtisii*, Plunkett mallee, grows 3–10 m (10–33 ft) tall and has multiple trunks. A fast-growing tree suitable for home gardens and street planting, it flowers profusely from an early age through late winter and spring. It is especially attractive to birds and insects. *E. deglupta*, kamerere, is one of the few eucalypts not native to Australia. It occurs naturally in some parts of New Guinea, Indonesia and the Philippines. Native to tropical forests with very high rainfall, it is fast growing and may reach 60–70 m (200–230 ft). It is a colonizing species in its habitats and is cultivated both for timber and wood pulp. This tree has a very colorful trunk as the bark peels in ribbons revealing green, blue, purple and red to orange shades. *E. erythrocorys*, illyarie or red

ABOVE The twisted, gray-streaked trunk of the snow gum, *Eucalyptus pauciflora*, is an imposing sight as it nears the end of its life.

cap gum, is one of the most striking eucalypts in cultivation. The buds have a bright red, waxy, four-sided cap, opening to the brightest yellow flower, providing a most eye-catching sight. It grows 4–10 m (13–33 ft) high and may even be grown in a very large tub. Although more adaptable than some Western Australian eucalypts, it does best in warm to hot areas where summer rain and humidity are low. It must have perfectly drained soil. *E. globulus*, Tasmanian blue gum or southern blue gum, may grow to over 50 m (160 ft) high in ideal conditions, but can be as low as 15 m (50 ft). There are a number of subspecies, though all are large trees. The young leaves are quite rounded and covered in blue-gray bloom, while adult leaves are sickle-shaped, dark green and up to 30 cm (12 in) long. This is an ideal shade and shelter tree for large gardens, parks and rural properties. *E. haemastoma*,

scribbly gum, is fairly small at 10–15 m (33–50 ft), often having a slightly bent or twisted trunk with characteristic scribbles formed by insects burrowing in the bark. It is an attractive small gum for home gardens and parks. The canopy is rather open, allowing understorey plants to flourish beneath. *E. macrocarpa*, mottlecah or rose-of-the-west, has the largest flower of any eucalypt. These are deep pink to crimson and appear on top of the untidy, sprawling growth of this mallee-type eucalypt. The foliage is silvery gray. This species does best in fairly arid areas and appears unable to tolerate summer rain or humidity. Drainage must be perfect. All parts of the plant are used in floral work, including the woody, flattish capsules which are often 7 cm (3 in) in diameter. *E. melliodora*, yellow box, is one of the best of all the honey-producing eucalypts. It is also grown for its durable timber. Although generally too large for suburban gardens, it is ideal in larger gardens, parks and rural areas. It may grow 10 to 30 m (33–100 ft) high and is adaptable to a wide range of soils. *E. microcorys*, tallow wood, is large, 20–40 m (65–130 ft) high, but its wide-branching habit makes it an ideal shade and shelter tree. The trunk is covered in reddish brown, fibrous bark and white blossom appears over a long period through spring and early summer. The timber is one of the best possible hardwoods available, with an extensive range of applications. *E. nicholii*, willow peppermint or narrow-leaved black peppermint, zone 8, is often planted by home gardeners in the mistaken belief that it is a small tree. Its general range is from 12 to 20 m (40–65 ft) high. The trunk is fibrous, gray-brown and the leaves are blue-green and very narrow. It is frost-tolerant and also tolerates exposed, windy sites. *E. pauciflora* subsp. *niphophila*, snow gum or white sally, zone 8, is now classified by some botanists as *E. niphophila*. *E. pauciflora* occurs in a range of habitats, from coastal regions to areas well over 1500 m (5000 ft). The subspecies appears to occur only above 1500 m (5000 ft) in alpine areas of its range. Snow gums may have single or multiple trunks, often bent or twisted in shape. In higher altitudes, the smooth trunks show decorative streaks and patches of pink, brown, white and green. It ranges in size from 8 to 20 m (26–65 ft) and has abundant blossom from mid-spring to midsummer. *E. pilularis*, blackbutt, grows 25 to 40 m (65–130 ft). It is fast growing on good soils in mild areas with good rainfall. The bark is fibrous and dark on most of the trunk, becoming smooth only on the upper branches. It is an important timber tree and is ideal for park and landscape planting. *E. pyriformis*, pear-fruited mallee, zone 9, is a small, decorative tree, 2–6 m (6–20 ft) high, with multiple trunks. It is ideal for home gardens and responds well to hard pruning and coppicing. It is best grown in fairly arid areas with low summer rainfall and is drought-tolerant when established. The buds, flowers and ribbed fruiting capsules are very ornamental and are used in floral arts and crafts. The flowers may be colored cream, yellow, pink or red. *E. robusta*, swamp mahogany, grows 20–25 m (65–80 ft) high, occurring naturally on saline soils in coastal estuaries or other waterlogged areas. It is fast growing and makes a good street, park or large garden tree. Unfortunately, its appearance is often ruined by sap-sucking insects, known as lace lerps, which feed on its foliage. *E. scoparia*, Wallangarra white gum, is a good choice for home gardens, normally growing from 8 to 12 m (26–40 ft). It has a smooth, light-colored trunk and graceful, narrow, drooping foliage. The canopy is high, letting other plants grow successfully underneath. It is also quite fast growing. *E. sideroxylon*, mugga or pink-flowered ironbark, zone 9, grows 10–30 m (33–100 ft) high. It is recognizable by its deeply furrowed, very dark bark and attractive, blue-green foliage. Flowering may be from midwinter to spring and flowers may be pink, red, white or yellow. The very hard wood is used in construction, and oil

TOP RIGHT The scribbly gum, *Eucalyptus haemastoma*, has a slightly contorted trunk and is so named because of the characteristic scribbles formed by insects burrowing in the bark.

RIGHT Mugga ironbark, *Eucalyptus sideroxylon*, has a dark, heavily ridged trunk and graceful, blue-green foliage.

ABOVE Coral gum, *Eucalyptus torquata*, flowers from a young age. It is used as a street tree in arid regions.

ABOVE *Eucharis x grandiflora* needs tropical conditions to produce its exquisite, scented white flowers.

can be distilled from its foliage. *E. torquata*, coral gum, is one of the most ornamental of all eucalypts. Flowering from a young age, the lovely blossom can be coral pink to red or occasionally white or cream. It grows 6–12 m (20–40 ft) and is useful in home gardens and parks and as a street tree. It is used widely in arid areas as it can tolerate either acid or alkaline soil. Ideally suited to arid inland conditions, it can also be grown in subtropical and cooler zones but is unlikely to do well in regions which have high humidity or high summer rainfall.

Eucharis (fam. Amaryllidaceae)
Amazon lily

This genus from the tropical Americas comprises 20 species of evergreen, bulbous plants grown as greenhouse specimens in cooler regions but outdoors in warm temperate to tropical areas, where they need semi-shade and a minimum winter temperature of 18°C (64°F). They do best, and look their best, in pots or tubs. These are some of the loveliest of all bulbous plants.

CULTIVATION In frost-prone climates, grow in an intermediate or warm greenhouse or conservatory. These bulbs need a good quality potting mix which drains freely, and plenty of water during the growing period. Feed with soluble liquid fertilizer. Provide an enforced resting period after flowering by withholding food and water, to encourage the formation of new flower spikes. Although a summer and a winter flowering are possible, this is very difficult to achieve. Propagate from offsets taken from bulbs after flowering.

CLIMATE At least zone 10.

SPECIES *E.* x *grandiflora*, from Colombia, is the best known species, producing delightful, white, scented flowers, 10 cm (4 in) across, with waxy, open petals, faintly tinged with green on the corona. There are usually two to four on each stem. The rich, deep green leaf blades grow to 50 cm (20 in) and the plant itself reaches 1 m (3 ft).

Eucomis (fam. Liliaceae)
Pineapple lily

Mainly native to South Africa, the 10 species of this small genus of bulbs make interesting feature plants for the garden. The flower spikes are quite distinctive, bearing a tuft of leaves at the crown, resembling a pineapple. A single flower spike rises from each rosette of thick leaves and is densely covered with small, six-petalled flowers ranging from cream and green shades to pinkish purple. Long-lasting, they make excellent cut flowers.

CULTIVATION These lilies are easy to grow both in the garden and in pots. In the garden, plant the bulbs 15 cm (6 in) deep in a well-drained, warm, sheltered position in full sun. During spring, they can be potted in a good quality potting mix. Water generously during summer but very seldom during winter. Once flower spikes appear, these plants can be fed with weak, liquid manure or soluble, organic plant food. Propagate from the side shoots or offsets which develop around the parent bulb. In very cold areas, grow these bulbs in a cool greenhouse or conservatory.

CLIMATE Zone 8.

BELOW A tightly packed flowering stem of pineapple lily, *Eucomis comosa*, can become heavy enough to topple over.

SPECIES *E. autumnalis* has long, strap-shaped, crinkly leaves from which arise 50–60 cm (20–24 in) long spikes of drooping, bell-shaped, greenish flowers, in late summer and fall. *E. bicolor*, to 75 cm (30 in), has green flowers with purple margins, in late summer, topped by a large tuft of leaves. *E. comosa*, pineapple lily, is striking with long, lance-shaped, crinkly leaves, spotted with purple on the undersides, and flower spikes comprised of masses of star-shaped, white flowers. The varieties produce pinkish purple flowers. *E. pole-evansii*, tallest of the species, grows to 2 m (6 ft), the top 60 cm (24 in) encircled by open, soft green flowers with cream centers.

Eucryphia (fam. Eucryphiaceae)

This small genus of six species of evergreen trees or shrubs from Chile and Australia are grown for their beautiful, large, white flowers, similar to single-flowered camellias. The trees are mainly columnar in shape and can be pruned after flowering if necessary. In cultivation, some of the species may be deciduous, depending on conditions.

CULTIVATION Eucryphias do best in a climate with cool to mild winters and humid summers. Most

BELOW above 'Ballerina' is a lovely cultivar of Tasmanian leatherwood *Eucryphia lucida*.

prefer a lime-free soil, and all need constant moisture and good drainage. Where possible, they should be sheltered from strong, drying winds. Choose a sunny site. Propagate from seed or semi-ripe cuttings.

CLIMATE There are species suited to various climatic zones.

SPECIES *E. lucida*, or Tasmanian leatherwood, zone 8, is a handsome evergreen from which is derived a pinkish colored timber, but it is better known for its excellent, unusually flavored honey. It has glossy, green, oblong leaves, silvery on the undersides, and open, pure white, four-petalled flowers, 2.5 cm (1 in) across. This species mostly reaches only 10 m (33 ft) under cultivation, but may be taller in the wild. *E. moorei*, plum wood, zone 9, also yields a pinkish timber, used in building and cabinet-making. It is a variable tree, 5–10 m (16–33 ft) tall, with pinnate leaves and 2.5 cm (1 in) flowers in late summer, which makes a pretty ornamental. *E.* x *nymansensis* 'Nymansay', zone 7, a natural hybrid, is a lovely, small, compact tree, which grows quickly, in time reaching around 10–15 m (33–50 ft), and flowers early. The leaves, which may be simple or compound on the same plant, are elliptic, toothed at the edges and deep green in color on the surface but lighter green beneath. The 6 cm (2½ in), white flowers have golden stamens. It will tolerate some lime.

Eugenia (fam. Myrtaceae)

Comprising over 500 species mostly from tropical America, these evergreen trees and shrubs, with attractive foliage, flowers and berries, are sometimes grown as ornamentals, though many are cultivated for their edible fruits. A number of Australian species formerly included in this genus have now been placed with *Syzygium*, as have species from other genera.

CULTIVATION In frost-prone climates, grow in a warm greenhouse or conservatory in pots of well-drained, soil-based potting compost.

ABOVE The fleshy, red fruits of Eugenia uniflora are shaped like tiny pumpkins. They are eaten fresh or made into jellies or jams.

Shade from direct, strong sun. Water regularly in summer, less frequently in winter. Outdoors grow in well drained, humus-rich soil and full sun. Propagate from seed.

CLIMATE At least zone 10.

SPECIES Most of these may be difficult to obtain in the US. *E. aggregata*, cherry of the Rio Grande, from Brazil, grows to around 5 m (16 ft). The orange-red berries ripen to a deep purple. The fruit can be eaten raw or used in pies. *E. brasiliensis*, Brazil cherry, grows to 15 m (50 ft), with white flowers, followed by dark red fruits, ripening to almost black. The fruit is eaten raw or used in jams, jellies and pies. *E. pitanga*, pitanga, is a low-growing shrub from Brazil and Argentina, with round, red, edible fruits. *E. reinwardtiana*, beach cherry, is the only Australian species left in this genus. A tall shrub to about 5 m (16 ft), it occurs on that country's north-eastern coast. It is most suitable for growing in tropical and subtropical coastal gardens. The fruits are edible. *E. uniflora*, Surinam cherry or Barbados cherry, is a shrub or small tree, widely cultivated in tropical regions for its fruit and as a hedging plant. White flowers are followed by yellow to red edible fruits. In its native areas, the leaves are crushed and used as insect repellant.

Euonymus (fam. Celastraceae)

Spindle tree

This northern hemisphere genus comprises around 170 species of evergreen and deciduous shrubs and small trees, mostly from eastern Asia and the Himalayas. The evergreen species are grown as hedges, edgings and borders, and respond well to regular clipping. The deciduous species have handsome foliage which colors beautifully in fall, and attractive four-lobed fruits which split open in fall to reveal brightly colored seeds. The flowers are small and may be greenish white or sometimes reddish brown.

CULTIVATION These hardy plants will adapt to most soils and climates, including coastal climates, though the deciduous species provide better fall color in areas with a dry fall and a cold winter. The soil must be well drained. Best results come from soils enriched with organic matter. Propagate from stratified seed sown in spring, or from semi-ripe cuttings taken in summer and fall, or by layering.

CLIMATE There are species suited to various climatic zones.

SPECIES *E. alatus*, winged spindle tree or cork tree, zone 3, so-called for its distinctive corky, 'winged' branches, is an attractive, compact, deciduous shrub from China and Japan. Slow growing, it reaches only about 2.5 m (8 ft). In fall, the finely toothed, dark green leaves, pointed at both ends, turn a very vivid, deep red, while the purplish berries split to reveal the orange-red seeds. *E. europaeus*, common spindle tree, zone 3, from Europe and Great Britain, is quite an ordinary deciduous shrub or small tree until fall when it colors a brilliant yellow and scarlet and the pinkish red seed capsules reveal large, orange seeds. Wood of this species was used to make spindles. Cultivars with differently colored seed capsules and leaves are sometimes available. *E. japonicus*, Japanese spindle tree, zone 7, is a hardy, spreading, evergreen shrub from China and Japan, with deep green, shiny

ABOVE A gold-variegated form of *Euonymus japonicus* can be used as a specimen plant or for hedging.

foliage, useful as a hedge or coastal plant. The dull pink, four-angled fruits contain orange seeds. Many variegated cultivars, with cream or gold markings, are available and more cultivated than the species. *E. latifolius*, zone 5, native to southern Europe and western Asia, is an attractive, deciduous shrub or small tree, to 5 m (16 ft), with glossy, deep green, finely toothed, pointed leaves coloring orange, red and purplish crimson in fall. Large, rose-crimson fruits remain on the tree after the leaves have fallen.

Eupatorium (fam. Asteraceae)

Hemp agrimony

There were previously hundreds of species in this genus but after reclassification, only about 40 remain. Mainly natives of eastern North America, only a few species are suitable for the garden. Although members of the daisy family, the tubular flowers form fluffy heads rather than the distinctive ray floret of the daisy. Species cultivated as ornamentals make good background plants in perennial borders, as their form is substantial and flower color unusual.

ABOVE *Eupatorium megalophyllum* adds bulk and height to the back of a border. It tolerates partial shade too.

CULTIVATION Any frost-tender species are grown in an airy, cool to intermediate greenhouse or conservatory with maximum light. Use soil-based potting compost. Outside, choose a position with well-drained yet moisture-retentive soil and full sun or partial shade. Propagate by division, or from seed or softwood cuttings according to species.

CLIMATE There are species suited to various climatic zones.

SPECIES *E. cannabinum*, hemp agrimony, zone 5, from Europe, is a frost-hardy, herbaceous plant, to 1.5 m (5 ft), with purplish lilac flowers in late summer. *E. megalophyllum*, zone 10, a native of Mexico, produces several erect, reddish purple branches. This shrub grows to 2 m (6 ft) high and wide and has broad, ovate, grayish green leaves and striking, flattened clusters of fluffy, violet-blue flowers during fall. *E. purpureum*, Joe pye weed, zone 4, is an herbaceous species from North America, with vanilla-scented leaves and a flattish head of pale purple flowers above a spiral of leaves. It grows to 2 m (6 ft). This species, also known as boneset or gravelroot, has a history of use in herbal medicine.

Euphorbia (fam. Euphorbiaceae)

This extremely large genus consists of about 2000 species of widely differing form, although the flowers of the various species are very similar. In fact, they have a distinctive, very compact inflorescence, known as a cyathium, and the colored part of some species, such as *Euphorbia pulcherrima* (poinsettia), is actually a set of bracts; the actual flower is the insignificant center. Euphorbias range in size and shape from the giant, candelabra type to small ground-hugging plants the size of tennis balls. Many form clusters of small heads and others have arms radiating from a central head. Some are confused with species of cactus. Many species are leafless; others have deciduous leaves. The seed capsules dry and pop open, dispersing the rather hard seeds far on hot days. Euphorbias are native to a range of habitats, including many parts of Africa, Madagascar, Europe, western Asia, eastern India, the Canary Islands and the Americas. All species may cause discomfort if eaten and the caustic sap can cause burning and irritation of the skin.

CULTIVATION Most non-succulent species require almost frost-free conditions outdoors, though they can be grown successfully in greenhouses

BELOW Snow on the mountain, *Euphorbia marginata*, is an annual that provides a mound of cool green and white.

where necessary. They are usually grown in pots as indoor plants or for transplanting. Older specimens should be pruned back heavily after transplanting. Prune deciduous species each year after flowering, both to encourage good blooms the following season and to maintain their shape. Propagate these species from cuttings, allowing the cut surface to dry for at least a few hours before planting. In frost-prone climates, most of the succulent species are grown in a cool to intermediate greenhouse or conservatory. Grow them in pots of well-drained, soil-based or cactus compost. They need maximum light and airy conditions. Keep dry in winter but water normally in the growing period. Hardy herbaceous perennials and shrubs need a sunny or partially shaded spot in the garden with well-drained, fertile soil. Propagate these by division in early spring or from stem-tip cuttings.

CLIMATE Depends on species; some require hot, tropical conditions, others tolerate frost.

SPECIES *E. candelabrum*, zone 9, from South Africa and Somalia, is a tree-like, succulent shrub to 10 m (33 ft). The many branches have undulating, winged margins bearing pairs of short, sharp thorns and tiny, rudimentary leaves on the young growth. *E. caput-medusae*, Medusa's head, zone 9, is a succulent from South Africa, with a thickened trunk from which radiate snake-like branches, the top half covered with deciduous, linear leaves, up to 15 mm (½ in) long. Beautiful, yellow inflorescences appear at the tips of young branches in summer. *E. characias*, zone 7, from Portugal and the western Mediterranean, is an evergreen shrub-like species popular for both its foliage and inflorescences which provide highlights or contrasts. These grow to over 1 m (3 ft), with blue-gray-green leaves and lime green, long-lasting inflorescences. The subsp. wulfenii is the form most often grown. *E. fulgens*, scarlet plume, zone 10, is a non-succulent shrub from Mexico, to 1 m (3 ft), with slender, pendulous branches and yellow flowers encased by small, fragrant, orange-red bracts, appearing after the

TOP Poinsettia, *Euphorbia pulcherrima*, is a popular Christmas-flowering pot plant in the US. Various colors are now available.

ABOVE The sharp lime green inflorescences of *Euphorbia characias* subsp. wulfenii light up the garden from early spring to early summer.

ABOVE .Pencil tree, *Euphorbia tirucalli*, makes a fine feature plant, with its thin, cylindrical, branched stems.

unbranched stems have large, ovate, pointed and toothed leaves, though it is mostly grown for its large, showy bracts appearing in fall and lasting through winter. The inflorescences can grow to 15–30 cm (6–12 in) across. Pink, salmon, yellow and white-flowered single and double forms are available, as well as dwarf forms for pot culture. *E. tirucalli*, caustic bush or pencil tree, zone 10, is a succulent, to 5 m (16 ft) tall, from eastern and southern Africa and the Arabian Peninsula. It has twiggy stems and tiny, deciduous leaves which fall quickly. Once used to make latex, its sap is caustic and poisonous.

Eupomatia (fam. Eupomatiaceae)
Copper laurel, bolwarra

The foliage, flowers and fruits of this genus of only two species from the east coast of Australia and New Guinea are beautiful, but the plants are rarely available elsewhere.

CULTIVATION In frost-prone climates, grow in an intermediate to warm greenhouse or conservatory. Soilless potting compost is suitable. Shade from direct strong sun. Water regularly in summer but less in winter. Propagate from cuttings in fall or from seed when ripe.

willow-like foliage has fallen. Frost-sensitive, it needs a warm, sheltered position. *E. griffithii*, zone 5, is an herbaceous perennial species to 90 cm (36 in), with mid to dark green, linear leaves and orange to scarlet inflorescences. Flowering lasts through summer. *E. marginata*, snow on the mountain, zone 4, is a non-succulent annual, native to North America, growing to 60 cm (24 in). It has white bracts and soft leaves with white margins. *E. milii* var. *splendens*, crown of thorns, zone 10, is a climbing or trailing plant from Madagascar. Almost leafless, it has bright scarlet bracts in spring or summer, the flowers persisting for months. This striking species is suitable as a pot plant in the home or greenhouse and may grow 1 m (3 ft) or so wide. *E. obesa* is a South African succulent which forms an unbranched, brownish green sphere, 12 cm (5 in) across, with a distinctly ribbed and furrowed surface. *E. pulcherrima*, zone 10, a native of Mexico, is the popular poinsettia, a familiar sight at Christmas in both hemispheres. A deciduous shrub, it grows to 3 m (10 ft) tall and nearly as wide. The long,

BELOW An unpruned plant of *Eupomatia laurina* displays the pretty pink new growth.

CLIMATE Zone 10.

SPECIES *E. laurina* is a shapely shrub or small tree, 3–6 m (10–20 ft) tall, with shiny, dark green, oval leaves, the young leaves and branches tinted with a pinkish copper color, and clusters of fragrant, greenish yellow flowers. The small, edible, fig-like fruits are tasty both to humans and native animals. It is a plant which grows well in shade and also makes a good screen or hedge plant.

Euryops (fam. Asteraceae)

This genus contains over 90 species of evergreen shrubs, mostly from southern Africa, and they are grown for their large, yellow, daisy-like flowers. They have soft, grayish green, finely divided foliage.

CULTIVATION These shrubs like a reasonably frost-free, mild to warm climate, light, well-drained soil and full sun. Frequent removal of spent flowers prolongs the bloom period. Prune after flowering to encourage a neat, rounded shape. In areas prone to hard frosts, grow in a cool, airy greenhouse. Propagate from semi-ripe cuttings in summer or from seed in spring under glass.

ABOVE *Euryops pectinatus* can provide a bright mound of color in the garden in summer and fall.

CLIMATE Zone 9 for most species.

SPECIES *E. pectinatus* is a vigorous, easy-care shrub useful for summer and fall color in rock gardens and borders, and does well in seaside gardens and windy conditions. It grows to 1 m (3 ft) high and wide, producing bright yellow daisies, 5 cm (2 in) across, and grayish, feathery foliage. *E. speciosissimus* (syn. *E. athanasiae*) grows quickly to 1.5 m (5 ft) and is covered in bright yellow flowers in summer. Prune well and propagate from seed.

Eutaxia (fam. Papilionaceae)
Small-leaf eutaxia

Mostly native to Western Australia, this genus comprises eight species of small, evergreen, showy shrubs closely related to Pultenaea and

BELOW *Eutaxia myrtifolia* (syn. *E. obovata*) does best in climates with hot, dry summers and wet winters but it can be grown under glass.

Dillwynia. They bear yellow or red pea flowers in summer or fall. These shrubs are unlikely to be available outside Australia.

CULTIVATION These shrubs must have perfect drainage and full sun. Advanced plants are hard to transplant. Propagate from the abundant seed or from fall cuttings struck in a cool frame or under glass in a 3:1 mixture of sharp sand and peat. Where hard frosts are likely, grow in a cool, airy greenhouse.

CLIMATE Zone 9.

SPECIES *E. microphylla*, originating in Australia, is a small, hardy, neat shrub to 1 m (3 ft), with small, opposite leaves, covered in late summer and early fall with pretty, tiny, yellow pea flowers. *E. myrtifolia* (syn. *E. obovata*), a bushy, rounded shrub, to 1 m (3 ft), has sharp-pointed leaves and orange-yellow, pea-type flowers. Easily grown, it can stand pruning.

Evolvulus (fam. Convolvulaceae)

Comprising about 100 species of annuals, perennials and subshrubs native to warm regions of North and South America, few of the genus are cultivated. One species is often cultivated as a groundcover in warm, frost-free regions and some are used as edging or border plants.

CULTIVATION Grow in well-drained soil in full sun. These plants tolerate poor soils and do not bloom as well in heavily enriched soils. Water regularly during dry summers but keep dry in winter. Established plants tolerate some drought. In frost-prone areas, grow in an airy, intermediate greenhouse with maximum light, in pots of soil-based potting compost.

CLIMATE Zone 9.

SPECIES *E. pilosus* (syn. *E. glomeratus*) is a trailing plant, growing less than 50 cm (20 in) high and spreading at least as wide. The small gray-green leaves are covered in silky hairs. It

ABOVE Useful as a groundcover or spillover plant, blue-flowered *Evolvulus pilosus* (syn. *E. glomeratus*) tolerates fairly harsh conditions.

has a long flowering period through summer. The flowers are funnel-shaped and usually bright blue, or may be mauve-pink or paler blue with a white eye.

Exocarpos (fam. Santalaceae)

This genus of shrubs and small trees extends from Southeast Asia to Hawaii. The leaves are often reduced to small scales and the roots generally attach themselves to other plants. Short spikes of very small, cream to yellow, summer to fall flowers are followed by small, seed-like nuts on fleshy stalks. These plants are rarely available outside their native countries.

CULTIVATION Because of its semi-parasitic nature, Exocarpos is not easy to grow and is difficult to establish. The seed does not germinate readily. These plants are best enjoyed in botanical gardens.

CLIMATE At least zone 9.

ABOVE With its slender, pendulous branches, *Exocarpos cupressiformis* may develop into a tall shrub or a small tree.

SPECIES *E. cupressiformis*, native cherry, is widely distributed in temperate Australia. It is an attractive, small tree, with fine, drooping foliage and cream flowers. The fruits are borne on fleshy, red stalks.

Exochorda (fam. Rosaceae)
Pearl bush

This genus consists of four hardy, deciduous shrubs from central Asia and China, which are transformed in spring or summer by the delicate white flowers clustered at the ends of the branches. Both their broad, shrubby form and abundant flowering make them very desirable garden plants.

CULTIVATION Related to Spiraea, these shrubs prefer a well-drained soil, a sunny position and a cool temperate climate. Propagate from softwood cuttings in early summer under glass.

CLIMATE Most are suited to zone 5.

SPECIES *E. giraldi*, with an arching habit, grows to 3 m (10 ft), and has pink-flushed young foliage and rounded, white flowers, 2.5 cm (1 in) across. *E. macrantha* 'The Bride', is an arching yet compact shrub to 2 m (6 ft) and bears white blossoms at the end of spring through to early summer. It is the most popular exochorda grown. Although this hybrid was raised over 50 years ago, it remains a most beautiful form. *E. racemosa*, zone 4, is another popular species. When properly grown and cared for, it makes a beautiful display, with its arching sprays of rounded, white flowers, 2–3 cm (about 1 in) across. It is often spreading in habit and may grow 3–4 m (10–13 ft) high. Prune lightly after flowering.

ABOVE The simple, white flowers of *Exochorda racemosa* are very appealing, the blossom being reminiscent of other members of the rose family.

F

Fagus to Fuchsia

Fagus (fam. Fagaceae)

Beech

Widely distributed through temperate areas of the northern hemisphere, beech is valued as an ornamental for its lovely foliage and fall color. It is also prized for its timber. These large, deciduous trees are grown in mixed woodland gardens and parks and as specimen trees. Common beech is used extensively for hedging in Britain.

CULTIVATION Although adaptable to a wide range of soils and conditions, beech prefers well-drained soil of moderate fertility. These trees can be planted in full sun or dappled shade, though copper beech needs full sun to produce the most intense foliage color. The yellow-leaved forms prefer partial shade.

CLIMATE Cool to cold climates.

SPECIES *F. grandifolia*, American beech, zone 4, is a spreading tree, to about 10 m (33 ft), that may be as wide as it is high. *F. sylvatica*, known as common beech, zone 5, may grow to 25 m (80 ft) high and 15 m (50 ft) wide. The dark green foliage is silky when young and turns a rich golden brown in fall. Nuts containing triangular seeds are also shed in fall. The form *purpurea* is the copper beech, recogniz-able by its deep burgundy to purple foliage which turns a brilliant copper color in fall. 'Aspleniifolia', fern leaf beech, has narrow leaves, deeply cut into slender lobes; 'Dawyck' is a very upright form, 7–8 m (23–26 ft) tall; 'Riversii', with very deep purple leaves, must be grafted to maintain its color; 'Zlatia' has yellow foliage when young which turns green through summer and colors a rich yellow in fall. *F. sylvatica f. pendula*, the weeping beech, is an outstanding specimen tree with pendulous branches from which thick curtains of foliage hang down.

Faradaya (fam. Verbenaceae)

From northern Australia, New Guinea and regions nearby, these plants, related to *Clerodendrum*, are well suited to warm climates. They are unlikely to be available outside their native countries.

CULTIVATION These plants like hot, wet, humid conditions and fertile, well-drained soil enriched with leaf litter compost or well-decayed manure. In cool and cold climates, grow in a warm greenhouse or conservatory with a humid atmosphere.

CLIMATE Subtropical and tropical climates only.

BELOW *Faradaya splendida* is a rainforest liana or climber which freely produces fagrant flowers.

ABOVE Wind-sculpted beeches, *Fagus sylvatica*, growing in a very exposed location.

SPECIES *F. splendida* is a vigorous species found in northern Queensland rainforests where it can pull itself up into the tree canopy to reach the light. The broad, glossy bright green leaves grow up to 30 cm (12 in) long and the fragrant, white, tubular flowers are borne profusely in terminal sprays. The short-lived flowers are followed by large, egg-shaped, glossy white fruits, each containing a single seed. In subtropical gardens it is sometimes seen as a spreading mounded shrub.

Farfugium (fam. Asteraceae)

There are only two species in this genus of plants from eastern Asia. Only one of these species is in common cultivation.

CULTIVATION Plant in a well-drained but moist soil, heavily enriched with manure or compost, preferably in dappled sunlight or light shade. Mulch with organic matter. Water regularly through spring and summer, but give only occasional waterings in winter to prevent the roots drying out completely. Propagate by division of the clumps in late winter or spring. These plants are susceptible to attack by snails, so take suitable precautions.

CLIMATE Best in cool, moist climates with light frost only. Zone 8.

BELOW *Farfugium japonicum* makes good groundcover in moist soils with partial shade.

SPECIES *F. japonicum* (syn. *F. tussilagineum*, *Ligularia tussilaginea*) and its gold-spotted cultivar 'Aureo-maculatum', or leopard plant, are the ones most commonly grown in the US. These plants reach about 50 cm (20 in) high, bearing daisy-like flowers amongst the large leaves. They are very handy as they make good feature plants for shaded locations.

x Fatshedera (fam. Araliaceae)
Tree ivy

A bigeneric hybrid of *Fatsia* and *Hedera* (ivy), x *Fatshedera* is an attractive plant and one easily cared for, with dark green, leathery, ivy-shaped leaves, to 25 cm (1 in) across, which grows to between 1 and 2 m (3–6 ft). The heavy, textured foliage resembles a large leaf ivy rather than Fatsia.

CULTIVATION Indoors, this plant needs light and warmth, and a regular application of liquid fertilizer. Propagate from small cuttings which will take root in water or sandy soil. In the garden, grow in partial shade in well-drained soil and mulch well. Give ample water in dry summers.

CLIMATE Zone 7. Good for cool, moist climates.

SPECIES x *F. lizei* has dark green leaves, while the foliage of the cultivar 'Variegata' is edged with cream-white. 'Annemieke' (syn. 'Lemon and Lime') has yellow-variegated leaves.

ABOVE The large, glossy foliage of x *Fatshedera lizei* is very handsome. Flowers seen here rarely appear on plants grown indoors.

Fatsia (fam. Araliaceae)
Japanese aralia

Allied to *Aralia*, the two or three species in the genus are native to eastern Asia. Attractive, evergreen plants grown worldwide as indoor specimens, they are valued for their large, deeply lobed, glossy, dark green leaves and their huge sprays of tiny, milky white flowers. They grow to a height of 2–4 m (6–13 ft).

CULTIVATION In cool climates, *Fatsia* can be grown outdoors, provided it is positioned in full shade or half shade and given protection from prevailing winds. Indoors, plant in good quality potting mix and water regularly in the summer months. Propagate from cuttings or seed.

CLIMATE Zone 8.

SPECIES *F. japonica* produces whitish flowers in fall, followed by black fruit. The leaves are about 40 cm (16 in) across. The cultivar 'Variegata' has cream-edged margins. Other named varieties have larger leaves, different variegations or a more compact habit.

ABOVE *Fatsis japonica* is grown for its handsome foliage. In cool regions it is sometimes grown outdoors along with annual bedding plants.

Faucaria (fam. Aizoaceae)
Tiger jaws

Native to South Africa, these stemless, mat-forming succulents are mostly covered

ABOVE The fleshy, gray-green leaves of *Faucaria tigrina* crowd into mounds of growth. The flowers are tucked in amongst the leaves.

with white, irregular spots. They have thick, fleshy, grayish green leaves, keeled towards the tip, and toothed margins. From late summer to fall, the large, stemless, golden yellow flowers, sometimes reddish on the outside, rarely white, open in the afternoon. They make very attractive pot plants for sunny windowsills.

CULTIVATION Grow in pots of cactus compost in an airy, intermediate greenhouse with maximum light. Water sparingly in winter, moderately in the growing season. Propagate from seed or stem cuttings.

CLIMATE Zone 9.

SPECIES *F. felina*, cat's jaws, has vivid green or reddish leaves, with indistinct, white dots, and golden yellow flowers, 5 cm (2 in) in diameter. *F. tigrina*, tiger jaws, has triangular, gray-green leaves covered with white dots and edged with white, recurved teeth. Large, golden yellow, daisy-like flowers bloom in fall, emerging from buds that are often reddish. This species which forms clumps is easy to grow.

Feijoa (now Acca; fam. Myrtaceae)
Pineapple guava

Native to Brazil and Argentina, these attractive, evergreen shrubs, with red and white flowers, are often used as hedges and ornamentals, and make very good windbreaks. They are also grown for their edible fruits which taste of pineapple and guava. The fruits are eaten raw or used in salads or jams.

CULTIVATION These plants need a well-drained, sandy loam, rich in organic matter. They fruit best in a moist, subtropical climate, although warmth, sun and moisture are also necessary for cultivation as an ornamental. In cool climates fruiting is better in a cool greenhouse or conservatory. Propagate from seed sown when ripe and germinate in a temperature of 16°C (61°F). Keep seedlings shaded and transplant when about 10 cm (4 in) high into the garden. Fruiting plants should be spaced 4–7 m (13–23 ft) apart. They can also be increased by layering or from semi-ripe cuttings taken from the ends of branches and struck under glass. Two plants are needed for cross-pollination. Wait for the fruits to fall, then store until they emit a pineapple-like aroma.

CLIMATE Zone 8.

SPECIES *F. sellowiana* (syn. *Acca sellowiana*) is a quick-growing, compact shrub to about 2 m (6 ft). It has oblong, gray-green leaves, white below, and red and white flowers with conspicuous, red stamens in summer. The oval, green fruits, tinged with red, grow to 5 cm (2 in) long. Cultivars which produce quality fruits include 'Beechwood', 'Coolidge' and 'Nazemetz'. These are self-fertile and therefore single trees will produce fruit.

Felicia (fam. Asteraceae)
Blue daisy

This South African genus comprises around 80 species of annuals and perennials widely grown for lovely, blue daisy flowers which bloom nearly all year if regularly dead-headed. Some species are attractive border or rockery plants as they trail and cascade. They can also be used as a groundcover, clipped as low hedges or grown in containers. The species below are frequently used for summer bedding. (*F. amelloides* can be grown as an annual.)

CULTIVATION Most species cannot tolerate frost and need to be kept indoors or in a glasshouse in colder climates. Any well-drained soil will do, but they must be grown in full sun for best flowering. Although tolerant of dry conditions, occasional deep watering in dry periods is necessary. Prune after spring and fall flowering to encourage blooms. Propagate from seed or from cuttings.

ABOVE The fruit of *Feijoa sellowiana* (syn. *Acca sellowiana*) should be collected when it falls. In cool climates, fruiting is better under glass.

ABOVE Grown as a low hedge, *Felicia amelloides* is smothered in flowers over a long period. Shearing after flowering should produce another show of daisies.

CLIMATE Zone 9.

SPECIES *F. amelloides*, blue daisy or blue marguerite, is a bushy, evergreen shrub, with a spreading habit. It grows up to 60 cm (24 in), producing blue daisy flowers among the round to oval, bright green leaves. In colder climates it makes an effective indoor plant. There are named varieties of this species, including a form with cream variegated leaves. *F. bergeriana*, the kingfisher daisy, is a mat-forming annual, with delicate, blue daisy flowers which open only in sunshine, so it needs a sunny spot. Summer flowering, it grows to just 20 cm (8 in).

Fenestraria (fam. Aizoaceae)
Baby's toes, window plant

The two species of this succulent genus are native to Namibia. They are clump-forming plants that offset from the base, producing upright, almost cylindrical leaves, each with a transparent window in the top. The window allows light to penetrate into the leaf to produce chlorophyll, the green pigment of the plant. In cultivation all, or most, of the leaves are visible, but in their habitat they are often buried in sand with only the window visible.

CULTIVATION In frost-prone climates, grow in pots of cactus compost in an airy, intermediate greenhouse or conservatory with maximum light. Keep plants dry over winter but carry out

ABOVE Stemless leaves of *Fenestraria aurantiaca* have windows at the top to allow light to penetrate.

moderate watering in the growing season. Outdoors, the plants need full sun and poor, very well drained soil. Propagate from seed or offsets.

CLIMATE Zone 10.

SPECIES *F. aurantiaca* grows 3–5 cm (1–2 in) high, forming clumps up to 15 cm (6 in) across. The flowers are daisy-like and usually bright yellow. Flowering time varies but is often late summer to fall.

Fennel (*Foeniculum vulgare*, fam. Apiaceae)

Fennel has a strong aniseed flavor which is often an acquired taste. All parts of fennel are used in food preparation, particularly in the Mediterranean region, although these ingredients are now also used in cooking in many other parts of the world. The seeds, leaves and stalks are used to flavor fish stews and stuffings, and the seeds add an especially delicious taste to bread. Freshly chopped leaves can be added to potato salad, green salads, meat sauces and cheese dishes. The bulb is very crisp and often eaten raw in salads, particularly after a meal, to cleanse the palate and aid digestion. It is also delicious cooked, served with olive oil and parmesan cheese or tomato sauce.

CULTIVATION Sow seed directly into shallow drills between spring and late summer, allowing 45 cm (18 in) between the rows. Thin seedlings to 30 cm (12 in) apart within each row. Use a well-drained soil, enriched with manure or organic matter, in a sunny location. Provide ample water to encourage growth and feed with a complete fertilizer. Weed control is essential. If grown for the swollen stem base, sow in late spring or early summer. Sowings of these bulb cultivars, especially bolt-resistant kinds, can also be made under glass in cell trays in spring and planted out in early summer. The leaves can be used about three months after sowing and should be picked when needed. When the stem base has reached about the size of a tennis ball, mound

ABOVE Fennel foliage adds an ornamental touch to the herb garden. It can of course be grown amongst flowering shrubs or perennials.

ABOVE *Ferocactus glaucescens* can be well displayed in a terracotta bowl. Terracotta seems to suit cactus and succulent plants.

up the soil to blanch the bulbous base and cut off any flower heads. About two weeks later, cut away the base from the roots, hang in the kitchen and use immediately. Seed is generally harvested in fall when the flower heads have ripened. Clip off the heads and sun dry them for a few days, shake out all the seeds, sieve out the rubbish and store the clean seed in airtight containers.

CLIMATE Zone 5, but Finocchio or Florence fennel is grown as a summer and fall annual in all climates.

SPECIES *F. vulgare*, a native of Europe, is an herbaceous perennial which grows to 90 cm (36 in). It has hollow fleshy stems, light green, feathery leaves, flat clusters of yellow flowers in summer and pale green seeds, ripening to a yellow-brown color in fall. The variety azoricum, or Finocchio (Florence fennel), is smaller than the species and is grown for the swollen, bulb-like stem base.

Ferocactus (fam. Cactaceae)
Barrel cactus

Originating from Mexico and the southern parts of North America, these medium to very large barrel-shaped cactuses have vicious spines and thick, prominent ribs. Large, bell-shaped, red, purple or yellow flowers are borne at the top. Most species are solitary growers but some are clump forming.

CULTIVATION In hard frost areas, grow in an airy, intermediate greenhouse or conservatory, in pots of cactus compost, and provide maximum light. Do not water in winter, but water regularly in the growing period. Propagate from seed and germinate at 20°C (68°F). Outdoors, plants need full sun and well-drained soil.

CLIMATE Zone 9.

SPECIES *F. cylindraceus* has a solitary stem, up to 3 m (10 ft), and yellow to orange flowers. The long, curved spines are generally a yellowish color, though sometimes red. *F. glaucescens* is a flattish, round plant, to 30 cm (12 in) across, with a blueish bloom. It has six to seven sharp ribs, yellow spines and yellow flowers. *F. latispinus* is popular, growing 25–30 cm (10–12 in) high. It has a flattened, round shape, acute ribs and white, red, pink, purple or yellow flowers. Some of the spines become broad and red, and the lowest ones are hooked.

Ferraria (fam. Iridaceae)

Black iris

This South African genus of ten species has the usual sword-like leaves of the iris, though the flowers are greenish brown, splashed with purple. They have a pungent, rather offensive smell, but are decorative. Each flower lasts a short time but they bloom for some months.

CULTIVATION Black irises are sensitive to frost and so are usually grown in an intermediate greenhouse. Use deep pots of soil-based potting compost. Provide maximum light. Do not water in the summer dormant period but water moderately in the growing period. Outdoors grow in well-drained soil with sun or partial shade. Propagate from offsets when dormant.

CLIMATE Zone 10.

SPECIES *F. crispa* has intricately marked, deep brown and yellow, upward-facing flowers, 7–10 cm (3–4 in) across, in spring and early summer. It grows to a height of 45 cm (18 in). The stem-clasping leaves become progressively smaller as they extend up the stem.

ABOVE The exotic flowers of *Ferraria crispa* will bloom even in shade but will be more prolific with some sun.

Festuca (fam. Poaceae)

Fescue

Originally from temperate Europe and Asia and tropical highlands, these hardy grasses have fine, wiry leaves. Hard-wearing and frost-resistant, they are ideal for cooler, temperate lawns and are often included in 'lawn seed' mixtures or mixed with bent grass. Some species are tufting ornamentals.

CULTIVATION For care of lawn species of *Festuca*, see the section on lawns. Blue fescue is a popular, tufting plant used in borders and rockeries. It needs full sun, well-drained soil Clip it back after flowering or when it is untidy. Clumps can be divided and divisions replanted at once.

CLIMATE Zone 5.

SPECIES *F. glauca*, blue fescue, with grayish blue leaves, is a thickly tufting dwarf useful for planting in rockeries. Clumps can grow 25 cm (10 in) wide and to 30 cm (12 in) tall in suitable conditions. Spikes of blue-green flowers appear in early to midsummer. Strong-colored cultivars include 'Blue Fox' and 'Sea Urchin'. *F. rubra*, red fescue, is a perennial and a parent of the fescue most commonly used for lawns in the US. It has clusters of dark green, almost blueish leaves. Subspecies rubra, with russet-colored foliage, grows to 45 cm (18 in) and is sometimes used in ribbon borders. Subspecies *commutata*, chewings fescue, has needle-shaped leaves and is quite often used in lawn mixes.

ABOVE Closely planted clumps of the tufty blue fescue, *Festuca glauca*, make a weed-proof edging for a garden bed.

Ficus (fam. Moraceae)
Fig

This large, diverse genus of around 800 species includes trees, shrubs and climbers, both evergreen and deciduous, widely distributed over the warmer areas of Australia, Southeast Asia, India and the Pacific islands, extending as far as the Mediterranean and Africa. Some start their life as epiphytes, eventually strangling their host with their strong aerial roots; others are popularly used as house plants; and some are grown for their fruit. In all species the flowers are monoecious and quite unusual as they are enclosed in what later becomes the fruit. They vary widely in foliage and habit, but all species have a milky sap. Most figs grow extremely large but in cool and cold climates they make fine pot plants for home, warm greenhouse or conservatory.

CULTIVATION In frost-prone climates, grow as pot plants. Use soilless or soil-based potting compost and provide good light, but shade from direct, strong sun. They like a humid atmosphere. *F. carica*, the common fig grown for its fruits, can be grown outside in zone 8 but needs sun, a sheltered spot and well-drained soil. Most figs can be propagated from semi-ripe cuttings in summer, rooted with bottom heat. *F. carica* can be grown from hardwood cuttings in winter. Some species, like *F. elastica*, can be propagated by air-layering.

CLIMATE Zone 10 for most species.

SPECIES *F. aspera* 'Parcelli', clown or mosaic fig, is a very showy shrub, with thin, dark green leaves, splashed with white. The fruits are striped cream and pink. *F. benghalensis*, banyan tree, a native of India, is renowned for its fascinating display of aerial roots which eventually form secondary trunks. It can grow to 30 m (100 ft) tall and much, much broader, sometimes having the appearance of a small forest. It is widely cultivated in the tropics for shade, and is considered sacred by the Hindus in India. *F. benjamina*, weeping fig or laurel

TOP The Moreton Bay fig, *Ficus macrophylla*, has a massive framework and very wide spread.

ABOVE The rounded crown and graceful weeping foliage of *Ficus benjamina* make this a lovely specimen or street tree.

fig, is a tropical, evergreen tree from India and Southeast Asia, often used as a potted indoor plant, but also grown outdoors where it can reach 15 m (50 ft) or more. The form 'Exotica' has wavy-edged leaves. It is known for its extremely invasive root system and should not be grown near foundations or underground pipes. *F. carica*, common fig or fig tree, zone 8, from the Mediterranean, has been cultivated for centuries for its delicious edible fruits which come in a variety of shapes and colors. It generally grows 3–5 m (10–16 ft). (See entry at Fig,

ABOVE The heavy-textured foliage of *Ficus elastica* 'Decora' is the main attraction of this large tree, often potted for indoor use.

Ficus carica.) *F. elastica*, India rubber plant, from tropical Asia, is widely cultivated for shade in tropical countries, though generally as a pot plant outside the tropics. Its new growth is contained in rosy sheaths which look very attractive against the glossy, dark green mature leaves. Cultivar 'Decora' has shiny, dark green leaves with an ivory midrib and red on the undersides; 'Doescheri' has leaves boldly variegated with cream, white and grayish green, and the central veins and leaf stalks are pink; 'Variegata' has light green leaves with white or yellow margins. *F. lyrata*, fiddleleaf fig or banjo fig, from tropical Africa, grows to 12 m (40 ft) outdoors, although it is often grown as an indoor or pot plant. The large, fiddle-shaped leaves are a bright, glossy green. *F. macrophylla*, Moreton Bay fig, occurs in coastal rainforests of eastern Australia where it reaches heights of 60 m (200 ft) with a vast spread. Too large for most gardens, it has been widely planted as a shade and park tree in many warm to mild regions. *F. microcarpa* var. *hillii*, to 20 m (65 ft) or more, makes a good street, park or shade tree, and is also grown as a standard, either in the garden or in a container. It has graceful, weeping branches and small, neat leaves. This variety will tolerate a temperate climate. *F. obliqua*, Australian strangler fig, grows huge under rainforest conditions, and has a buttressed trunk and aerial roots. *F. pumila*, creeping fig, zone 9, is an evergreen climber from Asia, with heart-shaped leaves and aerial roots, and is attractive growing on walls. Cultivar 'Minima' has small, slender juvenile leaves. *F. religiosa*, bo tree or sacred fig, occurs in India and throughout Southeast Asia. Quite similar to the banyan, though not as tall, it is a deciduous, fast-growing tree, widely planted in the tropics. The bo tree is sacred to Hindus, and Buddhists particularly, as Buddha received enlightenment under the shade of this interesting tree. *F. rubiginosa*, Port Jackson fig or rusty fig, from New South Wales, grows to 30 m (100 ft). It has a wide-spreading crown, buttressed trunk and pendulous branches. The small leaves are a rust color when they are young and the fruits are borne in pairs in the spring and the summer. Too large for most home gardens, it is a good street, park or shade tree for coastal areas. *F. superba*, sea fig, from Asia and Australia, grows to a large tree with very large leaves and dull purple fruits. Var. *henneana*, cedar fig, is a deciduous epiphyte native to northern Australia. *F. sycomorus*, sycamore fig or Egyptian sycamore, from Africa through to Lebanon, is the sycamore tree of the Bible. It grows to 18 m (60 ft), with rounded leaves and fruits.

Fig (*Ficus carica*, fam. Moraceae)

A familiar sight in the Mediterranean region of Europe, the common fig is grown for its fruits in the US in zone 8 and above, and is cultivated commercially in California, Texas and Louisiana. It is one of the oldest cultivated plants, featuring often in the mythology of the Egyptians, Romans and Greeks. It is known to have been cultivated around the Mediterranean since antiquity. It is grown both for its ornamental beauty and its fruit which, interestingly, contains the flower within it. The fruit is either oblong or pear-shaped and pulpy when ripe.

ABOVE The widely cultivated edible fig, *Ficus carica*, can bear heavy crops in a good season.

Figs are delicious eaten raw with prosciutto or soft white cheese, or poached and served with cream. They can also be baked or grilled. Fig and ginger jam is wonderful at breakfast on grainy toast.

CULTIVATION The common fig can be grown in the home garden under a wide range of climatic conditions, provided the soil is loose and friable enough to allow the shallow roots to penetrate and find moisture. It needs plenty of water in summer. Propagate from hardwood cuttings taken in winter. Space plants 5–7 m (16–23 ft) apart to allow for their dense foliage. Fruit is produced in two to four years. Figs are borne on new wood in spring and the main crop matures in summer or fall. Sometimes trees will produce two crops in a year, and even three in rare instances.

CLIMATE Zone 8.

SPECIES *F. carica* is a deciduous tree, 7–9 m (23–30 ft) tall, but often smaller under cultivation. There are many cultivars, mostly self-fertile, but they differ in respect of climatic adapability. There are cultivars for cool conditions near the coast, while others are suited to long hot summers. 'Brown Turkey' is very adaptable regarding climate; 'Kadota' is good for hot areas; and 'Mission' is suitable for desert areas.

Filipendula (fam. Rosaceae)
Meadowsweet

This small group of perennials is native to northern temperate zones. Cultivated as ornamentals, some species are used in scented oils, and some have medicinal properties.

CULTIVATION These plants like moisture and an open position in the garden, particularly near water. Propagate by division in spring, or from seed sown when ripe in a sandy loam. Most prefer partial shade and need protection from sun at the hottest time of day.

CLIMATE There are species suited to various climatic zones. Most are tolerant of very low temperatures and are best in cool, moist climates.

SPECIES *F. kamtschatica*, zone 3, grows to 2 m (6 ft), with large, lobed leaves and white or pale pink, fragrant flowers. *F. purpurea*, zone 6, grows to 1 m (3 ft), with fern-like foliage, red stems and fluffy heads of carmine pink flowers in summer. It is a useful border plant and excellent for cutting. The form albiflora has white

ABOVE Meadowsweet, *Filipendula* species, has many medicinal applications, although it is mainly cultivated for ornament.

flowers; 'Elegans' has white flowers with red stamens. *F. rubra*, queen of the prairie, zone 2, is a very attractive species, to around 3 m (10 ft), with plumes of peach-pink flowers. Cultivar 'Venusta' is smaller, with deep pink to reddish purple flowers. *F. ulmaria*, meadowsweet or queen of the meadows, zone 2, grows to 1 m (3 ft), with fern-like foliage and large heads of feathery, creamish white flowers. Cultivar 'Aurea' has golden yellow leaves; 'Flore Pleno' has double flowers. *F. vulgaris*, dropwort, zone 3, to 1 m (3 ft), has fern-like foliage and white, fragrant flowers. It tolerates slightly drier conditions and works well as a border plant. Cultivar 'Multiplex' has double flowers.

Firmiana (fam. Sterculiaceae)
Chinese parasol tree

This small genus of deciduous trees originates from Asia and Africa. Some are grown for their light timber but one species is especially known as an ornamental.

CULTIVATION These trees will do well in most normal soils but they must have some protection from wind. In areas prone to hard frosts, grow in a cool greenhouse or conservatory in large pots or tubs of soil-based potting compost. Can stand outside for the summer. Propagate from seed sown when ripe and germinate in a temperature of 13°C (55°F).

CLIMATE Zone 9.

SPECIES *F. simplex*, from eastern Asia, grows to 20 m (65 ft). It has handsome, three- to five-lobed leaves, 25–30 cm (10–12 in) across, and unusual, papery fruits in fall. The foliage turns yellow in fall. The yellowish to greenish white flowers are borne in terminal sprays on the tree's thin stems.

Fittonia (fam. Acanthaceae)
Nerve plant

Originating from Peru, these two species of beautiful, dwarf trailers are widely grown as indoor plants. The veins on the leaves are white, red or otherwise colored.

CULTIVATION Grow in a warm greenhouse or conservatory, or in a warm room in the home. Good subjects for terrariums. The plants can be grown in shallow pots or hanging containers and prefer soilless potting compost. Provide

ABOVE The large, lobed leaves of *Firmiana simplex* take on a papery texture as they color before falling in fall.

ABOVE Silver nerve plant, *Fittonia verschaffeltii* var. *argyroneura*, needs warmth and high humidity to thrive.

good light but shade from sun at all times. A humid atmosphere is essential. Do not over-water, especially in winter. Keep the compost only slightly moist. Propagate from tip cuttings in spring, rooting them in a close propagating case. Stems can be layered at any time.

CLIMATE Tropical climates only.

SPECIES *F. verschaffeltii*, known as nerve plant, painted net leaf or silvernet, is the most commonly grown species. It has dark green leaves veined with rose-red. Var. *argyroneura*, silver nerve plant, has clearly marked, white veins.

Flindersia (fam. Rutaceae)

Named after Matthew Flinders who first circumnavigated Australia, this genus of tropical, evergreen trees is mostly indigenous to Australia. These trees have pinnate leaves, dotted with the oil glands that are characteristic of the *Rutaceae* family, and mostly very showy terminal sprays of smallish flowers. The fruits are often interesting, from large, woody and boat-shaped, to the star-shaped variety of *F. australis*. This genus is unlikely to be available outside its native countries.

CULTIVATION Except in the tropics and subtropics, this genus would have to be grown in a warm, humid greenhouse or conservatory, using suitable large pots or tubs. Propagation is from the large seeds which are sown as soon as ripe, and they need bottom heat to germinate.

CLIMATE Tropical and subtropical.

SPECIES *F. australis*, crow's ash or Australian teak, mostly native to Queensland, may grow to 40 m (130 ft), though much less in cultivation. Valued for its durable timber, it is also widely used as a street or park tree. The ornamental, star-shaped woody fruits are used in dried arrangements. *F. brayleyana*, Queensland maple, is a tall forest tree yielding one of the world's best quality cabinet timbers.

ABOVE The heavily mottled trunk of *Flindersia maculosa* makes this tree a fine feature wherever it is planted.

F. maculosa, leopard wood, from the inland regions of Queensland and northern New South Wales, is a twisted, bushy, prickly shrub in its juvenile phase, maturing to a symmetrical small tree, with a fine, straight, slender trunk. It has distinctive, mottled bark and simple, delicate foliage which forms a fairly open crown.

Forsythia (fam. Oleaceae)

This small genus of deciduous shrubs, with all but one species native to China and Korea, is grown mainly for the profusion of yellow, star-shaped flowers that appear before the leaves in spring.

CULTIVATION *Forsythia* is easy to grow in ordinary garden soil, in full sun or dappled shade. Prune right after flowering, cutting back old flowered wood to younger shoots lower down. Never prune in winter or flowers will be lost. Propagate from softwood cuttings in spring or

ABOVE The appearance of the clear yellow flowers on *Forsythia suspensa* signals the end of winter.

early summer, from semi-ripe cuttings in late summer, or from hardwood cuttings in fall or winter.

CLIMATE Zone 5. Best in cool, moist climates. Flowering tends to be poor or absent if climate is too warm.

SPECIES *F.* 'Beatrix Farrand' is a popular hybrid with a bushy habit, 2 m (6 ft) high and wide, and large, deep yellow blooms from early spring. *F.* x *intermedia* is a compact shrub, to 1.5 m (5 ft) tall and wide and the large, yellow flowers appear from early spring. It is mainly the cultivars that are grown. 'Lynwood' grows to 2–3 m (6–10 ft), with large, broad-petalled flowers, 3 cm (1 in) across; 'Spectabilis' was developed in the last century and is still one of the most popular hybrids in this group, growing to 2.5 m (8 ft), with narrow-petalled flowers, 3 cm (1 in) across. *F. ovata* grows to 1.5 m (5 ft) tall with spreading habit. Generally starting to bloom in early spring, this shrub is soon covered with masses of small, cheery yellow flowers, 15 mm (½ in) long. *F. suspensa*, golden bells, is a rambling shrub, with very long, slender, arching branches; it may be trained against a wall or allowed to droop over

a fence. Clusters of bright yellow, pendulous flowers are followed by attractive, bright green, oval leaves. It grows to 3 m (10 ft).

Fouquieria (fam. Fouquieriaceae)
Ocotillo

From the desert areas of Mexico and southwestern United States, this genus comprises around ten species of spiny and succulent shrubs and trees. All species have thickened stems, masses of thorny branches and small, oval, bright green, deciduous leaves which appear after rain. The showy, bell-shaped flowers, often with rolled-back tips, appear in clusters at the ends of the branches in summer or fall, also after rain. They also come in red, cream, yellow, white or light purple. In the wild, some species are pollinated by humming birds.

CULTIVATION In climates prone to frost, grow in an airy, intermediate greenhouse or conservatory, in pots of cactus compost. Ensure maximum light. Do not water in winter but water

ABOVE *Fouquieria diguetii* is an unusual, spiny shrub from southern California and Mexico.

moderately during the growing period. Outdoors, plants need full sun and soil that is very well drained, but not too rich. Propagate from seed or softwood cuttings in spring, with bottom heat for both.

CLIMATE Zone 9.

SPECIES *F. columnaris* (syn. *Idria columnaris*), boojum tree, is a spiny tree, growing to 20 m (65 ft) in its habitat, with a thick, whitish trunk. The branches form at 90 degrees to the trunk and the small, roundish leaves are deciduous. Bell-shaped, creamy flowers, with a light honey fragrance, are produced in summer to fall. *F. splendens*, variously known as ocotillo, candlewood and flaming sword, is the most popularly cultivated species. It has a short, swollen trunk, thorny, arched branches and numerous, bright red flowers with rolled lobes which appear after rain.

Frankenia (fam. Frankeniaceae)

Native to coastal areas in temperate and subtropical climates, these low-growing or prostrate, evergreen subshrubs and perennials are somewhat heath-like in appearance, with thin stems and tiny leaves. In the right climate they can be grown in seaside gardens, particularly as groundcover.

CULTIVATION In frosty areas, grow in a cool greenhouse or conservatory. These shrubs tolerate

ABOVE *Frankenia pauciflora* is tolerant of saline soils and coastal exposure.

salty air and sandy soil. Propagate by division in fall or from seed sown under glass, or in seed beds in early spring. Transplant in fall.

CLIMATE Zone 9.

SPECIES *F. laevis* is a carpet-like, trailing species, with gray-green foliage which turns a reddish brown color in fall. In spring, it is dotted with stemless, rose pink, papery flowers. *F. pauciflora* is a widespread, prostrate, mat-like Australian native, with some erect branchlets, grayish green leaves and small, pink or white flowers. It can tolerate salt marsh conditions. *F. thymifolia*, to 4 cm (1½ in), has a prostrate, creeping habit and larger, pink flowers.

Fraxinus (fam. Oleaceae)
Ash

Found throughout the northern hemisphere, except in the coldest regions and the tropics, this genus comprises around 65 species of deciduous trees, many very ornamental, and making beautiful park and street trees. Some of the species are valued for their tough, pale

ABOVE The gold fall foliage of a fine ash tree, *Fraxinus species*, glows against a blue sky.

timber. They all have pinnate leaves, most of which color beautifully before falling, and winged fruits, called samaras. Masses of tiny flowers appear before the leaves open. Flower structure divides the genus into two sections, but this does not concern the gardener.

CULTIVATION *Fraxinus* will grow in most soils, even limestone soils, but prefers a well-drained, sunny position, though it will tolerate partial shade. Being deciduous, it is best to plant in late fall or early winter. Propagate from stratified seed sown in spring, except for *F. excelsior* 'Aurea' and *F. angustifolia* Raywood = 'Flame', which should be budded onto the seedlings of *F. angustifolia* or *F. americana* in the early summer.

CLIMATE There are species suited to various climatic zones.

SPECIES *F. americana*, white ash, zone 3, is a magnificent tree which is highly valued in its native habitat of North America. It reaches heights of 15–30 m (50–100 ft) and has a long, straight trunk. The leaves comprise seven to nine long, lance-shaped, dark green leaflets, paler on the undersides, which change to a purplish color before falling. Useful as a specimen tree, it yields valuable hardwood timber used for many purposes. *F. angustifolia*, narrow-leaved ash, zone 6, is a popular tree in drier climates, as it tolerates very dry, almost desert, conditions. It is a handsome tree, to 25 m (80 ft) tall. Cultivar Raywood = 'Flame', claret ash, is a hardy tree, 6–10 m (20–33 ft) tall. Its attractive foliage colors superbly in fall to a deep coppery red, even in lowland areas. *F. excelsior*, common ash or European ash, zone 4, grows 30–40 m (100–130 ft) tall in its habitat, although around half this size in cultivation. It has a rounded canopy, making it a lovely shelter or specimen tree for large gardens. It has distinctive, black buds from which both the leaves, comprising nine to eleven leaflets, and flowers emerge. The timber is well suited to carpentry. As an ornamental it is hard to better the golden ash, *F. excelsior* 'Aurea'.

The twigs and small branches are yellow and the lime to yellow foliage becomes deep gold in fall. *F. ornus*, manna ash or flowering ash, zone 6, grows 7–15 m (23–50 ft) tall, with gray buds and long, slightly toothed, sharply pointed leaflets. In late spring it is covered in sprays of strongly perfumed, dull white flowers, borne at the tips of the branches. The sweet sap, or 'manna' (not the 'manna' referred to in the Bible), was once used as a laxative.

Freesia (fam. Iridaceae)

Freesias are South African cormous plants, loved for their beautiful colors and delicious perfume. The many hybrids range in color from creamy white through yellow, orange, red, purple, brown, lavender and blue. Low-growing and hardy, they have slender, strap-like leaves and erect flower spikes extending above the leaves in late winter and early spring, depending on the climate. The funnel-shaped flowers grow to 5 cm (2 in) long, with about five to seven on each stem, and make good cut blooms.

CULTIVATION Except in frost-free or relatively frost-free climates, freesias are grown in an airy, cool greenhouse or conservatory as pot plants. Use pots of soil-based compost for the corms, which can be planted in late summer or early fall. Freesias need good light but shade from

ABOVE Rich creamy yellow freesias are a delight in the garden or as cut flowers.

direct sun. When flowering is over, watering is gradually reduced until the compost becomes dry. The corms are then stored dry and cool until planting time again. Freesias to be grown in the garden are planted in fall, 8 cm (3 in) deep, in a sunny position with well-drained soil. Freesias can also be grown from seeds sown in fall and germinated at 18°C (64°F).

CLIMATE Zone 9.

SPECIES *F. refracta* is a low, tufted plant, to about 30 cm (12 in), with creamy yellow, very fragrant flowers borne in one-sided spikes in late winter and spring. Modern hybrids, classed as *Freesia x hybrida*, come in a wide color range, including red, blue, mauve, pink and purple. Most have no scent. Large, yellow and plain white types generally have the best perfume.

Fremontodendron (fam. Sterculiaceae)
Flannel bush

This small genus of two or three species of trees and shrubs originates from the south-western parts of North America where they occur in dry canyons and woodlands and on mountain slopes. The stems and leaves are covered with silky brown hairs which may cause skin irritation. Their very decorative, yellow flowers

BELOW The clear yellow flowers of *Fremontodendron californicum* make a bright feature, however the foliage may cause skin irritation.

appear over a long period from late spring to late summer.

CULTIVATION Grow in very well drained, neutral to alkaline soil that need not be especially rich. Flannel bush flowers best in full sun and it needs protection from cold winds. The best position in the garden is against a sunny, warm wall. Established plants are tolerant of dry conditions. Plants trained against a wall can be spur pruned in late winter by cutting back the old flowered shoots to within three to four buds of the main framework branches. Propagate in late summer from semi-ripe cuttings.

CLIMATE Zone 8.

SPECIES *F. californicum* is an evergreen shrub to 5–6 m (16–20 ft) high and about as wide. It reaches to about 6 m (20 ft) in its native California. It has dark, lobed leaves and produces masses of saucer-shaped, bright, golden yellow flowers from late spring until well into fall. It can be grown in a shrub border or trained against a wall.

Freycinetia (fam. Pandanaceae)

Found from Southeast Asia to the Pacific Islands, the climbers or scramblers of this large genus have lance-shaped or linear leaves, small flowers and prettily colored, often fragrant bracts. The oblong, cone-like fruit is woody or rather fleshy, with many seeds. Not readily available outside its countries of origin.

CULTIVATION In frost-prone climates, grow in a warm, humid greenhouse or conservatory. They also make excellent house plants. Shade plants from direct sun. Water well in summer, more sparingly in winter. Propagate from suckers removed in spring and inserted in cuttings compost until well rooted.

CLIMATE At least zone 10.

SPECIES *F. australiensis* is a vigorous climber from the rainforests of northern Queensland,

ABOVE Needing some means of support, *Freycinetia excelsa* is similar to *F. australiensis*, but the flower bracts are deep orange.

with long, curved leaves and red bracts surrounding the flowers. It can be grown on trees in tropical and subtropical areas and elswhere as a potted plant. *F. banksii*, from New Zealand, will climb to 30 m (100 ft) or more. Multi-branched, it has narrow leaves, up to 1 m (3 ft) long and about 25 mm (1 in) wide. The flowers are enclosed by fragrant bracts, the inner ones being thick and white or pale lilac at the base, and edible with a sweet taste.

Fritillaria (fam. Liliaceae)

Fritillary

The name of this genus of bulbous plants from Western Europe, the Mediterranean, Asia and North America derives from Latin *fritillus*, meaning 'dice-box', as the checkered patterns on some of the species resemble the checkerboards associated with dice games. Few species are in general cultivation and these are found only in cooler climates. Few consider fritillaries beautiful but they are fascinating. Some species smell unpleasant. These plants, especially the crown imperial, are outstanding in a mixed bulb garden or with mixed perennials or annuals. They should be grouped to gain the best effect. The flowers are produced in spring or early summer, depending on species.

CULTIVATION Requirements differ according to species, but the easier and more popular species are best planted in fertile, well-drained yet moisture-retentive soil, and in sun. Small species can be planted on a rock garden, taller species in a mixed or shrub border. Propagation is from seed sown in fall and germinated in a garden frame. Allow them to freeze over winter or remove offsets from mature bulbs.

CLIMATE There are species suited to various climatic zones.

SPECIES The best known species is the spectacular crown imperial, *F. imperialis*, zone 4, with a cluster of orange, yellow or red, bell-shaped flowers hanging below a crown of green leaves, on stems 50–90 cm (20–36 in) high. *F. meleagris*, snake's head fritillary, zone 4, occurs in meadows throughout England and Europe and is easy to cultivate. The checkered flowers are purple or pink-purple. *F. pallidiflora*, zone 3, grows about 40 cm (16 in) high and has creamy flowers with a green base. *F. pudica*, yellow fritillary, zone 3, is a small grower, to about 15 cm (6 in), from western North America. The flowers can be flushed with red or orange.

ABOVE Always an object of interest, these are the very distinctive flowers of the crown imperial, *Fritillaria imperialis*.

Fuchsia (fam. Onagraceae)

Native to the rainforests of Central and South America, with a few species from New Zealand and Tahiti, the trees and shrubs of this large genus mostly produce wonderfully exotic flowers from summer through to late fall. Usually pendulous, the flowers have an elongated calyx tube, with four reflexed lobes or sepals and four petals, and stamens which frequently protrude beyond the petals. The colorful hybrids of *F. fulgens* and *F. magellanica* and their varieties are the most popular and the hybrid flowers can be divided into three classes: single, semi-double and double. These hybrids are either upright or trailing, the latter making a pretty display in hanging baskets. Some fuchsias are grown for their variegated or beautifully colored leaves rather than their flowers, which are not as showy as those on plants with plain, green foliage. The leaves are simple and alternate, opposite or whorled. The fruit is a berry. Frost-tender fuchsias are grown in a cool greenhouse or conservatory in frost-prone climates, and the hybrids are also used as summer bedding plants.

CULTIVATION Fuchsias are easily propagated from tip cuttings taken from late spring until early fall. Seed from the ripe berries can be used to propagate the straight species which need a well-drained soil enriched with organic matter and regular water during spring and summer. Feed with blood, fish and bone or slow-release fertilizer in the growing season. Regular tip pruning produces bushy growth which is able to bear more flowers. Hard prune at the end of winter. Cool summers with moist soil and a sheltered position in partial shade provide the best conditions for fuchsias in the garden. Provide a deep winter mulch to protect roots from hard frosts.

CLIMATE Zone 10 for the following species, unless otherwise indicated.

SPECIES *F. arborescens*, tree fuchsia, is a large shrub or small, bushy tree, with fleshy, shiny, dark green foliage. Beautiful clusters of

ABOVE Scarlet and deep magenta flowers on this hybrid fuchsia will give many weeks of color.

lavenderpink flowers are borne at the ends of the branches through summer. *F. fulgens* is a popular, medium-sized shrub with slightly succulent stems and large, almost heart-shaped, toothed leaves. A profusion of pendulous, scarlet flowers, with long calyx tubes, appear in terminal clusters. *F. magellanica*, ladies' eardrops, zone 6, the hardiest of the species, is a large, evergreen shrub, to 5 m (16 ft). Its pendulous flowers have red sepals, short, purplish petals and very prominent stamens. The many varieties available include the dwarf macrostema. *F. procumbens*, trailing fuchsia, zone 9, is one of the New Zealand natives. It is a prostrate evergreen, with small, heart-shaped, slender-stalked leaves. The small, erect flowers have purple and green, reflexed lobes and red calyx tubes. Bright red berries, up to 2 cm (1 in) in diameter, persist throughout fall and winter. *F. triphylla* is a small shrub with downy leaves, purplish underneath, and terminal clusters of pendulous, brilliant scarlet flowers. Cultivar 'Gartenmeister Bonstedt', a shrubby bush that flowers for much of the year, prefers more sun than the hybrid fuchsias. Many hundreds of hybrids are available in combinations of white, red and purple and various shades of these colors.

G

Gaillardia to Gypsophila

Gaillardia (fam. Asteraceae)

Blanket flower

Endemic to central and western United States and parts of South America, this genus comprises around 28 species of long-flowering annuals and perennials. They have rough, toothed or deeply divided leaves and will provide a continuous supply of ray-like flowers on single stalks for cutting during the summer.

CULTIVATION These hardy plants are easy to grow and can tolerate heat and drought. They need only a light, well-drained soil and plenty of sun. Propagate the annuals from seed, and the perennials by division or from root cuttings.

CLIMATE Zone 8, but zone 5 for G. x *grandiflora*.

SPECIES G. *amblyodon* is an annual, to 1 m (3 ft), with maroon summer flowers and oblong to lance-shaped, mostly entire leaves, to 8 cm (3 in). G. x *grandiflora* is a vigorous perennial which flowers from seed in its first year. A range of these hybrids is available, with flowers in tones of red, yellow and orange. Cultivar 'Burgundy' has wine red flowers, with a yellow band along the outer edges; 'Goblin' (syn. 'Gobolin') is a 30 cm (12 in) dwarf having yellow and red blooms. G. *pulchella* is an upright annual, which grows 45–60 cm (18–24 in), with crimson or yellow, ball-like flowers and hairy, lance-shaped, gray-green leaves. It is useful in borders, where it creates bright spots of color. There are several cultivars available some with double flowers.

Gai lum

(*Brassica olearacea* Alboglabra Group)

Chinese broccoli

Gai lum is used widely in Chinese cooking and can be boiled, steamed or stir fried. It is a good source of dietary fiber, folic acid and potassium, and has a high vitamin C content. Few varieties are grown, the main one being a Japanese cultivar, 'Kailaan'. It is similar in appearance to choy sum, although the leaves are rounder and the stalks, or petioles, are round and slender. The flowers are white. It is harvested just as the first flowers begin to open.

CULTIVATION This leafy vegetable needs well-drained soil enriched with organic matter. Dig in manure or compost four to six weeks prior to sowing seed. Apply a dressing of lime or dolomite to the soil before sowing unless the

ABOVE The strong colours of a *Gaillardia* hybrid will stand up to summer heat without fading.

ABOVE This crop of gai lum is about to be harvested as the first flowers are appearing.

soil is known to be alkaline. Space plants about 20 cm (8 in) apart. Give regular water to keep the crop growing quickly and ensure that the area is kept weed free. The first harvesting should be about seven to eight weeks after sowing.

CLIMATE Zone 8, but grown in all climates as a summer annual.

Galangal

(Kaempferia galanga, Alpinia galanga,
fam. Zingiberaceae)

Both of these plants have rhizomes that are used as a source of flavor and aroma. Both are used widely in the preparation of Asian dishes, especially Thai cuisine. *Kaempferia galanga* has attractive, rounded, strongly veined foliage and small, simple, white flowers. It is low growing and the rhizomes, or roots, multiply rapidly in tropical regions. Outside the tropics, this plant dies down completely with the onset of cool weather. *Alpinia galanga* has tall, upright, cane-like growth, typical of all species of *Alpinia*. It spreads by running rhizomes, rapidly forming large clumps under consistent warm, humid conditions.

ABOVE The spice, galangal, is derived from two different plants. This is *Alpina galanga*. Many species of *Alpina* are cultivated as ornamentals.

CULTIVATION In frost-prone climates, grow plants in a warm, humid greenhouse or conservatory, in pots of soil-based potting compost. Ensure good light but shade from direct sun. Water normally in growing season, but in winter keep Kaempferia dry during dormancy and water Alpinia only moderately. Propagate by division in spring.

CLIMATE Zone 10.

Galanthus (fam. Amaryllidaceae)
Snowdrop

In cool and cold parts of the US the first snow-drop the first snowdrop announces the beginning of spring, often appearing while snow is still on the ground. These delicate, little, white, nodding flowers appear in singles or doubles on slender stems above the flat, narrow, strap-like leaves. They are different from snowflakes, *Leucojum* species, in that some of the white petals, the three shorter ones, have green horse-shoe markings on them. Snowdrops are native to Europe and western Asia where they occur both in woodland and exposed rocky outcrops.

CULTIVATION Snowdrops need a cool, shady spot and a light soil. Plant the bulbs, 8 cm (3 in) deep and 5 cm (2 in) apart, in late summer. They are perfect for naturalizing under decidu-ous trees. They can be lifted, divided and replanted when they are in leaf, as soon as flowering is over.

CLIMATE Zone 6, unless otherwise indicated below.

SPECIES *G. caucasicus*, zone 5, to 15 cm (6 in), often flowers from late fall to early spring. *G. elwesii* is an early bloomer and a strong grower, to 20 cm (8 in). *G. nivalis*, the common or wild snowdrop, zone 4, which grows to around 10 cm (4 in), has single flow-ers, with green-tipped petals, and blue-green leaves. 'Flore Pleno', 10–15 cm (4–6 in), pro-duces double flowers. *G. plicatus*, Crimean snowdrop, to 20 cm (8 in), produces largish

ABOVE Snowdrops, *Galanthus species*, should be planted in generous drifts to create the most impact.

ABOVE This abundant show of flowers and buds on *Galtonia candicans* ensures that there will be a long floral display.

flowers with green markings. *G. plicatus* subsp. *byzantinus*, to 20–30 cm (8–12 in), has broad, dark green, 12 cm (5 in) long leaves and among the largest flowers of the species, with green marks at the base of the inner segments. Many named cultivars and hybrids of snowdrops have been produced, particularly in Europe, and specialist bulb growers should be able to offer some of these.

Galtonia (fam. Hyacinthaceae)

Similar to the hyacinth but much taller, these South African bulbous plants are grown for their delightful flower spikes of greenish white, bell-shaped flowers which bloom in summer. Excellent for the back of a border, only two species are regularly seen in cultivation.

CULTIVATION Plant galtonias in fall, about 8–10 cm (3–4 in) deep, and try not to disturb them. Grow in a moisture-retentive yet well-drained soil in full sun. If grown in cooler areas, they require a mulch to protect them from winter frost. Propagate from offsets or seed. These plants self-seed but take about three years to reach to a flowering size.

CLIMATE There are species suited to vairous climatic zones.

SPECIES *G. candicans*, summer hyacinth, zone 5, grows up to 1.2 m (4 ft), with leaves up to 1 m (3 ft) long and 5 cm (2 in) wide. The sweetly perfumed, summer flowers are pure white. A beautiful, double, white galtonia named 'Moonbeam' appeared by chance in a New Zealand garden amongst a group of the single *G. candicans*. It produces 30 or more blooms at a time on stems to 1.5 m (5 ft). This cultivar is not freely available outside its country of origin. *G. viridiflora*, zone 8, also blooms in summer, with palest green trumpet-shaped flowers.

Gardenia (fam. Rubiaceae)

Gardenias are one of the most popular plants for warm climate gardens worldwide because of their exquisite, white, beautifully perfumed blooms which contrast perfectly with their attractive, dark green foliage. Mostly from tropical Asia and Africa, there are around 200 species of gardenia. Throughout most of the US gardenias are grown in a warm greenhouse or conservatory but they can be grown outdoors in zone 10 or warmest parts of zone 9.

ABOVE The heavy-textured white flowers of gardenia will create a heady fragrance in a warm greenhouse or conservatory.

CULTIVATION These tender, evergreen shrubs are best grown in a warm greenhouse or conservatory, in large pots or tubs of acid (lime-free) potting compost. They need maximum light but shade from direct sun. Provide moderate humidity. Water normally in the growing period, using lime-free water, but very sparingly in winter. Liquid feed once a month in spring and summer. Propagate from semi-ripe cuttings in late summer.

CLIMATE Warmest parts of zone 9, zone 10 and tropical.

SPECIES *G. augusta*, Cape jasmine, from southern China, is the most commonly grown of the species. It grows to 2 m (6 ft) in height, with thick-petalled flowers, blooming naturally in summer. There are numerous cultivars including 'August Beauty' which freely produces large double flowers from spring to fall. It is quite a tall plant. More compact is the cultivar 'Mystery', with semi-double, white flowers. Double, pure white flowers grace the erect-growing 'Veitchii'. *G. thunbergia*, tree gardenia, from the forests of southern Africa, is an especially beautiful, though slow-growing, species, to 3.5 m (11 ft), which will thrive in any rich, well-drained soil. It has broad, glossy leaves and fragrant, single, white flowers.

Garlic *(Allium sativum*, fam. Alliaceae)

Believed to have its origins in the Mediterranean basin, this perennial, herbaceous plant has been known since antiquity. It is mostly treated as an annual in cultivation. The leaves are long and narrow, and the flowers pinkish white on long stems. The oval bulb has a membraneous cover enclosing a number of small, separate parts called cloves. Garlic is grown for the cloves which have a pungent flavor and odor and are used throughout the world for flavoring meats, vegetables, dressings, bread, sauces and salads. Garlic has been used medicinally for centuries and modern studies confirm its many useful properties.

CULTIVATION As fertile seeds are rarely produced, the plant must be propagated from the cloves. Garlic can be easily grown in areas which are suitable for onions. Plant in fall or spring, 8 cm (3 in) deep and 15 cm (6 in) apart within the row, and 30 cm (12 in) between rows. The bulbs are ready to harvest about six to eight months after planting, when the top growth becomes

ABOVE Bundles of garlic are hung in a dry, airy place to dry completely prior to cleaning and plaiting into ropes for storage.

dry and falls over. Pull bulbs out and dry out in a cool, airy place. When sufficiently dry, braid the tops together and hang up under cover to dry out further, ready for use. Other cultivation details are identical to those required for onions. In warm climates, fall plantings should be mature by the following summer. Cool climate early spring plantings will also be ready for harvesting in the summer but bulbs may not be as large as those from fall plantings.

CLIMATE Zone 8.

Garrya (fam. Garryaceae)
Silk tassel bush

Native to western North America, this small genus of winter-flowering shrubs is grown mainly for the unusual and very attractive catkins on the male plant. The female flower catkins are short and open and not nearly as striking, so it is worth seeking out a male plant. The long, pendulous catkins are light green and silky and last for several weeks in winter. Garrya is an ideal background or screen plant as it is quite a tall shrub. It also makes an interesting espalier when trained to show off its silky tassels. Garrya should be planted where its winter display can be a feature.

ABOVE Providing winter interest in the garden, the male tassel flowers of *Garrya elliptica* cascade like a beautiful curtain.

CULTIVATION Garryas will grow in any soil and do not require much sun. Propagate from semi-ripe cuttings in summer, rooting them in a heated propagating case.

CLIMATE Zone 8.

SPECIES *G. elliptica* is a shrub or small tree which may reach 5–6 m (16–20 ft), but is more often only 3–4 m (10–13 ft) tall. The leaves are elliptic to oval-shaped and around 7 cm (3 in) long; the silvery green catkins of the male plant grow to 30 cm (12 in). The female plant has long clusters of black fruits in fall.

Gasteria (fam. Liliaceae)

The name of this genus from South Africa derives from the Greek aster, a 'belly' or 'paunch', referring to the swollen, lower part of the flower. Comprising mostly stemless succulents which range in size from the tiny *G. bicolor* var. *liliputana*, with leaves only 2–3 cm (about 1 in) long, up to the large *G. acinacifolia* whose leaf spread reaches to 70 cm (28 in) in diameter, they are found growing under the shelter of shrubs which protect them from the hot sun. Some stemless species form a spiral rosette, but mostly the thick, rough, leathery leaves are distichous, that is they grow in layered ranks. All species readily form offsets which quickly make clumps. The leaves are mostly tongue-shaped and deep green in color, with a tubercled surface like sandpaper; some of the larger species have keeled leaves; most have white spots or splotches; and all end in a sharp, hard point. Loose, pendulous sprays of tubular flowers, with swollen bases, are borne on tall stems. They are pink to red, their petals edged in pale green.

CULTIVATION In cold and cool climates, grow in an airy, intermediate greenhouse or conservatory, in maximum light, but shade from direct sun. Grow in pots of cactus compost, available from good garden centers. The plants should be kept dry when they are dormant in winter, and watered moderately at other times. Propagate

ABOVE The fleshy, sword-shaped leaves of *Gasteria acinacifolia* have fine, transverse bands of small, greenish white spots.

from offsets or from leaf cuttings taken when the plants are in growth.

CLIMATE Zone 10.

SPECIES *G. acinacifolia*, the largest species, forms a spiralled rosette of thick, shiny, keeled leaves with lighter green blotches. The inflorescences are branched and very tall, two or three stems appearing at the same time. *G. bicolor*, a more upright plant, has keeled, splotched leaves which spiral upwards. It does not make offsets readily, but occasionally produces small plantlets on the flower stems. *G. bicolor* var. *liliputana*, with tiny, white-spotted leaves, forms clumps of tiny offsets very readily. This species has orange-green flowers in spring and summer. *G. carinata* var. *verrucosa*, a distichous plant, has long, tapering leaves which are covered with large, white tubercles.

Gaultheria (fam. Ericaceae)

Many of these evergreen shrubs are found in Central and South America, with some species from Asia and North America, and a few native to Australia and New Zealand. They have attractive, shiny leaves and berry fruit, some yielding aromatic oils, and pink or white, heath-like flowers. The smaller species are suitable for rock gardens.

CULTIVATION These plants like a well-drained, sandy, lime-free soil and partial sun. They should be kept moist at all times. Plant in fall or spring where they are to grow. Propagate by seed, suckers, cuttings or division.

CLIMATE There are species suited to various climatic zones.

SPECIES *G. antipoda*, zone 9, one of the New Zealand species, grows to around 1.5 m (5 ft), sometimes in trailing form. It has small, oblong leaves and persistent, single, white or pink, fragrant flowers in summer. The berries are red or white. *G. procumbens*, wintergreen or mountain tea, zone 4, is a trailing shrub, 5–15 cm (2–6 in) high, with white or pink flowers and bright red berries that produce an aromatic oil used in tobacco and medicinally. It is useful for growing in rockeries. *G. rupestris*, zone 7, from New Zealand, generally has an upright, branching habit, growing to a height and spread of 2 m (6 ft). It has oblong, leathery leaves and

BELOW Pale pink, urn-shaped flowers are borne on the arching stems of *Gaultheria shallon*, known as salal in the American North West.

clusters of white flowers. *G. shallon*, zone 6, from the north-west of the United States and western Canada, grows to 2 m (6 ft), with pretty pink or white flowers. Known locally as salal, it is used by florists quite often. It is generally known by them as lemonleaf.

Gaura (fam. Onagraceae)

Native to North America, there are about 20 species in this genus of herbaceous perennials. They look very pretty in informal or wild gardens, blooming from spring to fall. For this reason, they are becoming more popular, especially where low maintenance is a priority.

CULTIVATION Easy to grow, these plants prefer a light, sandy soil. Propagate from seed in early spring or by division of the clumps after the foliage has died down in winter. They are drought-tolerant once established, but prefer an occasional deep watering in summer.

CLIMATE Zone 8.

SPECIES *G. lindheimeri*, the most commonly cultivated species, is a bushy plant which grows to 1 m (3 ft). It has loosely branched, fine stems, lance-shaped, mid-green leaves and

ABOVE *Gaura lindheimeri* flowers appear to float on their long, slender stems.

small, delicate, white flowers, with pink calyx tubes, which give the plant a misty pink appearance. There is a pink-flowered form now available. This is known as 'Siskiyou Pink'.

Gazania (fam. Asteraceae)

These brilliantly colored, daisy-like perennials from South Africa have very tenacious roots, making them excellent soil binders on steep slopes. They will also hold and stabilize sand in seaside gardens. In rock gardens, they provide patches of color in summer and fall, opening with the morning sun and closing in the late afternoon, and also look attractive in pots or tubs. The flowers of the species come mostly in varying shades of yellow, with distinctive brown or black markings, and the entire or deeply lobed, long and narrow leaves form basal rosettes. Hybrids in various shades of pink, red, mahogany and cream are available. Some have attractive stripes.

CULTIVATION Gazanias are fairly tough plants and will grow well in a sunny position in most soils. Apply a slow-acting fertilizer prior to flowering. To rejuvenate, trim back the foliage and cut off the outside shoots and dead growth. If a number of different varieties are grown it is not uncommon to find new hybrids growing alongside the parent clump. In frost-prone climates, grow these frost-tender plants as

ABOVE *Gazania tomentosa* has silvery gray foliage and yellow flowers. It is very drought-tolerant once established.

summer annuals, planting out young plants in early summer. Raise plants from seed sown in a propagating case under glass, in late winter or early spring.

CLIMATE Zone 9.

SPECIES *G. x hybrida*, treasure flower, to 30 cm (12 in), is available in many colors including pink, beige, white and orange, often with attractive markings. *G. rigens,* growing to 30 cm (12 in), is probably the showiest of the species, with various shades of orange or yellow flowers, marked with black and white. *G. rigens* var. *uniflora* has smaller, yellow flowers.

Geijera (fam. Rutaceae)

Eight species of evergreen trees and shrubs native to New Guinea, Australia and New Caledonia, these often have a weeping habit and are mostly grown for their attractive shape. Dense clusters of small, ivory-colored flowers appear amongst the long, lance-shaped, dark green leaves in spring. The species below is available in the US.

CULTIVATION In frost-prone climates, grow in a cool to intermediate greenhouse or conservatory in soil-based potting compost. Provide maximum light and, as these plants are drought-tolerant, water only moderately in the growing season and sparingly in winter. Outdoors a dry spot in full sun is suitable. Propagate from seed sown in fall.

CLIMATE Zone 10.

SPECIES *G. parviflora*, wilga, from eastern and southern Australia, forms an attractive pyramidal shape, growing 5–6 m (16–20 ft) tall, and is valued for its aromatic hardwood. Its pendulous foliage is very graceful, the narrow, fragrant leaves growing to 15 cm (6 in) long. Open clusters of small, whitish flowers appear profusely in spring, followed by black seeds. It has been used as a fodder tree for sheep in drought conditions.

ABOVE These trees can be recognized by the strong peppermint smell of the foliage. The small flowers of *Geijera parviflora* sit on the branch tops.

Geissorhiza (fam. Iridaceae)

Comprising over 80 species from winter rainfall areas of South Africa, particularly Cape Province, these grow from very small bulbous corms and are slow to multiply. They grow actively through winter and are dormant in summer. The leaves may be long, sword-shaped and very narrow or thread-like. The funnel-shaped flowers are arranged on stems like freesias and ixias.

CULTIVATION Grow outside in warm areas in a well-drained position with full sun. Protect from excessive rain when dormant. In frost-prone areas, grow in a cool greenhouse or conservatory in maximum light, in pots of well-drained, soil-based potting compost. Do not water when dormant. Propagate by division when dormant.

CLIMATE Zone 9.

SPECIES *G. imbricata* has white blooms flushed with purple stripes on the outside. It flowers in spring, being one of the last of the group to flower. The flower stems grow to about 30 cm (12 in) high. *G. radians*, known as wine cups,

ABOVE The richly colored flowers of wine cups, *Geissorhiza radians* (syn. *G. rochensis*), are intricately patterned.

ABOVE *Gelsemium sempervirens*, Carolina jasmine, has cheery, yellow flowers in winter and spring.

bears deep blue to purple flowers in late winter to early spring. Growing naturally in damp grass, it seldom reaches more than 15 cm (6 in) high. *G. splendidissima* is a beautiful species, growing 20 cm (8 in) high, with bright violet-blue flowers.

Gelsemium (fam. Loganiaceae)
Carolina jasmine

This genus consists of three species of evergreen climbers, one of which is widely grown. The species known as Carolina jasmine is valued for its bright display of winter to spring flowers and ease of cultivation. It makes an attractive garden feature and can also be used as a container plant on patios and verandahs, or trained up posts and over pergolas. n frosty climates, it is best grown in a cool greenhouse or conservatory

CULTIVATION Gelsemium needs full sun for the best flowering. Grow in well-drained soil with added organic matter, or in good quality potting mix. Water regularly during dry summers. Provide lattice, wire or plastic netting, or climbing nets for support. Propagate from semi-ripe cuttings in summer and root in a heated propagating case.

CLIMATE Zone 9 at least.

SPECIES *G. sempervirens*, Carolina jasmine, has glossy, green, lance-shaped leaves and clusters of large, fragrant, yellow flowers from winter through to spring. It can grow quite vigorously in warm, humid areas. It is a decorative garden feature as well as being useful for pot culture.

Genista (fam. Papilionaceae)
Broom

Endemic to the Canary Islands, North Africa, southern Europe and western Asia, brooms are grown mainly for their pretty, fragrant pea flowers, although in the past, several of the species were commonly used for making dyes. Deciduous or almost leafless, they are hardy shrubs, well suited to drier climates, and vary rather widely in habit. The smaller species make excellent rockery and pot plants.

CULTIVATION Brooms thrive in light soils in sunny spots in the garden. Most require light pruning to improve their shape and to encourage good flowering. Do not prune into the old wood. Propagate from semi-ripe cuttings in summer, or from seed in spring.

CLIMATE There are species suited to various climatic zones.

ABOVE The very fragrant flowers of *Genista monosperma* (syn. *Retama monosperma*) appear on bare stems in early spring.

SPECIES *G. aetnensis*, Mount Etna broom, zone 8, from Sicily and Sardinia, has a rounded, weeping habit. This shrub grows to 6–8 m (20–26 ft). It is almost leafless, with fragrant, yellow flowers in summer. *G. hispanica*, Spanish gorse, zone 6, is a low-growing shrub, to 1 m (3 ft), useful for planting in rockeries or on dry, sunny embankments. The sparsely leaved branches are spiny and the golden yellow flowers are borne in dense clusters in spring. *G. tinctoria*, dyer's greenweed or dyer's broom, zone 3, from southern Europe and western Asia, has been used since ancient times as a source of yellow dye and for medicinal purposes. It is a deciduous shrub, to 1 m (3 ft), with non-spiny branches, bright green leaves and sprays of yellow flowers in summer. Cultivar 'Royal Gold', is a compact shrub, to 1 m (3 ft), with gold-yellow flowers.

Gentiana (fam. Gentianaceae)
Gentian

Grown for their intense blue flowers, and for the medicinal properties of their bitter roots, these perennials are found growing naturally in temperate, arctic or high tropical regions, mostly in Europe and Asia, with the largest number in China. They look wonderful in rockeries and borders.

CULTIVATION The seed of gentians must be sown fresh or it may take a year to germinate. Seed sown in spring of the previous year must be kept moist if it has not come up. Most species require well-drained, gritty soil, with added leaf mould or peat, although they sometimes have special requirements like most alpine plants. Most need a sunny position with plenty of summer moisture but should be kept dry in winter. All species need to be firmly anchored in the soil to avoid wind damage. Propagate species from seed, or divide root offsets in spring.

CLIMATE There are species suited to various climatic zones.

SPECIES *G. acaulis*, stemless gentian, zone 3, an alpine species, growing to 10 cm (4 in), is probably the most widely grown. It forms rosettes of

ABOVE Gardeners in cool climates are envied for their ability to grow the lovely alpine, *Gentiana acaulis*, the blue gentian.

glossy, green, narrow leaves and spring brings a mass of dark blue, tubular flowers, with green-spotted throats. Cultivar 'Alba' produces white flowers. *G. asclepiadea*, willow gentian, zone 6, grows to 1 m (3 ft), with dark blue flowers. Var. *alba* has white flowers. *G. farreri*, zone 5, is a prostrate plant with blue flowers, striped with white. *G. lutea*, great yellow gentian, zone 5, is one of the largest of the species, growing up to 2 m (6 ft), and uncommonly produces pale yellow flowers. It prefers damp conditions and is the major source of gentian root. *G. makinoi*, zone 6, from Japan, grows to about 60 cm (2 ft). The bell-shaped, pale blue flowers are spotted. *G. saxosa*, zone 8, from New Zealand, is a prostrate plant, to 15 cm (6 in), with loose rosettes of leaves and white, lobed flowers with brownish veins. *G. septem-fida*, crested gentian, zone 3, grows to 20 cm (8 in), with bright blue flowers. *G. sino-ornata*, zone 6, is a prostrate species, forming rosettes of leaves from which protrude deep blue flowers, paler at the base. It grows to 18 cm (7 in).

Geranium (fam. Geraniaceae)

Cranesbill, geranium

The name of this large genus of some 300 species of mostly perennials, found in temperate and alpine regions throughout the world derives from the Greek geranos, meaning 'a crane', as the seed pod shape resembles the bill of that bird. These are not the plants commonly known as garden geraniums and botanically known as pelargoniums. The true geranium is an adaptable addition to the rock garden or the front of a border. The flowers bloom from spring to summer in colors ranging from white to soft pink, mauve, magenta and blue. Most are singles, although there are one or two double-flowered forms.

CULTIVATION Geraniums are easily grown in almost any well-drained soil. Propagate by division or by seed. Some species seed freely, seed being spread when the ripe seed pod opens. Most can be grown in full sun but tolerate partial shade. Water regularly in growing season, only very occasionally in winter.

CLIMATE There are species suited to various climatic zones.

SPECIES *G. endressii*, zone 5, is a bushy plant, to 45 cm (18 in), with rose pink flowers. Cultivar 'Wargrave Pink', with deeper colored flowers, is very popular. *G. incanum*, zone 9, unusual in that it comes from warm South Africa, is commonly grown in rock gardens or hanging baskets. Its grayish green, deeply lobed leaves are aromatic, and its five-petalled flowers are usually red with deeper colored veins. *G. maderense*, zone 9, grows to 1 m (3 ft) or so and produces masses of magenta flowers, opening in succession. *G. nepalense*, zone 7, which blooms in fall, is useful when other species are past their flowering. *G. phaeum*, zone 5, dusky cranesbill or mourning widow, takes its common names from the almost maroonish black color of the flowers. *G. pratense*, zone 5, is a popular plant for perennial borders. It has fine foliage and deep blue or violet flowers. A number of good cultivars are available. *G. robertianum*, herb Robert, zone 6, is a pretty annual with dainty leaves which turn bright red in fall under dry conditions. *G. san-guineum*, bloody cranesbill, zone 5, has blood red flowers and deeply divided, dark green leaves. Var. *striatum*, with pink flowers veined with deep red, makes a good edging plant.

BELOW The spreading perennial Geranium 'Johnson's Blue' produces its royal blue flowers throughout summer.

Gerbera (fam. Asteraceae)

Barberton daisy, Transvaal daisy

Comprising around 30 species of tough perennials from Africa, Madagascar and Asia, gerberas are very popular cut flowers, gaining renewed popularity in recent years. The daisy-like blooms grow on long stems from a spreading rosette of long, rough-edged leaves.

CULTIVATION In frost-prone areas, grow gerberas as pot plants in an intermediate greenhouse or conservatory. Use soil-based potting compost, and provide good light. Outdoors, gerberas need warmth and full sun, and are unable to survive severe frosts. Space the plants at least 50 cm (20 in) apart as the long leaves spread widely. Gerberas must be planted with their crowns set above soil level. The soil must be very well drained; if there is any doubt about this, grow them in raised beds. Gerberas can be propagated by root division, best done after the plants have flowered for two years. Straight species can be raised from seed.

CLIMATE Zone 9.

SPECIES *G. jamesonii*, Transvaal or Barberton daisy, has orange flowers, about 8 cm (3 in) in diameter, on 30 cm (12 in) long stems. It is the parent species of the many hybrids, available in a dazzling color range, in single and double form, most larger than the original species.

Geum (fam. Rosaceae)

Avens

Regularly found growing in temperate regions of the northern hemisphere, this genus consists of around 40 species of hardy, perennial plants, valued for their attractive blooms and long-flowering period from late spring until early fall. The showy flowers, in double or single form, arise from basal rosettes of hairy, lobed leaves and come in shades of white, yellow and red.

CULTIVATION These plants will thrive in a position that receives morning sun but is shaded in the afternoon, in a moderately rich soil. Sow seed from fall until early winter in mild climates. Seedlings transplant easily, and should be spaced 30 cm (12 in) apart. Division of an existing clump in late winter is the easiest method of propagation. Water well during the growing season, especially in dry weather.

ABOVE *Gerbera jamesonii* has orange-scarlet flowers but there are hybrids in various colors, such as this rich red.

ABOVE *Geum* 'Mrs J. Bradshaw' is a bright red, double-flowered variety that has been popular for many years.

Although perennials, *Geum* species can be treated as annuals in warmer climates. Plants retained for further flowering should be cut back in late winter to early spring.

CLIMATE There are species suited to various climatic zones.

SPECIES *G. chiloense*, zone 7, 30–60 cm (12–24 in), has larger leaves and upright, scarlet flowers. Named geum cultivars (zone 7): 'Dolly North' has orange flowers; 'Fire Opal' has single, orange flowers overlaid with red; 'Prince of Orange' has bright orange flowers; and 'Red Wings' produces semidouble, bright scarlet flowers. 'Mrs J. Bradshaw', with small sprays of double scarlet flowers, and 'Lady Stratheden', with double, yellow-orange flowers, are the cultivars most grown. *G. coccineum*, zone 5, to 1 m (3 ft), produces single, red flowers with yellow filaments. *G. rivale*, Indian chocolate or purple avens, zone 3, to 60 cm (24 in), has nodding, dull orange-pink flowers, with purple calyces. *G. urbanum*, zone 6, cloveroot or herb Bennet, grows to 1 m (3 ft), with erect, toothed leaflets and yellow flowers with green calyces.

Ginger (*Zingiber officinale*, fam. Zingiberaceae)

Native to tropical Southeast Asia, ginger is widely cultivated for its aromatic rhizomes. It is used green (fresh) or preserved and crystallized. The dried and powdered rhizome is used extensively in drinks, cakes and biscuits. It is also prescribed for travel sickness. The preparation of ginger can be a rather elaborate process. Ginger for local consumption is grown and prepared in many Asian countries, while preserved ginger is a popular export from China. Plants in cultivation are sterile cultivars, with seed rarely being formed. Growing to about 60 cm (24 in) high, ginger has cane-like stems, long, lance-shaped leaves and yellow-green flowers.

CULTIVATION In frost-prone climates, ginger can be grown in a warm greenhouse or conservatory, either in large pots or tubs or in a soil border. Fresh ginger roots can be purchased

ABOVE The lush, green foliage of ginger will enhance any warm conservatory or greenhouse and the plant is easily grown.

from greengrocers or supermarkets. Cut large roots into sections, making sure that each section displays some good buds or 'eyes'. Plant in early spring just below the soil surface. Soil should be free draining and heavily manured a few weeks before planting. Water sparingly until the new growth is vigorous, but water thoroughly throughout the growing season. Plants can be lifted and roots harvested in mid to late fall. The time from planting to maturity will vary with the district and conditions.

CLIMATE Zone 10 and above. Can be grown outdoors only in the tropics and subtropics.

Ginkgo (fam. Ginkgoaceae)
Maidenhair tree

Ginkgo biloba is the only remaining species of this remarkable genus, known to have first appeared some 300 million years ago. It is even older than the ancient conifers and cycads, both of which belong to the same group as the *Ginkgo* genus. While the earliest fossils of the conifers and cycads bear little resemblance to their present forms, fossilized *Ginkgo* leaves are virtually identical to the modern species which has survived only because it has been cultivated around Buddhist temples in China and Japan. It is a truly beautiful tree, greatly valued for street and city plantings in temperate climates, as it is resistant to pollution and almost completely free of diseases and pests. It is easy to propagate and adapts to a wide range of soils.

CULTIVATION Ginkgos thrive in areas of high rainfall, with cold winters and warm, humid summers. They will grow in almost any soil, provided it is deep and the subsoil is sufficiently moist. Some shelter from hot, drying winds is necessary. Propagate from seed or by grafting onto seedling understocks.

CLIMATE Zone 4.

SPECIES *G. biloba*, a native of south-western China, is a medium to large, deciduous tree, reaching heights in ideal conditions of 25 m (80 ft), though seldom growing taller than 15 m

(50 ft) in a range of situations. They grow fairly slowly and have rather a spreading, low-branching habit. Their bark is quite corky and their fresh green foliage resembles large maidenhair leaves, coloring a golden yellow in fall, even in mild coastal areas. The large seeds of the fruits, known as 'ginkgo nuts', are edible and nutritious, though they emit an unpleasant smell once they have fallen. Cultivar 'Fastigiata' has a slender, conical growth habit, with upward-pointing branches.

Ginseng (*Panax species*, fam. Araliaceae)

The fleshy roots of several species of *Panax* have been used medicinally for centuries in various Asian countries. *P. ginseng*, from Korea and Manchuria, is used as a cancer treatment in China. It is now extremely rare in the wild and therefore expensive. It has almost reached extinction through overharvesting, and while it is possible to propagate this plant through tissue culture, commercial dealers in ginseng are generally not interested in this fairly uniform product. The most sought-after roots are those which resemble human shapes. American ginseng, *P. quinquefolius*, zone 3, is cultivated occasionally for export to Asia, but there seems to be no desirable alternative for devotees of the original ginseng root.

ABOVE With slightly ascending branches and fluted, fan-like leaves, *Ginkgo biloba* is a most distinctive tree.

ABOVE American ginseng, *Panax quinquefolius*, is sometimes cultivated as an ornamental foliage plant.

Gladiolus (fam. Iridaceae)

There are about 180 species of gladioli coming originally from various parts of Africa, Europe and the Middle East. Their name derives from the Latin gladius, a sword, which refers to the shape of their leaves. Gladioli are grown from corms, the compressed base of the stems, which produce two or three leaves and usually a one-sided flower spike. However, many hybrids have been developed which vary enormously in size, color and the arrangement of the blooms on the flower spike, the most well-known being the large-flowering types. Gladioli are not as easy to grow and care for as many other flowering plants as they may need regular spraying, but they are still very popular because they make a striking display in the garden and provide excellent cut flowers. They can also be grown in pots.

CULTIVATION Gladioli must be grown in a position that receives full sun. In milder areas, plant

BELOW Large-flowered hybrids of *Gladiolus* have a huge color range. Bright scarlet and a bi-colored purple and white are just two of them.

the corms in late winter; in cooler zones, plant in spring to early summer. They require very good drainage, so if the soil is heavy, build up the bed about 15 cm (6 in) above normal soil level and lighten the soil by adding sand. If the soil is very acid, apply a dressing of lime or dolomite at the rate of 60–120 g per square metre (2–4 oz per square yard). Compost or decayed cow manure may be added, as well as commercial rose fertilizer or other complete plant food. Plant corms in clumps about 8–10 cm (3–4 in) deep and 15 cm (6 in) apart. Several corms of the same variety look impressive when planted together. Water thoroughly and mulch after planting. In some areas, gladiolus thrips are a problem every season as they damage the foliage and flowers with their rasping and sucking action. Spraying with a registered pesticide may therefore be necessary. Flowers should be ready for picking 11 to 14 weeks after planting, though cold weather can slow growth and some varieties are slower to mature than others. Cut flowers just as the second bud on the spike is starting to open. Cut the stem, leaving as many leaves as possible. After the flowers have been cut, continue to give the plant the usual care. When the foliage yellows and dies, dig out the plants carefully and cut the remnants of withered leaves back to within two centimetres (about an inch) of the new corm, which will have formed above the old one. Dry corms in a warm, airy place, then clean off the remains of the old corms, dust with derris or other insecticidal dust and store in paper bags, labelled with their colors. When the new planting season comes around, any small cormlets present around the base of the new corms should be set out about 5 cm (2 in) apart in a separate area. The following year, the cormlets, after having been lifted and stored over winter, can be again planted out, spaced around 10 cm (4 in) apart. Cormlets should come true to color and type.

CLIMATE Zone 9 for most species.

SPECIES *G. communis* subsp. *byzantinus*, zone 7, originating from the Mediterranean, produces red or reddish purple flowers, with faint white markings. The leaves are about 30 cm (12 in) long and the flower spikes nearly three times as long. A white form is also available. *G. x colvillei* flowers in colors of white, deep pink or yellow and has given rise to many forms which also flower in late spring. *G. tristis* produces highly perfumed, pale yellow flowers, sometimes with purple bands on the upper petals. The flower stems are shorter, to 60 cm (24 in), and the leaves are quite slender. This species may be left undisturbed for some years. Species gladioli are becoming readily available, but most varieties grown are cultivars and hybrids.

Glaucium (fam. Papaveraceae)
Horned poppy, sea poppy

This genus comprises about 25 species of annual, biennial and perennial herbs, originally from Asia and the countries around the Mediterranean. Long, poppy-like stems arise from rosettes of basal leaves, often of silvery or blue-green, bearing a single flower, mostly in shades of red, orange or yellow, some with dark spots at the base of the petals.

CULTIVATION These poppies are easily propagated from seed sown where it is to grow. The flowers do best in a very open, sunny situation. The soil must be well drained but need not be rich; in

ABOVE Yellow-flowered *Glaucium flavum* grows naturally right on the seashore around the Mediterranean.

fact they do well in poor, low-nutrient soils. They dislike transplanting or disturbance.

CLIMATE Zone 7.

SPECIES *G. corniculatum*, a biennial, produces red or orange flowers, with a black spot at the base of each petal, and bristly fruit. *G. flavum*, a short-lived perennial from the Mediterranean regions, grows to 1 m (3 ft), with golden yellow to orange flowers, to 5 cm (2 in) across. The seeds yield an oil which is used commercially. *G. grandiflorum* is an attractive, ornamental species, with large, deep orange to rich crimson flowers having a dark spot at the base of the petals. Summer flowers are abundant.

Glechoma (fam. Lamiaceae)
Field balm, ground ivy

This genus consists of about a dozen species but only one is grown–a creeping, hardy perennial from Europe which makes an excellent ground-cover or hanging basket specimen. The variegated form is particularly attractive.

ABOVE Ground ivy, *Glechoma hederacea*, occurs naturally in woodlands throughout Europe.

CULTIVATION These tough, trailing plants can be used on dry banks or slopes, or as an undershrub cover. Propagate by division in spring or from cuttings in late spring. Grow in full sun or partial shade. Provide plenty of water during dry summers.

CLIMATE Zone 7.

SPECIES *G. hederacea* is a sturdy plant found growing naturally in damp woodlands. Considered a weed in some regions, it can become invasive. It has heart-shaped leaves and short spikes of lilac-blue or occasionally pink flowers in summer. The cultivar 'Variegata' is marked with a silvery white color.

Gleditsia (fam. Caesalpiniaceae)

Honey locust

Native to North America and Asia, these hardy, deciduous trees, with their attractive, spreading, fern-like foliage, are useful as shade, street and park trees. Their main drawback is their rather vicious thorns.

CULTIVATION While preferring good quality soil, gleditsias can adapt to a variety of conditions. Propagate species from seed which should be soaked in hot water before planting. Cultivars with special features are generally grafted onto seedling understocks. Best where supplementary irrigation is available, they will tolerate drought once well established. Many species are very hardy and will tolerate climates with very hard frosts.

CLIMATE There are species suited to various climatic zones.

SPECIES *G. aquatica*, swamp locust, zone 6, grows to 18 m (60 ft), with insignificant white flowers. The thorns are about 10 cm (4 in) long, but not as profuse as on other species. *G. japonica*, zone 6, is a spiny tree, to 20 m (65 ft), with purplish branches when young and very long, twisted seed pods. *G. sinensis*, zone 5, from China, to 13 m (42 ft), has cylindrical, branched spines. *G. triacanthos*, honey locust, zone 3, can reach to 30 m (100 ft), though seldom more than 15–20 m (50–65 ft) in cultivation. It has an open canopy, the fine foliage coloring golden yellow in fall, insignificant white flowers and long, twisted seed pods persisting throughout winter. The form inermis is a thornless, drought-resistant type. Cultivar 'Rubylace' has rich ruby red foliage and 'Sunburst' grows moderately slowly, with bright golden yellow foliage.

Gleichenia (fam. Gleicheniaceae)

This genus of ferns is found in swampy, wet areas from Africa and tropical Asia to Australia and New Zealand. They have long, creeping, intertwined rhizomes and upright, forked fronds, the leaflets varying from pouched and rounded to coarse or delicate and flat.

CULTIVATION These ferns are generally not available commercially. Propagation is generally by division of the rhizome, sometimes from spores. Keep the plants moist at all times, and feed occasionally with a liquid fertilizer. Species such as the dwarf *G. dicarpa* and the 3 m (10 ft) tall *G. microphylla* would need to be grown in a warm conservatory or greenhouse in cool and cold climates, if they are available.

ABOVE *Gleditsia triacanthos* 'Sunburst' is seen here in mid-spring, covered in fresh new growth. This is easier to site than the species as stems are thornless.

ABOVE *Gleichenia dicarpa* forms extensive thickets of growth in exposed, wet areas, such as moist cliff faces.

ABOVE *Globularia cordifolia* creates a pretty swathe of color with its small, lavender blue flowers.

CLIMATE Zone 10.

SPECIES *G. dicarpa*, pouched coral fern, from eastern Australia and New Zealand, takes its common name from the pouched leaflets and the whole fern's similarity to coral in form. The much-divided, upright fronds produce an attractive, rather unusual pattern. This species is a valuable fern in the wild, preventing erosion in creek beds by building up soil patches and filtering the water. *G. microphylla*, umbrella fern, is found throughout Australia and New Zealand. Similar in frond structure to *G. dicarpa*, it is a rather more delicate species, though still environmentally effective in its habitat.

Globularia (fam. Globulariaceae)
Globe daisy

These easy-to-grow, mat-forming perennials and small shrubs, found mainly in the Mediterranean, bear pretty, daisy-like flowers in summer. They are ideal for window boxes, pots and rock gardens.

CULTIVATION Globularias thrive in sun with good drainage. Propagate from seed or by division in spring, or from summer cuttings which strike easily in a sharp, sandy loam.

CLIMATE Most species can be grown in zones 5 or 6.

SPECIES *G. cordifolia*, zone 6, a prostrate, evergreen subshrub, with tiny, spoon-shaped leaves and fluffy, lavender blue flower heads. Var. *alba* has white flowers. *G. meridionalis*, zone 5, has blue flowers on long stalks. Cultivar 'Alba' has white flowers. *G. repens*, zone 5, the smallest species, to 2 cm (1 in), is a creeping, slow-growing shrub with tiny, blue flowers. *G. trichosantha*, globe daisy, zone 6, a perennial, grows to 20 cm (8 in). It forms clumps of leafy rosettes from which arise soft, blue, ball-like flowers in spring and summer.

Gloriosa (fam. Colchicaceae)
Gloriosa lily

Native to tropical Africa and India, this small genus of climbing vines bears strikingly beautiful flowers, mostly a combination of red and yellow, with wavy-edged petals. Gloriosa lilies climb by tendrils which extend from the leaf tips and need the support of a trellis or similar. They are herbaceous, dying back to the fleshy roots in fall, and remaining dormant till spring.

CULTIVATION Propagate from seed or offsets, or by careful division of the brittle tubers. Pot tubers

ABOVE Fluted, recurved petals give the flowers of the Gloriosa lily a floating effect. Growth is rapid in warm weather.

ABOVE A bright yellow flower nestles in the center of the thick, fleshy leaves of *Glottiphyllum linguiforme.*

in very well-drained, loamy soil between late winter and early spring, in an intermediate greenhouse in colder climates. Provide plenty of water up to flowering time, then reduce the amount given. Lift the tubers carefully in fall and store dry over winter. Under glass, the plants need to have maximum light.

CLIMATE Zone 10.

SPECIES *G. rothschildiana,* to 2 m (6 ft), has bright scarlet and yellow flowers. It is the best in cultivation and has the largest flowers. *G. superba,* to 2 m (6 ft), has red or purple flowers, edged with yellow, in summer and fall. The petal edges are wavy and the flowers have long, prominent stamens. Several cultivars are also grown, including the well-known 'Rothschildiana' with bright red and yellow flowers. The cultivar 'Citrina' has acid yellow flowers marked with purple-red, and 'Lutea' is also yellow.

Glottiphyllum (fam. Aizoaceae)

The 50 or so species of this South African genus of succulents are so similar that many may be hybrids. They are prostrate, almost stemless, with branched shoots of tongueshaped, very fleshy, glossy, dark green leaves. Sometimes the leaves are curved or tapered to a sharp point. The large, daisy-like yellow flowers, 8 cm (3 in) across, bloom in the summer through to late in winter. Occasionally, the flowers can be white.

CULTIVATION In areas prone to frost, grow in an intermediate greenhouse or conservatory, in pots of cactus compost, obtainable from good garden centers. Provide maximum light. Water moderately from the middle of summer to the end of winter, and keep the compost almost dry when the plants are dormant. Propagate from seed in spring with bottom heat. Alternatively, use stem cuttings taken towards the end of summer.

CLIMATE Zone 10.

SPECIES *G. fragrans* has thick, tongue-shaped leaves and large, fragrant, golden yellow flowers. *G. linguiforme,* the most commonly grown species, has glossy, bright green, tongue-shaped leaves and golden yellow flowers. *G. semicylindricum* has the same golden yellow flowers but its leaves are quite distinctive, projecting stiffly outwards. They are semi-cylindrical, slightly curved and pale green. In full sun, the margins become bright red.

Gloxinia

(see *Sinningia speciosa*, fam. Gesneriaceae)

Glycyrrhiza (fam. Papilionaceae)

Native to Europe, Asia, Australia and America, this genus consists of 20 species of temperate and subtropical perennial herbs grown for the juice from its roots, used in the production of licorice.

CULTIVATION Plant in a rich soil, deep enough for the large root system, in a sunny position. Cut down each year after flowering. The roots are ready for harvesting after three years. Propagate by division in early spring, or from seed sown in pots in fall or spring.

CLIMATE Zone 8.

SPECIES *G. glabra*, licorice plant, has a somewhat straggly habit, growing to a height and

BELOW *Glycyrrhiza acanthocarpa* is fairly similar in appearance to *C. glabra* which is cultivated for the licorice obtained from the roots.

spread of 1 m (3 ft). It has large, mid-green leaves and blue or violet, pea-like flowers on short, erect spikes in summer.

Godetia (see Clarkia)

Gompholobium (fam. Papilionaceae)
Wedge pea

Mostly from Western Australia, this genus comprises around 25 species of woody shrubs with pinnate leaves, and lovely red or yellow pea flowers in spring. Unfortunately, they are rarely available outside Australia.

CULTIVATION These Australian natives are well suited to warm rockeries, preferring a well-drained, sunny site. Propagate from heat-treated seed obtained from the fruit. The seed can be difficult to obtain. Outdoors grow in a well-drained sunny position. Sow seed in late spring to early summer.

CLIMATE Zone 9.

SPECIES *G. capitatum*, to 1 m (3 ft), has white, hairy new shoots, narrow, feathery leaflets and dense, terminal clusters of yellow flowers. *G. grandiflorum*, large wedge pea, from New

ABOVE *Gompholobium grandiflorum* grows naturally in open forest or heathland.

South Wales, is an erect, spindly shrub, to 1 m (3 ft), with narrow, glabrous leaflets and large, single, yellow flowers. *G. latifolium*, golden glory wedge pea, from eastern Australia, has the largest flowers of the genus in a bright yellow color. It grows vigorously to 1 m (3 ft), with olive-green foliage, the new growth having a bronze tone.

Goodenia (fam. Goodeniaceae)

An Australian native, *Goodenia* comprises over 170 species of small subshrubs and prostrate plants which have pretty yellow, white or blue flowers. Few of the species are cultivated, although most have good ornamental potential, being small, showy and fairly easy to propagate. The plants are unlikely to be available outside Australia.

CULTIVATION In frost-prone climates, these Australian natives need to be grown in a cool, airy greenhouse or conservatory. Grow in pots of well-drained, soil-based potting compost or in a soil bed. Outdoors grow in a sunny spot with moist yet well-drained soil. Provide maximum light. Propagate from cuttings, preferably taken in fall.

CLIMATE Zone 9.

SPECIES *G. affinis*, from South Australia and Western Australia, has woolly, gray leaves which form rosettes 8–10 cm (3–4 in) high, and yellow flowers. *G. hederacea*, a trailing plant good for groundcover, roots at the nodes. The yellow flowers bloom in spring and summer. *G. heteromera*, a prostrate plant also suitable as a groundcover, spreads with runners and has small, yellow flowers during summer and fall. *G. ovata* is a widely distributed, quick-growing shrub to 2 m (6 ft), with yellow flowers in spring and summer. *G. pinnatifida* is a small plant, less than 30 cm (12 in) high, with rosettes of leaves and yellow flowers throughout spring and summer.

Goodia (fam. Papilionaceae)
Golden tip, clover bush, yellow pea

This genus of three species of native Australian open shrubs is fast growing. They have yellow or orange pea flowers and soft foliage. The plants are unfortunately not likely to be available outside Australia.

CULTIVATION In frost-prone climates, these Australian natives need to be grown in a cool, airy greenhouse or conservatory. Grow in pots of well-drained, soil-based potting compost, or in a soil bed, and provide maximum light. Outdoors the drought-resistant goodias will do well in almost any sunny situation. Propagate from seed, which germinates very easily.

CLIMATE Zone 9.

BELOW *Goodia pubescens* is a compact-growing shrub with clear yellow pea-type flowers.

ABOVE In its natural habitat, *Goodenia bellidifolia* grows happily in damp ground in open, sunny spots.

SPECIES *G. lotifolia*, golden tip or clover bush, is a tall, vigorous, suckering plant, to 2.5 m (8 ft), which is suitable as a specimen, but can also be trimmed into a hedge. The spring blooms make attractive cut flowers, but are not long lasting. The light green foliage may be poisonous to stock. After some years of cultivation, *G. lotifolia* forms a thicket some metres in width and needs pruning for good flowering and shape. It recovers from trimming quickly. *G. pubescens* is a small, rounded shrub, to 1 m (3 ft), with yellow flowers in spring and summer, and fine, downy foliage.

Gooseberry

(*Ribes uva-crispa*, var. *reclinatum*, syn.

R. grossularia, fam. Grossulariaceae)

Believed to originate from temperate northern Africa, southern Europe and south-western Asia, the gooseberry is a hardy, deciduous, frost-resistant, bushy plant which grows to around 1 m (3 ft). This shrub has thorny stems and produces green, acid fruit, ripening to pale yellowish green, yellow, reddish yellow or red, depending on the variety. It is grown for its fruit which is picked soft for eating raw or while still hard if cooking it for pies, preserves or jams.

CULTIVATION Plant in a medium to heavy soil, with plenty of added organic matter. Make sure the soil is kept moist while plants are in active growth. Add a complete plant food every spring. Propagation is usually from 30 cm (12 in) cuttings of young wood, taken in early winter after the leaves have fallen, or by layering. If the gooseberry is to be grown as an untrained bush, plant the cutting with only the top bud above ground level; if a miniature tree form is desired, remove all but the top four buds from the cutting before planting it, with the lowest of these buds 10–15 cm (4–6 in) above ground level. During the next winter, cut shoots back to 15 cm (6 in). During the following winter remove the ends of any pendulous new branches, while retaining as many strong shoots as possible. The bush should be kept open to facilitate picking and to allow

ABOVE Gooseberry bushes can be very long lived. The fruit is especially popular for pies and other desserts.

good air circulation and maximum sun exposure for the fruit. Gooseberries are carried on the shoots of the previous year's growth, and on the shoots and spurs of old wood. To ensure the continuing production of young fruiting wood, prune back laterals to a few buds each winter. Strong shoots from low on the bush may be used eventually for the renewal of the framework.

CLIMATE Gooseberries are best in zones 6 to 8.

Gordonia (fam. Theaceae)

From Southeast Asia, except for one North American species, these evergreen, warm-temperate trees and shrubs have leathery leaves and bear beautiful, fragrant flowers, resembling the single camellia, in fall, winter and early spring. The flowering season depends on the climate where they are grown.

CULTIVATION In relatively frost-free climates, grow in a woodland garden, in acid to neutral, moisture-retentive soil with dappled shade or full sun. Shelter plants from cold winds. In frosty climates, grow in pots of acid, soilless potting compost in a cool greenhouse. Shade from direct sun. Propagate from semi-ripe cuttings in summer.

CLIMATE Zone 9 for most species.

ABOVE *Gordonia axillaris* is a lovely tree for small gardens, providing seasonal flowers and light shade all year round.

SPECIES *G. axillaris*, zone 8, from southern China and Hong Kong, is an evergreen species, growing to around 4–6 m (13–20 ft), with pure white or creamish white flowers, up to 7.5 cm (3 in) across, with golden stamens. Sometimes the petals are frilled at the edges. A lovely, small tree for the home garden, it is also used successfully as a street tree.

Gossypium (fam. Malvaceae)
Cotton

These shrubs are found in warmer regions of the world, one species being the cotton produced commercially for cotton and cotton seed oil. The leaves have spotted oil glands, and the open flowers are like small hibiscus and colored from white to yellow to purplish red, often spotted purplish red towards the base. The seeds are usually covered with down or loose lint.

CULTIVATION In frost-prone climates, grow cotton for its novelty value in a cool to intermediate greenhouse or conservatory. Cotton needs humid conditions and abundant moisture during the growing season, and prefers a compost of loam and peat. Propagate from seed sown in spring at a temperature no lower than 16°C (61°F). Small plants can be potted on as required during summer. Commercial cotton must be harvested during dry weather.

CLIMATE Zone 10, but grown as a summer annual.

SPECIES *G. arboreum*, tree cotton, to 4 m (13 ft), is widely cultivated in Asia. The flowers are yellow with a purplish red base. *G. barbadense*, sea island cotton, to 3 m (10 ft), has yellowish purple flowers. Var. *brasiliense*, kidney cotton, has larger flowers and fruit capsules. *G. herbaceum*, Levant cotton, is a hairy annual or perennial, to 2 m (6 ft), with yellowish purple flowers. *G. hirsutum*, upland cotton, is a shrub, to 2 m (6 ft), with creamish yellow flowers, turning purple with maturity. *G. sturtianum*, Sturt's desert rose, is the floral emblem of the Northern Territory in Australia. This Australian native is an erect or rounded shrub, to 2 m (6 ft), with mauve, red-centered, summer flowers. *G. thurberi*, wild cotton, is a shrub to 4 m (13 ft), with lobed leaves and whitish yellow flowers, purple on the undersides.

ABOVE Sturt's desert rose, *Gossypium sturtianum*, floral emblem of Australia's Northern Territory, is a decorative shrub for hot, arid regions.

Gourd (fam. Cucurbitaceae)

Gourds are the fruit of the various species of the *Cucurbit* family, the name applying particularly to those used for ornament, such as cultivars derived from *Cucurbita pepo* var. *ovifera*. They vary widely in shape, color, markings and size and make an attractive indoor decoration. Some species may be available only from specialist clubs or enthusiasts.

CULTIVATION These annuals should be treated like pumpkins, cucumbers, melons and other gourds in cultivation. Sow seed where the plants are to grow in late spring in rich soil in a sunny location, allowing space for their trailing habit. Otherwise they can be contained in a smaller area by training them onto a trellis. Alternatively, sow under glass in mid-spring and plant out in late spring or early summer. To assist fruiting, water with liquid manure until fruit is ready for harvest in early fall. To use the fruit as an ornament, cut it with some stem and leave to dry in a warm, dry place for several weeks.

CLIMATE Zone 10, but grown as a summer annual.

ABOVE Ornamental gourds come in a bewildering range of shape, size and color, making them popular for home decoration.

SPECIES *Cucumis anguria*, gooseberry gourd, with green, prickly fruits, is like ordinary cucumber in growth habit. *Cucumis dipsaceus*, hedgehog gourd, produces a burr-like fruit and is also similar to the cucumber in growth. *Cucurbita pepo* var. *ovifera*, yellow-flowered gourd, is a vine, producing an interesting range of small, decorative gourds. *Lagenaria siceraria*, trumpet or crookneck gourd, is a wide-spreading vine, to 10 m (33 ft), resembling a pumpkin vine. The fruits come in many unusual shapes. *Luffa cylindrica*, loofah, is a running, climbing vine, with long fruits, netted, fibrous and dry inside. *Tricosanthes cucumeria* var. *anguina*, snake gourd, is a wide-spreading, climbing vine with long, coiled or straight fruit, to 2 m (6 ft).

Granadilla

(*Passiflora quadrangularis*, fam. Passifloraceae)

Passion flower

This tendril-climbing vine from Brazil is related to the passionfruit, but has larger fruit and may not produce so profusely. It is a vigorous, ever-

ABOVE The large fruits of granadilla will become yellow or orange when fully ripe. The pulp is very sweet.

green climber with fragrant, intricate, red, purple, pink and white flowers in summer and fall. The greenish yellow, many-seeded fruit is eaten fresh or used to make soft drinks and jams.

CULTIVATION Grow in an intermediate to warm greenhouse or conservatory in cool and cold climates, ideally in a soil border, alternatively in a large tub of soil-based potting compost. Shade from direct sun. Prune in early spring by cutting back lateral shoots to within four buds of the main woody stems and branches. Propagate from semi-ripe cuttings in summer.

CLIMATE Zone 10.

Grape (*Vitis species*, fam. Vitaceae)

Known to have been cultivated since the fourth century BC in Syria and Egypt and since 2500 BC around the Aegean, the origins of the grape, *Vitis vinifera*, are uncertain. This species, sometimes called European grape, and its cultivars are now grown in many parts of the world both for table grapes and for wine. A number of American species, including *V. labrusca*, are grown both commercially and in home gardens. The many hybrids between *V. vinifera* and *V. labrusca* are now grown mainly as wine grapes. *V. labrusca* is very important commercially as a rootstock as it appears resistant to the insect pest, *Phylloxera*, which can wipe out enormous areas of vines. In some countries, strict quarantine requirements which restrict the importation and movement of grape vines between states and wine-growing regions are in force to try to keep vines free of this disastrous pest.

CULTIVATION Grapes are long-lived plants if provided with appropriate conditions. They tolerate cold winters if they have long, hot summers, with low rainfall. However, high humidity in summer can lead to bunch rot, berry splitting, downy and powdery mildew, and black spot. Late spring frosts can severely damage flowers and reduce crop potential.

ABOVE Grown for table grapes, this healthy vine shows masses of flower buds about to open. The vine provides shade too.

Grapes prefer a humus-rich, sandy soil, though any soil, except a heavy, waterlogged clay, is suitable, if it is well drained. Over-feeding will lead to excessive growth and reduction of crops. Grapes should be pruned during winter dormancy and may be trained along one or two horizontal wires to cover a wall or trellis, or into a bush or standard, which gives fewer but better bunches. In each case the aim is to produce a sturdy framework of trunk and branches which gives rise to annual shoots or canes. Cut these back in winter, leaving only a few buds to produce fruiting wood called spurs. The shoots from the buds on the spurs or rods bear the grapes in the following summer. The main trunk and branches will be formed in the first two or three years. Cut back the newly planted bush to two or three buds and the following winter cut out the weaker shoots. Tie the strongest shoots to a post and tip prune back to the desired height, 20–50 cm (8–20 in) for a standard, or to the height of the horizontal wire or the lowest horizontal on a trellis. If necessary, repeat this type of pruning the next year until the required height is reached. The two strongest shoots from this trunk should be trained along the horizontal wire or trellis in opposite directions and cut back; if a standard is required, three or four well-spaced canes should be pruned back to two or three buds on the trunk. The rest should be cut out. Grapes are produced on shoots of the current year's wood, which comes from the canes of the previous season's growth. Grapes do not ripen well after cutting so they should be left on the vine until they are ripe. Grapes may be attacked by mites, mealy bug and thrips. They are also very sensitive to spray drift from herbicides.

CLIMATE Zone 5 or 6.

SPECIES *V. vinifera* is a vigorous, deciduous vine which develops a twisted woody trunk, covered with bark which is shed in strips. It has long, flexible branches and coarsely toothed, lobed leaves. The small, greenish flowers are borne in drooping clusters and the pulpy oval fruits, usually containing two to four small, hard seeds, have either white or dark skins, covered with a white, powdery substance known as the bloom. Grapes may be eaten fresh, as table grapes, or they may be dried and sold as raisins, sultanas and currants. Grapes may be used also in wine and spirit making. Regarding suitable cultivars of American and European grapes for the home garden, bear in mind that there are scores of them, differing in climatic requirements, and availability will vary from one region to another. It is, therefore, best to buy locally available cultivars, as then you will know that they are right for your climate. There is a choice of grapes for both wine making and dessert.

Grapefruit (*Citrus x paradisi*, fam. Rutaceae)

Although the grapefruit possibly originated from Southeast Asia, the fruit we know today probably developed from a hybrid from the West Indies. It has long been an important commercial product and over time has been improved through breeding and selection so that it is now not so acidic. *Citrus x paradisi* is an evergreen tree which grows to around 5 m (16 ft). The large, round fruit have a white or pink, pulpy flesh and can weigh to 2 kilograms

ABOVE Although it may have a tendency towards biennial bearing, 'Wheeney' produces bumper crops of grapefruit in most years.

(4½ pounds). Recommended cultivars include 'Marsh', 'Ruby', 'Wheeney', and 'Star Ruby'. Grapefruit are a valuable source of vitamin C and are usually consumed fresh or as a juice.

CULTIVATION Grapefruit tolerates cold less than the orange but it can be grown outside in the warmer parts of zone 9. In lower zones it must be grown in an intermediate greenhouse or conservatory. Grow in large pots of soil-based potting compost. Ensure good light but shade from direct sun. Plants can be stood outdoors for the summer if desired. Outdoors, grapefruit will grow in any good soil, but needs good drainage. No citrus, in fact, can stand 'wet feet'. Plentiful water is required to fill out the fruit and keep the foliage in good condition. Grapefruit likes full sun but needs shelter from cold, winter winds. Propagate by budding of proven scions onto rootstocks resistant to soil-borne diseases. Container-grown trees can be planted out at almost any time but it is probably best to avoid midwinter. Plant established container-grown stock as they are ahead in growing time, should be well shaped, and not usually affected by transplanting. Little or no pruning is necessary, except to remove dead wood and broken branches, and to encourage a canopy of leaves to shade the fruit. Citrus are heavy feeders so a complete plant food should be applied in winter and late spring. It is not advisable to feed from late summer to fall as the new flush of growth will be most susceptible to attack by citrus leaf miner. Use organic mulches, too, but well clear of the trunk. Always spread fertilizer within the leaf drip zone, as it is here that the root hairs will absorb nutrients. For the home garden, allow a 2–3 m (6–10 ft) diameter area around each tree; on undulating land, space the trees along the contour to prevent soil erosion. Allow grapefruit to mature on the tree and gather with care so as not to bruise. Use secateurs to cut the stem, retaining part of the stem on the fruit. Insect pests may need to be controlled by sprays; fungi are the main problem in moister climates. Collar rot can be minimized by not injuring the scion and by planting trees so that the graft is well clear of the finished soil level.

CLIMATE Zone 9 (warmer parts) and zone 10.

Graptopetalum (fam. Crassulaceae)

These fleshy succulents, endemic to North America and Mexico, form mats of thick-leafed rosettes, from tiny plants to 80 cm (32 in) tall. While similar to related *Echeveria*, the bell-shaped flowers, borne on thin, nodding stems, are less dazzling in color. They hybridize readily with *Echeveria* species and there are several attractive and popular cultivars known as *Graptoveria*.

CULTIVATION In frost-prone areas, grow in an airy, intermediate greenhouse or conservatory, in pots of cactus compost. Ensure maximum light. Water sparingly in fall and winter. Outdoors grow in semi-shade in well drained, humus-rich soil. Outdoors, plants need well-drained soil in full sun, but they will tolerate partial shade.

CLIMATE Zone 9 (warmer parts).

ABOVE *Graptopetalum paraguayense* has pretty rosettes of succulent leaves with a pearly sheen.

SPECIES *G. filiferum*, from Mexico, is almost stemless, forming offsets from the base of the dense, pale green rosette. This species is a parent of a lovely hybrid known as 'Silver Star'. *G. pachyphyllum* is very small, to 3 cm (1 in) across, forming mats of dense rosettes of tiny, thick, fragile leaves, blueish green in color, developing red tips in the sun. *G. paraguayense*, the most commonly grown, has thick, prostrate stems and loose rosettes of marbled, grayish green to purplish leaves. The white flowers are spotted red.

Graptophyllum (fam. Acanthaceae)
Caricature plant

These 10 species of evergreen shrubs are native to the south-west Pacific and Australia. They are grown as foliage plants and in frosty climates make good house or conservatory plants. The leaves may be mottled, streaked or spotted with various colors. Some markings resemble rough drawings, hence the common name, caricature plant.

CULTIVATION Grow in a warm to intermediate greenhouse or conservatory, or warm room indoors. Use soil-based potting compost and

ABOVE Sometimes used indoors in very bright light situations, *Graptophyllum pictum* presents variably patterned foliage.

ensure good light but shade from direct sun. Plants need very little water in winter–keep compost only barely moist. Propagate in summer from semi-ripe cuttings, which need bottom heat to root.

CLIMATE Zone 10 (warmer parts).

SPECIES *G. pictum*, caricature plant, grows 1–2 m (3–6 ft) high, with glossy foliage veined and marked yellow, paler green, pink or red. Purple-crimson flowers appear in summer but these are not spectacular. The cultivar 'Tricolor' has purplish green leaves with creamy yellow and pink splashes. The stalks and leaf midribs are red.

Grevillea (fam. Proteaceae)

There are more than 250 species of these decorative, evergreen Australian plants, the largest genus in the family *Proteaceae*. They vary greatly in form, habit, leaf shape, flower structure and size, from tall rainforest trees (*G. robusta*) to prostrate rockery plants (*G. lavandulacea*). There are grevilleas with clusters of flowers, called the spider flower grevilleas, and those with elongated, spike-like, one-sided flowers, called the toothbrush grevilleas. Grevillea flowers have no separate petals, the long styles forming a major part of the clusters of flowers. Most grevilleas have brightly colored flowers, often during spring and summer in the northern hemisphere, and attractive foliage, and make beautiful ornamentals. Many smaller species can be used as pot plants. The low-growing species are particularly suitable for planting on banks and on tops of walls where their pretty flowers can be seen to full advantage. Other species make excellent cut flowers, and some are already grown commercially. A good deal of research has been carried out on these plants and there are several major groups of cultivars available, among them the 'Poorinda' and 'Clearview' range. These cultivars are now being grown extensively in various countries, especially in warm areas of the United States, South Africa and New Zealand. Grevilleas are easy to cultivate and ecologically beneficial, as long as soils are well drained. A large number of species are readily available from garden centers throughout the year.

CULTIVATION Propagate grevilleas from seed from the small, hooked capsules. The plant ejects the ripe seeds quickly, so tie a paper bag lightly around almost-ripe capsules to catch the seed. Seed may germinate erratically, some taking

BELOW *Grevillea* 'Robyn Gordon', probably the most widely grown of all grevillea cultivars, is rarely out of flower.

much longer than others. In favorable conditions, grevilleas will hybridize naturally but the plants produced may be sterile. These forms must be propagated from cuttings taken in summer or fall from healthy tips, about 6–8 cm (2–3 in) long, cut just below the leaf nodes. Remove the leaves carefully from the lower two-thirds. For species with large leaves, it is advisable to reduce the remaining leaf area by about a third by cutting off the leaf tips. Strike cuttings in a mixture of two parts coarse, sharp sand to one part peat moss. Keep moist and shaded. When potting on the small, established plants, avoid root disturbance by first immersing them in water. Plant at the same depth as they were in the cutting mix in a mixture of sandy loam and leaf mould or peat moss, with an added teaspoon of blood, fish and bone per small pot. The plants can be potted on a second time as they harden up, before being planted out. Grevilleas need good drainage, slightly acidic soil and a warm position. Most species are relatively disease-free, except for scale pests which can be fairly easily controlled with a white oil spray. In cold and cool climates, grow in an airy, cool greenhouse or conservatory, in pots of acid potting compost and in maximum light. Grevilleas dislike a lot of phosphorus in the soil

CLIMATE Zone 9 (warmer parts), unless indicated below.

SPECIES Many but not all of the following are available in the US. *G. acanthifolia* occurs naturally in the Blue Mountains of New South Wales and is one of the few grevilleas that can tolerate wetter soils and some shade. It varies in form from an upright shrub of about 3 m (10 ft) to a low, spreading one. It has stiff, deeply divided leaves, with sharply pointed lobes, and mauve to pink flowers of the toothbrush type. *G. alpina* varies a good deal in form, leaf shape and flower color and can tolerate very cold conditions. It generally has small, grayish green leaves and either red, yellow, pink or white flowers. *G. banksii*, a popular species from Queensland, named after Sir Joseph Banks, is an erect grower with large heads of red flowers throughout most of the year and deeply lobed, dark green leaves. It grows to 2–8 m (6–26 ft) tall. There is also a white-flowered form. *G. biternata* (syn. *G. curviloba*) generally takes a prostrate form. It has become a popular groundcover. It has fine, green, fern-like foliage and white flowers in spring. *G. buxifolia*, gray spider flower, endemic to sandstone areas of New South Wales, is an open, rounded, bushy

BELOW LEFT The golden, toothbrush flowers of *Grevillea robusta* are freely produced, almost covering the dark green foliage.

BELOW *Grevillea banksii* is one of the longest flowering species and is a parent of 'Robyn Gordon', which is in flower most of the year.

shrub, to 1.5 m (5 ft). The closely set leaves are oblong in shape and hairy, and the reddish brown flowers, borne in clusters, are also hairy, which gives them a grayish tinge. *G. x gaudichaudii*, a natural hybrid between *G. acanthifolia* and *G. laurifolia*, is a very useful groundcover plant. It is a vigorous grower, with coarsely lobed, sharply pointed leaves and reddish purple flowers of the toothbrush type, in spring and early summer. This species has been grafted onto *G. robusta* and the resulting weeping standard grevilleas make striking accents in the garden. *G. juniperina*, zone 8, spider flower, from eastern Australia, is a very hardy plant, with bright green, spiky leaves and red or yellow flowers in spring and summer. It is generally a tall shrub, though there is a prostrate form producing dull yellow flowers throughout most of the year. *G. lavandulacea*, zone 8, also varies in form, but is commonly low growing with grayish foliage and bright red flowers. The Poorinda Hybrids include 'Beauty', with scarlet flowers in late winter; 'Constance', with orange-red flowers throughout most of the year; 'Elegance', with orange and pink flowers; 'Firebird', which grows 1–2 m (3–6 ft), with bright red flowers; 'Pink Coral', with pink flowers; 'Queen', with apricot wheel-shaped flowers; 'Signet', with deep pink flowers; 'Splendor', with silvery foliage and red flowers. *G. robusta*, silky oak, from subtropical rainforests of east coast Australia, grows to 30 m (100 ft) tall. The golden yellow, toothbrush-type flowers bloom profusely in summer, almost covering the dark green, fern-like foliage. The flowers are rich in nectar and the beautiful timber produced from these trees is used in cabinet-making. It is a popular tree for large gardens and parks in temperate climates. *G. rosmarinifolia*, zone 8, rosemary grevillea or spider flower, is an attractive, useful shrub as it can be trimmed into a formal hedge. It grows to a height and spread of 2 m (6 ft). It has clusters of red, spider-like flowers with narrow, pointed leaves. Many forms are available. *G. thelemanniana* has both an upright and a prostrate form, the latter being the more commonly grown and available in two types, one

TOP Cream to pale yellow flowers of *Grevillea biternata* sit well above the finely divided foliage.

ABOVE The pale, creamy flowers of *Grevillea* 'Moonlight' stand out against the dark, gray-green foliage. This makes an excellent garden shrub.

with gray leaves and red flowers, the other with pale green foliage and softer red flowers. The gray-leafed form is more frost-tender. Both flower from late winter to spring. *G. tridentifera*, to 2 m (6 ft), has attractive, three-lobed, pointed leaves and soft, feathery, white flowers. Many Grevillea cultivars are sold under their cultivar names only, such as Grevillea 'Poorinda Constance' or Grevillea 'Canberra Gem'. The label should describe their future size and flower color. 'Robyn Gordon', with a height and spread of 1 m (3 ft), is probably the most commonly grown of all the cultivars. It produces red flowers for many months of the year. Other popular shrubby cultivars include 'Honey Gem', to 3 m (10 ft) high, with a spread of 2.5 m (8 ft), and rich gold flowers; 'Moonlight' to 2 m (6 ft) high and 3 m (10 ft) wide, with creamy white flowers; and 'Misty Pink' which reaches 3–4 m (10–13 ft) high. 'Bronze Rambler' is a useful grevillea cultivar widely used as a groundcover or spillover plant.

Griselinia (fam. Griseliniacea)

Of this small genus of six species of evergreen shrubs or trees, native to New Zealand and parts of Chile, only the species below are in general cultivation. They have a bushy habit and make an attractive hedge when trimmed. The foliage is glossy and leathery, the flowers are inconspicuous and the fruit is a black berry, borne only on female plants.

CULTIVATION Griselinias will adapt to poor soil, provided the climate is warm and they have lots of sun. Plant in early spring or fall and prune after flowering is finished. Propagate from cuttings in summer or from seed.

CLIMATE There are species suited to various climatic zones.

SPECIES *G. littoralis*, zone 7, a small tree from New Zealand, can tolerate salty winds, which

ABOVE The neat, dense foliage of *Griselinia littoralis* makes it ideal for screens, hedges and windbreaks.

makes it useful for seaside gardens. It has bright green, oblong leaves, to 8 cm (3 in), and insignificant flowers. The cultivar 'Variegata' has foliage streaked with white. *G. lucida*, zone 8, also from New Zealand, has darker green foliage. Var. *macrophylla* has much larger leaves.

Guava (*Psidium species*, fam. Myrtaceae)

These small, evergreen trees or shrubs from tropical America have now become naturalized in many other tropical regions. Guavas are grown as ornamentals and also for their delicious fruit, eaten raw or made into jellies and preserves.

CULTIVATION In frost-prone climates, guavas are grown in an intermediate greenhouse or conservatory, mainly as novelty foliage plants. They need large pots or tubs of well drained, soil-based potting compost. Shade from direct strong sun. Outdoors grow in a sheltered, sunny position with rich, moist, free-draining soil. Propagate from seed or cuttings, or by layering in spring.

CLIMATE Zone 10 and above.

SPECIES *P. guajava*, common yellow guava, is a small tree, to around 10 m (33 ft), which is useful as a shade tree for small gardens. It has smooth, greenish brown bark, a dense, bushy canopy, rather long, leathery leaves, and large white flowers in spring. The round or oval, yellow fruit is the largest of the species, growing between 25 and 100 mm (1–4 in) in diameter. It has a sweet, musky flavor and numerous, hard seeds. The flesh may be white, pink or red, depending on the variety, and can be served fresh or used to make jams and jellies. *P. littorale* var. *longipes* (syn. *P. cattleianum*), purple strawberry guava, grows to around 7 m (23 ft). It has smooth, attractively mottled bark, glossy and leathery, rounded leaves and single, white flowers in spring. The fruit is a purplish red color, with a reddish pulp and a flavor said to resemble strawberry. It is also used for jams and jellies. The fruit does not travel well.

ABOVE Yellow guava, *Psidium guajava*, bears large, sweet, succulent fruit. It is not difficult to cultivate in warm areas.

Guichenotia (fam. Sterculiaceae)

There are five species in this genus of small, evergreen shrubs, all native to Western Australia. The foliage has a soft, downy covering and the small, open, bell-shaped flowers are mostly mauve.

CULTIVATION In frost-prone climates, grow in an intermediate greenhouse or conservatory in pots of well-drained, soil-based potting compost. Ensure bright light. Outdoors they prefer a well-drained soil in an open, sunny spot. Propagate from semi-ripe cuttings in summer.

ABOVE The soft lavender bells of Guichenotia macrantha are actually the calyx of the very small flowers inside.

CLIMATE Zone 10.

SPECIES *G. ledifolia*, to around 70 cm (28 in), has small, mauve flowers. *G. macrantha* is similar to *G. ledifolia* but grows slightly taller. It is very showy in summer, with larger mauve flowers.

Guzmania (fam. Bromeliaceae)

Closely related to vriesias in appearance and cultural needs, these bromeliads are grown for the striking bandings and markings on their leaves and their long-lasting, colorful bracts. The leaves are smooth-edged and spineless. In their natural habitat of South America, they grow epiphytically but they can be grown in pots, or mounted on a tree branch. They need a warm greenhouse or conservatory, and also make good house plants.

CULTIVATION For pot cultivation, try to obtain a special compost for epiphytic bromeliads. Alternatively, use a soilless potting compost. On tree branches, pack roots with sphagnum moss. Plants need humidity and good light, but shade from direct sun. Mist spray daily and water well in the growing season. In winter do not spray, and keep compost only just moist. Propagate from large, rooted offsets in spring.

CLIMATE Zone 10.

ABOVE This hybrid of *Guzmania sanguinea* has a perfectly formed rosette of striped foliage, accented by a rosy red center.

SPECIES *G. lindenii* is a superb specimen, growing to 1 m (3 ft), with zigzag barring on the long leaves forming a perfect rosette. *G. lingulata* forms a plain green rosette, to about 45 cm (18 in) in diameter, and produces a red and yellow inflorescence. Var. *cardinalis* is more beautiful than its parent; minor forms a small, dark green rosette with bright red flower bracts. *G. musaica*, a tender species, has prominently barred leaves and a bright red or pink inflorescence. *G. sanguinea* is a small, stemless plant, with mottled leaves which are tinged with red and yellow when in flower. *G. zahnii* grows 50 cm (20 in). The copper-tinged coloring of the leaves is a very attractive feature against the yellow inflorescences.

Gymnocalycium (fam. Cactaceae)
Chin cactus

This large group of South American cactuses is very popular and their ease of culture makes them a good choice for novice growers. All species are small, and all are characterized by a chin-like protuberance below the areoles, hence their common name. The well-defined ribs are notched into tubercles. The spines vary from weak to very strong. The large, funnel-form, day-time flowers are self-sterile, and range in color from white through yellow to green and red.

BELOW The small, globular body of *Gymnocalycium denudatum* is crowned by a large, white, red-throated flower. Offsets are developing at the base.

CULTIVATION In cool and cold climates, grow these cactuses in an intermediate greenhouse or conservatory, in pots of cactus compost. Plants need maximum light but shade them from direct, strong sun. Water normally in the growing period, but withhold water in the winter resting period. Propagate in spring from seed, germinating them at 24°C (75°F), or from offsets.

CLIMATE Zone 10.

SPECIES *G. andreae* is a flattened, globe-shaped, dark green plant, with warty ribs. Large, sulphur yellow flowers appear at the crown in the spring and the summer. *G. baldianum* is a small, solitary, globe-shaped, gray cactus with a depressed apex and rounded ribs. The wine red flowers are 25 cm (10 in) in diameter. *G. mihanovichii* has a striped body, a number of greenish flowers and whorls of brownish yellow spines. There are unusual natural varieties in colors of red or yellow which are very attractive. *G. multiflorum* is a broadly globe-shaped, blueish green, ribbed plant, with deep furrows between the ribs, and comb-like spines. The short, pink flowers are about 25 mm (1 in) in diameter. *G. quehlianum*, a flattened, blueish green plant, has white flowers with a red-colored throat. *G. saglionis* is the largest of the species, and it is also one of the most attractive. It has thick, rounded tubercles, curved, reddish spines and white to pink, bell-shaped flowers.

Gynura (fam. Asteraceae)

From tropical Africa, India and Asia, this genus comprises about 40 species of subshrubs, semi-climbers and perennials, grown mainly for their decorative foliage. The unpleasant-smelling flowers are mostly borne in flat clusters, although sometimes singularly, and are predominantly orange, but occasionally purple.

CULTIVATION Gynuras make attractive house plants and can also be grown in a warm greenhouse. Use soil-based potting compost and shade from direct sun. Propagate from semi-ripe cuttings in summer.

ABOVE below 'Purple Passion', an improved form of *Gynura aurantiaca*, does well as a container plant, both indoors and out.

CLIMATE Zone 10.

SPECIES *G. aurantiaca*, velvet plant, from Java, is shrubby at first, and then with age becomes trailing or climbing in habit. The stem and leaves are covered with velvety, purple hairs and the flowers are a bright orange. *G. procumbens*, another climbing or scrambling plant, coming from Malaysia and the Philippines, grows to about 3 m (10 ft), with similarly hairy stems and leaves in a deep purple-red. The flowers are the usual orange.

Gypsophila (fam. Caryophyllaceae)

Mostly native to the Mediterranean and parts of Asia, this genus comprises around 125 species of annuals and perennials. Generally in the US the perennials are more popular than the annuals and they are better suited to cool climates. *G. paniculata* and its cultivars are particularly popular. By continuously sowing the seeds of the annuals in the ground where they are to bloom, it is quite possible to have a show of these attractive plants in all but the coldest months of the year.

CULTIVATION *Gypsophila* likes a full sun position, with shelter from strong winds. It prefers a limed soil, but will tolerate most soils, provided they are well drained. Propagate annuals from seed, sown in flowering positions from spring onwards. Perennial species are raised from seed sown in winter under glass, with a temperature of 18°C (64°F).

CLIMATE Zone 4, unless indicated otherwise below.

SPECIES *G. elegans*, zone 7, is a bushy annual, to 40 cm (16 in), with clusters of small, white flowers which provide a pretty display from summer to early fall. Cultivar 'Grandiflora Alba' produces larger, white flowers; 'Rosea' has rose pink flowers; 'Purpurea' has small, purplish flowers. *G. muralis* is a small annual, to 15 cm (6 in), with pink to white flowers. *G. paniculata* is a perennial, to 1 m (3 ft), with white or pinkish flowers. The cultivar 'Compacta Plena' has double flowers in white to palest pink; 'Flore-pleno' has double flowers. The best of the double forms of *G. paniculata* is 'Bristol Fairy', which is very popular as a cut flower and often used in wedding bouquets. *G. repens* grows to 15 cm (6 in), with white flowers. Cultivar 'Rosea' has deep rose flowers.

ABOVE *Gypsophila paniculata* 'Bristol Fairy' blooms over a long period and produces long-lasting cut flowers.

H

Habranthus to Hyssop

Habranthus (fam. Amaryllidaceae)
Rain lily

These flowering bulbs from temperate areas of South America can be confused with some species of *Hippeastrum*. They grow to 30 cm (12 in), with delicate pink, yellow or red flowers and strap-like foliage. Most produce their funnel-shaped flowers in summer and fall.

CULTIVATION If regular hard frosts occur, grow in a cool conservatory or greenhouse, in pots of soil-based compost. Plant in spring, 10 cm (4 in) deep. Provide maximum light. When bulbs are dormant, keep compost only slightly moist. Outdoors, grow in well-drained soil in full sun and plant bulbs shallowly so that the necks show above ground level. Propagate from offsets.

CLIMATE Zone 9 (warmer parts).

SPECIES *H. brachyandrus*, to 30 cm (12 in), has a solitary, delicate pink flower, ribbed in deep reddish purple. *H. robustus* has widely flaring, funnel-shaped flowers in light rose pink which appear with or just after the leaves. The flowers are produced one per stem. This species, from Brazil, grows to about 30 cm (12 in). *H. tubispathus*, from South America, grows to a height of 20 cm (8 in). The red and brown, funnel-shaped flowers are deep yellow inside.

ABOVE The pretty, pink flowers of *Habranthus robustus* appear with, or just after, the dark green, grassy leaves.

Haemanthus (fam. Amaryllidaceae)
Blood lily

These splendid, flowering bulbs from tropical and southern Africa generally have broad green leaves and clusters of most unusual flowers. Many plants in this genus are now classified as *Scadoxus*.

CULTIVATION In frost-prone areas, grow in an intermediate greenhouse or conservatory, in pots of soil-based potting compost. Plant in fall, the bulb neck showing above compost level. Ensure maximum light. When dormant, keep herbaceous species dry and evergreens slightly moist. For optimum flowering, allow bulbs to become pot-bound. Propagate from offsets.

CLIMATE Zone 10.

SPECIES *H. albiflos*, to 30 cm (12 in), has fleshy leaves and greenish white flowers and is the most commonly cultivated species. *H. coccineus*, to 25 cm (10 in), is quite spectacular, with purple-spotted stems and bright red flowers, with yellow stamens, surrounded by scarlet to pink bracts. *H. magnificus*, (now *Scadoxus puniceus*), giant stove brush, has 30–40 cm (12–16 in) long leaves and bright scarlet flowers.

ABOVE Large, round heads of scarlet flowers of *Haemanthus coccineus* appear on sturdy stems before the foliage emerges.

Hakea (fam. Proteaceae)

Needle bush, pincushion, sea urchin

There are around 140 species of evergreen trees and shrubs in this Australian genus. The leaves vary enormously, but are generally simple, alternate, or needle-like, lance-shaped or kidney-shaped. They can be entire or lobed, but are always stiff and leathery. The small, tubular flowers resemble *Grevillea* and are generally clustered in the leaf axils, sometimes forming a globular head. The mostly large, hard seed cases are in two sections, with beaks at the end. Hakeas are attractive to birds and relatively disease-free. Grown widely in Australasia, they are also popular in California and the Mediterranean. Some of the prickly species make good hedges, and tolerate pruning and trimming; fast-growing species like *H. salicifolia* are used for shelter and shade.

CULTIVATION Propagation is generally from the winged seeds, and color forms usually come true from seed. Best seed comes from mature, woody, year-old capsules. Store them in a paper bag in a warm spot. Within two weeks they will release the seed which should be sown in a well-drained potting mix, and germinated in a temperature of 18°C (64°F). Germination can take up to ten weeks. Seedlings should be potted on quickly, then planted out when they reach 20 cm (8 in). Hakeas can also be propagated from cuttings of half-ripe shoots taken in fall and struck in a sharp sand and peat mix of about 3:1, treated with fungicide as they are susceptible to damping-off. They prefer an open, sunny, well-drained spot as they do not like 'wet feet'. They are surface-rooting plants and most respond to light pruning after flowering. Most species respond well to a slow-release fertilizer. They take slight frost but in frost-prone climates, grow in an airy, cool greenhouse or conservatory, in pots of soil-based potting compost. Ensure maximum light and acid soil.

CLIMATE Warmer parts of zone 9, or zone 10.

TOP Spreading, low-growing *Hakea myrtoides* carries a prolific show of deep pink or red flowers in spring.

ABOVE The lovely *Hakea bucculenta*, from Australia, has very narrow leaves and rosy red flowers. It is very hard to grow in humid areas.

SPECIES Some of the following species are available in the US. *H. francisiana* (syn. *H. multilineata*), grass leaf hakea, from South Australia, is a tall, handsome shrub with long, narrow, downy, grayish green leaves and pink to deep red flowers, borne in cylindrical spikes. It may be difficult to grow in humid, coastal regions or in heavy soils. *H. laurina*, pincushion hakea, a native of Western Australia, is a fast-growing, small tree, to 6 m (20 ft), with narrow, lance-shaped, gray-green leaves. From late fall to midwinter, the tree bears ball-shaped, sweetly-scented, crimson flower heads, and long, cream styles, like a pincushion. *H. salicifolia* (syn. *H. saligna*), willow hakea, from New South Wales and Queensland, is a well-shaped, small tree growing quickly to 7 m (23 ft). It has long, narrow, tapering leaves, bronze-red when young, green when mature, and cream, fragrant flowers on long stems. *H. sericea*, (syn. *H. lissosperma*) from eastern Australia, is a large, bushy shrub, growing to 3–5 m (10–16 ft) tall, with sharply pointed, needle-like leaves and clusters of lightly perfumed, white or pale pink flowers in spring. *H. suaveolens* from Western Australia is a vigorous, rounded shrub, growing to 3 m (10 ft) and useful as a windbreak in coastal areas. It has prickly, needle-like leaves and produces terminal clusters of fragrant, white flowers. *H. victoriae*, royal hakea, an upright shrub from Western Australia, has marvellous, very ornate foliage, but it is hard to cultivate except in areas of low humidity. The kidney-shaped or roundish, gray-green leaves are heavily veined with gold and edged with fine teeth. The green turns to gold and red at the base of the leaves. Many of the attractive, flowering species are from Western Australia.

Halesia (fam. Styracaceae)
Snowdrop tree

Native to eastern North America and China, these five species of deciduous shrubs or small trees are grown mainly for their clusters of attractive white, bell-shaped flowers which appear during spring. These are superb plants for a woodland garden or shrub border.

CULTIVATION Halesias need a rich soil containing plenty of humus and which retains moisture, yet is well drained. It should be acid or neutral. Give partial shade or full sun with shelter from wind. Propagate from seed in fall in warmth, followed after eight weeks by a cold spell, or by layering in spring.

ABOVE Although the flowers are not long lasting, the lovely *Halesia carolina* is worth growing. It is popularly known as silver bell or snowdrop tree.

CLIMATE Zone 5.

SPECIES *H. carolina* is a spreading tree, to 6–8 m (20–26 ft), with slender, pointed leaves, downy gray underneath, which color yellow in fall. In mid to late spring it is covered in masses of drooping, bell-shaped, white flowers. Small winged fruits follow in fall. *H. monticola* is a fast-growing tree, to 12 m (40 ft), with a profusion of much larger white flowers. The form *rosea* has pink flowers.

Hamamelis (fam. Hamamelidaceae)
Witch hazel

Originally from eastern Asia and North America, these five to six species of deciduous shrubs or small trees, growing between 2 and 10 m (6–33 ft) tall, produce fragrant, yellow flowers that bloom in winter or very early spring on bare branches, before the foliage appears.

CULTIVATION *Hamamelis* prefers cool conditions and will do well in most soils, providing it has protection from hot winds and plenty of moisture. Propagate from seed, which takes up to two years to germinate, or by layering, which is also slow, at the end of summer. Most species are quite slow growing.

ABOVE In late winter, a profusion of flowers on the bare branches of this *Hamamelis x intermedia* cultivar fills the air with fragrance.

ABOVE A cultivar of *Hardenbergia violacea*, a light climber which produces masses of pea-like flowers in late winter and spring.

CLIMATE Best in cool, moist climates. Zone 5 for most species.

SPECIES *H.* x *intermedia* cultivars are the most popular witch hazels the US. They are 4 m (13 ft) high, shuttlecock-shaped shrubs with yellow fall foliage and scented, yellow, orange, copper or red flowers in the winter. A popular cultivar is 'Arnold Promise' with scented, yellow flowers. *H. japonica*, Japanese witch hazel, reaches 4 m (13 ft) in height and has long, spreading branches and small, sweetly perfumed, yellow flowers with twisted petals. The flowering branches are often used to great effect as indoor decoration. *H. mollis*, Chinese witch hazel, suited to zone 6, grows to 4 m (13 ft), producing extremely fragrant, golden yellow flowers in mid and late winter. The thick, mid-green leaves, which are downy on the undersides, color yellow in the fall. Many new cultivars are now becoming available.

Hardenbergia (fam. Papilionaceae)

This is a small genus of Australian twining shrubs or vines which make very attractive garden ornamentals or goundcovers. They also look quite beautiful in large pots, or trained on trellises or fences.

CULTIVATION In climates which are prone to frosts, hardenbergias are best grown in a cool,

airy greenhouse or conservatory, in pots of lime-free, well-drained, soil-based potting compost. Ensure they receive maximum light, but provide shade from direct strong sun. Outdoors, plant in acid or neutral soil in a sunny or partially shady position. Prune after flowering to contain the plant if necessary. Propagate in spring from seed that has soaked in hot water for a day. Germinate at 20°C (68°F).

CLIMATE Zone 9 (warmer parts) or zone 10.

SPECIES *H. comptoniana*, native lilac, from Western Australia, is a delightful plant, with compound, dark green leaves and very beautiful sprays of bright, mauve-purple, spring flowers. *H. violacea*, native sarsparilla, is also quite beautiful and can be used as a shrub, ground-cover, climber or twiner. The leaves vary from broadly ovate to quite narrow, with conspicuous veins. Masses of small, mostly bright purple pea flowers are produced in spring. The cultivar 'Alba' has white flowers; 'Rosea' has pink flowers.

Harpephyllum (fam. Anacardiaceae)
Kaffir plum, wild plum

There is only one species in this South African genus. An attractive evergreen tree, it is used as a lawn specimen or for street plantings.

ABOVE With its broad, spreading canopy, *Harpephyllum caffrum* makes a delightful specimen tree in a mild climate.

ABOVE *Harpullia pendula*, Australian tulipwood, is noted for its heavy crops of ornamental fruits. Grow as a foliage pot plant in frosty climates.

CULTIVATION Kaffir plum prefers a warm climate, so if frosts are a problem it should be grown as a small foliage plant in a cool to intermediate greenhouse or conservatory. Propagate from seed.

CLIMATE Should succeed in sheltered warm areas of zone 9, plus zone 10.

SPECIES *H. caffrum*, kaffir plum, is a dense, broadly domed tree, which grows to a height and width of 10–15 m (33–50 ft). It has a short, straight trunk, glossy, dark green leaves and small, white flowers. The small, red fruit makes a tasty jam.

Harpullia (fam. Sapindaceae)

This genus comprises around 26 species of dioecious or polygamous trees from India, Asia and Australia, growing 10–15 m (33–50 ft) tall. They are probably not available outside their native countries.

CULTIVATION In frosty cool and cold climates, this tree would have to be grown as a small specimen plant in an intermediate to warm greenhouse or conservatory. Propagate from seed or cuttings.

CLIMATE At least zone 10.

SPECIES *H. arborea*, from Malaysia and the Philippines, grows to 10 m (33 ft), with sprays of pendulous flowers and bright orange fruit. *H. pendula*, Australian tulipwood, produces a beautiful timber used in cabinetmaking. It grows 10–15 m (33–50 ft) tall. Its insignificant, yellow flowers are followed by striking red and yellow fruits.

Hatiora (fam. Cactaceae)
Drunkard's dream

This unusual genus of epiphytic cacti is native to Brazil.

BELOW Unopened buds on the stem segment tips of *Hatiora salicornioides* are like small, glowing torches.

CULTIVATION Grow in a warm greenhouse or conservatory, in hanging baskets, or mounted on a tree branch. Fill containers with an orchid compost or a cactus compost formulated for epiphytes. Give good light but shade from direct sun, and mist spray daily. In winter, keep the compost only barely moist. Propagate from cuttings in summer.

CLIMATE Tropical or subtropical.

SPECIES *H. salicornioides* has a bushy habit and grows to around 40 cm (16 in) in height and spread. It has thin, jointed, tube-like stems and the small, yellow, self-sterile flowers are borne at the tips of the stems in late winter to early spring.

Haworthia (fam. Aloaceae)

This genus comprises about 70 species of succulents, native to South Africa. All are neat, low-growing plants which form dense or open rosettes, although some species become more elongated, growing to about 20 cm (8 in) high. The foliage is either blunt or sharply pointed, and often marked in white. Long-lasting, insignificant, whitish green flowers are borne in loose sprays on tall, thin, pendulous stems. Flowering may be from spring to fall, depending on the species.

ABOVE In good conditions, *Haworthia attenuata* can form large colonies of rosettes. The white-dotted lower surface of the leaf is decorative.

CULTIVATION In frost-prone climates, grow in an airy, intermediate greenhouse or conservatory, in pots of cactus compost. Ensure good light but shade from direct strong sun. Water normally in growing period but allow the compost to become dry in winter. Propagate from offsets or leaf cuttings in spring.

CLIMATE Zone 10.

SPECIES *H. attenuata* is the most widely grown species. It forms a leafy, stemless, dark green rosette, which is about 6 cm (2½ in) across, and also produces numerous offsets. The horned undersurface of the leaves is banded with white dots or tubercles. *H. cymbiformis* forms mats of rosettes of pale green, very fleshy, boat-shaped leaves. This species is variable but the leaves may have translucent tips or stripes. *H. marginata* grows up to 12 cm (5 in) across, with smooth, rigid, sharply pointed, mid-green, keeled leaves with white margins. It produces very few offsets. *H. pumila* (syn. *H. margaritifera*) is similar to *H. attenuata* but has larger rosettes, 15 cm (6 in) across, and prominent tubercles scattered on both sides of the leaves. *H. tessellata* has smooth, shiny, dark green or blue-green recurved leaves, checkered with translucent lines which form tiny squares. *H. truncata* is the rarest of the species and is keenly sought by enthusiasts. It has unusual, rough, dark green, erect leaves which grow in closely packed rows like irregular steps. In its habitat, only the tips of the leaves appear above the ground.

Hazelnut (Corylus avellana, fam. Corylaceae)
Filbert

The hazelnut or filbert is grown commercially for the edible nut, although some of these trees, particularly those from Europe and western Asia, are grown as ornamentals, hedges or windbreaks. The highly nutritious nut has a smooth amber shell and is about half the size of a walnut. Hazelnuts are used to make a sweet spread and are also used in chocolate making. *Corylus avellana* and the cultivars grow to around 4 m (13 ft) in height. They are deciduous, monoecious shrubs or small trees, native to northern temperate zones with cooler climates. The cultivar 'Purpurea' has purplish bronze foliage; 'Aurea' has golden foliage; 'Contorta', with its attractive twisted branches, may be used for bonsai. The twisted stems are often used in floral work. The nuts are borne in terminal clusters. A number of cultivars have been produced specifically for their nuts and these are preferable to the straight species.

CULTIVATION Hazelnuts will grow on almost any soil, providing it is deep and well drained. Propagate from seed, from suckers or by layering. Plant in the early winter. It is best to plant several varieties to be sure of achieving better pollination. Not much pruning is required, except for the removal of inside wood, low branches, weak stems and dead wood. Well-grown trees or bushes take about five or six years to produce nuts and they will gradually increase their production with age. The nuts must be left on the tree until they are quite ripe. Frequent picking is necessary to prevent the brown-colored nuts from becoming discolored. Store them in bags, only after the fruit has completely dried, in a place which has a quite humid atmosphere.

CLIMATE Zone 4.

ABOVE In summer the foliage of hazelnuts is extremely dense. Trees must be closely planted as they are pollinated by wind.

Hebe (fam. Scrophulariaceae)
Veronica

These popular, evergreen, flowering shrubs are mostly indigenous to New Zealand and nearby islands. Many members of this genus were previously included with *Veronica* or *Parahebe*. Hebe makes pretty garden ornamentals or hedges, with its attractive foliage and small brushes of white, blue, crimson, pink or lilac flowers. Some species have broad leaves, while others have small, conifer-like foliage. Most species of hebe have a long flowering period.

CULTIVATION In the US, hebes are not hardy in all zones, preferring the less severe or milder climates. They will tolerate almost any soil, including the alkaline type. Many make excellent shrubs for seaside gardens, being tolerant of sandy soil and salt air. Growth will be more compact if pruned after flowering. Propagate from cuttings taken when flowering is finished.

CLIMATE Zone 8 for the following species, unless otherwise specified.

SPECIES *H. albicans* is a distinctive species, with densely packed, blue-gray leaves and white, summer flowers. It grows to 1 m (3 ft) and rarely needs trimming. *H. andersonii* grows to 2 m (6 ft), with white flowers, tipped in violet. Cultivar 'Variegata', to 2 m (6 ft), has cream-edged foliage and long spikes of lavender blue flowers. *H. buxifolia*, zone 7, is a neat, rounded shrub, to 1 m (3 ft), with glossy foliage and white, summer flowers. *H. colensoi*, zone 6, is a dwarf shrub, to 45 cm (18 in), very useful for growing in rockeries with pale green leaves and clusters of white flowers. *H. cupressoides*, zone 6, to 2 m (6 ft), has cypress-like foliage and can take dry conditions. *H. diosmifolia*, zone 7, is a popular species in New Zealand where it can reach to 6 m (20 ft), though more usually it grows to 1 m (3 ft). It has a mound-like shape, with narrow, glossy, bright green leaves and masses of either pink, or more frequently lavender blue, flowers for most of the year. *H. elliptica*, zone 7, grows to 2 m (6 ft), with

ABOVE Hebes are easy-care garden shrubs for many areas. There is a large range of flower colors, including this rich crimson-purple.

Hedera (fam. Araliaceae)

Ivy

This small genus of evergreen climbers has become naturalized in many parts of the world, although it comes originally from Europe, North Africa and Asia. Most species cling to supports by means of tiny, aerial roots; other species have a trailing habit and are widely grown as groundcover in either sunny or shady spots where grass will not grow. Ivy is also a popular indoor potted plant, requiring some sort of support such as driftwood. There is a great range of named cultivars with widely diverse patterns and color in the foliage.

CULTIVATION Ivy will grow in any soil, if drainage is efficient, and will adapt to sun or shade. It will tolerate dry conditions once the plants are established. *H. canariensis* will not tolerate severe cold. Ivy should not be allowed to climb up living trees as it will damage them and may ultimately kill them. To propagate a climbing type, take cuttings from parts of the plant with aerial roots and juvenile foliage. When propagating a fancy-leaf type, take the cuttings from immediately below the leaf nodes. The cuttings should measure about 20 cm (8 in) and it is best to take several from one stem. Remove the lower leaves, dip the cuttings into a softwood hormone powder and place in a mix of ver-

large, lilac flowers. Cultivar 'Variegata' (now correctly *H. franciscana* 'Variegata') has cream-edged leaves. *H. hulkeana*, New Zealand lilac, is an open, upright grower, with oval, glossy, dark green leaves, margined in red, and a profusion of small, lilac flowers in spring and early summer. It grows to 1 m (3 ft) and has parented many hybrids. *H. macrantha*, zone 6, is low-growing, to 60 cm (24 in), and suitable for rock gardens. The white flowers are the largest of the genus. *H. parviflora* var. *angustifolia*, zone 7, to 2 m (6 ft), has pale lilac flowers in summer. *H. pimeleoides* var. *glaucocaerulea*, zone 7, grows to 45 cm (18 in), with dusty blue leaves and masses of deep blue flowers. *H. salicifolia*, zone 7, a variable species, to 4 m (13 ft), has white flowers tinged with lilac. *H. speciosa*, zone 7, is a desirable species which grows to 2 m (6 ft), with large, glossy, dark green leaves and purple flowers. Many hybrids are from this species, including cultivar 'Blue Gem', a cross with *H. elliptica*, which grows well in coastal areas, to 1 m (3 ft), and has sea blue flowers; 'La Seduisante', with crimson flowers; and 'Midsummer Beauty', to 2 m (6 ft), with long spikes of lavender flowers. *H. vernicosa*, zone 7, grows to 1 m (3 ft), with small leaves and lavender, summer flowers.

ABOVE The variegated form of *Hedera canariensis* makes a dense groundcover. It tolerates the dry shade under a large tree.

miculite and sharp sand. Water thoroughly and leave to strike in a sheltered, warm spot.

CLIMATE There are species suited to various climatic zones.

SPECIES *H. canariensis*, Canary Islands ivy, zone 8, is a vigorous climbing species, with large, leathery, lobed leaves, about 20 cm (8 in) across, which turn bronze-green in winter. The cultivar 'Gloire de Marengo' has red stems and very showy, glossy leaves, marked with gray, dark green and cream. *H. helix*, English or common ivy, zone 5, a popular species, grows quite quickly up very tall trees if allowed. It has dark green, five-pointed leaves. There are numerous cultivars available in a variety of leaf shapes and markings, including groundcovers with ruffled or wavy-edged foliage. Popular cultivars of English ivy include 'Glacier', 'Luzii' 'Oro di Bogliasco', and 'Parsley Crested'. Var. *hibernica*, Atlantic ivy, zone 7, is a robust groundcover, particularly well suited to shady positions under trees. It has small, bright green, five-lobed leaves.

Hedycarya (fam. Monimiaceae)
Native mulberry

These small, evergreen trees and shrubs are native to Australia and New Zealand. They are rarely available outside their native countries.

ABOVE Although the flowers are insignificant, the fruits of *Hedycarya angustifolia* are very decorative. The timber is used in fine cabinetwork.

CULTIVATION Outdoors, these trees need moist soil and shelter from wind. When young they require partial shade. In frost-prone climates, grow in a cool, airy greenhouse or conservatory.

CLIMATE Zone 10.

SPECIES *H. angustifolia*, Austral mulberry, is a native of eastern Australia and grows 3–6 m (10–20 ft) in height. It has thin, shiny, light green leaves and insignificant, pale-colored flowers. It produces small, attractive, red or yellow fruits that resemble mulberries. *H. arborea*, from New Zealand, is similar, with bright red berry fruits. It grows to 5–10 m (16–33 ft) high.

Hedychium (fam. Zingiberaceae)
Ginger lily

Native to tropical Asia, the Himalayas and Madagascar, these 40 or so rhizomatous perennials are grown for their large, handsome foliage and unusual, flamboyant flowers. They are grown under glass in frost-prone climates but are often bedded out for the summer.

CULTIVATION Grow in a cool to intermediate greenhouse in pots of soil-based potting com-

BELOW The striking, yellow flowers of *Hedychium gardnerianum* have a strong perfume. This is a vigorous grower.

post. Shade from direct sun and ensure a humid atmosphere. Reduce watering considerably in winter. Outdoors they need a moist soil rich in humus, shelter, and partial shade or full sun. Propagate by division in spring.

CLIMATE Zones 9 or 10.

SPECIES *H. coccineum*, red or scarlet ginger lily, grows to 2 m (6 ft), with showy, scarlet flowers throughout summer. *H. coronarium*, white ginger lily or butterfly flower, grows to 1.5 m (5 ft), with large, glossy, dark green, succulent leaves. The exquisite, satiny, butterfly-like, white flowers are borne on 30 cm (12 in) long spikes and fill the air with their sweet scent in summer. They look very pretty in float bowls. *H. gardnerianum*, Kahili ginger, grows to 2.5 m (8 ft), with 45 cm (18 in) spikes of yellow and scarlet blossoms lasting right through summer. The flowers are heavily scented.

Helenium (fam. Asteraceae)

According to Greek legend, these flowers grew from the tears of Helen of Troy, hence the generic name. They are hardy perennials and produce summer and fall daisy flowers, with very prominent centers, and they are excellent for cutting. The flowers come in a range of fall shades.

CULTIVATION Heleniums prefer a rich soil and a sunny position. They are very hardy, making useful plants for holiday homes. Propagate from seed or by division of existing plants in fall. Water well while young.

CLIMATE Zone 3 for *H. autumnale*, Zone 7 for *H. bigelovii*.

SPECIES *H. autumnale*, sneezeweed, grows to 1.5 m (5 ft) and has yellow flowers with brown centers. 'Moerheim Beauty' and 'Wyndley' are two popular cultivars. 'Moerheim Beauty' produces flowers in shades of russet. *H. bigelovii*, to 1 m (3 ft), also has brown and yellow flowers.

Helianthemum (fam. Cistaceae)

Sun rose, rock rose

These evergreen or semi-evergreen, low-growing or prostrate shrubs are native mainly to Europe, particularly the Mediterranean, and are popular for rock gardens, raised beds and as groundcover, especially on banks.

BELOW *Helianthemum* 'Supreme', with its deep red flowers, forms a spreading mound of color in the garden.

ABOVE Russet to crimson flowers are abundant on *Helenium* 'Bruno'. The late summer to fall flowering bridges a seasonal gap.

CULTIVATION These plants love full sun and prefer an alkaline soil. They are generally short-lived but can be trimmed back to encourage new growth and more flowers. Propagate from cuttings taken in summer and planted in a sandy compost.

CLIMATE Zone 6 for most species and also hybrids.

SPECIES *H. appenninum*, to 45 cm (18 in), has a spreading habit. It is a short-lived species, with gray leaves and white flowers in summer. *H. nummularium*, zone 5, has a neat, prostrate habit, growing to 20 cm (8 in). The pretty, orange, red, pink or yellow, late spring flowers last for only one day. This species has produced many widely grown hybrids. *H. oelandicum* subsp. alpestre, to 12 cm (5 in), has mats of gray-green leaves and, in late spring and summer, a succession of yellow flowers.

Helianthus (fam. Asteraceae)
Sunflower

This genus comprises many annual and perennial plants with daisy-like flowers, usually yellow, but also in a range of orange and brown shades.

CULTIVATION Annual species are grown from seed sown in spring, while the perennials should be lifted and divided in fall or spring. Sunflowers prefer well-drained soil, enriched with organic matter, but can tolerate poorer soils. They need regular water in the growing season, but tolerate dry conditions well, although the flowers will be small.

CLIMATE There are species suited to various climatic zones.

SPECIES *H. annuus*, the annual sunflower, zone 6, is one of the most important oilseed crops in the world, with a wide range of applications in food and industry. It is also popular as a decorative annual for home gardens, appealing to adults and children alike. It can grow up to 3 m

ABOVE A giant sunflower provides a talking point in the garden. These tall growers need shelter from strong wind.

(10 ft), but many cultivars are available of various size, flower form and color. *H. decapetalus*, zone 5, is an easy-care perennial, 1.5–2 m (5–6 ft) high, with bright yellow flowers from late summer to fall. *H. x laetiflorus*, showy sunflower, zone 4, grows to over |2 m (6 ft) and is most suitable for low-rainfall areas. *H. tuberosus*, Jerusalem artichoke, zone 4, a native of North America, was eaten by indigenous American peoples long before European settlement.

Helichrysum (fam. Asteraceae)
Everlasting, immortelle

Formerly a very large genus of several hundred species, a great number have now been reclassified into other genera.

CULTIVATION Propagate from seed or cuttings. Firm tip cuttings will strike easily at almost any time of the year. These plants require perfect drainage as they rot easily. They will grow in sun or partial shade but need good air circulation. Grow tender species in a cool greenhouse.

ABOVE *Helichrysum petiolare* 'Limelight' has pale lime green, felty leaves. It is good for lighting up a shaded corner of the garden.

ABOVE This lovely species of *Heliconia* has white flowers peeping out from its brilliant scarlet bracts.

CLIMATE There are species suited to various climatic zones. A dry climate is best.

SPECIES *H. bellidioides*, zone 7, a perennial from New Zealand, grows 30–40 cm (12–16 in) and produces silvery green foliage and silvery white flowers. *H. petiolare*, zone 10, is a shrubby perennial, with a height and spread of 1 m (3 ft), grown for its attractive foliage. The rounded, felty leaves are silver-gray and the flowers are cream. It does well in partial shade. One cultivar has pale lime-colored foliage. *H. sibthorpii*, zone 7, from Greece, is a tiny plant, 5–8 cm (2–3 in) high, with white, woolly foliage and small, cream, glossy, daisy flowers.

Heliconia (fam. Heliconiaceae)
Lobster claw, parrot beak

There are between 100 and 200 species in this genus of showy plants from tropical America, South Pacific islands and the Moluccas. These plants grow from rhizomes and have large, paddle-shaped or spoon-shaped foliage, mostly similar to that of the banana. Brilliantly colored bracts enclose the true flowers, which are often pollinated by hummingbirds or bats in their habitats. The flowering stems may be upright or pendulous. Most flower in spring or summer. They can be used as specimen plants or in mixed foliage borders. In frost-prone climates, they are grown in a warm greenhouse or conservatory.

CULTIVATION Grow in large pots or tubs of soilless potting compost, ideally containing shredded bark. Plants need good light but shade from direct strong sun, and a humid atmosphere. Containers could be stood outdoors for the summer in a very sheltered, partially shaded spot. Propagate by division in spring.

CLIMATE Frost-free. Zone 10 at least.

SPECIES *H. bihai* varies in height from 1 m to 5 m (3–16 ft). The foliage is dark green and the upright inflorescence is white with green tips, and is surrounded by broad, red bracts with a yellow base. There are several named cultivars of this species. *H. nutans*, to 1–2 m (3–6 ft) tall, has a pendulous inflorescence, encased by orange-red bracts. The flowers have yellow sepals. *H. psittacorum*, parrot beak, grows up to 2 m (6 ft) high, with spoon-shaped or linear leaves. The floral bracts are orange-red, while the flowers are orange-red with green, banded tips.

Heliopsis (fam. Asteraceae)

These hardy, North American perennials make a bright display in garden borders and produce excellent cut flowers. The bright yellow, dahlia-like flowers, up to 8 cm (3 in) wide, contrast with the opposite, mid to dark green leaves.

ABOVE Clump-forming *Heliopsis helianthoides* adds a splash of gold to the garden. Flowers are great for indoor decoration too.

ABOVE The flowers of *Heliotropium arborescens* have a delicious, vanilla scent. It grows best in warm, sheltered gardens.

CULTIVATION Plant in average garden soil in sun, though they will benefit from added humus. Water in dry weather and feed in spring. They can be divided every three years.

CLIMATE Zone 4.

SPECIES *H. helianthoides*, to 1.5 m (5 ft), has rich gold flowers in summer. It is classed as perennial, but is often short-lived. Subsp. *scabra* grows to around 1 m (3 ft), with golden yellow blooms. Cultivar 'Patula', to 1.25 m (4 ft), has large, semi-double, golden orange flowers.

Heliotropium (fam. Boraginaceae)
Cherry pie

This large group of mostly perennials and shrubs, from the Americas and the Pacific and Canary Islands, are rarely cultivated. In frost-prone climates, they are used as summer bedding plants, being raised each year from seed or cuttings. They make good pot plants under glass.

CULTIVATION Heliotropes like a rich, well-drained soil and a sunny, protected situation. They need a minimum winter temperature of 7°C (45°F), ample water and feeding before flowering. Cut back the plant after flowering to encourage further blooms and to prevent strag-

gly growth. Propagate from seed sown in spring and germinated at 18°C (64°F). Increase named cultivars from semi-ripe cuttings in late summer, rooted with bottom heat.

CLIMATE Zone 10 and above.

SPECIES *H. arborescens* is lovely from late spring to fall, with clusters of lilac, fragrant flowers. It has the characteristic small, oval, crinkled leaves and grows to around 1 m (3 ft). There are numerous cultivars of *H. arborescens*, including some with dark purple blooms such as 'Black Beauty' and 'Iowa'.

Helipterum (see Rhodanthe)

Helleborus (fam. Ranunculaceae)
Hellebore, Christmas or Lenten rose

Native to central, eastern and southern Europe and western Asia, these perennials, mainly evergreen, are popular for their winter or early spring flowers. They look best when mass planted, say in a woodland garden or shrub border. They have divided, sometimes sharply toothed foliage, and bowl-shaped flowers in shades of white, cream, yellow, green, pink, red and purple.

CULTIVATION Hellebores need rich soil, much added organic matter, and at least part shade. Feed in spring and allow a year for plants to become established. Propagate species from seed sown in fall in a garden frame, or divide established clumps of species and hybrids in late summer or early fall. They hybridize well and produce interesting flower colors.

CLIMATE There are species suited to various climatic zones.

SPECIES *H. argutifolius*, zone 7, from Corsica and Sardinia, grows 1.2 m (4 ft). Taller spikes of green flowers appear above the coarsely toothed leaves. *H. foetidus*, zone 6, to 80 cm (32 in), has pale green flowers, tipped with purple. *H. lividus*, zone 7, is a deciduous species, to 45 cm (18 in), with purple or brown flowers, green when young. *H. niger*, Christmas rose, zone 3, to 30 cm (12 in), has white, saucer-shaped flowers, sometimes tinged with pink. *H. orientalis*, Lenten rose, zone 6, grows to 45–60 cm (18–24 in), but it is its wide range of cultivars which are grown, with flowers in shades of white, cream, yellow, pink, red and purple. The flowers of many are spotted

with a contrasting color. *H. viridis*, zone 6, is another deciduous species, which grows 30–45 cm (12–18 in), and produces unusual, pale green flowers.

Hemerocallis (fam. Hemerocallidaceae)
Day lily

These perennials from eastern Asia, China and Japan are very popular plants because of their abundance of showy, funnel-shaped, lily-like flowers in summer. While individual blooms last for only a day, one cluster may be in bloom for weeks during summer. The long, narrow leaves are a pale green color. Day lilies have been extensively hybridized and many cultivars are now available. Some are evergreen, others are completely deciduous in winter. There is a great range of plant sizes, from tall to dwarf forms. Flower size varies too.

CULTIVATION Day lilies are fairly hardy and most can be grown in full sun all day. Brightly colored varieties should be planted in half-shade to prevent the flowers from fading. None, however, should be grown in full shade. Plant in fall or spring in soil enriched with manure.

ABOVE Many fine day lily hybrids are in creamy yellow or orange shades, not surprisingly as many species exhibit these colors.

BELOW This very choice variety of *Helleborus* has massed flowers of rich, rosy pink. There are now many lovely hybrids available.

Established plants are fairly drought-tolerant but will be better with some regular watering. Propagate by division of existing plants, or from seed.

CLIMATE There are species suited to various climatic zones.

SPECIES *H. aurantiaca*, zone 6, to 1 m (3 ft), produces clumps of foliage, above which rise orange-yellow flowers on long stems. *H. citrina* zone 4, reaches just over 1 m (3 ft) and bears fragrant, lemon-yellow blooms. *H. fulva*, zone 4, has been cultivated for centuries and has produced many cultivars, including 'Flore Pleno' which grows to 1 m (3 ft), with double, brilliant orange flowers, marked with dark brown. *H. middendorffi*, zone 5, to 30–45 cm (12–18 in), has sweetly scented, deep yellow flowers. *H. minor*, zone 4, is a dwarf species, with fragrant reddish brown flowers, colored yellow inside. *H. thunbergii*, to 1 m (3 ft), produces fragrant, bright yellow flowers. Many hundreds of named cultivars of *Hemerocallis* are available with flowers in all shades of yellow, orange, red, pink, brown and purple. Most are hardy in zone 6.

Hemiandra (fam. Lamiaceae)
Snake bush

This small, Australian native genus has one species which is especially lovely and makes a pretty rock garden or pot specimen. It is grown in some warm areas including California

CULTIVATION Propagate from seed or by cuttings of half-ripe, young growth struck in a sharp sand and peat mix of about 3:1. Pot up in a well-drained, sandy loam mix. Plant out in a sunny position, with protection from wind.

CLIMATE Grows in warmer parts of zone 9.

SPECIES *H. pungens* generally grows 60–90 cm (24–36 in), but is often a prostrate or cascading plant. It has small, narrow, bright green leaves and a profusion of delightful, large, pinkish

ABOVE Sometimes difficult to cultivate, *Hemiandra pungens* is worth trying for its delicate pink to mauve flowers.

mauve flowers with bright pink spots on the throat in spring.

Hepatica (fam. Ranunculaceae)
Liverleaf

Found growing wild in woodlands of the northern temperate regions, these hardy, dwarf woodland perennials, which bloom in early spring, are particularly recommended for naturalising in woodland gardens. They look lovely planted in bold, informal drifts. Alternatively grow them on a rock garden.

BELOW A charming woodland plant, *Hepatica transsilvanica* thrives in moist, humus-rich soils. Flowers appear in early spring.

CULTIVATION They like a moist, even alkaline soil, and half-shade. Propagate by division of the roots and from seed sown in trays of sandy compost during fall.

CLIMATE These perennials need a cool, moist climate.

SPECIES *H. americana*, zone 4, is an almost stemless plant, to 15 cm (6 in), with deep lavender blue, pink or white flowers. *H. x media* cultivar 'Ballardi', zone 5, grows to 25 cm (10 in), with large, attractive, bright blue flowers. *H. transsilvanica*, zone 5, 10 cm (4 in) tall, has lavender blue blooms and is also available in a pink form.

Hesperis (fam. Brassicaceae)

This genus of fragrant biennials and perennials is suited to temperate climates. The species *H. matronalis* in particular is cultivated widely in parts of the US, where it has also become naturalized. The narrow foliage is quite unremarkable, though the fragrant blooms are very pretty, resembling those of stocks.

CULTIVATION These plants need well-drained, humus-rich soil and sun or partial shade. Plant in spring or fall, water well in dry weather and fertilize in early spring. Remove spent flower stalks in fall. *Hesperis* species self-sow.

CLIMATE Grows best in mild to cool, moist areas.

SPECIES *H. matronalis*, sweet rocket or Dame's violet, zone 3, is an erect perennial which grows to 1 m (3 ft) high. The white or lilac flowers are very fragrant on summer evenings. *H. tristis*, zone 6, a biennial which grows to 60 cm (24 in), is also very fragrant on summer nights. The flowers may be white, yellowish green, red or purple.

Heterocentron (fam. Melastomataceae)

Originating from mountainous areas of Mexico and Central America, these small, showy shrubs may be erect or prostrate. The bright green leaves are oval in shape and the attractive flowers are brightly colored.

CULTIVATION In frost-prone climates, grow in an intermediate greenhouse or conservatory, or as house plants. Use soil-based potting compost and ensure maximum light, but shade from direct strong sun. For bushy plants, pinch out growing tips. Propagate by division in spring.

CLIMATE At least zone 10.

SPECIES *H. elegans*, Spanish shawl, is a low-growing, evergreen species to 10 cm (4 in), with

BELOW A pretty woodland plant, *Hesperis matronalis* has become naturalized in several parts of the world.

ABOVE Once established, *Heterocentron elegans*, Spanish shawl, densely carpets the ground, rooting down into spaces between brick paving.

oval, mid-green leaves and magenta flowers in summer and fall. It makes a good hanging basket. Under glass, or in frost-free gardens, it makes good groundcover. It is a native of Mexico, and can also be found in Honduras and Guatemala.

Heuchera (fam. Saxifragaceae)
Coral bells

There are 55 species of mostly low-growing perennials in this genus from North America, mainly grown as groundcover. They are also well suited to growing in rockeries or at the front of garden beds. Many form rosettes of growth with foliage that is rather like that of the true geranium. Dainty, bell-like flowers are carried on tall stems high above the leaves. The flowers can be cut for the vase although they will last very much longer on the plant. All species flower in spring or summer.

CULTIVATION Grow in full sun to part shade in light soil enriched with organic matter. Partial shade is best in warm regions. They should be given ample water during dry spring or summer weather. Species can be grown from seed. The rosettes can be lifted and divided every three or four years to increase stock. Cultivars must be divided to maintain their character.

CLIMATE There are species suited to various climatic zones.

SPECIES *H. americana*, zone 4, grows 40–80 cm (16–32 in) high and has coppery green foliage and brownish green flowers. *H. micrantha*, zone 5, grows to 60 cm (24 in) and produces white flowers flushed with pink. *H. sanguinea*, coral bells, zone 3, is most often grown. With crimson flowers, it grows to about 60 cm (24 in). This species has been widely hybridized and there are cultivars with white, pink and deep red flowers. Some of the cultivars have quite pretty, marbled foliage.

Hibbertia (fam. Dilleniaceae)
Guinea flower

These hardy, decorative evergreens are among the best known of the native genera of the eastern coast of Australia. Though mostly shrub-like, there are some climbing species. They have shiny, dark green foliage and open, starry flowers, similar to the buttercup, ranging in color from golden yellow to apricot. A cluster of yellow stamens appears in the center of the five loose petals.

CULTIVATION In climates prone to frost, grow in a cool greenhouse or conservatory. Use a soil-based potting compost and ensure good light but shade from direct sun. Plants like a reasonably humid atmosphere. Prune lightly after flowering. Outdoors grow in well-drained soil with full sun or partial shade. Propagate from

ABOVE The tiny flowers of coral bells are displayed high above the foliage. Here it is used as edging for a rose bed.

ABOVE Twining around a dead tree branch, *Hibbertia dentata* is a light climber with clear yellow flowers.

semi-ripe cuttings in late summer, rooting them with bottom heat.

CLIMATE Zone 10.

SPECIES Not all of the following are available outside their country of origin. *H. astrotricha*, trailing guinea flower, has a spreading or trailing habit, densely packed, fine leaves and bright yellow, spring flowers. It grows to a height of 1 m (3 ft) and a spread of 2 m (6 ft). *H. bracteata* is a low-growing, branching shrub, to 35 cm (14 in), with yellow flowers. *H. dentata* is a low-growing species which sends out twining runners and bears yellow flowers, 2 cm (1 in) across. *H. montana* is a low shrub, with yellow flowers in early spring. *H. obtusifolia*, to 30–90 cm (12–36 in), has small, shiny, grayish green leaves and large, cup-shaped, yellow flowers. *H. procumbens* has a mat-like habit and produces bright yellow flowers. *H. scandens* is a vigorous climbing plant, sometimes growing up to 4 m (13 ft) high, though it can be equally well be trained as a groundcover. It has smooth, dark green foliage and bright golden yellow flowers which are sometimes fragrant. The capsule-shaped fruit has scarlet seeds. *H. stellaris*, from Western Australia, is fairly rare in the wild and very difficult to cultivate. This is a pity as it is one of the most beautiful of the species, having fine, bronze-tipped foliage, and a profusion of lovely, deep apricot to orange flowers which bloom over a long period. *H. stricta* has a prostrate habit and grows to 30 cm (12 in). The yellow flowers have hairy brown bracts.

Hibiscus (fam. Malvaceae)

There are around 200 species in this genus, varying from small, annual and perennial herbs through to woody shrubs and trees. Most come from the tropics, though a few originate from temperate regions of the world. The evergreen Asian hibiscus, *H. rosa-sinensis*, is one of the best known tropical flowers and, with good reason, the state flower of Hawaii, where many hybrids have been raised. *H. syriacus* is a much

ABOVE Cultivars of *Hibiscus syriacus* are grown in European gardens and come in shades of pink, red, blue and white.

hardier, deciduous type and will tolerate more adverse conditions than the evergreen species. Hibiscus flowers are mostly solitary and axillary, though in some species they are borne in sprays. Most blooms last for only one day, but modern hybrids of *H. rosa-sinensis* last much longer, even when cut. The flowers are usually large and showy, with a single stamen, and mostly marked with a deeper color at the base. Many come naturally in double forms and these have several stamens. In fact, the earliest recorded varieties of *H. rosa-sinensis* were doubles, hence the common name, rose of China. The fruit of the hibiscus is a dry capsule, often quite hairy and spiny. The leaves vary greatly according to the species, from the shiny, obtuse, entire leaves of *H. rosa-sinensis* to the deeply divided, hairy leaves of *H. diversifolius*.

CULTIVATION Hibiscus prefer a rich, well-drained, sandy loam, with added animal manure. They like full sun and shelter from cold winds, particularly in cooler districts. During the growing season, they need plenty of water and fertilizer to make sure the blooms are large and many. Regular pruning is necessary to encourage fresh, healthy growth which in turn produces the best blooms. *H. rosa-sinensis* should be reduced by one-third in early spring, in late

ABOVE The large, apricot-orange flowers of the Hawaiian hibiscus 'Surfrider' will continue to appear over many months.

spring for cooler districts; *H. syriacus* and *H. mutabilis* may be pruned back quite hard in winter; *H. moscheutos* needs the old canes removed; and other species should be trimmed after flowering. Hibiscus should not be planted in damp, poorly drained soils as they are prone to attack by *Phytophthora* root rot and collar rot. Insect pests such as aphids, whitefly, mealy bugs and scale insects may attack hibiscus and are particularly troublesome under glass. Before spraying, check that the chemical is suitable for hibiscus. Propagate from seed or from cuttings. Many annual and perennial species are grown from fresh, viable seed sown in spring. Some hibiscus have been found to germinate more readily if their seed is nicked with a razor blade. Sow seed in a commercial seed-raising mix, or sand and peat. Increase *H. mutabilis* from hardwood cuttings taken in winter; *H. syriacus* from hardwood cuttings taken in winter or from firm tip cuttings in summer; and *H. rosa-sinensis* from hardwood cuttings, about 15 cm (6 in) long, taken in late winter or early spring, or from semi-hardwood in summer or fall. Mild bottom heat can improve results. Some hybrids of *H. rosa-sinensis* are better if grafted by wedge or cleft graft onto rootstocks, such as *H. arnottianus* or *H. rosa-sinensis* cultivar 'Ruth Wilcox', in spring. Strike cuttings in a mixture of coarse, washed river sand and coir peat, or perlite and coir peat. Hormone powder will help root formation.

CLIMATE There are species of hibiscus suited to various climatic zones, from cold and cool to subtropical and tropical climates. In much of the US, *H. syriacus* is the usual garden plant and most others need to be grown under glass in an intermediate to warm greenhouse or conservatory.

SPECIES Some of the following species are unlikely to be available outside their native countries. *H. arnottianus*, zone 10, from Hawaii, is an evergreen shrub or small tree, to 6 m (20 ft), with ovate, entire, mid-green leaves and delicate, white, fragrant flowers with a central, red staminal column. *H. diversifolius*, zone 10, from Africa, Australia and the Pacific Islands, is an open, spreading shrub, to 3 m (10 ft), with deeply lobed, prickly leaves and very pale yellow flowers, to 18 cm (7 in) across, with purple centers. *H. heterophyllus*, native rosella, zone 10, is a free-flowering Australian native. A tall, evergreen shrub, to 6 m (20 ft), it has simple or divided leaves and mostly white to pale pink flowers, to 12 cm (5 in) across, with maroon centers. Yellow variations, with red centers, also occur. *H. insularis*, zone 10, from Norfolk Island, is a tall, evergreen, spreading shrub, to 4 m (13 ft), forming a tangle of woody stems at the base. It has small, entire leaves and pale cream to soft lemon flowers, 10 cm (4 in) across, fading to a dull pink. The center of the flowers is maroon. *H. moscheutos*, swamp rose mallow, zone 5, from south-eastern and eastern United States, is an herbaceous perennial which grows to 2.5 m (8 ft). It has ovate leaves and pink or rose flowers. The flamboyant 'Southern Belle' hybrids produce huge flowers, to 35 cm (14 in) across, in many colors, including red, white, lavender and pink. *H. mutabilis*, cotton rose or confederate rose mallow, zone 8, from China, may be a multi-branched shrub or small, deciduous tree, to 4 m (13 ft), with large, lobed leaves, hairy on the undersides, and double or single, white, fall flowers, 18 cm (7 in) across, turning to deep pink. *H. rosa-sinensis*, rose of

China, Chinese hibiscus or Hawaiian hibiscus, zone 9, is an evergreen shrub or small tree, highly valued for its colorful flowers which are produced over a very long period. The many hybrids of this species have greatly increased the color range as well as the size and quality of the blooms. The colors now range through reds, oranges, yellows, whites, pinks, browns and lavenders, as well as multi-colors, and are produced in single, semi-double and double flowers up to 30 cm (12 in) across. In warm temperate zones they flower from late spring to late fall, and in the tropics they produce blooms all year round. In cooler weather, the blooms will become smaller and deeper in color and sometimes double blooms will revert to single. The red flowers of *H. rosa-sinensis* yield a dye. Some cultivars tend to be considerably hardier than others, but most are frost-tender. The taller growing cultivars are used for street plantings, hedges and windbreaks; the lower growing types are used as specimens, low hedges or as container plants. Some may be espaliered and others can be grown as standards. A very adaptable plant, *H. rosa-sinensis* can tolerate salt air but not front-line coastal exposure. Hundreds of cultivars are available, and more are being introduced all the time. *H. sabdariffa*, Jamaican sorrel or rosella, zone 10, is a tropical annual or biennial, to 2 m (6 ft), with three-lobed leaves and small, yellow flowers. The calyx of the flower is used in jams and jellies. *H. schizopetalus*, zone 10, from tropical eastern Africa, is an evergreen shrub, to 4 m (13 ft), with rounded, toothed, deep green leaves and delicate red or orange-red flowers, suspended on long stems. The petals are finely cut and recurved, and the staminal column hangs well below the flower. *H. syriacus*, shrub althaea or rose of sharon, zone 5, is a beautiful, free-flowering, deciduous shrub or small tree, 3–5 m (10–16 ft) high, originally from China. A hardy species, it is useful for temperate-climate gardens as it flowers profusely from late summer into fall. Its leaves take various forms, but are usually three-lobed or toothed. Its cultivars come in cooler colors like blue, pink, purple and white, and may be single or double and up to 16 cm (6 in) across. The petal base is generally blotched with red or maroon. *H. tiliaceus*, cottonwood tree, zone 10, is a tropical, spreading, evergreen tree, to 12 m (40 ft), with large, heart-shaped, soft green leaves and yellow flowers, to 10 cm (4 in) across, with crimson centers, through the year.

BELOW There are many cultivars of *Hibiscus rosa-sinensis*, the Hawaiian hibiscus, which needs to be grown under glass in frosty climates.

Hicksbeachia (fam. Proteaceae)
Monkey nut

Of these two species of trees native to north and east Australia, only one is in cultivation. However, it is unlikely to be available in the US.

CULTIVATION In frost-prone climates, grow as a young foliage plant in an intermediate greenhouse or conservatory. It adapts well to pot culture. Use soil-based potting compost and water well in the growing period. Outdoors it needs well drained, humus-rich soil and a sunny spot.

CLIMATE Zone 10.

ABOVE The red nuts of *Hicksbeachia pinnatifolia* are edible but unlikely to be produced in small pot plants under glass.

ABOVE In this mass planting of showy *Hippeastrum* hybrids the red and white cultivar breaks up the mass of plain red blooms.

SPECIES *H. pinnatifolia*, monkey nut, is native to rainforests of eastern Australia. Growing to 10 m (33 ft), it has handsome, large, lobed leaves and sprays of creamy yellow flowers in summer. These are followed by red, oval-shaped, edible 'nuts'.

Hippeastrum (fam. Amaryllidaceae)

These magnificent, bulbous plants from tropical America are generally grown in pots and often grown on windowsills. The individual, trumpet-shaped blooms may be as much as 20 cm (8 in) across and are quite spectacular. They appear on tall, straight stems 30–60 cm (12–24 in) long, in winter and spring before the strap-like, mid-green leaves.

CULTIVATION Grow in a warm greenhouse or conservatory, or in a warm room in the home. Plant bulbs in fall, the top third exposed. Use soil-based potting compost. These bulbs need maximum light but shade from direct strong sun. Water normally when in growth but gradually reduce after flowering and dry off when plants become dormant. Plants flower best when pot bound so do not pot on until essential. Propagate from offsets in fall.

CLIMATE Zone 10.

SPECIES *H. aulicum*, to 60 cm (24 in), has crimson or purple flowers with green throats. *H. pratense* (now correctly called *Rhodophiala pratensis*) grows to 40 cm (16 in), producing bright red or purple-violet flowers. *H. psittacinum* has green and scarlet-striped flowers. *H. puniceum*, Barbados lily, to 45 cm (18 in), has bright red flowers with a green base. *H. reginae*, to 60 cm (24 in), has red and white flowers with greenish white throats. *H. reticulatum*, to 30 cm (12 in), has bright reddish mauve flowers with deeper markings. *H. striatum*, to 30 cm (12 in), has green and crimson flowers. Hybrids come in pure white, salmon and dark red, and in a variety of different-colored stripes.

Hoheria (fam. Malvaceae)
Lacebark

Originally from New Zealand, this small genus comprises deciduous and evergreen shrubs and trees with a slender, upright habit. They have alternate, simple leaves, often lobed when young, but are mostly grown for their attractive, terminal sprays of delicate, fragrant flowers. These lovely, summer-flowering ornamentals generally develop first as shrubs, becoming tree-like when adult, although they may still bear some juvenile leaves. Some species have been used medicinally by the Maori peoples.

CULTIVATION Lacebarks prefer deep, well-drained soil, enriched with organic matter, and a sheltered position. Propagate from cuttings of half-ripe shoots taken in summer or by layering. Plants grown from seed can vary considerably.

CLIMATE Zone 8.

SPECIES *H. angustifolia* grows into a tree of about 9 m (30 ft) tall, with clustered leaves, narrowly oval to sharply pointed, and sprays of white flowers. It is evergreen. *H. lyallii*, lacebark, is a deciduous, large shrub or small tree, 7–9 m (23–30 ft) tall. The young, oval leaves and branches are pubescent and fragrant, white flowers grow singly or in clusters. The common name is derived from the thick, fibrous bark. *H. populnea*, a mostly evergreen tree, to 9 m (30 ft), is quite smooth, with glossy, toothed, leathery leaves. The white flowers appear in clusters in late summer and early fall. The timber is used for furniture-making, the bark for ropes and cords. *H. sexstylosa*, ribbonwood, is a small tree, to 7 m (23 ft), similar to *H. populnea*, but with narrow, oval to lance-shaped leaves. Small clusters of sweetly scented, white flowers are borne profusely in late summer and fall.

BELOW *Hoheria iyallii* is considered one of New Zealand's most beautiful trees. Flowers are borne in profusion in summer.

Holmskioldia (fam. Verbenaceae)

Chinese hat plant

Native to warm, coastal areas of India, Madagascar and Africa, these shrubs are valued for their exotic red flowers and rapid growth.

CULTIVATION Except in tropical climates, grow in a warm greenhouse or conservatory, in pots or soil bed. Use soil-based potting compost for containers. Shade from direct sun but ensure good light. Provide supports for the stems. Prune after flowering to keep plant within bounds. Propagate from semi-ripe cuttings in late summer. They need bottom heat to root.

CLIMATE Tropical climates only.

SPECIES *H. sanguinea* is a vigorous, scrambling, evergreen shrub, growing to 3.5 m (11 ft) or more, and cultivated mostly for its clusters of quite unique flowers, formed from a narrow, red tube backed by a spreading, red calyx. The long, arching canes make it perfect for espaliering. There is also a yellow-flowered form available.

Homalocladium (fam. Polygonaceae)

This unusual, tropical evergreen shrub from the Solomon Islands is usually leafless when in

BELOW Regular pruning after flowering is needed to keep *Holmskioldia sanguinea* compact and flowering to its potential.

flower. It has stalkless clusters of small, greenish flowers and triangular-shaped, hard, dry fruits enclosed by a large, deep reddish purple calyx. This plant is grown for its foliage, rather than its flowers, which are not showy.

CULTIVATION Grow in a warm greenhouse or conservatory, or as a house plant, in frost-prone climates. It is unlikely to flower when pot grown. Use soil-based potting compost and provide good light, but shade from strong sun. Propagate from cuttings (stem sections) in summer, in a heated propagating case.

CLIMATE At least zone 10.

SPECIES *H. platycladum*, centipede or tapeworm plant, or ribbon bush, grows 2–3 m (6–10 ft) in cultivation but twice as tall in its habitat. It produces flat, jointed stems, the tiny greenish flowers appearing in clusters at alternate joints.

ABOVE *Homalocladium platycladum* is a most curious-looking, tropical shrub which can be grown as a house plant.

Horseradish

(*Armoracia rusticana*, fam. Brassicaceae)

This perennial herb belongs to the mustard family and has a long history of medicinal use. It forms a rosette of large, tough, toothed leaves, similar to spinach, and a thick, white taproot which is ground and used for culinary purposes, or dried and used in herbal remedies.

ABOVE Horseradish is easy to cultivate in almost any soil that is deep enough to allow good roots to develop.

Horseradish, with its sharp taste, is a delicious accompaniment to roast beef.

CULTIVATION Propagate from root cuttings, planted out in spring, about 30 cm (12 in) apart, in a moist, moderately rich soil. Dig the soil to a depth of about 60 cm (24 in) before planting. If the subsoil is very heavy, mix with coarse sand, incorporating organic matter and a supplement of blood, fish and bone. Water well and watch for snails. Allow only one strong shoot to grow. Harvest the root each year, or it will become woody and the plant will tend to become invasive.

CLIMATE Zone 5.

Hosta (fam. Hostaceae)
Plantain lily

There are around 40 species in this genus of hardy, herbaceous perennials, mostly native to Japan, with a few species from China and Korea. They are mainly grown for their clumps of large, decorative leaves which come in a variety of greens and blue-greens, sometimes with green, silver or gold markings. The sprays of nodding, funnel-shaped, lily-like flowers in blue, lilac, violet or white are borne on long stems, mostly high above the leaves, in summer. They look very pretty planted around water features or under trees. An extensive range of lovely cultivars is available.

CULTIVATION Plantain lilies are easy to grow, provided they have a moist, shady spot and rich soil. They can also be grown in tubs and pots if well watered. Grown in clumps, they help discourage weeds from becoming established. Add well-rotted manure and peat to the soil and mulch each spring with compost or manure. Plant in the fall or spring and water well during dry weather. Propagate by division of clumps in late winter or early spring. The species may be grown from seed but the cultivars must be divided.

CLIMATE Zone 6, or zone 5 if the root area is heavily mulched.

SPECIES *H. fortunei* has broad, green leaves and pale lilac flowers. The variety albopicta has yellowish white leaves, edged with green and darkening with maturity; the form aurea has yellow leaves which turn light green in summer; the variety aureomarginata has heart-shaped, deep green leaves, edged yellow. *H. lancifolia* grows to 60 cm (24 in), with narrow, dark green leaves and violet flowers which fade with age. It seldom sets seed. *H. plantaginea*, to 65 cm (26 in), has large, shiny, green leaves and fragrant, white flowers in fall. *H. plantaginea* var. *japonica* has more elongated leaves and flowers. *H. rectifolia*, to about 1 m (3 ft), has 30 cm (12 in) long leaves and produces cobalt blue or violet, bell-shaped flowers. *H. sieboldiana* var. *elegans*, to 75 cm (30 in), has grayish blue leaves and dense sprays of pale lilac flowers borne on stems usually shorter than the foliage. *H. sieboldii*, to 30 cm (12 in) high, has leaves edged in white or yellowish white and violet flowers. *H. undulata* var. *undulata*, to 90 cm (36 in) has wavy-edged leaves with a central white band and pale lavender flowers borne in dense clusters. The variety *univitatta* also has leaves bearing a central white band. *H. ventricosa*, to 1 m (3 ft), has long, heart-shaped, green leaves and deep violet flowers with darker veins.

Hovea (fam. Papilionaceae)

Blue or purple pea, rusty pod

Occurring both in western and eastern Australia, this genus comprises around 12 species of shrubs which are covered with masses of beautiful, blue pea-flowers in spring. Often found in forests as undershrubs, few are

BELOW In early spring, *Hovea longifolia* puts on a wonderful show of color, but the flowering period is all too short.

ABOVE Although grown primarily for foliage, hostas do have pretty flowers that stand above the leaves.

as yet cultivated in home gardens. They have oval-shaped leaves, sometimes hairy on the undersides.

CULTIVATION Hoveas like protection and do best in moist, partly shaded spots. They prefer a fairly deep, rich, sandy loam which has been mulched. In areas with hard frosts grow in a cool greenhouse or conservatory, in pots of soil-based compost. Provide airy, slightly humid conditions and good light. Propagate from seed which germinates easily if soaked in hot water overnight, then nicked carefully with a blade along the side. Plant in a 3:1 mix of coarse sand and peat.

CLIMATE Zone 9.

SPECIES Not all are available outside Australia. *H. acutifolia* is an erect, bushy shrub, to 1.2 m (4 ft), with oval, light green leaves, velvety underneath, and clusters of rich purple flowers from late winter to early spring. *H. elliptica* is a hardy species, to 2.5 m (8 ft), with an arched, branching habit. It is attractive in spring when covered with pretty, blue flowers. *H. hetero-phylla* is a dwarf species to 30 cm (12 in). It has a trailing habit and clusters of mostly lilac flowers. *H. lanceolata* is a lovely, quite hardy shrub, to 2 m (6 ft), mostly found in sheltered valleys. The flowers are lilac through to purple. *H. pungens*, to about 1 m (3 ft), is a small shrub with spiky leaves and violet flowers, marked with white at the base.

Hovenia (fam. Rhamnaceae)
Japanese raisin tree

There are only two species of trees in this genus from China and Japan, both of which are decid-uous. One is cultivated for its handsome foliage and sweet, edible fruit, formed by the base of the flower stem. The fruits are also used medic-inally and the timber is valued commercially.

CULTIVATION These trees are best grown in a shel-tered position, in well-drained soil rich in organic matter. Pruning is generally unneces-

ABOVE The curious-looking fruit of *Hovenia dulcis* is sweet and tasty. The tree canopy is light and fairly open.

sary. Propagate from seed sown in spring or from semi-ripe cuttings in late summer to early fall.

CLIMATE Zone 6.

SPECIES *H. dulcis*, Japanese raisin tree, is decid-uous and grows 10–15 m (33–50 ft) tall. The branches form an open, lacy effect and the broad leaves have finely serrated margins. These color yellow in fall. Cream flowers appear in early summer through to midsummer. The caramel brown fruits are formed from the thick-ened peduncle (flower stalk) and ripen in fall to early winter. They are valued as confectionery in Japan.

Howea (fam. Arecaceae)
Sentry palm

This genus comprises only two species, both from Lord Howe Island. The two species were first named *Kentia* and they have since been commonly known by that name. Both are graceful palms with arching feathered leaves and quite distinctive, long, smooth stalks. The inflorescence is also rather uncommon, consist-ing either of a simple, unbranched spike of light brown or green flowers, depending on whether it is a male or female plant, or branched spikes. The flowers are followed by fruits containing a large, very hard seed covered with thin, fibrous flesh. The traditional potted palms of hotel lobbies and palm courts were howeas for, apart from their elegance, they can tolerate less light and lower temperatures than many other palms, and are reasonably disease-free. They are slow growing and can be left in the same containers for years. Given appropriate conditions, they will also grow and seed most successfully outdoors. Growing these palms is, in fact, a major industry on Lord Howe Island.

CULTIVATION In frost-prone climates, grow these palms in a warm greenhouse or conservatory, or as house plants. They prefer soil-based potting compost enriched with shredded bark. Provide maximum light but shade from direct sun, and a humid atmosphere. Pot on only every few years, and in the interim years, topdress with fresh compost in the spring. Liquid feed monthly during the growing season. Water normally in the growing season but keep the compost only slightly moist in winter. These palms are likely to be attacked by scale insects and red spider mites, which need to be kept under control. Outdoors grow in well-drained soil with partial shade or full sun. Propagate from seed sown as soon as it has ripened and germinate it in a temperature of 26°C (79° F).

BELOW In its native Lord Howe Island, Howea belmoreana, sentry or curley palm, grows in large, dense colonies.

CLIMATE Warmest parts of zone 9, or zone 10.

SPECIES *H. belmoreana*, sentry palm or curly palm, is the less commonly grown species. Its closely ringed trunk rarely exceeds 6 m (20 ft) in height and about 15 cm (6 in) in diameter. The inflorescence is a single spike and the shiny, green fruits ripen to a grayish green color. *H. forsteriana*, Kentia palm or thatch-leaf palm, is widely grown both indoors and outdoors in Australasia, Europe and the United States. It has a slender trunk, to about 12 m (40 ft). The inflorescences are branching spikes and the fruits ripen from yellow to orange, to a dull, deep red.

Hoya (fam. Asclepiadaceae)

Most of the 200 or so species of this genus of succulents are climbers. They have a broad distribution from China and India, through Malaysia and Australia, to the islands of the South Pacific. Hoyas have fleshy, leathery, sometimes shiny leaves and clusters of fragrant, star-shaped flowers in white, cream, yellow, pink or red in spring to summer.

CULTIVATION In frost-prone climates, hoyas are grown in a warm greenhouse or conservatory, except for *H. carnosa*, which is best in cool conditions. Grow in pots of soil-based potting compost, enriched with shredded bark and leaf mould. Plants need good light but should be

ABOVE The pink, waxy buds of *Hoya carnosa* look quite artificial. Plants thrive when their roots are confined.

shaded from direct sun, and they like a humid atmosphere. The climbers will need support of some kind. Climbers can be lightly pruned after flowering. Propagate from semi-ripe cuttings in summer, rooting them in a heated propagating case, or by layering in spring.

CLIMATE Subtropical to tropical; at least zone 10.

SPECIES *H. australis*, wax plant, from Queensland and Fiji, has slender, twining stems, pairs of thick, shiny, oval, dark green leaves, 5–8 cm (2–3 in) long, and small, white flowers with red centers. *H. carnosa*, the most commonly grown species, is a native of China and India. A twining species, it has thick, fleshy leaves, to 9 cm (3½ in) long, and dense clusters of long-lasting, white or pale pink flowers with pinkish red centers. Variegated leaf forms are available. *H. lanceolata* subsp. *bella*, from India, is a shrubby species, with thin, drooping branches, up to 45 cm (18 in) long, and pairs of small, pale green, elongated, heart-shaped leaves. The clusters of small, waxy, white flowers, with purplish pink centers, last about a week. *H. macgillivrayi*, from the very north of eastern Australia, has striking large red flowers, to 6 cm (2½ in) across, in umbels of six to ten flowers. *H. rubida*, coming from the same area, has bright green, ovate leaves, to 12 cm (5 in) long, and waxy, dark red flowers, to 4 cm (1½ in) across. The fruit is long and thick.

Humulus (fam. Cannabaceae)
Hops

The two or three species of this genus of hardy, twining perennials are found in temperate regions of the northern hemisphere. These fast-growing plants have rough stems, broad leaves, small unisexual flowers and small, dry fruit with one seed. Hops are often seen climbing walls, balconies or pergolas, and if trained along wire or fences they can provide an effective windbreak. However, they are mostly associated with the production of beer which is made from the bitter resin of the mature female flower of *H. lupulus*.

ABOVE The golden form of *Humulus lupulus* is a very vigorous climber for cool climates. It needs a sturdy pergola or arch for support.

CULTIVATION Hops will grow well in almost any type of soil, but do best in a very rich soil. They prefer a temperate climate and require frequent watering during dry summers. Propagate from seed in spring germinated at 18°C (64°F), or from semi-ripe cuttings in summer, with basal heat.

CLIMATE Zone 5.

SPECIES *H. japonicus*, Japanese hops, from eastern Asia, is usually treated as an annual and grown from seed. It is a decorative plant, which grows to 4 m (13 ft), with long, sawtoothed, pale green leaves. Cultivar 'Variegatus' has foliage streaked and blotched with white. *H. lupulus*, common hops, from the temperate regions of Europe, has been introduced into many other areas where it is used purely for commercial beer production. It grows 6–9 m (20–30 ft) high and has long, serrated leaves and quite spiky fruits. The cultivar 'Aureus' is very popular and widely grown for its highly attractive golden foliage.

Hyacinthoides (fam. Hyacinthaceae)
Bluebell

These bulbous plants from Europe and north-western Africa are grown around the world and look very pretty in borders or rock gardens. They are probably seen at their best when allowed to naturalize under deciduous trees. They have long leaves growing from the base and attractively perfumed blue, white and pink, bell-shaped, spring flowers. The blue is the most commonly seen and is the most vigorous grower.

CULTIVATION Bluebells grow best in partial shade in a well-drained soil in a natural setting. Plant bulbs 10 cm (4 in) deep in fall. Propagate by division of the bulbs as the clumps become larger. Water regularly while the plants are in active growth.

CLIMATE Moist and cool. Zone 5.

SPECIES *H. hispanicus* (syn. *Endymion hispanicus*), Spanish bluebell, is the most widely grown species in warm to mild areas. It has strap-like leaves that may reach 50 cm (20 in) long and blue flowers. There are cultivars with white or pink flowers, while 'Excelsior' has pale violet flowers striped in blue. *H. non-scripta* (syn. *Endymion non-scriptus*), English bluebell, flowers right through the spring and, in cool climates, into the early summer. It has the same strappy, green foliage to about 40 cm (16 in) long, and produces nodding, blue-violet flowers. Cultivars are available with pink or white flowers.

ABOVE Bluebells are most appealing when allowed to naturalize, but this may be difficult to achieve in small gardens.

Hyacinthus (fam. Hyacinthaceae)
Hyacinth

Native to western and central Asia, this genus of bulbs contains only three species, but it is the cultivars of *Hyacinthus orientalis* that are grown by gardeners. They are valued for their often highly fragrant flowers which are produced in spring. As well as being grown in spring bedding schemes, they are also suited to patio containers, and growing in bowls indoors for winter or spring flowering.

CULTIVATION In the garden, hyacinths need a deep, reasonably fertile, well-drained soil in a position exposed to full sun or partial shade. Plant the bulbs in fall, 10 cm (4 in) deep and about 10 cm (4 in) apart. For winter blooms indoors, plant in bowls of soilless potting compost with the tops of the bulbs just visible above the compost, again in fall. It is possible to buy specially prepared hyacinth bulbs which flower early in winter, generally around Christmas time. After planting, keep the bowls of bulbs in a cool, completely dark place. After

BELOW Hyacinths are perennial favorites for their pretty appearance and lovely, light perfume.

six to eight weeks, when the bulbs have rooted, the pots should be kept at a room temperature of about 10°C (50°F). When the plants have flowered, the bulbs can then be planted out in garden beds. Bulbs can also be grown in water or moist, bulb fiber in specially designed, glass bowls. These bowls should be kept in a cool, dark place for about eight weeks until the roots have formed. They can then be placed in a reasonably light position in a greenhouse or warm room at about 18°–21°C (64°–70°F). After they have bloomed once, the bulbs can be planted out. Hyacinths forced indoors are unlikely to flower the following year. Propagate the species from seed sown in light soil in boxes which should be kept in a cold frame. It takes at least three years for the seedlings to come to flower. Hyacinths can also be propagated from bulblets or offsets removed from the old bulbs. These are best planted in open beds in the fall and take two to three years to bloom. Production of bulblets can be induced by scooping out a saucer-shaped depression in the bottom of a mature bulb so that about one-third or more of the bulb is removed. Place the wounded bulb in a dry, shady spot to dry the wounded area completely before planting it out. Plant in a free-draining, sandy loam and do not overwater.

CLIMATE Zone 7.

SPECIES *H. orientalis*, the common hyacinth, from Turkey, Syria and the Lebanon, is a favorite with gardeners. It grows 15–30 cm (6–12 in) high, with dense spikes of very fragrant, funnel-shaped flowers, which vary widely in color, and glossy, green, strap-like foliage. Most of the larger varieties have been raised from this species which is still cultivated in southern France as a source of perfume. Cultivars of *H. orientalis* are available in white, pale blue, deep blue, pink, red and yellow flowers.

Hydrangea (fam. Hydrangeaceae)

There are around 20 species in this genus of lush, showy, evergreen or deciduous shrubs

ABOVE A single shrub of *Hydrangea macrophylla* displays a range of colors. Flowers go through pretty shades as they age.

from temperate Asia and North America. They are grown for their spectacular, domed or flat flower clusters which consist of minute flowers surrounded by colored bracts which in the original species were red, pink, white or blue. They mostly flower in midsummer. Many hybrids are now available and these come in rich reds, soft and deep pinks, and purplish blues. They are generally less vigorous than the original species. Hydrangeas range in height from shrubs of 1 m (3 ft) tall to climbers which reach 18 m (60 ft). Most have large, oval leaves with serrated edges. Some are prolific bloomers. Both sterile and fertile florets are sometimes found on the one flower head, while flower heads of many of the cultivated forms are made up of mostly sterile florets. Hydrangeas come with double, semi-double, or serrated bracts. They can be grown indoors or outdoors.

CULTIVATION Hydrangeas need a rich, well-drained, but moisture-retentive soil, with added leaf mould, cow manure, peat moss or compost. They can be grown in full sun or partial shade but need protection from cold winds. They can grow for many years, provided they are pruned regularly and generally cared for. To produce blue or purple bracts from pinkish varieties, aluminium sulphate or other commercial preparations may be added monthly to acidify the soil. An annual addition of lime to the soil will tend to favor the production of pink or red tones. Weather conditions may affect flower color. Most newer hybrids are more color stable than the older types. Propagate from hardwood cuttings, 25 cm (10 in) long, planted singly in sandy soil in a sheltered position, in late fall. They will be well rooted by the fall of the following year. Some species can also be propagated by layering or by separating suckers. They can also be struck from tip cuttings during the growing season.

CLIMATE There are species suited to various climatic zones.

SPECIES *H. anomala* subsp. *petiolaris* is the climbing hydrangea, zone 5, a deciduous plant reaching at least 15 m (50 ft) and clinging to flat surfaces by means of aerial roots. Its flat heads of white flowers appear in summer. *H. arborescens*, zone 3, a rounded shrub, to 2.5 m (8 ft), has domed white flowers. Cultivar 'Grandiflora' has clustered, sterile flowers. *H. aspera*, zone 7, from southern and eastern Asia, is a much-branched, deciduous shrub, to 2 m (6 ft), with white, sterile flowers. Subspecies *sargentiana* is a beautiful, upright, deciduous shrub which grows to a height and spread of 3 m (10 ft). It has velvety, oblong, tapered leaves and late-flowering, blue to purple, usually fertile flowers. *H. heteromalla*, zone 6, a branching shrub, to 2 m (6 ft) or more, has both fertile and sterile white flowers. *H. macrophylla*, common hydrangea, from Japan, zone 5, is a deciduous shrub of neat, rounded habit, up to 2 m (6 ft) in height. It has flat heads of blue or pink flowers in mid to late summer. However, it is the many cultivars that are grown by gardeners. There are two groups of cultivars: the *Hortensias* or mophead hydrangeas, with large ball-shaped flower heads, consisting of sterile flowers, and the *Lacecaps*, with flat heads of fertile flowers, surrounded by large sterile flowers. There are many to choose from in each group. Flower colors may be blue, pink, red or white, or combinations. *H. paniculata*, zone 3, from China and Japan, is a deciduous shrub or small tree, to 7 m (20 ft), with yellowish white, conical flowers. Cultivar 'Grandiflora', with large, showy, white flowers, is most commonly grown. *H. quercifolia*, zone 5, from North America, is a bushy, deciduous shrub, to 2 m (6 ft), and has white flower cones, to 25 cm (10 in) long, and lobed leaves coloring attractively in fall.

Hymenocallis (fam. Amaryllidaceae)
Spider lily

This genus of summer-flowering bulbous plants, previously known as *Ismene*, has wonderfully exotic, spider-like flowers on quite tall stems. The white or yellow, sweetly scented flowers are quite large, about 10 cm (4 in) across. The bright green leaves are broad and strap-like. There are around 40 species, all from the West Indies and Andes region of South America.

CULTIVATION In frost-prone climates, grow the very tender species in a warm greenhouse, but grow the hardier species like *H. narcissiflora* in a cool greenhouse. Plant bulbs in fall with the top third exposed. Grow in pots of well-drained, soil-based potting compost. While dormant, evergreen species should be kept just moist, but deciduous species completely dry.

BELOW Massed groupings of *Hymenocallis* species are lovely in flower but the bright, bold foliage is also a significant feature.

Outdoors, grow in well-drained soil in full sun. Protect from winter rains. Propagate from seed or offsets.

CLIMATE Zone 10 for most species.

SPECIES *H. caribaea*, from the West Indies, grows to 70 cm (28 in) and produces fragrant, white flowers. *H. x festalis* is a lovely hybrid, with pure white, deliciously perfumed flowers. *H. littoralis* grows to 75 cm (30 in), with numerous long leaves and unusual, pure white flowers. *H. x macrostephana*, zone 9, a hybrid, has up to eight white, green-tubed flowers on each stem. *H. narcissiflora*, sacred lily of the Incas, Peruvian daffodil or basket flower, zone 9, tolerates light frost. It grows to 60 cm (24 in) and bears up to five scented, white flowers. *H. speciosa*, from the West Indies, has very fragrant, white flowers.

Hymenosporum (fam. Pittosporaceae)

Australian frangipani

The only species of this genus from the rainforests of tropical Australia is grown for its attractive, large, creamish yellow flowers and layered branching habit. In frost-prone climates, it makes a good subject for the intermediate conservatory, while outdoors, in the right climate, it can be planted as a specimen tree.

BELOW The scented flowers of *Hymenosporum flavum* range from cream through rich cream to yellow with age.

CULTIVATION Under glass, grow Australian frangipani in soil-based potting compost, with maximum light but shade from direct sun, and in airy conditions. Outdoors, a position in full sun is needed, plus well-drained soil containing plenty of humus. Propagate from seed in spring or semi-ripe cuttings in summer, both with basal warmth.

CLIMATE Warmer parts of zone 9.

SPECIES *H. flavum*, to 15 m (50 ft), is a fast-growing evergreen with glossy, bright green leaves. This tree is splendid in early summer with clusters of fragrant, tubular, cream flowers maturing to a rich yellow. These are followed by flat seed pods.

Hyophorbe (fam. Arecaceae)

Bottle palm

This genus of slow-growing feather palms is almost extinct in its native Mascarene Islands, but two of the species have been fairly widely cultivated in tropical regions of the world. They are used for coastal planting as they tolerate salt-laden winds. They are unusual, having short, stout trunks and neat crowns of only a few arching leaves. The inflorescences are borne at various times of the year, the buds enveloped by pointed, green bracts.

CULTIVATION In frost-prone climates, grow in a warm conservatory or greenhouse, in pots or tubs of soil-based potting compost. Provide maximum light, but shade from direct sun, and a humid atmosphere. Propagate from seed in spring, germinated at 27°C (81°F).

CLIMATE At least zone 10.

SPECIES *H. lagenicaulis*, bottle palm, has a gray, swollen trunk, to 70 cm (28 in) in diameter, but total height rarely exceeds 3 m (10 ft). The crown has only a few leaves, up to 1.5 m (5 ft) long, with two regular rows of leaflets pointing upwards. The dark fronds have a twist about half-way along their length. *H. verschaf-*

ABOVE The swollen trunks of *Hyophorbe lagenicaulis* make an impact on the tropical landscape and would be equally impressive under glass.

feltii, spindle palm, from Rodriguez, grows to 6 m (20 ft). The trunk, its middle diameter around 40 cm (28 in), tapers towards the top. The crown has five to ten leaves, up to 1.5 m (5 ft) long, with softer, less regularly placed leaflets.

Hypericum (fam. Clusiaceae)
St John's wort

There are over 400 species of annuals, perennials and shrubs in this genus which is endemic to temperate regions of the northern hemisphere. Many hybrids have also been developed. They range from large, spreading or arching shrubs to compact subshrubs to groundcovers. The foliage of shrubs and subshrubs is usually evergreen and often veined or dotted with black. The attractive, five-petalled flowers have masses of stamens at the center and come in various shades of yellow. They flower for much of the year. Most species are vigorous growers and are used in borders, rock gardens and mixed shrub plantings, or as groundcover.

CULTIVATION Plant in well-drained soil in a sunny position, though some, like *H. calycinum*, do better in shade. Some need the protection of a wall or fence. Most require little pruning, while some benefit from pruning in early spring. The method of propagation depends on the species and may be from seed, from cuttings struck in sandy soil in a cold frame, or by division or from suckers.

CLIMATE There are species suited to various climatic zones.

SPECIES *H. calycinum*, rose of Sharon or Aaron's beard, zone 6, a shrub to 60 cm (2 ft), has creeping stems and gold-yellow flowers, 5 cm (2 in) across. *H. forresti* (syn. *H. patulum* var. *forresti*), zone 5, is a shrub, to about 1 m (3 ft) high, suitable for very cold areas. *H. x inodorum*, zone 8, is an arching shrub of 1.5 m (5 ft), has fragrant leaves and flowers. *H. monogynum*, zone 9, a spreading, semi-evergreen shrub, grows to 1 m (3 ft) tall. *H. x moseranum* (*H. calycinum x H. patulum*), zone 7, an evergreen shrub, grows 30–60 cm (12–24 in) tall, with wide, saucer-shaped flowers. *H. olympicum*, zone 6, is either an upright or trailing shrub, to 25 cm (10 in). *H. patulum*, zone 6, an upright, evergreen shrub, with golden yellow flowers, grows to a height and spread of 1.5 m (5 ft). *H. perforatum*, known as perforate St John's wort, zone 3, is a troublesome weed, declared noxious in some coun-

ABOVE The cupped, golden flowers on this cultivar of *Hypericum patulum* are very clear against the dark foliage.

tries. *H. prolificum*, zone 4, is an evergreen shrub, to 2 m (6 ft), with small flowers.

Hypocalymma (fam. Myrtaceae)

These Western Australian shrubs are quite beautiful and make delightful garden ornamentals in warm climates, or attractive conservatory specimens in cooler areas. They flower profusely in colors ranging from white and shades of pink to cream and yellow. *Hypocalymmas* produce good cut flowers. Native habitats vary greatly so species should be selected to suit local conditions.

CULTIVATION All species need to be grown in well-drained soil. Most prefer shade in the hottest part of the day and dappled shade at other times. Under glass, grow in cool, airy conditions, in pots of soil-based potting compost, with extra grit added. Ensure plants receive maximum light, but shade them from direct strong sun. Propagate from seed in spring (do not cover seeds with compost) or from semi-ripe cuttings in late summer, both with basal warmth.

CLIMATE Warmer parts of zone 9.

ABOVE Arching stems on *Hypocalymma angustifolium* carry their small flowers neatly spaced. They flower in spring and summer.

SPECIES *H. angustifolium* is a hardy, spreading shrub, to 1 m (3 ft) tall, with fine foliage and deep pink flowers in spring and summer. It tolerates wet, swampy conditions. *H. cordifolium*, a spreading shrub, to 1 m (3 ft), has white spring flowers. The young growth is a reddish color, turning to light green as it matures. It tolerates poor drainage, but needs ample water in summer. Semi-shade is best. *H. robustum*, Swan River myrtle, to 60 cm (24 in), has masses of deep pink flowers, tipped with gold, in spring. It prefers light shade.

Hypoestes (fam. Acanthaceae)

This is quite a large genus of perennial herbs from tropical and subtropical regions of Southeast Asia, southern Africa and Madagascar, but only two species are commonly cultivated. They are grown for their attractive foliage, in frost-prone climates in a warm greenhouse or conservatory, as house plants, or as annual, summer bedding plants.

CULTIVATION Under glass or indoors, grow in pots of soil-based potting compost. Ensure good light but shade from direct sun. A humid atmosphere is recommended. Propagate in spring from seed germinated at 18°C (64°F) or from softwood or semi-ripe cuttings.

BELOW The polka-dot plant, *Hypoestes phyllostachya*, makes a good houseplant and is also used for summer bedding in a sunny or lightly shaded spot.

CLIMATE Subtropical to tropical. Zone 10 plus.

SPECIES *H. aristata*, from South Africa, is a shrub-like plant, to 1 m (3 ft), with terminal spikes of small, pink to purple, tubular flowers from summer to winter. *H. phyllostachya*, freckle-face, pink polka dot plant, measles plant or flamingo plant, from Madagascar, grows to about 1 m (3 ft), with attractive, pinkspotted, egg-shaped leaves. The small, mauve flowers are quite insignificant. This species is good to plant for summer bedding.

Hypoxis (fam. Hypoxidaceae)
Star grass

Mostly native to South Africa, but also found in North and South America, Australia and Southeast Asia, these cormous perennials are grown on rock gardens in warm climates, or in a cool greenhouse in frost-prone areas. They have long, slender leaves and in spring and summer produce small, star-shaped yellow or white flowers.

CULTIVATION Plant bulbs, smooth side downwards, in a well-drained soil, enriched with compost or manure, in fall. They need a sunny position and protection from excessive winter rain and frosts. When grown in pots in a greenhouse use a soil-based potting compost enriched with leaf mould and grit. Ensure good light. Do not water in winter when the corms are dormant. Propagate from offsets when dormant, or from seed in spring.

CLIMATE Zone 9.

SPECIES *H. hirsuta*, from North America, to 20 cm (8 in), has leaves the same length, and yellow flowers in late spring. *H. hygrometrica*, golden weather grass, is an Australian species which grows to only 15 cm (6 in). It has long, narrow leaves and the small, yellow flowers tend to close in cloudy weather. *H. stellata*, from South Africa, has yellow or pure white flowers, with greenish stripes and a distinctive, purplish black center, and long, smooth leaves.

ABOVE A pink-flowered form of hyssop makes a pretty, decorative plant. Flowers attract butterflies and bees.

It grows to about 25 cm (10 in). Var. *elegans* produces white flowers banded with dark blue to purple stripes.

Hyssop (*Hyssopus officinalis*, fam. Lamiaceae)

Used as a symbol of humility in religious paintings, hyssop has been known since antiquity in southern parts of Europe and central Asia. Its aromatic leaves are made into a tea used for respiratory problems and as an aid to digestion. They are also used fresh as a flavoring for soups and salads. Oil of hyssop, obtained from the roots, is used in some liqueurs and colognes. *H. officinalis* is a shrubby, perennial herb, to 45–60 cm (18–24 in) in height, with narrow, dark green leaves and small blue flowers. There are ornamental varieties, whose flowers are white, rose or red

CULTIVATION Plant in a reasonably fertile, well-drained, ideally alkaline soil in a sunny spot. Propagate from soft stem cuttings in summer or from seed in fall, germinated in a garden frame.

CLIMATE Zone 3.

IJ

Iberis to Justica

Iberis (fam. Brassicaceae)

Candytuft

Native to southern Europe and western Asia, this genus of about 30 annuals, perennials and subshrubs has adopted the ancient name for Spain. All of the species are low-growing and make excellent border or rockery plants. Their pretty, mostly fragrant flowers are widely used in floral arrangements.

CULTIVATION Iberis will grow well in any ordinary garden soil, provided it is adequately drained. They will tolerate either full sun or partial shade. Grow annuals from seed in situ, thinning the seedlings to 30 cm (12 in) apart. Flowers will bloom about two months after planting and the spent flower heads should be removed to encourage further production and to prevent plants from running to seed. Perennials are propagated by root division or from stem cuttings taken in summer after flowering. They can also be grown from seed, but flowering will take 12 months.

CLIMATE Zone 7.

ABOVE White candytuft, *Iberis amara* 'Iceberg' is a popular summer annual. In this garden setting, it is teamed with heartsease.

SPECIES *I. amara*, rocket candytuft, is an erect, bushy annual, to about 30 cm (12 in), with lance-shaped, mid-green leaves and domed heads of small, pure white flowers. Preferring partial shade and regular water, it is a favorite with florists. Some strains have large, hyacinth-flowered blooms and are more popular than the species. There are several others available, too. *I. sempervirens*, edging candytuft, is a low, compact, evergreen subshrub, to about 30 cm (12 in), suitable for edgings and rock gardens. The dense, rounded heads of white flowers complement the dense, dark green foliage. Flowering lasts for many weeks. *I. umbellata*, common candytuft, to about 30 cm (12 in), is the common annual and comes in pink, violet, purple, red, lilac or crimson. For cut flowers, pick when well formed but not overmature, early in the day. Plunge into water immediately. This species has no fragrance and has become naturalized in many areas.

Ilex (fam. Aquifoliaceae)

Holly

There are 400 species in this genus of mostly hardy, evergreen and deciduous trees which are found predominantly in temperate climates of the northern hemisphere. They are grown for their attractive, thick, dark green, leathery leaves and their cheerful berries which are produced mainly in winter. Some of the leaves have smooth margins, while others have distinctive, toothed, spiky edges. The small, insignificant, greenish white flowers are usually unisexual and the berry, though commonly red, can also be yellow or black. Although hollies will grow in warm areas, most need a cooler climate to do well and produce good crops of berries. Hollies make good hedges and windbreaks, and also pleasing specimen plants in lawns, shrub borders and woodland gardens.

CULTIVATION Propagate hollies from seed, cuttings or by grafting. Seed can take up to a year to germinate and the sex of the plants will

ABOVE The dark, glossy foliage of *Ilex aquifolium* shows off a cluster of red berries and some white flowers.

not be known until they flower some years later. However, this is not important if growing large numbers for hedges or screens. Cuttings or grafting, using seedling understock, are used to reproduce varieties and cultivars. Cuttings, 5–8 cm (2–3 in) long, are taken in fall from mature wood of the current season. Hollies will grow in most garden soils but need regular watering in summer when young. Prune in late winter to encourage dense growth.

CLIMATE Zone 6 for the species listed below.

SPECIES *I. aquifolium*, common or English holly, is popular in Europe and North America for the color it provides in winter. It has been very widely hybridized. It is the holly we associate with Christmas. A very hardy, rather slow growing, evergreen tree, to about 25 m (80 ft), it forms a roughly pyramidal shape. The spiky, deep green leaves become smoother with age. As the flowers are unisexual, berries are only found on female trees when there is a male tree close by to provide pollen. Holly makes a beautiful specimen tree and can also be used as a hedge. It can tolerate very cold winters and, once established, can also tolerate drought. The wood from this species is used for veneers and inlays. Some cultivars bear only male flowers, others only female, so if a crop of berries is required, it is necessary to grow a mixture of varieties. 'Silver Queen' is the best of the silvery cream, variegated forms, bearing male flowers only. The leaves are margined with creamy white. A silvery variegated cultivar like 'Argentea Marginata', with female flowers, could be chosen to grow with it. Other popular cultivars include 'Golden Queen', which is actually a male holly, with spiny leaves boldly edged with gold. A very fine holly, it will pollinate female cultivars. It makes a superb specimen tree in a lawn. 'Ferox', known as hedgehog holly because the upper surfaces of the leaves are prickly, is a compact holly, with purple bark, which does not produce berries. 'Ferox Argentea' is a slow-growing, variegated form with silvery white markings; 'Ferox Aurea' is slow growing, to around 2 m (6 ft), with golden variegations; 'J. C. van Tol' is a self-fertile, female holly producing heavy crops of berries. The clusters of bright, glossy, red berries, which remain on the bush throughout winter, and the deep green foliage make this a handsome garden specimen. *I. cornuta*, Chinese or horned holly, is a much-branched, evergreen shrub or small tree, which is self-fertile. It tolerates a warmer climate and produces larger berries than the common holly. *I. crenata*, Japanese or box-leafed holly, is a compact, evergreen shrub, with stiff branches, small, narrow, deep green leaves and small, black berries. In Japan it is favored for bonsai, and it is also used as a hedge and for topiary. There is a wide range of cultivars of both *I. cornuta* and *I. crenata*. There are numerous dwarf forms of *Ilex crenata* including 'Compacta', 'Helleri', 'Hetzii' and 'Morris Dwarf'. These would make good dense ground cover if mass planted in groups or drifts.

Illicium (fam. Illiciaceae)
Aniseed tree

Native to North America and Southeast Asia, this genus comprises around 40 species of evergreen shrubs grown for their striking, many-petalled, fragrant flowers and handsome foliage.

CULTIVATION Grow illiciums in partial shade or full sun, ensuring the site is sheltered from cold winds. The soil should be acid or lime-free, well drained yet moisture-retentive, with plenty of humus. Propagate from semi-ripe cuttings in summer or by layering in spring.

CLIMATE Zone 8 for most species.

SPECIES *I. anisatum*, Chinese or Japanese anise, is an aromatic shrub or small tree, growing slowly to about 8 m (26 ft). The oval, thick, fleshy, pointed leaves are glossy, dark green and the pale yellow flowers are borne in spring, even when these plants are young. The bark from this species is dried and used for incense in its native homelands, and the flowering branches are often used to decorate Buddhist graves in Japan. *I. floridanum*, purple anise, zone 9, from the south of North America, produces beautiful, star-shaped, deep purple flowers in early summer. It is a bushy, aromatic shrub, to about 3 m (10 ft), with deep green, lance-shaped, leathery leaves. *I. verum*, star anise, is a slow-growing tree, growing to around 20 m (65 ft), with long leaves, about 15 cm (6 in) long, and whitish pink spring flowers, turning purple. The unripe fruit is the source of a spice used in Chinese cooking and a distilled oil which has a long history of medicinal use.

Impatiens (fam. Balsaminaceae)
Balsam, busy Lizzie

Impatiens are so-called because of the impatience they display in growth and spread. Comprising about 800 species of annuals, perennials and small shrubs from tropical and subtropical Asia and Africa, these mostly succulent or soft-wooded plants provide a cheerful display from spring to early fall. They are easy to grow both in the garden and in pots or hanging baskets, indoors or out, and are now available in a multitude of colors.

CULTIVATION In climates which are prone to frost, grow in an intermediate to warm greenhouse or conservatory, or as house plants. The *I. walleriana* cultivars and New Guinea impatiens are grown mainly for their use as summer bedding plants, planted out when frosts are over. Under glass, grow in pots of soilless potting compost and shade from direct sun. Provide atmospheric humidity. Outdoors, plants are best in partial shade. Propagate from seed in early spring or from softwood cuttings in spring, both in a heated propagating case.

CLIMATE Must be grown in frost-free conditions. Zone 10 and above.

SPECIES *I. balsamina*, garden or rose balsam, is a bushy annual, to about 50 cm (20 in), with many different-colored flowers, from rose, scarlet and white to pink and yellow, in summer. The Camellia-flowered Series has large, double flowers and is very popular with gardeners, as are the dwarf strains. *I. hawkeri*, New Guinea impatiens, and its hybrids have a great variety of foliage and flower forms, and make popular container plants. *I. mirabilis*, to 2 m (6 ft), has very fleshy stems and a swollen caudex. The leaves are borne in terminal clusters and the large flowers are yellow. *I. repens*, golden dragon, is a trailing plant, often grown indoors, preferring a light spot.

BELOW The highly aromatic *Illicium anisatum* has pretty cream to yellow flowers. Grow in a sheltered spot to concentrate the fragrance.

ABOVE The double camellia-flowered, compact-growing strains of *Impatiens balsamina* are the most popular.

The flowers are bright yellow and slightly hairy on the outside. It benefits from a little liquid fertilizer every month. *I. sodenii*, pale perennial balsam, is an evergreen which grows 1–2.5 m (3–8 ft) and is very useful for planting in dry, frost-free, shaded situations. The pale lilac flowers are borne on thick, sappy stems. *I. walleriana*, busy lizzie or Zanzibar balsam, is the species most often seen in home gardens, either as a bedding or indoor plant. It grows to about 60 cm (24 in), flowering over a long period in shades of carmine, orange, scarlet, rose, lilac, purple, pink or white, with some variegations. It self-seeds freely. The more compact dwarf forms don't seed themselves and make better garden and container plants.

Incarvillea (fam. Bignoniaceae)

Originally from Asia, these annual or herbaceous perennials were introduced into Europe in the mid-19th century. It is mostly the perennials that are cultivated, some being stemless. They have fern-like foliage and showy, trumpet-shaped flowers in a variety of colors, from red, rose, pink and purple to white.

CULTIVATION These pretty plants like a sunny position and deep, rich soil. Although incarvilleas are quite hardy, they will not tolerate wet roots, so provide perfect drainage. Plant the fleshy, rooted crowns 10 cm (4 in) deep in spring, and, in climates subject to hard frosts, lay a permanent mulch around the plants. Propagate from seed in fall or spring, germinating it in a garden frame. Alternatively, divide plants or take basal cuttings in spring.

CLIMATE There are species suited to various climatic zones.

SPECIES *I. delavayi*, pride of China, zone 6, is a fleshy rooted, clump-forming perennial, to 45 cm (18 in), very attractive in borders or rock gardens. It has stemless, fern-like leaves, tall flower stems and blooms in deep pink to purple in spring. *I. mairei* var. *grandiflora*, zone 4, to 15 cm (6 in), flowers in early summer with large, deep rosy red blooms, with an orange tube and a throat blotched with white. *I. olgae* zone 7, is a rather shrubby plant, 60–90 cm (24–36 in) high, with clusters of pale pink flowers in early summer.

ABOVE The clustered, pink, trumpet-shaped flowers of *Incarvillea delavayi* make a splash of color in the spring garden.

Indigofera (fam. Papilionaceae)

Indigo

Found in tropical and subtropical regions throughout the world, this large genus of around 700 species includes annuals and perennials, as well as evergreen and deciduous shrubs and small trees. Many of the species cultivated are shrubs with dark, blueish green foliage and sprays of pea-like flowers which make an attractive display during spring. The colors of the flowers range from purple to pinkish lilac. *I. tinctoria* is the source of the dark blue dye, known as indigo, highly valued in times past.

CULTIVATION Indigoferas will grow in most garden soils, provided they are moist and well drained. The plants will flower more freely if regularly watered. Propagate from seed, which germinates more quickly if soaked overnight in warm water before sowing, as the seed coat is hard and waxy. They can also be propagated from cuttings and often from suckers.

CLIMATE There are species suited to various climates.

SPECIES *I. amblyantha*, zone 5, from Asia, is a shrub, to 2 m (6 ft), with pink flowers. *I. australis*, Australian indigo, zone 9, is one of the more tender species. It grows to about 1.5 m (4 ft) tall with bluish green, pinnate leaves and sprays of pink, purple or, very occasionally, white flowers. *I. decora*, zone 5, from China and Japan, is a small shrub, to 60 cm (24 in), with reddish new growth, light green, pinnate leaves and abundant sprays of pinkish white blooms during the warmer months of the year. It tends to spread by underground runners but these can be easily pulled out when young. *I. heterantha*, zone 7, a hardy, 2–3 m (6–10 ft) high shrub with a spreading habit, flowers profusely with lovely, rose-colored blooms.

Iochroma (fam. Solanaceae)

This genus consists of 15 shrubs and trees from tropical America, some of which have local medicinal uses. They are grown for their attractive foliage and clusters of tubular flowers which may be blue, purple, red, yellow or white. Most have a long flowering period through summer. Fruits are berries with an enlarged calyx.

ABOVE Flowering in sun or shade, *Indigofera australis* is very adaptable. Prune regularly for compact growth.

ABOVE An easy-care shrub for the conservatory, *Iochroma cyaneum* is not widely grown today. The deep indigo blue flowers last many months.

CULTIVATION In climates prone to frost, grow in an intermediate greenhouse or conservatory in pots of soil-based potting compost. Plants need good light but shade from direct sun. Propagate from seed in spring germinated at 18°C (64°F), or from semi-ripe cuttings in summer, rooted with bottom heat.

CLIMATE Warmest parts of zone 10 and above.

SPECIES *I. cyaneum*, a spreading evergreen shrub, grows to a height of 3–4 m (10–13 ft). The leaves are shiny green above, grayish beneath. Drooping trusses of the deepest violet-blue tubular flowers are carried through summer, with spot flowering possible until winter. Fruits are rare in cultivation.

Ipheion (fam. Alliaceae)

Native to South America, this small genus of low-growing, bulbous plants comprises around ten species. Pretty, blue or white flowers, often sweetly scented, appear among the grassy leaves in spring. The foliage dies down in summer, reappearing in fall, though lying on the ground in winter. When crushed, the leaves have an oniony smell.

ABOVE Spring star flower, *Ipheion uniflorum*, is one of the earliest bulbs to flower at the end of winter. Grow it in pots, rockeries or as edging.

CULTIVATION These bulbs need a warm, sheltered position in full sun with well-drained, yet moisture-retentive soil containing humus. In climates with hard frosts, ensure the plants are mulched in winter. Plant in fall, 8 cm (3 in) deep and 5 cm (2 in) apart. In climates with long periods of very hard frosts, grow in pots of gritty, soil-based potting compost in an unheated greenhouse or conservatory. Maximum light is needed. When dormant in summer, the compost should remain slightly moist. Propagate from seed sown in fall or spring and germinated in a garden frame. Alternatively, divide clumps in summer.

CLIMATE Zone 8.

SPECIES *I. uniflorum*, spring starflower, from Argentina, is the only species known in cultivation. It produces masses of star-shaped, blueish white flowers and looks wonderful planted in beds, borders, rockeries or containers. It grows to 20 cm (8 in), with slender, gray-green foliage.

Ipomoea (fam. Convolvulaceae)
Morning glory

Originating from tropical and warm-temperate regions of the world, this large genus comprises some 500 species of evergreen or deciduous, annual and perennial herbs and subshrubs, with a few succulents. Most species have a twining habit, but there are also prostrate and erect growers. These plants are particularly useful for covering fences, trellises and banks, and can also be grown in pots. Although they are very attractive and have stunning flowers, some of the species have become invasive weeds and some species are quite poisonous to stock. They should be kept out of the reach of children (*I. tricolor*, for example, can induce hallucinations).

CULTIVATION Ipomoeas are generally grown from the hard seed, which should be gently filed away from the scar to break the seed coat, before planting, to aid germination. Some of

ABOVE The large, white blooms of moonflower, *Ipomoea alba*, have fluted petals and a delicious scent.

the perennial species can be propagated from cuttings or layers. Mulch in early spring with a rich compost of decayed manure or leaf mould, particularly if the leaves have yellowed. In frost-prone climates, grow in an intermediate to warm greenhouse or conservatory, in soil-based potting compost. Provide maximum light but shade from direct sun. Alternatively, annuals or species treated as such can be grown outdoors in summer, in a well-drained, sunny, sheltered spot.

CLIMATE Zones 9 and 10.

SPECIES *I. alba*, moonflower, zone 10, from tropical regions, reverses the usual flowering pattern by opening buds at sunset and closing them at dawn. This beautiful, perennial vine, often grown as an annual, has richly perfumed, round, white flowers, 15 cm (6 in) across, striped with lime green. It grows quickly to about 4 m (13 ft). *I. horsfalliae*, cardinal creeper, zone 10, is very suitable for growing indoors in temperate climates. This lovely, perennial vine produces long, tubular, rosy red flowers almost all year round,

requiring a moist soil with plenty of organic matter. *I. indica* (syn. *I. acuminata*), purple winder or blue dawn flower, zone 10, is one of the most popular of the species, appearing particularly attractive in the early morning when the profusion of brilliant blue, trumpet-shaped flowers open. It is considered a weed in some warm countries. *I. pandurata*, wild sweet potato vine, zone 9, is a twining or trailing perennial with large, tuberous roots and white and purple flowers, about 10 cm (4 in) across. *I. purpurea*, common morning glory, zone 9, can be invasive in warm areas. In the US it is a popular, annual climber and has pink, purple, red, or white, trumpet-shaped flowers.

Iresine (fam. Amaranthaceae)

Bloodleaf

There are about 80 species of these quick-growing perennials, originally from South America, but only a few are in cultivation. Grown for their brilliantly colored foliage, they look very attractive in a mixed border. In cool climates, they are treated as annuals, as they die right down in winter, and are incorporated into summer bedding displays.

BELOW 'Aureoreticulata' is the most commonly grown cultivar of *Iresine herbstii*. This cultivar and the species are often grown together.

CULTIVATION Plants for summer bedding are propagated from stem-tip cuttings taken in late summer and rooted under glass. They are wintered in a warm greenhouse and propagated again in early spring to provide young plants for planting out when frosts are over. For best color, plant in a sunny position.

CLIMATE Zone 10 and above.

SPECIES *I. herbstii*, bloodleaf or beefsteak plant, an annual or short-lived perennial, grows to 2 m (6 ft), with beautiful, red and violet leaves. Pinch out flower spikes as they appear so the plant does not put its resources into setting seed and will continue to grow its decorative foliage. Cultivar 'Aureoreticulata' has greenish, yellow-veined leaves with red stems. *I. lindenii* has finer, spear-shaped, glossy leaves which are usually a deep, blood red color, but which become paler toward the center vein.

Iris (fam. Iridaceae)

The Iris is aptly called the rainbow flower as it is found in all colors of the rainbow and many combinations of those colors. It has been known since antiquity, and has found a place in myths, legends, medicine and religion, as well as in heraldry and magic. Irises comprise a very large plant group of over 300 species with many hundreds of cultivars, all with very varied habits and preferred conditions. Some, such as the Dutch iris, grow from bulbs. Others, such as the tall bearded iris and Louisiana iris (both hybrids of several species), Japanese iris (*I. ensata*, syn. *I. kaempferi*) and Siberian iris (*I. sibirica*), grow from rhizomes. Irises generally have stiff, sword-shaped leaves, 40–80 cm (16–32 in) high, while the flowers rise on straight stems above the foliage. Most flower in spring or early summer. Louisiana and Japanese irises, in particular, make lovely cut flowers with quite a long vase life. Growing requirements vary, with many needing excellent drainage, while others, such as the Siberian iris and Japanese iris, can tolerate permanently damp ground.

CULTIVATION All four types discussed below prefer to be grown in full sun, with some protection from strong wind. The soil should be well enriched with organic matter. For bearded irises, it may be necessary to lightly lime the soil. Bearded irises require well-drained soil, while the others prefer a soil with good moisture-retention and can be successfully grown in damp soil on the margins of ponds. Japanese irises are more exacting in their requirements and must have quite acid soil –they will not tolerate lime in any form. Bearded iris should be planted with the rhizomes about 20 cm (8 in) apart and only the roots buried. Divide existing clumps immediately after flowering in late spring to early summer, cutting the leaves off to a short fan. Japanese and Siberian irises are best planted in late winter or early spring, at about 15–20 cm (6–8 in) apart, with the crown of the plant at soil level. Lifting and dividing of these is best done in late fall or winter. Louisiana irises can also be planted in late winter or spring. Apply complete plant food as new growth starts in spring. Japanese irises, in particular, need additional manure or compost

ABOVE Lovely Louisiana irises prefer moist soil and full sun, but apart from these requirements are easy to grow.

in spring as well as fertilizer. All irises appreciate deep, regular watering during their growing and flowering period. Japanese, Siberian and Louisiana irises, especially, need plenty of water to keep the soil moist throughout the entire growing season from spring to fall. After flowering, cut off spent flower stems and remove any foliage that has died, especially at the end of the growing season. These irises are fairly free of problems but there are diseases that can affect them, such as fungal leaf spot, which can be treated with copper oxychloride, and rust. With the latter, remove affected leaves and spray if necessary with a suitable fungicide. The rhizomes can also rot but there is usually little that can be done beyond removal of the affected plants.

CLIMATE Zone 7 for most species.

Types Bearded irises are hybrids and come in an amazing range of single colors and bicolors. Their graceful, elegant flowers open one or two at a time on stems held well above the fans of stiff leaves. Planted en masse they can be a breathtaking sight. Even a small group of these irises are worth growing. Two species of iris are grown for the production of orris, used in perfumery. They are *I. germanica*, especially its variety florentina, and *I. pallida*. *I. germanica* is the 'fleur-de-lis' (literally 'lily flower') known to French history. Louisiana irises are

ABOVE Tall bearded irises look wonderful in mass plantings. Individual flowers are very delicate looking.

bred from irises native to Louisiana and Florida in the United States and have a rather flat form. Hybrids available today include an amazing range of colors of astonishing depth and richness. From pure white to the darkest purple, there is one to suit every gardener. These plants love moist soil and full sun. Japanese irises have been grown in Japan for centuries, although their exact origin is obscure. They are known for their beautiful, flat flowers, some having wavy or frilled margins. Many have flowers that are veined or netted in deep colors. The color range covers all the shades of blue, red and purple, with new shades appearing all the time. These irises are lovely as cut flowers. Siberian irises multiply well given the right conditions, especially plenty of moisture. The foliage of this group is narrower than that of some of the others and the color range is confined mainly to white and shades of blue and purple. Varieties are now available in pinks and reds.

Iris (*Iris xiphium hybrids*, fam. Iridaceae)
Dutch iris

Although known as Dutch iris, these hybrids were developed from the Spanish iris, *I. xiphium*, and other species. Widely grown as a cut flower, Dutch iris is a lovely garden subject, especially when planted en masse in solid blocks of color. It also makes a good container plant. The deep violet blue is probably the most popular color, but it also comes in golden yellow, white and other shades of blue and violet. All have a yellow or orange blotch on the petals. The flower stems may be more than 50 cm (20 in) high in good conditions. Dutch irises flower in the spring and summer. There is a range of lovely forms and colors.

CULTIVATION Dutch irises need full sun, with some protection from strong wind. The soil must be well drained, with decayed compost or manure dug in a month or so before the iris are planted. Plant the bulbs in fall, 8–10 cm (3–4 in) apart to a depth of 5 cm (2 in). Mulch

ABOVE The most popular color of Dutch iris is probably this rich royal blue, whether for garden display or as a cut flower.

soil surface with rotted manure or compost after planting. If soil has been well prepared, little or no fertilizer will be needed. In poor soil, a little blood, fish and bone can be applied once the leaves emerge. Water well after planting, then withhold water until the foliage appears. Give deep, weekly watering during the growth and flowering periods, and cease all watering once the foliage starts to die down. Bulbs may be left undisturbed for several years or until the floral display begins to deteriorate. If you wish to lift the bulbs, do so as soon as the foliage dies down and store the cleaned bulbs in a dry, airy place. Few problems are encountered by home gardeners but bulbs will rot easily if overwatered or if the soil is poorly drained.

CLIMATE Zone 7.

Isopogon (fam. Proteaceae)
Drumsticks

There are around 30 species in this Australian genus of evergreen shrubs. The leaves vary from long and narrow to broader and divided, and the unusual, rounded flower heads come mostly in yellow or pink and are followed by large, globe-shaped fruit cones.

CULTIVATION In climates which are prone to regular frosts, grow in an airy intermediate greenhouse or conservatory, in pots or tubs of soil-based potting compost, enriched with grit and leaf mould. Plants need maximum light but shade from strong, direct sun. Only moderate watering is required. In the garden, grow in acid to neutral soil in a sunny, sheltered position. Propagate from seed in spring after soaking in water for a day. Germinate at 24°C (75°F).

CLIMATE Warmer parts of zone 9.

SPECIES *I. anemonifolius*, drumsticks, from eastern Australia, is an upright shrub to about 2 m (6 ft) high. It produces tight, round, yellow flower heads on straight stems in spring. The light green, narrow, much-divided leaves grow to about 10 cm (4 in) long. *I. anethifolius*, from New South Wales, has attractive, soft foliage which colors a bronzy brown in winter, and terminal, yellow flower heads in spring

ABOVE Commonly known as drumsticks, *Isopogon anemonifolius* has pretty, yellow flowers that open slowly from the base.

and early summer. It grows to about 1 m (3 ft). *I. dubius* (syn. *I. roseus*), from Western Australia, is a small, erect, prickly shrub, to about 1 m (3 ft), with much-divided leaves and vivid pink flower heads. This species needs to be protected from frost. *I. trilobus*, barrel coneflower, has unusual, divided leaves and masses of yellow flower heads.

Isotoma

(syn. *Laurentia*, fam. Campanulaceae)

Of this small genus of tender annuals and perennials from Australia and tropical America, only one or two are in cultivation. *Isotoma axillaris* (syn. *Laurentia axillaris*) is becoming very popular for outdoor, summer display either for use in hanging baskets and or in patio tubs.

CULTIVATION Grow either as summer bedding plants or as pot plants in an intermediate conservatory. Raise from seed in spring and germinate at 18°C (64°F). Pot seedlings into soil-based potting compost. Alternatively, take softwood cuttings in summer. Plant out after frosts in a sunny position.

CLIMATE These tender annuals and perennials require zone 10.

BELOW Mat-forming *Isotoma fluviatillis* makes a good lawn substitute for areas that are not walked on frequently.

SPECIES Isotoma axillaris (syn. *Laurentia axillaris*), is a small, bushy perennial with a woody base, which produces masses of starry, blue flowers against a background of light green, narrow-lobed leaves from the spring to the fall. It is invariably grown as an annual and is now popular as a summer display plant. There are now several cultivars with flowers in various colors–pink and shades of blue, or white.

Itea (fam. Escalloniaceae)

Of the ten species in this genus of deciduous or evergreen shrubs or trees, most are from cooler regions of eastern Asia, with one species from North America. The leaves of some species are similar to those of the willow, while some resemble holly.

CULTIVATION Iteas prefer a slightly acid or peaty soil that is permanently moist, but not boggy, and a sheltered spot in the garden. Plant in late fall or early spring and propagate from cuttings taken in fall and placed in a sandy mix, with bottom heat. They can also be propagated from rooted suckers in early fall or from seed sown in the spring.

CLIMATE There are species suited to various climatic zones.

ABOVE Graceful tassels of lightly scented flowers make *Itea ilicifolia* an unusual shrub worth seeking out.

SPECIES *I. ilicifolia*, zone 7, is an attractive, evergreen shrub, 4–5 m (13–16 ft) high, with holly-like leaves and long, tassel-like stems of greenish white flowers in summer or fall. *I. virginica*, zone 6, sweetspire or Virginia willow, from North America, is a deciduous, upright, slender shrub, to about 3 m (10 ft), which colors a vivid red in fall. It produces thin spikes of fragrant, greenish white flowers in summer. The most widely grown of the species, it is suitable for massed or mixed planting, particularly in low, wet places.

Ixia (fam. Iridaceae)
African corn lily

Native to South Africa, this genus comprises around 45 species of cormous plants which produce an abundance of pretty, fragrant, starry flowers, about 5 cm (2 in) across, on long stems in spring to early summer. Hybrids are available in a lovely range of colors, including shades of red, pink, orange, yellow and cream, with dark centers. The blossoms open fully only in sunshine, forming an

BELOW *Ixia viridiflora* is prized by gardeners for its exquisitely shaded flowers that are somewhere between duck egg blue and pale green.

attractive cup shape when partly open, and closing in the evening and on cloudy days. The long, slender leaves die down to the ground in midsummer. Ixias are best in massed groups in the garden, but also make good pot plants and cut flowers.

CULTIVATION Where temperatures drop below freezing, grow in pots in a cool greenhouse. Pot corms in fall, in soil-based potting compost. Ensure maximum light and airy conditions. Keep compost completely dry when corms are dormant. Repot into fresh compost annually. Outdoors, plant corms 15 cm (6 in) deep in a warm, sunny, well-drained border.

CLIMATE Warmer parts of zone 9.

SPECIES *I. campanulata* grows to 30 cm (12 in), with dark purple or crimson flowers in spring to early summer. *I. maculata*, to 60 cm (24 in), is the most commonly grown species, with brown-centerd, orange-yellow flowers, spotted with black, along the ends of the stems in spring. *I. patens* grows to about 45 cm (18 in), producing pink flowers with green throats in spring. *I. viridiflora*, to 30 cm (12 in), is quite exquisite in full bloom. Pale, blueish green flowers, with purple-black centers, appear in spring.

Ixiolirion (fam. Amaryllidaceae)
Lily of the Altai

There are four species in this genus of bulbous perennials from western and central Asia which produce lovely sprays of delicately fragrant, lavender blue, star-shaped flowers in late spring or early summer. The stems are rather weak and the sparse, grass-like foliage dies down in the summer. They make attractive, long-lasting cut flowers.

CULTIVATION Plant these bulbs 15 cm (6 in) deep and 10 cm (4 in) apart in fall, in a warm, sunny border with well-drained soil. Provide an organic mulch to protect the bulbs from excessive rain in winter. Propagate from seed

ABOVE Bulbs of *Ixiolirion tataricum* need a good summer baking for their best flowering. This plant is not too well known, but should be more widely grown.

sown in a garden frame when ripe, or from offsets when corms are dormant. Ixiolirions can also be grown in pots in an unheated greenhouse.

CLIMATE Zone 7.

SPECIES *I. tataricum*, Tartar lily, the only species cultivated, has long-lasting, blue flowers in spring or early summer.

Ixora (fam. Rubiaceae)

Mostly native to Asia and Africa, with some species found in Australia, the Pacific Islands and America, this genus includes around 400 species of tropical evergreen shrubs and trees with spectacular, fragrant flower heads in white, yellow, orange, pink and red. In climates which are prone to frost, they are ideal subjects for growing in a warm greenhouse or conservatory.

CULTIVATION Under glass, these plants should be grown in pots of gritty, soilless potting compost. Add some leaf mould if it is available.

Plants need good light but they should be shaded from strong, direct sun, and they require a humid atmosphere. Be sparing with water in winter but water normally in the growing season. You may need to lightly prune in spring in order to restrict growth. Outdoors grow in a sunny or partially shaded, sheltered spot with well-drained soil. Propagate from semi-ripe cuttings in summer, rooting them in a heated propagating case.

CLIMATE Subtropical and tropical. Zone 10 plus.

SPECIES *I. chinensis* is a neat, compact shrub which grows to a height and spread of about 2 m (6 ft). The deep green leaves are narrowly pointed and the heads of tubular flowers are borne in profusion at the top of the shrub in spring and summer. It comes in white, yellow, pink, orange and red flowered forms. *I. coccinea*, flame of the woods or jungle flame, from tropical Asia, grows to 2–3 m (6–10 ft) in its habitat but only to about 1 m (3 ft) when it is cultivated. It produces dense clusters of brilliant, orange-red flowers throughout the entire summer and has broad, glossy, blunt leaves. A number of cultivars has been produced and these come in various colors.

ABOVE Rich red to orange flowers appear on *Ixora chinensis* over a long period throughout the warmer months. It makes a good greenhouse or conservatory plant.

Jacaranda (fam. Bignoniaceae)

There are some 45 species of trees in this genus from tropical America. One species, *J. mimosifolia*, is rightly considered one of the most beautiful flowering trees in the world. Deciduous only at the end of winter when it loses its fern-like foliage, it lies dormant until spring or early summer when it becomes a cloud of mauve-blue flowers. The flowers fall, forming a carpet of blue below. It makes a beautiful specimen or street tree, transforming the garden or street when in full bloom.

CULTIVATION In frost-prone climates, grow in a cool conservatory or greenhouse as a foliage plant, as it is unlikely to flower when pot grown. Use rich, soil-based, potting compost. Plants need maximum light and airy conditions. Water normally in the growing period but reduce considerably in winter. Outdoors, in suitable climates, grow in full sun with well-drained soil. Propagate from seed in spring or from semi-ripe cuttings in summer, with basal warmth for both.

CLIMATE : Warmest parts of zone 9.

BELOW The glorious canopy of lavender-blue flowers on *Jacaranda mimosifolia* is even more outstanding if the leaves have fallen before flowering begins.

SPECIES *J. mimosifolia*, from Argentina and Bolivia, is a broadly spreading tree, to 10 m (33 ft) tall, with fine, fern-like foliage, dense clusters of funnel-shaped, mauve-blue flowers and flat, round seed pods that appear in fall. Pink and white varieties exist but are rarely seen.

Jackfruit (*Artocarpus heterophyllus*, fam. Moraceae)

This is a fast-growing, tropical tree which may reach 15 m (50 ft) in three to five years. It bears huge, edible fruits, up to 90 cm (36 in) long in ideal conditions. The fruit is eaten raw or cooked, but the ripe fruits and the flowers have a strong, unpleasant odor typical of plants pollinated by flies. The timber is used for quality furniture. Originally native to India and Malaysia, it has now spread to most tropical areas.

CULTIVATION Outside the tropics, grow in a warm, humid greenhouse or conservatory, in large pots or tubs of soil-based potting compost. It is unlikely to fruit when thus grown. Propagate from root suckers or semi-ripe cuttings.

CLIMATE Tropical areas only.

ABOVE The heavy, barrel-shaped jackfruit is carried on major branches. Trees are grown both for their fruit and their excellent timber.

Jasione (fam. Campanulaceae)

Sheep's bit

These hardy annuals and perennials from the Mediterranean have simple leaves and dense, dome-shaped flowers in varying shades of blue. They are well suited to growing in sunny rock gardens.

CULTIVATION Grow in a sunny spot with well-drained soil which ideally should be sandy. Propagate from seeds sown in a garden frame in fall, or by division in spring (for perennials).

CLIMATE Zone 5 for most species.

SPECIES *J. humilis*, a perennial with blue flowers, grows to 20 cm (8 in). *J. laevis* (syn. *J. perennis*) is a hairy perennial, to 30 cm (12 in), with spherical, clear blue flowers on unbranched stems, borne well above a tufted rosette of foliage. *J. montana*, zone 6, an annual to 45 cm (18 in), has pale blue to lilac flowers.

ABOVE The flowers of *Jasione laevis* resemble those of pincushion flower, Scabiosa species, although they are not related.

Jasminum (fam. Oleaceae)

Jasmine

This large genus comprises both climbers and shrubs that may be either evergreen or deciduous. It is mostly the climbers that have the beautiful, sweet fragrance and they have become a

ABOVE In late winter and spring, the heavy perfume of *Jasminum polyanthum* pervades the air. Flowering is abundant.

favorite with American gardeners. The petals of some of the scented species are used in perfumes and teas. The star-shaped flowers come in shades of pink, yellow and white and the leaves are simple, trifoliate or pinnate and may be either opposite or alternate.

CULTIVATION These fast-growing plants need annual pruning to control them. In cold and cool climates, grow the hardy species outdoors in full sun or partial shade, tender species in a cool to intermediate greenhouse or conservatory.

CLIMATE There are species suited to various climatic zones.

SPECIES *J. azoricum*, zone 9, is an evergreen climber, from Madeira, with opposite leaves and fragrant, white flowers in late summer. It grows to 4–5 m (13–16 ft). *J. laurifolium* f. *nitidum*, zone 10, from the South Pacific, is a slender-stemmed climber, 2–3 m (6–10 ft) tall, with glossy, solitary leaves and sprays of white flowers. *J. mesnyi*, zone 9, from China, is an evergreen, semi-climbing shrub with lovely, semi-double, yellow flowers. It has long, arching branches, so it needs plenty of room to be seen to best effect, and dark green, trifoliate leaves. This species grows to around 3 m (10 ft) and needs a frost-free climate. *J. nudiflorum*, zone 6, is a rambling, deciduous shrub from China, which grows to a height of 3.5 m (11 ft) and produces single, yellow flowers in winter. *J. officinale*, common jasmine, zone 7, from China, is a deciduous or semi-evergreen, shrubby climber which can grow as tall as 9 m (30 ft). The clusters of deep pink buds are followed by deliciously fragrant, white flowers in summer and fall. The form affine has a rather straggly habit but produces the most beautiful, white, scented flowers. This climber grows to 3 m (10 ft) and can be easily trained to beautify walls, doorways and other architectural features. *J. polyanthum*, zone 9, is another tall climber from China, to 3 m (10 ft). It is an attractive, evergreen species, with fern-like foliage and intensely perfumed, white flowers. It can become rampant and invasive in warm areas, but makes a pretty pot plant in cooler regions. *J. rex*, king jasmine, zone 10, from Thailand, grows to 2.5 m (8 ft) and bears white summer flowers. *J. sambac*, Arabian jasmine, zone 10, is an evergreen climber with very fragrant, white flowers. The double cultivar 'Grand Duke of Tuscany' has been grown for centuries. The flowers of both species and cultivars are used to flavor tea.

Jubaea (fam. Arecaceae)
Chilean wine palm, coquito palm

This single-species genus of palms from the coastal regions of Chile is the most cold-tolerant of all southern hemisphere palms, appearing at its best in temperate climates. It has become rare in its homeland where it has been constantly cut down to harvest the sweet sap distilled to make palm honey.

CULTIVATION Chilean wine palm is very slow growing, preferring a sunny position and a reasonably deep, moist soil. Propagate from fresh seed. Germination will take several months.

CLIMATE Zone 9.

SPECIES *J. chilensis* is a feather palm which grows up to 20 m (65 ft) tall. It is slow growing

ABOVE Chilean wine palm, *Jubaea chilensis*, has a massive trunk and a feathery crown. This distinctive palm is grown as a specimen or in avenues.

in its early years but grows more rapidly once it has formed a trunk. It has a huge trunk, often over a metre in diameter, which in old palms tapers just below the crown. The trunk is smooth, dull gray in color, and is patterned lightly with diamond shapes. The large crown is formed from a dense mass of long, arching, dark green leaflets with a thick midrib. It produces many short, yellow inflorescences and large fruits, the flesh of which tastes rather like that of the coconut.

Juncus (fam. Juncaceae)
Rush

These mainly rhizomatous plants grow in cool, marshy areas throughout the world and may have little ornamental value. However, a few species are attractive enough to plant at the edge of a garden pond or in permanently boggy ground.

ABOVE Growing in shallow water or boggy soil, *Juncus effusus* makes an effective accent plant for a water feature.

ABOVE Immature juniper berries are a pretty blue before they mature to black.

CULTIVATION These plants do best in a clay soil which retains moisture. Plant during late winter to spring and propagate by division. With variegated plants, any green stems that appear should be removed as soon as they appear or the whole plant may revert to green. All plants have a better appearance if the old foliage is cut back at the end of winter.

CLIMATE Zone 4.

SPECIES *J. effusus*, Japanese common or soft rush, from Eurasia, North America, Australia and New Zealand, is a perennial which grows up to 2 m (6 ft), though sometimes much shorter. It has soft, green stems and yellowish brown flowers. This species is cultivated in Japan to make traditional matting. Cultivar 'Vittatus', to 1 m (3 ft), has leaves striped yellow or white. The popular form spiralis has spiralling stems.

Juniper berry

(*Juniperus communis*, fam. Cupressaceae)

Juniper berries have been used for centuries as a culinary and medicinal herb. Juniper branches were burnt in homes and streets during times of plague in the belief that this would purify the air. The crushed berries are used to flavor meat and game and also to make sauces for use with cold meats. The berries or the distilled oil have long been used to flavor gin and other spirits. Berries develop on female trees of the common juniper, *J. communis*, which is an upright tree growing 5–10 m (16–33 ft) tall in good conditions. It has prickly, gray-green leaves, silvery on the undersides. This tree and its numerous cultivars are extensively grown as ornamentals. Male trees bear small yellow cones, while female trees bear the small berries that are green at first, ripening to blue and then black. Ripening of berries can take up to three years and berries are still mostly picked by hand.

CULTIVATION Junipers can be grown in almost any kind of soil but growth will be more vigorous in good soils. Generally grown from seed, they can also be grown from firm tip cuttings taken from fall through to early winter. These plants need regular watering during their first two or three years and thereafter in very hot, dry summers. All trees benefit from mulching with organic matter and, if the soil is very poor, all-purpose fertilizer can be applied in spring.

CLIMATE Zone 3.

Juniperus (fam. Cupressaceae)
Juniper

Mostly found in temperate and subarctic regions of the northern hemisphere, although extending into the tropical mountains of Southeast Asia, eastern Africa and Central America, this genus comprises around 60 species of conifers ranging from very tall trees to prostrate shrubs, all of which are long lived and become woody with age. The cones, commonly known as 'berries', distinguish junipers from other members of the cypress family. They are blueish black or reddish in color and the seed-bearing scales are fused together, forming a fleshy structure. The juvenile leaves are needle-like, often developing with maturity into cypress-type leaves: short, scale-like and pressed closely to the branchlets. The unpleasant smell emitted by the adult leaves of some species when crushed helps to distinguish this genus from *Cupressus*. Junipers are extremely useful plants: apart from their aesthetic appeal, they are probably the hardiest and most trouble-free of all the conifers.

CULTIVATION As junipers are generally very hardy, they thrive in much of the US. They are best grown in a position full with full sun, although they will perform well in partial shade. They also do well in the dappled shade of trees, and indeed groundcover junipers are often planted under trees and large shrubs. The soil should be well drained. Chalky soils are particularly suitable, though not essential, for the plant's well-being. These plants will also take dry sandy or gravelly soils. Pruning is not essential but they can be trimmed annually if neat, bushy, compact plants are required. They tolerate trimming better than most conifers and many will even re-sprout from lopped ends of quite large branches. Nearly all junipers can be used as bonsai subjects. Propagate from cuttings taken in summer or early fall from the current year's growth, with a heel of the previous year's wood. Dip cuttings in a hormone rooting powder, plant in a sand and peat propagating mixture and cover with an inverted glass jar or plastic bag to ensure humid conditions. Seed can also be used if available, but it requires cold treatment to ensure good germination. Cultivars must be grown from cuttings to retain their character.

CLIMATE There are species suited to various climatic zones.

SPECIES *J. bermudiana*, Bermuda cedar, zone 9, from the Bermudas, is a large, spreading tree, rarely seen outside botanical gardens. The beautiful forests in its native habitat have long been denuded. *J. chinensis*, Chinese juniper, zone 4, from China, Japan and Mongolia, is generally a bushy tree up to 20 m (65 ft) tall, with fine, dark green, cypress-like foliage. The hard, brownish seed cones, about 1 cm ($\frac{1}{3}$ in) in diameter, have a waxy bloom. Cultivar 'Aurea' is an upright shrub, to 10 m (33 ft) or more, with golden yellow foliage in winter and spring, becoming greener in summer; 'Kaizuka' (syn. 'Torulosa') is a slender tree, 5–6 m (16–20 ft) tall, with a narrow trunk, deep green, adult-type, corkscrew-like foliage, and strongly ascending, sharply pointed, lateral branches; 'Keteleeri', has a narrow, pyramidal habit, growing to 10 m (33 ft) high, with adult-type, dark green foliage and masses of cones; 'Stricta' has a slender, columnar habit, with blueish, less prickly foliage, especially when young, and some adult-type foliage. *J. communis*, common juniper, zone 3, from northern Europe, Asia and North America, may be a slim, upright tree up to 10 m (33 ft), or a spreading shrub with a height and spread of 3–5 m (10–16

BELOW The billowing foliage of shore juniper, *Juniperus conferta*, spills over a wall. It makes dense groundcover.

ABOVE *Juniperus squamata* 'Blue Star' has dense, blue-tinted foliage. This compact grower does best in cool regions.

ft). It has juvenile-type foliage, with bands of blueish white stomata on the inside faces. This species is the source of juniper berries, the fleshy fruits used for flavoring gin. Cultivar 'Depressa Aurea' is a dwarf shrub to 50 cm (20 in) tall and 1.5 m (5 ft) across, with gracefully pendulous branch tips which color bronze-gold in winter, yellow in spring and greener in summer. 'Compressa' is a miniature which is column-shaped, rarely exceeding 50 cm (20 in) in height, with densely packed, dark green, small, prickly leaves. 'Hibernica', Irish juniper, the oldest and best known cultivar, grows to around 5 m (16 ft), forming a dense column of dull, blueish green foliage when young but taking on a broader conical shape with maturity. *J. conferta*, Japanese shore juniper, zone 5, native to bleak, coastal areas of northern Japan and eastern Siberia, is a popular groundcover species in the US and it will thrive in seaside as well as inland gardens. It is a prostrate species spreading to 2.5 m (8 ft) or more, eventually becoming a solid mat to a height of 30 cm (12 in). The juvenile foliage is fresh green in color. It grows vigorously, but can be contained by trimming. *J. deppeana*, alliga-

tor juniper, zone 8, from Mexico and southern North America, grows to 15 m (50 ft) or more in its habitat, but rarely taller than 6 m (20 ft) in cultivation. The bark of the trunk is divided into squarish shapes, hence the common name. It forms a conical shape, with a pointed crown and cypress-like foliage in a beautiful, silvery blueish gray color. It prefers a relatively cool and dry climate. *J. horizontalis*, creeping juniper, zone 4, from the north of North America, makes an excellent groundcover as it is very tough and spreads rapidly. Cultivars are available in a range of attractive colors, including 'Bar Harbor', which has small, erect, densely packed branches, the foliage turning a dull, deep mauve in winter; 'Douglasii', a very vigorous type, with a tangle of leading shoots and blueish gray foliage in summer, turning dull purplish in winter. *J. x pfitzeriana*, zone 3, covers a group of cultivars probably parented by *J. chinensis* and *J. sabina*. All are spreading shrubs, and one or two semi-prostrate. Good cultivars include 'Gold Coast', 'Kuriwao Gold', 'Old Gold', and 'Pfitzeriana Aurea'. These all have gold or yellow foliage and are among the most popular cultivars of pfitzer juniper. Grow in full sun for best foliage color. *J. procumbens*, Japanese garden juniper, zone 8, from Japan, is a prostrate, shrubby species, to 60 cm (24 in) high, the main branches being borne parallel to, and slightly above, the ground. Thick, flaky, pale brown bark covers the main branches. It has tufts of prickly, light green foliage and brown or black berries. *J. sabina*, savin, zone 3, a shrub from the mountains of Europe and Asia, grows 3–4 m (10–13 ft) in height. Variety 'Tamariscifolia' is the type most grown in the US. It forms a dense mound of fine foliage, to 1 m (3 ft) high and 1.5 m (5 ft) across. The very small leaves are a dull, blueish green. This species will tolerate relatively warm and dry conditions. *J. scopulorum*, Rocky Mountain juniper, zone 3, is native to the mountains of western North America. In its habitat, it forms a tree, to 12 m (40 ft), similar to *J. virginiana*. In the US one of the most popular cultivars is 'Skyrocket', which forms an extremely narrow column, to a height of about

6 m (20 ft). It is quite fast growing, so soon forms a pleasing specimen garden tree, decked in feathery, gray-green foliage. *J. squamata*, zone 5, from the eastern Himalayas, is known mainly by its juvenile cultivar 'Meyeri', long cultivated in Chinese gardens and introduced to the west about a century ago. It is a beautiful form, with an erect, open habit, strong branches, pendulous at the tips, covered with steel blue, needle-like leaves. It generally grows to about 1.5 m (5 ft) but can reach 10 m (33 ft) with age. *J. virginiana*, pencil cedar, zone 7, from eastern North America, grows 20 m (65 ft) in its habitat, though usually under 10 m (33 ft) in cultivation. It is a pyramid-shaped tree, with dull, grayish green foliage. Mature trees often exhibit juvenile foliage, especially around the lower parts of the tree. Cultivars worth growing include 'Gray Owl', a sizeable shrub to 3 m (10 ft), high with a spread of 3–4 m (10–13 ft). The horizontal branches are clothed in silvery gray foliage. 'Hetzii' carries its branches in upward-pointing tiers, and reaches a height of 5 m (16 ft), with a similar spread. It has an open habit of growth and blue-gray foliage.

Justicia (fam. Acanthaceae)

Native to tropical and subtropical regions of the world, and temperate parts of North America, this genus of perennials and small shrubs now includes many species from *Jacobinia* and all of the species from *Beloperone*. Most have strikingly beautiful flowers which bloom over long periods.

CULTIVATION Except in subtropical and tropical climates, these plants should be grown in an intermediate greenhouse or conservatory in pots of rich, soil-based potting compost. Provide good light but shade from direct strong sun, and ensure a humid atmosphere. Pinch out young plants to make them bushy; in late winter lightly prune older plants to keep them compact and shapely. Outdoors grow in well-drained yet moist soil and in partial shade. Propagate from semi-ripe cuttings in summer, rooting them in a heated propagating case.

ABOVE *Justicia carnea* is an easy-care, evergreen shrub for the intermediate greenhouse or conservatory and produces its flamboyant flowers over a long period in summer and fall.

CLIMATE Tropical and subtropical. Warmest parts of zone 10.

SPECIES *J. adhatodoides* (syn. *Duvernoia adhatodoides*) has elliptical leaves, up to 20 cm (8 in) long and fragrant, bell-shaped, white flowers with purple markings on the throat. It grows to 3 m (10 ft) high and makes a good filler plant for the back of borders. *J. brandegeana* (syn. *Beloperone guttata*), shrimp plant, is one of the most widely grown of the species. An evergreen shrub, it grows to 1 m (3 ft) and has soft, ovate leaves and pendulous flower spikes, 15 cm (6 in) long. The bracts are red or brown and the small, tubular flowers are white with red spots. The cultivar 'Yellow Queen' has light green bracts with a yellowish tinge. *J. carnea* is a very handsome, evergreen shrub, growing to 3 m (10 ft), with stunning, hooded, deep pink flowers and rough, deep green leaves, purple on the undersides. There is also a white-flowered form. *J. rizzinii*, to 60 cm (24 in), has drooping, scarlet flowers, tipped with yellow, and small, narrow leaves. Flowering from fall to the end of spring, this is an evergreen species with soft foliage and stems, and in the UK is considered a particularly outstanding plant for the greenhouse or conservatory.

K

Kaempferia to Kunzea

Kaempferia (fam. Zingiberaceae)

The 50 species of rhizomatous perennials in this genus are native to India, southern China and Southeast Asia. They grow in forests as understorey plants. Some are used as flavorings and spices, as well as for scent and medicine. The foliage is attractive, marked or marbled in contrasting colors. Flowers may be pink, white or lilac. These plants die back completely in winter. Except in tropical climates, they are grown in a warm greenhouse or conservatory. Some spread rapidly, so are best confined to pots.

CULTIVATION These are best grown in soil-based potting compost in large pots or tubs. They need good light but should be shaded from direct sun. When the plants are growing, provide a humid atmosphere and water well. When they are dormant in winter, do not water the plants. Propagate by division in spring.

CLIMATE Tropical regions.

SPECIES *K. galanga* has rather horizontal foliage, to 15 cm (6 in) long, and fragrant, white flowers spotted with violet at the base. It is grown for its rhizome which is used as a flavoring in Asian dishes as well as for its scent. *K. pulchra* grows up to 15 cm (6 in), with dense, prettily marked foliage and simple, pale lilac flowers in summer. *K. rotunda*, Resurrection lily, also grows to about 15 cm (6 in). The leaves are silvery green above and purple beneath. Small spikes of white flowers with lilac tips appear in summer.

Kalanchoe (fam. Crassulaceae)

This very variable genus of around 125 species is widely distributed in tropical areas, especially tropical Africa and Madagascar. It now includes plants formerly classified with *Bryophyllum*. Many species are cultivated in the US either under glass or as house plants. They have opposite, fleshy, deeply lobed or pinnate leaves and bear terminal flower clusters which appear in late winter or spring.

CULTIVATION Except in warm frost-free climates, grow in an intermediate greenhouse or conservatory, in pots of gritty, soil-based, potting compost. They need maximum light but should be shaded from direct, strong sun. When they are in growth, water moderately, and in winter keep compost barely moist. Propagate from stem cuttings, from plantlets which develop on leaves, or from offsets. Sow seed in spring and germinate at 21°C (70°F).

CLIMATE Warmer parts of zone 10.

SPECIES *K. beharensis*, feltbush, probably the largest species, is a spreading shrub. The fleshy, heart-shaped leaves, up to 30 cm (12 in) long and about 20 cm (8 in) wide, are wavy-edged and covered with thick, brown felt which fades to green with age. The leaf scars on the thick stems become very hard and pointed, resembling large rose thorns. This species rarely flowers in cultivation. *K. blossfeldiana*, flaming Katy, from Madagascar, is a small, shrubby perennial, to 30 cm (12 in), with red-margined, deep green leaves and dense sprays of small, bright red flowers which last for several weeks. Hybrids come in red to pink, orange to yellow, and almost white flowers. *K. delagoensis* (syn. *K. tubiflora*), from Madagascar, has become naturalized in some parts of the world. It has

ABOVE Small, simple, lilac flowers appear amongst the heavily veined leaves of *Kaempferia pulchra*.

ABOVE There are several kalanchoe hybrids, of which this red cultivar is an example. They make good pot plants, while the pendent kinds make effective, hanging basket plants.

reddish brown, spotted, cylindrical leaves, grooved on the upper sides, and bright orange-red, bell-shaped flowers. *K. fedtschenkoi* is a popular succulent, to 50 cm (20 in), with many branches and trailing stems. It has glossy, blueish green, lobed leaves and sprays of lovely, purple or red, tubular flowers. *K. manginii* looks very attractive in a hanging basket, pro-ducing drooping stems of small, green leaves, edged with red, and a profusion of bell-shaped, red or pink flowers. *K. pinnata*, air plant, from tropical Africa and nearby islands, has become naturalized in many parts of the world. It pro-duces large, fleshy leaves on a stout, somewhat striped, purplish green stem and large, pendu-lous, bell-shaped flowers in green, with purple tips. Plantlets develop from the margins of the leaves. This species grows to 1 m (3 ft) tall. *K. pumila*, from Madagascar, is a very beautiful plant, with gray, ovate leaves, covered in a white powder, and violet-pink flowers with rolled back petals. It grows to only 20 cm (8 in) high. *K. tomentosa*, panda plant, to 50 cm (20 in), has felt-like stems and leaves, with brown markings on the edges. The pale yellow flowers are rarely seen in cultivation.

Kale

(*Brassica oleracea Acephala* Group, fam. Brassicaceae)

Curly kale

Curly kale has attractive, curled and crimped leaves which are cooked as a vegetable or used in salads. There are also decorative cultivars which have colored foliage.

CULTIVATION Grown as a cool-season annual for fall and winter cropping, seeds are sown in late spring in an outdoor seed bed. Transplant seedlings to cropping positions when 8–10 cm (3–4 in) high, spacing them about 60 cm (24 in) apart each way. Pick leaves as required. Frost often improves the flavor.

CLIMATE Zone 8 is best, but very hardy kales should survive zone 7.

ABOVE Ornamental kales can be used in flower borders or patio containers.

Kalmia (fam. Ericaceae)

Calico bush

Native to North America and Cuba, where they grow in woodlands and damp meadows, these beautiful, evergreen shrubs, related to rhododendrons, produce unusual flowers in spring or early summer. They resemble blobs of icing sugar when they are in bud.

CULTIVATION Ideal for woodland gardens and shrub borders, kalmias like dappled shade and need acid, humus-rich, moisture-retentive soil. Keep permanently mulched with chipped or shredded bark. Propagate by layering in spring or from semi-ripe cuttings in summer.

CLIMATE Cool and moist. There are species which are suited to various climatic zones.

SPECIES *K. angustifolia*, sheep laurel, zone 2, is an open, quite twiggy shrub, to 1 m (3 ft), with saucershaped, pink flowers and oval leaves. This species is poisonous to animals. The form rubra is very popular and produces dark red blooms. *K. latifolia*, calico bush, zone 5, grows to about 3 m (10 ft) high. It is the most popular species in the US and is grown mostly for its delightful flowers. The pale pink flowers have unusually arranged stamens and the deep green, oval leaves are quite leathery. It grows to about 3 m (10 ft). Some good cultivars include 'Fresca', with flowers banded in purple; 'Nipmuck', with virtually white flowers developing from red buds; 'Ostbo Red', with pale pink flowers from bright red buds; and 'Silver Dollar', which has big white blooms.

Kennedia (fam. Papilionaceae)

Native to Australia, most of these 15 species of climbing or scrambling plants are from Western Australia. They produce bright pink or scarlet, pea-like flowers and the leaves consist of three leaflets. In climates that are prone to frosts, Kennedia species are very good and unusual plants which will suit the conditions of cool to intermediate greenhouses and conservatories, as they adapt well to either pot or tub culture.

CULTIVATION Under glass, grow in a gritty, well-drained, soil-based potting compost. Plants need maximum light, but should be shaded from direct strong sun. Be very sparing with water in winter but water normally in the growing period. Provide supports for the stems of climbers, and in late winter, prune back side shoots to within four buds of the main stems.

ABOVE One of the loveliest of North America's woodland shrubs is *Kalmia latifolia*. It loves humus-rich soil.

ABOVE Large, colorful flowers of Kennedia coccinea are outstanding against the leathery foliage of this scrambling plant.

Propagate from seed in spring, after soaking the seeds in water overnight (pour boiling water over them). Outdoors grow in moist yet well-drained soil and partial shade. Germinate at 21°C (70°F).

CLIMATE Zone 10.

SPECIES *K. coccinea*, coral vine, is a vigorous climber, with a profusion of bright, orange-red or scarlet flowers in spring and early summer. The young growth is rather hairy. *K. macrophylla* is a twiner, with large, light green, trifoliate leaves and long sprays of large, scarlet flowers, yellow at the base, in spring. *K. microphylla* is a dense, mat-forming groundcover with small, shiny, dark green leaves and rich pinkish red flowers in spring. *K. nigricans*, black coral pea, is a vigorous climber with large, shiny green leaves and unusual, black and yellow pea flowers in spring. *K. prostrata*, running postman, is a trailing species which spreads to 1.5 m (5 ft). It produces large, scarlet flowers in spring and summer. *K. rubicunda*, dusky coral pea or red bean, is an extremely vigorous species that spreads rapidly. It has oval, hairy leaves and striking, dull rusty red flowers in late spring and early summer.

Kerria (fam. Rosaceae)

There is only one species in this genus of spring-flowering shrubs from China and Japan. With delightful, yellow flowers, they are perfect for brightening a shady corner of the garden and for cutting.

CULTIVATION These hardy shrubs do well in a moist, well-drained soil in either sun or partial shade, but require hard pruning after flowering to avoid straggliness. Cut back shoots that have flowered to young shoots lower down. Propagate from semi-ripe cuttings in summer, or from hardwood cuttings in fall or winter, rooting them in a garden frame or greenhouse. Divide established clumps in fall or winter.

CLIMATE Zone 4.

ABOVE *Kerria japonica* 'Pleniflora' is a large shrub and can make a good screen.

SPECIES *K. japonica* is a multi-stemmed shrub to 2.5 m (8 ft), with single, round, golden flowers clustered along the stems, and bright green, ovate, finely serrated leaves. Often grown is cultivar 'Pleniflora', with bright yellow, double flowers.

Keteleeria (fam. Pinaceae)

Native to central and southern China and Taiwan, this genus of tall, fir-like, evergreen trees has stiff, narrow leaves and large cones.

CULTIVATION Tolerant of only very light frost, keteleerias do best in mild climates. They require a moist, well-drained, peaty soil. They should not be pruned but allowed to develop their own attractive form. Propagate by seed.

CLIMATE Warmer parts of zone 9.

SPECIES *K. fortunei* is a handsome tree, growing to 12–24 m (40–80 ft) tall. It has horizontal branches, sharply tipped leaves and cones

ABOVE Like the firs, *Keteleeria fortunei* has upright-growing cones. These delicate, blue-green cones are a feature.

ABOVE It is easy to see how *Kigelia pinnata* got the name of sausage tree. The woody fruits persist for months.

10–18 cm (4–7 in) long, borne on reddish twigs. The foliage is a rich, dark green. This species makes an imposing lawn specimen.

Kigelia (fam. Bignoniaceae)
Sausage tree

This genus comprises only one species of evergreen tree, native to woodlands and more open country of tropical Africa. It is often grown as a curiosity, either as a specimen or shade tree, in tropical gardens. In the US, it is sometimes grown under glass for its foliage only.

CULTIVATION Grow in a warm greenhouse, in a large pot or tub of soil-based potting compost. Shade from direct strong sun. It may be necessary to prune lightly in late winter. Propagate from seed sown in spring and germinated at 22°C (72°F).

CLIMATE Warmer parts of zone 10, and above.

SPECIES *K. pinnata*, sausage tree, grows 10–15 m (33–50 ft) high. The pinnate leaves are dark green and leathery. The very dark burgundy flowers, suspended on long stems, emerge from yellowish buds. Their unusual odor is attractive to bats, their natural pollinators. The woody, cylindrical fruits, 30–50 cm (12–20 in) long, are beige-brown when ripe, lasting on the tree for many months.

Kingia (fam. Xanthorrhoeaceae)
Drumhead, grass tree

This single-species genus from Western Australia is a member of the grass tree family, thought to be one of the oldest still in existence. It is difficult to cultivate, slow growing and hard to transplant but, if successful, adds an exciting textural quality to a garden. It is unlikely to be available outside Australia.

CULTIVATION In most of the US, this plant must be grown in a warm greenhouse or conserva-

ABOVE Very slow growing *Kingia australis* produces a ring of drumstick-like flowering heads amongst the upper leaves.

tory, in a large pot or tub of sandy, soil-based potting compost, which must be very well drained. It needs maximum light but shade from strong, direct sun. Outdoors grow in light, well-drained soil and full sun or light shade. Although seed germinates easily, seedlings may take many years to develop. The tree has a deep and complex root system and does not take kindly to being disturbed.

CLIMATE Zone 10.

SPECIES *K. australis* grows extremely slowly to around 6 m (20 ft). With age, it forms a cylindrical-shaped trunk, topped by a tuft of 60 cm (24 in) long, needle-like leaves, resembling a grass skirt. The ball-shaped heads of creamy colored flowers are borne singly on shortish, erect stalks, forming a circle within the leaves.

Kiwi fruit

(*Actinidia deliciosa*, fam. Actinidiaceae)

Chinese gooseberry

Native to China and widely grown in the North Island of New Zealand, this twining, deciduous vine is a vigorous grower and needs a strong trellis for support and ease of harvesting. Unrelated to the English gooseberry, the fruit does have a similar, appealing taste and is now marketed to countries around the world. It is delicious raw and is also used in sweets, jams and pickles.

CULTIVATION This dioecious plant needs one male plant to pollinate up to ten female plants. It can be propagated from seed, though it is not possible to distinguish the male and female seedlings until they flower. The fruit types from the female seedlings can also be very variable. A better method is to graft a scion from proven stock onto a seedling root stock, about 8 cm (3 in) long. Plant the stock about 5 cm (2 in) deep, and stake and protect from winds. Plant

ABOVE Kiwi fruits mature slowly and can remain on the vine for many weeks.

out at any time during the dormant season near a trellis or pergola. It needs a light, well-drained soil with added organic matter and some liquid fertilizer, as the plant is a heavy feeder. As the plant has a shallow root system, the soil must not be allowed to dry out. Mulching around the vines helps retain moisture and aids weed control which is essential. Train and prune regularly to prevent unmanageable growth and to improve fruit size and quality. In winter, prune established plants by thinning out congested growth. Also prune some of the three-year-old lateral growths to within one bud of the main stems, and reduce others to several buds. The crop is harvested in mid-fall when the fruit is firm enough to handle, but not hard. At this stage, the flesh is green to whitish, reasonably firm and juicy, and the flavor is fully developed. It can be stored in a cool location without refrigeration for up to eight weeks. Kiwi fruit appears to be relatively pest- and disease-free.

CLIMATE Zone 8.

VARIETIES Some good cultivars include 'Chico', 'Hayward', 'Tomuri' (often used to pollinate 'Vincent'), and 'Vincent' which is suitable for milder winter climates.

Knightia (fam. Proteaceae)

Maori honeysuckle, rewarewa

Native to New Zealand, this tall, columnar tree grows 12–20 m (40–65 ft) high. The trees yield a fine timber and appear to have some fire-resistance.

CULTIVATION The only species cultivated, *K. excelsa* prefers a well-drained soil and will tolerate fairly dry conditions. In climates prone to frost, grow in a cool greenhouse. Propagate from seed sown in spring.

CLIMATE Warmer parts of zone 9.

SPECIES *K. excelsa* has long, leathery, toothed leaves, dense sprays of bisexual, deep reddish brown, summer flowers which attract birds,

ABOVE The slender tree, *Knightia excelsa*, may be multi-trunked. The young leaves and shoots are covered with brown, felty hairs.

and winged seeds. It is grown for its timber, used in cabinet-making, and its beautiful flowers, which generally take several years to appear.

Kniphofia (fam. Asphodelaceae)

Red hot poker

These striking, erect-growing perennials from southern Africa, with handsome flower spikes borne on long, bare stems, make an attractive garden display, particularly as background plants. Numerous cultivars make better garden subjects than straight species. Most have flowers in shades of scarlet, yellow, cream and green, with many in two tones.

CULTIVATION Kniphofias prefer light, well-drained soil and need plenty of water in hot weather. Once established, they tolerate drought well. Propagate from seed (new plants take up to three years to flower), or by division of the roots in spring. Cultivars must be divided.

CLIMATE There are species suited to various climates.

SPECIES *K. caulescens*, zone 7, growing to 1.2 m (4 ft), has rosettes of long leaves on a woody stem and dense, 15 cm (6 in) long spikes of flowers that turn from red to yellow. *K. foliosa*, zone 9, with 1 m (3 ft) long, sword-shaped leaves and bright yellow flowers on 30 cm (12 in) spikes, is from Ethiopia and grows to 1 m (3 ft). *K. northiae*, zone 7, recognized by its very long, blueish leaves which sometimes reach 150 cm (60 in), grows to 1.5 m (5 ft) and bears 30 cm (12 in) spikes of yellow flowers, which are red in bud. *K. pumila*, zone 9, which grows to 60 cm (24 in), has orange flowers and blueish foliage. *K. uvaria*, zone 5, one of the most popular species, has coral red flowers and grows 1.2 m (4 ft) tall. Many hybrids of *Kniphofia*, in various flower colors, are available.

ABOVE Also known as torch lilies, *Kniphofia* species are dramatic with their bright color and stature.

Koelreuteria (fam. Sapindaceae)
Golden rain tree

These graceful, deciduous trees from eastern Asia are grown for their lovely foliage, flowers and decorative fruit. They are thought to have inspired the willow pattern design. These trees are well suited to milder US climates and flower best where summers are hot.

CULTIVATION Koelreuterias prefer warm, dry conditions and a reasonably rich soil, and need to be planted in full sun. They can be propagated from seed sown in fall and germinated in a garden frame, or from root cuttings in winter under glass.

CLIMATE There are species suited to various climatic zones.

SPECIES *K. paniculata*, zone 5, to 10–12 m (33–40 ft) tall, makes a delightful garden addition, with long, showy sprays of deep yellow flowers in summer, followed by papery, bladder-like, pinkish brown pods. The large, compound leaves color gold in fall. This is the most

ABOVE With bright sunny, fall days *Koelreuteria paniculata* takes on rich, tawny gold and orange colors.

ABOVE The scarlet-orange flowers on *Kohleria eriantha* echo the red-margined leaves. The leaves have a velvety texture.

commonly cultivated species. Two other handsome species *K. bipinnata*, zone 8, and *K. elegans*, zone 9, which grow to 15 m (50 ft) in their habitats, are also cultivated.

Kohleria (fam. Gesneriaceae)

This small genus of rhizomatous perennials and shrubs comes from tropical America.

CULTIVATION In the US, these tender plants are grown as pot plants in warm greenhouses and conservatories. Rhizomes are started into growth in spring. Use acid, soilless potting compost. Plants need a growing temperature of at least 21°C (70°F). Ensure a humid atmosphere during the growing period and shade plants from direct sun. Plants die down in fall, when stems should be removed and rhizomes kept virtually dry over winter. Propagate by division in spring.

CLIMATE Tropical only.

SPECIES Several species and hybrids are grown. Highly regarded and readily available is *K. eriantha*, with oval, dark green leaves which have

red hairs along the edges, and clusters of tubular, reddish-orange flowers with yellow spots. The plant grows to a height of 1.2 m (4 ft).

Kohl rabi

(*Brassica oleracea*, *Gongylodes* Group, fam. Brassicaceae)

Kohl rabi is a biennial but is treated as a cool-season annual. The edible, turnip-like, swollen stem grows and develops above the ground. There are green-stemmed and purple-stemmed cultivars available. Either type can be cooked and eaten as a vegetable, or served raw in salads. The taste is a pleasant combination of cabbage and turnip.

CULTIVATION Plant in a moderately rich, well-drained soil, with added organic matter, in full sun. Sow seed direct in cropping position, from mid-spring to late summer, to ensure a succession. Sow in rows 30 cm (12 in) apart and space plants at 25 cm (10 in). Protect early sowings with cloches or fleece. Give plenty of water and liquid fertilizer to encourage growth. Harvest the tubers when they have reached the size of a tennis ball. If allowed to grow larger, they will

ABOVE The purple of the bulbous stem of kohl rabi is echoed in the purple mid-vein of the leaf.

become stringy and tough. Keep the area weed free to avoid competition.

CLIMATE Zone 8 and above; grown in all climates as a summer crop.

Kolkwitzia (fam. Caprifoliaceae)

Beauty bush

This single-species genus from China is very similar to *Abelia*, although it is deciduous. It is a lovely shrub, particularly in full bloom in spring or early summer.

CULTIVATION Plant in a rich soil in full sun, in fall or spring. After flowering, cut back flowered stems to younger shoots lower down. Propagate from semi-ripe cuttings in summer.

CLIMATE Zone 4.

SPECIES *K. amabilis* grows 3–3.5 m (10–11 ft) tall, with graceful, arching stems and profuse clusters of pink, trumpet-shaped flowers, which are followed by dry, bristly fruits. It has a suckering habit, though it never gets out of hand.

ABOVE The aptly named beauty bush, *Kolkwitzia amabilis*, is a good choice at the back of a border or as a specimen.

Kopsia (fam. Apocynaceae)

This genus consists of 25 species of evergreen trees and shrubs, most of which are native to Southeast Asia and Malaysia. Fairly fast growing, their flowers are similar to those of frangipani, to which they are related.

CULTIVATION In frost-prone climates, these tropical plants are grown in a warm greenhouse or conservatory. Give good light, but shade from direct strong sun. Grow in a large pot or tub of well-drained, soil-based potting compost. Water well in summer but keep only slightly moist in winter. Outdoors grow in full sun with well-drained, humus-rich soil. Propagate from seed in fall or spring or from semi-ripe cuttings in summer, both with bottom heat.

CLIMATE Subtropical and tropical. Zone 10 and above.

SPECIES *K. flavida*, from New Guinea and Java, grows 10–12 m (33–40 ft) high, with long, oval leaves, deep green above, yellowish below. Fragrant, white, spring flowers have yellow throats. *K. fruticosa* is shrub-like, growing 6–8 m (20–26 ft) high. It has thin, shiny, textured leaves and clusters of pale pink, fragrant flowers with red throats, in spring.

ABOVE The flowers of *Kopsia fruticosa* have just a hint of pink and appear in the spring. A good warm conservatory shrub.

Kreysigia (fam. Liliaceae)

This pink-flowered lily, the only species in the genus, is found in coastal rainforests of northern New South Wales and south-eastern Queensland. It makes an attractive pot plant, but is unlikely to be available outside its native Australia.

CULTIVATION Grow in a warm, humid greenhouse or conservatory in frost-prone climates. It needs well-drained, soil-based potting compost. Outdoors this plant requires well-drained soil and a warm, humid situation. Propagate from seed, cuttings or by division.

CLIMATE Subtropical to tropical only.

SPECIES *K. multiflora* is a small, suckering plant, producing a number of slender stems from a fibrous-rooted rhizome. It has broad, stemless leaves and fine, long spikes of spring flowers, then capsule-shaped fruit containing yellow seeds.

ABOVE *Kreysigia multiflora* needs to be grown under glass in frost-prone climates but then may not flower well.

Kumquat (*Fortunella* species, fam. Rutaceae)

Originally from China and eastern Asia, the kumquat is the smallest citrus cultivated, in tree size and fruit. It is grown both for decorative value and for its edible fruit. It is an evergreen shrub, to 3.5 m (11 ft), with small leaves, sometimes variegated, sweetly perfumed, white flowers, and orange-yellow, aromatic fruit, a little larger than a cherry. The fruit is eaten raw and is delicious made into jams and preserves.

CULTIVATION Kumquats are sensitive to frost, and in frost-prone climates should be grown in pots in a cool greenhouse or conservatory. Soil-based potting compost is recommended. Provide full light (but shade from direct strong sun) and an airy atmosphere. Where plants can be grown outside, they need a spot in full sun with fairly rich, well-drained, yet moisture-retentive soil. Propagation is from seed sown under glass in spring, or from semi-ripe cuttings

ABOVE Ripening Nagami kumquats. They are sweet enough to be eaten raw.

in summer. They will need basal warmth to root. Lightly prune plants to ensure a good shape and an open center. When pruning, bear in mind that they fruit on the previous year's wood.

CLIMATE At least zone 9.

SPECIES *F. japonica*, round or Marumi kumquat, has a sweet rind. *F. margarita*, oval or Nagami kumquat, can be eaten fresh.

Kunzea (fam. Myrtaceae)

Mostly found in heathlands in temperate areas of Australia, this genus of around 24 species of attractive, evergreen shrubs has brush-like flowers, mistakenly called bottlebrushes, a name which refers to Callistemon species. The flowers on all species are fluffy and may be pink, red, yellow or white. The small leaves are delightfully aromatic. Kunzeas are grown in a cool greenhouse or conservatory in cool climates and they adapt well to pot culture. The plants can be moved outdoors for summer and are ideal for shrub borders in warm climates.

CULTIVATION Under glass, grow in pots of acid, sandy, soil-based potting compost. Give maximum light and airy conditions. Water normally in the growing period, but keep compost only slightly moist in winter. In the garden, in favorable climates, grow in full sun, in neutral to acid, well-drained, sandy soil. Prune lightly after flowering to maintain shape. Propagate from seed sown in spring (do not cover with compost), or from semi-ripe cuttings in summer, both with basal warmth.

CLIMATE Zone 10, but may be worth trying in warmest parts of zone 9.

SPECIES *K. affinis*, from Western Australia, grows to 2 m (6 ft), with terminal clusters of beautiful, bright pink flowers, with small, greenish anthers. *K. ambigua*, from eastern Australia, has stiff foliage and white, or occasionally pink, flowers with a honey fragrance. It

ABOVE *Kunzea recurva* var. *montana* has creamy yellow flowers. It makes a dense, rounded shrub in full sun.

grows well coastally, reaching up to 3 m (10 ft) high. *K. baxteri*, crimson kunzea, is a superb, ornamental shrub, to 3 m (10 ft) high, with vivid crimson flowers almost year round. In cultivation, this plant may not bloom for several years. *K. capitata* is an adaptable plant, to 1 m (3 ft), with fine, woolly foliage and mauve-pink to purple, terminal flowers. *K. parvifolia*, from south-eastern Australia, produces masses of pink-lilac, fluffy balls in late spring or early summer. *K. recurva*, from Western Australia, has fine foliage and pink flowers from spring to early summer. Var. *montana* has fine foliage and yellow, spring flowers.

L

Laburnum to Lysimachia

Laburnum (fam. Papilionaceae)

Bean tree, golden chain tree

Originating from temperate regions of Europe and western Asia, this genus comprises two species of ornamental, deciduous trees grown for their attractive foliage, abundant sprays of yellow, spring flowers, followed by brown pods.

CULTIVATION Almost any soil will do, but these plants prefer full sun. They can be trained over pergolas and arches or on walls, and respond well to pruning in winter. Propagate species from seed and varieties and cultivars by grafting and budding onto stock species, or by layering.

CLIMATE Zone 5 for the following.

SPECIES *L. anagyroides* grows to 5 m (16 ft), with sprays of golden flowers in late spring to early summer. Cultivar 'Pendulum' is a weeping form. It is a long-lived tree, often trained over arches or pergolas. The timber is sometimes used as an ebony substitute in inlaid work. All parts of the plant are poisonous. *L.* x *watereri*, golden chain tree, is a hybrid of *L. alpinum* and *L. anagyroides*, producing very long, drooping sprays of golden flowers. Cultivar 'Vossii' has even longer flower trusses.

Laccospadix (fam. Arecaceae)

Atherton palm

Native to the coastal rainforests of northern Queensland in Australia, *Laccospadix* is a feathered palm related to *Howea*, the young plants particularly being quite similar in appearance and cultivation needs. In its natural habitat, it is generally found as an understorey plant. Because it originates from areas of reasonable altitude, it is more cold-tolerant than many tropical palms, and may do well in more temperate regions. However, it is not readily available outside its native Australia.

CULTIVATION In frost-prone climates, grow in an intermediate to warm greenhouse or conservatory in a pot or tub of soil-based potting compost. Provide maximum light, but shade from direct sun. Propagate from seed, which must be sown fresh. Germinate at 27°C (81°F). Germination can be rapid (for a palm), as little as six weeks in ideal conditions. This palm is generally slow growing.

CLIMATE Zone 10 plus.

ABOVE *Laburnum anagyroides* is effective used over pergolas or arches where its bright flowers can be seen from below.

ABOVE *Laccospadix australasica* is not well known outside its native Australia but would make a good conservatory plant in frost-prone climates.

SPECIES *L. australasica*, the single species, usually forms clumps of up to about ten stems, 5 cm (2 in) or so in diameter and 2–3 m (6–10 ft) tall, but sometimes has only a single stem to 15 m (50 ft) tall and 15 cm (6 in) in diameter. The leaves grow up to 2 m (6 ft) long and ascend steeply, and the narrow, deep green leaflets sit in two, neat rows. Erect flower spikes, arising from among the leaf bases, are followed by juicy-fleshed fruits which ripen through yellow to bright scarlet.

Lachenalia (fam Hyacinthaceae)

Cape cowslip

Originally from South Africa, lachenalias are small bulbs planted for fall to spring display. When mass planted, the upright spikes of small, white, yellow or red, tubular flowers resemble marching soldiers. While red, yellow and white flowers are familiar, there is a surprising color range amongst the numerous species. In the new types being grown, colors include pink, purple and cream. The strap-like leaves are sometimes spotted at the base. In frost-prone climates, these bulbs make ideal pot plants for the cool greenhouse or conservatory. The flowers retain their color after drying, and are good cut blooms.

CULTIVATION Under glass, grow the bulbs in pots of soil-based potting compost, planting in late summer or early fall, 10 cm (4 in) deep. Give maximum light. Water normally when in full growth but ease off as the leaves die down, and do not water when bulbs are dormant. Resume watering when growth starts in fall. Propagate by detaching bulblets when repotting.

CLIMATE Zone 10.

SPECIES *L. aloides* grows to 30 cm (12 in). The leaves are sometimes spotted and the flower spikes comprise drooping, yellow bells with red tips. Var. *aurea* has orange flowers; var. *conspicua* has orange flowers with purple veins and yellowish tips; var. *luteola* has lemon flowers with green tips; 'Nelsonii' has yellow flowers

ABOVE *Lachenalia aloides* is a popular species and makes a good pot plant for the cool conservatory, flowering in winter and early spring.

with green tinges; var. *quadricolor* has red flowers which graduate to greenish tips, and have a purplish color inside. *L. bulbifera* has orange flowers, colored purple inside, and grows to 25 cm (10 in). *L. liliiflora* grows to 30 cm (12 in), with white, cylindrical flowers. *L. mutabilis* has blueish green flowers which turn brown with age. This species grows to 30 cm (12 in). *L. orchioides* grows to 40 cm (16 in) high. The leaves are often spotted with purple and the flowers are colored pale blue, shading to greenish yellow. Var. *glaucina* has flowers which are shaded blue to a purplish tone.

Laelia (fam. Orchidaceae)

Closely related to *Cattleya*, *Encyclia*, *Sophronitis* and other orchid groups, this large, tropical American genus has been widely hybridized. The contribution of *Laelia* to such hybrids is dazzling colors: yellow, scarlet, reddish orange and copper.

CULTIVATION In frost-prone climates, grow in a cool to intermediate greenhouse or conservatory. These orchids are mainly epiphytic so can be grown in slatted, wooden orchid baskets

ABOVE *Laelia anceps* is native to Mexico. The pink and purple form is most often seen but there are other color forms known.

filled with compost formulated for epiphytic orchids, and suspended from the greenhouse roof; small species can be mounted on pieces of bark and hung up in the greenhouse. During the summer, shade the plants from direct sun and water normally, feeding with liquid fertilizer every seven to ten days. Mist spray the plants daily. During the winter, the plants will need maximum light and far less water. Propagate by division when plants become pot bound and need potting on. With some species, leafless pseudobulbs can be removed and potted singly.

CLIMATE Must be totally frost-free.

SPECIES *L. anceps* is easy to grow, producing large, showy, upright flowers in rose to purple in late fall to winter. The erect stems grow to 60 cm (24 in) and the flowers are about 10 cm (4 in) across. *L. autumnalis*, from Mexico, likes cool growing conditions as it occurs naturally at quite high altitudes. The stems grow up to 1 m (3 ft) in length, each bearing from five to ten, large, purple flowers in fall through to winter. *L. cinnabarina*, from Brazil, carries sprays of bright orange-red flowers in winter. *L. lundii*, a dwarf type from Brazil, grows only 12 cm (5 in) high and thrives in a small pot.

The lilac flowers appear in winter and are usually about 3–4 cm (1–1½ in) across. *L. tenebrosa*, also from Brazil, produces large flowers in summer, variable in color but often copper to yellow, suffused with lavender.

Lagenaria (fam. Cucurbitaceae)
Bottle gourd

Originating from tropical South America and Africa, this genus comprises six species of vine. Many of the fruits, or gourds, come in unusual shapes and are useful for decorative dried arrangements, while native peoples use them as utensils and containers.

CULTIVATION Easily grown as an annual, these vines need a warm, sheltered situation and some kind of support. Water and fertilize well while gourds are forming. Propagate from ripened seed sown in spring. Do not subject plants to frost.

CLIMATE Zone 10; grown outdoors as a summer annual in all climates.

SPECIES *L. siceraria*, calabash or bottle gourd, has climbing tendrils and white flowers in summer, followed by ornamental gourds of

ABOVE A potted *Lagenaria siceraria* displays some well-formed gourds that will have very hard shells when fully ripe.

many colors, shapes and sizes, including round, striped, oval, dumb-bell and cylindrical. Cultivar 'Hercules' Club' produces long, club-shaped gourds.

Lagerstroemia (fam. Lythraceae)
Crape myrtle

Native to East and Southeast Asia, as well as some of the islands in the western Pacific, these lovely evergreen and deciduous shrubs and trees are grown for their showy clusters of frilly flowers which appear in late summer or fall. The common name is derived from the crinkly nature of the flowers. In frost-prone climates, grow in a cool to intermediate greenhouse. Where the climate is warmer, grow as specimen plants in the garden or as hedges. *L. indica* is a frost-tolerant species suited to zone 7.

CULTIVATION Under glass, grow in pots or tubs of soil-based potting compost, in maximum light. They can be stood outside in summer. In the garden, crape myrtles prefer well-drained, fertile soil, enriched with organic matter. They are able to tolerate dry periods, although it is advisable to water them through spring and summer to ensure good flowering. Prune in winter if necessary. In humid climates, powdery mildew can be a problem. Propagate from cuttings taken in summer, or from large hardwood cuttings of about 15–25 cm (6–10 in), taken in winter. Root them under glass in pots of cuttings compost. Some varieties will sucker from the roots, especially if cut back hard, and these can be detached and grown on during spring and summer.

CLIMATE There are species suited to various climatic zones.

SPECIES *L. fauriei*, zone 9, is a deciduous species with white flowers which comes from Japan. *L. floribunda*, zone 10, is a small tree with pink or white flowers. *L. indica*, crape myrtle or pride of India, zone 7, is a deciduous shrub or small tree, to 6 m (20 ft), with roundish leaves and profuse clusters of white, pink, lilac or purplish

ABOVE Large trusses of bright pink, frilly flowers on crepe myrtle persist over several weeks in late summer to fall.

flowers in late summer and fall. There are numerous cultivars, some of which originated in North America, but they are not all readily available. However, it is worth looking out for such kinds as 'Catawba', with purple blooms; the deep red cultivar 'Dallas Red'; the deep pink-flowered 'Miami', which has a long flowering period in summer and fall; 'Sioux', with especially large, pink flowers; and 'White Dwarf', whose name describes it well. This cultivar forms a low bush about 1 m (3 ft) in height. The dwarf shrubby 'Petite' series with flowers in various colors is particularly popular with gardeners. *L. speciosa*, Queen's crape myrtle, zone 10, can reach 25 m (80 ft) in its habitat, and is highly prized in its native India, Sri Lanka and Burma for its timber. It has long, leathery leaves with red-brown undersides and showy clusters of large, purple, pink or white flowers from summer to fall.

Lagunaria (fam. Malvaceae)
Norfolk Island hibiscus

This single-species genus, native to coastal Queensland and Lord Howe and Norfolk Islands of Australia, makes a very useful street tree in the right conditions. It is also a fine specimen tree for large gardens.

ABOVE Pale pink flowers of *Lagunaria patersonii* are pretty against the gray-green foliage. Flowers are borne

CULTIVATION In frost-prone climates, grow in pots of soil-based potting compost in a cool greenhouse. Give good light. In the garden, Lagunaria needs well-drained soil and full sun. Young plants require protection from frost, but once established, this plant tolerates light frost. Propagate from seed (being mindful of the hairs on the seed capsule which can cause irritation to the skin), or from cuttings taken in fall.

CLIMATE Zone 10, but also warmer parts of zone 9.

SPECIES *L. patersonii* grows 10–15 m (33–50 ft) high, making a tall and narrow shape or becoming wide and spreading, depending on conditions. It has oval, pale gray-green leaves and hibiscus-like, generally pink, open flowers over a long period. The fruits contain bright red seeds. The irritant hairs on the seed capsule give rise to another common name, cow itch tree. This is a particularly good tree for exposed coastal sites.

Lambertia (fam. Proteaceae)
Honey flower

These Australian shrubs produce striking, red, orange or yellow flowers and an abundance of nectar which attracts birds to the garden. The foliage is very stiff and sometimes sharply pointed or prickly. Lambertias are quite slow growing, but make excellent garden shrubs, flowering for a long period from spring to summer. In frost-prone climates, they can be grown as pot plants in a cool to intermediate greenhouse or conservatory.

CULTIVATION Under glass, grow these plants in an acid, soil-based potting compost, in maximum light. In the garden, plant in a well-drained, light, acid to neutral soil. Choose a sheltered position in full sun. Propagate from seed in spring or semi-ripe cuttings in summer, both in a heated propagating case.

CLIMATE Zone 10, or warmer parts of zone 9.

SPECIES *L. ericifolia* grows 3 m (10 ft) in height, with showy, orange-red flowers and narrow, stiff foliage. This Western Australian species is not suitable for humid areas. *L. formosa*, mountain devil, native to eastern Australia, is the most widely cultivated species. It produces clusters of large, bright red flowers almost year round. Their foxy 'faces' make the seed capsules

ABOVE *Lambertia formosa* flowers, also known as mountain devils, attract birds with their nectar.

useful for making children's toys. *L. ilicifolia*, holly-leafed lambertia, has stiff, gray-green foliage and yellow blooms. *L. multiflora*, many-flowered honeysuckle, produces yellow or red flowers for much of the year.

Lamium (fam. Lamiaceae)

Dead nettle

These rhizomatous perennials, from Europe and Asia, are very useful groundcover plants for shaded areas of the garden, such as under trees and shrubs. The kidney-shaped leaves are often variegated with silver, and the two-lipped flowers appear in late spring and summer.

CULTIVATION Most species prefer cool, moist situations and do well planted under trees. Propagate by division in early spring or fall, or from stem tip cuttings in early summer.

CLIMATE There are species suited to various climatic zones.

SPECIES *L. galeobdolon*, zone 6, with yellow flowers, is known as yellow archangel. It comes from Europe. Forms with silver-variegated leaves are commonly grown. It can be rather invasive in warm climates. *L. maculatum*, zone 4, to 30 cm (12 in), has purple, pink or white flowers. The leaves have a central white rib. Cultivar 'Aureum' produces leaves blotched with yellow, and the foliage of 'Beacon Silver' and 'White Nancy' is heavily marked with silver.

Lampranthus (fam. Aizoaceae)

Originally from Cape Province in South Africa, this genus consists of 200 species of prostrate, perennial succulents, grown for their profusion of sparkling, summer and fall flowers. These branching plants have rounded to three-angled, shiny, bright green, blunt or tapered leaves. The glossy, 5 cm (2 in) wide, daisy-like flowers, range from pure white through yellow, orange, red and pink to purple. In frost-prone climates, grow in an intermediate greenhouse or use as summer bedding plants.

CULTIVATION These succulents are easy to grow, requiring only full sun to open the flowers. They are useful groundcovers and soil-binding plants. Trim occasionally after flowering as they can become straggly. Under glass, grow in pots of cactus compost in maximum light. Keep plants only slightly moist in the winter. Propagate from seed or stem cuttings in the spring with basal warmth.

ABOVE Rich orange and yellow flowers make this *Lampranthus* species a bright splash of color.

ABOVE Some *Lamium maculatum* cultivars have leaves attractively marked in silver and can provide dense groundcovers.

CLIMATE Warmer parts of zone 9.

SPECIES *L. amoenus* has semi-cylindrical leaves, which turn a reddish color in full sun, and purplish red flowers. *L. aureus* grows to around 40 cm (16 in), with vivid, golden-orange flowers and threeangled, blueish green, tapering leaves. *L. candidus* has white flowers which turn pinkish with age. *L. coccineus* is a dazzling sight in summer, with its intensely red, iridescent blooms. The gray-green leaves are tubular. *L. purpureus* has shiny, rounded leaves and abundant pink-purple flowers. *L. roseus* has masses of pale pink flowers and *L. specta-bilis* very large, purplish red flowers.

Lantana (fam. Verbenaceae)

A large genus of well-known shrubs, native to tropical and South Africa and tropical America, many of the species have bright, attractive flowers. Some are prickly, and most have foliage that is slightly rough.

CULTIVATION In frost-prone climates, grow in an intermediate greenhouse or conservatory, or use as summer bedding plants. Under glass, grow in pots of soil-based potting compost, in bright light. When bedded outdoors, the plants need a sunny position. Prune lightly in late winter for a compact habit. Propagate from semi-ripe cuttings in summer.

ABOVE Trailing lantana *L. montevidensis* makes an easy-care, spillover plant for walls and banks.

CLIMATE Zone 10, or possibly warmer parts of zone 9.

SPECIES *L. camara* is a dense shrub which grows to 3 m (10 ft) high. It has now been declared a noxious weed in many warmer parts of the world and so must be controlled. The characteristic, four-angled stems bear recurved prickles, the clusters of small flowers are pale cream with dark yellow centers changing to lilac, and the green fruits turn black with maturity. The seeds of these fruits are easily distributed by birds. There are several useful and colorful dwarf, sterile cultivars of *L. camara* to grow instead of the species. These mainly grow to around 50 cm (20 in) high, and flower in white, yellow, orange, pink, red or mauve. *L. montevidensis* is a hardy, trailing plant whose leaves darken in cold weather. It has long-lasting, mauvish purple flowers and is good for banks or for trailing over walls.

Lapageria (fam. Philesiaceae)
Chilean bellflower

This lovely, climbing plant originates from Chile and is that country's native emblem.

CULTIVATION Where frosts are likely, grow in a cool conservatory or greenhouse. Grow in a pot

ABOVE The lovely Chilean bellflower, *Lapageria rosea*, has rich, rosy red flowers. Beneath is a flower of the white form.

or tub of acid, soilless potting compost with added grit. Good light is needed but shade from direct sun. Outdoors, grow against a sheltered wall with partial shade, in moist yet well-drained, acid to neutral soil which contains plenty of humus. Propagate by layering in the spring or from semi-ripe cuttings, taken in the summer.

CLIMATE Warmer parts of zone 9.

SPECIES *L. rosea* grows with suppport 3–5 m (10–16 ft) high and produces a profusion of deep pink to red, bell-shaped flowers with a waxy, translucent appearance. It has a long flowering period through summer and fall. The leaves are a glossy, bright green. Var. *albiflora* has white flowers.

Larix (fam. Pinaceae)
Larch

Native to the colder areas of the northern hemisphere, this genus comprises ten species of deciduous, fast-growing conifers which can be distinguished from *Cedrus*, which looks similar, by their small, linear leaves, mostly in dense

ABOVE The weeping, needle-like foliage of the Japanese larch, *Larix kaempferi*, is silhouetted against a clear sky.

rosettes, and their small, many-scaled cones. These fairly large trees are grown for their graceful form and attractive, needle-like foliage, and are cultivated for their strong, durable timber. The leaves color yellow in fall, before falling. Larches are suited to cold and cool parts of the US but not to warm climates. They are too large for ordinary, private gardens.

CULTIVATION If the climate is suitable, these trees have no particular requirements. They prefer full sun and well-drained soil. Propagate from seed, which germinates readily.

CLIMATE Zone 4 for most. Zone 2 for *L. laricina*.

SPECIES *L. decidua* (syn. *L. europaea*), European larch, from the mountainous areas of central Europe, grows to 30 m (100 ft) or more, with a pyramidal crown and light green leaves. *L. kaempferi*, Japanese larch, is a large, vigorous tree, growing 30 m (100 ft) tall, with a spread of 10 m (33 ft). It has soft, needle-like leaves in gray-green to blue-green and is popular in suitable climates. *L. laricina*, tamarack, from North America, is a small to medium conifer, 18–25 m (60–80 ft) tall, with bright green leaves.

Latania (fam. Arecaceae)
Latan palm

Of these three species of dioecious fan palms, native to the Mascarene Islands, two are widely grown in the tropics. All are medium-sized, single-trunked palms. The trunk reaches 15 m (50 ft) high and is 20–25 cm (8–10 in) in diameter. The broad base of the stems of these palms splits into two halves, and the very heavy, stiff, palmate leaves form a substantial crown. The large, sparsely branched, flowering stems develop slightly fleshy fruits if the flowers are fertilized. The latans are dramatic but fairly slow growing. In their early growth stage, the deep reddish or orange-yellow of the ribs contrasts with the dark green of the leaf blades.

CULTIVATION In frost-prone climates, grow in a warm greenhouse or conservatory. Grow in

ABOVE The striking, fan fronds of the blue latan palm, *Latania loddigesii*, spread out stiffly from the crown.

pots of sandy, soil-based potting compost and add some leaf mould if available. Ensure maximum light, but shade from direct sun. Outdoors grow in full sun with fairly rich, well-drained soil. Propagate from fresh seed, sown one seed per pot, and germinated at 26° (79°C). Normally, germination is rapid (for a palm), occurring in two to four months.

CLIMATE Warmer parts of zone 10.

SPECIES *L. loddigesii*, blue latan, from Mauritius, has rather glaucous adult leaves, about 1.5 m (5 ft) long. *L. lontaroides*, red latan, from Reunion, has gray-green leaves with reddish stalks. Young palms have red leaves and bright red petioles. *L. verschaffeltii*, yellow latan, from Rodrigues, has pale green, slightly yellowish leaves with yellow edges.

Lathyrus (fam. Papilionaceae)
Wild pea

These annuals and perennials, many of which are climbers, originate from Europe, Asia, North America, South America and east Africa. The pea-shaped flowers bloom profusely during spring and summer, and range in color from a reddish purple, through shades of rose and pink, to mauve and white. *L. latifolius* and cul-

tivars of *L. odoratus* are the most commonly grown kinds in the US.

CULTIVATION The perennials are easily grown in almost any soil. They enjoy sun and tolerate fairly dry conditions. Propagate from seed or cuttings, or by division of the plants in spring. The climbing species need the support of a sunny wall or trellis. The annuals like sun, but they do best in a deep, moist soil. Propagate from seed sown in fall for spring and early summer flowering. All respond to regular feeding with a balanced liquid fertilizer when buds are forming.

CLIMATE There are species suited to various climatic zones.

SPECIES *L. grandiflorus*, everlasting pea, zone 6, from southern Europe, is a perennial climber, to about 2 m (6 ft), with large, rose-purple flowers. *L. japonicus*, beach pea, zone 3, is a perennial, trailing plant, with sprays of purple flowers, often seen along the shores of seas and lakes of Europe, North America and parts of Asia. *L. laetiflorus*, zone 8, a perennial climber, to around 3 m (10 ft), produces pale lavender

ABOVE Sweet pea, *Lathyrus odoratus*, is a favorite with home gardeners, for garden display and as a cut flower.

flowers veined with purple. *L. latifolius*, zone 5, from Europe, has become naturalized in many areas, including North America. A perennial climber, to 3 m (10 ft), it has clusters of fragrant, pale pink to purple flowers. The cultivar 'Albus' has pure white flowers. *L. odoratus*, sweet pea, zone 7, from Italy, is a vigorous, climbing annual whose pretty, fragrant flowers come in many colors. It grows to about 3 m (10 ft) and provides excellent cut flowers. Many varieties are cultivated for summer flowering, and dwarf forms grow in pots and hanging baskets. There are heat-resistant cultivars available for warm climates. *L. splendens*, zone 8, often called pride of California, is a perennial sub-shrub, to about 3 m (10 ft), with clusters of pink, violet or magenta, summer flowers.

Laurelia (fam. Monimiaceae)

Of these three species of evergreen trees, one originates from New Zealand and the other two from Chile. They all have very aromatic, leathery leaves, the fragrance of which is similar to that of the bay laurel.

CULTIVATION Grow in well-drained, but moisture-retentive, soil in sun or semi-shade, with shel-

ABOVE The hairy tufts on seeds of *Laurelia novae-zelandiae* aid in their dispersal over a wide area.

ter from winds. Propagate during summer from semi-ripe cuttings.

CLIMATE Zone 9.

SPECIES *L. novae-zelandiae*, with oblong, coarsely toothed leaves, reaches heights of 35 m (100 ft) in its native habitat of New Zealand. *L. sempervirens*, from Chile, grows to around 25 m (80 ft). Its tufted seeds are blown long distances by the wind. The fruits are used as a spice.

Laurus (fam. Lauraceae)
Bay laurel, sweet bay

The ancient Greeks used the leaves of this tree to form the wreaths which crowned the heroes of battle or sport and those who attained the baccalaureate, awarded for excellence in learning or the arts. Both species are medium-sized, evergreen trees with highly aromatic leaves.

CULTIVATION Propagate from seed or from cuttings of ripe wood. Laurel does best in a rich, moist soil in a sunny position, although it tolerates frost and partial shade. Control scale insects, which often attack laurels, with a systemic insecticide.

CLIMATE Zone 9 for *L. azorica*, zone 8 for *L. nobilis*.

ABOVE A free-standing bay laurel hedge acts as backdrop for an elegant urn. Bay laurel is a very versatile plant.

SPECIES *L. azorica*, Canary Island laurel, grows 10 m (33 ft). It has 12 cm (5 in) long leaves and tiny, greenish cream flowers. *L. nobilis*, sweet bay, from the Mediterranean, has dense, dark green leaves, which are used in cookery, and small, starry, fragrant, yellow flowers in the spring. Small, round, green berries follow the flowers, and ripen to a purplish black in the fall. Growing about 12–15 m (40–50 ft) tall in its native habitat, it is usually smaller in cultivation and is often grown in tubs as a standard or shaped as topiary.

Lavandula (fam. Lamiaceae)
Lavender

There are around 28 species of these delightful aromatic shrubs, often grown as low hedges. From the Mediterranean, the Canary Islands, North Africa and India, their tiny lavender and purple flowers are densely clustered on erect spikes which protrude above the fragrant, grayish green leaves. The dried flower spikes are used for scenting household linen. Oil of lavender, used in perfume, is obtained from *L. angustifolia* and *L. stoechas*.

CULTIVATION Lavender thrives in a sunny, well-drained situation. A slightly alkaline soil suits them best. Prune back as soon as the flowering season is over. It is preferable to renew these plants from cuttings every few years, though they can be grown from seed. Some species can be propagated by division.

CLIMATE Dry climates preferred. There are species suited to various climatic zones.

SPECIES *L. angustifolia* (syn. *L. spica*), common or English lavender, zone 5, from the Mediterranean, flowers in mid and late summer, depending on climate. Good garden cultivars include 'Hidcote', a compact type, to about 50 cm (20 in), with dark purple flowers; 'Loddon Pink', growing to around 40 cm (16 in), with soft pink flowers; 'Munstead', to 40 cm (16 in), with blueish purple flowers; and 'Nana Alba', a small, rounded bush with white flowers. *L. dentata*, zone 9, grows to about 1 m (3 ft), with soft gray, toothed leaves and small lavender flowers in mid and late summer. *L. lanata*, zone 8, from Spain, has violet flowers. Foliage and stems are covered with white hairs. *L. stoechas*, French lavender, zone 8, has deep purple summer flowers and smooth leaves. From the Mediterranean, it grows to 60 cm (24 in). Sub-species pedunculata has wide, silvery leaves and long spikes of pale blue, summer flowers. Common names for various lavender species vary from place to place.

Lavatera (fam. Malvaceae)

All 25 species of these annual, biennial and perennial, herbaceous plants and sub-shrubs bear mallowlike flowers in white or rose-purple tones. They are found in many parts of the world, including the Mediterranean, Macronesia, Asia, Australia and California.

CULTIVATION Lavateras are easy to grow but prefer warm, dry conditions. Propagate annuals from seed sown in mid to late spring, where the plants are to grow. Grow the perennials from cuttings taken in summer, or from seed sown in seed boxes, in late winter or early spring.

CLIMATE There are species suited to various climatic zones.

ABOVE A narrow path between massed lavenders allows foliage to be brushed in passing, releasing the lovely fragrance.

ABOVE Soft, pretty flowers are borne over many weeks on the annual *Lavatera trimestris*. There are many lovely cultivars.

SPECIES *L. arborea*, tree mallow, zone 8, from the Mediterranean, is a biennial or short-lived perennial which grows to 3 m (10 ft). It has longish leaves and reddish purple flowers which may appear in the first year. *L. assurgentiflora*, zone 9, is a semi-evergreen or deciduous shrub from California, to 2 m (6 ft), with 15 cm (6 in) long leaves and rosy purple flowers. *L. trimestris* (syn. *L. rosea*), zone 7, is a branching annual, to 1.5 m (5 ft), with pink, summer flowers. Various cultivars are available, such as the well-known 'Loveliness', with dark pink flowers; the white-flowered 'Mont Blanc'; pale pink 'Pink Beauty'; and the rose-pink 'Silver Cup'. There are numerous shrubby, evergreen hybrids such as 'Rosea', with pink flowers, *L.* 'Barnsley' with white, red-eyed flowers all summer; rich pink *L.* 'Bredon Springs'; and very deep pink *L.* 'Burgundy Wine'.

Leek (*Allium porrum*, fam. Alliaceae)

The leek was cultivated as early as 2500 BC by the Sumerians and was probably introduced to England by the Romans. However, it is the Welsh with whom it is generally associated as it has been part of their culture since the 12th century and is still their national symbol. Mostly treated as an annual, it is grown for its stem, which has a mild, onion-like flavor. The French have immortalized the leek in dishes like vichyssoise. *Allium porrum* is a bulbous plant, similar to the onion, but the leaves are broad and flat and the bulb is a tubular shape. A good seed catalogue will list numerous cultivars.

CULTIVATION Propagate from seed sown in early spring, either in an outdoor seed bed or in modules in a heated greenhouse. Plant out when seedlings are 6–8 cm (2½–3 in) tall. For long, well-blanched stems which will be very tender, plant in deep holes so that only the tops of the leaves are showing. Water in well. Space plants about 20 cm (8 in) apart, in rows about 45 cm (18 in) apart. Leeks like a rich, loamy soil and plenty of water in dry periods in the growing season. Keep weeds controlled and apply a complete fertilizer in bands along the rows at a rate of about 60 grams per metre (two ounces per yard).

CLIMATE Zone 6.

ABOVE Young leeks can be harvested and eaten at this stage but many people prefer them to develop thicker stems.

Lemon (*Citrus limon*, fam. Rutaceae)

Thought to have originated in India, Citrus limon was relatively late to cultivation when compared with many other plants. Around the 12th century it was introduced to Spain by the Arabs and from there it was carried through the Mediterranean and eventually to most tropical and subtropical regions. Although attractive in appearance, with fragrant, white flowers, it is grown chiefly for its acid, juicy fruit. The juice is high in vitamin C, and often used to treat colds. It makes a delicious, refreshing drink. Lemon juice is used in salad dressings, cakes, icings and biscuits, and is mandatory with fish. A commercial oil is extracted from the rind, while citric acid is produced from the pulp. Lemon can also be used to remove rust or ink stains, and is an ingredient in perfumes, cosmetics and furniture polish.

CULTIVATION In areas prone to hard frosts, grow in pots or tubs in an airy, cool to intermediate greenhouse or conservatory. Use soil-based potting compost, and provide maximum light, but shade from strong sun. Outside, the lemon tree does best in a mild to warm climate. Plant in any reasonable, well-drained garden soil, in full sun. Keep the area free of weeds or long grass, and feed regularly with animal manure or chemical fertilizer. The lemon is usually grafted onto an understock resistant to disease.

ABOVE Meyer lemons have very smooth skin. The rind is difficult to grate but the flesh is very juicy.

Remove shoots below the graft. Little pruning is required. The fruit is produced on the previous year's wood. If branches are weak or too long, cut them back. Lemons are ready for use when yellow; if they are to be stored, pick as soon as they start to change color, usually in winter. Retain the swollen end of the stem and store in a cool, dark, well-ventilated place. Lemons keep better than other citrus fruit.

CLIMATE Zone 10 and warmer parts of zone 9.

SPECIES *C. limon* is a small, evergreen tree, with short spines, which grows to around 4–5 m (13–16 ft). It has oblong, leathery, deep green leaves, pointed at the end, and fragrant, waxy, white flowers. The fruit is oval to oblong in shape, with finely pitted rind. Cultivar 'Eureka' is an almost spineless tree with rounded or sharply pointed, dark green leaves, and is almost continuously in fruit. 'Lisbon' is a more upright tree, with lighter green leaves. *C.* x *meyeri* 'Meyer', known as Meyer's lemon, is thought to be a hybrid of *C. limon* and *C. sinensis*. It is the hardiest lemon available, of compact habit, and has rounded, smooth, thin-skinned fruits. The fruits are very juicy and less acid than those of 'Eureka'.

Lemon balm (*Melissa officinalis*, fam. Lamiaceae)

Lemon balm

Native to southern Europe and some parts of Asia, this hardy perennial is grown for the fresh, lemon-flavored fragrance of the leaves. Used mostly in herbal teas for soothing benefit, the leaves are also added to stews, sauces and soups as a substitute for lemon. Only one of the three species has been cultivated. *M. officinalis* has small, greenish white flowers and leaves resembling nettle. It grows to about 70 cm (28 in). The cultivar 'Aurea' has gold-flecked leaves.

CULTIVATION Suited to warm and cool climates, though not to the tropics, balm will grow in

ABOVE Lemon balm leaves make delicious tea and add flavor to salads, poultry and fish. Plants make good groundcover.

ABOVE Lemon grass grows very vigorously at the height of summer but dies down as cool weather approaches.

any garden soil, but likes a sunny aspect. It spreads rapidly, dying down in winter and shooting again in spring. Propagate from seed, sown in early spring, or by division of the roots at the end of summer or in early fall.

CLIMATE Zone 4.

Lemon grass

(*Cymbopogon citratus*, fam. Poaceae)

Native to tropical regions of the Old World, this genus includes over 50 species of perennial, clump-forming grasses. The species called lemon grass is grown commercially for its aromatic oil, used in perfumery and aromatherapy. The leaves are commonly used in Thai cookery.

CULTIVATION Lemon grass is best grown in well-drained soil, enriched with manure or compost, in full sun. Keep well watered through the growing season. Propagate by division of the clumps in late winter or spring. It can also be grown from seed. In cool and cold climates, it is grown in pots of soil-based potting compost in a warm greenhouse. Ensure good light and a reasonably humid atmosphere.

CLIMATE Zone 10.

SPECIES *C. citratus*, lemon grass, forms dense clumps or tufts to about 1.5 m (5 ft) high. The sword-shaped leaves are almost 1 m (3 ft) long and the foliage is highly scented. *C. exaltatus* is an attractive grass, native to many areas of Australia. It grows to less than 1 m (3 ft) high and its foliage is strongly lemon scented. *C. nardus*, citronella grass, is similar to *C. citratus* and is the source of citronella oil.

Lemon verbena

(*Aloysia triphylla*, fam. Verbenaceae)

This perennial, deciduous shrub has branching, woody stems. The leaves are narrow and the terminal spikes of white or lilac flowers appear in summer. It grows up to 2 m (6 ft) high. Both the fresh and the dried leaves are used as a garnish for fruit drinks, to flavor milk puddings, and for making tea. The dried leaves and flowers are used in potpourri.

CULTIVATION Grow in light to medium, moderately rich, well-drained soil in full sun, and give protection from wind. Lemon verbena will not tolerate excessive cold or severe frosts.

ABOVE Lemon verbena is a straggly grower but worth growing for its highly fragrant foliage. Prune regularly to keep growth vigorous.

ABOVE *Leonotis leonurus* produces its colorful hooded flowers in fall and winter. It is not hardy but thrives under cool glass.

Propagate from semi-ripe cuttings in summer, rooted under glass.

CLIMATE Zone 8.

Leonotis (fam. Lamiaceae)

Mainly from South Africa, this genus consists of 30 species of evergreen, flowering shrubs and herbaceous plants. Only one species seems widely cultivated, and it was popular in Victorian era gardens.

CULTIVATION In frost-prone climates, grow in a cool conservatory or greenhouse in pots of soil-based potting compost. Ensure maximum light. Prune hard, almost to soil level, in early spring. Outdoors, grow in a sunny, sheltered spot in well-drained soil and prune old flowered stems in spring. Propagate from semi-ripe cuttings in summer.

CLIMATE Zone 9 if relatively frost-free, otherwise zone 10.

SPECIES *L. leonurus* derives its common names, lion's ear or lion's tail, from the tawny color of the hooded flowers which form a spiral up the stem. They also come in an orange-red color and bloom for a long period, from fall to early winter. This square-stemmed shrub grows to 2 m (6 ft). There is also a creamy white-flowered form.

Leontopodium (fam. Asteraceae)

Widely distributed throughout mountainous regions of the world, from Europe through to China and South America, these low-growing, tufted, woolly perennials include the Swiss edelweiss. There are around 30 species.

CULTIVATION Leontopodiums, especially the Swiss edelweiss, are grown as alpines on rock gardens mainly in the north. They need well-drained, alkaline to neutral soil and full sun. Support a pane of glass over plants in winter to protect them from excessive rain. Propagate from seed sown when ripe.

CLIMATE Zone 5 for most species.

SPECIES *L. alpinum*, edelweiss, from mountainous parts of Europe, grows to 30 cm (12 in),

ABOVE The charming Swiss edelweiss can be grown only in cool regions. Both flowers and leaves have a woolly texture.

with grayish leaves covered with white down, and star-shaped, cream flowers surrounded by white bracts. They resemble a short-petalled flannel flower. *L. haplophylloides*, zone 6, from China, is a lemon-scented plant which grows to around 35 cm (14 in). It has grayish white foliage and the flowers are similar to those of the edelweiss. *L. japonicum*, native to China, Korea and Japan, has darkish green leaves and light gray flower heads. It grows to about 50 cm (20 in).

Lepidozamia (fam. Zamiaceae)

Australia is home to only four genera of cycads, one of which is *Lepidozamia*, which includes the tallest types in the world. They also have the largest cones. There are only two species, both found in rainforests of the east coast. Rather like palms, they have fairly slender, straight, generally unbranched trunks, with long, pinnate leaves radiating from the top of the trunk. The leaves have relatively long, bare stalks. Like all cycads, they are dioecious, and both sexes bear a solitary terminal cone at least 60 cm (24 in) long. Until recently, lepidozamias have been grown only by botanical gardens and cycad enthusiasts, but these plants are now appearing more often in specialist nurseries.

Their dark green, glossy, leathery foliage and elegant symmetry make them attractive subjects for indoor use while they are young.

CULTIVATION In areas prone to frost, grow as pot plants in an intermediate to warm conservatory or greenhouse, or in a warm room in the house. Grow in a gritty, soil-based potting compost, enriched with chipped bark. Keep only slightly moist in winter. Shade from direct sun but ensure good light. Outdoors plants need a semi-shaded, sheltered situation, free from frost. Propagate from seed sown in spring and germinated at 24°C (75°F). Germination and growth are very slow.

CLIMATE Zone 10.

SPECIES *L. hopei*, from steep slopes of the lush rainforests of northern Queensland, can reach 10 m (33 ft) or more in height, mature plants forming a trunk and large crown. The leaves

ABOVE *Lepidozamia peroffskyana*, scaly zamia, is faster growing than some cycads but still takes many years to form a distinct trunk.

can grow as long as 3 m (10 ft) and the leaflets are 20–30 cm (8–12 in) long and flared at the base. *L. peroffskyana*, from the eucalypt forests of southern Queensland and northern New South Wales, where it is can reach 12 m (40 ft) in height, is much smaller in cultivation, at around 2–4 m (6–12 ft). The crown is renewed every year and can be 3 m (10 ft) across. New leaves appear together, and leaflets are shorter than those of *L. hopei*.

Leptospermum (fam. Myrtaceae)
Tea-tree

There are around 80 species in this genus of attractive, evergreen shrubs and trees, mostly from Australia and New Zealand, with a few from Malaysia. Tea trees are among the most popular of the Australian shrubs grown in the US. In warmer regions they are grown in the garden, but in cooler and cold climates they are happy to be grown under glass. In Australia, the leaves of the Manuka were used for brewing a type of tea by the sailors from the Endeavour and the early settlers, hence the common name, tea-tree. These fine-foliaged trees bear very pretty, five-petalled, open flowers in colors ranging from white through many soft pinks to dark red, followed by round, woody capsules

ABOVE *Leptospermum scoparium* Nanum Group is low growing and ideal for small greenhouses and gardens.

which may remain on the branches for some years before releasing hundreds of very fine seeds. The flowers produce an abundance of nectar which attracts both bees and birds to the garden. Tea-trees provide brilliant spring and summer color, and shelter for birds, and compact forms may be planted fairly close together to make attractive hedges or windbreaks. Many improved cultivars have been developed. Tea-trees are also grown commercially for their essential oils and timber, which is valued for its strength. Adopted in the early days of settlement for building and fencing, it is now used mostly for rustic garden furniture and brush-wood fencing.

CULTIVATION In frost-prone climates, the frost-tender and half-hardy species are grown in a cool conservatory or greenhouse. Use soil-based potting compost and ensure maximum light, with shade from direct strong sun. Light pruning may be necessary after flowering to ensure a compact shape. The hardy species can be planted against a sheltered wall which receives sun for much of the day. Outdoors any well-drained soil is suitable, except very alkaline ones, plus a position in full sun. Feed with blood, fish and bone fertilizer annually, in spring. Both under glass and outdoors, scale insects can be a problem in some areas. Propagate from seed in spring or fall, and germinate at 15°C (59°F). Take semi-ripe cuttings in summer and root them in a heated propagating case.

CLIMATE Warmer parts of zone 9 for most species, unless otherwise specified below.

SPECIES Not all of the following may be available outside their countries of origin. *L. juniperinum*, prickly tea-tree, is a very attractive species, with light green, pointed leaves and small, white flowers in early spring. *L. laevigatum*, coastal tea-tree, can be seen in the sand dunes along the east coast of Australia. Growing into a tall, bushy shrub or small tree, to 6 m (20 ft), it often has a gnarled trunk. The leaves are a grayish color and the flowers are white. It is useful as a quick-growing hedge or low shelter in coastal areas, as it is highly resistant to salt spray and wind. *L. nitidum*, shining tea-tree, to about 2 m (6 ft), is very attractive, with shiny, oval leaves, large, white flowers and reddish new growth. Cultivar 'Copper Sheen' is a lower growing shrub, the copper to dark red foliage contrasting well with the creamy yellow flowers in early spring. *L. petersonii*, lemon-scented tea-tree, is a fast-growing shrub or small tree from the eastern states of Australia, with highly fragrant, lance-shaped leaves and snow white flowers in spring and early summer. Growing to a height of 5 m (16 ft) and a spread of 2.5 m (8 ft), this attractive species is widely cultivated. It is also grown commercially for the oil, citral, a lemon essence. *L. scoparium*, Manuka, zone 8, comes from New Zealand and Australia, where it is found in poor soils along the banks of rivers. Phenol, an oil, is obtained from this species. Many beautiful hybrids in a wonderful color range, in single- and double-flowered forms, have been produced from this white-flowered shrub. *Leptospermum* hybrids are now grown in many other parts of the world, including South Africa, Europe and the US. Cultivar 'Nicholsii', the first red-flowering form to be discovered, early in the twentieth century, is still very popular. 'Chapmanii', with rose-colored flowers, was the first form of *L. scoparium* to break from the common white. Manukas, as this species and its cultivars are called in New Zealand, make excellent, long-lasting cut flowers. All grow to about 2 m (6 ft) in height and width. Var. *rotundifolium*, round-leaf tea-tree, is an attractive, spreading bush, with shiny, round leaves and white, pink or lilac flowers. *L. squarrosum*, peach blossom tea-tree, has sharply pointed foliage and large, pink flowers in fall. It has an open growth habit and reaches about 4 m (13 ft) in height.

Leschenaultia (fam. Goodeniaceae)

These exceptionally beautiful, small shrubs are all native to Western Australia. Tubular flowers with spreading lobes bloom over a long period,

ABOVE The glowing orange flowers of *Leschenaultia formosa* make an outstanding show in spring and summer.

generally in late spring and summer. The shimmering blue of *L. biloba* is unforgettable; others have striking, red flowers. Where frosts occur, grow these prostrate or low-growing plants in a cool or intermediate conservatory or greenhouse. Outdoors in suitable climates, use them as groundcover.

CULTIVATION In a greenhouse or conservatory, grow in pots of gritty, soil-based potting compost with added coir fiber. Plants need maximum light, airy conditions, good light and shade from direct strong sun. Prune lightly after flowering to maintain shape. Outdoors grow in very well-drained soil in full sun. Propagate from softwood cuttings in spring, rooting them in a heated propagating case.

CLIMATE Zone 10.

SPECIES *L. acutiloba* grows to 25 cm (10 in) high, with cream flowers flushed with blue. *L. biloba*, blue leschenaultia, is a spreading plant, growing to about 50 cm (20 in) high, and renowned for its lovely, bright blue flowers. Cultivar 'Blue Flash' has white and blue flowers.

L. formosa, red leschenaultia, may be prostrate or nearly prostrate and is possibly the easiest species to grow. It produces an abundance of scarlet flowers. *L. macrantha*, wreath leschenaultia, is an unusual, yet beautiful plant, yellow and red flowers enclosing a central mass of grayish blue leaves to form a wreath in late spring and summer. *L. tubiflora* is a choice species with small, upright flowers in cream, pink or red, or sometimes a combination of these colors.

Lettuce (*Lactuca sativa*, fam. Asteraceae)

One of the most popular salad vegetables, lettuce is also used in some European countries for soup. Originating from the Middle East and the Mediterranean, many cultivars have now been developed. Those most favored in the US may be divided by shape into three groups: loose heads of cutting lettuce, head lettuce whose leaves fold inwards, and those with long, upright, spoon-shaped leaves (romaine or cos lettuce). There is now a great range of loose-leaved lettuces on the market, most grown hydroponically. Although naturally a cool

ABOVE Cut-leaf lettuce is one loose-leaf or non-hearting lettuce used in salads, both for appearance and flavor.

weather plant, cultivars have also been developed to grow in warm weather, and types are now available to suit all seasonal conditions. It is best to buy cultivars which are sold in your region or country as then you will be sure they are suited to your climate.

CULTIVATION Lettuce plants can be grown in a wide range of moderately rich, well-drained soils, preferably with a pH of 6 or more. Sow seed directly into drills 30 cm (12 in) apart, then cover with 1 cm (⅓ in) of fine soil and keep moist. Thin plants to 15–30 cm (6–12 in) apart, depending on the type, and provide plenty of moisture, but avoid wetting the leaves as much as possible. If using a liquid fertilizer to encourage growth, it should be high in nitrogen. As lettuce is quick growing, sow successively every two weeks. Start sowing in early spring and continue through summer and into early fall, choosing cultivars suited to the sowing and cropping seasons. Bear in mind that lettuce seed will not germinate in temperatures above 25°C (77°F).

CLIMATE Zone 6. Lettuce is grown as a seasonal annual in all climates. Ideal range is 10°–20°C (50°–68°F), but not above 25°C (77°F).

SPECIES *Lactuca sativa* is an annual with large, roundish leaves forming a close head. The erect stem grows to 1 m (3 ft) and carries small, pale yellow flowers. Seed catalogues list many cultivars of lettuce. There are cultivars specially bred for summer, fall, winter or spring cropping. In cool and cold climates winter and spring cropping generally takes place in a cold or slightly heated greenhouse, depending on the particular cultivar. However, there are cultivars which will stand the winter outdoors.

Leucadendron (fam. Proteaceae)

This genus comprises around 80 species of dioecious, evergreen trees and shrubs from South Africa. All have stiff, leathery, upright leaves, and the flower heads are surrounded by bracts (modified leaves) which are often very colorful.

ABOVE Flowers of *Leucadendron* species are long lasting on the plant and make excellent cut flowers. They bloom prolifically when conditions are right.

CULTIVATION In climates which are prone to frost, grow in an airy, intermediate conservatory or greenhouse. Grow in pots of acid potting compost; add extra grit and peat or peat substitute. Give maximum light. Keep the atmosphere dry. Outdoors grow in full sun in perfectly drained, acid soil which should be low in nutrients, especially phosphorus. Propagate from semi-ripe cuttings in summer, rooted in a heated propagating case.

CLIMATE Zone 10.

SPECIES *L. argenteum*, silver tree, grows to 9 m (30 ft) and has long, velvety, silvery leaves. *L. grandiflorum*, which grows to about 2 m (6 ft), has reddish flower heads, surrounded by pink bracts, in late summer. *L. salignum* is a shrub, to 1 m (3 ft) high, with golden yellow flower heads on the male trees and greenish ones on the female trees, surrounded by yellow bracts, in summer. Many species and cultivars are grown for the cut flower market.

Leucanthemum (fam. Asteraceae)
Shasta daisy

The 25 species in this genus are native to Europe and the mountains of northern Asia. This group includes quite a variety of plants, including both annuals and perennials. Habitats cover alpine regions, damp meadows and open grasslands. The best known are herbaceous perennials, good garden plants providing excellent cut flowers.

CULTIVATION Grow in well-drained soil in full sun, with protection from strong wind. Dig in plenty of compost or manure three to four weeks before planting. Keep well watered in spring and summer to ensure good-sized plants and flowers. Give complete plant food with growth in spring and give soluble liquid fertilizer in late spring to early summer to encourage flowering. Propagate by dividing clumps in late winter or spring. Discard the old, central growth, replanting only the younger outer divisions, each with its own roots and shoots.

CLIMATE Zone 5.

SPECIES *L.* x *superbum*, Shasta daisy, is a clump-forming perennial with dark green,

ABOVE An unusual, very tall cultivar of Shasta daisy 'Phyllis Smith' towers above a red-flowered *Achillea* species.

toothed, basal leaves, 15–25 cm (6–10 in) long. The large, daisy-like flowers are white and may be single or double. They appear during summer on flower stems 50 cm (20 in) or more tall and make excellent cut flowers. Double-flowered forms include 'Esther Read', 'Wirral Supreme' and 'Horace Read'. 'Everest' or 'Mount Everest' is the largest of all the single-flowered forms. An attractive, dwarf form, 'Silberprinzesschen' (syn. 'Little Princess'), is suitable for edging garden beds and has flowering stems 25–30 cm (10–12 in) high.

Leucojum (fam. Amaryllidaceae)
Snowflake

This small genus of bulbous plants originates from western Europe, the Middle East and North Africa. The dainty, bell-shaped, nodding flowers look like large snowdrops and, as with most species, appear in spring. Ideal for mass planting in woodland gardens and shrub borders.

CULTIVATION Plant these bulbs at a depth of 8 cm (3 in) and leave undisturbed for a few years. They like deep, well-drained soil and a warm, semi-shaded position. The fall-flowering species should be planted out in midsummer and the spring- and early summer-flowering species in fall. Once the leaves emerge, give regular, deep watering and continue until the foliage starts to die off.

ABOVE Naturalized clumps of *Leucojum aestivum* make a charming picture in late winter. A site under deciduous trees is ideal.

CLIMATE Zone 5 for most species, zone 4 for *L. aestivum*.

SPECIES *L. aestivum*, summer snowflake, from southern Europe, grows to about 60 cm (24 in) high and has slightly fragrant, white flowers, tipped with green. These appear in late spring. This species likes a steadily moist, humus-rich soil. *L. autumnale* grows to 20 cm (8 in), with white flowers tinted with pink in fall. The leaves follow the flowers. *L. vernum*, from Europe, grows to 30 cm (12 in), with white flowers tipped with green.

Leucopogon (fam. Epacridaceae)
White beard heath, native currant

Many of these small shrubs are difficult to cultivate, but can sometimes be successfully grown in rockeries or pots. There are around 150 species, mostly native to Australia, with some in Malaysia and New Caledonia. They have stiff, ornamental foliage and hairy flowers, generally white or pink. Most flower in summer. The orange or red fruits of some species are edible.

ABOVE *Leucopogon microphyllus* has tiny leaves and small flowers clustered on the stem tips. Some of the Leucopogon species produce fruits which are able to be eaten.

CULTIVATION Where frosts occur, grow in a cool conservatory or greenhouse in pots of acid, soil-less, potting compost. Ensure good light. Outdoors, grow in moist, acid soil containing plenty of humus, in partial shade or full sun. Propagate from semi-ripe cuttings in summer.

CLIMATE Zone 10, or warmer parts of zone 9.

SPECIES Not all of these are available outside their native countries. *L. ericoides* is a small shrub from eastern Australia, growing to about 1 m (3 ft) high. Fairly common on heathland and coastal dunes, it has grayish foliage, pink buds and pinkish white flowers. *L. fraseri*, Otago heath, is a prostrate to low, spreading shrub, 30–60 cm (12–24 in) high, with pinkish flowers and edible, orange-yellow berries. *L. juniperinus* grows 60–90 cm (24–36 in) high, with prickly foliage and white flowers. *L. linifolius* is a lovely, leafy shrub, with clusters of fluffy, white flowers. *L. milliganii* is a prostrate, spreading, alpine species from Tasmania, with bright red berries. *L. strictus* is a small shrub from Western Australia, with attractive, reddish pink flowers.

Leucospermum (fam. Proteaceae)
Pincushion

Grown for their showy, red, orange or yellow flower heads, these woody, evergreen shrubs also bear smooth, pale-colored fruits. This South African genus of around 40 species is related to *Leucadendron*. Some species are grown for the cut flower trade because of their good vase life.

CULTIVATION In frost-prone climates, grow in a cool to intermediate conservatory or greenhouse, in pots of acid, soil-based potting compost, to which has been added extra grit and peat. Outdoors grow in well-drained, acid soil low in phosphorus, in a warm sunny position. Ensure maximum light. Propagate from semi-ripe cuttings in summer with basal warmth.

CLIMATE Warmer parts of zone 10 and above.

ABOVE In the right climate, *Leucospermum tottum* makes a magnificent show. Flower color may be red or red-pink.

SPECIES Not all of these are available outside their country of origin. *L. bolusi*, bolus pincushion, reaches about 2 m (6 ft) high, with dense, short, leathery leaves and flower heads borne in terminal clusters. Consisting of many prominent, orange stamens, the flower heads grow to around 10 cm (4 in) in diameter. *L. cordifolium* is a shrub which grows to 2 m (6 ft) high and, in good conditions, 2–3 m (6–10 ft) wide. It flowers over a long period, from early spring through to midsummer. The large flower heads may be orange, scarlet or yellow. This species is probably the most commonly cultivated for the cut flower market. *L. reflexum*, rocket pincushion, has small, gray, leathery leaves and large, deep red flower heads, tipped in yellow. It grows up to 4 m (13 ft) high. *L. tottum*, firewheel pinchusion, grows 60 cm (24 in) tall, with spiky, dome-shaped, red or red-pink flower heads from mid-spring to late summer.

Leucothoe (fam. Ericaceae)

Comprising around 50 species of deciduous or evergreen shrubs, this small genus has a broad distribution, from eastern Asia to Madagascar, to North and South America. The simple leaves are glossy green in color, the flowers vary from white to pink, and the fruit is a many-seeded

ABOVE Arching stems of dainty, white flowers adorn the glossy, ribbed foliage of Leucothoe fontanesiana in spring.

capsule. With handsome foliage and prettily shaped flowers, they look lovely growing under tall trees. Some species have a suckering habit.

CULTIVATION Any average soil that is moist and free of lime will do, but these shrubs do best in shade, with shelter from strong wind. Propagate from seed in spring in a garden frame, or from semi-ripe cuttings in summer, with basal warmth.

CLIMATE Zone 5 for most species. Zone 6 for *L. grayana*.

SPECIES *L. davisiae*, Sierra laurel, grows naturally in mountainous regions of central California. It is an evergreen with quite long flower sprays in early summer. *L. fontanesiana*, switch ivy, is an evergreen, spreading shrub from North America, to about 2 m (6 ft) high, with longish leaves and sprays of white flowers in spring. *L. grayana*, from Japan, is a deciduous species to about 1 m (3 ft) high, with onesided flower clusters during summer and early fall. *L. racemosa*, sweet bells, is a deciduous shrub with variable leaves and one-sided terminal sprays, from spring to late summer, usually growing to height and width of about 1.5 m (5 ft).

Lewisia (fam. Portulacaceae)

Originating from western North America, this genus consists of 20 species of evergreen or herbaceous perennials that form rosettes or tufts of fleshy leaves. They grow from thick roots and are useful in rock gardens or wall crevices. These small, decorative plants have pink, red, purple, yellow, white or orange flowers in spring or early summer.

CULTIVATION Lewisias like a deep, loose, gritty, acid to neutral soil with perfect drainage. Herbaceous species need full sun, evergreens light shade. They are easiest to grow tucked in pockets of a dry stone wall so there is never too much free water around their roots. Propagate from seed sown in spring or fall, or by root division. Some species can be grown from offsets.

CLIMATE Cool to cold climates only.

SPECIES *L. brachycalyx*, zone 5, grows to 8 cm (3 in) high, with rosettes of fleshy leaves and delicate, white or pale pink flowers. *L. columbiana*, zone 5, to 25 cm (10 in) high, has bright magenta-pink or sometimes paler pink flowers, with dark red veins. *L. cotyledon*, zone 6, is an evergreen with dark leaves and small sprays of striped pink to purple flowers which may also be cream to yellow or apricot.

ABOVE *Lewisia cotyledon* is the species most often cultivated. Despite the many cultivars on the market, the original species is hard to beat.

There are a number of very pretty hybrids of this species. *L. rediviva*, zone 4, from high altitudes of British Columbia, California and Utah, is a deciduous species, producing rather grassy leaves which die back before or during flowering. The flowers are rosy pink or white. *L. tweedyi*, zone 5, is an evergreen forming rosettes of mid-green foliage. Growing 15–20 cm (6–8 in) high, these plants bear white or salmon pink flowers in spring or early summer. Hybrids of this species have pretty colors.

Liatris (fam. Asteraceae)
Blazing star, gay feather

These hardy perennials from eastern North America make attractive borders, with feathery spikes of white, lavender or purple flowers. Unusually, the flowers open from the top downwards. There are over 40 species, most of which occur in prairies or open woods.

CULTIVATION These plants need well-drained yet moisture-retentive soil, ideally light or sandy, and a position in full sun. Propagate by division in early spring, or from seed sown in fall in a garden frame.

CLIMATE Zone 3 for most species. Zone 5 for *L. aspera*.

SPECIES *L. aspera*, to 2 m (6 ft), has glossy foliage and purple flower spikes. *L. pychnostachya* grows 1.5 m (5 ft) high, producing violet blooms on thick spikes. It has a long flowering period, from midsummer to early fall. *L. spicata*, to 1.5 m (5 ft), is grown for its cut flowers. With erect, grass-like, mid-green leaves and crowded, fluffy spikes of purple flowers in summer or early fall, it prefers moist conditions.

Libocedrus (fam. Cupressaceae)

This is a genus of six species of evergreen conifers from New Zealand, New Caledonia and the south-western part of South America. The young leaves are short and needle-like, while mature leaves are scale-like. The male and female cones are on the same tree. Characteristic of this genus is the feather-like shape of the flattened branchlet sprays.

CULTIVATION These trees like cool, humid conditions and a reasonably deep, fertile, well-drained soil. Young trees prefer semi-shade and

ABOVE Backlighting shows the uncommon habit of *Liatris spicata* flowers flower buds open from the top of the spike down.

ABOVE This *Libocedrus plumosa* shows tracery of adult scale leaves on branchlets and maturing blue-purple cones.

some shelter. Propagate from seed or cuttings which strike fairly readily.

CLIMATE Zone 8 for the species listed.

SPECIES *L. bidwillii*, kaikawaka, sometimes reaches 20 m (65 ft) or more in its mountainous habitat in New Zealand, while cultivated it is often only a rounded, bushy shrub or small, column-shaped tree. The branchlets are less flattened than in other species. *L. plumosa*, kawaka, is found in sheltered, less elevated forests of New Zealand, where it reaches 30 m (100 ft). Cultivated, it is generally narrowly upright, growing slowly to around 10 m (33 ft), with beautiful, long, fern-like branchlet sprays in glossy, olive green. Grown commercially for its deep red, attractively grained timber, in the garden it is an excellent specimen or container plant.

Licuala (fam. Arecaceae)

This large genus of over 100 species of palms extends from Southeast Asia to Vanuatu and Australia. Although many are small, understorey palms, some species grow quite large. The best known feature of some of the most commonly cultivated species is their large, pleated, almost circular leaves. Many species, however, have deeply divided, ribbed leaf segments with blunt, slightly toothed ends. Trunks may be solitary or in clumps and the inflorescences are generally on long, arching stems. The orange or red fruits that form after flowering create a most decorative display. All species require warm conditions for optimum growth, and in frost-prone climates they make good pot or tub plants for the warm greenhouse or conservatory, especially those with a clustering habit.

CULTIVATION Under glass, grow in pots or tubs of soil-based potting compost, fortified with extra peat and grit. Ensure good light (but shade from direct sun), and a humid atmosphere. Outdoors, grow in partial shade. Propagate in spring from seed or suckers.

CLIMATE Zone 10, but also warmer parts of zone 9.

SPECIES *L. grandis*, a native of the New Hebrides, grows to only about 3 m (10 ft) high. It has large, pleated, undivided leaves, arranged in several crowded tiers, and crimson fruits. It is one of the most beautiful of all palms, making an outstanding feature in tropical gardens. *L. ramsayi*, the Queensland species, is found in swampy, lowland rainforests where it may grow to 15 m (50 ft) tall. It has a pale grayish brown trunk, 15 cm (6 in) diameter, and translucent, fresh green leaves on slender stalks. The circular leaf blades are about 1 m (3 ft) across, the slender, arching inflorescence has cream flowers, and the small fruits are orange-red. It grows very slowly when young and is quite difficult to cultivate. *L. spinosa*, from Southeast Asia, has densely clumping stems, 6–8 cm (2½–3 in) in diameter, and 3–5 m (10–16 ft) tall. These canes carry spirals of leaves divided into narrow, wedge-shaped segments. The shiny, bright orange fruits are borne on a slender, arching inflorescence, to 3 m (10 ft) long. This species is easily cultivated and makes a good tub plant.

ABOVE New fronds of *Licuala ramsayi* are fully circular, but split as they mature.

Ligularia (fam. Asteraceae)

Hardy, herbaceous perennials from temperate Europe and Asia these large, daisy-like summer flowers are usually yellow or orange.

CULTIVATION Grow in a sheltered spot in moist soil and full sun. Propagate by division in spring or from seed sown outdoors in fall or spring.

CLIMATE Cool to cold climates for all.

SPECIES *L. dentata*, zone 4, from China and Japan, is useful for growing at the edges of a pool. It reaches around 1 m (3 ft) high. Cultivar 'Desdemona' has large leaves tinged with purple, and orange flowers; 'Othello' has large leaves and orange flowers. *L. hodgsonii*, zone 5, from Japan, is a smaller species, only 90 cm (36 in) high, with distinctive, rounded leaves. *L. japonica*, zone 5, also a native of Japan, does well around the margins of a pool, growing to 1–1.5 m (3–5 ft) tall. *L. przewalskii*, zone 4, growing to about 2 m (6 ft), produces spikes of small, yellow flowers and stems tinged with purple.

ABOVE Tall stems of massed, yellow daisy-like flowers appear in summer on clump-forming perennial *Ligularia stenocephala*.

Ligustrum (fam. Oleaceae)
Privet

From Europe, Asia, North Africa and Australia, this genus comprises around 50 species of evergreen, partially evergreen and deciduous shrubs and trees. Due to its dense habit, privet has been and still is used extensively as a hedge plant, but there are many species which are well worth growing in the shrub border as specimens. Even the usual hedging species are very pleasing in appearance when grown as specimen shrubs. Privet generally has oval, green leaves and sprays of small, strongly scented, white flowers in the summer, followed by black berries.

CULTIVATION Privet will thrive in almost any conditions and grows very rapidly. The roots are invasive, spreading far into the garden and causing damage to pipes and building structures. Propagate from seed sown in spring or fall in a garden frame, or from semi-ripe or hardwood cutting, in summer and winter respectively.

CLIMATE Most conditions, except hot tropics.

SPECIES *L. japonicum*, zone 7, from Japan, grows 3–4 m (10–13 ft), with large leaves and long, dense sprays of flowers. Cultivar

BELOW Golden privet makes a fine, easy-care hedge. It tolerates a wide variety of soils and growing conditions.

'Rotundifolium' has almost round leaves. It is often used for hedging. *L. ovalifolium*, zone 6, from Japan, has oval leaves. Cultivar 'Aureum', golden privet, grows to a height of 4 m (13 ft) and can be used as a background plant to small annuals or can be trimmed to a small, formal shape. The glossy, green, oval leaves have yellow margins and color best in full sun. Cut out any green shoots as they appear, otherwise it will revert to the normal green form. *L. vulgare*, common privet, zone 5, grows to about 4.5 m (15 ft) and is often used as a hedge. The powerful perfume and the pollen of this species' flowers can cause an allergic reaction, so it should be regularly clipped to avoid flowering.

Lilium (fam. Liliaceae)

The first illustrations of liliums were done on Cretan pottery around 2000 BC, while bulbs have been found in mummy cases in Egypt, presumably included with the dead because the bulbs at that time were used for food and as medicine. The earliest known type is the Madonna lily (*L. candidum*), from the Mediterranean, which symbolizes purity. Today, lilium societies throughout the world distribute the latest information on breeding and culture and members exchange ideas and plants. The genus Lilium, containing the true lilies, is distinguished from other bulbous plants by the fleshy scales of the bulb that are not enclosed by a protective skin or tunic. Most of the lilies grown today are hybrids.

CULTIVATION Liliums can be grown both in acid or slightly alkaline soil, but they all need good drainage, some sun and some shade, and a cool root run. Late varieties need more shade as they flower when the sun is at its hottest. If the ground has been well manured, further feeding is generally unnecessary; if not, add a generous amount of compost and a handful of complete fertilizer to a square metre (yard). If growing in pots, use a good quality potting mix with some additional coir peat or aged cow manure. Do not allow lilium bulbs to dry out. Before planting, put them in a mesh bag and hose thoroughly to remove dirt and diseased scales. Except for *L. candidum*, which must be planted with the top near the surface of the soil, plant the bulbs to a depth of about 10 cm (4 in), a little deeper for particularly large bulbs. After planting, give the bulbs a thorough soaking. During the growing season, water deeply once a week, although potted plants may need watering every two days unless in a very sheltered position. Bulbs may be left for years in one spot in the garden, provided that the soil is nourished and kept cool in the heat of summer. Even the best soils need plenty of organic matter added to them periodically, otherwise fewer blooms will be produced each year. Liliums can be propagated by several methods. If left alone, bulbs will naturally divide, forming two and sometimes more bulbs. In some species, stem bulbs will form at the base of the stem, above the bulb but under the ground. When these are removed at the end of the growing season and planted individually, they will usually grow and occasionally produce a single bloom during the next flowering season.

BELOW This vivid, orange-scarlet Asiatic lily gives real zest to the summer garden.

Some liliums form bulbils in the leaf axils; when they are ready to fall in fall, they may be removed and planted in seedling trays, often producing leaves before winter. Flowering should occur in two years. Propagation by scales taken from the bulbs is another method. After rinsing the bulbs, remove the scales and place in a plastic bag with damp peat so that there is air for the developing bulblets. Tie the top of the bag to keep the moisture in and put in a warm, dark spot; in about three weeks, small bulblets should have formed. These can be treated as small plants. They will be identical to the parent bulb from which the scales were taken and may flower after two years. Liliums can also be raised from seed. Sow seed in pots or seed trays as soon as it is ripe, using seed compost, and germinate in a garden frame. Loosely fill the seed tray with mix, sow the seed and firm down. Sprinkle a thin layer of mix or vermiculite over the seed. Water gently. Asiatic types (those which send up a leaf on germination) appear in about three weeks. Oriental varieties (those which form a bulblet before the first leaf appears) will show the first leaf in spring if sown in fall. Asiatic seedlings will usually flower in two years; Oriental ones in three years. Liliums are subject to attack by slugs, snails and aphids. When shoots emerge in spring, snails and slugs may eat them, causing the bulb to die. Use snail baits as needed and watch for aphids which can be gently hosed off the plants.

CLIMATE There are species suited to various climatic zones.

SPECIES *L. auratum*, golden-rayed lily, zone 6, from Japan, was introduced to England in the mid-19th century and has been widely grown ever since. This magnificent species has large, white, heavily perfumed flowers, spotted with purplish red flecks, with a golden stripe running from the throat to the edge of each petal. Stems grow 1–2 m (3–6 ft) tall and may bear up to 20 blooms. *L. candidum*, Madonna lily, zone 6, has sparkling, pure white, trumpet-shaped, glorious, fragrant flowers, during mid-

ABOVE Easy to cultivate, *Lilium longiflorum* carries several perfumed, white, trumpet flowers on each stem. This is lovely in the garden or as a cut flower.

summer. One of the earliest recorded species, it is still sought after, but quite difficult to grow as it is prone to fungal disease. *L. henryi*, zone 5, from central China, is a vigorous grower, with small, pendulous, reflexed, orange flowers. The stems grow up to about 2 m (6 ft), sometimes bearing as many as 40 blooms. *L. longiflorum*, Easter lily from Japan, zone 9, is a vigorous grower with beautiful, white, highly fragrant, trumpet-shaped flowers which are widely used in the cut flower market. This lily is not very hardy and is often grown in pots under glass. Height is up to 1 m (3 ft). *L. regale*, regal lily, zone 5, from western China, was introduced to England in the early 1900s. Reasonably easy to grow, it reaches a height of over 2 m (6 ft). The large, trumpet-shaped, summer flowers are a pale rose-purple on the outside, the white inside blending to yellow at the base of the throat. *L. rubellum*, zone 6, is an Oriental species, flowering early, to 50 cm (20 in) tall, with beautiful, pink flowers. This species has been used extensively in hybridizing. General nurseries may carry a small range of lilium bulbs, but to get a good selection, contact a specialist grower. Many of these specialists advertize in popular garden magazines.

Lime (*Citrus aurantiifolia*, fam. Rutaceae)

The lime tree is a distinctly tropical fruit tree, probably originally from India and Southeast Asia, and introduced into many tropical areas of the world. Grown for its highly flavored, very acid fruit, which is rich in Vitamin C and citric acid, it is widely used in Thai cooking and makes a delicious drink for hot weather. It has elliptic-ovate leaves, to 7 cm (3 in) long, white flowers and greenish yellow, ovoid fruit which is smooth and thin-skinned, rather like a small, unripe lemon. There are numerous cultivars of lime. The one most favored for growing outdoors in California is 'Bears', which can be grown wherever oranges thrive. Another well-known lime is 'Mexican'.

CULTIVATION The requirements are similar to those of the lemon (see Lemon, *Citrus limon*), but the lime is very cold-sensitive and prefers the warmth, high rainfall and humidity of tropical climates. Except in subtropical and tropical climates, grow in pots or tubs in an intermediate to warm greenhouse or conservatory. Use soil-based potting compost, and provide maximum light but shade from strong sun. In the open, lime does best in a sheltered, sunny position, with well-drained soil.

CLIMATE Subtropical and tropical only; suited to the warmest parts of zone 10 and above.

Limonium (fam. Plumbaginaceae)
Statice, sea lavender

Mainly perennials and subshrubs, sometimes treated as annuals, only a handful are in general cultivation. This is a large genus of plants with a wide distribution through dry, arid and maritime regions of the northern and southern hemispheres. The papery flowers, borne on strong, flattened stems, come in many colors, and are often used in dried floral arrangements. Limoniums are useful in mixed borders and are also a good choice for seaside gardens as they are salt-tolerant.

CULTIVATION Grow in a sunny position with well-drained soil. Tender kinds (those recommended for zone 9) can be grown in a cool, airy greenhouse. Perennials treated as annuals can be raised from seed, sown in spring under glass. Germinate at 18°C (64°F). Plant out after frosts. Perennials can be propagated by division in early spring, or from seed, sown outdoors in spring.

ABOVE These well-formed limes are close to maturity. Fruit must be picked before turning yellow to avoid stem-end rot.

ABOVE Papery, purple flowers on *Limonium latifolium* stand high above a rosette of rounded, fleshy leaves.

CLIMATE Zone 9 for most species listed below. Zone 5 for *L. latifolium*.

SPECIES *L. latifolium* is a perennial, to 60 cm (24 in), with clusters of purple to royal blue flowers for a long period over summer, and large, basal leaves in rosettes. *L. macrophyllum* is a perennial, to about 70 cm (28 in), with white or yellow flowers. *L. perezii* is a perennial subshrub, to 60 cm (24 in), with yellow flowers with blue calyces. *L. sinuatum*, a perennial which is often treated as an annual, grows to 50 cm (20 in). It produces dense rosettes of dark green leaves, and blue or cream flowers in summer and early fall. A wide range of colors is available in hybrid mixes.

Linaria (fam. Scrophulariaceae)
Toadflax

This large genus of annuals and perennials, mostly from the northern hemisphere, are grown for their long-lasting, colorful flowers which resemble tiny snapdragons. Often used as bedding plants in parks and gardens, they generally have narrow, flax-like leaves. Some species have a long history of use in herbal medicine.

ABOVE Long, slender flower spikes are carried on *Linaria purpurea* through summer into early fall.

CULTIVATION These easy-care plants will grow in almost any soil, provided it is not compacted. If the soil is acid, add lime at the rate of about 225 g per square metre (8 oz per square yard) and a little complete plant food. Propagate from seed sown where the plants are to grow, barely covered with a fine layer of sieved soil or sand. Thin seedlings to about 50–75 mm (2–3 in) apart. Water generously in the early stages and apply a complete fertilizer monthly once the plants are well established. After flowering, cut back hard to obtain a second crop of blooms.

CLIMATE There are species suited to various climatic zones.

SPECIES *L. dalmatica*, zone 5, is a perennial, to 1 m (3 ft), with yellow flowers. Cultivar 'Canary Bird' has deeper yellow flowers. *L. maroccana*, zone 6, an annual, is the species most often grown. It has slender growth, to 45 cm (18 in), and needs generous planting for effect. The same plant produces variously colored flowers. Cultivar 'Excelsior', to 45 cm (18 in), with blue, orange, pink, purple or yellow flowers, looks very attractive in borders or massed plantings. 'Diadem' has bright violet flowers, marked with white. 'Fairy Bouquet' is a compact plant of about 20 cm (8 in), with larger flowers than the 'Excelsior' hybrids. 'Northern Lights' grows to 40 cm (16 in), with similar flower colors to 'Excelsior', as well as red and bronze. The annual *L. reticulata* 'Aureopurpurea', zone 7, grows to 45 cm (18 in) and produces purple and yellow flowers. *L. vulgaris*, common toadflax, zone 4, grows to 1 m (3 ft), with bright yellow flowers. This species tends to become invasive in warm areas.

Linospadix (fam. Arecaceae)

Walking stick palm

Ten species of these small, delicate palms occur in rainforests of northern Queensland, Australia and New Guinea as understorey plants, with a single species coming from southern Queensland and New South Wales. They are feather palms, but have no crownshaft and the inflorescences are simple, unbranched spikes. The stems are seldom taller than 3 m (10 ft) or thicker than 4 cm (1½ in)and in all but one species, which has a solitary stem, they produce a cluster of stems. The pinnate leaves are rarely more than 1 m (3 ft) long and the leaflets often vary in width. Wiry flower spikes bear tiny, greenish flowers, followed by small, bright scarlet fruits with crisp, juicy, edible flesh surrounding a small, soft seed. The fruits may be densely packed on the spikes, bending them downwards. They are not widely grown, but highly recommended.

BELOW above *Linospadix monostachya* is a small, slender palm which adapts well to pot or tub culture under glass.

CULTIVATION Except in subtropical and tropical climates, grow in a warm, humid conservatory or greenhouse, in pots or tubs of soil-based potting compost. Plants need good light, but shade from direct sun. Liquid feed regularly in the growing season to encourage rapid growth. Grow in a shady spot with well drained yet moist, humus-rich soil. Propagate from fresh seed germinated in 24°C (75°F). It may take several months to germinate. Some suckering species may be increased by division of the clumps.

CLIMATE Subtropical and tropical only; warmer parts of zone 10.

SPECIES *L. minor* grows mainly at low altitudes in North Queensland. The stems are around 2 m (6 ft) in height and 2.5 cm (1 in) in diameter, and the leaves are about 60 cm (24 in) long, with sparse leaflets. *L. monostachya*, the southern species, has one stem, to 3 m (10 ft) or sometimes 4 m (13 ft) tall and 2.5–4 cm (1–1½ in) in diameter. The leaves, to 1 m (3 ft) long, are variable in width and number. The very ornamental, fruiting spikes ripen in late summer or fall, hanging well below the leaves. *L. palmerana* occurs at the base of the highest Queensland mountains. In the young plant, the leaves are only 20–30 cm (8–12 in) long, each with only two pairs of broad leaflets, making it extremely pretty. At maturity, it reaches 1.5 m (5 ft) tall, with several narrow stems and small leaflets of mixed widths.

Linum (fam. Linaceae)

Flax

These hardy perennials, annuals and shrubs are found in temperate regions of the northern hemisphere. Most occur in Europe, especially around the Mediterranean. Apart from the economically valuable *L. usitatissimum*, which is the source of linseed oil and which supplies flax used for making linen, there are several ornamental garden plants suitable for rock gardens and borders. The abundant flowers may be blue, red, white or yellow.

ABOVE Although individual flowers are short-lived, *Linum perenne* continues to bloom over a long period in summer.

CULTIVATION Grow in any well-drained soil and shelter from strong wind. Give regular summer water, but keep fairly dry in winter. Propagate from seed or cuttings.

CLIMATE There are species suited to various climatic zones.

SPECIES *L. flavum* 'Compactum', zone 5, a perennial to 15 cm (6 in), has dense heads of golden yellow flowers during summer. In cool areas, protect from excess winter wet. *L. grandiflorum*, zone 7, the choicest annual species, produces reddish pink flowers in summer. There are several choice cultivars of this species. *L. monogynum*, zone 8, from New Zealand, a white-flowering form, grows to 60 cm (24 in) high. *L. narbonense*, zone 5, a perennial, grows to 60 cm (24 in), with large, sky blue flowers with a white eye, in spring and summer. Cultivar 'Heavenly Blue' is slightly smaller and useful for rockeries. *L. perenne*, zone 7, is a vigorous, upright perennial, to 30 cm (12 in), with open, pale blue, funnel-shaped flowers in midsummer. Varieties with white or pink flowers are also available.

Liquidambar (fam. Hamamelidaceae)
Sweetgum

These large, pyramidal trees are renowned for their beautiful, fall foliage which changes from tones of yellow ochre, to orange, pink, red and purple before the maple-like leaves fall. Liquidambar, in fact, is one of the few deciduous trees to produce brilliant fall color in mild areas. The aromatic resin from some species is used in perfumery and medicine, and the timber is also very fine. They grow upwards of 10 m (33 ft).

CULTIVATION Liquidambars will do well in most soils in temperate areas, provided they have ample summer water. Propagate from seed, which may not germinate until the second year. Selected varieties are grafted or budded onto seedling understocks.

ABOVE Liquidambars show a diverse range of fall color, often with many different tones displayed on the one tree.

CLIMATE There are species suited to various climatic zones.

SPECIES *L. formosana*, zone 7, from Taiwan, grows to 12 m (40 ft) in ideal conditions, and has large, three-lobed leaves, bronze-tipped when young. *L. orientalis*, zone 8, native to south-west Asia, has coarsely toothed, five-lobed leaves which color up in fall. This tree is one source of the gum resin, storax, thought to be the Biblical balm of Gilead. *L. styraciflua*, zone 5, from the east of the United States, has a broadly conical to spreading habit, growing to 30 m (100 ft). It has five- to seven-lobed leaves and retains its foliage longer than other species. Cultivar 'Burgundy' was selected in California for rich red fall leaf color which can persist into winter.

Liriodendron (fam. Magnoliaceae)
Tulip tree

There are only two species in this genus of large, graceful, deciduous trees. Their unusual, four-lobed leaves distinguish them from all other trees, while their beautiful flowers are also unique, being greenish yellow in color, with orange or yellow at the base of the petals and prominent stamens. They flower in midsummer and have bright gold fall foliage.

CULTIVATION Tulip trees do best in very rich, damp soil in a temperate climate, but their large size makes them suitable only for large gardens. Propagate from seed.

CLIMATE Best in cool, moist climates.

SPECIES *L. chinense*, Chinese tulip tree, zone 8, has a broadly columnar habit, growing to 25 m (80 ft). The striking, olive green flowers are colored pale yellow at the base. *L. tulipifera*, zone 4, from eastern North America, grows 30 m (100 ft) in its habitat and has fragrant, large, pale lime flowers, usually carried near the top of the tree, with a broad orange band at the base. This species is more commonly grown, reaching 20–30 m (65–100 ft) in cultivation. Timber of this species, called yellow poplar in America, is used in cabinet-making. The leaves of cultivar 'Aureomarginatum' are widely edged with deep yellow. It is lower growing than the species.

Liriope (fam Convallariaceae)
Lily turf

Native to Japan and China, these small, evergreen, herbaceous perennials form clumps of grass-like foliage and bear small flowers, ranging from purple to white. They make stylish garden borders and are also suitable for rockeries or as groundcover in shady places.

CULTIVATION Lily turf will grow in sun but prefers semi-shade and well-drained, moderately fertile soil. Propagate by division of the plants in late winter or early spring.

CLIMATE There are species suited to various climatic zones, but all are quite hardy.

SPECIES *L. exiliflora*, zone 7, to 45 cm (18 in), has dark green foliage and violet flowers. *L. muscari*, zone 6, 30–45 cm (12–18 in) high, has dense tufts of dark green leaves and deep

BELOW A red garden seat around a large *Liriodendron tulipifera* provides a focal point in this lovely garden.

ABOVE The variegated leaf form of *Liriope muscari* shows its late summer flowers. Plant in groups for the best effect.

purple flowers. Cultivar 'Variegata' has yellow-striped leaves. *L. spicata*, zone 4, with a creeping habit, grows only to 25 cm (10 in). The flowers are lilac or white.

Lithodora (fam. Boraginaceae)

These seven species of small shrubs or trailers from south-west Europe and Asia Minor are grown for their brilliant blue flowers, mainly as spillover or groundcover plants.

CULTIVATION Lithodora needs well-drained soil, slightly alkaline, but acid for *L. diffusa*, and full sun. Propagate from semi-ripe cuttings in spring.

CLIMATE Zone 7.

SPECIES The usual Lithodora grown is *L. diffusa* 'Heavenly Blue'. A prostrate plant, good for groundcover, it produces rich, royal blue flowers in late spring and summer. *L. oleifolia*, from the Pyrenees in France, is a small shrub, to 25 cm (10 in), with light blue flowers in summer.

Lithops (fam. Aizoaceae)
Living stone, pebble plant, stoneface

Originating from South Africa and Namibia, these fascinating plants consist of a top-shaped body composed of an opposite pair of swollen, fleshy leaves joined at the base, with a narrow

BELOW These curious succulents are easily overlooked when not in flower. The yellow flower of *Lithops turbiniformis* is startling against the dull background.

ABOVE The brilliant, royal blue flowers of *Lithodora diffusa* decorate and soften a low stone wall.

fissure dividing them for half their length. The apex of each is the flattened 'stone face', sometimes completely translucent and sometimes with small 'windows' or translucent spots. Patterns, markings and dots are reproduced from generation to generation, only the main body color varying slightly at times. They form clumps slowly, increasing by one or two bodies each year. The white or yellow, daisy-like flowers, which emerge from the fissure in late summer or fall, are quite large, completely covering the small plant when fully open. For several days, they open about midday and close at sunset.

CULTIVATION These tender succulents are grown in an intermediate greenhouse or conservatory. Grow in deep pots of cactus compost, which should be readily available from good garden centers. If available, add some leaf mould to the compost. The plants need maximum light and airy conditions. Carry out normal watering from the start of summer to the end of fall but do not water the plants for the rest of the year, when they are resting. Propagate from seed sown in spring. Germinate at 24°C (75°F). Detach and pot up offsets in summer.

CLIMATE Must be frost-free. Warmer parts of zone 10, and above.

SPECIES *L. aucampiae* has large, reddish brown bodies with darker brown windows covering most of the flat top. The flowers are yellow. *L. divergens* has a very wide fissure between the leaves, a greenish pink, slightly wrinkled body, crescent-shaped, green windows on the inward-sloping tops, and yellow flowers. *L. fulviceps* is coffee-colored, with dark blue and orange dots and yellow flowers. *L. julii* has a grayish green body with darker veining, a dotted line on the edges of the fissure, and white flowers. *L. karasmontana* is gray, with brown windows and lines and white flowers. *L. olivacea* is green, with an olive green window on each leaf, and yellow flowers. *L. turbiniformis* has a dark brown body, with darker markings and yellow flowers.

Littonia (fam. Colchicaceae)

These eight species of unusual, climbing plants have nodding, bell-shaped, orange flowers in summer. The central vein of the leaves extends to form a tendril by which the climber attaches itself to other plants or objects.

CULTIVATION In frost-prone climates, grow in an intermediate conservatory or greenhouse in pots of gritty, soil-based potting compost. Plant the tubers in fall. Ensure maximum light. Water normally in the growing period, then reduce watering as the leaves die down, and keep almost dry in winter. Outdoors, grow in full sun and well-drained soil. Plant 15 cm (6 in) deep. Propagate from seed, or by division of the clump in winter.

CLIMATE Warmer parts of zone 9.

SPECIES *L. modesta*, from South Africa, is the only species cultivated. This herbaceous perennial has masses of attractive, yellow-orange summer flowers and grows to 2 m (6 ft).

ABOVE Not commonly cultivated, climbing lily *Littonia modesta* is rewarding to grow in a container or in the warm-climate garden.

Livistona (fam. Arecaceae)
Cabbage palm

There are around 30 species in this genus of fan palms, native to Australia, New Guinea and Southeast Asia. The species vary in size from dwarf, understorey palms less than 2 m (6 ft) high, with stems 5 cm (2 in) thick, to those reaching 30 m (100 ft), with huge crowns. Most are single-trunked, sometimes covered with the remains of old leaf-bases, though many have only faintly marked, gray or brownish trunks when mature. The leaves are generally fairly deeply divided into long, narrow segments. The inflorescences develop from among the leaf-bases. Drooping sprays of small, creamish yellow flowers are surrounded by brown or reddish brown bracts. The flowers have both male and female parts, though some species never set fruit. The purple-black fruits may be round or oblong, with a hard seed. Their elegant foliage makes them excellent for outdoor landscaping, and they can be used indoors when young.

CULTIVATION In climates prone to frost, grow these palms in an intermediate to warm greenhouse, or as house plants in a warm room. Grow in pots of soil-based potting compost. Plants need good light but shade from direct sun. Water normally during the growing season but much less during winter. Outdoors grow in well-drained yet moist soil and in full sun or light shade. Propagate from seed sown in the spring and germinated at a temperature of 24°C (75°F). Germination can be rapid, often under two months, although some species take up to six months. The seedlings are very deep rooting, so sow one seed per pot to avoid disturbance.

CLIMATE Zone 10.

SPECIES Not all of these species are available outside their native countries. *L. alfredii*, Millstream palm, occurs only in oasis areas of the very dry Pilbara area of Western Australia. It is slow growing, to about 12 m (40 ft), and is rarely seen outside specialist collections. This elegant, ornamental palm does well in very hot, dry regions, though it must have permanent water at its feet. *L. australis*, cabbage palm, is found along the east coast of Australia, from southern Queensland to Victoria. The 'cabbage', or fleshy part of the leaves of this palm was eaten by the early explorers as a vegetable substitute and the leaves were woven into baskets and hats by the early colonists. Easy to cultivate, it is one of the taller species, reaching heights of 25 m (80 ft). The glossy, olive green, fan leaves are fairly deeply divided, with drooping tips. The dull, brownish black, round fruits are about 2 cm (¾ in) in diameter. *L. benthamii*, from far northern Queensland the Northern Territory, and Papua New Guinea, is a tropical, lowland species, occurring in swampy creeks on the margins of rainforests close to the sea. Growing 10–15 m (33–50 ft), it has folded, deeply divided leaves. It makes a very ornamental indoor plant when young. *L. chinensis*,

BELOW Large sprays of rich cream flowers arch out over the crown of the cabbage palm, *Livistona australis*.

Chinese fan-palm, thought to have originated from southern China, is one of the most popular ornamental palms for tropical and temperate regions. It has a rough trunk and a heavy, round crown of very large, pale, dull green leaves with long, weeping tips. The elongated fruits are a beautiful, blueish gray color. In warm temperate areas, it reaches 6–8 m (20–26 ft) tall over many years, while in tropical areas, it is faster growing to about 15 m (50 ft) tall. *L decipiens*, from coastal central Queensland, is similar to *L. australis* in size and color, but its leaves are divided right down to the midrib into numerous, very long, narrow segments, part of which hang down vertically. The delicate, curtain-like effect created makes this one of the most beautiful of all the species. *L. mariae*, from central Australia, is another species found only in oasis areas of very dry country. However, it is quite similar to *L. alfredii* but resembles *L. australis* in size and growth habit. Its most striking characteristic is the deep, reddish purple color of the young plants, which develops best in full sun in hot, dry conditions and fades to green after a height of 1–2 m (3–6 ft) is reached. This species is easily cultivated, at least when young, and grows more rapidly than most others. *L. rotundifolia*, from Indonesia and the Philippines, is a tall, tropical species which is very attractive when young. The leaves form an almost circular shape and the tips of most of the broad segments are only slightly pendulous. Var. *luzonensis* has a very attractive trunk which is smooth, shiny and reddish brown between the prominent, white or gray rings formed by the leaf scars.

Lobelia (fam. Campanulaceae)

There are over 300 species of annuals and herbaceous perennials in this genus, found in most tropical and temperate regions of the world. Their range of habitats is most diverse, from marshes to woodlands, mountain slopes to near deserts. The leaf shape and flower formation are variable, but the leaves are generally dark green. The flowers can be brilliant blue,

ABOVE The aptly named cardinal flower, perennial *Lobelia cardinalis*, has tall spikes of flowers which are the color of a cardinal's robes.

red, yellow or white. Because of the intensity of color, they look their best in massed plantings or in borders and rockeries. A number of species have medicinal uses.

CULTIVATION Most of the annuals are frost-sensitive, while the perennials are quite hardy and thrive in cooler regions. All prefer a rich, moist soil. Most species prefer a sunny situation, but some do well in partial shade. An application of liquid fertilizer prior to flowering will increase the intensity of the flower color. Propagate annuals from seed sown in spring under glass and plant out when frosts are over. Perennials can be lifted and divided in late winter or spring.

CLIMATE There are species suited to various climatic zones.

SPECIES *L. cardinalis*, cardinal flower, zone 3, is native to North America. This herbaceous perennial grows to 1 m (3 ft) high, with bright red flowers in summer to early fall. It thrives in moist ground. *L. erinus*, edging lobelia, zone 10, is a small annual, to 15 cm (6 in), used for edging garden beds and also for pots and hanging baskets. Many cultivars are available including 'Cambridge Blue' and 'Crystal Palace' with blue flowers on compact plants. Good trailing cultivars, ideal for hanging baskets, are 'Blue Cascade', 'Hamburgia' and 'Sapphire'. *L. inflata*, Indian tobacco, zone 3, is a hairy annual, cultivated for the alkaloids in the leaves which help chest ailments. *L. laxiflora*, zone 9, is a shrubby grower, very easily grown, to 1 m (3 ft), with tubular, red flowers with yellow lobes. *L. siphilitica*, blue cardinal flower, zone 5, is a perennial, to 1 m (3 ft), with crowded sprays of summer, blue flowers. *L.* x *speciosa*, zone 3, covers a group of hybrid perennials, all growing to about 1 m (3 ft). Named cultivars with bright pink or red flowers are popular for perennial borders.

Lobularia (fam. Brassicaceae)

Sweet Alison, sweet alyssum

This small genus of annuals and perennials is native to the Canary Islands and the Mediterranean. Only one species is common in

BELOW White sweet Alison, *Lobularia maritima*, is teamed with purple violas and bright green parsley to make a stunning display.

cultivation. It is highly popular as a summer bedding plant, when it is often used for edging beds, and is also used in patio containers and hanging baskets in combination with other summer bedding plants. This species is hardy and can also be grown on rock gardens, and it is especially useful for seaside gardens.

CULTIVATION The usual way to raise sweet alyssum is to sow the seed in late spring where the plants are to flower. Alternatively, it can be treated as a tender bedding plant and sown under glass in mid-spring. The young plants are then planted out when frosts are over, together with other bedding plants. Sweet alyssum prefers a light, well-drained soil and a sunny position. It needs little care, but it is worth trimming off the dead flowers to encourage more to follow. It is best to trim the plants immediately after the first flush of flowers.

CLIMATE Zone 7.

SPECIES *L. maritima* is a mound-shaped, compact plant, growing between 5 and 20 cm (2–8 in) high. Narrow, mid-green leaves are all but obscured by masses of tiny flowers in rounded heads. The flowers are lightly scented and mainly white in the species, but there are a number of cultivars available in shades of pink, lavender and purple, such as 'Oriental Night', 'Rosie O'Day' and 'Violet Queen'. Pure white still appears to be the most popular color, well-known cultivars being 'Carpet of Snow', 'Little Gem' and the large-flowered 'Tetra Snowdrift'.

Loganberry

(*Rubus Loganberry* Group, fam. Rosaceae)

This blackberry-like plant is a vigorous, shrubby grower with long, trailing canes, bearing many prickles. It has toothed leaves, gray and felty on the undersides, and short clusters of large, white flowers. The red, acidic fruit is composed of small segments and is similar in flavor to the raspberry. It is served fresh or stewed or made into preserves or jams. The loganberry is a

ABOVE Loganberries dislike extremes of temperature but are delicious fruits to grow where space and climate permit.

hybrid and was raised in California. It is thought to be a cross of a *Rubus ursinus* cultivar and a raspberry.

CULTIVATION The loganberry will grow almost anywhere but it is not suitable for very cold climates, zone 7 being the minimum it will tolerate. It does best in a sunny position in a rich, loamy soil; poorer soils should be enriched with organic matter and complete fertilizer. Give plenty of water during the summer months. Mulching with manure is beneficial. Tie the long canes to a trellis or wire as they will take root where they touch the ground. Fruit is produced in the second year, and all fruiting canes and the weakest of the new canes should be cut back to ground level in winter, leaving only four to six new canes to bear fruit the following season. Propagate from young cane tips. Bent down and buried in the soil in summer, they will make roots and a new shoot. Cut the shoot from the old cane and replant in early spring.

CLIMATE Zone 7.

Lomandra (fam. Lomandraceae)
Mat-rush

Native to Australia, this genus of small, tufted, grass-like plants are widely distributed, though few species are cultivated. They have long, sword-like or grassy leaves. The mostly cream flowers on long spikes are short-lived, but the clusters of rounded, yellow fruit capsules remain decorative for a long time. Bracts, which are often spiny, are a lasting feature of the inflorescence. They are best grown in a cool conservatory or greenhouse in climates prone to frost, especially if the climate is also damp or wet.

CULTIVATION Under glass, grow in well-drained soil-based potting compost. Plants need maximum light. Outdoors, plant in a sunny position with well-drained soil. Propagate from seed sown as soon as ripe and germinate at a temperature of 18°C (64°F). Alternatively, divide established clumps in spring.

CLIMATE Zone 9.

SPECIES Not all of these species are available outside Australia. *L. longifolia* is the best

ABOVE Much seed is produced on the decorative seed head of *Lomandra longifolia* after the flowers have fallen.

known. *L. effusa*, scented mat-rush, is reed-like, to 1 m (3 ft), with narrow, twisted, blueish green leaves and graceful, branched sprays of white or yellow, tissuey flowers. *L. filiformis*, wattle mat-rush, to 25 cm (10 in), has tufts of stiff, blueish leaves and yellow, ball-shaped, wattle-like flowers, which give the species its common name. *L. gracilis*, frayed mat-rush, grows to 25 cm (10 in), with narrow, twisted leaves, fraying into fine threads near the base. *L. leucocephala* has tufting, grayish leaves and large, globular, white flowers embedded into the frayed bracts. The highly perfumed flowers are usually borne in terminal heads. *L. longifolia* is tussock forming, to 70 cm (30 in) high and 1 m (3 ft) wide. Native to eastern and southern Australia, this tough, useful plant, with very decorative inflorescences, has many applications in the home garden and larger landscape. The strappy leaves have an arching habit. It is the most widely grown of the species. *L. multiflora*, many-flowered mat-rush, grows in narrow tufts, with slender, widely branched sprays of drooping, yellow, white or brown flowers.

Lomatia (fam. Proteaceae)

These Australian and South American, woody plants vary from low shrubs to large trees. They have mostly finely divided leaves and small flowers which attract birds. Few species are in general cultivation, although many have great ornamental qualities. Their foliage is ideal for dried arrangements.

CULTIVATION Lomatias prefer a light, slightly acidic, loamy soil, but can be grown in sun or partial shade. Water well in summer, decreasing the amount substantially in winter. Propagate from seed contained in the capsules, or from cuttings taken in late summer to fall struck in a mix of three parts sharp sand to one part peat or vermiculite. In frost-prone climates, ensure plants are well protected from frost, say in a sheltered woodland garden or cool greenhouse.

CLIMATE Zone 9, or possibly zone 8.

ABOVE Ideal for growing in light shade under tall trees, *Lomatia myricoides* is suitable for a range of climates.

SPECIES *L. fraxinifolia*, native to higher altitudes of Queensland rainforests, grows to 20 m (65 ft) in its habitat, but half that size in cultivation. The glossy foliage is very attractive and its trusses of cream flowers appear in late summer or fall. *L. ilicifolia*, holly lomatia, is a good garden species, with holly-shaped leaves and white flowers. *L. myricoides* is a graceful shrub, 3–5 m (10–16 ft) high, with narrow, toothed leaves and cream flowers in summer. It is a good understorey plant beneath trees, and is also used as a screening plant. *L. silaifolia*, crinklebush or wild parsley, is an upright, stiff shrub, to 1–2 m (3–6 ft) high, with lacy foliage. It is grown for the use by florists in dried floral arrangements. *L. tinctoria* grows to 1 m (3 ft) or more, with lacy, light green, divided leaves. This species does well in cool areas.

Lonicera (fam. Caprifoliaceae)
Honeysuckle

This genus comprises around 180 species of deciduous and evergreen shrubs and climbers from the northern hemisphere. Grown for their masses of delicate, sweetly scented flowers, the climbers are perfect for covering fences, arches,

ABOVE Vigorous and sometimes invasive, *Lonicera japonica* produces an abundance of yellow flowers in spring and summer.

arbors and walls, while the shrubby varieties can be trained into pretty hedges. Generally they flower in winter, spring and summer. Most species are hardy and some can become invasive in warm climates.

CULTIVATION Honeysuckle can be grown in most soils, but most prefer regular water in summer and full sun. For hedging, plants should be no more than 50 cm (20 in) apart. Prune in early spring. Climbing varieties require a wire or trellis. Propagate evergreens from semi-ripe cuttings in summer, deciduous species from winter hardwood cuttings, or all by layering in spring.

CLIMATE Zone 5, unless otherwise stated below.

SPECIES *L.* x *brownii*, scarlet trumpet honeysuckle, has coral red flowers that are yellow inside. It flowers during summer. *L. caerulea*, zone 2, a deciduous shrub, to 1.5 m (5 ft) high, with yellow flowers and blue berries. *L. caprifolium*, Italian woodbine, grows to 5 m (16 ft), with highly fragrant, yellow flowers, tinted with purple on the outside of the petals. It flowers in summer and fall. *L. flava*, yellow honeysuckle, is a deciduous climber, to 3 m (10 ft), with

yellow, scented flowers. *L. fragrantissima*, from China, is a semi-deciduous shrub, with sweetly perfumed, cream flowers in winter. *L.* x *heckrottii* flowers in summer, with rich, pinky red blooms, colored yellow on the insides. *L. hildebrandiana*, giant honeysuckle, zone 9, an evergreen or semi-evergreen climber from Burma and China, grows 20–25 m (65–80 ft) tall, with creamy flowers that turn orange with age. *L. japonica*, Japanese honeysuckle, zone 4, an evergreen or semi-evergreen climber from eastern Asia, has fragrant, white flowers sometimes flushed with purple, in spring and summer. Very vigorous, it can grow to 10 m (33 ft) tall. *L. nitida*, zone 7, an evergreen species, to about 2 m (6 ft) high, with thick foliage, is clipped for topiary and small, formal hedges. *L. periclymenum*, deciduous European woodbine, zone 4, bears abundant clusters of fragrant, white or yellow flowers, flushed with purple, in midsummer. *L. sempervirens*, trumpet honeysuckle, zone 3, is an evergreen climber, to 5 m (16 ft), with yellow and red flowers.

Lophomyrtus (fam. Myrtaceae)

Natives of New Zealand, these two species of small, evergreen trees are generally slow growing, reaching only about 6 m (20 ft). Grown for their decorative, leathery foliage, varying in color from dark green to a coppery shade, they have small, white flowers and dark red berries.

CULTIVATION In frost-prone climates, grow in a cool conservatory in pots of soil-based potting compost. The plants need good light, but shade from direct sun. Outdoors, choose a partially shaded spot with well-drained yet moist, slightly acid soil, with plenty of humus. Propagate from semi-ripe cuttings in summer.

CLIMATE Zone 9.

SPECIES *L. bullata*, with long, puckered, coppery-colored leaves, tiny white flowers similar to those of the myrtle, and reddish purple berries grows to 6 m (20 ft). *L.* x *ralphii*, generally 2–5 m (6–10 ft) tall, has smaller, greener

ABOVE The small, rounded leaves of *Lophomyrtus x ralphii* 'Variegata' are attractively variegated cream and green.

leaves, small, white flowers in summer, and red berries.

Lophostemon (fam. Myrtaceae)
Brush box

There are just four species in this genus, the most well-known being brush box, formerly known as *Tristania conferta*. Brush box is a handsome tree but is too tender to be grown outside in frost-prone climates. However, as a young plant it makes a pleasing foliage specimen for a cool or intermediate greenhouse or conservatory, but it is unlikely to flower.

CULTIVATION In the greenhouse or conservatory, grow in pots of acid, well-drained, potting compost and ensure maximum light, but shade from direct sun. Keep compost only slightly moist in winter. Outdoors grow in well-drained, acid soil with full sun or partial shade. Propagate either from seed in the spring or alternatively, from semi-ripe cuttings in summer, providing bottom heat for both.

CLIMATE Zone 10.

SPECIES *L. confertus* (syn. *Tristania conferta*), brush box, is native to forests on the eastern coast of Australia. In nature, it is a majestic tree, often growing to over 40 m (130 ft) in height,

ABOVE This row of variegated brush box is showing fresh, red-brown trunks following the shedding of the old bark in early summer.

but in cultivation rarely exceeding 15–20 m (50–65 ft). The foliage is a dark, glossy, green and a profusion of cream flowers appears from mid to late spring through early summer. The trunk is gray-brown as it matures, but shedding bark each year reveals a smooth, reddish brown trunk. The timber is very high quality and is often used in flooring and wood panelling. Cultivars 'Perth Gold' and 'Variegata', with cream to yellow leaf variegations, are much smaller trees, and are ideal for growing under glass.

Loquat (*Eriobotrya japonica*, fam. Rosaceae)

Native to China and widely cultivated in Japan and other subtropical regions, this evergreen tree grows 6–8 m (20–26 ft) tall. In cooler areas, it is grown as a foliage plant. It has dark green, glossy leaves, to 30 cm (12 in) long, with rusty hairs on the undersides, and clusters of cream, fragrant flowers in fall, followed in winter to spring by the oval to pear-shaped, thin-

ABOVE The loquat, *Eriobotrya japonica*, will only fruit in warm conditions, but it is a good foliage plant in cooler climates.

skinned, deep yellow fruit. Not as sweet or rich as many other tropical fruits, it is eaten fresh or stewed, or made into jam.

CULTIVATION Loquats require warmth in order to thrive and set fruit. They will tolerate occasional dry conditions once established, but do best with occasional, deep watering in the warmer months. They will grow in any ordinary, free-draining garden soil, but prefer full sun. Trees can be pruned in spring to remove straggly stems. The loquat is not recommended as a garden tree, except in areas with cold winters, as the fruit acts as a host to fruit fly at a time when no other fruit is setting. Outdoors, grow against a warm, sunny wall, but in climates prone to hard frosts, grow in a cool, light and airy greenhouse in a tub of soil-based potting compost. The plant can be stood outdoors for the summer. Propagate from semi-ripe cuttings in summer.

CLIMATE Zone 8.

VARIETIES As well as the species, there are several fruiting cultivars including 'Champagne', bred for warm regions, 'Gold Nugget' and 'MacBeth'.

Loropetalum (fam. Hamamelidaceae)

This single-species genus originates from China and Japan.

CULTIVATION An ideal shrub for a sheltered, woodland garden or shrub border, it needs partial shade and a moisture-retentive, yet well-drained soil, containing plenty of humus. Propagate from semi-ripe cuttings in summer in a heated propagating case, or from seed sown as soon as ripe in a garden frame.

CLIMATE Zone 8.

SPECIES *L. chinense* grows to 4 m (13 ft) in mild conditions, with attractive, evergreen foliage and profuse clusters of cream flowers, similar to those of witch hazel, in late winter or spring.

BELOW The dainty, cream, fringed flowers of *Loropetalum chinense* contrast with the small, leathery leaves.

Lotus (fam. Papilionaceae)

There are about 100 species of annuals, perennials and sub-shrubs in this genus, which is mostly native to Europe, including the Mediterranean, but also other parts of the world, including Africa, Asia and America. They have pea-like flowers and a low, sometimes creeping, habit, making them suitable as groundcover or for rockeries and hanging baskets. Some species are used as pasture, while others are quite toxic.

ABOVE *Lotus berthelotii* is best grown over a wall or in a hanging basket where its fine, silvery foliage can cascade.

CULTIVATION These plants prefer full sun and well-drained, sandy soil. Water regularly in warm months but keep much drier in winter. Propagate from seed or cuttings.

CLIMATE There are species suited to various climatic zones. Grow tender species in a cool greenhouse.

SPECIES *L. australis*, zone 9, an Australian native shrub with pale pink flowers, grows to 60 cm (24 in) high. *L. berthelotii*, zone 10, from the Canary Islands, has silvery branches, with fine, needle-like leaves, and scarlet flowers in spring and early summer. It is grown as a groundcover, although it looks best in a basket or as a spillover plant on a wall, as this allows the pretty foliage and flowers to be seen to advantage. *L. corniculatus*, bird's foot trefoil, zone 5, is widespread in various parts of the world. It is low growing, with yellow flowers tipped with red. A double-flowered form, 'Plenus', is a compact plant, more suited to ornamental growing. *L. jacobaeus*, St James' trefoil, zone 9, grows to 1 m (3 ft), with streaked yellow and purple-brown flowers.

Lovage (*Levisticum officinale*, fam. Apiaceae)

Lovage is one of the tallest herbs, capable of growing to more than 2 m (6 ft). It has clusters of yellow flowers and dark green, compound leaves. Delightfully fragrant, the stems and leaves are used in salads, soups and stews. It is also grown for medicinal purposes. Lovage makes a useful windbreak in herb gardens.

CULTIVATION This herb will grow in most garden soils, provided they are well drained and enriched with organic fertilizer, in either sun or semi-shade. It prefers some shade in hot climates. Propagate from seed sown in spring or fall.

CLIMATE Zone 4.

ABOVE Lovage is said to taste of both celery and parsley but with a peppery tang, making it a versatile herb.

Luculia (fam. Rubiaceae)

These mainly fall- and winter-flowering, deciduous or evergreen shrubs from the Himalayas and China have pointed, bronzy green, oval leaves and fragrant, pink or white flower heads. Admired by gardeners, they are often hard to grow and are known to suddenly die for no apparent reason.

ABOVE Sometimes temperamental, *Luculia gratissima* is one of the loveliest of all shrubs with pretty flowers and a sweet scent.

ABOVE *Luffa cylindrica* has large, yellow flowers typical of the Cucurbit family. This young fruit will enlarge greatly before reaching maturity.

CULTIVATION In frosty climates, grow in a cool to intermediate conservatory or greenhouse, in pots or tubs of soil-based potting compost. Provide maximum light, but shade from direct sun. Plants may need to be pruned lightly after flowering to retain compactness. Outdoors grow in well-drained soil in a sunny, sheltered position. Propagate from seed in spring or from semi-ripe cuttings in summer, both in a heated propagating case.

CLIMATE Zone 10.

SPECIES *L. grandifolia*, to 5 m (16 ft) tall, is deciduous and may be spreading or upright. It has much larger leaves and clusters of fragrant, white flowers in summer. *L. gratissima*, a native of the Himalayas, is generally evergreen, growing to 5 m (16 ft). It has sweetly scented, rose-pink flowers during fall and early winter.

Luffa (fam. Cucurbitaceae)
Loofah

A fascinating, tendril-climbing vine, *Luffa* is found in many tropical areas. Its large, club-shaped fruit, dry, when mature, to become loofahs, or vegetable sponges.

CULTIVATION This plant requires warm, moist conditions and is propagated from seed.

CLIMATE Zone 10 and above, but grown as a summer annual in various climates.

SPECIES *L. acutangula* has club-shaped fruits, to 30 cm (12 in) long, used as food in Asian countries. *L. cylindrica* grows to 3 m (10 ft), with attractive, green foliage, yellow flowers and large fruit, edible when young. Known as sponge gourd, this is the species most grown.

Lunaria (fam. Brassicaceae)
Honesty

This genus includes only three species of perennials and biennials, often grown as annuals. They are cultivated for the pretty purple or mauve flowers and the curious, translucent, circular seed pods which are often used in dried floral arrangements. These plants tend to self-seed freely.

ABOVE A choice purple cultivar of the annual *Lunaria annua*. As it reseeds freely this plant can become weedy.

CULTIVATION This hardy plant will grow in most conditions, but needs space to spread. It prefers some shade, especially in warmer areas. Propagate from seed in late spring, or *L. redeviva* by division in spring.

CLIMATE Zone 8.

SPECIES *L. annua*, from the Mediterranean, has an erect habit, to 80 cm (32 in), with scented, purple, white or pink flowers. There is a variegated form with leaves edged in white. The perennial *L. redeviva* grows to around 90 cm (36 in) and has scented, pale lilac flowers.

Lupinus (fam. Papilionaceae)
Lupine

Originating from a varied range of habitats in North America and the Mediterranean, this large genus consists of over 200 species of annuals, herbaceous perennials and shrubs. The annuals are grown for their dark green foliage and tall stems bearing showy blooms in a range of wonderful colors, including pink,

yellow, white and blue. The perennial Russell lupines, achieved by crossing *L. arboreus* with *L. polyphyllus*, are also beautiful and very popular in cool-climate gardens. They have very strong stems and large clusters of magnificently colored flowers.

CULTIVATION Lupines do best if grown in reasonably fertile, well-drained, light or sandy, acid soil, and they will perform well in a sunny or partially shady spot. However, if the soil is too rich the lupines will produce too much foliage and not enough flowers. Propagate annuals from seed and perennials by division of established clumps or from cuttings. Mulch with compost during spring and cut back the old flower stalks after flowering. Lupines are also grown as green manure and dug in when flowering commences.

CLIMATE There are species suited to various climatic zones.

SPECIES *L. albus*, white or field lupine, zone 9, an annual with white flowers, is grown as a green manure crop, or natural fertilizer.

BELOW Russell lupines are great favorites for the perennial border in cool climates, adding both vertical accents and color.

ABOVE Deep indigo blue lupines fix nitrogen in the soil through their roots.

L. arboreus, tree lupin, zone 8, is a shrubby type, to 2 m (6 ft) or more, with yellow, white or purple, scented flowers. *L. hartwegii*, zone 10, is a slightly hairy annual to 1 m (3 ft), with blue, white and green flowers in summer and fall. It does best in drier, warmer areas. *L. luteus*, yellow lupine, zone 6, an annual from the Mediterranean, grows to about 50 cm (20 in) and flowers in early summer. *L. nootkatensis*, zone 4, from the United States, is a perennial, to 1 m (3 ft), with blue or pink flowers. *L. perennis*, zone 4, also from the United States, flowers in late spring in blue, pink or white. It grows to around 50 cm (20 in). *L. polyphyllus*, zone 3, with blue, pink or white flowers, grows to 1.5 m (5 ft). *L. subcarnosus* and *L. texensis*, zone 8, both annuals from Texas, have blue flowers known as blue bonnets.

Lycaste (fam. Orchidaceae)

Widespread in the tropical Americas and the West Indies, these orchids are mainly epiphytic, with some terrestrial. Attractive, long-lasting flowers are borne singly on stems arising from the pseudobulb base.

CULTIVATION Grow in a cool to intermediate greenhouse or conservatory in pots of proprietary bark-based orchid compost, or as epiphytes, by mounting them on pieces of bark hung from the roof. In summer, the plants need regular watering, a very humid atmosphere and shade from direct sun. In winter, keep compost almost dry and ensure good light. Propagate by division in spring.

CLIMATE Tropical only.

SPECIES *L. aromatica* has fragrant flowers, 7–8 cm (about 3 in) across, in yellow tinged with green, in spring and summer. The lip is orange. *L. deppei* blooms in spring and summer. The flowers, 7–8 cm (about 3 in) across, have green sepals flecked with red-brown, white petals, and a deep yellow lip with red markings. *L. skinneri*, the national flower of Guatemala, has numerous cultivars. It has

ABOVE *Lycaste deppei*, from Central America, is easy to cultivate, flowering best when kept very dry through winter.

large, beautiful flowers, to 15 cm (6 in) across, in a waxy white, tinged with rose. The lip is sometimes dotted with purple.

Lychee (*Litchi chinensis*, fam. Sapindaceae)

Lychee fruits are available fresh, canned, frozen or dried. The wrinkly, red fruits contain a sweet, white, edible flesh and a large seed. Lychees are native to southern China and are slow-growing evergreens, reaching 10–12 m (33–40 ft) high and wide in ideal conditions. They are subtropical trees that demand warm, humid summers and cool, frost-free winters. Fruit bearing is very dependent on the weather because, although trees need ample soil moisture, especially at flowering time, rain during this period may destroy the flowers before they have been pollinated. Bee and other insect activity is also severely reduced during rain. Although there is an enormous number of named varieties in commercial cultivation, home gardeners are likely to be restricted to a few such as 'Brewster', 'Groff', 'Kwai Mi' and 'Mauritius'. Lychees may start bearing after about six years, but seedling trees may take up to 20 years to start cropping.

CULTIVATION Except in frost-free climates, the lychee has to be grown under glass, usually as a young foliage plant as fruits are unlikely to be produced. A cool to intermediate greenhouse or conservatory is suitable, growing the plant in a large pot or tub of soil-based potting compost. Ensure good light, but shade from direct sun. Outdoors grow in well-drained soil in a sunny, sheltered position. Propagate from seed germinated with bottom heat provided.

CLIMATE Zone 10.

Lychnis (fam. Caryophyllaceae)
Campion, catchfly

Widely distributed throughout temperate and cold zones of the northern hemisphere, there

ABOVE This heavy crop of lychees is half ripe. This is a most rewarding fruit to grow if conditions are suitable.

ABOVE above Maltese cross, *Lychnis chalcedonica*, is a tall-growing perennial, providing summer color in the garden.

are around 20 species of these five-petalled biennials and herbaceous perennials, mostly with red flowers. They are grown in mixed borders and rock gardens.

CULTIVATION Easily grown in most well-drained garden soils, Lychnis is tougher than many herbaceous perennials and can tolerate both dry conditions and frost. Propagate from seed; the perennial species can be divided.

CLIMATE Zone 4.

SPECIES *L. chalcedonica*, Maltese cross, a lovely perennial with clusters of bright scarlet flowers, grows to 90 cm (36 in). *L. coronaria*, rose campion, from south-east Europe, grows to about 1 m (3 ft), with magenta flowers. There is also a white-flowered form, 'Alba'. *L. flos-jovis*, flower of Jove, is an erect perennial, to 1 m (3 ft), with pink or red flowers. *L. viscaria*, catchfly, reaches about 45 cm (18 in) and has deep green leaves and sticky stems topped with pink-purple flowers. There are numerous cultivars available, some with double flowers.

Lycopodium (fam. Lycopodiaceae)
Tassel fern, club moss

These evergreen fern allies, many of which are Australian natives, include the epiphytic tassel fern.

CULTIVATION In frosty climates, grow in a warm greenhouse or conservatory. Use them in slatted, wooden orchid baskets hung from the roof. Fill with peat-based, soilless potting compost with added sphagnum moss (chopped) and pieces of charcoal. Provide good light, but shade from direct sun. When the plants are growing, mist spray them daily and water normally. Keep the compost only slightly moist in winter.

CLIMATE Warmest parts of zone 10, and above.

SPECIES *L. dalhousieanum*, blue tassel fern, is a beautiful, Australian species, with large, hang-

ABOVE Tassel ferns, *Lycopodium species*, produce curtains of pendulous fronds. Hanging baskets must be used to display these beauties.

ing, greenish blue stems. It is reputedly hard to cultivate. *L. phlegmaria*, common tassel fern, grows in a range of habitats in north-eastern Queensland. It is one of the easiest tassel ferns to cultivate, with its tolerance of cooler temperatures and variable conditions. *L. squarrosum*, water tassel, native to India and Australia, has very pale green, hanging stems.

Lycoris (fam. Amaryllidaceae)
Spider lily

There are 11 species in this genus of attractive, bulbous plants from China, Japan and Burma. The clustered flowers are borne on tall stems, and come in red, yellow, pink and white. All

ABOVE The long stamens give golden spider lily, *Lycoris aurea*, an airy look. It needs a sheltered spot to grow well.

species have long, curving exserted stamens which explain the significance of the common name. The strap-like leaves are about 2 cm (¾ in) wide and in the range of 30–40 cm (12–16 in) long.

CULTIVATION Most species prefer a frost-free climate with wet winters and dry summers, although some do well in colder areas. Plant in fall in full sun or dappled sunlight in a well-drained soil, with added organic matter. They need regular watering while flowering and throughout winter when the foliage is in active growth. Restrict water in summer. Propagate from offsets of bulbs in fall, after flowering. Plant with the neck of the bulb at, or just below, soil level. If summers are regularly very wet, these bulbs are best grown in a cool greenhouse.

CLIMATE The species below are suitable for zone 8.

SPECIES *L. aurea* grows 30–40 cm (12–16 in) high, with bright golden flowers in spring and summer. It is widely cultivated for the cut flower market. *L. radiata*, to 40–50 cm (16–20 in) and a good garden subject, produces bright red flowers in fall. *L. squamigera*, resurrection lily, grows to 60 cm (24 in), with fragrant, rosy pink, summer flowers.

Lygodium (fam. Shizaeaceae)

Native to tropical and subtropical rainforests, these ferns number about 45 species. Although lygodiums have underground rhizomes, they are called climbing ferns as the fine, wiry frond stalks can climb to considerable heights. The leaflets are quite variable.

CULTIVATION In frost-prone climates, grow in a warm greenhouse, in pots of soil-based potting compost, with added peat and chopped up

ABOVE This unusual, tender fern, *Lygodium japonicum*, is a climber and needs some means of support.

sphagnum moss, plus a few charcoal lumps. Give good light, but shade from direct sun. Mist spray plants each day when in full growth. Propagate by division in spring.

CLIMATE Zone 10 and above. Subtropical and tropical.

SPECIES *L. japonicum*, widespread in Asia and also in parts of Australia, is a very attractive species which twists and climbs to a height of several metres (yards). It has quite deeply divided, lobed pinnae. *L. microphyllum* (syn. *L. scandens*), climbing maiden hair, has simple, triangular pinnae, spaced alternately on the twining stalks. With a wide natural range, it is fairly easily to cultivate.

Lysichiton (fam. Araceae)

These two species of herbaceous, marsh or swamp plants are grown for their beautiful blooms, which have showy spathes that fall away as the flowers mature, and bold, showy foliage. Once these plants become well established, they tend to suppress weed growth.

CULTIVATION Plant in swampy areas or beside a garden pool. Propagate from seed or remove offsets from main clumps in spring or summer.

CLIMATE Zone 6.

SPECIES *L. americanus*, yellow skunk cabbage, has large, dark green leaves and yellow, arum-like flowers. Its common name refers to its extremely unpleasant odor. *L. camtschatcense*, white skunk cabbage, from Japan, is odorless, and has handsome, pure white spathes enclosing small, yellow flowers.

Lysimachia (fam. Primulaceae)
Loosestrife, creeping jenny

There are around 150 species of these herbaceous and evergreen perennials, native to

BELOW A clump of yellow skunk cabbage, *Lysichiton americanus*, is popular for bog gardens and poolsides.

ABOVE *Lysimachia nummularia*, known as creeping jenny, is a pretty groundcover. This golden form must have sun to maintain its foliage color.

Europe, Asia, North America and South Africa. Many are upright and slender, but the genus also includes the well-known creeping jenny, perfect for hanging baskets or groundcover. Some species have medicinal uses in their areas; others are used in teas.

CULTIVATION These plants prefer a rich, moist soil. Some grow well in shady, damp spots beside water features. Propagate by division in the spring or fall or, alternatively grow from seed.

CLIMATE There are species suited to various zones. All are very hardy.

SPECIES *L. atropurpurea*, zone 6, from Greece and Asia Minor, grows to 60 cm (24 in), with purple, summer flowers. *L. clethroides*, goose-

BELOW Purple loosestrife, *Lythrum salicaria*, is a perennial which flowers in the summer, is suitable for moist soils, and is very easily grown.

neck loosestrife, zone 4, from China and Japan, has curved spikes of white flowers to 1 m (3 ft) in height. *L. nummularia*, creeping jenny, zone 4, is a creeping perennial with yellow flowers. The cultivar 'Aurea' has golden, coin-shaped foliage. *L. punctata*, garden loosestrife, zone 5, is a clump-forming perennial which grows to around 1 m (3 ft) high. It has mid-green leaves and, in summer, boasts a profusion of bright yellow, starry flowers. It is at its best planted in drifts or groups and is also useful for growing beside pools. *L. vulgaris*, zone 5, from Europe and Asia, grows 1–1.5 m (3–5 ft), with yellow, summer flowers.

Lythrum (fam. Lythraceae)
Loosestrife

This genus comprises around 30 species of annuals and hardy herbaceous perennials, found in most temperate regions of the world. Bushy plants, they are useful for the back of borders where the soil is moist and rich. The lovely flowers, mostly in shades of pink or purple, appear in summer.

CULTIVATION Both annuals and perennials require a rich, moist soil, so are often used around pools or streams. Some species self-seed freely, so spent flower stems should be cut off as flowers fade. Propagate by division.

CLIMATE Zone 3. These plants are very hardy.

SPECIES *L. alatum* grows to 1 m (3 ft) or more, and produces beautiful, purplish crimson flowers. *L. salicaria*, purple loosestrife, can be seen growing beside lakes, ponds and waterways throughout Europe and temperate parts of Asia. It grows to 1 m (3 ft), the whole plant turning into a blaze of purple in the summer and then dying back in the winter. Selected forms with flowers in shades of rich pink or rose are more popular and are grown more widely than the straight species. *L. virgatum*, to 1m, is also more often seen as the cultivars 'Morden Gleam' (rose-pink), 'Morden Pink' (magena), and 'Morden Rose' (rose red).

M

macadamia to Myrtus

Macadamia (fam. Proteaceae)

Several species of this small genus of 11 species of nut-bearing, evergreen trees come from the warm, eastern coastal areas of Australia. The dense, dark green, leathery leaves are arranged in whorls and the long, pendulous spikes of small flowers are followed by the round fruit containing the hard-shelled nuts. These trees are grown commercially in Australia, not only for their delicious nuts, but also for the high quality oil yielded by the kernel and the substances contained in the hull which are used for tanning leather. The trees are variable producers and unseasonal dry spells during spring and early summer will reduce the crop and affect the size and quality of the fruit. These trees are difficult to propagate by vegetative methods, and are now generally being increased by new grafting methods.

ABOVE Macadamias are now grown commercially for their edible nuts in various parts of the world, but only in frost-free climates.

CULTIVATION These trees are sensitive to frost, so in climates prone to frost they should be grown as young foliage plants in an intermediate greenhouse or conservatory. It is unlikely they will bear nuts under glass. Grow in pots of soil-based potting compost and provide bright light, but shade from direct sun. They are deep-rooted trees and so would be best in deep containers or even planted in a soil border. Outdoors grow in deep soil with a high organic content and in full sun.

CLIMATE Warmer parts of zone 10 and above.

SPECIES *M. integrifolia* is a large, round-headed tree which grows to around 18 m (60 ft) tall. When young, the leaves are coarsely toothed, generally becoming entire at maturity and growing 10–30 cm (4–12 in) long. The smooth-shelled nut is 1–3 cm (⅓–1 in) in diameter. *M. ternifolia* grows to 5 m (16 ft) tall, with small, bitter, inedible nuts. *M. tetraphylla* is a large, handsome, round-headed tree, distinguishable by its finely serrated leaves, 10–50 cm (4–20 in) long. It reaches heights of around 18 m (60 ft). The rough-shelled nuts are 1–4 cm (⅓–1½ in) in diameter. Selected, heavy-bearing varieties with good-quality nuts are available from specialist growers.

Macfadyena (fam. Bignoniaceae)

Native to tropical America, this small group of woody vines is grown for their beautiful, bright yellow, bell-shaped flowers, borne singly or in small clusters. The leaves are quite unusual, having two leaflets plus a terminal leaflet with a claw-like tendril.

CULTIVATION These climbers are frost-tender, so grow them in an intermediate greenhouse or conservatory if frosts are a problem. Use soil-based potting compost. Ensure good light but shade from direct sun. After flowering, prune back lightly to keep plant in its allotted space. Outdoors grow in well-drained soil with full sun or partial shade. Propagate from semi-ripe cuttings in summer in a warm propagating case.

ABOVE *Macfadyena unguis-cati*, cat's claw, is a vigorous climber with flamboyant, spring and summer flowers.

ABOVE The pale lilac flowers of *Mackaya bella* are pretty but this is worth growing for its dark, glossy foliage alone.

CLIMATE Warmer parts of zone 10 and above.

SPECIES *M. unguis-cati*, cat's claw, cat's claw trumpet, is a vigorous climber which can grow to 10 m (33 ft) tall, and therefore needs to be grown in a large conservatory. It flowers profusely in spring and summer. The flowers are about 10 cm (4 in) across; the fruit, which resembles a bean pod, grows to 30 cm (12 in) or more long; and the leaves are lance-shaped or oblong.

Mackaya (fam. Acanthaceae)

From South Africa, this beautiful, evergreen shrub is prized for its clusters of lovely, bell-shaped flowers that bloom from spring to fall. The large flowers are delicately colored in pale lilac with dark red veining on each lobe. The oval, pointed leaves are a glossy, dark green.

CULTIVATION In frost-prone climates, grow in an intermediate greenhouse or conservatory in a pot of soil-based potting compost, with maximum light, but shade from direct sun. Outdoors, choose a sunny or partially shaded spot with well-drained, slightly acid or neutral soil (slightly alkaline soil is also suitable). Prune lightly in spring to maintain a shapely plant. Propagate from seed in spring or from semi-ripe cuttings in summer, both with basal warmth.

CLIMATE Warmest parts of zone 9, or zone 10.

SPECIES *M. bella* is the only species, and it grows to a height of 2 m (6 ft). Upright at first, it may eventually spread to 1.5 m (5 ft) or more. It makes a good conservatory or greenhouse plant.

Macleaya (fam. Papaveraceae)

Grown mainly for their attractive, veined, lobed leaves, these plants make excellent specimen or border plants. They can be extremely vigorous as they spread from underground rhizomes. The feathery, white flowers are borne in graceful, branching, terminal clusters.

CULTIVATION *Macleaya* likes rich, moist soil and full sun or dappled shade. Propagate from suckers in late fall or spring. If transplanting a clump, remove all roots from the soil as new plants will grow even from very small pieces of root left in the ground.

ABOVE The curious-looking fruit of *Maclura pomifera* smells good but it contains a very caustic, milky sap.

ABOVE Dying back to the ground in winter, *Macleaya cordata* makes rapid growth in spring. The lobed leaves are very decorative.

CLIMATE There are species suited to various climatic zones but all are very hardy.

SPECIES *M. cordata*, plume poppy, zone 3, is a native of China and Japan. This perennial grows to about 3 m (10 ft), exuding an orange-colored sap when cut. The leaves are white underneath and the fluffy flowers are a pale cream. *M. microcarpa*, zone 5, is similar to *M. cordata*, but it does not grow as tall. Cultivar 'Kelway's Coral Plume' produces coral pink buds from which emerge buff to pink flowers.

Maclura (fam. Moraceae)

This genus consists of 12 species of trees and shrubs native to Asia, Africa and America. They may be evergreen or deciduous and are usually thorny. They can be grown in shrub borders, or *M. pomifera* may be grown as a hedge. Fruits are only produced in climates with long, hot summers.

CULTIVATION These plants can be grown in almost any type of soil as long as it is well drained. They prefer a position in full sun. Although they benefit from regular summer watering, they are fairly tough and easy to grow. Pruning is not usually necessary. Propagate from seed in a garden frame, or from semi-ripe cuttings in summer, rooted with basal warmth.

CLIMATE Zone 5.

SPECIES *M. pomifera*, Osage orange or bow wood, is native to Arkansas and Texas in the United States. This deciduous tree grows 10–15 m (33–50 ft) high. Its wood bends easily and it is made into bows by the Osage people indigenous to the natural range of the tree. The timber has also been used in fencing and for railway sleepers. Its broad, oval leaves are shiny green above, paler beneath, coloring bright yellow in fall. The branches and stems are thorny. In spring, the tree carries pendulous sprays of greenish yellow flowers which are fairly inconspicuous. The fruit that develops later is large, 10–12 cm (4–5 in) across, and green, ripening to a pale yellow. Although the fruit has a pleasant smell, it should not be eaten. This species makes an excellent, impenetrable hedge and hence is ideal for garden boundaries.

Macropidia (fam. Haemodoraceae)
Black kangaroo paw

This unusual, Western Australian plant is closely related to the other kangaroo paw,

ABOVE Black kangaroo paw has strange, felty-textured flowers that contain bird-attracting nectar.

ABOVE The heavily veined leaves of *Macropiper excelsum* are almost circular. This is an important medicinal plant for the Maori people of New Zealand.

Anigozanthos, differing mainly in the color of its flowers which are a combination of black and greenish yellow. It is unlikely to be available outside Australia.

CULTIVATION *Macropidia* is sensitive to frost so should be grown in an airy, cool to intermediate conservatory or greenhouse, in pots of gritty, lime-free, soil-based potting compost. Provide maximum light but shade from direct, strong sun. This plant does not relish a humid atmosphere. Keep the compost only slightly moist in winter. Propagate from ripe seed, germinated at 10°C (50°F), or by division in spring.

CLIMATE Zone 10.

SPECIES *M. fuliginosa* is the only species. This tufted plant grows to 50 cm (20 in) high, with strap-shaped or sword-like leaves.

Macropiper (fam. Piperaceae)

These shrubs or small trees originating from New Zealand and the South Pacific resemble the pepper tree. They have alternate leaves, axillary spikes of small, unisexual flowers that protrude from the foliage, and fruit which is colored yellow to bright orange.

CULTIVATION Macropipers are sensitive to frost and they should be grown in an intermediate greenhouse or conservatory in climates prone to frost. They like a rich, well-drained, soil-based potting compost and good light, but shade from direct sun. Keep the compost steadily moist. Outdoors grow in partial shade in a rich, well-drained soil. Propagate from seed in the spring or alternatively from semi-ripe cuttings in the summer, with bottom heat for both.

CLIMATE Zone 10.

SPECIES *M. excelsum*, kawa kawa or pepper tree, from New Zealand, is an attractive, bushy shrub or small tree. It has dark green, heart-shaped, aromatic leaves, tiny yellow to orange flowers, and clusters of small, round, orange fruits.

Macrozamia (fam. Zamiaceae)
Burrawang, Zamia palm

This genus comprises 14 species of cycads, all natives of Australia, varying from very large plants to dwarf, trunkless types with only a few leaves showing above ground. These have large, swollen, underground stems, tapering into thick taproots, twisted midribs and often much-divided leaflets which point in different directions. The cones are borne among the leaves, the cone scales ending in a single, strong, sharp spine. The seeds under the female scales are shed at maturity by disintegration of the whole cone. None of the species is commonly cultivated, but *M. communis* is probably the usual species grown. Most others are found only in botanical gardens or enthusiasts' collections. Some species are quite rare and threatened in their natural habitats. Efforts are being made to conserve them.

CULTIVATION These cycads are frost-tender so in frost-prone climates should be grown in an intermediate to warm greenhouse or conservatory. Grow in deep pots of gritty, soil-based potting compost and provide maximum light but shade from direct sun. Atmospheric humidity should be low to moderate. Keep the compost only slightly moist in winter. Outdoors grow in deep, light, well-drained soil in partial shade. Propagate from ripe seed

ABOVE This burrawang, *Macrozamia communis*, carries several male cones in its crown. The shiny, dark foliage is sometimes mistaken for a palm.

germinated at 25°–30°C (77°–86°F). Early growth is very slow.

CLIMATE Zone 10.

SPECIES *M. burrawang*, from coastal New South Wales, is a variable species–sometimes almost trunkless, at other times with a small trunk about 30 cm (12 in) high, and occasionally a little higher and covered in old leaf bases. The shiny, dark green leaves are gracefully arching and grow 1.5 m (5 ft) or more long. The numerous, straight, sharp-pointed leaflets are borne in two regular rows. The male cones, up to 45 cm (18 in) long, are curved outward. *M. miquelii*, from coastal Queensland and northern New South Wales, is like *M. communis* but has fewer leaves and smaller, shorter-spined cones. *M. moorei*, from southern Queensland and northern New South Wales, is by far the largest species, with a huge trunk up to 7 m (23 ft) tall in the wild, though generally about 2–4 m (6–13 ft) in cultivation. It has a thick crown of elegantly arching, rich green leaves up to 3 m (10 ft) long. The cones are similar to those of *M. communis*. It could easily be mistaken for a palm at first glance. *M. pauli-guilielmi*, from southeastern Queensland and northern New South Wales, is quite variable, though generally trunkless, with only a few, erect leaves up to 1 m (3 ft) long, twisted midribs and spidery leaflets up to 30 cm (12 in) long and 5 mm (⅕ in) wide. The cones are small and usually solitary. It makes an interesting ornamental.

Magnolia (fam. Magnoliaceae)

This popular genus consists of over 100 species of mostly deciduous trees and shrubs which are grown for their large, beautiful flowers. Magnolias are grown as lawn specimens and amongst other trees; the smaller species are popular as container plants.

CULTIVATION Magnolias should be protected from strong winds to ensure they look their best when in flower. They prefer a light loam which is slightly acid. They need plenty of water in summer, while a thick mulch of decayed leaf mould, aged cow manure or straw will help to control evaporation. If transplanting, move before the new growth begins. Propagate species from seed in fall, sown outside; deciduous and evergreen species and cultivars from semi-ripe cuttings in late summer; named cultivars by budding or grafting; all magnolias by layering in spring.

CLIMATE There are species suited to various climatic zones.

SPECIES *M. campbellii*, zones 8–9, from the Himalayas, is a deciduous tree growing as tall as 25 m (80 ft) in its habitat. It likes a sheltered situation. The beautiful, fragrant, erect blooms appear on leafless branches from late winter to mid-spring. The flowers are pink and white inside and pink on the outside of the petals. Subspecies *mollicomata*, zone 8, is similar, but hardier, and flowers earlier. It grows 15–25 m (50–80 ft) tall. *M. delavayi*, zone 9, is an evergreen, spreading tree, to 9 m (30 ft) tall, which is less hardy than other species. It has large leaves, to 25 cm (10 in) long, and fragrant, creamy white flowers. *M. denudata* (syn. *M. heptapeta*), yulan or lily tree, zone 6, has been cultivated in China for many centuries. A deciduous shrub or tree, it grows to around 15 m (50 ft). In spring it produces masses of erect, fragrant, white flowers on leafless branches. *M. grandiflora*, laurel magnolia or bull bay, zone 6, is an attractive, evergreen tree from the south of the United States which reaches heights of 30 m (100 ft). It is fairly slow growing, developing a broad crown with age. The large, white, cup-shaped flowers have purple stamens and a sweet perfume, and appear in summer; the leaves are glossy green on top and rust-colored and hairy on the undersides. The flowers are followed by cone-like fruit. *M. hypoleuca*, zone 6, is a hardy, deciduous tree which can grow as tall as 15 m (50 ft). The cream or ivory, fragrant flowers appear at the same time as the leaves.

ABOVE The large, cupped, white flowers of *Magnolia grandiflora* have a heavy texture. This close-up shows the detail of the flower structure.

M. kobus, zone 5, is a deciduous tree, 10–20 m (33–66 ft) tall, with small, generally upright, creamy white flowers which are borne on leafless branches. *M. liliiflora* (syn. *M. quinquepeta*), zone 6, is a deciduous, bushy shrub, with a height and spread of up to 3.5 m (11 ft). Narrow, fragrant flowers, purple outside and white inside, are borne amongst the oval, dark green leaves from mid-spring to midsummer. Cultivar 'Nigra' has large, dark purple flowers, colored pale purple to pink on the inside. *M. x loebneri* (*M. kobus* x *M. stellata*), zone 5, is similar to *M. stellata* but it has larger leaves and 12-petalled flowers. This deciduous tree grows to around 10 m (33 ft) tall and has a spreading habit. *M. sieboldii*, zone 7, is a hardy shrub or tree, to 9 m (30 ft), with a spreading habit. The fragrant, cup-shaped, white flowers appear in midsummer and are followed by crimson fruit. *M. x soulangeana* (*M. denudata* x *liliiflora*), zone 5, is a hardy, deciduous tree, to 4.5 m (15 ft), with large, purple flowers, white on the inside, which appear before and after the leaves emerge. Cultivar 'Alba' has pure white flowers; 'Alexandrina' produces large flowers

ABOVE *Magnolia* x *soulangeana* is a glorious sight in full bloom. This lovely tree is underplanted with ferns.

flushed with purple at the base; 'Lennei' has rose-purple flowers, colored white on the inside; 'Rustica Rubra' is a more vigorous grower, with rosy purple, goblet-shaped flowers; *M. stellata*, zone 4, from Japan, is a spreading, deciduous shrub, growing between 3 and 8 m (10–26 ft) tall. The white, fragrant, many-petalled flowers appear from early spring to mid-spring before the dull green, oval leaves. It flowers when quite young. Cultivar 'Rosea' has pink flowers; 'Waterlily' is a fine, many-petalled form.

Mahonia (fam. Berberidaceae)

There are 70 species in this genus of evergreen shrubs with handsome foliage, clusters of fragrant, yellow flowers and dark blueish black fruit which generally has a whitish or blue-gray bloom. The fruit can be made into a delicious jelly. Many of these plants make good hedges and windbreaks, while some species are excellent groundcovers.

CULTIVATION *Mahonia* needs a well-drained soil and a sunny position. *M. aquifolium* is the easiest to cultivate and suits most soils. Propagate from seed sown in fall, from suckers detached from the parent plant in spring or fall, or from half-ripe cuttings struck in sandy peat in late summer or fall.

CLIMATE Zone 6, unless otherwise indicated below.

SPECIES *M. aquifolium*, holly mahonia, holly barberry or Oregon grape, zone 5, from western North America, is a dense, bushy shrub which grows to around 1 m (3 ft) high. The oval-shaped leaves are divided into pairs of glossy, deep green leaflets, which take on a purple tone during the cooler months. The tight clusters of small yellow flowers appear in spring and are followed by attractive, globular fruits. *M. japonica* zone 7 is an upright, spreading shrub, to about 2 m (6 ft), with narrow, spiny, deep green leaflets and long, loose, drooping sprays of fragrant flowers in winter. *M. japonica* Bealei Group grows to 2 m (6 ft), with pinnate leaves divided into pairs of

ABOVE *Mahonia aquifolium* has holly-like leaves and is crowned in spring with spikes of yellow flowers, followed by blue-black fruits.

dull, grayish green leaflets, colored yellowish green on the undersides, with spiny margins. The yellow flowers are borne in upright sprays in winter. *M. lomariifolia*, zone 8, from central and western China, is somewhat taller than most species, growing 3–5 m (10–16 ft) high. The leaves of this showy shrub are divided into many narrow, rigid, dark green leaflets. Tight clusters of deep yellow blooms appear during late fall and winter. *M. repens*, zone 5, from the west of the United States, has a creeping habit, growing no taller than 30 cm (12 in). It has spiny leaflets and clusters of small, fragrant, yellow flowers in spring. The cultivar 'Rotundifolia' has rounded leaflets with few serrations and is much taller than the species, growing to 1.5 m (4 ft).

Malcolmia (fam. Brassicaceae)

Virginia stock

This genus of over 30 annuals and perennials is native to the Mediterranean region, extending east to Afghanistan. Only one annual species is common in cultivation. It is a popular filler plant for garden beds as it can be sown between other annuals, bulbs or shrubs. It is also a good container plant.

CULTIVATION Grow in full sun or partial shade in a well-drained soil. Very acid soils should be dressed with lime before the seed is sown. Sow seed where it is to grow, from late spring onwards, and repeat the sowings every few weeks to ensure a succession of flowers. These stocks self-sow themselves very freely and consequently, once they are sown, they may well remain in the garden permanently. For something different, try sowing the seeds between cracks and gaps in paving, or even in a gravel path or other gravelled areas.

CLIMATE Zone 8, but grown as a summer annual in all climates. Not suitable for hot humid climates.

SPECIES *M. maritima*, Virginia stock, is native to the Mediterranean. A spreading, low-

ABOVE For quick cover, nothing beats Virginia stock, *Malcolmia maritima*, as it takes only a few weeks from sowing to flowering.

growing annual, it rarely reaches more than 20–30 cm (8–12 in) high, with small, oval, gray-green leaves and masses of small, four-petalled flowers in mauve, pink and white. Not suitable for cutting, these plants are discarded once the flowers fade. It is excellent for quick garden effect and does well in coastal gardens.

Malpighia (fam. Malpighiaceae)

There are around 45 species in this genus of decorative, mostly evergreen shrubs, originating chiefly from tropical America. They are grown for their clusters of unusual flowers, with five, slender-stalked petals, in white, rose or red, and their attractive, spiny-toothed foliage. The fruits come in shades of orange, red or purple.

CULTIVATION Except in frost-free climates, grow in an intermediate to warm conservatory or greenhouse, in pots of soil-based potting compost. Plants need maximum light but shade from direct sun, and normal watering in summer with much less in winter. Outdoors grow in an open, sunny position in well

ABOVE The pale, fringed petals of *Malpighia coccigera* stand away from the flower center. The small leaves of the shrub make it ideal for clipping.

drained, humus-rich soil. Lightly prune in spring to maintain shape. Propagate from seed or cuttings.

CLIMATE Warmest parts of zone 10 and above.

SPECIES *M. coccigera*, holly malpighia, from the West Indies, is a lovely, ornamental shrub, to 1 m (3 ft) high, with shiny, holly-like leaves and a profusion of pink flowers, followed by edible red berries. *M. glabra*, acerola or Barbados cherry, grows to 2 m (6 ft) high, with red or pink, star-shaped flowers, followed by edible red fruit, about the size of a cherry, high in vitamin C. The dark green leaves are smooth along the edges.

Malus (fam. Rosaceae)
Crab apple

This genus comprises around 35 species of hardy, deciduous, small trees or large shrubs grown mainly for their lovely, spring blossom. There is a great range of cultivars grown purely for their blossom, though they also color well in fall. The showy, decorative fruit is mostly edible and is used for making jams and jellies. Many varieties grown for their fruit are descendants of *Malus pumila*, the wild or original apple, one of the earliest known fruits. Extensively hybridized to achieve better flavor and larger fruit, they are best grown in cool, temperate climates. Crab apples make pretty specimen trees and are ideal for small gardens.

CULTIVATION *Malus* likes well-drained soil, reasonably rich in humus. It is best grown in full sun with shelter from very strong wind. Species can be raised from seed but generally plants are grafted or budded onto seedling understocks. Most home gardeners do not bother raising their own plants but prefer to buy four-year-old trees from a garden center or nursery which will generally produce some flowers and fruits in the first year from planting. Best planting time is fall or winter. Ornamental *Malus* do not require pruning, except for the removal of any dead or diseased wood.

CLIMATE There are species suited to various climatic zones but all are very hardy to moderately hardy.

SPECIES *M.* x *arnoldiana*, zone 4, is an elegant New Zealand hybrid, growing to about 2 m (6 ft) high, with lovely pink flowers and yellow

ABOVE Always a favorite, *Malus floribunda* opens its pretty, pale blossoms from rich crimson buds.

fall fruit. *M. baccata*, zone 2, from Asia, grows to 5 m (16 ft), with white flowers. Var. *mandschurica* has sweetly fragrant, white flowers and red, cherry-like fruit. *M. floribunda*, zone 4, grows 5–8 m (16–26 ft) high, acquiring a broad, umbrella shape with maturity. Bright red buds open to pale pink flowers. The fruits are small. This species does well in warmer areas. *M. x zumi* var. *calocarpa*, zone 5, grows to 7m and has a pyramidal habit, white flowers and shiny, bright red fruits held into winter. *M. ioensis*, prairie crab, zone 2, is a leafy tree, with a shrubby growth habit. A native of North America, it looks beautiful in late spring with masses of delightfully fragrant, pinkish flowers. It produces one of the finest crab apples, yellowish in color. Cultivar 'Plena', Bechtel's crab, has double pink flowers. *M. x magdeburgensis*, zone 4, is a small hybrid, with dense clusters of semi-double, rose-colored flowers. *M. x purpurea* 'Eleyi', zone 4, grows 6–8 m (20–26 ft) tall, with pinky purple flowers followed by cherry-sized, purple-red fruits. It does quite well in warmer areas. *M. spectabilis*, Chinese apple, zone 4, grows to 8 m (26 ft), with pink, semi-double flowers and yellow fruit. Cultivar 'Flore Pleno' has clusters of rose-colored, double flowers. *M. tschonoskii*, zone 6, from Japan, is a pyramidal tree, to 12 m (40 ft), with pinkish white flowers, brownish yellow fruit and brilliant fall foliage. *M. yunnanensis*, zone 6, to 9 m (30 ft), has white to pale pink flowers and small, red fruit. Among the hybrids, *M.* 'Dorothea', zone 4, to 7m, has rose-pink, semi-double flowers followed by small yellow fruits. *M.* 'John Downie', zone 2, to 6m, bears white flowers followed by large red fruits.

Malva (fam. Malvaceae)
Mallow

There are around 30 species of annuals, biennials and perennials in this genus which is native to Europe, North Africa and temperate parts of Asia. These hardy, summer-flowering plants may be smooth or hairy, prostrate or

ABOVE Hollyhock mallow, *Malva alcea*, flowers all through summer, carrying a profusion of pastel, fluted flowers.

upright. Most have divided, lobed leaves and showy flowers which may be saucer-shaped or funnel-like. These may be clustered or solitary.

CULTIVATION Mallows grow in most garden soils, though the annuals need a sunny aspect. Propagate from seed sown where the plants are to grow. Perennials can be propagated from basal cuttings in spring as they do not divide successfully.

CLIMATE There are species suited to various climatic zones, but all are very hardy.

SPECIES *M. alcea*, zone 4, is a hardy perennial, often grown as an annual. It grows to around 1 m (3 ft) high, with rose-purple flowers. *M. moschata*, musk mallow, zone 3, from Europe, is a pretty perennial, useful for herbaceous borders and for naturalizing in wild gardens. Both the leaves and spreading stems are hairy and the early summer flowers are white or rose-mauve. All parts of the plant have a musky odor, particularly in warm conditions. It grows to 1 m (3 ft) high. The form *alba*, with white flowers, has a bushy, branching habit. *M. sylvestris*, high mallow, zone 5, is a biennial grown as an annual. It is a troublesome weed in some countries, as are some other species of *Malva*. The foliage is distinctive for its sparse, spreading hairs, and the darkly veined, rose-purple flowers appear from early spring to late summer. It grows to 1 m (3 ft) high or more.

Malvaviscus (fam. Malvaceae)

Native to Central and South America, these evergreen shrubs, which are sometimes vine-like in habit, are grown for their beautiful, red, hibiscus-like flowers which may be solitary or borne in terminal clusters. Sometimes the leaves are divided into palm shapes.

CULTIVATION Where frosts occur, grow in an intermediate to warm greenhouse in pots of soil-based potting compost. Although the plants need good light, they should be shaded from direct sun. Outdoors, in suitable climates, grow in any well-drained soil in a sunny or partially shady spot. Prune lightly after flowering to maintain a good shape. Propagate from seed in spring or semi-ripe cuttings in summer, with bottom heat for both.

CLIMATE Warmest parts of zone 9 and above.

SPECIES *M. arboreus* is an evergreen, rounded shrub, to 3 m (10 ft) high, with bright green, soft-haired, oval lobed leaves, with toothed margins. The solitary, red, erect flowers have protruding stamens. *M. arboreus* var. *mexicanus*, Turk's cap or cardinal's hat plant, grows 2–3 m (6–10 ft) high and produces scarlet, trumpet-shaped flowers resembling a partly opened hibiscus, over many months.

Mammillaria (fam. Cactaceae)
Pincushion cactuses

This genus of over 150 species of freely flowering cactuses originates from the tropical Americas and the Caribbean. Generally small and clump-forming, they have a wide range of spine colors. All have a ring of flowers around the crown of the plant. Flowering times vary greatly. This cactus group is popular with growers and collectors as it is easily grown and flowers reliably.

CULTIVATION In areas prone to frost, grow in pots in an airy, intermediate conservatory or greenhouse. These cactuses also make good house plants. Use a proprietary cactus compost and ensure maximum light, but shade from strong, direct sun. Water normally from spring to fall and keep virtually dry during the winter. Propagate in spring from seed germinate at 20°C (68°F) or from offsets in spring.

ABOVE Bright scarlet flowers over a long period make *Malvaviscus arboreus* var. *mexicanus* a standby in warm gardens.

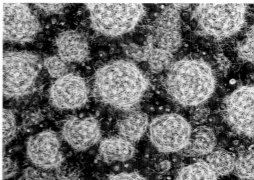

ABOVE Maturing red fruits of *Mammillaria prolifera* encircle each rounded stem. This species readily forms large colonies.

CLIMATE Zone 10.

SPECIES *M. bocasana*, snowball cactus, is a silky-haired, clump-forming species with hooked spines and small, cream flowers. *M. camptotricha*, bird's nest cactus, has a clustering habit. The yellowish spines are long and twisted, and the small, white flowers are scented. *M. elongata* has clustering, finger-shaped bodies with different colored spines. It produces cream flowers. *M. hahniana* is covered with long, white hairs and produces purplish red flowers in a perfect ring. *M. longiflora* has a small body, but large, pink, long-tubed flowers. *M. prolifera* is a clustering type, known as little candles, with tiny stems, cream flowers and red berries. *M. senilis* is a slow grower, eventually forming clumps, covered with white spines and producing scarlet, long-tubed flowers in spring.

Mandarin (*Citrus reticulata*, fam. Rutaceae)
Tangerine

Mandarins make excellent home garden trees as they are smaller than some other citrus and often foliaged almost to the ground. They produce a round, orange-colored fruit with sweet pulp and thin skin. While the fruit is mostly eaten fresh, it does have a place in the kitchen alongside other citrus, particularly in sweets.

CULTIVATION Mandarins are frost-tender but are hardier than other citrus and take some frost. However, where frosts are severe, grow in a cool, airy greenhouse or conservatory in pots or tubs of soil-based potting compost, with good light, but shade from direct sun. Plants can be stood outside for the summer. In the garden, mandarins need a sheltered spot with full sun, and well-drained, acid to neutral soil.

CLIMATE Warmer parts of zone 9.

VARIETIES *Citrus reticulata* is a small tree, to about 3 m (10 ft), with quite narrow leaves and slightly winged leaf stalks. 'Satsuma' orange is

ABOVE Mandarins are hardier than other citrus and can be grown outdoors in relatively frost-free gardens, or in a cool conservatory if hard frosts are a problem.

a Japanese cultivar grown commercially. There are many cultivars from which to choose. Fruit flavor and time of maturity varies greatly. The cultivars 'Clemantine', 'Dancy', 'Kara' and 'Kinnow' are well known.

Mandevilla (fam. Apocynaceae)

Mostly from tropical America, these fast-growing, climbing shrubs are grown for their masses of beautiful, showy, trumpet-shaped, jasmine-scented flowers borne in small to large clusters. The smooth-edged leaves grow in a circle around the stem. There are around 100 species. Those commonly available are frost-tender and are grown in an intermediate greenhouse or conservatory in frost-prone climates.

CULTIVATION When pot grown under glass, use a soil-based potting compost. Ensure maximum light, but provide shade from direct strong sun. Prune in late winter by cutting the side shoots back to within four growth buds of the main stems. Outdoors grow in a sunny, sheltered spot with well-drained soil. Propagate in spring from seed germinated at 20°C (68°F), or from semi-ripe cuttings in summer, with basal warmth.

CLIMATE Zone 10.

SPECIES *M. x amabilis*, a woody climber, has large, showy, pale pink flowers changing to deep rose. *M. x amabilis* 'Alice du Pont' is the best known and produces masses of bright pink flowers in summer. It grows to 6 m (20 ft) in height. *M. laxa* (syn. *M. suaveolens*), Chilean jasmine, from Argentina, is a deciduous climber, with slender, dark green, pointed leaves and heavily perfumed, white, trumpet-shaped flowers. *M. sanderi* (syn. *Dipladenia sanderi*) is a smooth, woody twiner with opposite, leathery leaves and rose pink, funnel-shaped flowers. Several cultivars with deep pink or red flowers are available. *M. splendens*, a woody twiner from Brazil, climbing to 3 m (10 ft) high, has silky stems and small clusters of rose pink, funnel-shaped flowers.

Manettia (fam. Rubiaceae)

This genus of about 80 evergreen, twining plants originates from tropical America. They usually have simple, opposite leaves, sometimes toothed or fringed, and tube- or funnel-shaped flowers, borne either singly or in clusters. The flowers are usually red, pink or yellow, but sometimes bicolored. They must be grown in an intermediate greenhouse in frost-prone climates.

CULTIVATION When pot grown under glass, use soil-based potting compost. Ensure maximum light, but provide shade from direct sun. In late winter, prune the side shoots back to within four buds of the main stems. Outdoors grow in full sun or partial shade with rich, well-drained soil. Propagate in spring from seed germinated at 18°C (64°F), or from semi-ripe cuttings in summer, with bottom heat.

CLIMATE At least zone 10.

SPECIES *M. cordifolia*, firecracker vine, is a light, evergreen vine with heart-shaped to

ABOVE Chilean jasmine, *Mandevilla laxa*, delights with both its appearance and its lovely fragrance.

ABOVE A light, twining climber with small, red and yellow flowers, *Manettia luteorubra* is suitable for growing in pots.

oblong leaves and bright red, solitary flowers which usually grow from the leaf axil. *M. luteorubra* (syn. *M. bicolor*), Brazilian firecracker, is an attractive, evergreen climber, to about 2 m (6 ft). It has opposite, tapering leaves and tubular, red flowers, tipped with yellow.

Mango (*Mangifera indica*, fam. Anacardiaceae)

Although there are over 40 species in the genus *Mangifera*, only one is well known in tropical climates. The mango is native to Asia, from northern India through to Malaysia. It is grown as a major fruit crop in many tropical and subtropical regions such as South America, the West Indies and Australia. The trees are large and can grow to 20 m (65 ft) in height and around 12 m (40 ft) wide in the tropics. They are often planted for shade and the fruit is a bonus. A number of cultivars have been produced but not all are readily available outside the tropics. Mangoes are mainly eaten fresh, though they are also canned. Mango is used to flavor ice cream and for jams and preserves.

ABOVE In warm, humid climates mango trees bear heavy crops of delicious fruit. This bountiful tree fills a suburban garden.

CULTIVATION Except in the tropics and subtropics, mango must be grown in a large pot in a warm greenhouse or conservatory. In such conditions, it would be as a novelty foliage plant and unlikely to fruit. Use a rich, soil-based potting compost. Give maximum light but shade from strong sun and provide a humid atmosphere. Mangoes, especially the fruiting cultivars, are propagated commercially by grafting. The species can be raised from seed, sown as soon as available in a heated propagating case. Where conditions allow growing outdoors, the soil must be well drained and contain plenty of humus. Feed young trees with a high-nitrogen fertilizer, established trees with a balanced fertilizer in spring, summer and fall. Trees will usually start setting fruit in their third year but do not come into regular heavy bearing for at least ten years. Fruit maturity may be difficult to judge, but skin color will change from darkish green to a greenish yellow. Fruits should be cut, not pulled, from the tree. Mangoes are susceptible to various local pests and diseases, including powdery mildew.

CLIMATE Warmest parts of zone 10 plus tropical climates.

Mangosteen

(*Garcinia mangostana*, fam. Guttiferae)

Mangosteen is described as one of the best of all tropical fruits, yet, until recently, it was cultivated rarely outside its native Malaysia and Indonesia. It is unlikely to be available outside the tropics. It is a decorative, evergreen tree, growing about 8–10 m (26–33 ft) high, with dark, leathery leaves and pretty, rose pink flowers. The smooth fruits have purple skins enclosing a few seeds in a succulent, white pulp.

CULTIVATION The mangosteen is not grown outside the tropics and in any case it would not fruit well. In other climates, it would need to be grown as a young foliage plant in a warm, humid greenhouse or conservatory. Plants are

ABOVE Mangosteen fruits must be a deep reddish purple before they are fully ripe. These fruits have a long way to go.

ABOVE Known as cassava, manioc or tapioca, *Manihot esculenta* is one of the staple foods of several tropical regions.

grown from seed, which should be sown in individual pots to avoid root disturbance when potting or transplanting. Germinate in a warm propagating case. Seeds are viable for only a short time after removal from the fruit. In suitable climates, young trees usually start producing fruit after about eight years.

CLIMATE Suited to the tropics only.

Manihot (fam. Euphorbiaceae)

These shrubs and trees, mostly from tropical America, are grown quite widely as ornamentals in many tropical climates, but in most of the US would need to be grown as young foliage plants under glass. In some parts of the world, several species, most notably *M. esculenta*, are grown commercially for the starch from their roots, used to produce the grain, tapioca. Some species, however, are poisonous. All species are monoecious, and all produce a milky sap. The alternate leaves are usually palm-shaped and deeply divided. The flowers have no petals and are borne in axillary clusters.

CULTIVATION Grow in a warm greenhouse or conservatory in a large pot or tub of sandy, soil-based potting compost. Ensure good light but shade from direct sun. Propagate from cuttings or by division.

CLIMATE Zone 10 and above.

SPECIES *M. dulcis*, sweet cassava, is a shrub which has fiddle-shaped leaves and sweet, tuberous, edible roots. *M. esculenta*, cassava, manioc tapioca, is a shrub, reaching to 3 m (10 ft), grown primarily for its commercial uses. It has soft, pithy stems and large, leaves, deeply divided into narrow, finger-like segments. Its roots contain a large amount of poisonous prussic acid, but this is destroyed by the cooking process. *M. dulcis* contains very little prussic acid.

Maranta (fam. Marantaceae)

This genus from tropical America comprises about 30 species of perennial, evergreen, clump-forming plants, grown mostly for their decorative leaves, though some species are also very striking when in bloom. They make very attractive house plants. Arrowroot comes from the thick, starchy rhizome of *M. arundinacea*.

CULTIVATION Outside tropical climates, marantas need to be grown in a warm greenhouse or conservatory or in a warm room in the home. Use a soil-based or soilless potting compost, and, as the plants have only shallow root systems, grow them in half-depth pots or pans. They need good light (but shade from direct sun) and a humid atmosphere throughout the year. They should be mist sprayed daily in the growing period. Propagate in spring, either by division or from basal cuttings rooted in a heated propagating case.

CLIMATE Tropical only.

SPECIES *M. arundinacea*, arrowroot, grows up to 2 m (6 ft) high, with green, tapering leaves and white flowers. Cultivar 'Variegata' has leaves marked dark green, light green and yellow. *M. bicolor*, to 40 cm (16 in), has oval-shaped, olive green leaves with brown spots, a lighter, central stripe on top and light purple below. The white flowers are marked with purple and the tubers are borne at the base. *M. leuconeura*, prayer plant, grows to 30 cm (12 in). The satiny, deep green, silver-veined foliage is purple on the underside. The

white flowers of this species are spotted with purple. Var. *erythroneura* has very dark green leaves, dark red on the undersides, with bright red veins and midribs and a light green, zigzag central band. Var. *kerchoveana* has light green leaves which are blueish gray on the undersides, boldly marked with brown, but eventually turning green.

Marattia (fam. Marattiaceae)

Distributed throughout the tropics, this genus comprises around 60 species of ferns. They have large, fleshy rhizomes, resembling those of *Monstera*, and thick, waxy stalks. The large fronds are bipinnate to tripinnate, and the coarse, fleshy, waxy leaflets are shiny on top and duller below. These ferns are unlikely to be available to home gardeners.

CULTIVATION Outside the tropics, this fern will grow only in a warm, humid greenhouse. Propagate *M. salicina* from a mature, tuberous growth obtained from the base of a fully grown plant. Place in a pot with the rhizome

BELOW *Maranta leuconeura* var. *kerchoveana* is a popular greenhouse or house plant but it needs plenty of warmth and humidity.

ABOVE The long, graceful fronds of *Marattia salicina* make a lovely foliage feature. Variety howeana, native to Lord Howe Island, is pictured here.

top protruding just above the soil surface. Keep reasonably damp. The tuber may take around two years to grow. In protected situations, the growth rate will be reasonable after the first frond appears. Move to its permanent position when the pot is outgrown. This fern needs considerable space to develop. Although it produces spores, propagation from these is difficult if not impossible, .

CLIMATE Tropical only. Warm, humid conditions are required.

SPECIES *M. salicina*, potato fern, is native to north-east Queensland in Australia, Norfolk Island, New Zealand and the South Pacific. It is also known as horseshoe fern, king fern and para. In the wild, it thrives in very damp, shaded rainforest situations. The rhizomes have many thick, waxy roots and thick, fleshy, upright to drooping stems, swollen at the base. The arching, glossy, green fronds are very attractive and grow to 4 m (13 ft) long.

Marjoram, sweet

(*Origanum majorana*, fam. Lamiaceae)

Sweet marjoram and oregano (or wild marjoram) are so closely related that it is difficult to separate them. The plants are very similar in appearance, marjoram leaves being a little softer than those of oregano and gray-green in color. Growth tends to sprawl, to about 30 cm (12 in) high. The small, white flowers of both are also very similar. Their cultivation needs are identical and both have similar culinary uses, although marjoram has a sweeter, more spicy flavor. Marjoram is an ingredient in mixed herbs, along with thyme and sage, and is used to flavor poultry, egg dishes, fish, vegetables and sauces. Its flavor and aroma are slightly more subtle than oregano (wild marjoram). Marjoram is used also as an infusion, in herbal baths and herb pillows.

CULTIVATION These plants can be grown in any well-drained soil, but must be sited in full sun.

ABOVE A golden form of wild marjoram, or oregano, is a feature of this border, and provides leaves for culinary use.

They can be grown from seed, sown in spring, or from cuttings, taken from late spring through summer. Fertilizer is generally not required and plants grown 'hard' often have the best flavor. Water heavily when the soil is dry, but do not overwater. Harvest leaves for drying just before the plants are in full bloom in late summer or fall. Cut stems and hang in bunches in a cool, airy place. When the bunches are partially dry, tie net or muslin around them so that the dried leaves will not fall to the ground. The dried leaves should be stored in air-tight jars. Cutting stems for drying may be all the pruning that is needed, but these plants tend to become very woody after three or four years and should be replaced.

CLIMATE Zone 7.

Marrow (*Cucurbita pepo*, fam. Cucurbitaceae)

Summer squash, vegetable marrow

One of the oldest domesticated plants, marrow is known to have been cultivated in Mexico for several thousands of years. Often described in seed lists as either bush or trailing types, these plants mostly have large, lobed leaves that are rough and like sandpaper to touch. Marrows may be green, white or striped, and either cylindrical or round. Although they do not have a strong flavor, they are often eaten boiled, but they are tastier stuffed with a savory meat or vegetable mixture and baked.

CULTIVATION These plants usually need plenty of space to spread. The soil must drain well and preferably contain plenty of organic matter. Sow seeds in spring once the soil has warmed. It is best to sow three seeds in one place, and to select the strongest plant and discard the others once growth is active. In frost-prone climates, sow under glass in mid-spring, one seed per pot, and plant out when frosts are over. All-purpose plant food can be applied once plants are in active growth. Give ample water during the growing season. All vegetables need to be grown quickly to produce their best. Once plants start to flower and bear, check them carefully each day and harvest the fruit at the preferred stage. In warm weather, fruits can develop very rapidly indeed.

CLIMATE Zone 10, but grown as a summer annual in all climates.

ABOVE The large leaves of a vegetable marrow shade its bright yellow flowers. Vines need plenty of room to spread.

Marsilea (fam. Marsileaceae)
Nardoo, water clover

There are about 65 species of these aquatic or bog ferns, some of them floating plants, that bear a strong resemblance to clover. They are non-flowering and reproduce from spores. Most are native to tropical regions, Africa especially, but several species are originally from Australia. A very small number occur naturally in Europe. Although most are grown in pools, some species can be grown in the ground or in containers, in constantly wet soil or potting mix.

CULTIVATION In climates prone to frost, grow *Marsilea* in a warm conservatory or greenhouse. It can be grown in water of almost any depth, but does well in quite shallow pools. It can be planted directly into silt at the bottom of a pond or in a container placed in a pond. It can also be grown in permanently boggy ground. The plant's color and appearance will vary depending on its growing conditions. It will grow in sun or shade. *Marsilea* is generally propagated by division, but in nature its natural increase is from spores.

CLIMATE Warmer parts of zone 9 or zone 10.

ABOVE The small, clover-like leaves of *Marsilea angustifolia* form a dense cover over a pond surface.

SPECIES *M. angustifolia*, narrow leaf nardoo, is a small species that needs to be grown in shallow water. *M. drummondii*, common nardoo, has pretty leaves that may be russet-toned when grown in shallow water, or greener and covered with silvery hairs if grown in boggy ground. This and other species can be grown in a container, provided it is placed in a deep saucer of water to keep the growing medium quite damp. *M. mutica*, rainbow nardoo, has the most colorful foliage of all. It is a rich green, patterned in crimson and deep ochre. This species can be grown in water of almost any depth but will not adapt to cultivation in the ground.

Masdevallia (fam. Orchidaceae)

In the wild, these epiphytic orchids are found mostly at high altitudes in the north of South America, in areas with high light intensity. There are around 300 species, and many variations exist within the genus. The lovely, dainty flowers are generally characterized by their unusual shape, appearing rather like a triangle balanced on a slender stem. They often have long, slender tails at each apex.

ABOVE The triangular shape of this rosy Masdevallia hybrid is emphasized by its long, slender-tailed sepals.

Most striking are the iridescent petals which change color with different angles.

CULTIVATION In frost-prone climates, grow in an airy, intermediate greenhouse or conservatory, in proprietary, bark-based orchid compost formulated for epiphytes. Small pots make the best containers. Plants need good light (but shade from direct sun) and a humid atmosphere in summer. Water well in summer but in winter keep the compost only slightly moist. Propagate from side shoot cuttings.

CLIMATE Frost-free zone 10 and above.

SPECIES *M. coccinea* produces beautiful, bright purplish red flowers on erect, 40 cm (16 in) long stems in summer. The iridescent effect is very pronounced in flowers in this color range. *M. trochilus* is more tolerant of warmer conditions than others of the genus. The flowers are reddish brown and yellow. Many lovely hybrids are grown today, including some with bicolored or spotted flowers.

Matricaria (fam. Asteraceae)

There are about five species of annuals in this genus, most species having been moved to other genera. However, they are not often grown and are not too well known to home gardeners. Some are rather invasive and many are aromatic. They have pinnate leaves and the single flower heads are borne at the ends of branches. Named for the Latin word for womb, *Matricaria* was used in the past to treat female disorders. It was also used in herbal medicines prescribed for digestive ailments, fever and insomnia.

CULTIVATION Easily grown, these plants do best in shallow soil enriched with compost and complete fertilizer before planting. Seed is best sown in spring where the plants are to flower. Being annuals, the plants are discarded at the season's end. Dead-heading plants regularly may encourage production of more flowers over a longer period.

ABOVE Scentless mayweed, *Matricaria inodora*, (syn. *Tripleurospermum inodorum*) has small, white, daisy flowers like the better known *M. recutita*, sweet false chamomile.

CLIMATE Zone 8 or 9.

SPECIES *M. africana* (syn. *Oncosiphon africanum*) is an erect or spreading annual, to 30 cm (12 in), with daisy-like flowers. *M. aurea* is a many-branched, erect or spreading annual, to around 30 cm (12 in), with yellow discs and no petals. *M. matricarioides*, pineapple weed, is an erect, very aromatic annual, to 30 cm (12 in), with yellow to green discs. This species is a common weed in many parts of the world. *M. suffruticosa* (syn. *Oncosiphon suffruticosum*) is a very aromatic, upright annual, to 45 cm (18 in), with bright yellow discs. *M. recutita*, often known as sweet false chamomile, is an annual with small, daisy-like flowers.

Matthiola (fam. Brassicaceae)
Stock

Native to the Mediterranean region, this genus of annuals, biennials and perennials belongs to the same plant family as cabbages and cauliflowers. Originally they were poor quality, shrubby biennials with purple flowers only, but today many improved hybrids are available in a range of colors. Some are very fragrant and are grown for their cut flowers. Stock cultivars are divided into column types, which produce the largest flowers and only one stem, and double-flowering types. Double-flowering stocks do not always produce double flowers, though varieties are available which do produce double, fragrant flowers with long stems. Dwarf types grow to around 30 cm (12 in) and the taller types to about 75 cm (30 in). Stocks look their best in massed groups or as border plants, blending well with pansies, violas and alyssum. They have soft, gray-green foliage and densely clustered flowers in shades of white, pink, lilac, purple and deep red. Most seed contains a mixture of the many colors now available.

CULTIVATION Plant in any reasonable, well-drained garden soil, but not where stocks have been grown in the previous year. Dig soil well and dress with lime and a complete fertilizer, adding some well-decayed manure or compost.

ABOVE Both single- and double-flowered stocks come in the same color range. Single flowers are often strongly fragrant.

Raise plants from seed sown in spring. Night-scented stock is sown in situ. Successional sowings, a few weeks apart into summer, will ensure a long season of flowers. Stocks to be bedded out for the summer, such as the Ten Week stocks, are sown under glass in early spring and planted out when the frosts are over. The column stocks are sown outdoors in midsummer, and planted out in the following spring. Protect them with cloches over winter in cold areas. Stocks can be planted in formal beds with other bedding plants, or they can be grown in more informal groups and drifts in a mixed or herbaceous border. Plants need a sunny position and protection from wind. Tall stocks will need to be supported, perhaps with twiggy sticks. All stocks need plenty of water during the growing season if the weather is dry. Remove spent blooms to encourage further flowering. Stocks make excellent cut flowers and the stems should be cut as soon as a few flowers have opened; they will then last for a long time indoors.

CLIMATE Stocks are quite hardy and are suitable for zone 6.

SPECIES *M. incana* and its cultivars generally grow 30–60 cm (12–24 in) or more high, depending on the variety. The flowers come in various hues: lavender, purple, pink and red, or in white. Cultivars are classified by flower type. *M. longipetala* subsp. *bicornis*, night-scented stock, produces single, perfumed flowers, in various shades of pink to purple in summer and is at its most fragrant at night. It prefers a cool, semi-shaded position and is a pretty edging or rockery plant.

Maurandya

(syn. *Asarina*, fam. Scrophulariaceae)

Only one of the two species of climbing plants in this genus from Mexico is often seen in cultivation. This twining climber should be provided with wire, trellis or lattice for support.

ABOVE *Maurandya barclayana* will produce its rich purple to magenta flowers even in partial shade.

CULTIVATION Where regular frosts occur, grow in a cool greenhouse or conservatory or as a summer annual outdoors. *Maurandya* will grow in any type of well-drained soil, but growth will be vigorous if the soil is enriched with organic matter. It can be grown in full sun to partial shade. Provide ample water during dry spring or summer weather, but allow to dry out between waterings during the cooler months. Pruning should be confined to training or restraining too vigorous growth. Propagation is from seed or from firm stem cuttings, taken from late spring through summer.

CLIMATE Zone 10, or warmest parts of zone 9.

SPECIES *M. barclayana* (syn. *Asarina barclaiana*) is a twiner that may grow 2–5 m (6–16 ft) high, depending on conditions. The lobed leaves are vaguely triangular or heart-shaped. The tubular to trumpet-shaped flowers are bright pink to purple and appear mainly through summer into fall.

Mazus (fam. Scrophulariaceae)

Native to China, Malaysia, Australia and New Zealand, these prostrate perennials, closely related to *Veronica*, are useful for groundcover or rockeries. Most species are matforming, rooting readily where the stems touch moist soil. These are sometimes used as lawn substitutes.

CULTIVATION These plants prefer a moist, sandy soil, although they will tolerate all but very hot, dry conditions. Propagate by division in spring or from seed sown in spring or fall and germinated in a garden frame. They can also be grown from seed sown in early spring and kept moist in warm weather.

CLIMATE Zone 6, unless otherwise indicated below.

SPECIES *M. japonicus* is a trailing, perennial herb with stems up to 30 cm (12 in) long. It has toothed, oval leaves and blue flowers. The lower lip of the flowers is spotted brown and bearded. *M. pumilio*, zone 7, from Australia and New Zealand, is a dwarf, creeping type, forming a dense mat and with pinkish blue flowers with yellow throats in late spring and summer. *M. radicans*, from New Zealand, has strong stems, thick, upright branches and narrow, oval leaves. The lovely, white flowers have yellow throats. *M. reptans*, zone 3, produces rose to lavender flowers, the lower lip spotted in white, yellow or purple.

Meconopsis (fam. Papaveraceae)

Asiatic poppy

This genus from the Himalayas, western China and Europe produces brightly colored, poppy flowers. Most species are quite challenging to grow and need a cool, moist climate to succeed. They are generally grown in woodland gardens or in shrub borders.

CULTIVATION Grow in a slightly acid to neutral, moisture-retentive yet well-drained soil, with plenty of organic matter such as leaf mould. Choose a sheltered position with partial shade, and plant in bold groups or drifts. Mulch with organic matter. Propagate from seed sown as soon as ripe in a garden frame.

CLIMATE There are species suited to various climatic zones, but all need cool, moist climates.

SPECIES *M. aculeata*, zone 7, from the Himalayas, grows to 60 cm (24 in), with lovely

BELOW *Mazus pumilio* is a carpeting plant used as a soil-binding groundcover. It will take light foot traffic.

ABOVE Providing the bluest of blue flowers, *Meconopsis betonicifolia* is very demanding to grow, even in cool, moist climates.

blue or sometimes mauve, summer flowers. *M. betonicifolia*, blue poppy, zone 7, can grow to nearly 2 m (6 ft) tall. It is one of the most exquisite of the species, with satiny, pure sky blue flowers with yellow stamens in summer. The oblong, hairy, mid-green leaves form basal rosettes. *M. cambrica*, Welsh poppy, zone 6, from western Europe, has cheerful, yellow or orange flowers that often pop up in unlikely places, such as between bricks. It grows from seed to 45 cm (18 in) high. Var. *aurantiaca* has orange flowers; 'Flore Pleno' has double orange and yellow flowers. *M. delavayi*, zone 8, from China, grows to 25 cm (10 in), with deep purple flowers. It is a good choice for rockeries. *M. grandis*, zone 5, to about 1 m (3 ft), has deep blue flowers in midsummer. *M. quintuplinervia*, harebell poppy, zone 8, from Tibet and western China, is a perennial, to 45 cm (18 in), with pale purple flowers. It can be propagated by division.

Medinilla (fam. Melastomataceae)

Although there are about 150 species in this genus of tropical plants, few are in general cultivation. They occur in the tropics from Africa, through the Philippines and Borneo, to the Pacific regions. Most are shrubs, but there are also some scrambling climbers in the group.

CULTIVATION Outside the tropics, grow as pot plants in a warm greenhouse or conservatory. Use soil-based potting compost. The plants need bright light, but shade from direct sun. A very humid atmosphere is essential. Water normally in the growing season but ease up considerably in winter. Propagate from semi-ripe cuttings in summer, rooting them in a heated propagating case. An easier method is to air layer plants in summer.

CLIMATE Strictly for tropical regions, these plants prefer more than 20° C (68°F), even at night and in winter.

SPECIES *M. magnifica* is the only species commonly in cultivation. It bears long sprays

ABOVE The pink flowers of *Medinilla magnifica* appear in spring and summer and are followed by black fruits, as shown here.

of beautiful pink to coral flowers over many months. The flower spray is topped with several, pink bracts. An evergreen shrub growing to about 2 m (6 ft) high, it has glossy, dark green leaves that may be up to 30 cm (12 in) long. The rather angular stems are ribbed or winged.

Medlar (*Mespilus germanica*, fam. Rosaceae)

The medlar has been grown for its fruits in its native Europe for centuries, although it has never been very popular. It can be eaten fresh only when very ripe, with the pips removed, or cooked to make pies, jellies or spreads. This deciduous tree is regularly grown as an ornamental, being very pretty in flower. The white flowers resemble roses, the leaves are oblong and toothed, and the round, brown fruit is about 5 cm (2 in) across. Fall color is good in cool areas.

CULTIVATION Plant in a sunny position, in good soil. Prune only to shape and remove dead or spindly shoots. Propagate from seed, although germination is slow, or by grafting onto pear, quince, hawthorn or seedling medlar.

CLIMATE Zone 6.

Megaskepasma (fam. Acanthaceae)
Brazilian red cloak

There is only one species in this genus, an evergreen shrub from Venezuela. Sometimes grown in warm regions such as Florida.

CULTIVATION Outside the tropics or subtropics, grow in a warm greenhouse in pots of soil-based potting compost. The plant needs maximum light but should be shaded from direct strong sun. A very humid atmosphere is essential. Be sparing with water in winter, but water regularly in the growing season. Prune lightly after flowering to maintain a shapely specimen. Outdoors grow in dappled shade and humus rich, well-drained soil. Propagate in spring from seed germinated at 21°C (70°F),

ABOVE Although often grown for their unusual edible fruit, medlars make outstanding ornamentals for cool climate gardens.

or from semi-ripe cuttings in the summer, rooting them in a heated propagating case.

CLIMATE Tropical, but should flourish in warmer parts of zone 10.

SPECIES *M. erythrochlamys* is an evergreen shrub which grows 2–3 m (6–10 ft) high. It has strongly veined, opposite leaves and, from early fall to winter, bears upright spikes of white to pale pink flowers, surrounded by rich crimson bracts. The crimson bracts persist for many weeks, long after the flowers have fallen.

Melaleuca (fam. Myrtaceae)
Honey myrtle, paperbark

These evergreen trees and shrubs are mostly indigenous to Australia, although a few species are found in New Guinea, coastal Southeast Asia and New Caledonia. There are around 140 species in the genus which is closely related to *Callistemon* (bottlebrush), but distinguishable by the colorful, bunched stamens of the brush flowers. Melaleucas make beautiful ornamentals, with their attractive, neat foliage, compact growth habit and dazzling spring and summer flower displays. They are

ABOVE Grown in an open sunny position, *Melaleuca armillaris* forms a dense, rounded shrub or small tree.

ABOVE Melaleucas are like callistemons but have bunched stamens in various bright colors during spring and summer.

needle-like, flat or scale-like. It is widely used in floral art.

CULTIVATION Under glass, grow in pots of soil-based potting compost. Ensure airy conditions and maximum light, but shade from direct strong sun. Do not be too free with the watering in the growing season as very wet compost is disliked, and be even more sparing in winter. In the garden, plant in a sunny, sheltered spot with well-drained soil. Shade is appreciated during the hottest part of the day. If necessary, prune after flowering to restrict size. Propagate from seed in spring or from semi-ripe cuttings in summer, with basal warmth for both.

CLIMATE Warmest parts of zone 9, or zone 10.

SPECIES Not all of these are available outside their country of origin. *M. armillaris*, bracelet honey myrtle, is a small to medium-sized, spreading tree, growing to 10 m (33 ft) tall and 3–6 m (10–20 ft) wide. It has dark green, needle-like foliage and small, whitish cream brushes. A fast-growing species, it is very useful as a hedge plant. *M. bracteata*, black tea tree, has attractive foliage and cream, terminal flowers. It is a good choice for coastal gardens as it is very suitable for wet situations. Cultivar 'Golden Gem' grows to 2 m (6 ft), with variegated yellowish foliage; 'Revolution Green', with very fine, light green foliage, makes a useful screen plant. *M. decussata*, totem pole, is a hardy species which grows 2–5 m (6–16 ft) tall, with upright, small-leafed foliage and mauve brushes in spring. *M. ericifolia*, swamp paperbark, can be used to improve the drainage of difficult sites. It is bog- and salt-resistant, and has fine, dark green foliage and white brushes in spring. *M. fulgens*, showy honey myrtle, is a shrub to 2 m (6 ft) high, with an erect, open habit. In spring and summer, it is covered with beautiful, scarlet brushes, tipped in gold. *M. hypericifolia* is a rounded shrub to around 3 m (10 ft) high, with drooping branches, oval leaves and bright orange-red flowers. *M.*

recommended for relatively frost-free climates, or for the cool conservatory or greenhouse, where frosts are a problem. They are widely used in landscaping because of their tolerance of pollution, salt winds and saline soils. They can also withstand wet, boggy conditions and cold. None of the species do well in hot, very dry situations. All species respond well to pruning and clipping. The Western Australian species make outstanding garden shrubs, some growing into spreading, flat-topped bushes, forming natural hedges. *M. alternifolia* and *M. linariifolia* yield fragrant oils with antiseptic properties, used in a range of products. Saplings from some species, like *M. ericifolia* and *M. squarrosa*, are used to make rustic garden furniture and brushwood fencing. The timber of most of the tree-size species is unaffected by moisture and is invaluable for posts and boatbuilding. The bark of these trees is used to make bark paintings and to line hanging baskets. The flowers are useful for attracting birds to the garden and are long lasting when cut. In many different colors, they are produced in clusters or singly, either along the stem or terminally. The capsular fruits contain many tiny seeds. The foliage is very variable and may be *incana* is an outstanding shrub grown for its soft, grayish, weeping foliage and dainty, creamy yellow spring flowers. *M. laterita*, robin red breast shrub, grows 2–3 m (6–10 ft) high, with thick foliage and bright orange-red brushes from summer to fall. *M. nesophila*, one of the Western Australian species, is a hardy, bushy, erect shrub, to about 5 m (16 ft), with lovely, mauvish pink flowers, gold-tipped stamens and gray-green, oval leaves. *M. pulchella*, claw honey myrtle, is a small, hardy shrub, with soft foliage and bright, purplish pink, claw-shaped flowers from summer to fall. *M. steedmanii* is a very attractive shrub, to 2 m (6 ft) high, with thick, grayish foliage and large, bright red flowers, tipped with gold. *M. styphelioides*, prickly-leafed paperbark, grows to about 9 m (30 ft) tall, with a white, papery trunk and small cream-colored brushes. In a suitable climate this is a good shade tree.

Melastoma (fam. Melastomataceae)

This genus of around 70 species of evergreen, tropical shrubs or small trees is from Southeast Asia, the Philippines, India and South America. They are grown for their lovely foliage, flowers and berries.

ABOVE *Melastoma denticulatum* flowers mainly in summer, but sporadically through the year. Its resemblance to the related Tibouchina species is striking.

CULTIVATION Outside the tropics, grow in a warm greenhouse or conservatory, in pots of soil-based potting compost. Provide good light but shade from direct strong sun. Keep the atmosphere moderately humid. After flowering, prune back lightly to restrict size. Propagate from seed in spring or from semi-ripe cuttings in summer, both with basal warmth.

CLIMATE Tropical only.

SPECIES Not all are available outside their countries of origin. *M. denticulatum*, from Queensland and coastal northern New South Wales, is a soft, bushy shrub, with heavily veined, reddish green leaves and large, pink flowers. *M. malabathricum*, Indian rhododendron, originates from India, Asia, New Guinea and Australia. Growing to around 2 m (6 ft) high, it has large, purple to soft pink flowers, handsome foliage and reddish fruits. *M. polyanthum*, gooseberry laurel, grows to 3 m (10 ft), with soft, veined leaves and small, terminal clusters of pink, rose-lilac or reddish purple flowers and round fruits.

Melia (fam. Meliaceae)

Only one species of this small genus of shrubs and trees from the rainforests of Asia, India and Australia is widely cultivated. It is grown in most warm countries of the world as a shade tree or ornamental. The timber is used for making furniture, while the bark and leaves are used medicinally in some countries.

CULTIVATION In frost-prone climates, grow in an intermediate conservatory or greenhouse as a foliage specimen, as it may not flower under glass. Use soil-based, potting compost. Ensure maximum light, but shade from direct strong sun. Prune back in late winter to restrict size if necessary. Outdoors, plant in a rich, well-drained, moist soil in a sunny situation. Propagate from seed in spring or softwood cuttings in summer, with bottom heat for both.

ABOVE Chains of yellow berries persist on white cedar *Melia azedarach* through fall and winter.

CLIMATE Zone 10.

SPECIES *M. azedarach*, Persian lilac or white cedar, is a deciduous tree which grows 12–20 m (40–65 ft) tall. Sprays of fragrant, lilac flowers in late spring are followed by large, deep green, pinnate leaves and yellow berries. The berries are extremely toxic if eaten. Var. *australasica*, white cedar, an Australian native to 12 m (40 ft), is widely grown in warmer areas of Australia as a street tree. Very adaptable, it can withstand drought as it matures. Cultivar 'Umbraculiformis', Texas umbrella tree, produces pendulous foliage in the shape of an umbrella, giving this tree its common name.

Melianthus (fam. Melianthaceae)
Honeybush

Native to South Africa, these large, unusual shrubs are grown for their luxuriant foliage, although the leaves have an unpleasant smell if bruised. They have a suckering habit so their spread may need to be controlled. The flowers, which have calyces filled with nectar, are borne on long spikes in spring and summer. The fruit is contained in a seed bag which bursts when squeezed. *Melianthus* is generally suited to large gardens only.

ABOVE The striking, gray-green foliage of *Melianthus major* creates a strong architectural effect in the garden.

CULTIVATION In climates with hard frosts, grow in pots of soil-based potting compost in a cool greenhouse. They can be stood outside for the summer. Outdoors, grow in a sheltered, sunny position. Propagate from seed or softwood cuttings in spring, with bottom heat for both.

CLIMATE Zone 9.

SPECIES *M. major* is a sprawling shrub, with a height and spread of 2–3 m (6–10 ft), which makes a striking accent plant. The luxuriant foliage is grayish green and the tubular flowers are a brownish red color. The nectar-rich flowers are very attractive to birds.

Melicytus (fam. Violaceae)

Native to New Zealand and some Pacific regions, these small trees and shrubs are grown for their lovely, toothed foliage and attractive, bright blue berries, borne along the branches. Male and female trees are required for fruit production.

ABOVE Masses of violet-blue berries adorn the branches of *Melicytus ramiflorus* through fall.

CULTIVATION *Melicytus* will grow in any reasonably rich, well-drained soil and can be planted in either a sunny or a shaded site. Although at their best if sheltered, some species will tolerate strong winds. Propagate from seed sown in spring under glass or from semi-ripe cuttings in summer. In frost-prone climates, grow in a cool greenhouse.

CLIMATE Warmer parts of zone 9.

SPECIES Not all of these are available outside their countries of origin. *M. lanceolatus*, which grows 5–6 m (16–20 ft) tall, has bright green, willow-like foliage. It can tolerate cold conditions. *M. macrophyllus* has very attractive, toothed foliage. *M. ramiflorus*, mahoe, grows to 10 m (33 ft), its trunk clothed in white bark. The green flowers are followed by a profusion of violet-blue berries.

Melocactus (fam. Cactaceae)

Turk's cap

Originating from tropical coastal areas of northern South America, Mexico and the West Indies, these cactuses are mostly barrel-shaped, with sharp ribs, strong, deep green spines, and a densely spined crown from which the flowers and fruit appear. The small, violet to red flowers are diurnal and open at the crown center. The pink fruit is generally more visible. All of these cactuses look quite similar when young. Once the bristly head has been produced, they cease to grow in height.

CULTIVATION Grow in a warm greenhouse or conservatory in pots of well-drained cactus compost. Ensure maximum light. Water in moderation during the growing season but apply very little in winter. Too much water will cause plants to rot. Propagate from seed in spring. Germinate at 21°C (70°F).

CLIMATE Warmest parts of zone 10.

SPECIES *M. bahiensis*, a small, free-flowering plant, is the most widely grown species. *M. communis* (syn. *M. intortus*) grows to 1 m (3 ft) in ideal conditions. *M. matanzanus*, to 30 cm (12 in), has a bright orange-red head and bright pink to red flowers, followed by pink seed pods.

ABOVE *Melocactus bahiensis*, from Brazil, has a curious-looking, flattened, red crown on top of its spiny body.

Melon (fam. Cucurbitaceae)

Cantaloupes, honeydews, musk melons and watermelons are not all of the same genus *Cucumis*, but the plants are very similar. They are grown as annuals, with stems to 2 m (6 ft) or more in length, rough lobed leaves and separate male and female flowers. Cantaloupes and musk melons are roundish with orange flesh, while the honeydew is also roundish in shape, but has green flesh. The seeds are contained in the hollow centers of these fruits. Watermelons may be round or oval-shaped, the red flesh being embedded with the black or variegated seeds. All of these melons are watery, refreshing summer fruits which are eaten raw. The jam melon is the exception. It is also a vine, but the melon has a hard, white flesh which is made into jam. Melon and lemon, or melon and pineapple are popular jam combinations.

CULTIVATION All of these melons are grown from seed and require lots of sun, a warm growing season and frost-free conditions for at least five months. However, the jam melon tolerates slightly cooler conditions. While melons require a fairly rich soil, avoid high-nitrogen fertilizers as they may cause excessive leaf growth at the expense of the fruit. The soil

ABOVE Honeydew melon is popular for summer breakfasts or in mixed fruit plates. The flesh is pale green with a delicate flavor.

should be just slightly acid. Seeds will not germinate in cold soil, so avoid early spring sowing. They are usually sown in groups of six to eight seeds, 1.5–3 m (5–10 ft) apart, depending on the variety. The seeds should be planted, pointed end down, 2–3 cm (about 1 in) deep, and the seedlings thinned, retaining only the strongest two or three, to about 20 cm (8 in) apart. These plants require ample water during the growing period. Pinch out the terminal tips after the stems have reached 2 m (6 ft) to reduce the spread of the plants and hasten the setting of the fruit. If there are not enough bees in the garden, hand pollination may be necessary. The female flowers can be recognized by the immature fruit behind the petals. The pollen from the male flower is easily transferred with a child's paintbrush. Weed matting or hay makes a clean bed for the fruit and also acts as a mulch for controlling weeds. Where the growing season is short, sow seed individually in peat pots in a heated greenhouse in mid-spring and plant out when frosts are over. Or, sow directly at that time and cover with cloches. Many melons are prone to powdery mildew and watermelon is susceptible to wilt. Select varieties with resistance to these diseases. It is sometimes difficult to know when melons are ripe. Musk melon types are ready when they leave the vine at the slightest touch and have the characteristic aroma. Watermelons will have a flat, dead sound when tapped. They should be harvested before the adjacent tendrils are quite dead.

CLIMATE Zone 10, but grown as summer annuals in all climates.

SPECIES *Cucumis melo* is a trailing vine with soft, roundish leaves and small, yellow flowers. The Cantalupensis Group, cantaloupe, produces roundish fruit with a hard, rough rind; the Inodorus Group, honeydew, has large, round fruit with a smooth rind and green or white flesh; the Reticulatus Group, musk melon, also has roundish fruit with netted rind and orange flesh. Choose cultivars that are resistant to powdery mildew. *Citrullus lanatus*, watermelon, is a vigorous annual vine. Frost-sensitive and sun-loving, it produces large fruit, varying in size and shape, but generally with red flesh. If possible, choose cultivars that are resistant to wilt. Var. *citroides*, jam melon, has small fruit, the hard white flesh being used for making jam.

Mertensia (fam. Boraginaceae)

Blue bells

This genus comprises some 50 species of perennials from temperate countries of the northern hemisphere. These plants may be prostrate or clumping, with some species forming neat mounds. The simple, smooth-edged leaves are blue-green in color and the blue, bell-shaped flowers form drooping clusters.

CULTIVATION Mertensias combine well with azaleas, ericas and rhododendrons, and make a colorful addition to semi-shaded areas of rock gardens. They grow well in the open but must have a lime-free soil and plenty of water in spring. The flowers last longer if these plants are grown in cool, shady spots. Propagate from seed or by division of the roots in fall.

CLIMATE There are species suited to various climatic zones, but all are very hardy.

SPECIES *M. ciliata*, zone 4, originally from the west of the United States, is a woodland species, growing to 60 cm (24 in) high, with rose-colored buds, followed by clusters of bright blue flowers on upright stems. *M. primuloides*, zone 5, a native of the Himalayas, is a dwarf, growing to only 15 cm (6 in) high and producing deep indigo blue flowers. Varieties with white and yellow flowers are available. *M. pulmonarioides*, Virginia cowslip or blue bell, zone 3, native to eastern United States, is probably the most popular species. It grows to about 45 cm (18 in) high and has intense blue flowers in mid and late spring.

Meryta (fam. Araliaceae)

Of this genus of about 30 species of tropical and subtropical trees from New Zealand, Polynesia, Melanesia and Australia, only one is commonly cultivated.

CULTIVATION In frost-prone climates, merytas should be grown in an intermediate to warm greenhouse or conservatory in pots of soil-

ABOVE Blue bells or Virginia cowslip, *Mertensia pulmonarioides*, is a pretty, woodland garden plant ideal for planting under deciduous trees.

ABOVE *Meryta sinclairii* , New Zealand puka, makes a good pot plant under glass with its glossy, prominently veined leaves.

based potting compost. Provide good light but shade plant from direct sun, otherwise the leaves will scorch. Keep well watered through the growing season. Outdoors grow in a shady, sheltered spot with well-drained yet moist soil. Propagate from the black, fleshy seeds, or from semi-ripe cutting, in summer, both with bottom heat.

CLIMATE Zone 10.

SPECIES *M. sinclairii*, New Zealand puka, can grow as tall as 8 m (26 ft), though it is sometimes grown as a pot plant. The large, attractive, glossy leaves radiate spirally from a single stem. They grow 30–50 cm (12–20 in) long and have pale, prominent veins. The yellow flowers and stem stalks are marked with brown. After flowering, grape-sized fruits are set. These are very slow to mature. A white and gold, variegated leaf form, known as 'Moonlight' is worth seeking out.

Mesembryanthemum

(fam. Aizoaceae)

Ice plant

Naturalized throughout many hot, dry regions of the world, this genus includes both annual and biennial succulents. Mostly prostrate in habit, all are covered with soft protuberances and appear as though covered with dew. This feature gave rise to the common name. The flowers vary in color from white and creamy yellow to pink and red.

CULTIVATION These plants are easy to grow and work well in rockeries and as groundcovers. Propagate from stem cuttings or from seed. Grow in full sun in any well-drained soil. Water regularly to establish and then only occasionally as they are very drought-tolerant. In frost-prone climates they can be bedded out for the summer.

CLIMATE Zone 9.

SPECIES *M. crystallinum*, a biennial succulent from southern Africa, has become naturalized in other parts of the world, including the Mediterranean and the south-west coast of North America. It has a carpet-forming habit, dense, spoon-shaped leaves and cream, self-fertile flowers. *M. nodiflorum* occurs in many countries, including southern parts of Europe, northern Africa and North and Central America. It has grayish green leaves and stems, and white flowers.

Metasequoia (fam. Taxodiaceae)

Dawn redwood

The single species in this genus of conifers is extraordinary as it was known from fossil remains before it was discovered in a valley in Central China in 1945. The survival of this once widespread genus in one discrete area makes it truly a 'living fossil'. Dawn redwood is now one of the more popular conifers because of its ornamental qualities, rapid growth, tolerance of a wide range of conditions and general hardiness.

CULTIVATION To achieve an attractive shape, plant in deep, reasonably fertile soil and give protection from winds. If abundant water is supplied to the roots, it will grow vigorously, although it does quite well even on a normal, well-drained site. It enjoys cold climates, but

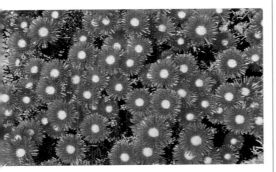

ABOVE The ideal groundcover or soil binder for hot, dry sites, *Mesembryanthemum* flowers so profusely that foliage is obscured.

ABOVE Dawn redwood, *Metasequoia glyptostroboides*, breaking into soft new spring leaf is a pretty sight.

cannot tolerate unseasonal spring frosts. Propagate from seed sown outdoors in fall. Alternatively, propagate from semi-ripe cuttings in summer or from hardwood cuttings in winter, under glass with basal warmth.

CLIMATE Zone 5.

SPECIES *M. glyptostroboides*, the only species, has fresh green, fern-like foliage, like that of the redwood. In cooler climates, the leaves turn a yellowish bronze color in fall. It is a deciduous tree which sheds whole branchlets rather than single leaves. The bark of young trees is a rich reddish-brown, which peels off in thin flakes and becomes grayish brown and fibrous with age. *Metasequoia* generally has an erect, tapering growth habit, with large numbers of small, rather contorted side branches. It grows to between 20 and 40 m (65–130 ft), depending on conditions and climate, and produces cones after about 15 years.

Metrosideros (fam. Myrtaceae)

New Zealand Christmas tree, Pohutukawa

Mostly native to New Zealand and Pacific Islands, this genus consists of around 60 species of evergreen trees and shrubs, grown for their rich, dark green foliage and bright scarlet, brush-like flowers, some of which appear at Christmas in their native countries. They are very useful plants as they are salt-resistant and attract birds to the garden. In frost-prone climates, grow in a cool greenhouse or conservatory.

CULTIVATION Under glass, grow in pots of acid, soil-based potting compost. Provide maximum light, but shade from direct sun. Water normally in the growing season but reduce considerably in winter. Outdoors, grow in a sunny, sheltered spot in well-drained, acid to neutral soil. Propagate from seed in spring (do not cover with compost) or semi-ripe cuttings in summer, both with basal warmth.

CLIMATE Warmest parts of zone 9, or zone 10.

SPECIES *M. carmineus* is a climber with round leaves and clusters of bright red flowers. *M. excelus*, New Zealand Christmas tree, is very beautiful, with its wide, spreading canopy and profusion of scarlet flowers in summer. The leaves are a shiny, deep green with white,

BELOW The bright red, brush-like flowers of *Metrosideros excelsus* emerge from gray-coated buds.

downy undersides. It grows to around 15 m
(50 ft). The cultivar 'Aureus' is a lovely, yellow-
flowered form. *M. fulgens* is also a climbing
type but its flowers are orange-red and borne
in terminal clusters. Cultivar 'Aurata' produces
yellow flowers. *M. kermadecensis* grows to
around 12 m (40 ft), with red flowers for most
of the year. Cultivar 'Variegatus' has grayish
green leaves with creamy white margins.
Cultivar 'Sunninghill' is another variegated
form with golden yellow markings on the
leaves. In New Zealand, especially, there is a
wide range of named cultivars of both
M. excelsus and *M. kermadecensis*.

Michelia (fam. Magnoliaceae)

This genus of around 45 species of evergreen,
flowering shrubs and trees comes originally
from tropical and subtropical Asia and is
closely related to the magnolia. The timber of
several species is used in carving and fine
furniture work, and the essential oil from the
flowers of *M. champaca* is used in perfumery.

ABOVE Large, pure white flowers will emerge from these
buds of *Michelia doltsopa*. This is known as Wong-Lan
amongst the Chinese community.

This species is often grown around Hindu and
Jain temples.

CULTIVATION Grow in a cool greenhouse or
conservatory in frost-prone climates, in acid,
soil-based compost. Outdoors, grow in well-
drained yet moist, acid to neutral soil
containing plenty of humus, in a sheltered
spot, with full sun or partial shade. Propagate
by layering in spring or from semi-ripe cuttings
in summer.

CLIMATE Zone 9.

SPECIES *M. champaca* is an upright tree, to
25 m (80 ft) in its habitat, rarely reaching more
than 10 m (33 ft) in cultivation. Very fragrant,
creamy yellow flowers appear from
midsummer to fall. *M. doltsopa* grows to 10 m
(33 ft) in cultivation, with scented, cream
flowers in spring and early summer and bright,
glossy green foliage. *M. figo*, port wine
magnolia, has a shrubby growth habit. The
leaves are glossy and the very small, cream
flowers are tinged with purple and richly
perfumed. Growing to 5 m (16 ft), it makes a
good screen or hedge plant.

Microcoelum

(syn. *Lytocaryum*, fam. Arecaceae)

Originating from Brazil, this genus comprises
only two species of small feather palms. They
are small, graceful palms with slender trunks.

CULTIVATION Although this genus is mostly
grown as an indoor plant because of its slow
growth habit, it is possible to cultivate it
outdoors if it is given protection from strong
sun. It is best grown as an understorey plant
amongst other tall palms or trees.

CLIMATE Warmer parts of zone 9.

SPECIES *M. weddellianum* (syn. *Lytocaryum
weddellianum*), Weddell palm, has a solitary,
smooth, gray stem, 2–3 m (6–10 ft) tall and

ABOVE Small, graceful *Microcoelum weddellianum* (syn. *Lytocaryum weddellianum*) is very versatile, making an excellent palm for shaded gardens or for container growing.

ABOVE *Micromyrtus ciliata* has very tiny, white flowers that redden with age. It is a good filler shrub for borders.

5 cm (2 in) in diameter. However, it takes well over 10 years to reach this height and width. One of the most elegant of all small palms, it has gracefully arching leaves, about 1 m (3 ft) long, with many, very narrow, regularly spaced leaflets, shiny green on top, whitish on the undersides. The very small inflorescence is enclosed in a narrow bract covered in rust brown hairs. The oval fruits are yellowish green in color.

Micromyrtus (fam. Myrtaceae)
Fringed heath myrtle

There are 16 species in this Australian genus of small, heath-like shrubs with tiny leaves and lovely, little flowers. Used widely by florists, the cut flowers remain fresh for up to two weeks. The fruit is a small nut surrounded by the calyx which falls from the shrub when ripe. Easy to cultivate, these shrubs form a neat, compact shape, with a height of 1 m (3 ft) and a width of 2 m (6 ft). It is unlikely to be available outside Australia.

CULTIVATION Although they are usually frost-tolerant, these plants prefer full sun and a well-drained, sandy loam. Where hard frosts occur, grow in a cool, airy greenhouse or conservatory in pots of soil-based potting compost. Propagate from semi-ripe cuttings in summer, with bottom heat.

CLIMATE Warmer parts of zone 9.

SPECIES *M. ciliata*, fringed heath myrtle, is the species usually cultivated. This spreading shrublet grows into an erect form outdoors in dry areas. A profusion of pinkish white flowers appears in spring; they turn red with age. *M. rosea*, from Western Australia, is a very attractive species, 1–2 m (3–6 ft) high, with deep pink flowers.

Microsorum

(syn. *Polypodium*, fam. Polypodiaceae)

This fairly large genus of ferns comprises about 40 species, several being natives of Australia and New Zealand. They have creeping rhizomes, mostly covered with dark scales, and smooth, solid stems. The thinly textured fronds are variable, and may be upright to pendent and entire to divided. In frost-prone climates, grow these ferns in a warm greenhouse or conservatory.

ABOVE Fronds of *Microsorum diversifolium* are variable in shape and texture. This mature frond shows developing spore cases.

CULTIVATION Under glass, grow in pots of peaty, soilless potting compost, with good drainage. Water regularly. Propagate by division of the rhizome, retaining a couple of fronds and some of the root. Peg down firmly or anchor with a piece of sandstone to avoid movement. They can also be grown from spores, but this is a much slower process.

CLIMATE Zone 10.

SPECIES *M. diversifolium*, kangaroo fern, is distributed through much of south-eastern Australia, New Zealand and Norfolk Island. The variable fronds are often deeply lobed and may grow 40–50 cm (16–20 in) high. This fern has a creeping habit, growing well among rocks in damp conditions. It will also scramble up the trunks of tree ferns. *M. membranifolium*, pimple fern, is from the tropical rainforests of north-eastern Queensland. The largest of the Australian species, it has solid, mostly erect, pinnate fronds, about 1 m (3 ft) long when mature, with broad lobes and distinctive veining. When young, the fronds are pale green, becoming deeper in color with age. *M. punctatum*, from north-eastern Queensland and other tropical areas, has simple, erect, pale green fronds which taper to the base and are rounded at the tip. This tropical species needs plenty of heat in order to flourish. *M. scandens*, fragrant fern, from eastern Australia and Norfolk Island, has fine, green stems and upright to pendent fronds, some being entire, others divided, with many lobes and rippled margins. This species is one which does well among rocks or on tree fern trunks, and it makes an effective climber.

Millettia (fam. Papilionaceae)

These 90 species of tropical trees, shrubs, lianes and climbers, mostly from Africa and Asia, include three Australian species, among them the lovely native wisteria, *M. megasperma*. In climates which are prone to frost, grow in a cool to intermediate conservatory or greenhouse.

CULTIVATION In the greenhouse or conservatory, grow in a pot of soil-based potting compost. Ensure maximum light, but shade the plant from direct strong sun. If necessary, prune after flowering to restrict size. Outdoors grow in a sunny spot with rich, moist, well-drained soil.

ABOVE A vigorous climber in the wild, *Millettia megasperma* will adapt to container growing under glass, although it is not readily available in the US.

Propagate from semi-ripe cuttings in summer, or from seed when available, both in warmth.

CLIMATE Zone 10.

SPECIES Not all of these are available outside their countries of origin. *M. caffra*, from South Africa, is a tree growing to 9 m (30 ft), with silky, hairy leaves and trusses of purplish to reddish, pea flowers. *M. megasperma*, native wisteria, is a vigorous climber, similar to wisteria, producing sprays of mauve to dark purple, pea flowers in the spring, followed by large, cylindrical pods, up to 15 cm (6 in) in length, containing red seeds. *M. ovalifolia*, from Burma, is a small tree to 5 m (16 ft), with shiny leaves and purple or blue flowers.

Miltonia (fam. Orchidaceae)
Pansy orchid

There are 20 species in this genus of vibrantly colored orchids from tropical South America. The flowers are usually quite impressive, with a very large lip. In some species they are solitary, but mostly there are several flowers to a stem. Many beautiful hybrids are available.

CULTIVATION Grow in an intermediate greenhouse or conservatory in pots of epiphytic orchid compost, which should be available from specialist orchid growers. Alternatively, as they are epiphytes, grow in slatted wooden orchid baskets hung up in the greenhouse. They can also be grown completely epiphytically by mounting them on slabs of bark and surrounding the roots with sphagnum moss. In summer, these orchids need a humid atmosphere, shade from direct sun, and regular watering. In winter, give maximum light but much reduced watering.

CLIMATE Tropical only.

SPECIES *M. phalaenopsis* (syn. *Miltoniopsis phalaenopsis*), from Columbia and Ecuador, produces inflorescences with three to five

ABOVE This hybrid *Miltonia* has large, velvety, red flowers with a very striking central pattern.

flowers in white with purple streaks on the lip, in fall. *M. regnellii*, from Brazil, has similar inflorescences in fall. The sepals and petals are white, and the lip is light rose streaked in purple, with white margins. *M. spectabilis*, also from Brazil, flowers in fall. The solitary, erect, long-lasting blooms have reddish purple sepals and petals, and a lip of rose with purple markings.

Mimosa (fam. Mimosaceae)

Most of the 400 or so species of perennial shrubs, trees and woody vines in this genus are tropical in origin, with the largest number

ABOVE The sensitive plant, *Mimosa pudica*, rapidly folds its leaves when touched, and hence is a curiosity for children.

being native to the tropical Americas. They have feather-like foliage and round heads of small flowers with long stamens.

CULTIVATION Mimosa must be grown in a sunny position. They do not tolerate frost. Propagate from seed sown in late winter or early spring or from cuttings taken from young growth. Where frosts are a problem, grow in an intermediate greenhouse or conservatory.

CLIMATE Warmest parts of zone 9, or zone 10.

SPECIES *M. pudica*, sensitive plant, touch-me-not or humble plant, grows 30–45 cm (12–18 in) high, and has sensitive foliage and flowers which droop if handled. The lilac-pink flowers appear in summer. This species can be invasive and has become a problem weed in some tropical countries.

Mimulus (fam. Schrophulariaceae)
Monkey flower, musk

There are about 150 species in this genus of annual or perennial plants and shrubs, found in most temperate zones of the world, though widespread in North America. The trumpet-like flowers come in many colors, including yellow, orange, red, wine purple, copper and white, with spots of contrasting

ABOVE Generally grown as annuals, mimulus hybrids display an amazing range of colors and patterns.

shades. The smaller types make useful border plants and also work well in verandah boxes or hanging baskets. Some species thrive in boggy or permanently wet soils. The numerous, named hybrids are normally grown as summer bedding plants.

CULTIVATION The majority of mimulus enjoy a moisture-retentive soil which contains plenty of humus. It should not be allowed to dry out at any time. They grow equally well in either full sun or dappled shade. Propagate from seed sown in spring under glass, especially for the summer bedding types. Germinate at 13°C (57°F). Perennials can be divided in spring or raised from softwood cuttings in summer.

CLIMATE There are species suited to various climatic zones.

SPECIES *M. aurantiacus*, zone 8, from North America, is a compact, evergreen, perennial shrub, to 1 m (3 ft), grown for its attractive, yellowish orange flowers, with prominent apricot lips. *M. cupreus*, zone 8, an annual, 20–30 cm (8–12 in) high, has yellow to bright copper flowers. *M. fremontii*, zone 9, an annual, to 20 cm (8 in), produces crimson to purple flowers. *M. guttatus*, zone 6, is a perennial, 30–45 cm (12–18 in) high, with yellow flowers spotted in red. *M. moschatus*, monkey musk, zone 7, is a prickly, hairy perennial, to 30 cm (12 in), with yellow flowers. *M. ringens*, zone 3, a perennial which grows to around 1 m (3 ft), has violet to pink or white flowers. Named hybrids of numerous species (*M. x hybridus*, zone 6) are available.

Mina (syn. *Ipomoea*, fam. Convolvulaceae)

Native to Central and South America, these herbaceous, twining or climbing plants have bright green, lobed leaves. The flowers form a slightly irregular, curved tube. Some botanists include this plant with *Ipomoea*.

CULTIVATION Grow as an annual and propagate from seeds sown in spring. Sow seed,

ABOVE Called Spanish flag because of its color combination, *Mina lobata* is a fast-growing climber that can be supported by light wire or lattice.

ABOVE Aromatic spearmint, *Mentha spicata*, is the mint species most familiar as a culinary herb.

germinated at 18°C (64°F), at one seed per pot. Plant out after frosts in a warm, sunny, sheltered spot, with some means of support, such a trellis.

CLIMATE Zone 9, but grown as a summer annual in all zones.

SPECIES *M. lobata*, (syn. *Ipomoea lobata*), the only species generally cultivated, is a showy climber, producing long sprays of orange-red flowers, tipped with gold, through summer and fall.

Mint (*Mentha species*, fam. Lamiaceae)

These rambling, perennial herbs spread by rhizomes and are easily grown in almost all soil types and climatic conditions, apart from the very hottest and driest. They have prostrate or erect, branched stems and terminal spikes of small, white or purple flowers. The aromatic, volatile oils are stored mostly in the oval-shaped leaves. There are a number of widely grown species, each with a distinctive flavor

and aroma. Mint adds a delicious taste to cool, summer drinks. Mint sauce, served with lamb, is made from spearmint, or common mint.

CULTIVATION Mint prefers a moderately rich, moist soil and some shade. Grow in pots or in a corner of the garden as it can be very invasive. Water regularly during summer. Propagate from cuttings or root divisions, making fresh plantings every few years. Pennyroyal, a useful groundcover, may be cut back with a mower after flowering to keep it at about 2.5 cm (1 in) high. Cut mint in the morning before the dew has dried. To dry, tie in small bunches and hang in a spot with a maximum temperature of 30°C (86°F). Once dried, strip the leaves from the stems and store in air-tight containers.

CLIMATE There are species suited to various climatic zones.

SPECIES *M. x piperita*, peppermint, zone 3, is an erect plant, to 60 cm (24 in), with slightly reddish stems, and grown mostly for its oil. The oval, toothed, pointed leaves are sometimes hairy on the undersides. Small, purple flowers are borne in terminal spikes. *M. pulegium*, pennyroyal, zone 7, has a prostrate habit, with small leaves, about 1 cm (⅓ in) long, and clusters of mauve flowers.

Pennyroyal can be invasive, in which case it should be treated as a weed. *M. spicata*, spearmint or common mint, zone 3, has erect stems to 60 cm (24 in), oval, toothed, almost stalkless leaves, about 5 cm (2 in) long, and loose spikes of purple flowers. *M. suaveolens*, applemint, zone 6, has sturdy, upright stems to 60 cm (24 in), with hairy, roundish leaves and dense spikes of purplish white flowers. Variegated applemint is one of the many varieties of these species.

Miscanthus (fam. Poaceae)

These ornamental, perennial grasses originate from eastern Asia, South Africa and the Old World tropics. They are increasingly popular with gardeners in various parts of the temperate world and several species and many cultivars are grown in borders or as accent plants. The silky, fan-shaped flower heads are very decorative and some are used in dried arrangements.

CULTIVATION *Miscanthus* will grow in any soil, provided it is in a sunny position and well watered. Best results come from soils enriched with organic matter. Propagate from seed sown in late winter or spring, or by division in late winter or early spring. Variegated forms must be divided. Cut back to ground level once growth starts to die back in late fall. In very mild areas, these plants may remain evergreen but will benefit from cutting back in fall or late winter.

CLIMATE There are species suited to various climatic zones.

SPECIES *M. sacchariflorus*, Amur silvergrass, zone 8, very decorative and silky, grows 2–3 m (6–10 ft) tall. Cultivar 'Aureus' has goldstriped leaves. *M. sinensis* 'Variegatus', zone 4, grows to 2 m (6 ft), with silvery, variegated foliage and long, plumed flower heads. Cultivar 'Gracillimus' is a smaller type, with narrow, arching foliage; 'Zebrinus', zebra grass, grows to about 1.2 m (4 ft) and has green foliage, with yellow horizontal bands.

Molucella (fam. Labiatae)

One of the four species is thought to have originated from the Moluccas, hence the genus name. These attractive, soft-wooded annuals produce 60 cm (24 in) long spikes of light green, bell-shaped calyces enclosing the tiny, white flowers. They are long lasting and also useful in dried arrangements.

ABOVE *Miscanthus sinensis* 'Variegatus' forms a generous clump of leaves. Flower spikes rise high above the leaves in late summer to fall.

ABOVE The unusual, green, bell-like flowers of *Molucella laevis* are equally decorative in the garden or vase.

CULTIVATION Molucellas do well in any soil, provided they are planted in a warm spot and are well watered. Sow seed in early spring under glass or in late spring in flowering position. Space plants 30 cm (12 in) apart each way.

CLIMATE Zone 8.

SPECIES *M. laevis*, bells of Ireland, grows to around 1 m (3 ft), and has distinctive, shell-like calyces. *M. spinosa*, growing to 1 m (3 ft), has spined calyces.

Monstera (fam. Araceae)

Native to the tropical Americas and the West Indies, this genus of sturdy, evergreen climbers has large, glossy green, leathery, irregularly divided leaves, quite often perforated, and large, arum lily-like, boat-shaped flowers. The unusual fruit matures from the center of the flower structure. The aerial roots produced along the stem attach themselves to available support which must be very sturdy.

CULTIVATION *Monstera* is a popular house or conservatory plant which needs warm conditions. Grow in a pot of soil-based potting compost. Shade from direct sun but ensure good light. Provide humidity. If necessary, prune in spring to reduce size. Propagate from leaf cuttings in summer with basal warmth. Air layer in spring or summer.

CLIMATE Best in tropical climates, but also subtropical.

SPECIES *M. acuminata*, shingle plant, is from Central America. It has flattened stems and 25 cm (10 in) long leaves. *M. adansonii* produces 90 cm (36 in) long leaves and smaller, more slender fruit than *M. deliciosa*. *M. deliciosa*, Swiss cheese plant, has deeply divided, dark green leaves, 45–60 cm (18–24 in) across, and large, edible fruit, with a fruit salad taste. The dissected leaves have oval to elliptical holes between some of the lateral veins. In its natural habitat, it is a robust climbing plant.

ABOVE The elongated fruit of *Monstera deliciosa* will ripen slowly over many weeks. Fruit should not be eaten until it is completely ripe.

Whether grown indoors or outside, these plants generally develop aerial roots. These should be trained down into the pot or soil.

Moraea (fam. Iridaceae)
Butterfly iris, peacock iris

These cormous perennials are native to tropical South Africa. The leaves and flowers are very similar to those of *Iris* to which it is closely related. *Moraea* mostly grows from corms, though a few species grow from rhizomes. Free-flowering during the spring and early summer months, the blooms range in color from pure white to shades of lilac.

CULTIVATION In climates pone to frost, tender species are grown in pots in a cool greenhouse, hardier ones in the garden in a well-drained, sheltered, sunny spot. Plant in fall or spring about 8 cm (3 in) deep. Under glass, do not water plants from midsummer to fall, while

ABOVE Flowers of peacock iris, *Moraea aristata*, appear to float above the grassy foliage. The peacock blue eye of the flower is iridescent.

they are dormant. Propagate from offsets during the dormant period.

CLIMATE Zone 9 for most species, zone 8 for *M. spathulata*.

SPECIES *M. angusta*, from South Africa, grows to 30 cm (12 in), with dull, brownish yellow flowers. *M. fugax*, also from South Africa, has fragrant flowers in mauve or white and grows to 60 cm (24 in). *M. spathulata*, from South Africa, grows to 60 cm (24 in) and has bright yellow flowers with purple edges. *M. villosa* is variable, but the flowers are mostly purple with a deeper, peacock blue eye.

Mucuna (fam. Papilionaceae)
Scarlet jade vine, New Guinea creeper

This tropical genus of around 100 species consists of climbing plants or lianes, many native to tropical Asia and the Pacific Islands. Few species are in general cultivation, but those that are have spectacular flowers. The stems of these plants are often covered with irritant hairs. The seeds of some species are used in medicinal drugs, while others are planted as fodder crops.

CULTIVATION Outside the tropics and subtropics, these plants need to be grown in a warm

ABOVE A spectacular cascade of scarlet flowers distinguishes *Mucuna bennettii*, a vigorous, tropical liane or climber.

greenhouse or conservatory in pots of soil-based potting compost. Provide good light, but shade from direct sun. After flowering, prune side shoots back to within four buds of the main stems. Propagate from seed sown in spring and germinate at 21°C (70°F).

CLIMATE Strictly for tropical regions.

SPECIES *M. bennettii*, a native of New Guinea, is a quick-growing climber which can reach 20 m (65 ft) into the tops of the rainforest canopy in its habitat. It has compound leaves, with elliptic to oval leaflets. Short, dense flower clusters are made up of numerous, bright scarlet, boat-shaped flowers which make a very showy display, mostly during the summer months. *M. pruriens*, native to tropical Asia, has become widely naturalized in the tropics. Its stems are covered in rough hairs when young, though these become smooth in time. Its flowers are deep purple or pale lilac to white and may be produced through spring and summer. It is an annual or it may live for a few years.

Muehlenbeckia (fam. Polygonaceae)

Wire plant

Native to Australia, New Zealand and South America, this genus comprises around 15 species of semi-woody creepers and climbers. They have small leaves, 1–2 cm (⅓–¾ in) long, and small, greenish white, insignificant flowers. Most are very vigorous growers.
CULTIVATION Muehlenbeckias are hardy and will grow in any soil, in a sunny position. Propagate from seed germinated at 21°C (70°F) and sown as soon as available, or from semi-ripe cuttings in summer.

CLIMATE Zone 8.

SPECIES *M. australis*, from New Zealand, has a tangled appearance, growing to about 8 m (26 ft) high. Small, greenish flowers are followed by black, glossy fruit. *M. axillaris* has a matted, sprawling growth habit, wiry stems and small, rounded leaves. The small flowers are greeny yellow. *M. complexa*, wire vine, from New Zealand, is a scrambling shrub, to about 3 m (10 ft), with thin, wire-like stems and tiny flowers. All species are recommended for covering stumps, earth banks and garden walls.

ABOVE Small, yellow-green flowers are produced in the leaf axils of *Muehlenbeckia axillaris*. Growth is fairly prostrate.

Mulberry (*Morus*, fam. Moraceae)

Mulberry trees have probably been cultivated for many thousands of years. The black mulberry, *Morus nigra*, which may have originated from western Asia, was certainly known to the early Greeks and Romans who grew it for its delicious, juicy, black fruit. The white mulberry, *M. alba*, from China, was grown mainly for its leaves which were used to feed silkworms. The red mulberry, *M. rubra*, is native to North America, the red fruit ripening to dark purple. These trees are deciduous, with entire or lobed, toothed leaves and small flowers. Mulberries are eaten fresh or made into jam.

CULTIVATION Plant in any well-drained garden soil in a sunny position. Avoid growing mulberry trees near paths or clothes lines as the fruit is very juicy and leaves long-lasting stains. Propagate from hardwood cuttings taken during the dormant period. Seedling trees often appear in gardens as the fruit is eaten by birds.

CLIMATE Zone 5.

SPECIES *M. alba*, white mulberry, is a large tree, growing 12–18 m (40–60 ft) tall, with clusters of white, cylindrical fruits up to 2.5 cm (1 in) long which turn pink and then red. This

BELOW This mulberry tree has been trained as an ornamental standard. It is underplanted with snow-in-summer.

ornamental species has spreading, pendulous branches. The common or black mulberry, *M. nigra*, is a large, spreading tree, 15 m (50 ft) tall, with rough, dark green leaves. The juicy, dark red fruit is delicious, but stains the hands and clothes. There are several good fruiting cultivars including the semi-dwarf 'Black Beauty' which grows no more than 4.5m in height. *M. rubra* is very ornamental but the fruit can be poor.

Murraya (fam. Rutaceae)

There are four species in this genus of small trees or shrubs which originate from parts of India, Southeast Asia and Australia. They have attractive, glossy, green leaves and fragrant, white flowers, and make useful hedging and screening plants. In frost-prone climates, they make good container plants for the intermediate to warm greenhouse or conservatory.

CULTIVATION Under glass, grow in well-drained, soil-based potting compost. Provide good light, but shade from direct strong sun. Water well during the growing season, but far less in winter. Outdoors grow in full sun or very light shade in rich, well-drained soil. Propagate from seed sown in spring or from semi-ripe cuttings in summer, both with bottom heat.

CLIMATE Zone 10.

SPECIES *M. koenigii*, curry leaf, is a small tree, native to India and Sri Lanka. The leaves are used in curries in places where the plant grows naturally. *M. paniculata*, orange jessamine, is an attractive shrub, 5–7 m (16–23 ft) high, with glossy foliage and heavily scented, white flowers which may appear several times a year. Its normal flowering time is summer, but it often blooms after periods of heavy rain.

Musa (fam. Musaceae)

This genus of large, evergreen, suckering perennials is best known as the edible bananas, *M. acuminata* and *M. x paradisiaca* (see entry on Banana). Native to tropical Asia, *Musa* species have been cultivated for hundreds of years, some for leaf fiber, a few as ornamentals.

CULTIVATION In frost-prone climates, grow in large pots or tubs or in a soil border in a cool or intermediate greenhouse or conservatory. Use soil-based potting compost for containers and provide bright light, but shade from strong sun. The plants can be stood outside for the summer. Outdoors, a warm, sheltered spot with moist, yet well-drained, deep, fertile soil is required. Propagate from suckers in spring.

ABOVE Reminiscent of orange blossom, the flowers of *Murraya paniculata* are not long lasting but appear in flushes.

ABOVE A bold foliage plant for warm gardens, *Musa velutina* produces decorative bunches of rose pink bananas.

CLIMATE Zone 10. *M. velutina* should survive in zone 9.

SPECIES *M. ornata*, flowering banana, grows to about 3 m (10 ft) and has blue-green foliage. The yellow to orange flowers are enclosed in pink to purple, showy bracts and appear at various times of year. The fruits with black seeds are yellow to green in color. *M. velutina*, growing to around 1.5 m (5 ft), has mid-green leaves. Both the flowers and bracts are a mix of pale and deep pink. The fruits are rich pink on the outside, splitting to reveal black seeds. This is an attractive ornamental for warm climate gardens.

Muscari (fam. Hyacinthaceae)
Grape hyacinth

These 30 species of mainly spring-flowering, bulbous plants originate from the Mediterranean and south-western Asia. The spikes of small, rounded, bell-shaped flowers mostly range from sky blue to lavender blue, though they are occasionally seen in yellow. The foliage is rush-like. They look very decorative when mass planted in garden borders.

CULTIVATION Plant the bulbs in a well-drained soil at summer's end or early in fall. They grow in almost any position, but prefer semi-shade. They increase rapidly and should be lifted and replanted periodically to avoid overcrowding. Do not lift these bulbs until all the foliage has died down naturally.

CLIMATE There are species suited to various climatic zones.

SPECIES *M. armeniacum*, zone 4, grows to 25 cm (10 in) high, with deep violet flowers. Several cultivars are available. *M. azureum*, zone 8, grows 15–20 cm (6–8 in) high, with tubular, bright blue flowers. Cultivar 'Album' has white flowers; 'Amphibolis' bears light blue flowers. *M. comosum*, tassel hyacinth, zone 4, grows to 45 cm (18 in), with greenish brown flowers at the base of the stem and a profusion of smaller, purplish blue flowers above.

ABOVE Royal blue grape hyacinths make a lovely color contrast with the bright yellow daffodils planted behind them.

Cultivar 'Plumosum', feather hyacinth, has feathered reddish purple flowers. *M. macrocarpum*, zone 7, to 15 cm (6 in) high, has yellow flowers with purple lobes. *M. neglectum*, zone 4, to 15 cm (6 in), has fragrant, dark blue flowers in dense spikes.

Mushroom

Many forms of mushroom are in cultivation today. Mushrooms are a popular addition to many dishes. They are eaten raw in salads, or cooked in sauces, soups, side dishes and stuffings. The field mushroom is *Agaricus campestris*, while *Agaricus bisporus* is the cultivated mushroom sold in the shops. There are many types of fungi quite similar in appearance. However, while many are edible, some are extremely poisonous, so it is not safe to eat wild gathered mushrooms unless their identity is known. Today, mushrooms are grown commercially in special premises, whereas they were once grown in disused railway tunnels and cellars. Apart from the common mushroom, there are many fancy varieties grown for the boutique market. These include oyster mushrooms, chanterelles or egg mushrooms, straw mushrooms (*Volvariella volvacea*) and shiitake mushrooms (*Lentinus edodes*).

CULTIVATION Mushrooms need still air, high humidity and a constant temperature to grow

ABOVE Mushrooms are grown in large bags of specially formulated compost 'seeded' with spawn.

ABOVE This unusual cultivar of Mussaenda appears to be totally white. The large white flower bracts obscure the tiny flowers.

well. Home-growers are probably best to grow their mushrooms from pre-packed mushroom 'farms' sold in garden centers. These are easily managed and produce very satisfactorily. Mushrooms can be harvested at the preferred size but often the bulk of the crop is ready at one time.

CLIMATE Cool, damp conditions are preferable.

Mussaenda (fam. Rubiaceae)

Native to tropical Africa, Asia and the Pacific Islands, this genus consists of around 100 species of evergreen shrubs and climbers. Though the flowers are insignificant, the large, leaf-like, often brightly colored sepals make an attractive display against the green of the foliage. The fruit is a berry.

CULTIVATION Outside the tropics and subtropics, grow in a warm greenhouse in pots of soil-based potting compost. Provide good light, but shade plants from direct sun. Prune climbers in winter by cutting back the side shoots to within four buds of the main stems. Propagate from semi-ripe cuttings in summer, in a heated propagating case.

CLIMATE Zone 10 at least.

SPECIES *M. erythrophylla*, Ashanti blood, from tropical Africa, is a sprawling, evergreen shrub that is a climber in its habitat, where it grows to about 10 m (33 ft) tall. In cultivation it can be maintained as a shrub, 2–3 m (6–10 ft) high. The large, bright green, oval leaves are hairy underneath, and the yellow flowers, with large, scarlet sepals, appear in summer. There is also a dwarf form. *M. frondosa* from India, is an erect shrub which grows to a height and breadth of about 3 m (10 ft). The yellow-orange, summer flowers are overshadowed by the large, white sepals. The pale green leaves are oval in shape.

Mustard (*Sinapis alba*, fam. Brassicaceae)

There are several species of mustard, but only one is widely grown: the white mustard, *Sinapis alba*. This is the mustard used in the seedling stage with common garden cress (*Lepidium sativum*) for making salads and sandwiches. *Sinapis alba* is an annual with bright green leaves. If allowed to grow to maturity it would reach about 60 cm (24 in) in height, but it is used in the seedling stage when 8–10 cm (4–5 in) high. It is a native of the Mediterranean, North Africa and central Asia.

CULTIVATION Mustard is normally grown indoors or under glass. Sow two days after cress for the

ABOVE The bright yellow flowers of *Sinapis alba* make mustard a decorative crop to grow. The seed capsules are a distinctive shape.

ABOVE The gently curving stems of *Myoporum floribundum* are laden with starry, white flowers. This lovely shrub is rare in the wild.

two to be ready together. Sow seed thickly in a tray, on the surface of soilless seed compost or on a thick pad of blotting paper. Keep constantly moist. Another way to grow white mustard is as a cut-and-come-again salad crop in the garden. Sow seed in spring and cut young plants as required for their leaves. They will re-sprout and can then be cut again.

CLIMATE Zone 6.

Myoporum (fam. Myoporaceae)

There are 32 species in this genus of trees, shrubs and groundcovers, many of which are natives of Australia, though some originate from New Zealand, China and Japan. They are useful as ornamentals and screens and for shade and windbreaks. Of those most cultivated, two are excellent groundcovers.

CULTIVATION Grow *Myoporum* in an intermediate greenhouse in areas with hard frosts. Outdoors, it does best in full sun with well-drained, yet moisture-retentive soil. Propagate from semi-ripe cuttings in summer, with basal warmth.

CLIMATE Zone 9.

SPECIES Not all are available outside their native countries. *M. debile* is a prostrate plant, with drooping stems and leaves, and large green, purple or red, edible fruit. *M. insulare*, boobialla, is a dense bush or tree, with smooth leaves, white flowers with purple dots and round, purple fruits. This species tolerates coastal exposure. *M. laetum*, ngaio, a native of New Zealand, grows to 5 m (16 ft) tall. It produces large, white flowers with purple spots in summer, followed by reddish purple fruits. The young leaves are brownish green. *M. montanum* grows to 3 m (10 ft) with white flowers spotted in purple and round, white to purple fruits. *M. parvifolium*, creeping boobialla, from southern and western Australia, is a prostrate species, growing to 15 cm (6 in) high and a spread of 80 cm (32 in). It has dark green, narrow leaves and clusters of white, tubular flowers in summer, followed by round, reddish purple berries. *M. platycarpum*, sugarwood, grows 2–10 m (6–33 ft) high, producing white flowers, followed by white to purple fruits. The bark sometimes exudes a sugary material, accounting for its common name. Its timber is quite fragrant.

Myosotidium (fam. Boraginaceae)
Chatham Island forget-me-not

There is only one species in this genus which is endemic to the Chatham Islands, off the coast of New Zealand.

ABOVE The lovely *Myosotidium hortensia* is fairly demanding in its cultural requirements, but is well worth the effort.

ABOVE The well-loved forget-me-not, *Myosotis sylvatica*, is at its best naturalized under deciduous trees.

CULTIVATION This lovely plant can be difficult to grow if conditions are not right. It must be grown in humus-rich soil that drains well but retains some moisture at all times. As it is shallow-rooted, mulching with compost or aged manure is helpful. It prefers semi-shade and must be well watered in the growing season. Feed it with weak solutions of fish emulsion or seaweed extract. Propagate from seed sown in fall. Established clumps self-seed.

CLIMATE Zone 8. Best in cool, moist climates.

SPECIES *M. hortensia* has large, glossy, rounded to heart-shaped, heavily veined leaves. Plants may grow to about 40 cm (16 in) tall, while the sturdy flower stems rise to about 60 cm (24 in). In late spring to early summer, it bears large heads of deep blue flowers that may be paler around the edges. After flowering, winged seeds develop. This evergreen perennial forms clumps, often producing a thick rootstock along the soil surface. This should not be disturbed.

Myosotis (fam. Boraginaceae)

Forget-me-not

This genus comprises around 50 species of annuals, biennials and perennials. Those commonly cultivated come from temperate zones of Europe, Asia and America. There are also Australasian species. The dainty flowers may be blue, pink or white. They make good bedding plants and are useful for rock gardens and borders, and as groundcover under trees.

CULTIVATION Forget-me-nots do well in fertile, well-drained soil in moist, semi-shaded situations. Sow seed of annuals and biennials to be used for spring bedding in early summer in a garden frame or outdoor seed bed. Perennials are sown in spring in situ. Once established, they tend to reproduce readily by self-seeding.

CLIMATE There are species suited to various climatic zones. Best in cool moist climates.

SPECIES *M. australis*, zone 8, from New Zealand, with yellow or white summer flowers, grows to 45 cm (18 in). *M. azorica*, zone 9, to 45 cm (18 in), has blue flowers with white eyes in summer. Var. *alba* has white flowers. *M. scorpiodes* (syn. *M. palustris*), zone 5, has bright blue, summer flowers with pink, white or yellow centers. It grows 15–30 cm (6–12 in) high. This species is a marginal aquatic plant that grows from a creeping rootstock, making it a good soil binder. *M. sylvatica*, zone 5, grows 30–60 cm (12–24 in) high and has blue flowers with yellow eyes in spring. This is the species best known and widely used for spring bedding. Cultivars have white, pink or blue flowers.

Myroxylon (fam. Papilionaceae)

Native to tropical America, this genus consists of two species of slender, graceful, evergreen trees, grown for their timber and their attractive, white flowers, resembling butterflies, and glossy, green foliage. They are also the source of true balsam, used in medicines and cosmetics. An abundance of winged fruits appear in late summer.

CULTIVATION Outside the tropics, grow myroxylons in a warm humid greenhouse. Propagate from scarified seed.

CLIMATE Tropical only.

SPECIES *M. balsamum*, from Venezuela, is the more common species.

ABOVE *Myroxylon balsamum*, the source of balsam for ointments and medicinal syrups, also yields a fine timber.

Myrtus (fam. Myrtaceae)
Myrtle

This genus comprises only two species of densely foliaged, evergreen shrubs, grown for their shiny foliage and pretty, starry, white flowers. The small leaves have a delightful fragrance when crushed. These plants respond well to clipping, so make good hedging plants.

CULTIVATION Myrtle is best grown in full sun but it can be grown in partial shade. It will grow in almost any kind of well-drained soil but does best in humus-enriched soils. It needs regular watering to establish but established plants tolerate dry conditions well. Prune plants after flowering to maintain a compact, bushy shape. If used for hedging, they may need shearing two or three times during the growing season. Myrtle is easily propagated from firm tip cuttings, taken from late spring through to late summer but can also be grown from seed.

CLIMATE Zone 8.

SPECIES *M. communis*, common myrtle, from the Mediterranean, is an erect shrub, growing to around 3 m (10 ft). It has pointed, aromatic leaves and fragrant, white flowers from midsummer to early fall, which are followed by black, edible berries. This species has been used ornamentally and ritually since ancient times. It is the classic myrtle of Ancient Greece, evident in the myrtle wreaths in ancient art and jewellery. It had many medicinal uses. The oil was extracted for cosmetics and perfume and the dried berries were used as spice. Cultivar 'Variegata' has green leaves with white margins.

ABOVE Rich, blue-black berries form on *Myrtus communis* after the plant has flowered. When the shrub is clipped for hedging, the fruits are not generally seen.

N

Nandina to Nyssa

Nandina (fam. Berberidaceae)
Sacred bamboo

This single-species genus, whose natural habitat spreads from India through to eastern Asia, is somewhat like bamboo. Popular with landscape gardeners, it makes an effective accent plant or informal hedge, and can also be grown in large tubs. It is frequently used in Japanese-style gardens.

CULTIVATION This hardy, quick-growing shrub can be grown in any soil, either in sun or semi-shade, provided it has sufficient water. Propagate from seed sown in fall in a garden frame, or from semi-ripe cuttings in summer.

CLIMATE Zone 7.

SPECIES *N. domestica*, heavenly bamboo, is an upright, evergreen shrub, which grows up to 1.5–2 m (5–6 ft). Long sprays of small, white, summer flowers are followed by red berries. The fern-like foliage may become bronze or red in fall. There are several cultivars, including 'Harbor Dwarf' with fiery winter foliage, which grows under 1m and makes excellent ground cover. 'Moyer's Red' has bright red winter foliage.

ABOVE Through autumn and winter, the pretty foliage of *Nandina domestica* is decorated with sprays of bright red berries.

Narcissus (fam. Amaryllidaceae)
Daffodil

Native to the northern hemisphere, mainly central Europe and the Mediterranean region, with one species extending through to China and Japan, these lovely, bulbous plants are very popular with gardeners throughout warm to cool areas of the world. Daffodils are probably the best known and most widely grown of all bulbs, and to many they are a true indicator of spring. They look wonderful mass planted in the garden but they also make great pot plants and excellent cut flowers. In large gardens in cool climates, they are often naturalized in grass. The jonquils, or Jonquilla group of narcissus, are particularly attractive with their heads of several, small, often highly scented flowers. They flower in mid to late spring. There are over 50 known species and thousands of cultivars. Experts divide the genus into 12 groups, depending on the flower form and size. Home gardeners should know what conditions they need to grow narcissus successfully.

BELOW Bright, golden daffodils bring a lift to winter and spring gardens. Not all types flower well in warm areas.

ABOVE 'Erlicheer' is a ruffled double jonquil, flowering in winter or spring. The rich cream flowers are highly scented.

CULTIVATION Plant in well-drained soil, rich in organic matter, though jonquils will tolerate poorer soils. Both grow best in a sunny spot, but will tolerate shade for part of the day. Some protection from strong wind is desirable. Plant bulbs of tall daffodils about 15 cm (6 in) deep and 10–15 cm (4–6 in) apart, and those of the dwarf kinds 8 cm (3 in) deep and 8–10 cm (3–4 in) apart, in late summer or early fall. Give a thorough watering after planting, but do not water again until foliage appears. Water regularly during growth and flowering. Feed with blood, fish and bone or complete plant food after flowering has finished. Spent flowers should be removed and foliage allowed to die off naturally. If drainage is good, bulbs may be left in the ground and divided every three years or so. Narcissus do have a few problems. One of the most serious, as there is no cure, is virus, particularly one which causes yellow streaking of the foliage and stunted growth. If this is noticed, dig up and destroy the bulbs. Various fungi can cause bulbs to rot. Slugs and snails are a particularly serious problem in many gardens. They will eat the foliage as well as the blooms and are most active during wet or damp weather.

CLIMATE Best in cool climates; zone 6, unless otherwise specified below.

FORMS The foliage of the trumpet forms grows 30–40 cm (12–16 in) high, while the flowers may be taller. The most popular daffodil is the bright yellow, trumpet-shaped bloom, but there are many white, cream and pink cultivars and others with two tones. Many have a delightful perfume. Modern hybrids with split trumpets are also available. The Large-cupped and Small-cupped daffodils are popular and have cup-shaped coronas rather than trumpets. Often the flowers are bi-colored. *N. bulbocodium* and *N. cantabricus*, zone 8, are known as hoop-petticoat daffodils. They have narrow, almost cylindrical foliage and yellow or white flowers. Small-growing hybrids of the species *N. cyclamineus* and *N. triandrus*, angel's tears, zone 4, often have reflexed petals. The flowers of the lovely *N. poeticus*, pheasant's-eye or poet's narcissus, zone 4, are fragrant and mainly white, with a flat central corona, edged with red. The Tazetta group, zone 8, has stems bearing four to eight flowers, as do those of the Jonquilla group, zone 4. Jonquils produce yellow, orange, white or cream flowers on stems 30–40 cm (12–16 in) high. Some of the most popular Tazetta cultivars are 'Paper White', with white flowers, and 'Grand Soleil d'Or', with yellow petals and orange cups. The Jonquil cultivar 'Erlicheer' is a rich creamy double, with a very strong fragrance. They look lovely planted in groups in the garden or crowded into pots. They are very tough, often surviving in old gardens after everything else has perished, although flowering may be poorer.

Nectarine (see Peach)

Nelumbo (fam. Nymphaeaceae)

American lotus

The two species of these large, herbaceous, aquatic plants are among the most spectacular of all water plants, with their very large, almost circular leaves and beautiful, fragrant, showy flowers which emerge from the water in summer. They are ideal for large ponds but in frost-prone climates, the frost-tender *N. nucifera* needs a warm greenhouse or conservatory.

CULTIVATION Lotus plants grow vigorously, so should not be overplanted. If growth becomes congested, the plants should be divided. Lotus can be grown from rhizomes planted in early spring in a large pond with a layer of soil on the bottom. They can also be grown from seed which may germinate better if scarified. Roll the seeds in a ball of clay and drop them into the pond, a practice adopted in ancient Egypt.

CLIMATE Subtropics to tropics, although *N. lutea* can be grown in zone 6.

SPECIES *N. lutea*, golden lotus, is from North America, where it was formerly cultivated as an edible crop by the native Americans. The leaves are 30–60 cm (12–24 in) in diameter and the fragrant, pale yellow flowers are 25 cm (10 in) across. *N. nucifera*, sacred lotus, with origins in India, China and Tibet, is sacred to several religious groups, including the Buddhists and Hindus. The leaves grow to almost 1 m (3 ft) in diameter and the pink

flowers are beautifully fragrant. Cultivated in Asia for its edible roots and seeds, it is known to have been widely grown by the Egyptians after its introduction about 500 BC. There, the seeds were ground to make flour. A number of named cultivars bear pink, red and white flowers, both singles and doubles.

Nemesia (fam. Scrophulariaceae)

Comprising over 60 species of annual and perennial, herbaceous plants and subshrubs from tropical and South Africa, *Nemesia* gives color to rockeries, borders and window boxes.

CULTIVATION The annuals, which are often grown for summer bedding, are raised from seed sown in spring under glass. Germinate at 15°C (59°F). Plant out after frosts, in a sunny spot with well-drained soil. They are best in slightly acid soil which retains moisture. They need shelter from strong winds. Keep well watered in dry summer periods to maintain the flower display.

CLIMATE Zone 9, but grown as summer annuals in all climate zones.

BELOW Massed nemesias in mixed colors are a cheerful sight in summer, whether used in bedding schemes, at the front of borders or in patio containers.

ABOVE The delicately shaded flower of the sacred lotus is an important symbol in several Asian countries.

SPECIES *N. strumosa*, an annual, grows to 40 cm (16 in) high and produces an abundance of brightly colored flowers, borne in terminal sprays, throughout summer. There are numerous cultivars available, including some in a wide range of bright, mixed colors. Those with bicolored flowers are also recommended, such as the blue and white 'KLM', and 'Mello Red and White' (color as name). *N. versicolor* is an annual species with a large color range and both tall and dwarf forms.

Nemophila (fam. Hydrophyllaceae)
Baby blue eyes

These 11 species of annuals are mainly native to western and south-western North America. The species *N. menziesii* is probably the most widely grown and is used for edging borders and filling patio containers.

CULTIVATION Raise from seed sown where the plants are to flower, in early spring or, in mild climates, in fall. Once in the garden they may self-sow. Nemophilas can be grown in any well-drained, yet moisture-retentive soil, provided it is reasonably fertile, and in a sunny or partially shaded spot. Keep well watered

BELOW *Nemophila menziesii* has cool blue and white flowers which contrast well with other, brighter flowering annuals.

during dry summer spells to maintain flower display.

CLIMATE Zone 7.

SPECIES *N. menziesii*, baby blue eyes, has small, bright blue flowers with white centers and ferny foliage. It grows 15–20 cm (6–8 in) high and flowers in summer.

Neoporteria (fam. Cactaceae)

These small, globe- to cylindrical-shaped cactuses, native to Chile, Peru and Argentina, have green to brown bodies. They have ribbed stems covered in spines, which are variable in color and form. The funnel-form flowers are diurnal and come in shades of pink through to yellowish cream. The buds are hairy and the fruit is pink. Most bloom in the period late spring to fall.

CULTIVATION Grow in an intermediate greenhouse or conservatory in pots of cactus compost. Give maximum light. Do not water during winter.

CLIMATE Zone 10.

SPECIES *N. curvispina*, from Chile, grows to about 15 cm (6 in) and is heavily ribbed. Yellow flowers, sometimes with a reddish tint,

ABOVE Spines on this variety of *Neoporteria subgibbosa* vary in color. Those on the top of the crown are black.

appear from spring to fall. *N. horrida* is a short, green, cylindrical plant with sharp ribs, strong brown spines turning gray, and pinkish yellow flowers. *N. subgibbosa*, also from Chile, can grow as high as 1 m (3 ft). It has either an upright or prostrate growth habit and pink or red flowers, generally in fall. *N. umadeave* is a globose, green plant with ribs cut into tubercles. It has strong, curved, cream spines with dark tips and the bell-shaped flowers are yellow.

Neoregelia (fam. Bromeliaceae)

There are over 70 species of these striking, mainly terrestrial bromeliads which occur naturally in forests of South America. Grown for their large rosettes of thick, shiny leaves, they are among the most popular of the bromeliads. The variable coloring of the leaves intensifies if the plant is given the right amount of light, taking on different colors at the time of flowering. A pincushion of tiny flowers appears in the heart of the plant, sometimes surrounded by bracts.

CULTIVATION Grow in pots in a warm, humid greenhouse or conservatory. The plants need a very free draining, soilless potting compost, such as coarse orchid compost. Special bromeliad compost may be available in some

ABOVE right The bromeliad *Neoregelia carolinae* and its cultivars (one seen here) turn red in the center at flowering time.

areas. If plants might topple over, place pebbles or gravel in the pots to keep them stable. Most species prefer dappled shade, though the rich colors may be diminished if there is too much shade. The central cup of the rosette should be kept filled with water. Collect rain water for use on bromeliads if your water supply is known to have a high chalk content. Propagate plants from offsets of pups which should be removed from the parent when about one-third the size of the parent.

CLIMATE At least zone 10.

SPECIES *N. ampullacea* is a tiny plant with blue flowers and leaves banded in burgundy. *N. carolinae*, the most commonly grown species, forms a compact rosette of roughly 25 cm (10 in) long leaves. The center of the rosette colors crimson to cerise at flowering time, when deep violet flowers appear in the cup. Var. *tricolor* has cream- and green-striped foliage that takes on a pinky flush at flowering, when the center of the rosette turns crimson. *N. concentrica* has broad leaves, to 60 cm (24 in) long, patterned in purple or burgundy. *N. fosteriana*, which has burgundy foliage, is often used in hybridizing. *N. marmorata* has wide leaves, to about 30 cm (12 in) long, marbled in red on both sides. *N. spectabilis*, painted fingernail, has red-tipped, olive green leaves, banded in gray on the undersides.

Nepenthes (fam. Nepenthaceae)
Tropical pitcher plant

This genus consists of around 70 species of unusual, insectivorous plants, occurring naturally in moist habitats from India through to northern Australia. Most are scrambling plants, climbing by means of tendrils to reach up to 5 m (16 ft) with support, and becoming woody with age. The inflorescence is fairly insignificant. The main feature of the plants is the pendulous, insect-trapping pitcher, formed from adapted leaves. Each pitcher has a cap or lid which prevents water entering the container. Insects attracted by nectar enter the

ABOVE This pitcher plant has its lid wide open, revealing the red-spotted throat of the inner pitcher, which invites insects to enter.

pitcher and cannot escape because of the slippery, waxy, inner surface. They are also hampered by the lid. The insects' bodies break down and are absorbed into the plant as food. These plants can be grown in tropical gardens as curiosities and make unusual container plants for greenhouses. Many hybrids between species have been developed.

CULTIVATION Most of these plants prefer very warm, humid conditions with temperatures from 21°C (70°F) upwards. A few species like humid conditions with lower temperatures. They need perfect drainage and constant moisture, but need to be kept relatively dry in winter. Nepenthes can be grown in slatted, wooden orchid baskets, in live sphagnum moss, or in a mix of chipped bark, perlite and coir. Propagate from cuttings of firm tip growth taken in early spring and place in a coarse orchid compost in a warm greenhouse, where they should take root in four to six weeks. Pot into small pots of sphagnum moss. They can also be raised from seed sown in spring, but this is difficult. A liquid fertilizer may be used once the plant is established. The tiny seedlings carry a miniature pitcher on each leaf.

CLIMATE Tropical only.

SPECIES *N. ampullaria* is a scrambling or prostrate plant, with fringed, greenish pitchers. *N.* x *atrosanguinea* produces cylindrical, fringed pitchers in a reddish purple color with yellowish markings. *N.* x *balfouriana*, from Indonesia, has long, fringed, cylindrical pitchers in pale green, sometimes marked with purple or rust. It can grow up to 6 m (20 ft). *N. mirabilis*, from Southeast Asia, southern China and Australia, grows between 2 and 10 m (6–33 ft), with large leaves. The attractive pitchers are reddish green in color. *N. rafflesiana* is a straggling climber, with dark green leaves and long, pale green pitchers mottled in dark brown to purple. *N. superba* has very large, long pitchers in green, with purple blotches around the lip.

Nepeta (fam. Lamiaceae)

This genus comprises over 200 species of perennials, often used formerly as folk medicine. Now mainly grown as groundcover and edging plants, they have attractive flowers and aromatic foliage. Hybrids come in a range of colors.

CULTIVATION *Nepeta* can be grown in any ordinary, well-drained soil, provided it is planted in a sunny situation. As it can be rather invasive, it should not be grown close to other smaller plants. Cut back dead fall growth in late winter or early spring when new growth begins, and trim to remove dead stems. Propagate from seed sown in spring, by division in spring, or from cuttings taken from new growth in summer after flowering. Young shoots strike readily in a sandy compost and can be planted out the following spring.

ABOVE are numerous hybrids of *Nepeta*, generally with larger and more colorful flowers than the species, all flowering during the summer.

CLIMATE Zone 3, but zone 4 for *N. racemosa*.

SPECIES *N. cataria*, catmint or catnip, is a perennial with upright, branching stems, growing to 1 m (3 ft). It has gray-green leaves and whorls of white flowers with mauve spots, from late spring to fall. This sweet-smelling herb is very attractive to cats. The leaves are used for tea. *N. x faassenii* is a bushy, clump-forming hybrid growing to around 45 cm (18 in). It has long leaves and masses of small, light lavender-blue flowers throughout summer. There are numerous other hybrids of *Nepeta*, generally with larger and more colorful flowers than the species. *N. racemosa* (syn. *N. mussinii*) is a green bush, growing to 30 cm (12 in) high, with sprays of blue flowers.

Nephrolepis (fam. Oleandraceae)
Sword fern

Mostly found on the edges of rainforests in the tropics, these ferns are grown extensively as indoor plants around the world. There are about 30 species, as well as numerous popular cultivars. They have short, scaly, upright rhizomes, crowded stems and hair-like runners. The fishbone-shaped fronds vary from erect to pendent, and the sickle-shaped leaflets are often much divided. These fast-growing ferns make good pot plants for the home or the intermediate greenhouse or conservatory.

CULTIVATION Under glass or indoors, grow these ferns in soil-based potting compost to which some well-rotted leaf mould has been added if available. Ensure good light, but shade from direct sun which may cause scorching of the fronds. Provide a humid atmosphere, but at the same time, airy conditions. Plants need moderate amounts of water in the growing season, but far less in winter. Feed every three or four weeks during the spring and summer with weak liquid fertilizer. Propagate by detaching and potting rooted runners in spring.

CLIMATE Subtropical to tropical. *N. cordifolia* will survive in zone 10.

SPECIES *N. cordifolia*, southern sword fern, has become naturalized in most tropical and many subtropical regions of the world. It is very vigorous, producing fleshy tubers along its

ABOVE A lovely Boston fern grows in partial shade below a rhododendron. Both enjoy the humus-rich soil and shade.

wiry running roots. *N. exaltata*, sword fern, is a tropical American species which has also naturalized itself in many areas of the world. *N. exaltata* 'Bostoniensis' is the well-known Boston fern which is widely used as a houseplant. There are many other cultivars of this species , some with finely divided or heavily ruffled fronds, others with extremely long, pendulous fronds that can only be grown in hanging baskets.

Nerine (fam. Amaryllidaceae)

There are about 30 species in this genus of bulbous plants from South Africa. The attractive, spider-like flowers borne at the end of long stems appear in fall in colors ranging from white through various shades of pink to deep crimson and scarlet. The leaves are strap-like.

CULTIVATION These plants need perfect drainage and a hot, sunny position. Plant bulbs with their necks above ground during late summer or early fall. Water while plants are in active growth, but keep dry during dormancy. Nerines will flower best if undisturbed. In frost-prone climates, grow tender species in a cool,

ABOVE *Nerine bowdenii* is the species most often cultivated. It has pink, crinkly petals and long, protruding stamens.

airy greenhouse, in pots of soil-based potting compost.

CLIMATE Zone 9, but zone 8 for *N. bowdenii*.

SPECIES *N. bowdenii* grows to about 30 cm (12 in), with rose pink flowers. *N. filifolia* has fine, grass-like foliage that grows 15–20 cm (6–8 in) high and delicate, little, pink or white flowers in fall. *N.* 'Fothergillii Major' is a vigorous grower, to 60 cm (24 in), with large, bright scarlet flowers in fall. *N. flexuosa* has pale pink flowers, and grows to 50 cm (20 in). Cultivar 'Alba' has white flowers. *N. masonorum* grows to only 20 cm (8 in), producing rose-pink flowers with darker stripes. *N. sarniensis*, Guernsey lily, is a delightful species, to 40 cm (16 in), bearing trumpet-shaped flowers with prominent stamens in colors from pink to rose, crimson and scarlet.

Nerium (fam. Apocynaceae)
Oleander

This genus comprises only one species, an evergreen shrub which will grow almost anywhere (except in cold climates) and tolerates a range of conditions from hot semi-arid to coastal, providing it has sun for most of the day. It is toxic to both animals and human beings if ingested. Oleanders are widely grown for their attractive flowers in single or double form in white, pink, cream and red, through summer and fall. They have leathery, dark green, spear-shaped leaves.

CULTIVATION In frost-prone climates, grow in pots of soil-based potting compost in a cool, airy greenhouse or conservatory. Plants can be stood outside for the summer. These shrubs are perfect for harsh conditions as they will withstand long periods of drought in inland areas and also provide effective windbreaks in coastal gardens. Prune fairly heavily in early winter and remove all straggly canes. They can be grown quite successfully as small standards by allowing only one main stem to develop as

ABOVE Pink-flowering oleanders are often used in street plantings as they cope well with the often hostile growing conditions.

a trunk and removing all side growth. Propagate from cuttings of top shoots, about 8 cm (3 in) long, taken in late summer and fall.

CLIMATE Zone 9.

SPECIES *N. oleander*, native to the Mediterranean and western China, produces deep pink to white flowers. It generally grows to a height and width of about 3 m (10 ft). The many cultivars offer variegated foliage, single or double flowers, and colors ranging from white to salmon, pale and deep pink, cerise and crimson. There are also some good dwarf forms available.

Nicotiana (fam. Solanaceae)

Named for Jean Nicot, a French consul in Portugal, who introduced the tobacco plant to Portugal and France in the 16th century, this genus consists of around 70 species of annuals and perennials, native to tropical and North America and Australia. The genus includes both commercial tobacco species, as well as a number of tall-growing ornamentals. Many of the species produce sprays of long-tubed flowers which open only at night to emit their fragrance, while the newer strains offer flowers which remain open but have little perfume. The summer flowers may be white, pink, crimson, wine or scarlet.

CULTIVATION These plants will grow in any average garden soil but prefer full sunlight. They are frost sensitive. Propagate from seed sown in spring in seed boxes. When transplanting, allow around 15 cm (6 in) between seedlings.

CLIMATE Zone 9 or 10, but grown as summer annuals in all climatic zones.

SPECIES *N. alata* (syn. *N. affinis*) is a perennial, often grown as an annual. The cream flowers are fragrant at night. This species grows to about 1.5 m (5 ft). *N. langsdorffii* is a popular, annual species. It is a strong grower to 1.5 m (5 ft) and is sticky, with a branching habit of growth. In summer, it bears clusters of pendulous, tubular, pale green flowers. Also with green flowers, yellow-green this time, is the popular annual, *N. 'Lime Green'*, which is much used for summer bedding. The most popular nicotianas for summer bedding are cultivars of the annual

ABOVE The white, tubular flowers of *Nicotiana sylvestris* are echoed by the white snow-in-summer growing below.

N. x *sanderae.* These come in many colors and attain 30-45 cm (12–18 in) in height. Among the best known are the Domino Series and the Nicki Series. *N. suaveolens* grows to 1.5 m (5 ft) high, with white flowers, purplish green on the outside. *N. sylvestris* grows to 1.5 m (5 ft) high, with fragrant, white flowers. *N. tabacum* is the most commonly cultivated commercial tobacco plant. It grows to 2 m (6 ft) high, with very large, hairy leaves and inconspicuous, pink flowers.

Nidularium (fam. Bromeliaceae)

Native to forests of the tropical Americas, *Nidularium* is an important member of the large bromeliad family. The strap-like leaves radiate from a central cup which houses the submerged inflorescence. The flowers, generally red, white or blue, are enclosed by short bracts which flush spectacularly during flowering.

CULTIVATION Outside the tropics or subtropics, grow in a warm, humid greenhouse or conservatory or as house plants. Grow in pots of soilless potting compost, one formulated for bromeliads if available. The plants need good light, but should be shaded from direct sun.

ABOVE So-called blushing bromeliad, *Nidularium fulgens* has small flowers that form in the cup of the red rosette.

Keep the 'cup' filled with lime-free water in the growing season. Water sparingly in winter.

CLIMATE Warmest parts of zone 10 and above.

SPECIES *N. billbergioides* has an unusual form, with an upright rosette of orange bracts at flowering time. *N. fulgens*, sometimes known as friendship plant or blushing bromeliad, forms a rosette of red bracts around white and violet flowers at flowering time. It has strap-shaped, softly toothed, mottled, yellow-green leaves. *N. innocentii*, a parent of a number of good hybrids, has soft green leaves, with reddish undersides, and white flowers surrounded by red bracts. Var. *lineatum* has fine stripes along its leaves; *striatum*'s leaves feature narrow, cream stripes, while the flower bracts are reddish purple.

Nierembergia (fam. Solanaceae)
Cup flower

Native to Argentina, Mexico and Chile, this genus consists of more than 20 species of perennials and sub-shrubs with fine foliage. Masses of blue, and occasionally white, cup-shaped flowers appear in summer and again in fall, if cut back after the first flush. They generally grow to about 25 cm (10 in), with some reaching 1 m (3 ft), and suit borders and rock gardens. The perennials are often grown as annuals for summer bedding.

CULTIVATION These plants will grow in poor soils, but really thrive in better soils. They prefer a sunny situation and require ample water during dry weather. Raise plants from seed sown in spring under glass and germinated at 15°C (59°F). Plant out when frosts are over. Take cuttings of perennials in summer. *N. repens* can be divided in spring.

CLIMATE Zone 9. Zone 10 for *N. caerulea.*

SPECIES *N. caerulea* produces masses of lavender-blue flowers with yellow throats. Cultivar 'Purple Robe' is a small, bushy

ABOVE *Nierembergia repens* is a lovely, creeping plant for rock gardens. Its creamy white flowers appear over a long season.

ABOVE An easy-care annual, *Nigella damascena* has light, feathery foliage and bright blue flowers that fade as they age.

CLIMATE Zone 7.

perennial with purple flowers, best grown as an annual. *N. repens*, a creeping plant rooting at the nodes, has large, cream flowers. *N. scoparia* is one of the shrubby species, growing to around 45 cm (18 in) high. It has pale blue flowers, edged in white.

Nigella (fam. Ranunculaceae)

Love-in-a-mist

There are 14 species of annuals in this genus, which spreads from the Mediterranean across to Asia. The summer flowers are mainly light blue and are almost hidden by the delicate, misty, fern-like foliage, hence the common name of the most often grown species.

CULTIVATION These plants can be grown in any well-drained soil, but need a position in full sun to flower well. Propagate from seed sown where the plants are to grow. Sow in spring for normal summer flowering, or in fall for earlier flowering the following year. In cold or wet climates, cover the seedlings with cloches over winter. Thin seedlings to 20–30 cm (8–12 in) apart. They self-seed freely.

SPECIES *N. damascena*, love-in-a-mist, grows 30–60 cm (12–24 in) high, with blue flowers followed by inflated, roundish, green seed pods, both of which are used in floral decoration. Cultivar 'Miss Jekyll' has bright blue flowers; 'Oxford Blue' has blue flowers which change from light to dark as they mature; Persian Jewels Series come in shades of pink, carmine, lavender, purple and white. *N. hispanica*, 30–60 cm (12–24 in) high, has deep blue flowers with red stamens. Its cultivar 'Curiosity' is similar, but also has a black center.

Nolina (fam. Agavaceae)

These tree-like succulents are native to Mexico. The bark-covered trunk is 3–6 m (10–20 ft) tall, slender at the top and very swollen at the base. The long, narrow, leathery, tapering leaves form clusters at the top of the trunk and are sometimes pendulous. The small flowers are borne in large sprays.

CULTIVATION In frost-prone climates, these plants need to be grown in an intermediate

ABOVE The stiff leaves of *Nolina longifolia* are used as brooms in its native Mexico. Plumes of flowers arch out from the plant base.

greenhouse or conservatory. Use soil-based potting compost. Provide maximum light. Water in moderation during the growing season and reduce even more in winter. Outdoors grow in full sun with well-drained soil (established plants take arid conditions). Propagate in spring from seed germinated at 21°C (70°F), or from offsets in spring.

CLIMATE Zone 10.

SPECIES *N. bigelowii* (syn. *Dasylirion bigelowii*) has a reasonably short trunk. The old leaves hang from the trunk like a grass skirt. The sprays of greenish colored flowers are borne on 3 m (10 ft) tall stems. *N. recurvata* (see *Beaucarnea recurvata*).

Nomocharis (fam. Liliaceae)

From the Himalayas, Tibet, Burma and western China, this genus consists of seven species of bulbous perennials related to fritillaries and lilies. The attractive, summer flowers may be saucer-shaped or bell-like and come in a variety of shades, spotted with contrasting colors. The petals are often fringed and the stamens decorative and prominent.

CULTIVATION Plant bulbs in a woodland garden or shrub border in fall or spring, 15 cm (6 in) deep. They need acid, moisture-retentive, yet well-drained soil containing plenty of humus, and partial shade. Full sun is suitable in really cool climates. Propagate from seed sown in fall or spring. Germinate seed at 10°C (50°F). Nomocharis can also be propagated from bulb scales in late summer.

CLIMATE Zone 7.

SPECIES *N. aptera*, from China, grows between 45 cm and 1 m (18–40 in) high. It has pink flowers with a maroon eye and crimson spots. *N. farreri*, from Burma, grows to 1 m (3 ft), with pink flowers spotted maroon and crimson. *N. pardanthina*, from western China, has white or pink flowers spotted purple and red. It grows to 1 m (3 ft). *N. saluenensis* grows between 45 cm and 1 m (18–40 in). The white flowers are tinged with rose and spotted in purple on the outside.

ABOVE Lovely *Nomocharis pardanthina*, a bulbous perennial from China, likes cool, moist conditions and humus-rich soils.

Nopalxochia (fam. Cactaceae)

Native to Mexico, these epiphytic cactuses have round, bushy main stems and flat branches with wavy edges. The rather large, self-sterile, funnel-form flowers are diurnal. These cactuses are useful for growing in baskets.

CULTIVATION In frost-prone climates, grow in an intermediate greenhouse or conservatory or as house plants. These cacti are good in hanging containers, but can be grown in ordinary pots. They need an acid, soilless potting compost which must be very well drained. Provide good light (but shade from direct sun), and a humid atmosphere. Water plants normally during the growing season, but keep only slightly moist in winter. Propagate from cuttings of the stem sections in summer, or from seed in spring, both in a warm propagating case.

CLIMATE At least zone 10.

SPECIES *N. phyllanthoides* has a profusion of rose pink flowers. Cultivar 'Deutsche Kaiserin', also with rose pink flowers, is a popular choice. The many cultivars are more spectacular in bloom than the species.

BELOW The pink, orchid-like flowers of *Nopalxochia phyllanthoides* 'Deutsche Kaiserin' are quite unlike those of any other cultivar.

Normanbya (fam. Arecaceae)
Queensland black palm

This single-species genus of feather palm is confined to a small area in the north of Queensland. The common name refers to the trunk, which is gray, but has a layer of hard, black fibers. This palm is not likely to be available outside its native Australia.

CULTIVATION This palm needs humid, frost-free conditions and shelter from strong wind. It also requires a well-drained soil with a high organic content, and should be kept mulched, at least in its early years. Young palms must have shade for their first few years. Slow-release fertilizer or blood, fish and bone should be applied in early spring and again in early summer. Give regular, deep waterings through spring and summer but much less often during the cooler months. This palm can be grown indoors when young, but often does poorly as the humidity is too low. Germination of seed can be erratic, taking three months or even longer.

ABOVE The arching fronds of *Normanbya normanbyi* show the jagged leaflets. This palm is carrying a heavy crop of fruit.

CLIMATE Warmest parts of zone 10 and above.

SPECIES *N. normanbyi* is a very handsome palm which grows 15–20 m (50–65 ft) tall in the tropics. It has a distinctive, pale gray trunk and arching, pendulous feathery fronds. The leaflets have jagged ends and are rich green on the upper side and gray-white beneath. They grow from every direction, giving a slightly foxtail effect. For this reason, it is sometimes confused with the foxtail palm, *Wodyetia bifurcata*. The short sprays of numerous, white or pinkish flowers emerge from beneath the crownshaft. After flowering, oval to pear-shaped fruits form. These generally ripen during summer, maturing to a pink or rich red color.

Nothofagus (fam. Fagaceae)
Southern beech

Native to the southern hemisphere, this genus comprises over 30 species of evergreen and deciduous trees and shrubs with dark green leaves, often with toothed margins. Though much smaller, the attractive foliage is similar to that of their relative, the true beech. They make beautiful shade and ornamental specimens for cool climates, though most are too large for gardens, and can also be clipped to provide hedges. They are also grown for their timber.

CULTIVATION These trees need acid soil and a position in full sun. Propagate from cuttings or by layering, although seedlings can often be found under mature trees. These often transplant successfully–trees up to 3 m (10 ft) tall will safely transplant, if ample soil is attached to the roots and they are staked when young for protection from wind. They can be grown in pots and make unusual bonsai subjects.

CLIMATE Zone 9 unless otherwise indicated below.

SPECIES *N. antarctica*, Antarctic beech, zone 7, from South America, is a deciduous tree which

ABOVE Although slow-growing, *Nothofagus cunninghamii* is worth a place in warm temperate gardens. The small, shiny leaves are appealing.

grows to 30 m (100 ft) tall. *N. cunninghamii*, myrtle beech, is an imposing, evergreen tree from south-eastern Australia which can attain a height of 50 m (160 ft) in its habitat, but usually grows 20–30 m (65–100 ft) in cultivation. It has dense sprays of small, shiny, toothed leaves. The young foliage is a reddish bronze color. A dwarf, alpine form is available. *N. fusca*, New Zealand red beech, has a slender growth habit and round, wavy leaves with a bright brownish red tone which color attractively in winter. *N. gunnii*, deciduous beech, zone 8, is an attractive, mountain species, and one of the few deciduous Australian trees. It is a small grower, to about 3 m (10 ft), with lovely, golden fall foliage. The leaves are small, round and furrowed. *N. moorei*, from alpine and mountainous regions of Australia, has a huge trunk covered with brown, scaly bark and distinctive, triangular-shaped, greenish bronze foliage. It grows to 20 m (65 ft) tall.

Notholirion (fam. Liliaceae)

Originating from Asia, these six species of bulbous perennials are similar to true lilies, though they differ in the formation of the bulbs.

CULTIVATION Plant bulbs 15 cm (6 in) deep in the fall for summer flowering in moist, well-drained soil, preferably in semi-shade. Propagate from the small bulbils which form at the base of the flower stems when the main bulb has died off after flowering, or by lifting and dividing the bulbs in early fall.

CLIMATE Zone 8.

SPECIES *N. bulbiferum* has beautiful, pinkish lavender, funnel-shaped flowers, tipped in green. It grows up to 1 m (3 ft) high. *N. campanulatum*, to 1 m (3 ft) high, has pendulous, crimson flowers, tipped in green. *N. thomsonianum* bears a tall spike of fragrant, pinkish mauve flowers from a rosette of basal leaves. This species is easily cultivated but does not always flower well.

BELOW Best grown in regions with cool summers, *Notholirion campanulatum* likes plenty of water while in active growth.

Notocactus (syn. Parodia, fam. Cactaceae)

Originating from Brazil, Uruguay and Argentina, these popular cacti are mostly globular in shape, though a few are column-shaped. They have distinct, often notched, ribs and varied spines. The self-fertile, diurnal flowers, which grow from the top of the plant, are funnel-shaped, with red or purple stigmas. The buds and fruits are woolly. Still generally sold as *Notocactus*, botanists now include this in the genus *Parodia* (see entry at *Parodia*).

CULTIVATION These mostly small cacti are easy to grow but need an intermediate greenhouse or conservatory in frost-prone climates. Grow in pots of well-drained cactus compost, available from good garden centers. Provide maximum light (but shade from direct strong sun), and a dry, airy atmosphere. Apply water in moderation during the growing season and keep dry in winter. Propagate in spring from seed germinated at 21°C (70°F).

CLIMATE Warmest parts of zone 9 and above.

SPECIES *N. concinnus* is a small, tubby cactus, with deep yellow flowers. *N. herteri*, prized for its hot pink to purple flowers, is squat and must be about tennis ball size before it will flower. *N. leninghausii* is a columnar cactus that may grow to 90 cm (36 in) high in ideal

ABOVE A clustering colony of *Notocactus leninghausii* thrives in rough, coarse soil.

conditions. It has large, yellow flowers. *N. uebelmannianus* is another squat grower, generally with large, purple flowers although there is a yellow-flowered form. All species are slow to produce offsets.

Nutmeg (*Myristica fragrans*, fam. Myristicaceae)

There are more than 100 species of *Myristica*, extending through parts of Southeast Asia and into Australia. However, *Myristica fragrans* is the only species common in cultivation and both nutmeg and mace come from this large tree which is native to the Moluccas. It may grow 15–18 m (50–60 ft) tall. Male and female flowers are carried on separate trees, one male tree being planted in commercial plantations to pollinate about ten female trees. The fruit at maturity is fleshy and pale yellow and splits to reveal a fleshy, red covering, mace, enclosing the woody seed, nutmeg. Nutmeg is dried and sold whole for grating or in powdered form. It is used for flavoring both savory and sweet dishes. Most commercial production is in Indonesia and parts of the West Indies.

CULTIVATION Nutmeg trees can be grown outside only in tropical climates. Elsewhere, they can be grown as young foliage plants in pots in a warm greenhouse, but plants may not be available outside the tropics. Use a soil-based potting compost. Shade from direct sun. Propagate from seed sown when available in a warm propagating case.

CLIMATE Suitable for tropical regions only.

Nuytsia (fam. Loranthaceae)

Western Australian Christmas bush, fire tree

As this beautiful plant is semi-parasitic, it requires a host plant in cultivation, like most other members of this family of mistletoes. In summer in its native country, this unusual tree provides a splendid display of brilliant orange flowers. Not available outside its country of origin and difficult to grow, it would be worth looking out for in botanical gardens.

CULTIVATION *Nuytsia* can be easily propagated from the ripe, winged seeds. Sow seed in a sharp, sandy peat mix of 3:1. While the seedlings are quite small, add a tuft of couch grass to the potting mix. Plant out when still young, together with the host (which may be any other plant), in a full sun position. Water

BELOW This young nutmeg tree will grow very large in time, yielding nutmet, mace and oil of nutmeg which has medicinal applications.

ABOVE *Nuytsia floribunda* is a parasitic small tree or shrub and hence very difficult to grow. It is arguably one of the world's most beautiful flowering trees.

well, particularly in the early stages of growth. They may not bloom for several years and maintaining plants in cultivation can be very difficult.

CLIMATE Zone 9.

SPECIES *N. floribunda*, the only species, is an evergreen tree of around 9 m (30 ft) tall. It has spreading branches and slender leaves, sometimes developing a broad trunk. The flowers are borne in longish clusters towards the end of the branches. It is considered by many to be one of the most glorious flowering trees in the world.

ABOVE The many-petalled flowers of this hybrid tropical water lily are a most unusual shade, between magenta and purple.

Nymphaea (fam. Nymphaceae)
Water lily

Water lilies are without doubt the best known and most widely grown of all aquatic plants. Species occur naturally throughout the world, both in tropical and cold regions, but many more hybrids than species are in general cultivation. They are broadly classified as either hardy (cold tolerant) or tropical. The two groups do not cross pollinate so they cannot be interbred for color. Most hardy varieties are day blooming, as are many tropicals, but some tropicals also flower at night. Water lilies have a glorious color range, including white, cream, yellow, orange, pink, rich crimson, blue and purple. Tropical varieties include blues and purples not found naturally amongst the cold-tolerant types. Many water lilies have plain, dark green leaves, but a great number have leaves that are heavily splashed or blotched in deep maroon or purple. In cool and cold climates, hardy water lilies flower in summer and sometimes into fall. Tropical varieties will not come into bloom before summer, except in the true tropics. In cool regions, flowering usually commences in late spring or early summer and continues through summer. All water lily blooms make beautiful cut flowers. Water lilies are grown worldwide, in small ponds and large ornamental lakes, from the tropics to the cool

zones. Water lily pools have been enjoyed for centuries in Arabic and Moorish gardens, and also by the Chinese and Japanese, but they did not become popular in Europe until the late 19th century. At this time, wealthy collectors built heated glasshouses containing pools in which a range of tropical water lilies was grown. Prior to this, the only variety that could be grown outdoors in cool to cold climates was the white *Nymphaea alba*. Water lilies were immortalized by the French Impressionist painter, Claude Monet, in a series of large-scale paintings done in his own garden at Giverny in France. Today, these gardens are visited by thousands of people every year.

CULTIVATION Water lilies thrive and flower profusely only in full sun. Most will grow in water 30–50 cm (12–20 in) deep, although true miniatures prefer water of only 10–15 cm (4–6 in) depth. In the tropics, very vigorous types can be grown in water 1–2 m (3–6 ft) deep. In cool regions, there must be sufficient depth of water above the crown of the hardy water lilies to prevent them from freezing. All water lilies like to be grown in still water, away from fountains, pumps and cascades. They are usually potted in a mix of three parts of good quality soil to one part of very well decayed cow manure. After potting, the top of the soil should be covered with a layer of gravel or pebbles. Potted plants should be lowered into the pond very gently and slowly in order to avoid dislodging the plants or the mix. Propagate by lifting and dividing the rhizomes and removing offsets in late winter or early spring, depending on the district. In frost-prone climates, tropical water lilies need to be grown in a pool in a heated greenhouse or conservatory, with a minimum winter temperature of 10°C (50°F).

CLIMATE There is a water lily to suit every climatic zone, but advice should be sought from an expert grower to ensure that the right choice is made.

SPECIES *N. alba*, zone 5, from Eurasia, has dark green leaves, crimson beneath, and slightly scented, white flowers. *N. caerulea*, zone 10, the so-called blue lotus, from tropical and North Africa, has star-shaped, pale blue flowers. *N. capensis*, the Cape water lily, zone 10, has very fragrant blue flowers. *N. gigantea*, the Australian water lily, zone 10, which is native to tropical Australia and New Guinea, has very large leaves, up to 50 cm (20 in) across, and large, blue to purple flowers. It spreads up to 3 m (10 ft) in tropical waters. *N. odorata*, zone 3, a fragrant American species with white flowers, is being used today in hybridizing work, as is the dwarf species, *N. tetragona*, which is suited to zone 2. Small forms are becoming increasingly popular because they are well suited to growing in small ponds with shallow water. Few straight species of water lily are grown today, except by specialist growers and collectors. This is due to the vast range of beautiful hybrids available. Home gardeners should visit specialist growers to see what is available and to seek advice on their culture.

Nyssa (fam. Nyssaceae)

Native to eastern Asia and eastern North America, this genus consists of five species of deciduous trees, grown both for their timber and for their brilliant fall foliage.

CULTIVATION Nyssas prefer acid to neutral, moisture-retentive yet well-drained soil, and a sheltered position with full sun or partial shade. They do not like transplanting, so plant small specimens and then leave well alone. Propagate from seed sown outdoors in fall, or from semi-ripe cuttings in summer.

CLIMATE Zone 3.

SPECIES *N. aquatica*, cotton gum or tupelo gum, can grow to 30 m (100 ft) in its native United States, but is mostly around 15–20 m (50–65 ft) cultivated. It is essentially a swamp grower and tolerates floods. The small flowers are very attractive to bees. *N. sylvatica*, tupelo or sour gum, is also a native of the United States and can grow to 30 m (100 ft) in its habitat. Generally seen around 15–20 m (50–65 ft) in cultivation, it has a distinctive, horizontal branching habit. The glossy foliage turns brilliant scarlet or crimson in fall.

ABOVE Tupelo or sour gum, *Nyssa sylvatica* makes a brilliant specimen in fall. Note the horizontal, slightly weeping branches.

O

Ochna to Oxypetalum

Ochna (fam. Ochnaceae)

Bird's eye bush, Mickey Mouse plant

There are around 90 species of deciduous and evergreen, tropical trees and shrubs in this genus with origins in Africa and Asia. They have leathery leaves, trusses of yellow flowers, scarlet sepals and decorative berries.

CULTIVATION In frost-prone climates grow in an intermediate greenhouse in pots of soil-based potting compost. Prune lightly after flowering to restrict size. Outdoors grow in a sheltered, sunny spot with moist yet well-drained soil. Propagate from seed in spring or semi-ripe cuttings in summer, both with bottom heat.

CLIMATE Zone 10.

SPECIES *O. atropurpurea*, carnival bush, is an evergreen shrub, native to South Africa. Growing to around 1.5 m (5 ft), it has fine, oval, pointed leaves that change from bronze in spring to glossy green in summer, and purple sepals. *O. serrulata*, a native of southern Africa, grows around 2 m (6 ft) high. It has narrow oblong leaves and bright yellow flowers, followed by green berries. The berries ripen to black, providing contrast with the waxy flower calyces (or sepals) which mature to bright red.

ABOVE *Ochna serrulata* produces an abundance of flowers and seed. Berries ripen to black before falling.

The fruits are very attractive to birds which disperse their seed widely. The seedlings have a very long tap root, making removal difficult once these plants are more than a few centimetres high. This is the best known and most widely grown species.

Ochroma (fam. Bombacaceae)

Balsa

Native to tropical America, this evergreen tree has a smooth trunk, broad, green leaves, some measuring 30 cm (12 in) across, and large, white, showy flowers. In its native habitat, the flowers are pollinated by bats. Not grown by private gardeners. May be found in some botanic gardens.

CULTIVATION *Ochroma* is very fast growing in warm regions. Propagate from seed.

CLIMATE Zone 10.

SPECIES *O. pyramidale* (syn. *O. lagopus*), balsa, is the only species, sometimes reaching a height of 30 m (100 ft). Its timber is the lightweight balsa wood, with a wide range of commercial applications.

ABOVE Originating in the foothills of the Andes, *Ochroma pyramidale* is the source of balsa wood. The seeds are encased in a mass of silky hairs.

Odontoglossum (fam. Orchidaceae)

This large genus of over 100 species of epiphytic and rock-dwelling orchids is from South and Central America. The roots of some species grow in the leaf mould at the base of trees. Most produce long sprays of attractive, ruffled flowers, widely varied in colors and markings. The many, fine hybrids are more likely available than the species.

CULTIVATION Grow in an intermediate greenhouse or conservatory in small pots of bark-based orchid compost. In summer, provide good light (but shade from strong sun), and a humid atmosphere. Water regularly. In winter, considerably reduce watering and humidity. Propagate by division when plants outgrow their pots.

CLIMATE At least zone 10.

SPECIES *O. apterum*, from Mexico, has white flowers with reddish brown spots in spring. *O. cirrhosum*, from Ecuador, has white flowers with crimson or purple spots, also during spring. *O. grande* (syn. *Rossioglossum*

grande), tiger orchid, from Guatemala, has large, yellow and brown flowers 10–20 cm (4–8 in) across, in fall.

Odontonema (fam. Acanthaceae)

Originating from tropical America, this genus comprises about 20 species of shrubs, with clusters of long, slender, tubed flowers in red, yellow or white.

CULTIVATION In frost-prone climates, grow in a warm conservatory or greenhouse in pots of soil-based potting compost. Prune back after flowering to restrict size if necessary. Outdoors odontonemas need a rich, moist, well-drained soil and sunny position.

CLIMATE Warmest parts of zone 10 and above.

SPECIES Some species may be difficult to obtain. *O. barlerioides*, to 1 m (3 ft) high, has attractive, slender leaves and dense clusters of tubular flowers. *O. callistachyum* is a more shrubby species, to 5 m (16 ft) high, with smooth, shiny leaves and clusters of red flowers. *O. schomburgkianum*, also shrubby, grows to only 2 m (6 ft), with long leaves and clusters of red flowers.

ABOVE *Odontoglossum crispum*, from Colombia, has white or delicately shaded pink flowers, with red spotting on the lip.

ABOVE Sometimes called red justicia, *Odontonema callistachyum* prefers a sheltered position in filtered sunlight.

Oenothera (fam. Onagraceae)

This genus consists of over 100 species of hardy annuals, biennials and perennials from North America, now grown widely in other parts of the world. In summer, a profusion of delicate flowers appears, releasing a beautiful fragrance mainly at night. The flowers are most commonly yellow, though white, pink and red are also seen. The trailing species are a good choice for rock gardens, while more shrubby varieties are useful for borders. Some species have become troublesome weeds in some countries.

CULTIVATION Plant in any garden soil in a sunny position. Most species grow from seed, while the peren-nial species are propagated from cuttings. Some species tend to be invasive.

CLIMATE Zone 5, unless otherwise specified below.

SPECIES *O. acaulis* is a trailing perennial, with white flowers, turning pink with age, throughout summer. *O. biennis*, evening primrose, zone 4, is the main plant from which the popular essential oil is extracted. This biennial produces fragile, yellow blooms, flowering and releasing its fragrance only in the evening. It grows to 1 m (3 ft) or more. *O. fruticosa*, zone 4, is a perennial plant, to 60 cm (24 in), with rich yellow flowers. *O. fruticosa* subsp. *glauca* has a branching habit and pale yellow flowers from late spring to late summer. The leaves are usually gray-green, and the plant grows to 90 cm (36 in). *O. macrocarpa*, a trailing perennial, to 15 cm (6 in), has bright yellow flowers, sometimes spotted in red. *O. perennis* is a perennial, to 50 cm (20 in), with yellow flowers. *O. speciosa*, white evening primrose, is an attractive, clump-forming perennial, bearing masses of pink-tinted, white flowers from summer to fall. It grows 30–60 cm (12–24 in) high. The pink-flowered form 'Rosea' is popular in cottage gardens.

Okra

(*Abelmoschus esculentus*, syn.

Hibiscus esculentus, fam. Malvaceae)

Gumbo, lady's fingers

Native to tropical Asia, *Abelmoschus esculentus* grows to 2 m (6 ft) or more, with very broad leaves and yellowish white, purple- or red-blotched flowers. The tapering, cylindrical,

ABOVE *Oenothera fruticosa*, popularly known as sundrops, produces yellow, cup-shaped flowers from late spring through summer.

ABOVE Young, upright okra pods are at the ideal stage for picking. Picked when young, they make good eating.

green pods grow to 20 cm (8 in). Okra has long been an important ingredient in the cuisine of southern USA and the Caribbean, as well as in curries in other parts of the world. The pods release a mucilaginous glue when cooked which is used to thicken stews.

CULTIVATION Okra needs a reasonably fertile, well-drained soil, an open, sunny situation and ample water in dry periods. Repeated applications of liquid fertilizer will encourage okra's growth. Sow seed 2–3 cm (about 1 in) deep in warm soil where it is to grow. Space dwarf plants 30–40 cm (12–16 in) apart and taller varieties 45–90 cm (18–36 in) apart, leaving adequate space between rows. Okra likes the same conditions and treatment as tomatoes and cucumbers. Therefore, in cool climates it would be best grown in a greenhouse. Daily collection of the young, tender pods will encourage the production of more seed pods.

CLIMATE Zone 9, but grown as a summer annual in all climates, under glass in cool areas.

Olearia (fam. Asteraceae)

Daisy bush

Native to Australia and New Zealand, this genus includes around 100 species of evergreen shrubs and trees, grown for their silky foliage and pretty clusters of daisy-like flowers. Many make good shelter plants for seaside gardens. Different species have their origins in a wide range of habitats and conditions so there is one to suit almost any situation.

CULTIVATION Daisy bushes thrive on almost any type of soil, as long as it is well drained. Most prefer a position in full sun, although some will take a little shade. Keep plants well mulched with leaf litter or compost, making sure that the mulch is well clear of the stems. Avoid digging close to the plants, otherwise their surface roots may be damaged. Plants should be pruned regularly after flowering. Propagate from seed or strike from cuttings taken from late spring to early fall.

ABOVE Compact-growing *Olearia tomentosa* blooms in spring or summer. It tolerates exposed, coastal conditions.

CLIMATE Zone 8.

SPECIES Not all species will be available outside their native countries. *O. argophylla*, musk daisy bush, is a small tree, native to south-eastern Australia, with large leaves and clusters of white flowers. It grows 3–8 m (10–26 ft) high. *O. chathamica*, a native of New Zealand, is a very pretty species suitable for growing in cold areas. It reaches about 2 m (6 ft) high, with felted leaves, woolly underneath, and dense clusters of pale mauve flowers with deep purple centers. *O. cheesemanii*, also from New Zealand, grows to 3 m (10 ft), with shiny, green leaves covered in silky hairs on the undersides and a profusion of white flowers. *O. lirata*, snow daisy bush, from eastern Australia, is a tall shrub, to 6 m (20 ft), bearing a mass of white blooms during flowering. *O. phlogopappa*, Otway daisy bush, from south-eastern Australia, grows to 2 m (6 ft) high. The leaves are narrow and the small flowers, in white, pink, lilac, blue or purple, completely cover the bush in spring. *O. pimeloides*, from all states of Australia except Tasmania, is a rounded shrub which grows 1 m (3 ft) in height and width and bears large, white, single-stemmed flowers.

O. ramulosa, from all states of Australia except Western Australia, grows to 2 m (6 ft), with clusters of small, white flowers. *O. teretifolia*, from south-eastern and southern Australia, grows to 1.5 m (5 ft), with clusters of small, white or pale blue flowers. *O. tomentosa*, from south-eastern Australia, is a compact shrub, less than 1 m (3 ft) high, with large, white or blue flowers.

Olive (*Olea europaea*, fam. Oleaceae)

Olea includes some 20 species of evergreen trees and shrubs, including the common olive, *Olea europaea*, which is native to the Mediterranean, and cultivated for several thousand years for the extraction of olive oil as well as for its fruit. These trees have small, leathery, green leaves and creamy white flowers, followed by the fruit. They are adaptable, very long lived, and cultivated in many regions of the world. The oil is extracted from the ripe fruit and is used in food preparation, medicine and the manufacture of toiletries and cosmetics. Both the green fruits and the fully ripened, black fruits are preserved and pickled, either plain or stuffed with pimento, nuts or anchovies.

ABOVE European olives make attractive ornamentals, their silvery gray foliage blending well with many color schemes.

CULTIVATION In climates subject to hard frosts, grow in a cool greenhouse or conservatory in a large pot or tub of soil-based potting compost. Where it is possible to grow olives outdoors, winters must be cool enough to provide the chilling needed to induce flowering, but temperatures of less than –9°C (16°F) can kill these trees. Long, hot summers are necessary for proper growth and development of the fruit. Inland areas where humidity is low appear to be more suitable than coastal regions. Deep, well-drained soils are ideal and olives grow well in soils that are slightly alkaline or even with some salinity. Although these trees are droughttolerant once established, adequate water is needed throughout the growing season to ensure good fruit development. Seedling-grown trees may take eight to ten years to produce a crop, while some types may produce only every second year. Propagation is by budding in late summer to early fall, grafting in spring or from semi-hardwood cuttings taken from midsummer onwards. Olives are relatively free from pests and diseases but they are prone to attack by scale insects, especially when grown under glass.

CLIMATE Zone 9.

SPECIES *Olea europaea* is a tree growing 6–12 m (20–40 ft) tall, with narrow, leathery leaves which are dull green above and silvery beneath. The insignificant flowers are cream in color and are followed by the fruits. Traditionally grown varieties include 'Sevillano', 'Verdale' and 'Manzanillo', while 'Mission' and University of California selections (marketed as 'UC' followed by a number) are newer varieties which have a wider range of climatic tolerance as well as possessing good bearing characteristics. Varieties grown more specifically for oil extraction include 'Bouquetier' and 'Correggiola'. *Olea europaea* subspecies *africana* grows around 8 m (26 ft) in height and has darker, glossy, green leaves and fleshy fruit which is edible but without the flavor and succulence of the European olive. It has become naturalized in many areas and can become quite invasive.

Omalanthus (fam. Euphorbiaceae)

Native poplar

Native to Australia and other tropical areas, these shrubs are grown for their unusual flowers, which have no petals and form tassel-like clusters. The simple, alternate leaves are often interestingly colored. This genus is unlikely to be available outside its native countries.

CULTIVATION Outside the tropics, grow in a warm greenhouse with a steady temperature, in pots of rich, soil-based potting compost. Water freely during the growing season but less during the winter. It can be propagated quite easily from seed under glass, or from cuttings during spring and summer.

CLIMATE Tropical.

SPECIES *O. populifolius*, native bleeding heart, forms a large shrub or small tree, to about 4 m (13 ft). The heart-shaped leaves are dark green with paler veining, turning red with age. There are usually some red leaves on the shrub during the entire year. Borne in tassels, the yellow flowers are individually very small and insignificant.

ABOVE *Omalanthus populifolius*, native bleeding heart, from Australia, needs to be grown in a warm greenhouse or conservatory in cool and cold climates.

Oncidium (fam. Orchidaceae)

Originating from Central and South America, this very large genus of over 450 orchids is quite variable. Some have pseudobulbs; some do not. Those usually grown are epiphytes. A number of the most commonly grown species are referred to as 'dancing ladies' and provide long-lasting cut flowers. Grow in an intermediate greenhouse or conservatory with a minimum temperature of 13°C (55°F).

CULTIVATION These orchids can be grown in pots or hanging orchid baskets containing bark-based orchid compost, or mounted on slabs of bark and hung up in the greenhouse. In the growing season, provide a humid atmosphere and good light, but shade from direct sun, and water frequently. In winter, ensure maximum light and keep plants dry, except for those without or with only tiny pseudobulbs, which should be kept moist. Propagate plants by division when they outgrow their pots.

CLIMATE Tropical or subtropical.

SPECIES *O. cheirophorum*, a true miniature with a profusion of bright yellow flowers, needs only a 10 cm (4 in) pot. *O. flexuosum* is a fast

ABOVE above Native to Brazil, *Oncidium sarcodes* has its intricately patterned flowers spaced along the stems.

grower. Grow it in an orchid basket or on a slab of bark. Its many sprays of yellow flowers are marked with red-brown. *O. lanceanum* has long sprays of yellowish brown flowers, marked with reddish brown. The lip is in shades of purple and the leaves are patterned in reddish brown. *O. sphacelatum* produces long sprays of many hundreds of small, yellow flowers, marked with red-brown. Species orchids are rarely available as there are many more appealing cultivars.

Onion (*Allium cepa*, fam. Alliaceae)

The onion is probably one of the most well known of all vegetables. Onions and garlic were used by the ancient Egyptians and today are used both as separate vegetables and as flavoring throughout the world. Onions are eaten raw, cooked as accompaniments to meats, or added to stews, curries, sauces and soups. They come in a range of shapes– round, flattened or globular–and the skin color may be white, brown, yellow, red or purple. Some varieties have a strong, pungent flavor, while others, like the red- or purple-skinned Spanish onion, are quite sweet. Although true perennials, they are grown as annuals and are classed as early, mid-season or late for purposes of harvesting.

ABOVE Onions close to maturity push their bulb tops up above the soil. Foliage should yellow before bulbs are pulled.

Failure with onion-growing is often caused by planting the wrong variety for the season. Some varieties do not store well, and it is important to select the type that best suits your purpose.

CULTIVATION Sow seeds in well-drained soil that has been liberally dressed with manure or compost about two weeks before planting. Unless the soil is known to be alkaline, apply about half a cup of lime or dolomite per square metre (yard) to the planting area. Sow seed in spring in drills about 2 cm (¾ in) deep in rows 30 cm (12 in) apart. Thin seedlings first to about 5 cm (2 in) apart and then later to about 10 cm (4 in). The thinnings can be used to flavor soups or salads. Onions can also be grown from sets (tiny bulbs) planted in spring and, for novice gardeners, are easier than sowing seeds. Weed control is essential and should be ongoing. All-purpose fertilizer can be applied in bands along the sides of the rows if growth is quite slow. If the soil has been well prepared, this may not be necessary. Onions for immediate use can be pulled or dug out at any stage. Do not pull onions for storage until the tops have browned and toppled over. Pull plants over to expose the bulbs to the sun, or spread them on trays to dry in the sun or in a dry, airy, sheltered place. When the outside skin is quite dry, cut off the stems 2–5 cm (1–2 in) above the bulb. Make sure bulbs are dry before storing, or they may rot.

CLIMATE Onions are very hardy and are suited to zone 5 and above. Climates with hot, dry summers are best, but not essential.

Ophiopogon (fam. Convallariaceae)
Lilyturf, mondo grass

Originating from the Philippines, China and Japan, some of these 20 species of low-growing, evergreen, stemless perennials have become very popular in recent years as groundcover and edging plants. They also make attractive pot plants. The foliage is grass-like, the flowers vary from white to mauve and the tiny berries can be blue or blueish green.

ABOVE The variegated form of *Ophiopogon jaburan* is pretty massed in pots or in the ground. Summer brings its purple flower spikes.

CULTIVATION Tolerant of a wide range of soils, these plants will grow in sun or shade. Better foliage color is obtained in shade or partial shade. Regular watering during hot weather maintains best appearance. Propagate by division of the plants in late winter or spring.

CLIMATE Zone 7, unless otherwise specified below.

SPECIES *O. jaburan*, snakebeard, from Japan, grows to 60 cm (24 in), with white flowers and violet-blue berries. Cultivars with variegated leaves and purple flowers similar to grape hyacinth are available *O. japonicus*, mondo grass, grows to 35 cm (14 in), with dark green foliage, white or mauve flowers and blue berries. *O. planiscapus*, zone 6, to 20 cm (8 in), has slender foliage, and produces white or mauve flowers and blue berries. Cultivar 'Nigrescens' has foliage which becomes almost black at maturity.

Opuntia (fam. Cactaceae)

There are about 200 species in this genus which has a wide geographical spread, from southern Canada, throughout the Americas, and south to the Straits of Magellan. Many local, common names have been adopted, more familiar ones being prickly pear, cholla and tuna. Opuntias are jointed or segmented cactuses with mainly padded, flattened joints and they may be cylindrical or rounded in shape. Some, such as the prickly pear or Indian fig, *Opuntia ficus-indica*, have edible fruit. This species is grown for its fruits in many tropical and subtropical parts of the world. In some places it has become naturalized. There are also large numbers of smaller species of various shapes and sizes popular with cactus enthusiasts. Many make good container plants. Opuntias flower in spring or summer, depending on the species and district. Many have yellow flowers. Berry-like fruits that form after the flowers have faded are edible in some species. Long grown as living fences in their native areas, many were introduced to other countries for this purpose with devastating results. Species like *O. aurantiaca*, *O. stricta* and *O. vulgaris* became appalling weeds in Australia, Africa and India. After years

ABOVE Grizzly bear cactus, *Opuntia erinacea* var. ursina, is well sited against this terracotta-colored wall.

of concentrated effort, many infestations are under control but constant vigilance is needed to prevent prickly pear from getting out of hand.

CULTIVATION These plants are easily propagated from stem segments separated from the parent plant and can also be grown from seed sown in spring. In frost-prone climates, grow in a cool greenhouse or conservatory in pots of cactus compost, with maximum light. Keep dry in winter and water normally at other times. Outdoors, grow in a sunny, well-drained spot.

CLIMATE Mostly zone 9.

SPECIES *O. basilaris*, beaver tail, grows about 40 cm (16 in) high, with purple-gray flat pads and red-purple flowers in summer. *O. bigelovii*, known as teddy bear cholla (pronounced 'choya'), is densely covered with spines that appear furry. It grows 1–2 m (3–6 ft) high. *O. erinacea* is a clump-forming cactus with flattened, blue-green pads. Var. *ursina*, with masses of fine, hair-like spines, known as grizzly bear cactus, is the more popular. *O. ficus-indica*, Indian fig, is almost tree-like, growing 3–5 m (10–16 ft) high, with large, segmented, paddle-shaped leaves and bright yellow flowers that mature into deep red or purple fruit. *O. microdasys* has dark green pads dotted with white areoles, and bristles that may be white, yellow or brown. The form that is brown-bristled is known as teddy bear ears. *O. tunicata* makes a small, spreading bush, 60 cm (24 in) high and 1 m (3 ft) wide. It has thick, creamy, satiny spines and bright, yellow flowers in summer.

Orange (Citrus, fam. Rutaceae)

The orange is thought to be one of the oldest cultivated fruits, having been known for the last 3000 years. Probably originating from tropical Asia, it was cultivated in China before reaching Europe. The first orange to reach Europe was *Citrus aurantium*, introduced by the Crusaders and still widely cultivated, espe-

ABOVE The Seville orange grown here in a home garden provides plenty of fruit for making marmalade.

cially in Spain. Columbus brought the orange to the New World and, by the 17th century, trees were established in Florida. The orange now grows in warmer areas of all continents and is a very important item in international markets. Grown chiefly for its fruit and juice which are valuable sources of Vitamin C, it is eaten fresh, as well as being made into marmalades and preserves, and used in cakes, salads, and meat and vegetable dishes. Some types are used in the manufacture of perfume. The deliciously scented blossom is widely used at weddings.

CULTIVATION In climatic zones below zone 9, grow in a cool to intermediate greenhouse or conservatory in pots or tubs of soil-based potting compost, with shade from direct strong sun. The plants can be stood outdoors for the summer. In areas where oranges can be grown in the garden, plant the trees in ordinary garden soil, with effective drainage, in a full sun position. In very windy or frosty districts, some protection is necessary. Give regular, deep watering during flowering and fruit setting to ensure good quality fruit. Citrus trees have many surface roots, so avoid growing competing plants such as grass under them. Mulch well to aid moisture retention, but keep mulch well clear of the trunk. Feed in late winter, and again in early and late summer. Flowering takes place in spring and summer and is followed by the fruits, which can take many months to mature and ripen. Flowers and fruit may be present on the tree at the same time. Little pruning is needed once established. Citrus bark is very susceptible to sunburn, so trees should not be pruned in summer. As the fruit is produced on the previous year's wood, any damage to the wood by frost, disease or negligence can cause the loss of the crop in the following year. Hand clip the fruit, leaving a bit of stem on it and taking care not to bruise the rind as this spoils the appearance and can set up conditions for moulds and rots to develop.

CLIMATE Zone 9 or 10. Best in warm, frost-free, low humidity climates.

SPECIES *Citrus aurantium*, sour or Seville orange, is cultivated or naturalized in many parts of the world. It originally came from Southeast Asia, being introduced to Europe by the Spanish. Seville oranges have a flattened shape and are most widely used in marmalades and preserves. This species is grown as a street tree in several areas of southern Spain and is also being more widely used as an ornamental in parts of the United States, such as Florida, California and Arizona. *C. sinensis*, sweet orange, is an evergreen tree which grows to about 8–12 m (26–40 ft) and bears round, orangecolored, edible fruit. Its sweet, juicy pulp is contained in a smooth outer skin or rind. The pulp and juice are eaten and the essential oil of orange is extracted from the rind. Of the many varieties and cultivars available today, the 'Washington' navel is probably still the favorite eating orange, followed by 'Valencia'. There are many other cultivars but it is best to buy those that are offered locally. Blood oranges are very popular in Mediterranean countries and again there are several cultivars.

Oregano (*Origanum vulgare*, fam. Lamiaceae)

Oregano and marjoram are very similar in appearance and both have similar culinary uses. Oregano, however, has a coarser texture and a somewhat stronger flavor than the herb we know as marjoram. The light green foliage is somewhat firmer. The small, white flowers of both are almost impossible to tell apart. Described as a subshrub, it is generally a sprawling plant which grows 30–90 cm (12–36 in) high. In mediaeval times it was used as a strewing herb and for making scented bags and pillows. Today it has extensive culinary use, added to pizza and pasta, rice dishes and meat and vegetable dishes. Its pungency increases on drying. It is an important ingredient of many traditional dishes of the countries around the Mediterranean, such as Italy and France.

CULTIVATION Oregano can be grown in any well-drained soil, but must have full sun all day. It can be grown from seed sown in spring, or from cuttings taken in later spring through summer. Fertilizer is not needed and plants grown 'hard' have a better flavor. Water heavily when the soil is dry but do not overwater. Harvest leaves for drying just before the plants reach full bloom in late summer or fall. Cut stems and

ABOVE Oregano grows rapidly in warm conditions. Pick the leaves for storage as the plants near their flowering peak.

hang in bunches in a cool, airy place. When the bunches are partially dry, tie net or muslin around them so the dried leaves do not fall to the ground. Store dried leaves in airtight jars. Cutting stems for drying may be all the pruning that is needed, but plants generally need replacing every three or four years, or even less, as they become sparse or woody.

CLIMATE Zone 5.

Ornithogalum (fam. Hyacinthaceae)

There are around 80 species of bulbous plants from Africa, Europe and Asia in this genus. They have slender leaves and attractive, star-shaped, fragrant flowers in white or silvery white, mainly in spring. Some species tolerate very cold conditions, while others need warm growing areas.

CULTIVATION These plants do well in most conditions and soils, in either sun or partial shade. The more tender species can be easily grown in mild conditions, but need a greenhouse or glassed-in verandah in cold, frosty climates. Propagate from seed or by division of offsets.

ABOVE The pyramidal flower heads of *Ornithogalum thyrsoides* open slowly, providing a long floral display. The flowers are elegant in arrangements.

CLIMATE There are species suited to various climatic zones, some being tender, others hardy.

SPECIES *O. arabicum*, zone 9, is a tender species, to 60 cm (24 in), which can be grown in cooler districts, provided it is protected from frost. The white flowers have black centers. *O. balansae*, zone 6, from Asia, grows to 5 cm (2 in) high, with white flowers, striped in green. *O. nutans*, zone 6, from southern Europe, is a hardy perennial, to 50 cm (20 in), with silvery flowers, lightly marked with green. *O. pyrenaicum*, zone 6, originally from southern Europe, grows to 90 cm (36 in) and produces yellow spring flowers, tinted with green. *O. thyrsoides*, chincherinchee, zone 9, a tender species native to South Africa, is popular as it provides good flowers for cutting. The sprays of beautiful, pure white flowers with showy, yellow stamens are borne on long stems.

Orthosiphon (fam. Lamiaceae)

Cat's whisker

There are about 40 species of these evergreen shrubs and perennials native to tropical regions of Africa, Asia and Australia. Few are cultivated as ornamentals, although they have great potential. Some species are suitable for container growing.

ABOVE The long, white, whiskery stamens on *Orthosiphon stramineus* give this flower a rather curious appearance.

CULTIVATION Outside the tropics, grow in a warm greenhouse or conservatory in pots of well drained, sandy, soil-based potting compost. They need ample water through the growing season, but should be kept drier in winter. Propagate from seed or cuttings taken from late spring through to early fall. Provide bottom heat for both.

CLIMATE Zone 10 to tropical.

SPECIES *O. stramineus*, the cat's whisker or whisker plant, grows to about 1 m (3 ft) high. It has squarish stems and opposite, mid-green leaves, toothed on the margins. The summer flowers are the palest blue to white and are carried upright on the tips of the stems. The long stamens curving out from the flower provide the whiskered effect.

Osbeckia (fam. Melastomataceae)

This genus of about 60 species of small shrubs is native to semi-tropical regions of many countries, including Africa, Australia and India. The majority of the species have slender, veined leaves and prominent flowers that vary from pink and violet to a rich, purplish red. The genus is very similar in appearance to *Tibouchina*, but with smaller leaves and flowers. Osbeckias are not readily available and are generally seen only seen in botanical gardens.

CULTIVATION Outside the tropics or subtropics, grow osbeckias in a warm greenhouse or conservatory, in pots of acid, soil-based potting compost. Provide good light, but shade the plants from direct, strong sun. Prune in late winter to restrict size, if necessary. Propagate from seed or semi-ripe cuttings, with bottom heat for both.

CLIMATE Tropical or subtropical.

SPECIES *O. stellata* is one of the cultivated species, found over a wide area from India to China. It is an upright to spreading shrub to 1.8 m (6 ft), with oval, deep green leaves which

ABOVE A species of *Osbeckia*. These tropical shrubs are related to Tibouchina but not as well known.

have conspicuous veins. Throughout summer it produces loose clusters of shallow, bowl-shaped flowers in shades of purple, rosy lilac, pink, or sometimes even white.

Osmanthus (fam. Oleaceae)

Native to Asia, the United States and Hawaii, this genus consists of 15 species of evergreen shrubs and trees. The flowers of most species are not showy, but the perfume is outstanding. The leaf shape and flowers vary according to species.

CULTIVATION Any garden soil will suit, though a sunny, sheltered spot is essential. Propagate from cuttings taken in late summer. Pruning is generally not necessary beyond a little shaping.

CLIMATE There are species suited to various climatic zones.

SPECIES *O. americanus*, zone 9, a native of the southern United States, grows up to 15 m (50 ft), with large, glossy leaves and creamy white, fragrant flowers. *O. delavayi*, zone 7, is a delightful shrub, to 2 m (6 ft) or more, with clusters of white, sweet-scented flowers, followed by purplish black berries. *O.* x *fortunei*, zone 7, a hybrid from Japan, grows to 3 m

ABOVE The flowers of *Osmanthus fragrans* are small, but wonderfully fragrant. Grow in a sheltered corner to confine the scent.

ABOVE *Osteospermum* copes with dry soil and hot, dry conditions. It is tough and useful as a groundcover for large areas.

(10 ft) high, with holly-like leaves and fragrant, white blooms. *O. fragrans*, zone 7, is a tender, compact shrub to 6 m (20 ft), with little clusters of pretty, small, fragrant, white flowers in fall, or in spring and summer, and finely toothed, oblong leaves with slender points. The flowers are used by the Chinese to flavor tea. Many describe the fragrance as that of sweet ripe apricots. *O. heterophyllus*, zone 6, is a hardy shrub, quick-growing to 5 m (16 ft) tall, with broad, holly-like leaves and clusters of white, fragrant, fall flowers.

Osteospermum (fam. Asteraceae)

Mainly from South Africa, this genus comprises 70 species of annuals, perennials and sub-shrubs. Growing no more than 1 m (3 ft) high, with attractive, daisy-like flowers that open only in sunlight, they are often used as summer bedding and patio-container plants, or, in frost-free climates, as groundcover.

CULTIVATION Osteospermums need warm, dry conditions and full sun for the flowers to look their best. They are easily propagated from cuttings. Established plants are very drought-tolerant.

CLIMATE Zone 9, but used as summer annuals in all climatic zones.

SPECIES *O. amplectans* grows to 1 m (3 ft), with smallish leaves and attractive, yellow flowers with yellow and purple centers. *O. ecklonis*, the most popular species, looks at its best mass planted in the wild garden or as a specimen in the rock garden. This perennial, shrub-like species grows to 1 m (3 ft) and produces white flowers, pale blue on the reverse, with a dark blue center. *O. fruticosum* is a shrubby perennial, to 60 cm (24 in), with narrow leaves and white and purple flowers. *O. jucundum*, a perennial, trailing species, grows to only 40 cm (16 in) high, with shiny, dark green foliage and a profusion of cerise flowers in spring. There are now many cultivars and hybrids available and these are probably more popular with home gardeners than the species.

Owenia (fam. Meliaceae)

These six species of Australian native trees produce a milky sap and small flowers, followed by acid fruit which is eaten by the Aborigines. They are unlikely to be available outside Australia.

ABOVE Although the flowers of *Owenia venosa* are small, the fruits that follow are large and succulent. This tree has great potential for use in arid regions.

CULTIVATION In frost-prone climates, grow in an intermediate to warm greenhouse or conservatory. Outdoors grow in a sunny spot with well-drained soil. Propagation may be successful from semi-ripe cuttings in late summer, rooted in a mix of three parts coarse sand to one part peat or vermiculite. If propagating from seed, make sure it is fresh. However, seed-raising is difficult and treatment is needed to break dormancy of the seed. Many of the usual methods have not proved very successful.

CLIMATE Zone 10 and above.

SPECIES *O. acidula*, sour plum or emu apple, is native to Queensland and New South Wales and generally grows to about 8 m (26 ft). It may be tree-like or shrubby in form, and has pendulous branches and reddish, acidic, thirst-quenching fruit.

Oxalis (fam. Oxalidaceae)

Widely distributed, the largest number of species come from South Africa and South America, although this genus also contains the ubiquitous weeds of American gardens, orna-

ABOVE *Oxalis purpurea* 'Alba' has silky, white flowers through fall and winter. It is not considered invasive.

mentals and perennial, tuberous or bulbous plants. They have tripartite leaves which fold up at night, a caustic sap with a sour taste, and spring or summer flowers. All of the weed species produce many bulbils, from which they are generally propagated.

CULTIVATION Grow the bulbous and tuberous species in sandy soil in full sun, and keep dry during the winter resting period. Because some of these species can be invasive, it is a good idea to contain them by growing in pots. Propagate the bulbous and tuberous species from the ripe seed which is expelled with great force from the seed capsules. The tuberous-rooted types can be grown from the bulbils they produce in spring or summer.

CLIMATE There are species suited to various climatic zones.

ABOVE *Oxalis obtusa*, from South Africa, has pretty, pink flowers with a yellow eye. This is not an invasive species.

ABOVE *Oxydendrum arboreum* carries sprays of white flowers in the summer and brilliant foliage color in the fall season.

SPECIES *O. adenophylla*, zone 5, has pink or mauve flowers. *O. carnosa*, zone 10, a succulent from Chile and Bolivia, grows to 10 cm (4 in) high. It has a tuberous root, thick, fleshy stems which become woody and somewhat gnarled, and yellow flowers in groups of three or four. *O. gigantea*, zone 9, from Chile, is a succulent shrub, to 2 m (6 ft) high, covered in fine hairs. It has drooping side branches, oval leaf lobes and yellow flowers. *O. hirta*, zone 9, has bright pink flowers in winter. *O. lobata*, zone 8, produces bright yellow flowers in late summer and fall. *O. pes-caprae*, soursob, zone 9, is a stemless perennial. The leaves are generally marked with small, purple spots and the flowers are yellow. It is a common weed of cereal crops in some countries. *O. purpurea* 'Alba', zone 8, has large silky white flowers in winter. There is also a burgundy-leaved form of *O. purpurea* with striking, hot pink flowers. *O. succulenta*, zone 9, a succulent from Chile and Peru, has a short, thick-branched, scaly stem and small, deciduous leaflets on thick, fleshy stalks. Many small, yellow flowers grow on the forked stalks. Some of the more attractive oxalis species worthy of cultivation include *O. adenophylla*, *O. hirta*, *O. lobata* and *O. purpurea*.

Oxydendrum (fam. Ericaceae)

Native to the Americas, this genus contains only one species of deciduous tree, generally grown as an ornamental or lawn specimen.

CULTIVATION Plant in a well-drained, lime-free soil mulched with leaf mould or cow manure. Keep well watered during spring and summer. For propagation, use cuttings, layers or seed.

CLIMATE Zone 5. Best in a cool, moist climate.

SPECIES *O. arboreum*, sourwood, grows to 15–20 m (50–65 ft), with green, bitter-tasting leaves, around 15 cm (6 in) long, that turn crimson during fall, and sprays of white, bell-shaped flowers during summer. It is sometimes grown to attract bees.

Oxylobium (fam. Papilionaceae)
Shaggy pea

These small, open-growing evergreen shrubs are native to Australia. Although most species are poisonous to stock, they make small, attractive garden shrubs as they have interesting

ABOVE *Oxylobium ilicifolium* is an erect, sometimes straggly, shrub, with interesting holly-shaped leaves and bright yellow pea flowers during spring.

foliage and brightly colored, pea flowers. They are worthwhile growing in hot, dry conditions.

CULTIVATION In climatic zones below 9, grow in a cool, airy greenhouse. Outdoors, oxyloblums prefer hot, dry, sandy soils, but will grow in any ordinary garden soil in a sunny position. Propagate from the hard-coated seed, first placing it in boiling water and allowing it to stand for a day. The resulting, swollen seed will germinate readily. Cuttings also strike easily. Do not transplant established shrubs.

CLIMATE Zone 9.

SPECIES Not all of the following species are available outside Australia. *O. ellipticum*, common shaggy pea, is an alpine species, to 2.5 m (8 ft) high, with yellow and brown flowers. *O. ilicifolium* has holly-like leaves and bright yellow flowers. It grows to 2 m (6 ft). *O. lanceolatum*, to 3 m (10 ft), produces sprays of orange flowers. *O. procumbens* is a dwarf species, which makes a very good groundcover, with oval- to heart-shaped leaves and clusters of orange-red flowers. *O. scandens*, a prostrate or climbing species, has yellow flowers. *O. robus-*

tum is a small tree, to 4 m (13 ft), with orange-yellow, spring and summer flowers.

Oxypetalum (syn. *Tweedia*, fam. Asclepiadaceae)

The species grown, *O. caeruleum* (syn. *Tweedia caerulea*), a native of South America, Brazil and Uruguay, has sky blue, summer flowers.

CULTIVATION In frost-prone climates, grow in a cool to intermediate greenhouse, in a pot of soil-based potting compost. Provide good light. In late winter, cut back old flowered shoots to within three or four buds of their base. Outdoors grow in a warm frost-free situation in light, well-drained soil. Can also be grown as an annual – sow early spring. Propagate from seed or softwood cuttings, both with bottom heat.

CLIMATE Zone 10.

SPECIES *O. caeruleum* (syn. *Tweedia caerulea*) is a shrubby, twining climber, to around 1 m (3 ft) high. It has hairy, pale green foliage and pretty, powder blue, starry flowers, and boat-shaped, green seed pods.

ABOVE Flowers of *Oxypetalum caeruleum* are an uncommon shade of blue. These flowers emerge from pink-flushed buds.

P

Pachyphytum to Pyrus

Pachyphytum (fam. Crassulaceae)

There are around 12 species of low-growing, branched, perennial succulents in this interesting and attractive genus from Mexico. They have loose rosettes of very thick, smooth, rounded leaves, sometimes covered with thick, white powdery meal. The inflorescence is borne on a single, thick stem which straightens up as the flowers open. The flowers of some species are similar to those of *Echeveria* but shorter. Other species have flowers that appear hooded because the thick calyx is much longer than the petals.

CULTIVATION In frost-prone climates, grow in an intermediate greenhouse or conservatory, in pots of well-drained cactus compost. Plants need maximum light but shade from strong sun. When plants are in growth, water in moderation, but keep compost quite dry in winter. Propagate from seed in spring, or from leaf or stem cuttings in summer. Provide bottom heat for both.

CLIMATE Warmest parts of zone 10.

SPECIES *P. compactum* is a very compact plant, with dense, flattened, blueish mauve leaves, which come to a point at the end. The flowers are reddish orange, with blueish tips and pink sepals. *P. hookeri* has green, spindle-shaped leaves and red flowers, with green tips and short, pinkish sepals. *P. oviferum* is the most beautiful of the species, resembling sugared almonds. It has very white, egg-shaped leaves and drooping clusters of very hooded, dark red flowers from the end of winter to early spring. Fine hybrids of *Pachyphytum* and *Echeveria*, known as x *Pachyveria*, have been produced.

Pachypodium (fam. Apocynaceae)

Mostly native to Madagascar, these upright, perennial succulents range in size from low-growing forms to trees up to 10 m (33 ft) tall. All have the characteristic swollen stems and are very fleshy. Most have spines. The leathery leaves are arranged spirally on the stems. The white, yellow or red flowers are borne at the ends of the stems, sometimes before the leaves appear. These plants are usually cultivated by the specialist grower or collector.

CULTIVATION Outside the tropics, grow in a warm greenhouse or conservatory in pots of cactus compost. Give maximum light. Water in moderation when in growth and keep dry in winter. Propagate from seed in spring, germinated at 21°C (70°F).

ABOVE Commonly called the sugar-almond plant, *Pachyphytum oviferum* has pale green leaves that are covered with a white, powdery bloom.

ABOVE Curious-looking *Pachypodium lamerei* has a grey, spiny trunk topped with leathery leaves.

CLIMATE Tropical only.

SPECIES *P. lamerei*, Madagascar palm, can grow eventually to about 6 m (20 ft). It is, of course, not a palm but its appearance may give that impression. It should reach flowering size of about 1 m (3 ft) after 10 years or so. The swollen trunk is gray-brown and covered in sharp spines. The very fragrant, white flowers, with gold throats, resemble those of frangipani. They appear from midsummer through to early fall. *P. namaquanum*, ghost man, has a thick, fleshy stem, to 3 m (10 ft) high, and covered in thorns. The narrow, wavy leaves, about 12 cm (5 in) long, form tufts at the top of the trunk. This species produces many purple-red flowers, striped yellow inside. *P. succulentum*, from South Africa's Cape Province, is a shrub-like succulent, with sturdy, very thorny branches and slightly hairy leaves. The small flowers range in color from pink to crimson, sometimes with red stripes.

Pachysandra (fam. Buxaceae)

Native to eastern Asia and North America, some of these glossy green creeping perennials make good groundcovers for semi-shaded areas of the garden. Only three species are in general cultivation.

ABOVE Revelling in moist, humus-rich, soil, *Pachysandra terminalis* makes a pretty groundcover for cool to mild regions.

CULTIVATION Plant in a moist, partially shaded position and propagate from cuttings taken in summer, or by division of the plants during spring. Give ample water during spring and summer.

CLIMATE Zone 5.

SPECIES *P. procumbens*, from North America, grows 20–30 cm (8–12 in) high, with broadly ovate leaves and mostly greenish cream (occasionally purplish pink) flowers. *P. terminalis*, from China and Japan, has leathery, ovate leaves, toothed at the tips, and terminal spikes of white flowers, marked with pink, in early summer. It grows to 30 cm (12 in). Cultivar 'Variegata' has leaves streaked with white.

Pachystachys (fam. Acanthaceae)

Originating from tropical America and the West Indies, this genus consists of 12 species of small, evergreen shrubs and perennials, sometimes included in the genus *Jacobinia*. The large leaves are distinctly veined and the large,

ABOVE The yellow bracts of *Pachystachys lutea* are far more decorative than the tiny, white flowers that emerge from them.

attractive flowers are borne on thick, terminal spikes. They come in bright red, yellow or purple. The flower bracts are often more colorful than the flowers themselves.

CULTIVATION Outside the tropics and subtropics, grow in a warm, humid greenhouse or conservatory, in pots of soil-based potting compost. Provide good light, but shade from strong sun. Trim lightly after flowering to maintain a good shape. Propagate from softwood cuttings, with basal warmth.

CLIMATE Warmest parts of zone 10 to tropical.

SPECIES *P. coccinea*, cardinal's guard, is a small, bushy shrub, to 1.5 m (5 ft), with dark green leaves, 20 cm (8 in) long and about 10 cm (4 in) wide, and red flower spikes, to 15 cm (6 in). *P. lutea* grows to 1 m (3 ft), with 15 cm (6 in) long leaves and shorter spikes of yellow and white flowers. This species is sometimes grown as a house plant.

Paeonia (fam. Paeoniaceae)
Peony, paeony

This genus, originating from temperate parts of Europe, China and North America, was formerly considered a member of the Ranunculaceae family, but is now in its own family. Comprising around 33 species, the genus is divided into herbaceous perennials and tree types. Cultivars of the herbaceous plants are mainly derived from *P. lactiflora*, while the tree peony cultivars are usually derivatives of *P. suffruticosa*. Both types flower in spring to early summer. Most of the perennials have large, exquisite, ruffled flowers ranging from pink, mauve and purple to white and yellow, and some have huge, poppylike, single flowers. Both the perennial and tree peonies are widely grown in the US and are among the most popular hardy garden plants. The tree peony originated from China and was introduced into Korea and Japan between the sixth and eighth centuries. By careful selection, the Japanese tree peony has developed quite

ABOVE The sumptuous flowers of *Paeonia* 'Bowl of Beauty' sit aloft stems 90 cm (36 in) high. This is a popular cultivar.

differently from its antecedent in China. It has a wider color range and a more robust character. The tree peony is deciduous in winter; the flowers are similar to those of the herbaceous type, but usually about 30 cm (12 in) across, and may also be single or double. In cultivation the tree peony grows only to shrub proportions, usually reaching 2–2.5 m (6–8 ft) high.

CULTIVATION Plant the herbaceous species in deep, well-drained soil and enrich with well-rotted compost during fall. They will grow in sun or semi-shade. Propagation is best by division during late fall or early spring, but they will grow from seed. Plants may remain undivided for up to ten years. Tree peonies will grow in any soil, provided it is well drained. They prefer a sheltered situation. Dress with blood, fish and bone in spring.

CLIMATE Zone 6, unless otherwise specified below.

SPECIES *P. delavayi* is a tree type, growing to about 2 m (6 ft), with dark maroon flowers. *P. emodi*, zone 8, from India, grows to 1 m (3 ft) high, producing single, white flowers. *P. lacti-*

ABOVE *Paeonia officinalis* 'Rubra Plena' is a popular cultivar that flowers in the early and middle parts of summer.

flora, to 1 m (3 ft) high, has single, fragrant, white flowers, to 10 cm (4 in) across. Many cultivars have been produced from this species in shades of white, pink, red and purple in single, semi-double and double forms. *P. lutea*, from China, has saw-toothed leaves and single, yellow flowers. This tree-type species grows to about 2 m (6 ft). *P. mlokosewitschii*, from the Caucasus, grows to 90 cm (36 in), with pale green leaves, hairy on the undersides, that darken with maturity, and single, open, pale yellow flowers, to 12 cm (5 in) across. *P. officinalis*, zone 8, from Europe, is believed to have been used medicinally by the ancient Greeks. It grows to 60 cm (24 in), with lobed leaves and single, bright red, rose-like flowers. Subspecies *humilis* has dark pink to red flowers. Cultivar 'Alba Plena' produces double, white flowers; 'Rosea Plena' double, pink flowers; and 'Rubra Plena', double, crimson flowers. *P. peregrina*, zone 8, from southern Europe, has deeply divided leaves and cup-shaped, deep red flowers. It grows to 60 cm (24 in). Many glorious cultivars have been produced from most of the species, and are generally more available than the species. *P. suffruticosa*, zone 5, from China, bears single, cup-shaped flowers in white, pink, red or purple. Both flowers and leaves are very large. Many beautiful cultivars of this tree type are available.

Pandanus (fam. Pandanaceae)
Screw pine

Occurring mostly in countries around the Pacific and Indian Oceans, but not the Americas, this group of large plants has many practical uses for the indigenous peoples of these regions. The leaves are used for thatching, basketry, mats, cordage and chair seats, while some species provide edible fruits. Recognized by their stilt roots and large rosettes of vaguely palm-like leaves, they are a common sight on tropical coasts, although some species occur naturally in forests. In their habitats, these trees may grow between 6 and 15 m (20–50 ft) high, becoming strongly branched with age. They have long, sword-like leaves that bend and droop at the ends. Male and female flowers are produced on separate plants, so trees of both sexes are needed to produce the large, pineapple-like fruits. Outside the tropics or subtropics, grow pandanus for its foliage as a house plant or in a warm greenhouse or conservatory.

ABOVE The large, distinctive fruits of *Pandanus tectorius* are edible. Male flowers of this species are fragrant.

CULTIVATION Under glass or in the home, grow in pots of soil-based potting compost. Plants need good bright light (but shade from direct strong sun), and a very humid atmosphere. Propagate from seed sown as soon as available (newly ripened seed is best) and germinate at 21°C (70°F). Soak seed in tepid water for a day before sowing. Alternatively, propagate from suckers in spring.

CLIMATE Warmest parts of zone 10 to tropical.

SPECIES Not all are available outside their native countries. *P. cookii*, from Queensland in Australia, grows 6–9 m (20–30 ft) tall , with slender, wide-spreading branches and sparse, fairly narrow leaves, 1–2 m (3–6 ft) long. The egg-shaped fruit is a dull, deep pink when ripe. *P. monticola*, from high rainfall forests of northern Queensland, is an unusual species, with very slender, scrambling branches and long, very narrow, deep green leaves. It has yellowish fruits which are different from those of other Australian species. *P. pedunculatus*, from eastern Australia and south-western Pacific islands, is similar in habit to *P. tectorius*. *P. tectorius* occurs mainly in seashore areas of Southeast Asia and Polynesia, although it is sometimes found in coastal Queensland and on nearby Barrier Reef islands. A much-branched, spreading plant, it grows to a height and width of around 8 m (26 ft). The fruits are an orange-red color when ripe. Two variegated cultivars which make good house or conservatory plants are 'Sanderi', which has leaves with a narrow, golden yellow, central stripe, and 'Veitchii', which has leaves with white-striped margins.

Pandorea (fam. Bignoniaceae)

Native to Australia, Malaysia and New Caledonia, this small genus of evergreen, twining climbers was named after the Pandora of Greek mythology. Grown for their beautiful, bell-shaped flowers and glossy, pinnate leaves, most species are fairly easy to cultivate and make excellent trellis plants. Except in warm climates, grow in an intermediate greenhouse or conservatory.

ABOVE *Pandorea pandorana* 'Snow Bells' is a vigorous climber which blooms prolifically in winter and spring.

CULTIVATION Under glass, grow in a large pot of soil-based potting compost. Provide good light, but shade from direct, strong sun. Give regular water in the growing season but reduce considerably in winter. Prune after flowering to keep plant within allotted space. Outdoors grow in full sun with moist yet well-drained soil. Propagate from seeds in spring or from semi-ripe cuttings in summer, both in a heated propagating case (or carry out layering in spring).

CLIMATE Warmest parts of zone 10 to tropical.

SPECIES *P. doratoxylon* is a shrubby climber found in most of the states of Australia, with large clusters of yellow flowers from late winter to late summer. *P. jasminoides*, bower plant, is a lovely species from a coastal rainforest habitat. The white, trumpet-shaped flowers, with deep red throats, appear from spring to summer. Cultivar 'Alba' has larger, pure white flowers; 'Rosea' has large, pinkish red flowers, with purple throats. *P. pandorana*, wonga-wonga vine, is a robust climber which has dense, terminal sprays of white to yellow flowers with red to purple spots and stripes inside the throat. There are various forms, including the beautiful 'Snowbells', which produces masses of pure white flowers. The fruits are flattened capsules, containing numerous seeds which ripen to brown.

Papaver (fam. Papaveraceae)
Poppy

Consisting of around 80 species, these delightful annuals and perennials are very popular, bedding and border plants. They have long stems and delicate, cupped flowers in a range of oranges, yellows and reds, pink, cream and white in summer. These plants produce a milky sap and capsule-shaped fruit, containing many fine seeds.

CULTIVATION Poppies prefer a rich, light, well-drained soil, a full-sun position, and protection from wind. Poppies are easily raised from seed. Sow the seeds of annuals and biennials outdoors in spring. Seedlings dislike disturbance, so do not transplant them. Seeds of perennials are sown at the same time but ideally in seed trays in a garden frame. Pot up seedlings and then plant them out when they are large enough. Perennial poppies can also be propa-

ABOVE Blood red Flanders poppies, *Papaver rhoeas*, light up this border in summer and contrast well with the green and gray foliage of other plants.

gated by division in spring or by root cuttings taken in winter. Cut the flowers of poppies for indoor floral displays early in the morning and plunge the ends of the stems into boiling water for about 15 seconds, before arranging the blooms in a vase.

CLIMATE There are species suited to various climatic zones.

SPECIES *P. croceum*, Iceland poppy, is a biennial, usually grown as an annual. It forms a rosette of pale green foliage from which emerge tall flower stems carrying saucer-shaped blooms in shades of yellow, red, orange, cream, pink or white in summer. There are many cultivars of Iceland poppy: 'Champagne Bubbles' has a wide range of soft colors, including pink and red and several shades of yellow; 'Oregon Rainbows' has quite large blooms in mixed colors, some being picotees and bicolors; and 'Wonderland' is a low grower in single or mixed colors. *P. orientale*, Oriental poppy, is a tall-growing perennial with long, toothed and divided

ABOVE Mass plantings of Iceland poppies, *Papaver croceum*, are guaranteed to lift the spirits in summer. There are several cultivars in mixtures of colors.

leaves and large, orange to scarlet flowers, with purple-black centres. There are many beautiful cultivars available, including 'Cedric Morris', with large, pink, frilly flowers, and 'Picotee', with white flowers, and almost pleated petals, margined in pinky orange. Flowering occurs from late spring to midsummer. *P. rhoeas* is an annual known to many as the Flanders poppy. Naturalized in many parts of the world where it may also be known as the field or corn poppy, it has saucer-shaped, deep red flowers, often marked in black at the base, during summer. Cultivars of this species are available, some having double flowers in red, white or pink. The famous Shirley poppies are a selection of this species, with single or double flowers, in various colors. *P. somniferum*, the opium poppy, has very large flowers in pink, white, red or mauve. Double forms sold as 'Paeony flowered' have very frilly blooms in a lovely range of colors.

Paphiopedilum (fam. Orchidaceae)
Slipper orchid

These orchids are mainly native to Southeast Asia, with some occurring in the Himalayas, through to China, and south to Papua New Guinea. They come from diverse habitats, from areas at sea level to mountainous areas with altitudes of over 2000 m (6500 ft). Many species are threatened in the wild so few are offered for sale, but an enormous range of cultivars and hybrids is available from specialist growers.

CULTIVATION Grow paphiopedilums in an intermediate greenhouse with minimum temperature of 13°C (55°F). Grow them in small pots with bark-based orchid compost (formulated for terrestrial orchids), available from specialist growers. In summer, plants need good light (but shade from direct sun), a humid atmosphere, and frequent watering. Feed every seven to ten days. In winter, plants need maximum light, reduced humidity, and much reduced watering (keep compost slightly but steadily moist). Propagate from side shoot cuttings.

ABOVE Large hybrids of slipper orchids have an intricate flower structure. The flowers are shiny and waxy, and look almost artificial.

CLIMATE Tropical.

SPECIES *P. bellatulum*, from Thailand and Burma, has creamy white, summer flowers, heavily spotted with maroon, and checkered leaves. *P. concolor*, from Burma and southwestern China, is a dwarf species, mostly with pale yellow, summer flowers, finely spotted with purple. *P. insigne* is a cool-growing species with long-lasting, yellowish green flowers, marked with brown and white. The lip is a yellowish brown color. Flowering is in late fall to early winter. *P. niveum*, from Thailand, has white flowers, faintly dotted with purple, in summer. *P. parishii* is a native of Thailand, Burma and south-western China. Dark purple and green flowers, with long, twisted, pendulous petals and green lips, appear in the summer. *P. philippinense*, from the Philippines, produces long sprays of drooping, hairy, reddish purple flowers, with white sepals and yellow lips, from summer to fall.

Paradisea (fam. Asphodelaceae)

The two species in this genus are native to moist woodlands and meadows of southern Europe. Clump-forming perennials, their flowers are fragrant and make lovely cut blooms.

ABOVE *Paradisea liliastrum* will bloom prolifically in suitable conditions. Like all lilies, these make lovely cut flowers.

ABOVE Spires of pale blue or white flowers of *Parahebe derwentiana* appear in greatest profusion when grown in shade in cool districts.

CULTIVATION These plants like a well-drained soil and a moist, semi-shaded situation. They grow well in cooler, coastal regions, with some wind and sun protection. Propagate by division in early spring. Plant the rhizomes 15–20 cm (6–8 in) deep and then leave undisturbed.

CLIMATE Zone 7.

SPECIES *P. liliastrum*, St Bruno's lily, from mountainous areas of southern Europe, is a herbaceous perennial, growing to about 40 cm (16 in) high, from a rhizomatous rootstock. White, funnel-shaped flowers are borne on long, thin stems in early summer. The strap-like leaves are grayish green in color. Cultivar 'Major' grows twice as high as the species, also producing much larger flowers. *P. lusitanicum*, from Portugal, may grow over 80 cm (32 in) in height. Its white, summer flowers are borne in large numbers on strong stems.

Parahebe (fam. Scrophulariaceae)

Once classified with *Veronica*, this genus of around 30 species of small, dense, evergreen shrubs mostly from New Zealand, with a few that are native to Australia and New Guinea, is very closely related to *Hebe*. *Parahebe* species differ from *Veronica* in their fruit, which is a flattened capsule. They look very pretty grown in rock gardens and borders, flowering from summer through to late fall.

CULTIVATION *Parahebe* will grow in any well-drained soil. Propagate by division during spring, or by firm tip cuttings taken in summer. Cut back established plants after flowering is complete. Although frost-tolerant, they prefer shelter from strong wind in cold areas.

CLIMATE Zone 8 for most species.

SPECIES *P. catarractae*, waterfall veronica, from New Zealand, has a semi-prostrate habit, becoming more upright with maturity. It bears small sprays of white, funnel-shaped flowers, tinged with purple. *P. linifolia*, from New Zealand, is a dwarf, branching shrub, growing to about 25 cm (10 in), with white to pale pink flowers. *P. lyallii*, from New Zealand, is a many-branched, semi-prostrate shrub, with terminal spikes of small, white to pink flowers and oval, serrated, leathery, green leaves. *P. perfoliata*, digger's speedwell, zone 9, is a tender species from south-eastern parts of Australia. Growing 50–100 cm (20–40 in) in height, it has long sprays of lovely, dainty, blue to purple flowers and attractive, grayish blue foliage, tinged with purple when young.

Parodia (fam. Cactaceae)

Native to mountainous regions of South America, these small to medium cactuses are generally globe-shaped. Many are solitary growers, while others produce offsets to form clumps. The stems are ribbed, and brightly colored spines often protrude from the tubercles. The spines are variable and may be bristly and soft, or strong, and straight or hooked. The funnel-shaped flowers, which may be yellow, orange or red, protrude from the woolly crown of the plant, even when still quite young. (See also entry for *Notocactus*.)

CULTIVATION These cactuses are easy to grow, but need an intermediate greenhouse or conservatory in frost-prone climates. Grow in pots of well-drained cactus compost. Provide maximum light (but shade from direct strong sun), and a dry airy atmosphere. Apply water in moderation during the growing season, but keep dry in winter. : Outdoors grow in well-drained soil and full sun but with shade during the hottest part of the day. Propagate in spring from seed germinated at 21°C (70°F).

ABOVE Parodias are generally small, globe-shaped, densely spiny cactuses which produce large, brightly colored flowers in spring or summer.

CLIMATE Warmest parts of zone 9 and above.

SPECIES *P. aureispina* is a medium-sized plant with notched ribs, yellow spines, the central one hooked, the others bristly, and golden yellow flowers, 4 cm (1½ in) in diameter. *P. chrysacanthion* is a smaller type, densely covered with fine, yellow spines. The golden yellow flowers are only 2 cm (¾ in) in diameter. *P. maassii* has a large number of spirally arranged ribs and yellow, needle-like spines. The flowers are a coppery or red color 3 cm (1 in) across. *P. nivosa* is a round to egg-shaped cactus, growing to only 15 cm (6 in) in height. Difficult to cultivate and frost-sensitive, it has a pure white, woolly crown and rich red flowers, to about 5 cm (2 in) in diameter. *P. penicillata* is a large plant, about 30 cm (12 in) high, which has tufts of stiff white, yellow or brown spines and produces beautiful, red flowers. Its form becomes cylindrical with age.

Paronychia (fam. Illecebraceae)

This genus of 50 small, annual and evergreen, perennial creepers is widely distributed throughout the world. Only a few are cultivated, mainly as groundcovers. Two of the species, *P. argentea* and *P. capitata*, are used medicinally in some parts of the world.

CULTIVATION Plant in any type of soil, provided it is well drained. *Paronychia* can be grown in semi-shade or in warm, dry rockeries. Propagate from seed sown in early spring, or by division of the plants in spring.

CLIMATE Zone 6 or 7.

SPECIES *P. argentea*, a perennial from southern Europe, is a mat-forming plant, to 30 cm (12 in) wide, with heads of tiny flowers, surrounded by silvery bracts, in summer. It was formerly used in folk medicine. *P. argyrocoma*, a perennial from North America, grows to 30 cm (12 in). Silvery hairs cover the entire plant and tiny flowers appear in dense clusters. *P. capitata*, a compact perennial from the Mediterranean,

ABOVE Dense flower clusters of *Paronychia argentea* decorate the plant in summer. This plant does well where summers are hot and dry.

ABOVE Through all its stages of fall color change, *Parrotia persica* is an attractive asset to the garden.

forms a grayish green mat. Tiny, green, spring flowers are contained in the silvery bracts. *P. sessiliflora*, a perennial from North America, has mat-like growth and yellowish green foliage. *P. virginica*, also a perennial from North America, grows to 45 cm (18 in) high. It has branched sprays of tiny flowers in short, silver bracts.

Parrotia (fam. Hamamelidaceae)
Persian ironwood

Native to south-western Asia, particularly the area around the Caspian Sea, this genus consists of only one species. It is a lovely, small but spreading tree used as a lawn specimen or in an open position in a woodland garden or shrub border.

CULTIVATION Grow in well-drained soil in full sun. Sun is essential for obtaining the best fall foliage colors. Pruning is generally unnecessary beyond initial training to establish one single trunk. Propagate from seed sown in fall in a garden frame, from semi-ripe cuttings in summer, or by layering in spring.

CLIMATE Zone 5.

SPECIES *P. persica*, Persian ironwood or Persian witch-hazel, is a small, deciduous, spreading tree, growing between 6 and 10 m (20–33 ft) tall. It produces dense heads of bright red, petal-less flowers in spring. The 12 cm (5 in) long leaves appear after the flowers, turning brilliant yellow, orange and finally red in fall.

Parsley (*Petroselinum crispum*, fam. Apiaceae)

Originating from southern Europe, parsley is now found in most regions of the world. Valued as both a sacred and a medicinal plant by the ancients, it is now known to contain iron, vitamin A and vitamin C. The oil from this plant is used in drugs that have been developed for the treatment of malaria, and parsley tea is reputed to be beneficial, especially for diabetics. But it is as a culinary herb that it is best known, and is generally considered an essential item in the herb garden. Delicious when used with butter and lemon when cooking fish, it is equally pleasing in salads, egg dishes, sauces, soups and stews. Parsley is complementary to other herbs, and combines with chervil, chives and tarragon to make up what is called *fines herbes*.

ABOVE Parsley is included in many recipes and is used as a garnish for hot and cold dishes. Its bright, emerald green is also utilized in the ornamental garden.

CULTIVATION Sow seed in spring in 1 cm (⅓ in) deep drills, directly where it is to grow, or in modules under glass. Plant out when large enough to handle, and space seedlings 20–30 cm (8–12 in) apart. Use a rich, well-drained soil that retains moisture. Parsley can be grown in either partial shade or in full sun. Sow fresh seed each year to obtain better quality plants. The seed is slow to germinate, sometimes taking between three and six weeks. Once established, occasional applications of nitrogen fertilizer or soluble liquid fertilizer will assist strong, leafy growth.

CLIMATE Zone 6.

VARIETIES *Petroselinum crispum* is an aromatic biennial, treated as an annual in the garden, which produces a thick taproot and a rosette of tightly curled, serrated, bright green foliage on long stalks. The small yellow flowers are borne in umbrella-like clusters. There are two main types of parsley cultivated, the most popular being curled-leaved. Flat-leaved or French parsley is considered to have a better flavor. There are numerous cultivars of both types. Another type is Hamburg parsley, sometimes called turnip-rooted parsley, *P. crispum* var. *tuberosum* has roots which resemble parsnips and leaves which can be used in the same way as ordinary parsley. The roots are used as a cooked vegetable and have a delicious flavor.

Parsnip (*Pastinaca sativa*, fam. Apiaceae)

A native of eastern Europe, the parsnip belongs to the same family as vegetables and herbs such as fennel, parsley, celery, chervil and carrots. All requiring a long, cool season to develop, they are nevertheless easy to grow and keep well. The parsnip is a biennial, cultivated as an annual. The long, tapered, highly flavored root is the part we eat, although it also contains a volatile oil and can be used in the production of wine and beer. Known to the ancient Greeks and cultivated since the Middle Ages, parsnips are an essential part of the perfect roast dinner.

CULTIVATION Parsnips grow well in regions with cold and cool winters but are also suited to milder climates. A deeply dug, well-drained bed, heavily fertilized from a previous crop, will produce the best results. Sow fresh seed in mid-spring, in 1–2 cm (⅓–¾ in) deep drills, spaced 30 cm (15 in) apart. Sow groups of three to four seeds, 15 cm (6 in) apart. Keep the soil steadily moist until the seeds germinate, which may take around two weeks. The groups of seedlings are thinned out, leaving the strongest one at each station. The top growth of parsnips is frost-tender and will be killed back, but the

ABOVE These parsnips are close to maturity. Harvest when the roots are a moderate size; do not wait until they are coarse and stringy

roots can remain in the ground all winter; pull them as needed. In fact, the flavor of parsnips is improved by frost. The roots can also be lifted and stored for several months in boxes of damp sand, in a cool place.

CLIMATE Zone 6.

VARIETIES Parsnips are subject to a disease known as parsnip canker but resistant cultivars are available, and these, of course, should be grown in preference to cultivars that are non-resistant. There are many cultivars of parsnip but they vary from one country to another. It is best to buy from a reputable mail-order seed company.

Passiflora (fam. Passifloraceae)
Passion flower

There are around 500 species of these showy tendril climbers, including the familiar passionfruit, primarily from the tropical Americas. The flower of *Passiflora* was viewed by the Spanish missionaries who accompanied the conquistadores to South America as a symbolic representation of the Passion and Crucifixion of Jesus. The ten petals represented the ten apostles, the five stamens and five sepals were seen as the five wounds of Christ, and the blue to purple corona recalled the crown of thorns. The flowers come in a range of colors, including pink, white, blue, purple and scarlet, depending on the species. Many are grown for their brilliant, showy blossoms, while some species, such as *P. edulis* (passionfruit), *P. laurifolia* and *P. quadrangularis*, are cultivated for their delicious fruit. In frost-prone climates, most species need to be grown in an intermediate to warm greenhouse or conservatory.

CULTIVATION Under glass, grow in a soil border, or in a large pot or tub of soil-based potting compost. Give maximum light, but shade from direct strong sun. Outdoors, plant in well-drained, yet moisture-retentive soil. Plants will thrive in full sun or partial shade but need pro-

ABOVE Scarlet-flowered passion flower, *Passiflora coccinea*, provides a continuous display of bright flowers over several months.

tection from cold winds. Plants can be pruned in early spring by cutting back all side shoots to within three or four buds of the main stems. Propagate from semi-ripe cuttings in summer, rooted with bottom heat, or by layering in spring.

CLIMATE There are species suited to various climatic zones.

SPECIES *P.* x *alatocaerulea*, zone 9, used in perfume, has white and pink to purple flowers. *P.* x *allardii*, zone 9, produces flowers with pale pink petals and a deep blue corona. *P. antioquiensis*, banana passionfruit, zone 9, is a vigorous species, with bright red flowers. Cultivated banana passionfruit is more often *Passiflora mollissima*, zone 8. *P. cinnabarina*, red passion flower, zone 10, produces flowers with scarlet petals and sepals and a yellow corona, in spring. *P. coccinea*, red or scarlet flowering passionfruit, zone 10, is a vigorous plant with bright scarlet flowers, borne over a long period from midsummer into fall. *P. mixta*, zone 10, has pink to orange-red sepals and petals and a lavender to purple corona.

P. racemosa, zone 10, bears crimson flowers with a purple corona, banded in red or white. *P. vitifolia*, zone 10, produces small, scarlet flowers with a red to bright yellow corona and delicious-smelling, ovoid, yellow-green fruit.

Passionfruit

(*Passiflora edulis*, fam. Passifloraceae)

Purple granadilla

A native of Brazil, the common passionfruit is now grown in most of the warmer regions of the world, and in countries like Australia and New Zealand it is an important economic crop. The delicious, pulpy flesh of the fruit is eaten raw and also widely used in tarts, fruit salads and other sweets. In climates prone to frosts, it can be grown in an intermediate to warm greenhouse or conservatory.

CULTIVATION Under glass, grow in a soil border, or in a large pot or tub of soil-based potting compost. Provide maximum light but shade from direct strong sun. Bear in mind that this plant can take up a lot of space, even when trained into the roof of the greenhouse. The plant should be pruned in early spring by cutting back all side shoots to within three or four buds of the main stems. Propagate from semi-ripe cuttings in summer, rooted with bottom heat, or by layering in spring. Under glass, there are several pests that may attack it, particularly scale insects, mealy bugs, red spider mites and whitefly.

CLIMATE Zone 10.

SPECIES *Passiflora edulis*, passionfruit, is an evergreen, tendril climbing vine, with dark purple to nearly black fruit, about 7 cm (3 in) long, containing a pleasantly flavored, tart, yellowish pulp and many, soft, black seeds. Both the pulp and the seeds are edible. *P. mollissima*, banana passionfruit, is a vigorous plant. It is one of the hardier passifloras and can be grown outdoors in zone 8, provided it is in a sunny position and very well sheltered from

ABOVE Both the flowers and foliage of *Passiflora edulis* are decorative. This species grows easily and crops well in warm climates.

cold drying winds. This species produces heavy crops of long, yellow, very acid fruit, containing more pulp than other types. *P. quadrangularis*, granadilla, is widely cultivated in tropical areas for its large, edible fruits, which can grow to over 20 cm (8 in) long. The flowers are extremely decorative, so this vine is worth growing for its floral display alone.

Patersonia (fam. Iridaceae)

Native iris, native flag

Most of these 13 species of iris-like plants originate from Australia, although there are species native to Papua New Guinea, Borneo and Sumatra. Clump-forming perennials with underground rhizomes, they have narrow, upright, grass-like leaves and lovely, blue to light purple flowers on long stems, from papery bracts. Like iris, the flowers can occasionally be yellow or white. While usually lasting less than a day, a succession of blooms appear over a long period in spring and summer. In frost-prone climates, grow them in a cool to intermediate greenhouse or conservatory.

ABOVE The delicate flowers of *Patersonia glabrata* last only one day, but new ones appear daily over many months.

CULTIVATION Under glass, grow in pots of well-drained, soil-based potting compost. Plants need maximum light, but do not subject them to direct strong sun. They need regular watering in the growing season, but should be kept only slightly moist in winter. Outdoors these plants need a sandy, well-drained soil and full sun. Propagate in spring from seed germinated at 18°C (64°F), or by division in fall. Plants benefit from division every four years.

CLIMATE Zone 10.

SPECIES Not all are available outside their countries of origin. *P. fragilis*, from eastern and southern parts of Australia, is a small, tufting plant with grass-like leaves, 15–40 cm (6–16 in) long. The mauve to purple flowers are borne on stems shorter than the foliage, in spring and early summer. *P. glabrata*, from eastern Australia, with violet, three-lobed flowers, in spring and summer, is very similar to *P. fragilis*. *P. longiscapa*, purple flag, is a species from south-eastern Australia, with purplish mauve flowers, from spring to summer. Tolerating damp soils, it will grow anywhere there is sufficient moisture. An excellent, white-flowered

form is also available. *P. occidentalis*, from Western Australia, grows 30–60 cm (12–24 in) high and has large purple flowers, in spring and summer. *P. sericea*, from eastern Australia, grows to 30 cm (12 in) or more. The deep purple flowers, which fade to mauve, are produced in summer. The whole plant tends to be covered in fine, woolly hairs.

Paulownia (fam. Scrophulariaceae)

Native to China and eastern Asia, these six species of large, deciduous, spreading trees are grown for their beautiful, jacaranda-like flowers and handsome foliage. Similar to *Catalpa* in many ways, they differ in having alternate leaves, rather than opposite leaves. The blueish violet to white flowers are borne in spiky clusters prior to the foliage.

CULTIVATION Paulownias do well in any reasonably rich, light soil, with some protection from wind. They are generally very fast growing. Although these trees enjoy cool climates, the flower buds can be damaged by late spring

ABOVE Delicately shaded flowers of *Paulownia tomentosa* in close-up. On tall trees it is hard to appreciate the detail.

frost. These trees can be grown as shrubs by pol-larding them in early spring each year. They will produce very large leaves but will not flower. Propagate from seed sown in spring or fall, or from root cuttings in winter, both in a garden frame.

CLIMATE Zone 6 for *P. fortunei*; zone 5 for *P. tomentosa*.

SPECIES *P. fortunei*, from China, grows in a con-ical shape to between 6 and 13 m (20–43 ft), generally spreading with age. The ovate leaves, to 25 cm (10 in) long, are downy on the under-sides, and the light purple flowers have purple and white throats. *P. tomentosa*, princess tree or Royal paulownia, originates from China. In Asia, it is grown for its timber, which is used in cabinet-making. The most commonly culti-vated species, it may reach a height of 15 m (50 ft). It has large, downy, heart-shaped leaves, up to 30 cm (12 in) long, and highly fragrant, blueish violet flowers. This is a very adaptable species and will take a polluted atmosphere in its stride.

Pavetta (fam. Rubiaceae)

There are around 400 species of evergreen shrubs or trees in this genus from tropical and subtropical parts of the world, including the Philippines and Africa. They have opposite leaves, white or green flowers and fleshy, pea-like fruits. The flowers appear in summer, and with some care will continue to bloom annu-ally for many years.

CULTIVATION In cold and cool climates, grow in an intermediate to warm greenhouse or conser-vatory. Grow in a pot of gritty, well-drained soil-based potting compost. Provide good light (but shade from direct strong sun), and a very humid atmosphere. In late winter, prune as necessary to restrict size. Outdoors grow in a sunny spot with well-drained yet moist soil. Propagate from seed in spring or from semi-ripe cuttings in summer, both in a heated propagat-ing case.

ABOVE Masses of buds are yet to open on pretty *Pavetta lanceolata*. Long stamens extend from the simple, white flowers.

CLIMATE Warmest parts of zone 10 to tropical.

SPECIES Not all are available outside their native countries. *P. borbonica* is grown for its dark green foliage, mottled with light green, and displaying a salmon-red midrib. The leaves grow to around 25 cm (10 in) long. *P. capensis* (syn. *P. caffra*), from South Africa, is a shrub, growing to 2 m (6 ft) high. It has white branches, white flowers and shiny, black fruit. *P. indica* is a small shrub from India, southern China, south-western Asia and northern Australia. The leaves grow to about 25 cm (10 in) long and the white, fragrant flowers are borne on slender stalks. *P. natalensis*, from South Africa, is a showy shrub, growing to around 2.5 m (8 ft) or more. It has shiny, green leaves, about 10 cm (4 in) long, and clusters of spidery, white flowers.

Pawpaw (Carica papaya, fam. Caricaceae)
Papaya

While the name 'pawpaw' is mostly used worldwide, both pawpaw and papaya are common names for the same species, *Carica papaya*. A native of South America, this tree is now grown in most tropical and subtropical

ABOVE Pawpaws crop well when several trees are planted together to ensure that there is good cross polination.

with bottom heat. Trees produced for fruiting are generally grafted. Gardeners in the right climate for growing pawpaws outside for fruit should bear in mind that the trees are mostly dioecious, so a male plant is necessary to pollinate the separate female plant, though at times the flowers can be bisexual. In the tropics, dioecious plants may bloom about five months after the seed has been sown and will bear eight months later, between 20 and 50 fruits at any one time.

CLIMATE Tropical, but can be grown in warmest parts of zone 10.

Pea (*Pisum sativum*, fam. Papilionaceae)

Of European origin, the garden pea is one of the oldest cultivated vegetables. It is said to have been introduced to Britain by the Romans. Until the late 16th century and the development of the edible-podded pea (also known as mange tout, sugar pea or snow pea) by the Dutch, it was only eaten dried. It was also found to be a good fodder and green manure crop, and was the first vegetable crop to be mechanized. Peas may be eaten raw, or boiled with a sprig of mint, then tossed in butter, to accompany poultry and meat. They are also used in soups and stocks. Edible-podded peas are favorites in stir-fries, and pea shoots are prized by the Cantonese.

CULTIVATION Peas are grown as annuals and are best in cool, humid climates. A suitable temperature range is 12°–18°C (54°–64°F). The seeds need a soil temperature of at least 10°C (50°F) to germinate. Peas are either round seeded or wrinkle seeded. Round-seeded peas are the hardiest and the wrinkle seeded kinds have the sweetest flavor. In mild climates, early peas can be sown in mid to late fall and over-wintered under cloches. Alternatively, start sowing from late winter or early spring, the earliest sowings again under cloches. Successional sowings can then be made at monthly intervals until the middle of summer. Seeds are sown in drills 2.5 cm (1 in) deep and 5 cm (2 in) apart.

regions of the world for the delicious fruit, which varies substantially in size. The thick flesh ranges in color from yellow to orange and contains numerous inedible seeds. It is usually eaten raw, but can also be used in jams, pickles and chutneys. Papaya juice is also delicious. *C. papaya* grows rapidly to about 6 m (20 ft). The soft stems contain no woody tissue and the crown is comprised of a cluster of lobed, palmate leaves and yellow flowers.

CULTIVATION Outside the tropics and warm subtropics, grow as a foliage plant in a warm greenhouse or conservatory. It will do well in a large pot or tub of rich, well-drained, soil-based potting compost. Ensure good light (but shade from strong sun), and a humid atmosphere. It can be propagated from seed or cuttings, both

ABOVE Grown in full sun, peas bear heavy crops. Pick often to ensure a long and productive life from the vines.

Leave enough space between the rows for access. Peas grow in any fertile, well-drained soil and in an open, sunny position. It is best to rotate them with other crops, avoiding growing them in exactly the same spot more than once every three or four years. This prevents diseases from building up in the soil. The plants will need to be supported, either with twiggy sticks or with pea and bean netting, supported with stakes. Keep moist at all times and pick the pods regularly, while they are young and tender.

CLIMATE Zone 6.

VARIETIES There are many cultivars of garden peas, including edible-podded kinds, and the best advice is to buy those that are offered locally by seedsmen. There are early, second early and maincrop cultivars of garden peas, a classification that relates to time of maturity. Early peas are the best choice if there is not much space available to grow all types. Height of peas varies from about 45 cm to 1.5 m (18–60 in). The dwarf kinds are often the first choice with home gardeners, as they need the least elaborate supports, but tall-growing kinds give the heaviest yields.

Peach (Prunus persica, fam. Rosaceae)

Probably originating in China and cultivated there since around 2000 BC, the peach is recorded in Chinese literature as early as 551 BC. One of the most widely grown fruits, it is renowned for its juiciness and delicious flavor, as is the nectarine, a variety of *Prunus persica*. The fruit can be eaten fresh, canned or preserved in thick syrup, or made into scrumptious tarts and sweets. Poached peaches and nectarines are exquisite.

CULTIVATION Peaches must be grown in full sun, with protection from strong wind. In colder areas, avoid planting on low ground because late frosts may damage the spring blossom. Soil should drain well and preferably contain plenty of organic matter. Trees are usually planted during their dormant season, from early winter onwards. Plant in holes that are large enough to take the roots without cramping. Bare-rooted trees should have their roots trimmed to about 20 cm (8 in) in length, and any damaged roots should be removed. A light dressing of complete fertilizer can be placed around the tree, well out from the trunk. Trees start to make root growth long before any sign of top growth is evident. Water well at this stage to settle the soil. Once growth starts, give regular, deep waterings and mulch the area to conserve moisture, making sure that the mulch does not come into contact with the trunk. Established trees are usually fed in late winter, five to six weeks before flowering, and again about six weeks after the blossom has fallen. Newly planted trees should be cut back to encourage strong growth in the first season. During the next two years, in spring, prune to encourage the growth of strong main and secondary limbs. Peaches flower and fruit on wood made the previous season so, every winter, trees should be lightly pruned to develop an open vase shape, which will allow sun to reach all parts of the tree and will ensure good air circulation. During the first few years, it may also be necessary to do some thinning and tip pruning in summer. Trees usually start to crop well after

ABOVE The rosy flush on these well-formed peaches shows that they are close to full maturity.

three to four years. There are a number of pests that may be a problem with peaches and nectarines. In warm, dry climates red spider mites may infest the plants. Aphids may also attack new shoots and cause distortion. In warm climates, peaches and nectarines may be attacked by fruit fly. The worst disease and hard to control is peach leaf curl. It is prevented by spraying trees annually with a copper fungicide, first as soon as the leaves have fallen, and again in mid and late winter.

CLIMATE Best in zones 8 to 10.

VARIETIES Peaches are covered with a downy fuzz and the white or yellow flesh surrounds the central stone, hence the name 'stone fruit'. Peaches may be clingstone, where the flesh clings to the stone, or slipstone, where the flesh comes away cleanly and easily from the stone. There is an enormous number of varieties in cultivation in the world today, both commercially and in home gardens. Peaches and nectarines are self-fertile and therefore single trees can be planted, which is useful where space is limited. The choice of available cultivars varies from country to country, so it is best to buy those offered by local nurseries or fruit special-

ists; then you will know that they will suit your climate. In the US natural or genetic dwarf peaches and nectarines which form large bushes are popular. There are many cultivars available. Dual-purpose or flowering and fruiting peaches, developed in Southern California, can also be recommended. They produce an attractive flower display as well as good crops of fruits.

Peanut

(*Arachis hypogaea*, fam. Papilionaceae)

Believed to have originated from tropical Brazil, *Arachis hypogea* is now grown commercially, being an important source of food and oil in many warmer regions of the world. In frost-prone climates, it should be grown in a heated greenhouse, with a humid atmosphere, as a growing temperature of 20°–30°C (68°–86°F) is required. The peanut is an annual, to about 30 cm (12 in) high, but with a spreading habit of growth. It produces yellow, pea-like flowers during summer. After pollination and pod (shell) set, the stem elongates and bends, forcing the young pods into the ground, where they mature and ripen. When fully developed and ripe, they must be dug like any other root

ABOVE Peanuts develop on plant roots. These must be dug and left to dry before picking. In some regions they are called groundnuts.

crop. The seeds within the pods are the peanuts. High in protein, the nut can be eaten raw or roasted, or used in confectionery and cooking.

CULTIVATION Peanuts can be grown in the home garden or greenhouse border. They are propagated from seed in spring, which is the raw nut inside the shell of an unroasted peanut. They need warm conditions and the soil must be light and friable. If necessary, the plants can be grown on a mound or ridge. Once growth is under way, plants need regular watering but the ground should never be sodden. The crop takes four to five months from sowing to harvest.

CLIMATE Zone 9, but can be grown in cooler climates under glass.

Pear

(*Pyrus communis*, *Pyrus pyrifolia*, fam. Rosaceae)

Pears have their origins in Europe, the Caucasus and China. They have been cultivated since ancient times, though quality forms were not developed until the 19th century. Today, many thousands of varieties can be found in many parts of the world, particularly Europe and North America. Though some trees have ornamental value, the pear is grown mainly for its fruit. Pears are eaten fresh and are delicious poached or made into tarts. They create an interesting surprise in a tossed salad, particularly combined with walnuts and blue cheese. Commercially, they are canned and dried.

CULTIVATION As pear trees are deciduous, purchase bare-rooted trees and plant in winter, during dormancy. Container-grown stock can be planted out at any time of year, but winter to early spring is probably the best time. Pears prefer deep, fertile, well-drained soil, so plenty of organic matter should be dug in about a month before planting. Plant at the same depth at which they were growing in either the ground or the container. Water well to settle the soil, but do not apply fertilizer at this time.

ABOVE European pears, such as this old dessert cultivar 'Conference', are best suited to cool climates.

Fertilizer can be applied to the root zone once growth is under way, at the end of winter or in early spring. In subsequent years, apply complete plant food in late winter and mulch during the growing season with manure or compost. Trees should be kept moist when in active growth. Prune in winter to an open vase shape, or to develop the central leader system. Pear trees should begin bearing in four to five years and should continue for many years. The most serious pests of pears are caterpillars, which eat the leaves, and aphids, which can damage and weaken shoot tips. Several diseases attack pears; undoubtedly the most troublesome is scab disease.

CLIMATE European pears are best in zones 6 to 8, but Asian pears are better in warmer climates.

VARIETIES *Pyrus communis*, European pear, is a very large tree, often growing 10–12 m (33–40 ft) in good conditions. However, varieties of pear for cultivation at home and commercially are budded or grafted onto rootstocks that are less vigorous. 'Anjou' is a well known, late-maturing cultivar with fruits of good flavor. 'Beurre Bosc' is a very hardy pear, best in cooler climates, whose fruits have a fine flavor. 'Clapp's Favorite' is also very hardy and bears early, sweet fruits. 'Doyenne du Comice' has large fruits of excellent flavor. 'Seckle' is very popular and bears small, sweet, mid-season fruits. Most European pears are not self-fertile and need a pollinator to ensure good cropping. Obtain advice from a fruit specialist on which varieties to grow together. Asian pears, bred from *Pyrus pyrifolia* and *Pyrus ussuriensis*, are becoming more widely grown around the world and are better suited to warmer, sunnier climates, their chilling requirements being less than those of the European pear. Cultivars of Asian pears can be pollinated by European pears, although they are partially self-fertile.

Pecan

(*Carya illinoinensis* syn. *C. pecan*, fam. Juglandaceae)

Native to southern and central North America, down to Mexico, the pecan can be grown over a wide area as it is a perfectly hardy tree. It is grown commercially in some countries, particularly in the United States, for its nuts or pecans, which are eaten raw, as well as being used for flavoring ice cream and in the renowned pecan pie. It also makes a handsome garden tree and can be planted as a lawn specimen.

CULTIVATION Pecans like a deep, well-drained, slightly acid loam and ample water during the growing season. Propagation is by grafting, and planting should occur during winter dormancy. Grafted trees will produce nuts after five years, but do not reach full production until about the tenth year. Harvest by laying ground sheets to collect the fallen nuts, or by shaking the branches. Pecans are subject to attack from certain bugs, beetles and birds, mites and scale insects.

CLIMATE Zone 6.

VARIETIES *Carya illinoinensis* (syn. *Carya pecan*) is a long-lived, deciduous tree, which may reach a height of 30 m (100 ft) in its habitat, generally around 10 m (33 ft) in cultivation.

ABOVE Tassels of male flowers on pecans produce copious quantities of pollen. Female flowers appear on top of the tassel clusters.

The tree has both male and female flowers, which produce clusters of the fruits which are contained in green husks. As the fruit matures, the outer husk splits into four sections, revealing a smooth, thin-shelled nut which ripens in fall. Numerous cultivars are available and these are mainly self-fertile, although some need a pollinator. Cultivars should be chosen to suit the climate.

Pedilanthus (fam. Euphorbiaceae)
Slipper flower, zig-zag plant

These succulent, clumping shrubs from the West Indies, California and Mexico have erect, jointed, cylindrical branches to 1 m (3 ft) high, alternate, deciduous leaves and showy, red bracts enclosing small flowers, in summer. They can be grown in warm rockeries and make good feature plants for succulent gardens. In most of the US, they are generally grown as house plants, or in a warm greenhouse or conservatory.

CULTIVATION In the greenhouse or conservatory, grow in pots of well-drained, gritty, soil-based potting compost. Provide good light, but shade plants from direct sun. During the winter, the

ABOVE It is unusual to see such a fine display of scarlet-bracted flowers on *Pedilanthus tithymaloides*. This is often grown for its foliage alone.

compost should be kept only slightly moist. Apply water in moderation during the rest of the year. Outdoors grow in well-drained soil with full sun or partial shade. Propagate from cuttings taken from the tops of the stems, in summer. Provide bottom heat for rooting. Plain green species can also be raised from seed sown in spring. Seed should be germinated at 21°C (70°F).

CLIMATE Frost-free and tropical only.

SPECIES *P. macrocarpus*, from Mexico, has green, cylindrical, branching stems, to 1 m (3 ft) high and about 1 cm (⅓ in) thick, with tiny leaves and red flowers with red bracts. *P. tithymaloides*, zig-zag plant, from the West Indies, is probably the best-known species and makes a good pot plant for the home, greenhouse or conservatory. Growing to 2 m (6 ft) high, it has unusual, thin, dark green stems that change direction in a zig-zag fashion and larger, mid-green leaves. The cultivar 'Variegatus' has green leaves, flushed with white and pink.

Pelargonium (fam. Geraniaceae)

Geranium

The plants that most of us call geraniums in fact belong to the genus *Pelargonium*. Most of the 250 species are native to South Africa, while the true *Geranium* species, or cranesbill geraniums, originate from a number of countries, including Europe. Several species and numerous hybrids of *Pelargonium* are old garden favorites and are also popular as potted plants. There is quite a range of sizes and growing habits amongst these plants and some are grown for their foliage value alone. In warm climates, these plants grow rapidly and quickly become rangy but, in cooler regions, they grow more slowly and are ideally suited to bedding schemes, edgings and container-growing. They continue to be amongst the most popular and best known of plants.

CULTIVATION In frost-prone climates, grow as summer bedding plants or as greenhouse pot plants. For best results, grow in locations which receive full sun all day. The soil must be very free draining but need not be rich. Acid soils should be limed before planting, by adding 100 grams of lime or dolomite per square metre (3½ oz per square yard) before planting. Geraniums need regular water to establish but, once established, they should be watered only as the soil dries out. It is better to underwater than overwater. Slow-release fertilizer or pelleted poultry manure may be applied in spring, but excess

BELOW Grown for its boldly patterned, colorful leaves, this cultivar of *Pelargonium* x *hortorum* has flowers which are quite insignificant.

ABOVE Regal Pelargonium bears large trusses of flowers in late spring and early summer. The delicate pink, frilly petals are highlighted by dark blotches.

fertilizer, especially high-nitrogen types, can result in weak, soft growth. Plants should be well maintained by cutting off spent flower heads and by regular tip pruning. Prune plants fairly hard in early to mid-fall. Propagate from tip cuttings taken at almost any time of year. *Pelargonium* grown as pot plants under glass should be grown in well-drained, soil-based potting compost. Ensure maximum light and an airy atmosphere, but shade the plants from direct strong sun.

CLIMATE Zone 10. *Pelargonium* prefers warm to hot, dry climates.

SPECIES *Pelargonium* x *domesticum*, Lady Washington pelargonium, Martha Washington geranium, regal geranium, has a shrubby habit. The leaves are fluted and slightly hairy, with stems becoming woody with age. The large, velvety flowers usually have a distinct blotch or feathering on the petals. The color range includes white, salmon, apricot, crimson and various shades of mauve or purple. *P.* x *hortorum* is the garden or zonal geranium. The rounded, lobed leaves mostly have concentric zones of color, forming the characteristic horseshoe mark. Some varieties are grown mainly for their very decorative, colorful foliage, and many

of these have fairly insignificant flowers. The blooms are borne in rounded heads made up of many individual flowers that may be of single, double or rosebud form. The color range covers white through pink, red, apricot, lavender and magenta, and includes some bi-colors. *P. peltatum*, the ivy geranium, has a trailing or climbing habit. The slightly fleshy leaves are ivy shaped and not zoned. Free-flowering, these geraniums come in a lovely color range, including white, pink, red, lilac and several outstanding bi-colors. Scented-leaf geraniums, grown for their aromatic foliage and diverse range of form and leaf shape, include *P. graveolens*, rose-scented geranium, *P. odoratissimum*, apple-scented geranium, and the peppermint geranium, *P. tomentosum*. These are best grown as greenhouse or conservatory pot plants in frost-prone climates. Grow them in intermediate conditions.

Pellaea (fam. Adiantaceae)

This genus comprises around 80 species of ferns, which are native to tropical and subtropical Australia, New Zealand, America and South Africa. Most have short, creeping rhizomes and firm, dark green to light green leaflets, glossy above and paler beneath. The leaflets vary from linear to roundish oval to sickle-shaped, and the young fiddle heads (fronds) are folded over rather than rolled up, as they are in many other ferns. Pellaeas are suitable for growing in the garden and also for containers.

CULTIVATION There are hardy species which can be grown in the garden in moist soil with partial shade, and tender species (those described here) which, in climates prone to frosts, need to be grown as pot plants in a cool to intermediate greenhouse or conservatory. They grow well in pots of soilless potting compost. Shade plants from direct sun but provide good light. Outdoors plant in rich soil in a sunny position. Propagate by division in spring.

CLIMATE Zone 10 for most of the following species.

ABOVE The rich green, coin-shaped leaves of *Pellaea rotundifolia* look best when congested. Do not divide

SPECIES *P. falcata*, sickle fern, from India and Australasia, has pinnately divided fronds and sickle-shaped leaflets on short stalks. A tough species, it does well in rocky or damp situations and is also suited to pots. *P. paradoxa*, from Queensland and New South Wales, is like *P. falcata*, but the fronds are shorter and the leaflets fewer and broader, with a rounded base. It can be hard to cultivate. *P. rotundifolia*, button fern, from New Zealand, has creeping, wiry rhizomes. The stems are covered in brown scales and the glossy leaflets are round to oval and widely spaced on short stalks. The upright to pendulous fronds are clump-forming. This species is quite tolerant of dry situations, but slow growing. It tolerates temperatures down to -5°C (23°F) so can be grown outside in zone 6, where it makes good groundcover in moist, acid, open woodland conditions.

Peltophorum (fam. Caesalpiniaceae)

These eight species of tall, evergreen, tropical trees are grown in tropical and subtropical regions for shade and for their flowers. Terminal sprays of yellow to golden, fragrant flowers with roundish petals appear in summer, followed by long, brown seed pods. The alternate, fern-like leaves are a deep glossy green. The trees grow quickly but may take five years to flower.

CULTIVATION In frost-prone climates, grow in an intermediate greenhouse or conservatory, in a large pot or tub of gritty, soil-based potting compost. Provide maximum light but shade from strong sun. Prune to restrict size. Propagate from seed in spring after soaking in hot water. Germinate at 21°C (70°F).

CLIMATE Warmest parts of zone 10 to tropical.

SPECIES *P. dasyrachis* is grown for shade in coffee and cacao plantations of its native Thailand, Malaysia and Sumatra. *P. dubium*, from Brazil, is a large, handsome tree, to 15 m (50 ft), with rust-colored, hairy branches and simple or branched sprays of rust flowers. *P. pterocarpum*, yellow flame or yellow flamboyant, native to India, Malaysia and Australia, is cultivated in many tropical countries. It grows to about 15 m (50 ft), and has very hairy, rusty branches, fern-like foliage and attractive, rust-red, flattened seed pods. The fragrant flowers, with crinkly, red-striped, yellow petals are borne in clusters, in early summer. The powdered bark is used medicinally, for tanning and as a yellow-brown dye in batik making.

ABOVE *Peltophorum pterocarpum* rightly deserves the name 'yellow flamboyant', which well describes its floral display.

Pennisetum (fam. Poaceae)

There are around 80 species in this genus of annual and perennial grasses, found in tropical and warm temperate zones. They have cylindrical spike-like or brush-like inflorescences and narrow spikelets, surrounded by spirals of hairy bristles. Some species are cultivated as cereal or fodder crops, while others are used as border and lawn plants. Some are very invasive in various parts of the world.

CULTIVATION All species prefer a sandy, well-drained soil and a sunny position, but most do well in a range of soils and situations. Most species are propagated from seed while some, such as *P. latifolium* and *P. setaceum*, are increased by division of the rootstock.

CLIMATE There are species suited to various climatic zones.

SPECIES *P. alopecuroides*, zone 7, grows to over 1 m (3 ft) high, producing 15 cm (6 in) 'foxtail' inflorescences in late summer and fall. It is grown as an ornamental grass and is an effective addition to the perennial border. It is a potential weed in warm areas. *P. clandestinum*, kikuyu grass, zone 10, is used both as lawn and pasture grass and covered in the section on lawns. *P. latifolium*, zone 9, from Argentina, grows to 2 m (6 ft) high, with broad leaves and pendulous flower spikes. It makes a good greenhouse or border plant. *P. purpureum*, elephant or Napier grass, zone 9, a tropical African species, is used commercially for fodder and paper-making. A robust grass, it grows to 2–7 m (6–23 ft) high. *P. setaceum*, fountain grass, zone 9, is a tufted perennial from tropical Africa. Growing to 1 m (3 ft) high, it has long, narrow leaf blades, feathery, purple-pink spikes and is a useful feature plant. *P. villosum*, zone 8, from north-east, tropical Africa, is a loosely tufted perennial, to 60 cm (24 in), with broad spikes and tawny or purple inflorescences. It can be invasive.

Penstemon (fam. Scrophulariaceae)
Beard tongue

This genus comprises over 250 species of perennials and shrubs, all native to North America, except for one species from north-eastern Asia. Many hybrids are also available, so there is a wide color range, from white and yellow to pink, red, maroon, blue and purple. The tall

ABOVE Ornamental *Pennisetum alopecuroides* makes quite a feature in the garden. Avoid seed spread by cutting off 'foxtails' before seed sets.

ABOVE Pale pink lupins and the rich, rosy red flowers of a hybrid *Penstemon* provide a long flowering display in the garden.

varieties make excellent border plants, while the dwarf types look very colorful as bedding plants.

CULTIVATION Plant in a loose, gravelly soil or a mixture of leaf mould, peat and loam. They require good drainage and an open, sunny situation. A weekly application of liquid fertilizer to the summer bedding species will produce good flowers. Species can be propagated from seed, in spring, under glass. All can be propagated from softwood or semi-ripe cuttings in summer, rooted with bottom heat. Divide established clumps in spring.

CLIMATE There are species suited to various climatic zones.

SPECIES *P. azureus*, zone 8, grows to 75 cm (30 in), with attractive, deep blue or purple flowers. *P. barbatus*, zone 3, produces sprays of delightful, scarlet, tubular flowers, from mid-summer to early fall. This perennial grows up to 2 m (6 ft) high. There are several cultivars available. *P. cobaea*, zone 4, is a parent of some of the most popular hybrids. It has large, showy, purple or white flowers. *P. fruticosus*, zone 4, with lavender-blue flowers, forms a dense clump and is also a parent of several popular varieties. *P. heterophyllus*, zone 8, a shrub to 60 cm (24 in) high, has blue to purple flowers. It is an excellent border edging plant. *P. hirsutus*, zone 3, is a perennial, to 1 m (3 ft), with purple or violet flowers, also producing several lovely cultivars. *P. triphyllus*, zone 5, to 75 cm (30 in) high, has lavender to lilac-blue flowers and a staminode with thick, yellow hairs. Garden cultivars include 'Apple Blossom', 'Firebird', 'Garnet', 'Lady Hindley' and 'Sour Grapes'.

Pentas (fam. Rubiaceae)

From tropical Africa and Madagascar, this genus includes around 30 species of perennials and shrubs with opposite leaves and clusters of attractive, delightfully colored flowers. In frost-prone climates they make good pot plants in an intermediate greenhouse or conservatory.

ABOVE With regular removal of spent flower heads, *Pentas* cultivars will bloom for months. They cut well for posies too.

CULTIVATION Under glass, grow in soil-based potting compost with extra grit added. Give good light but shade plants from direct sun. Prune in late winter to restrict size, if necessary. Remove dead flower heads regularly. Propagate from softwood cuttings all year round and root them in a heated propagating case.

CLIMATE Warmest parts of zone 10 to tropical.

SPECIES *P. bussei*, red star cluster, is rather straggly, with ribbed, ovate leaves and scarlet, spring flowers, and grows to 1 m (3 ft) or more. *P. lanceolata*, Egyptian star cluster, is a compact shrub to 2 m (6 ft) tall, from the Arabian peninsula to tropical east Africa. It makes a good greenhouse pot plant and in warm climates can be bedded out for the summer. It is grown for the bright green, hairy, oval leaves and large clusters of starry flowers, in pink, lilac, purple or magenta, which bloom for months. Many varieties are available, some with two-toned flowers.

Peperomia (fam. Piperaceae)

This extremely large genus of mainly succulent perennials is found in the tropics worldwide.

Many species come from Central and South America. Mostly low-growing or creeping, they have rounded, decorative, waxy leaves, sometimes variegated, and spikes of green or whitish flowers. Some species with succulent leaves have 'windowed' strips on the leaves, allowing light to the tissue deep within the leaves. They are attractive as house plants, in hanging baskets and terrariums.

CULTIVATION Grow as house plants, or in a warm greenhouse or conservatory. Grow in small pots, or plant trailing species in hanging baskets. A soilless potting compost is suitable. Plants need good light (but shade from direct sun), and a humid atmosphere in spring and summer. Do not apply too much water in the growing season and in winter, keep the compost only slightly moist Those with very thick, fleshy leaves are fairly drought-tolerant and take drier conditions. Propagate from seed in spring, or from leaf or stem cuttings in spring and summer. Provide bottom heat for all. Divide clump-forming species in spring.

CLIMATE Tropical only.

SPECIES *P. argyreia*, watermelon peperomia, a popular ornamental to 20 cm (8 in), has thick, silver-gray leaves with dark green veins and reddish leaf stalks. *P. bicolor* has deep green leaves, purplish underneath, and silver-gray veins. It grows to 25 cm (10 in). *P. caperata* 'Emerald Ripple', is a handsome species, with small, heart-shaped, crinkly leaves and whitish, branching flower spikes. It grows to 15 cm (6 in). *P. dolabriformis*, a succulent, has fleshy leaves and the characteristic, windowed margins. *P. glabella*, to 15 cm (6 in), has trailing, red stems and oval, veined leaves. Cultivar 'Variegata' has leaves variegated with cream. *P. obtusifolia*, pepper face, is a popular perennial upright species, to 15 cm (6 in) or more, with large, fleshy, dark green leaves with purple edges, purplish stems and white flowers on red stems. Several cultivars have been produced from this species, including 'Green and Gold' and 'Variegata'. *P. scandens* is a trailing type, to 60 cm (24 in) or more, with heart-shaped leaves. Cultivar 'Variegata' has yellow-margined leaves and pink leaf stalks.

Pericallis x hybrida

(syn. *Senecio* x *hybridus*, fam. Asteraceae)

Cineraria

Originally from the Canary Islands, this versatile hybrid group can be treated as annuals, biennials or perennials. However, plants treated as annuals and raised fresh from seed each fall produce lovely single bloom, daisy-like flowers,

ABOVE Lime green flower spikes of *Peperomia caperata* 'Emerald Ripple' stand high above the dark, crinkly leaves.

ABOVE Cinerarias, *Pericaliis* x *hybrida*, are popular pot plants for the greenhouse, conservatory or windowsill.

with leaves gray-white underneath. They make a colorful display in a cool greenhouse or conservatory, or as house plants. They are grown to flower in the winter and spring.

CULTIVATION To grow them as annual pot plants, sow seed in spring to early summer and germinate them at 18°C (64°F). Seedlings are potted on until in 12.5–15 cm (5–6 in) pots. Use soil-based potting compost. Ensure maximum light, but shade from direct sun. Do not overwater as they dislike very wet compost. Compost should be steadily moist. Liquid feed once a fortnight when in full growth. Dead-heading will ensure a longer flowering period. When flowering is over, the plants are discarded. Cinerarias are susceptible to several problems, including white fly, red spider mites, thrips and aphids. They may also be attacked by leaf miner, the species found on chrysanthemums.

CLIMATE Warmest parts of zone 9, but generally grown under glass.

SPECIES *P.* x *hybrida* (syn. *Senecio* x *hybridus*) ranges in height from 20 to 90 cm (8–36 in). *Pericallis* has a richness and brilliance of color found in few other plants grown as annuals. The color range includes every shade of blue, pink, red, purple, cerise, magenta and white. Ray florets are sometimes bi-colored. The many cultivars include tall, semi-dwarf and dwarf. Most popular for pot plants are the dwarf cultivars. Most dwarf and semi-dwarf kinds have large flower heads.

Pernettya (syn. *Gaultheria*, fam. Ericaeae)

Originating mainly from the Americas and Australasia, these low-growing, evergreen shrubs, now correctly called *Gaultheria*, have simple, alternate, quite leathery leaves and white, bell-shaped, generally solitary flowers. Most species have brightly colored berries in winter.

CULTIVATION Plant in a sunny position in a well-drained, acid soil in either spring or fall. Water

ABOVE Bright pink fruits on *Pernettya mucronata* are longer lasting and more striking than its small, spring flowers.

regularly through spring and summer. Propagate from seed, cuttings of half-ripe wood, layers or suckers.

CLIMATE There are species suited to various climatic zones.

SPECIES *P. lanceolata*, zone 7, from Tasmania, is a small, compact shrub, to 45 cm (18 in), with glossy leaves, rounded, white flowers and deep pink berries. *P. macrostigma*, zone 8, from New Zealand, is a twiggy, prostrate, straggly shrub, to 50–60 cm (20–24 in), with leathery leaves and white flowers in summer and fall, followed by red fruits. *P. mucronata*, zone 6, native to cooler areas of South America, grows to about 1 m (3 ft), with white or pink, bell-shaped flowers in late spring. Several cultivars of this species are grown. *P. tasmanica*, zone 7, from Tasmania, is a carpeting species, with tiny, dark green leaves and clusters of small, white flowers, followed by cream, pink or red berries.

Persimmon (*Diospyros kaki*, fam. Ebenaceae)

Diospyros kaki has its origins in China but is known to have been cultivated in Japan since the eighth century. It is a small, deciduous ornamental tree, with a spreading habit, which grows to about 10 m (33 ft). It is renowned for its brilliant display of fall color. The mature fruits may be rounded or flattish and either red or yellow-orange. They have a high vitamin C content and are usually eaten fresh, though they can be cooked. Some fruits are very astringent, but there are several non-astringent varieties as well. The major commercial producers of persimmons are China, Brazil, Japan and Korea.

CULTIVATION To fruit well, the persimmon needs a long, hot summer, hence it may not crop well in cooler regions, where it could be grown in a cool greenhouse to improve its chances of fruiting. This tree prefers a well-drained loam, but any well-drained soil will do. It is important to water well, particularly during dry periods in the growing season. Fertilize with a complete plant food, starting with about 450 g (1 lb) per tree per year until five years old, then using around 2 kg (4½ lb) per tree per year. The fruit ripens from midsummer to early fall. It can be picked in the firm, yellow-orange stage and placed in a sunny position to ripen. This helps to avoid the fruit fly to which it is susceptible. If persimmons are frozen, any astringency dis-appears on thawing. Named varieties are available from both general and specialist nurseries.

CLIMATE Zones 8 to 9.

VARIETIES There are numerous cultivars of persimmon available including 'Chocolate' which is very sweet; 'Fuyu' with very firm flesh; the similar 'Goshu' (also known as 'Giant Fuyu'); the popular 'Hachiya' with very large fruits which are astringent until fully ripe; and 'Tamopan' which is also astringent until completely ripe. Cultivars are grown as grafted trees.

Persoonia (fam. Proteaceae)
Geebung

There are around 60 species of these attractive, compact shrubs or small trees, all of which originate from Australia. Their leaves vary in shape and the short spikes or sprays of open, bell-shaped, usually yellow flowers are followed by edible, though rather astringent, berries containing a one- or two-celled nut. Persoonias are unlikely to be available outside Australia.

ABOVE Ripening persimmons, *Diospyros kaki,* vie for attention with the tree foliage as it colors up in fall.

ABOVE Unusual, yellow flowers and needle-like foliage are features of *Persoonia chamaepitys,* a species not often seen in cultivation.

CULTIVATION In frost-prone climates, grow in an airy, cool greenhouse or conservatory in pots of acid, soil-based potting compost. Shade from strong, direct sun. Outdoors, grow in acid, sandy soil with good drainage, in a sunny position. Provide adequate water during hot dry weather. Pruning is generally unnecessary. Cuttings are difficult to root.

CLIMATE Zone 9 if relatively frost-free.

SPECIES *P. acerosa*, mossy geebung, is a small or prostrate shrub, to 2 m (6 ft), with yellow flowers crowded at the ends of the branches. *P. chamaepitys* is an attractive, prostrate, spreading plant, with soft, needle-like, bright green leaves and clusters of showy, bright yellow flowers. *P. lanceolata*, to 2 m (6 ft), has narrow leaves and small, yellow flowers. *P. levis*, broad-leafed geebung, is a spreading shrub, to 4 m (13 ft), with thick, bright green, oval leaves and yellow flowers arising from the leaf bases. The fruits are edible but quite astringent. *P. pinifolia*, pine-leafed geebung, is the most attractive of the species and the most commonly cultivated. Delicate, bright green, pine-like foliage appears all year round, and sprays of small, yellow flowers appear in spring or summer. The berries ripen to red or purple tones in late summer or fall, persisting for many months. The foliage is used as a filler in floral arrangements. *P. subvelutina*, velvety geebung, is an elegant, tall shrub, with downy foliage and red fruits, found in mountainous regions.

Petasites (fam. Asteraceae)

This genus comprises 15 species of hardy, herbaceous, spreading perennials, native to Europe, Asia and North America. Only two of the species are cultivated, and even these can be invasive. Sweetly scented flowers are borne in erect sprays.

CULTIVATION Grow in any garden soil, in a spot where there is plenty of room to spread. All species thrive in moist soils and in full or par-

ABOVE *Petasites fragrans* is often grown beside water features in large gardens, where its spreading habit is not a problem.

tial shade. Propagate from seed or by division in fall.

CLIMATE Cool to warm southern temperate and mild, inland areas.

SPECIES *P. fragrans*, winter heliotrope, zone 7, from southern Europe, has winter flowers and leathery, leaves, downy on the undersides, both of which are strongly fragrant. The leaves of winter heliotrope often appear after the flowers. *P. japonicus* var. *giganteus*, giant butterburr, zone 5, from Japan, grows to 1.5 m (5 ft). Although valued for its huge leaves, the pale whitish yellow flowers are not particularly attractive. The thick stalks can be cooked and eaten.

Petrea (fam. Verbenaceae)
Purple wreath

Native to Mexico and the West Indies, and extending into South America, this genus consists of tropical, evergreen or deciduous shrubs, trees and woody climbers. They have starry, purple or violet flowers and simple, opposite leaves. Outside the tropics or subtropics, these plants are grown in an intermediate to warm greenhouse or conservatory.

CULTIVATION When growing in the greenhouse, pot into soil-based potting compost. Ensure maximum light but shade from direct, strong sun. Climbing species will need supports for their stems. Prune in late winter to keep plant in allotted place. Outdoors grow in a sunny spot with rich, moist yet well-drained soil. Propagate by layering in spring, or from semi-ripe cuttings during summer, in a heated propagating case.

CLIMATE Warmest parts of zone 10 to tropical.

SPECIES *P. arborea* is a vine-like tree or shrub, to 8 m (26 ft) high, with trails of violet flowers, growing to 15 cm (6 in) long. *P. racemosa* is either a shrub or a twining shrub which grows to 4 m (13 ft). The deep purple, blue or lilac flowers are borne in 30 cm (12 in) long trails in summer. *P. volubilis*, purple wreath or Queen's wreath, grows to 10 m (33 ft) or more high in ideal conditions. It is one of the loveliest of all climbing plants. In summer, it is covered with a mass of purple and lilac flowers. Cultivar 'Albiflora' has white flowers.

ABOVE The lovely tropical climber *Petrea volubilis* flowers abundantly and over a long period in a warm greenhouse or conservatory

Petrophila (fam. Proteaceae)
Conesticks

The Proteaceae family includes *Banksia*, *Hakea* and *Grevillea*, as well as this genus of about 40 species of shrubs. Native to Australia, mostly Western Australia, they have very attractive, variable foliage and dense terminal spikes of cone-like flowers, followed by woody, cone-like fruits. Both the foliage and the woody cones are used in floral work. In the wild, these shrubs grow mainly on sand, gravel and granite soils. They are not readily available outside their native Australia.

CULTIVATION In frost-prone climates, grow in an airy, cool greenhouse or conservatory in acid, well drained, soil-based potting compost. Outdoors, these plants must have perfect drainage and acid to neutral soil. Coarse, sandy or gravelly soils suit them well and their root zone should be mulched with decayed leaf mould. Check that the mulch does not pack around the stem or the plants will rot. Most species prefer full sun, but some will do well in light, dappled shade. Plants can be watered during the growing season, however, established plants are very drought-tolerant. If fertilizer is needed, use low-phosphorus, slow-

BELOW Well suited to poor, sandy soils, *Petrophila heterophylla* is sparsely branched with intricate, creamy

release types. Propagate from seed. Germination may be erratic and may take from six to eight weeks.

CLIMATE Warmest parts of zone 9.

SPECIES *P. acicularis* is a low-growing shrub, to about 60 cm (24 in), with red, spring flowers. *P. biloba*, 1–2 m (3–6 ft) high, has large, pink and gray flowers in late winter and lobed, pointed leaves. *P. canescens* (syn. *P. sessilis*) is an upright-growing shrub which may reach around 3 m (10 ft) at maturity. The finely divided leaves are creamy yellow and the flowers are borne during spring to early summer. The cones are 3–4 cm (about 1½ in) long and gray and woody. *P. linearis* has thick, entire leaves and pink flowers. *P. pedunculata* is a stiff, upright shrub, to about 3 m (10 ft), with divided leaves and stalkless, yellow flower heads in spring. *P. pulchella* grows to 2 m (6 ft), producing pale yellow flowers in spring and summer. *P. teretifolia* may sometimes be a dwarf form, though it mostly grows to around 1 m (3 ft). It has sharp, dark green leaves and loose terminal clusters of soft, velvety pink and gray flowers.

Petunia (fam. Solanaceae)

Originating from warm areas of the Americas, this genus of about 40 species of bright annuals and perennials is closely related to the tobaccos and a member of the same family as the potato. Among the most popular flowers in the world, they add color to the porch or verandah when planted in hanging baskets or pots, and also make delightful bedding plants.

CULTIVATION Plants for bedding out in summer are raised from seed in a heated greenhouse. Sow seed in mid-spring and germinate at 18°C (64°F). Transplant seedlings to seed trays and grow on under glass. Plant out when frosts are over, in late spring or early summer, after hardening in a garden frame. Plants need well-drained soil, full sun and wind protection. Remove dead heads to encourage more flowering.

ABOVE A lovely cultivar of the annual petunia has lilac flowers, richly adorned with maroon to crimson veining.

CLIMATE Zones 9 to 10; grow as summer annuals in all climatic zones.

SPECIES *P. hybrida*, or hybrid petunia, is thought to be derived from *P. axillaris* and *P. integrifolia*. The flowers may be single or double, fluted, saucer- or trumpet-shaped, and come in a great range of colors, including many bi-colors and those with a contrasting edge. There are a great many cultivars of petunias and these are inclined to vary from one country to another. Consult mail-order seed catalogues to find out what is available. Most catalogues list a comprehensive range of cultivars. The hybrid petunias are split into two groups. The Multiflora petunias are generally bushy plants, although some have a trailing habit. They have comparatively small flowers but the plants are very free flowering and make a tremendous show of color. The Multifloras are favorites for summer bedding, as well as patio containers, and most tolerate wet weather quite well. The Grandiflora petunias have much larger flowers and they are not as tolerant of inclement weather. They are good for containers like hanging baskets and window boxes, particularly when sheltered from the elements.

Phaius (fam. Orchidaceae)

Found in tropical habitats in Southeast Asia, Australia and the Pacific Islands, this genus consists of 30 species of terrestrial orchids, only a few of which are commonly cultivated. The flowers are carried on tall, upright stems and are often quite spectacular.

CULTIVATION Grow in a warm greenhouse or conservatory in pots of proprietary orchid compost (formulated for terrestrial orchids). Deep pots are needed to accommodate the extensive root system. Summer requirements include a very humid atmosphere, copious watering, and good light, but shade from direct sun. Liquid feed about once a week. In winter, ensure maximum light and reduce watering and humidity. Propagate by division when plants outgrow their pots.

CLIMATE Tropical.

SPECIES *P. tankervilliae*, from Australia and Asia, is a magnificent, tall species, with long, glossy leaves and interesting flowers, with red-brown sepals and petals, a white back and a magenta lip. Between four and twelve flowers are produced in summer on stems up to 1 m (3 ft) high.

Phalaenopsis (fam. Orchidaceae)
Moth orchid

For sheer, breathtaking beauty there is probably no other orchid to rival the moth orchid. They are native to tropical regions of Southeast Asia, the Himalayas, through the Philippines to New Guinea and Australia. Thousands of hybrids have been developed by breeders around the world. They are epiphytic orchids, growing from flat, fleshy roots. The leaves may be plain green or mottled, and individual plants carry from two to six leaves. The flower stems may be upright or arching and pendulous, and may carry from one or two to over 50 blooms. The flowers come in every color except blue, and flowers of hybrids are striped, barred, spotted and mottled.

CULTIVATION These orchids need a minimum winter temperature of 18°C (64°F) and high humidity, so a heated greenhouse is required in temperate climates. As they do not have pseu-

ABOVE *Phaius tankervilliae* occurs naturally in paperbark swamps, so it likes a moist potting mix. The flowers are sometimes 10 cm (4 in) across.

ABOVE A massed display of flowering Phalaenopsis hybrids is hard to surpass. The flowers are long lasting on the plant or when cut.

dobulbs (only minimal water being stored in the thick leaves) they must not be allowed to dry out. Use a proprietary orchid compost (formulated for epiphytic orchids) and grow in slatted, wooden orchid baskets. Most of the roots will, however, tend to live in the humid open air, clinging to adjacent walls or posts. Light intensity should be relatively low and controlled with shadecloth. Good ventilation is essential.

CLIMATE Humid, tropical climates.

SPECIES *P. amabilis* is widely distributed through Southeast Asia, extending into northeastern Queensland. A profusion of large, white flowers are borne on long stems at almost any time of year. *P. amboinensis*, from the Moluccas and Borneo, produces yellow flowers, with brown or purplish markings, from spring to summer. *P. schillerana*, from the Philippines, has mottled leaves and large, rosy purple flowers, borne on long stems, in winter. *P. stuartiana*, also from the Philippines, has similarly mottled leaves. This species has many flower stems bearing white flowers, with white and yellow lower sepals and lip, in winter to spring. *P. violacea*, from Malaysia and Borneo, is summer-flowering. The flowers have white dorsal sepals and petals, tinted in green, with purple dots at the base, and purple and white lateral sepals. The lip is a bright violet. The Borneo native has a larger flower.

Phebalium (fam. Rutaceae)

Not widely cultivated, these attractive, aromatic shrubs have starry, white, yellow or pink flowers, often in terminal clusters. All 40 species are Australian natives, except *P. nudum*, which is from New Zealand. All are woody shrubs of varying sizes. The flowers may be white, pink or yellow.

CULTIVATION In frost-prone climates, grow in a cool greenhouse or conservatory in pots of acid, soilless potting compost. Provide good light, but shade from direct strong sun. Pruning may

ABOVE *Phebalium squameum*, satinwood, is a large shrub which produces white, starry flowers throughout spring and summer.

be needed after flowering to restrict size. Outdoors grow in a sunny spot with acid, humus rich, moist yet well-drained soil. Propagate from semi-ripe cuttings during summer, in a heated propagating case.

CLIMATE Warmest parts of zone 10 and above.

SPECIES *P. ambiens* grows to 2 m (6 ft) high, with light green, stem-clasping foliage and white flowers. *P. dentatum* has narrow, silvery foliage and masses of cream, spring flowers. *P. nottii* is a rounded shrub, 1–2 m (3–6 ft) high, with small, narrow, dark green leaves and terminal clusters of mauve-pink flowers. *P. nudum*, New Zealand naked phebalium or maire hau, is beautiful and highly aromatic, with red bark and flat-topped clusters of white flowers. *P. squameum*, satinwood, is a large shrub or even a small tree, with dark green leaves, scaly on the undersides, and white, starry flowers in spring and summer.

Philadelphus (fam. Hydrangeaceae)
Mock orange

There are about 60 species in this genus from North and Central America, eastern Europe and Asia. One of the most popular of the flowering shrubs, they have simple, ovate leaves and pretty, strongly scented, white or cream flowers. Many *Philadelphus* grown in gardens are hybrids and they flower mainly in early summer. They can be grown in mixed shrub borders, as specimens or as screening plants.

CULTIVATION Easily grown, these shrubs prefer moist, well-drained soil and a sunny position. Prune immediately after flowering, by cutting out the flowered shoots back to the old wood. This will result in a profusion of blooms in the following summer. Remove very old canes from the base to allow for the growth of new, young canes. Propagate from softwood cuttings rooted with bottom heat, or from hardwood cuttings in winter, in a garden frame.

CLIMATE There are species suited to various climatic zones.

SPECIES *P. coronarius*, zone 5, is an erect, rounded shrub, growing to a height and spread of about 3 m (10 ft). It has toothed, oval, bright green leaves and terminal sprays of cream flowers. This species needs a sheltered position. Cultivar 'Aureus' has bright yellow new growth. *P. delavayi*, zone 6, from China, grows to 3 m (10 ft), with dense clusters of pure white flowers, in early summer. *P.* x *lemoinei*, lemon mock orange, zone 5, is an erect shrub, to around 2 m (6 ft), with arching branches and downy leaves. Pure white, very fragrant flowers are freely produced in small clusters. *P.* 'Manteau d'Hermine', zone 7, bears a profusion of scented, double cream flowers on smooth shoots. *P. mexicanus*, Mexican mock orange, zone 9, to 4 m (13 ft) high, is suited to all but the coldest areas, requiring some shelter. It has very fragrant, solitary, cream flowers. *P. microphyllus*, zone 6, grows to 1 m (3 ft) high, with small, snowy white flowers on leafy shoots. Its growth is compact and upright. *P.* 'Virginal' is a very popular cultivar, growing to 3 m (10 ft) with clusters of fragrant, double, white flowers.

Philodendron (fam. Araceae)

This is a large genus of some 500 species of climbing, and often epiphytic, plants, native to tropical America and widely grown indoors. Adaptable and fast-growing, they are able to survive in a variety of environments, some flourishing with low humidity and little natural light. In their habitat, the climbing species reach to the top of the tallest trees, but can be grown in pots if provided with support. Using a modestly sized container will encourage them to become very bushy. While they have unusual, arum-like flowers, they are grown mostly for their glossy foliage which varies substantially in shape, size and color. Many species have been hybridized to produce a range of good cultivars.

CULTIVATION Grow in a warm greenhouse or conservatory, or as house plants. They thrive in soilless potting compost. Good light is needed, but shade from direct sun. Provide a humid atmosphere. Water well when in full growth, but far less in winter. Climbers can be supported on poles covered with sphagnum moss, which should be kept moist. Propagate from leaf-bud or stem-tip cuttings in summer, and root them with bottom heat. Alternatively, layer in spring.

ABOVE Always reliable, *Philadelphus species* and hybrids adapt to a range of climates and conditions. The fragrant white flowers are greatly admired.

ABOVE In the tropics, *Philodendron bipinnatifidum* climbs high into tree canopies.

CLIMATE Tropical.

SPECIES *P. bipinnatifidum*, formerly and better known as *P. selloum*, has very large, deeply divided leaves. It is generally shrub-like, but is semi-climbing in the tropics. It is widely used as a house plant but it can become very large and take up considerable space. *P. crassinervium*, a climber, has red-margined leaves with purple stalks, and yellow and green flowers. *P. domesticum*, elephant's ear, has triangular leaves. *P. scandens*, heartleaf philodendron, is a climber with long, trailing stems and dark green leaves.

Phlebodium (fam. Polypodiaceae)

This genus of ferns is found from Florida through to Central and South America. One species, *Phlebodium aureum*, the golden polypody, is widely grown. In frost-prone climates, it needs a warm greenhouse or conservatory.

ABOVE *Phlebodium aureum* is a vigorous grower in summer weather. Tall fronds provide good background for softer, daintier ferns.

CULTIVATION In the greenhouse, grow in a pot of soil-based potting compost with added leaf mould and chipped bark. Ensure that plants receive good light, but shade them from direct sun. Do not overwater but keep the compost steadily moist. Far less water is needed in winter. Propagate in the spring by dividing established plants.

CLIMATE Warmest parts of zone 9 to tropical.

SPECIES *P. aureum*, golden polypody or rabbit's foot fern, takes its name from the thick, hairy rhizomes that creep along the soil surface. Tall, deeply lobed fronds on strong stems may grow to 1 m (3 ft) high. The variety sold as 'Glaucum' or var. *aureolatum* has distinct, blue-green foliage. Many other cultivars are hard to identify except by fern experts. Mature fronds produce conspicuous, round, golden yellow spore cases on the underside of the fronds. These tend to self-sow freely.

Phlomis (fam. Lamiaceae)

Originating from southern Europe, northern Africa and Asia, this genus consists of about 100

ABOVE The bright flowers of *Phlomis fruticosa* contrast well with the gray-green, velvety leaves. It thrives in hot, dry summers.

species of perennials and shrubs rather similar to sage. The flowers may be yellow, white or lilac, and form circular whorls near the tops of the tall stems. The leaves are large and wrinkled, and highly aromatic. *Phlomis* can withstand coastal conditions with poor soil, and fairly severe drought.

CULTIVATION These shrubs can be grown in any type of well-drained soil. Once they are established, they can tolerate long periods without any rain at all. Propagate from seed sown in spring, or from cuttings in late summer.

CLIMATE Zone 7, but zone 9 for *P. chrysophylla*.

SPECIES *P. chrysophylla*, from south-western Asia, is an evergreen, growing 70 cm to 1 m tall (28–40 in), with broad, gray-green leaves and yellow, summer flowers. *P. fruticosa*, Jerusalem sage, the best known variety, is a mounded evergreen, with wrinkly, gray-green leaves that may grow to 1 m (3 ft) in ideal conditions. The golden yellow flowers grow in whorls up the stem in late spring or summer. *P. russeliana* (syn. *P. samia*) is an upright-growing perennial with slightly hairy, oval leaves and hooded, pale primrose flowers, from late spring through

most of summer. In all of the species, the dried flowering stems remain decorative after the flowers have fallen.

Phlox (fam. Polemoniaceae)

This genus includes around 67 species, all but one native to North America and Mexico. These annuals, perennials or alpines, with their fragrant, colorful flowers, are grown around the world for their spring to summer and fall displays. Excellent edging and border plants, they also make attractive hanging baskets and window boxes.

CULTIVATION Easily grown, phlox prefer rich, well-drained soil and plenty of water during the growing season. They need a warm, sunny situation, protected from strong wind. Feed with all-purpose fertilizer during the growing season. Propagate the perennial species from root cuttings or by lifting and dividing about every three years. Grow the annuals from seed, sown in spring once the soil has warmed, or raise in a heated greenhouse. Pinch out the growing tips of the first shoots to ensure compact, bushy growth. Regular removal of spent flowers will prolong the flowering display. Propagate the

ABOVE Perennial phlox, *Phlox paniculata*, brings a bright splash of color to the summer garden, year after year.

alpine species by layering or by root division. Plant in a fairly rich, moist soil in sunny, protected rockery crevices. Drainage must be excellent to avoid rotting of the roots, especially in winter.

CLIMATE There are species suited to various climatic zones.

SPECIES *P. carolina*, thickleaf phlox, zone 5, is an herbaceous perennial, growing to about 1 m (3 ft), with purple to pink flowers. *P. divaricata*, wild Sweet William, zone 4, is a creeping, spreading perennial, rooting down as it grows. It bears lavender, violet or white flowers in early summer. *P. douglasii*, zone 5, is an evergreen perennial that forms a mound about 20 cm (8 in) high, producing pink, white or lavender flowers in late spring or summer. *P. drummondii*, zone 6, is the familiar, annual phlox which grows 10–40 cm (4–16 in) high, depending on variety. Numerous strains of this annual are available, most with flowers in shades of white, pink, red, purple or lavender, some with a contrasting eye. *P. paniculata*, zone 4, is a popular, herbaceous perennial which grows 40–80 cm (16–32 in) high. Many cultivars are listed, but the following are some of the better known: 'Blue Boy', with mauve-blue flowers; 'Brigadier', with orange-red flowers; 'Bright Eyes', which has pale pink flowers with a red eye; 'Mia Ruys', which is pure white; and 'Prince of Orange', with dark orange blooms. *P. subulata*, zone 3, may be known as alpine phlox or moss phlox. This is an evergreen perennial that may be mound- or mat-forming. It is at its best in rockeries, where it has room to spread. There are many named cultivars, the late spring or early summer flowers being pale blue, white, pink, purple or red.

Phoenix (fam. Arecaceae)

Date palm

Distributed widely throughout tropical and warm regions of Africa, Asia and southern China, this well-known genus of feather palms

ABOVE Multi-stemmed *Phoenix reclinata* makes an outstanding landscape feature as it matures into large clumps.

comprises around 17 species. *Phoenix* can be distinguished from other palm genera by the sharp, strong spines of the lower leaflets and the pattern of old leaf bases. The palm-like inflorescences are borne among the leaf bases and the oblong fruits ripen to yellow, orange, red, purple or black, depending on species. They are among the hardiest of palms and look striking in larger landscapes.

CULTIVATION These palms are easy to grow, but in frost-prone climates are best grown as pot plants in a warm greenhouse or conservatory. Outdoors, all need sun, but young plants can survive in quite deep shade. All the larger species can tolerate strong winds. Most are not suitable for use as container plants as their powerful roots tend to push out through the bottom of the pot. They should therefore be planted out at an early stage of growth. An exception is *P. roebelenii*, which is less vigorous and often container grown. Although most are from the tropics, all seem to do well in climatic zones considerably cooler than those in which they occur naturally. Propagate from seed, which germinates reasonably quickly. These palms are dioecious.

CLIMATE Warmest parts of zone 9 and above.

SPECIES *P. canariensis*, Canary Island date, is now widely cultivated in many parts of the world, and mature specimens are often found in parks and streets in warm-climate countries. It is generally too large for the home garden as it grows up to 20 m (65 ft) tall, with a solitary stem, about 70 cm (28 in) in diameter, rough-surfaced and patterned with diamond-shaped leaf scars. It has a massive crown, with crowded, forward-pointing, dull, deep green leaflets. In midsummer, the female plants bear orange fruits among the leaf bases. *P. dactylifera*, date palm, is the source of the edible date, and is thought to be a native of northern Africa and the Arabian peninsula. In various warm and tropical parts of the world, including California and Arizona, it is grown commercially for its fruit. It has a rough trunk, growing to about 30 m (100 ft) tall and 30–40 cm (12–16 in) in diameter. As it suckers from the base, old trees may have several trunks. The leaves are very long, narrow and quite sparse, with forward-pointing, grayish green leaflets. Fruit color varies from pale yellow to reddish. *P. reclinata*, African wild date, found throughout tropical and southern Africa, is a very ornamental species. Multistemmed even when young, it eventually forms a clump of about 20 slender trunks, up to 15 m (50 ft) tall, with new sucker growths appearing continuously at the base. The crown is relatively small, with shorter leaves than those on other species and glossy, bright green, sparser leaflets. Fruits are bright orange-yellow. This palm is a spectacular subject for large, grassed areas. *P. roebelenii*, pygmy date palm, originally from Laos, the smallest species generally cultivated, grows to around 3 m (10 ft) tall. The single, slightly crooked trunk is narrow at the bottom, broadening near the top, and covered with peg-like projections, representing the old leaf bases, each beautifully round-tipped and symmetrical. The crown has densely packed leaves to about 1.5 m (5 ft) long, the lower ones pendulous, and evenly spaced, narrow, glossy green leaflets. The female inflorescences bear a profusion of small, black fruits.

Phormium (fam. Agavaceae)

New Zealand flax

There are only two species in this genus, both natives of New Zealand. Now grown for the dramatic impact of their sword-like foliage, particularly in larger vistas, flax was used in times past by the Maori peoples for making rope and twine, the fibers being among the strongest in the known plant world, and for medicinal purposes. The leaves were used for weaving mats and baskets. Extremely hardy, these large, clumping plants have long leaves, sometimes up to 5 m (16 ft) in their habitat, in colors ranging from light greenish yellow to deep blueish green, occasionally with yellow or red margins, and sprays of lily-like, summer flowers on tall stems. These interesting plants suit a wide range of habitats, from cool regions to seaside areas.

ABOVE A fine, green and gold cultivar of *Phormium tenax* makes a striking centerpiece for a display of annuals.

CULTIVATION Propagate species from ripened seed and cultivars by division of the clumps, in late winter to early spring. These very adaptable plants will grow in any well-drained soil, but prefer an open, sunny position. Provide plentiful water during the warmer months, but little during winter.

CLIMATE Zone 8.

SPECIES *P. cookianum* (syn. *P. colensoi*), mountain flax, grows up to 2 m (6 ft) high and wide, occurring naturally in drier woodland areas. It has arching leaves and yellow-green flowers, followed by twisted seed capsules, to 15 cm (6 in) long. *P. tenax*, New Zealand flax or New Zealand hemp, is the most commonly grown species. It grows up to 4 m (13 ft) high, with long, stiff, upright leaves and dull red, spiky flowers, followed by fruiting capsules, to about 8 cm (3 in) long. A number of cultivars are available, including Purpureum Group, with bronze-purple leaves; 'Rubrum', with red leaves; 'Veitchianum', whose leaves are boldly striped with cream; and 'Variegatum', whose leaves are striped with creamy yellow and white. Newer cultivars are classed by the dominant foliage color, for instance, bronze-leaved hybrids or red, yellow, orange or pink-leaved hybrids. There are many beautiful forms from which to choose.

Photinia (fam. Rosaceae)

Comprising around 60 species from eastern and Southeast Asia, the Himalayas and western North America, this genus of evergreen and deciduous trees and shrubs is grown for its beautiful new foliage or fall color. The new growth of many varieties is bright pinky red. The simple, glossy, toothed leaves turn red as the weather cools and the clusters of insignificant, pungent, white, spring flowers are followed by red or dark blue berries. Photinias are popular hedging plants, at their best in mild areas.

CULTIVATION A position in full sun ensures good foliage color and compact growth. The soil

ABOVE *Photinia glabra* 'Rubens' is prized for its pinky red, new growth. Here it is decked with cream flowers too.

must be well drained and preferably enriched with organic matter. Photinias will not tolerate heavy, waterlogged soils. Mulch plants with well-decayed compost or manure and give complete plant food in spring and midsummer. Plants grown as hedges must be regularly fed and mulched because of the intense root competition. Regular, deep watering during dry spring or summer conditions is essential. Any hard pruning should be done in late winter but regular, light shearing should ensure an almost continuous display of the bright pinky red new growth. Species can be grown from seed and all can be grown from firm tip cuttings taken during summer.

CLIMATE Zone 8, but zone 7 for *P. serratifolia*.

SPECIES *P.* x *fraseri* 'Robusta' is a fast-growing, evergreen shrub, to around 5 m (16 ft), with bronze-red young leaves, becoming large with age. The flowers are larger than those of other types. *P.* x *fraseri* 'Rubens', red-leaf photinia, is an evergreen shrub growing 4–5 m (13–16 ft) high. The new foliage is a brilliant red, maturing to green. *P. serratifolia*, Chinese hawthorn, is a small, evergreen tree, growing to around 7 m (23 ft), though it can be clipped to form a hedge. The serrated, dark green leaves have a bronze tint in spring, and the small white flowers are followed by small, red berries which are attractive to birds.

Phygelius (fam. Scrophulariaceae)

These two species of evergreen shrubs from South Africa are grown for their attractive, red, summer flowers, similar to those of *Penstemon* (beard tongue), and dark green, oval leaves. They thrive in shade in warm regions, but prefer sun in cooler zones.

CULTIVATION Plant in a light, moist soil enriched with organic matter, including chalky soils, in a warm, sunny, sheltered spot. If growing in cool climates, provide protection from very cold, strong wind. If damaged by frost or wind, the rootstock will probably rejuvenate in spring. Propagate from cuttings of semi-ripened shoots taken in fall and struck in a sharp sand and peat mix of 2:1, by seed sown in early spring, or by division of the rootstock in early spring, before new growth begins.

CLIMATE Zone 8.

ABOVE 'Yellow Trumpet', a cultivar of *Phygelius aequalis*, is distinctive in varying from the usual salmon or red flowers.

SPECIES *P. aequalis* grows to 1 m (3 ft) high, with salmon pink, tubular flowers, orange and purple inside. Cultivar 'Yellow Trumpet' has creamy yellow flowers. *P. capensis*, Cape fuchsia, grows to 2 m (6 ft), with sprays of orange to dark red flowers which can reach 1 m (3 ft) long. Cultivar 'Coccineus' is a hardier, improved form with brighter, scarlet flowers. Hybrids between the two species have resulted in plants like 'Moonraker', with creamy yellow flowers, and 'African Queen', which has striking red flowers with orange-red lobes.

Phyllodoce (fam. Ericaceae)

These eight species of small, evergreen shrubs originate in the alpine regions of Europe and Asia. They are best suited to growing in pockets of cool-climate rockeries. The small, leathery leaves are long, slender and slightly downy on the undersides. The bell- or urn-shaped flowers are mostly in shades of pink or purple. They appear in late spring to early summer and are very reminiscent of heather which is in the same botanical family.

CULTIVATION These plants should be grown in acid or lime-free soil which is able to retain

ABOVE Neat, dark, leathery leaves are a perfect complement to the dainty bell-like flowers of *Phyllodoce nipponica*.

moisture, yet is free draining. Add organic matter such as leaf mould or peat before planting. Site them in semi-shade. Propagate from seed in spring under glass, or from semi-ripe cuttings in summer. Plants can also be layered in spring.

CLIMATE Best in cool to cold climates.

SPECIES *P. aleutica*, zone 2, from Asia and Alaska, grows to 25 cm (10 in), with small, solitary, urn-shaped, yellow flowers. *P. caerulea*, zone 2, to 15 cm (6 in), has a tufting habit. The solitary, pitcher-shaped flowers are purple-pink in color *P. empetriformis*, zone 3, is also a tufting plant, to 30 cm (12 in), with small, pitcher-shaped, bright reddish purple flowers. *P. nipponica*, zone 3, from Japan, is a small plant with small, whitish pink, bell-shaped flowers.

Phyllostachys (fam. Poaceae)

This genus of bamboo is one of the running or monopodial types. Underground runners or rhizomes may travel 3–4 m (10–16 ft) in a growing season and become an invasive nightmare. However, in cooler climates, many species do not spread fast and remain as manageable clumps. These are very attractive plants that may be used as features and for screening. Many species make lovely displays if grown in large, decorative tubs. Containers must be set on a solid base, not on the ground, as plants will send roots into the earth through drainage holes.

CULTIVATION Most of these bamboos can be grown in full sun or partial shade. Although tolerant of quite poor soil, they do require good drainage. Soils or potting mixes enriched with organic matter produce better looking foliage and growth. Keep plants well watered during the growing season to maintain a good appearance. Feeding is unnecessary as a rule, but container-grown plants should be given slow-release fertilizer or liquid fertilizer during the growing season. Propagate from a section of the

ABOVE Often used as a feature plant in courtyards, the black canes of *Phyllostachys nigra* will always attract interest.

rhizome that contains a node, or by dividing a section of the plant. This is best done in late winter to spring.

CLIMATE Zone 8 for most species.

SPECIES *P. aurea*, golden bamboo, is also known as fishpole bamboo, although it is not the source of split cane rods that come from the Tonkin bamboo, *Pseudosasa amabilis*, which is rarely cultivated as an ornamental. Golden bamboo may grow to 6–10 m (20–33 ft) high. It has slender, golden canes and pretty, green and gold foliage. *P. bambusoides*, madake or giant timber bamboo, from China and Japan, is a very hardy species with large leaves. It grows to 20 m (65 ft) in height. The young shoots are edible. Cultivar 'Castillonis', kimmeichiku, from Japan, grows to 12 m (33 ft), with bright gold stems, striped with green. In their native countries, they are used for a wide variety of construction purposes. *P. nigra*, black bamboo or kurochika, is a beautiful species, which is highly prized by gardeners. The stems turn black when mature, and provide striking landscape contrast. A very fast growing species, it reaches maturity within a season, growing to about 7 m (23 ft) in height. Var. *henonis*, hakichu, from Japan, grows to 12 m (40 ft), the new stems being bright green.

Physalis (fam. Solanaceae)

This genus of some 80 species, originally from Asia, Australia, Mexico and North America, includes the beautiful Chinese lantern plant, with its brilliant red, air-filled calyces, and Cape gooseberry, with its small, yellow, edible fruits. The fruits enclosed in the 'lanterns' retain their color when dried and make good Christmas decorations. All species make excellent pot or tub plants.

CULTIVATION These plants like rich, well-drained soil and a sunny or partially shaded position, with protection from wind. Water well during summer and feed with liquid fertilizer. The Cape gooseberry is a perennial, but is grown as a summer annual in a cool greenhouse in cool and cold climates. Sow seeds in spring in a heated propagating case. Pot up seedlings, then when large enough, plant out in a soil border or in large individual pots. Propagate the hardy perennials by division every three years, or raise them from seeds sown in spring, in a garden frame.

CLIMATE There are species suited to various climatic zones.

SPECIES *P. alkekengi*, bladder cherry or Chinese lantern plant, zone 6, is a hardy perennial which grows to 60 cm (24 in) tall, and produces cream, bell-shaped flowers. The very showy fruit consists of a single, scarlet berry enclosed in a bright red, papery calyx. Cultivar 'Gigantea' has very large calyces; 'Pygmaea' is a dwarf form, which grows to 20 cm (8 in). *P. ixocarpa*, tomatillo, zone 8, is an annual from Mexico, growing to over 1 m (3 ft) and producing yellow flowers and purple, sticky, edible fruit. *P. peruviana*, Cape gooseberry, zone 9, is an attractive plant with gray-green leaves, which produces yellow, edible fruits. The summer flowers are blotched with shades of yellow and purple. The dwarf Cape gooseberry, *P. pruinosa*, zone 5, is an annual, which grows to around 50 cm (20 in), and produces yellow, bell-shaped flowers and edible, yellow fruits.

Physocarpus (fam. Rosaceae)
Ninebark

Grown for their flowers, handsome foliage and unusual fruits, these ten species of hardy, deciduous shrubs are natives of Asia and America. The species in general cultivation are all native to the United States. The bark of the branches peels off in winter, to reveal a brightly colored, patterned surface. The serrated, lobed leaves are prominently veined and the small flowers form decorative clusters along the branches. These shrubs are useful for borders and as specimen plants.

CULTIVATION *Physocarpus* likes a moist, loamy soil and will grow in full sun or partial shade. Prune straggly growth in spring. Propagate from ripe seed sown in a light seed compost, or from summer cuttings of semi-hardwood struck in a sandy peat mix. Rooted suckers can also be divided from the main growth.

ABOVE *Physalis alkekengi*, Chinese lantern, is grown for its unusual, lantern-like seed capsules which can be dried for indoor decoration.

ABOVE Suckering to form small colonies, common ninebark, *Physocarpus opulifolius*, is reliable for shrub borders or screens.

CLIMATE There are species suited to various climatic zones.

SPECIES *P. bracteatus*, zone 6, grows to 2 m (6 ft), with white, summer flowers. *P. capitatus*, zone 6, to 3 m (10 ft), has an upright habit and produces white, summer flowers. *P. malvaceus*, zone 6, grows to 2 m (6 ft), and has white, summer flowers. *P. monogynus*, zone 5, grows to 1 m (3 ft), with pink flowers. *P. opulifolius*, common ninebark, zone 2, from the United States, is a very attractive species and probably the most commonly cultivated. It has rounded, heart-shaped leaves, white to pink flowers and reddish, inflated fruits. It grows to 3 m (10 ft). Cultivar 'Luteus' has bright yellow leaves when young.

Physostegia (fam. Lamiaceae)
Obedient plant

Native to North America, these hardy perennials make a striking display in borders and wild gardens. The attractive, terminal flower spikes may be pale pink, magenta or white, and make good cut flowers.

CULTIVATION Most garden soils will be suitable, with full sun or partial shade. Propagate by divi-

ABOVE An easy-care perennial, *Physostegia virginiana* flowers reliably every year. The flowers cut well for indoor decoration.

sion of the clumps or from seed. After flowering, cut plants back, as old stems can look shabby.

CLIMATE Zone 4.

SPECIES *P. virginiana*, obedient plant, is the most widely grown of the species, seldom reaching over 1.5 m (5 ft). The hinge-like structure of the flower stalks allows them to be moved and 'obediently' stay in place. The leaves are lance-shaped and serrated, and the flowers may be magenta, pink or white. Cultivar 'Alba' has white flowers; 'Gigantea' grows to 2 m (6 ft) high; and 'Vivid' has deep purple-pink blooms.

Phytolacca (fam. Phytolaccaceae)

The 25 or so species of perennials, shrubs and trees in this genus from temperate to warm and tropical climates, including the Americas and Asia, are valued for their colorful fall leaves and ornamental fruits, which are generally colored black or deep red. The perennials usually have colorful stems. Several species contain poisonous alkaloids.

CULTIVATION All species do best in well-drained soil with some organic matter. The tree species benefit from mulching, especially in their early years. Most can be grown in full sun or partial shade. They should be given ample water in spring and summer but allowed to dry out between waterings in cooler months. Fertilizer is generally not necessary unless the soil is extremely poor. Propagation is from seed obtained from fully ripe berries.

CLIMATE Zone 4 for *P. americana*, zone 9 for *P. dioica*.

SPECIES *P. americana*, pokeweed, a shrubby perennial from North America, grows to 3–4 m (10–13 ft). It has reddish stems, long oval leaves and white or pink flowers, in summer. Deep blackish red berries then form on stems up to 30 cm (12 in) long. The plant is poisonous if eaten but has long been used medicinally by native Americans. Its medicinal properties are

under continuing investigation. A rich purple dye is extracted both from roots and berries. *P. dioica*, zone 9, a large, evergreen tree, has a shady spreading canopy. Native to parts of South America, it may grow to 15–20 m (50–65 ft). Most noticeable are its thick trunk and its flaring base of wide, spreading roots, which protrude well above the soil surface. Not widely cultivated today, it was formerly grown as a shade tree in parts of southern Europe.

Picea (fam. Pinaceae)
Spruce

There are around 40 species of evergreen conifers in this genus from mountainous regions of the northern hemisphere. Widely cultivated for their lovely form and evergreen foliage, they are distinguishable from other members of Pinaceae by their short, needle-like leaves which are arranged spirally on the branches, and vary from bright green to blueish in color. Unlike firs (*Abies*), which they most closely resemble, they have pendulous cones. Fast-growing to a conical or columnar shape, spruces make handsome ornamentals for cooler climates. There are a number of attractive dwarf cultivars, suitable for smaller gardens. Several species yield excellent timber.

BELOW Slender, pendulous cones on *Picea smithiana* emphasize the graceful, weeping habit of this lovely tree.

ABOVE The canopy of this old *Phytolacca dioica* is thinning, but the tree remains distinctive with its massive trunk base.

ABOVE This mature spruce has a broad, conical shape, with its foliage extending right down to the ground.

CULTIVATION Spruces need good rain all year round, cool winters, and deep, fertile soil. Propagation is generally from seed, which germinates easily. The dwarf cultivars must be propagated from cuttings to maintain their characteristic shape and foliage. Some forms of blue spruce are propagated by grafting.

CLIMATE Cool to cold.

SPECIES *P. abies*, common or Norway spruce, zone 3, is native to Northern and Central Europe, where it can reach 60 m (200 ft) tall. In cultivation, it usually grows to about 20 m (65 ft) It has a very straight trunk, with a long, narrow, central leader, downward-sweeping, irregularly spaced side branches and pendulous branchlets. Popular dwarf cultivars are 'Clanbrassiliana', which grows to 1.5 m (5 ft) and has short leaves; 'Globosa Nana', with a very tight, compact habit, to 80 cm (32 in) high; and 'Nidiformis', which is a flat-topped shrub, to about 1 m (3 ft) high, with short leaves *P. glauca*, white spruce, zone 3, from Canada, grows to 30 m (100 ft) when mature, but grows rather slowly. In the US, the superb dwarf cultivar, var. *albertiana* 'Conica', is better known. It grows up to 1 m (3 ft) high in a perfect cone shape. *P. omorika*, Serbian spruce, zone 4, from Serbia and Bosnia, has a very narrow, upright growth habit, deep blueish green foliage and pendulous branches. This striking tree can reach 20 m (65 ft) in cultivation. *P. pungens*, Colorado or blue spruce, zone 3, from the west coast mountains of North America, forms a pyramidal shape, growing to around 30 m (100 ft) in the wild. It has blueish green, pointed needles and gray bark. Cultivar 'Glauca', known as blue spruce, is more often grown. It is a conical, symmetrical tree, 7–10 m (23–33 ft) tall, with stiff, spreading, crowded branches. It prefers a cool climate and a dry atmosphere. 'Koster' is another attractive, blue cultivar. *P. smithiana*, Himalayan spruce, zone 7, from the western Himalayas, is a vigorous species with a conical habit and graceful, pendulous branches.

Pieris (fam. Ericaceae)

Originating from North America, the West Indies, eastern Asia and the Himalayas, this genus includes seven species of fairly dense, evergreen shrubs or small trees, grown for attractive flowers and foliage. They have leathery, green leaves and sprays of tiny, white, urn-shaped, waxy flowers, similar to lily-of-the-valley, which appear in abundance during spring. *Pieris* make excellent border and specimen plants, and also look very effective in tubs or pots.

CULTIVATION Grow in slightly acid, well-drained, peaty soil, in a shady spot with some shelter from strong winds. Water frequently, especially during summer months, and trim straggly shoots after flowering. Propagate species from seed and cultivars from semi-ripe cuttings, in summer, rooted in a heated propagating case.

CLIMATE Cool and moist. Zone 7 for most species, but zone 6 for *P. japonica*.

ABOVE *Variegated pieris*, clipped to form a low hedge, borders a path, and softens the effect of the wall on the other side.

SPECIES *P. formosa*, a native of western China, grows to 4 m (13 ft) and produces a display of bronze young growth during spring. *P. formosa* var. *forrestii*, from China, has large clusters of flowers and scarlet young growth. It grows to 2 m (6 ft) high. *P. japonica*, lily-of-the-valley bush, from Japan, is a lovely shrub, growing to around 4 m (13 ft) in cultivation. It has pendulous sprays of large, heather-like, white flowers. Many cultivars are available. 'Christmas Cheer' has pink-stalked, white flowers with pink tips; 'Flamingo' has deep rose pink buds. opening to deep pink; 'Purity' is a compact form, growing to about 1 m (3 ft), with pure white flowers; and 'White Cascade' has long sprays of white flowers, over a long period. 'Variegatus' develops dark green foliage with cream margins. The cultivars 'Valley Rose' and 'Valley Valentine' are comparatively recent introductions but have proved their garden worth and so can be recommended. The former is a dwarf plant decked with pink and white blooms, while the latter produces dark red flowers from equally dark buds. Both of these were bred in Oregon.

Pilea (fam. Urticaceae)

Found in tropical regions around the world, this genus comprises more than 600 species of perennials, grown both indoors and outdoors for their handsome foliage. These plants may be succulent or woody, and growth may be upright or creeping and mat forming.

CULTIVATION Outside warm and tropical climates, grow as house plants or as pot plants in a warm greenhouse or conservatory. They do best in half pots or pans of soilless potting compost. Provide good light (but shade from direct sun), and a humid atmosphere. Allow compost to become dry on the surface before watering. Propagate in spring from cuttings made from the stem tips. Provide basal warmth for rooting.

CLIMATE Warmest parts of zone 10, to tropical.

SPECIES *P. cadierei*, aluminium plant, grows to 30 cm (12 in) and has dark green leaves with silvery markings. *P. microphylla*, artillery plant, grows to 35 cm (14 in). The foliage densely clothes the stems and the flower buds burst to release their pollen. In warm areas, this species can be invasive. *P. nummularifolia*, creeping Charlie, is a creeping type, suitable for hanging baskets.

ABOVE *Pilea microphylla*, artillery plant, has very tiny leaves and is a popular house plant.

Pimelea (fam. Thymelaeaceae)
Rice flower

There are around 80 species in this genus of small, evergreen shrubs, mainly native to Australia and New Zealand. Related to *Daphne*, they are grown for their showy, terminal flower heads in white, cream, yellow, pink or red. The flowers of many species are fragrant and the fruits are generally elongated and nut-like, but may be berry-like and succulent. Sharp hairs on the seeds can be irritating to the skin.

CULTIVATION In climates prone to frost, grow in a cool greenhouse or conservatory in pots of acid, sandy potting compost. Ensure maximum light. In the garden, the plants need an acid or neutral, well drained soil and full sun. Propagate from semi-ripe cuttings in summer, rooting them in a heated propagating case. Lightly trim plants after flowering.

CLIMATE Warmest parts of zone 9, or zone 10.

SPECIES *P. ferruginea*, pink or rosy rice flower, from Western Australia, is the most popular species in cultivation. A compact grower to about 1 m (3 ft), it has small, neat leaves in opposite rows, and rounded heads of pink flowers through spring into early summer. Named cultivars of this species are available. *P. ligustrina*, from 1.5 to 2 m (5–6 ft) high, has larger leaves and white flowers. *P. linifolia*, slender rice flower, is from the eastern and southern states of Australia. Growing to 60 cm (24 in) high, it has white flowers in summer and sometimes in other seasons. *P. prostrata* is a mat-forming species from New Zealand, which is useful as a groundcover or rockery plant. Growing only 15 cm (6 in) high, it has white flowers, followed by tiny white berries. *P. rosea*, pink rice flower, is a rounded shrub, with a height and breadth of about 60 cm (24 in). It has bright pink flowers, although they may occasionally be pale pink or white, in summer. Western Australia's *P. spectabilis* grows to between 70 cm and 1.5 m (28–60 in) high. It has large, showy, flower heads, in white, opening from deep pink buds. The most spectacular species, it is not easy to grow outside its preferred climate. *P. suaveolens*, also from Western Australia, grows to about 70 cm (28 in) high, with large, fragrant, yellow-green flowers.

Pineapple

(*Ananas* species, fam. Bromeliaceae)

Native to South America, this fascinating, perennial plant has stiff, sword-like leaves borne in rosettes on short fleshy stems. Grown for its fruit, the pineapple is an important commercial crop in many tropical countries, but in the US it is grown only as a novelty for its foliage. It needs a warm greenhouse.

CULTIVATION Pineapples can be grown in pots using soilless potting compost. Plants need maximum light and a humid atmosphere. In the growing season, water the plants well and feed with a liquid fertilizer about once a week. Reduce watering considerably in winter. Propagate from rooted offsets in summer. Alternatively, propagate from the tuft of leaves at the top of the fruit. Cut it off and treat it like a cutting, rooting it in cuttings compost in a warm propagating case.

BELOW This pretty species of *Pimelea* has its creamy flowerheads framed by a broad, pale green calyx.

ABOVE A large pineapple, close to maturity, sits in a nest of broad leaves.

CLIMATE Tropical only.

SPECIES *Ananas nanus*, the smallest of the species, produces decorative, edible fruit, to 10 cm (4 in) or more long. *A. bracteatus* var. *tricolor* is a larger, improved variety with white, yellow, green- and red-striped leaves. It is slow to reproduce. *A. comosus*, considered by early European visitors to South America as the finest fruit of all, grows to around 75 cm (30 in). It has long, narrow leaves and dense heads of reddish flowers which develop into the large, fleshy fruit, bearing a rosette of leaves at the top. Some varieties of this species have prickles on the edges and tips of the leaves. A green- and yellow-striped variety, *A. c.* var. *variegatus*, makes an attractive pot plant.

Pine nut (*Pinus pinea* 'Fragilis' fam. Pinaceae)

The seeds of the Mediterranean stone pine are the pine nuts most commonly available for various culinary applications. They can be eaten raw or roasted and salted, but are more frequently used in pasta and vegetarian dishes, as well as in soups and stews. They are also sometimes used in confectionery. The stone pine grows into a large, flat-topped tree that may reach 20 m (65 ft) or more in height. The roundish cones must ripen fully in hot sun for the cone scales to open and release the seeds. The seeds are encased in a tough outer covering that must be crushed to remove the seeds. Other pines with edible nuts include the Mexican nut pine, *Pinus cembroides*; the arolla pine, *P. cembra*, from Central Europe; and the Russian *P. cembra* ssp. *sibirica*.

CULTIVATION These trees are grown from seed sown as soon as it is ripe. Plant in any well-drained soil and water regularly through their first two or three years. However, they are remarkably drought-tolerant once established. Growth is fairly rapid for a conifer and young trees will have an upright habit, developing the broad umbrella-shaped crown with maturity. Trees should not be pruned.

CLIMATE Best in a Mediterranean climate with hot, dry summers and cold, wet winters. Zone 8.

ABOVE The stone pine, *Pinus pinea*, is the most common source of the edible pine nut. Mature trees have tall, bare trunks.

Pinus (fam. Pinaceae)

Pine

This well-known conifer group comprises over 100 species. Except for one species, which can be found as far south as Indonesia, they are native to the northern hemisphere. The pines are renowned for their commercial uses, in particular the production of timber and paper, while the resin of some species yields turpentine. The needles are used as mulch and the cones and bark for fuel. Although regarded as trees of far northern regions, such as Canada or Scandinavia, the greatest number of species is found in warm temperate and subtropical parts of North America. The bristlecone pine (*P. aristata*), from the Rocky Mountains, has some of the oldest known specimens in the world. Over 6000 annual rings have been counted on contorted specimens of this species, growing on windswept mountain tops. Also in the United States is the tallest known species, *P. lambertiana*, which has been known to reach over 80 m (260 ft). Pine leaves or 'needles' are borne on short shoots in a fixed number, this being one of the most distinctive identifying characteristics of *Pinus*. The number relevant to each species is noted below. Most pines are two- to five-needled and rarely one. In some species, there can be a variation in number. Full maturity of cones and seeds is achieved over many months, so that at any time of year, three successive stages of seed-cone development can be seen along the branches. Pines are often grown for special purposes, such as screens, windbreaks, timber production and Christmas trees. There are some highly ornamental species, although most are reasonably attractive. There is a species of pine to suit almost every climate, from the tropics to very cold zones.

CULTIVATION As the various species of pine originate from a vast range of climates and habitats, their requirements in cultivation vary widely. However, most like full sun, the only exception being where a species is grown in a hotter or drier climate than it has adapted to. In such instances, partial shading is advisable, as this provides cooler conditions and humidity. Propagate from seed sown at any time of year in mild climates, or in spring in areas with cold winters. Use a light, sandy germinating medium, barely cover the seeds, and place in a warm, shady position. Germination mostly occurs very rapidly. Pot seedlings into open-bottomed tubes or black polythene bags to avoid coiling of the roots. If large numbers of trees are required, plant seedlings in rows in a well-tilled plot of soil and transplant bare-rooted to their permanent positions when about 20–30 cm (8–12 in) high. Bare-rooted planting is normally done in winter and should only be used in regions with cool, wet winters. Container-grown plants can be planted out at any time, but preferably from winter to early spring. Watering is generally unnecessary, unless pines are established under very harsh conditions, as their roots rapidly penetrate to the subsoil. Staking of young trees is rarely required. Pines generally respond well to feeding, superphosphate giving good results where

ABOVE An unusually contorted trunk makes this specimen of *Pinus pinaster* a focal point of this Japanese-style garden.

ABOVE Easily recognized from a distance, *Pinus patula* should be sited so its distinctive form can be appreciated.

soils are deficient in phosphorus. Pruning is not normally required for these symmetrical trees; however, twin leading shoots should be reduced to a single growth to avoid a weak point in the long term.

CLIMATE Choose a pine to suit your area.

SPECIES *P. bungeana*, lacebark pine, zone 5, from central China, is a slow grower but capable of reaching over 15 m (50 ft) in ideal conditions. It is prized for its flaky bark which sheds in patches to reveal a pure white trunk. It has short, stiff, shiny, green needles in groups of three, and shiny, gray twigs. The small, rounded cones are pale brown in color. *P. canariensis*, Canary Island pine, zone 9, grows up to 30 m (100 ft) tall. It has a very straight trunk, with dull reddish brown bark, broken into large plates. The very fine, straight, dull green needles, 25 cm (10 in) long, are borne in threes, and the brown cones are oval shaped. *P. contorta*, shore pine or lodgepole pine, zone 7, from western United States, Canada and Alaska, is best suited to cool climates. It is a pyramidal 'Christmas tree' type, with a long central leader and densely packed,

short, twisted needles, in twos. *P. coulteri*, big-cone pine, zone 7, from the mountains of California and Mexico, is known for its huge cones, which grow to 35 cm (14 in) long and 15 cm (6 in) wide. It is a broad-crowned, heavy-branched tree, with stiff, blueish green needles in threes. *P. densiflora*, Japanese red pine, zone 5, is often used in bonsai in Japan. Generally it is a medium-sized pine with soft, twisted needles like those of *P. radiata*, normally borne in twos. This lovely tree has attractive, orange-red, flaking bark and egg-shaped, yellow-purplish cones. It is suitable for cool areas with high rainfall. *P. elliottii*, slash pine, zone 8, from the south-east of the United States, is useful for warmer, summer-rainfall areas. It makes a fine tree, with deeply furrowed, red-brown bark on its straight trunk and densely packed, straight needles, to 25 cm (10 in) long, in bundles of two or three. This species is used for screens and windbreaks, as well as for avenues, in warm climates. It is also grown for its timber. *P. halepensis*, Aleppo pine, zone 8, from the eastern Mediterranean, tolerates most conditions and is a good choice for dry areas. Generally, it grows to less than 10 m (33 ft) high, sometimes forming a large shrub. Young trees are a broad, pyramidal shape, becoming more rounded with maturity. It has fine, straight, dull green needles, to 10 cm (4 in) long, in pairs. This species has attractive, reddish brown, scaly bark, while the young shoots are gray-green in color. The egg-shaped cones are reddish brown. *P. lambertiana*, sugar pine, zone 7, from Oregon and California, is a very handsome pine with a very tall, straight, slender, smooth, gray trunk. The needles are borne in bundles of five and are around 10 cm (4 in) long. The slightly curved cones are unusual, growing up to 45 cm (18 in) long, with thin, rounded, overlapping scales. This is one of the 'white pine' group, all of which make fine ornamentals but require good soil and prefer cool climates with high rainfall. *P. montezumae*, zone 6, from Mexico, is a variable species which has been divided into a number of varieties. The fine needles, 15–25 cm (6–10 in) long, are generally in bundles of five, but occasionally

ABOVE This close-up shows the soft, drooping needle leaves of *Pinus patula* and clusters of small, male cones.

they may be in bundles of four to six. They are blue-green or gray-green, and variable in habit. This species is suitable for a wide range of temperate and subtropical climates. *P. monticola*, western white pine, zone 6, from south-west Canada and western United States, is related to and rather like *P. lambertiana*, differing mainly in the size of its cones, which are much smaller. As a young tree it is quite lovely, its needles, borne in bundles of five, being shiny, dark green on the outer face with bands of bright blueish white on the two inner faces. In its habitat, this tree can reach heights of 65 m (215 ft). *P. mugo*, dwarf mountain pine, zone 3, from central and southern Europe, one of the few naturally dwarf pines, may be a spreading shrub or a small tree, preferring a cool temperate climate. The branch tips point upward and the stiff, curved, olive green needles are borne in pairs, in dense rosettes. Its windswept appearance makes it an appealing bonsai sub-

ject. This species and some of the more compact cultivars and wild forms also make good rockery plants. The Pumilio Group is often a semi-prostrate mound of closely packed needles, though it can grow to 2 m (6 ft). Cultivar 'Gnom' has a rounded, compact habit, rarely exceeding 1 m (3 ft) in height. *P. nigra*, black pine, zone 5, from central and southern Europe, has an open, conical habit, rarely exceeding 15 m (50 ft) in cultivation. It has a straight trunk, dark, furrowed bark and stiff, twisted, dark gray-green needles, in pairs, 10–15 cm (4–6 in) long. *P. palustris*, long-leaf or pitch pine, zone 7, from the south-east of the United States, is regarded as a most useful timber tree. Adult trees are similar to *P. elliottii* but they have heavier, more twisted limbs. The young plants are distinctive as they pass through a stemless, tufted stage for the first five to ten years, with the growing point at or below ground-level, and densely crowded, floppy needles, up to 40 cm (16 in) long. The stem then elongates, but stays unbranched for a height of up to 4 m (13 ft) or more, the seedling tree appearing as a straight pole, clothed in long, soft, bright green needles. This species does well in swampy areas, though it requires a long, hot, humid summer to make good growth. It is not widely cultivated, due to slow early development. *P. patula*, Mexican weeping pine, zone 8, is known mainly as an ornamental in the US. Probably the most elegant pine, it is a vigorous, broadly pyramidal tree, usually 10–15 m (33–50 ft) tall, with fine, soft, mid-green needles drooping from the branches. Needles grow in threes to about 20 cm (8 in) long. This species does well in warm temperate areas, though it tolerates cold conditions. *P. pinaster*, maritime pine, zone 8, from south-west Europe and the Mediterranean, can grow up to 25 m (80 ft) tall in cultivation. It is an important source of turpentine. The maritime pine has a short, often slightly crooked trunk and a rounded crown. Its attractive, reddish brown, fissured bark, with its jigsaw pattern, is very distinctive. The curved, twisted, shiny, gray-green needles, 10–20 cm (4–8 in) long, are borne in pairs. Suitable for exposed sites, this species does well in sandy, gravelly or hard clay soils of relatively low fertility. On such sites, especially near the sea, it makes a stunted, crooked, often very striking, small tree. Climatically it is suited to milder parts of the US. *P. pinea*, stone pine or Roman pine, zone 8, from southern Europe and Turkey, was considered the 'true' pine in Roman times, grown for its edible seeds, or pine nuts, as opposed to *P. pinaster*, the wild or 'false' pine. It has a characteristic growth habit, growing only 15–20 m (50–65 ft) tall, with a straight, often leaning trunk and a flat, umbrella-like crown of dense, deep green foliage. The slightly twisted needles, about 10 cm (4 in) long, are borne in pairs, and the abundant, rounded cones, 10–15 cm (4–6 in) long, have very thick, woody, brown scales. Its climatic preferences are similar to those of the cluster pine, but it is not quite so tolerant of poor soils. *P. ponderosa*, western yellow pine, zone 6, is a native of western North America, where it is valued for its timber. It can grow up

BELOW Scots pine, *Pinus sylvestris*, is restricted to growing in cool areas. This mature cone has alrerady opened to shed its seeds.

to 70 m (230 ft) tall in its habitat, but is generally much smaller in cultivation. It is quite slender and upright, with an open habit. Its distinctive bark forms a mosaic of different-colored plates. The stiff, straight, pale green leaves are borne in threes and are 15–25 cm (6–10 in) long. Preferring heavy soils, this species does well in cooler areas of the US. *P. radiata*, Monterey pine, zone 7, is a native of California, where it makes a rather crooked tree of only moderate size. However, in some forest plantations it has been known to reach heights of over 50 m (160 ft) and diameters of 1 m (3 ft) or more. This species is distinguished from most other pines by the rich, dark green foliage shade, the furrowed, gray bark and the rather soft, twisted needles, 7–10 cm (3–4 in) long, in groups of three. It is a particularly good pine for coastal planting. *P. roxburghii* (syn. *P. longifolia*), Chir or longleafed Indian pine, zone 9, is very similar to its relative, *P. canariensis*, differing mainly in its slightly more spreading, roundtopped habit and the richer red color of its bark. It has light green, drooping needles, to 30 cm (12 in) long, which grow in bundles of three, and oval cones with reflexed scales. This is a beautiful Himalayan species, its range extending from Afghanistan to Bhutan, but sadly, it is not often grown, possibly because it needs a warm climate. *P. thunbergii*, Japanese black pine, zone 6, is similar to *P. radiata*, but it has stiffer, slightly thicker and deeper grayish green needles, borne in pairs. Its irregular branches and purplish black bark, and its capacity to stand trimming and pruning, have made it an important bonsai subject in Japan. It does well in sandy soils and in coastal conditions in cooler climates.

Piper (fam. Piperaceae)
Pepper

Native to many tropical regions of the world, this genus comprises more than 1000 species of climbing shrubs and trees, including *P. nigrum* which is grown commercially for its black and white pepper. Only a few of the species are in general cultivation, usually as ornamentals.

CULTIVATION Grow in a warm greenhouse or conservatory in pots of soil-based potting compost, with shade from direct sun and a humid atmosphere. Propagate from seed in spring, or semi-ripe cuttings in summer, both with bottom heat.

CLIMATE Zone 10 to tropical.

SPECIES *P. betle*, from India, is a climbing shrub with green flowers and fleshy, red fruits. The leaves of this species are packed into a plug and masticated like chewing gum. *P. kadsura*, Japanese pepper, is a deciduous shrub which climbs by aerial roots. *P. methysticum*, from the Pacific Islands, is a shrub growing to 2–6 m (6–20 ft). It is widely cultivated, especially in Fiji, for the preparation of the drink, kava-kava. *P. nigrum*, common pepper, from Malaysia and India, is an attractive climbing shrub with glossy, green leaves and green fruit which matures to red, then to black. Black pepper is made by grinding the whole fruit, while white pepper is made from the inside of the fruit.

ABOVE Long chains of green fruits on *Piper nigrum* will ripen to red, then black, before being harvested as peppercorns.

Pisonia (fam. Nyctaginaceae)

Native to tropical and subtropical regions, including South America, this genus comprises about 50 species of evergreen shrubs and trees. They are grown for their foliage and are mainly used as house or pot plants for the warm greenhouse or conservatory.

CULTIVATION In the greenhouse or home, grow in pots of soil-based potting compost. Plants need good light, but shade from direct sun. Propagate from semi-ripe cuttings in summer, or from seed in spring, with bottom heat for both.

CLIMATE Tropical.

SPECIES *P. alba* is a shrub-like species known as lettuce tree in Malaysia and the Philippines. It has striking, light green foliage. Mostly grown as an ornamental, the leaves are also eaten raw or cooked. Plants range from 3 to 5 m (10–16 ft) in height. *P. umbellifera*, parapara or bird catcher tree, grows from 2.5 to 10 m (8–33 ft) tall. It may be shrubby or tree-like, with shiny, oval leaves, 10–40 cm (4–16 in) long, and tiny, pink or yellow flowers with a sticky calyx, which is capable of trapping small birds. There is a variegated form, 'Variegata', which has wavy-margined leaves, tinged with pink, especially when young.

ABOVE Insects and small birds are unable to escape the extremely sticky calyces of *Pisonia umbellifera*.

Pistachio (*Pistacia vera*, fam. Anacardiaceae)

The edible pistachio grows on a deciduous tree 8–10 m (26–33 ft) high. Native to western Asia and Iran, it is widely cultivated in the Mediterranean and western US and other regions with similar climates. Male and female flowers are borne on separate trees, so trees of both sexes are needed to produce nuts. Trees bear nuts after about five years. Many have a biennial cropping habit: they bear a very heavy crop one year and a very light one the next. Nuts are harvested in fall. The nut is eaten raw or salted. It is also used in confectionery and to flavor ice cream.

CULTIVATION These trees can be grown from seed, but better results come from trees that have been budded with selected, heavy-bearing varieties. They are usually planted in winter while they are dormant. They need well-drained soil, preferably enriched with organic matter. Apply complete plant food in spring and again in late summer. Prune only to remove any weak growth or to head back very vigorous growth. Trees produce flowers, and therefore nuts, on the previous season's growth.

CLIMATE Warmest parts of zone 9. The ideal climate has hot summers and cool winters.

ABOVE Large clusters of nuts are produced on pistachio trees during good seasons. These are close to maturity.

Pistacia (fam. Anacardiaceae)
Pistachio, mastic tree

This genus of nine species of evergreen and deciduous trees is native to the Mediterranean, Asia, southern United States and Central America. Some are cultivated for their edible nuts, resins and oils.

CULTIVATION In frost-prone climates, tender species should be grown in a cool greenhouse. All need well-drained soil and prefer a warm, sunny position. Most prefer a Mediterranean climate of hot, dry summers and cool to cold, wet winters. *P. chinensis* tolerates quite cool climates but is unsuitable for very cold zones. *P. vera* needs a hot, dry summer to flower well and set good crops of nuts. All will grow from seed, but selected varieties are propagated by budding and grafting.

CLIMATE Warmest parts of zone 9 for most species. *P. chinensis* will grow in zone 8.

SPECIES *P. chinensis*, from China and Taiwan, is a deciduous tree which grows to 20 m (65 ft) in its habitat, but only to around 10–12 m (33–40 ft) in cultivation. It is a very ornamental

BELOW A lovely, small tree for home gardens or street plantings, *Pistacia chinensis* is seen here in all its fall glory.

tree with dark green, compound leaves which color to brilliant red, gold or orange in fall. *P. lentiscus*, from the Mediterranean, is an evergreen which grows to about 5 m (16 ft). This is the mastic tree, producing resin which has been used for chewing gum since classical times. Mastic is also used in dentistry and as a varnish for oil paintings. *P. terebinthus* is a deciduous tree, native to the Mediterranean, which grows to around 5 m (16 ft). It was formerly used as a source of turpentine. *P. vera*, pistachio nut tree, is a deciduous tree from western Asia and Iran, growing 8–10 m (26–33 ft) tall. This is the source of the edible nut, delicious eaten raw and also used in confectionary and ice cream.

Pitcairnia (fam. Bromeliaceae)

This genus of around 260 species of grass-like bromeliads is from the tropical Americas, the West Indies and West Africa. Most are terrestrial plants, forming mounds of foliage, from which appear stems of long-lasting flowers in red, orange or yellow. The long, narrow leaves are almost spineless in some species, but many are heavily spined.

ABOVE The flowers of pitcairnias are surrounded or enclosed by highly colorful bracts. The inflorescence of this species resembles an Olympic torch.

CULTIVATION Grow in a warm greenhouse or conservatory in pots of soilless potting compost. Plants need good light (but shade from direct sun), and a humid atmosphere. Keep plants only slightly moist in winter. Propagate from well-developed, rooted offsets in spring or summer.

CLIMATE Tropical.

SPECIES These are not readily available outside their countries of origin. *P. corallina*, from Colombia and Peru, is hard to grow, but produces trailing clusters of lovely, red flowers. It grows to 1 m (3 ft). *P. flammea* grows well in fairly heavy shade. It has narrow, spineless, sword-shaped leaves up to 90 cm (36 in), long and soft scarlet flower spikes. *P. paniculata* has large, erect sprays of striking, red and yellow flowers, borne on long, slightly drooping stems. It is fast growing in spring.

Pithecellobium (fam. Leguminosae)

This genus comprises about 20 species of tropical and subtropical trees and shrubs, generally grown as ornamentals, though some yield tannin and commercial timber. They have

ABOVE Studded with savage thorns, the trunks of *Pithecellobium dulce* are quite safe from attack by any predator.

thorny stems, pinnate leaves, and heads or spikes of funnel shaped, five-lobed flowers, followed by flat, curved seed pods.

CULTIVATION Outside the tropics and subtropics, grow in a warm greenhouse, although plants are unlikely to be available outside countries of origin. Grow in a rich, well-drained potting compost and water well in growing season. Keep barely moist in winter. Propagate from seed or by air layering.

CLIMATE Warmest parts of zone 10 to tropical.

SPECIES *P. arboreum*, from Mexico, Central America and the West Indies, grows to a height of 20 m (65 ft). It has thick bark, long, slender leaves, and white flowers. *P. dulce*, Manila tamarind or Madras thorn, from Central America, was introduced to tropical regions of Asia as a shade tree or thorny hedge. It is very useful in those areas, producing edible fruit and seed oil from which soap is made. The bark also yields tannins and the timber is suitable for fire wood.

Pittosporum (fam. Pittosporaceae)

Native to many subtropical and tropical regions, this genus of about 200 species is particularly abundant in Australia and New Zealand. It provides some of the best, most useful garden shrubs and trees, with small, fragrant flowers in spring. Species are used for shade, shelter and hedges, as well as for ornamental garden specimens. They are also fairly widely grown in the US in zone 9, and some are hardy enough for zone 8. In frost-prone climates, the tender species can be grown in a cool greenhouse.

CULTIVATION In the greenhouse or conservatory, grow in pots of soil-based potting compost. Provide maximum light and airy conditions. Stand plants outdoors for the summer. In the garden, grow in any well-drained, moisture-retentive soil, in a sunny position. Shelter from wind. Green-leaved pittosporums will tolerate

ABOVE Decorative clusters of berries are a feature of *Pittosporum rhombifolium*. Orange when mature, these last for months.

partial shade. Hedges can be trimmed in spring and summer. Propagate from fresh seed under glass, or from semi-ripe cuttings in summer, with bottom heat.

CLIMATE Zone 9 for most species.

SPECIES *P. crassifolium*, karo, a native of New Zealand, is a tall shrub or small tree, to 5 m (16 ft) high. It has leathery, oval, deep green leaves and terminal clusters of fragrant, star-shaped, reddish purple, early summer flowers. The fleshy fruit is oval in shape and greenish white in color. Cultivar 'Variegatum' grows to 3 m (10 ft) high, with gray to bright green leaves, edged in creamy white. It tolerates exposed coastal conditions and salty winds. *P. eugenioides*, tarata or lemon wood, also from New Zealand, is a lovely, fast-growing large shrub or small tree, to about 12 m (40 ft). Densely foliaged, the wavy-edged, shiny, yellow-green leaves emit a lemon aroma when crushed. This species has a grayish white, smooth trunk and produces clusters of small, yellow flowers in summer, followed by large clusters of oval, green fruit which persist through fall and winter. Cultivar 'Variegatum', growing to 4.5 m (15 ft), is an

BELOW *Pittosporum eugenioides* 'Variegatum' makes a dense billowing hedge, screen or windbreak.

excellent, creamy yellow-variegated foliage form, and is the most popular with gardeners. *P. phillyreoides*, weeping pittosporum, is a graceful tree, to around 10 m (33 ft), with shiny, dark green leaves on pendulous branches. The yellow flowers are borne singly or in small clusters at the ends of the branches, and are followed by deep yellow fruits which ripen to a reddish brown. *P. rhombifolium*, orange-berried pittosporum, a native of the rainforests of eastern Australia, may grow to 20 m (65 ft) but is generally about 10 m (33 ft) in cultivation. It has glossy, oval leaves and clusters of small, creamy white flowers, followed by bright orange berries. The berries are very decorative and are persistent on the tree for many months. It is an ideal small tree for the home garden and is widely planted as a street tree in some areas. *P. tenuifolium*, kohuhu, zone 8, from New Zealand, grows into a small tree or tall shrub of around 10 m (33 ft). The attractive, silvery green, wavy-edged leaves contrast with the blackish stems and bark. Small, purple, deliciously scented flowers appear in spring, followed by round, green fruits, ripening to black. Many forms make excellent, hardy garden plants. *P. tobira*, Japanese mock orange, zone 8, from Japan and China, is a slow-growing shrub or small tree, up to 5 m (16 ft) high, mainly grown for its attractive, wavy, leathery, dark green leaves, and creamy yellow flowers with a lovely fragrance of orange blossom. Clusters or orange-yellow fruit follow the flowers. Particularly hardy and wind-resistant, it also tolerates coastal exposure. It is often cultivated as a tub plant, especially in Europe. *P. undulatum*, Australian mock orange, is a tree, to 12 m (40 ft) tall, with wavy, dark green leaves and small, whitish cream to yellow, spring and summer flowers with a very strong, daphne-like perfume. The fruit is a yellow berry.

Planchonella (fam. Sapotaceae)

There are around 60 species in this genus of trees native to tropical and subtropical areas of Malaysia, northern Australia, New Zealand and Polynesia. The timber from these reasonably tall trees is used for carving and fine woodwork. The New Zealand species, *P. novo zelandica*, is probably the most suitable for growing as an ornamental. This genus is unlikely to be available outside the countries of origin.

CULTIVATION Outside the tropics or subtropics, grow in a warm greenhouse or conservatory, as planchonellas cannot tolerate frost. Grow in well drained, soil-based compost. Outdoors grow in well drained, loamy, humus-rich soil in

ABOVE Mature, black fruits of *Planchonella australis* cut open to reveal the soft, pink-flushed pulp, containing the shiny, black seeds.

a warm, sunny, sheltered position. Propagate from ripe seed, from cuttings, or by layering.

CLIMATE Zone 10 to tropical.

SPECIES *P. australis*, black apple, grows to over 30 m (100 ft) in its rainforest habitat. It has glossy leaves, clusters of small, white flowers, and black plum-like fruit. This tree yields a milky sap. *P. laurifolia* grows into a tall tree in its natural, rainforest habitat. It has mottled, scented bark, shiny leaves and plum-like fruits. *P. novo zelandica*, tawapou, is a handsome specimen tree, to 5 m (16 ft), with glossy, dark green leaves, white flowers and large woody seeds.

Platanus (fam. Platanaceae)
Plane tree, sycamore

Most of the six or seven species in this genus of large, deciduous trees from the northern hemisphere are native to North America and Mexico, with one from south-east Europe. They look somewhat like maples, but have very large, lobed leaves, opposite on the stems. Tolerant of pollution, they are widely planted as street trees and also as avenue plantings on large properties.

CULTIVATION All species tolerate a wide range of conditions, but prefer to be grown in deep, good quality soils. They do best in areas where rainfall is reliable or where ample water is available. They can be pruned, but it is much better to allow them to attain their natural, broad-domed shape. Plane trees are easily propagated from seed, but they are very commonly grown from hardwood cuttings of dormant wood, taken in winter.

CLIMATE There are species suited to several climatic zones.

SPECIES *Platanus* x *hispanica*, zone 5, London plane, so-called for its extensive planting in that city, is also extensively grown in many other cities throughout the world. It is a large

ABOVE Gold and tawny fall leaves deck these imposing London planes, *Platanus* x *hispanica*. Tolerant of pollution, they make fine street trees.

tree, to 35 m (115 ft), with a heavy trunk of mottled cream and blue-gray, flaking bark. The rounded fruits and leaves shed hairs which can cause respiratory problems in susceptible people. *P. occidentalis*, zone 4, known as eastern sycamore or buttonwood in its native United States, is a broad, spreading tree that can grow over 45 m (145 ft) tall. *P. orientalis*, zone 6, oriental plane, from south-eastern Europe and western Asia, grows 30 m (100 ft) or more. Superficially similar to the London plane, the leaf lobes are very much narrower. This species is also popular as a street tree or for growing in parks and large gardens.

Platycerium (fam. Polypodiaceae)
Staghorn fern, elkhorn fern

Commonly found in tropical rainforests of Southeast Asia, Africa, South America and Australia, this genus of 17 species of ferns contains both epiphytic and lithophytic (rock-growing) types. The frond structure varies, but always comprises two forms, fertile and infer-PP

ABOVE *Platycerium bifurcatum*, common staghorn fern, is made up of individual overlapping plants, each of which will grow if separated from the mass.

tile. The backing, or nest, leaves are infertile, helping to attach the fern to its host, and providing moisture and food to the roots of the fern. The fertile fronds overhang the base of the plant and produce spore material. When they die off, they are replaced by new fronds.

CULTIVATION These ferns produce offsets or plantlets on the outside of the nest leaves, resulting in the continual growth of the clump. These can be carefully cut off, attached to boards or logs, and kept moist until established and then placed in permanent positions. *P. superbum,* however, must be propagated from spores and, for the novice grower, this is quite difficult. Elkhorns and staghorns can be grown on boards, terracotta, hardwood logs, a tree trunk, or on hanging baskets lined with bark or moss. They grow slowly, taking around four years to produce the fertile fronds. Outside the tropics, grow in an intermediate greenhouse or conservatory.

CLIMATE Tropical.

SPECIES *P. bifurcatum*, common staghorn fern, is an Australian species, which is native to New South Wales and Queensland. The nest leaves are large, wavy-edged and rounded. The fertile fronds protrude outward into two forks, often with several lobes, carrying the spore cases on the underside. These fronds become pendulous with age. *P. superbum*, staghorn fern, is a beautiful species, and much larger than *P. bifurcatum*. The large, light gray-green backing leaves form a circular shape, while the fertile fronds extend outwards and become pendulous like those of the common staghorn fern. Spore cases develop on the frond undersides. A frayed appearance is created when the spore cases burst to reveal masses of hanging threads.

Platycodon (fam. Campanulaceae)
Balloon flower

From China and Japan, this is a single-species genus of perennials, suitable for growing in borders or clusters. The dwarf varieties look attractive in rockeries.

CULTIVATION *Platycodon* needs a rich, fertile soil and a sunny position. It can be grown from seed or cuttings, or by division of the clumps, which is best carried out in spring.

ABOVE The stems of *Platycodon* often need light staking so that the flowering stems do not lie on the ground.

CLIMATE Zone 4.

SPECIES *P. grandiflorus*, balloon flower, grows to 60 cm (24 in) high, producing balloon-like buds that open to purple-blue, bell-shaped flowers, during late summer. The serrated leaves are an attractive blueish green color. Many lovely cultivars are available.

Platylobium (fam. Papilionaceae)

There are around six species in this small genus of native Australian evergreen shrubs, grown for their attractive foliage and brightly colored, pea-shaped flowers which appear in summer or fall.

CULTIVATION These easy-care plants will grow in any well-drained soil. To propagate, pour boiling water over the hard, black seeds, produced in broad, flat seed pods, and leave them to soak overnight. Those that swell are fertile, and will germinate rapidly if planted in sandy soil. Once established, these plants tolerate dry conditions. Where frosts are a problem, grow in a cool, airy greenhouse or conservatory.

CLIMATE Zone 9.

ABOVE Flowers of *Platylobium formosum* are borne singly. Known as handsome fat pea this plant produces either yellow or red flowers.

SPECIES These are not readily available outside their native country. *P. alternifolium* is a trailing, prostrate species with broad, soft leaves and bright yellow or red flowers. *P. formosum*, handsome flat pea, is an upright shrub, to 1 m (3 ft), with heart-shaped leaves, yellow or red flowers, and a hairy calyx. *P. triangulare* is also a prostrate grower, but it has triangular, ivy-shaped leaves. The yellow flowers are borne in pairs and the calyces are hairy.

Plectranthus (fam. Lamiaceae)

The 350 species of herbaceous plants and shrubs in this genus, which is related to *Coleus*, are found in many tropical and subtropical regions of the world. Most species have toothed, aromatic foliage and attractive, small flowers. The plant stems are square in section.

CULTIVATION Outside the tropics, grow in an intermediate to warm greenhouse or conservatory in pots of soil-based potting compost. Shade plants from direct sun, but ensure good light. Propagate from cuttings prepared from the stem tips, in spring or summer, or from seed sown as soon as available. Provide bottom heat for both.

CLIMATE Tropical.

ABOVE *Plectranthus saccatus* is a vigorous, subshrub, growing to 60 cm (24 in) high. Lavender-blue flowers appear through the warm months.

SPECIES *P. amboinicus*, five spice, grows up to 30 cm (12 in) high. It has very aromatic, fleshy leaves, covered in fine hairs, and bears mauve-blue flowers on spikes. This species has long been cultivated for culinary use in India, Southeast Asia and tropical America. *P. argentatus* has silvery green, very furry leaves and mauve-blue flowers. It is fast growing and makes a good groundcover for semi-shaded areas. *P. australis* grows 60–80 cm (24–32 in) high, with fleshy leaves and purple flowers. *P. oertendahlii*, candle plant, has attractive foliage, deep green above and purple-crimson beneath. Sprays of pale pink to mauve flowers appear in early fall. This species is useful as a groundcover and also for hanging baskets.

Pleione (fam. Orchidaceae)

Both epiphytic and terrestrial types are found in this genus of 16 species of orchids, which are found from India through to Taiwan and Thailand. The flowers come in many colors, but are often white, pink, cerise, mauve or purple.

ABOVE Lovely, small terrestrial orchids, *Pleione* species and hybrids have fringed lips, mostly in a contrasting color.

CULTIVATION These orchids are usually grown in pans in a cold (unheated) greenhouse. Use a proprietary orchid compost, formulated for terrestrial orchids. The plants are best repotted every year, before flowering commences. Water well in spring and summer but keep only slightly moist in winter. Provide good light, but shade from direct strong sun. Propagate by division when repotting. Retain only young pseudobulbs for repotting.

CLIMATE Zone 9.

SPECIES *P. humilis* is found growing on trees in its habitat at altitudes of 2500 m (8125 ft). The flower stalk rises from the base of the pseudobulb and the flowers are pure white, with a fringed lip, colored primrose inside. *P. limprichtii*, from Tibet, produces pink to purple flowers with a large, pink, fringed lip, spotted with brown. *P. praecox* grows on oak and rhododendron trees at quite low altitudes. The light purple flowers have white mid-veins on the petals, and a fringed lip, blotched with yellow.

Plum (fam. Rosaceae)

Cultivars of the European group (the species mentioned below) are commonly grown plums. The Japanese plums (Prunus salicina cultivars) grow best in the warmer climate of the west. In severe climates a group of hybrids produced from American wild plums, Japanese plums and other species is grown. Believed to have originated from the temperate zones of Eurasia, the plum has been cultivated for longer than any other fruit, apart from the apple. It is also said that Alexander the Great introduced the plum into Greece from Syria or Persia, where the damson plum has been growing for a very long time. The plum is grown not only for its fruit but also as an ornamental, because of its variously colored flowers and foliage.

CULTIVATION European plums like heavy clay soils, while Japanese plums prefer a lighter soil. Good drainage is essential for both and ade-

ABOVE Plum blossom makes a pretty addition to the spring garden with the added promise of fruit to come.

quate water is necessary once the fruit has begun to develop. Propagate by budding onto different rootstocks. Though the flowers are bisexual, it is best to plant another recommended variety for pollination. Few plums set good crops without cross-pollination. It is essential to select the right pollinator for optimum cropping, but a fruit nursery will be able to advise on this. Pruning in the early years involves shaping the tree to develop strong leaders and an open centre. As the plum is borne on the same short stems or spurs, year after year, pruning is needed to bring on new fruiting wood. Reduce the number of stems to prevent overcropping and improve fruit quality. Tip prune the branches to keep the tree from becoming too tall, cut out dead wood, and keep the centre of the tree open. Pruning is done in early summer to avoid infection from the disease known as silver leaf. All large wounds should be painted with proprietary pruning paint. Contact your local nursery for more information on the varieties grown in your area. The plum can be attacked by brown rot, birds, borers, fruit fly, rust, shot hole and bacterial canker. Shot hole is very common in humid areas.

CLIMATE European plums are best in zones 6 to 8. Japanese plums are ideal for zone 9. Hybrids of the American and Japanese plums are suited to the north central US.

SPECIES *Prunus domestica*, common or European plum, is a mostly deciduous and low-growing tree, with a broad spread. It is the earliest fruit tree to blossom, flowering before the foliage appears. Oval or globe-shaped, the edible fruit is either clingstone or freestone, with juicy flesh which is generally yellow in color. There are many cultivars and a good fruit nursery will be able to offer a wide selection suitable for your area. For instance, the greengage types are truly delicious and well worth growing, having round, green fruits which are very sweet and therefore good for dessert. Also consider the transparent gages where the actual stone can be seen through the flesh. These are also good for dessert. Then there are the prune type of plums, which have dark purple skins and very sweet flesh. These are normally grown for drying. Damsons are also grown in the US, being selections from *P. insititia*. The small fruits are very tart and are mainly used for jams and jellies. The trees are small and compact, and there are several, self-fertile cultivars available, ideal where space is limited. The Japanese plums are from *P. salicina*, and are also known as salicine plums. These have round fruits, usually quite large, with skin color purple, red or yellow. They are most widely grown in California. There is a number of self-fertile cultivars which should be considered where space is at a premium. When buying the hardy hybrids bear in mind that there can be problems with pollination, so do check out their pollination requirements at a fruit nursery.

Plumbago (fam. Plumbaginaceae)
Leadwort

Of this genus of 15 species of shrubs, climbers, perennials or annuals, native to tropical and

ABOVE Sky blue flowers of *Plumbago auriculata* will cover this shrub from late spring, right through summer.

ABOVE This glorious, red frangipani, or plumeria, is an outstanding cultivar and also has scent which is characteristic of this genus.

warm regions of the world, only a few are in general cultivation. They make good cool to intermediate conservatory plants in frost-prone climates.

CULTIVATION In the conservatory, grow in pots of soil-based potting compost in good light, but shade from direct sun. In the garden, grow in a sunny, sheltered spot with well-drained soil. Prune climbers in late winter by cutting back side shoots to within three buds of the main stems. Propagate from semi-ripe cuttings in summer.

CLIMATE Warmest parts of zone 9 at least.

SPECIES *P. auriculata*, from South Africa, is a semi-climbing shrub bearing spikes of sky blue flowers at the ends of its trailing stems, throughout summer into fall. Growing vigorously in warm climates, to 3 m (10 ft) high, it also has a less rampant, white-flowered form.

Plumeria (fam. Apocynaceae)

Frangipani

Originally from Central America, this genus consists of seven species of trees, the scent of which is unforgettable. In frost-prone climates, it is a good subject for the warm greenhouse or conservatory. The frangipani is a symbol of eternity for Buddhists because branches continue to flower even when cut.

CULTIVATION In the conservatory or greenhouse, grow in pots of sandy, soil-based potting compost. Ensure maximum light, but shade from strong sun. Keep the compost only slightly moist in winter, but water well at other times. Propagate from stem-tip cuttings in early spring.

CLIMATE Tropical only.

SPECIES *P. rubra* var. *acutifolia*, from Mexico, is more commonly grown than the species. The white flowers have yellow markings on the throat and a deliciously sweet perfume. The form *lutea* has yellow flowers but the outside is often flushed light red. Many hybrids have been produced in a range of colors, some of which may have been spontaneous hybrids.

Podalyria (fam. Papilionaceae)

Only two of these 20 species of evergreen shrubs from South Africa are in general cultivation. The pea-shaped flowers are fragrant and showy, while the foliage has a silky texture. In climates prone to frosts, these plants should be grown in a cool greenhouse.

CULTIVATION Propagate from seed or cuttings. Soak seed overnight in warm water before sowing. Plant in open, free-draining soil, in full sun. Tip prune to encourage bushy growth and remove spent flower heads, unless seed is to be collected.

CLIMATE Zone 9 or 10.

SPECIES *P. calyptrata*, sweet pea bush, is fast growing to 2 or 3 m (6–10 ft). The silver-green foliage is covered with fine, soft hairs. Pink to mauve flowers appear from spring to early summer. *P. sericea*, to about 1 m (3 ft), occurs naturally on dry, gravelly soils in its native South Africa. The silky, silver-gray foliage is very attractive. Mauve-pink flowers appear from winter to mid-spring.

ABOVE Now restricted to a few areas in the wild, the New Zealand totara, *Podocarpus totara*, produces a most durable timber.

ABOVE The silvery foliage of *Podalyria calyptrata* is itself a decorative asset to the garden, even without the pretty pink flowers.

Podocarpus (fam. Podocarpaceae)
Plum pine, plum yew, yellow-wood

Botanically, this genus belongs to the conifers, even though its seeds are generally not carried in cones, but singly or in small groups at the ends of branchlets, mostly on short stalks, which are often swollen and fleshy. Some species, however, have seed-bearing organs, more like normal cones. In some species, the leaves are narrow and flattened, those of tropical types growing as long as 30 cm (12 in); in others the leaves are small and needle-like and crowded along the branchlets. There are around 100 species of *Podocarpus*, originating from tropical and temperate rainforests of Australasia, southern and eastern Asia, South America and southern Africa. The species range from tall, forest trees to almost prostrate, sub-alpine shrubs. Several are grown widely as shade trees for streets, parks and larger gardens; others are used in rockeries. Most are tender and need to be grown in an intermediate to warm greenhouse or conservatory in frost-prone climates.

CULTIVATION *Podocarpus* species vary in their requirements. The tall-growing species, originally from dense forest habitats, like a very sheltered position and deep, fertile, moist soil. Other species, such as *P. salignus*, are very hardy, tolerate pollution and are suitable for inner-city conditions. Most are fairly slow growing but this can be an advantage. Propagate from seed, which in most species has a short viability, or by cuttings, which are more easily struck than for most conifers.

CLIMATE There are species suited to various climatic zones.

SPECIES *P. elatus*, brown pine or plum pine, zone 10, from eastern Australia, grows in its habitat to around 35 m (100 ft), though seldom reaches more than 15 m (50 ft) in cultivation. It has flaky brown, bark and very leathery, deep green leaves, to 8 cm (3 in) long. The seeds are borne singly on rounded, black, edible fruits. Its dense canopy makes it an excellent shade or street tree. As the plum pine responds well to heavy pruning, it is also useful as a hedging plant. *P. ferrugineus* (syn. *Prumnopitys ferruginea*), miro, zone 9, is a native of New Zealand, where it is found in rainforests. The small leaves are quite yew-like and the bright red seeds are large and oval in shape. In cultivation, it is a slow-growing, small tree of slender, upright habit. *P. macrophyllus*, zone 7, from mountainous regions of China and Japan, rarely grows larger than a shrub outside its habitat. It grows into an irregularly columnar shape and has densely crowded, narrow leaves, about 10 cm (4 in) long, very thick and leathery. Very slow growing, it makes a good container plant and a thick hedge. It is best suited to cooler temperate climates. *P. totara*, totara, zone 9, has a magnificent trunk, 3 m (10 ft) in diameter, covered with reddish brown bark, which matures to a grayish brown color. It was formally an important timber tree in its native New Zealand. It has a rather narrow, bushy crown, stiff, sharply pointed, bronze-green leaves, and crimson fruits. In cultivation it seldom exceeds 8 m (26 ft) tall.

Podranea (fam. Bignoniaceae)

Originating from southern Africa, this genus includes only two species of climbing plants, which are closely related to *Pandorea*.

ABOVE Easy-care and fast-growing, *Podranea ricasoliana* is ideal for quickly covering unsightly fences or sheds.

CULTIVATION These lovely plants need a well-drained soil with plenty of organic matter, and a sunny situation. Wire, trellis or lattice must be provided to support these twiners, and ample water given during the warm months. In frost-prone climates, grow in a cool greenhouse in pots of soil-based potting compost. Prune back side shoots after flowering. Propagate from seed or cuttings.

CLIMATE At least zone 9.

SPECIES *P. ricasoliana* is a compact evergreen climber, to about 4 m (13 ft), grown for its beautiful, scented, funnel-shaped flowers in pink, with red-striped petals, which appear from winter through to summer. It has a leathery, twisted stem and dark green, fern-like leaves.

Polemonium (fam. Polemoniaceae)

There are 25 species of hardy, herbaceous perennials in this genus from North America and Eurasia. Only a few species are generally cultivated, making a very pretty display as a

ABOVE Both the foliage and flowers of Jacob's ladder, *Polemonium caeruleum*, are attractive. It does well in the ground and in containers.

massed garden bed, or in borders or rockeries. Sometimes grown as a container plant, they also make effective hanging basket subjects. The foliage is mainly fern-like and the flowers appear in summer.

CULTIVATION These plants will grow well in good soil, in temperate conditions. Flowering does not last long, but the plants seed freely. Propagate from seed or by division of the clumps.

CLIMATE There are species suited to various climatic zones.

SPECIES *P. caeruleum*, Jacob's ladder, zone 2, from temperate parts of Europe, is the most commonly cultivated species. Growing to 90 cm (36 in) high, it has pretty, sky blue flowers. *P. carneum*, zone 6, growing to 90 cm (36 in), has salmon-colored flowers. *P. elegans*, zone 5, is a dwarf species, growing to 15 cm (6 in), with blue flowers. *P. foliosissimum*, zone 3, to 75 cm (30 in), has blue, cream or white flowers. *P.*

foliosissimum var. *flavum*, zone 3, grows to 90 cm (36 in), producing red flowers with yellow centres. *P. reptans*, zone 4, to 60 cm (24 in), has either blue or white flowers.

Polianthes (fam. Agavaceae)
Tuberose

These 13 herbaceous perennials are native to Mexico. They are known to have been cultivated in pre-Columbian times, but the species are not now known in the wild. The white to pink flowers are borne in racemes.

CULTIVATION In frost-prone climates, grow in a warm greenhouse or conservatory, or outdoors for the summer. In the greenhouse, grow in pots of soil-based potting compost, planting the tubers in spring. Provide maximum light. In summer, be careful not to overwater but liquid feed every two weeks. When the foliage starts to die back, start to reduce watering and keep the compost dry over winter. In the garden plant in spring, in well-drained soil and

ABOVE Tuberose, *Polianthes tuberosa*, is a good cut flower and is heavily scented. A single stem will perfume a room.

in a sunny position. Except in frost-free climates, the tubers are lifted in fall and stored over winter in slightly moist peat or sand, in a frost-free greenhouse. Propagate from offsets during the dormant period, or from ripe seed which has been germinated at 21°C (70°F). Offsets, which are used to replace old, deteriorating mother tubers, may take two years to reach flowering size.

CLIMATE Warmest parts of zone 9.

SPECIES *P. tuberosa* grows to more than 1 m (3 ft) high, with slender leaves often as long as 30 cm (12 in). The waxy, white flowers are highly scented, the oil being used in perfumery. Polianthes are often grown as cut flowers.

Polygala (fam. Polygalaceae)
Milkwort

This large genus of some 500 species of trees, shrubs, annuals and herbaceous perennials are indigenous to most regions of the world. Few species, however, are in general cultivation.

CULTIVATION These plants will grow in most soils and conditions, but generally do best in full sun, with ample water. Propagate from cuttings, seeds or suckers.

BELOW *Polygala* x *dalmaisiana* is a hybrid of garden origin, one of its parents being the species *Polygala myrtifolia*

CLIMATE Depends on the species selected, as they come from a wide range of habitats.

SPECIES *P. calcarea*, zone 7, is a prostrate, evergreen perennial, with a creeping habit. The flowers are mainly blue, but may also be white. *P. chamaebuxus*, zone 6, grows to only 10 cm (4 in), with sprays of tiny, yellow, pea-like flowers, in spring and early summer. *P.* x *dalmaisiana*, zone 9, is an evergreen shrub to 2.5 m (8 ft) with purple or rose-magenta flowers in summer and fall. *P. myrtifolia*, zone 9, to 2 m (6 ft), bears green-white, purple-veined flowers, from spring to fall. *P. paucifolia*, zone 2, is a shrubby, low-growing species, to 15–18 cm (6–7 in) high, which produces pinkish purple flowers. It is suitable for growing in rockeries. *P. vayredae*, zone 6, from Spain, grows to 20 cm (8 in) and has purplish flowers.

Polygonatum (fam. Convallariaceae)
Solomon's seal

This genus consists of over 50 species of hardy herbaceous perennialso found in many temperate regions of the world. *P. biflorum* and *P. odoratum* are the two most commonly cultivated, and these are valued for their graceful,

ABOVE Clusters of narrow, bell-like flowers are suspended from the stems of *Polygonatum multiflorum*, which enjoys woodland conditions.

leafy stems and white blossoms. These are superb plants for moist woodland gardens and shrub borders.

CULTIVATION *Polygonatum* needs a moisture-retentive, yet well-drained soil, well supplied with humus, and a position in sun or semi-shade. Propagate by division in spring.

CLIMATE Best in cool, moist climates.

SPECIES *P. biflorum*, to 1 m (3 ft) or more, produces green and white flowers in late spring and summer. *P. odoratum* flowers towards the end of spring and into early summer, producing white, green tipped, scented flowers on stems at least 80cm high. There is a cultivar with white-edged leaves called 'Variegatum'. *P. multiflorum*, to 90 cm (36 in), has similar flowers, again in late spring.

Polygonum (fam. Polygonaceae)

Most species in this genus have now been placed into other genera: *Fallopia* and *Persicaria*. Those described here include a vigorous, deciduous climber, a hardy perennial and a hardy annual. Plants generally have alternate leaves and sprays, spikes or rounded heads of small

ABOVE In cool climates, *Polygonum capitatum* is cultivated as a rockery or groundcover plant. It can be invasive in warm areas.

flowers, generally in pink or red but also white, which are produced in summer and fall.

CULTIVATION These hardy plants will grow in any ordinary garden soil, but favorable conditions will result in better plants. Propagate perennials by division, annuals from seed, and climbers from hardwood cuttings in fall.

CLIMATE There are species suited to various climatic zones.

SPECIES *P. baldschuanicum* (syn. *Fallopia baldschuanica*), zone 4, is an aggressive, deciduous climber with long-stalked, pale green, heart-shaped leaves and masses of tiny, white, pink-flushed flowers, carried in sprays, in late summer and fall. *P. capitatum* (syn. *Persicaria capitata*), zone 8, is a fast-growing, perennial groundcover, striking roots from the nodes on the stem. It has deep green leaves, with brown markings, becoming bronze in fall, and globular heads of tiny, pink flowers. *P. orientale* (syn. *Persicaria orientalis*), Prince's feather, zone 6, an annual to almost 1.5 m (5 ft) high, has long, bright pink flowers. It is sometimes grown for the cut flower trade.

Polypodium (fam. Polypodiaceae)

The 75 species in this genus of ferns are found in many regions, with the greatest number originating in tropical America. Most are epiphytic, with creeping rhizomes. The fronds are variable and may be simple or pinnate, sometimes lobed, and upright or pendulous. There has been much discussion in classifying this genus, as species have often been included in different genera by botanists. The most outstanding examples of the genus are some of the cultivars.

CULTIVATION Plant the hardy species on rock gardens or in shrub borders, in well-drained soil which contains plenty of humus. *P. cambricum* does best in alkaline soil. Provide partial shade or full sun and protection from winds. In frost-prone climates, the tender

ABOVE This graceful *Polypodium* species cascades from the crown of a tree fern. The dappled shade provided by the fern is ideal for its growth.

species are grown in a warm greenhouse or conservatory in pots of soilless potting compost. The easiest method of propagation is to divide established plants in spring. Alternatively, sow spores as soon as ripe.

CLIMATE There are species suited to various climatic zones.

SPECIES *P. cambricum*, southern polypody, zone 6, is a terrestrial fern, native to Britain and Europe. Fronds are divided with rather broad leaflets. This fern is suited to cooler climates or sheltered, cool areas of other regions. *P. formosanum*, caterpillar or grub fern, zone 9, is an epiphytic fern from Japan, China and Taiwan. It has gray-green, creeping rhizomes and the long narrow fronds are pale green. Grown outdoors in warm climates, it needs greenhouse conditions in cool zones. *P. loriceum*, caterpillar fern, zone 10, originates from the tropical Americas, Mexico and the West Indies. The greenish white rhizome creeps across the surface, the stems are short, and the thin, divided

fronds are long, spreading and drooping. The narrow lobes taper at the tips and have wavy edges. The circular spore cases on the lobes bear masses of golden yellow spores. This beautiful fern is easy to grow and an excellent choice for a large basket. *P. vulgare*, common polypody, zone 3, is native to Britain, Europe and Asia. It has long, divided fronds and is suitable for growing outdoors even in very cold climates.

Polyscias (fam. Araliaceae)

There are about 100 species in this genus of tropical shrubs and trees, native to Asia, the Pacific region and Africa. In frost-prone climates, they are grown as ornamentals in a warm greenhouse or conservatory or as house plants in a warm room. They are valued for their attractive, often finely divided foliage. Flowers are generally cream or green and of no ornamental value. In their places of origin, some are used medicinally and for perfume, while others are used to stupefy fish to guarantee a good catch.

CULTIVATION Grow in pots of soil-based, potting compost in good light, but shade plants from direct sun. During the growing season, the plants appreciate a humid atmosphere. Outdoors plant in well drained, humus-rich soil in partial shade or full sun and water well in

ABOVE The delicate, lacy foliage of *Polyscias filicifolia* makes this a popular plant for container-growing, indoors or out.

summer. Propagate from semi-ripe cuttings in summer or alternatively, from seed in spring. Provide basal warmth for both.

CLIMATE Zone 10 to tropical.

SPECIES *P. filicifolia*, fern leaf aralia, grows 2–2.5 m (6–8 ft) high. The very fine, lacy foliage makes it an ideal specimen plant, although it is grown as a hedge in some regions of the world. It is also grown as an indoor plant, but requires plenty of bright indirect light. Variegated forms are sometimes available. *P. guilfoylei* is a tall shrub, 4–8 m (13–26 ft) high, native to various parts of Polynesia. The large, compound leaves often have white splashes or margins. Cultivar 'Victoriae' is a compact grower with finely divided leaves, distinctly edged in white.

Polystichum (fam. Dryopteridaceae)
Shield fern

These 200 species of ferns are distributed worldwide. The upright rhizomes are covered in scales, sometimes forming a short, trunk-like structure with age. The arching fronds are simply or severally divided, and form a crown. Proliferous buds, or bulbils–those which produce new plants vegetatively–may be found at the tips of fronds. These tough, wiry ferns make excellent garden subjects or container plants.

CULTIVATION In frost-prone climates, the tender species are grown in an intermediate to warm greenhouse or conservatory. Outdoors, the hardy species like very well drained soil which contains plenty of humus, and full or partial shade. They are good in a shrub border or woodland garden. Most species can be propagated from the bulbils which can be removed from the parent plant, and potted or planted in the garden when sufficiently mature. Others may be propagated from spores. Clumps can be lifted and divided in late winter or spring.

CLIMATE There are species suited to various climatic zones.

ABOVE This hardy fern, *Polystichum retrorsopaleaceum*, is a native of Japan, and a good subject for shady, woodland gardens.

SPECIES *P. formosum*, broad shield fern, zone 10, is from eastern Australia. The short, thick rootstock and stems are covered with dull brown scales; the coarse, dark green fronds are broader at the centre than the other species; and the leathery leaflets are deeply toothed. Propagation is from spores only. *P. proliferum*, mother shield fern, zone 10, from eastern Australia, has a solid rhizome, covered in dark brown, shiny scales, forming a short trunk. The large, divided fronds are light green when young, darker green with age, and produce tiny plantlets near the tips. This species is very easily grown from proliferous buds on the fronds. *P. setiferum*, soft shield fern, zone 7, is one of the most widely grown species, adapting well to a wide range of conditions. It originates in woodlands of Britain and Europe. Fronds are tall and arching, and generally over 75 cm (30 in) long. Numerous cultivars are grown. Some produce offsets or bulbils along the mid-veins, making propagation simple.

Pomaderris (fam. Rhamnaceae)

Native to Australia and New Zealand, this genus comprises around 45 species of evergreen shrubs. Only a few of the species are in cultivation, though these shrubs have good horticultural

ABOVE Woolly pomaderris, *Pomaderris lanigera*, blooms prolifically in spring and summer, with clusters of yellow flowers.

potential and are impressive when in flower, in late spring and summer. They have hairy, alternate leaves and rounded fragrant flower heads, mostly in yellow, cream or white, and are interesting foliage plants and ornamentals.

CULTIVATION Pomaderris an be propagated from the seed, contained in the fruit, which will germinate readily if sown in sand. It can also be propagated from semi-hardwood cuttings taken from late spring to fall. These are easy-care plants which will thrive in most situations in the garden, provided there is good drainage and shelter from strong winds. Trimming is necessary only to maintain a compact shape. In frost-prone climates, grow in a cool, airy greenhouse or conservatory in pots of soil-based potting compost. Provide bright light.

CLIMATE Warmest parts of zone 9.

SPECIES Not all available outside countries of origin but *P. apetala* is grown in California. *P. andromedifolia* grows 1–3 m (3–10 ft) high. The leaves are dark green above and velvety brown underneath. The cream flowers are borne in dense clusters. *P. apetala*, tainui or native hazel, occurs in New Zealand and Australia and is grown mainly for its soft and hairy foliage. It reaches around 5 m (16 ft). In spring, it is covered in long clusters of yellow flowers. *P. ferruginea*, rusty pomaderris, grows to 2 m (6 ft), and has oval leaves and rich yellow flowers. *P. kumeraho*, golden tainui, is a native shrub of New Zealand which grows to 3 m (10 ft). In spring, its slender branches are covered in blueish green foliage and masses of tiny, yellow flowers, in large clusters. This species was used by the Maoris in the treatment of asthma and other bronchial problems. *P. lanigera* grows to 2 m (6 ft), with rusty green leaves and rounded clusters of yellow flowers. *P. pilifera* is a spreading shrub, growing to 1.5 m (5 ft) in height. The green leaves are striped with white at the midrib and masses of bright yellow flowers appear in irregular clusters during spring. *P. rugosa* grows to 3 m (10 ft), with rusty green leaves and white flowers.

Pomegranate

(*Punica granatum*, fam. Punicaceae)

Punica granatum is a small, attractive, deciduous tree or shrub originally from south-eastern Europe, northern Africa and Asia. It is grown as much for its bright green, glossy foliage, which turns gold in fall and its dazzling red flowers, as for its edible fruit. There is also a dwarf pomegranate which grows to about 2 m (6 ft). It is frequently grown as a low hedge or as a specimen. There are a number of very attractive forms with double flowers, grown purely for the beauty of the flowers, as most are sterile and produce no fruit. The pomegranate is about the size of an apple. The crimson-colored, juicy pulp has a bittersweet flavor and contains large numbers of seeds, relative to the amount of flesh. Grenadine, a syrup fermented from the juice, is used to make cordials, confectionery and preserves. The rind and flowers are used in medicine for their astringent properties, and the tannin is used for staining leather. The

ABOVE Dwarf pomegranate is often grown purely for ornament. Its fruits, though small, are edible.

ABOVE Producing the largest fruit of the citrus family, pomelo or shaddock must have very warm, humid conditions to thrive.

pomegranate was a symbol of hope, fertility and eternity in Jewish and Christian tradition, and figures in the Song of Solomon. Mythology suggests that it was the fruit given to Venus by Paris.

CULTIVATION Although pomegranates can tolerate a wide climatic range, they need dry summer heat to set fruit and deep regular watering. In frost-prone climates, grow in a cool greenhouse in a tub of soil-based potting compost. Outdoors, plant in deep, loamy slightly alkaline soil, spacing trees 4–5 m (13–16 ft) apart, and hedges 2–2.5 m (6–8 ft) apart. Prune lightly in winter. Old neglected trees can be heavily pruned if they need rejuvenating. Propagate from seed or hardwood cuttings, or by layering. Double-flowered forms must be grown from cuttings.

CLIMATE Zone 9.

Pomelo (syn. Pummelo)

(*Citrus maxima*, fam. Rutaceae)

Shaddock

Believed to be originally from southern China, Malaysia and Polynesia, *Citrus maxima* (syn.

C. grandis) is a tender, tropical tree which grows 5–9 m (16–30 ft) high. It has thin, blunt spines, characteristic, winged leaf stalks and large, white flowers. The round to pear-shaped fruit is very large, sometimes weighing up to 9 kg (20 lb), and yellow to orange in color. It may be one of the ancestors of the grapefruit. The pomelo has coarse, segmented, acidic flesh used mostly for preserving in India and parts of Asia. A good cultivar is the pink-fleshed 'Chandler'.

CULTIVATION Outside the subtropics or tropics, grow in an intermediate greenhouse or conservatory in a large pot or tub of slightly acid, soil-based potting compost. Provide humidity in summer. Outdoors grow in rich soil in a warm sunny position.

CLIMATE A very tender species. Requires zone 10.

Poncirus (fam. Rutaceae)

Closely related to *Citrus*, this single-species genus is originally from China, but widely grown in Japan and often used as hedging in some countries. It is also used as a rootstock for cultivated citrus.

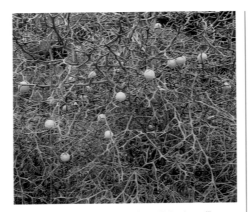

ABOVE The yellow fruits of *Poncirus trifoliata* hang like lanterns amidst a thicket of narrow, thorny twigs and branches.

ABOVE This variety of the edible sweet corn, *Zea mays*, produces the type most suitable for popping.

CULTIVATION This shrub or small tree will adapt to any ordinary, well-drained soil. It needs a sheltered position with full sun. If it is grown as a hedge, trim after flowering, but not too hard or fruits will be lost. Propagate from seed in fall in a garden frame, or from semi-ripe cuttings in summer, in a heated propagating case.

CLIMATE Zone 6.

SPECIES *P. trifoliata* is a fast-growing, deciduous shrub or small tree with flattened stems, long, stout spines and trifoliate leaves with winged leaf stalks. The fragrant, white, five-petalled flowers appear just before new spring growth and they are followed by the fragrant, round, yellow fruit which is not usually eaten.

Popcorn (*Zea mays*, var. *praecox*, fam. Poaceae)

Zea mays var. *praecox* is an erect, monoecious annual, probably from Mexico or Central America. A variety of maize or Indian corn, popcorn is grown for the small cobs with mostly pointed, pinkish white kernels which we recognize as the popcorn some love to eat. Popcorn is eaten in a variety of ways, such as seasoned with butter and salt and as a cereal with milk and sugar. Since the introduction of Japanese hull-less varieties, the quality of popcorn has improved enormously.

CULTIVATION Grow and propagate as for sweet corn. Like sweet corn, it must be grown in blocks, not rows, to ensure good pollination.

CLIMATE Zone 7, but grown as a summer annual.

Populus (fam. Salicaceae)
Poplar

The 35 species of these widely grown deciduous trees are found throughout the northern hemisphere. In the US, they are mainly grown in rural areas and large gardens as windbreaks and tall screens. They are also excellent for avenue plantings. The broad, alternate leaves come in various tonings and the pendulous, catkin flowers appear in spring while the tree is still bare. Color in fall is usually golden.

CULTIVATION All poplars grow quickly and easily, preferring cool temperate climates with regular rainfall. Plant in deep, moist, well-drained fertile soil in full sun. All need ample water in the growing season. Most poplars are extremely vigorous and they should be planted where there is ample room for their enormous root systems–at least 18 m (60 ft) away from drains and paths. Propagate from 30 cm (12 in) long hardwood cuttings in early winter. Those that tend to sucker very freely, particularly the silver-leaved types, may be grafted on non-suckering rootstock. All species will transplant easily at any size. No pruning is necessary. Poplar rust damages a great many species and cultivars. Control is impossible on large trees. For new plantings, seek out varieties which have resistance to rust.

CLIMATE There are species suited to various climatic zones. All are very hardy.

SPECIES *P. alba*, white or silver poplar, zone 3, is a beautiful tree from Europe, North Africa and central Asia, growing over 20 m (65 ft) high. It has broadly oval, dark green leaves,

ABOVE These tall, narrow spires of *Populus nigra* 'Italica', in their fall gold, make an imposing avenue planting.

covered in white or gray down on the undersides. The leaves turn a rich gold in fall. This species can tolerate low-level drought, salt-laden winds and poor alkaline soils. The form *pyramidalis* has an erect, columnar habit, growing to 30 m (100 ft) or more when fully mature. *P. balsamifera*, balsam poplar, zone 2, from North America, grows up to 30 m (100 ft) and has glossy, almost yellow branches and oval, shiny leaves, which are white on the reverse side. *P.* x *canadensis*, zone 4, is very upright, with rounded, triangularshaped leaves. It grows over 20 m (65 ft) and the trunk has heavily furrowed bark. *P. deltoides*, cottonwood, zone 2, from eastern North America, grows up to 30 m (100 ft) and spreads to about half the height. It makes a lovely shade tree for rural properties, but is relatively short lived and very brittle in high winds. The very large, almost triangular, glossy, green leaves are veined with yellow. *P. nigra*, black poplar, zone 2, from Europe and central Asia, grows 15–30 m (50–100 ft), with a broad head of foliage. The diamond-shaped leaves are bronze when young, changing to a bright green as they mature. In fall, they turn a pale yellow before falling. This species is best known by one of its cultivars, 'Italica', or Lombardy poplar, which grows in the shape of a spire and has narrower, heart-shaped leaves. This poplar is quite widely planted in rural areas for its use as a windbreak. *P. tremula*, aspen, zone 2, from Europe, Asia and northern Africa, grows to about 25 m (80 ft), with a dark gray, fissured bark. The fine, rounded leaves are borne on very fine branchlets, so they rustle in the lightest breeze. They are colored bronze-red when young, deep green when mature. In fall, they color yellow. *P. tremuloides*, the quaking or American aspen, which grows to 15–20 m (50 65 ft), has similar leaves to *P. tremula* and they too rustle in the slightest breeze. *P. yunnanensis*, zone 5, is a broad-growing tree with leaves bright green above and grayish green beneath. The leaf stalk and mid-vein is red. Growing to around 20 m (65 ft), the yunnan poplar is useful for shade. It does better than many other species of poplarin warm districts with lower rainfall .

Portulaca (fam. Portulacaceae)

These succulent plants are widespread through tropical and warm parts of the world. Most of the 40 species are annuals, but some are perennials. Erect to sprawling, the stems branch and rebranch and sometimes become quite woody. The fleshy leaves grow in whorls and the flowers are cup-shaped, with wavy-edged petals, in red, pink and yellow to white.

CULTIVATION Raise from seed sown in spring, under glass in climates which are prone to frost. *Portulaca* will thrive in any well-drained soil in full sun. It can tolerate exposed, windy sites and, once established, it will tolerate dry conditions well. It is an ideal choice for troughs, tubs, pots and hanging baskets, as well as for open-ground growing.

CLIMATE Warmest parts of zone 10, but grown as a summer annual in all climates.

SPECIES *P. grandiflora*, rose moss or sun plant, is the well-known prostrate garden annual from which a number of brightly colored cultivars, in single and double forms have been developed. Flowers come in colors of yellow, red, pink, purple and white. They open in the sun and close when it is overcast or dark. New strains that remain open in dull weather are now available. These plants rarely grow more than 15 cm (6 in) high. The blooms are not suitable for cut flowers. *P. oleracea*, purslane, is the original annual purslane which is believed to have originated from India, but has since spread to many countries. It is cultivated as a salad crop, or as a leaf vegetable for cooking, when it is known as summer purslane. There are both green- and yellow-leaved types available.

Portulacaria (fam. Portulacaceae)

Elephant bush

This single-species genus from South Africa is not too well known but will appeal to succulent enthusiasts. A succulent, evergreen, many-branched shrub, in its native habitat it is often used as a fodder plant.

CULTIVATION *P. afra* will grow just about anywhere. It makes an attractive pot plant or bonsai specimen and does well in the garden, provided it receives protection from frost. In climates which are prone to frost, grow it in a warm greenhouse or conservatory. In its hot, dry habitat, it produces clusters of tiny, pink flowers, followed by small, pinkish berries. However, it is said that the plant will flower

BELOW The elephant bush, *Portulacaria afra*, is grown like any other succulent plant in a warm greenhouse or conservatory.

ABOVE In bright sun, annual portulaca provides a brilliant show of color. These plants are good for binding sandy soils.

only when it is old and has been left completely dry for several weeks, or even months, through the winter. Its flowers should appear in summer. Propagation may be from seed but is very easy from cuttings at almost any time of year.

CLIMATE Zone 10.

SPECIES *P. afra*, to 2 m (6 ft) high, has a thick, fleshy, silvery brown trunk. The branches are horizontally arranged, rather brittle, and sometimes twisted. The small, fleshy, round leaves are glossy green and flat. The infrequent flowers are borne in bundles on a thick stem and are a pretty salmon pink, coloring the whole bush. The cultivar 'Foliisvariegatus' has leaves variegated with yellow.

Posoqueria (fam. Rubiaceae)

There are about 12 species of deciduous, flowering trees or shrubs in this tropical American genus, only a few of which are cultivated. The leaves are rather large, thick and shiny, and the flowers are tubular and fragrant, and ranges in color from white to scarlet. After it has flowered, it produces large, fleshy berries containing many seeds.

BELOW The very distinctive flowers of *Posoqueria latifolia* give this small tree the name 'needle flower'. Both flowers and fruit are fragrant.

CULTIVATION In climates which are prone to frost, grow in an intermediate greenhouse or conservatory, in pots of gritty, soil-based potting compost. Shade from direct sun and provide moderate humidity. Prune lightly after flowering in order to maintain shape. Outdoors grow in sun or partial shade and well drained, humus-rich soil. Propagate from semi-ripe cuttings in summer, with bottom heat.

CLIMATE Zone 10.

SPECIES *P. latifolia*, needle flower tree, from Mexico and South America, grows to about 6 m (20 ft). The elliptical leaves are about 15 cm (6 in) long, the flowers are white and the fruit is yellow and edible but not very tasty. Both flowers and fruit are fragrant.

Potato (*Solanum tuberosum*, fam. Solanaceae)

One of the most important food crops in the world, and the staple food of temperate climates, the potato is produced in nearly every country. Cultivated in Central and South America as long as 4000 years ago, and introduced to Europe by the Spanish conquistadores in the 16th century, it took some 200 years to become a popular food in Europe. At the beginning of the 20th century, there were more than 1000 known varieties, while today fewer than 100 varieties are in cultivation. However, there has been renewed interest in recent years in many of the more unusual cultivars, and so more of these are becoming available to home gardeners. These are all varieties of *Solanum tuberosum*, the low-growing perennial, cultivated for its starchy, edible tubers (the swollen ends of underground rhizomes). The potato is grown throughout the US. Filling and quite nutritious, it is a versatile vegetable which can be served boiled, mashed, fried, baked or layered with cream or yoghurt, and cooked in curries, soups and stews.

CULTIVATION Propagate by planting 'seed potatoes', using the small, whole tubers or pieces obtained by cutting the tuber into sections,

ABOVE Flowering of potatoes indicates that they are nearing maturity and can usually be harvested a few weeks later.

each with one or two buds (eyes). Tubers can be selected from an existing crop or from purchased potatoes, but it is much better to buy certified seed potatoes, as these are guaranteed to be disease-free. (True potato seed, which forms inside the fleshy green or purple fruits, resembling tiny tomatoes, is used only for breeding.) Next, the seed tubers are encouraged to form sturdy shoots before planting, a process known as chitting or sprouting. In late winter spread the tubers out on trays, with the 'eyes' facing upwards, and keep them in a cool, frost-free place with good light. When shoots are 2.5 cm (1 in) long, the tubers can be planted. Chitting takes about six weeks. Planting is carried out in spring, starting in early spring with the early cultivars. These are followed by second-early potatoes, then finally the maincrop cultivars. Plant tubers 10-12 cm (4–5 in) deep and 35 cm (14 in) apart, in rows spaced 45 cm (18 in) apart. Maincrop cultivars are planted 75 cm (30 in) apart in rows spaced 80 cm (32 in) apart. This allows access for weeding, feeding and earthing up. Shoots should emerge within three to four weeks. At this stage, they are very frost-tender. Use a well-drained soil that is slightly acid and contains some organic matter. When plants are about 25 cm (10 in) high, they should be earthed up, in other words the soil should be mounded on each side of the plant. This helps smother weeds, and, more importantly, prevents the tubers from turning green. Potatoes need a plentiful supply of nutrients and regular watering if the weather is dry. Complete fertilizer can be laid in bands alongside the rows. Harvesting can begin as plants die down, but new potatoes can be dug from about four weeks after flowering. These must be used quickly as they do not store well. Green coloring on potatoes is poisonous and unplanted seed pieces should be destroyed or buried deeply and not fed to livestock. Pests that may attack potatoes include potato cyst, eelworm, wireworms, cutworms and slugs. Among the diseases that may be encountered is potato blight. This is a serious and frequent, fungal disease that is worse in warm, humid conditions. Common scab is another frequent disease, most troublesome if the soil is alkaline. Copious watering deters it. It is best not to grow potatoes on the same piece of ground more than once in every four years, to prevent a build up of soil-borne pests and diseases. Crop rotation is therefore advisable.

CLIMATE Zone 10, but grown as an annual, summer crop in all climates.

Potentilla (fam. Rosaceae)
Cinquefoil

There are around 500 species in this genus, most originating from temperate and very cold zones of the northern hemisphere. They can be divided into two broad groups: herbaceous, low-growing types to about 30 cm (12 in) high; and small shrubs, to about 1.5 m (5 ft) high. Most species are perennials; only a few are annuals. Some have a long history of use in herbal medicine. The flowers of the species have five petals and come in a variety of colors, from yellow through to pink and red. The strawberry-like, green leaves are quite smooth on top, white-downy below. Cultivars of some species have double flowers. The hybrid cultivars make excellent border plants, flowering

ABOVE *Potentilla atrosanguinea*, the Himalayan cinquefoil, flowers over a long period, through summer and fall. It is an excellent plant for the mixed border.

freely from spring to fall, with the main display in summer.

CULTIVATION Easy to grow, potentillas like a sunny, well-drained position. They set seed freely and may be propagated by sowing seed in early spring. A temperature of 13°–18°C (55°–65° F) is necessary for germination. Hybrids will not come true from seed, but roots may be divided to produce new plants. Potentillas that produce runners will spread by rooting at the nodes on the runners. Shrubs can be propagated from semi-ripe cuttings in late summer, rooted in a garden frame.

CLIMATE There are species suited to various climatic zones.

SPECIES *P. atrosanguinea* var. *argyrophylla*, zone 5, up to 1 m (3 ft) high, has toothed, oval leaves, gray-white and silky beneath, and yellow, summer flowers, about 3 cm (1 in) across. *P. atrosanguinea*, zone 5, produces deep red flowers, the leaves being not as sharply toothed. This species and its varieties are excellent, hardy perennials for the mixed or herba-

ceous border, and flower over a very long period throughout summer and fall. *P. fruticosa*, shrubby cinquefoil, zone 2, is a densely leaved shrub, to 1.5 m (5 ft), with bright yellow flowers, 3 cm (1 in) across. This species will do well in most conditions. There are many cultivars available. *P. nepalensis*, zone 5, from the Himalayas, grows to 90 cm (36 in) high, with red stems and green leaves, prominently veined on both sides. A profusion of deep red or pink flowers appears on the slim, branching stems throughout summer. Cultivar 'Miss Willmott' is a dwarf type, bearing numerous, magenta flowers. *P. recta*, zone 4, from central and southern Europe, grows 30–50 cm (12–20 in) high, with green leaves, up to 10 cm (4 in) long, and numerous, yellow flowers in early summer. In some countries, it has become a garden escape.

Pratia (fam. Campanulaceae)

Distributed throughout many countries with warm climates, from South America to New Zealand, Australia, Asia and Africa, these carpet-forming perennials are useful for rock gardens and damp, shady places in the garden. There are around 25 species in the genus. All have branching stems, small, starry flowers and little, lobed leaves.

ABOVE *Pratia pedunculata* forms a dense, low groundcover when grown in partial shade, in moisture-retentive soil.

CULTIVATION Pratias are grown in partial or full shade. They need plenty of moisture and will not withstand drying out. The best method of propagation is division of established plants in spring or fall. Make sure newly planted divisions do not dry out.

CLIMATE Zone 7 for most species.

SPECIES *P. angulata*, from New Zealand, has white, starry flowers in summer, followed by purple fruits. *P. concolor* has tiny, toothed, oblong leaves and blue, starry flowers. It suits wet soil and can become invasive. *P. macrodon*, mountain pratia, from New Zealand, has tiny, round leaves, yellow or white flowers, and purple fruit. *P. nummularia*, zone 9, from tropical Asia, has tiny, round leaves and lilac, rose or yellowish green flowers with yellow throats and purple lower lips, followed by small, purple fruits. *P. pedunculata* has small, round, toothed leaves and starry, blue flowers. It makes a good groundcover. *P. purpurascens*, white root, is a spreading, lobelia-like plant, with long-stalked, lilac and blue flowers. It can be invasive, especially in turf.

Prickly pear

(*Opuntia ficus-indica*, fam. Cactaceae)

Indian fig

Many species of *Opuntia* are grown as ornamentals, but this species is cultivated for its edible fruit. It is an almost tree-like cactus, growing 3–5 m (10–16 ft) high, with large, segmented, paddle-shaped leaves. It bears bright yellow flowers along the rims of the segments, and these mature into deep red to purple fruit. The succulent fruits are known and enjoyed in many parts of the world. To prepare fruit for eating, wash and scrub with a brush, to remove spines. Slice off the top and the bottom, slit the skin and peel. The fruit is eaten raw, sometimes sliced and sprinkled with lemon or lime juice, and the pulp is used in jams.

CULTIVATION In frost-prone climates, grow in a

ABOVE The fleshy fruits of prickly pear are produced abundantly each year in suitable climates.

cool greenhouse or conservatory in pots of cactus compost, with maximum light. Keep dry in winter and water normally at other times. Outdoors, grow in a sunny, well-drained spot. Propagate from the paddle-shaped segments. Separate from the parent plant, allow the cut end to dry for a few days, then insert in cuttings compost, under glass.

CLIMATE Best in zone 10 and above.

Primula (fam. Primulaceae)

The genus name is a contraction of the Latin *primula veris*, meaning 'the first of spring', and in times past the flowering of primulas was thought to signal the arrival of spring. This large genus includes about 400 species, mostly from the temperate regions of the northern hemisphere. Characteristic of the genus are the pretty flowers, borne in clusters on long stems above a basal rosette of leaves. The natural flower colors have been extended through extensive breeding so that flowers are now available in various shades of carmine, pink, white, red, yellow and blue. Some species have blooms with centres of a contrasting color. Primulas are mainly perennials, but are often

ABOVE The many colors of polyanthus, *Primula* x *polyantha*, provide a cheerful garden display from late winter through spring

cultivated as annuals. They generally require a moist, cool position, and many dislike alkaline soils.

CULTIVATION Primulas do extremely well in cool to mild regions of the US. Some species do have particular growing requirements, but generally primulas will adapt to most garden soils and to sun or shade, provided there is sufficient moisture available. The tender primulas used as annual pot plants (*P.* x *kewensis*, *P. malacoides* and *P. obconica*), are grown in a cool greenhouse or conservatory. Raise them from seed sown in spring and pot into soilless potting compost. Grow in light and airy conditions, but shade from direct sun. Hardy primulas can be raised from seed sown as soon as ripe, or in spring, in a garden frame. Perennials can be divided in fall or early spring.

CLIMATE There are species suited to various climatic zones.

SPECIES *P. auricula*, zone 3, growing to 20 cm (8 in), has thick, often mealy leaves, to 10 cm (4 in) long. The flowers of the wild form appear in spring. They are yellow, sometimes fragrant, and are borne in clusters. The wild form, however, is not generally cultivated but hybrids from it are. Auriculas have had a great following through fanciers' clubs, particularly in Europe, over the past two centuries. Formally shaped flowers, often with gold 'lacing' and patterns, are popular. *P. denticulata*, zone 5, from the Himalayas, grows to about 30 cm (12 in), with 20 cm (8 in) long, somewhat mealy leaves. The flowers are borne in dense clusters in very early spring, in white through to mauve and purple, with yellow centres. A number of very decorative cultivars are available. *P.* x *kewensis*, zone 9, a hybrid of *P. floribunda* and *P. verticillata*, appeared in one of the glasshouses in the Royal Botanic Gardens, Kew, in 1897, and first bloomed in 1899. It grows to about 45 cm (18 in) high, with 20 cm (8 in) long leaves and fragrant, bright yellow flowers, borne in clusters up the plant stem, in late winter and spring. *P. malacoides*, zone 9, the commonly cultivated annual primula, from China, grows 30–45 cm (12–18 in) high. The 20 cm (8 in) long leaves are slightly hairy, pale green on top, and a little powdery on the undersides. The flowers come in various shades of rose and lavender through to white and appear in many-flowered clusters borne either singly or in groups up the stem. This species is well suited to pots. *P. obconica*, zone 9, from China, grows to 30 cm (12 in). It has hairy, scalloped leaves, about 25 cm (10 in) long. These can be irritating to sensitive skin. The flower clusters may be light purple, lilac, carmine or pink, sometimes with a yellow centre. The many cultivars often have flowers which are much larger than those of the wild species. *P.* x *polyantha*, zone 6, is a complex hybrid of several species of *Primula*. Producing large, brightly colored flowers, it is used as a potted plant or in massed garden displays, from winter to spring. It is mostly grown as an annual in warm climates, but is perennial in cool regions. *P. veris*, cowslip, zone 5, to 30 cm (12 in), is native to much of Europe, Britain and Asia. The oval, stemless leaves, to around 20 cm (8 in) long, are hairy underneath. The deep yellow, fragrant flowers are almost flat, and are borne in dense clusters. This species is one of the parents of polyanthus. *P. vulgaris*, English primrose, zone 6, native to much of Europe, is another parent of polyanthus. It grows to 15 cm (6 in), with wrinkled, lanceshaped, toothed leaves, to 20 cm (8 in) long. The flowers are mostly pale yellow, though occasionally purple or blue, and are borne singly. There is a very large number of herbaceous perennial primulas known commonly as candelabra primulas. These are delightful, colorful plants for cool-climate gardens and are worth seeking out from local and mail order nurseries. Most are woodland plants, revelling in moist soil and shade or filtered sunlight. Many of these species are native to China and the Himalayas.

Prostanthera (fam. Lamiaceae)
Mint bush

This genus of around 50 species of shrubs is native to Australia and is found growing naturally in a range of habitats. It belongs to the same botanical family as the common culinary herb, mint, hence the common name. The species vary in shape, size and growth habit, but all have showy, spring and summer flowers in almost every color, from red, purple, lilac, mauve and pink through to greenish yellow, cream and white, and highly aromatic foliage, with a minty smell. The flowers are trumpet-shaped and sometimes have striped or spotted throats. The fruit is a small nut. If planted alongside paths or walkways so that the foliage is brushed when passing, they will exude a a highly aromatic scent. In garden situations, in their natural environment, they are extremely fast growing, flowering from the first year with bright displays, but often proving to be short lived, sometimes dying quite suddenly and unexpectedly. In the right situation, however, these shrubs are not necessarily short lived, with some specimens still flowering after 15 years. In the garden, the

ABOVE Mint bush, *Prostanthera* species, is a lovely sight in full bloom. It is enjoyed both for its flowers and the minty aroma of its foliage.

bright colors of these bushes can be used to great effect and contrast, one of the most dramatic effects being the combination of purple mint bush (*P. ovalifolia*) and the yellow-gold of one of the wattles (*Acacia*) which flower simultaneously in late spring. To enjoy this effect in climates prone to regular hard frosts, one would need to employ a cool greenhouse or conservatory. The other species would also have to be grown in a greenhouse or conservatory situation.

CULTIVATION Under glass, grow in pots of soil-based potting compost. Provide good light and airy conditions. In the garden, if you have a suitable climate, prostantheras can be grown in a variety of soil types, but thrive in a lightly textured, well-drained soil. Newly planted speci-mens need care and attention until they are well established. Fall is a good time to plant, leaving the winter months for becoming estab-lished, and spring for rapid growth. Prostantheras generally prefer morning sun with afternoon shade, although many species tolerate light shade all day. The root systems of these plants are shallow, so planting in a shel-tered position amid rocks, larger shrubs and trees is worthwhile, to prevent their being blown over in strong winds or rain. Most species will flower in the first year. Most also benefit from regular pruning, especially straight after flowering. From the time of planting, tip pruning should be undertaken to encourage the development of a compact, bushy shape. Regular tip pruning is more effective than occa-sional heavy cutting, as cutting into older wood can often set back the plant severely or even kill it. The root system of this plant is close to the surface, so avoid disturbing soil near the plant. A mulch of coarse river sand or decayed leaf mould will help reduce weeds and maintain moisture, as will the placement of large rocks around the roots. Prostantheras can be propa-gated from seed or cuttings. Growing from cut-tings is the easiest method for these plants, as they flower earlier and are true to type. Cuttings of side shoots taken in late spring after flowering, or in early fall, are best. Place cut-tings in a propagating case, with bottom heat and keep the compost moist at all times. Since cuttings are easy to strike, it is a good idea to have new plants always under way, especially if cultivating some of the more spectacular flow-ering forms. Prostantheras will take light frosts and are fairly free from the usual insect pests and diseases, possibly due to the aromatic oils contained in the foliage. *Phytophthora* root rot is possibly the cause of most plant failures. This fungus thrives in warm weather, in water-logged soils.

CLIMATE Warmest parts of zone 9.

SPECIES Not all are available outside their coun-try of origin. *P. baxteri*, from Western Australia, grows to 1 m (3 ft) high, with sparse foliage and pretty, white flowers, with violet stripes in spring. *P. cuneata*, alpine mint bush, a native of the mountainous areas of south-eastern Australia, grows to a height of 1 m (3 ft) and a spread of 1.5 m (5 ft). It has rounded, shiny foliage. Large, white flowers, tinged with purple, bloom profusely in early summer. This species is suitable for shady situations. Cultivar 'Alpine Gold', with brilliant yellow young leaves and gold variegated margins, is worth trying. *P. incana*, velvet mint bush, spreads to a height and width of 2 m (6 ft). The small, oval leaves are soft, gray and hairy. The lavender, spring flowers have purple throats and are borne in ter-minal sprays. A white flowering form is also available. *P. incisa*, cut leaf mint bush, is a low, compact, bushy shrub with dense, light green, fan-shaped leaves. In spring, this shrub is covered with lilac lobed flowers. *P. lasianthos*, Victorian Christmas bush, is a fast-growing, tall shrub to small tree, native to cool, moist, forest habitats of eastern Australia. It has grayish green, lance-shaped, toothed leaves and creamy white flowers, tinged with pink or pale blue, and marked with purple and orange in the throats. The lovely flower sprays appear from spring through to midsummer. *P. nivea*, snowy mint bush, is a large, spreading shrub with flat-tened, light green, aromatic leaves and a pro-fusion of white flowers, borne in sprays, in late spring. This species likes a cool, damp situation. Var. *induta*, a compact type from the moun-tains of south-eastern New South Wales, has sil-very foliage and large, bright lavender-blue flowers in late spring. *P. ovalifolia*, purple mint bush, is the most commonly grown species and probably the most beautiful: it produces a spec-tacular, spring display of bright purple flowers. The small, oval leaves are dark green on top and grayish green on the undersides. Both the foliage and the stems are strongly aromatic. This species grows to around 2.5 m. *P. rotundifolia*, purple mint bush, grows to a height of 2 m (6 ft) and a width of 1.5 m (5 ft). An abundance of purplish blue flowers covers this shrub in spring. The dense, oval, dark green leaves emit a very strong, mint perfume.

Protea (fam. Proteaceae)

This spectacular genus of some 115 species of evergreen shrubs and small trees is originally from South Africa and is renowned for the great diversity of form among the species. Proteas are valued for their amazing flower heads, which have been described as glorified artichokes. They are actually large, dense clusters of bright, stiff, overlapping bracts, surrounding a bisexual flower. The leaves are usually stemless, tough and leathery. In frost-prone regions, proteas are grown in a cool greenhouse or conservatory. Many species of protea are grown for the cut flower trade.

CULTIVATION In the greenhouse or conservatory, grow proteas in large pots or tubs of acid, soil-based potting compost. Provide maximum light and airy conditions. Do not overwater plants: keep them steadily moist in the growing period and water far less in winter. Feed once or twice in summer with a liquid fertilizer, low in phosphorus. Outdoors, if the climate is suitable, grow proteas in acid to neutral, well-drained soil of low fertility. Choose a sheltered position which receives full sun. Do not feed. Pruning is not generally required. Propagate from seed in spring or as soon as ripe, germinated at 18°C (65°F), or from semi-ripe cuttings, rooting them with bottom heat.

CLIMATE Warmest parts of zone 9 to zone 10.

SPECIES *P. cynaroides*, king protea, is South Africa's floral emblem. Growing to 2 m (6 ft) high, it is characterized by its large, open flower heads and red-stemmed, shiny, green leaves, which are oval and leathery. The central dome of pink flowers is surrounded by downy pink bracts. Flowering occurs from the end of spring through to summer. *P. eximia*, ray-flowered protea, is an upright grower to 4–5 m (13–16 ft), with silvery green, broad, oval leaves. The flowers have deep pink outer bracts surrounding paler pink central flowers, tipped with purple. *P. grandiceps*, peach protea, is a spreading shrub, growing to around 1.5 m (5 ft) tall, with oval leaves, sometimes edged with red. The rose or purplish red flower heads are 12 cm (5 in) deep and 15 cm (6 in) across, with a grayish white, hairy fringe. *P. latifolia*, broad-leaf protea, grows to 2 m (6 ft) with silvery green foliage and pink, carmine or green flower heads, 15 cm (6 in) across, in summer. *P. neriifolia*, oleander-leafed protea, is another popularly grown species, reaching about 1.5 m (5 ft) high. The narrow, oblong, gray-green leaves are about 15 cm (6 in) long. Goblet-shaped flower heads open at the tips of the branches from spring through to summer. They are rose pink to brown in color, with a black fringe. The dried flower heads last for many months. *P. pulchella* grows to 1.5 m (5 ft) high, with lance-shaped, prominently ribbed leaves, 18 cm (7 in) long, and reddish pink flower heads, with black silky tips. *P. repens* (syn. *P. mellifera*), honey protea, one of the easiest and most widely cultivated proteas, is very attractive to bees. Growing to 3 m (10 ft) high, it has narrowly

ABOVE *Protea repens*, known as honey protea or sugarbush, has creamy white petals, tipped with deep pink or scarlet.

oblong leaves and fragrant flower heads in white, pink or red, in spring and summer.

Prunella (fam. Lamiaceae)
Self-heal

Prunella has a long history of use in herbal medicine, being especially recommended for throat problems and for healing wounds. The generic name is thought to have derived from a German word, itself corrupted from medieval Latin *brunella*, a name for tonsillitis. Widely grown in the US, this genus of around seven species of hardy perennials is originally from Eurasia, northern Africa and North America. It may become invasive if not controlled, and is especially suitable for wild gardens, for instance in shaded positions, where the soil is moist. Spikes of colorful flowers appear in summer.

CULTIVATION Prunellas can be grown in most soils in sun or shade. These vigorous, spreading plants seed freely. Propagate from seed or by division of the clumps in alternate years, to keep growth under control.

ABOVE In cool climates *Prunella vulgaris*, or self-heal, may bloom from early summer until late fall. It is known to have astringent properties.

CLIMATE Zone 5 for *P. grandiflora*; zone 3 for *P. vulgaris*.

SPECIES *P. grandiflora*, large self-heal, zone 5, is 15 cm (6 in) high, with a spread of at least 1 m (3 ft). It makes a good groundcover or rock garden plant. It is slightly hairy, with purple flowers. Cultivar 'Alba' has white flowers; 'Rosea' has rose-red flowers; 'Rubra' has deep red flowers. *P. vulgaris*, self-heal or sickle wort, zone 3, is a creeping plant, with a spread of 50 cm (20 in), sending out runners that form dense clumps of dull green, wedge-shaped foliage. The blueish violet or purple flowers are borne on spikes about 10 cm (4 in) high.

Prunus (fam. Rosaceae)

This is a large genus of shrubs and trees grown both for ornament and fruit. Most are deciduous and most are native to the northern hemisphere, particularly Europe and Asia. *Prunus* contains many of the most delicious, edible stone fruits (apricots, cherries, peaches, plums and nectarines) and some of the most beautiful flowering trees, for example, the Japanese flowering cherries. Some species are grown for their superb fall foliage; others for their brightly colored, summer leaves. The variety in growth

BELOW *Prunus subhirtella* becomes an airy cloud of pale blossom when it flowers in spring. Blooming may be intermittent from fall to spring

habits makes it possible to select one suitable for any position in the garden. Most of the species and all of the cultivars described here are grown for their attractive flowers, which appear from early to late spring, unless otherwise stated.

CULTIVATION Although fairly adaptable, *Prunus* species do better in areas with cold winters. Most of those grown for their spring flowers and fall foliage thrive in cool and cold climates, where they have complete winter dormancy. Some *Prunus*, though, such as the ornamental forms of peach, *P. persica*, are better in somewhat milder climates, and in positions sheltered from cold winds. Plant all *Prunus* in well-drained garden soil, enriched with well-rotted organic material, and water well prior to planting. Because the deciduous species are fully dormant in winter, they can be transplanted easily as quite large specimens. Branches should first be pruned by one-third and damaged roots should be removed by clean cuts with secateurs. Feed once a year with a complete plant food and renew mulch. Most *Prunus* species require little or no pruning, except to remove wayward branches and dead wood. *P. glandulosa* needs to be pruned back immediately after flowering. This species and its cultivars are generally cut almost to ground level, which results in regrowth of slender stems clothed with new, red-tinted, green leaves. They will flower the following year. *P. persica* suffers, as all peaches do, from infestations of peach leaf curl, the symptoms of which are unsightly, blistered and misshapened leaves. To control, apply a copper compound at leaf-bud swell. If not treated early, it will be another year before effective treatment can be carried out. Most of the ornamental species are budded onto seedling stock of the same or similar species in summer, and many, such as the weeping kinds (*P. subhirtella* 'Pendula' and *P.* x *yedoensis* 'Pendula'), are grown on tall standards by this method, the branches drooping almost to ground level and providing a spectacular curtain of spring flowers. The lovely, upright *P. campanulata* is also budded, but it seeds

ABOVE *Prunus glandulosa* has delicate-looking single flowers. Cut back hard after flowering to promote new flowering wood for the next season.

freely, sometimes producing lovely, pale pink forms. *P. glandulosa* is propagated from soft basal cuttings in spring; *P. laurocerasus* and *P. lusitanica* are propagated from semi-ripe cuttings in late summer or fall, or from hardwood cuttings in winter.

CLIMATE Best in cool to cold, moist climates; some species do well in warmer areas.

SPECIES *P. armeniaca*, zone 6, apricot, is the species grown for the popular stone fruit, ornamental apricots being derived from *P. mume*. *P. avium*, zone 4, wild cherry, from western Asia and Europe, is thought to be one of the parents of the modern fruiting cherries. It is a broad, spreading tree, which grows to around 20 m (65 ft) high. The pointed, dark green leaves turn red, crimson and yellow before falling. Cultivar 'Plena' grows to a height and spread of around 12 m (40 ft), with a rounded habit and green, oval to lance-shaped

ABOVE The bright cerise-pink flowers of Taiwan cherry, *Prunus campanulata*, appear in early spring.

leaves that color well in fall. The semi-double, white flowers are borne in large clusters. *P.* x *blireana*, zone 5, cherry plum, grows 4 m (13 ft) tall and 3 m (10 ft) wide, forming a vase shape. The reddish purple leaves change to deep green in summer and the dainty, double flowers are rose pink, appearing in early to mid-spring, before the foliage emerges. *P. campanulata*, zone 8, Taiwan cherry, is slow-growing, to 10 m (33 ft) high, with a slender, upright habit. The green leaves are ovate to lance-shaped, coloring well in fall. This species looks spectacular in spring, when the bare branches are covered with clusters of bell-shaped, cerise flowers. *P. cerasifera*, zone 4, cherry plum, has been cultivated in the Mediterranean region for many years, both as an ornamental and for its fruit. Numerous ornamental cultivars have been developed, including 'Nigra', which grows 4 m (13 ft) high and 3 m (10 ft), wide in a vase shape. It has blackish purple leaves and single, pale pink flowers. *P. cerasus*, zone 6, sour cherry, is grown for its fruit. *P. dulcis* (syn. *P. amygdalus*), zone 7, almond, originating from central Asia, is known to have been cultivated by the Greeks and Romans. Even the wild fruiting form has great flowering beauty, and lovely, ornamental hybrids are available.

P. glandulosa, zone 4, dwarf flowering almond, reaches 1 m (3 ft) tall and wide with upright, suckering growth. The new growth of the green, ovate leaves is tinged with pink and the single, pink flowers are followed by deep red, fleshy fruit. Cultivar 'Alba Plena' has double, white flowers; 'Sinensis' has double, pink flowers. *P. laurocerasus*, zone 7, cherry laurel, from eastern Europe and south-west Asia, and *P. lusitanica*, zone 7, Portugal laurel, are two of the best known, evergreen ornamentals. Both have glossy green, leathery leaves and upright spikes of small, sweetly scented, white flowers followed by red berries, which ripen to black. Both make excellent hedging and screening plants, being a familiar feature of the Mediterranean landscape. They tolerate frequent clipping and withstand a wide range of climatic conditions, including cold winds and dryness, once established. *P. mume*, zone 7, Japanese or ornamental apricot, is a deciduous tree, 6–8 m (20–26 ft) high, with a rounded crown. It is the first of the *Prunus* species to flower, flowers often appearing in late winter. Species blooms are single and may be white or red, but there are many lovely, double-flowered forms. *P. padus*, zone 4, bird cherry, grows 15 m (50 ft) tall and 10 m (33 ft) wide, with an open, spreading habit. The broad, green leaves are lance-shaped and the single, white, fragrant flowers appear in pendulous clusters. *P. persica*, zone 8, peach, has been known in its native China for almost 5000 years. It grows to 5 m (16 ft) tall and 4 m (13 ft) wide, in a vase shape, and is easily recognized by its profusion of pinkish red blooms. The mid-green leaves, to 15 cm (6 in) long, appear after the blossoms. Many of the ornamental hybrids have double flowers and set no fruit. Cultivar 'Versicolor' has double, white flowers striped with red, or occasionally deep rose; 'Alba Plena' produces double, pure white flowers; 'Rosea Plena' bears double, deep rose pink flowers. *P. serrulata*, zone 6, Japanese flowering cherry, zone 6, grows 8–9 m (26–30 ft) high and is the parent of many beautiful hybrids, with variable growth habits and flowers. There are many fine cultivars of

ABOVE Flowering cherry plum, *Prunus* x *blireana*, is a lovely tree for small gardens. The blossom appears before the leaves.

Japanese flowering cherries. 'Amanogawa' has an upright, poplar-like form and has semi-double, pale pink flowers; 'Fugenzo', with double, pale pink flowers, has a spreading growth habit; 'Kanzan' also has a spreading habit, bearing double, rich pink flowers; 'Kiku-shidare-zakura' (syn. 'Cheal's Weeping Cherry') has a weeping habit, producing double, deep pink, frilled flowers; 'Okumiyaku' has a wide, spreading form with a flattened crown and double, white flowers, from pink buds; 'Shirofugen', also of wide, spreading habit, has double flowers which are pink in bud opening to blush white; 'Shirotae' (syn. 'Mt Fuji' or 'Kojima') has a broad, spreading habit, with semi-double, sometimes single, white, drooping flowers; 'Tai-Haku', the great white cherry, has a very tall, strong growth habit, reaching 6 m (20 ft), with very large, single, snow white flowers, borne in pendulous clusters; 'Ukon' has an open, spreading habit with maturity, producing interesting pink-tinged greenish cream flowers. *P.* x *subhirtella* 'Pendula' (syn. *P.* x *subhirtella* 'Pendula Rosea'), zone 6, weeping rosebud cherry, is usually grown on standards, 1–3 m (3–10 ft) tall. The pendulous branches arch gracefully and the broad, lance-shaped, green leaves turn golden yellow in fall.

The new growth is a pinkish bronze and the small, single flowers are pale pink. *P.* x *yedoensis*, zone 6, yoshino cherry or traditional cherry of Japan, grows to a height of 15 m (50 ft) and a width of 10 m (33 ft), into a large, round-headed, striking tree with broad, lance-shaped, green leaves. The leaves color well in fall, following the massed display of fragrant, white or pale pink flowers. It makes an excellent lawn specimen or avenue tree.

Pseuderanthemum (fam. Acanthaceae)

This genus of 60 species of tropical shrubs and perennials is not well known outside the tropics, though some species are popular greenhouse and conservatory plants. While the flowers are attractive, these shrubs are grown mainly for their showy, colorful foliage. Some have origins in the tropical Americas, but many are native to the Pacific Islands.

CULTIVATION Grow in a warm conservatory or greenhouse, in pots of soil-based potting compost. Give good light (but shade from direct sun), and a humid atmosphere. Pruning may be needed in spring to restrict size. Propagate from semi-ripe cuttings in summer, with basal warmth.

CLIMATE Tropical.

ABOVE This plain, green-leaved species of *Pseuderanthemum* has simple, white flowers, flushed with pink.

SPECIES *P. atropurpureum*, from Polynesia, grows 1–1.5 m (3–5 ft) high. Foliage is brilliant green or deep purple, splashed or spotted with white, pink, purple, yellow or green. Tubular, white flowers spotted pink to purple, appear in summer. *P. reticulatum*, golden net bush, has deep green leaves, veined with pale yellow. It grows to around 1 m (3 ft) high and bears white flowers with deep pink to red throats, in late spring through summer.

Pseudobombax (fam. Bombacaceae)

Native to the tropical Americas, this genus consists of around 20 species of medium-sized trees, with large flowers in white, red or purple. CULTIVATION In frost-prone climates, grow as foliage plants in pots in a warm greenhouse or conservatory. It is unlikely they will flower under glass. Use soil-based potting compost, and provide maximum light. Outdoors these trees need sun and deep, well-drained soil with a high organic content.

CLIMATE Zone 10 and above.

SPECIES *P. ellipticum*, shaving brush tree, from Central America, grows to 9 m (30 ft) and has interesting, greenish gray bark. The white to pink flowers appear on bare branches in spring, before the leaves. Many stamens extend beyond the flower petals, giving the shaving brush effect. *P. grandiflorum*, from Brazil, grows to about 40 m (130 ft), with deep purple-red flowers.

Pseudopanax (fam. Araliaceae)

This genus comprises 12 to 20 species of evergreen trees and shrubs, grown for their interesting sword-shaped foliage. Natives of New Zealand and South America, these shrubs can grow to 6 m (20 ft), and some even higher, particularly in cool climates.

CULTIVATION Where hard frosts occur regularly, grow in a cool greenhouse or conservatory, in pots of gritty, soil-based potting compost. Ensure maximum light, but shade from direct strong sun. In the garden grow in a sunny, sheltered spot with well-drained soil. Propagate from seed in spring or from semi-ripe cuttings in summer, with bottom heat for both.

CLIMATE Zone 9.

SPECIES *P. chathamicus*, from the Chatham Islands, grows to 6 m (20 ft), the fairly broad adult leaves reaching up to 20 cm (8 in) long.

ABOVE *Pseudobombax ellipticum* is aptly named 'shaving brush tree' for its large brush-like staminate flowers.

ABOVE The stiff, sword-like leaves of *Pseudopanax crassifolius* make this an unusual plant for a garden feature.

P. crassifolius, lancewood, is a New Zealand species which can grow as tall as 15 m (50 ft). The plant changes dramatically as it matures. Initially, it has a single stem with stiff, sword-like leaves, to 1 m (3 ft) long; older plants become branched with a rounded canopy; and finally the leaves become compound and leathery, to about 30 cm (12 in) long. *P. ferox*, also from New Zealand, grows to 6 m (20 ft), with narrow or sword-shaped leaves. *P. lessonii* is more shrub-like, the mature leaves having three to five leaflets. The leathery leaves are a rich green, sometimes tinged with bronze-purple. There are many different forms of this species.

Pseudotsuga (fam. Pinaceae)
Douglas fir

Only one of the six species of this genus of conifers is in general cultivation. *P. menziesii* is a majestic tree, occurring naturally in a belt of magnificent, coniferous forest on the North American west coast. The name Oregon pine (or Oregon) is given to the timber of this species, exported from North America in huge quantities. The Douglas fir is recommended for planting only in the largest gardens and in parks and arboreta. Apart from one species from Mexico and California, the other four species are all from eastern Asia. This distribution of North America and eastern Asia is the same for a number of tree genera, including *Thuja, Calocedrus, Liriodendron* and *Magnolia*.

CULTIVATION The Douglas fir does best in cool areas with very high rainfall in deep, fertile, well-drained soil. Under such conditions, saplings can grow by 2 m (6 ft) a year in their rapid-growth phase. Propagation is from seed only, obtainable from the cones freely carried on even quite young trees. Germin-ation is reliable and quite rapid. After planting out, young trees normally require no staking or trimming.

CLIMATE Zone 6.

SPECIES *P. menziesii* is very similar to the true firs (*Abies*). Like them, it has short, flattened,

ABOVE The cones of *Pseudotsuga menziesii* are unique, with their conspicuous bracts outside the cone scales. This majestic tree is for large gardens and parks only.

needle-like leaves, which are blueish green and fragrant. However, its cones are pendulous like those of the spruces, with thin, brownish, persistent scales. In the wild, it grows into a huge tree, sometimes exceeding 90 m (36 in). Its sturdy trunk is clothed in dark reddish brown, corky bark.

Pseudowintera (fam. Winteraceae)

Previously classified under the genus *Drimys*, all three species of shrubs or small trees are originally from New Zealand, occurring naturally in both lowland and alpine forests. These shrubs are best suited to warm-climate gardens. In cooler areas, grow in a cool greenhouse.

CULTIVATION In the greenhouse, grow in pots of soil-based potting compost, in good light. In the garden, grow in acid to neutral, moist yet well-drained soil containing plenty of humus, in a sheltered, sunny position. Propagate from semi-ripe cuttings, rooted in heat.

CLIMATE Zone 9.

SPECIES *P. axillaris*, pepper tree, is a small, evergreen tree with black bark and glossy, alternate

ABOVE *Pseudowintera colorata* has very interesting winter foliage, as dark scarlet to purple pigments blotch the green leaves.

ABOVE Quick-growing *Psoralea affinis* adapts to almost any kind of soil in warm regions.

leaves. The greenish white flowers occur in the leaf axils or in scars of fallen leaves. The red berries follow the flowers in winter. *P. colorata*, New Zealand alpine pepper tree or horopito, is the most commonly cultivated species. It is a stiff, symmetrical shrub, to 3 m (10 ft), suitable for zone 8 if well sheltered. The green foliage is blotched with scarlet and purple in winter, and is silvery gray on the undersides. It lasts well when cut in winter. The aromatic bark and greenish flowers, which appear from spring to summer, were used medicinally by the Maoris.

Psoralea (fam. Papilionaceae)
Scurfy pea

The 130 species in this genus of fragrant shrubs and perennials, grown mainly for their flowers, are found mostly in North and South America and South Africa.

CULTIVATION Psoraleas do best in a warm temperate climate. In cooler areas, grow in pots in a cool greenhouse or conservatory, using soil-based potting compost. In the garden, choose a spot in full sun, with moderately fertile soil.

Trim plants after flowering to reduce seed set, as they tend to self-sow. *P. pinnata*, especially, needs pinching during the growing season and pruning after flowering for compact, tidy growth. Propagate from seed.

CLIMATE Warmest parts of zone 9.

SPECIES *P. affinis*, to 3 m (10 ft), produces blue or purple, summer flowers. *P. pinnata*, to 3 m (10 ft), is a fast-growing shrub with a profusion of blue and white flowers, in summer. It is the most commonly cultivated species.

Pteris (fam. Pteridaceae)
Brake fern

Native to shady, damp gullies of tropical and subtropical rainforests, these ferns can also be found growing in sunny rock crevices. This large genus comprises about 280 species of terrestrial ferns, with short creeping rhizomes which form clumps, and variously divided fronds. Popular with growers are cultivars with unusual leaflet formation, and the many variegated forms.

ABOVE Silver brake fern, *Pteris argyraea*, is one of the loveliest species in cultivation. It is an ideal fern for the greenhouse or conservatory.

CULTIVATION Grow in an intermediate greenhouse or conservatory in pots of soil-based potting compost. Add some leaf mould if available, plus lumps of charcoal. Shade plants from direct sun, and provide a humid atmosphere. Outdoors grow in shade and moist soil. Propagate by division in spring.

CLIMATE Zone 10 to tropical.

SPECIES *P. argyraea*, silver brake, is one of the most beautiful of the entire genus. It is very large, reaching up to 2 m (6 ft) in the wild. The short, creeping rhizomes form a large crown, the stems are brown with papery, brown scales at the base and the fronds grow to 1 m (3 ft) or more. The silvery white strip running down the centre of the leaflets contrasts dramatically with the deep green of the margins. *P. cretica* is found in many tropical and subtropical regions of the world, and many cultivars and natural varieties of this species are available. Cultivar 'Albolineata' is a very beautiful fern, the leaflets displaying a very broad, silvery white stripe. It makes an excellent pot or basket subject, both for indoors and outdoors. *P. ensiformis* is a smaller, daintier species from Southeast Asia, extending east to Polynesia. The short, creeping rhizomes form clumps and the finely divided fronds are erect when young, becoming pendulous with age. Cultivar 'Victoriae' is an attractive, variegated form; 'Evergemiensis' is similar, but the sterile fronds are larger and more decorative. *P. tremula*, Australian brake, is found in many parts of Australia and New Zealand. It has tufted, upright rootstocks which form a crown and upright stems which are dark at the base, becoming lighter at the tip of the fronds. The fronds have finely toothed margins and are very large in mature ferns. The spores are very fertile, causing the fern to spread rapidly. This tenacious fern tolerates a wide range of conditions and makes a good rock garden subject. *P. tripartita*, giant brake fern, occurs in north-eastern Queensland and throughout the lowland tropics of the world. It has solid rootstocks which form a trunk in mature specimens. The stems are long and green, and the fronds are large, forming three branches. It can be grown in the garden in suitable climates. *P. umbrosa*, jungle brake, native to Australia's eastern states, is a many-branched fern with long stems. The large, upright fronds vary from light to dark green in color, depending on the amount of sunlight they receive. Very similar to *P. cretica*, this species is suitable for growing in large pots and in the garden. *P. vittata*, ladder or Chinese brake, is found in many tropical and subtropical regions of the world. The rootstocks are very short and solid with pale scales, the stems are brown at the base, and the fronds are up to 1 m (3 ft) long, composed of simple, oblong to lance-shaped leaflets.

Pterocarya (fam. Juglandaceae)
Wingnut

This is a small genus of ten species of deciduous, ornamental trees native to the Caucasus and several parts of Asia. Most are fast growing. They are grown for their very attractive, pinnate foliage and the long, pendulous strings of winged nuts which are carried over much of the

ABOVE The long strands of greenish yellow flowers on *Pterocarya fraxinifolia* are followed by nuts that mature in fall.

summer. Although adaptable to a range of soils and growing conditions, their roots are shallow and sometimes produce suckers.

CULTIVATION Suitable for most soils, they do best in deep, fertile soils that are kept reasonably moist in summer. Regular summer watering is essential. Trees can be propagated from seed, suckers, or by layering.

CLIMATE Best in cool, moist climates. Zone 7.

SPECIES *P. fraxinifolia*, Caucasian wingnut, grows to 30 m (100 ft) in its native habitat but in cultivation will more likely be 12–15 m (40–50 ft). The long leaves are made up of numerous leaflets and the long strings of winged nuts that develop after the flowers have fallen are suspended on long, string-like stems that can be 45 cm (18 in) long. *P. stenoptera*, Chinese wingnut, also grows to around 30 m (100 ft) high in its native China, but about half that in cultivation. It also has long, compound leaves, and its winged nuts are carried on stems about 30 cm (12 in) long.

Pterostylis (fam. Orchidaceae)
Greenhoods

This genus comprises some 60 species of tiny, terrestrial orchids from Australia, New Zealand,

ABOVE The blunt greenhood, *Pterostylis curta*, is seen here with the unusual, hood-like flower formation characteristic of all the greenhood orchids.

New Guinea and New Caledonia, though few species are in general cultivation. They are known for their unusual, hood-like flower formation, from which their common name has evolved.

CULTIVATION Grow in an intermediate greenhouse or conservatory, in shallow pots of terrestrial orchid compost. Be careful with watering as these orchids do not like overwatering.

CLIMATE Zone 10.

SPECIES *P. grandiflora* grows 15–25 cm (6–10 in) high, with a solitary, erect, translucent, green flower with reddish brown bands.

Ptilotus (fam. Amaranthaceae)
Mulla mulla

There are around 100 species in this genus of perennials which are found in semi-arid regions of all states of Australia, except Tasmania. Pretty, greenish or pinkish brushes, sometimes

ABOVE The woolly flowers of *Ptilotus* species come in gray, silver, lavender or pale pink shades.

lightly fragrant, dot the sandy deserts of inland Australia after rain. The soft, hairy foliage is grayish white in color. Very attractive when mass planted, they are suitable for growing in rockeries and pebble gardens.

CULTIVATION In frost-prone climates grow in an airy cool greenhouse or conservatory, in pots of soil-based potting compost. Ensure maximum light. Water very sparingly in winter, normally at other times. In the garden, grow in very well-drained soil with full sun. Propagate in spring from seed germinated at 16°C (61°F).

CLIMATE Zone 9.

SPECIES These are not easy to obtain outside their native Australia. *P. exaltatus*, pussytails or lambs tails, is a robust, drought-resistant perennial, 60–90 cm (24–36 in) high, with woolly, gray to lavender, upright, brush flowers, with long silvery hairs. *P. grandiflorus* has an upright growth habit, reaching 15–30 cm (6–12 in) high. The large, pinkish, silvery flowers appear in summer. *P. obovatus*, growing to 45 cm (18 in), has grayish, hairy leaves and small, fluffy, pinkish white flowers, in spring and summer. *P. polystachyus* is a stiffly erect plant, to 1 m (3 ft), with rough, grayish leaves and erect, slender, greenish white flower spikes.

There is also a red form. *P. spathulatus* is a low-growing, tufted plant with pale greenish to cream flowers on upright stems.

Ptychosperma (fam. Areacaceae)

Mainly found in Papua New Guinea and the surrounding islands, this genus of 28 species of small to medium-sized, feather palms also includes two or three species from northern Australia. There are both solitary and multi-trunked types, but all have a well-developed, slender crownshaft, at least when fully mature. The leaves may be divided into only a few, or many, leaflets which may be narrow and linear or fishtail-shaped. All leaflets have toothed apexes. Flowers and fruits are borne on large, spreading sprays below the crownshaft.

CULTIVATION Where frosts occur, grow in a warm greenhouse or conservatory. These palms also

ABOVE *Ptychosperma macarthurii*, Macarthur palm, adapts well to cultivation in pots, in a warm greenhouse or conservatory.

make good house plants. Use soil-based potting compost. Ensure good light (but shade from direct sun), and provide a humid atmosphere. Keep well watered during the growing period, but reduce in winter. Outdoors plants need partial shade and plenty of water. Propagate from seed sown in spring and germinated at 24°C (75°F). Seed usually germinates very easily, taking from six to twelve weeks.

CLIMATE Warmest parts of zone 10 to tropical.

SPECIES *P. elegans*, solitaire palm, from northern Queensland, is the best known of the species. It has a smooth, solitary, prominently ringed trunk, to about 8 m (26 ft) tall and up to 12 cm (5 in) in diameter. The leaves are gracefully recurved, to about 2 m (6 ft) long, with crowded, broad leaflets. The large, spreading inflorescences appear through much of the year, with heavy crops of scarlet fruits, developing after the small white flowers fall. *P. macarthurii*, Macarthur palm, from rainforest areas of northern Queensland, is a clumping species with up to 20 or so closely crowded trunks. Its trunks are more slender and its leaves slightly smaller than those of *P. elegans*; otherwise it is fairly similar to that species. Many of the species from New Guinea and Indonesia are cultivated in tropical botanical gardens.

Pulmonaria (fam. Boraginaceae)
Lungwort

Grown for their delightful flowers, some of these hardy, European and Asian, dwarf perennials also have attractive, silver-spotted leaves. The flowers generally appear very early in the year, in late winter or early spring, and are mainly in shades of blue. They are excellent for woodland gardens and groundcover.

CULTIVATION Grow in any ordinary, moist garden soil, well supplied with humus, in partial shade or even full shade. Propagate from seed or by division, in spring. They can be divided every few years. *Pulmonaria* works well planted with

ABOVE The royal blue flowers of lungwort appear before the new leaves. The spotted foliage can make a dense groundcover under trees.

other early spring-flowering plants, such as primroses, and it can be allowed to naturalize under deciduous trees.

CLIMATE Cool climates are best. Zone 4.

SPECIES *P. angustifolia*, blue cowslip, has blue, tubular-shaped flowers, sometimes tinged with pink, which emerge from basal rosettes of mid-green foliage, in spring. It grows to a height and spread of around 30 cm (12 in). *P. officinalis*, lungwort or Jerusalem cowslip, grows to 30 cm (12 in), with pink to violet flowers and leaves spotted with white. This plant was formerly used in folk medicine to treat diseased lungs.

Pultenaea (fam. Papilionaceae)
Bush pea, eggs and bacon

Comprising around 100 species, this genus of native Australian shrubs provides a wonderful display of brightly colored, pea-shaped flowers in yellow, orange, brown or red flowers, throughout spring or summer. Some have a light perfume. The foliage is variable, from prickly to soft, downy gray, providing year-round interest. There are several dwarf and prostrate species which are ideal for rock gardens and trailing down banks or walls, and as

ABOVE Bronze bush pea, *Pultenaea villosa*, has soft, slightly hairy foliage. It bears masses of yellow flowers from spring to summer.

flowers in spring. *P. microphylla*, spreading bush pea, may be prostrate or upright, with narrow, hairy, triangular-shaped leaves and yellow and brown flowers. *P. pedunculata*, mat bush pea, is a low-growing, trailing shrub with unusually bright green foliage. The yellow, orange or red flowers cover this shrub from late spring to early summer. It makes an excellent rockery plant or groundcover. *P. stipularis* grows about 1 m (3 ft) high. The foliage is very decorative, resembling soft pine leaves. Large heads of bright yellow flowers appear in spring. *P. villosa*, bronze bush pea, grows to 2 m (6 ft), and produces yellow flowers amongst the soft, brownish green, pendulous foliage.

Pumpkin

(*Cucurbita species*, fam. Cucurbitaceae)

Originally thought to have come from Mexico and Central America, pumpkins are annual vines or bushes, grown for their edible fruit. They can be used once the outer skin begins to harden; immature fruit has poor flavor and will not keep. Fruit intended for storage should be thoroughly ripe–when the fruit stalk turns brown and begins to wither. Leave about 8 cm (3 in) of stalk attached to the fruit for handling and prevention of entry of disease organisms into the fruit.

CULTIVATION Grow in a warm, sunny spot, with protection from strong winds. Most varieties need at least five months of frost-free weather. If space is limited, bush types are more suitable. As soon as the soil warms up in spring, sow seeds direct in drills or hills. In areas with a short growing season, sow seed in pots, keep in a warm place and transplant when the soil has warmed. The soil should be enriched with organic matter, well-drained and moist. When the vines are around 1.5–2 m (5–6 ft), pinch off the tips to produce more laterals and increase the number of female flowers. Weed control is essential. Before the fruit can develop, pollination must take place. Bees are the best pollinators although hand pollination is very success-

groundcover. Some species tend to be short-lived. In climatic zones lower than 9, grow in an airy, cool greenhouse or conservatory.

CULTIVATION *Pultenaea* species produce abundant seed which is easy to propagate. Soak in hot water and allow to stand overnight. Sow in sandy loam. Most species can also be propagated from tip cuttings of semi-ripe growth, preferably taken in fall. *Pultenaea* can be grown in any well-drained, light garden soil which is slightly acidic. It does well in soil enriched with leaf mould. Under glass, grow in pots of acid, soil-based potting compost.

CLIMATE Zone 9.

SPECIES Few are available outside their native Australia. *P. cunninghamii* is grown for its lovely, blueish gray foliage. It rarely grows more than 1 m (3 ft) high, producing large, yellow to orange-red flowers. *P. daphnoides* is an upright grower, to 3 m (10 ft). The large, yellow flowers are borne terminally and the foliage is olive green. *P. flexilis* grows to 4 m (13 ft) high, with pale green foliage and clusters of bright yellow flowers, in spring. *P. juniperina*, prickly bush pea, is a graceful, spreading shrub, 1–3 m (3–10 ft) high, with pointed, lance-shaped leaves and a profusion of fragrant, soft, orange

ABOVE This smooth-skinned orange pumpkin should not be picked until the stalk withers and browns.

ful. The home gardener should cut off the male flower and rub the pollen onto the stigma of the female flower (just above the ovary). (This can also be done with a small brush.) When this portion starts to expand, both pollination and fertilization have taken place. Female flowers have a distinct rounded swelling under the base of the petals. Aphids, red spider mites, and powdery mildew may be a problem.

CLIMATE Zone 9 at least, but also grown as a summer annual in all climatic zones.

SPECIES *Cucurbita maxima*, *C. moschata*, *C. pepo* and *C. pepo* var. *pepo* are the species from which all today's cultivars derive. Pumpkins generally have a round, flattened fruit with a hard rind, though the color may be shades of green, yellow or orange. The flesh is mostly orange or yellow. The plant is usually a running vine but bush types, which need less space, have been developed. There are numerous cultivars of pumpkin but their availability varies from place to place. Most retail seed companies generally include a few in their mail-order catalogues. Probably the best known cultivars among the large-fruited pumpkins are 'Atlantic Giant' and 'Mammoth'. These are particularly popular with exhibitors in vegetable shows and competitions. There are also small and mini-pumpkins whose flesh is generally sweeter and with finer grain.

Puya (fam. Bromeliaceae)

There are around 160 species in this genus of large, showy bromeliads from highland areas of South America. Because of their size, they are generally grown in parks and public gardens, rather than home gardens, where they offer a spectacular display when in bloom. The strap-like leaves radiating from the centre are usually narrow and heavily barbed. Puyas are terrestrial and their natural habitat is among rocks. In areas prone to frost, grow in a cool greenhouse or conservatory.

CULTIVATION In the greenhouse, grow in pots of soilless potting compost. Plants need maximum light. Keep compost only slightly moist in winter; water more freely at other times. Where they can be grown outdoors, choose a sunny spot with well-drained soil. Propagate from seed germinated at 21°C (70°F).

CLIMATE Zone 10 to tropical.

SPECIES *P. berteroniana*, from Chile, produces what many believe is the world's most beautiful flower–a single, yucca-like inflorescence, covered with scores of metallic blue flowers, with orange stamens. *P. spathacea*, from Argentina,

ABOVE The shiny leaves on this young *Puya berteroniana* are already well armed with spines. Plants will be up to 1 m (3 ft) high at maturity.

to 1 m (3 ft) or more, has dark blue flowers on a branched, red-stemmed stalk. *P. venusta* is not quite as large as some of the species and suits home gardens. The inflorescence combines purple and deep rose pink to create a stunning effect.

Pyracantha (fam. Rosaceae)
Firethorn

These evergreen shrubs are originally from Asia and the Mediterranean, but are now grown in temperate climates everywhere, for the brilliant red or orange berries which follow the clusters of small, white flowers, covering the branches in spring. The berries can persist through winter. Firethorns make good hedges, screens and fill-in plants.

CULTIVATION These hardy shrubs will grow well in most soil types, in sun or shade. They do, however, need an open, sunny position if they are to flower and fruit satisfactorily. They prefer regular watering through summer, but established shrubs tolerate dry periods well. Propagate species from seed sown in fall, in a garden frame, or from semi-ripe cuttings in summer, in a heated propagating case.

CLIMATE Zone 7 for most species, zone 6 for *P. coccinea*.

ABOVE The brilliant scarlet berries of *Pyracantha* species often persist through winter, providing welcome color.

SPECIES *P. angustifolia*, from western China, grows to 3 m (10 ft) or more and has graceful, horizontal branches, narrow, green leaves, gray on the undersides, and large, shiny, orange berries. *P. coccinea*, from southern Europe, is one of the most popular of the species. It is a very leafy, large shrub, which grows 2–5 m (6–16 ft) high, with arching branches and scarlet berries. Cultivar 'Lalandei' produces orange-red berries. *P. crenulata* is a shrub or small tree, to 6 m (20 ft), with orange-red berries. *P.* 'Watereri' is a widely grown hybrid, to about 2.5 m (8 ft), with a dense habit, deep green foliage, and brilliant red fruits.

Pyrostegia (fam. Bignoniaceae)

Related to bignonias, these South American, evergreen climbers are very strong growers, supporting themselves by tendrils. They provide rich midwinter color. In their natural environment, flowers are pollinated by hummingbirds.

CULTIVATION Outside the subtropics and tropics, grow in an intermediate greenhouse or conservatory in a large pot or tub of soil-based potting compost. If available, add extra grit and some leaf mould. Ensure maximum light. Support

ABOVE Lighting up late winter days are the bright orange flowers of flame vine, *Pyrostegia venusta*. The dark foliage is a good foil for the bright flowers.

the stems and train into the roof area. Outdoors grow in full sun with rich, well-drained soil. Prune after flowering by cutting back sideshoots to within four buds of the main stems. Propagate from seed sown in spring, or from semi-ripe cuttings in summer, both in a heated propagating case.

CLIMATE Zone 10.

SPECIES *P. venusta* (syn. *P. ignea*), flame vine, the most commonly cultivated species, is grown mainly for its brilliant display of fiery orange, tubular-shaped flowers, in pendulous clusters.

Pyrus (fam. Rosaceae)

Pear

Native to temperate Eurasia and North Africa, this genus comprises around 30 species of deciduous trees, some of which are grown for their edible fruit and others for ornamental value. The ornamentals have glossy, green leaves which color superbly in fall and clusters of open, cup-shaped, white flowers, in spring. Any fruit is usually small and hard.

CULTIVATION These hardy trees will grow in most soils, provided they have a sunny position, but require ample moisture and rich, deep soil to thrive. Bare-rooted trees are available in fall and winter; container-grown plants may be planted out throughout the year. Propagate species from seed outdoors in fall, cultivars by budding in summer, or by winter grafting.

CLIMATE Zone 4 for most species, zone 5 for *P. calleryana*.

SPECIES *P. calleryana*, Callery or Chinese wild pear, is a pretty tree, 10–12 m (33–40 ft) high, with broad, oval leaves which give brilliant fall color. The pure white, spring blossom is very showy but has a slightly unpleasant odor. *P. salicifolia*, willow leaf pear, is a tree, 8–10 m (26–33 ft) high, with slightly leathery, gray-green leaves. More popular than the species is

the weeping *P. s.* 'Pendula', a superb specimen tree and ideal for small gardens. *P. ussuriensis*, Manchurian pear, is a broad, cone-shaped tree, growing 12–15 m (40–50 ft). The shiny green foliage turns rich crimson in fall. The tree is covered in white blossom in spring.

TOP *Pyrus ussuriensis*, or Manchurian pear, colors brilliantly in fall. This tree is just starting to turn.

ABOVE Pear blossom is white, smothering the tree in mid-spring. Pears have great ornamental value, with their spring blossom and rich fall color.

QR

Quandong to Ruta

Quandong

(*Santalum acuminatum*, fam. Santalaceae)

The quandong, native to the drier regions of Australia's mainland states, is now in commercial production in that country. The trees have pendulous foliage and grow to around 5 m (16 ft) high. The edible fruits are slightly tart but make an unusual addition to jams, jellies and fruit pies. The fruits provided a good dietary supplement to the inland's early settlers and are still eaten by the Aborigines. Stones of the fruit were used in games like Chinese Chequers and also used to make necklaces in the 19th century. The fruits, which have a high vitamin C content, can be eaten fresh or cooked. The quandong is unlikely to be available outside Australia.

CULTIVATION This tree is a partial parasite and needs other plants to sustain it, especially in its early years. Where the climate is suitable, it must be grown in full sun, in an open, sandy or gravelly soil. Give regular water to establish, then only occasional deep waterings during flowering and fruit setting. It is not really suitable for growing under glass in frost-prone climates.

CLIMATE Zone 10. Arid.

Quassia (fam. Simaroubaceae)

This genus of about 35 species of trees and shrubs is from tropical America, Africa and Southeast Asia, and, unlikely to be available outside these countries. In their native areas, the trees have many uses, but only one species is widely known. Medicinal oils and insecticides are extracted from many of the species. Although they have ornamental value, with very showy flowers, they are most often planted for practical purposes.

CULTIVATION In frost-prone climates, grow as a foliage plant in a warm greenhouse or conservatory, in a large pot of soil-based potting compost. Outdoors, plant in full sun in deep, well-drained soil enriched with organic matter. Give ample water during the spring and summer. Propagate from seed, germinated in a heated propagating case.

CLIMATE Tropical regions only.

ABOVE Quandongs in cultivation bear much heavier crops than those growing in their arid natural habitat.

ABOVE The bitterwood, *Quassia amara*, has attractive foliage and flowers but can be grown outside only in tropical climates.

SPECIES *Q. amara*, bitterwood or Surinam quassia, is an evergreen shrub to small tree, growing 8–10 m (26–33 ft) high. The compound leaves, consisting of several leaflets, grow to about 25 cm (10 in) in length. Flowers are showy and bright scarlet. Its wood is the source of the bitter drug, quassia.

Quercus (fam. Fagaceae)

Oak

This large genus of around 600 species comprises both deciduous and evergreen trees, which sometimes live to a great age and grow to an impressive size. Most are from temperate regions, but a surprising number are natives of tropical and subtropical regions, from Mexico through to Southeast Asia. They have alternate leaves, mostly lobed and leathery, but sometimes thin and glossy. The male flowers appear as yellow catkins in spring, while the female flowers are small and insignificant, and develop into the distinctive acorns, enclosed by a cup-shaped base. When ripe, the acorn (the nut) drops from this cup to the ground, from where it may be carried away by birds and ani-

ABOVE Oaks produce abundant catkins of male flowers in spring. This is the holm oak, *Quercus ilex*, of the Mediterranean.

mals. Grown for their handsome appearance and valuable timber, the oaks are ideal as street trees or for parks and very large gardens. The foliage of many deciduous types colors vividly in fall. Evergreen species are often slower growers than the deciduous types.

CULTIVATION All oaks thrive on deep, moist, rich soils and like plenty of water in summer. Propagate from the acorns sown in fall. Plant in tall containers, as they soon develop a vigorous taproot. Acorns can also be planted where they are to grow. If transplanted from open ground, leave a ball of soil around the roots, as the roots are slow to recover if left bare. Cultivars are grafted or budded onto the common oak.

CLIMATE Most oaks prefer a cool, moist climate, but there are species that enjoy warm to hot climates.

SPECIES *Q. canariensis*, Algerian oak or Canary oak, zone 7, from North Africa, the Canary Islands and the Iberian Peninsula, will tolerate warmer conditions than many species. A semi-evergreen to 30 m (100 ft), it has coarsely toothed, shiny leaves that are glabrous on the undersides. *Q. cerris*, Turkey oak, zone 7, from central and southern Europe and Turkey, is a very impressive, deciduous tree, growing to 30 m (100 ft). It has oblong, very coarsely toothed leaves, tinged with gray when young, and dark green and downy when mature. *Q. coccinea*, scarlet oak, zone 4, from eastern North America, is a deciduous tree, to 25 m (80 ft), with deeply lobed, glossy, bright green leaves. The leaves color a brilliant scarlet in fall, remaining longer on the tree than those of other species. *Q. ilex*, holm oak, zone 7, native to areas around the Mediterranean, is a dense, round-headed, evergreen tree with dark gray, scaly bark and leathery, rather narrow leaves, both entire and toothed. This species can be grown in exposed, coastal conditions. It grows up to 18 m (60 ft) tall. *P. palustris*, pin oak, zone 5, from eastern and central United States, matures to a height of around 25 m (80 ft). It is a deciduous, graceful tree with pale green, deeply lobed foliage which colors red in fall, remaining on the tree for some time, though the color is often poor in warmer areas. *Q. robur*, English or pedunculate oak, zone 5, is a massive, round-headed tree, growing between 12 and 30 m (40–100 ft) in cultivation, and possibly one of the most famous of the oaks. The shortstalked leaves have rounded, shallow lobes. The rich green spring foliage deepens in summer and changes to dull gold or brown in fall. This species is the source of fine timber and one of Europe's most valuable timber trees. Cultivar 'Concordia', known as the golden oak, is one of the smallest, growing to only 10 m (33 ft). The golden yellow spring foliage persists into summer. *Q. rubra*, red oak, zone 3, from the east of North America, is a deciduous species, growing up to 25 m (80 ft). The oblong leaves have large, triangular, pointed lobes. This species colors beautifully in fall to a rich red-brown color. *Q. suber*, cork oak, zone 8, is the main source of commercial cork. An evergreen growing to 18 m (60 ft), it has ovate, lightly toothed or entire leaves, glossy green above, gray and downy beneath. The thick, rough, silvery gray bark yields the cork. *Q. virginiana*, live oak or southern oak, zone 8, from the south-east of the United States and Mexico, grows up to 18 m (60 ft) tall. This beautiful species is a dense, evergreen tree of rounded habit. The oblong to rounded leaves are entire or sparsely toothed near the apex, glossy, dark green above and white and downy below. This species makes an excellent shade tree.

Quince (*Cydonia oblonga*, fam. Rosaceae)

Native to western Asia, the quince has been cultivated since antiquity and has long been naturalized in the Mediterranean region. It was a symbol of love, happiness and fertility in Greek and Roman times. This tree is grown for its fruit which is generally used to make jams, jellies and preserves, being virtually inedible raw. The common quince is a slow-growing, deciduous tree, to around 6 m (20 ft), with rather crooked branches, but it is an exquisite sight when the pale pink blossom appears in spring. This is fol-

ABOVE Quinces are ripe when their skin is pale yellow, usually in mid-fall. These fruits have a way to go.

lowed by the hard, apple-like, deliciously smelling, greenish yellow fruit which is covered with a light brown felt. Recommended cultivars are 'Apple', 'Cooke's Jumbo', 'Pineapple' and 'Smyrna'.

CULTIVATION This tree fruits best when the summers are long and hot. In cold climates, it is best grown against a warm, sheltered wall. It prefers fairly moist soil, provided the drainage is adequate. Propagate from long, hardwood cuttings, which tend to sucker, or from named varieties budded onto quince seedlings. Quince is often used as a dwarfing rootstock for fruit trees, especially the pear. Set out plants when they are one or two years old. Fruit bearing will begin in the second or third year. Hand-pick fruit with care when it is mature and well colored, as it bruises easily. Prune in winter while the plant is dormant. Quinces grown against a wall can be fan trained and will then need annual pruning. The old, fruited side shoots are cut back to within three to four buds of the main framework branches. The fruits will then be produced on these 'spurs'. Quince is susceptible to a number of diseases, including fireblight, quince leaf blight, and mildew.

CLIMATE Zone 5.

Quisqualis (fam. Combretaceae)

Rangoon creeper

This genus comprises around 17 species of showy, vigorous climbers from the tropics, including Africa and Indo-Malaysia. They have entire, oblong to elliptical leaves which are borne on slender stems. The base of the leaf stalk remains after the leaf falls, hardening into a thorn-like hook which the plant uses to support itself as it climbs. An abundance of white, tubular flowers, borne in terminal clusters, is produced in the summer and fall. The flowers change color as they age.

CULTIVATION Outside the warm subtropics and tropics, grow the Rangoon creeper in a warm greenhouse or conservatory. Use soil-based potting compost. Provide maximum light, but shade the plant from direct strong sun. The plant should be kept only slightly moist in winter, but during the growing season must be watered normally. Liquid feed every four weeks in the summer. Provide supports for the stems. Prune in late winter to keep the plant within bounds and to remove any very old wood. Outdoors grow in well-drained soil and full sun. Propagate from seed sown in a heated propagating case, during spring. Alternatively, take softwood cuttings in spring, again rooting

them in warmth, or layer a stem in spring. If suckers are produced, detach and pot at the start of the growing season.

CLIMATE Warmest parts of zone 10 to tropical.

SPECIES *Q. indica*, Rangoon creeper, is the most commonly grown of the species. Shrubby when young, it reaches 9 m (30 ft) when it is fully grown. White, red and pink flowers may be borne together on the one plant. Flowers will emerge white but they age to pink or red. They are strongly fragrant, particularly so at night.

Radicchio

(*Cichorium intybus*, fam. Asteraceae)

Red chicory

Red chicory is a hardy, perennial salad vegetable which is usually grown as an annual. The plant has a low habit of growth, forming a rather tight heart of leaves, the outside leaves being red-green in color and with a very bitter taste. The inner leaves are not so well colored and are usually whitish. They are crispy and not quite so bitter. The leaves are used rather like lettuce in salads, and are usually shredded. However, they may also be used as a cooked vegetable.

BELOW The long-tubed flowers of *Quisqualis indica* are seen here at various stages of maturity. Flowers open white, then age to pink and red.

BELOW Red chicory is used rather like lettuce in salads and is grown in a similar way. It is usually harvested in fall and winter.

CULTIVATION Radicchio or red chicory is suitable for a wide range of climates, as it is very hardy. There are numerous cultivars with various degrees of frost-tolerance, and some are incredibly hardy. There are also F1 hybrids available with a very uniform habit of growth. And they have tighter hearts than older, non-hybrid cultivars. Radicchio will grow in any fertile, well-drained garden soil. Dig it well before sowing and incorporate bulky organic matter. Radicchio is generally grown for use in the fall or winter. Seed is sown outside from early summer to midsummer, where the plants are to grow. Plants should have a spacing of up to 35 cm (14 in) apart each way. Either harvest single leaves or the entire plant. In very cold areas, place cloches over the plants in late fall. Alternatively, plants can be lifted carefully, with some soil around their roots, and replanted in an unheated greenhouse.

CLIMATE Zone 3.

Radish (*Raphanus sativus*, fam. Brassicaceae)

Of unknown origin but cultivated since antiquity for its tasty root, the radish is probably the easiest vegetable to grow–and the quickest. It was popular in ancient China and is often used grated to accompany Japanese dishes.

ABOVE A lone, red radish pushes up amongst a good crop of white radishes. White radishes are popular in Asian cuisine.

CULTIVATION Propagate from seed which is sown in shallow drills and lightly covered with rich soil, preferably well manured from a previous crop. The better the soil, the better the radish. Radishes can be sown at almost any time of year but prefer cool conditions. They must be grown quickly, and they require plenty of water. When the second leaf appears, thin out the plants to 3–5 cm (1–2 in) between small radish plants and 5–7 cm (2–3 in) between larger, or winter, radishes. They may be planted between rows of plants which grow more slowly like cabbage, parsnip or sweet corn. Successive plantings every two weeks will result in a constant supply. Small radishes may be ready for harvest in four to six weeks, but the long, white radishes used in Asian cuisine mature in eight to ten weeks.

CLIMATE Zone 6.

VARIETIES *Raphanus sativus* is an annual, with mauvish white flowers and a thick, round or elongated edible root. Radishes come in different shapes and sizes and may be divided into two groups: quick-growing, small radishes and large winter radishes, which take two to three months to mature. The small radishes may be round to long and tapering and either red or white, while winter radishes are generally long and tapering or cylindrical, and may be red-, white- or dark-skinned. There are many cultivars of small, summer radish, as a quick look at any good seed catalogue will reveal. 'Cherry Belle', for instance, is a particularly popular one. There are also long-rooted, white radishes known as mooli types, for summer use, but these are not so readily available. Among the large-rooted winter types are 'Long Black Spanish' and 'White Chinese', and again, these are not so freely available as the small, summer radish.

Rambutan

(*Nephelium lappaceum*, fam. Sapindaceae)

Rambutan is the fruit of a large, evergreen tree which is indigenous to Malaysia but is now

ABOVE Rambutans ripen erratically so they must be picked frequently. The fruit must be a rich red to be fully ripe.

ABOVE The heavy-textured flowers of *Randia benthamiana* have completely recurved petals and a sweet fragrance.

widely cultivated in the tropical lowlands of Central America, the Philippines and Australia. Some call it the hairy lychee. Trees may grow to around 15 m (50 ft) or more in height, with a dense canopy of pinnate leaves. Fruits are carried in clusters of ten or twelve, and at maturity are about 5 cm (2 cm) long, bright red and covered with soft, fleshy spines. The fruit is eaten fresh, on its own or in fruit salads. It can be dried or canned, much the same as the lychee. Unlikely to be available in the US.

CULTIVATION Not really suitable for growing under glass in frost-prone climates. Outdoors, these trees need deep, rich, fertile soil and high rainfall. They may be grown from seed, but are more commonly propagated by bud grafting, which ensures that good cropping and other features are maintained.

CLIMATE For tropical regions only.

Randia (fam. Rubiaceae)

Previously a genus of 200 to 300 species, these have now been split into several groups. *Randia* species are tropical, evergreen trees and shrubs, sometimes quite spiny, with trumpet-shaped flowers and berry fruit. Many are cultivated as ornamentals, but some are grown for their edible fruit.

CULTIVATION Outside the tropics, if plants are available, grow in a warm greenhouse or conservatory, in pots of soil-based potting compost. Water well in the growing season. Propagate from cuttings of young shoots in spring, ideally with bottom heat.

CLIMATE Tropical only.

SPECIES *R. benthamiana* and *R. fitzalanii* are two Australian species in cultivation. Both may grow 6–8 m (20–26 ft) high and are known as native gardenia because of their perfumed, white flowers. *R. formosa*, from tropical South America, is a spineless shrub with ovate leaves and white flowers, in the shape of slender trumpets.

Ranunculus (fam. Ranunculaceae)

This large genus of 400 species of annuals and perennials is widely grown throughout the

ABOVE *Asiatic ranunculus* are available in a wide color range. These bright primary-colored types are outstanding.

world. The leaves are variable, some entire, some deeply divided, while the flowers range in color from white to yellows and reds. Cultivated varieties include pinks and oranges as well. One species, *R. asiaticus*, and its cultivars are popular bedding plants and make excellent cut flowers. Ranunculus are poisonous if eaten and are rarely, if ever, grazed by stock.

CULTIVATION *R. asiaticus* and its cultivars require deep, well-drained soil, enriched with plenty of organic matter, and a sunny position, sheltered from strong wind. If necessary, about 100 g (3½ oz) of complete fertilizer to each square metre (yard) of soil should be dug in some weeks before planting. Propagate from seed sown in summer and transplant seedlings when about 5 cm (2 in) high, setting them 15–20 cm (6–8 in) apart. Flowering should occur in late spring to early summer. Alternatively, commercially grown tubers are available in mixed or separate colors, usually producing more robust plants. Set tubers, claws down, in a bed, 15–20 cm (6–8 in) apart and about 4–5 cm (about 2 in) deep, between late summer and early fall. Young plants need weekly watering once growth begins and may

be given weak liquid fertilizer when the flower buds appear. The tubers are lifted when the foliage has died down and are stored in a cool, dry, airy place until the following fall. Flowers may be poorer in the second or third season. In frost-prone climates, Asiatic ranunculus, which is half-hardy, can be grown in pots in a cool greenhouse or conservatory. Most of the Australasian species are from alpine regions and are suitable for cultivation as rockery plants. Most are water loving and are especially suitable for cool-climate cultivation. Propagate from cuttings placed in a sharp sand and peat mix of 2:1. Alternatively, the clumps can be divided in spring or fall. Many of these species make good groundcover plants for damp and shady spots.

CLIMATE There are species suited to various climatic zones.

SPECIES *R. acris*, meadow buttercup, zone 5, from Great Britain and Europe, is a hairy plant with very long flower stems which can be up to 90 cm (36 in) and on which balance the lovely, golden, cup-shaped flowers. *R. asiaticus*, Asiatic ranunculus or Persian buttercup, zone 9, from the Mediterranean region and south-west Asia, is parent to many beautiful hybrids and cultivars. It is a tuberous perennial, grown as an annual, with segmented leaves and erect flower stalks. Masses of large, multi-petalled, single or double flowers appear in late spring and early summer on 35 cm (14 in) stems. These beautiful blooms come in many colors, from yellow, orange and red to pink and white. *R. collinus*, zone 8, is a mat-forming Australian, alpine species, with wedge-shaped leaves and almost stalkless, yellow flowers. *R. lappaceus*, common or native buttercup, zone 9, originates from both Australia and New Zealand, where it is often found in damp or marshy places. This fibrous-rooted perennial has deeply lobed leaves and shining, yellow, cup-shaped flowers. *R. rivularis*, zone 9, found in most states of Australia, is a water-loving, mat-forming perennial, growing to around 1 m (3 ft) across, with shining, yellow flowers in summer.

Raoulia (fam. Asteraceae)

Scabweed or cushion plant

This genus comprises 25 species of dwarf, carpeting plants, most originating from New Zealand. They have a neat, compact growth habit, forming thick cushions of silky, silvery white foliage. The small, daisy-type flowers in yellow or white appear in spring or summer. Raoulias make lovely rock garden ornamentals for cooler climates.

CULTIVATION These alpine plants require perfect drainage and a sunny situation, and will not do well in humid climates. Plant in moist, well-drained, acidic soil that has been well composted. Propagate by division in spring or by young rosettes treated as cuttings in the summer. Root them in a shaded garden frame.

CLIMATE Zone 7.

SPECIES *R. australis*, golden scabweed, makes a carpet of silvery foliage, spread over 25 cm (10 in). In summer it produces tiny, fluffy yellow blooms. *R. eximia* is a cushion-forming plant, to a height of 35 cm (14 in) and a spread of 1 m (3 ft). The velvety, white foliage is in the form of tiny rosettes. *R. glabra*, a smaller, cushion-forming plant, spreading to only 40 cm (16 in), has green foliage and small, white or yellow flowers. *R. haastii* spreads cushion-like to 1 m (3 ft) across, with hairy, light green foliage, turning chocolate brown from winter through to spring. *R. mammillaris*, vegetable sheep, forms rounded, dense, white cushions, to 50 cm (20 in) across. The tiny, white flowers are sunk deep in the foliage. *R. subsericea* is a prostrate, mat-forming perennial, with silvery foliage, tinted pale green and gold, and tiny, white flowers. The stems creep and strike roots. *R. tenuicaulis* is a mat-forming plant, to 1 m (3 ft) across, with creeping stems, white foliage and tiny, yellow flowers.

Raspberry (*Rubus idaeus*, fam. Rosaceae)

Difficult though it is to believe, raspberries still grow wild all over Europe. This plant bears white flowers that develop into the sweet, aromatic fruits that are mostly red, but can also be purple, black or yellow. The latter are occasionally available in specialist markets. Raspberries may be eaten fresh, or they can be made into delicious jams and tarts. They are also available in canned or frozen form. Owing to the perishable nature of the fruit, fresh raspberries tend to be quite expensive.

CULTIVATION Raspberries are very hardy so can be grown easily in cool and cold climates. They

ABOVE A vertical rock face with its perfect drainage, is the ideal place for this silvery blue *Raoulia hookeri*.

ABOVE Fresh raspberries are a treat. However, they ripen erratically and so a row of plants is needed to supply a good quantity.

prefer well-drained soil, with added organic matter, and it must not be allowed to dry out. They also need a sunny position and protection from strong winds. The best planting time in temperate climates is late fall, but spring is better in cold climates. Set plants 40 cm (16 in) apart in rows spaced 2 m (6 ft) apart, and running north to south. Canes of plants that fruit in the summer are cut back to 20 cm (8 in) after planting, and fall-fruiting raspberries are cut to soil level. Provide posts and horizontal wires in order to support the weight of the canes. Tie in the canes as required. Once they start fruiting, raspberries should be pruned annually. Summer-fruiting raspberries have the old, fruited canes cut right down to soil level immediately after the berries have been harvested. Fall-fruiting raspberries have all their canes pruned down to the ground in winter. Feed annually in early spring with a balanced fertilizer, and apply a mulch. Water as necessary in summer. Raspberries are prone to numerous diseases and pests but undoubtedly the most serious are viruses as there is no cure for these. They are spread by aphids, so keep these pests under control. Buy virus-free plants from a nursery and if plants subsequently become infected dig up and destroy them.

CLIMATE Zone 3.

VARIETIES *Rubus idaeus*, European raspberry, is a slightly prickly, deciduous perennial which sends up canes of 1.5–2 m (5–6 ft) in height every two years. The canes fruit in the second year. However, fall-fruiting raspberries fruit on the current year's canes. There are many cultivars of the European raspberry available, some fruiting in summer and others fruiting in fall. It is important to buy certified stock from a reputable fruit specialist to ensure that the plants are free from virus.

Ravenala (fam. Strelitziaceae)
Traveller's palm

Native to Madagascar, but now widely grown throughout the tropics, the only species in this

ABOVE The leaf stalks of traveller's palm, *Ravenala madagascariensis*, appear woven like a fan. The soft, red flowers belong to a *Mussaenda* species.

genus is most distinctive. It is a medium-sized, tree-like plant with a short trunk, the huge leaves on long stalks spreading like a fan from the trunk. Clusters of white flowers are freely produced from the leaf bases, in summer.

CULTIVATION This foliage plant likes rich, moist conditions and a minimum winter temperature of 16°–18°C (61°–64°F). Outside the tropics, grow in a warm greenhouse or conservatory, in a large pot or tub of soil-based potting compost. Provide maximum light and a humid atmosphere. Propagate in spring, from seed germinated at 21°C (70°F), or from rooted suckers.

CLIMATE Tropical.

SPECIES *R. madagascariensis*, the only species, has acquired the common name, 'traveller's palm', because the water collected in the base of the boat-shaped leaves has sometimes been used as emergency drinking water by travellers in countries where these remarkable plants are grown. Despite the common name, it is totally unrelated to the palm. It grows to 9–12 m (30–40 ft) tall, with leaves up to 4 m (13 ft) long held on overlapping long stalks, and bears a few, white flowers in summer. The fruit is a capsule, containing seeds which have a fleshy, bright blue coat.

Rebutia (fam. Cactaceae)
Crown cactus

There are more than 40 species in this genus of cactuses from Bolivia and Argentina, all small and cluster forming. They have low, rounded tubercles and hairy, needle-like spines. The sometimes self-fertile flowers emerge from the base of the tubercles in late spring to early summer, and may be vivid orange, pink, purple, red or yellow, and sometimes white. They last up to several days and are followed by fleshy fruits, becoming papery with age. Plants regularly produce offsets.

CULTIVATION In frost-prone climates, grow in an intermediate greenhouse or conservatory in pots of proprietary cactus compost. Provide full light and a dry, airy atmosphere. Do not water in winter but water in moderation during the rest of the year. Propagate in spring from seed germinated at 21°C (70°F), or in spring from offsets .

ABOVE Very satisfying to grow, *Rebutia* species readily form colonies, and flower without a fuss.

CLIMATE Zone 10 and above.

SPECIES *R. albiflora* is composed of tiny plants with soft, white spines which grow very quickly to fill their pot. It has white flowers with a pink stripe down the middle of the petals. This species is self-sterile but flowers profusely. *R. aureiflora* has clusters of deep green-purple bodies, covered in short, bristly, brown to gray spines. An abundance of golden-orange flowers, to 4 cm (1½ in) across, appears at the end of spring, from around the base of the plant. *R. kupperana* has a purplish green body, with stiff, dark brown spines, and deep red flowers, 4 cm (1½ in) in diameter. *R. minuscula* is a dark green cactus, depressed at the apex, with spiralled tubercles and weak, yellow spines. The 2 cm (¾ in) flowers are crimson. *R. senilis*, firecrown cactus, is a flat, bristly cactus with white spines and crimson flowers, to 4 cm (1½ in). Var. *kesselringiana* produces green buds, followed by yellow flowers.

Regelia (fam. Myrtaceae)

This genus from Western Australia contains only five species, but all have superbly colored

ABOVE *Regelia ciliata* has pink to purple, fluffy flowers. This small, decorative shrub does best in hot, dry climates.

flowers and attractive, neat foliage. They make beautiful ornamentals, are reasonably fast growing, and are able to withstand fairly long, dry periods.

CULTIVATION *Regelia* species like a hot, dry climate, without too much humidity, and need excellent drainage. In climate zones below 9 grow in a cool, airy greenhouse or conservatory, in pots of soil-based potting compost. Propagate from firm tip cuttings, taken in fall. *R. inops* will germinate readily from the small seed contained in the round, greyish capsules found around the old wood stems, but other species may be less reliable.

CLIMATE Warmest parts of zone 9.

SPECIES Not readily available outside Australia. Flowering times relate to natural habitats. *R. ciliata* is a leafy, spreading shrub, about 1 m (3 ft) high and 2 m (3 ft) wide. The stems are stiff and the mid-green leaves are small and hairy. The deep mauve-pink to bright purple flowers are borne in dense clusters over a long period, from winter through to summer. This species grows reasonably quickly. *R. inops* is a variable, dense shrub, 1–2 m (3–6 ft) high, with rigid, triangular, dull green leaves. Clusters of bright pinkish purple flower heads appear in spring. This lovely species grows moderately quickly. *R. velutina* (syn. *R. grandiflora*) is an outstanding species, but requires extremely good drainage. It has an attractive growth habit, reaching 2–3 m (6–10 ft), lovely, greyish blue foliage arranged in neat rows up the branches and beautiful, bright red flowers, with golden anthers, borne profusely on short spikes, in spring and summer. It is a moderate to fast grower.

Rehmannia (fam. Scrophulariaceae)

These ten, herbaceous perennials, often grown as biennials, were formerly considered to be in the family Gesneriaceae, which they resemble. Originally from China, they are grown for their lovely, pink to mauve or yellow flowers,

ABOVE Chinese foxglove, *Rehmannia elata*, has flaring, trumpet-shaped flowers. All parts of the plant are slightly hairy.

which resemble foxgloves. The leaves are borne in basal rosettes.

CULTIVATION In the garden, grow in well-drained yet moisture-retentive soil, containing plenty of organic matter. Choose a sheltered, sunny site. Where winters are damp and mild, lift and pot up plants in fall, using soil-based potting compost, and winter in a cool greenhouse. Alternatively, plants can be grown permanently under glass. Propagate from seed germinated at 15°C (59°F) in early spring, soft basal cuttings in spring, or root cuttings in fall.

CLIMATE Zone 8.

SPECIES *R. elata*, Chinese foxglove, grows up to 1.5 m (5 ft) high, and in summer bears pinkish purple flowers with a yellow throat, spotted with red. The sticky *R. glutinosa* grows to only 30 cm (12 in) and has red-brown and yellow flowers, in spring and summer.

Reinwardtia (fam. Linaceae)
Yellow flax

Originating from India and China, this genus comprises only one species, a showy, evergreen

ABOVE The cheerful, yellow flowers of *Reinwardtia indica* brighten late fall and winter days. It is an adaptable, easy-care plant.

shrub with oval or elliptic, alternate leaves and single or clustered, yellow, winter flowers.

CULTIVATION In frost-prone climates, grow in an intermediate greenhouse or conservatory, in pots of soil-based potting compost. Provide good light (but shade from direct strong sun), and a slightly humid atmosphere. In the garden, plant in rich soil with an open, sunny aspect, although these plants will tolerate partial shade. Water regularly during the growing season. Pinch back stems frequently to encourage compact, bushy growth and prune back hard in late spring, after flowering, to ensure vigorous, shapely growth. Propagate from soft tip cuttings in early summer.

CLIMATE Zone 9 if relatively frost free; otherwise zone 10.

SPECIES *R. indica*, yellow flax, grows to 1 m (3 ft) high, with bright green, smooth, oval leaves and bright yellow flowers, which appear from fall to the end of spring.

Reseda (fam. Resedaceae)

Mignonette

The 55 species of this genus of mostly small perennials and annuals are from Europe, and in particular, the Mediterranean. The genus contains species used since earliest times for dyes and essential oils. The flowers are not showy, but are sweetly perfumed.

CULTIVATION Grow in well-drained soil, in sun or part shade. In warm climates, sow in fall; in cool areas, spring sowing is best. Give regular water in the growing season.

CLIMATE Zone 6.

SPECIES *R. lutea*, wild mignonette, is an annual or perennial growing to 50 cm (20 in), and *R. luteola*, dyer's rocket or weld, is a biennial to 1.75 m (6 ft); both are sources of yellow dye. They were used by the ancient Romans and have been cultivated for centuries as dye plants. *R. odorata*, mignonette, is an annual, 30–60 cm (12–24 in) high. The highly fragrant, but unspectacular flowers are green and pink. It has long been cultivated for oil for use in perfumery. There are red- and yellow-flowered forms that are showier, but lack the fragrance.

ABOVE The pale green, conical flower spikes of mignonette, *Reseda odorata*, have a strong perfume once they mature and open fully.

Rhagodia (fam. Chenopodiaceae)

There are 11 species in this Australian native genus. They have little ornamental value but are useful as fodder plants, sand binders and sometimes groundcover, especially in dry areas. Several rhagodias occur naturally in very arid parts of the country, but more grow wild in cooler regions.

CULTIVATION In frost-prone climates, grow in a cool, airy greenhouse or conservatory in pots of soil-based potting compost. Provide good light. Outdoors, they are best grown in full sun and in well-drained soil. Propagate from seed or from firm tip cuttings.

CLIMATE Zone 9 to 10.

SPECIES *R. baccata*, coastal saltbush, is an upright shrub, to 1.2 m (4 ft), which grows well in temperate, coastal areas. It is a useful sand binder. Although flowers are not very decorative, these are followed by red berries that persist for many months. *R. nutans* is a prostrate, spreading, evergreen perennial with arrow-shaped leaves and red, sometimes yellow, berries. This species is drought-resistant and is therefore useful groundcover in arid or very dry areas. *R. parabolica*, fragrant salt bush, grows naturally in sheltered, rocky valleys, where it reaches around 2.5 m (8 ft).

ABOVE Coastal saltbush, Rhagodia baccata, bears characteristic, red berries that persist over many months.

Rhamnus (fam. Rhamnaceae)
Buckthorn

This is a genus of some 150 species of mainly deciduous, small trees and shrubs, mostly found in northern hemisphere temperate zones, although a few species are natives of Brazil and South Africa. Grown for their foliage and fruit, rather than their insignificant, green flowers, some species are also grown for their commercial value, as a source of dye, or used medicinally. In the US, they are grown in shrub borders or in woodland gardens. Some, such as *R. frangula* and the spiny *R. cathartica*, both deciduous, make excellent hedges.

CULTIVATION *Rhamnus* will grow in any well-drained yet moisture-retentive garden soil, from poor to reasonably fertile. They can be grown in full sun or in a position with partial shade. Very little pruning is required, but if they are being grown as a hedge, then trim annually, in late winter or early spring. Propagate from semi-ripe cuttings in summer, or by layering in spring.

CLIMATE There are species suited to various climatic zones.

SPECIES *R. alaternus*, Italian buckthorn, zone 7, from the Mediterranean, is a large, evergreen,

ABOVE Italian buckthorn, *Rhamnus alaternus*, bears masses of berries amongst its terminal leaves. The berries are black at maturity.

multi-stemmed shrub, 4–6 m (13–20 ft) high. It has small, dark, glossy, green leaves and blue-black fruits. It makes an excellent hedge or screening plant. Cultivar 'Argenteovariegata' has narrow leaves, marbled with gray, and edged with creamy white. *R. californica*, coffee berry, zone 7, is an evergreen shrub, to 2 m (6 ft). The red fruit turns black on ripening. This species adapts to a wide range of growing conditions. *R. cathartica*, zone 3, from Europe and parts of Asia, is a deciduous species with spines at the ends of the branches, and black fruit. *R. purshiana*, cascara sagrada, zone 7, is a tall, deciduous shrub, to 6 m (20 ft), native to the north-western United States, where it grows as an understorey plant in tall forests. The bark is the source of cascara sagrada, a medical drug. The common name is from the Spanish word for 'sacred bark'. Early Spanish missionary priests came to learn its uses from the American native tribes in California. It has been used since the end of the 19th century as a laxative.

Rhapis (fam. Arecaceae)
Lady palm

Originating from southern China through to Thailand, this genus contains around 12 species of low-growing, slender-stemmed fan palms. Generally, they form large clumps of bamboo-like stems, covered with fine mats of fibers which arise from the base of the leaves. The leaves are very deeply divided, almost to the base, and are borne on very slender stalks. The small inflorescence is tinged with cream or pink. In cultivation, they rarely set fruit. *Rhapis* can be grown in the ground in a sheltered, shaded area but makes a lovely container plant, for use indoors or out. Its slow growth is an advantage for container growing, but it also accounts for the high price of established clumps purchased from nurseries. Its elegant appearance lends itself to most decorating styles.

CULTIVATION In climates prone to frost, grow as house plants, or in an intermediate to warm greenhouse. They are best in pots of soilless

ABOVE Slender lady palm, *Rhapis humilis*, forms large clumps as it ages. The varied heights of its fronds create a pretty effect.

potting compost. Ensure good light, but shade plants from direct sun. If the climate is suitable for outdoor cultivation, plant in any good, well-drained garden soil that does not dry out. Plants are best in shade, such as the dappled shade cast by large trees. Water well during dry periods. Propagate by division of established clumps in spring, or by removing a rooted offset, which should be established in warmth. Sow seed in spring and germinate in a temperature of 26°C (79°F).

CLIMATE Warmest parts of zone 9.

SPECIES *R. excelsa*, lady palm, from southern China, grows to 2–3 m (6–10 ft) tall, often forming a dense clump of many stems, up to 2–3 m (6–10 ft) across, with maturity. The glossy, deep green leaves are deeply divided into a number of segments. The stems are covered in a coarse, ragged mat of dark gray fibers. *R. humilis*, slender lady palm, grows to 4–5 m (13–16 ft) tall, with a narrower spread. The leaves are slightly paler green and not so shiny, with a larger number of slightly pendulous segments. The mat of pale, greyish brown fibers covering the stems is tighter.

Rhipsalidopsis

(syn. *Hatiora*, fam. Cactaceae)

Botanists have now put this genus into *Hatiora* (see entry at *Hatiora*). The species described here include the Easter cactus. Epiphytic cactuses from Brazil, they have flat, segmented stems and somewhat trumpet-shaped, brightly colored flowers.

CULTIVATION Grow in a warm greenhouse or conservatory, in hanging baskets, or mounted on a tree branch. Fill containers with either orchid compost or cactus compost formulated for epiphytes. Plants need good light (but shade from direct sun), and a humid atmosphere (mist spray daily). In winter, keep the compost only barely moist. Propagate from cuttings in summer.

CLIMATE Tropical or subtropical.

SPECIES *R. gaertneri*, (syn. *Hatiora gaertneri*), Easter cactus, has flattened joints, 2–8 cm

ABOVE On this lovely specimen of *Rhipsalidopsis gaertneri*, every flattened leaf tip bears a brilliant scarlet flower.

(¾–3 in) long, and bright red, spring flowers. *R. rosea* (syn. *Hatiora rosea*) has long-lasting, pink flowers in spring, followed by four-sided fruits. Most plants in cultivation are hybrids.

Rhipsalis (fam. Cactaceae)

Most species in this large, cactus genus are from tropical America, but one species is found in Sri Lanka, Malagasy, and along the eastern and western coasts of Africa. Bushy and mostly drooping, these epiphytic cactuses have thin, pale green branches which may be cylindrical, angled or flat. The flowers may be shades of white, cream, pink and yellow and the fruit is a small white, pink or purple berry.

CULTIVATION In frost-prone climates, grow in an intermediate to warm greenhouse, in pots or hanging baskets. Use a proprietary cactus compost formulated for epiphytes. Shade from direct sun and ensure a humid atmosphere. Mist spray daily in summer. Propagate from stem segments in spring.

CLIMATE Zone 10 to tropical.

ABOVE Epiphytic *Rhipsalis micrantha* has found a niche high in a large tree from which its growth can cascade.

SPECIES *R. cereuscula* is a darker green than most species, with very short joints. The white, terminal flowers are followed by white fruit. *R. crispata* has flat, wavy, leaf-like, notched joints. The creamy yellow flowers are produced from the areoles in the notches. *R. dissimilis* is a much-branched, variable plant, some areoles bearing bristles, others smooth. The red buds open to white flowers with rosy pink, outer petals and are followed by purple fruit. *R. houlletiana* has long, saw-toothed, flat joints on thin, cylindrical, erect stalks that curve downwards. Short-lived, yellowish white flowers appear from areoles and the fruit is a carmine color. *R. paradoxa*, chain cactus or link plant, has very long, chain-like or plaited branches. During late spring, small, trumpet-like, cream flowers appear along the margins of the branches and are followed by the small fruits.

Rhodanthe

(syn. *Helipterum*, fam. Asteraceae)

Everlasting or paper daisy

This group of annual or perennial plants was formerly classified with *Helipterum*. Those species transferred to the genus *Rhodanthe* are Australian. These plants are grown massed for garden display and for the papery flower heads which can be dried and kept for long periods.

CULTIVATION Grow as annuals, raising plants from seed. In frost-prone climates, sow under glass in early spring. Germinate at 15°C (59°F). Plant out when frosts are over. Where frosts are not a problem, sow in flowering positions in mid-spring. Plants prefer a very well drained, poorish soil and a position in full sun. If you want to cut the flowers for drying, do so before they have opened completely. Bunches can be hung upside down in a dry, airy place to continue drying.

CLIMATE Zone 9. Best in areas with low humidity and hot, dry summer weather.

SPECIES *R. anthemoides* is a perennial, occurring in most Australian states, often in alpine

ABOVE This cream form of *Rhodanthe chlorocephala* combines well with any foliage or flower color.

areas. It grows around 50 cm (20 in) high and bears white, paper daisies in summer. *R. floribunda*, a white summer-flowering annual, occurs naturally in New South Wales, South Australia, Western Australia and the Northern Territory. *R. manglesii*, from Western Australia, has white or pink, paper daisy flowers in summer. This free-flowering annual is frequently grown as a bedding plant, producing a spectacular and long-lasting display. It grows about 30 cm (12 in) high. *R. chlorocephala* subsp. *rosea*, also known as *Acroclineum roseum* and *Helipterum roseum*, is another popular, summer-flowering annual with papery flowers in pink, white or almost red. Both *R. chlorocephala* subsp. *rosea* and *R. manglesii* are grown for the cut flower trade.

Rhododendron (fam. Ericaceae)

This very large genus of 700–800 species of evergreen and deciduous shrubs and trees originates mainly in temperate areas of the northern hemisphere, especially Southeast Asia and the Himalayas. They are also found in the highlands of New Guinea, and some originate from North America and Europe. Thousands of cultivars and hybrids have been bred since the 19th century, these being more popular than the species. Rhododendrons are among the most

ABOVE The Vireya rhododendrons give a strong, tropical air yet are easy to grow in a cool greenhouse or conservatory.

ABOVE RIGHT Tree-like, broad-leafed rhododendrons form a tall screen in this cool garden. They give many weeks of color in cool, moist climates.

popular of all flowering shrubs. They can be divided into the following groups: the hardy, broad-leaf rhododendrons, the tender, Vireya rhododendrons and the hardy azaleas.

CULTIVATION Rhododendrons need a well-drained soil with a high organic content. Dig in copious quantities of well-decayed organic matter before planting and mulch well with organic matter. All must have acid or lime-free soil. They should not be planted too deeply as they are surface-rooting plants. Spread the roots, cover with soil and top with leaf litter, old manure or compost. Rhododendrons need shelter from strong wind and prefer morning sun and afternoon shade, or the light shade provided by tall trees. Rhododendrons do need some sun in order for the flower buds to form. They will not develop in permanent shade. Keep well watered in the warmer months and in dry, windy weather. Rhododendrons must never be allowed to dry out or they will suffer and drop their leaves. Broad-leaf rhododendrons may be in flower any time between late winter and late spring, depending on the vari-

ety. In their habitats, Vireyas flower from late summer through to early winter, but in cultivation, flowering time is variable and plants may flower more than once a year. Azaleas flower in the spring. The tall, deciduous kinds usually bloom in late spring and continue into early summer. Dwarf, evergreen azaleas such as the Kurume hybrids, bloom in mid to late spring. Rhododendrons do not generally need feeding and in any case, fertilizers which are alkaline, such as blood, fish and bone, should be avoided. If it is considered necessary to feed rhododendrons, apply a proprietary, slow-release fertilizer in spring. Little or no pruning is needed. If it is necessary to improve the shape of a plant, it should be done immediately after flowering. Dead flower heads can be removed by twisting them off. Propagate evergreen rhododendrons from semi-ripe cuttings in late summer, rooted with bottom heat. Hormone rooting powder increases the chances of rooting. Cuttings of many can be slow to form roots. Deciduous azaleas can be propagated from softwood cuttings in spring, again with bottom heat, but these are even more tricky. Far better for propagating rhododendrons is to layer young stems, in spring. This is a slow process, and may take a year, but is almost guaranteed to produce a new plant. Rhododendrons are susceptible to various pests and diseases, including root weevil larvae which eat the roots and can cause severe damage. The adults eat the edges of the leaves but this is not considered serious, only unsightly. Vireyas under glass may be attacked by scale insects and whitefly.

CLIMATE With such a vast range of species and hybrids, it is possible to give only general guidelines as to suitable climates. The broad-leaf rhododendrons and azaleas vary in their hardiness, but they are suited only to temperate (cool temperate for the majority) and cold climates. In climates prone to frost, grow Vireya rhododendrons in a cool conservatory or greenhouse. They adapt well to pot culture.

TYPES *Broad-leaf rhododendrons* are generally evergreen shrubs that range from less than 1 m (3 ft) to tall, tree-like species, with the greatest range around 3–4 m (10–13 ft) in height. Most have rather leathery leaves, often somewhat hairy on the undersides. Flowers are borne in large, showy trusses in white, pink, red, blue, mauve, purple, cream, yellow and orange. Some are fragrant. An enormous range of species and cultivars is available. Broad-leaf rhododendrons are cool-climate plants. They may be grown as specimens but look spectacular when mass planted. *Vireya rhododendrons* are evergreen shrubs, rarely growing more than 2 m (6 ft) high. Some are open in habit, others more compact and densely foliaged. The glossy leaves are mid-green. Flowering is variable and may be more than once a year. Colors range from white, yellow, apricot and salmon through to pinks and bright red. There are many cultivars, mostly in 'sunset' shades. Vireyas do well as understorey plants, but can be planted in a mixed shrub border. They are suitable for container growing and some also do well in hanging baskets. Azaleas, which are really types of rhododendron, can be divided into deciduous and evergreen types. Their showy clusters of flowers provide a reliable show of color in spring, year after year. There are various groups of deciduous azaleas, best known being the Ghent hybrids, the Knap Hill-Exbury Hybrids, and the Mollis hybrids. Their strongly colored flowers come in red, yellow and orange shades, although some come in pastel shades, plus cream and white. Many cultivars are fragrant. The best-known evergreen hybrid azaleas are the Kaempferi and Kurume hybrids, which are generally dwarf to small plants in pink, red and also white.

Rhodohypoxis (fam. Hypoxidaceae)
Rose grass

Closely related to *Hypoxis*, this genus consists of six species, only one of which is in widespread cultivation. All are native to the south-east corner of South Africa.

CULTIVATION This is an ideal rock-garden plant in climates with only light or infrequent frosts. In more frosty climates, it is best grown in an alpine house. In the garden, it needs well-drained, lime-free soil containing plenty of humus, and a position in full sun. Protect from winter rain with a sheet of glass or cloche. Under glass, grow in pans of acid, gritty, soil-based potting compost with some leaf mould added. Provide maximum light and an airy atmosphere. Keep only slightly moist in winter. Propagate by division in fall.

CLIMATE Zone 9.

SPECIES *R. baurii* is a small, tuberous, herbaceous perennial, with tufted, grassy foliage, to about 10 cm (4 in) long, covered with pale

ABOVE Rose grass, *Rhodohypoxis baurii*, is a delightful little plant for filling pockets between rocks. Flower tones vary as they age.

hairs. Masses of rose-colored flowers with pale undersides appear during the summer. Varieties are available with white and pale pink to deep crimson flowers.

Rhodoleia (fam. Hamamelidaceae)

There are around seven species of small, evergreen trees in this genus originating from Asia. Only one is generally cultivated and is grown for its attractive foliage and flowers which bloom from late winter through spring.

CULTIVATION This tree prefers warm temperate or subtropical areas, but will thrive in any well-drained soil. Grow in a sunny or semi-shaded position, provided it is sheltered from strong wind. In frosty climates, grow in a cool greenhouse in pots of soil-based potting compost. Lightly prune after flowering. Propagate from seed or cuttings in late spring or late fall.

CLIMATE Zone 9.

SPECIES *R. championii*, from China and Hong Kong, grows 3–5 m (10–16 ft) high, with oval, leathery leaves borne at the branch tips and clusters of deep rose pink flowers. The blooms have a silky texture and prominent, decorative stamens.

ABOVE *Rhodoleia championii* produces the loveliest, deep rose flowers.

Rhoeo (syn. *Tradescantia* fam. Commelinaceae)
Moses in the basket

Botanists have now placed species from this genus into *Tradescantia* (see entry at *Tradescantia*) but most people still know this plant as *Rhoeo*. It is a fleshy perennial from central America that is grown in an intermediate greenhouse or conservatory, or as a house plant, in frost-prone climates.

CULTIVATION In the greenhouse or home, grow in pots of soilless potting compost. Plants need good light (but shade from direct sun), and a humid atmosphere. Carry out normal watering in the growing season but keep only just moist in winter. Cut out tips of shoots to encourage a bushy habit. Propagate in spring or summer from cuttings obtained from the tops of the stems, and root them in warmth.

CLIMATE Zone 10.

SPECIES *R. spathacea* (syn. *Tradescantia spathacea*) is an evergreen plant grown for its attractive dark green foliage, colored bright purple on the underside. The upright, linear leaves are 30 cm (12 in) long and 5 cm (2 in) wide. The insignificant, white flowers emerge from small, boat-like structures at the base of the leaves.

BELOW The tiny, white flowers in boat-shaped structures of *Rhoeo* give this scrambling plant its common name of Moses in the basket.

Cultivar 'Vittata' has leaves striped longitudinally with pale yellow.

Rhoicissus (fam. Vitaceae)

Cape grape

There are around ten species of evergreen climbers in this genus which originates from tropical and South Africa.

CULTIVATION In frost-prone climates, grow as a house plant, or in an intermediate greenhouse or conservatory. Plants grow best in soil-based potting compost, with maximum light, but shade from direct strong sun. Keep only slightly moist in winter, but water normally at other times. Outdoors grow in a warm, sunny, sheltered spot with moist yet well-drained soil. Provide supports for stems and prune in spring to keep plants within bounds, if necessary. Propagate from semi-ripe cuttings in summer, with basal warmth.

CLIMATE Zone 10 to tropical.

SPECIES *R. capensis*, Cape grape, has large leaves and produces clusters of edible, glossy, reddish purple fruits. This species climbs by means of tendrils and produces tubers. It is a very vigorous climber to about 5 m (16 ft) high and needs plenty of space to develop, but is amenable to pruning to keep it under control.

ABOVE The vigorous new growth of *Rhoicissus capensis* is soft and pink. Vines become very congested as the stems grow over one another.

Rhombophyllum (fam. Aizoaceae)

These clump-forming, succulent perennials all have yellow, summer flowers. Superficially they resemble the related *Lampranthus* species as well as *Mesembryanthemum* species, known as ice plants.

CULTIVATION Where frosts occur, grow in an intermediate greenhouse or conservatory, or as a house plant. Grow in pots of proprietary cactus compost. Provide maximum light and a dry atmosphere. Water sparingly in the growing season, but keep dry in winter. Propagate from seed sown in spring germinated at 21°C (70°F), or from rooted offsets, in spring or summer.

CLIMATE Zone 10.

SPECIES *R. dolabriforme*, from Cape Province, becomes shrubby with age. The stems are woody and the grass green leaves are wedge-shaped, with a two-lobed tip dotted with transparent spots. The flowers are about 4 cm (1½ in) across. A white-flowered form, which blooms over many months, has been developed. *R. neli* is similar to *R. dolabriforme*, but the two-lobed leaves are not wedge-shaped.

ABOVE *Rhombophyllum dolabriforme* has an odd growth habit: dotted, succulent leaves arch out from a central stem.

They are greyish green, with very small, darker colored spots. *R. rhomboideum* has a very different leaf formation. It forms a loose rosette of smooth, dark greyish green leaves, spotted in white, which are quite flat on the upper surface. The golden yellow flowers, 3 cm (about 1 in) across, are tinged with red.

Rhopalostylis (fam. Arecaceae)
Nikau palm

The three species of medium-sized feather palms in this genus grow up to about 10 m (33 ft) tall, with closely ringed trunks topped by a crownshaft from which the leaves arise. These have very short stalks, thick midribs, and dense, erect, green leaflets. The flowers are borne in short, stiff inflorescences, the many branches turning an interesting mauve color at flowering time. Red, berry-like fruits follow the flowers.

CULTIVATION These palms will grow outdoors in the warmest parts of zone 9 or 10, but in other

ABOVE The unusually stiff, upright growth of the fronds is a distinguishing feature of *Rhopalostylis sapida*, a native of New Zealand.

climates are best grown in pots of soil-based potting compost in an intermediate greenhouse or conservatory. They are slow growing and outdoors need sheltered, frost-free conditions with well-drained soil and partial shade. Propagate in spring from fresh seed, germinated in warmth.

CLIMATE Warmest parts of zone 9 or 10.

SPECIES *R. baueri*, from Norfolk Island, is the larger of the two species in cultivation and is still fairly common in the remnant vegetation of the island. It has a trunk about 20 cm (8 in) in diameter and slightly arching leaves to about 3 m (10 ft) long. The inflorescence can be up to 80 cm (32 in) long and pendulous when weighed down with fruit. Young plants often have reddish tones in their foliage. *R. sapida*, Nikau palm, from New Zealand, is the most southerly wild palm. The stiff, straight leaves emerging from the crownshaft are responsible for its common name, 'feather duster palm'. The trunk grows to 15 cm (6 in) in diameter, the leaves to about 2 m (6 ft) long, and the cream to mauve inflorescences to 40 cm (16 in). The leaves were used by Maoris for building their huts. This species is probably more cold-tolerant than *R. baueri*.

Rhubarb

(*Rheum* x *cultorum*, fam. Polygonaceae)

Rhubarb is very simple to grow and absolutely delicious. Cultivated for its large, thick, red or green leaf stalk (the leaf is highly poisonous), rhubarb is cooked and used for pies and cakes, or simply eaten with cream. It is sometimes cooked with apples. Although known for many centuries, and probably a native of northern Asia, it was originally used only for medicinal purposes.

CULTIVATION Rhubarb likes climates with warm to cool, moist summers. Any well-drained garden soil will do, providing it contains plenty of animal manure. Rhubarb is best in full sun

ABOVE Rhubarb grows vigorously in rich, well-prepared soil. Harvest stems often to keep new growth coming.

and must have frequent, deep watering. As the plants will remain in the soil for some years, their bed should be well prepared in advance by digging in plenty of manure. Rhubarb is purchased as pot-grown plants from garden centers. These are usually available for planting in winter or spring. As rhubarb is a gross feeder, it requires regular applications of liquid or granular, complete fertilizer, mulching and stringent weed control. Whenever a flowering head appears, cut it off. Harvest very few leaf stalks during the first year, but more can be taken in the second year as new growth appears from the crown. To harvest, pull the stalk with a jerking movement away at an angle; never cut it. Many gardeners place a 40–60 cm (16–24 in) high tin, plastic or timber pen around their plants to encourage longer stems and smaller leaves. When plants reach three or four years old, the crowns tend to become woody and growth becomes crowded and less vigorous. At this stage, it is best to lift the plants, divide the roots so that each piece has one healthy bud (or 'eye'), and replant pieces about 1 m (3 ft) apart in a newly prepared location. In mild climates, lifting can be done in early winter; in colder regions, early spring is best.

CLIMATE Rhubarb is very hardy and should survive in zone 3.

VARIETIES There are many cultivars of rhubarb, so buy whatever is available in your area. Popular cultivars include red-stalked 'Cherry', 'Macdonald' and 'Strawberry', and green-stalked 'Victoria'. Four to six plants are usually sufficient for a home garden.

Rhus (fam. Anacardiaceae)
Sumac

There are over 200 species of shrubs, small trees and occasionally climbers in this diverse genus, including both deciduous and evergreen types. They are often grown as ornamentals for their attractive, rich, fall foliage in shades of bronze, orange, yellow, red and purple. The dried leaves of some species yield tannin; others are a source of waxes and lacquers; some cause dermatitis on sensitive skins. Most species are from temperate and subtropical areas of the northern hemisphere, including North America, eastern Asia and South Africa. The plant known as poison ivy was formerly *Rhus toxicodendron* but is now known as *Toxicodendron radicans*. It is a little-grown shrub or climber, and although poisonous, is used in alternative medicine.

ABOVE *Rhus trichocarpa*, a native of China and Japan, is a large, spreading, deciduous shrub or tree, notable for its spectacular, fall foliage tints.

CULTIVATION *Rhus* species do best in temperate zones, but most will tolerate a range of conditions as long as there is adequate moisture. Grow in a sunny position for best fall foliage color. Propagate from seed in spring after chilling for three months. Propagate in winter from root cuttings or rooted suckers.

CLIMATE There are species suited to various climatic zones.

SPECIES *R. glabra*, zone 2, the smooth sumach from North America, is a popular shrub, growing to 2.5 m (8 ft) in height and spread, with smooth stems. It bears green-yellow flowers, followed by red fruits (on female plants). *R. typhina*, staghorn sumac, zone 3, from eastern North America, grows 8–10 m (26–33 ft). The greenish flowers are followed by distinctive, dull crimson, hairy fruits, with a velvety appearance. The fruits are a source of tannin. Cultivar 'Dissecta' has finely divided leaves. *R. verniciflua*, Japanese varnish tree, zone 9, grows to 20 m (65 ft), with white flowers and yellowish green fruit. Cultivated in Japan for commercial lacquer, it is poisonous to touch.

Ribes (fam. Grossulariaceae)
Currant

Originating from cool temperate zones of both the northern and the southern hemispheres, this genus consists of about 150 species of low-growing, deciduous and evergreen shrubs. Included in *Ribes* genus are attractive ornamentals, as well as the species producing delicious gooseberry and currants. Some species have beautiful fall foliage, in brilliant reds and oranges, and lovely, spring flowers; others with reddish brown branches, provide a feature in the winter garden.

CULTIVATION Grow in any fertile, well-drained soil in a position which receives plenty of sun. Propagate deciduous species from hardwood cuttings, evergreens from semi-ripe cuttings, in summer.

ABOVE Deciduous flowering currant, *Ribes sanguineum*, is an attractive ornamental for cool gardens. Several good cultivars have derived from this species.

CLIMATE There are species suited to various climatic zones.

SPECIES *R. americanum*, American black currant, zone 2, grows to 1.5 m (5 ft), with cream flowers, followed by black fruits. This species is grown for its brilliantly colored fall leaves. *R. x gordonianum*, zone 6, to 2 m (6 ft), is a sterile hybrid with pendulous sprays of bronze-red and yellow flowers. *R. malvaceum*, zone 7, from California, grows to 2 m (6 ft), and bears pendent sprays of pink or purple flowers and purple fruit. *R. odoratum*, zone 5, Buffalo currant, to 2 m (6 ft), is grown mainly for the deliciously spicy, clove-like scent released by the yellow flowers borne in long sprays. The three-lobed, glossy leaves color beautifully in fall. The fruit is black. *R. sanguineum*, zone 6, growing to 2 m (6 ft), is a popular species, native to North America, with drooping spikes of white, pink or crimson flowers in spring, and blue-black fruits. The aromatic lobed leaves are borne on graceful, arching stems. There are a number of good cultivars of this species: 'Brocklebankii', with yellow foliage and light pink flowers; 'King Edward VII', with deep red blooms; 'Pulborough Scarlet', with deep red blooms with white centers; and 'White Icicle', with white blooms. *R. speciosum*, zone 7, to 2 m (6 ft), has rich red, drooping, fuchsia-like flowers. *R. viburnifolium*, zone 9, is an evergreen species from North America, to 2.5 m (8 ft). It has rose red flowers, red fruits, and leaves which smell of turpentine.

Ricinocarpos (fam. Euphorbiaceae)
Wedding bush

These attractive flowering shrubs are all natives of Australia. While several species are worth growing, many are difficult to cultivate. They are unlikely to be available outside their native country. It is a variable genus–in leaf structure, number of flower petals and the presence or otherwise, of male and female flowers on the same bush. The leaves vary greatly between species, sometimes even on the same shrub, but are generally dark green in color. The large, waxy, mostly white, fragrant flowers generally appear in spring in the plant's natural habitat.

CULTIVATION In frost-prone climates, grow in an intermediate greenhouse or conservatory in pots of acid, well-drained, sandy, soil-based potting compost. Shade from direct, strong sun. Outdoors these shrubs need a well drained, acid, light, sandy soil, with protection from wind and some shade. Propagate from ripe seed in warmth–it does not germinate easily–or from cuttings in fall, and rooted with bottom heat.

CLIMATE Zone 10.

SPECIES *R. bowmanii*, pink wedding bush, grows up to 1 m (3 ft) high. The small leaves are quite stiff. The flowers are broad and star shaped and may be pale pink through to deep pink, with red stamens. *R. cyanescens*, from Western Australia, is a rounded shrub, wider than it is high, with narrow leaves and white flowers. *R. glaucus*, also from Western Australia, grows less than 1 m (3 ft) high, with small, glossy leaves and numerous, large, white flowers. *R. pinifolius*, wedding bush, is the most commonly grown. A compact shrub, to 2 m (6 ft), it produces terminal clusters of lovely, white to cream, long-stalked flowers, with yellow stamens. The foliage is variable, but is generally soft and pine-like. *R. speciosus* has shiny leaves, dull on the undersides, and showy, white, starry flowers, in spring and early summer. It grows 1–3 m (3–10 ft) high.

Ricinus (fam. Euphorbiaceae)
Castor oil plant, castor bean

This single-species genus is grown mainly in its Asian habitat for the oil yielded by the seeds, which is used medicinally and for manufactur-

ABOVE In its native Australia, *Ricinocarpos pinifolius* flowers from late winter and throughout spring.

ABOVE Grown for its ornamental foliage in cool climates, the castor oil plant has become a widespread weed in many warm regions.

ing soaps and varnishes. The large, bright green, deeply divided, veined leaves are very decorative, and a number of variously colored leaf forms are available. Woolly sprays of greenish cream flowers are borne in summer. This frost-tender, evergreen shrub is usually grown as an annual, often included in summer bedding schemes, in patio containers, and in subtropical borders.

CULTIVATION In frost-prone climates, propagate from seed sown in spring and germinated at 21°C (70°F). Plant out when frosts are over. In milder climates, sow in spring where the plants are to grow.

CLIMATE Zone 9 to tropical.

SPECIES *R. communis* grows to around 2 m (6 ft) in cool climates where it is usually treated as an annual, and 5–10 m (16–33 ft) in the tropics. The flowers have no petals, but masses of stamens. Cultivars include 'Carmencita', 'Impala' and 'Red Spire', all of which display rich foliage and stem color and often heavy fluting of the leaves, and 'Zanzibarensis', which has very large, green leaves, prominently veined in white.

Robinia (fam. Papilionaceae)
Locust

Originally from North America, these 20 species of deciduous flowering shrubs and trees are useful for street plantings as they grow very rapidly and are able to withstand pollution. They are also grown as ornamentals for their fresh, green foliage and decorative, pea-like flowers which may be white, pink or mauve. Most species have thorned branches and flower in summer.

CULTIVATION Robinias will grow in any soil, ideally reasonably fertile, but will also succeed in poor and very dry conditions. The ideal soil is moisture-retentive yet well drained. Choose a position in full sun, but sheltered from wind, as these trees have very brittle wood. Some

ABOVE The pendulous, scented flowers of *Robinia pseudoacacia* resemble those of wisteria. This species flowers from early summer to midsummer.

species, particularly *R. pseudoacacia*, sucker freely and this may be a problem if the suckers appear in lawns. Avoid digging around the trees as this can disturb the roots and cause suckering. Propagate species from seed sown in fall, from root cuttings in winter or from rooted suckers in early spring. Cultivars are budded in summer.

CLIMATE There are species suited to various climatic zones.

SPECIES *R.* x *ambigua*, zone 3, is a small tree with pink flowers and compound leaves. Cultivar 'Bella-rosea' produces deep pink flowers. *R. hispida*, rose acacia, zone 5, looks very pretty in summer when covered with masses of deep rose pink flowers. The leaves are long and fern-like. It grows to 2 m (6 ft). *R. pseudoacacia*, false acacia or black locust, zone 3, grows to about 25 m (80 ft) in its habitat, but only to about 10 m (33 ft) in cultivation. It has graceful, prickly branches and fern-like leaves. The fragrant, white, pea-like flowers are very attractive to bees and are followed by reddish brown seed pods. Many cultivars are available: some have colored foliage, others have pendulous growth habits and variable flowering habits.

Cultivar 'Frisia', golden robinia, is the variety most commonly grown in the US. It is thornless, with golden foliage. *R. viscosa*, clammy locust, zone 3, grows to around 13 m (42 ft). The foliage colors attractively in fall to a golden yellow. The long clusters of lovely, rose pink flowers, with red calyces, are attractive to bees.

Rocket

(*Eruca vesicaria* subsp. *sativa*, fam. Brassicaceae)

Arugula

Rocket is a popular addition to green salads for its peppery flavor. Although it has been cultivated in Europe for centuries, it has only recently become well known in other parts of the world. The seeds are processed into an oil which is a good substitute for rape seed or canola oil. The plant can grow up to 60 cm (24 in) high, but is usually harvested for salads when the leaves are young and tender. The leaves are deeply lobed and, if flowers are allowed to develop, these are creamy yellow, with purplish veins. It is grown as an annual, but can be overwintered in very warm regions.

CULTIVATION Sow seed in spring or fall, the first leaves being ready to harvest after five to six weeks. Plants tend to run to seed if grown through the summer. Plant in well-drained soil enriched with organic matter. A light dressing of lime should be added to very acid soils just before sowing. Keep plants growing vigorously with regular watering and by feeding with soluble plant food. Cut or pinch out flower buds as they start to form to keep plants in vegetative growth.

CLIMATE Zone 7.

Romneya (fam. Papaveraceae)
Matilija poppy

This tall, shrubby, herbaceous perennial from California and Central America bears large, white, sweetly perfumed, poppy-like flowers in summer through to fall.

CULTIVATION Plant in a light, well-drained soil in a sunny spot. Propagate from seed sown in early spring, or from suckers and root cuttings taken in winter.

CLIMATE Zone 7.

SPECIES *R. coulteri*, the only species, grows to over 2 m (6 ft), and produces satiny, white, fragrant flowers. The deeply divided foliage is colored an attractive gray-green. Var. *trichocalyx* is similar to the species, but it produces larger flowers with hairy calyces.

ABOVE Rocket leaves add a tang to mixed salads. It is easy to cultivate in the home garden.

ABOVE Crimped, white petals surround a mass of golden stamens on the lovely *Romneya coulteri*. It sometimes suckers in ideal conditions.

Romulea (fam. Iridaceae)

From the Mediterranean region and South Africa, this genus consists of 80 species of cormous, herbaceous plants whose flowers bear some resemblance to those of *Crocus*.

CULTIVATION Grow in a rock garden, in a sunny position with well-drained soil. Plant the corms in fall. Tender species are best grown in pots in a cool greenhouse or alpine house. Plant them in pots of gritty, soil-based potting compost. When the plants are dormant in summer they must be kept dry, but water normally when in growth. Propagate from seed in fall under glass, or from offsets in summer or fall.

CLIMATE There are species suited to various climatic zones.

SPECIES *R. bulbocodium*, which is popularly known as satin flower, zone 8, from the Mediterranean, grows no more than 10 cm (4 in) and in spring produces trumpet-shaped, purple flowers, each with a yellow or white throat. It is a good rock-garden plant which will multiply rapidly if conditions are suitable. *R. rosea*, zone 9, from South Africa, is consid-

ered a weed of turf in some warm countries, but is also a good garden plant, with its pretty pink or purple flowers. *R. sabulosa*, zone 9, another South African native, grows to 10 cm (4 in) and bears red flowers, marked with pink and white, in late spring.

Rondeletia (fam. Rubiaceae)

There are around 150 species in this genus of exotic, evergreen shrubs mainly from tropical America and the West Indies. Very few are in general cultivation. They have decorative, prominently veined foliage. Masses of white, pink or red flowers are borne in large trusses, in summer or fall. Outside the tropics or subtropics, they are grown in an intermediate to warm greenhouse.

CULTIVATION In the greenhouse or conservatory, grow in pots of soil-based potting compost. Plants need maximum light. Shade from direct, strong sun. Outdoors plant in a warm, sunny position with well-drained soil. Cannot tolerate heavy frost. Propagate from semi-ripe cuttings in summer, rooting them in a heated propagating case.

CLIMATE Zone 10 to tropical.

BELOW Large trusses of fragrant, pink flowers are produced in abundance during the summer on *Rondeletia amoena*. In frost-prone climates, grow this shrub under glass.

ABOVE Satin flower, *Romulea bulbocodium*, is a small, cormous perennial ideal for sunny rock gardens. It flowers in spring and early summer.

SPECIES *R. amoena*, from Mexico and Guatemala, is the species most often grown in the UK and Europe. Growing to around 3 m (10 ft), with a bushy crown, it has rounded clusters of fragrant, salmon to rose pink flowers at the branch tips. *R. odorata*, to 2.5 m (8 ft), has orange-red, fragrant, fall flowers. *R. strigosa* is a smaller species, to 1.5 m (5 ft) high, with bright crimson flowers.

Rosa (fam. Rosaceae)

Rose

Throughout history, the rose has been a symbol of life and love. It was known to the ancient Egyptians, the Greeks and the Romans, who grew roses in vast numbers. The Greek poet Sappho in 600 BC called it 'the queen of flowers'. Over the centuries, the rose has gained many other symbolic meanings and it has had many uses. It is still used in the preparation of a range of cosmetics, food and medicine. *Rosa* is from the same family as peaches, raspberries, *Cotoneaster* and *Spiraea*, and contains about 100 species. Wild roses grow around the Mediterranean, throughout the Middle East, Europe, North America and Asia, with the greatest number found in China. In Europe, during the Middle Ages, the apothecary's rose, *R. gallica* var. *officinalis*, was highly valued by apothecaries because of its ability to retain its scent. Indeed, it was a major source of rose oil and medicine in Europe during that period. Later, in England, the Lancastrians adopted this rose as their emblem. In the late 18th century, the introduction into Europe of the repeat flowering roses from China saw the beginning of rose hybridizing on a large scale, and this has continued to this day. Roses are lovely mass planted or as specimens. They may be grown as formal, standard bushes, trained to weep to the ground from stems 2 m (6 ft) or more high. Or they may simply form part of a mixed shrub border. Miniatures and polyantha roses are sometimes grown in containers, while hardy species, such as *R. rugosa*, are often used as hedges. Whole gardens have been

ABOVE The early Austin rose, 'Charles Austin', has the many-petalled, rounded flowers typical of these English roses.

devoted to roses and they are always popular for planting in parks and municipal gardens. In large home gardens there may be special rose beds, while in the small garden, a rose bush or two can be surrounded by annuals, perennials or bulbs.

CULTIVATION Although some roses tolerate a degree of shade, the best situation is in full sun; many disease problems can be avoided if they are grown there. Good air circulation is important too, but some shelter from very strong wind is desirable, so that flowers are not damaged. They need well-drained soil that has been prepared by adding large amounts of well-rotted manure or compost a few weeks before planting. Lime or dolomite should be added to soils known to be very acid. Roses have big root systems and should be thoroughly soaked once or twice a week during the growing season. To feed, use a complete plant food in late winter or very early spring. Feed again after the first flowering flush, and again in mid to late summer. Timing and severity of pruning depends on the type of rose. Those flowering once only are pruned after the summer blooming. Repeat-flowering types are pruned in winter in milder areas, or in early spring in very cold areas. Prune to an outward-pointing leaf bud to keep the center of the bush open. Refer to a rose text-book for full details of pruning as it is quite a complex subject. Many roses strike fairly read-ily from cuttings of dormant wood taken in winter, or very early spring. Others are more difficult and need to be budded onto rootstocks of species roses. Unfortunately, roses may suffer from a number of diseases and are attacked by a range of insects, although some species and older roses do not succumb so readily. Roses are susceptible to the diseases of black spot, mildew, rust, canker and oak root fungus, while pests include aphids, scale insects, caterpillars, red spider mites, leaf-cutting bees and deer.

CLIMATE The hardiness of roses is variable. Many tolerate extreme cold, while others are killed by frost. However, the majority of roses, including the modern hybrids, are fully hardy and suit-able for zone 5. The modern hybrids, though, will need winter protection in regions where temperatures frequently fall below -12°C. This is achieved by mounding up the base of the plants (the lower 30cm) with soil (not from the rose bed) and then, as soon as the mounds are

BELOW Introduced in 1894, 'Francis Dubreuil' is a beautifully formed tea rose. It is as rich a red as any rose could be.

frozen, covering them with straw or similar material. This prevents alternate freezing and thawing, which is very damaging. Alternatively use proprietary styrofoam rose cones.

VARIETIES *Rosa* includes the wild species, as well as Gallica, Damask, Alba, Moss, Centifolia, Portland, China, Tea, Noisette and Bourbon roses. In the 19th century, the Hybrid Musk, Hybrid Perpetual and finally the Hybrid Tea roses were developed. It was from these that all the modern roses have come. Since the 1970s, there has been great interest in what are known as 'English' roses, which were bred by David Austin. These are recurrent-flowering roses and they have the many-petalled form, lovely fra-grance and full vigor of the much older roses. Roses are loved for their form and color and many are very fragrant. They can be evergreen or deciduous, and most varieties have prickled stems. In the right climate, they can be very long lived, although they do not live as long in warmer climates. They reach maturity in three to five years and flower in two or three years. Some flower just once a year, in summer, but the display is often spectacular, while many others produce successive flushes of bloom in summer and fall. Some varieties produce bril-liant red hips in fall after flowering and are grown for this quality alone. Flowers may be single, double or many petalled and there is a wide range of colors: white, cream, yellow, apri-cot, orange, every shade of pink and red, mauve and blue, and bicolored. Roses may be less than 25 cm (10 in) tall, or grow to 2 or 3 m (6–10 ft) or more. There are miniatures, shrubs, ground-covers (with miniature or normal-sized flow-ers), climbers and ramblers.

Roselle (*Hibiscus sabdariffa*, fam. Malvaceae)
Jamaica sorrel

The fleshy part of this fruit is used for making jams and preserves, which are quite delicious, though not widely eaten. Believed to have orig-inated from tropical Africa, *Hibiscus sabdar-iffa* is a fast-growing annual or biennial, which reaches to 1–2 m (3–6 ft) high. It has large,

ABOVE The fruit of roselle is ready to pick three weeks after flowering. Only the fleshy red scales are used for preserves.

three-lobed leaves, red leaf stalks and yellow, hibiscus-type flowers, followed by the fruit which may be red or yellow.

CULTIVATION In frost-prone climates, this tender plant can be grown like tomatoes, either under glass or in the garden. Sow seed in spring, pot up the seedlings, and plant out when 15 cm (6 in) high. To plant into the garden, wait until frosts are over, then place them 60 cm (24 in) apart in rows 1 m (3 ft) apart. The first heads may be harvested about three weeks after flowering. Once harvesting has begun, collect the heads every week so that the fruit is not fully mature and woody. The roselle is relatively pest-free.

CLIMATE Zone 10 to tropical, but will grow as a summer annual in all zones.

Rosemary

(*Rosmarinus* species, fam. Lamiaceae)

Rosemary has long been steeped in myth and symbolism, being reminiscent of friendship in particular. The two species originate from the Mediterranean, where rosemary has traditionally been widely used in cooking. It adds a delicious flavor to lamb, pork, fish and vegetable dishes. Rosemary oil is used in soaps, perfumes and shampoos.

CULTIVATION Rosemary needs an open, well-drained soil and a sunny situation. It does well in rocky, dry coastal areas, but needs shelter in cold regions. Prune after flowering to retain shape and encourage new growth. Propagate from seed sown in spring or from semi-ripe cuttings in summer, both in a garden frame.

CLIMATE Best in areas of low humidity, with hot, dry summers and cool to cold winters. Zone 7 or 8.

SPECIES *R. officinalis*, common rosemary, is a shrubby, evergreen perennial, to 2 m (6 ft), with upright, branching stems. The needle-like leaves are dark green on top, silvery on the undersides, and very fragrant. The pale blue flowers are borne in terminal clusters. It is popular for borders, rockeries and container growing. Var. *albiflorus* has white flowers;

BELOW Rosemary revels in the reflected heat of the pavers and stone walls in this garden. It adapts to a range of landscape uses.

'Benenden Blue' has blueish violet flowers; 'Tuscan Blue' has blue-violet flowers. *R. officinalis* Prostratus Group is a dwarf rosemary to 20 cm (8 in) high, with a spreading prostrate habit and blue flowers. It is less hardy than the species. This is ideal for covering sunny banks or for a rock garden.

Rosularia

(syn. *Umbilicus*, fam. Crassulaceae)

From North Africa, southern Europe and Central Asia, these succulents form rosettes of crowded, hairy, pale green leaves, with sprays of red or yellow summer flowers. Offsets at the base form small clumps.

CULTIVATION Plant in a moderately rich, well-drained soil and give winter protection. Water in summer during growth and flowering, but keep fairly dry in winter. Propagate from seed or offsets, or by division of the roots in spring.

CLIMATE Zone 7.

SPECIES *R. aizoon* (syn. *R. pallida*), from Turkey, has very hairy leaves and large, whitish

ABOVE Forming large colonies of tight, gray-green rosettes, *Rosularia aizoon* is ideally displayed in a shallow, terracotta bowl.

yellow flowers. *R. paniculata*, from Iran, has 4 cm (1½ in) long leaves and white to pink flowers, borne on very long stems. *R. platyphylla*, from Russia, has very hairy leaves and stems and cream flowers. *R. serrata*, from the eastern Mediterranean, has gray-green, toothed leaves and white or light pink flowers.

Rothmannia (fam. Rubiaceae)

There are around 30 species in this genus of lovely, evergreen shrubs or small trees, native to tropical Africa, South Africa, Madagascar and Asia, and once classified with *Gardenia*. Widely grown in warm and tropical climates around the world, they all have attractive, glossy, green, lance- to oval-shaped foliage, and stalkless, bell-shaped flowers, some highly perfumed. The flowers appear in spring through to summer and are followed by fleshy, rounded fruit.

CULTIVATION Outside the tropics or subtropics, grow in an intermediate to warm greenhouse or conservatory in pots of acid (lime free), soil-

ABOVE *Rothmannia globosa* is guaranteed to flower prolifically every year. The flowers are followed by clusters of round, black fruits.

based potting compost. Plants need good light, but shade from direct, strong sun. They may need pruning in late winter to restrict size. Propagate in spring from seed germinated at 16°C (61°F), or from semi-ripe cuttings in summer, rooting them in a heated propagating case.

CLIMATE Tropical or subtropical.

SPECIES *R. capensis*, Cape gardenia, is a small tree, growing to 12–14 m (40–46 ft), with oval leaves, slightly wavy along the margins. The beautiful, cream flowers have reddish spotted throats and a sweet scent. *R. globosa*, tree gardenia, is very popular in some countries with warm climates. A shrub or small tree, from South Africa, it grows 3–6 m (10–20 ft) high, with oval to lance-shaped leaves. In summer, it is covered with masses of long, waxy, highly scented, creamy white flowers, sometimes tinted with pink. *R. longiflora* from tropical Africa is a shrub or small tree, to 5 m (16 ft), with many branched stems and long flowers, reddish purple on the outside, white on the inside, with purplish red spotted throats.

Roystonea (fam. Arecaceae)
Royal palm

Comprising about 12 species, these tall, striking, feather palms grow naturally only in the Caribbean region, from southern Florida through to parts of South America. They have massive, smooth, whitish brown, erect trunks and may grow up to 40 m (130 ft) when mature. The trunks are topped by very long, smooth, green crownshafts from which emerge huge fronds up to 7 m (23 ft) in length and 2 m (6 ft) wide. The crowded leaflets are a deep, rich green. The upward-pointing, white inflorescences are followed by small, brown or purple, berry-like fruits. In climates that are prone to frost, grow these palms as young plants in a warm conservatory or greenhouse.

CULTIVATION Grow in pots of soil-based potting compost, under glass. Ensure maximum light,

ABOVE The Cuban royal palm, *Roystonea regia*, is an imposing avenue palm in the tropics, but it can be grown under glass in frost-prone climates.

but shade plants from direct, strong sun. Outdoors grow in full sun with moist, rich, well-drained soil. Propagate from seed sown in spring and germinated at 26°C (79°F).

CLIMATE Zone 10 to tropical.

SPECIES *R. regia,* Cuban royal palm, reaches 30 m (100 ft) when fully grown, though is more usually seen around 20 m (65 ft). Unusually for a palm and distinctive of the species, the trunk is straight but swollen in the middle, tapering to the crownshaft, and often narrower near the bottom. The fronds grow to at least 4 m (13 ft). *R. regia* is the only species commonly in cultivation.

Rudbeckia (fam. Asteraceae)
Coneflower, black-eyed Susan

Native to North America, these 15 species of annuals and perennials are easy to grow in almost any conditions. They are bright, flowering plants adding color in summer and fall, and

ABOVE There are numerous cultivars of black-eyed Susan, *Rudbeckia hirta*, and they bring welcome color from mid-summer to early fall.

good cut flowers. Only a few are widely cultivated.

CULTIVATION Soil must be well drained but need not be rich, although better results will be obtained from better quality soils. Grow in full sun, preferably with protection from strong wind. All can be grown from seed and perennials can also be propagated from division of existing clumps.

CLIMATE There are species suited to various climatic zones.

SPECIES *R. hirta*, black-eyed Susan, zone 4, is a short-lived perennial, but usually grown as an annual from a spring sowing. It reaches about 1 m (3 ft) tall. The daisy-type flowers are yellow to orange and the raised cone of disc flowers in the center is colored very dark brown. Cultivated varieties are available. *R. laciniata*, zone 3, is a perennial, to 1.5–2.5 m (5–8 ft). Bright yellow, daisy flowers appear in late summer and fall. 'Hortensia' (syn. 'Golden Glow'), with its double flowers, is the most commonly grown form.

Ruellia (fam. Acanthaceae)

There are about 150 species in this genus of perennials, shrubs and subshrubs, found in tropical and North America, Africa and Asia. They are grown for their large, showy flowers and decorative foliage.

CULTIVATION In climates prone to frosts, grow as pot plants in a warm conservatory or greenhouse. Use soilless potting compost. Provide good light (but shade from direct sun), and a very humid atmosphere. If young shoots are pinched out bushy plants will result. Prune back old, flowered stems when flowering is over. Propagate in spring from seed germinated at 21°C (70°F), or from softwood cuttings in spring.

CLIMATE Warm zone 10 to tropical.

SPECIES *R. elegans*, a perennial sub-shrub from Brazil, grows to 60 cm (24 in). The bright scarlet flowers grow to about 5 cm (2 in) long and

ABOVE *Ruellia* species make good pot plants in frost-prone climates, where they should be grown in a warm greenhouse or conservatory.

are borne in groups of two to three blooms. *R. macrantha* is a shrub, to 2 m (6 ft), with large, prominently veined, pinkish lavender flowers, borne in the axils of the upper, oval leaves. *R. portellae* is a prostrate annual or perennial, to 30 cm (12 in). Rosy pink flowers, about 4 cm (1½ in) long, are borne singly.

Rumohra (fam. Davalliaceae)
Leather fern

This spreading fern is found only in the southern hemisphere–in parts of Australia, New Zealand, South America and South Africa.

CULTIVATION In climates prone to frost, grow in a warm conservatory or greenhouse. This fern is epiphytic so it can be grown in a hanging slatted, wooden orchid basket filled with soil-based potting compost, with added chipped bark and leaf mould. Alternatively, use a half pot or pan. It can also be grown on a slab or bark, hung up in the greenhouse. Plants need good light (but shade from direct sun), and a humid atmosphere. Outdoors grow in sun or partial shade with moist soil. Propagate from pieces of rhizome complete with roots.

CLIMATE Zone 10 to tropical.

SPECIES *R. adiantiformis* is the only species in cultivation. It has a long, creeping rhizome with light brown scales. The large, upright to pendent fronds are triangular in shape, with a wide base, leathery and glossy green above, and lighter green below. Spore cases are carried on the undersides of the leaflets on either side of the mid-vein. This is quite a tall-growing fern at up to 1.5 m (5 ft), and it has a spread of about 1 m (3 ft).

Ruschia (fam. Aizoaceae)

There are over 350 species in this large genus, found in a broad range of habitats in its native South Africa. These are succulent plants that bear shiny flowers resembling those of *Mesembryanthemum* or *Lampranthus*. They vary widely in size and shape, ranging from tiny clumps, with little foliage to huge, spread-

ABOVE In frosty areas, grow *Rumohra adiantiformis*, the leather fern, epiphytically in a warm greenhouse or conservatory.

ABOVE Several species of *Ruschia* bear lavender to purple, daisy-type flowers that carpet the fleshy leaves in summer.

ing mats of wiry stems, densely covered with fleshy leaves.

CULTIVATION In frost-prone areas, grow in pots of cactus compost in an intermediate greenhouse. Ensure maximum light and a dry atmosphere. Do not water plants in winter. Plants can be bedded out for the summer. Propagate in spring from seed germinated at 21°C (70°F) or from cuttings in summer.

CLIMATE Zone 10.

SPECIES *R. acuminata* is a shrubby species which can be upright or prostrate. It has oval, blueish-green leaves and light pink or white flowers. *R. dualis* is a small, clump-forming plant, with thickened leaves and deep pink flowers. *R. evoluta* is a mat-forming plant with blue-tinged leaves. The flowers are a most brilliant pink. *R. rubricaulis* is a shrubby plant, with red stems and larger, mauve flowers.

Ruscus (fam. Ruscaceae)

Originating from western Europe, North Africa, Madeira, the Azores and Iran, these six species of dwarf, evergreen shrubs are useful for woodland gardens and other shady parts of the garden. Their rootstocks travel underground to form colonies. They are often found growing in dense shade, particularly amongst the roots of trees, although they will also grow in sunny spots. The leaves are actually flattened stems and the unisexual flowers are either solitary or borne in clusters in the center of the modified leaves. The female plants produce attractive, shiny, red berries.

CULTIVATION These shrubs grow easily in any garden soil, thriving in shaded areas. Both sexes should be planted together for production of the berries. Propagate from seed sown outdoors as soon as ripe, or by division in spring.

CLIMATE Zone 7.

SPECIES *R. aculeatus*, box holly or butcher's

ABOVE *Ruscus* x *microglossum* is not common in cultivation, but it has become naturalized in many places. The tiny flowers can be seen in the center of the modified leaves.

broom, is a hardy shrub, to 1 m (3 ft), with erect, branching stems. The tiny, green, star-shaped flowers are followed by large, red berries. Dried sprays are used in floral decoration. This species occasionally produces hermaphrodite forms.

Russelia (fam. Scrophulariaceae)
Coral plant

There are around 50 species in this genus of evergreen shrubs, native to Cuba, Mexico and Colombia. They have pendulous branches and are almost continuously in flower, hence suitable for hanging baskets. The flowers come in red, mottled red, pink or white. They are also popular greenhouse plants in cold areas. In warm regions, they are used as spillover plants on banks and walls, forming good groundcover.

CULTIVATION Russellias can be grown in a cool to intermediate greenhouse or conservatory in frost-prone climates. Grow in pots or baskets of soil-based potting compost. Provide good light, but shade from strong sun. Water well in summer but less in winter. In the garden, plants need well-drained soil with plenty of humus,

ABOVE *Russelia equisetiformis* is shown at its best when allowed to spill over a wall or bank.

and a sheltered position, with full sun. Lightly trim in mid-spring to ensure shapely plants. Once russellias are growing strongly, they tolerate long, dry periods well. Propagate in spring from softwood cuttings in a heated propagating case, or by layering stems.

CLIMATE Zone 9 to 10.

SPECIES *R. equisetiformis*, coral plant, fountain plant or fountain bush, is a smooth shrub, to 1.2 m (4 ft), with pendulous branches and small, red, narrowly tubular flowers, borne in small clusters along the stems. A native of Mexico, it is cultivated widely in warm areas of the world. *R. sarmentosa*, from Central to South America, grows to 2 m (6 ft) high, with 8 cm (3 in) long, ovate, toothed leaves and dense clusters of red flowers.

Ruta (fam. Rutaceae)

Originally from the Mediterranean through to south-west Asia, this genus contains about eight species of pungently aromatic, perennial herbs and sub-shrubs. One of the species, commonly known as rue or herb of grace, is grown in herb gardens for its medicinal properties rather than for culinary usage, as it has a strong odor and bitter taste. However, its cultivars and other species are grown for their striking, greyish green, lacy foliage and bright yellow, four-petalled flowers, borne in terminal clusters. All are strongly aromatic.

CULTIVATION *Ruta* can adapt to poor soils, but prefers an open, sunny position and good drainage. Prune mature plants to maintain a neat shape. Propagate from seed sown in spring, or by root division. Cultivars are best propagated from 15 cm (6 in) long, firm shoots struck in late summer or early fall.

CLIMATE *R. graveolens* can be grown in zone 5.

SPECIES *R. graveolens*, rue, from the Mediterranean, yields an essential oil containing rutin, used to treat blood pressure. With attractive foliage and clusters of small, yellow summer flowers, it is an attractive garden plant, often grown in mixed borders. Handle with care as it may cause dermatitis. Cultivar 'Jackman's Blue' has attractive foliage with a marked blue color; 'Variegata', to 45 cm (18 in), has grayish green leaves with white margins.

ABOVE The intense, blue-green foliage of *Ruta graveolens* is highlighted by small, citrus yellow flowers.

S

Sabal to Syzygium

Sabal (fam. Arecaceae)
Palmetto

Sabal comprises some 15 species of fan palms, native to southern North America and the Caribbean. They may have tall, upright trunks or very short, mainly underground, stems. The fan-type fronds are deeply segmented. These are borne on stout, spineless leaf stalks which often persist on the trunk for many years. When grown in parks and botanical gardens, the stalks are often trimmed, giving these palms quite a distinctive appearance. The much-branched inflorescence consists of creamy flowers enclosed by tightly overlapping, smooth, green bracts. The rounded fruits ripen to dark brown or almost black. Sabals are not difficult to grow, doing well in a wide range of conditions and climates, from temperate to tropical. They will also adapt to exposed, coastal conditions. Like most other fan palms, they are fairly slow growing. Palmetto fronds have traditionally been used as roof thatching.

CULTIVATION Sabals prefer deep soils, with groundwater close to the surface, but will adapt to less favorable conditions. Adult palms like full sun, while younger specimens tolerate quite deep shade. Most of the species are tropical, but *S. palmetto* and *S. minor* can tolerate low temperatures in winter, though they need long, hot summers. Deep-rooted from an early age, they make better growth in the ground than in containers. *S. minor* can be grown satisfactorily as a container plant, though it is not a very handsome subject. It is better used in massed plantings, where its coarse leaves create interesting textures. In frost-prone climates, grow in pots in a cool to intermediate greenhouse, using soil-based potting compost. Plants can be stood outside for the summer. Propagate in spring from seed germinated at 21°C (70°F).

CLIMATE Zone 9–10.

SPECIES *S. blackburniana* (syn. *S. umbraculifera*), from the West Indies, is the largest species, with a trunk to about 15 m (50 ft) high and 50 cm (20 in) diameter, becoming smooth and pale gray with age. The very large, pendulous leaves are borne on thick, green leaf stalks, about 2.5 m (8 ft) long. This species makes an outstanding feature plant. *S. minor*, dwarf palmetto, is found over a large part of southern United States. This species has a stem that is mostly underground and the dull green fronds emerge from the trunk to a height of about 1 m (3 ft). As they age, the leaves tend to collapse from a point around the top of the leaf stalk. The inflorescence is quite striking, consisting of small, white, fragrant flowers and rising vertically to about 2 m (6 ft). Masses of pea-sized, dark brown fruits appear along the branchlets. *S. palmetto*, common palmetto or cabbage palmetto, is spread from southeast North America through to Cuba and the Bahamas, growing to 25 m (80 ft) in the wild but generally about 10 m (33 ft) in cultivation. It has a sturdy trunk, about 40 cm (16 in) in diameter, bearing markings of old leaf bases, and a rounded, compact crown. The fan-type fronds are borne on short, stout leaf stalks. The name is Spanish for 'little palm', a name given by early Spanish settlers in Florida.

ABOVE *Sabal palmetto* forms a strong element in the landscape. Note the slight twist on the large fan fronds.

Saffron (*Crocus sativus*, fam. Iridaceae)

Saffron is the most costly of all herbs and spices as it comes from the stigma of the saffron crocus flower, and about 150,000 flowers are needed for 1 kg (about 2 lb) of pure saffron. It has been used since classical times as a spice and in cosmetics, and was formerly used as a dye and in medicine. It is mentioned in the Song of Solomon in the Bible and is thought to have originated from Asia Minor. Today, most saffron is processed in Spain although it is cultivated in southern Europe and parts of Asia and India. It is a small plant, growing from an underground corm. It produces both its leaves and pretty, pale lilac flowers in fall. Saffron is prized for cooking and coloring food, and is used in cakes and breads, paella, bouillabaisse and many Indian dishes.

CULTIVATION Plant corms in late summer to early fall, in free-draining sandy soil. Flowers appear in early fall and the stigmas are picked by hand. These are dried in the sun or in ovens at very low temperatures before being stored in airtight containers. Plants must not be cut or lifted until the foliage has died down naturally. If the soil is very well drained, corms can be left in the ground until the following season, otherwise they must be lifted and stored in a dry, airy place.

CLIMATE Zone 6.

ABOVE Saffron crocus flowers in autumn. Thousands of flowers are needed to produce a worthwhile quantity of saffron.

Sage (*Salvia officinalis*, fam. Lamiaceae)

Originating from the Mediterranean, sage has been known since ancient times, and it is in Italy that this lovely herb is put to best use: the leaves are sautéed in olive oil until crisp and used to flavor stews. The English, on the other hand, prefer to use sage in traditional stuffings for roast duck or goose. While widely used in the kitchen, the leaves are also valued for their medicinal properties. *Salvia officinalis* is a hardy perennial, growing between 60 cm (24 in) and 1 m (3 ft), with branching stems, attractive, grayish green leaves and mauve or purple flowers, borne at the ends of the stems in summer. The aromatic leaves are slightly bitter.

CULTIVATION Grow in a well-drained sandy soil, in raised beds if possible, in an open sunny location. Water young plants liberally, decreasing the quantity as the plant matures. Propagate from seed in spring, or from semi-ripe cuttings in summer, rooted with bottom heat. Sprinkle seed over a prepared seed box and cover lightly with soil. Plant out when about 10 cm (4 in) high, spacing them 60 cm (24 in) apart within and between rows. If propagating from cuttings, use a very coarse mix and plant out when well rooted. Pinch out

ABOVE One of the culinary mainstays, sage is a herb that must be grown in full sun, in perfectly drained soil.

growing tips during the first year to encourage bushiness, and harvest in summer, just before the plant flowers. The leaves may be dried in an oven at a very low temperature. When completely dry, remove the stems and store leaves in air-tight containers. Renew plants from seed or cuttings every three to four years. Sage can also be grown successfully in containers.

CLIMATE Zone 5. Best in a Mediterranean climate of hot, dry summers and cool, wet winters.

Saintpaulia (fam. Gesneriaceae)
African violet

Although there are some 20 species in this genus of perennial, herbaceous plants, only one is generally cultivated, either as a greenhouse or indoor plant. It has broad, dark green leaves covered with fine, downy hairs and delicate, five-lobed, semi-succulent flowers with yellow anthers.

CULTIVATION African violets should be grown in a warm greenhouse or conservatory or as house plants. They need warm, shady, moist conditions and a light, soilless potting compost. Temperatures should be no cooler than 13°C (55°F). The ideal temperature range is 18°–25°C (64°–77°F). Water should be room temperature and should not touch the leaves. Place pot in a dish filled with pebbles and cover the pebbles

ABOVE The original species of African violet, *Saintpaulia ionantha* has deep purple flowers. Today's range of cultivars is varied in form and color.

with water so that, while the pot is not actually standing in the water, humidity constantly surrounds it. Direct sunlight or sudden changes of temperature will damage this tender plant. Established plants require regular feeding, with weak, liquid fertilizer, in spring and summer. Propagate from leaf cuttings placed in wet sand, or suspended over water.

CLIMATE Tropical.

SPECIES *S. ionantha*, the species most commonly called African violet, has dark green, heart-shaped leaves and violet flowers. Cultivars are many and varied, with flower colors ranging from pale violet through to pink, white and bi-colors, and foliage that is smaller and paler, or in fancy forms. They now also include single and double flowers with plain or ruffled petals. Increasingly popular is a great range of miniature forms with the same colors as the standard types.

Salix (fam. Salicaceae)
Willow

Occurring in cold and temperate regions of the northern hemisphere, including most northern European countries, this genus consists of around 300 species of deciduous trees and shrubs. The alternate, bright green leaves are generally slender and lance-shaped. The small flowers are borne in fluffy catkins, the male being yellow and the female, green and less conspicuous. Grown for their timber, willows also make attractive ornamentals or specimens, particularly in areas where drainage is poor, and have a great range of traditional uses in farming and gardening. Fast-growing, they have tough yet flexible stems that are used in basket-weaving. Shrubby willows with brightly colored stems are often grown for winter effect.

CULTIVATION Willows are easy to grow, most species preferring moist, heavy soils. All species do well near water or in poorly drained areas. Some benefit from stooling or pollarding annually to encourage the attractive stem or branch

ABOVE Growing in ideal conditions beside a small lake, *Salix babylonica* and *S. babylonica* var. *pekinensis* 'Tortuosa' are two very different willows.

ABOVE The soft, velvety catkins of *Salix caprea*, pussy willow or goat willow, are favorites of children and adults.

coloration. Propagate from hardwood cuttings, which can be quite long young stems, and root outdoors in moist soil; 30–40 cm (12–16 in) soft tip cuttings will root readily in water. Larger growing species should not be planted near buildings or drains as the roots are extremely vigorous.

CLIMATE There are species suited to various climatic zones.

SPECIES *S. alba*, white willow, zone 2, from Europe and central Asia, is an elegant tree, to 25 m (80 ft), its branches weeping at the ends. The silky foliage is blue-green on the undersides. It makes a good windbreak. Cultivar 'Aurea' has yellow-green branches; var. *caerulea* is the cricket bat willow, valued for its timber, which is used to make cricket bats; subsp. *vitellina*, the golden willow, has golden yellow stems; and subsp. *vitellina* 'Britzensis' has brilliant orange-red young stems. *S. babylonica*, weeping willow, zone 5, from China, may be confused with *S. alba* 'Tristis', the weeping species now often cultivated. A graceful, weeping tree with long, slender leaves, it grows to 15 m (50 ft) or more. *S. babylonica* var. *pekinensis* 'Tortuosa' has twisted and curled shoots and stems that show up particularly well in winter. The leaves are also twisted.

It makes an unusual specimen tree for a lawn, and grows to 15 m (50 ft). *S. caprea*, pussy willow, zone 5, grows well in poor drainage areas but its extensive root system may be a problem. It grows to 8 m (26 ft), the leaves being oval in shape. The attractive, silky male catkins make the leafless twigs popular for indoor decoration. The cultivar 'Kilmarnock', known as the Kilmarnock willow, is a very popular, small, weeping tree growing to a height of 2 m (6 ft), with a similar spread. It is ideal for small gardens. *S. cordata*, furry willow, zone 2, grows to 2.5 m (8 ft), with silky leaves and long, slender catkins. *S. fragilis*, crack willow, zone 5, from north-western Asia and Europe, is one of the larger species, growing to 20 m (65 ft) or more, its brittle branches forming a broad crown. The toothed leaves color yellow in fall. *S. lanata*, woolly willow, is a shrub, to 1 m (3 ft), with silvery foliage. *S. purpurea*, purple osier, zone 5, is one of the best known of the shrubby species, growing to around 5 m (16 ft). The leaves are blueish green, the young shoots reddish purple, and the catkins silvery green. *S. x sepulcralis* var. *chrysocoma*, golden weeping willow, zone 6, is widely grown. The young shoots are deep yellow and hang right down to the ground. It is a large tree, with a height and spread of about 15 m (50 ft).

Salpiglossis (fam. Solanaceae)

Of these two species of annual, biennial or perennial plants from the Andes, only one species is in general cultivation, and it is usually grown as an annual.

CULTIVATION *Salpiglossis* can be grown as summer display plants outdoors in warm sunny climates, or as pot plants in an intermediate greenhouse in cooler areas. Sow seeds in spring, germinated at about 21°C (70°F). Under glass, grow in pots of soil-based potting compost, in good light, but shade from sun. In the garden, grow in a sunny, sheltered spot with well-drained, moisture-retentive soil.

CLIMATE Zone 8.

SPECIES *S. sinuata*, painted tongue, is very showy, producing large, striking, trumpet-shaped flowers in brilliant red, orange-yellow, purple or blueish violet, often veined with a contrasting color. It grows 60–75 cm (24–30 in) high. There are numerous cultivars of this species but the dwarf kinds are preferred by gardeners. These include Bolero Hybrids which are noted for their very large flowers, and Splash hybrids which are particularly free flowering.

ABOVE Massed *Salpiglossis sinuata* form a rich tapestry of burgundy, red and pink, with the occasional yellow flower.

Salsify

(*Scorzonera hispanica*, fam. Asteraceae;
Tragopogon porrifolius, fam. Asteraceae)

Vegetable oyster

From southern Europe, northern Africa and Asia, salsify is grown for its oyster-flavored tap roots, which can be roasted, boiled or made into soup. Its leaves are eaten in salads.

CULTIVATION *Salsify* prefers a light, deep soil which has been worked and manured for a previous crop. Plants are raised from seed sown between early and late spring where the plants are to grow. Sow 1 cm (⅓ in) deep, in rows spaced 45 cm (18 in) apart. The seedlings are thinned out to stand 10 cm (4 in) apart. Keep well watered and weeded during the summer and start to harvest from early fall. If desired, all roots can be lifted and stored in containers of moist sand in a shed or garage.

CLIMATE Zone 6.

SPECIES *Scorzonera hispanica*, black salsify, has a fleshy, black-skinned taproot. *Tragopogon porrifolius* is a hardy biennial, to over 1 m (3 ft), which is treated as an annual unless seed is required. The edible, white root is 30 cm (12 in) long, and the small flowers are purple.

ABOVE *Tragopogon porrifolius*, salsify, is grown for its thick roots, which are cooked as a winter vegetable.

Salvia (fam. Lamiaceae)

Sage

Salvia is a huge plant group of over 900 species, comprising shrubs, herbaceous perennials and annuals. Salvias are often associated with red or purple flowers, but there are also species with cream, yellow, white, blue and pink flowers. Many have highly aromatic foliage, with scents ranging from the delicious to the outright unpleasant. The foliage of pineapple sage (*S. elegans*, 'Scarlet Pineapple'), for example, has a delicious perfume, while bog sage (*S. uliginosa*) smells rather unpleasant. Culinary sage, *S. officinalis*, is also one of this group. Most salvias are extremely easy to grow and, once established, need little more than occasional, deep watering in hot weather and some cutting back after flowering. Tall-growing salvias are ideal for the back of borders or as fillers between shrubs. Others of varying heights are suitable for edges or mixed with annuals, bulbs and other perennials. Many salvias have a very long flowering period, through summer into fall. Some species, like *S. leucantha*, flower in winter through to spring. Summer to fall flowering of salvias makes them an asset, as they continue to bloom after many perennials have finished. However, none of them make good cut flowers.

CULTIVATION Many species prefer full sun all day, but quite a number will tolerate semi-shade or shade for part of the day. Several can be grown in dappled shade, under trees. Any well-drained soil is suitable, while mulching with decayed manure in early spring will improve the condition of the soil. Water regularly to establish; once established, they can be drought-tolerant, although occasional, deep soakings during dry periods will encourage better growth and blooming. However, poorly drained soils and overwatering may kill these plants. Apply complete plant food or pelletted poultry manure in spring in poor soil, but too much fertilizer will result in all foliage and few flowers. Tip prune after each flowering flush to promote further blooming. In late fall or early winter, cut plants off just above ground level. To avoid lifting and dividing the clumps, wait until new growth begins in spring, then simply thin out crowded

ABOVE The tender Mexican sage, *Salvia leucantha*, is a vigorous grower, its purple and white flowers rising above white-backed leaves in winter and spring.

ABOVE Annual *Salvia splendens* bears its scarlet flowers over months. Cut back after the first flush for a second blooming.

growth. Propagate from seed or cuttings. In frost-prone climates, the frost-tender species can be grown in a cool greenhouse or conservatory, or planted out for the summer. Grow in pots of well drained, soil-based potting compost and ensure maximum light, but shade from direct sun. Keep humidity low.

CLIMATE There are salvias suited to various climatic zones, but many are frost-tender.

SPECIES *S. azurea*, zone 4, a perennial, grows to over 1 m (3 ft) high, with intense, deep blue flowers. *S. elegans* 'Scarlet Pineapple', pineapple sage, zone 10, is a tall, attractive plant with long, textured leaves, which smell of pineapple when crushed. The bright red flowers are quite striking. *S. farinacea*, mealy cup sage, zone 9, is a short-lived perennial, 30–50 cm (12–20 in) high, often better treated as an annual. It has deep purple or white flowers with a woolly, white coating. *S. guaranitica*, zone 9, is very easy to grow, reaching in excess of 1 m (3 ft). It has flowers in the intense blue of *S. azurea*. *S. involucrata*, zone 9, is a vigorous plant, growing to about 1.2 m (4 ft), with bright rosy pink flowers over a very long period. *S. leucantha*, Mexican sage, zone 10, is a very useful perennial, the velvety purple and white flowers blooming in winter and spring. The leaves are green with white, felty undersides. This species is also very vigorous, growing 1 m (3 ft) tall, and spreading rapidly by means of underground stems. *S. microphylla*, zone 9, has bright red flowers. *S. officinalis*, common sage, zone 5, is one of the most difficult to grow, demanding perfect drainage and disliking humidity and excessive summer rain. The foliage is gray and rather wrinkled and the flowers are generally pale violet. *S. patens*, zone 9, to 60 cm (24 in) high, produces intense, deep blue flowers. *S. uliginosa*, bog sage, zone 9, bears bright blue flowers, with a touch of white, from summer into fall. This long flowering period makes it a useful perennial, despite its rather offensive smell. It can also be rather invasive. It is easy, however, to pull out unwanted plants.

Samanea (fam. Leguminosae)

Monkey pod, rain tree, saman

The monkey pod is the best known of these species of generally fast-growing trees and shrubs, native to tropical America and Africa. The leaves are compound with eight pairs of leaflets, and the flowers are tufty in rounded heads. These are followed by curved pods, the seeds of which are enclosed in pulp. Unlikely to be available outside countries of origin.

CULTIVATION Outside the tropics, samaneas are grown in a warm greenhouse or conservatory in pots of soil-based potting compost. Provide maximum light but shade plants from strong, direct sun. Water normally in the growing season, but reduce considerably in winter. Pruning may be needed in late winter to restrict size. Propagate from seed sown in spring and germinated at 15°C (59°F). First soak seeds in warm water for 24 hours. Take semi-ripe cuttings in summer and root with bottom heat.

CLIMATE For tropical regions only.

SPECIES *S. saman*, (syn. *Albizia saman*), monkey pod or rain tree, is fast growing, developing into a tree with a short, massive trunk and a canopy much wider than it is high. These

ABOVE Flowers of *Samanea saman* burst out of tight clusters of buds. The creamy flowers have long, pink, fluffy stamens.

trees grow to 20 m (65 ft) or more, folding their leaves when it rains, allowing plants beneath to be thoroughly watered. In the dry season, they shed much of their foliage. Yellowish flowers with long pink stamens appear in late spring or summer, followed by dark pods that split along one side as they mature.

Sambucus (fam. Caprifoliaceae)

Elder, elderberry

Found in most temperate regions of the world, this genus includes around 20 species of mostly deciduous shrubs and trees. All have feathery foliage, clusters of creamy white flowers, and red, blue or purple-black berries. In some species the berries are poisonous, although those of *S. nigra* are edible and have been used to make elderberry wine for many centuries. The fruit of the American elder, *S. canadensis*, is also used in wine, jams, jellies and pies.

CULTIVATION Elders do well in any reasonably well drained, moist soil, in either sun or partial shade. The golden varieties require pruning for best spring effect. Propagate from seed or cuttings, hardwood cuttings being slow but reliable.

CLIMATE There are species suited to various climatic zones.

SPECIES *S. callicarpa*, zone 6, a native of California, grows to 6 m (20 ft) and has very decorative, red berries. *S. canadensis*, American elder, zone 3, grows about 3 m (10 ft) high. White flower heads are followed by berries ripening to purple-black. Cultivar 'Aurea' is striking if grown in sun, where its golden foliage is best seen. *S. nigra*, common elder, zone 5, the most widely cultivated species, is a small, shrubby tree, to 10 m (33 ft), with clusters of cream flowers in summer, followed by black berries. Cultivar 'Albovariegata' has variegated leaves and 'Aurea', golden leaves. *S. racemosa*, European red elder, zone 4, grows to 4 m (13 ft), with feathery foliage, large clusters of cream flowers, and scarlet berries. 'Plumosa Aurea' has golden yellow foliage.

ABOVE The small creamy flowers on *Sambucus nigra* are massed in flat plates on the top of the branches.

Sanchezia (fam. Acanthaceae)

There are about 20 species in this genus of shrubs with origins in tropical America. They have opposite leaves and spikes or sprays of mostly colorful flowers, borne on stem tips or in the leaf axils. Outside the tropics, grow as pot plants in a warm conservatory or greenhouse.

CULTIVATION In the greenhouse, grow in pots of soil-based potting compost. Ensure plants have

ABOVE Grown for its handsome foliage, *Sanchezia speciosa* has rich green leaves, strongly veined in white.

good light, but shade from direct, strong sun. Water normally when in full growth, far less in winter. Pruning may be needed in late winter to restrict size. Propagate from softwood cuttings in spring or semi-ripe cuttings in summer, rooting both in a heated propagating case.

CLIMATE Warmest parts of zone 10 to tropical.

SPECIES *S. speciosa* is the most frequently cultivated species. It is a bushy shrub, growing to a height and width of about 1.5 m (5 ft). The oval to lance-shaped leaves are bright green, with prominently marked veins of white, cream or yellow. Spikes of flowers appear mainly in summer. These are yellow with red bracts that often persist long after the flowers have fallen.

Sandersonia (fam. Colchicaceae)
Chinese lantern lily

This is a genus containing only one species. Now rare in its native South Africa, this perennial climber, which grows from tubers, is an unusual subject for frost-free gardens or, where frosts occur, for an intermediate conservatory or greenhouse.

ABOVE The quaintly shaped lantern flowers of *Sandersonia aurantiaca* have a lovely satin sheen that reflects the light.

CULTIVATION If growing in pots under glass, plant tubers in gritty, well drained, soil-based potting compost. Plant about 7 cm (3 in) deep in early spring. Ensure plants receive maximum light, but shade them from direct, strong sun. Water normally and liquid feed monthly when in full growth, but as the plants die down, start reducing water and keep completely dry during the dormant period. If growing in the garden, choose a sunny spot with well-drained soil containing plenty of humus. Keep off excessive rain over winter. Propagate by division while dormant, or from ripe seed germinated at 21°C (70°F).

CLIMATE Zone 9 if relatively frost free.

SPECIES *S. aurantiaca*, Chinese lantern lily, grows 80 cm (32 in) high. The linear to lance-shaped leaves are stem-clasping, and the satiny, rich gold to orange flowers are carried on slender, drooping stems. These may need light support to prevent them from toppling over. This is an excellent cut flower.

Sanguinaria (fam. Papaveraceae)
Bloodroot

The genus name is derived from the Latin sanguis, meaning 'blood', which refers to the color of the plant's sap. An herbaceous perennial from North America, the leaves are blueish gray and the flowers are pure white with yellow anthers.

CULTIVATION This lovely, woodland plant prefers a semi-shaded, moist spot in a well-drained soil. Propagate by division after flowering.

CLIMATE Zone 3. Cool, moist climates only.

SPECIES *S. canadensis* is a delightful, low-growing plant, to 20 cm (8 in), with kidney-shaped leaves and white flowers. Cultivar 'Plena' has more showy, double flowers.

ABOVE Charming little *Sanguinaria canadensis* has simple, pure white flowers. It is strictly a cool-climate plant.

ABOVE The delicate, greenish white flowers of *Sansevieria trifasciata* contrast with the tough leaves. They are also nectar-rich and fragrant.

Sansevieria (fam. Agavaceae)
Mother-in-law's tongue

Comprising around 70 species, as well as many different varieties and forms, these succulent plants originate from arid areas in Africa (tropical and subtropical), Malagassy and southern Asia. All have short, thick, creeping rhizomes from which arise tough, upright, sword-shaped fibrous leaves, from which hemp fiber is manufactured. The leaves of many species are spotted, blotched or banded in various patterns. Mature plants bear sprays of small greenish white flowers borne on fairly tall stems. Sansevierias are popular and resilient indoor plants.

CULTIVATION Easy to grow, these plants require very little water and moderately rich, well-drained soil. They can be grown in either sun or shade. Their thick rhizomes fill pots quickly, so sansevierias may need repotting annually. Indoors, sponge the leaves to remove dust. Propagate from leaf cuttings, segments of the rhizome with a node, or from seed sown in spring or summer.

CLIMATE Zone 10 or tropical.

SPECIES *S. cylindrica*, from Africa, has tall, cylindrical, sharp-pointed, dull green leaves and tubular, pale pink or white flowers. *S. trifasciata*, mother-in-law's tongue, from western Africa, has stiff, straight, erect leaves, ending in a blunt point and banded in grayish green and dark green. Cultivar 'Hahnii', believed to be a sport of *S. trifasciata*, is a vase-shaped plant with wider, shorter leaves marked horizontally with deep green. Cultivar 'Laurentii' is like *S. trifasciata*, but has cream to yellow bands down the leaf sides.

Santalum (fam. Santalaceae)
Sandalwood

Native to Australia, Southeast Asia and the Pacific, these evergreen trees and shrubs are generally grown either for their fruit or the perfumed 'sandalwood' from which precious and sacred ornaments have been made for centuries by the Chinese and Indians. The timber also yields an essential oil which has medicinal uses. With their red fruits and pendulous foliage, they can also make attractive garden ornamentals and tub specimens. However, being partial parasites on the roots of other plants, cultiva-

ABOVE Native to dry, arid regions of inland Australia, *Santalum lanceolatum* is a small tree, growing to about 7 m (23 ft). Like the related quandong, its fruits are edible.

tion can be difficult. It is unlikely that this genus is available outside its countries of origin.

CULTIVATION Outside the tropics, sandalwoods need to be grown in a warm greenhouse, but are generally considered outside the scope of the home gardener. The seeds of all species, except *S. lanceolatum*, have hard shells which require nicking before being placed, nick downwards, in a sharp sand and peat mix of 3:1, in a partially shaded spot. Plants need to be kept moist in summer. Santalum species need a host when small, so plant with another small shrub or grass and transplant together.

CLIMATE Zone 10 to tropical.

SPECIES *S. acuminatum*, quandong, is a small tree, native to Australia, to 5 m (16 ft) high, with a dense crown of pale green leaves. The small white flowers are followed by edible fruits, to 3 cm (1 in) in diameter, which change from green to bright red when ripe. The nut kernels and the fruits of this species were eaten by Aborigines, who buried the fruit to improve the flavor. *S. album*, white sandalwood, is native to Timor and other Indonesian islands and is now cultivated in India and in Hawaii for export. Growing to 5 m (16 ft), it has small flowers which turn red as they mature, and black, cherry-like fruits. *S. freycinetianum*, iliahi tree, from Hawaii, is cultivated there for export. *S. lanceolatum*, plum or cherry bush, or northern sandalwood, is a small tree with lovely, pendulous foliage and edible, round, black fruits. *S. spicatum*, fragrant or Swan River sandalwood, threatened with extinction, is the most commercially important species, as the oil is used as a fixative for perfumes. This small, bushy tree, to 3–4 m (10–13 ft) high, has blueish green foliage and small, yellow fruits.

Santolina (fam. Asteraceae)

Lavender cotton

Endemic to the Mediterranean, this genus consists of 18 compact, evergreen shrubs, generally with gray, aromatic foliage and circular, daisy-like flower heads in summer. They make good border or rockery plants.

CULTIVATION Santolinas are easy to grow, requiring only full sun and well-drained soil. Prune after flowering to remove old flower heads and to prevent plants from becoming leggy. Propagate from cuttings from late spring to fall.

CLIMATE Zone 7.

SPECIES *S. chamaecyparissus*, lavender cotton, is a many-branched, dwarf shrub, to 60 cm

ABOVE Clipped for compact growth, *Santolina chamaecyparissus* grows happily in a raised bed, mulched with gravel.

(24 in), with silver-gray, aromatic foliage. Masses of yellow blooms cover this bush in summer. Used as low hedging, it also has insecticidal properties and a long history of use in folk medicine as an antiseptic. *S. rosmarinifolia* subsp. *rosmarinifolia* (syn. *R. virens*) has bright green, feathery foliage and yellow flower heads.

Sapium (fam. Euphorbiaceae)
Tallow tree

These evergreen or deciduous trees and shrubs are found in warm and tropical regions around the world. The genus comprises around 100 species. Some yield the raw latex used in the manufacture of rubber, while *S. sebiferum* contains a white, waxy seed covering which is made into soap and candles. In the garden, sapiums are useful as ornamentals or for shade.

CULTIVATION These plants do best in well-drained soil enriched with organic matter, in full sun. They are easily grown from seed.

CLIMATE Zone 9.

SPECIES *S. sebiferum*, Chinese tallow tree, is the most commonly cultivated. Native to warm regions of China and Japan, it is a fast-growing, attractive tree, to 10 m (33 ft), with a spreading crown. The soft, heart-shaped leaves color red in fall and the small, greenish yellow flowers are borne in catkins in spring. This species has become naturalized in some countries.

Sapodilla (*Manilkara zapota*, fam. Sapotaceae)

Native to the West Indies and Central America, sapodilla is most important commercially for the latex or chicle gum in its bark that is tapped like rubber. This provides the basis for chewing gum. It is cultivated for this purpose in several Central American countries, but is also grown for its fruit in many tropical countries. The fruit is chopped and used in sweet dishes, or served with lime juice and other salad vegetables. It is borne on slow-growing, evergreen trees that may be 5–15 m (16–50 ft) tall. The leaves are dark and leathery and the small, green and brown flowers are carried in clusters in the leaf axils. Trees begin bearing after about five years. Mature fruit is 5–8 cm (2–3 in) across and has a rough, corky, rusty brown skin when it is fully ripe. It must be fully ripe when eaten to avoid unpleasant tannins and milky juice. Ripe fruit has honey-colored pulp that is translucent, sweet and fragrant. Hard, shiny seeds are in the fruit center.

CULTIVATION In frost-prone climates, grow as a young foliage plant in a warm greenhouse or conservatory, in pots of rich, sandy, soil-based

ABOVE New growth on *Sapium sebiferum* is pinky red. The heart-shaped leaves on layered branches form a shady canopy.

ABOVE The unattractive, rough, rusty-looking skin of tropical sapodilla gives no indication of its luscious flesh.

potting compost. Outdoors, sapodillas tolerate poor soil, but will do best in well-drained soil that is rich in organic matter. Established trees tolerate dry conditions and are very wind-resistant, often being grown in fairly exposed coastal areas. They may be propagated from seed but do not come true to type, so seedlings are best used as stocks for grafting of reliable varieties.

CLIMATE Warmest parts of zone 10 to tropical.

Saponaria (fam. Caryophyllaceae)

Soapwort

Both the generic name and the common name refer to the juice of the leaves of S. *officinalis*, which lathers like soap when placed in water. The 20 species of annuals, biennials and perennials are all from Europe and south-west Asia, some being regarded as weeds.

CULTIVATION Saponarias require a sunny situation, but will thrive in almost any soil. Propagate annuals from seed and perennials from cuttings or by division.

CLIMATE There are species suited to various climatic zones.

ABOVE Bouncing Bet, *Saponaria officinalis*, has been used for centuries as a cleaning agent and in folk medicine. It is used today in skin lotions and shampoos.

SPECIES S. *caespitosa*, zone 7, is a low-growing perennial, to 15 cm (6 in), producing masses of pink flowers which are larger than those of most other species. S. *ocymoides*, zone 4, also a perennial, grows to 10 cm (4 in). With its trailing habit, it is used for growing in rock gardens or on banks and walls. It forms a carpet of small, deep pink, five-petalled flowers, borne in sprays, in summer. S. *officinalis*, bouncing Bet, zone 4, is a vigorous, spreading perennial, to 60 cm (24 in) high, with sprays of pink, summer flowers. Cultivar 'Rubra Plena' has double, red flowers and 'Alba Plena' has double, white flowers.

Sapote, black

(*Diospyros digyna*, fam. Ebenaceae)

Chocolate pudding fruit

Related to the persimmon, black sapote produces round fruits, about 5–12 cm (2–5 in) in diameter. Fruits are olive green, becoming almost black at maturity, with a very sweet, dark chocolate flesh that can be scooped from the fruit and eaten fresh. The tree is an evergreen, to 8–15 m (26–50 ft) high, with elliptical leaves about 20 cm (8 in) long and small, white, fragrant flowers. Black sapote is native to Mexico and Central America, although it is now naturalized in many parts of tropical Asia.

BELOW Black sapote fruits must be picked much darker than the unripe fruit pictured here. They should be dark brown to black before they are harvested so that the delicious, creamy flesh can be enjoyed.

CULTIVATION In climates prone to frost, grow in a warm greenhouse or conservatory as a young foliage plant. Use pots of rich, soil-based potting compost. Water well during the growing season. Outdoors this tree grows best in well-drained soil of high fertility. Propagation is from seed in spring, or by shield budding in summer.

CLIMATE Warmest parts of zone 10 to tropical.

Saraca (fam. Leguminosae)

Known for their brightly colored flowers, this genus comprises 11 species of trees from Southeast Asia. Grown as ornamentals in tropical and subtropical regions, one of the species is thought to be the tree under which Buddha was born. The flowers are used in temple offerings, and some species were formerly used in local medicines.

CULTIVATION In climates which are prone to frost, saracas are occasionally grown as pot plants in warm greenhouses or conservatories. They should be grown in well-drained, soil-based potting compost. Shade the plants from direct sun. Water well during the growing season, but keep them drier at other times. Outdoors these trees require the shade and protection of taller trees, and moist yet well-drained soil. Trees are

propagated from seed, but tend to be slow growing in their early years.

CLIMATE Warmest parts of zone 10 to tropical.

SPECIES *S. indica* (syn. *S. asoca*), the Asoka or sorrowless tree, grows 8–10 m (26–33 ft) tall. The branchlets are pendulous, with the young foliage being quite limp. The compound leaves are made up of three to six pairs of long, tapering leaflets. The flowers make a spectacular show, opening orange-yellow and then deepening to a rich red as they age. Their fragrance is evident only at night. The pods containing the seeds develop after the flowers have faded. *S. thaipingensis* also grows 8–10 m (26–33 ft) in height. The leaflets are broader than those of *S. indica* and the massed flower heads are yellow.

Sarcochilus (fam. Orchidaceae)

There are 16 species in this genus of epiphytic orchids, found mostly in rainforests and moist gullies of eastern Australia, with one species occurring in New Caledonia. These very beautiful, highly perfumed orchids are easy to grow and make an attractive addition to any orchid collection. Flowering usually occurs in fall and

ABOVE Some very choice hybrids of *Sarchochilus* have been produced from various species. They also have the advantage of being easy to grow.

BELOW Native to the Malay Peninsula, *Saraca thaipingensis* carries its yellow flowers on branch tops above the drooping leaves.

winter in the northern hemisphere, but some species flower at other times.

CULTIVATION Grow in an intermediate to warm greenhouse or conservatory, in pots of epiphytic orchid compost. Alternatively, grow in hanging, slatted wooden orchid baskets, or mount plants on slabs of bark or cork hung up in the greenhouse. Provide high humidity and shade from direct sun, and water very sparingly when plants are resting.

CLIMATE Zone 10.

SPECIES *S. ceciliae*, fairy bells, is a dainty species with thick, narrow leaves and creeping stems that form dense clumps. The tiny, bell-shaped, highly fragrant flowers are usually pink and are borne on upright sprays. *S. falcatus*, orange blossom orchid, is a lovely species with flattish leaves and sprays of white to cream, highly fragrant flowers, often marked in yellow or orange on the lip. *S. fitzgeraldii*, ravine orchid, has branching stems that form a mat with age. The 20 cm (8 in) long sprays bear highly scented flowers, mostly in white, though sometimes pink, marked with red on the base. *S. hartmannii* is a variable species, like *S. fitzgeraldii*, with stiff, channelled leaves and slightly longer sprays of white flowers, the base marked with pink to maroon spots. Some very choice hybrids are available from specialist growers.

Sarcococca (fam. Buxaceae)
Sweet box

Originating in Asia, this genus consists of 11 species of evergreen shrubs, grown mostly for their attractive foliage and sweetly perfumed, though insignificant flowers, which appear in late winter through to spring. These low, dense shrubs are useful border plants and may also be grown as understorey plants under taller trees and shrubs.

CULTIVATION Sweet boxes need moist yet well-drained soil with plenty of humus, partial or full shade, and a sheltered position. Propagate

ABOVE The red berries of *Sarcococca ruscifolia* persist through many months. This hardy plant is tolerant of dry shade, pollution and poor soil.

by division in late winter or from semi-ripe cuttings in summer.

CLIMATE There are species suited to various climatic zones.

SPECIES *S. confusa*, zone 6, a dense shrub, to 2 m (6 ft), has attractive foliage and small, white flowers, followed by black berries. *S. hookeriana*, zone 6, forms a dense clump of upright, somewhat arching stems which grows to around 2 m (6 ft). Small, fragrant, white flowers are followed by black berries. *S. ruscifolia*, zone 8, forms a dense clump to about 1 m (3 ft) high, with cream, scented flowers and red berries.

Sarracenia (fam. Sarraceniaceae)
Pitcher plant

These eight species of insect-trapping, carnivorous plants from swampy areas of eastern North America are grown mostly as curiosities. The pitchers are beautifully veined and decorative. Each leaf is folded over on itself, forming a pitcher which traps the insects.

CULTIVATION In climatic zones lower than those recommended, grow in shallow pots in a cool greenhouse or conservatory, in a mix of sphag-

ABOVE *Sarracenia alata*, or yellow trumpet, grows naturally on swamp margins in many areas of the United States.

num moss, leaf mould and sharp sand. Stand pots in shallow trays of water during the growing season. In winter, keep barely moist. Always use lime-free water. In the garden, grow in a sunny position with moist, acid soil containing plenty of humus. Propagate by division in spring.

CLIMATE There are species suited to various climatic zones.

SPECIES *S. flava,* yellow pitcher plant, zone 7, is a tall-growing species with leaves over 1 m (3 ft) long. The leaves are greenish yellow with crimson throats, and the flowers are yellow. *S. leucophylla*, zone 8, is another tall species, also growing over 1 m (3 ft). The leaves are green and the white lid is veined with purplish red. The flowers are deep crimson or purple. *S. psittacina.* parrot pitcher, zone 8, has green leaves, to 20 cm (8 in) long, veined with red, that tend to lie horizontally. *S. purpurea*, common pitcher plant, zone 3, has 30 cm (12 in) long leaves, which also tend to lie down rather than stand upright. They are green with purple-red veining.

Sasa (fam. Poaceae)
Kuma bamboo grass

Native to eastern Asia, these small species of bamboo are all rhizomatous plants. Sprouts come up some distance apart and grow into single, erect stems. Cultivars are available with variations in stem and leaf colors. Suitable for growing in tubs, Sasa may be invasive if left to grow wild.

CULTIVATION Grow in well-drained soil, in sun or shade. Add compost or manure to the soil before planting. This plant is frost-tolerant. Propagate by dividing clumps in late winter or early spring.

CLIMATE Zone 8.

SPECIES *S. veitchii*, dwarf bamboo or kuma bamboo grass, is a small, hardy bamboo, growing to just over 1 m (3 ft). The thick leaves whiten at the margins in fall. A smaller form, known as minor, is available.

Savory (*Satureja* species, fam. Lamiaceae)

Comprising around 30 species of herbaceous plants from temperate parts of the northern hemisphere, the genus includes the two herbs, summer and winter savory. The leaves are used both fresh and dried in cooking, and the dried leaves are sometimes included in pot-pourri.

ABOVE The very ornamental dwarf bamboo, *Sasa veitchii*, grows from a running rhizome, so may need confining with root barriers.

ABOVE Winter savory, *Satureja montana*, has strongest flavor when grown in full sun with no added fertilizer.

CULTIVATION Grow both species from seed in rich, well-drained soil in a sunny situation, although winter savory may also be grown from cuttings or by division. Replace plants every few years.

CLIMATE Zone 8 for *S. hortensis*; zone 6 for *S. montana*.

SPECIES *S. hortensis*, summer savory, zone 8, is a bushy annual, to about 30 cm (12 in) high, with narrow, dark green leaves and pale lilac or white, tubular flowers in late summer. The leaves have a sweet, spicy flavor and are used to flavor bean dishes, vinegar and salad dressings. *S. montana*, winter savory, zone 6, is a perennial shrub, to 30 cm (12 in) high, with dark green, pointed leaves and small, white to lilac, tubular flowers in summer. It has a stronger flavor than summer savory and is used to flavor meats like chicken and pork.

Saxifraga (fam. Saxifragaceae)

This genus consists of well over 300 species of lovely, dwarf perennials which are found in temperate and alpine areas throughout the world. Many cultivars have been developed and these make attractive additions to cool-climate rock and alpine gardens. Although the genus has been divided into 16 groups to aid identification, there is still some dispute over which species are actually grown. Many are cultivated in the US, particularly by rock-garden specialists. The leaves are variable and may be linear or geraniumlike, or often variegated, while some form succulent rosettes. The flower clusters are mainly pink to purple, white, cream or yellow, and are usually borne on spikes above the low, sometimes clump-forming foliage.

CULTIVATION Requirements vary widely, some species needing shade and moist soil, others requiring full sun and very well drained soil. Some need acid soil, others alkaline conditions. Gardeners wishing to grow saxifrages should consult a specialist book on alpines to ascertain plant needs. Most are propagated by division or offsets in spring.

CLIMATE There are species suited to various climatic zones.

SPECIES *S. paniculata*, zone 2, from central Europe, forms mats of longish, gray-green leaves, carried in rosettes. The plant flowers in early summer, bearing panicles of cream-white

BELOW *Saxifraga stolonifera* is grown for its attractive, heavily veined foliage. The tiny, white flowers are a bonus.

blooms. It grows to a height of about 15 cm (6 in) and will spread to about 30 cm (12 in). There are numerous varieties and cultivars available. Grow in a well-drained, alkaline soil, in full sun. *S. rosacea*, zone 6, is one of the mossy saxifragas, forming clumps of bright green leaves of variable shape only 8 cm (3 in) high. The usually white, open flowers are borne in spring. Cultivars provide masses of flowers in a range of red, bright carmine and pink. *S. stolonifera*, Aaron's beard, mother of thousands, roving sailor or strawberry geranium, zone 8, is a native of Japan. It has geranium-like, olive green leaves, attractively veined in silver, and long spikes of white, spring flowers. Ideal for growing in a hanging basket, it prefers an acid soil and semi-shade. It forms clumps of about 30 cm (12 in) in height. The main feature of the many cultivars is the prettily variegated leaves. *S. umbrosa*, zone 7, grows to a height and spread of around 20 cm (8 in), forming rosettes of fleshy leaves. A profusion of tiny, starry, white flowers appears on tall stems in spring. Grow this species in shade with moist soil. Cultivars of this and other species are available. Consult local garden centers and mail order growers for types suited to local conditions.

ABOVE Large, gold-tipped stamens protrude from the starry, scarlet flowers of *Scadoxus multiflorus* subsp. *katherinae*, an unusual, bulbous plant.

Scadoxus (fam. Amaryllidaceae)
Blood lily

There are nine species of bulbous plants, with striking and unusual flowers, in this genus from tropical Africa. Formerly included with the genus *Haemanthus*, these nine species have been separated out after varied cell structure was identified. In frost-prone climates, grow these bulbs in an intermediate to warm conservatory or greenhouse.

CULTIVATION In the greenhouse, grow in pots of soil-based potting compost. Plant the bulbs shallowly in fall, with the necks showing above compost level. Ensure maximum light, but shade plants from direct sun. Water normally when in full growth, but as the leaves start dying, gradually reduce watering, and keep the compost dry while the plants are dormant in fall and winter. Propagate from offsets when dormant, or from seed sown when ripe and germinated at 21°C (70°F).

CLIMATE Zone 10.

SPECIES *S. multiflorus* is a bulbous perennial producing rounded heads of red, summer flowers followed by small, orange berries. Subspecies *katherinae* has foliage with distinctly wavy margins. *S. puniceus* has large basal leaves that form a tall stem of sheathed leaf stalks. In spring or summer, yellow-green to pink or scarlet flowers appear.

Scaevola (fam. Goodeniaceae)
Fan flower

Most of the around 90 species of small shrubs, perennials and vines belonging to this genus are Australian natives, although some are found in subtropical and tropical regions of Asia, Polynesia, Africa and America. Many of the cultivated Australian species have distinctive, fan-shaped, blue flowers, the five petals being arranged on only one side. These are borne in profusion over many months, but mainly in spring and summer. They make excellent plants for massed displays, rockeries and for trailing over embankments, and are also suitable for pots. In the US, the frost-tender scaevolas are becoming increasingly popular for summer bedding and for summer display in patio containers and hanging baskets. They can also be grown in a cool greenhouse or conservatory.

CULTIVATION Propagate from seed sown in spring and germinated at 21°C (70°F) or propagate from softwood cuttings in spring or summer, in a heated propagating case. If growing under glass in pots, use soil-based potting compost and provide bright light, but shade from direct sun. For outdoor display, plant out when frosts are over in well-drained but moisture-retentive soil, in a sunny or partially shady spot.

CLIMATE Zone 10.

SPECIES *S. aemula*, fairy fan flower, a native of Australia, is a prostrate, mat-forming plant with blue or purple-blue flowers in summer. *S. albida* is a spreading plant about 30 cm (12 in) high, producing white, pale blue or mauve flowers from spring through to summer. *S. calendulacea* is a groundcover plant, growing naturally on sand dunes where it is a useful sand binder. The blue flowers seem to appear throughout the year. *S. crassifolia*, from Western Australia, is a rounded shrub, about 1 m (3 ft) high and wide, with thick, serrated, dark green leaves and bright blue or mauve flowers. *S. frutescens*, beach naupaka, from Polynesia and northern Australia, is a spreading shrub, to 3 m (10 ft) high. The leaves are fleshy and the white flowers, streaked with purple, are followed by white fruits. *S. ramosissima*, from New South Wales, has a scrambling habit, spreading to 1 m (3 ft), and growing to 25 cm (10 in) tall. It produces large, blueish purple, summer flowers. *S. striata*, from Western Australia, is a low-growing, bushy shrub, to 30 cm (12 in), with a spreading habit. The deep purple flowers have a yellow throat.

Schefflera (fam. Araliaceae)

There are around 700 species in this genus of fast-growing shrubs or small trees, which occur naturally in tropical and warm regions of the world. Very popular outdoors in subtropical and tropical climates as ornamental foliage plants, some are elsewhere well known as indoor plants. The glossy, green leaves hanging from the tops of the stems form an umbrella shape. Most species have long spikes of white or greenish white flowers, although they may be red, followed by dense clusters of purple to red berries.

CULTIVATION In frost-prone climates, grow as house plants or in a warm greenhouse or conservatory. Use soil-based potting compost. Plants need good light, but shade from direct sun. Outdoors grow in full sun or partial shade and moist yet well-drained soil. Propagate from seed sown in spring and germinated at 21°C (70°F), or from semi-ripe cuttings in a heated propagating case, in summer.

CLIMATE Zone 10 or tropical for most species. *S. heptaphylla* can be grown in zone 9.

ABOVE The intense, cerise-purple flowers on this *Scaevola striata* help to explain the increasing popularity of the scaevolas.

ABOVE Umbrella tree, *Schefflera actinophylla*, grows rapidly in warm climates. Its flowers attract parrots and honeyeaters.

SPECIES *S. actinophylla*, umbrella tree, occurs naturally in rainforests of northern Australia. Growing to 10 m (33 ft) tall, this tree has deep, glossy green leaves, long spikes of crimson flowers borne at the top of the plant from late summer to early spring, and masses of dark purple to red berries. This species will not tolerate heavy frosts. It is widely grown as an indoor plant. *S. digitata*, patete, from New Zealand, is a small tree, 4–8 m (13–26 ft) high. The glossy, dark green leaves have sheathing stalks and the spikes of green flowers are followed by small, purplish black berries. The soft wood of this tree was used by the Maoris for fire wood. *S. heptaphylla*, from Asia, is a tall shrub or small tree in cultivation, but grows to 12–25 m (40–80 ft) in its habitat. The leaves are borne in eights and the white flowers are followed by purplish fruits.

Schinus (Fam. Anacardiaceae)
Pepper tree

This genus contains around 25 species of evergreen trees, all natives of South America, and all of graceful habit. These deliciously aromatic trees are mostly grown as shade or street trees. They are not generally recommended for the smaller garden as they have strong surface roots.

CULTIVATION In climates prone to hard frosts, grow as pot plants in an intermediate greenhouse or conservatory, using soil-based potting compost. Provide good light, but shade from direct sun. Outdoors, grow in well-drained yet moisture-retentive soil, in full sun. Propagate from seed in spring or semi-ripe cuttings in summer, both in a heated propagating case.

CLIMATE Zone 9 or 10.

SPECIES *S. molle*, pepper tree or Peruvian mastic tree, is probably the best known species, a native of South America and growing to 25 m (80 ft) in height. It has a wide-spreading crown and weeping branches clothed with green, pinnate leaves, and pendulous trusses of white-yellow flowers in winter through to summer. The fruits are reddish pink. Trunks of old trees become gnarled and furrowed. *S. terebinthifolius*, Brazilian pepper tree, is a smaller tree of about 6 m (20 ft), with stiffer, more upright branches. Drooping sprays of tiny white, summer flowers are followed by clusters of bright red berries.

ABOVE The pendulous growth of *Schinus molle* gives light shade and is suitable for growing outdoors in zone 9.

Schizanthus (fam. Solanaceae)

Butterfly flower, poor man's orchid

Native to Chile, these ten species of spring- and summer-flowering annuals are valued for their rather exotic flowers and pale green, fern-like foliage. In cool climates, grow these frost-tender plants as pot plants in a cool greenhouse or conservatory, or treat them as tender, summer bedding plants.

CULTIVATION For summer flowering sow seed in mid-spring, germinated at 16°C (61°F) or sow in late summer for winter-flowering pot plants. Under glass, grow in pots of soil-based potting compost and provide good light, but shade from sun. In the garden, plant out when frosts are over in a sunny and sheltered position with well-drained, yet moist soil.

CLIMATE Zone 10.

SPECIES *S. pinnatus* has produced many of the hybrids that we grow today. Most popular are dwarf cultivars. A good seed catalogue should list several. Also worth growing is *S.* x *wiseto-nensis* which is similar to *S. pinnatus*.

Schizophragma (fam. Hydrangaceae)

From China and Japan, these four species of summer-flowering climbers are closely related to *Hydrangea*. For cool areas only, they are sometimes more spectacular than the climbing Hydrangea species, *H. anomala* subsp. *petio-laris*, and are useful for covering pergolas, tree trunks and walls.

CULTIVATION These climbers like a rich, moist loam with added manure or leaf mould. They will thrive in partial shade or full sun. Plant in fall or spring, mulch the root area, and train the plant as it grows onto the chosen support. Remove the spent blooms wherever possible, as well as dead or straggly branches. Propagate from cuttings from early to late summer. Layers of mature growth will also strike in about 12 months.

CLIMATE Zone 5 for *S. hydrangeoides*, although zone 7 is needed for *S. integrifolium*.

SPECIES *S. hydrangeoides*, Japanese hydrangea vine, from Japan and Korea, is a very vigorous plant, which climbs by means of aerial roots. It

ABOVE The richly colored flowers of *Schizanthus* hybrids are backed by soft, ferny leaves. Plants come in a broad palette of colors.

ABOVE The flowers of *Schizophragma hydrangeoides* closely resemble those of many hydrangeas. Provide a wall or other very strong support.

can reach to 10 m (33 ft) or more. The hairy, serrated, deep green leaves have red stalks, and the flattened flower heads, which are 25–30 cm (10–12 in) across, are made up of tiny, cream flowers that are surrounded by ornamental, cream bracts. *S. integrifolium* is a native of China and also reaches heights of at least 10 m (33 ft). It has oval, deep green leaves, sometimes with finely toothed edges, and in summer produces 30 cm (12 in) wide heads of cream-white flowers, with large, cream bracts around the edge.

Schlumbergera

(formerly *Zygocactus*, fam. Cactaceae)

Christmas cactus, crab cactus

These epiphytic cactuses from Brazil include the Christmas cactus and the similar crab cactus. They are both popular and easily grown pot plants for the home or intermediate greenhouse or conservatory, flowering in fall and winter.

CULTIVATION Grow in cactus compost formulated for epiphytes. Plants can be grown in hanging baskets if desired. Provide good light, but shade from direct sun. Maintain a humid atmosphere. Water normally, but keep only slightly moist in the winter and spring following flowering. Propagate in summer from cuttings of stem sections rooted with bottom heat.

CLIMATE Zone 10. Must be frost-free.

SPECIES *S.* x *buckleyi* is the familiar Christmas cactus, which produces bright red blooms in the winter. Rather similar and often confused with that hybrid is *S. truncata*, the crab cactus, but the stem sections have toothed edges, resembling a crab's claw. The flowers in shades of pink, red, orange and white are produced in fall and winter.

Sciadopitys (fam. Sciadopityaceae)

Japanese umbrella pine

In appearance this is one of the most attractive of all conifers. Native to Japan, this tree is often planted around temples.

CULTIVATION The Japanese umbrella pine needs a slightly acid to neutral, reasonably fertile and

ABOVE The fall- and winter-flowering schlumbergeras come in a range of dazzling colors and are easily grown as pot plants in the home or greenhouse.

ABOVE Whorls of lovely, shiny leaves like the spokes of an umbrella make *Sciadopitys verticillata* a highly sought-after plant.

well-drained, yet moist soil. Choose a position in partial shade, or in full sun with shade in the hottest part of the day. Propagate from semi-ripe cuttings in summer, rooted with bottom heat, or from seed in spring, in a garden frame.

CLIMATE Zone 6.

SPECIES *S. verticillata*, the only species, is a very tall tree in its native habitat, but in culti-vation is very slow growing, rarely achieving more than tall shrub dimensions. Sections of its branches clothed with dense whorls of upward-facing leaves, or needles, alternate with bare sections up to 15 cm (6 in) long and about 1 cm (⅓ in) thick, covered with brown, flattened scale leaves. The glossy, dark green, soft needles are quite distinctive, being 10–15 cm long (4–6 in), 2–3 mm (¹⁄₁₀ in) wide, blunt-tipped, and very ornamental. This plant's extremely slow growth in its earlier years makes it a per-fect tub plant or bonsai subject. In an estab-lished garden, in a cool, moist climate, it would be possible to see a specimen of at least 10 m (33 ft) tall and roughly conical in habit, possi-bly bearing cones.

Scilla (fam. Hyacinthaceae)
Squill

There are about 90 species in this genus of bul-bous plants, native to Europe and temperate parts of Africa and Asia. They are rather like hyacinths, bearing spikes of either single or clustered flowers.

CULTIVATION These bulbs make a pretty display under deciduous trees or in rock gardens. Easily grown in almost any soil, in cool climates, they tolerate sun or semi-shade and can be left in the ground for several years. Propagate by dividing clumps or from offsets when dormant, or from seed sown when ripe in a garden frame. Plants grown from seed may not flower for up to five years.

CLIMATE There are species suited to various climatic zones.

ABOVE *Scilla peruviana* tends to grow lax and flop over when conditions are too shady. However, the royal blue flowers can still be enjoyed.

SPECIES *S. bifolia*, zone 6, grows to 15 cm (6 in) high, with blue, star-shaped flowers, sometimes white, in early spring. It is good for mass plant-ing in cool temperate climates. *S. mis-chtschenkoana* (syn. *S. tubergeniana*), zone 6, to only 10 cm (4 in) high, has pale blue, almost white flowers, with darker central markings, in late winter to early spring. *S. peruviana*, Cuban lily or hyacinth of Peru, zone 8, is in fact native to the Mediterranean. Growing to 25 cm (10 in), it has rounded clusters of deep mauve flowers, from late spring to early summer. The strap-like foliage is a glossy olive to dark green. This species prefers a warm temperate climate. *S. siberica*, zone 5, Siberian squill, grows to 20 cm (8 in), producing loose clusters of bright blue flowers in early spring. Cultivars of this species are available.

Scleranthus (fam. Caryophyllaceae)

This small genus of ten species of mostly alpine, cushion-forming plants are found worldwide. They make interesting additions to alpine or rockery gardens and attractive groundcovers. They can be grown between paving slabs or stones.

CULTIVATION *S. biflorus* is probably the best known species and this and others will need seeking out from alpine specialists. These plants need sharply drained, sandy soil which is able to retain adequate moisture. Make sure the soil is free from perennial weeds before planting, as the weeds not only spoil the appearance of these plants, but may in fact smother them. Propagate from seed, or by division of the plants in either spring or fall.

CLIMATE Zone 7.

SPECIES S. *biflorus*, knawel or green rocks, a native of eastern Australia and New Zealand, forms a rounded cushion of bright green, moss-like foliage, spreading to about 35 cm (14 in). Tiny, bright green flowers appear in spring. This perennial plant is suitable for rockeries or as groundcover, with an attractive appearance whether massed or as a feature plant. S. *brockiei* is an open, tufted perennial from New Zealand, with tiny, narrow, soft leaves and pairs of minute, stalkless flowers without petals. S. *pungens*, from South Australia, is a cushion-forming plant, spreading to about 40 cm (16 in), with slender, stiff leaves, 1 cm (⅓ in) long, and white flowers held amongst the foliage. S. *uniflorus*, from New Zealand, is a compact, tufted perennial which grows to 20 cm (8 in) across. The tiny, leathery leaves are quite rigid and pressed close to the stems, and the solitary flowers are stalkless.

Scutellaria (fam. Lamiaceae)
Skullcap

Some species in this genus of around 300 species of annual or perennial, herbaceous plants are shrub-like, although stems do not become very woody. Scutellarias are mostly native to mountainous and temperate regions of the world, though a few species are indigenous to the tropics. Many are suitable for mixed borders and some small species are suited to rock gardens.

CULTIVATION Scutellarias are best grown in a light, very well-drained soil. Gravelly or sandy types are especially suitable. Soil should be either alkaline or neutral. Choose a position in full sun, although plants will also tolerate dappled shade, as cast by trees, provided it is not too heavy. Small species can, if desired, be grown in an alpine house. In this instance, grow in pans or half pots of well-drained, soil-based potting compost. Ensure good light and provide an airy atmosphere. Propagate from seed sown in fall in a garden frame, by division in early spring, or from soft, basal cuttings in spring.

CLIMATE Depends on the species.

ABOVE *Scleranthus biflorus* forms emerald green cushions as it spreads over and between rocks. It needs ample moisture but must not sit in water.

ABOVE *Scutellaria indica* is a useful, small species for the rock garden or mixed border. It flowers profusely in summer.

SPECIES *S. alpina* is a hardy, spreading perennial from Europe and Central Asia, growing to 15 cm (6 in) high. It has toothed, oval leaves and purple flowers in mid to late summer. *S. costaricana*, from Costa Rica, grows between 45 cm and 1 m (18–40 in) high, with almost heartshaped leaves and clusters of orange-scarlet flowers with yellow throats, in early summer. In cool climates, this species requires greenhouse conditions. *S. indica* is a hardy perennial from China and Japan which grows to 30 cm (12 in). It has small, hairy leaves and light purplish blue or slate-blue flowers, in summer through to early fall. Var. *parvifolia*, with lilac-blue flowers, attains a height of 25 cm (10 in) and a spread of about 30 cm (12 in).

Sedum (fam. Crassulaceae)

Stonecrop

This large genus comprises more than 300 succulent species which occur mostly in northern temperate regions, but having some which are native to tropical areas. Ranging in size from tiny, mat-forming groundcovers to dwarf, shrub-like plants, they may be annuals, perennials or subshrubs. The plants are very variable and the leaves may be a variety of shapes and sizes, but they always come in crowded whorls. The five-petalled, star-like flowers, borne mostly in clusters, may be white, yellow, reddish pink or violet. Many are grown in the open garden but a great number are popular as potted plants.

CULTIVATION Grow the hardy species in a well-drained rock garden or border, in full sun. In climates prone to frost, tender species are grown in an intermediate greenhouse or conservatory, or as house plants, in well-drained, gritty, soil-based potting compost. Provide maximum light and an airy atmosphere. Keep plants only slightly moist in winter. Propagate from seed in spring, by division in spring, or from softwood cuttings in summer.

CLIMATE There are species suited to various climatic zones.

ABOVE In the large *Sedum* genus, many species have yellow, starry flowers, those emerging from the base of the rosettes standing well above the leaves.

SPECIES *S. acre*, zone 5, known as wall pepper in Europe, has several varieties and forms, all with small, pale yellow flowers. *S. adolphii* and *S. nussbaumeranum*, zone 9, both from Mexico and closely related, are very alike and often confused. The former has a fleshy, branching stem with alternate, thick, yellowish green leaves, 3.5 cm (1½ in) long, with reddish margins, which taper to a point. The flowers are white. *S. nussbaumeranum* differs only in that the leaves are not margined in red. *S. bellum*, zone 9, another Mexican species, forms a tight rosette of white, mealy leaves, which sends up a leafy, flowering stem in the winter growth period, although the dense, white flowers do not appear until the following winter. The rosette dies after it produces tiny, basal offsets, which then take a summer rest. *S. morganianum*, burro's tail or donkey's tail, zone 9, is a well-known species from Mexico, which sends out long, pendulous stems with blueish green, curved and pointed, thick leaves and terminal, rosy red flowers. *S. multiceps*, zone 8, from Algeria, is a small, erect plant with the appearance of a miniature Joshua tree (*Yucca brevifolia*). *S. pachyphyllum*, pink baby's toes or jelly beans, is so called because of the pink tips on the ends of the thick, cylindrical, glaucous, blue leaves. *S. rubrotinctum*, zone 8, which is from Guatemala, is a prostrate plant with glossy, green leaves just like jelly beans, which turn a reddish color in the sun. The flowers are bright yellow. Cultivar 'Aurora' is very attractive, with pink leaves striped longitudinally in light green. *S. sieboldii*, zone 9, from Japan, is another of the species which rests in rosette form when dormant, sending out drooping, red stems of blueish, almost circular leaves with serrated margins, borne in whorls, which turn red in fall. The pink flowers form small, flat cymes. There is a variegated leaf form which makes an excellent basket specimen. *S. spathulifolium*, zone 7, which comes from British Columbia and California, forms mats of small, flat, blue rosettes, about 2.5 cm (1 in) across, with yellow flowers. *S. spectabile*, zone 7, grows to a height and spread of about 50 cm (20 in). It has large, spoon-shaped leaves and large cymes of pink flowers. The leaves die back to dormant rosettes for the resting season. Several cultivars of this sedum are available. Because of its flowering in late summer to fall, it is a great asset in the garden. *S. stahlii*, zone 9, coral beads, is a prostrate plant which has red leaves and produces bright yellow flowers.

Selaginella (fam. Selaginellaceae)
Little club moss

A large group of primitive plants, there are about 700 species distributed throughout tropical and subtropical regions of the world, with some occuring in temperate climates. Although moss-like in appearance, they reproduce from spores, like ferns. They are shallow rooted and low growing, creeping along the ground, making good groundcovers for damp, shady spots. They also do well in pots and hanging baskets. Colors of foliage include both light and

ABOVE A popular container plant, *Selaginella kraussiana* 'Aurea' has fine, distinctly gold growth. Allow foliage to overflow the pot.

dark green, gold and blue-green shades. Although they tend to multiply freely in suitable conditions, they are not difficult to pull out if they are unwanted.

CULTIVATION Most of the species listed here need to be grown in an intermediate to warm greenhouse or conservatory, in pots of soil-based potting compost containing some leaf mould, if it is available. Ensure good light (but shade from direct sun), and a humid atmosphere. Keep compost moist at all times. Outdoors, grow in a partially shady spot, with moist soil containing plenty of humus. Propagate by division in spring.

CLIMATE Zone 10, but *S. braunii* will survive in zone 8.

SPECIES Garden centers mainly carry plants of cultivated varieties rather than the species, as enthusiasts tend to collect a range of foliage forms and colors. *S. braunii*, from China, has small, silvery green leaves and a compact form. It is cultivated outdoors in mild regions in sheltered-shade positions. *S. kraussiana*, spreading club moss, is the species many people consider a pest, although it is decorative. It is an African species which has become naturalized in most warmer parts of the world. There is a golden form 'Aurea' and a more compact variety cushion type known as 'Brownii'. *S. pallescens*, known as moss fern or sweat plant in the United States, is native to North and South America. It can be grown outdoors in the tropics or subtropics, but requires greenhouse conditions elsewhere. *S. uncinata*, rainbow fern or peacock moss, has a metallic sheen of blue-green lighting up the foliage. Originally from China, it has become naturalized in warm and tropical areas.

Selenicereus (fam. Cactaceae)
Queen of the night

Originating from tropical America and the Caribbean, these epiphytic climbing, or somewhat pendulous cactuses have long, sinuous branches, producing aerial roots. The stems are ribbed and spiny. The very large, perfumed, mostly white flowers are nocturnal. The buds are woolly and brown.

CULTIVATION Outside the tropics, these cactuses should be grown in a warm conservatory or greenhouse, in pots or hanging baskets of cactus compost formulated for epiphytes. Species with climbing stems need supports. Provide bright light (but shade from direct sun), and a humid atmosphere. Water normally when in full growth, but keep the compost only slightly moist in winter. Propagate in summer from cuttings of stem sections, rooting them with bottom heat.

CLIMATE Tropical.

SPECIES *S. grandiflorus*, queen of the night, the most commonly grown species, has cream or white, sweetly scented flowers, 20–25 cm (8–10 in) long, which are quite spectacular. The slender, blueish green stems bear short, yellow spines. *S. hamatus* has four-angled stems with

ABOVE Flowers of the exquisite *Selenicereus grandiflorus* open at dusk but fade by the following morning.

hook-like projections along the edges. The large, white flowers, 30 cm (12 in) across, are borne sparingly. *S. macdonaldiae*, with the largest flower of all cactuses, is also known as queen of the night. Its white flowers have almost no fragrance.

Sempervivum (fam. Crassulaceae)
Houseleek, hen and chickens

Endemic to mountainous and high areas of Europe, western Asia and Morocco, these ornamental, succulent rosettes make good cover for walls, banks and rock gardens. The plants are steeped in folklore. In days past, these plants had many, many uses, from protection against lightning and curing warts and corns to, curiously, helping a maiden select a husband. Her suitors would be presented with a young plant each and the one who had the best plant after a period of time was the right choice!

CULTIVATION Grow in very well drained, gritty soil, which can be quite poor, in a sunny position. Hairy species can be grown in pans of gritty, soil-based compost in an alpine house, to protect them from excessive rain. Propagate in spring or summer from young offsets, or from seed in spring.

ABOVE Flowers of *Sempervivum* species develop on thick, upright stems. This rosette will die after flowering, but its many offsets will continue to grow.

CLIMATE There are species suited to various climatic zones.

SPECIES *A. arachnoideum*, cobweb houseleek, zone 5, from the European Alps, is a dainty, little plant, criss-crossed with fine, white hairs. Rarely growing more than 8–10 cm (3–4 in) high, it has pink to crimson flowers in summer. *S. ciliosum*, zone 6, from Greece, has produced several varieties. All have fine hair on the edges of the leaves and form neat rosettes. All have greenish yellow flowers. *S. marmoreum*, zone 5, from the Balkans and southern Russia, forms flattish rosettes, spreading to form wide mats. The leaves are olive green, tinged red or brown. The red flowers have white tips. *S. tectorum*, zone 4, the most common European species, has many varieties and forms, all with red-tipped leaves and pink flowers.

Senecio (fam. Asteraceae)

This huge genus comprises over 1000 species, with a broad distribution throughout the world, and includes annuals, perennials, evergreen shrubs and climbers. They are variable in size, shape and habit. The daisy-like flowers, mostly in yellow but sometimes red, orange, blue or purple, are borne in clusters.

CULTIVATION These plants need a reasonably fertile, well-drained soil, full sun and protection from frost. In frost-prone climates, grow tender species (including those listed) in a cool to intermediate, light, airy greenhouse or conservatory, in pots of well-drained, soil-based potting compost. Succulent species need to be grown in a large, shallow container so that their roots have a free run. Tip prune shrubby types regularly to encourage bushy growth. Propagate from cuttings.

CLIMATE Zone 9 for most species listed here; zone 10 for *S. macroglossus*.

SPECIES *S. articulatus*, candle plant, from South Africa, is a succulent plant with jointed stems which take on red colors in sunlight. It has gray-green leaves and yellowish flowers rather like dandelions. *S. cruentus* (syn. *Pericallis cruenta*), from the Canary Islands, is

BELOW Dusty miller, *Senecio cineraria*, zone 9, is grown primarily for the foliage contrast of its decorative, gray leaves.

a perennial with purple flowers. *S. macro-glossus*, Cape or Natal ivy, is a twining climber from South Africa, with ivy-like leaves. There is also a variegated leaf form. The daisy-type flower heads are pale yellow. *S. petasitis*, velvet geranium, is a shrub to 2.5 m (8 ft) high and 3 m (10 ft) wide. The large, geranium-like leaves and stems are clothed in soft hairs. From late winter to spring, yellow flower heads appear on red stalks. *S. rowleyanus*, string of beads, string of pearls or green beads, from Namibia, is a succulent with small, creamy flower heads. This species makes a good basket plant, as the bead-like leaves on long stems trail gracefully over the side. *S. serpens*, blue chalk sticks, is a groundcovering succulent with fleshy, upright leaves. The stems and foliage are an unusual, intense shade of blue.

Senna (fam. Caesalpiniaceae)

Senna, cassia

This genus is found in tropical and temperate regions throughout the world. The evergreen or deciduous shrubs and trees have pinnate leaves, showy, mostly yellow flowers, and flattened or cylindrical, sometimes winged, pods. Dried pulp from some species' pods yields the medicinal drug, senna. Many species now in this genus were formerly classified as Cassia.

CULTIVATION In areas prone to frost, grow in an intermediate to warm conservatory or greenhouse, in pots of soil-based potting compost. Ensure maximum light and a moderately humid atmosphere. Never overwater plants and in winter be even more sparing. Pruning may be needed to restrict size, but only lightly prune *S. artemisioides* as it dislikes pruning, and never cut into the old wood of this species. Prune after flowering. Propagate in spring from seed germinated at 21°C (70°F), or from semi-ripe cuttings in summer, with basal warmth.

CLIMATE Zone 10 or tropical.

SPECIES *S. artemisioides*, silver cassia, an Australian native, to 1.5 m (5 ft), is low-branch-

ABOVE The fine foliage of silver cassia, *Senna artemisioides*, is highlighted by small, clear yellow flowers.

ing, with silvery gray leaves, pale yellow flowers and flattened pods. *S. candolleana* (syn. *S. bicapsularis*), a shrub to 3 m (10 ft), has thickish leaves comprising three to five pairs of leaflets and bright yellow flowers in late summer and fall. The slender pods are bean-shaped. *S. didymobotrya* is a shrub growing to 3 m (10 ft) high. The flower spikes, to 30 cm (12 in) long, are held on the stem tips. Yellow blooms appear intermittently, but the main flowering period is fall and winter. *S. multijuga* is a decorative small tree, growing 6–8 m (20–26 ft) high. Its very long leaves contain between 18 and 40 leaflets and the large, yellow flowers are followed by flattened pods.

Sequoia (fam. Taxodiaceae)

Redwood, coastal redwood

S. sempervirens is the only species in this genus and is famous for being the world's tallest tree, some specimens reaching heights of around 110 m (360 ft). Occurring on the west coast of the United States, particularly in California and Oregon, it is valued for its timber, which is used in internal woodwork in houses as well as for outdoor furniture.

ABOVE Redwood, *Sequoia sempervirens*, makes a magnificent lawn specimen for a large garden. It prefers a cool, moist climate.

CULTIVATION To achieve its full potential, *Sequoia* needs a cool climate with substantial rainfall throughout the year and a deep, fertile, well-drained soil, although it does adapt to warmer climates. Under favorable conditions, it makes quite fast growth, reaching about 10 m (33 ft) in ten years. Propagate in spring from seed germinated in a garden frame, or from semi-ripe cuttings in late summer, with bottom heat.

CLIMATE Zone 7.

SPECIES *S. sempervirens* is a tall, conical tree with very thick, reddish brown, furrowed bark, which is highly aromatic. The branches are borne in horizontal tiers, sometimes drooping slightly. The bright green, flattened leaves, about 2 cm (¾ in) long, are borne on the smaller side branches. The egg-shaped cones are carried at the ends of the small branches. The small, flattened seeds are released each year as the cones mature. There are several cultivars in different sizes and foliage color.

Sequoiadendron (fam. Taxodiaceae)
Giant sequoia, giant redwood, big tree

Native to the Sierra Nevadas in California and closely related to *Sequoia*, *Sequoiadendron giganteum*, the only species in this genus, is also a huge tree, although shorter than its relative, at about 80 m (260 ft). It holds the record, however, for yielding more timber than any other tree. Both are very long-lived, surviving 1000 years or more. It is distinguishable from *Sequoia* by its smaller leaves that are spirally arranged, rather than in two rows and flattened. Its cones are also larger.

CULTIVATION *Sequoiadendron*'s requirements are similar to those of *Sequoia*, but it does not tolerate warmer conditions as well and it is more tolerant of drier climates.

CLIMATE Zone 7.

ABOVE This slow-growing, stately tree, *Sequoiadendron giganteum*, is one to plant for posterity. Trees live an incredibly long time.

SPECIES *S. giganteum* (syn. *Wellingtonia gigantea*) is a dense, conical tree, growing to about 30 m (100 ft) in cultivation, while reaching 80 m (260 ft) in the wild. Its huge trunk, quite stout at the base, is covered in rough, deeply furrowed, reddish brown bark. The lowest branches are pendulous, often touching the ground, with upturned tips. The foliage is dark green and slightly prickly. It is a magnificent tree for large parks and gardens.

Serenoa (fam. Arecaceae)
Saw palmetto

This low-growing fan palm, native to the south-east of North America is most unusual, as the stems tend to be prostrate and creeping, eventually forming large colonies.

CULTIVATION *Serenoa* will grow in any soil, provided it is well drained, but prefers full sun or semi-shade. It does not tolerate frost, so in climates prone to frost, grow in an intermediate greenhouse, in a pot of soil-based compost. Propagate from seed or suckers.

CLIMATE Zone 9.

SPECIES *S. repens*, the only species, is rather like *Sabal minor*, which occurs in the same region of North America. It is distinguishable from that species by its toothed leaf stalks, its semi-prostrate, above-ground trunks, its more conspicuous white flowers, and its larger, egg-shaped, black fruits. The upright, fan-shaped leaves range in color from green to blueish green to silver. This interesting palm is well suited to exposed, coastal situations.

Serissa (fam. Rubiaceae)

This genus comprises one species of evergreen shrub from Southeast Asia. The oval, leathery leaves release an unpleasant odor when crushed, while the flowers are small and quite attractive. Grown outdoors in tropical and temperate climates, it needs greenhouse conditions in cooler climates. Grow in an intermediate greenhouse or conservatory. It can be used for bonsai.

CULTIVATION In the greenhouse, grow in pots of soil-based potting compost. Plants need maximum light, but shade from strong, direct sun. Water plants in moderation and keep only slightly moist in winter. Outdoors grow in a sheltered spot in full sun with moist yet well-drained soil. Propagate by layering in spring or from semi-ripe cuttings rooted in heat, in late summer.

CLIMATE Zone 10 to tropical.

ABOVE Saw palmetto, *Serenoa repens*, is very unusual for a palm, as its growth is almost prostrate.

ABOVE *Serissa japonica* 'Variegata' makes a good greenhouse pot plant, and is also sometimes used for bonsai.

SPECIES *S. japonica* (syn. *S. foetida*) is a small, rounded shrub, growing 30–60 cm (12–24 in) high, with small leaves and white flowers borne in the leaf axils. Cultivar 'Variegata' has cream-edged leaves and *S. j. rosea* has pink flowers.

Sesbania (fam. Papilionaceae)
Scarlet wisteria

There are about 50 species of shrubs, small trees and perennials in this genus from tropical and subtropical climates. The most commonly cultivated are the larger species with colorful flowers. The bark and leaves of some species have medicinal uses.

CULTIVATION In climates prone to frost, grow in an intermediate to warm greenhouse or conservatory, in pots of soil-based potting compost. Provide maximum light. If necessary, lightly prune in spring to maintain a good shape. Outdoors grow in a sunny, sheltered spot with moist yet well-drained soil. Propagate in spring from seed germinated at 16°C (61°F) or from semi-ripe cuttings in summer, with basal warmth.

CLIMATE Zone 10 or tropical.

SPECIES *S. drummondi* is a tall shrub, to 6 m (20 ft), with long leaves and yellow flowers.

BELOW Chains of vermilion pea flowers appear on *Sesbania tripetii* during summer. It is native to Brazil and Argentina.

S. emerus grows 5 m (16 ft) high, with yellow flowers which are spotted in dark purple. *S. grandiflora*, scarlet wisteria tree, is a much larger, but short-lived type, growing to 12 m (40 ft), producing red-pink or white flowers and fern-like leaves. *S. tripetii*, Brazilian glory pea or scarlet wisteria, has pendulous clusters of vermilion flowers.

Setaria (fam. Poaceae)

Found in warmer parts of the world, this genus includes around 100 species of annual and perennial grasses. Many yield bird seed and are also used as fodder grasses, while some species are valued as decorative additions to floral arrangements.

CULTIVATION Grow annual species from seed sown in a sunny spot in late spring or early summer; the perennials may be propagated from seed or by division. They need a warm situation but will do well in any reasonably fertile soil.

CLIMATE There are species suited to various climatic zones. Zone 9 for *S. drummondii*.

SPECIES *S. italica*, Italian millet, zone 6, is an annual grass, to 1.5 m (5 ft), with bristly leaves.

BELOW Palm grass, *Setaria palmifolia*, has finely ribbed leaves with a pleated look. It makes a tall groundcover for large areas.

S. palmifolia, palm grass, zone 10, is a perennial and the most decorative of the species. The almost 2 m (6 ft) long stems are clothed with smooth, broad leaves resembling some palm leaflets. This species can be grown under glass in frosty climates.

Shallot

(*Allium cepa* Aggregatum Group, fam. Alliaceae)

Eschalot, scallion

Closely related to chives, garlic, leek and onion, this plant is believed to have originated in the Middle East and then been introduced to Europe during the Crusades. The leaves and bulblets are chopped into salads, while the bulblets give a garlic flavor to cooked dishes. The shallot is a herbaceous, upright, perennial plant, treated as an annual. Growing to 45 cm (18 in), it has dark green, hollow, round leaves and greenish white flowers.

CULTIVATION Prepare soil by digging in well-aged manure or compost a fortnight before planting. At planting time, add a light dressing of lime or dolomite–about half to one cup per square metre(square yard). True shallots produce clusters of bulbs which should be separated and planted singly, spaced about 10 cm (4 in) apart, in rows 30 cm (12 in) apart. Plant shallots in the period early winter to early spring, with the tips just showing above soil level. Water after planting, but do not water again until new growth appears. Keep weeds under control as they compete for food and moisture, and dense weed growth can smother the plants and inhibit growth. Harvest the crop 16–20 weeks after planting. Pull the shallots, and place in an airy place out of the sun to dry the outer skin, which will then be easy to remove.

CLIMATE Zone 5.

Silene (fam. Caryophyllaceae)

Campion, catchfly

This genus consists of about 500 species of annuals, biennials and perennials, native mainly to the northern hemisphere. The greatest number is found in the Mediterranean region. Many are grown in rockeries or borders, while some are considered weeds. Those cultivated generally include the white- to pink-, red- and purple-flowered forms. Most flower from late spring through summer.

CULTIVATION Silene prefers a light, sandy soil and a sunny position. Propagate annuals from seed

BELOW Perennial *Silene schafta* is studded with dainty, pink flowers in summer and fall. It suits informal meadow plantings.

ABOVE Shallots have hollow, rounded leaves and the bulbs form in clusters.

and perennials by division, or from basal cuttings.

CLIMATE Zone 7 for most species; zone 6 for *S. dioica*.

SPECIES *S. dioica*, red campion, native to North Africa and most of Europe, is a rosette-forming perennial with 30–90 cm (12–36 in) long flower stems. The flowers are bright pink. There are several cultivars, including 'Rosea Plena', a pretty, double form. *S. laciniata* is a perennial, to 1 m (3 ft) high, with scarlet flowers. *S. pendula*, an annual growing to 40 cm (16 in) high, produces pale pink to white flowers during summer. *S. schafta*, from the Caucasus, is a mat-forming perennial, producing deep magenta or pink flowers in summer and fall.

Silver beet

(*Beta vulgaris* subsp. *cicla*, fam. Chenopodiaceae)

Swiss chard

Once very popular, silver beet is not eaten as much as spinach today. However, it is a delicious vegetable. The stems can be blanched and tossed in olive oil or made into a scrumptious gratin with blue cheese. The leaves can be steamed and simply tossed in butter or olive oil, or used as the basis of a frittata or salad. Silver beet is easy to grow and crops over a long period.

CULTIVATION Silver beet needs perfect drainage, abundant water and regular applications of nitrogen fertilizer to encourage leaf growth. While it adapts to a range of soils, it thrives in good quality soils. Propagate by seed sown in situ; if sown in pots, transplant when plants are about 8–10 cm (3–4 in) high. In cool districts, sow seed from spring to early summer, while in warmer districts, seed can be sown at almost any time of year. Plants started in spring will continue to crop until the following spring. When plants sown direct are about 10 cm (4 in) tall, thin to 30–45 cm (12–18 in) between plants, and 60–75 cm (24–30 in) between rows. Begin to harvest eight to ten weeks later, taking only two or three leaves from each plant. Remove by snapping or twisting off leaves, or by cutting close to the base. Silver beet is relatively free of most insect pests and diseases, but leaf spot may cause problems in humid areas. If this appears, remove worst-affected leaves and avoid overhead watering. Keep plants growing rapidly and harvest often.

CLIMATE Zone 5.

VARIETIES *Beta vulgaris* subsp. *cicla* is an upright-growing biennial best treated as an annual. Branching from ground level, it has white leaf stalks and deep green, mostly crinkled leaves. There are several forms with variously colored stems. These are very decorative and can even be grown in the flower garden. Try the cultivar 'Ruby Chard' which has brilliant red stems, somewhat like red-stemmed rhubarb.

Sinningia (fam. Gesneriaceae)

Gloxinia

Originating in tropical America, these beautiful plants often have attractive foliage, but they are mainly grown for their striking flowers, which come in shades of red, blue, purple and pink,

BELOW With regular water and fertilizer, silver beet grows rapidly. Pick leaves frequently to keep plants productive.

ABOVE This striking, two-toned gloxinia has flaring, crimson petals edged in white. Today's range of colors is vast.

sometimes spotted or fringed with white. Outside the subtropics or tropics, they are grown as pot plants in the warm greenhouse. They also make good house plants, best on a light windowsill. Most sinningias are deciduous perennials, growing from tubers and dying down in winter. However, there are some deciduous or evergreen, shrubby species. Most flower during the summer, the blooms typically being bell- or trumpet-shaped.

CULTIVATION The tubers of perennial sinningias are started into growth in early spring. Put them into trays of moist peat or peat substitute and provide plenty of warmth. When shoots appear, pot up tubers individually, using soilless potting compost. Plants need good light (but shade from direct sun), and a very humid atmosphere. In fall, the tubers are gradually dried off and stored over winter in a cooler place, and kept completely dry. Sinningias can also be raised from seed sown in spring and germinated at 21°C (70°F). Do not cover with compost. Another propagation method is from leaf

cuttings in spring or summer, in a heated propagating case.

CLIMATE Warmest parts of zone 10 or tropical.

SPECIES *S. canescens* (syn. *S. leucotricha*) is an upright grower with woolly, silver foliage and stems. Salmon to orange-red or pink flowers appear in small clusters in summer. *S. cardinalis*, cardinal flower, has hairy leaves marked with a darker green around the veins. The scarlet flowers are tubular and appear on short stalks above the foliage. *S. regina*, violet slipper or Cinderella slipper, from Brazil, has dark, velvety green leaves, veined in white above but red underneath. The violet flowers have a long, open bell shape. *S. speciosa*, florists' gloxinia, bears violet to red or white flowers in the wild, but a wider range of colors, including spotted varieties, in cultivation. Most of the florists' gloxinias are hybrids of *S. speciosa*. Their large, bell-shaped flowers have a rich range of colors.

Smithiantha (fam. Gesneriaceae)

Native to Mexico, this genus consists of four species of summer-flowering, tender perennials grown for their attractive, velvety foliage and terminal clusters of nodding tubular flowers.

CULTIVATION Outside the subtropics or tropics, grow as pot plants in an intermediate to warm

ABOVE *Smithiantha* 'Orange King' is worth growing for its foliage alone. It flowers in summer through to fall.

greenhouse or conservatory. They also make good house plants. Pot or repot the rhizomes in spring, using shallow pots of soilless potting compost. Plants need good light (but shade from direct sun), and a very humid atmosphere. Do not overwater them. Gradually dry off plants in fall and keep the rhizomes completely dry during the winter. Store them in a cooler place. Smithianthas can be propagated from seed sown in spring and germinated at 18°C (64°F).

CLIMATE Warmest parts of zone 10 or tropical.

SPECIES *S. cinnabarina* grows to 60 cm (24 in) high, producing red flowers, spotted yellow or white in the throat. The heart-shaped, deep green leaves have purple-streaked veins. *S. multiflora*, to 75 cm (30 in), has velvety, dark green leaves and white or cream flowers, with yellow throats. *S. zebrina* grows to 75 cm (30 in) high and has velvety, dark green leaves, with veins marked purple or brown. The scarlet and yellow flowers have spotted markings in the throat. Many fine hybrids of various species have been bred, including 'Orange King', with brilliant orange-red flowers through summer, and handsome deep green leaves, heavily marked in burgundy.

Solandra (fam. Solanaceae)
Chalice vine

These climbing, woody shrubs or vines have alternate, simple, entire leaves which are leathery and glossy. The large, funnel-shaped flowers are often fragrant, especially at night.

CULTIVATION Outside the warm subtropics or tropics, grow in an intermediate to warm greenhouse or conservatory. Grow in a large pot of soil-based potting compost. Provide maximum light, but shade from direct sun. The stems will need supports of some kind and can be trained into the roof. Prune in late winter to keep plant within its allotted space. Outdoors solandras like fertile soil and full sun. Propagate from seed in spring germinated at 18°C (64°F) or from

ABOVE *Solandra maxima*, a vigorous climber with very large, summer flowers, is spectacular in a large conservatory.

semi-ripe cuttings in summer, with basal warmth.

CLIMATE Warmest parts of zone 10 or tropical.

SPECIES *S. grandiflora*, the most commonly grown species, is a large, coarse vine, growing to 10 m (33 ft). It has large, glossy leaves and white solitary flowers which turn a brownish yellow color. *S. guttata*, gold cup or trumpet plant, is a climbing shrub from Mexico that blooms intermittently throughout the year. The pale yellow flowers have purple throats. *S. maxima*, golden chalice vine, is similar to *S. guttata*, but grows higher, reaching about 4–5 m (13–16 ft). It is also a native of Mexico. The 20 cm (8 in) long, chalice-shaped flowers are yellow and are conspicuously lined with purple.

Solanum (fam. Solanaceae)

In this genus there are about 1500 species of annuals, perennials, shrubs, trees and climbers, found in temperate and tropical regions throughout the world. Many species are native to tropical America. They may be evergreen, semi-evergreen or deciduous. Edible vegetables like the potato and eggplant are part of this genus, while many species are grown for their ornamental foliage, flowers and decorative berries. They are useful, quick-growing plants for both garden and pots. Many species are extremely poisonous if eaten.

CULTIVATION In the garden, solanums require a well-drained, alkaline or neutral soil, in a sunny position. In frost-prone climates, the tender species are grown in a cool to intermediate greenhouse in pots of soil-based potting compost. Climbers will need side shoots pruned back to three buds after flowering. Shrubs can be lightly trimmed in spring. Propagate in spring from seed germinated at 21°C (70°F), or for shrubs and climbers, from semi-ripe cuttings in summer, with basal warmth.

CLIMATE Zone 9 or 10 for the species listed.

SPECIES *S. aviculare*, kangaroo apple, zone 9, is native to Australia and New Zealand. It is a fast-growing but short-lived shrub, to 3 m (10 ft) high. The large, soft leaves are dark green to blueish green. The starry, blue to purple flowers, 4 cm (1½ in) in diameter, appear from spring through to fall, followed by green berries

BELOW The white-flowered *Solanum jasminoides* 'Album' is a vigorous climber, which flowers throughout summer and fall. It is not too hardy.

which ripen to yellow and red. *S. capsicastrum*, Christmas or winter cherry, zone 10, is often grown in pots. This shrub from Brazil has dark green, oval leaves, white flowers, and orange-scarlet berries. *S. jasminoides*, potato vine, zone 9, is a popular, quick-growing South American climber, covered in clusters of blueish white flowers for many months. *S. lanceolatum*, zone 10, is a prickly shrub growing about 2.5 m (8 ft) tall, with long, narrow leaves, large, lavender-blue flowers, and round, orange fruits. *S. pseudocapsicum*, zone 9, is known as Jerusalem cherry. There are a number of named cultivars suitable for pots. Their attractive, colorful fruits are poisonous. *S. rantonnetii*, zone 10, from Paraguay and Argentina, is a roundish, evergreen shrub with pendulous branches and glossy, bright green, oval foliage. Lovely, violet-blue flowers in summer and fall are followed by red fruits. Named varieties have larger flowers. *S. seaforthianum*, zone 10, a South American twining climber, grows to 6 m (20 ft), with deeply cut leaves and large clusters of starry, blue, summer flowers with yellow stamens, followed by small, scarlet berries. *S. wendlandii*, potato vine or paradise flower, zone 10, is a vigorous climber from Costa Rica. The bright green leaves are prickly and branched clusters of lilac-blue flowers are followed by large, round or oval fruits. *S. wrightii*, the potato tree, zone 10, from Brazil is fast growing to 5 m (16 ft). It has large, lobed leaves and scented, pale violet flowers in spring.

Soldanella (fam. Primulaceae)

These 11 or so species of alpine, perennial herbs are natives of mountain regions of Europe. Only a few species are cultivated, usually in rock gardens. Flowering very early in spring, they often push up and flower through the snow. The simple leaves, borne on long stalks, are usually rounded in shape, and the flowers are bell-shaped, with fringed lobes above the leaves.

CULTIVATION These plants need a cool, moist yet well-drained soil containing plenty of humus, and a position in partial shade, or full sun with

ABOVE One of the earliest of alpines to flower, *Soldanella hungarica* has dainty, lilac flowers with fringed petals.

ABOVE Baby's tears, *Soleirolia soleirolii*, forms a dense mat of growth, which creeps over soil or rocks.

shade during the hottest part of the day. Mulch with sharp sand or grit and ensure some protection from heavy rain in winter. Propagate from seed sown in a garden frame in fall, or by division after flowering in spring.

CLIMATE Zone 6. Cool climates are best.

SPECIES *S. hungarica* grows to 10 cm (4 in) high, with kidney-shaped leaves and lilac flowers. *S. minima*, to 10 cm (4 in), has round to oval leaves and white or pale blue flowers. *S. montana* is a mound-forming perennial, to 25 cm (10 in), with rounded, heart-shaped leaves with hairy stalks. The clusters of blue to lilac flowers appear in early spring. *S. villosa* has round leaves with hairy stalks and pale violet flowers.

Soleirolia (fam. Urticaceae)
Baby's tears

Indigenous to the Mediterranean, this creeping, monoecious perennial is an attractive ground-cover but can become invasive. The small, alternate, round leaves are bright green and the tiny, inconspicuous flowers are borne singly in the leaf axils. This genus was previously known as *Helxine*.

CULTIVATION Propagate by division in spring. Grow in shade or sun and in any garden soil. Can be damaged by hard frosts. In cold climates, grow under glass as a pot plant.

CLIMATE Zone 8. Cool to warm temperate climates.

SPECIES *S. soleirolii*, baby's tears, Irish moss or mind-your-own-business, is a delicate, carpeting plant with slightly hairy stems and tiny, round leaves with short leaf stalks.

Solidago (fam. Asteraceae)
Golden rod

In times past, healing properties have been attributed to these hardy herbaceous perennials from North America and Europe. Some species are quite vigorous and spreading. The alternate, simple leaves may be entire or toothed, and the daisy-type flowers are borne in sprays. Several species and numerous hybrids are grown in the US.

CULTIVATION These easy-care plants can become invasive especially in warm climates. *S. canadensis* can be invasive, although the new cultivars have helped to overcome this problem. Solidagos can be grown in almost any garden soil, in sun or partial shade. Tall types may require staking. Propagate by division of the clumps every three years, in spring and fall.

ABOVE Golden rod, *Solidago species*, has several forms, all with similar, golden flowers. This cultivar is a compact grower, to about 60 cm (24 in).

They can also be raised from seed sown in situ. Flowering will occur in the second year.

CLIMATE There are species suited to various climatic zones. All are very hardy.

SPECIES *S. canadensis*, to 1.5 m (5 ft), has a rhizome but no crown. Sprays of bright yellow flowers appear in late summer. *S. virgaurea*, European golden rod, is a hardy, upright perennial, 1 m (3 ft) high, with dense, terminal sprays of fluffy, yellow flower heads in late summer and fall. Var. *minuta* grows to 30 cm (12 in) and makes a suitable rock garden plant. There are many cultivars and hybrids of golden rod including dwarf or low-growing kinds which are the most popular with gardeners. A very well-known compact hybrid is *S.* 'Goldenmosa' which grows to 75cm with pale yellow flowers.

Sollya (fam. Pittosporaceae)
Bluebell creeper

Both species of this genus of hardy shrubs or climbers are native to south-western Australia.

The fresh, neat, bright green foliage and pretty, open, bell-shaped flowers make sollyas excellent garden or conservatory shrubs. They can be pruned to a compact bush or left to climb or cascade, in favorable conditions. They have a variety of uses, as flowering shrubs, cover for fences, stumps, trees and trellises, as hanging basket or pot plants, or as trailers for embankments.

CULTIVATION Sollyas tolerate a wide range of conditions, including partial shade. Light, well-drained soil and a warm, protected position produce vigorous growth and long flowering periods. In frost-prone climates, grow in a cool greenhouse in pots of soil-based potting compost. Shade from direct strong sun. Propagate from seed in spring, germinated at 16°C (61°F) or from softwood cuttings in early summer.

CLIMATE Warmest parts of zone 9.

SPECIES *S. heterophylla*, bluebell creeper, has neat, oval to lance-shaped leaves and pendulous clusters of bluebell-like flowers during spring and summer. The flowers are a clear, sky blue but may also be lavender-blue. Oval, fleshy, blue fruits develop after flowering.

BELOW Small, bell-shaped flowers dot the dense foliage of *Sollya heterophylla* any time through spring and summer.

Sophora (fam. Papilionaceae)
Kowhai

Widely distributed in temperate regions of the northern hemisphere, this genus of 50 evergreen and deciduous trees and shrubs also includes a few species from New Zealand. Mostly open, many-branched trees, they have alternate, feathery leaves and drooping clusters of pea-type flowers in spring or summer, followed by bean-like seed pods. They make good shade trees or lawn specimens.

CULTIVATION Sophoras are suitable for cool climates, but will tolerate hot conditions if they receive enough water in summer. Most prefer moist, well-drained soil, but will grow in sun or partial shade. Any tender species (zone 10 in list) can be grown in an intermediate greenhouse in frost-prone climates. Propagate from seed when ripe, in a garden frame, or from semi-ripe cuttings in summer, with basal warmth.

CLIMATE There are species suited to various climatic zones.

SPECIES *S. chrysophylla*, zone 10, from Hawaii, is a compact, deciduous shrub, to 3 m (10 ft).

BELOW The cream flowers of the Japanese pagoda tree, *Sophora japonica*, appear in late summer or fall. The small, pea-shaped flowers are scented.

The leaves are composed of a number of pairs of leaflets, and the bright yellow flowers are borne in short clusters. *S. japonica*, Japanese pagoda tree, zone 5, from central China, is a lovely, deciduous tree, growing up to 20 m (65 ft). The leaves are composed of blueish leaflets and the cream flowers are borne in long trusses. The timber, bark and fruit yield a yellow dye. Cultivar 'Pendula', weeping pagoda tree, with drooping branches, is sometimes grafted onto standards; 'Tortuosa' has twisted branches. *S. microphylla*, zone 8, from New Zealand, is an evergreen tree, growing to 5 m (16 ft). The leaves, comprised of small, dark green leaflets, have a fern-like appearance. The flowers, mostly deep yellow in color, are borne in dense clusters in summer. There are many popular cultivars, such as 'Earlygold', 'Goldies Mantle' and 'Goldilocks'. *S. prostrata*, zone 8, is a low-growing or upright shrub, also from New Zealand, which may be 60 cm to 3 m (2–6 ft) high. The flowers range from orange to brownish yellow and occasionally bright yellow. *S. tetraptera*, Kowhai or New Zealand laburnum, zone 8, is New Zealand's national floral emblem. Reaching up to 12 m (40 ft), though generally smaller, this tree develops a slightly pendulous habit. The leaves are comprised of large numbers of silky, gray-green leaflets, is borne on interlocking branches. A profusion of golden yellow flowers are borne in drooping clusters, in spring. *S. tomentosa*, silverbush, zone 10, is a tall shrub or small tree with loose clusters of pale yellow flowers.

Sorbus (fam. Rosaceae)
Mountain ash, rowan, whitebeam

This genus includes more than 100 deciduous trees and shrubs, found throughout temperate regions of the northern hemisphere. Many are grown for their colorful display of fall foliage. The trees are small to medium in height and are of two main types. The rowan or mountain ash types have pinnate leaves, comprising varying numbers of leaflets, while the whitebeams have simple leaves. Mountain ash types color red and orange in fall. The terminal clusters of

ABOVE Mature rowans, *Sorbus aucuparia*, carry large, conspicuous bunches of bright berries through fall into winter. The foliage colors well too.

small, white flowers appear in late spring and are followed by red, orange, pink, yellow or white berries in fall. Many species have edible fruits that have a range of culinary and medicinal uses. The timber of some species is used for carpentry, while the bark has been used in tanning. The fruit is very attractive to birds.

CULTIVATION *Sorbus* need soil with good drainage, and a position in sun or partial shade. The mountain ash types grow best in acid to neutral soils, while the whitebeams prefer alkaline or chalky soils, and tolerate dry conditions. Propagate from seed sown in fall, outdoors. Cultivars are budded in summer or grafted in late winter.

CLIMATE There are species suited to various climatic zones.

SPECIES *S. americana*, zone 2, is a variable species, to 9 m (30 ft), with green, sword-shaped leaflets, grayish green on the undersides, and dense clusters of flowers, followed by small, round, bright red fruit. *S. aria*, whitebeam, zone 5, is a European tree, growing to 15 m (50 ft). The simple, oval leaves are green above and felty white below. It produces clusters of very small, bright red, speckled berries. Cultivar 'Majestica' has very large leaves which are pure white on the undersides. *S. aucuparia*, rowan or mountain ash, zone 2, is the most commonly grown species. It is an erect tree, to 15 m (50 ft) in its native habitat, usually smaller in cultivation. It has a narrow crown and pinnate leaves which color rich gold or red in fall. The dense clusters of flowers are followed by very decorative, small, scarlet fruits. Cultivar 'Fructu Luteo' produces yellowish orange fruit which is not attractive to birds. *S. domestica*, service tree, zone 6, grows to around 20 m (65 ft), and is long-lived. It has pinnate leaves and sprays of white flowers, followed by pear-shaped, edible fruit ripening to bright yellow, crimson or orange-scarlet. The bark is used in tanning. This species can be identified by the large fruit.

Sorrel (*Rumex scutatus*, fam. Polygonaceae)
French sorrel

Sorrel is the common name for a number of sharp-tasting herbs of the genus *Rumex*, used medicinally and in cooking. The tender, young leaves are added to soups and salads and are used in sauces served with fish, chicken and boiled potatoes. *Rumex scutatus*, French or

BELOW Common in European grasslands, sorrel has been used since ancient times as a culinary and medicinal herb.

leaf-shield sorrel, is less bitter than other species and is the one most often used in cooking. It has large, heart-shaped leaves. If available, the cultivar 'Silver Shield' is a better choice than the species.

CULTIVATION Sow seed in spring in 1 cm (⅓ in) deep drills. Thin out when large enough to handle. Grow in fertile soil, with plenty of moisture around the roots. Apply side dressings of nitrogen fertilizer or liquid-soluble fertilizer every three to four weeks during the growth period to encourage leafy growth.

CLIMATE Zone 6.

Sowerbaea (fam. Asphodelaceae)
Vanilla lily

All five species of this genus are Australian natives, found growing in moist situations. Small, tufted perennials with a fibrous root system, they resemble clumps of grass when not in flower. The flowers have a strong, vanilla perfume. Sowerbaeas are suitable for rockeries and as container plants.

CULTIVATION Vanilla lily needs deep soil but can be grown in full or partial sun. It does best in permanently damp soil. In climatic zones below zone 9, grow in pots of soil-based compost, in a cool greenhouse. Propagate from seed or by division of the clumps in early spring.

BELOW With flowers like shooting stars, *Sowerbaea laxiflora* likes to be grown in a moisture-retentive soil, in full sun.

CLIMATE Zone 9.

SPECIES *S. juncea* is a small, tufted plant, 25–30 cm (10–12 in) high with grass-like leaves and pinkish violet blooms, clustered at the tops of the long stems. It grows naturally in eastern Australia, often at the edge of swamps. *S. laxiflora*, from Western Australia, growing to 45 cm (18 in), is clump-forming. It has upright, grass-like leaves and nodding, bright pinkish mauve flowers in summer. It generally produces fewer blooms than *S. juncea*.

Sparaxis (fam. Iridaceae)
Harlequin flower

There are six or so cormous plants in this African genus. They have linear leaves and erect, branched stems bearing bell-shaped flowers, enclosed in large, colorful spathes. The flowers come in brilliant shades of red, orange or purple, or white and cream, with black and yellow centers. With its abundance of spring or summer flowers, *Sparaxis* looks best mass planted.

CULTIVATION In frost-prone climates, *Sparaxis* is best grown in pots in a cool greenhouse or conservatory. Plant the corms in fall, 10 cm (4 in) deep, in well-drained, gritty, soil-based potting

BELOW In frost-prone climates, the cormous *Sparaxis tricolor* makes a colorful display in a cool greenhouse or conservatory.

compost. Ensure good light, but shade plants from direct, strong sun. Carry out moderate watering during the growing season and after flowering, gradually dry off the plants. During dormancy, in summer, the compost should be kept completely dry. Outdoors, grow in full sun and in well-drained soil. Propagate from offsets during the dormant period.

CLIMATE Zone 10.

SPECIES *S. fragrans* has tall flowering stems, to 60 cm (24 in). Each bear three or four flowers, ranging in color from purple to yellow and cream, many being given varietal names. *S. pillansii*, to 60 cm (24 in), has pink flowers with dark yellow centers, near-white filaments and dark purple anthers. *S. tricolor*, velvet or harlequin flower, to 45 cm (18 in) high, is the most commonly grown species. The flower spikes are borne on drooping stems. The very showy flowers may be red or pink through to orange-red, with dark purple markings on the base and a yellow throat, or pale pink or white with a purple base and yellow throat. The leaves are lance-shaped.

Sparrmannia (fam. Tiliaceae)

African hemp

There are three species of evergreen shrubs and small trees in this genus from tropical and tem-perate parts of southern Africa and Madagascar. The large, soft leaves vary from simple to lobed, and the flowers are borne in clusters on long stalks. The fruit is a spiny capsule.

CULTIVATION In areas where frosts occur, grow in an intermediate conservatory or greenhouse in large pots of soil-based potting compost. In the growing period, water liberally and liquid feed every four weeks. Reduce watering in the winter. Provide maximum light, but shade from direct, strong sun. Prune back in late winter to control size. Outdoors grow in a sunny, sheltered spot with moist yet well-drained, fertile soil. Propagate from seed sown in spring and germinated at 18°C (64°F), or from semi-ripe cuttings in summer, with basal warmth.

CLIMATE Zone 10 or tropical.

SPECIES *S. africana*, African hemp, is a fast-growing, spreading shrub, 3–6 m (10–20 ft) high. The white flowers, borne in clusters, have prominent, yellow and reddish-purple stamens. The main flowering is in spring to early summer, but it flowers sporadically all year round. The leaves may be oval to heart-shaped or lobed. Cultivar 'Flore Pleno' is a double-flow-ered form. *S. ricinicarpa* grows to 3 m (10 ft), with variable leaves and white or purple-tinged flowers, with prominent yellow stamens, produced intermittently throughout the year.

Spartium (fam. Papilionaceae)

Spanish broom

A single-species genus of deciduous shrub from the Mediterranean, *Spartium* is now widely grown in many parts of the world, and has become naturalized in many places with a Mediterranean climate. It is upright-growing, with rush-like branches. The leaves are very small, often falling early leaving the green branches almost bare. Masses of yellow, fra-grant flowers are borne at the branch ends from the beginning of summer to early fall.

BELOW 'Flore Pleno', a double-flowered form of *Sparrmannia africana*, has large, lobed leaves that are slightly furry.

ABOVE *Spartium junceum*, Spanish broom, is a good choice for a hot, dry situation and also thrives in seaside gardens.

CULTIVATION While *Spartium* can be grown in any garden soil, it prefers a well-drained soil in a sunny position. Prune after flowering to maintain compact shape. Propagate from seed sown in spring or fall. Seed can be germinated in a garden frame.

CLIMATE Zone 8.

SPECIES *S. junceum* is a quick-growing shrub, to 3 m (10 ft) high, with cylindrical branches. The blueish green leaves are linear to lance-shaped and the fragrant, yellow, pea-shaped flowers are a source of yellow dye.

Spathiphyllum (fam. Araceae)
Peace lily, Madonna lily

Most of the 36 species originate in Central and South America, while one species is found in the islands of Southeast Asia. With their interesting leaf shapes and fragrant, white flowers with white and green spathes, they are one of the most popular indoor plants.

CULTIVATION Spathiphyllum is pot grown, except in the tropics and subtropics, where it may be grown in open ground. Potting mix should be slightly moisture-retentive but well drained. Indoors, grow these plants in bright, indirect light. They will tolerate low light levels, although flowering will be poor in those conditions. They need to be kept moist through the warmer months, but allowed to dry out somewhat between waterings in cool weather. They like a humid atmosphere. The white flowers will age to green and should be cut off once they start to brown. Repotting, when necessary, should be done in warmer months. Propagate by division of older clumps or from seed.

CLIMATE Tropical.

SPECIES Few true species are in common cultivation. This very popular and easy-care indoor plant is mainly known from its several cultivars. *S.* 'Mauna Loa' is one of the best known, a vigorous plant up to 1 m (3 ft) in height when in flower. It has shiny, deep green foliage and scented, white spathes in spring and summer.

ABOVE The sail-like flowers of *Spathiphyllum* cultivars are freely produced in humid conditions, in reasonably bright light.

The species *S. wallisii* is also grown, with deep green foliage and wavy edges. The spathes are white and scented and produced over a long period in spring and summer. Height is up to 70 cm (28 in) when in flower.

Spathodea (fam. Bignoniaceae)

This native of tropical Africa is a handsome, evergreen tree, grown for its showy flowers and ornamental foliage. It makes an excellent street tree in subtropical and tropical areas and a striking specimen tree for gardens. In cooler climates, it can be grown in a pot in a warm greenhouse, but it is unlikely to flower.

CULTIVATION In the greenhouse, grow in a large pot of soil-based potting compost. Even better would be to plant it in a soil bed. Ensure good light (but shade from direct strong sun), and provide a humid atmosphere. In the growing season, carry out liberal watering and liquid feed every four weeks. In winter, reduce watering. In the garden, plants need a sunny spot with moist, yet well-drained soil. Propagate from seed in spring, germinated at 21°C (70°F), from semi-ripe cuttings in warmth, or by air layering in summer.

CLIMATE Warmest parts of zone 10 or tropical.

SPECIES *S. campanulata*, African tulip tree or flame of the forest, grows to 20 m (65 ft) in its native habitat, but is usually about 10–15 m (33–50 ft) in cultivation. The pinnate leaves grow to 40 cm (16 in) long. The flared, funnel-form flowers are a brilliant scarlet-orange and are borne in long trusses on the tips of the branches. Flowering is from late spring through summer, with the main show usually being in mid to late summer. The flowers are followed by a pod to 20 cm (8 in) long.

Spathoglottis (fam. Orchidaceae)

These 40 species of terrestrial orchids are generally found in mountainous regions of tropical Asia through to Australia and the Pacific. The genus name refers to the tongue-like shape of the lip.

CULTIVATION Grow in pots of terrestrial orchid compost in a warm greenhouse. Water well in the growing season and shade from strong, direct sun. When growth has ceased and the pseudobulbs are fully developed, reduce watering.

CLIMATE Tropical.

SPECIES *S. aurea* has a leafless stem, to 60 cm (24 in) long, bearing golden yellow flowers

ABOVE The fine gold edging on the flame-colored flowers of *Spathodea campanulata* emphasize their

ABOVE *Spathoglottis plicata*, a terrestrial orchid, bears pretty, star-shaped flowers. It needs to be grown in a warm greenhouse or conservatory.

with crimson spots at the lip. *S. plicata* is a very variable species, growing in grassy lowlands in its habitat. The broad leaves are about 75 cm (30 in) long and the flowers, 3–4 cm (1–1½ in) across, are borne on long stems. They are usually a deep purple-pink shade and appear five or six at a time. In tropical climates, it blooms through most of the year.

Spinach

(*Spinacia oleracea*, fam. Chenopodiacea)

Spinach

A number of vegetables are known as 'spinach'. True spinach (*Spinacia oleracea*) is very popular in many counties. This pot herb is grown for its edible leaves, which have many uses. A warm spinach salad is delicious, and spinach is often an important ingredient in gnocchi, quiches and roulades, as well as Middle Eastern dishes. It is an excellent source of fiber, vitamins and iron. It is believed spinach was first grown by the Persians in the 6th century and it was introduced to Europe by the Arabs in the 11th century.

CULTIVATION Spinach is an annual vegetable which can be grown in any well-drained, yet most soil in an open, sunny situation. It is raised from seeds sown in cropping positions during the period late winter to midsummer. It does not perform too well in very warm climates, soon running to seed. However, there are special cultivars available for summer sowing. Prepare 2 cm (¾ in) deep drills at 30 cm (12 in) apart. Sow seed 5 cm (2 in) apart in the drills and thin seedlings to 15 cm (6 in) apart. Seeds can be sown at intervals of three weeks to ensure a succession of leaves. Harvesting can start about eight weeks from sowing. Very hardy cultivars can be sown in early fall for leaves in early spring.

CLIMATE Zone 5.

VARIETIES There are many cultivars available for sowing at different times of year: spring, summer and fall. Make sure you choose a cultivar suitable for a particular sowing time.

Spinach, New Zealand

(*Tetragonia tetragonioides*, fam. Tetragoniaceae)

Native to Australia, New Zealand and the Pacific Islands, *Tetragonia tetragonioides* was collected by Sir Joseph Banks during his Pacific voyages with James Cook, and it was he who introduced it to England. This perennial, somewhat succulent, trailing plant is grown for its leaves, especially in summer, when other green

ABOVE Spinach can be grown successfully only in cool conditions. It has softer, smaller leaves than silver beet.

ABOVE New Zealand spinach is grown for its tender, succulent leaves. Being frost-tender, it is grown as a summer annual.

vegetables tend to run to seed. It is low-growing, with leaves smaller than those of true spinach. Freshly picked leaves are sweet and tender.

CULTIVATION This vegetable will grow in poor, sandy soil in fairly deep shade, although sunny conditions will produce a better quality plant. Propagate from seed sown in spring. Soak seed before planting at a depth of about 2.5 cm (1 in), and keep moist until seedlings come up. Space them 30–60 cm (12–24 in) apart within rows, allowing about 1 m (3 ft) between rows, as this plant spreads out to form a mat. Applications of liquid fertilizer when plants are actively growing will assist leaf formation. New shoots are produced after young shoots and leaves have been picked.

CLIMATE Zone 9. New Zealand spinach is frost-tender, but can be grown as a summer annual.

Spiraea (fam. Rosaceae)
Bridal wreath, May bush

Native to Europe, Asia, North America and Mexico, this genus comprises over 80 species of deciduous shrubs, grown for their lovely floral display and fall foliage color. Some flower early in spring, while others bloom in summer, the flower clusters generally being pink or white. Many hybrids are available, some of which make good ornamentals. If allowed to develop naturally without pruning, these shrubs grow into attractive, bushy plants with drooping or arching branches. Spiraeas are easy care garden shrubs and a fairly wide range of species, plus some excellent culivars and hybrids, is available in the US.

CULTIVATION These easy-care shrubs like a reasonably rich soil with plenty of sun and water. The addition of compost or manure in spring will improve plant growth. Care should be taken to avoid spoiling the natural arching or pendulous form of these shrubs, but they can be pruned to thin out old growth and to shorten over-long canes. Propagate from seed, suckers or cuttings of young shoots struck in sandy soil in a frame, or by layering.

CLIMATE There are species suited to various climatic zones.

SPECIES *S. cantoniensis*, zone 6, from China, has a graceful, spreading habit, growing 1–5 m (3–16 ft) high. It produces dense clusters of small, white flowers along its branches and is very showy when in bloom in early summer. The narrow, dark green leaves are blue-green on the undersides. Cultivar 'Flore Pleno' is a double-flowered form. *S. japonica*, zone 5, from China and Japan, is one of the most popular species, a 2 m (6 ft) high shrub with pink or white, summer flowers. However, it is mainly the cultivars that are grown, such as 'Anthony Waterer', with deep pink blooms, 1.5 m (5 ft) high; 'Bumalda', also with deep pink flowers, 1 m (3 ft) high; and the popular 'Goldflame', with reddish young foliage which changes to yellow and then green, and deep pink flowers, 80 cm (32 in) high. *S. nipponica* 'Snowmound', zone 4, is a popular, arching shrub to 1.2 m (4 ft), smothered with pure white flowers in midsummer. *S. prunifolia*, bridal wreath, zone 4, from China, is very popular in Japan. It is an upright-growing shrub,

ABOVE Small, white flowers smother the crown of *Spiraea cantoniensis* in early summer. This plant looks best if allowed to develop a natural, arching shape.

1–2 m (3–6 ft) high, with double, white flowers. The leaves color orange in fall. *S. thunbergii*, zone 4, from China, with clusters of small, white flowers borne on slender, arching branches and lance-shaped, finely toothed, light green leaves which color pink and orange in cooler areas. It grows to 1.5 m (5 ft) high. *S.* x *vanhouttei* (*S. cantoniensis* x *S. trilobata*), zone 4, grows to 2 m (6 ft) high and bears clusters of small, white flowers.

Sprekelia (fam. Amaryllidaceae)
Jacobean lily

This striking, bulbous plant from Mexico can be grown outdoors in warm climates, but needs greenhouse conditions in cooler areas.

CULTIVATION In areas where frosts occur, Sprekelia is best grown in an intermediate conservatory or greenhouse. Grow in pots of soil-based potting compost. Plant the bulbs in fall, making sure the top one-third is showing above compost level. Provide maximum light and carry out moderate watering in the growing period. Liquid feed fortnightly when flowering is over, to build up the bulbs. When the leaves start dying down, reduce water and when dormant (sometime in summer and fall), keep barely moist. Bulbs should be repotted every three years into fresh compost. Outdoors grow in full sun with well-drained soil. Propagation is from offsets taken during the dormant period.

CLIMATE Warmest parts of zone 10 to tropical.

SPECIES *S. formosissima*, Jacobean lily, has stunning, bright crimson, lily-like blooms on 30 cm (12 in) stems. They make excellent cut flowers. The broad, strappy leaves develop together with the twolipped flowers in spring. It is also known as 'Aztec lily' because of its origins and as 'orchid amaryllis' because the flower is sometimes thought to resemble an orchid.

Sprengelia (fam. Epacridaceae)
Swamp heath

This small genus of about four heath-like flowering shrubs related to Epacris, are all natives of Australia. Their natural habitat is moist, peaty marshes, sometimes at high altitudes. They have stiff, stem-clasping, dark green leaves and attractive, star-shaped, tubular flowers surrounded by leaf-like bracts. Sprengelias are not likely to be available outside their native

ABOVE Jacobean lily, *Sprekelia formosissima*, grows well both in pots and in the garden. The crimson flowers are simple but very striking.

ABOVE Pink swamp heath, *Sprengelia incarnata*, grows naturally in open heathland in eastern Australia. It flowers in winter and spring in its natural habitat.

Australia and in climates prone to frosts would need to be grown in a cool greenhouse or conservatory.

CULTIVATION Propagate from seed sown in late spring, although this may be very slow to germinate. It can also be grown from firm tip cuttings taken in fall. These may take some months to form roots. Under glass, grow in pots of acid, soilless potting compost and provide light, airy conditions. In the garden, plant in a moist, sunny situation in peaty, acid soil.

CLIMATE Warmest parts of zone 9.

SPECIES *S. incarnata*, pink swamp heath, is a stiff-foliaged shrub which grows to 1 m (3 ft) or more. Its dense sprays of starry flowers are contained in bracts. The pointed petals are pink. *S. monticola*, rock sprengelia, is a small, almost prostrate plant, with a spreading habit, usually found on damp rock ledges at higher altitudes. The starry flowers are pinkish white. *S. sprengelioides* is a shrub which occurs naturally in swampy, coastal areas. It has a variable growth habit, to 1 m (3 ft) high, and small, blunt leaves. The large, white flowers are borne at the ends of the stems.

Spring onion

(*Allium cepa* and *Allium fistulosum*, fam. Alliaceae)

There is some confusion as to which species is referred to by the common name of spring onion. Spring onions are often called shallots and vice versa. *A. cepa* covers spring or bunching onions that are small types of the common onion, with long necks and very small bulbs. These may be known as Japanese bunching onions, Chinese small onions, scallions (a term also used for shallots) and Welsh onions. (There is, however, no valid connection between this last species and Wales.) Spring onions, whatever their botanical origin, are used mainly in salads and stir fries. *A. fistulosum*, grown in China for centuries, resembles very coarse chives, with hollow leaves and very little

ABOVE These spring onions are close to maturity and can be harvested as needed for culinary use. Leeks are growing behind them.

swollen base. Several varieties of these vegetables in common cultivation are hybrids of the two species.

CULTIVATION These plants need well-drained soil, heavily enriched with organic matter. Manure or compost should be dug into the ground a couple of weeks before sowing. Add lime or dolomite to the soil before sowing unless the soil is known to be alkaline. Approximately half a cup per square metre (square yard) is needed. Seed can be sown direct in spring and thinned once plants are about 10 cm (4 in) high. Space 5–10 cm (2–4 in) apart. Thinned seedlings can be used to flavor salads or soups. It is important to keep the crop weed-free and to water regularly. Plants should be fertilized with high-nitrogen plant food to ensure rapid growth. Mound up the soil around the plant bases as they grow, to blanch the bases of the stems. Harvest as required. Spring onions do not store well for more than a few days.

CLIMATE Zone 5.

Spyridium (fam. Rhamnaceae)

Dusty miller, silver spyridium

This genus comprises around 30 species of Australian native shrubs. They are quite small,

ABOVE Hardy in well-drained soils, *Spyridium parvifolium* has small flowers framed by white, leaf-like bracts.

with downy, gray leaves and shoots and almost stalkless, white flowers, surrounded by bracts. Though ornamental and suited to coastal gardens, few species are cultivated. They are unlikely to be available outside Australia.

CULTIVATION Spyridiums are excellent sand-binding plants, preferring a well-drained, sandy soil in a sunny spot. In frost-prone climates, grow in a cool, airy greenhouse or conservatory in pots of gritty, well-drained soil-based potting compost.

CLIMATE Warmest parts of zone 9.

SPECIES *S. cinereum*, from Victoria, is a prostrate groundcover. Leaf-like white bracts surround the flower heads. *S. globulosum*, from Western Australia, is an upright-growing shrub, to 1 m (3 ft). The oval to oblong leaves have white undersides, and roundish, white flower heads appear from winter to fall in its natural habitat. *S. parvifolium* has foliage which is white and silky on the undersides. The flower heads are white.

Stachys (fam. Lamiaceae)

Woundwort, hedge nettle, betony

Comprising about 300 species of annuals and perennials, this genus has a broad distribution in temperate and subtropical areas of the world. Some species are weeds, while others are grown as ornamentals, or cultivated for their edible tubers.

CULTIVATION The perennial species of Stachys are frost-tolerant and grow in any ordinary, well-drained soil in full sun or very light shade. Most species are easily grown from seed, or by division in spring or fall. Species from Mediterranean climates, like *S. byzantina*, dislike high humidity.

CLIMATE Zone 5.

SPECIES *S. affinis*, Chinese artichoke, is an upright, hairy plant, to 45 cm (18 in), with white or pink flowers. The edible tubers are white, knotty and elongated, and are produced freely just below the ground. They are cultivated like Jerusalem artichokes. *S. byzantina* (syn. *S. lanata*), from the Middle East and the Caucasus, is probably the most often cultivated species. It is known as lamb's ears. A perennial with soft, silvery gray, heavily felted leaves, it is mainly grown as a border or edging plant. Pink to purple flowers grow on stems that may be over 50 cm (20 in). Cultivar 'Silver Carpet' is a non-flowering form which is used as a groundcover. *S. macrantha*, betony, is a perennial, bearing purple-pink flowers on stems 30–60 cm (12–24 in) high. Several cultivars are available. *S. officinalis*, wood betony

ABOVE This drive is bordered by clumps of silvery lamb's ears, *Stachys byzantina*, backed with clusters of *Nepeta* species.

or bishop's wort, grows from a woody rhizome, with flowering stems up to 60 cm (24 in) high. The summer flowers are purple to crimson. This herb has been used since ancient times in folk medicine, once being considered the panacea for all ills.

Stachyurus (fam. Stachyuraceae)

Native to east Asia and the Himalayas, these ten species of hardy, deciduous shrubs and small trees produce sprays of flowers which develop before the leaves, usually in winter or early spring. The stems may be red or reddish brown.

CULTIVATION Plant in acid, moist soil with good drainage and containing plenty of humus. Choose a sheltered position in full sun or partial shade. Propagate from semi-ripe cuttings in summer, rooted with bottom heat, or from seed in a garden frame in fall.

CLIMATE Zone 7. Best in cool, moist climates, but can be grown in warm temperate zones.

SPECIES *S. chinensis* is a bushy shrub, to 2 m (6 ft), with red stems and pale greenish yellow, bell-shaped flowers, borne in drooping sprays up to 10 cm (4 in) long. *S. praecox*, from Japan,

BELOW Tassels of pale yellow-green flowers deck the bare branches of *Stachyurus praecox* in late winter and early spring.

is the most commonly grown species. A loosely branched shrub to 4 m (13 ft), it has reddish brown stems and pendulous sprays of pale yellow flowers. Like *S. chinensis*, the leaves develop a red tint in fall.

Stanhopea (fam. Orchidaceae)

These evergreen, epiphytic orchids are natives of Central and South America, with a single leaf arising from the small pseudobulb. The waxy, fragrant flowers are borne in pendulous clusters. Sometimes known as 'upside-down orchids', they must be grown in hanging containers as the flowers emerge from the base of the pseudobulb.

CULTIVATION Grow in a warm greenhouse in slatted, wooden orchid baskets, using a proprietary orchid compost formulated for epiphytes. Provide a humid atmosphere and, in summer, shade from strong sun. During the growing period, water regularly but be very sparing during the dormant period, which is invariably in early summer. Propagate by division when pot-bound.

CLIMATE Warmest parts of zone 10 or tropical.

BELOW Generally found only in specialist collections, *Stanhopea oculata* produces flowers in varied shades of yellow.

SPECIES *S. oculata* produces large, light yellow to orange flowers, spotted in maroon, on 15 cm (6 in) long stalks in summer. The lip is yellow and mauve in parts. *S. tigrina*, probably the best known species, has large, unusual, yellow and brown flowers in summer which are quite pungent. *S. wardii* is also quite widely grown. It has yellow flowers, spotted plum and purple.

Stapelia (fam. Asclepiadaceae)
Carrion flower, star flower, starfish plant, toad flower

These unusual clump-forming succulents are widely distributed throughout tropical and South Africa. The fleshy, four-angled stems have toothed edges and grow 20–30 cm (8–12 in) high. The stems are smooth and velvety and the flowers emerging from the base of the plant are quite bizarre. These are variable and may be rounded, star-shaped, flat or bell-shaped, often with a ring towards the center. However, they smell of rotting flesh which attracts insects, particularly blowflies, to the center of the flower to assist pollination.

ABOVE Starfish or toad flower, *Stapelia variegata*, is a curiosity now classified in the genus Orbea by many botanists.

CULTIVATION In cool and cold climates, grow in an intermediate to warm greenhouse, in pots of very gritty, soil-based potting compost, with a layer of grit on top to provide good surface drainage. Plants need a dry atmosphere and maximum light, but shade from direct, strong sun. Do not overwater at any time, but keep only slightly moist during the winter resting period. Outdoors, plant in a very well drained soil, in a sunny spot. Propagate in spring or summer from rooted offsets or stem cuttings.

CLIMATE Zone 9 to 10.

SPECIES *S. gigantea*, from southern Africa, has upright, velvety, light green stems, to 20 cm (8 in), and huge, flattened flowers, to 35 cm (14 in) across, with long, sharply tapering lobes. They are pale yellow and covered in red hairs, barred with red ridges. Long, white hairs cover the recurved margins. *S. hirsuta*, from Cape Province, has velvety dark green stems and star-shaped flowers, 12 cm (5 in) across, with brownish red, silky hairs in the center and on the edges of the spreading lobes, which are marked with horizontal red and yellow ridges.

Staphylea (fam. Staphyeaceae)
Bladder nut

There are about ten species of hardy, deciduous shrubs in this genus from temperate regions of the northern hemisphere. They have attractive leaves, terminal sprays of white flowers, and produce unusual, inflated fruit.

CULTIVATION Bladder nuts do well in moist, loamy soil in a sunny or partially shaded situation. If they are watered moderately when young and increasingly during growth, these shrubs will flower sooner. Prune immediately after flowering by cutting back old flowered shoots to younger shoots or buds lower down. Propagate from seed sown in a garden frame in fall, or from semi-ripe cuttings in summer, rooting them in a heated propagating case. Alternatively, carry out layering in spring.

ABOVE In spring to early summer, *Staphylea pinnata* bears large trusses of scented, white flowers. It is native to Europe, Turkey and the Caucasus.

CLIMATE Zone 6.

SPECIES *S. holocarpa*, from China, is a shrub or tree, 7–8 m (23–26 ft) tall, the rose to white flowers developing before the leaves. Cultivar 'Rosea' has pink flowers and the young foliage is attractively flushed with bronze. *S. pinnata*, European bladder nut, grows to 5 m (16 ft). The white flowers are borne in nodding sprays about 10 cm (4 in) long.

Star anise (*Illicium verum*, fam. Illiciaceae)

Native to south-eastern China and north-eastern Vietnam, this is a slow-growing tree that may reach 15 m (50 ft) in ideal conditions. It has elliptical leaves, up to 15 cm (6 in) long, and pretty, star-shaped flowers that are cream, ageing to pink, then maroon. The flowers resemble some species of magnolia and the genus *Illicium* was previously in the Magnoliaceae family. The unripe fruits are used as a culinary spice and oil is distilled from the fruit to flavor liqueurs. Star anise has some medicinal applications.

CULTIVATION These trees need well-drained, acid soil, rich in organic matter. They can be grown

ABOVE Unripe fruits of star anise are harvested as culinary spices.

in full sun or partial shade, but should be sheltered from strong wind. In climatic zones below 9, grow in a cool greenhouse or conservatory in pots of acid, soil-based potting compost.

CLIMATE Zone 9. Tolerates light frost.

Star apple

(*Chrysophyllum cainito*, fam. Sapotaceae)

With origins in the West Indies and Central America, this is a large tree which grows to a height of 9–15 m (30–50 ft) and a spread of 6–8 m (20–26 ft). It has large, elliptic leaves which are shiny green above and covered with gold hairs on the undersides. The flowers are white, but very small and almost inconspicuous. Fruit is set after about seven years and from the tenth year, bearing is usually prolific. Fruits are rounded and, depending on the variety, the skin color may be green with pink or yellow flushes, or a dark purple-brown. Its common name comes from the fact that when the fruit is cut in half the inside appears star-shaped. Inside, the fruit is divided into segments of white, pulpy flesh, surrounded by a drier type of flesh. All of this is edible. However, don't bite into the fruit as the skin contains a latex which may cause severe mouth irritation. Fruit should be cut open and the sweet jelly-like flesh spooned out. Although it can be eaten alone, it

ABOVE The fruit of the star apple must ripen to a deep purple-red before it is ready to eat. It has a very refreshing taste alone or mixed with other fruits.

is more often mixed together with chopped or segmented oranges, to be eaten raw or made into drinks.

CULTIVATION Outside the tropics, grow as a young foliage plant in a warm greenhouse or conservatory, in pots of soil-based potting compost. Provide a humid atmosphere. Water well when in full growth. Propagate from seed, which germinates in about six weeks in a heated propagating case. If growing outdoors, plant in well-drained soil of high fertility. Fruit should not be allowed to ripen on the tree but should be picked when the skin is still smooth but deep purple in color. Ripen in a warm room indoors. Very ripe fruit is dull, wrinkled and soft to the touch.

CLIMATE Suitable for the tropics only as trees need high temperature and high humidity all year.

Star fruit

(*Averrhoa carambola*, fam. Oxalidaceae)

Carambola

Cultivated throughout the tropics, the origin of this species is uncertain, with opinion divided between Brazil and Malaysia. Introduced into Europe in the late 18th century, it never became popular like some of the exotic fruits brought there around the same time. The tree is a small evergreen, 14 m (46 ft) high, with compound leaves bearing small, purple flowers in short sprays along the branches. Fruits are borne in profusion. They are 8–12 cm (3–5 in) long and ribbed, making five corners which, cut in section, resemble stars. The outer fruit is waxy yellow and contains the yellow flesh. Fruits are eaten fresh or made into drinks, jams and preserves. They have a high content of vitamins A and C. The juice of the fruit removes stains from the hands or clothing.

CULTIVATION Outside the subtropics and tropics, grow as a young foliage plant in a warm greenhouse or conservatory, in pots of soil-based potting compost. Provide a humid atmosphere and shade plants from strong, direct sun. Outdoors grow in sun and well drained, humus-rich soil. Plenty of water needed. Propagate from seed sown in a warm propagating case. Budded trees are best for fruit production.

CLIMATE Needing high temperature and high humidity, these trees are best suited to the trop-

BELOW This abundant crop of star fruit will be picked when the fruit is deep yellow to orange. Star-shaped slices of this fruit make a pretty garnish.

ics, but may be grown in suitable microclimates in the subtropics. Zone 10.

Stenocarpus (fam. Proteaceae)

Native to Australia and New Caledonia, these evergreen trees are grown for their striking flowers and foliage. The smooth, shiny, alternate leaves may be entire or lobed. The flowers are somewhat like the grevilleas from Australia. Growth is moderate to slow, most species taking up to seven years to flower.

CULTIVATION In frost-prone climates, grow in an intermediate greenhouse or conservatory, but bear in mind that plants may not flower when grown in pots. Use soil-based potting compost in containers. Provide good light, but shade from direct, strong sun. Pruning may be needed in late winter to control size. Outdoors grow in a sunny, sheltered spot with moist yet well drained, humus-rich soil. Propagate from seed in spring, germinated at 21°C (70°F), or from semi-ripe cuttings, in a heated propagating case, during summer.

CLIMATE Zone 10 or tropical.

SPECIES S. *salignus*, scrub beefwood, is an upright-growing shrub or small tree, with narrow, alternate, elliptical leaves. The fragrant, greenish yellow flowers are borne in dense, roundish clusters, making an attractive display against the dark green foliage. The fruit is a long, flattened pod. S. *sinuatus*, firewheel tree, found in rainforests of Australia's east coast, is the most commonly grown species. It is an attractive tree, growing 10–20 m (33–65 ft) in the wild and around 9 m (30 ft) in cultivation. It has shiny, dark green, lobed leaves and spectacular, orange to red flowers, arranged in a wheel-like shape. In its natural habitat, this species attracts honeyeaters and other birds.

Stephanandra (fam. Rosaceae)

These four species of deciduous shrubs from eastern Asia are grown mainly for their attractive foliage which colors delightful shades of orange in fall. The light brown, bare branches are very ornamental in winter.

CULTIVATION Stephanandras like a rich, moist, loamy soil and full sun. To achieve good fall color, they need plenty of water and cool conditions. Prune annually in early spring by cutting out thin, damaged or diseased shoots, as well as about half the remaining shoots, to allow new growth as much room as possible. Propagate from semi-ripe cuttings in summer

ABOVE *Stenocarpus sinuatus*, firewheel tree, is spectacular in flower, but unfortunately it is shy to bloom when container-grown.

ABOVE The attractive foliage of *Stephanandra tanakae* is embellished with sprays of small, white or yellow-green flowers in early summer.

or hardwood cuttings in winter. Plants can also be propagated from rooted suckers removed in winter.

CLIMATE Zone 5 for *S. incisa*; zone 6 for *S. tanakae*.

SPECIES *S. incisa*, lace shrub or cutleaf stephanandra, from Japan and Korea, grows to a height and spread of 2 m (6 ft). The deeply incised leaves are borne on long, graceful, curving stems and the tiny, white flowers form loose sprays. *S. tanakae*, 3 m (10 ft) high, has yellowish green flowers on arching, brown stems, clothed with lobed, toothed leaves.

Stephanotis (fam. Asclepiadaceae)
Madagascar jasmine, wax flower

Only one species of this genus of evergreen, climbing plants, from the Malay Archipelago to Malagasy, is commonly cultivated. The glossy, dark green leaves contrast well with the clusters of small, white, waxy flowers, making stephanotis a popular choice of florists, particularly for bridal decorations.

CULTIVATION Outside the tropics, grow in a warm greenhouse or conservatory. Stephanotis also makes a good house plant. Grow in a pot of soilless or soil-based potting compost. Shade from direct, strong sun but ensure good light. Provide a humid atmosphere and supports for stems. If necessary, prune in late winter to restrict size. Propagate from semi-ripe cuttings in summer, in a heated propagating case.

CLIMATE Tropical.

SPECIES *S. floribunda* grows to around 4 m (13 ft). The elliptical leaves are thick, smooth-edged and shiny and the deliciously fragrant, white flowers make a lovely display from spring to fall.

Sterculia (fam. Sterculiaceae)
Indian almond tree

Grown as ornamental and shade trees in sub-tropical and tropical regions, the main disadvantage of *Sterculia* is the offensive odor released by leaves of some species. Most species are fast growing and deciduous, with colorful calyces taking the place of flower petals.

CULTIVATION In climates which are prone to frosts, grow in a warm to intermediate greenhouse or conservatory in pots of rich, soil-based

ABOVE Sweetly scented, heavy-textured flowers are borne abundantly on established plants of *Stephanotis floribunda*, grown in a warm greenhouse or conservatory.

ABOVE The fruits of *Sterculia quadrifida* are far more decorative than its flowers. The seeds contained within the long red seed pods are edible.

potting compost. Outdoors grow in a warm sunny spot (must be frost free) with rich, moist yet well-drained soil. Propagate from ripe seeds germinated in warmth, or from semi-ripe cuttings with bottom heat.

CLIMATE Zone 10 or tropical.

SPECIES *S. foetida*, Indian almond, originating from India and warmer parts of Asia, grows to 20 m (65 ft) tall. The leaves are long and divided, and the calyces are purple, red and yellow. The dark red seed pods grow to about 8 cm (3 in) long. The leaves of this species give off the characteristic, unpleasant odor. *S. quadrifida*, koralba or peanut tree, is a medium-sized, rainforest tree with a rounded crown. The small, entire leaves are dull green, while the 8–10 cm (3–4 in) long, red seed pods are woody, opening on one side to reveal the edible seeds. *S. rubiginosa*, from India and Indonesia, is a shrub or tree growing to 6 m (20 ft) high, with long leaves, white on the undersides, and drooping sprays of red calyces. The seed pods grow to 8 cm (3 in) in length. *S. villosa*, from India, is characterized by its white bark. It has large, velvety, lobed leaves and the silky calyces are pink inside. These are borne in sprays at the branch tips.

Sternbergia (fam. Amaryllidaceae)

Fall crocus

Native to southern Europe to central Asia, these eight species of dwarf bulbs bear charming, crocus-like flowers in fall through to spring. Suitable for rock gardens and the front of warm borders, they can also be grown in pans in an alpine house or bulb frame.

CULTIVATION Plant bulbs in late summer, 15 cm (6 in) deep, in well-drained soil in a sunny position. When growing in pans, use a gritty, soil-based potting compost, which should be kept dry during the summer dormancy period. Propagate from offsets when dormant, or from seed when ripe.

ABOVE *Sternbergia lutea*, with its yellow, fall flowers, is one of the joys of this season in suitable climates

CLIMATE These bulbs prefer areas with hot, dry summers, followed by cool to cold winters.

SPECIES *S. colchiciflora*, zone 5, has yellow, stemless, fragrant flowers which bloom in fall, before the leaves appear. *S. lutea*, zone 7, from the Mediterranean, is the most commonly grown species. The buttercup yellow flowers are produced in late fall, at the same time as the glossy, strap-shaped leaves. This is thought to be the lily-of-the-field referred to in the Bible.

Stewartia (fam. Theaceae)

This is a small genus of nine species of deciduous trees or shrubs, native to eastern Asia and eastern North America. Related to camellias, they are cultivated as ornamentals for their flowers and foliage, as well as for their attractive, peeling bark.

CULTIVATION These plants can be grown in full sun or light shade, depending on climate. They require a regular supply of water during the growing season and prefer a slightly acid soil, rich in humus. Soil must drain well. Mulch root zone with decayed manure or compost. Little or no pruning is required, except to thin out old trees. Propagate from seed sown in fall in a garden frame, or from semi-ripe cuttings, rooted with bottom heat. Layering in spring is more reliable.

ABOVE The flowers of *Stewartia pseudocamellia* have crimped petals surrounding the central stamens. The foliage colors well in fall.

CLIMATE Zone 5. Best in cool, moist climates.

SPECIES *S. pseudocamellia* is the best known species. It is native to Japan, where trees can grow to 15 m (50 ft) or more. In cultivation, they are more likely to be 8–10 m (26–33 ft) at maturity. The peeling bark, in gray and pinkish or reddish brown, is an outstanding feature. The leaves are oval and glossy green, and the cup-shaped, white flowers have a central mass of golden stamens.

Sticherus (fam. Gleicheniaceae)

Fan or umbrella fern

This genus consists of about 100 species of ferns from tropical and southern temperate regions of the world. They have fine, creeping, slender rhizomes, stiff, upright stems and regularly branched fronds, which form a shape like the frame of an umbrella. The simple or lance-shaped leaflets are pale green through to deep green, producing a pretty growth pattern due to the regular branching of the fronds. In frost-prone climates, these ferns are grown in an intermediate greenhouse or conservatory.

CULTIVATION Generally grown in pots, these ferns need a large one to allow the long, creeping rhi-

zomes room to spread. Use a fibrous peat mixed with coarse sand and well-rotted leaf mould that drains well. Water regularly, but do not fertilize. As these ferns grow naturally in and along creek beds, they will grow well in the ground provided they are positioned in a damp situation with protection above. Propagation from spores is slow, as is the initial growth rate. However, they can be grown from a length of rhizome containing a few small, young fronds, during the growth period.

CLIMATE Zone 10.

SPECIES *S. flabellatus*, shiny fan fern, is a native of eastern Australia, New Zealand and New Guinea. The rhizomes are covered in brown scales and the long stems are dark brown to black. The fronds are 1.5 m (5 ft) long and the leaflets are a glossy, dark green on top, paler on the undersides, and have finely serrated margins. This species prefers to be grown in the ground, provided it has ample moisture. It is slow to recover after transplanting. *S. lobatus*, spreading fan fern, from the east coast of Australia, has firm rhizomes covered in brown scales. The sturdy stems are glossy brown and the fronds, to 2 m (6 ft) long, are dull green, with paler undersides. *S. tener*, silky fan fern, from eastern Australia has a very long, wiry, brown-scaled rhizome and sturdy stems growing to 2 m (6 ft).

ABOVE A tough little fern, *Sticherus flabellatus* has stiff, shiny foliage, much appreciated by florists.

Stigmaphyllon (fam. Malpighiaceae)

There are approximately 100 species in this genus of twining, woody, tropical climbers from tropical America, where they are found covering branches at the tops of tall trees, bearing attractive, yellow flowers. The small, heart-shaped leaves are covered with fine, silky hairs.

CULTIVATION In areas prone to frost, grow in an intermediate to warm conservatory or greenhouse, in a pot of soil-based or soilless potting compost. Shade plant from direct strong sun, but ensure good light. Stems will need supports. If needed, prune in late winter to control size. Propagate by layering in spring or from semi-ripe cuttings in summer, rooted in a warm propagating case.

CLIMATE Tropical.

SPECIES *S. ciliatum*, golden vine, is the only species widely cultivated. Fast-growing in the tropics, it may be rather slow elsewhere. It is covered with clusters of yellow flowers in fall. *S. lingulatum*, golden vine, produces large clusters of small, yellow flowers. *S. littorale*, often found near water, has round leaves and golden flowers, borne in large clusters.

BELOW Petals of the yellow-flowered *Stigmaphyllon ciliatum* are arranged like spokes on a wheel. In frost-prone climates, this climber can be grown in a warm greenhouse.

Stokesia (fam. Asteraceae)

Stokes' aster

A native of south-eastern North America, this late-flowering perennial provides good cut flowers from late summer to fall. It is easy to grow and looks its best in mass plantings. It is also suitable for container growing.

CULTIVATION Stokesias are excellent for mixed or herbaceous borders. They thrive in light, well-drained yet moist, acid soil in a sheltered, sunny position. Avoid wet or heavy soils. In areas with hard frosts, protect roots with a deep mulch over winter. Propagate by division in spring, from seed in fall (germinate in a garden frame), or from root cuttings in winter.

CLIMATE Zone 7.

SPECIES *S. laevis*, the only species, is a perennial, 30–45 cm (12–18 in) high, which forms basal rosettes of narrow, divided leaves. Flower colors range from mauve through pink to purple. Cultivars are available in other colors, including white and rose pink.

BELOW One of the great stand-bys of a perennial display is Stokes' aster, *Stokesia laevis*. With regular dead-heading, this easy-care plant produces masses of flowers.

Strawberry (*Fragaria* species, fam. Rosaceae)

Fragaria chiloensis, believed to be from Chile, was introduced to France early in the 18th century. It was then crossed with *F. virginiana*, producing the first of the modern cultivars with larger flowers and fruit. The low-growing *Fragaria* hybrids (*Fragaria x ananassa*) not only provide the succulent red fruit which is everyone's favorite, but also decorative ground-covers for the rock garden. The delicious wild strawberry, *Fragaria vesca*, has been cultivated in Europe for centuries, spreading to other parts of the world as it was improved in size and bearing qualities. Strawberries are eaten fresh with pure, thick cream, and home-made strawberry jam is a must for a Devonshire tea. They are also delicious when used to decorate cakes and tarts. Strawberries are popular as they are easy to grow and do not require much space. With the many cultivars available, it is possible to have strawberries through summer and fall.

CULTIVATION Strawberries need a well-drained soil, preferably a sandy loam, and a site in full sun. Prepare the bed well before planting. Dig well and fertilize with half a cup of blood and bone per square metre (yard). Incorporate some well-decayed manure or compost into the top soil layer. Raising the bed ensures perfect drainage. Strawberries can be grown from runners, but it is best to plant virus-free stock from certified growers. The best planting time is late summer. However, everbearing strawberries are planted in summer, fall or spring. Remove the outside leaves of new plants and trim them. Spread the roots and plant so the base of the crown is just above soil level. Set the plants in rows, with about 30 cm (12 in) between plants and 40 cm (16 in) between rows. In frost-prone climates, late spring frosts can kill the flowers, so if there is a risk, it is advisable to cover the rows of plants with cloches or fleece during flowering. If the plants are kept covered after fruit set, then fruits will ripen earlier. Weed control is essential at all times. To make this easier, black polythene sheeting or weed matting, obtainable from nurseries, can be laid over the beds, with holes cut out for the plants. The sheeting acts as a mulch, represses weeds, and keeps the fruit clean and off the ground. However, ensure the ground is thoroughly soaked before laying the plastic. As the plants develop, remove the runners to avoid weakening the plants and to prevent unwanted spreading. Keep plants well watered, taking care to direct water to the planting holes. To harvest the strawberries, nip off just behind the star-shaped calyx. About every two or three years, replace with new stock rather than old runners. The strawberry is more prone to pest and disease attack than most other fruit, one of the main predators being birds which will pick off the fruit before it is fully ripened. To prevent this, place a fine, wire mesh over the strawberry bed once flowering begins. Mites, thrips, gray mould, mildew and leaf spot can cause problems. Gray mould attacks not only the fruit, but also the flowers and stems, and can be the cause of poor fruit set.

CLIMATE Zone 4. Choose varieties to suit your climate.

SPECIES *Fragaria x ananasa* is a perennial, evergreen, herbaceous groundcover, spreading by means of runners. It has compound leaves

ABOVE Healthy-looking strawberry plants are starting to flower, signalling the start of the fruiting season.

comprised of three leaflets, with toothed margins and small, white flowers. The red fruit is fleshy. Some cultivars bear fruit 5 cm (2 in) or more in length. Strawberries are classified into different types. June-bearing cultivars produce one crop per year, in late spring, early summer or later in the summer. These are the most popular strawberries. Everbearing cultivars crop on and off over a long period, in summer and through into fall. Plants of these are often replaced annually. Usually the first flush of flowers is removed. Cultivars of June-fruiting and everbearing strawberries are constantly being developed and improved, so study catalogues of mail-order fruit specialists for details of the latest cultivars and to find out which are suitable for your area. *F. vesca*, the wild strawberry, which includes alpine strawberries, is native to Europe and several cultivars are available. The deep red fruit is generally smaller than that of the strawberry grown for the commercial market and is produced over a long period in summer and fall.

Strelitzia (fam. Strelitziaceae)
Bird of paradise

These five species of evergreen perennials, indigenous to South Africa, are valued for their spectacular flowers, reminiscent of exotic birds.

BELOW Truly one of the most bizarre but also most spectacular of flowers is produced by *Strelitzia reginae*. The floral display is very extended.

They make excellent feature plants. All species have large, banana-like leaves and the familiar, large flowers with sharp, arrow-like petals. Clumps may reach very large proportions with age.

CULTIVATION Strelitzias require warm, frost-free conditions, moist yet well-drained soil and a sunny spot. In frost-prone climates, grow in large pots or tubs in an intermediate to warm greenhouse or conservatory. Move these outside for the summer if desired. Use soil-based potting compost. Shade plants from strong, direct sun, but ensure good light. Good ventilation is required. Plants need liberal watering when in full growth, plus liquid feeding every four weeks. Water far less in winter. Propagate in spring by removing and potting up rooted suckers.

CLIMATE Zone 10.

SPECIES *S. alba* is a clump-forming species to at least 10 m (33 ft) in height, and in spring produces white flowers from purplish spathes. *S. nicolai* is another very large, clump-forming species, growing to about 10 m (33 ft) in height. This also flowers in spring and has striking, white and blue flowers from deep reddish spathes. The best known is *S. reginae*, bird of paradise flower, with spectacular, orange and blue flowers in winter and spring from green spathes flushed with orange and purple. This species grows to around 2 m (6 ft) high.

Streptosolen (fam. Solanaceae)
Orange browallia, marmalade bush

Originating in Columbia and Peru, this single-species genus is an evergreen, sprawling shrub, valued for its attractive foliage and brilliant orange flowers.

CULTIVATION In frost-prone climates, grow in a cool or intermediate conservatory or greenhouse. Grow in pots of soil-based potting compost. Provide maximum light, but shade plants from strong, direct sun. If growing outside, plant in a sunny, sheltered spot in reasonably

ABOVE Producing abundant flowers, *Streptosolen jamesonii* is rarely out of flower from late spring to late summer.

ABOVE Grown for its vividly colored foliage, *Strobilanthes dyeranus* has purple and green leaves, overlaid with silver.

rich, well-drained, yet moist soil. Prune lightly in late winter to maintain a well-shaped plant. Propagate from semi-ripe cuttings in late summer, in a warm propagating case, or by layering in spring.

CLIMATE Zone 9 to tropical.

SPECIES *S. jamesonii* grows to around 2 m (6 ft) high, producing masses of orange, trumpet-shaped flowers amongst the narrow, oval leaves, from late spring to late summer.

Strobilanthes (fam. Acanthaceae)

There are about 250 species of attractive perennials and shrubs in this genus from tropical Asia. They may be deciduous or evergreen and generally have tubular, hooded flowers. Only a few species are grown. Outside the tropics, grow in a warm greenhouse or conservatory.

CULTIVATION Grow in pots of soil-based potting compost, under glass. Shade plants from strong, direct sun, but ensure good light. If necessary, shrubby species can be lightly pruned in spring to ensure a good shape. Propagate in spring from seed or softwood cuttings, in a warm propagating case.

CLIMATE Tropical.

SPECIES *S. anisophyllus* (syn. *Goldfussia anisophylla*), from India, grows between 90 cm and 1.5 m (36–40 in) high, with bronze-green foliage and lovely, light blue flowers. It flowers in winter and spring but can bloom sporadically through the year. *S. dyeranus*, from Burma, is a shrubby species, to 1 m (3 ft) high, with metallic-looking foliage, purple green and deep rose above and dark red to purple beneath.

Strongylodon (fam. Papilionaceae)
Jade vine

This genus of about 20 species of shrubs or climbers is found in Southeast Asia, with a number native to the Philippines. Only one species is grown, but this is not easy to obtain. It is among the most beautiful of all climbing plants.

CULTIVATION Outside the tropics, grow in a warm greenhouse, in a large pot or tub of acid, soil-based potting compost. Even better, grow in a bed of acid soil. Shade from direct, strong sun, but ensure good light. A humid atmosphere is essential. The stems will need supports. If necessary, prune in late winter to control size. Propagate by

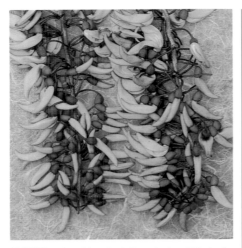

ABOVE There is nothing else in the natural world that quite matches the extraordinary color of *Strongylodon macrobotrys* in bloom.

air layering in spring, or from ripe seed sown as soon as available and germinated at 30°C (86°F).

CLIMATE Tropical.

SPECIES *S. macrobotrys*, jade vine or emerald creeper, is a strong-growing twining climber that may extend for 15 m (50 ft) or more in ideal conditions. The new leaves are bronze to pink, turning deep green as they mature. The long, pea-type flowers are massed in sprays that may be 40–80 cm (16–32 in) in length. The flowers are an exquisite shade of turquoise, and appear from late winter through spring.

Stylidium (fam. Stylidiaceae)
Trigger plant

There are around 135 species in this genus of soft or woody, perennial plants, mostly from Australia, but some species occur in Southeast Asia and also New Zealand. They form rosettes of mostly grassy leaves, from which long, thin stems emerge, bearing spikes of unusual, lopsided flowers. The long, bent column contain-

ing the anthers and the stigma hangs outside the little blooms like a handle. When it is touched by an insect, it springs across and dusts it with pollen. These unusual plants can be 'triggered' by tickling the flower with a pointed stick. In frost-prone areas, grow in a cool or intermediate greenhouse or conservatory. Outdoors, plant in a mixed border.

CULTIVATION In the greenhouse, grow in pots of soil-based potting compost. Ensure maximum light and airy conditions. Very little water is needed in winter. In the garden, plant in a sunny spot with well-drained soil. Propagate by division in spring, or from ripe seed germinated at 18°C (64°F).

CLIMATE Zone 9.

SPECIES *S. bulbiferum*, from Western Australia, spreads by runners, forming mats of growth 15 cm (6 in) high. Red, pink to almost white flowers are borne in summer on reddish stems. *S. calceratum*, a native of Victoria, grows to 10 cm (4 in) high, with rosettes of tiny, oval leaves, thread-like stems and clusters of small,

ABOVE The sensitive column of the trigger plant can be seen protruding from the centre of these small, mauve flowers.

pinkish white flowers. *S. graminifolium* is probably the best known species, a native of eastern and southern Australia. It has grass-like tufts of leaves, slender, erect stems, to 15 cm (6 in) high, and pale pink to deep red-pink flowers. *S. laricifolium* is the tallest of the species from eastern Australia, growing to 1 m (3 ft) high, and producing pink flowers.

Styphelia (fam. Epacridaceae)
Five corners, golden heath

These 14 species of low, heath-like shrubs are native to Australia. They have stiff, prickly, pointed leaves and pretty, bell-shaped flowers which generally appear in summer. They have recurved, tubular flowers, hairy inside, with long stamens. *S. tubiflora* was one of the first Australian plants to be grown in Europe. These small, ornamental shrubs are suitable as garden plants, or for growing in rockeries and pots. In frost-prone areas, grow in a cool greenhouse or conservatory.

CULTIVATION In the greenhouse, grow in pots of acid, soilless potting compost. Provide light, airy conditions. Avoid overwatering, especially in winter. In the garden, plant in a sunny position in acid to neutral, well-drained soil, containing plenty of humus. Propagate from semi-ripe cuttings in summer, in a warm propagating case.

CLIMATE Zone 9 to 10.

SPECIES *S. adscendens*, golden heath, is low and spreading, with grayish green, toothed leaves and greenish yellow flowers. *S. longifolia* is a small, erect shrub with spear-shaped leaves and green and yellow flowers with pointed calyces. *S. triflora*, five corners, is a dwarf shrub with grayish green foliage and pink to red flowers, with yellow lobes and calyces and pink bracts. *S. tubiflora*, red five corners, is an attractive species with small, flat leaves and long, crimson flowers with green, fringed bracts. *S. viridis*, green five corners, has blunt leaves and green flowers with short, smooth lobes.

Styrax (fam. Styracaceae)
Snowbell, storax

This is a genus of about 120 species of evergreen or deciduous trees and shrubs, native to Europe, Asia and North America. Several species, predominantly the tropical Asian species, contain resins with a long history of medicinal use. One is the original source of friar's balsam, while others are used as antiseptics, and in the making of cough medicines and toiletries. Several cool-climate species are grown as ornamentals, as they produce a lovely display of flowers, mainly in summer.

CULTIVATION *Styrax* are best grown in a sheltered spot, with full sun or partial shade. The soil should be acid to neutral, well drained yet moisture-retentive, and contain plenty of humus. The easiest method of propagation is by layering in spring, but semi-ripe cuttings can be taken in summer and rooted in a warm propagating case. Percentage rooting is usually low.

BELOW *Styphelia tubiflora* has long stamens protruding from waxy, red tubular flowers. The flowers appear in summer.

ABOVE *Styrax officinalis* is the original source of friar's balsam. It bears masses of snowy white, bell flowers in early summer.

CLIMATE There are species suited to various climatic zones.

SPECIES *S. americanus*, the American snowbell, zone 7, is a deciduous shrub that grows to a height and width of 2 or 3 m (6–10 ft). The dark green leaves, to 8 cm (3 in), are oblong in shape and pretty, white, nodding flowers appear singly or in small groups from early to midsummer. *S. japonicus*, the Japanese snowbell, zone 5, is a graceful, deciduous tree, growing to 8–10 m (26–33 ft) high. Its glossy, green foliage turns rich red or yellow in fall. The white, sometimes pale pink, flowers are bell shaped, appearing along the undersides of branches in summer. *S. officinalis*, storax, zone 9, can be shrubby or tree-like, growing 6–8 m (20–26 ft) high. Its white, bell-like flowers are borne in small clusters on the branch tips in early summer. Native to the Mediterranean, it is the original source of friar's balsam. A distinctive variety of this species occurs naturally in northern California.

Swainsonia (fam. Papilionaceae)

There are around 50 flowering subshrubs and perennials in this genus, mostly native to Australia. They have lovely, long, feathery foliage and very showy pea flowers in long sprays. These quick-growing shrubs have a long flowering period from spring to summer, if conditions are favorable, and make attractive additions to the garden, providing excellent cut flowers. The low-growing species are suitable for rockeries and for pots and baskets. In areas prone to frosts, grow in a cool conservatory or greenhouse. There have been some changes in botanical classification: the plant listed here as *S. formosa* is listed in the US and Europe as *Clianthus formosus* (see entry on *Clianthus*).

CULTIVATION Most species grow readily from seed sown in fall or spring. Seeds need treatment and should be either nicked carefully with a blade, or abraded with sandpaper, before soaking for 24 hours in cold water. They can also be grown from cuttings and need a sunny, well-drained situation. Most plants in this genus will

ABOVE To cultivate Sturt's desert pea, *Swainsona formosa* or Clianthus formosus, requires very dry climates.

collapse if drainage is not perfect, if they are overwatered, or if conditions are too humid. Swainsonas improve in form if cut back each winter, new shoots being pendulous or climbing. In frost-prone areas, grow in an airy, cool or intermediate greenhouse in pots of well-drained, soil-based potting compost.

CLIMATE Warmest parts of zone 9.

SPECIES *S. formoa* (syn. *Clianthus formosus*), Sturt's desert pea or glory pea, is the floral emblem of South Australia. It is a prostrate, spreading plant with soft, gray-green, ferny foliage. The beak-like, scarlet flowers borne in upright clusters have black to brown, shiny bosses, or bumps, in the middle. It is an annual or short-lived perennial, germinating quickly after rain in its habitat. It is drought-tolerant once established and is most suitable for growing in containers like hanging baskets or up-ended terracotta pipes, filled with potting compost. These plants will not tolerate any root disturbance. *S. galegifolia*, Darling pea, from New South Wales and Queensland, grows to 1 m (3 ft), with smooth, light green, pinnate foliage. The flowers range from bright mauve to pink and red, sometimes tinged with brown or yellow. 'Albiflora' has pure white flowers; 'Splendens' has brilliant crimson flowers; and 'Violacea' has rose-violet flowers. *S. grayana* grows 1 m (3 ft) high, with grayish green, pinnate leaves that are woolly underneath. The mauve, pink or red flowers are marked in white at the bottom of the main petal, and the sepals are tinged with white. The large blooms make good cut flowers. *S. procumbens* is a dwarf species, growing to only 30 cm (12 in), with a spreading habit. The large, bright mauve or rose-purple flowers tend to fade as they mature.

Swede

(*Brassica napus*, Napobrassica Group, fam. Brassicaceae)

Rutabaga

Known as rutabaga in the US, this vegetable, which is related to cabbages, cauliflowers and

ABOVE Swedes or rutabagas close to maturity. They are harvested in fall and winter and can be lifted and stored if desired.

kales, is grown for its edible, succulent roots. The yellow or white rutabaga (from the Swedish rotabagge) became known as Swedish turnip, or swede. It is larger and sweeter than the turnip, more cold-tolerant, and more easily stored. While rutabaga and turnips are often considered lesser vegetables, they can be delicious if cooked correctly. Braised in a good stock and finished on top of the stove, rutabaga makes an excellent accompaniment to duck, beef or lamb. Alternatively, it can be steamed or baked, or added to stews.

CULTIVATION Rutabaga is essentially a cool weather crop, grown throughout the winter in most areas. Seed is sown in late spring or early summer where plants are to grow, in drills 2 cm (¾ in) deep, the rows spaced 45 cm (18 in) apart. Thin the seedlings to 25–30 cm (10–12 in) apart. Rutabaga need well-drained soil that has been deeply dug and enriched with organic matter. They also require regular watering during the growing season. Band the rows with a complete fertilizer before sowing, and give regular applications of liquid fertilizer, to encourage vigorous growth. Hearts of swedes tend to discolor and brown if there is a deficiency of boron in the soil. Ensure that the soil is kept at a steady level of moisture, as very dry soils further restrict the availability of boron. Use fertilizers which contain trace elements to help avoid this problem. Plants will mature in four to five months. Lift them and store in sand in a cool, dry place, or leave in the ground over winter, as frost is said to improve the flavor.

CLIMATE Zone 7.

VARIETIES The species itself is a native of Europe, but only cultivars are grown. There are several available and they will be listed in good seed catalogues. The flesh is generally yellow and the skin is buff and purple in color.

Sweet cicely

(*Myrrhis odorata*, fam. Apiaceae)

This herbaceous perennial from Europe has been grown for centuries for culinary use. It grows 1 m (3 ft) high, with a fleshy taproot, thin, branching stems, and soft, lacy leaves. The small, white flowers are borne in terminal

ABOVE Sweet cicely is a pretty, aromatic herb with mainly culinary uses. In earlier times, extracts from the roots were used to treat wounds and snake or dog bites!

clusters and the ridged seeds are dark brown. The leaves, seeds and roots add a licorice flavor to salads, and the roots can also be cooked as a vegetable.

CULTIVATION Sweet cicely is best grown in a position which has light, dappled shade cast by trees. It will grow in any well-drained, yet moist soil. Propagate from seed that is sown in clumps and spaced about 60 cm (24 in) apart, in fall or in early spring. When the seedlings appear, thin to one seedling from each clump. Alternatively, the roots can be divided either in fall or late winter.

CLIMATE Zone 5.

Sweet corn

(*Zea mays* var. *saccharata*, fam. Poaceae)

With origins probably in Mexico or Central America, sweet corn was part of the staple diet of the Central and Southern American native peoples prior to the arrival of the Spanish. It was introduced to Europe by Christopher Columbus in the 17th century and quickly became popular there. Hugely popular in the United States, it is generally served in the UK and Europe simply boiled, or perhaps barbecued, with butter and freshly ground pepper. However, a good sweet corn and crab meat soup is hard to beat, and sweet corn fritters are quite delicious. Milled corn can be used in breads, cakes and pancakes.

CULTIVATION Sweet corn produces separate male and female flowers, and cobs will not form unless pollination takes place. Corn must be planted in blocks, rather than in rows, for the pollen to be carried by wind, as it will not travel for more than a short distance. In the garden, choose a block in full sun and ensure that the soil is well drained and reasonably rich. While corn plants tolerate wind, they will not grow in cold conditions. Enrich soil before planting by digging in a handful of complete fertilizer with a high nitrogen content or poultry manure to

decreases, the starch content rises, and the grain becomes floury in texture. The main pest is corn earworm but gardeners generally tolerate this and simply cut off affected ends of cobs.

CLIMATE Zone 7, but grown as a summer crop in all climatic zones.

VARIETIES *Zea mays* var. *saccharata* is an erect, monoecious annual, widely grown in both tropical and temperate regions. At maturity, cobs are borne in the axils of the broad leaves. The male flower with the pollen is the tassel at the top of the cob, the kernels are the ovaries and the cob itself makes up the female flower. Each kernel has a silk thread running to the outside of the cob, through which pollen grains move into the ovary to effect fertilization. Cob and kernels are protected by a green, leafy covering husk. Modern varieties have been bred for higher yields, increased sugar content, less starch, greater disease-resistance, and general hardiness. There are many cultivars available, including some that are classed as supersweet.

ABOVE Sweet corn is wind-pollinated so must be close planted in blocks to ensure that pollen is carried from the male to the female flowers.

each square metre (yard) block. An additional side dressing of nitrogenous fertilizer when the corn is 15–20 cm (6–8 in) high is also recommended. Sow seed in spring, 5 cm (2 in) deep, direct into the prepared bed, spacing plants 30–45 cm (12–18 in) apart. By placing two seeds in each space, the weaker one can be removed when the seedlings are 10 cm (4 in) high. In frost-prone climates, cover the young plants with cloches for frost protection, or sow seeds in a heated greenhouse in late spring, singly in individual small pots, and plant out the young plants as soon as frosts are over. Gently remove all weeds as they appear, and provide ample water. During maturation, the kernels reach a critical point called the 'milk stage' when the kernel is composed of around 70 per cent watery sap and reaches its optimum sugar content. The corn is ready for harvesting and eating if a milky sap spurts out when a kernel is pressed with the fingernail. If left longer on the plant, the moisture content of the kernels

Sweet potato

(*Ipomoea batatas*, fam. Convolvulaceae)

Indigenous to the tropical Americas and the East Indies, sweet potato is widely cultivated in warm and temperate parts of the world for its edible, tuberous roots. This vegetable is becoming more widely used. It can be served baked with a roast dinner, or boiled and mashed. It can be made into soups, fritters and chips, and is served in a variety of interesting ways with other vegetables and meats. It is a valuable source of vitamin A and also contains vitamin C.

CULTIVATION The sweet potato is an herbaceous perennial, but is grown as a summer annual. It is a fast-growing climber. In cool climates, this vegetable is generally grown in a warm, humid greenhouse, ideally in a soil border or bed, but it can also be grown in grow bags or large pots and tubs. The tubers should be planted in

ABOVE These large root tubers of sweet potato have been dug and washed. Sweet potato varieties may have white, cream or orange flesh.

ABOVE *Symphoricarpos* species make ideal hedges and screens, and are tolerant of pollution, exposed sites and poor soil. The white berries persist even after the leaves have fallen.

spring, about 7 cm (3 in) deep and 30 cm (12 in) apart. If growing in a soil border or bed, tubers are generally planted in raised soil ridges. Alternatively, and a better option in cooler climates, plants can be raised from seed sown in spring and germinated at 24°C (75°F). Plant out young plants when about 15 cm (6 in) high. Sweet potatoes grown from tubers can be harvested within three to four months. Those grown from seed will be ready in about five months.

CLIMATE Outdoor cultivation in warmest parts of zone 9.

Symphoricarpos (fam. Caprifoliaceae)
Snowberry

These 16 species of deciduous shrubs, mostly from North America, are often grown as ornamentals for their attractive foliage and distinctive berries, which are borne on bare branches in fall and winter. The flowers are quite inconspicuous.

CULTIVATION Snowberries can be grown in almost any garden soil, in full sun or partial shade. Pruning may be required in winter, to thin out some of the older canes. Propagate by division, or from seed, cuttings or suckers.

CLIMATE There are species suited to various climatic zones.

SPECIES *S. albus* (syn. *S. racemosus*), snowberry, zone 3, is striking, with clusters of pure white berries in fall and winter. It grows to 1 m (3 ft). *S. x chenaulti*, zone 4, is smaller, with red berries spotted in white. *S. microphyllus* (syn. *S. montanus*), zone 7, grows to 2 m (6 ft), with pink berries which are quite translucent. *S. orbiculatus*, Indian currant or coralberry, zone 2, is very dense and twiggy, but quite decorative. Masses of small, bright pink berries persist after the leaves have fallen. Cultivar 'Foliis Variegatis' has gold-variegated foliage.

Syncarpia (fam Myrtaceae)
Turpentine tree

The five species of trees in this genus, from coastal forests of eastern Australia, are very handsome. They are grown for their timber used for heavy-duty constructions (such as wharves), being resistant to marine borers,

ABOVE Occurring naturally in Australia, *Syncarpia glomulifera* or turpentine tree, flowers there from mid-spring to early summer.

white ants and fire. They are planted in the south of the US as shade trees but they are not suitable for the average garden as they are too large, and cannot be recommended for growing under glass in frost-prone climates.

CULTIVATION Turpentines prefer a rich, moist, well-drained soil. They have low frost-tolerance. Propagation is from ripened seed, which germinates readily.

CLIMATE Zone 9.

SPECIES *S. glomulifera*, turpentine tree, grows up to 60 m (200 ft) in the wild, but less than 20 m (65 ft) in cultivation. The trunk is clothed in red-brown, deeply furrowed bark. It has dense, glossy, dark green foliage and sprays of white flowers, followed by woody fruits fused into a spiky, ball shape. This species smells of turpentine. *S. hillii*, another tall species, with larger, glossy leaves, is grown mostly for its timber which is exceptionally durable.

Syngonium (fam. Araceae)

These 30 species of tropical climbing plants originate in tropical America and the West Indies. They have very attractive foliage and climb by means of aerial roots, which are produced on the stems. They make good house plants and are also ideal for warm greenhouses and conservatories.

CULTIVATION When growing these plants in pots indoors, or under glass, use a rich, soilless potting compost. Shade from direct sun, but ensure good light, and provide a humid atmosphere. Water normally in summer, but reduce watering considerably in winter. Moss-covered poles can be used to provide support. Propagate from leaf-bud or stem-tip cuttings in summer, in a warm propagating case.

CLIMATE Tropical.

SPECIES *S. podophyllum*, goose foot plant, from Central and South America, has large, spear-shaped leaves which are borne on long stalks.

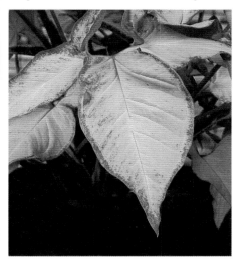

ABOVE Syngoniums are tropical climbers, similar to philodendrons, and are grown for their handsome foliage, which is often variegated, especially in the cultivars.

Variegated forms, with cream or silver markings, are available. Some of these have been given the name 'white butterfly'. This is perhaps in reference to the leaf shape. These 'butterfly' types are the ones that are the most popularly used as indoor plants.

Syringa (fam. Oleaceae)
Lilac

Native to eastern Asia and south-east Europe, this genus of around 20 species of deciduous shrubs has pale green, opposite leaves and small, showy flowers, which may be lilac, purple, pink, white or red, massed in loose heads. They make lovely, ornamental shrubs, especially for cooler regions. Their spring flowers are beautiful in a vase, filling the air with delightful fragrance.

CULTIVATION Lilacs require a moderately rich, well-drained garden soil with a fairly high lime content. They require a position in full sun for optimum flowering. They need regular, deep watering during the warmer months of the year. Mulch during the summer months to conserve soil moisture. Remove flower heads as soon as they begin to fade, to encourage flowering the following year. Propagate species from seed sown in fall or spring, in a garden frame. Cultivars can be propagated by layering in spring or from slightly firm, softwood cuttings in early summer, rooted in a heated propagating case.

CLIMATE Zone 5 unless otherwise specified.

SPECIES *S.* x *chinensis*, zone 4, to 3 m (10 ft), has fragrant, lilac flowers. Cultivar 'Alba' has white flowers; 'Saugeana' produces flowers tinged with red. *S.* x *hyacinthiflora*, zone 4, a French hybrid with broad leaves, has been widely hybridized, with many fine cultivars available. Some may be worth trying in warmer areas. *S. pubescens* subsp. *microphylla* has a spreading, shrubby habit, growing to 2 m (6 ft), with lilac flowers. *S. pubescens* subsp. *microphylla* 'Superba' is another small shrub, with rose-pink flowers until fall. The branches are tinged with purple and the leaves are velvety and slightly hairy. *S.* x *reflexa*, from China, is taller, to 4 m (13 ft), with large leaves and a profusion of deep pink flowers. *S. reticulata*, Japanese tree lilac, forms a squat, broad-crowned tree, growing to 9 m (30 ft). The creamy white flower clusters make a lovely, spring display against dark green foliage. The flowers smell of musk. Var. *mandshurica*, amur lilac, grows to 4 m (13 ft). *S. vulgaris*, common lilac, from south-eastern Europe, grows to about 4 m (13 ft), with a tree-like habit and true lilac flowers in white through to pale mauve. They have a delightfully sweet, yet strong, fragrance. Named cultivars are available in single and double flowering forms, in lovely colors. Some have been bred for resistance to leaf-spotting diseases.

Syzygium (fam. Myrtaceae)
Lilly pilly

These evergreen shrubs and trees are found in tropical and subtropical rainforests of Australia and Southeast Asia. They include the Australian lilly pilly and the clove tree from the Moluccas, as well as several species formerly included in the genus Eugenia. Grown for their lovely foliage (which is often pink or red when

BELOW This lovely, double-flowered, purple lilac is one of the many colorful and fragrant cultivars available today.

ABOVE *Syzygium wilsonii* is a winner on all counts: its new growth is a soft salmon pink and its flowers, magenta.

young), flowers and berries, they make attractive shade trees, ornamentals and specimens, and can be trimmed into a dense hedge. Outside subtropical and tropical climates, syzygiums can be grown in an intermediate to warm conservatory or greenhouse.

CULTIVATION Syzygiums prefer a rich, moist, well-drained soil enriched with organic matter, and full sun, and tolerate only light frosts. In the greenhouse or conservatory, grow in pots of soil-based potting compost. Ensure really good light, but shade from strong, direct sun. Syzygiums do not like too much water: apply water in moderation during growth, and reduce further in winter. Propagate from seed in spring germinated at 26°C (79°), from semi-ripe cuttings in summer, in a heated propagating case, or by layering in spring.

CLIMATE Subtropical to tropical.

SPECIES *S. aromaticum*, clove tree, has elliptical leaves, dotted with glands and clusters of yellow flowers, borne at branch ends. This species is the source of the well-known spice, which is the sun-dried flower bud. *S. coolminianum* (syn. *S. oleosum*), blue lilly pilly, native of eastern Australia, is a shrub or small tree, to 5–6 m (16–20 ft) high, with pale bark and a pendulous growth habit. The crushed leaves are highly aromatic and the cream flowers, borne in open sprays, are followed by blueish violet, round berries. *S. floribundum*, another Australian species, grows to 10–20 m (33–65 ft), with a weeping habit. The flowers are yellow and the berries, greenish white. *S. francisii* is a large, spreading Australian native, growing to heights of 40 m (130 ft), with small sprays of flowers and round, purple fruits. *S. jambos*, rose apple, a tree from the Malay Archipelago, 10–12 m (33–40 ft) high, has glossy, dark green leaves and large, rounded clusters of greenish white flowers, followed by fragrant, yellow, edible fruit which taste of rosewater. *S. luehmannii*, from eastern Australia, grows to 30 m (100 ft) in the wild, but only 8–10 m (26–33 ft) in cultivation. It has an upright habit and produces small clusters of creamy white flowers, followed by red, pear-shaped fruit. *S. paniculatum*, Australian rose or brush cherry, to 10–15 m (33–50 ft) high, has dense clusters of creamy white flowers and edible, rose-purple berries. *S. pycnanthum*, wild rose apple, from the Malay Archipelago, is a shrub or small tree, to 4 m (13 ft), with glossy leaves, showy clusters of pink flowers, and dark, reddish purple berries. *S. wilsonii* is shrub-like, to 2 m (6 ft). New growth is salmon pink and the powder puff flowers are magenta.

ABOVE Brush cherry, *Syzygium paniculatum*, bears masses of fleshy, edible berries after its fluffy, cream flowers have fallen.

TU

Tabernaemontana to Ulmus

Tabernaemontana (fam. Apocynaceae)

Widely grown in tropical and subtropical regions, these 100 or so species of flowering shrubs or small trees are similar to gardenias. All species produce a milky sap. They are used as ornamentals and as informal hedging in warm climates. Outside the tropics, grow them in a warm greenhouse or conservatory.

CULTIVATION Grow in pots of soil-based potting compost in the greenhouse or conservatory. Plants need very good light and should not be overwatered, especially in winter. If necessary, prune back lightly in late winter to maintain a good shape. Propagate from seed in spring or from semi-ripe cuttings in summer, both in a warm propagating case. Plants can also be layered in spring.

CLIMATE Tropical.

SPECIES *T. divaricata*, known as crape jasmine or moonbeam, occurs naturally in northern India, southern China and northern Thailand. Growing to 2.5 m (8 ft), it has oval, clusters of fragrant, white flowers. *T. grandiflora*, (syn. *Stemmadenia grandiflora*), from Venezuela, grows to 2.5 m (8 ft), with yellow flowers.

ABOVE The flower petals of *Tabernaemontana divaricata* are slightly twisted. The floral fragrance is very strong in still, warm conditions.

Tagetes (fam. Asteraceae)

Marigold

There are two types of marigold commonly grown, French and African, both natives of Mexico and Central America. These upright-growing, branching annuals are easy to cultivate and are grown for their attractive foliage and brightly colored, orange or yellow flowers, borne singly or in small, terminal clusters. Most flowers have a very strong smell. Both types are suitable for cutting, but the leaves should be removed from the stems to water level before arranging in the vase.

CULTIVATION Marigolds are grown as summer bedding plants and, in frost-prone climates, are raised from seed sown under glass in early to mid-spring, and germinated at 21°C (70°F). The young plants are planted out when frosts are over. In areas free from frost, sow in flowering positions in mid to late spring. Marigolds need a position in full sun, with reasonably fertile, well-drained soil. Plants should have dead flowers removed regularly to encourage a long period of flowering. If the weather is dry, water well and regularly.

CLIMATE Warmest parts of zone 9, although grown as summer annuals in all climatic zones.

SPECIES *T. erecta*, African marigold, has a stiff, upright habit and toothed, feathery leaves.

ABOVE Single-flowered French marigolds, seen in summer and fall, have a range of colours.

ABOVE African marigolds, *Tagetes erecta*, are tall growers. The large flowers feature rows of rolled, almost quilled, petals.

ABOVE The tree tomato, *Cyphomandra betacea*, can be grown in an intermediate greenhouse or conservatory in frost-prone areas. The fruits are edible.

Flowers have been bred in a range of forms, from double or ball types to more open semi-doubles with looser, more open flower heads of pale to deep golden yellow and various shades of orange. Plants may bloom from late spring until early fall if dead-headed regularly. Tall strains grow to 70–100 cm (28–40 in) high, medium to 45–70 cm (18–28 in), and the compact dwarf forms to 30–40 cm (12–16 in). *T. patula*, French marigold, is similar to the African type, but is lower growing, with a more branching habit. The smaller flowers range from dark red to yellow and bloom in summer and fall, making them particularly useful as cut flowers. Of the many cultivars available with single, double or crested flowers, most are dwarf plants around 15 cm (6 in) tall. *T. tenuifolia*, signet marigold, is also used for summer bedding, but is not as popular as the other two types. There are many cultivars, all dwarf, bushy plants with masses of small, single flowers in yellow or orange, from the end of spring to fall.

Tamarillo

(*Cyphomandra betacea*, fam. Solanaceae)

Tree tomato

This South American plant, related to *Solanum melongena* (eggplant), is grown both for its edible fruit and its ornamental qualities. It is a perennial, woody, tree-like shrub, growing to around 3 m (10 ft) high. The 8 cm (3 in) long, egg-shaped fruit has a smooth, dull red skin. It may be eaten raw, although, with its acidic taste, it is better poached and served with pure, rich cream.

CULTIVATION In areas prone to frost, grow in an intermediate conservatory or greenhouse in pots of soil-based potting compost. Ensure good light, shade from direct sun, and provide a humid atmosphere. Liquid feed monthly in summer. Pruning may be required in late winter to control size. Outdoors grow in a sheltered spot with full sun and rich, well-drained soil. Propagate in spring from seed germinated at 18°C (64°F), or from semi-ripe cuttings in summer, with basal warmth.

CLIMATE Warmest parts of zone 10 to tropical.

Tamarind

(*Tamarindus indica*, fam. Caesalpiniaceae)

This single-species genus of evergreen tree, a native of eastern Africa, has become naturalized in Southeast Asia. Grown mostly for its tart fruit (eaten fresh or used in chutneys and curries), it

ABOVE Tamarind trees carry their flowers on top of the branches, amongst the divided leaves. In its native Africa, trees are browsed by animals.

makes a good garden or park tree, with decorative, graceful foliage and attractive form. Tamarindus indica grows to about 20 m (65 ft) in ideal conditions, but is generally much smaller. It has fern-like leaves and small clusters of pale yellow to brown flowers in summer, followed by the 20 cm (8 in) long, dark brown seed pods.

CULTIVATION In frost-prone climates, grow in an intermediate to warm greenhouse or conservatory, perhaps as a young foliage plant, in pots of soil-based potting compost. Outdoors tamarinds like full sun, deep soil and plenty of moisture. Propagate from seed in a warm propagating case, but bear in mind that seedlings are prone to damping off, and seedling trees take a long time to bear fruit.

CLIMATE Warmest parts of zone 10 to tropical.

Tamarix (fam. Tamaricaceae)

Tamarisk

Native to western Europe and the Mediterranean region, and eastern Asia through to India, this genus consists of 54 species of mostly deciduous shrubs and small trees. With graceful, feathery foliage, some species make lovely ornamentals, while others are useful windbreaks, particularly in coastal areas. A few, once established, tolerate soil salinity and arid conditions. The small, white or pink flowers are borne on slender spikes.

CULTIVATION *Tamarix* species need a sunny position and will thrive in any well-drained soil, even dry conditions. They are best pruned annually to keep them fairly low and bushy. On spring-flowering species, prune old, flowered stems back to young shoots after flowering; prune late summer-flowering species in early spring, cutting back all previous year's shoots to a permanent woody framework. Propagate from hardwood cuttings in winter.

CLIMATE There are species suited to various climatic zones.

SPECIES *T. africana*, zone 8, from the Canary Islands, is a bushy shrub or small tree with black to dark purple bark. *T. aphylla*, athel, zone 8, is an evergreen tree with gray bark,

BELOW Tamarisks bear flowers in various shades of pink. These small trees are suitable for a wide range of climates.

from northern Africa and the Mediterranean. Growing to 10 m (33 ft), it has fine, grayish green foliage and pink flower spikes, borne at the branch tips. This species makes an good windbreak. *T. parviflora*, zone 5, from southeastern Europe, is a graceful shrub or small tree, with dark brown to purple bark and arching branches. Growing 5–6 m (16–20 ft) tall, it is pretty in spring, covered with masses of small, rose-pink flower spikes. *T. ramosissima* (syn. *T. pentandra*), zone 2, a small tree to 6 m (20 ft), has distinctive, blue-green foliage which contrasts with the dark brown to purple stems, bark and branches. Probably the most widely grown species, it too is lovely when in flower, the rose pink blooms being borne in abundance during late summer.

Tanacetum (fam. Asteraceae)

Tansy, feverfew

Amongst this group of around 70 species of aromatic annuals, perennials and subshrubs are several cultivated over the centuries for medicinal use and as insecticides. A number of species are grown purely as ornamentals today, although some are still widely grown for use in herbal teas, for flavoring, and for their insect-deterrent properties.

BELOW Common tansy, *Tanacetum vulgare*, grows rapidly in any kind of soil in full sun. These plants have insect-repellent properties.

CULTIVATION All species are best grown in full sun. Any type of soil is suitable, as long as it is well drained. Cut back the perennials in fall or early spring (but with *T. coccineum*, after the first flush of flowers), to encourage more blooms. Propagate from seed in spring, under glass. Perennials can be propagated by division in early spring, or from soft, basal cuttings or softwood cuttings in spring or early summer.

CLIMATE There are species suited to various climatic zones.

SPECIES *T. balsamita*, alecost or costmary, zone 6, is grown for its very aromatic foliage (see entry under *Costmary*). *T. coccineum*, zone 5, is an herbaceous perennial, 40–70 cm (16–28 in) high, with fine, feathery foliage and masses of daisy-like flowers, in early summer. This species has several cultivars, all making good cut flowers. *T. parthenium*, feverfew, zone 6, is a short-lived perennial, to about 45–60 cm (18–24 in), often grown as an annual. It flowers profusely in summer, the entire plant being covered with small, white, yellow-centered, daisy-type flowers. Leaves may be lobed or divided. This species can self-seed freely. Cultivars of *T. parthenium* are available. All parts of the plant are strongly aromatic and it has been cultivated for centuries for tonics and for reducing fever. *T. vulgare*, common tansy, zone 4, to 60–90 cm (24–36 in) high, is popular. It has feathery foliage and flat clusters of round, yellow flowers during summer. The leaves are said to smell like lemon and camphor. Tansy has a long history of use as an insect-repellent and is reputed to rid dogs of fleas. It has a number of culinary uses, as well as its many applications in folk medicine.

Tangelo (*Citrus x tangelo*, fam. Rutaceae)

Tangelo is a cross between mandarin and grapefruit. The fruit is a rich, bright orange, with a smooth skin, many varieties having a pronounced neck segment. It is very juicy, and different varieties have very distinctive flavors.

ABOVE Tangelo 'Minneola' is a good variety for the home garden. The fruit is very juicy, with a distinctive flavor.

The cultivar 'Minneola' was bred in the US in 1931. It matures in mid to late winter and has a distinctive, but slight, grapefruit flavor. 'Seminole' has the same parentage as 'Minneola', but is later maturing, ripening in spring. Both mandarin and grapefruit flavors can be detected in the fruit. The fruit of tangelos does not peel as easily as a mandarin. Other varieties include 'Orlando' and 'Sampson'.

CULTIVATION Like all citrus, tangelos must have perfectly drained soil, preferably enriched with organic matter, and full sun exposure. Trees should be sheltered from strong winds. They are not grown on their own roots, but budded on to selected rootstocks resistant to root rotting fungi and some virus diseases. In the growing season, give regular, deep waterings. Fertilize with a complete plant food containing trace elements in late winter and late spring, or early summer. Pruning is rarely needed beyond thinning out the canopy and removing crossing branches. Prune in cooler weather, as pruning in hot weather may expose previously shaded branches to sun scald. Tangelos can be grown in zone 9, but in cooler zones, grow in a cool or intermediate greenhouse, in pots of soil-based potting compost. Plants need maximum light, but shade from direct strong sun. They can be stood outside in summer if it is warm and sunny. Outdoors tangelos must have perfectly drained soil enriched with organic matter, and a sheltered position in full sun.

CLIMATE Zone 9. Trees can tolerate light frosts but must be protected when young.

Taro (*Colocasia esculenta*, fam. Araceae)

Taro is an important food crop throughout the tropics and is extensively grown in the Pacific Islands, and in many Asian countries. It is known as 'dasheen' in some countries. Grown mainly for its edible tubers, the young leaves are also eaten. Plants grow from a tuberous rhizome and vary from 1 to 2 m (3–6 ft) tall. It has large leaves, 40–50 cm (16–20 in) in length. Flowers are arum-like, with a yellowish spathe. In frost-prone and cool climates, grow in a warm greenhouse, in a soil bed or large container, and provide high humidity.

CULTIVATION Plant tubers 5–8 cm (2–3 in) deep in early spring. Soil should be well drained but enriched with manure or compost. Provide

ABOVE Cut taro root is seen here with its large-leaved plant, *Colocasia esculenta*. This is easy to cultivate in warm, humid conditions.

abundant water during the growing season. Tubers are ready to harvest in six to seven months. Propagate plants from small, subsidiary tubers or from division of the rootstock.

CLIMATE Warmest parts of zone 10 to tropical.

Tarragon

(*Artemisia species*, fam. Compositae)

Native to central and eastern Europe and Russia, tarragon is probably best known as the essential ingredient in bearnaise sauce. It is used to flavor fish and chicken, and is often found in vinegars. With its subtle flavor and aroma of aniseed, French tarragon, *Artemisia dracunculus*, is more popular than Russian tarragon, *A. dracunculus dracunculoides*.

CULTIVATION Tarragon is easy to grow, thriving in a warm, sunny position in light, well-drained soil enriched with organic matter. It can also be grown in window boxes and tubs. Mulch around the plant during summer and protect from excessive winter rain. Propagate by division in early spring or fall, from cuttings in early summer, or from seed in spring. The leaves are ready for picking in summer. Hang the leafy stalks in bunches or spread over a rack in a cool, airy place to dry. Store ground leaves in airtight containers, away from light.

CLIMATE Zone 3.

SPECIES *Artemisia dracunculus*, French tarragon, is a somewhat shrubby, clump-forming, hardy perennial, to about 1.2 m (4 ft) in height, with erect, branching stems, highly aromatic foliage, and heads of very light yellow flowers in summer. *A. dracunculus dracunculoides*, Russian tarragon, is a slightly larger, more vigorous plant, with coarser leaves, less delicately flavored than those of French tarragon.

Tasmannia (fam. Winteraceae)
Pepper bush

Grown for their attractive foliage, flowers and fruit, this Australian genus of six species of shrubs or small trees was previously classified under *Drimys*. The bright green leaves are borne on red stems and masses of greenish

ABOVE French tarragon has a delicate, aniseed flavor. It is an essential component of fines herbes, along with chervil, chives and parsley.

ABOVE Mountain pepper, *Tasmannia lanceolata*, is an Australian native. The fruit and seeds, and sometimes the leaves, have a hot flavor.

white flowers are followed by small, black berries. In cold climates, the foliage colors well in winter, remaining on the plant. It makes an attractive addition to floral arrangements.

CULTIVATION Best grown in well-drained, yet moist soil in a sheltered position, with full sun or partial shade. In frost-prone climates, grow in a cool greenhouse in pots of soil-based potting compost. Propagate from semi-ripe cuttings in late summer, with bottom heat.

CLIMATE Zone 9 or 10 for the species listed below.

SPECIES Few of these are likely to be available outside their native Australia. *T. insipida*, pepper bush, is a neat shrub, to 5 m (16 ft). Creamy white, summer flowers are followed by purple fruits. *T. lanceolata*, mountain pepper, occurs in mountain forests and in coastal Tasmania. It is a rounded shrub to 2 m (6 ft). The round, black fruits have red stems. *T. purpurascens*, a sub-alpine shrub, grows 2 m (6 ft) high. The round fruits are purplish black in color. *T. stipitata* is a rainforest shrub, growing to 4 m (13 ft). The flowers are white or cream and appear in early summer.

Taxodium (fam. Taxodiaceae)

Bald cypress, swamp cypress

There are only three species in this genus of conifers from eastern North America and the highlands of Mexico. Unlike most other conifers, they are deciduous, but instead of shedding their leaves, they shed small branchlets with the leaves attached. These trees are grown for their fresh, emerald green foliage and lovely fall tones of yellowish or coppery brown. They produce numerous, small pollen cones in drooping sprays at the branch ends, while the roundish seed cones are borne in clusters on stouter branchlets. Taxodiums make outstanding specimen trees where space permits.

CULTIVATION These conifers prefer a well-drained site, though they will adapt to poorly drained

ABOVE This large, pyramidal bald cypress, *Taxodium distichum*, is growing in a shallow waterway.

conditions. *T. distichum* is best suited to cooler areas and *T. mucronatum* to warmer climates, but both can be grown in a range of climates, preferring sheltered, humid conditions with plenty of sun. They can be grown in most soil types, except very shallow, rocky, or alkaline soils. Their growth is faster and more luxuriant if planted on pond or stream banks. Propagate from hardwood cuttings in winter, under glass, or from seed sown in spring, in a garden frame. In very cold climates, protect young plants from severe frosts.

CLIMATE Zone 5 for *T. distichum*; zone 8–9 for *T. mucronatum*.

SPECIES *T. distichum*, bald cypress, from eastern North America, can grow to heights of 45 m (145 ft) in the wild, but is mostly around 20 m (65 ft) in cultivation. It has a pyramidal crown, spreading to around 7 m (23 ft). The tiny, slender leaves are closely arranged in two flat rows and, in cooler climates, color a deep, rusty brown in fall. *T. mucronatum*, Montezuma cypress, is similar to *T. distichum*, with identical leaves, but differs in growth habit, with a huge trunk and widely spreading branches. Huge specimens can be seen in its native Mexico, the most famous being the great tree of Tulé.

Taxus (fam. Taxaceae)
Yew

These slow-growing evergreen conifers occur naturally in northern hemisphere temperate climates. Young trees are conical in shape, developing over a long period a domed crown and huge trunk. The flat, green, needle-like leaves are borne spirally, appearing to be in two rows. Male and female flowers are found on separate trees. Only two species of *Taxus* are commonly in cultivation, both suitable only for cool temperate areas. However, a number of named cultivars are grown. Yews are grown as hedges and windbreaks, and are also used in topiary. Most parts of these trees are poisonous to humans and animals if ingested.

CULTIVATION Yews will grow in any type of well-drained soil, including acid or alkaline types. They will also grow well in full sun or complete shade, but the golden-leaved cultivars produce their best color in a sunny spot. Hedges are trimmed in summer and fall. Propagate from semi-ripe cuttings in late summer or fall, in a garden frame.

CLIMATE Zone 6 for *T. baccata*, zone 5 for *T. cuspidata*.

SPECIES *T. baccata*, English yew, is a native of Europe, western Asia and northern Africa, and has long had religious associations. It is a popular topiary subject. English yew grows up to 25 m (80 ft) in the wild, but is generally much smaller, reaching around 10 m (33 ft), in cultivation, with a huge, short trunk. In today's gardens, the yew is mainly known in the form of a number of cultivars. 'Aurea' is a dense shrub, growing to around 2 m (6 ft), with many short, crowded shoots clothed in spirally arranged leaves. Young leaves are a pale golden yellow, becoming greenish yellow by winter. 'Fastigiata', Irish yew, is columnar in habit, with spirally arranged, deep green leaves. Generally around 2 m (6 ft) high, it does mature to greater heights. 'Fastigiata Aurea' has a similar growth habit, but the foliage is splashed with golden yellow. 'Fastigiata Aureomarginata' is also similar, but the bright golden yellow new foliage matures to green, leaving narrow bands of yellow around the margins. *T. cuspidata*, Japanese yew, is quite a large tree in its habitat, but is generally 8–10 m (26–33 ft) high in cultivation. This species has a much greater cold-tolerance than *T. baccata*. Faster growing, yet little different from *T. baccata*, its small, narrow, dull green leaves are arranged in V-shaped rows. Var. *nana* is more commonly grown. It is a low, spreading shrub, growing to 1.5 m (5 ft) high, though much wider, with dark green foliage.

Tecoma (fam. Bignoniaceae)
Trumpet bush

Comprising 12 species of showy, evergreen shrubs, climbers and trees, this genus is native to southern North America, South America,

ABOVE Yew, *Taxus baccata*, lends itself to formal shaping. This formal hedge screens the verandah from the street.

ABOVE *Tecoma stans*, yellow bells, has tubular, bright yellow flowers from the end of winter through to summer. Grow under glass in frosty climates.

and South Africa. Sprays of bright yellow to orange, tubular flowers are followed by bean-like fruits. The leaves are composed of a number of leaflets, which are generally serrated.

CULTIVATION Tecomas are frost-tender, so should be grown in a cool to intermediate conservatory or greenhouse in climates which are prone to frost. Plant in a large container of soil-based potting compost, or in a soil bed. Provide maximum light. Outdoors grow in full sun with rich soil. Prune back after flowering or in early spring to control size and maintain a good shape. Propagate from semi-ripe cuttings in summer, in a warm propagating case.

CLIMATE Warmest parts of zone 10 to tropical.

SPECIES *T. castaneifolia*, a native of Ecuador, is a shrub or small tree with serrated leaflets and yellow flowers. *T. garrocha* grows to 2 m (6 ft), with smooth, toothed leaflets and very striking, yellow or salmon-colored flowers with a scarlet tube. *T. stans*, yellow bells, is a large shrub or small tree, growing to 6 m (20 ft). It may be heavily pruned after flowering to maintain a compact shape. The bright yellow flowers, borne in sprays at the branch tips, bloom from the end of winter through to summer. The leaflets have deeply serrated margins.

Tecomaria (fam. Bignoniaceae)

This erect shrub, native to South Africa, is grown for its striking, brightly colored, funnel-shaped flowers which may be orange, yellow or scarlet.

CULTIVATION This species is frost-tender, so should be grown in a cool conservatory or greenhouse in frost-prone climates. Plant in a large container of soil-based potting compost, or in a soil bed. Provide maximum light. Outdoors grow in full sun or partial shade, and well drained, humus-rich soil. Prune back in early spring to control size and maintain a good shape. Propagate from semi-ripe cuttings in summer, in a warm propagating case.

CLIMATE Zone 10.

SPECIES Botanists have now included *Tecomaria capensis*, Cape honeysuckle, in the

ABOVE *Tecomaria capensis* (syn. *Tecoma capensis*), Cape honeysuckle, is frost-tender, but is a good shrub for a cool greenhouse or conservatory.

genus *Tecoma* (see entry under *Tecoma*). It is a straggling shrub to 2–6 m (6–20 ft). Clusters of tubular, orange-red to scarlet flowers appear in the summer. The deep green leaves are composed of a number of leaflets, serrated along the margins. There are several cultivars, including the low-growing 'Apricot', with orange blooms; 'Aurea' with yellow blooms; and 'Lutea', to 2 m (6 ft), with deep yellow blooms.

Telopea (fam. Proteaceae)
Waratah

The spectacular, scarlet flower of this Australian genus formed part of many legends of the Aboriginal peoples, who named it 'waratah'. The generic name, which comes from a Greek word meaning 'seen from afar', alludes to the brilliant color of the flowers, which stands out from the surrounding foliage. Early writers and artists were attracted to the waratah, one describing it in glowing terms as follows: 'The most magnificent plant which the prolific soil of New Holland affords is, by common consent, both of Europeans and natives, the Waratah'. Indigenous to open forests of south-eastern Australia, the waratah belongs to the same family as banksias, grevilleas and proteas. It is the largest of all native Australian flowers, growing to 12 cm (5 in) in diameter. The 'flower' is a head of many small, curved, tubular flowers, massed together in a close, spiral arrangement, and the leathery, green, long-stalked leaves are borne alternately on the stems. The seeds are contained in very large, leathery pods, to 12 cm (5 in) long. The very showy waratahs found in Tasmania and Victoria can be grown in cool climates, provided the situation is frost-free.

CULTIVATION Waratahs prefer deep, friable, well-drained, acid soil, to which a large quantity of decayed leaf mulch has been added prior to planting. Most species require plenty of moisture, especially in summer, but soil drainage must be good. Most also like a semi-shaded situation, with protection from wind, thriving if grown under tall trees. Once established,

ABOVE A cultivar of waratah, *Telopea speciosissima*. This shrub blooms in the spring and is a good subject for a cool greenhouse or conservatory.

waratahs respond to slow-release fertilizers. Low-nitrogen, low-phosphorus types are recommended. Waratahs flower only once every five years in the wild, but with good cultivation and pruning, they will flower annually. This is particularly true of cultivars. They make excellent, long-lasting cut flowers and are also attractive in dried arrangements. If left on the plant, cut back the flower stems to about half the length of each stalk after the flowers have died. Pruning is recommended to encourage blooms for the following season. Cut some stems right back to the ground every four to five years. The setting of seed will interrupt the next season's flowering, as one waratah bloom is capable of producing as many as 250 seeds. Propagate from seed sown in early spring, or from leaf bud cuttings taken in late spring, though these may be slow to strike. In frost-prone climates, grow in a cool greenhouse or conservatory in pots of acid, sandy, soil-based potting compost. Ensure excellent light.

CLIMATE Frost-free. Zone 9–10.

SPECIES *T. mongaensis*, Braidwood waratah, is an upright shrub, 2–4 m (6–13 ft) high, with a spreading, suckering growth habit. The dull, dark green leaves, to 15 cm (6 in) long, are smooth and leathery. Flowering occurs when the plants are about two years old, the deep red, showy blooms appearing throughout spring. The flower heads are flattish and up to 12 cm (5 in) in diameter. *T. mongaensis* x *T. speciosissima*, a hybrid, has been developed to obtain the best qualities of both species. It has less showy flowers than *T. speciosissima*, but the color is a darker red, and the growth is more compact, with smaller, smoother leaves. *T. oreades*, Gippsland waratah, is a taller shrub or small tree, to 6 m (20 ft), with a slender, upright, branching habit. It has smaller, looser, red flower heads, to 8 cm (3 in) across, and smooth, oval to lance-shaped leaves. *T. speciosissima*, the floral emblem of New South Wales, is the most spectacular species. This vigorous, many branched shrub grows to about 3 m (10 ft) and has stiff, leathery, dark green leaves, serrated at the edges. The magnificent, scarlet flower heads are 10–15 cm (4–6 in) in diameter, sometimes surrounded by prominent bracts. These spring blooms make excellent cut flowers. 'Wirrimbirra White' is a rare, white-flowering form. *T. oreades* x *T. speciosissima*, a hybrid to 3 m (10 ft), has masses of red flower heads in spring. *T. truncata*, Tasmanian waratah, from wet, mountainous regions, is suitable for growing in cool climates. Growing about 2–3 m (6–10 ft), it has smaller, flatter heads of scarlet flowers. The smooth, oblong leaves are around 10 cm (4 in) long and the dense flower heads have silky, hairy bracts.

Templetonia (fam. Papilionaceae)

These 11 species of attractive, Australian native shrubs have large pea flowers which may be red, yellow or purple. They are quite variable, some being spiny with alternate leaves, others being almost leafless. They flower from fall to spring and the blooms are followed by flat, leathery pods. Templetonias are frost-tender and need to be grown in a cool to intermediate

ABOVE The large red pea flowers of *Templetonia retusa* appear from winter to early spring. This may be hard to cultivate in humid regions.

conservatory or greenhouse in frost-prone climates.

CULTIVATION In the greenhouse, grow in pots of soil-based potting compost. Ensure maximum light but shade from strong, direct sun. Outdoors templetonias do best in a sunny, well-drained position. Propagate in spring from seed which is first soaked in boiling water and allowed to stand for 24 hours. Germinate at 16°C (61°F).

CLIMATE Zone 10.

SPECIES *T. aculeata* is a prickly, almost leafless shrub, with purple, yellow or brown flowers from late winter through much of spring. *T. retusa*, cockie's comb or coralbush, is native to limestone soils in South and Western Australia. It is also resistant to exposed, coastal conditions and salt spray. Growing to 1.5 m (5 ft) high, this ornamental shrub has grayish green, wedge, or heart-shaped leaves and masses of large, scarlet flowers during winter. *T. sulcata*, centipede bush, has flattened stems, which replace the leaves and yellow or brown flowers.

Terminalia (fam. Combretaceae)

Found in tropical and subtropical regions of India, Southeast Asia, Australia and southern Africa, this genus includes some 200 species of evergreen and deciduous trees and shrubs. The leaves are quite unusual, in that they grow in clusters at the branch ends. The flowers are rather insignificant, but the berry fruits are showy and valued as a source of tannin. Many species are grown for timber, dyes, inks, gum and oils.

CULTIVATION Outside subtropical or tropical climates, grow in a warm conservatory or greenhouse, in pots of sandy, soil-based potting compost. Provide maximum light and a humid atmosphere. Outdoors these trees and shrubs like a humid climate and rich, deep, well-drained soil. Propagate in spring from seed ger-minated at 21°C (70°F), or by layering in spring.

CLIMATE Warmest parts of zone 10.

SPECIES *T. bellirica*, myrobalan, grows to 25 m (80 ft) in its native India, where it is cultivated for its timber and fruit, which is an important source of tannin. *T. catappa*, tropical or Indian almond, is native to many tropical regions, where it may grow to over 20 m (65 ft). Widely grown in tropical areas, it thrives in coastal regions. The fruits are also a valuable source of tannin. *M. chebula*, known as myrobalan, is another tree cultivated for its tannin. This can grow to over 30 m (100 ft) in its native Sri Lanka, India and Malay Peninsula.

Tetradenia (fam. Lamiaceae)

This genus is not well known outside its countries of origin. It is native to South Africa and Madagascar and consists of five species of shrubs and perennials, all of which are aromatic and somewhat succulent. In frost-prone climates, grow these frost-tender plants in an intermediate to warm greenhouse or conservatory.

BELOW Some of the leaves of *Terminalia catappa* turn bright red before they fall These trees tolerate coastal exposure.

BELOW *Tetradenia riparia*, misty plume bush, is a frost-tender shrub with fluffy, mauve or white flowers. These appear in winter in its native South Africa.

CULTIVATION Under glass, grow in pots of soil-based potting compost and provide good light, but shade from direct, strong sun. Outdoors grow in a sheltered position with partial shade. Prune back hard after flowering to encourage a compact shape and new growth. Avoid over-feeding, as this will promote leafy growth at the expense of flowers. Propagate from cuttings in spring and root them in a heated propagating case.

CLIMATE Zone 10 or tropical.

SPECIES *T. riparia*, misty plume bush, musk bush or nutmeg bush, grows to around 2 m (6 ft) high. The sprays of fluffy, mauve or white flowers are 20–40 cm (8–16 in) long, and the foliage is highly aromatic. It is a native of South Africa, where it flowers during the winter.

Tetrapanax (fam. Araliaceae)
Rice paper plant

Comprising only one species of evergreen shrub or small tree, this genus is native to China and Taiwan. It is grown for its large, fan-like leaves and loose, showy clusters of creamy white, fluffy flowers, which bloom during fall. The pith of the stems is used for making rice paper in China.

ABOVE *Tetrapanax papyriferus* needs plenty of room for its wide, spreading leaves to grow. The hairs on the leaves may cause skin irritation.

CULTIVATION *Tetrapanax* needs well-drained soil and a sunny, sheltered position. It dies back to the ground in frost, but generally produces new growth in spring. In hard-frost areas, grow in a cool greenhouse or conservatory. Propagate by removing rooted suckers in spring.

CLIMATE Zone 8.

SPECIES *T. papyrifer* (syn. *T. papyriferus*) rice paper plant, grows to around 7 m (23 ft). The large, lobed leaves are densely covered in woolly hairs when young, and turn rust colored as they age. Cultivar 'Variegata' has cream to white leaves tinged with shades of green.

Tetratheca (fam. Tremandraceae)

Occurring naturally in moist, damp places throughout Australia, this genus of small shrubs produces masses of starry, mostly bright pink flowers with dark centers in spring and summer. Where frosts occur, grow in a cool, airy conservatory or greenhouse.

CULTIVATION In the greenhouse, grow in pots of acid potting compost. Provide good light, but shade from direct sun. In the garden, they need well-drained, acid soil in a sunny or partially shaded spot. Propagate from semi-ripe cuttings in summer, with basal warmth.

ABOVE *Tetratheca shiressii* has a lax growth habit, wiry stems and pretty, pink flowers in spring and summer.

CLIMATE Zone 9–10.

SPECIES *T. ciliata*, pink bells, from the southern states of Australia, is an erect shrub, wider than it is high, with small, rounded, soft leaves, arranged in whorls, and reddish pink flowers. A white-flowered form is in cultivation too. *T. denticulata*, Sydney pink bell, has small leaves, arranged in whorls and bright pink flowers. *T. ericifolia* grows to only 20 cm (8 in) high, with whorls of small, dark green leaves and bright magenta flowers. *T. juncea* is a wiry bush less than 30 cm (12 in) high, with leafless stems and large, bright pink flowers. *T. pilosa*, black-eyed Susan, produces bright mauve to magenta flowers. The light green leaves are variable. *T. shiressii* has small, oval-shaped leaves and large, bell-shaped, bright pink flowers. It has an open growth habit, growing to 60 cm (24 in) high. *T. thymifolia* produces a number of stems from ground level and has small, round, hairy leaves and bright, pinkish purple flowers. White-flowered forms are occasionally seen.

Teucrium (fam. Lamiaceae)
Germander

There are around 300 species in this genus of aromatic, evergreen and deciduous shrubs and subshrubs, and herbaceous perennials, widely distributed throughout the world, though mostly in areas around the Mediterranean. The genus name appears in both Latin and Greek ancient botanical works and several species of germander have a long history of use in herbal medicine. The soft-wooded, perennial species are useful for rock gardens and border plantings, while the shrubs make attractive, small hedges. Most species are summer flowering.

CULTIVATION Teucriums like full sun and well-drained, sandy soil, which is ideally alkaline or neutral. Gravelly or stony soil of low fertility is good for the small species, as in these conditions they remain more compact. *T. fruticans* should be pruned in early spring by cutting back all stems to within a few buds of the

ABOVE *Teucrium fruticans*, shrubby germander, has gray-green, aromatic foliage and light blue flowers in summer. It makes a good, low hedge.

ground. Propagate from seed sown in a garden frame in fall, or from softwood or semi-ripe cuttings in summer, in a heated propagating case.

CLIMATE There are species suited to various climatic zones.

SPECIES *T. chamaedrys*, wall germander, zone 5, from Europe, is low growing, spreading to about 75 cm (30 in) wide and 30–60 cm (12–24 in) high. It has small, deeply serrated, dark green leaves, sometimes hairy on the undersides. Sprays of reddish purple or rose pink flowers appear in mid to late summer. *T. fruticans*, shrubby germander, zone 8, from southern Europe, grows to 1 m (3 ft) high. The pretty, pale lavender flowers are borne in terminal sprays amongst aromatic, oval, gray-green foliage. This species tolerates poor, dry conditions and is often hedged at heights under 1 m (3 ft). *T. marum*, cat thyme, zone 9, is a low-growing shrub, to 30–50 cm (12–24 in), with stems covered in thick, white hair and small, lance-shaped leaves. The purple flowers are borne in clusters. Native to the islands of the western Mediterranean, this species is favored by cats. *T. scorodonia*, wood sage or sage-leaved germander, zone 6, is a dwarf shrub generally well under 1 m (3 ft) high. The heart-shaped leaves are gray-green and wrinkly and the yellow-green flowers are borne in tall spikes from midsummer to early fall. It has been used since mediaeval times as a tonic and other remedial purposes.

Thalictrum (fam. Ranunculaceae)
Meadow rue

This genus includes 130 species of herbaceous perennials, mainly from northern hemisphere temperate areas, though some also occur in tropical America and Africa, and South Africa. The cultivated species are very decorative, with their fern-like foliage and delicate flowers, which mainly come in pink or purple, and sometimes yellow or white.

CULTIVATION Grow in sun or partial shade, and ensure that these plants are kept well watered, particularly during dry weather. They prefer a humus-rich soil that drains well. Propagate from seed sown in spring in a sandy compost, or by division of the clumps in late winter or spring.

BELOW Meadow rue, *Thalictrum aquilegifolium*, carries pinkish purple flowers above pretty, fern-like foliage in late spring to early summer.

CLIMATE There are species suited to various climatic zones.

SPECIES *T. aquilegifolium*, feathered columbine, zone 6, from Europe and northern Asia, grows to about 1 m (3 ft). Fluffy sprays of pinkish purple flowers appear in late spring to early summer amongst gray-green leaves, divided into toothed leaflets. A number of cultivars are available in flower colors of white, deep purple or deeper pink tones. *T. chelidonii*, zone 7, a native of the Himalayas, grows to 1 m (3 ft) high. The mauve flowers, in late summer to early fall, are a little larger than those of most species. *T. dasycarpum*, zone 6, from North America, is an upright grower, to about 2 m (6 ft). The stems are often purplish in color, the leaves are prominently veined and hairy on the undersides, and the flowers are purple. *T. delavayi* (formerly *T. dipterocarpum*), zone 7, from western China, grows to 1 m (3 ft), with fine, small, triangular leaves, sometimes tinged blue. Masses of nodding, lilac flowers, with prominent, yellow stamens, are borne in loose sprays in summer. Cultivar 'Album' has pure white flowers. *T. flavum*, zone 6, from Europe and Asia, grows to just over 1 m (3 ft), with glossy, gray leaves divided into two or three leaflets, and fragrant, soft yellow, summer flowers.

Thelymitra (fam. Orchidaceae)
Sun orchid

These 50 species of terrestrial orchids are found mainly in Australia, though they extend to New Zealand, New Caledonia, New Guinea, Indonesia and the Philippines. Thelymitra species are generally known as sun orchids as many open only for a few hours in the middle of the day. Unlike most orchids, the sepals and petals are alike and there is no lip.

CULTIVATION In frost-prone climates, grow in pots of terrestrial orchid compost in an intermediate greenhouse or conservatory. Provide maximum light, to ensure the flowers open. During the growing period, water freely, but taper off towards fall, as growth dies down, and

ABOVE As its name suggests, *Thelymitra ixioides*, the sun orchid, will not open its lovely flowers in cloudy or overcast weather.

keep plants virtually dry in winter, apart from the occasional watering to prevent desiccation of the tubers. Propagate from seed sown as soon as ripe.

CLIMATE Zone 10.

SPECIES These are unlikely to be available outside their countries of origin. *T. ixioides* occurs naturally in temperate regions of Australia and New Zealand. It has a single, stem-clasping leaf, the stem bearing three to nine flowers, 4–5 cm (1½–2 in) in diameter. They are mostly violet, but may be mauve, blue, pink and occasionally white, and are usually marked with darker dots. This is the species most often grown, but *T. pauciflora* and *T. venosa* are worth trying.

Theobroma (fam. Sterculiaceae)

Native to tropical America, these 20 species of evergreen trees include *T. cacao*, from which cacao is obtained to be used in the manufacture

ABOVE Young trees of Theobroma cacao grow in the shad of larger trees. The fruit pods emerge directly from the trunk or branches.

of one of the world's most popular foods, chocolate. In fact, the genus name comes from two Greek words which mean 'food of the gods'. Cacao is derived from the seeds of the large fruits, which are fermented, roasted and ground.

CULTIVATION Outside the tropics, grow as a young foliage plant in a warm, humid greenhouse or conservatory, in pots of soil-based potting compost. Shade from direct sun. Propagate from seed sown in spring in a heated propagating case. Alternatively, increase from semi-ripe stem cuttings in summer, rooted with bottom heat.

CLIMATE Tropical.

SPECIES *T. cacao* grows to around 10 m (33 ft), with leathery, oval leaves about 30 cm (12 in) long. Small, creamy yellow flowers are borne for much of the year. The large seed pods grow to 30 cm (12 in) in length, ripening to a reddish brown. The many seeds are immersed in a sticky pulp.

Thevetia (fam. Apocynaceae)

There are eight species of ornamental trees or shrubs in this genus, all of which have their ori-

ABOVE *Thevetia peruviana* is an excellent shrub for the warm greenhouse or conservatory, as it bears its yellow or apricot flowers from late spring until fall.

gins in tropical America. Only one species is in general cultivation and it makes an attractive, long-flowering pot plant for the conservatory. Related to oleander and frangipani, these plants are poisonous if any part of them is ingested and the milky sap may cause skin irritations.

CULTIVATION Outside the tropics, grow in a warm greenhouse or conservatory in pots of soil-based potting compost. Plants need maximum light and airy conditions. Water well when plants are in full growth, but keep much drier in winter. If necessary, prune in late winter to restrict size. Propagate in spring from seeds germinated at 21°C (70°F), or from semi-ripe cuttings in summer, rooted in a heated propagating case.

CLIMATE Tropical.

SPECIES *T. peruviana*, sometimes called yellow oleander, is an evergreen shrub or small tree, growing 3–8 m (10–26 ft) high. The long,

narrow, glossy, green leaves are carried more densely towards the branch tips. The funnel-shaped flowers are fragrant and may be apricot, orange or clear yellow. These are carried towards the tips of the stems and may be seen from late spring through to fall. After flowering, seeds are formed in the green, fleshy fruit that matures to black when fully ripe.

Thomasia (fam. Sterculiaceae)

Paper flower

The 30 species in this genus of small, long-lived shrubs are natives of Western Australia, with one extending to the eastern states. The leaves are soft and velvety, and papery, bell-shaped flowers are produced over long periods, mainly in late winter and spring in the plants' natural habitats. The blooms range from white to deep pink and purple. The genus is unlikely to be available outside Australia.

CULTIVATION In frost-prone climates, grow in a cool to intermediate greenhouse or conservatory in pots of sandy, well-drained, soil-based potting compost. Ensure good light, but shade plants from direct, strong sun. Water in moderation during the growing period, but sparingly when resting. Outdoors thomasias need deep, sandy, well-drained soil and full sun to partial

ABOVE Many species of *Thomasia* have mottled nodding flowers. Most species are difficult to grow in humid areas with rain in summer.

shade. Propagate from seed soaked in boiling water and allowed to stand for 24 hours. Germinate in a heated propagating case. They can also be propagated from semi-ripe cuttings in summer, rooted with bottom heat.

CLIMATE Zone 10.

SPECIES *T. grandiflora* is a spreading shrub, less than 1 m (3 ft) high, but 1.5 m (5 ft) wide. It has small, dark green, crinkly leaves. The pinkish purple, mostly pendent flowers have black centers and appear from late winter to late spring. *T. macrocarpa*, large-fruited thomasia, is a spreading shrub with felty, heartshaped leaves, which are toothed at the margins. A profusion of mauve to purple flowers appears throughout spring. *T. petalocalyx* is native both to western and eastern Australia. It grows 60 cm (24 in) high and has small, oblong leaves, wavy around the margins. Small sprays of lilac-pink flowers with dark anthers are most abundant in early spring. *T. sarotes* grows to only 60 cm (24 in) high, with a spread to 1 m (3 ft). It has soft, dull blue-green leaves, rolled at the margins. From late winter through to spring, spikes of purple flowers appear on the branch tips. In its native habitat, it flowers for much of the year.

Thrinax (fam. Arecaceae)
Thatch palm

Originating in the West Indies and the southeast of the United States, this small genus comprises seven species of fan palms. Only one species, *T. parviflora*, is commonly cultivated. These palms are sensitive to frost, so where frosts occur, they should be grown as pot plants in a warm greenhouse or conservatory. Alternatively, they can be grown as house plants.

CULTIVATION In the greenhouse or conservatory, grow in pots of soil-based potting compost. Ensure good light, but shade plants from direct sun. Outdoors these palms like well-drained soil and warm, sunny, humid conditions. Propagate from seed sown in the spring germinated at a temperature of 26°C (79°F).

ABOVE The leaves of *Thrinax parviflora* have long been used as thatch in the West Indies, especially in its native Jamaica.

CLIMATE Warmest parts of zone 10.

SPECIES *T. morrisii*, grows to about 10 m (33 ft). Being a small palm it is ideal for growing in containers. The young leaves of this species are densely covered with white scales on the undersides. It is native to Florida and the West Indies, where it is known as the key palm. *T. parviflora*, thatch palm or palmetto thatch, grows to about 10 m (33 ft), with a very narrow trunk. It is native to Jamaica, where it has been used as a source of thatch. *T. radiata* is native to the Caribbean and Florida, where it is normally found in coastal areas. It tolerates salt-laden winds and is ideal for planting in subtropical and tropical zones.

Thryptomene (fam. Myrtaceae)

Of this genus of 40 species of Australian evergreen shrubs, only a few are commonly cultivated. They have long, graceful, arched branches which are clothed with tiny, aromatic leaves. They flower over a long period from winter through to summer, producing masses of small, white or pink, starry flowers. They are frost-tender shrubs, and in frost-prone climates are grown in a cool greenhouse or conservatory.

CULTIVATION Thryptomenes need acid or lime-free soil, so when pot grown under glass, use an acid, soil-based or soilless potting compost. Ensure maximum light and airy conditions. Outdoors grow in a sunny spot with well-drained soil. After flowering, cut back old flowered stems, but not into the old wood. Propagate in spring from seed germinated at 16°C (61°F). Do not cover with compost. Otherwise, propagate from semi-ripe cuttings in summer, with basal warmth.

CLIMATE Zone 10.

SPECIES Few of these are likely to be available outside their native Australia. *T. baeckeacea*, from Western Australia, has tiny, aromatic leaves and produces small, deep pink flowers in spring and summer. *T. calycina*, bushy heath myrtle or jam tart, from western Victoria, is a rounded or spreading shrub, growing to 1–2 m (3–6 in) high, with slightly pointed, dark green foliage and an abundance of red-centered, white flowers, borne in tapering sprays in spring or summer. This species is valued for its cut flowers. *T. ericaea* is a small, stiff shrub from South Australia, with tiny, overlapping leaves and white flowers. *T. saxicola* is the species which is most commonly grown. It is a compact plant, growing to 1 m (3 ft) high, with rounded leaves and pink or white flowers. Cultivar 'F.C. Payne' is recommended. It has tiny, green leaves and a profusion of light pink flowers, which appear in spring or summer, though it may also flower at other times of year. This form produces good cut flowers. *T. stenocalyx*, coming from Western Australia, grows to 1.2 m (4 ft), with oval leaves. It is the only species which produces yellow flowers. *T. stenophylla* is a low, spreading shrub which has very tiny, dense leaves and pink, summer flowers.

Thuja (fam. Cupressaceae)
Arbor-vitae

Native to temperate North America and eastern Asia, this genus consists of five species of conifers, columnar to pyramidal in shape. Their straight trunks are clothed in deeply furrowed, fibrous bark. They have aromatic, flattened, scale-like leaves and small, oval cones covered in overlapping scales. Several of the species are cultivated for their timber.

CULTIVATION Thujas will grow in any well-drained soil, provided it holds adequate moisture and is reasonably deep. They must have a position in full sun (particularly the colored-foliage cultivars), and a spot that is sheltered from wind. The majority of species are suitable for growing as formal hedges, and these should be trimmed in spring and again in late summer. The species can be raised from seed sown in spring, in a garden frame. All thujas can be propagated from semi-ripe cuttings, from late summer to mid-fall, rooting them in a heated propagating case.

CLIMATE Wide moisture and temperature range, but most prefer cool, moist climates.

BELOW *Thryptomene saxicola* 'F.C. Payne' is a fast-growing shrub with a long flowering period. It is suitable for growing in pots in a cool conservatory.

ABOVE The foliage of Western red cedar, *Thuja plicata*, is soft and pendulous. It is a well-known source of fine timber.

SPECIES *T. occidentalis*, American arbor-vitae, zone 3, from eastern North America, grows to about 20 m (65 ft), with a pyramidal crown and a thick trunk covered in reddish brown, peeling bark. The yellow-green leaves, blueish underneath, color bronze in fall. A vast number of cultivars is available. 'Ellwangerana Aurea' grows only 2–4 m (6–13 ft) high, and is broadly pyramidal to rounded in shape. The golden yellow foliage colors bronze-gold in winter. 'Ericoides' is a dwarf plant, growing to 50 cm (20 in), with loose, soft, crowded branches and soft, needlelike young foliage, maturing to brownish green. 'Globosa' has a dense, compact habit, growing to around 1 m (3 ft), with bright green foliage. 'Lutea' is very slow-growing, to about 3 m (10 ft), with a conical habit and golden yellow foliage, becoming a paler shade of yellow in winter. 'Pyramidalis' has a symmetrical, narrow, compact habit and is useful for formal plantings. 'Rheingold' is similar to 'Ellwangerana Aurea', but more rounded, tapering to a slight point at the center. The foliage is rich gold throughout winter. *T. orien-*talis, Chinese arbor-vitae, zone 6, is a native of China, but has long been cultivated in Japan. When young, it is a conical shape with dense foliage, maturing to a rather open, untidy shape, with protruding side branches. It is distinguished by its vertical, flat foliage sprays. This species has also given rise to many cultivars. 'Aurea Nana' has a neat, rounded habit, growing to 1 m (3 ft) high. The dense branchlets are green with gold tips. 'Beverleyensis' has a columnar habit, growing to around 3 m (10 ft). The gold-tipped foliage becomes a bronze-yellow in winter; 'Juniperoides' (syn. 'Decussata') has a rounded shape, growing less than 2 m (6 ft) in height. The dense, gray-green summer foliage matures to a rich purple in winter. 'Rosedalis' is a dwarf, oval form, growing to 1 m (3 ft), with small, soft, dense leaves. It changes color from pale yellow in spring to a bright light green in summer, and then to brownish purple in winter. *T. plicata*, western red cedar, zone 5, from western North America, grows up to 60 m (200 ft) in its habitat, but generally to around 25 m (80 ft) in cultivation. It is well known for its valuable timber. It is fast growing, with a broad, pyramidal form over many years, becoming more columnar with age. The foliage is a rich green color and highly aromatic. There are numerous cultivars, including 'Stoneham Gold', a cone-shaped plant to 2 m (6 ft), with rich gold young foliage turning to deep green, and 'Zebrina', cone-shaped to 15 m (50 ft), whose leaves are banded with light yellow.

Thujopsis (fam. Cupressaceae)

Closely related to thujas, this single-species genus from Japan yields durable timber, used both in general construction and for finer cabinetwork. While similar in several features to thujas, the leaves are larger and coarser and the cones are smaller and woody.

CULTIVATION This conifer needs a well-drained, yet moist soil and a sheltered, sunny position. Propagate from seed or cuttings as for thujas (see entry under *Thuja*).

ABOVE *Thunbergia grandiflora*, blue trumpet vine, has light to deep blue flowers in summer. It is a fast-growing, evergreen, twining climber.

ABOVE left A close look at the foliage of *Thujopsis dolabrata* reveals the neat, interlocking scale leaves.

CLIMATE Zone 7. Ideal for cool, moist climates.

SPECIES *T. dolabrata* is fairly slow growing, but makes a handsome specimen tree. It has a variable growth habit, making a narrowly pyramidal, open tree of around 20 m (65 ft), or sometimes a spreading shrub. The flattened, scale-like, dark green leaves are silvery white below and the cones are blueish gray. Cultivar 'Nana' is a dwarf, spreading, flat-topped shrub, with green foliage, becoming bronze in winter; 'Variegata' is slow growing, to 10 m (33 ft) high, with bright green foliage, splashed with white.

Thunbergia (fam. Acanthaceae)

There are about 100 species of flowering annual or perennial climbers, dwarf plants and shrubs in this genus, mostly occurring in warm regions of central and southern Africa, with some species from Madagascar, India and Asia. With their showy, brightly colored, funnel-shaped flowers, they make very attractive container or hanging basket plants.

CULTIVATION All thunbergias are frost-tender. In frost-prone climates, grow them in an intermediate to warm greenhouse or conservatory, in pots of soil-based potting compost. They need good light, but shade from direct, strong sun. Supports will be needed for the climbing stems. Climbers may need pruning in early spring to control size. *T. alata* is often grown outdoors as a summer annual, in a sheltered, sunny position with well-drained soil. Outdoors in suitable climates all thunbergias need a sunny spot with well-drained soil. Propagate in spring from seed germinated at 18°C (64°F), from semi-ripe cuttings in summer with basal warmth, or by layering in spring.

CLIMATE Zone 10 or tropical.

SPECIES *T. alata*, black-eyed Susan, is a twining, perennial climber, to 3 m (10 ft) high, from tropical Africa. It has mid-green, triangular or heart-shaped leaves, to about 8 cm (3 in) long, serrated at the margins. From summer through to fall, it is covered with a profusion of cream to deep orange flowers with purple or brown throats. It is well suited to hanging baskets or pot culture. Cultivar 'Alba' has white flowers with dark throats; 'Aurantiaca' has bright orange flowers with dark throats; and 'Bakeri' has pure white flowers. *T. erecta*, king's mantle or bush clock vine, is an upright or scrambling shrub from tropical Africa, to 2 m (6 ft) high. It has smooth, oval leaves, about 8 cm (3 in) long, and purple flowers, with a deep yellow or white throat. In warm climates, it blooms for much of the year. *T. grandiflora*, blue trumpet vine or clock vine, from India, is a climber, to 5 m (16 ft) high, grown for its lovely, drooping clusters of bright blue flowers, with creamy white throats, produced during summer and fall. It has toothed, heartshaped leaves, up to 20 cm (8 in) long. *T. mysorensis*, from India, is the most spectacular species. This vigorous climber bears long trusses of flowers, making it a perfect choice for a tall conservatory. The yellow and reddish brown hooded flowers are produced in spring.

Thyme (*Thymus* species, fam. Lamiaceae)

There are over 300 species in this genus of aromatic, evergreen, low-growing shrubs or perennial herbs from Europe or Asia. However, only a handful are used for culinary purposes. *Thymus* species are usually prostrate or creeping, and both the leaves and the flowers are mostly very small. They are well suited to alpine gardens, rockeries and borders. Some prostrate species and cultivars are used as lawns, releasing the wonderful aroma of thyme when walked upon. Thyme is one of the herbs used in a bouquet garni, and is often used in stock and soups. Generally cooked with foods,

ABOVE A carpet of *Thymus serpyllum* in flower is most attractive . Bees love working the flowers and thyme honey is popular in some countries.

it goes well with rabbit, chicken, lamb and fish.

CULTIVATION Grow thymes in well-drained, alkaline soil, in full sun. Propagate by division of the clumps in early spring, or from cuttings. Pick the leaves just before flowering, on dry days if possible, to ensure the best flavor. Hang to dry in a shaded, airy place. When dry, strip the leaves from the stems and store in air-tight containers, away from light.

CLIMATE There are species suited to various climatic zones.

SPECIES *T.* x *citriodorus* (*T. pulegioides* x *T. vulgaris*), lemon thyme, zone 7, is of garden origin. It is a much-branched shrub, the stems growing to 30 cm (12 in) high, with narrow, lance-shaped leaves and clusters of pale lilac flowers. The entire plant smells and tastes of lemon. *T. herbabarona*, caraway thyme, zone 7, from Corsica and Sardinia, is a prostrate shrub with erect flower stems, to 12 cm (5 in) high. The lance-shaped leaves have a very strong smell of caraway when crushed. The light pink flowers are borne on an oblong inflorescence. *T. polytrichus* (syn. *T. praecox*), zone 7, from southern Europe, is a creeping, prostrate-growing perennial, to only 5 cm (2 in) high. It has small, dark green, leathery leaves and pale to deep purple flowers through summer. Subspecies *britannicus* var. *albus* has white flowers. *T. pseudolanuginosus* (syn. *T. lanuginosus*), woolly thyme, zone 6, is a mat-forming perennial, growing to scarcely more than 1 cm (⅓ in) high. It has tiny, hairy leaves and sparse, pale pink flowers. *T. serpyllum*, wild thyme, zone 5, is a mat-forming perennial from central and northern Europe, with stems to 10 cm (4 in) high. It has small leaves and tiny, purple flowers. *T. vulgaris*, common or garden thyme, zone 7, is the species most often grown as a culinary herb. It has tiny, gray-green leaves and purple flowers. Both stems and leaves have the warm, spicy flavor of thyme. There are several cultivars including 'Argenteus', popularly known as the silver thyme because of its silver variegated foliage.

Thysanotus (fam. Asphodelaceae)

Fringed lily

There are over 40 species of lily-like, clump-forming plants in this mainly Australian genus, with two from New Guinea. They have lovely, fringed flowers in many shades of blue and purple. Most species have sparse, grassy foliage and erect, occasionally twining flower stems. The roots may be rhizomatous or tuberous. Fringed lilies are frost-tender and need to be grown in a cool to intermediate greenhouse or conservatory in frost-prone climates.

CULTIVATION Under glass, grow in pots of well-drained, soil-based potting compost. Provide maximum light but shade plants from direct, strong sun. Outdoors grow in sun or partial shade with well drained, humus-rich soil. Propagate from seed sown as soon as ripe and germinate in a heated propagating case. Tuberous species may be increased by division of clumps while dormant.

CLIMATE Zone 10.

SPECIES These are unlikely to be available outside their countries of origin, and flowering times given are local and may be different under cultivation in the northern hemisphere. *T. juncifolius*, rush fringed lily, has twining stems bearing purple flowers in spring and summer. *T. multiflorus*, mauve fringed lily, is a very showy species with grass-like, gray foliage and mauve-purple flowers held high above the foliage. *T. patersonii* is a weak, twining plant with large, blueish mauve flowers. *T. tuberosus*, common fringed lily or fringed violet, grows to 20 cm (8 in), with wiry, branched stems and large, purple flowers lasting one day only. Flowers may appear from mid-spring through to midsummer. The grassy foliage arises from tuberous roots.

Tiarella (fam. Saxifragaceae)

Foam flower

Native to woodland areas of North America, with one species from Asia, this genus includes around seven species of slender, perennial, herbaceous plants which enjoy shaded situations. Sprays of tiny, pink or white flowers appear in spring and summer and the leaves often color red in fall.

CULTIVATION These perennials like a moist soil containing plenty of humus, such as leaf mould, and either partial or complete shade. They are ideal for creating groundcover in woodland gardens or shady places in shrub borders. Propagate from seed in fall or spring in a garden frame, or by division in early spring.

ABOVE Flowers of the fringed *Thysanotus tuberosus* are exquisite in close-up.

ABOVE Spikes of white or pale pink flowers stand above the attractive, lobed leaves of *Tiarella wherryi.*

CLIMATE Zone 3 for most species; zone 6 for *T. wherryi*.

SPECIES *T. cordifolia*, foam flower, from eastern North America, has lobed, heart-shaped leaves, with flower stems to 30 cm (12 in) long, and cream-white, summer flowers. It spreads with running stems or stolons. *T. laciniata*, from north-west North America, has long flower stems, to 35 cm (14 in), irregularly toothed, segmented leaves, and white flowers. *T. wherryi* is a clump-forming perennial from the Appalachian Mountains of eastern United States. The heart-shaped leaves are three lobed and the flowers are carried on stems, 15–30 cm (6–12 in) long, in late spring to early summer. Flowers are usually white but may occasionally be pink.

Tibouchina (fam. Melastomaceae)
Glory bush, lasiandra

All 350 species of these evergreen trees, shrubs and subshrubs and herbaceous perennials occur in South America, mostly in Brazil. Most flower profusely from late summer through fall, with some continuing into winter, in colors generally of blue, purple or white. They can be grown

ABOVE Each year in summer and fall, *Tibouchina granulosa* displays its rich purple to magenta flowers.

as specimen plants or in mixed shrub borders. Some can be grown in containers. In frost-prone climates, they can be grown in an intermediate greenhouse or conservatory.

CULTIVATION In the greenhouse, grow in pots of soil-based potting compost. Shade plants from direct, strong sun, although good light is needed. Outdoors grow in a sunny spot with well drained, humus-rich soil. If necessary, prune in late winter to control size, or to maintain shape. Propagate from seed in spring, germinated at 16°C (61°F), or from semi-ripe cuttings in summer, in a heated propagating case.

CLIMATE Warmer parts of zone 10.

SPECIES *T. granulosa* is a tree growing to 10–12 m (33–40 ft), but is more usually seen as a shrub, 3–5 m (10–16 ft) high. It has heavily veined, oblong or lance-shaped, hairy leaves, to 20 cm (8 in) long. The reddish purple or violet flowers are about 8 cm (3 in) across. *T. laxa*, climbing lasiandra, a semi-climbing shrub, grows to about 2 m (6 ft). It has hairy branches and oval leaves about 5 cm (2 in) long. The sparse, violet-purple flowers, about 10 cm (4 in) across, are borne in clusters. *T. mutabilis* is a small tree, growing to 6 m (20 ft), with lance-shaped or oblong leaves up to 10 cm (4 in) long, and reddish, purple or white flowers, about 8 cm (3 in) in diameter, with purple stamens. *T. organensis* is a shrub, up to 6 m (20 ft) in height, with oval, gray-green, velvety leaves, to 15 cm (6 in) in length. The flowers, with a satiny texture, are blue-purple and about 12 cm (5 in) in diameter. *T. urvilleana*, glory bush or lasiandra, is a large shrub or small tree, growing to a height of about 5 m (16 ft). It has oval leaves, about 10 cm (4 in) long, and striking, purple flowers, 12 cm (5 in) across.

Tigridia (fam. Iridaceae)
Peacock flower, tiger flower

Native to Mexico and Guatemala, this genus consists of over 20 species of bulbs. They have somewhat grassy or sword-like foliage and

ABOVE The carnival colors of *Tigridia pavonia* make a bright splash. The flowers last only one day, but appear in succession over a long period.

highly colorful, six-petalled flowers in summer. There are three long petals and three short ones. Individual flowers do not last long but are produced in succession over a long period. Tigridias are frost-tender, so in frost-prone climates grow them in a cool greenhouse or outdoors for the summer; lift them in fall and store dry over winter in a frost-free greenhouse.

CULTIVATION Plant bulbs in spring, about 10 cm (4 in) deep. In the greenhouse, grow in pots of gritty, soil-based potting compost and provide maximum light. Dry off in winter when they are dormant. In the garden, grow in very well-drained, sandy soil in a sunny position.

CLIMATE Zone 10.

SPECIES *T. pavonia*, from Mexico, grows to 60 cm (24 in), sometimes with branching stems. The fairly stiff, sword-shaped leaves are 45 cm (18 in) long and similar to those of gladiolus. The flowers are in various colors, including red, orange, pink, yellow or white, and are usually boldly marked with contrasting colors in the center. The flower is 15 cm (6 in) in diameter. There are many cultivars of different colors available. Each flower lasts only one day, but there is a succession of blooms over a long period.

Tilia (fam. Tiliaceae)
Linden, lime

Native to cool temperate regions of the northern hemisphere, this genus includes between 40 and 50 species of ornamental, deciduous trees, cultivated since ancient times. Both quick growing and long lived, they are known to survive for hundreds of years. Often grown as street and screening trees in cooler climates, they have a regular, pyramidal habit when young, with clusters of small, yellow-green, fragrant flowers, followed by rather inconspicuous fruits. Several species yield soft but strong wood, used for making musical instruments.

CULTIVATION Limes need a deep, well-drained yet moist soil, preferably alkaline, but acid is acceptable. They take sun or partial shade, but are not very wind-tolerant. Propagate from seed sown outdoors in fall, or from rooted suckers in fall. Cultivars can be budded in summer.
CLIMATE There are species suited to various

BELOW Small flowers peep out from amongst the dense, heart-shaped foliage of *Tilia* x *europaea* in summer.

climatic zones.

SPECIES *T. americana*, American linden or bass-wood, zone 3, from eastern North America, grows to 40 m (130 ft). It has a straight trunk, smooth when young, clothed with deeply fissured bark when mature. The oval, dull green leaves, 10–20 cm (4–8 in) long, have toothed margins. The drooping clusters of flowers are followed by small, hairy fruit. This species has given rise to many cultivars. *T. cordata*, small-leaved linden, zone 3, grows to 30 m (100 ft). The rounded, finely toothed leaves are about 6 cm (2½ in), across and the flowers are borne in spreading clusters. The small, gray fruit is slightly ribbed. Timber of this species is used for wood carving. *T. x europaea*, common lime, zone 4, grows to 30 m (100 ft). It has a sturdy trunk and a dense, shapely crown of dark green, heart-shaped foliage. Clusters of pale yellow flowers appear in midsummer, followed by small, rounded fruits. The bark, timber and flowers of lime have all been used over many centuries. Lime flower tea is still popular as a refreshing and soothing beverage. *T.* 'Petiolaris' weeping linden, zone 6, grows to about 25 m (80 ft), with pendulous branches and oval leaves that are hairy underneath. The flower clusters are followed by warty-skinned fruits. *T. platyphyllos*, large-leaved linden, zone 5, from Europe and south-west Asia, to 40 m (130 ft), has a straight, gray trunk and dark green, heart-shaped, hairy leaves, to 12 cm (5 in) long, with toothed edges. The clusters of pale yellow flowers are followed by small, pear-shaped, ribbed fruits. Its many cultivars include 'Rubra', with bright red young twigs. *T. tomentosa*, silver linden, zone 6, from south-western Asia and southern Europe, has a broad, pyramidal shape, to 30 m (100 ft). This species has upright-growing branches and round, serrated leaves, to 10 cm (4 in) long with white hairs on the undersides. The clusters of greenish, summer flowers are followed by small, rough, oval fruit. This species tolerates dry conditions and pollution, but its nectar may be toxic to bees.

Tillandsia (fam. Bromeliaceae)
Air plant

The 400 natural species of this genus from the tropical Americas have the greatest diversity of shape and growth of all the bromeliads. Some of their inflorescences are brilliant, with flowers in shades of red, pink, blue and purple. While many species have the typical bromeliad, rosette shape, others, like *T. usneoides* are rambling in habit. Tillandsias range from tiny to large, bulky plants and are mainly epiphytic although some are terrestrial. The epiphytes have poorly developed root systems and absorb moisture and nutrients through their foliage. Outside the tropics and subtropics, grow in an intermediate greenhouse.

CULTIVATION In the greenhouse, mount the epiphytes on slabs of bark or on a tree branch. Generally they will not grow in pots. Provide good light (but shade from direct sun) and a humid atmosphere. From spring to fall, mist spray daily with soft water and liquid feed every four weeks. Terrestrial species need the same conditions but grow in pots of soilless potting compost. Outdoors grow in bright light but

ABOVE Starbursts of silver-gray are seen in many species of *Tillandsia*, a large and variable, bromeliad genus.

avoid direct strong sun. Propagate from well-developed offsets, in spring.

CLIMATE Warmest parts of zone 10 to tropical.

SPECIES These are epiphytic unless otherwise stated. *T. cyanea* is a small tufted plant, to 25 cm (10 in), forming a rosette of grass-like, arching leaves. It has a spectacular, vivid pink, paddle-shaped flower head, borne on a long stem, from which emerge bright blue flowers. Rock-dwelling *T. grandis*, the largest known species, produces flowering stems, to 2 m (6 ft) high, bearing very large inflorescences in yellows and greens. This species forms a large rosette. *T. ionantha* is an attractive, miniature species, forming a rosette to 7 cm (3 in) high, with green leaves tinged with red at flowering, and dark blue flowers. *T. lindenii* is a variable species, growing up to 50 cm (20 in) high, with bright pink bracts and purple-blue flowers. *T. streptophylla* has numerous leaves arising from a swollen base, with beautiful, mauve-blue flowers on a pink-stemmed inflorescence. It grows to 45 cm (18 in). *T. usneoides*, Spanish moss, a rambling species, is seen commonly from Florida south to Argentina, hanging in long, epiphytic tresses from trees.

Tithonia (fam. Asteraceae)
Mexican sunflower

This is a small group of tender annuals, perennials and shrubs, native to Mexico and central America. One species is commonly cultivated as an annual, while another, *T. diversifolia*, is a shrub that has become naturalized in many parts of the tropics.

CULTIVATION Tithonias will grow in any type of well-drained soil, but they do best in full sun with protection from strong wind. Regular watering is needed for establishment but, once growing, they will tolerate dry periods well. In frost-prone climates, raise the annual species in spring from seed germinated at 18°C (64°F) under glass, and plant out when frosts are over.

ABOVE Tall-growing *Tithonia rotundifolia* grows in almost any kind of soil. With regular dead-heading it flowers through summer and into fall.

In frost-free areas, sow direct in flowering positions, in spring.

CLIMATE Zone 10.

SPECIES *T. rotundifolia*, Mexican sunflower, is a colorful, sturdy annual, growing to 1 m (3 ft) or more. It has slightly hairy leaves and orange-red flowers, for a long period through summer into fall. There are named cultivars, but few show much improvement on the species. Mexican sunflowers are best grown in massed plantings, so plants can support each other. The flowers cut well for indoor use.

Todea (fam. Osmundaceae)
King fern

This genus consists of only two species of ferns, widely distributed through South Africa, Australia, New Zealand and New Guinea. They are large ferns that can develop massive trunks. The stalks are usually about one-third the length of the fronds, which are borne profusely. Spores are borne along the veins on the lower leaflets of fronds growing from the crown center. The fiber of the trunks is sought after by orchid growers.

CULTIVATION In climates prone to frost, grow in an intermediate to warm conservatory or

ABOVE *Todea barbara*, king fern, has massive fronds of 2–3 m (6–10 ft). The lower leaflets bear spores along the veins.

greenhouse. Grow in a pot of soil-based potting compost, with added leaf mould, bark and charcoal. Shade from direct sun and ensure a humid atmosphere. Outdoors grow in a shady spot with moist yet well-drained soil. Propagate from ripe spores germinated at 21°C (70°F).

CLIMATE Warmest parts of zone 10.

SPECIES *T. barbara* is a majestic, Australian species also occuring on islands north of New Zealand. Several crowns grow upwards to produce a solid, black, fibrous trunk. The fronds are bipinnate, with glossy, green, lance-shaped leaflets, toothed at the margins, and can grow 2–3 m (6–10 ft) long.

Tolmiea (fam. Saxifragaceae)
Pickaback plant

This single-species genus is from the west coast of the United States. A popular indoor plant which can be grown both in pots and hanging baskets, it tolerates poor light.

ABOVE The soft green, lobed leaves of *Tolmiea menziesii* are slightly hairy. Grow outdoors in woodland conditions or indoors in moderate light.

CULTIVATION Tolmieas can be grown both indoors and outdoors. In the garden, they need a mild climate, a moist, rich soil, and a shaded situation. If growing indoors, use a rich potting mix and keep moist. Propagate by division or by potting up the plantlets.

CLIMATE Zone 7.

SPECIES *T. menziesii* grows 30–60 cm (12–24 in) high, with long, hairy stems, to about 10 cm (4 in), bearing greenish purple flowers. It has bright green, hairy, ivy-shaped leaves, toothed at the margins. Plantlets are produced on the leaves and these will root if the leaves are pegged down into the soil, thus resulting in new plants.

Tomato

(*Lycopersicon esculentum*, fam. Solanaceae)

Like many other foods, the tomato was introduced to Europe by the Spanish explorers in the early 16th century. However, it was not widely used there, except in Italy and southern France, until the 1800s, which means it is one of the more recent crops to be grown and used on a wide scale. The tomato is a juicy, round, or egg-shaped fruit and a valuable addition to our diet, being rich in vitamin C (which is not destroyed

ABOVE A lovely, bush-ripened tomato will have flavor and juiciness quite unlike any grown for the mass market.

by heat) and containing carotene, starch, water and fiber. It ranges in color from yellow to dark red. Tomatoes have a myriad of uses. They are delicious in salads, particularly with oil, basil and bocconcini, and cooked, in soups, sauces and casseroles.

CULTIVATION Tomatoes are frost-tender perennials. In frost-prone climates, they are grown as an annual, summer crop by home gardeners, either in an intermediate greenhouse or in the garden. Plants are raised from seed sown in early spring, under glass, and germinated at 18°C (64°F). Pot up seedlings into small pots. Plant outdoors when frosts are over, or plant under glass in a border, grow bags or 25 cm (10 in) pots. Plants should be about 15 cm (6 in) high by planting time. If growing in rows, either under glass or in the garden, space rows 60 cm (24 in) apart. Plant rows can be 45 cm (18 in) apart for tall cultivars, or 60 cm (24 in) apart for bush cultivars. Outdoors, tomatoes need a fertile, moisture-retentive soil and a sheltered position, in full sun. Under glass, containers can be filled with rich, soil-based or soilless potting compost. Ensure maximum light. Bush types need no support but tall cultivars need bamboo canes or some other means of support and should be tied in regularly with soft garden twine. Tall types should have side shoots regularly removed. Water regularly and freely and start feeding with a proprietary, liquid tomato fertilizer as soon as fruits set. Pollination can be achieved, particularly under glass, by gently shaking the flower trusses. Under glass, tall cultivars are generally stopped after about four fruit trusses have formed. In the greenhouse, ventilate and shade to maintain a steady temperature of about 21°C (70°F). Avoid wildly fluctuating temperatures.

CLIMATE Zone 10, but grown as a summer annual in all climates. Must be grown in warm, frost-free conditions.

VARIETIES Bush tomatoes are best for outdoors, while tall cultivars are usually preferred for greenhouse cultivation. There are many cultivars of tomato, and they vary from place to place. Choose cultivars best suited to local conditions (consult retail seed catalogues and the seed displays in garden centers). Colors vary from red and orange to yellow, and sizes range from tiny, cherry tomatoes to giant, beefsteak types. There are plum- and pear-shaped cultivars which make an unusual addition to salads. Choose, where possible, cultivars that are resistant to diseases, as tomatoes are prone to a number of problems.

Toona (fam. Meliaceae)

The six species in this genus occur naturally from Southeast Asia through to northern Australia. They are important timber trees, although they are also grown as ornamental, shade trees. Some suit the home garden as specimen trees while others are suitable only for parks and very large gardens.

CULTIVATION These trees should be grown in deep, humus-rich soil that drains well. Best grown in sun, they will tolerate shade for part of the day. They need a plentiful water supply during the growing season, and mulching the root area with organic material is most beneficial. Propagation is from seed.

ABOVE The Australian red cedar, *Toona ciliata*, is one of very few deciduous Australian natives.

CLIMATE There are species suited to various climatic zones.

SPECIES *T. ciliata* (syn. *T. australis*), Australian red cedar, zone 9–10, is a large, deciduous tree native to Queensland and northern New South Wales. Growing to 40 m (130 ft) in its habitat, this tree was logged almost to extinction for its magnificent timber in earlier times. In cultivation, it is unlikely to exceed 20 m (65 ft). Its long, pinnate leaves have leaflets that are 8–10 cm (3–4 in) long. Small, white or pink flowers are produced in spring. *T. sinensis* (syn. *Cedrela sinensis*), Chinese cedar, zone 6, is a beautiful, deciduous tree, 10–12 m (33–40 ft) high, often planted as a feature so that its lovely spring foliage can be seen to advantage. The new, spring foliage is a strong pink, gradually maturing in late spring to its summer green. The fall color is orange-yellow. The scented, white, summer flowers are borne in pendulous sprays to 25 cm (10 in) long.

Torenia (fam. Scrophulariaceae)
Wishbone plant

Indigenous to tropical Asia and Africa, these 40 species of lovely, summer-flowering annuals and perennials make attractive subjects for borders and hanging baskets. The flowers are in the same color range as pansies–purple, blue, violet and yellow. The light to dark green leaves are oval to elliptical, with toothed margins.

CULTIVATION Torenias are frost-tender. The annuals, like *T. fournieri*, can be grown as pot plants in a cool greenhouse, or used for summer bedding. Raise plants from seed in mid-spring, germinated at 18°C (64°F). When danger of frost is over, plant out in partial shade, in well-drained yet moist soil.

CLIMATE Zone 9 to 10.

SPECIES *T. atropurpurea*, from the Malay Archipelago, grows to 60 cm (24 in), with single, purplish red flowers. *T. baillonii* is a shrubby annual, with purple and yellow flowers. *T. fournieri* is an annual species with a more erect growth habit, 20–30 cm (8–12 in) high. The flowers are multi-colored, in violet,

BELOW *Torenia fournieri*, wishbone plant, is a useful annual, making a good pot plant for the cool greenhouse or an attractive summer bedding plant.

purple and yellow. The long flowering period is from mid to late summer into fall. *T. hirsuta* is an annual with a spreading habit. The flowers have hairy calyces and deep blue corollas.

Torreya (fam. Taxaceae)

There are seven species in this genus of evergreen, coniferous trees and shrubs, native to North America and Asia. Some are grown for their oil-rich seeds and timber.

CULTIVATION Torreyas are best grown in rich, well-drained yet moist soil in a sheltered position, with full sun or partial shade. Propagate from ripe seed in a garden frame, or from semi-ripe cuttings, rooted with bottom heat.

CLIMATE Zone 7 for most species; zone 8 for *T. taxifolia*.

SPECIES *T. californica*, Californian nutmeg, grows to 20 m (65 ft) or more, with glossy, linear leaves, resembling those of yew, arranged in two ranks on the branchlets. Male and female flowers are borne on separate trees, followed by small, woody fruits. This very ornamental tree suits high-rainfall areas. *T. nucifera*, kaya or Japanese torreya, grows to over 20 m (65 ft). It is cultivated for its edible seeds, which are rich in oil. The timber is also very fine. *T. taxifolia*, stinking cedar, is from Florida, where it grows about 12 m (40 ft) high. The common name is from the fruits which smell most unpleasant when bruised.

Toxicodendron (fam. Anacardiaceae)

Native to Asia and America, the genus Toxicodendron has become widely naturalized and is declared a noxious weed in many parts of the world. Severe allergic reactions can be caused by contact with this tree. The sap appears to be the most toxic, but sensitive people can have bad reactions from any contact. Despite the glorious display of fall color, this tree should be treated with caution. It has long been cultivated in Japan for the berries, which are a source of wax, and the stems, which yield a natural lacquer.

CULTIVATION These trees will grow in sun or part shade and in any type of well-drained soil. They are very hardy, but do particularly well with regular, summer water. They propagate readily

BELOW *Toxicodendron succedaneum* has drooping leaflets that color bright scarlet in fall. Contact with this tree can cause severe allergic reactions.

BELOW Japanese torreya or kaya, *Torreya nucifera*, produces edible seeds and oil used in cooking in its native Japan.

from seed, and unwanted seedlings sometimes appear, as the berries are attractive to birds.

CLIMATE Zone 8.

SPECIES *T. succedaneum* is a small, deciduous tree, 6–10 m (20–33 ft) tall. Its compound leaves, 20–25 cm (8–10 in) long, are generally composed of 11 lance-shaped, dark green leaflets. The leaves end with a single leaflet and the leaflets fold along the midrib in the shape of a boat. In fall, the somewhat drooping foliage colors to brilliant scarlet. Creamy white or yellow-green flowers appear in summer, followed by large clusters of waxy, brown fruits, which persist on the tree through fall and winter.

Trachelospermum (fam. Apocynaceae)
Star jasmine

These 20 species of evergreen, twining, shrubby vines from eastern Asia and parts of America are slow growing during the early stages, but quite vigorous once established. They are grown for their lovely, starry flowers, quite similar to those of jasmine, and their heady perfume. Star jasmine can be grown over fences, trellises or archways, or trimmed regularly to form a small hedge.

BELOW Year-long glossy foliage and fragrant flowers from mid to late summer make *Trachelospermum jasminoides* an ideal climber or groundcover.

CULTIVATION Grow in a well-drained, loamy soil in full sun or partial shade. Prune back straggly branches in fall. Propagate in summer from semi-ripe cuttings, with basal warmth.

CLIMATE Zone 8.

SPECIES *T. asiaticum*, from Korea and Japan, grows to 7 m (23 ft) high, with clusters of fragrant, off-white flowers. *T. jasminoides*, star jasmine, from China, grows up to 7 m (23 ft) high, with clusters of white, fragrant flowers and lance-shaped leaves. It has a long flowering period, from mid to late summer. There are numerous cultivars of *T. jasminoides*, including some with variegated foliage.

Trachycarpus (fam. Arecaceae)
Windmill palm, Chusan palm

These six species of ornamental, mostly single-stemmed fan palms are indigenous to China and the Himalayas. One species, *T. fortunei*, is quite rare amongst palms in that it can be grown in cooler climates. The trunks are generally clothed in rough fiber and their large, fan-shaped leaves, borne on reasonably short stalks, are deeply divided into segments. Recurved inflorescences, comprising small yellowish flowers, are followed by dark blue berries.

BELOW These young specimens of *Trachycarpus fortunei* have yet to develop trunks. This is the hardiest of all palms.

CULTIVATION These palms can be grown in situations of full sun to light, broken shade and adapt to any free-draining soil. Propagation is from seed. They are shallow rooted and transplant easily. Young plants make excellent tub specimens.

CLIMATE Temperate. Zone 8 for *T. fortunei*; zone 9 for *T. martianus*.

SPECIES *T. fortunei*, Chusan palm or Chinese windmill palm, probably from China, was introduced to Europe in the 19th century. Growing to about 20 m (65 ft) tall, it is valued for its exotic qualities and cold-tolerance. Its trunk is covered by dense mats of brown fiber from the old leaf bases. The leaves are dark green above, blue-green below, and almost 1 m (3 ft) in diameter, with quite broad segments. The fruits are dark blue. *T. martianus*, from the eastern Himalayas, is very similar but loses its fibrous leaf bases more quickly, leaving a smooth, white-tinged trunk, about 15 m (50 ft) in height.

Trachymene (fam. Apiaceae)

Related to carrots and parsnips, this genus includes some 12 species of showy, annual or

ABOVE *Trachymene glaucifolia* is a wild parsley belonging to the same family as carrots, celery and parsnips.

perennial plants, native to Australia and the South Pacific islands. The small, dense flower heads are white, pink or blue, and make a pretty massed display in summer. Some species make good cut flowers.

CULTIVATION In frost-prone areas, sow seed in the middle of spring, under glass and germinate at 15°C (59°F). Plant out young plants when frosts are over. Alternatively, sow in flowering positions at the end of spring. Bear in mind that seeds take several weeks to germinate. Grow plants in sandy, well-drained soil in a sheltered, sunny position. Remove spent flowers to extend the flowering period.

CLIMATE Zone 9.

SPECIES It is unlikely that all of these are available outside their native Australia. *T. coerulea*, Rottnest Island daisy or blue lace flower, from Western Australia, is the most widely grown and probably the most reliable of the species. It grows to 45 cm (18 in), with dainty, pincushion heads of tiny, bright blue, summer flowers. *T. cyanopetala* is a small, spreading plant, with lobed, hairy leaves and minute, deep blue flower heads in summer. *T. incisa* is a perennial, native to New South Wales and parts of Queensland. The pretty foliage is finely dissected, and rounded heads of white flowers are borne on stems up to 50 cm (20 in) tall.

Tradescantia (fam. Commelinaceae)

There are about 70 species of perennials in this genus from the Americas. *T. fluminensis*, wandering Jew, is popular for the greenhouse or as a house plant, while the hardy *T. Andersoniana* Group and *T. virginiana* are popular plants for the mixed or herbaceous border.

CULTIVATION In the greenhouse or conservatory, grow in pots of soilless potting compost and shade from direct sun. In the garden, grow in moisture-retentive soil in a sunny or partially shaded position, and cut back stems after flowering. Propagate the tender species from soft tip

ABOVE The flowers of *Tradescantia virginiana* look like small, purple irises. Growing well in filtered sunlight, this plant will produce flowers during the summer.

ABOVE *Trevesia palmata* has a very complex leaf structure. Outside the tropics it is grown as a greenhouse or houseplant.

cuttings in spring or summer, and the hardy perennials by division, in early spring.

CLIMATE There are species suited to various climatic zones.

SPECIES *T. fluminensis*, zone 9, wandering jew, is an invasive species with succulent stems and white flowers that root down at the nodes. This species and its cultivars are grown as container or basket plants in cool climates. The hardy *T. Andersoniana* Group, zone 7, which contains many cultivars, and *T. virginiana*, common spiderwort or widow's tears, zone 7, are widely grown. These plants are ideal in perennial borders, where they will flower over a long period. *T. virginiana* has deep purple flowers, while the garden cultivars grown produce flowers in white, various shades of pink or red, and pale violet to the deepest purple.

Trevesia (fam. Araliaceae)

This genus of 12 species of evergreen shrubs or small trees, which comes from tropical regions of Asia has large, palmate leaves, with prickly, red hairs on the new growth, and produces long clusters of white flowers during spring and summer.

CULTIVATION In frost-prone climates, grow in a warm greenhouse or conservatory. Provide a humid atmosphere and shade plants from direct, strong sun. Grow in pots of soil-based potting compost. Water sparingly in winter. Propagate from firm tip cuttings.

CLIMATE Tropical.

SPECIES *T. palmata*, a small tree native to India, is the only species commonly cultivated outside the tropics, where it is grown as an indoor plant. Usually around 6 m (20 ft), it has large, palmately lobed leaves, up to 60 cm (24 in) wide, and clusters of greenish white flowers. Because of the young growth, it has a prickly appearance.

Trifolium (fam. Papilionaceae)
Clover

Commonly found in most temperate and subtropical regions of the world, this genus consists of around 230 species of annuals and herbaceous perennials. Some clovers are important fodder crops and are also grown as green manure cover crops because of their ability to fix nitrogen in the soil. Clovers flower in spring or summer, and are very attractive to bees.

ABOVE Subclover, *Trifolium subterraneum*, is cultivated as green manure or forage.

ABOVE Simple, three-petalled flowers emerge from the leafy clusters of *Trillium grandiflorum*. All plant parts are in groups of three.

CULTIVATION These plants prefer a well-drained soil and a sunny situation. Propagate from seed or by division.

CLIMATE There are species suited to various climatic zones.

SPECIES *T. incarnatum*, red clover, zone 7, grows to 50 cm (20 in) and produces brilliant crimson flowers. *T. repens*, white clover, zone 4, forms a carpet of green foliage with fluffy, creamy white flowers. It is considered a lawn weed by many. *T. subterraneum*, known as subclover, zone 7, is used as a green manure or forage crop. The white flowers, streaked with deep pink, are borne in small clusters.

Trillium (fam. Trilliaceae)

Wake robin, birthroot

These hardy perennials are grown for their beautiful, three-petalled, spring flowers, which may be white, yellow, green, pink or purple, depending on the species. There are 30 species in this genus, which is found mainly in North America, with some species native to eastern Asia.

CULTIVATION Trilliums require a shady woodland setting, with moisture-retentive yet well-drained soil rich in humus, such as provided by leaf mould or peat. The soil should be slightly acid or neutral. Provide a permanent mulch of leaf mould or chipped bark. Propagate from seed sown as soon as it is ripe in a garden frame. Germination and subsequent growth is very slow. Divide after flowering, but bear in mind that divisions take some time to become established.

CLIMATE There are species suited to various climatic zones. Most species prefer cool to cold, moist climates.

SPECIES *T. erectum*, birthroot, zone 4, from North America, grows to 60 cm (24 in) high. Its nodding, deep rose-purple flowers have an unpleasant scent. *T. grandiflorum*, wake robin, zone 5, also from North America, is a lovely plant, to 45 cm (18 in) high. Its white flowers turn pink as they mature, and are held above the deep green foliage. There is a double form of this species, 'Flore Pleno', and a distinct, pink form, known as 'Roseum'.

Tristaniopsis (fam. Myrtaceae)

These 30 species of trees and shrubs are native to Southeast Asia and Australia. One species is grown in the sub-tropics and tropics as a street or garden tree, but in climates prone to frosts, it would need to be grown in a warm greenhouse or conservatory.

ABOVE *Tristaniopsis laurina* becomes a small tree which, in frost-prone climates, would require a warm greenhouse.

ABOVE *Triteleia laxa*, 'Koningin Fabiola' (syn. 'Queen Fabiola'), has rich purplish blue, white-centered flowers.

CULTIVATION Under glass, grow in a pot of soil-based potting compost. Shade from direct, strong sun. Water well in the growing period, sparingly in winter. Outdoors grow in full sun or partial shade with deep, humus-rich soil. Propagate from seed sown in a warm propagating case.

CLIMATE Zone 10 or tropical.

SPECIES *Tristaniopsis laurina* (syn. *Tristania laurina*), water gum, is a small tree found in coastal forests in eastern Australia. It can grow to 10–15 m (33–50 ft) high, but is often seen at around 8 m (26 ft). The leaves are slightly leathery, glossy green above and paler below. This tree has smooth, light brown bark which peels off in strips, and it produces clusters of showy, rich yellow flowers. In the plant's natural habitat, the flowers attract insects and birds as they are rich in nectar.

Triteleia (fam. Amaryllidaceae)

There are 15 species of cormous perennials in this genus from western North America. They have long, narrow, somewhat grassy foliage, and in summer, heads of trumpet-shaped flow-ers. They tolerate frost so can be grown in sunny border. Blooms last well as cut flowers.

CULTIVATION Triteleias are best planted in a light, well-drained soil in a warm, sunny position. Plant corms in fall, about 8 cm (3 in) deep. Water plants as needed during growth. Propagate by dividing established clumps in the dormant season, or sow seed when ripe and germinate at 16°C (61°F).

CLIMATE Zone 8.

SPECIES *T. ixioides* (syn. *Brodiaea ixioides*), golden brodiaea, has golden flowers, with darker markings down the petal centers and tooth-like filaments beyond the petals. *T. laxa* (syn. *Brodiaea laxa*) has pale or deep violet flowers on stems to 50 cm (20 in) high. The one or two leaves grow to 30 cm (12 in). Cultivar 'Koningin Fabiola' (syn. 'Queen Fabiola'), bred in Europe, is probably the form most grown.

Tritonia (fam. Iridaceae)

Native to South Africa, these 30 species of cor-mous plants are grown for their showy flowers, appearing in mid to late spring or summer.

ABOVE A rich, salmon red variety of *Tritonia crocata* flowers in mid-spring. Tritonia flowers last well in the vase.

CULTIVATION In frost-prone climates, grow in a cool greenhouse or conservatory, in pots of well-drained potting compost. Plant corms 10 cm (4 in) deep, in fall. When the plants become dormant sometime after flowering, they should be kept warm and dry. Watering is resumed when growth commences. *T. disticha* is frost-hardy and in mild areas, can be grown outdoors in a sunny spot with well-drained soil. Propagate from offsets or from seed germinated at 16°C (61°F).

CLIMATE Zone 9.

SPECIES *T. crocata* has wiry stems, up to 50 cm (20 in) high, bearing spikes of bright yellow, freesia-like flowers. The erect, green leaves are sword-shaped. There are several cultivars available, with flowers in various colors. *T. disticha* produces flowers in various shades of red or pink in summer, on stems to 1 m (3 ft) high. Subsp. rubrolucens is worth growing for its long display of pink flowers.

Tropaeolum (fam. Tropaeolaceae)
Nasturtium

With distribution from Chile to Mexico, these annuals and perennials are grown for their

ABOVE Flame nasturtium, *Tropaeolum speciosum*, is an herbaceous perennial that will scramble up through shrubs.

brightly colored flowers, from pale yellow and orange through to deep red. Of the 90 species, most have a climbing, spreading habit. Nasturtiums contain a fragrant mustard oil used as a seasoning, while the flowers are added to salads for decoration. The leaves are used as a green salad vegetable, and flower buds and unripe fruits can substitute for capers.

CULTIVATION Nasturtiums will grow in almost any soil, although an over-enriched soil encourages foliage growth rather than flowers. *T. peregrinum*, however, requires a rich soil. Plant either in full sun or semi-shade and water frequently. Propagate from seed. Annual garden nasturtiums are sown in mid-spring, outdoors where they are to flower. Seed of perennials is best sown, as soon as ripe, in a garden frame.

CLIMATE There are species suited to various climatic zones.

SPECIES Hybrids of *T. majus*, the annual garden nasturtium, zone 10, are bushy or trailing plants. The many named cultivars have bright, summer flowers in red, orange, yellow or cream, and either double or single. The dwarf cultivars are the most popular with gardeners and are freely available. A dwarf form with variegated foliage and flowers in mixed colors has been bred and is known as Alaska Series. Well worth growing if available. *T. peregrinum*, canary creeper, zone 9, grows to 2.5 m (8 ft) high, with lobed gray-green leaves and rich yellow, fringed flowers. *T. speciosum*, flame nasturtium, zone 8, is an herbaceous, perennial climber, to 3 m (10 ft), with long, spurred scarlet flowers. *T. tuberosum*, zone 8, from Peru, has tuberous roots and cupshaped, orange and yellow flowers.

Tulbaghia (fam Alliaceae)

Native to tropical and South Africa, this genus includes over 20 species of mainly herbaceous perennials, growing from bulbs or rhizomes. They form clumps of grassy foliage, smelling of garlic or onions, and heads of mainly purple or white flowers from late spring to fall.

CULTIVATION In frost-prone areas, grow in a cool greenhouse or conservatory, in pots of soil-based potting compost. Provide maximum light. Keep the compost virtually dry when the plants are dormant. Water normally at other times. Outdoors, grow in a sunny spot with well-drained soil. Propagate from ripe seed sown in a garden frame, or alternatively, by dividing the clumps in spring.

CLIMATE Zone 9.

SPECIES *T. capensis*, from South Africa, grows to 60 cm (24 in), with green-purple flowers. *T. simmleri* (syn. *T. fragrans*), sweet garlic or pink agapanthus, grows to 40 cm (16 in). It has large flower heads in purple shades. There is also a white form. *T. violacea*, from South Africa, grows to 60 cm (24 in), with lilac flowers. It is known as society garlic, having a strong onion smell.

Tulipa (fam. Liliaceae)
Tulip

There are over 100 species of tulips, and many hundreds of hybrids. Most modern tulips are the result of extensive breeding programmes

ABOVE The foliage of *Tulbaghia violacea* has a pungent smell. This tough plant flowers reliably every year.

ABOVE A blood red tulip of the 'parrot' type shows the frilled and cut petals characteristic of this group.

ABOVE This mass planting of tulips is backed by Virginian stock. Tulips are popular for spring displays in parks and large gardens.

begun in the late 16th century in Europe, and continuing today. Tulips were all the rage 400 years ago as more species were introduced to Europe from Turkey, Iran and central Asia. Tulip species range in height from about 15 cm to around 60 cm (6–24 in), but most hybrids are probably 30–40 cm (12–16 in). They make excellent container plants or cut flowers. Flowers of the species can be bright, clear red or yellow, or cream with pink or red markings. Hybrid tulips may also be red, yellow, pink, white, apricot or deep mauve, with plain or frilled petals, some of the frilled or cut petal types being known as 'parrot' tulips. Tulips with 'broken' colors are known as 'Rembrandt' tulips–the flowers are plain-colored with streaks, flares or flames of other colors. This is caused by a virus carried by aphids so keep these tulips away from other types. Tulip bulbs are available in garden centers in late summer and early fall; for a wider choice, contact specialist growers. Species tulips are rarely available except from specialists. With selection, it is pos-

sible to have tulips in flower from early to very late spring.

CULTIVATION Tulips need full sun for at least half the day, and some wind protection. The soil should have a high organic content and be very well drained. If soil is known to be very acid, add lime or dolomite before planting at the rate of about 100 grams per square metre (3 oz per square yard). In warmer zones, place bulbs in the refrigerator crisper drawer for about six weeks before planting. This is unnecessary in areas with long, cold winters. Plant out in fall: early fall in cold areas; late fall in warmer areas. Plant bulbs 10–15 cm (4–6 in) deep and 10–12 cm (4–5 in) apart. Apply liquid fertilizer when buds appear and again after flowers fade. Water well after planting. Once leaves appear, give a deep watering every week or ten days if it is very dry or windy. Water regularly in dry times, especially once buds appear. Tulips flower between late winter and mid to late spring, depending on variety and climate. If cutting blooms for the house, choose those not fully open and cut early in the morning. After flowering, remove spent flower stems, give liquid plant food and continue regular, deep watering until leaves begin to yellow. If space is not needed, bulbs can remain in the ground in cold areas. To lift bulbs, dig carefully after the foliage yellows. Allow bulbs to dry (out of the sun), clean them and store in a cool, dry, airy place. Next fall, plant as is or remove the large mother bulb (which should bloom) from the center, for planting where required. The smaller offsets, which may not flower for another year or two, may be planted in less prominent positions. In warm areas, bulbs will not reflower; dig them up and discard. Tulips are susceptible to tulip breaking virus, carried by aphids, and a disease known as 'fire' which is a type of botrytis or gray mould. Both can be controlled. If plants become infected with gray mould, avoid planting tulips in the same spot for a couple of years.

CLIMATE There are species suited to various climatic zones. Best grown in temperate to cold climates.

SPECIES Popular species include *T. batalinii*, zone 5, with primrose yellow flowers; *T. clusiana*, the lady tulip, zone 7, whose white flowers are striped with deep pink on the outside; *T. kaufmanniana*, the waterlily tulip, zone 7; and *T. tarda*, zone 5, which has petals of rich yellow tipped with white. Most gardeners grow named hybrids which are in the 15 divisions of the *Tulipa* genus. Those most popular for spring bedding include the Darwin Hybrids and the Lily-flowered Group.

Turnip

(*Brassica rapa*, Rapifera Group, fam. Brassicaceae)

While somewhat scorned by those of Anglo-Saxon origin, the turnip is well thought of by French, Japanese and Middle Eastern cooks. The swollen root of the turnip is used as a cooked vegetable, generally boiled or steamed. Alternatively, it can be braised or pickled, or made into dumplings. The tender, green leaves can be sautéed or steamed.

CULTIVATION Turnips must be grown rapidly and are best when pulled and eaten just before full maturity. Grow from seed sown direct in early spring through to fall. Any well-drained garden

ABOVE Turnips, like swedes, push themselves out of the ground at maturity. There are numerous cultivars available.

soil is suitable, but soil enriched with manure is ideal. Sow seed 1 cm (⅓ in) deep in rows 30 cm (12 in) apart and thin seedlings to 10–15 cm (4–6 in). Water regularly and thoroughly. Applications of liquid fertilizer will keep plants growing rapidly. Early maturing varieties may be ready to pull in eight to ten weeks, while later maturing types should be forked up. Roots should not become too large or they will be tough. Twist off the tops and store in a cool, dry place, or in perforated plastic bags in the refrigerator. To have a continuous crop, make successive sowings over a few weeks. Turnips are susceptible to various pests and diseases, including flea beetles and clubroot.

CLIMATE Zone 6.

VARIETIES *Brassica rapa* is a hardy, cool-climate biennial, treated as an annual. The numerous cultivars include early types, which are very suitable for spring and summer cropping, and hardier, later types for fall and winter cropping.

Typha (fam. Typhaceae)
Cat tail, bulrush, reedmace

These dozen or so species of hardy, herbaceous perennials are often found growing in swamps and marshes of tropical and temperate parts of the world. Often known as bulrushes, they are more correctly known as reedmaces. Their rush-like foliage is used in the making of baskets and woven chairs.

CULTIVATION Typhas grow well at the edge of shallow water. Most are vigorous growers and they will spread quickly, so care should be taken to keep them under control, especially in warm climates. Cut off the flower heads before they dry out, to avoid unwanted spread. Propagate by dividing clumps in late winter or spring.

CLIMATE Zone 3 for the species below.

SPECIES *T. angustifolia*, lesser bulrush, grows to 2 m (6 ft), with narrow foliage and pale brown

ABOVE Bulrushes, *Typha* species, have velvety, brown flower spikes. These are suitable for planting in shallow water, in large ponds or lakes.

flower spikes, male and female being separated by a small section of stem. *T. latifolia*, bulrush, cat tail, may grow over 2.5 m (8 ft). It has narrow foliage and dark brown flowers.

Ulmus (fam. Ulmaceae)
Elm

There are over 40 species in this genus of handsome, deciduous trees, from temperate regions of the northern hemisphere. They make lovely shade trees, although the larger species are usually only suitable for large gardens and parks, as their roots are fairly invasive. The toothed leaves are asymmetrical at the base, with prominent lateral veins, those of most species coloring yellow in fall. Both the inconspicuous flowers and the winged fruits are borne in clusters.

CULTIVATION Elms do well in cool, moist climates. They prefer deep soils that are well drained but retain moisture, and require ample water through the growing season. Propagation is from seed sown outdoors in fall, and from semi-ripe cuttings in summer, rooted with bottom heat. Cultivars are usually budded or grafted. Dutch elm disease, which is transmitted by the elm bark beetle, has now almost wiped out many elm species in North America and Europe. The American elm, *Ulmus americana*, and the English elm, *U. procera*, are very susceptible and should not be planted. The disease is caused by a fungus and is transmitted by elm bark beetles which breed in the bark of dying elms and carry the spores to new growth of healthy trees, where the adult beetles feed on the soft young bark. The fungus enters and blocks the tree's sap, causing branches to die from lack of water. Progress of the disease is very rapid, with large trees dying mostly within one or two months. There is ongoing research to develop species or hybrids with resistance to the disease.

CLIMATE Elms are very hardy. There are species which are suited to various climatic zones.

SPECIES *U. americana*, American elm, zone 2, from North America, is a majestic tree, growing to 40 m (130 ft) in the wild, but much smaller in cultivation. It has a rounded crown and a

ABOVE The lovely tracery of branches is seen in the frame of this bare weeping elm, *Ulmus glabra* 'Pendula'.

ABOVE The conspicuous, green fruits of *Ulmus glabra*, wych elm, mature soon after the flowers.

ABOVE A young Chinese elm, *Ulmus parvifolia*, is the centerpiece of an island bed in a driveway.

trunk covered with deeply fissured, gray bark. The leaves are 15 cm (6 in) long. This species yields fine timber, but it is now nearly extinct in its habitat. There are several cultivars. *U. glabra*, wych elm or Scotch elm, zone 5, is not often grown now. This species can grow as tall as 35 m (115 ft) and has large, rough, oval leaves, to 15 cm (6 in) long. This is a non-suckering species. Cultivar 'Lutescens', golden elm, grows to about 15 m (50 ft). It is an attractive tree, providing good foliage contrast with other green trees. 'Pendula' grows to 20 m (65 ft), with long, leafy branches drooping to the ground. *U. minor* (syn. *U. carpinifolia*), smooth-leafed elm, zone 5, is native to Europe, western Asia and North Africa. Growing to around 30 m (100 ft) in its habitat, it is unlikely to exceed 15–20 m (50–65 ft) in cultivation. The glossy, oval leaves are 5–10 cm (2–4 in) long and the late winter flowers appear in thick clusters before the leaves appear. Cultivar 'Variegata' has pretty foliage, irregularly splashed and spotted in creamy white. *U. parvifolia*, Chinese elm, zone 5, is a shapely tree, 12–20 m (40–50 ft) tall, with spreading branches and an attractively mottled trunk, in shades of dark gray, red-brown and cream. The dark green foliage is evergreen in all but very cold regions. It is a native of China and Japan. *U. procera*, English elm, zone 6, is a magnificent tree which can grow to heights of 45 m (145 ft), but more often 20–30 m (65–100 ft). Unfortunately, it is one of the species that has succumbed to Dutch elm disease in the northern hemisphere. It has a rounded crown and smallish, rounded leaves. It suckers badly unless grafted onto *U. glabra* stock. Cultivar 'Argenteovariegata' has leaves spotted or striped with yellow and white; 'Louis van Houtte', with leaves colored butter yellow, is not often available. *U. pumila*, Siberian elm, zone 3, from eastern Siberia and northern China, is a hardy species with rapid growth. With broad, erect habit and sometimes shrubby, it grows to 4–12 m (13–40 ft). The dense foliage is deep golden yellow in fall. It appears resistant to Dutch elm disease, and is being used to breed new hybrid cultivars.

V

Vanda to Vriesea

Vanda (fam. Orchidaceae)

There are about 40 species in this genus of epiphytic orchids, native to India, Southeast Asia, the Philippines and Australia. Vandas are widely cultivated by orchid enthusiasts and grown commercially for the cut flower market. They have been extensively hybridized.

CULTIVATION Grow in an intermediate to warm greenhouse or conservatory. Plant in slatted, wooden orchid baskets filled with a proprietary orchid compost, formulated for epiphytic orchids. Ensure very good light, but shade from direct strong sun. During the growing season in summer, water regularly, but when resting in winter, reduce watering. Plants will benefit from being mist sprayed daily in the growing season to create a humid atmosphere, and from liquid fertilizer every two weeks. Outdoors grow in a sunny or partially shaded, sheltered position and provide plenty of moisture. Propagate from offsets in spring. Alternatively, cuttings, formed of sections of stem, can be taken in spring.

CLIMATE Tropical.

ABOVE Valued for its beautiful, violet-blue flowers, *Vanda Rothschildiana* is not difficult to grow if given plenty of warmth and humidity.

SPECIES *V. coerulea*, from northern India, Burma and Thailand, is highly sought after for its clear blue flowers, this being an unusual color in orchids. This species is now rare and threatened in the wild. Some plants show a tessellated or checkered pattern. This species has given rise to the famous *V. Rothschildiana*, which is violet-blue, with deeper veining. *V. tessellata* has yellow-green or blueish flowers chequered in brown. It comes from India, Sri Lanka and Burma. *V. tricolor*, with origins in Laos and Indonesia, has scented, yellow flowers patterned in reddish brown. The lip of the flower is reddish violet, striped with purple.

Veitchia (fam. Arecaceae)

These 18 species of striking feather palms are found in tropical forests of Fiji, the Solomon Islands and the Philippines. Most have a smooth, solitary, pale gray trunk and an umbrella-shaped crown, comprised of bright green, arching fronds divided into narrow leaflets. The inflorescences are followed by dense clusters of red or orange, egg-shaped

ABOVE Native to the Philippines, *Veitchia merrillii* is very ornamental, especially when carrying its fruit clusters.

fruits. They are suitable for growing outdoors in the subtropics and tropics, but in other climates should be grown in a warm greenhouse or conservatory.

CULTIVATION When grown as pot plants under glass, use a gritty, soil-based potting compost. Provide maximum light, but shade from direct, strong sun. Propagate from seed sown in spring and germinated at 24°C (75°F). Seed should germinate in about three months.

CLIMATE Warmest parts of zone 10 to tropical.

SPECIES *V. joannis*, from Fiji, grows 30 m (100 ft) tall. The gently arching fronds are divided into large numbers of leaflets. Large, stiff sprays of light red fruits appear under the crown after flowering. *V. merrillii*, Manila palm, native to the Philippines, is the species most cultivated. Growing to only 7 m (23 ft) tall, it has a slightly tapering, ringed trunk and a neat crown of feathery, bright green leaves. The quite small inflorescences are followed by clusters of bright red fruits.

Veltheimia (fam. Hyacinthaceae)

These unusual, South African natives have strappy leaves, wavy at the edges, and dense, erect spikes of drooping, tubular flowers.

CULTIVATION Where frosts occur, grow in an intermediate greenhouse, in pots of well-drained, sandy, soil-based potting compost. Plant the bulbs in fall with the top part (the neck) showing above the compost. Plants must have maximum light, including sun. When in full growth, water regularly, but start to reduce as soon as the leaves die down, and keep the compost only slightly moist when the bulbs are dormant (summer and fall). Allow plants to completely fill their pots before potting on. Outdoors grow in full sun or partial shade and well-drained loamy or sandy soil. Propagate from offsets in late summer.

CLIMATE Zone 10.

ABOVE *Veltheimia capensis* has very unusual, tubular flowers that are salmon pink, tipped in green.

SPECIES *V. bracteata* has heads of pink-purple flowers, sometimes tinged with yellow. They appear in spring on stems up to 45 cm (18 in) high. The flowers of *V. capensis* are usually pink with green tips, but they may be white, spotted with red. These also appear in spring on stems 45 cm (18 in) high.

Veratrum (fam. Melianthaceae)
False hellebore

With a wide distribution through southern Europe, Asia and North America, this genus includes at least 40 species of herbaceous perennials. The flowers come in a range of colors and are borne in sprays or spikes. Some species contain poisonous alkaloids, but have a history of medicinal use.

CULTIVATION *Veratrum* may be grown in full sun or partial shade, but likes a fairly rich, moist soil. It needs plenty of summer watering. To propagate, divide in early spring or sow ripe seed in fall, in a garden frame.

CLIMATE There are species suited to various climatic zones.

ABOVE *Veratrum viride*, known as Indian poke, carries spres of yellowish green flowers from early to midsummer.

ABOVE Verbascums give strong vertical accents in the garden. Here, this variety's yellow flowers contrast with silver foliage.

SPECIES *V. album*, white hellebore, zone 5, is widely distributed in Europe, across Siberia to northern Asia. Growing to 2 m (6 ft) high, it bears dense sprays of cream flowers in summer. *V. californicum*, corn lily, zone 5, from North America, grows to 2 m (6 ft), with whitish green flowers. *V. nigrum*, zone 6, is a perennial plant from southern Europe and Asia, growing to 1.2 m (4 ft). The large, pleated leaves are arranged spirally on the uprightgrowing stems, which carry long, narrow spikes of deep purple or reddish brown flowers, from late summer. *V. viride*, zone 3, to 2 m (6 ft) tall, has greenish white flowers. It is native to eastern North America.

Verbascum (fam. Scrophulariaceae)

Mullein

There are well over 300 species in this genus of annuals, biennials, perennials and subshrubs, from temperate areas of Europe, North Africa and Asia. The leaves are mainly simple and the flowers, borne in sprays or spikes, may be yellow, pink, purple, brownish or white. Several species are grown for their lovely, grayish green foliage and columnar shape. The many attractive cultivars generally provide better garden plants than the species. Use them as accent plants, or to provide height in borders.

CULTIVATION *Verbascum* will grow in any reasonable garden soil, provided it is well drained, but prefers a sunny situation. Propagate species from seed sown in spring; hybrids are increased by division or from root cuttings, in fall.

CLIMATE There are species suited to various climatic zones.

SPECIES *V. bombyciferum*, zone 6, biennial, from the Middle East, grows to 2 m (6 ft), with golden yellow flowers. The stems and leaves are covered in silver hair. *V. dumulosum*, zone 8, a spreading perennial from the Middle East, grows to 30 cm (12 in), with hairy, gray, felted foliage and pale yellow flowers. *V. olympicum*, zone 6, from Greece, is a biennial, growing to 1.5 m (5 ft). The large leaves, densely covered with white hairs, form rosettes, from which come spikes of bright yellow flowers in summer. *V. phoeniceum*, zone 6, a biennial or perennial, grows to 1.5 m (5 ft), with reddish purple flowers. There are cultivars in white, pink, lilac and purple. *V. thapsus*, zone 3, a biennial, flannel plant, grows to 1–2 m (3–6 ft) and has a very woolly appearance and yellow flowers. This species can be invasive.

Verbena (fam. Verbenaceae)
Vervain

Verbenas are native mainly to North, Central and South America, although some species are native to southern Europe. The genus contains about 250 species of annuals, perennials and subshrubs. They may be erect or prostrate and have mainly toothed leaves and heads or spikes of tubular flowers, opening out at the mouth. Most are frost-tender and are grown for their long display of showy flowers. The *V. x hybrida* cultivars are highly popular for summer bedding. *V. rigida* is also used for this purpose.

CULTIVATION In frost-prone climates, grow tender species in a cool to intermediate greenhouse or conservatory, in pots of gritty, soil-based potting compost, and provide good light. Summer bedding and other garden plants should be planted in a sunny spot with well-drained soil. Bedding plants are raised from seed sown in early spring, under glass, and germinated at 21°C (70°F). Plant out after frosts. All species can also be raised from seed in spring. Perennials can be divided in spring.

CLIMATE Zone 9 for most species, but zone 4 for *V. canadensis*.

SPECIES *V. canadensis*, rose verbena, is a creeping perennial, to 45 cm (18 in), with reddish purple, lilac, rose or white flowers. *V. x hybrida*, common garden verbena, is an annual bedding plant, 30–60 cm (12–24 in) high, with cultivars in many colors, including red, mauve, violet, white and pink, some with a white eye. The flowers appear in dense clusters from summer to fall. It also makes a pretty container plant. *V. peruviana* is a semi-prostrate perennial, from South America, mainly grown as annual groundcover, with dense heads of scarlet flowers. *V. rigida* is a perennial from South America, growing to 60 cm (24 in). Useful for rockeries, it has magenta or purpleviolet flowers. This species is often used for summer bedding. There are several cultivars including the white 'Alba' and the violet-blue 'Lilacina'.

ABOVE Modern cultivars of *Verbena x hybrida*, garden verbena, come in many pleasing colors including peach shades.

ABOVE There are many attractive varieties of annual verbena in both mixed and single colors, and available as seeds or seedlings.

Vernicia (syn. *Aleurites*, fam. Euphorbiaceae)

Tung oil tree

This genus is now correctly *Aleurites* (see entry under *Aleurites*). The species below, *V. fordii* (syn. *Aleurites fordii*), is native to central Asia and is widely cultivated as a source of tung oil, which is used in paints and quick-drying varnishes, but it is also grown as an ornamental. It is not easily available outside its country of origin.

CULTIVATION Grow in a sunny position, in well-drained, acid soil. *Vernicia* is tolerant of quite poor soil as long as drainage is good. Watering should be plentiful during the growing season, although established trees tolerate dry periods well. In frost-prone climates, grow as a young foliage plant in a cool to intermediate greenhouse or conservatory. Propagate from seed sown in warmth.

CLIMATE Zones 9 to 10 or tropical.

SPECIES *V. fordii* (syn. *Aleurites fordii*) grows 8–10 m (26–33 ft) high and is evergreen. Its large, heart-shaped leaves may be lobed or entire on the margins. The funnel- or bell-shaped flowers are white to cream, with red to orange streaks in the throat, and appear in early to mid-spring. They are held above the foliage so are quite prominent. The large, rounded fruits, 4–5 cm (2 in) across, contain the poison. The large, rounded fruits are poisonous but rich in oil.

Veronica (fam. Scrophulariaceae)

Speedwell

This large genus of annual and perennial plants is predominantly from Europe and western Asia, but a few species are from Australia and New Zealand, though most of these are now in the genera *Hebe* and *Parahebe*. Taller growing species make pretty bedding or border plants; low or dwarf types are attractive rockery or groundcover plants.

CULTIVATION The majority of species are very hardy. The border types can be grown in fertile, well-drained yet moist soil in full sun or partial shade. The dwarf, alpine species are best suited to sunny rock gardens with well-drained soil. Propagate from seed in fall in a garden frame, or by division in early spring. Raise shrubby types from softwood cuttings in spring, under glass.

CLIMATE There are species suited to various climatic zones. Most prefer cooler climates.

ABOVE Mat or cushion-forming species of *Veronica* make good groundcover or edging plants. They are also useful in rock gardens.

ABOVE Tung oil trees, *Vernicia fordii*, are grown in plantations to achieve a good yield of the oil-rich seeds.

ABOVE The fine, white spires of a *Veronica longifolia* cultivar are conspicuous amongst these dark blue salvias and Oriental poppies.

SPECIES The European perennial *V. austriaca* subsp. *teucrium*, zone 6, forms mats of growth, but produces flower spikes up to 90 cm (36 in) high, bearing rich blue flowers in summer. There is a number of excellent cultivars available. *V. chamaedrys*, germander speedwell, zone 3, is another spreading perennial from Europe, with 45 cm (18 in) spikes of blue, white-eyed flowers, in summer and fall. *V. cinerea*, zone 5, from the Mediterranean, is a prostrate, evergreen subshrub with white, woolly leaves and rich blue flowers, in early summer. *V. gentianoides*, zone 4, is a tufted perennial, growing between 15 and 60 cm (6–24 in) high, with a basal rosette of leaves and pale blue flowers with darker veins. Cultivar 'Variegata' has white-variegated leaves. *V. longifolia*, zone 4, is an upright perennial, 60 cm to 1.2 m (24–48 in) high, with pointed, toothed leaves and clusters of lilac flowers. Cultivar 'Alba' has white flowers. *V. pectinata*, zone 3, from mountainous regions, is a mat-forming plant, with gray foliage and deep blue

flowers, with white centers. Cultivar 'Rosea' has pink flowers. *V. prostrata*, zone 5, is an alpine, mat-forming perennial, growing to only 15 cm (6 in) high, but with a wide spread. The leaves are variable, but always toothed, and in spring and early summer, this plant is dotted with pretty blue flowers borne in spikes. *V. repens*, zone 5, is a mat-forming, creeping perennial, with pale blue flowers. Other color forms are also available. *V. spicata*, zone 3, is a perennial, growing to a height of 30–60 cm (12–24 in) and a spread of around 50 cm (20 in). The spreading stems carry slightly hairy leaves, and the dense flower sprays are usually blue. There are cultivars in other colors.

Verticordia (fam. Myrtaceae)
Feather flower

These 50 or so species of flowering shrubs, mostly from Western Australia, are considered among the most beautiful in the world. The name, *Verticordia*, is derived from the Latin for 'to turn the heart', and these exquisite shrubs certainly have this effect. The flowers come in shades of scarlet, pink, mauve, deep red, purple, golden yellow, orange, cream and white, and are known as 'feather flowers'. Flowering is profuse, almost covering the shrubs in spring and summer, with the delicate, feathered margins of

ABOVE The flowers of *Verticordia plumosa* vary from pale to rose pink. Feather flowers make a stunning spring show in suitable climates.

both the petals and sepals adding to their striking appearance. The leaves are small and neat. Verticordias have great horticultural value as garden plants and as cut flowers. Dried flowers retain their natural colors for about 18 months or even longer Verticordias are not easy to cultivate, even in their habitat, but experimental work on the genus is continuing in Australia and southern California. In frost-prone climates, verticordias, which are frost-tender, are best grown in an intermediate greenhouse or conservatory.

CULTIVATION In the greenhouse, grow in pots of acid, sandy, oilless potting compost. The plants need maximum light and good ventilation. Do not overwater plants, particularly in winter, as most species are native to low rainfall areas. When feeding in the growing season, use a fertilizer which has a low phosphate content. Outdoors, in the right climate, grow in acid soil with very good drainage, and in an open, sunny position. Mulch with gravel. Propagate from seed in spring, germinated at 18°C (64°F)–but bear in mind that germination rates may be poor–or from semi-ripe cuttings in summer, rooted in gentle heat.

CLIMATE Zone 10.

SPECIES These are not readily available outside their native Australia. *V. acerosa* grows to 60 cm (24 in), with tiny leaves and yellow flowers. *V. brownii* to 60 cm (24 in), has tiny leaves and masses of creamy white flowers. *V. chrysantha* is a small grower, with masses of bright, golden yellow flowers. *V. conferta* is a tiny, rounded shrub, with blueish green foliage and cup-shaped, bright red flowers, which cover the whole plant during late summer and fall. *V. densiflora* is an upright-growing shrub, to 60 cm (24 in), with thick foliage and dense clusters of pink to purple flowers, from spring to early fall. *V. grandis*, scarlet feather flower, is a most spectacular species. It is an open, spreading shrub with roundish leaves and stem-clasping, brilliant red flowers, frilled at the base. *V. mitchelliana* is a spreading shrub, to 50 cm

(20 in), with blueish green foliage and brilliant, deep red flowers, with prominent yellow styles. *V. multiflora* is a very small, open shrub, with bright green, sharpish leaves and dense clusters of flat, golden yellow flowers, during late spring. *V. nitens*, orange feather flower, is an open shrub, growing to about 1.2 m (4 ft). The blueish green foliage is quite succulent and the bright orange flowers are borne in abundance. *V. plumosa* has a delightful massed display of cup-shaped, pink flowers in spring through to summer. This leafy shrub, with blueish green foliage, grows to 60 cm (24 in). *V. serrata* is a taller species, to 1 m (3 ft), and bears flattened flowers in bright golden yellow to orange, in spring and summer. The thick, toothed leaves are bright green.

Viburnum (fam. Caprifoliaceae)

There are around 150 species in this genus, the majority from Asia and North America. These shrubs or small trees originate from both temperate or subtropical regions and may be deciduous or evergreen. Mostly grown for their showy flowers, some are cultivated for outstanding fall color or brightly colored berries, which often persist into fall and winter. The evergreen species are often grown as hedging

ABOVE *Viburnum plicatum* 'Mariesii' carries its lacecap flowers on horizontal, tiered branches in late spring or summer.

plants. Viburnums have simple, opposite leaves and mostly fragrant, dense, white flower heads. With some species, male and female plants are required for berry production, while others benefit from planting a second shrub to encourage cross-fertilization.

CULTIVATION Viburnums may be grown in any reasonably rich, moist soil, but prefer a deep, well-drained, fertile loam, with plenty of water in summer. Grow them in sun or partial shade. For a more compact, dense bush, prune lightly after flowering. Propagate from seed sown in fall, or from cuttings taken in summer. Viburnums may also be increased by layering or grafting.

CLIMATE There are species suited to various climatic zones. Most are very hardy.

SPECIES *V.* x *bodnantense*, zone 7, is a deciduous shrub, to 3 m (10 ft) high. The oval, deep green leaves are paler on the undersides, coloring shades of orange, red and purple in fall. The scented flowers are deep rose in bud, opening to pale pink from fall to spring, and fading to white. *V.* x *burkwoodii* (*V. carlesii* x *V. utile*), zone 5, is generally evergreen, to 2 m (6 ft), with an open habit. The clusters of flowers are pink in the bud in early spring, later opening to white. *V.* x *carlcephalum* (*V. carlesii* x *V. macrocephalum*), zone 5, is an upright-growing, deciduous shrub, to 2.5 m (8 ft), which is very similar to *V. carlesii*. Large, rounded heads of fragrant, white flowers, tinged with red, appear in spring, and the leaves color brilliantly in fall. *V. carlesii*, zone 5, native to Korea, is a densely foliaged, deciduous shrub, to 2 m (6 ft), with a spreading habit. The oval leaves are finely toothed at the margins and the fragrant flowers are borne in dense clusters, opening in pale pink from mid to late spring, ageing to white. This species bears large clusters of red fruits, ripening to blueish black. *V. japonicum*, zone 7, is a slow-growing evergreen, to 2 m (6 ft), with attractive, glossy, green, thick leaves and fragrant, white flowers, followed by red berries. This species is very sim-

ABOVE The flowers of *Viburnum carlesii* are white or white-flushed pink and very fragrant. Fall foliage color can be very good.

ilar to *V. odoratissimum*. *V. macrocephalum*, Chinese snowball tree, zone 6, is a deciduous or evergreen shrub, growing to 3 m (10 ft), with dark green, leathery, oval leaves coloring red and yellow in fall. In spring, the large, round, white flower heads, up to 15 cm (6 in) across, completely cover this shrub in a very showy display. *V. odoratissimum*, sweet viburnum, zone 9, is an evergreen shrub or small tree, to 6 m (20 ft), suitable for warm to hot climates. Its thick, leathery, rounded leaves are glossy green and the small, white, tubular flowers, borne in dense clusters, are very fragrant. The red berries ripen to black. *V. opulus*, common snowball or European guelder rose, zone 3, is a beautiful, deciduous shrub from Europe and North Africa grown for its flowers, fall color and clusters of translucent red berries, which persist after the leaves have fallen in fall. The pure white, lacy flowers appear in clusters during spring, and its leaves resemble those of the maple. This species grows up to 4 m (13 ft) high. *V. plicatum forma tomentosum*, zone 5, is a compact, rounded, deciduous shrub, growing to 3 m (10 ft). Flat, rounded clusters of white flowers appear along the horizontal branches in late spring or summer and are followed by red berries. The leaves color well in fall. *V. plicatum* 'Mariesii' flowers profusely, the branches displaying a tiered growth habit. *V. rhytidophyllum*, zone 6, is a fast-growing evergreen, up to 3 m (10 ft) high, with long, dark green, deeply veined leaves, felted on the undersides. The large, flat clusters of creamy flowers appear at the branch ends in spring. These are followed by oval, red berries, maturing to black. *V. suspensum*, zone 9, an evergreen to 2.5 m (8 ft), has oval, glossy, green leaves, paler beneath, and fragrant, creamy white to pink flowers, followed by red berries. *V. tinus*, laurustinus, zone 7, is a densely foliaged, evergreen shrub, to 3 m (10 ft) high, although it may be taller. The oval, glossy, dark green leaves may develop reddish purple tones in cold weather. The pink buds in late winter open to white, and are followed by black berries. Native to the Mediterranean, this species is grown as a hedging or screening plant.

Victoria (fam. Nymphaeaceae)

Giant water lily

This genus of two species of large, aquatic plants was named for Queen Victoria. In the mid to late 19th century, wealthy growers in the UK built special glasshouses to accommodate them. One of the species, *V. amazonica*, which occurs naturally in the Amazon, is the largest water lily in the world. Living in water or mud, these water lilies are prickly on all except the upper leaf surface. The leaves grow 2 m (6 ft) in diameter in cultivation, but often much larger in the wild. Large, projecting veins containing air cells enable them to float. The large, white, highly perfumed flowers open only at night, sinking to the bottom after pollination and being replaced by large, berry-like fruits.

CULTIVATION In frost-prone climates, grow in a warm greenhouse or conservatory. They can be grown as annuals from seed sown in early spring. A large pool of water and a minimum water temperature of 27°C (81°F) are needed to

ABOVE Like great platters, the giant leaves of *Victoria cruziana* float on the surface of a still pond.

grow these water lilies. Each plant needs about a cubic metre (yard) of richly composted soil, and crowns should be no more than 30 cm (12 in) below the water surface. Propagate from seed sown in pots set in shallow water. Germination occurs in about three weeks, when the seedlings should be transferred to larger pots until mature enough to plant out.

CLIMATE Warmest parts of zone 10 or tropical.

SPECIES *V. amazonica* (syn. *V. regia*), Amazon or royal water lily, produces leaves 2 m (6 ft) in diameter, with a reddish color underneath and upturned margins, accentuated on larger leaves. The white flowers mature to pink, opening partially the first night and fully on the second night. *V. cruziana*, Santa Cruz water lily, has green leaves which are hairy and purple on the undersides, and white, summer flowers. This species may be grown at slightly lower temperatures than *V. amazonica*.

Vietnamese mint

(*Persicaria odorata*, fam. Polygonaceae)

This widely distributed, warm-climate perennial, which is not very well known outside its

ABOVE Vietnamese mint has a very strong flavor and must be used with discretion so as not to overpower the other ingredients.

countries of origin, can be grown as an annual. It has been used in herbal medicine and, in earlier times the seeds were used as a pepper substitute. The leaves have little aroma but a strong flavor, so should be used sparingly. It is used mainly in Asian dishes. Vietnamese mint grows into a small shrubby bush with mid to dark green, lance-shaped leaves and long sprays of pink flowers from summer to mid-fall.

CULTIVATION Vietnamese mint should be grown where it will receive full sun for at least half a day. Naturally occurring in damp places, it needs copious watering throughout the growing season. Soil should have a high organic content. If there is plenty of organic matter in the soil, no extra fertilizer will be required. It is grown from seed sown in spring, or from cuttings taken from late spring through summer. Leaves are harvested as required. Plants may be perennial in warm regions so should be cut back hard in late winter to early spring to produce vigorous, new growth. It can be raised or grown permanently under glass in cold areas.

CLIMATE Zone 9 to 10.

Vigna (fam. Papilicnaceae)
Snail flower

There are about 150 species in this genus of upright or twining plants native to a range of tropical regions. Most species are widely cultivated pulses, forage and green manure crops, although some are cultivated in the home garden. One climbing species is grown as an ornamental. In cool and cold climates, it can be grown as an annual in a warm greenhouse or conservatory.

CULTIVATION Raise plants from seed sown in spring and germinated at a temperature of 18°C (64°F). In the greenhouse grow in pots of soil-based potting compost. Provide maximum light, but shade from strong, direct sun. Provide support for the climbing stems, which can be trained into the roof area If the climate is suitable for outdoor growing, plant in well-drained yet moist soil, in a sunny position. Plants can be grown over a pergola.

CLIMATE Zone 10 or tropical.

SPECIES *V. caracalla*, snail flower, is a fast-growing climber that grows up to 6 m (20 ft) or so in the tropics, but only 2–3 m (6–10 ft) elsewhere. Through summer and into fall, curious-looking flowers appear. These are purple to pink

ABOVE *Vigna caracalla*, snail flower, an evergreen, perennial climber, produces unusual, snail-like flowers in summer and fall.

and white, coiled and convoluted, resembling snails. Perennial in tropical regions, these plants die down during winter elsewhere, but regenerate the following spring. *V. radiata*, mung bean, is generally not cultivated by home gardeners except as a sprouting seed. It is cultivated in some tropical countries for its edible seeds and pods. *V. unguiculata*, cowpea, is grown for forage, green manure, and also for food. Subspecies *sesquipedalis*, known as snake bean, yard-long bean and asparagus bean, must be grown on a trellis of sufficient height to allow beans to develop properly. They may grow to 90 cm (36 in) long in ideal conditions.

Viminaria (fam. Papilionaceae)
Rush broom

This single-species genus is found in moist, temperate areas of Australia. It is similar to Spanish broom but tolerates a wider range of conditions. It is a shrub or small tree with a single trunk, long, slender branches almost devoid of leaves, and golden yellow, pea flowers. *Viminaria* is a useful ornamental for home and public gardens.

CULTIVATION Propagate from seed, which has been first placed in boiling water and allowed to stand for 12 hours. Provide a germination temperature of 21°C (70°F). Plant in moisture-retentive soil in full sun or partial shade. In areas which are subject to hard frosts, grow in a cool greenhouse.

CLIMATE Zone 9.

SPECIES *V. juncea* is a tall shrub, growing to 5 m (16 ft), with fresh green, flattened stems instead of leaves. The small, golden yellow, pea flowers with a light, clover fragrance, appear along the branches in late spring and summer. The fruit is a small pod with only one seed.

Vinca (fam. Apocynaceae)
Periwinkle

Native to Europe, these small, climbing or trailing, evergreen shrubs have long, tough runners and may become rampant if not controlled. However, with their pretty, five-lobed, blue to purple flowers, they make attractive groundcover and spillover plants. They are also suitable for window boxes.

CULTIVATION An ordinary garden soil and full sun provide the best conditions for flowering, but these plants can also adapt to a shaded spot. Allow to spread, then cut back in early spring. Propagate by division or from the rooted layers in fall or early spring.

ABOVE The growth of mature *Viminaria juncea* is dense and twiggy. As it withstands exposed conditions, it makes a good windbreak.

ABOVE Periwinkle, *Vinca major*, makes a dense, weed-suppressing groundcover. Established plants tolerate dry conditions.

CLIMATE There are species suited to various climatic zones.

SPECIES *V. major*, greater periwinkle, zone 7, has several, metre (yard) long stems, glossy, dark green, oval leaves and tubular, blue flowers, to 5 cm (2 in) across, in spring and summer. This tenacious vine can reach weed proportions in warm climates if not controlled. Cultivar 'Variegata' has yellowish white leaf margins. *V. minor*, lesser periwinkle, zone 4, is similar to *V. major*, but more prostrate. The stems are also more slender. It, too, has oval, glossy, dark green leaves and blue flowers in spring and summer. The form alba has white flowers; 'La Grave' has large, single, blue flowers; and 'Azurea Flore-pleno' produces double, blue flowers. Cultivars with variegated leaves are also available.

Viola (fam. Violaceae)

Pansy, violet, viola

Of the 500 species of hardy annuals or perennials in this genus, most are from temperate parts of the northern hemisphere, with a few from Australia and New Zealand. Most viola species are best mass planted as annual displays, garden edging, in rockeries or containers. In semi-shade or damp spots, violets make fragrant groundcovers.

CULTIVATION Plant violas in full sun or partial shade, depending on species and climate. Species grown as annuals generally need full sun. They do best in humus-rich soil that drains well. Water regularly and thoroughly in hot or windy weather, but keep much drier during winter. Regular removal of spent flowers will prolong the flowering display. Many are propagated from seed, especially those grown as annuals. Some perennial species can be propagated from tip cuttings taken in summer. Clumps of perennial forms can also be divided.

CLIMATE There are species suited to various climatic zones.

SPECIES *V. betonicifolia*, wild violet, zone 9, is an Australian species with a wide distribution. A tufted plant, it has blue-purple flowers and oblong leaves. *V. cornuta*, viola or horned violet, zone 7, is a tufted plant, to 30 cm (12 in), with oval, toothed leaves and large stipules. The common garden viola is a hybrid of this

BELOW LEFT The English or sweet violet, *Viola odorata*, is a native of Europe and produces its sweetly fragrant flowers at the end of winter and into spring.

BELOW With regular removal of spent flowers, velvety pansies will flower over a long period. Some cultivars flower in summer, others throughout winter.

ABOVE *Viola tricolor*, wild pansy or heartsease, is a European annual or biennial, flowering from spring to fall. It self-seeds freely so plants are always available.

ABOVE RIGHT *Viola hederacea*, Australian violet, makes excellent groundcover in a suitable climate.

species and originally had small flowers of one or two colors but with recent breeding it is becoming more like a true pansy. Many color forms are available in single or mixed strains. New cultivars of garden violas are appearing all the time, so consult a good retail seed catalogue to find out what is suitable for an area. *V. fili-caulis*, zone 9, from New Zealand, has glossy, heart-shaped leaves and yellow flowers on very slender stems. *V. hederacea*, Australian violet, zone 9, makes a useful groundcover. It has round leaves and delicate, blueish purple and white flowers on short stems. *V. lutea*, zone 5, is a leafy plant, to 20 cm (8 in), with creeping stems. The flowers may be yellow, purple, or purple and yellow. *V. odorata*, English or sweet violet, zone 8, from Europe, is the best known species, grown both in the home garden and commercially for perfume manufacture and floristry. A tuft-forming, spreading perennial, it has oval, toothed leaves and fragrant flowers, to 2 cm (¾ in) or more across, in deep violet, blue or white, with a short spur. The various forms

and cultivars available include the white 'Alba' and double-flowered 'Alba Plena'. There are also double cultivars in other colors. *V. septen-trionalis*, zone 4, a perennial from North America, grows to 15 cm (6 in) high, with toothed, oval to heart-shaped, hairy leaves and large, blueish purple, sometimes white, flowers. *V. tricolor*, wild pansy or heartsease, zone 4, from Europe, is an annual, to 30 cm (12 in). The leaves are oval to lance-shaped and the flowers are in combinations of purple, white, blue and yellow. Several cultivars are available, including the almost black 'Bowles' Black'. *V. x wittrockiana* cultivars, pansies, zone 7, are from crossing the species *V. altaica*, *V. cornuta*, *V. lutea* and *V. tricolor*. The pansy is a favorite annual for bedding and borders and for container growing. The flowers have a velvety texture and the color range is vast. Many are two or three toned and have attractive markings. Low growing, to a maximum of 25 cm (10 in), the leaves are heart-shaped, with slightly lobed margins. With regular dead-heading, they have a long flowering period. There is a huge cultivar range for summer and winter–spring flowering. A good seed catalogue will list a comprehensive selection.

Virgilia (fam. Pap lionaceae)

These South African trees are very fast growing, though rather sho-t lived, resulting in the adoption of local common names such as 'tree in a hurry'. In spring and summer, they provide a beautiful display of pea flowers. The alternate leaves are composed of a number of leaflets, and the fruit is a fla- pod.

CULTIVATION Outdoors, grow in acid or neutral, well-drained soil in a sunny spot. In frost-prone climates, grow in a cool greenhouse or conservatory. Propagate from seed soaked in hot water for 24 hours before sowing, and germinated at 15°C (59°F).

CLIMATE Zone 9 to 10.

SPECIES *V. divaricata* is an evergreen tree, to 9 m (30 ft), with deep green foliage and fragrant, usually deep pink flowers in spring. *V. oroboides* (syn. *V. capensis*), Cape lilac, is an evergreen tree, to 10 m (33 ft). The firm, pale green leaves are rather silky underneath, and fragrant, pink or purple flowers appear in clusters in spring and summer. It is inclined to become straggly with age.

Vitex (fam. Verbenaceae)

This genus includes some 250 species of deciduous and evergreen trees and shrubs, with a wide geographical distribution. They are found in tropical, subtropical and temperate regions of the world and are grown for their sprays of small, tubular flowers, which may be white, yellow, red or blueish purple. They have opposite, palmate, divided leaves composed of a number of leaflets, and small, berry-like fruits.

CULTIVATION *Vitex* species generally do well in any well-drained soil. *V. agnus-castus* is more cold-tolerant than other species and can be grown in cool or warm climates. *V. trifolia* will tolerate coastal exposure and can be grown in

ABOVE *Virgilia oroboides* carries clusters of two-toned, pink flowers in spring and summer.

ABOVE Chaste tree, *Vitex agnus-castus*, bears stiff spikes of dusky, lavender flowers above the star-shaped leaves.

quite poor, sandy soil. Propagate from seed in spring, germinated at 15°C (59°F), or from semi-ripe cuttings in summer, with bottom heat. These plants can also be increased by layering.

CLIMATE There are species suited to various climatic zones.

SPECIES *V. agnus-castus*, chaste tree or sage tree, zone 7, is a deciduous, rounded shrub or small tree, 3–5 m (10–20 ft) tall, with dense, erect sprays of lilac or blue, summer or fall flowers. The form *alba* has white flowers. *V. lucens*, pururi, zone 9, from New Zealand, is an evergreen tree, to 20 m (65 ft) high. The glossy, green leaves are composed of a number of leaflets, and the rosy pink flowers are borne in dense clusters. In the past, it was highly valued for its durable timber. *V. trifolia*, zone 10, occurs naturally both in eastern Australia and Southeast Asia. It is an evergreen shrub or small tree, to 6 m (20 ft), with mid-green leaves composed of three leaflets which are hairy underneath. The blue to purple flowers are borne in 20 cm (8 in) long clusters. The flowers are fragrant.

Vitis (fam. Vitaceae)

Grape vine, vine

These deciduous, woody climbers are grown both for their fruit and their richly colored, fall foliage. Climbing by means of tendrils which they coil around supports, they make very attractive ornamentals. The leaves may be simple or palmate, and the insignificant flowers are followed by the decorative fruits.

CULTIVATION Grape vines tolerate most soils, but do best in a humus-rich soil in full sun or partial shade. Be careful to allow sufficient room for growth when training vines over walls or trellises. Prune when completely dormant to prevent bleeding of the sap. Propagate from layers in late fall or from hardwood cuttings taken in winter.

ABOVE The scarlet, fall leaves of *Vitis coignetiae* are brilliant against this pale, stone wall.

CLIMATE There are species suited to various climatic zones.

SPECIES *V. amurensis*, zone 7, is a very vigorous climber with large, three- to five-lobed leaves and small, black fruit. The fall foliage ranges from orange-scarlet to deep red. *V. coignetiae*, crimson glory vine, zone 5, is a fast-growing climber, to 15 m (6 in) high, with large, slightly lobed leaves, up to 30 cm (12 in) across, coloring orange-red in fall. The black fruits are generally inedible. This species tolerates a wide range of climatic conditions. *V. vinifera*, wine or European grape, zone 6, climbs by means of few tendrils, bearing large clusters of fruit, varying in size and color. It is best to choose fruiting grapes according to local climate. As well as the European grape, there is also the American *V. labrusca*, suited to zone 5. There are many cultivars of each.

Vriesea (fam. Bromeliaceae)

These large bromeliads originate in tropical America. Most are epiphytes, although some larger species are terrestrials. Plants form the typical, rosette shape. Their short, broad, strap-like leaves are spineless, with smooth margins. Recurved at the tips, they can be barred or patterned. Their stunning inflorescences range from inflated, feather-shaped heads to erect spears.

CULTIVATION In frost-prone climates, grow in a warm greenhouse or conservatory. Vriesias also make good house plants. While most are epiphytic in their habitats, they are usually grown in pots. Use well-drained, soilless potting compost. Alternatively, grow as epiphytes by mounting plants on slabs of bark, or on a tree branch. When plants are in full growth keep their 'vases' filled with water and water the compost regularly. Provide a humid atmosphere by mist-spraying plants daily. Liquid feed monthly when in full growth. Reduce watering in the winter. Always use soft or lime-free water when watering or misting. Propagate from well-developed, rooted offsets, in spring.

CLIMATE Warmest parts of zone 10 or tropical.

SPECIES *V. fenestralis*, a classic vriesea, grows to 1 m (3 ft), with a fine tracery of lines on both sides of the leaves, which are heavily spotted in maroon. *V. hieroglyphica*, to at least 1 m (3 ft), is a highly prized species, with intricate markings on the leaves, deep green above, purple below. Yellow flowers with greenish yellow bracts appear on very tall stems, usually in summer. *V. splendens*, known as flaming sword, grows to 1 m (3 ft). The leaves are banded with purple, deep brown or deep green, and the spearlike inflorescence is orange, red and yellow.

ABOVE *Vriesea psittacina* is aptly named 'parrot feather' for its feather-like inflorescence. This is an easy species to cultivate.

ABOVE Many vriesias offered by garden centers are hybrids, such as this attractive plant with 'interwoven' bracts.

W

Wachendorfia to Wollemia

Wachencorfia (fam. Haemodoraceae)

Native to South Africa, this genus includes over 20 species of tuberous, perennial plants that are grown for their brightly colored flowers.

CULTIVATION Where frosts occur, grow these tender plants in a cool conservatory or greenhouse. Ideally, plant in a soil bed. Alternatively grow in pots of sandy, soil-based potting compost, with some leaf mould added. Ensure maximum light. Water freely when in full growth, but keep the compost only slightly moist when plants are dormant. In the garden, plant in moist soil, in a sunny spot. Propagate in spring, either from seed or by dividing clumps.

CLIMATE Zone 10.

SPECIES *W. hirsuta*, to 45 cm (18 in), has hairy leaves and red buds, opening to yellow flowers. *W. paniculata* grows to 45 cm (18 in), with spikes of yellow, funnel-shaped, summer flowers, which become red with maturity. *W. thyrsiflora*, red root, is an attractive plant, growing to over 1 m (3 ft) high. Bright, golden yellow flowers are borne in upright spikes, in early summer. This species forms large clumps and tends to self-seed. The red sap in the tubers was used as a dye in Africa.

Wahlenbergia (fam. Campanulaceae)
Rock bell

There are around 150 species in this genus, most of which originate in the southern hemisphere. Most are perennials with pretty blue, white or red, campanula-type flowers in summer, and soft, delicate foliage. Wahlenbergias make lovely pot and rockery plants and also look attractive in massed displays.

CULTIVATION Outdoors, grow these plants in a sandy, well-drained soil which contains plenty of humus. Choose a spot sheltered from wind and with partial shade. Plants can also be grown in an alpine house if the climate is unsuitable. Plant them in pans of well-drained, sandy, soil-based compost, with added leaf mould. Propagate in spring, either from seed germinated at 15°C (59°F), or by division.

ABOVE *Wachendorfia thyrsiflora*, red root, needs to be grown in a cool greenhouse or conservatory in frost-prone areas, and is best planted in a soil bed.

ABOVE *Wahlenbergia gloriosa*, Australian bluebell, tolerates several degrees of frost. It can be grown in sun or part shade.

CLIMATE There are species suited to various climatic zones.

SPECIES *W. albomarginata*, zone 7, is a tufted, rhizomatous perennial from colder areas of New Zealand. Its flowers are large and pale blue, or occasionally white. *W. gloriosa*, Australian or royal bluebell, zone 9, is one of the most beautiful native Australian plants. It is a matting or tufting alpine type, with spreading, underground stems and very large, blueish purple flowers, to 2.5 cm (1 in) across. This species is the floral emblem of the Australian Capital Territory. *W. gracilis*, zone 10, is an annual species from New Zealand, to 30 cm (12 in), with variably toothed leaves and large flowers, mostly white, sometimes blue or purple. *W. stricta*, zone 9, is quite widely grown. It is a variable species with small, soft blue, occasionally white, flowers. Forming clumps, 30–40 cm (12–16 in) high, it occurs widely in Australia.

ABOVE This venerable walnut tree is the focal point of this large garden, providing summer shade and a bountiful supply of nuts.

Walnut

(*Juglans nigra* and *Juglans regia*, fam. Juglandaceae)

Walnuts are large, deciduous trees producing edible nuts. The ball-shaped fruits are smooth and green and contain the nuts, which have dark brown, generally thin, furrowed shells. Walnuts are eaten raw or used in confectionery and cakes, and are delicious served with blue cheese or goat's cheese. Immature nuts can be pickled or candied. Some species of walnut are grown commercially for their beautiful timber.

CULTIVATION Trees should be planted in winter, while dormant. They should be placed no less than 5 m (16 ft), and preferably 7 m (23 ft), from other trees. They need deep, friable, well-drained soil and a plentiful supply of water during the growing season, either from deep, subsoil moisture or from regular irrigation. Feed trees in early spring with complete plant food. Pruning, if required, must be done during winter dormancy. Little pruning is generally needed except to train trees to a single main trunk, or to raise the crown by removing some of the lower branches. As trees grow and begin cropping, it is desirable to have a clear trunk to a height of at least 1.5 to 2 m (5–6 ft), to allow access to nuts as they fall. Walnuts can be grown from seed, but the quality of trees will be variable. To maintain good strains, trees are budded or grafted onto seedling understocks.

CLIMATE Zone 4 for *J. nigra*; zone 5 for *J. regia*.

SPECIES *Juglans nigra*, black walnut or American walnut, zone 4, grows to 30 m (100 ft) in its native territory, but very much smaller in cultivation. Like *J. regia*, this species has edible nuts. The fine timber of this species is used in furniture-making. Walnuts are slow growing but handsome trees. *J. regia*, English or Persian walnut, zone 5, is a deciduous tree, 30 m (100 ft) high, with oblong leaflets, to 15 cm (6 in) in length, and pendulous clusters of small flowers borne on the previous year's wood. There are many fruiting cultivars available, such as 'Concorde', 'Eureka', 'Franquette' and 'Payne', but choose to suit your climate.

Washingtonia (fam. Arecaceae)

Washingtonia palm, cotton palm,
thread palm

There are only two species in this genus of fan
palms, from the south of the United States and
Mexico. They are among the hardier palms and
are extensively planted in California and
Florida. These, tall, vigorous palms have a
single, upright trunk and a fairly compact
crown. The large, fan-shaped leaves are similar
in width and length and are divided into
drooping, strap-like segments. The leaf stalks
are of moderate length and edged with spines.
A most distinctive feature is the dense, gray-
brown skirt of dead leaves that forms around
the trunk, sometimes totally enclosing it. The
long, slender inflorescences, comprised of
small, delicate, white flowers, extend out well
beyond the leaves and are followed by small,
brown, egg-shaped fruits. Below climatic zone
9, grow in an intermediate greenhouse or conservatory, or as a house plant.

CULTIVATION In the greenhouse or home, grow in
pots of sandy, soil-based potting compost.
Ensure good light, but shade from strong, direct
sun. They need only moderate watering, and
should be kept only slightly moist throughout
winter. In the garden, these palms need a sunny
position, with well-drained soil. Propagate in
spring from seed germinated at 24°C (75°F).

CLIMATE Warmest parts of zone 9.

SPECIES *W. filifera*, desert fan palm or cotton
palm, occurs naturally in south-western United
States and into Mexico, and is the more
drought- and frost-tolerant of the two species.
The stout trunk is generally up to 15 m (50 ft)
tall and the crown is fairly broad and open. The
huge, grayish green leaves are divided into
many fine, long segments, between which
long, stiff, white threads appear. These are very
prominent, even from a distance, and give rise
to the common name 'cotton palm'. If the dead
leaves are removed as the palm grows, the

ABOVE Living up to its name of 'skyduster', this particular
Washingtonia robusta is about 80 years old.

trunk below will be smooth and pale gray. The
long inflorescences are followed by brown to
black fruits. *W. robusta*, thread palm or
Mexican washingtonia, is a native of western
Mexico. This species is better suited to growing
in the tropics, but it does not appear to like
constant high humidity or year-round rainfall.
It is much taller than *W. filifera*, with a trunk
up to 25 m (80 ft) high, tapering towards the
top. The glossy, mid-green leaves, borne on
fairly short stalks, are less deeply cut, and form
a compact crown. If the leaves are removed, the
leaf bases leave a criss-cross pattern on the
trunk. With this species, the white threads
between the segments generally occur only on
young plants. The inflorescences are smaller
than those of *W. filifera*, but the pea-sized,
dark brown fruits are borne in abundance.

Water chestnut

(*Eleocharis dulcis*, fam. Cyperaceae)

Widely cultivated in China and Southeast Asia, water chestnuts are an important part of the diet in those countries. The sweet, crunchy, edible tubers are eaten raw or cooked, although most people in the US would be more familiar with the canned product.

CULTIVATION Water chestnuts are grown in shallow water, in the same way as rice, in very rich soil with some added lime. They need full sun and high temperatures. Therefore, in cool and cold climate they would need to be grown in a warm greenhouse. Sowing to maturity takes about seven months and during this period they need frost-free conditions. Tubers should be planted in spring, 50 cm (20 in) apart, and kept quite moist until the plants are about 10–15 cm (4–6 in) high. At this stage, the area must be flooded and the water maintained at this level. In fall, the area is drained to harden off the tubers. The tubers are then dug up and stored.

CLIMATE Zone 9.

ABOVE In this home garden, an old bath has been recycled as the ideal container in which to grow water chestnuts.

Watsonia (fam. Iridaceae)

These beautiful, South African natives have long, tapering leaves and stalkless flowers borne in spikes. Flower colors range from white through many shades of pink, red, orange and lavender. There are around 50 species in this genus, all cormous plants, some growing up to 1.5 m (5 ft).

CULTIVATION In the garden, grow in a warm, sunny position with well-drained soil. In frosty climates, grow in a cool greenhouse, or treat summer-flowering species as for gladioli, lifting in fall and storing over winter. Propagate by division in spring.

CLIMATE Zone 9.

SPECIES *W. borbonica* (syn. *W. pyramidata*) is one of the larger, more attractive species, with its tall spikes of rose red, funnel-shaped flowers. *W. coccinea* grows to only 30 cm (12 in), with

ABOVE Watsonia meriana has deep rose pink flowers. Its compact growth makes it suitable for small gardens.

blood red, tubular flowers, in winter and spring. *W. marginata* produces its lilac-pink flowers, marked with purple and white, in spring and early summer. It reaches 2 m (6 ft) tall. *W. meriana* grows to about 50 cm (20 in), forming a neat clump of sword-shaped leaves. The summer flowers are a pretty shade of deep, rosy pink. Most of the watsonias grown in gardens are hybrids of mixed origin.

Weigela (fam. Caprifoliaceae)

These popular, deciduous shrubs are grown for their prolific flower display, in late spring and early summer. There are ten species, native to eastern Asia.

CULTIVATION These shrubs do well in most conditions, but prefer an open, sunny position and fertile soil. Prune after flowering by cutting back the old, flowered stems to young shoots or growth buds lower down. Every few years, cut out completely some of the oldest stems. Propagate either from semi-ripe cuttings in summer, with basal warmth, or hardwood cuttings in winter, in a garden frame.

CLIMATE Zone 5 for most species; zone 6 for *W. japonica*.

ABOVE A pretty, deciduous shrub for mixed borders, *Weigela florida* performs well even in poor soils.

SPECIES *W. florida* is grown for the magnificent, late spring and early summer display of trumpet-shaped, rose pink flowers borne on slender, arching branches. It grows 2–3 m (6–10 ft) high. There are several cultivars including 'Java Red' with red-flushed leaves, and 'Variegata' with white-edged foliage. *W. japonica* grows to 3 m (10 ft), the white buds opening to red in spring. *W. praecox*, to 2.5 m (8 ft), has scented, pink flowers, yellow inside. Most weigelas grown are named hybrids and there are many from which to choose.

Westringia (fam. Lamiaceae)

There are about 26 species of evergreen shrubs in this Australian genus. Many grow naturally in coastal regions. In their native country, they are widely planted for their flowers and foliage, but in frost-prone climates, they need to be grown in a cool greenhouse or conservatory. The dark green or silvery green foliage is generally fairly dense, and the pretty, tubular flowers appear for a long period, but are particularly profuse in summer or fall. Colors range from white and pale mauve to purple, some having red or yellow spots near the throat.

CULTIVATION In areas which are prone to frost, grow under glass in pots of sandy, soil-based potting compost. Add some leaf mould if it is available. Ensure maximum light and provide an airy atmosphere. Keep only slightly moist in winter. Outdoors westringias prefer an open, sunny position but will adapt to most well-drained soils. Lightly prune in early spring to maintain a neat shape. Propagate from seed in spring, germinated at 18°C (64°F), or from semi-ripe cuttings in summer, rooted in a heated propagating case.

CLIMATE Zone 10.

SPECIES *W. eremicola* is an upright shrub, growing to 1.5 m (5 ft) high, with white to mauve-pink, summer or fall flowers. It is a good choice for the home garden, although not showy in flower. *W. fruticosa*, Australian rose-

ABOVE *Westringia fruticosa*, Australian rosemary, can be grown in a cool greenhouse, where it will flower over a long period, from the end of spring to the beginning of fall.

mary, is a spreading shrub, growing to 2 m (6 ft) high, with fresh, rosemary-like foliage and producing white flowers with purple spots in the throat, from the end of spring to the beginning of fall. In the right climate, it can be grown to provide an attractive, informal hedge. It responds well to regular, light pruning. *W. glabra* is a small shrub, growing to 1.5 m (5 ft), with small, glossy leaves and clusters of lilac to purple flowers. *W. longifolia* is an open shrub, growing to 2 m (6 ft) high, with light green, linear leaves and flowers which are generally white. Blue-flowered forms, however, are seen occasionally. *W. rigida* is a small, stiff shrub, to 50 cm (20 ft), with large, almost white to pale lavender flowers, with spotted throats. Frost-tolerant, this species is not as decorative as some others.

Wisteria (syn. *Wistaria*, fam. Papilionaceae)

There are ten species or so in this genus of deciduous climbers, which have twining stems, soft, light green, much-divided leaves, and trusses of delicate, pea-shaped flowers.

Sometimes fragrant, flowers may be shades of blue, mauve, pink and white, and are followed by bean-like fruit. Wisteria is a garden favorite in a range of climates, providing summer shade and an attractive display in late spring and early summer. It is native to China, Japan, Korea and central and southern United States.

CULTIVATION Wisteria can be grown in almost any soil, provided it is well drained. However, it does need full sun, protection from wind and a strong support. Established wisterias need regular pruning to prevent congested growth. Train a permanent framework of stems to the shape desired, then spur prune to this. In midsummer, cut back the new, lateral shoots to within five or six buds of the main framework. Then, in midwinter, prune the plants back further, to within two or three buds of the framework. Wisterias can also be trained as standards. Propagation is by layering in spring.

ABOVE Trained against an old wall, this very fine, double-flowered cultivar of *Wisteria sinensis* is spectacular in late spring and early summer.

ABOVE *Wisteria floribunda* produces long trusses of flowers that can be up to 1 m (3 ft). This is the white form 'Alba'.

CLIMATE Zone 5 for most, but zone 8 for *W. japonica*, zone 6 for *W. macrostachya*.

SPECIES *W. brachybotrys*, from Japan, is known as silky wisteria or Yama Fuji. It has short, broad trusses of delightfully scented flowers that are deep violet, marked in yellow and white. Two outstanding cultivars are 'Shiro Kapitan', with large, white, fragrant flowers, and 'Murasaki Kapitan', which produces dark blue flowers, conspicuously marked with white. The flowers have little scent. *W. floribunda*, Japanese wisteria, has long stems, 10 m (33 ft) or more in length. The trusses of fragrant flowers can grow up to 1 m (3 ft) long, but are usually about half this size. They may be blueish violet, pink or white. The velvety fruit is about 15 cm (6 in) long. Cultivar 'Alba' or 'Shiro Noda' bears white flowers; 'Carnea' or 'Kuchibeni' has palest pink flowers; 'Macrobotrys' has very long trusses of mauve-blue flowers; 'Rosea' or 'Honbeni', rose wisteria, has rose pink flowers; and 'Violacea Plena' bears double, violet-blue flowers. *W. frutescens* a native of eastern and central North America, has trusses of lilac or purple flowers, followed by 10 cm (4 in) long fruit. *W. japonica*, from Japan and Korea, has 30 cm (12 in) long trusses of greenish white flowers, sometimes borne in pairs, followed by smooth fruits. *W. macrostachya*, Kentucky wisteria, from swampy areas of central North America, bears trusses of lilac or blue flowers, about 30 cm (12 in) long, followed by 12 cm (5 in) long fruit. *W. sinensis*, Chinese wisteria, is a very vigorous plant, sometimes growing to 10 m (33 ft) or more high. The trusses of mauve-blue flowers are 30 cm (12 in) long and appear before the leaves in spring. The flowers have only a light fragrance. Cultivar 'Alba' has very fragrant, white flowers.

Wodyetia (fam. Arecaceae)
Foxtail palm

This genus contains a solitary species of feather-leaved palm endemic to north-eastern Australia. It was named for Wodyeti, an Aboriginal bushman, the last male of his tribe, who had a

BELOW *Wodyetia bifurcata*, foxtail palm. This delightful effect can only be achieved in the tropics or subtropics. Elsewhere, grow under glass.

vast knowledge of the region. Identified only during the 1980s, it is extensively cultivated in the tropics and subtropics; however it is becoming rare and threatened in its habitat because of unscrupulous collectors.

CULTIVATION Outside the subtropics and tropics, the foxtail palm should be grown in a warm greenhouse or conservatory, in pots of soil-based potting compost. Provide good light but shade from direct, strong sun. Water well during the growing season, but reduce considerably in the winter. Outdoors these palms prefer a position in full sun, with deep, well-drained soil. Propagate from seed, which may germinate erratically, in a warm propagating case.

CLIMATE Subtropical and tropical.

SPECIES *W. bifurcata*, foxtail palm, grows to between 6 and 15 m (20–50 ft) tall. The narrow leaflets are arranged in a circular fashion on the stem–the so-called foxtail effect. The trunk has distinctive, closely spaced rings. Greenish flowers on a branched inflorescence emerge from the crownshaft base, followed by bright, orange-red fruits.

Wollemia (fam. Araucariaceae)
Wollemi pine

The discovery of this conifer in Australia in 1994 made international headlines. It was a chance discovery by a field officer of the National Parks and Wildlife Service in the Wollemi National Park west of the Great Dividing Range in New South Wales. It is a 'living fossil', its nearest relatives being known only from fossil records of the Cretaceous and early Tertiary periods. However, it is related to others of the Araucariaceae family, namely *Agathis* and *Araucaria*. With fewer than 40 adult trees known in the wild, it is one of the rarest plants in the world. It has been the focus of intense research since its discovery and is now being propagated and may be available for cultivation within a few years.

CULTIVATION Best grown in partial shade, in well-drained soil heavily enriched with humus, this tree should be given plentiful water during the warmer months, but kept much drier during winter. Little information exists about feeding, but slow-release fertilizer should be suitable. It has been propagated in the laboratory by tissue culture and from cuttings. In frost-prone climates, a cool greenhouse would be the best place to grow this conifer.

CLIMATE Best in areas with cool, moist winters and warm summers.

SPECIES *W. nobilis*, the Wollemi pine, grows to around 30 m (100 ft) in its habitat. It is an evergreen tree with an upright growth habit and unusual, spongy, knobby bark. Foliage is variable from the top to the bottom of the tree–from flattened trusses of leaves lower down, to short, rigid leaves in four rows, all directed upwards, higher. Male and female cones are carried separately on the same tree.

BELOW Discovery of the Wollemi pine in 1994 made headlines. This stem of rigid leaves bears a mature male cone at its tip.

XYZ

Xanthorrhoea to Zygopetalum

Xanthorrhoea (fam. Xanthorrhoeaceae)

Black boy, grass tree

This unusual and fascinating genus of around 15 species is native only to Australia. Actually very primitive plants, they are unlike any other known plant. They are slow-growing, long-lived, grass-like plants, which survive sometimes for several centuries and are thought to be among the oldest living plant species. They have a stem both above and below the ground, the stem above the ground being palm-like and topped with a thick clump of long, arching, tough, wiry leaves. Young plants are simply tufts of leaves, some taking around twenty years to form a trunk. The flower spikes are composed of densely packed, small, white to yellow flowers, followed by seed capsules which are carried along the length of the spike. Flowering times in the plants' natural habitats are extremely varied and often dependent on previous bushfires.

ABOVE A natural, sandstone outcrop in a bushland garden forms the perfect background for a grass tree (Xanthorrhoea species).

Grass trees are becoming better known and a few species are available. Where frosts occur, they have to be grown in a cool to intermediate greenhouse or conservatory.

CULTIVATION In the greenhouse or conservatory, grass trees can be grown in deep containers of sandy, soil-based potting compost, which must be very well drained, as they are prone to root rot. Ensure maximum light, but shield from direct, strong sun. Outdoors grass trees need deep, sandy soil with sharp drainage and full sun to partial shade. Propagate from seed in a warm propagating case. Germination can take up to a year and young growth is generally very slow.

CLIMATE Zone 10.

SPECIES X. arborea is a woody plant, with a 2 m (6 ft) high trunk, grayish green leaves and a long, thick flower spike. X. australis has a dark trunk and narrow, green leaves, the old leaves forming a skirt if allowed to remain on the plant. The long flower spike is partly bare. It has been known to grow to 4–5 m (13–16 ft), in length but is more usually less than 2–3 m (6–10 ft). X. macronema has an underground trunk and narrow glossy leaves, up to 1 m (3 ft) long, that are ribbed with sandpapery, rough margins. The short, chunky flowering spike is carried on a tall, slender stem. Flowers are yellow, with long, protruding stamens, and much larger than those of many other species. X. media generally has an underground trunk, but this may sometimes be up to 80 cm (32 in) above ground. The glossy, green leaves are very narrow and the narrow flowering spike, 30–80 cm (12–32 in) long, is carried on a stalk up to 2 m (6 ft) high. X. minor is a very small species, with short clumps of slender leaves. The trunks are underground and rarely seen. The flowers are strongly fragrant and may cover a good proportion of the 30–60 cm (12–24 in) long flower spikes. X. preissii, from Western Australia, has a 5 m (16 ft) high trunk, topped with a rounded tuft of leaves. The cream-colored flowers are crowded at the top of the 2 m (6 ft) long flower spikes, which extend high above the crown. They appear in spring. *X. resinosa* produces a clump of blue-tinged leaves from its trunk, which is mostly below ground level. The dense flower spike has a dark brown, velvety appearance because of dense hairs on the floral bracts.

Xanthostemon (fam. Myrtaceae)

The 45 species in this genus of evergreen trees and shrubs are native to tropical, north-eastern Australia, New Caledonia and parts of South-east Asia. Some species are grown for their timber, others as ornamentals. They are unlikely to be available outside their native countries.

CULTIVATION Outside the tropics and subtropics, grow in an intermediate to warm greenhouse or conservatory, in pots of well-drained, soil-based potting compost. Add some leaf mould if available. Provide good light but shade from direct, strong sun if necessary, to prevent leaf scorch. Water well during the growing season, but reduce in winter. Outdoors grow in full sun or partial shade and well drained, humus-rich soil. Propagate from seed in spring or from semi-ripe cuttings in summer, with bottom heat for both.

ABOVE *Xanthostemon chrysanthus*, golden penda, flowers in winter in its natural habitat. In frost-prone climates, it would have to be grown in a greenhouse.

CLIMATE Zone 10 or tropical.

SPECIES *X. chrysanthus*, golden penda or black penda, from north-eastern Queensland, grows to about 8 m (26 ft) in cultivation, but much taller in its rainforest habitat. It has oval, glossy leaves up to 15 cm (6 in) long. Mature leaves are mid to dark green, while new growth is pinky red. The showy flowers are large, rounded heads of bright, citrus yellow stamens. In their natural habitat, these appear mainly in winter but will be produced at other times in the northern hemisphere.

Xylomelum (fam. Proteaceae)
Woody pear

There are about four species of shrubs or trees in this genus from warm, dry areas of Australia. Leaves are leathery and sometimes serrated, and the dense flower spikes are similar to those of its relatives, grevilleas and hakeas. Flowers are creamy white, often clothed in rusty hairs. The large, woody fruits are in the shape of a pear. These plants are unlikely to be available outside their native Australia. In frost-prone climates,

ABOVE Two large, winged seeds are encased in the woody fruits of *Xylomelum pyriforme*. The seeds are released after fire or death of the plant.

they would need to be grown in an intermediate to warm greenhouse or conservatory.

CULTIVATION Under glass, grow in pots of acid, gritty, well-drained, soil-based potting compost. Provide maximum light. Outdoors grow in a sunny spot with well drained, acid, sandy soil. Propagate from the winged seeds which are released from the fruit when ripe. Germinate in a heated propagating case. The seeds generally germinate readily, but subsequent growth is quite slow. The young plants need ample moisture in the early growth stages.

CLIMATE Zone 10 or tropical.

SPECIES *X. angustifolium*, sand plain woody pear, from Western Australia, grows 3–5 m (10–16 ft) high, with narrow leaves and creamy yellow flowers, in summer, followed by pale gray fruits covered in soft, gray down. *X. occidentale*, western woody pear, from sandy, open woodlands of Western Australia, is a tree, to 8 m (26 ft), with a spreading crown. The trunk is covered with dark brown, flaky bark. The large, wavy-edged leaves are prickly at the margins and the creamy yellow, summer flower spikes are followed by large, 'pear' fruits, which grow up to 15 cm (6 in) long and persist on the tree for some time. *X. pyriforme*, woody pear, from eastern Australia, is a shrub or small tree, 3–9 m (10–30 ft) high, with leathery, lance-shaped leaves, cream flowers surrounded by rusty hairs, and large, gray, velvety fruits.

Xylosma (fam. Flacourtiaceae)

There are about 100 species of evergreen trees and shrubs in this genus, with a wide distribution through tropical and subtropical regions. Many originate in tropical America, but species also occur in Polynesia, New Caledonia, China, Japan and other parts of Southeast Asia. These plants are dioecious, with male and female flowers on separate trees. In suitable climates, they are grown as screening and hedging plants, but in frost-prone climates, they need to be grown in a cool to intermediate greenhouse.

ABOVE In a frost-free climate, *Xylosma congestum* makes an attractive, formal hedge. Elsewhere, grow under glass as a foliage plant.

CULTIVATION Best grown in full sun, these plants will tolerate partial shade. They prefer a humus-rich soil that drains well. They need ample moisture in summer, but can be kept much drier in winter. Little pruning is required, except for regular tip pruning for hedges or screens. Under glass, grow in pots of soil-based potting compost, in good light. Propagate from semi-ripe cuttings in summer, with bottom heat.

CLIMATE Zone 9.

SPECIES *X. congestum*, a small tree or shrub native to China, is about 5 m (16 ft) high, with shiny, oval, dark green leaves, with slightly serrated margins. Young growth is reddish. Flowers are small and insignificant. If both male and female trees are present, small, black berries will develop on the female trees.

Yam, white

(*Dioscorea alata*, fam. Dioscoreaceae)

In the large genus of *Dioscorea* there are several species used as food, but none is more widely

ABOVE *Dioscorea alata*, white yam, is a vigorous, twining climber that produces a single, huge tuber.

grown than *D. alata*, known variously as white yam and water yam. Native to tropical Asia, this perennial, twining vine produces thick, edible, tuberous roots, a staple food in many tropical regions. Tubers can reach 2 m (6 ft) in length and 40 kg (90 lb) or more in weight. There are many cultivars in countries where the yam is cultivated. Yams are peeled and cooked in various ways, including boiling, mashing and roasting. Tubers have a high starch content, but contain little else in the way of nutrients. They store better than many other tropical root crops. Many species of *Dioscorea* are poisonous, containing alkaloids which, in some instances, have medical applications.

CULTIVATION Yams should be grown in full sun, in deep fertile soil that drains well. They need a plentiful water supply through the growing season. Plants are generally propagated from sections of the tuber containing a good eye, from which growth emerges. This is most often the top section of the tuber. They can also be propagated from small bulbils that develop in the leaf axils, or from cuttings. Outside the subtropics and tropics, grow in a warm greenhouse, in which case the best planting time is spring.

CLIMATE Zone 10 and tropical.

Yucca (fam. Agavaceae)

Native to drier regions of Central and North America, these exotic, evergreen plants add a dramatic touch to a garden. They form rosettes of long, dagger-like leaves, usually tipped with a sharp spine, some species developing a trunk with age. Most have very striking inflorescences of drooping, white, bell-shaped flowers. In the past, in their native lands, yuccas have provided fiber for clothing, rope and twine, and the leaves have been used for basket-making and thatch. The young flowering shoots, fruits and flowers of some species were also used as food. Today, saponins obtained from the green fruits and seeds of some species are used to make soap, dental powders and pastes. In its

BELOW The tall flower spike of *Yucca whipplei* makes an outstanding feature in the landscape. These plants die slowly after flowering.

ABOVE The flowers of *Yucca* species are often egg-shaped and fragrant. Plenty of viable seed is set if the flowers are allowed to die off naturally.

homeland, *Y. filifera* is a source of paper pulp. Some species die after flowering, but by this time offsets will have been produced.

CULTIVATION Yuccas are easy plants to grow in the right climate, and thrive in well-drained, sandy soil, in full sun. In unsuitable climates, tender species can be grown in a cool greenhouse. Propagate in spring from rooted suckers.

CLIMATE There are species suited to various climatic zones.

SPECIES *Y. aloifolia*, Spanish bayonet or dagger plant, zone 9, is a tall, branched shrub, up to 8 m (26 ft) high, developing a trunk when mature. It has the typical stiff, erect leaves and a tall, thick inflorescence composed of large, cream flowers, held above the foliage. *Y. brevifolia*, Joshua tree, zone 8, is a tree-like species, the short leaves forming tufts at the ends of twisted branches. It is very slow growing, to around 13 m (43 ft). Rarely seen in cultivation outside south-western United States, it has greenish white flowers on a long, erect flower spike. *Y. filamentosa*, Adam's needle, zone 7, has a short trunk and a tall, narrow flower spike.

Threads of curly fiber peel away from the leaf margins. *Y. whipplei*, Our Lord's candle, zone 8, is a spectacular species, but dies after flowering. It is a stemless type, to 1 m (3 ft) high, with very stiff, narrow, blue-green leaves. The inflorescence of scented white flowers stands above the foliage, on stems to 2 m (6 ft) high.

Zamia (fam. Zamiaceae)

Native to tropical and other warm areas of America, these 30 species of cycads superficially resemble palms, but are not related to them in any way. They come from a range of habitats, including rainforests, open forests and savannah grasslands. These plants bear cones, the male and female types being on separate plants. Some species yield a starch-like sago. Only a few species are cultivated.

CULTIVATION In climates prone to frost, grow in a warm conservatory or greenhouse. *Zamia* also makes a good house plant. Grow in pots of sandy, soil-based potting compost and add some leaf mould to it if available. Plants need maximum light, but should be shaded from direct, strong sun. Outdoors grow in full sun with shade during hottest part of day, or in partial shade. Well-drained soil needed. Propagate from seed sown in spring and germinated at 24°C (75°F).

ABOVE Sculptural plants like *Zamia furfuracea* look best when several are grouped together.

CLIMATE Zone 10 to tropical.

SPECIES *Z. furfuracea*, from Florida and Mexico, is the main species grown. It is sometimes described as the cardboard palm. The leaves may be as long as 1 m (3 ft) and are composed of heavily textured, leathery leaflets, covered in fine brown hairs when young. Trunks grow to only 15 cm (6 in) or so. Male cones are narrow and cylindrical, while female cones are barrel-shaped, 20 cm (8 in) long and 5–7 cm (2–3 in) wide.

Zantedeschia (fam. Araceae)
Arum or calla lily

These six species of rhizomatous perennials from tropical and South Africa are identifiable by their classic, lily-type flowers, which are very familiar to most home gardeners. The glossy, green leaves are arrow-shaped.

CULTIVATION In frost-prone climates, grow the tender species in an intermediate greenhouse or conservatory. *Z. aethiopica* can be grown outdoors in cool climates, and is often planted in shallow water–up to 30 cm (12 in) deep–at the edge of a pool. Under glass, grow zantedeschias in a soil bed, or in pots of soil-based potting compost. Provide maximum light, but shade plants from strong, direct sun. During winter, keep the soil or compost only slightly moist.

Water well at other times. In the garden, grow in a sunny spot, with moist soil containing plenty of humus. Propagate by division in spring.

CLIMATE Zone 9 for most species; zone 8 for *Z. aethiopica*.

SPECIES *Z. aethiopica*, white arum lily, is the commercial arum lily, with large, white flowers, with yellow spadices, and spathes 25–30 cm (10–12 in) long. Growing 1 m (3 ft) high, it has become naturalized in many warm parts of the world. Cultivar 'Childsiana' is a dwarf, free-flowering type. The form 'Green Goddess' grows to 1.5 m (5 ft) and the green and white flowers are very popular with florists. *Z. albo-maculata* produces white-spotted leaves and pale yellow, white or sometimes pale pink flowers, with purple markings on the inside. It grows to 60 cm (24 in). *Z. elliottiana*, golden calla lily, grows 50–90 cm (20–36 in) high. It has dark green leaves, splashed with silver, and rich yellow flowers. This species has lovely cultivars in sunset shades. *Z. rehmannii*, pink arum lily, pink calla, to 60 cm (24 in), has rosy pink to purple, or pink-edged, white flowers.

Zauschneria (fam. Onagraceae)

This is a genus of four species of subshrubs and perennials from western North America. They are good plants for sunny rock gardens.

ABOVE Golden calla lily, *Zantedeschia elliottiana*, has golden yellow flowers that peep over the attractive, silver-splashed leaves.

ABOVE Californian fuchsia, *Zauschneria californica*, is a clump-forming perennial. It flowers for a long time and is frost-tolerant.

CULTIVATION Zauschnerias will grow in any well-drained soil, but prefer a sandy loam and full sun. Propagate in spring, either from seed in a garden frame, or from basal cuttings in a heated propagating case.

CLIMATE Zone 8.

SPECIES *Z. californica*, Californian fuchsia, grows to about 30 cm (12 in) in height, with a spread up to 50 cm (20 in). The small leaves are lance-shaped and the brilliant scarlet flowers are borne in loose spikes during summer or fall. The hardier subsp. *latifolia* has broader leaves.

Zelkova (fam. Ulmaceae)

This genus of five or six species of fine, deciduous trees or shrubs occurs naturally from the Mediterranean to the Caucasus and eastern Asia. Similar to elms, to which they are related, they are grown in gardens for their graceful, spreading shape and beautiful fall color. They are also cultivated for their timber in China and Japan. Zelkovas have smooth bark, coarsely ser-

rated leaves and insignificant, but fragrant, flowers. Male and female flowers are borne separately on the same tree.

CULTIVATION Zelkovas grow best when planted in a deep, fairly rich soil which is well drained, yet able to retain sufficient moisture. They will be equally happy in a sunny or partially shady position. In cold climates, try to plant in a sheltered position. Propagate from seed sown outside in fall, or from semi-ripe cuttings in summer, rooted with bottom heat.

CLIMATE Zone 5; zone 6 for *Z. sinica*.

SPECIES *Z. carpinifolia* is a slow-growing though long-lived tree, 20–30 m (65–100 ft) tall when mature. It has a dense, rounded crown and slender, upright branches. *Z. serrata*, Japanese zelkova, is an elegant, spreading tree, growing to about 30 m (100 ft) in its habitat, but generally 10–15 m (33–50 ft) in cultivation. The smooth bark is dappled gray and brown. *Z. sinica*, from China, grows to 18 m (60 ft). The leaves are pink and hairy when young, and the bark peels to reveal rust-colored patches.

Zephyranthes (fam. Amaryllidaceae)
Rain flower, wind flower, zephyr flower

This genus contains about 70 species of bulbs from North and South America. They are grown for their somewhat crocus-like flowers, produced any time from spring to fall, and often appearing with the grassy foliage. They are good for a rock garden. Where frosts occur, the tender species are generally grown in a cool greenhouse.

CULTIVATION Plant 10 cm (4 in) deep in pots of sandy, soil-based potting compost. Provide maximum light. During the dormant period, once the leaves have died down, keep only barely moist, but water regularly at other times. In the garden, grow in a sunny spot with well-drained soil. Propagate from ripe seed germinated at 18°C (64°F), or from offsets, when dormant.

ABOVE The wide, spreading crown of this old *Zelkova serrata* is thinning to reveal its lovely framework of branches.

ABOVE The simple, white flowers of *Zephyranthes candida* are very appealing amongst the shiny, grass-like foliage.

ABOVE *Zieria arborescens* is a large, spreading shrub with highly aromatic foliage and sprays of starry flowers.

CLIMATE There are species suited to various climatic zones.

SPECIES *A. atamasco*, Atamasco lily, zone 8, grows to around 30 cm (12 in) high. The pretty, white flowers, flushed with pink, appear in spring. *Z. candida*, zone 8, is a vigorous species, growing to about 18 cm (7 in). The pure white, cup-shaped flowers, sometimes flushed with pink, look very attractive amongst the grass-like foliage in fall. *Z. citrina*, zone 10, to about 15 cm (6 in), produces golden yellow flowers in fall. *Z. grandiflora*, zone 9, grows to around 30 cm (12 in), with lovely rose pink, late summer and early fall flowers. *Z. rosea*, zone 10, grows to only 18 cm (7 in), with rose pink flowers in fall. These latter species are very similar. Other species are available, some with smaller flowers.

Zieria (fam. Rutaceae)

Occurring naturally in eastern Australia, these 40 species of evergreen shrubs make attractive plants for warm temperate to subtropical gardens. Most have very fragrant foliage, the translucent dots on the leaves containing an aromatic oil. The starry flowers are similar to those of boronias and eriostemons to which

Zieria is related. These plants are unlikely to be available outside their native Australia, and in frost-prone climates, would need to be grown in a cool greenhouse.

CULTIVATION In the garden, grow in a very well-drained, sandy soil which is rich in humus. Choose a sunny position although plants will take partial shade. Under glass, grow in pots of well-drained, soil-based potting compost, and ensure good light and an airy atmosphere. Propagate from seed as soon as ripe, or from semi-ripe cuttings in summer, with bottom heat for both.

CLIMATE Warmest parts of zone 9.

SPECIES *Z. arborescens* is an attractive, spreading shrub to about 4 m (13 ft). The foliage is highly aromatic and makes a good background for the sprays of white, starry flowers. *Z. compacta* is a rounded shrub, growing to a height and width of around 1 m (3 ft), with clusters of white flowers. *Z. cytisoides* has gray, downy leaves and pink flowers. *Z. laevigata* grows to 1 m (3 ft), with angular branches, glossy, green leaves, and white or pale pink flowers. *Z. smithii* is a smooth-stemmed shrub with white flowers.

ABOVE A swathe of dwarf zinnias in shades of red and pink cut through a planting of mixed petunias. Dwarf zinnias can be grown on more exposed sites than the tall forms.

Zinnia (fam. Asteraceae)

With their range of very brightly colored flowers, zinnias make an attractive display when mass planted, while the dwarf types are decorative in borders. There are around 20 species in this genus of annuals and perennials, with a wide distribution through drier parts of the Americas and Mexico. Zinnias, which are frost-tender, are widely grown as summer bedding plants.

CULTIVATION In frost-prone climates, raise bedding plants from seed in early spring, under glass, germinated at 18°C (64°F) and plant out when frosts are over. If there is no risk of frost, seeds can be sown where they are to grow, in late spring. Zinnias grow best in a fairly rich soil, well drained yet moisture-retentive with plenty of humus. Full sun ensures optimum flowering. Remove dead flowers to encourage a long flowering period.

CLIMATE Zone 10, but grown as summer annuals in all climatic zones.

SPECIES *Z. elegans* is an upright-growing annual that may reach 80 cm (32 in) or more high. It is sometimes known as 'youth and old age' because of its habit of producing new flowers and growth that mask the old, faded blooms. It has stiff, stem-clasping leaves, and the large flowers have rows of overlapping petals (ray florets). The species has purple flowers and is rarely grown, its many cultivars being preferred. There is a vast color range, including yellow, red, pink, cream, white and purple. There is even a green cultivar called 'Envy'. Most cultivars have double flowers, but some are single or semi-double. There are tall-growing kinds up to 80 cm (32 in) in height, medium growers, to 60 cm (24 in), and small growers, about 15–40 cm (6–16 in). The annual *Z. haageana*, Mexican zinnia, grows to 60 cm (24 in), with brilliant orange flower heads. There are several cultivars, including dwarfs in mixed colors as well as the original orange, and these are ideal for summer bedding. The cultivar 'Persian Carpet', 40 cm (16 in) high, is grown worldwide.

Zucchini (*Cucurbita pepo*, fam. Cucurbitaceae)

Courgette

Zucchini or courgette has become a popular vegetable some parts of the world only over the past few decades but it has long been used by the French and Italians in such dishes as ratatouille and baked Mediterranean vegetables. It also makes a delicate accompaniment to meats, when steamed and tossed in a little butter. Zucchini may be dark green, pale green or yellow, and are best picked when about 10 cm (4 in) long.

ABOVE Zucchini flowers can be used as a culinary delicacy or left on the plant to mature into fruit.

CULTIVATION Grow this vegetable in full sun. The soil must drain well and should contain plenty of organic matter. Sow seeds in spring once the soil has warmed up. It is often best to sow three seeds in one place, and to select the strongest plant and discard the others once growth is active. In frost-prone climates, sow under glass in mid-spring, one seed per pot, and plant out when danger of frost is over. Space plants 90 cm (36 in) apart each way. Apply an all-purpose plant food once the plants are in active growth. Give ample water during the growing season. Check fruiting plants daily and harvest the fruits as soon as they are a suitable size. In warm weather, fruits can develop rapidly.

CLIMATE Zone 10, but grown as a summer annual in all climates.

VARIETIES Zucchini is a bushy annual and many cultivars have been produced by plant breeders. The fruits generally come in various shades of green, but there are also yellow cultivars which, unpeeled, add attractive color to meals.

Zygopetalum (fam. Orchidaceae)

Native to Central and South America and Mexico, this genus comprises around 20 species of mostly epiphytic orchids. They are generally easy to cultivate and their fragrant flowers appear in fall, winter and spring.

CULTIVATION Grow in an intermediate to warm greenhouse, either in pots, or slatted, wooden orchid baskets hung up in the greenhouse. Fill containers with a proprietary orchid compost formulated for epiphytes. When the plants are in full growth they need very high humidity, liberal watering and good light, but shade from direct sun. Liquid feed every seven to ten days. Reduce watering considerably in winter and ensure maximum light.

CLIMATE Tropical.

SPECIES *Z. mackaii*, from Brazil, is the most widely grown species. It has fragrant, green flowers, to 6 cm (2½ in) across, veined heavily with brown. The white lip is spotted heavily in violet. This is an easy species to grow, as well as being desirable for its fall to early winter flowers.

BELOW The unusual flowers of *Zygopetalum mackaii* are heavily scented and appear during fall and winter.

Index

A

Abelia 8, 513
A. x grandiflora 8
A. x grandiflora
'Francis Mason' 8
A. x grandiflora
'Variegata' 8
A. schumannii 8
A. uniflora 8
Abeliophyllum 8
A. distichum 9
Abelmoschus esculentus
644
Abies 9, 703, 748
A. alba 9
A. balsamea 9
A. cephalonica 10
A. firma 10
A. grandis 10
A. homolepis 10
A. lasiocarpa 10
A. magnifica 10
A. pinsapo 10
A. spectabilis 10
Abutilon 10
'Variegatum' 11
A. x hybridum 10
A. x hybridum 'Kuller's
Surprise' 10
A. x hybridum 'Yellow
Gem' 10
A. x hybridum 'Souvenir
de Bonn' 10
A. x hybridum 'Eclipse'
10
A. x hybridum 'Boule
de Neige' 10
A. x hybridum 'Jubilee'
10
A. x hybridum
'Tunisia' 10

A. x hybridum 'Sydney
Belle' 10
A. x hybridum
'Emperor' 10
A. x hybridum
'Carmine' 10
A. megapotamicum 10
Abyssinian banana 357
Acacia 11, 740
A. baileyana 12
A. beckleri 12
A. binervia 12
A. browniana 12
A. cardiophylla 12
A. decora 12
A. drummondii 12
A. ericifolia 13
A. iteaphylla 13
A. longifolia 13
A. melanoxylon 13
A. myrtifolia 13
A. podalyriifolia 13
A. pravissima 13
A. pubescens 13
A. pycnantha 13
A. ulicifolia 'Brownii'
13
Acacia baileyana 11
Acalypha 13
A. wilkesiana 14
laciniata 'Variegata' 14
'Marginata' 14
'Metallica' 14
'Triumphans' 14
Acanthopanax 14
A sieboldianus 15
A. henryi 15
A. simonii 15
Acanthus 15
A. mollis 15
A. spinosus 15

Acca 392
Acca sellowiana 393
Acer 16
A. buergerianum 17
A. campestre 17
A. cappadocicum 17
'Aureum' 17
'Rubrum' 17
A. carpinifolium 17
A. davidii 17
A. ginnala 17
A. griseum 17
A. hookeri 17
A. monspessulanum 17
A. negundo 17
'Elegans' 17
'Variegatum' 17
A. palmatum 17
'Atropurpureum' 17
A. pensylvanicum 17
A. saccharinum 17
A. saccharum 17
A. saccharum subsp.
nigrum 17
A. trifidum 17
Achillea 17
A. ageratifolia 17
A. chrysocoma 17
A. filipendulina 17
A. millefolium 18
A. ptarmica 18
'The Pearl' 18
A. tomentosa 18
'Aurea' 18
Achimenes 18
A. longiflora 19
Acmena 19
A. australis 19
A. hemilampra 19
A. smithii 19
Acokanthera 20

A. oblongifolia 20
Aconitum 20
A. lycoctonum 21
A. napellus 21
Acorus 21
A. calamus 21
'Variegatus' 21
A. gramineus 21
'Pusillus' 21
Acradenia 21
A. frankliniae 21
Actinidia 22
A. arguta 22
A. chinensis 22
A. deliciosa 22
A. kolomikta 22
A. polygama 23
Actinidia deliciosa 509
Actinodium 23
A. cunninghamii 23
Actinostrobus 23
A. pyramidalis 24
Actinotus 24
A. helianthi 24
A. minor 24
Adansonia 24
A. digitata 24
A. gregorii 25
Adenandra 25
A. amoena 25
A. coriacea 25
A. fragrans 25
A. uniflora 25
Adenanthos 25
A. argyreus 26
A. barbigerus 26
A. cuneatus 26
A. cunninghamii 26
A. flavidiflorus 26
A. meisneri 26
A. obovatus 26

A. pungens 26
A. sericeus 26
Adenium 26
  A. obesum 27
  A. obesum subsp.
    oleifolium 27
Adiantum 27
  A. aethiopicum 28
  A. capillus veneris 28
  A. formosum 28
  A. hispidulum 28
Aechmea 28
  A. caudata 29
    'Variegata' 29
  A. chantinii 29
  A. fasciata 29
  A. Foster's Favorite
    Group 29
  A. lueddemanniana 29
  A. orlandiana 29
  A. racinae 29
  A. tillandsioides 29
  Var. *purpurea* 29
Aeonium 29
  A. arboreum 30
    'Atropurpureum' 30
  A. canariense 30
  A. haworthii 30
  A. lindleyi 30
  A. lindleyi var.
    viscatum 30
  A. tabuliforme 30
  A. tortuosum 30
Aerides 30
  A. crassifolia 31
  A. crispa 31
  A. flabellata 31
  A. odorata 31
Aeschynanthus 32
  A. bracteatus 32
  A. ellipticus 32

A. lobbianus 32
A. pulcher 32
A. speciosus 32
Aesculus 32
  A. hippocastanum 32
  A. indica 33
  A. pavia 33
  A. x *carnea* 32
  A. x *carnea* 'Briotii' 32
Aethionema 33
  A. coridifolium 33
  A. grandiflorum 33
    'Warley Rose' 33
African corn lily 493
African hemp 840
African lily 33
African violet 800
Agapanthus 33
  A. africanus 34
  A. praecox subsp.
    orientalis 34
Agapetes 34
  A. serpens 34
Agastache 35
  A. foeniculum 35
  A. mexicana 35
  A. rugosa 35
Agathis 35, 941
  A. australis 35
  A. robusta 35
Agave 36
  A. americana 37
    'Marginata' 37
    'Medio-picta' 37
    'Striata' 37
  A. attenuata 37
  A. parviflora 37
  A. sisalana 37
  A. victoriae-reginae 37
Ageratum 37
  A. houstonianum 37, 38

Aglaonema 38
  A. commutatum 38
    'Pseudobracteatum'
    38
    'Treubii' 38
  A. costatum 38
Agonis 39
  A. flexuosa 39
    'Variegata' 39
  A. juniperina 39
  A. linearifolia 39
  A. marginata 39
  A. parviceps 39
Ailanthus 39
  A. altissima 40
  A. vilmoriniana 40
Aiphanes 40
  A. caryotifolia 40
Air plant 897
Ajuga 40
  A. reptans 41
    'Atropurpurea' 41
    'Multicolor' 41
Akebia 41
  A. quinata 41
  A. trifoliata 41
Albany daisy 23
Alberta 41
  A. magna 42
Albizia 42
  A. julibrissin 42
  A. lebbeck 42
  A. lophantha 43
Alcea 43
  A. rosea 43
Alchemilla 43
  A. alpina 44
  A. mollis 43, 44
  A. xanthochlora 44
Alder 49
Alecost 278

Alectryon 44
  A. coriaceus 44
  A. excelsus 44
  A. forsythii 44
  A. subcinereus 45
  A. tomentosus 45
Aleurites 45, 919
  A. cordata 45
  A. moluccana 45
Alkanet 60
Allamanda 45
  A. cathartica 46
    'Hendersonii' 46
    'Nobilis' 46
    'Williamsii' 46
  A. schottii 46
Allium 46
  A. aflatunense 47
  A. cyaneum 47
  A. macleanii 47
  A. moly 47
  A. narcissiflorum 47
  A. neapolitanum 47
  A. senescens 47
Allium *cepa* 648, 830,
  846
Allium fistulosum 846
Allium porrum 529
Allium sativum 413
Allium schoenoprasum
  237
Allocasuarina 47, 205
  A. decaisneana 47
  A. littoralis 47
  A. stricta 47
  A. verticillata 47
Alloxylon 47
  A. flammeum 48
  A. pinnatum 48
Alloxylon flammeum 356
Allspice 48, 181

Almond 48
Alnus 49
 A. cordata 49
 A. glutinosa 50
 A. incana 50
  'Aurea', 50
 A. rubra 50
 A. tenuifolia 50
Alocasia 50
 A. cuprea 51
 A. macrorrhiza 51
 A. odora 51
 A. x argyraea 50
 A. zebrina 51
Aloe 51
 A. arborescens 52
 A. aristata 52
 A. distans 52
 A. ferox 52
 A. polyphylla 52
 A. saponaria 52
 A. variegata 52
 A. vera 52
Alonsoa 52
 A. warscewiczi 52
Aloysia triphylla 531
Alphitonia 52
 A. excelsa 53
Alpine fir 10
Alpinia 53
 A. calcarata 53
 A. purpurata 53
Alpinia galanga 411
Alstroemeria 53
 A. aurea 54
 A. haemantha 54
 A. ligtu 54
Alternanthera 54
 A. dentata
  'Rubiginosa' 55
 A. ficoidea 55

A. philoxeroides 55
Althaea 55
 A. officinalis 55
Alyogyne 56
 A. hakeifolia 56
 A. huegelii 56
Amaranthus 56
 A. caudatus 57
 A. hypochondriachus
  'Erythrostachys' 57
 A. tricolor 57
  'Splendens' 57
Amaryllis 57, 285
 A. belladonna 57
Amazon lily 378
Amberboa moschata 217
Amelanchier 58
 A. canadensis 58
 A. laevis 58
 A. lamarckii 58
 A. x grandiflora 58
American cowslip 336
American lotus 623
Amherstia 58
 A. nobilis 59
Ammobium 59
 A. alatum 59
Ampelopsis 59
 A. aconitifolia 60
 A. brevipedunculata 60
Anacardium occidentale
 201
Anchusa 60
 A. azurea 60
  'Loddon Royalist'
   60
  'Morning Glory' 60
Androsace 60
 A. lanuginosa 61
 A. pubescens 61
 A. sarmentosa 61

Anemone 61
 A. blanda 61
 A. coronaria 61
 A. hupehensis 61
 A. nemorosa 61
Anethum graveolens 329
Angel's trumpet 151
Angelica 62
Angelica archangelica 62
Angiopteris 62
 A. evecta 62, 63
Angophora 63
 A. bakeri 63
 A. costata 64
 A. floribunda 64
 A. hispida 64
 A. subvelutina 64
Angraecum 64
 A. eburneum 64
 A. eichlerianum 64
 A. infundibulare 64
 A. sesquipedale 64
Anigozanthos 65, 266,
 575
 A. bicolor 65
 A. flavidus 65, 66
  'Pink Joey' 66
 A. humilis 66
 A. manglesii 65, 66
 A. preissii 66
 A. viridis 66
Aniseed 66
Aniseed tree 483
Annona 298
Annona cherimola 232
Annona reticulata 298
Annona squamosa x
 cherimola 298
Anomatheca 66
 A. laxa 67
  'Alba' 67

Anopterus 67
 A. glandulosus 67
 A. macleayanus 67
Anthemis 67
 A. cretica subsp. cretica
  68
 A. marschalliana 68
 A. tinctoria 68
  'Wargrave' 68
Anthriscus cerefolium
 234
Anthurium 68
 A. andraeanum 68
  'Rubrum' 68
 A. crystallinum 68
 A. scherzerianum 68
Antigonon 68
 A. leptopus 69
  'Album' 69
Antirrhinum 69
 A. majus 69
Aphelandra 69
 A. squarrosa 70
Apium graveolens var.
 dulce 213
Apium graveolens var.
 rapaceum 213
Apple 70
Apple myrtle 63
Apricot 72
 'Alfred' 73
 'Bredase' 73
 'Earliril' 73
 'Early Moorpark' 73
 'Farmingdale' 73
 'Goldcot' 73
 'Hemskirke' 73
 'Moongold' 73
 'Moorpark' 73
 'Sungold' 73
 'Veecot' 73

P. armeniaca 72
Aptenia 73
  A. c. 'Variegata' 73
  A. cordifolia 73
  A. lancifolia 73
Aquilegia 74
  A. vulgaris 74
Arabis 74
  A. albida 75
  A. alpina 74
  A. alpina subsp.
    caucasica 75
  'Flore Pleno' 75
  'Variegata' 75
Arachis hypogaea 677
Aralia 75, 392
  A. elata 75
  'Variegata' 75
Araucaria 75, 941
  A. araucana 76
  A. bidwillii 76, 77
  A. columnaris 76
  A. cunninghamii 76
  A. heterophylla 76, 77
  A. hunsteinii 77
Araucaria *cunninghamii*
  158
Arbor-vitae 890
Arbutus 77
  A. menziesii 78
  A. unedo 78
  A. x andrachnoides 77
Archidendron 78
  A. grandiflorum 78
  A. sapindoides 78
Archontophoenix 78,
  196
  A. alexandrae 78
  A. cunninghamiana 78
Archontophoenix
  cunninghamiana 196

Arctotis 79
  A. acaulis 79
  A. x hybrida 79
Ardisia 79
  A. crenata 80
  'Alba' 80
Areca 80
  A. catechu 80
  A. triandra 80
Arenga 81
  A. australasica 81
  A. engleri 81
  A. pinnata 81
  A. tremula 81
Argentine trumpet vine
  254
Argyranthemum 81
  A. frutescens 82
Arisaema 82
  A. amurense 82
  A. dracontium 82
  A. speciosum 82
Aristolochia 83
  A. durior 83
  A. elegans 83
  A. littoralis 83
  A. macrophyllya 83
Aristotelia 83
  A. racemosa 83
  A. serrata 83
Armeria 84
  A. maritima 84
Armoracia rusticana 468
Arnica 84
  A. angustifolia subsp.
    alpina 84
  A. chamissonis 84
  A. montana 84
Aronia 84
  A. arbutifolia 85
Artemisia 85

  A. absinthium 85
  A. absinthium
    'Lambrook Silver'
    86
  A. dracunculus 85
  A. lactiflora 85
  A. ludoviciana 85
  'Powis Castle' 86
Artemisia species 877
Arthropodium 86
  A. candidum 86
  A. cirrhatum 86
Artichoke, globe 86
Artichoke, Jerusalem 87
Artocarpus altilis 148
Artocarpus heterophyllus
  495
Arugula 785
Arum 87
  A. italicum 87
  A. maculatum 88
  A. palaestinum 88
Arum lily 949
Aruncus 88
  A. dioicus 88
Arundinaria 88
  A. gigantea 89
  A. pygmaea 89
Asarina 592
Asarum 89
  A. canadense 89
  A. caudatum 89
  A. europaeum 89
Ash 403
Asiatic poppy 593
Asparagus 89, 90
  A. densiflorus 90
  A. densiflorus 'Myersii'
    90
  A. densiflorus
    Sprengeri Group 90

  A. meyeri 90
  A. officinalis 90
  A. plumosus 90
  A. setaceus 90
Asparagus fern 89
Asparagus officinalis 90
  'Jersey Giant' 91
  'Martha Washington'
    91
Asperula 91
  A. orientalis 91
  A. tinctoria 91
Asphodel 91
Asphodelus 91
  A. acaulis 92
  A. albus 92
  A. cerasiferus 92
Aspidistra 92
  A. elatior 92
  'Variegata' 92
Asplenium 92
  A. australasicum 93
  A. bulbiferum 93
  A. flabellifolium 93
  A. flaccidum 93
  A. lyalli 93
  A. nidus 93
Astartea 94
  A. fascicularis 94
  A. heterantha 94
Aster 94
  A. amellus 95
  A. novae-angliae 95
  A. novi-belgii 95
  Callistephus chinensis
    94
Astilbe 95
  A. chinensis 96
  A. grandis 96
  A. japonica 96
  Astilbe x *arendsii* 96

Astrantia 96
  A. major 97
  A. maxima 97
  A. minor 97
Astroloma 97
  A. ciliatum 97
  A. compactum 97
  A. conostephioides 97
  A. humifusum 98
  A. pallidum 98
  A. pinifolium 98
Astrophytum 98
  A. asterias 98
  A. capricorne 98
  A. myriostigma 98
  A. ornatum 98
Atherton palm 518
Athrotaxis 98
  A. cupressoides 98, 99
  A. laxifolia 99
  A. selaginoides 99
Athyrium 99
  A. filix-femina 99
  A. nipponicum
    'Pictum' 99
Atriplex 99
  A. cinerea 100
  A. halimoides 100
  A. holocarpa 100
  A. muelleri 100
  A. nummularia 100
  A. paludosa 100
  A. prostrata 100
  A. semibaccata 100
  A. spinibractea 100
  A. spongiosa 100
Aubergine 353
Aubrieta 100
  A. deltoidea 101
    'Argenteovariegata'
      101

'Aureovariegata' 101
Aucuba 101
  A. japonica 101
    'Crotonifolia' 101
    'Picturata' 101
    'Serratifolia' 101
    'Variegata' 101
Aurinia 101
  Alyssum saxatile 102
  Aurinia saxatilis 102
Australian frangipani
    476
Australian fuchsia 273
Austromyrtus 102
  A. acmenioides 102
  A. dulcis 102
  A. tenuifolia 102
Avens 421
Averrhoa carambola 851
Avocado 102
  'Duke' 103
  'Fuerte' 103
  'Hass' 103
  'Rincon' 103
  'Wurtz' 103
Azalea 103
Azara 103
  A. integrifolia 103
  A. lanceolata 103
  A. microphylla 103

B
Babiana 106
  B. plicata 106
  B. rubrocyanea 106
  B. stricta 106
    Var. sulphurea 106
Baboon flower 106
Baby blue eyes 625
Baby's tears 835
Baby's toes 394
Backhousia 106
  B. anisata 106
  B. citriodora 107
  B. myrtifolia 107
  B. sciadophora 107
Bacon and eggs 317
Baeckea 107
  B. behrii 107
  B. crenatifolia 107
  B. linifolia 107
  B. preissiana 107
  B. ramosissima 107
  B. virgata 107
Bald cypress 878
Balloon flower 718
Ballota 107
  B. nigra 108
Balm of Gilead 9, 211
Balsa 642
Balsam 484
Balsam fir 9
Bamboo 88, 108
Bamboo palm 226
Bambusa 108
  B. glaucescens 109
  B. multiplex 109
  B. ventricosa 109
  B. vulgaris 109
Banana 109, 614
  M. acuminata 110
  M. x paradisiaca 110

Banksia 110, 343, 689
  B. asplenifolia 110
  B. baueri 110
  B. baxteri 111
  B. caleyi 111
  B. canei 111
  B. dryandroides 111
  B. ericifolia 111
  B. integrifolia 111
  B. marginata 111
  B. media 111
  B. petiolaris 111
  B. praemorsa 111
  B. prionotes 111
  B. robur 111
  B. serrata 110, 111
  B. spinulosa 112
Baobab 24
Baptisia 112
  B. australis 112
  B. bracteata 112
  B. leucantha 112
  B. perfoliata 112
  B. tinctoria 112
Barbarea 112
  A. biennial 113
  B. rupicola 113
  B. verna 113
  B. vulgaris 113
Barberry 126
Barberton daisy 421
Barklya 113
  B. syringifolia 113
Barleria 113
  B. cristata 114
  B. obtusa 114
Barrel cactus 395
Barringtonia 114
  B. asiatica 114
Basil, sweet 114
  'Citriodorum' 115

'Dark Opal' 115
'Purpurascens' 115
Basket flower 25
Bauera 115
  B. capitata 115
  B. rubioides 115
    Var. alba 115
  B. sessiliflora 115
Bauhinia 116, 221
  B. carronii 116
  B. corymbosa 117
  B. galpinii 117
  B. hookeri 117
  B. scandens 117
  B. variegata 117
  B. x blakeana 116
Bay laurel 527
Bay tree 117
Bean tree 518
Bean, broad 118
Bean, common 118
Bean, Lima 119
Bear's breech 15
Beard tongue 683
Beaucarnea 119
  B. recurvata 119
  B. stricta 119
Beaufortia 119
  B. decussata 120
  B. orbifolia 120
  B. purpurea 120
  B. sparsa 120
  B. squarrosa 120
Beaumontia 120
  B. grandiflora 121
Beauty bush 513
Bee balm 127
Beech 390
Beet 121
Begonia 121
  B. 'Cleopatra' 124

B. acutifolia 123
B. bowerae 124
B. coccinea 124
B. foliosa 123
  Var. miniata 123
B. heracleifolia 124
B. incarnata 123
B. maculata 124
B. masoniana 124
B. metallica 124
B. rex 124
B. sanguinea 124
B. scharffii 123
B. semperflorens 123, 124
B. socotrana 123, 124
  'Gloire de Lorraine' 124
B. x tuberhybrida 123
  Fibrous-rooted begonias 122, 123
  Rhizomatous begonias 122
  Tuberous begonias 121, 123
Belamcanda 124
  B. chinensis 124
Belladonna lily 57
Bellflower 186
Bellis 125
  B. perennis 125
Beloperone 501
Berberidopsis 125
  B. corallina 126
Berberis 126
  B. darwinii 126
  B. linearifolia 126
  B. thunbergii f. atropurpurea 126
    'Atropurpurea Nana' 126

'Aurea' 126
B. wilsoniae 127
B. x rubrostilla 126
Bergamot 127
  M. didyma 127
    'Cambridge Scarlet' 127
    'Croftway Pink' 127
Bergenia 127
  B. ciliata 128
  B. cordifolia 128
  B. crassifolia 128
  B. purpurascens 128
  B. x schmidtii 128
Beschorneria 128
  B. tubiflora 128
  B. yuccoides 128
Beta vulgaris 121
Beta vulgaris subsp. cicla 831
Betony 847
Betula 128
  B. nigra 129
  B. papyrifera 129
  B. pendula 129
    'Dalecarlica' 129
    'Fastigiata' 129
    'Purpurea' 129
    'Youngii' 129
  B. populifolia 129
Big tree 827
Bignonia 129, 254
  B. capreolata 130
Billardiera 130
  B. bicolor 130
  B. cymosa 130
  B. erubescens 130
  B. longiflora 130, 131
  B. ringens 131
  B. scandens 130, 131
Billbergia 131

B. horrida 132
B. leptopoda 132
B. nutans 132
B. porteana 132
B. pyramidalis 132
B. zebrina 132
Billy buttons 282
Birch 128
Bird flower 288
Bird of paradise 858
Bird's eye bush 642
Birthroot 906
Bishop's cap 98
Bismarck palm 132
Bismarckia 132
  B. nobilis 132
  B. orellana 133
Bitter cress 192
Bitter cucumber 132
Bitter gourd 132
Bitter melon 132
Bitter pea 317
Bittersweet 212
Bixa 133
Black boy 944
Black iris 396
Black kangaroo paw 574
Black wattle 172
Black-eyed Susan 791
Blackberry 133
Bladder nut 849
Bladder senna 262
Blandfordia 134
  B. grandiflora 134
  B. nobilis 134
  B. punicea 134
Blanket flower 410
Blazing star 541
Blechnum 134
  B. camfieldii 135

B. cartilagineum 135
B. chambersii 135
B. minus 135
B. nudum 135
B. patersonii 135
B. penna-marina 135
B. wattsii 135
Bleeding heart 324
Blood lily 446, 815
Bloodleaf 488
Bloodroot 806
Bloodwoods 276
Blue bells 601
Blue daisy 393
Blue pea 469
Blue spiraea 199
Bluebeard 199
Bluebell 472
Bluebell creeper 836
Blueberry 135
  V. angustifolium 136
  V. corymbosum 136
Bog arum 170
Bok choy 136
Boltonia 137
  B. asteroides 137
    Var. *latisquama* 137
    'Nana' 137
Bolwarra 384
Bombax 137
  B. ceiba 138
Bonewood 356
Borage 138
Boronia 115, 138
  B. heterophylla 139
  B. ledifolia 139
  B. megastigma 139
  B. pinnata 139
  B. serrulata 139
Bossiaea 139
  B. heterophylla 139

B. linophylla 139
Bottle gourd 520
Bottle palm 476
Bottle tree 143
Bottlebrush 173
Bougainvillea 139
  B. x *buttiana* 140
    'Barbara Karst' 141
    'Crimson Lake' 140
    'Golden Glow' 140
    'Hawaiian Gold'
      140
    'Louis Wathen' 140
    'Mrs Butt' 140, 141
    'Mrs McClean' 140
    'Scarlet Queen' 141
    'Temple Fire' 141
  B. glabra 141
    'Magnifica Traillii'
      141
    'Magnifica' 141
    'Sanderiana' 141
  B. spectabilis 141
    'Bridal Bouquet' 141
    'Easter Parade' 141
    'Killie Campbell'
      141
    'Klong Fire' 141
    'Lateritia' 141
    'Limberlost Beauty'
      141
    'Mary Palmer' 141
    'Orange King' 141
    'Pagoda Pink' 141
    'Scarlet O'Hara' 141
    'Snow Cap' 141
    'Surprise' 141
    'Thai Gold' 141
Bouvardia 141
  B. jasminiflora 142
  B. leiantha 142

B. longiflora 142
  B. ternifolia 142
Bowenia 142
  B. serrulata 142
  B. spectabilis 142
Box 161
Boxwood 161
Boysenberry 143
Brachychiton 143
  B. acerifolius 144
  B. discolor 144
  B. populneus 144
  B. rupestre 144
Brachyglottis 144
  B. bidwillii 145
  B. Dunedin 145
  B. elaeagnifolia 145
  B. repanda 145
Brachyscome 145
  B. iberidifolia 145
  B. multifida 145
Brachysema 145
  B. aphyllum 146
  B. celsianum 146
  B. praemorsum 146
Bracteantha 146
  B. bracteata 146
    'Dargan Hill
      Monarch' 147
Brahea 147
  B. armata 147
  B. brandegeei 147
  B. dulcis 147
  B. edulis 147
Brake fern 749
Brassavola 147, 208
  B. cucullata 148
  B. nodosa 148
Brassica napus 863
Brassica olearacea 410
Brassica oleracea 149,

154, 164, 209
Brassica oleracea
  Acephala Group 505
Brassica oleracea,
  Gongylodes Group
  512
Brassica parachinensis 240
Brassica rapa 136, 138,
  911
Brazilian red cloak 595
Breadfruit 148
Breynia 148
  B. disticha 149
    'Rosea Picta' 149
  B. nivosa 149
Bridal wreath 844
Broccoli, sprouting 149
Brodiaea 149
  B. californica 150
  B. coronaria 150
  B. elegans 150
  B. minor 150
  B. stellaris 150
Bromelia 150
  B. balansae 151
  B. pinguin 151
  B. serra 151
Broom 307, 418
Browallia 151
  B. americana 151
    'Caerulea' 151
    'Nana' 151
  B. speciosa 151
Brugmansia 151
  B. arborea 151
  B. sanguinea 152
  B. suaveolens 152
  B. x *candida* 151
Brunfelsia 152
  B. americana 152
  B. australis 152

B. latifolia 152
B. pauciflora 152
Brunnera 153
  B. macrophylla 153
    'Dawson's White'
    153
Brunonia 153
  B. australis 153
Brunsvigia 153
  B. josephinae 154
Brush box 559
Brussels sprouts 154
Bryophyllum 504
Buckeye 32
Buckinghamia 154
  B. celsissima 155
  B. ferruginiflora 155
Buckthorn 772
Buckwheat 155
Buddleja 155
  B. alternifolia 156
  B. davidii 156
    'Black Knight' 156
    'Charming' 156
    'Dubonnet' 156
    'Ile de France' 156
    'Magnifica' 156
    'Nanho Blue' 156
    'Pink Pearl' 156
    'Variegata' 156
  B. farreri 156
  B. officinalis 156
  B. salvifolia 156
Buffalo-wood 159
Bugbane 244
Bugleweed 40
Bugloss 60
Bulbine 156
  B. alooides 157
  B. bulbosa 157
  B. frutescens 157

B. semibarbata 157
Bulbinella 157
  B. floribunda 158
  B. hookeri 158
  B. rossii 158
Bulbophyllum 158
  B. globuliforme 158
  B. lobbii 158
  B. longiflorum 159
Bulrush 911
Burchellia 159
  B. bubalina 159
Burnet 159
Burning bush 326
Burrawang, 575
Bursaria 160
  B. longisepala 160
  B. spinosa 160
Bush pea 753
Bushman's poison 20
Busy Lizzie 484
Butia 160
  B. capitata 161
  B. yatay 161
Butter knife bush 293
Butterfly bush 155
Butterfly flower 818
Butterfly iris 611
Butterfly pea 252
Butterfly tree 116
Buxus 161
  B. balearica 161
  B. microphylla 161
    var. *japonica* 161
  B. sempervirens 161
    'Suffruticosa' 161
Buxus sempervirens 373

C
Cabbage 164
Cabbage palm 553
Cabbage tree 269
Caesalpinia 165
  C. coriaria 165
  C. echinata 165
  C. ferrea 165
  C. gilliesii 165
  C. pulcherrima 165
  C. spinosa 165
Cajanus 165
  C. cajan 166
Caladium 166
  C. x bicolor 166
Calamintha 166
  C. grandiflora 166
  C. nepeta 166
  C. sylvatica 167
  Nepeta species 166
Calandrinia 167
  C. balonensis 167
  C. burridgei 167
  C. ciliata 167
  C. grandiflora 167
  C. umbellata 167
Calanthe 167
  C. triplicata 168
  C. veitchii 168
  C. vestita 168
Calathea 168
  C. argyraea 168
  C. louisae 169
  C. majestica
    'Roseolineata' 169
  C. makoyana 169
  C. mediopicta 169
  C. picturata 'Argentea'
    169
  C. veitchiana 169
  C. zebrina 169

Calceolaria 169
  C. Herbeohybrida
    Group 169
Calendula 169
  C. officinalis 170
Calico bush 506
California poppy 371
Californian lilac 210
Californian red fir 10
Calla 170
  C. palustris 170
Calla lily 949
Calliandra 170
  C. haematocephala 171
  C. selloi 171
  C. tweedii 171
Callicarpa 171
  C. americana 171
  C. bodinieri 171
    var. *giraldii* 171
  C. dichotoma 172
  C. japonica 172
Callicoma 172
  C. serratifolia 172
Callisia 172
  C. elegans 172
  C. fragrans 172
    'Melnickoff' 173
Callistemon 173, 180,
  263, 595
  C. acuminatus 173
  C. brachyandrus 173
  C. citrinus 173, 174
    'Burgundy' 174
    'Candy Pink' 174
    'Endeavour' 174
    'Mauve Mist' 174
    'Red Clusters' 174
    'Reeves Pink' 174
  C. linearis 173, 174
  C. macropunctatus 174

C. pallidus 174
C. paludosus 174
C. phoeniceus 174
C. pinifolius 74
C. rigidus 17
C. salignus 173, 174
C. shiressii 174
C. sieberi 174
C. speciosus 174
C. viminalis 173, 174
  'Captain Cook' 174
  'Hannah Ray' 175
C. viridiflorus 175
Callistephus 175
Callistephus chinensis
  175
Callitris 175
C. columellaris 176,
  177
C. endlicheri 176
C. oblonga 177
C. preissii 177
C. rhomboidea 177
Calluna 177
  'Alba Plena' 177
  'Alba' 177
  'Aurea' 177
  'Blazeaway' 177
  'Cuprea' 177
  'Golden Feather' 177
  'Red Haze' 177
  'Robert Chapman'
  177
  'Searlei Aurea' 177
C. vulgaris 177
Calocedrus 177, 748
C. decurrens 178
C. formosana 178
C. macrolepis 178
Libocedrus decurrens
  178

Calocephalus 178
C. brownii 178
Calochortus 178
C. amabilis 179
C. luteus 179
C. macrocarpus 179
C. nitidus 179
C. uniflorus 179
C. venustus 179
Calodendrum 179
C. capense 179
Calostemma 180
C. purpureum 180
Calothamnus 180
C. quadrifidus 181
C. sanguineus 181
C. villosus 181
G. gilesii 181
Caltha 181
C. leptosepala 181
C. palustris 181
  'Flore Pleno' 181
Calycanthus 181
C. floridus 182
C. occidentalis 182
Calytrix 182
C. alpestris 183
C. tetragona 183
Camass 183
Camassia 183
C. cusickii 183
C. leichtlinii 183
C. quamash 183
Camellia 183
C. japonica 184, 185
  'Emperor of Russia'
  184
  'Great Eastern' 184
  'Moshio' 184
  'The Czar' 184
C. reticulata 185

C. saluensis 185
C. sasanqua 184, 185
  'Jennifer Susan' 185
  'Plantation Pink'
  185
  'Shishigashira' 185
C. sinensis 183
C. x williamsii 185
  'Donation' 186
  'E. G. Waterhouse'
  186
  'Elsie Jury' 186
  'Water Lily' 186
Campanula 186
C. cochleariifolia 187
  'Alba' 187
C. glomerata 186
C. x haylodgensis 187
  'Warley White' 187
C. isophylla 186, 187
  'Alba' 187
C. latifolia 186
C. medium 186
  'Calycanthema' 186
C. persicifolia 186
  'Alba' 186
  'Blue Gardenia' 186
  'Moerheimii' 186
  'Telham Beauty' 186
C. portenschlagiana
  187
C. poscharskyana 187
C. rapunculus 186
C. rotundifolia 187
Camphor tree 245
Campion 565, 830
Campsis 187
C. grandiflora 187
C. radicans 187
C. x tagliabuana 187
  'Madame Galen' 188

Canavalia 188
C. ensiformis 188
C. maritima 188
C. rosea 188
Candytuft 482
Canna 188
C. flaccida 189
C. indica 189
Cannon-ball tree 281
Cantua 189
C. bicolor 189
C. buxifolia 189
Cape chestnut 179
Cape cowslip 519
Cape gooseberry 190
Cape grape 779
Caper bush 190
Capparis 190
C. mitchellii 190
C. spinosa 190
  Var. *inermis* 190
Capsicum 191, 235
C. frutescens 191
Capsicum annuum 191
Capsicum annuum 191,
  235
Capsicum frutescens 235
Carambola 851
Caraway 191
Cardamine 192
C. pratensis 192
Cardamom 193
Cardiocrinum 193
C. giganteum 193
Carex 194
C. comans 194
C. elata 'Aurea' 194
C. morrowii 'Variegata'
  194
C. secta 194
Carica papaya 674

Caricature plant 436
Carissa 194
  C. bispinosa 194
  C. macrocarpa 194
Carmichaelia 195
  C. flagelliformis 195
  C. odorata 195
  C. williamsii 195
Carnation 323
Carnegiea 195
  C. gigantea 196
Carob 219
Carolina jasmine 418
Carpentaria 196
  C. acuminata 196
Carpenteria 196
  C. californica 197
Carpinus 197
  C. betulus 197
    'Columnaris' 197
    'Fastigiata' 197
    'Incisa' 197
    'Pendula' 197
    'Purpurea' 197
  C. caroliniana 197
Carpobrotus 197
  C. acinaciformis 198
  C. edulis 198
  C. glaucescens 198
Carrion flower 849
Carrot 198
Carum carvi 191
Carya 199
  C. aquatica 199
  C. cordiformis 199
  C. glabra 199
  C. illinoinensis 199
Carya illinoinensis 679
Carya pecan 679
Caryopteris 199
  C. clandonensis 200

C. incana 200
  'Candida' 200
C. incana x *C. mongholica* 200
C. x *clandonensis* 200
Caryota 200
  C. mitis 201
  C. rumphiana 201
  C. urens 201
Cashew 201
Cassava 202
Cassia 202, 826
  C. brewsteri 203
  C. fistula 203
  C. grandis 203
  C. javanica 203
Cassinia 203
  C. aculeata 204
  C. arcuata 204
  C. denticulata 204
  C. fulvida 204
  C. leptophylla subsp. *fulvida* 204
  C. quinquefaria 204
  C. uncata 204
Cassiope 204
  C. lycopodioides 204
  C. mertensiana 204
  C. tetragona 204
Cast-iron plant 92
Castanea sativa 234
Castanospermum 204
  C. australe 205
Castor bean 783
Castor oil plant 783
Casuarina 205
  C. cristata 206
  C. cunninghamiana 206
  C. equisetifolia 206
  C. glauca 205, 206

Cat tail 911
Cat's whisker 652
Catalpa 206, 673
  C. bignonioides 207
    'Aurea' 207
    'Nana' 207
Catananche 207
  C. caerulea 207
    'Alba' 207
    'Bicolor' 207
Catchfly 565, 830
Catharanthus 207
  C. roseus 208
Cattleya 208, 519
  C. amethystoglossa 209
  C. bowringiana 209
  C. labiata 209
Cauliflower 209
Ceanothus 210
  C. cyaneus 210
  C. dentatus 210
  C. impressus 210
  C. thyrsiflorus 210
    'A. T. Johnson' 210
    'Burkwoodii' 210
    'Marie Simon' 210
  C. x *veitchianus* 210
    'Emily Brown' 210
    'Joyce Coulter' 210
    'Julia Phelps' 210
    'Yankee Point' 210
Cedar 211
Cedrela 210
  C. odorata 211
  C. sinensis 211
Cedronella 211
  C. canariensis 211
Cedrus *211*, 525
  C. atlantica 212
    'Aurea' 212
  C. deodara 212

    'Aurea' 212
  C. libani 212
Celastrus 212
  C. angulatus 213
  C. orbiculatus 213
  C. scandens 213
Celeriac *213*
Celery 213
Celery root 213
Celmisia 214
  C. argentea 215
  C. coriacea 215
  C. gracilenta 215
  C. lyallii 215
  C. sessiliflora 215
  C. spectabilis 215
Celosia 215
  C. argentea var. *cristata* 215
Celtis 215
  C. australis 216
  C. occidentalis 216
  C. sinensis 216
Centaurea 216
  C. cyanus 216
  C. dealbata 216
  C. macrocephala 216
  C. montana 216
    Var. *alba* 216
  C. moschata 216
Centella 217
  C. asiatica 217
  C. cordifolia 217
  Hydrocotyle asiatica 217
Century plant 36
Cephalocereus 217
  C. senilis 217
Cephalotaxus 217
  C. fortunei 218
  C. harringtonia 218

'Fastigiata' 218
Cerastium 218
  C. alpinum 219
    Var. lanatum 219
  C. glomeratum 218
  C. tomentosum 219
Ceratonia 219
  C. siliqua 219
Ceratopetalum 219
  C. apetalum 220
  C. gummiferum 220
Ceratostigma 220
  C. plumbaginoides 220
  C. willmottianum 220
Cercidiphyllum 220
  C. japonicum 221
Cercis 221
  C. canadensis 221
    'Alba' 221
    'Plena' 221
  C. chinensis 221
  C. f. albida 221
  C. japonica 221
  C. occidentalis 221
  C. siliquastrum 221
Cereus 221
  C. peruvianus 222
  C. uruguayana 222
Ceropegia 222
  C. dichotoma 222
  C. haygarthii 222
  C. linearis subsp.
    woodii 223
  C. sandersonii 223
Cestrum 223
  C. 'Newellii' 223
  C. elegans 223
    Var. smithii 223
  C. fasciculatum 223
    Var. coccineum 223
  C. nocturnum 223

C. parqui 223
Chaenomeles 223
  C. japonica 223, 224
  C. speciosa 224
    'Alba' 224
    'Cardinalis' 224
    'Moerloosei' 224
    'Nivalis' 224
    'Rosea Plena' 224
    'Rubra Grandiflora'
      224
    'Simonii' 224
  C. x superba 224
    'Crimson and Gold'
      224
Chalice vine 833
Chamaecereus 351
Chamaecyparis 224,
    294, 295
  C. lawsoniana 224
    'Allumii' 225
    'Ellwoodii' 225
    'Erecta Aurea' 225
    'Fletcheri' 225
    'Minima Aurea' 225
    'Minima Glauca'
      225
    'Minima' 225
    'Nana' 225
    'Silver Queen' 225
    'Wisselii' 225
  C. obtusa 225
    'Crippsii' 225
    'Fernspray Gold'
      226
  C. pisifera 226
    'Boulevard' 226
    'Filifera Aurea' 226
    'Plumosa
      Compressa' 226
    'Squarrosa' 226

C. thyoides 226
    'Andelyensis' 226
    'Ericoides' 226
Chamaecyparis
    nootkatensis 294
Chamaedorea 226
  C. costaricana 227
  C. elegans 227
  C. erumpens 227
  C. microspadix 227
Chamaerops 228
  C. humilis 228
Chamelaucium 228
  C. uncinatum 229
Chamomile 229
  Anthemis nobilis 229
  Chamaemelum nobile
    229
  Matricaria recutita 229
Chasmanthe 229
  C. aethiopica 230
  C. floribunda 230
Chatham Island forget-
    me-not 617
Chayote 238
Cheilanthes 230
  C. distans 230
  C. tenuifolia 230
Cheiranthus 231
  C. cheiri 231
  Cheiranthus cheiri 231
  Erysimum cheiri 231
Chelone 231
  C. glabra 232
  C. lyonii 232
  C. obliqua 232
Chenopodium 232
  C. bonus-henricus 232
Cherimoya 232
Cherry 233
  P. avium 233

P. cerasus 233
Cherry pie 458
Chervil 234
  A. cerefolium 234
Chestnut 234
  C. sativa 234
Chilean bellflower 524
Chilean glory flower
    348
Chilean lantern tree
    284
Chilean wine palm 497
Chilli 235
Chilli pepper 191
Chimonanthus 235
  C. praecox 236
Chin cactus 442
China aster 175
China fir 292
Chinese broccoli 410
Chinese gooseberry 509
Chinese hat plant 467
Chinese lantern 10
Chinese lantern lily
    806
Chinese parasol tree
    400
Chinese tsai shim 240
Chinese white cabbage
    136
Chionanthus 236
  C. retusus 236
  C. virginicus 236
Chionodoxa 236
  C. cretica 237
  C. luciliae 237
  C. nana 237
  C. sardensis 237
Chives 237
Chlidanthus 237
  C. fragrans 237

Chlorophytum 238
  C. capense 238
  C. comosum 238
    'Variegatum' 238
Chocho 238
Chocolate pudding
  fruit 810
Choisya 239
  C. ternata 239
    'Sundance' 239
Chokeberry 84
Chorisia 239
  C. insignis 239
  C. speciosa 239
Chorizema 240
  C. cordatum 240
Choy sum 240
Christmas bells 134
Christmas cactus 819
Christmas rose 458
Chrysalidocarpus 241
  C. lutescens 241, 242
  C. madagascariensis
    242
Chrysanthemum 242
  C. carinatum 243
  C. x morifolium 242
  Chrysanthemum x
    morifolium 243
  Chrysanthemum
    balsamita 278
Chrysocoma 243
  C. coma-aurea 244
Chrysophyllum 244
  C. cainito 244
  C. oliviforme 244
  Chrysophyllum cainito
    850
Chusan palm 903
Cichorium endivia 356
Cichorium intybus 763

Cimicifuga 244
  C. americana 244
  C. racemosa 245
  C. rubifolia 245
  C. simplex 245
    'Brunette' 245
Cineraria 245, 685
Cinnamomum 245
  C. camphora 245
  C. zeylanicum 245
Cinquefoil 736
Cissus 245
  C. antarctica 246
  C. discolor 246
  C. hypoglauca 246
  C. quadrangularis 246
  C. rhombifolia 246
    'Ellen Danica' 246
Cistus 246
  C. x cyprius 247
    'Albiflorus' 247
  C. incanus 247
    'Doris Hibberson'
      247
    'Peggy Sammons'
      247
    'Silver Pink' 247
  C. ladanifer 247
Citharexylum 247
  C. fruticosum 247
  C. spinosum 247
Citrus 731
Citrus aurantiifolia 546
Citrus bergamia 127
Citrus limon 530, 546
Citrus maxima 731
Citrus reticulata 583
Citrus x tangelo 875
Citrus x paradisi 435
Clarkia 247
  C. amoena 248

Cleistocactus 248
  C. straussii 248
Clematis 248
  C. alpina 249
    'Columbine' 249
    'Pamela Jackman'
      249
    'White Moth' 249
  C. aristata 249
  C. armandii 250
  C. flammula 250
  C. foetida 250
    'Barbara Jackman'
      250
    'Comtesse de
      Bouchaud' 250
    'Gipsy Queen' 250
    'Jackmani Superba'
      250
    'Lady Betty Balfour'
      250
    'Lincoln Star' 250
    'Nellie Moser' 250
    'Perle d'Azur' 250
  C. macropetala 250
  C. montana 249, 250
    Var. rubens 250
  C. pubescens 249
  C. recta 250
    'Purpurea' 250
  C. rehderiana 250
  C. stans 250
  C. tangutica 250
  Jackmanii hybrids
    249
Cleome 250
  C. hassleriana 250
  C. lutea 250
Clerodendrum 251,
  390
  C. bungei 251

  C. speciosissimum 251
  C. splendens 251
  C. thomsoniae 251
  C. ugandense 251
Clethra 251
  C. alnifolia 252
    'Rosea' 252
  C. arborea 252
  C. barbinervis 252
Clianthus 252
  C. puniceus 252
Clianthus formosus 252
Clitoria 252
  C. cajanifolia 253
  C. laurifolia 253
  C. ternatea 253
Clivia 253
  C. miniata 253, 254
  C. nobilis 254
Clove 254
Clover 905
Clover bush 430
Club moss 566
Clytostoma 254
  C. callistegioides 255
Coastal redwood 826
Cobaea 255
  C. scandens 255
    alba 255
Coccoloba 255
  C. diversifolia 255
  C. uvifera 255
Cochlospermum 256
  C. gossypium 256
  C. religiosum 256
Coconut 256
Cocos nucifera 256
Codiaeum 257
  C. variegatum var.
    pictum 257
Coelogyne 258

C. cristata 258
C. flaccida 258
C. massangeana 258
C. pandurata 258
Coffea 258
C. arabica 258, 259
C. canephora 259
C. liberica 258, 259
Coffee 258
Colchicum 259
C. agrippinum 259
C. autumnale 259
'Album' 259
C. byzantinum 259
C. speciosum 259
'Autumn Queen' 259
'The Giant' 259
'Waterlily' 259
Coleonema 260
C. album 260
C. pulchrum 260
'Sunset Gold' 260
Diosma alba 260
Coleus 260, 71
C. blumei 261
Solenostemon
scutellarioides 261
Coleus blumei 260
Colocasia esculenta 876
Coltsfoot 261
C. Tussilago farfara 261
Columbine 74
Columnea 261
C. gloriosa 262
C. hirta 262
C. microphylla 262
Colutea 262
C. arborescens 262
C. x media 262

Colvillea 262
C. racemosa 263
Combretum 263
C. erythrophyllum 263
C. loeflengi 263
C. paniculatum 263
Comfrey 263
Symphytum officinale 264
Common daisy 125
Cone plant 264
Coneflower 349, 791
Conesticks 689
Congea 264
C. tomentosa 264
Conophytum 264
C. bilobum 265
C. calculus 265
C. fenestratum 265
C. pictum 265
Conospermum 265
C. brownii 266
C. ephedroides 266
C. mitchellii 266
C. triplinervium 266
Conostylis 266
C. aculeata 266
C. bealiana 266
C. setigera 266
C. stylidioides 266
Consolida 266
C. ajacis 267
C. orientalis 267
Convallaria 267
C. majalis 267
'Fortin's Giant' 268
Convolvulus 268
C. cneorum 268
C. incanus 268
C. mauritanicus 268
C. sabatius 268

C. tricolor 268
Copper laurel 384
Copper leaf 13
Copperleaf 54
Coprosma 268
C. x kirkii 269
C. repens 269
'Argentea' 269
'Marble Queen's' 269
'Picturata' 269
'Variegata' 269
Coquito palm 497
Coral bells 462
Coral berry 79
Coral plant 794
Coral tree 369
Coral vine 68
Cordyline 269
C. australis 269
'Veitchii' 270
C. fruticosa 270
C. stricta 270
C. terminalis 270
Coreopsis 270
C. gigantea 270
C. grandiflora 270
Early Sunrise' 270
C. lanceolata 270
C. tinctoria 270
C. verticillata 270
Coriander 270
Coriandrum sativum 270
Cornus 271
C. alba 271
C. capitata 271
C. florida 271
Var. pluribracteata 272
C. kousa 272
C. mas 272

C. nuttallii 272
Corokia 272
C. buddlejoides 272
C. cotoneaster 272, 273
C. macrocarpa 273
C. x virgata
'Cheesemanii' 272
C. x virgata 'Red Wonder' 273
C. x virgata 'Yellow Wonder' 273
Coronilla 273
C. emerus 273
C. valentina 273
Correa 273
C. alba 273
C. backhousiana 273
C. glabra 273
C. pulchella 274
C. reflexa 274
Corydalis 274
C. cava 274
C. lutea 274
C. nobilis 274
C. ochroleuca 274
C. sempervirens 274
'Rosea' 274
Corylopsis 275
C. glabrescens 275
C. pauciflora 275
C. sinensis 275
C. spicata 275
Corylus 275
C. avellana 275
'Aurea' 275
'Contorta' 276
'Crazy Filbert' 276
'Harry Lauder's Walking Stick' 276
C. chinensis 276
C. colurna 276

C. maxima 276
'Purpurea' 276
Corylus avellana 451
Corymbia 276, 374
C. calophylla 276
C. citriodora 276
C. ficifolia 277
C. maculata 277
C. papuana 277
C. ptychocarpa 277
E. citriodora 276
E. ficifolia 277
E. maculata 277
E. papuana 277
E. ptychocarpa 277
Eucalyptus calophylla 276
Corynocarpus 277
C. laevigatus 278
'Albovariegatus' 278
Cosmos 278
C. atrosanguineus 278
C. bipinnatus 278
'Candystripe' 278
'Sea Shells' 278
Sensation Series 278
C. sulphureus 278
Costmary 278
Cotinus 279
C. coggygria 279
'Royal Purple' 279
'Velvet Cloak' 279
C. obovatus 279
Cotoneaster 280, 787
C. conspicuus 280
C. franchettii 280
C. frigidus 280
C. glaucophyllus 280
C. horizontalis 280
C. lacteus 280
C. microphyllus 280

C. pannosus 280
C. salicifolius 280
Cotton 432
Cotton palm 936
Cotyledon 280
C. buchholziana 281
C. macrantha 281
C. orbiculata 281
Var. *oblonga* 281
Courgette 952
Couroupita 281
C. guianensis 282
Crab apple 580
Crab cactus 819
Cranesbill 420
Crape myrtle 521
Craspedia 282
C. chrysantha 282
C. globosa 282
C. uniflora 282
Crassula 282
C. arborescens 283
C. ovata 283
C. schmidtii 283
Crataegus 283
C. crus-galli 283
C. laevigata 283
'Paul's Scarlet' 283
'Plena' 283
'Rosea Flore Pleno' 283
C. phaenopyrum 283
C. x *lavallei* 283
Creeping jenny 568
Cress 284
Barbarea verna 284
Lepidium sativum 284
Nasturtium officinale 284
Crinodendron 284
C. hookerianum 285

C. patagua 285
Crinum 285
C. asiaticum var. *sinica* 285
C. bulbispermum 285
Var. *album* 285
C. moorei 285
C. x *powellii* 285
Crocosmia 286
C. aurea 286
C. x *crocosmiiflora* 286
'Emily McKenzie' 286
'Gerbe d'Or' 286
'Golden Fleece' 286
'Golden Glory' 286
'Jackanapes' 286
'Lucifer' 286
'Rheingold' 286
C. masoniorum 286
Crocus 286, 786
C. biflorus 287
C. chrysanthus 287
'Blue Pearl' 287
'Cream Beauty' 287
'E. A. Bowles' 287
'Snow Bunting' 287
C. imperati 287
C. kotschyanus 287
C. sativus 287
C. serotinus subsp. *salzmannii* 287
C. speciosus 287
'Albus' 287
'Cassiope' 287
'Oxonian' 287
C. tommasinianus 287
'Barr's Purple' 287
'Ruby Giant' 287
C. vernus 287
'Jeanne d'Arc' 287

'Little Dorrit' 287
'Pickwick' 287
'Queen of the Blues' 287
'Remembrance' 287
Crocus sativus 286, 799
Cross vine 129
Crossandra 287
C. infundibuliformis 288
Crotalaria 288
C. agatiflora 288
C. cunninghamii 288
C. laburnifolia 288
C. spectabilis 288
Croton 257
Crowea 288
C. exalata 289
C. saligna 289
Crown cactus 769
Crown vetch 273
Crucifix orchid 359
Cryptanthus 289
C. acaulis 289
'Ruber' 289
C. fosterianus 289
C. zonatus 289
'Zebrinus' 289
Cryptomeria 290, 292
C. japonica 290
'Compressa' 290
'Elegans Aurea' 290
'Elegans Compacta' 290
'Elegans' 290
'Globosa Nana' 290
Ctenanthe 291
C. lubbersiana 291
C. oppenheimiana 291
'Tricolor' 291
Cucumber 291
Cucumis sativus 292

Cucumber, African
   horned 292
Cucumis metuliferus 292
Cucumis sativus 291
Cucurbit 433
Cucurbita pepo 588, 952
Cucurbita pepo var.
   ovifera 433
Cucurbita species 754
Cumquat 292
Cunninghamia 292
   C. lanceolata 293
Cunonia 293
   C. capensis 293
Cup and saucer vine
   255
Cup flower 631
Cuphea 294
   C. hyssopifolia 294
   C. ignea 294
Cupid's dart 207
Cupressaceae 177
x *Cupressocyparis* 294
   x *C. leylandii* 294
      'Castlewellan' 294
      'Leighton Green'
         295
      'Naylor's Blue' 295
Cupressus 175, 176,
   295, 499
   C. arizonica var. *glabra*
      295
   C. cashmeriana 295
   C. funebris 295
   C. glabra 295
   C. lusitanica 296
      Glauca Pendula'
         296
   C. macrocarpa 296
      'Donard Gold' 296
      'Goldcrest' 296

'Golden Pillar' 296
'Horizontalis Aurea'
   296
'Lutea' 296
C. sempervirens 295,
   296
   'Swanes Gold' 296
C. sempervirens
   'Stricta' 296
C. torulosa 296
Cupressus macrocarpa
   294
Curly kale 505
Currant 297, 782
   Ribes nigrum 297
   Ribes rubrum 297
Curry leaf 297
Cushion bush 178
Cushion plant 767
Cussonia 298
   C. paniculata 298
   C. spicata 298
Custard apple 298
   'African Pride' 299
   A. cherimola 299
   Annona reticulata 299
   Annona squamosa x
      cherimola 299
   'Pink's Mammoth'
      299
Cyathea 299
   C. australis 300
   C. cooperi 300
   C. cunninghamii 300
   C. dealbata 300
   C. medullaris 300
Cycas 300
   C. media 301
   C. revoluta 301
Cyclamen 301
   C. coum 302

C. hederifolium 302
C. persicum 302
C. repandum 302
Cydonia oblonga 762
Cymbalaria 302
   C. hepaticifolia 302
   C. muralis 302
Cymbidium 302
   C. canaliculatum 304
   C. finlaysonianum 304
   C. lowianum 304
   C. madidum 304
   C. pumilum 304
   C. suave 304
Cymbopogon citratus 531
Cynara scolymus 86
Cynoglossum 304
   C. amabile 304
   C. nervosum 304
Cyperus 304
   C. alternifolius 305
   C. involucratus 305
   C. papyrus 305
Cyphomandra betacea
   873
Cypress 295
Cypress-pine 175
Cypripedium 305
   C. calceolus 306
   C. reginae 306
Cyrtanthus 306
   C. brachyscyphus 306
   C. elatus 306
      'Alba' 306
   C. mackenii 306
      Var. *cooperi* 306
   C. speciosa 306
      'Alba' 306
      'Delicata' 306
Cyrtomium 306
   C. falcatum 307

'Butterfieldii' 307
'Rochfordianum'
   307
Cytisus 307
   C. multiflorus 307
      'Burkwoodii' 307
      'Cornish Cream'
         307
      'Lilac Time' 307
      'Lord Lambourne'
         307
      'Pomona' 307
   C. scoparius 307
   C. x praecox 307
      'Albus' 307

D

Daboecia 310
D. azorica 310
D. cantabrica 310
'Atropurpurea' 310
'Bicolor' 310
'Praegerae' 310
Dacrydium 310
D. cupressinum 310
D. franklinii 311
Daffodil 622
Dahlia 311
Dais 312
D. cotinifolia 312
Daisy bush 645
Dampiera 312
D. diversifolia 312
D. linearis 312
D. purpurea 312
D. rosmarinifolia 312
D. stricta 313
D. wellsiana 313
Dandelion 313
Daphne 313, 706
D. cneorum 314
D. genkwa 314
D. odora 314
'Auriomarginata' 314
D. x burkwoodii 314
Darwinia 314
D. citriodora 314
D. fascicularis 315
D. leiostyla 315
D. macrostegia 315
D. meeboldii 315
Dasylirion bigelowii 633
Date 315
Date palm 696
Daucus 316
D. carota 316

Daucus carota subsp. sativus 198
Davallia 316
D. denticulata 316
D. fejeensis 316
D. pyxidata 317
Davidia 317
D. involucrata 317
Var. vilmoriniana 317
Daviesia 317
D. brevifolia 317
D. cordata 318
D. horrida 318
D. mimosoides 318
Dawn redwood 602
Day lily 459
Dead nettle 523
Delonix 318
D. regia 318
Delphinium 267, 318
D. elatum 319
D. grandiflorum 319
Dendrobium 319, 320
D. bigibbum 320
D. chrysotoxum 320
D. densiflorum 320
D. falcorostrum 320
D. fimbriatum 320
D. kingianum 320
D. nobile 320
D. speciosum 320
Dendrocalamus 320
D. giganteus 321
D. strictus 321
Derris 321
D. elliptica 321
D. microphylla 321
D. robusta 321
D. scandens 321
Desert candle 364

Desert lime 363
Desert rose 26
Deutzia 321, 322
D. gracilis 322
D. longifolia 'Veitchii' 322
D. scabra 322
'Candidissima' 322
'Pride of Rochester' 322
D. x magnifica 322
Dianella 322
D. caerulea 323
D. ensifolia 323
D. intermedia 323
D. laevis 323
D. revoluta 323
Dianthus 323
D. alpinus 323
D. barbatus 323
D. caryophyllus 323
D. chinensis 323
D. deltoides 323
D. gratianopolitanus 323
D. plumarius 324
D. subacaulis 324
Dicentra 324
D. cucullaria 324
D. formosa 324
D. spectabilis 324
'Alba' 324
Dichelostemma 150
Dichorisandra 324, 325
D. thyrsiflora 325
Dicksonia 325
D. antarctica 325
D. fibrosa 326
D. squarrosa 326
Dictamnus 326
D. albus 326

Var. purpureus 326
Dictyosperma 326
D. album 327
Dieffenbachia 327
D. amoena 327
D. maculata 327
'Rudolph Roehrs' 327
D. seguine 327
Dierama 327, 328
D. pendulum 328
D. pulcherrimum 328
Dietes 328
D. bicolor 328
D. grandiflora 328
D. robinsoniana 328
Digitalis 329
D. ferruginea 329
D. grandiflora 329
D. lanata 329
D. lutea 329
D. purpurea 329
Dill 329
Dillwynia 330
D. glaberrima 330
D. hispida 330
D. retorta 330
D. sericea 330
Dionaea 330, 331
D. muscipula 331
Dioscorea 331, 946, 947
D. alata 331
D. elephantipes 331
D. trifida 331
Dioscorea alata 946
Diospyros 331
D. digyna 332
D. ebenum 331, 332
D. kaki 332
D. virginiana 332

Diospyros digyna 810
Diospyros kaki 686
Diploglottis 332, 333
  D. australis 333
Diplolaena 333
  D. angustifolia 333
  D. grandiflora 333
Disa 333
  D. uniflora 334
Disanthus 334
  D. cercidifolius 334
Dischidia 334
  D. nummularia 335
  D. rafflesiana 335
Dittany 326
Diuris 335
  D. aurea 335
  D. longifolia 335
  D. punctata 335
Dodecatheon 336
  D. alpinum 336
  D. clevelandii 336
  D. hendersonii 336
  D. meadia 336
  D. pulchellum 336
Dodonaea 336
  D. adenophora 337
  D. boroniifolia 337
  D. cuneata 337
  D. lobulata 337
  D. viscosa 337
    'Purpurea' 337
Dog's tooth violet 370
Dogwood 271
Dolichos 337
  D. lablab 337
  D. lignosus 337
  Dipogon lignosus 337
  Lablab purpureus 337
Dombeya 337
  D. burgessiae 338

D. tiliacea 338
Donkey orchid 335
Doodia 338
  D. aspera 338
  D. media 338
Doronicum 338
  D. austriacum 339
  D. columnae 339
  D. cordatum 339
  D. plantagineum 339
Dorotheanthus 339
  D. bellidiformis 339
Doryanthes 339
  D. excelsa 339
  D. palmeri 340
Doryphora 340
  D. aromatica 340
  D. sassafras 340
Double tails 335
Douglas fir 748
Dove tree 317
Dracaena 340
  D. deremensis 341
    'Massangeana' 341
  D. draco 341
  D. fragrans 341
  D. godseffiana 341
  D. marginata 341
  D. surculosa 341
Dracophyllum 341, 342
  D. longifolium 342
  D. paludosum 342
  D. secundum 342
Drimys 342, 748, 877
  D. winteri 342
Drosera 342
  D. binata 342
  D. capensis 343
  D. macrantha 343
  D. petiolaris 343
  D. spathulata 343

Drumhead 508
Drumsticks 491
Drunkard's dream 450
Dryandra 343
  D. floribunda 343
  D. formosa 343
  D. polycephala 343
  D. praemorsa 343
  D. speciosa 343
Dumb cane 327
Duranta 343
  D. erecta 343, 344
  D. repens 344
Durian 344
Durio zibethinus 344
Dusty miller 846
Dutch iris 490
Dutchman's breeches 324
Dutchman's pipe 83
Dyckia 344
  D. brevifolia 344
  D. fosteriana 345
  D. remotiflora 345
Dysoxylum 345
  D. fraserianum 345
  D. muelleri 345
  D. oppositifolium 345
  D. spectabile 345

E

Earth star 289
Eccremocarpus 348
  E. scaber 348
Echeveria 348, 436, 660
  E. agavoides 348
  E. derenbergii 349
  E. elegans 349
  E. gibbiflora 349
  E. leucotricha 349
  E. pulvinata 349
  E. secunda 349
Echinacea 349
  E. angustifolia 349
  E. purpurea 349
    'Alba' 349
Echinocactus 349
  E. grusonii 350
  E. ingens 350
  E. platyacanthus 350
Echinocereus 350
  E. chloranthus 350
  E. enneacanthus 350
  E. knippelianus 351
  E. pectinatus 351
  E. reichenbachii 351
  E. triglochidiatus 351
Echinops 351
  E. bannaticus 351
    'Blue Globe' 351
    'Taplow Blue' 351
  E. ritro 351
  E. sphaerocephalus 351
Echinopsis 351
  E. backebergii 352
  E. chamaecereus 352
  E. cinnabarina 352
  E. huascha 352
  E. lageniformis 352
  E. spachiana 352
Echium 352

E. candicans 352
E. fastuosum 352
Edgeworthia 353
E. chrysantha 353
E. papyrifera 353
Eggplant 353
Eggs and bacon 753
Elaeagnus 354
E. angustifolia 354
E. pungens 354
'Maculata' 354
'Marginata' 354
Elaeis 354
E. guineensis 355
Elaeocarpus 355
E. cyaneus 355
E. grandis 355
E. kirtonii 355
Elder 805
Elderberry 805
Eleocharis dulcis 937
Elephant bush 734
Elettaria cardamomum
193
Elkhorn fern 717
Elm 912
Embothrium 356
E. coccineum 356
Var. *lanceolatum*
'Norquinco' 356
Emmenosperma 356
E. alphitonioides 356
Emu bush 363
Encyclia 519
Endive 356
Ensete 357
E. ventricosum 357
Entelea 358
E. arborescens 358
Epacris 358
E. impressa 359

E. longiflora 359
E. microphylla 359
Epidendrum 208, 359
E. ibaguense 359
Epimedium 359
E. diphyllum 360
E. grandiflorum 360
E. pinnatum 360
E. x rubrum 360
E. x versicolor 360
E. x youngianum 360
'Niveum' 360
'Roseum' 360
Epiphyllum 360
E. crenatum 360
E. hookeri 360
E. oxypetalum 360
Epipremnum 361
E. aureum 361
'Marble Queen' 361
'Tricolor' 361
E. pictum 'Argyraeum'
361
Episcia 361
E. cupreata 362
'Metallica' 362
E. dianthiflora 362
E. lilacina 362
Eranthemum 362
E. pulchellum 362
Eranthis 362
E. hyemalis 363
E. x tubergenii 363
'Guinea Gold' 363
Eremocitrus 363
E. glauca 363
Eremophila 363
E. alternifolia 363
E. bignoniiflora 364
E. longifolia 364
E. maculata 364

E. oppositifolia 364
E. scoparia 364
Eremurus 364
E. olgae 364, 365
E. robustus 364
E. spectabilis 365
E. stenophyllus 365
Erica 365
E. arborea 365
E. baccans 365
E. carnea 365
'Springwood Pink'
365
'Springwood White'
365
E. cinerea 365
E. erigena 365
E. hiemalis 366
E. lusitanica 366
E. mediterranea 365
E. x darleyensis 365
Erigeron 366
E. alpinus 366
E. aureus 366
E. glaucus 366
E. karvinskianus 366
E. speciosus 366
E. x hybridus 366
'Dignity' 366
'Pink Triumph' 366
'Quakeress' 366
'Vanity' 366
'Wuppertal' 366
Eriobotrya japonica 559
Eriostemon 366
E. australasius 367
E. buxifolius 367
E. myoporoides 367
'Clearview Pink'
367
E. verrucosus 367

Erodium 367
E. manescavii 367
E. reichardii 367
E. trifolium 368
Eruca vesicaria subsp.
sativa 785
Eryngium 368
E. agavifolium 368
E. amethystinum 368
E. maritimum 368
E. planum 368
Erysimum 231, 368,
369
E. asperum 369
E. kotschyanum 369
E. linifolium 369
Erythrina 369
E. acanthocarpa 369
E. caffra 369
E. crista-galli 369
E. vespertilio 370
E. x sykesii 369
Erythronium 370
E. americanum 370
E. dens-canis 370
'Pink Perfection'
370
'Purple King' 370
'Snowflake' 370
E. grandiflorum 370
E. hendersonii 370
E. oregonum 370
Escallonia 370
'Apple Blossom' 371
'Donard Brilliance'
371
'Donard Seedling' 371
E. bifida 371
E. iveyi 371
E. rubra var.
macrantha 371

'C. F. Ball' 371
E. x exoniensis 371
Eschalot 830
Eschscholzia 371
E. californica 372
Etlingera 372
E. elatior 372
Eucalypt 372
Eucalyptus 276, 372,
373, 374, 375
E. caesia 375
E. camaldulensis 375
E. cinerea 375
E. cladocalyx 375
'Nana' 375
E. curtisii 375
E. deglupta 375
E. erythrocorys 375
E. globulus 376
E. haemastoma 376
E. macrocarpa 376
E. melliodora 376
E. microcorys 376
E. nicholii 376
E. niphophila 376
E. pauciflora 376
E. pauciflora subsp.
niphophila 376
E. pilularis 377
E. pyriformis 377
E. regnans 374
E. robusta 377
E. scoparia 377
E. sideroxylon 377
E. torquata 378
Eucharis 378
E. x grandiflora 378
Eucomis 378
E. autumnalis 379
E. bicolor 379
E. comosa 379

E. pole-evansii 379
Eucryphia 379
E. lucida 380
E. moorei 380
E. x nymansensis
'Nymansay' 380
Eugenia 380
E. aggregata 380
E. brasiliensis 380
E. pitanga 380
E. reinwardtiana 380
E. uniflora 380
Euonymus 381
E. alatus 381
E. europaeus 381
E. japonicus 381
E. latifolius 381
Eupatorium 381
E. cannabinum 382
E. megalophyllum 382
E. purpureum 382
Euphorbia 382
E. candelabrum 383
E. caput-medusae 383
E. characias 383
E. fulgens 383
E. griffithii 384
E. marginata 384
E. milii var. splendens
384
E. obesa 384
E. pulcherrima 384
E. tirucalli 384
Euphorbia pulcherrima
382
Eupomatia 384
E. laurina 385
European fan palm 228
European silver fir 9
Euryops 385
E. athanasiae 385

E. pectinatus 385
E. speciosissimus 385
Eutaxia 385
E. microphylla 386
E. myrtifolia 386
E. obovata 386
Everlasting 456, 775
Everlasting daisy 146
Evolvulus 386
E. glomeratus 386
E. pilosus 386
Exocarpos 386
E. cupressiformis 387
Exochorda 387
E. giraldi 387
E. macrantha 'The
Bride' 387
E. racemosa 387

F
Fagopyrum esculentum
155
Fagus 390
F. grandifolia 390
F. sylvatica 390
'Aspleniifolia' 390
'Dawyck' 390
'Riversii' 390
'Zlatia' 390
F. sylvatica f. pendula
390
Fairy fishing rod 327
Fall crocus 259, 854
Fallopia 727
False baeckea 94
False cypress 224
False hellebore 917
False indigo 112
False pak-choi 240
Fan fern 855
Fan flower 815
Faradaya 390
F. splendida 391
Farfugium 391
F. japonicum 391
'Aureo-maculatum'
391
F. tussilagineum 391
x Fatshedera 391
x F. lizei 391
'Annemieke' 391
'Lemon and Lime'
391
'Variegata' 391
Fatsia 391, 392
F. japonica 392
'Variegata' 392
Faucaria 392
F. felina 392
F. tigrina 392

Feather flower 921
Feijoa 392
  F. sellowiana 393
    'Beechwood' 393
    'Coolidge' 393
    'Nazemetz' 393
Felicia 393
  F. amelloides 393, 394
  F. bergeriana 394
Fenestraria 394
  F. aurantiaca 394
Fennel 394
  F. vulgare 395
Ferocactus 395
  F. cylindraceus 395
  F. glaucescens 395
  F. latispinus 395
Ferraria 396
  F. crispa 396
Fescue 396
Festuca 396
  F. glauca 396
    'Blue Fox' 396
    'Sea Urchin' 396
  F. rubra 396
  Subspecies *commutata* 396
Feverfew 875
Ficus 397
  F. aspera 'Parcelli' 397
  F. benghalensis 397
  F. benjamina 397
    'Exotica' 397
  F. carica 397
  F. elastica 397, 398
    'Decora' 398
    'Doescheri' 398
    'Variegata' 398
  F. lyrata 398
  F. macrophylla 398
  F. microcarpa var. *hillii*

398
  F. obliqua 398
  F. pumila 398
    'Minima' 398
  F. religiosa 398
  F. rubiginosa 398
  F. superba 398
    Var. *henneana* 398
  F. sycomorus 398
  Ficus carica 398
Fiddlewood 247
Field balm 425
Fig 397, 398
  F. carica 399
    'Brown Turkey' 399
    'Kadota' 399
    'Mission' 399
Filbert 275, 451
Filipendula 399
  F. kamtschatica 399
  F. purpurea 399
    'Elegans' 400
  F. rubra 400
    'Venusta' 400
  F. ulmaria 400
    'Aurea' 400
    'Flore Pleno' 400
  F. vulgaris 400
    'Multiplex' 400
Fir 9
Fire tree 637
Firethorn 756
Firmiana 400
  F. simplex 400
Fishtail palm 200
Fittonia 400
  F. verschaffeltii 401
    Var. *argyroneura* 401
Five corners 861
Flamboyant tree 318
Flame nettle 260

Flame tree 143, 321
Flame violet 361
Flannel bush 405
Flannel flower 24
Flax 548
Flax lily 322
Fleabane 366
Flindersia 401
  F. australis 401
  F. brayleyana 401
  F. maculosa 401
Floss flower 37
Flowering maple 10
Flowering quince 223
Foam flower 894
Foeniculum vulgare 394
Forget-me-not 618
Forsythia 401
  F. 'Beatrix Farrand' 402
  F. x *intermedia* 402
    'Lynwood' 402
    'Spectabilis' 402
  F. ovata 402
  F. suspensa 402
Fouquieria 402
  F. columnaris 403
  F. splendens 403
  Idria columnaris 403
Foxglove 329
Foxtail lily 364
Foxtail palm 940
Fragaria 857
Fragaria chiloensis 857
Frangipani 722
Frankenia 403
  F. laevis 403
  F. pauciflora 403
  F. thymifolia 403
Fraxinus 403, 404
  F. americana 404

F. angustifolia 404
F. angustifolia Raywood = 'Flame' 404
F. excelsior 404
F. excelsior 'Aurea' 404
F. ornus 404
Freesia 404
  F. refracta 405
  Freesia x *hybrida* 405
Fremontodendron 405
  F. californicum 405
French sorrel 838
Freycinetia 405
  F. australiensis 405
  F. banksii 406
Fringed heath myrtle 605
Fringed lily 894
Fritillaria 406
  F. imperialis 406
  F. meleagris 406
  F. pallidiflora 406
  F. pudica 406
Fritillary 406
Fuchsia 407
  F. arborescens 407
  F. fulgens 407
  F. magellanica 407
  F. procumbens 407
  F. triphylla 407
    'Gartenmeister Bonstedt' 407
Fumitory 274

G

Gaillardia 410
  G. amblyodon 410
  G. x grandiflora 410
    'Burgundy' 410
    'Goblin' 410
    'Gobolin' 410
  G. pulchella 410
Gai lum 410
  'Kailaan' 410
Galangal 411
Galanthus 411
  G. caucasicus 411
  G. elwesii 411
  G. nivalis 411
    'Flore Pleno' 411
  G. plicatus 41
  G. plicatus subsp.
    byzantinus 412
Galtonia 412
  'Moonbeam' 412
  G. candicans 412
  G. viridiflora 412
Garcinia mangostana
585
Gardenia 412, 290
  G. augusta 412
    'August Beauty' 413
    'Mystery' 413
    'Veitchii' 413
  G. thunbergia 413
Garland lily 180
Garlic 413
Garrya 414
  G. elliptica 414
Gas plant 326
Gasteria 414
  G. acinacifolia 414, 415
  G. bicolor 415
  G. bicolor var.
    liliputana 414, 415

G. carinata var.
  verrucosa 415
Gaultheria 415, 686
  G. antipoda 415
  G. procumbens 415
  G. rupestris 415
  G. shallon 416
Gaura 416
  G. lindheimeri 416
    'Siskiyou Pink' 416
Gay feather 541
Gazania 416
  G. x hybrida 417
  G. rigens 417
  G. rigens var. uniflora
    417
Geebung 687
Geijera 417
  G. parviflora 417
Geissorhiza 417
  G. imbricata 417
  G. radians 417
  G. splendidissima 418
Gelsemium 418
  G. sempervirens 418
Genista 418
  G. aetnensis 419
  G. hispanica 419
  G. tinctoria 419
    'Royal Gold' 419
Gentian 419
Gentiana 419
  G. acaulis 419
    'Alba' 420
  G. asclepiadea 420
    Var. alba 420
  G. farreri 420
  G. lutea 420
  G. makinoi 420
  G. saxosa 420
  G. septemfida 420

G. sino-ornata 420
Geraldton wax 228
Geranium 420, 680
  G. endressii 420
    'Wargrave Pink' 420
  G. incanum 420
  G. maderense 420
  G. nepalense 420
  G. phaeum 420
  G. pratense 420
  G. robertianum 420
  G. sanguineum 420
    Var. striatum 420
Gerbera 421
  G. jamesonii 421
Germander 885
Geum 421, 422
  G. chiloense 422
    'Dolly North' 422
    'Fire Opal' 422
    'Lady Stratheden'
    422
    'Mrs J. Bradshaw'
    422
    'Prince of Orange'
    422
    'Red Wings' 422
  G. coccineum 422
  G. rivale 422
  G. urbanum 422
Ghost gums 276
Giant bamboo 320
Giant fern 62
Giant fir 10
Giant redwood 827
Giant sequoia 827
Giant water lily 923
Ginger 422
Ginger lily 53, 454
Ginkgo 422
  G. biloba 423

'Fastigiata' 423
Ginkgo biloba 422
Ginseng 423
  P. ginseng 423
  P. quinquefolius 423
Gladiolus 424
  G. x colvillei 425
  G. communis subsp.
    byzantinus 424
  G. tristis 425
Glaucium 425
  G. corniculatum 425
  G. flavum 425
  G. grandiflorum 425
Glechoma 425
  G. hederacea 426
    'Variegata' 426
Gleditsia 426
  G. aquatica 426
  G. japonica 426
  G. sinensis 426
  G. triacanthos 426
    'Rubylace' 426
    'Sunburst' 426
Gleichenia 426
  G. dicarpa 426, 427
  G. microphylla 426, 427
Globe daisy 427
Globe thistle 351
Globe tulip 178
Globularia 427
  G. cordifolia 427
    Var. alba 427
  G. meridionalis 427
  G. repens 427
  G. trichosantha 427
Gloriosa 427
  G. rothschildiana 428
  G. superba 428
    'Citrina' 428
    'Lutea' 428

'Rothschildiana' 423
Gloriosa lily 427
Glory bower 251
Glory bush 895
Glory of the snow 236
Glory pea 252
Glottiphyllum 428
　G. fragrans 428
　G. linguiforme 428
　G. semicylindricum 428
Gloxinia 429, 831
Glycyrrhiza 429
　G. glabra 429
Goat's beard 88
Godetia 429
Gold dust 101
Golden chain tree 518
Golden heath 861
Golden rain tree 511
Golden rod 835
Golden tip 430
Golden tuft 101
Golden wand lily 157
Gompholobium 429
　G. capitatum 429
　G. grandiflorum 429
　G. latifolium 430
Goodenia 430
　G. affinis 430
　G. hederacea 430
　G. heteromera 430
　G. ovata 430
　G. pinnatifida 430
Goodia 430
　G. lotifolia 431
　G. pubescens 431
Gooseberry 431
Gordonia 431
　G. axillaris 432
Gossypium 432
　G. arboreum 432

G. barbadense 432
　Var. brasiliense 432
G. herbaceum 432
G. hirsutum 432
G. sturtianum 432
G. thurberi 432
Gourd 433
　Cucumis anguria 433
　Cucumis dipsaceus 433
　Cucurbita pepo var.
　　ovifera 433
　Lagenaria siceraria 433
　Luffa cylindrica 433
　Tricosanthes cucumeria
　　var. anguina 433
Granadilla 433
Grape 434
　V. labrusca 434
　V. vinifera 434, 435
Grape hyacinth 615
Grape vine 928
Grapefruit 435
　'Marsh' 435
　'Ruby' 435
　'Star Ruby' 435
　'Wheeney' 435
Graptopetalum 436
　G. filiferum 436
　　'Silver Star' 436
　G. pachyphyllum 436
　G. paraguayense 436
Graptophyllum 436
　G. pictum 437
　　'Tricolor' 437
Graptoveria 436
Grass tree 341, 508,
　944
Grecian fir 10
Greenhoods 751
Grevillea 437, 447, 689
　'Bronze Rambler' 440

'Clearview' 437
G. acanthifolia 438,
　439
G. alpina 438
G. banksii 438
G. biternata 438
G. buxifolia 438
G. curviloba 438
G. x gaudichaudii 439
G. juniperina 439
G. laurifolia 439
G. lavandulacea 437,
　439
　'Beauty' 439
　'Constance' 439
　'Elegance' 439
　'Firebird' 439
　'Pink Coral' 439
　'Queen' 439
　'Signet' 439
　'Splendor' 439
G. robusta 437, 439
G. rosmarinifolia 439
G. thelemanniana 439
G. tridentifera 439
Grevillea 'Canberra
　Gem' 439
Grevillea 'Poorinda
　Constance' 439
　'Honey Gem' 440
　'Misty Pink' 440
　'Moonlight' 440
　'Poorinda' 437
　'Robyn Gordon' 439
Griselinia 440
　G. littoralis 440
　　'Variegata' 440
　G. lucida 440
　　Var. macrophylla 440
Ground ivy 425
Guava 440

P. cattleianum 440
P. guajava 440
P. littorale var. longipes
　440
Guichenotia 441
　G. ledifolia 441
　G. macrantha 441
Guinea flower 462
Gum tree 372
Gumbo 644
Guzmania 441
　G. lindenii 442
　G. lingulata 442
　　Var. cardinalis 442
　G. musaica 442
　G. sanguinea 442
　G. zahnii 442
Gymnocalycium 442
　G. andreae 442
　G. baldianum 442
　G. mihanovichii 442
　G. multiflorum 442
　G. quehlianum 442
　G. saglionis 442
Gynura 442
　G. aurantiaca 443
　G. procumbens 443
Gypsophila 443
　G. elegans 443
　　'Grandiflora Alba'
　　　443
　　'Purpurea' 443
　　'Rosea' 443
　G. muralis 443
　G. paniculata 443
　　'Bristol Fairy' 443
　　'Compacta Plena'
　　　443
　　'Flore-pleno' 443
　G. repens 443
　　'Rosea' 443

H

Habranthus 4–6
H. brachyandrus 446
H. robustus 446
H. tubispathus 446
Hackberry 215
Haemanthus 446, 815
H. albiflos 446
H. coccineus 446
H. magnificus 446
Hakea 447, 689
H. francisiana 447
H. laurina 447
H. lissosperma 448
H. multilineata 447
H. salicifolia 447, 448
H. saligna 448
H. sericea 448
H. suaveolens 448
H. victoriae 448
Halesia 448
H. monticola 448
Hamamelis 448
H. x intermedia 449
'Arnold Promise' 449
H. japonica 449
H. mollis 449
Handkerchief tree 317
Hard fern 134
Hardenbergia 449
H. comptoniana 449
H. violacea 449
'Alba' 449
'Rosea' 449
Hare's foot fern 316
Harlequin flower 839
Harpephyllum 449
H. caffrum 450
Harpullia 450
H. arborea 450

H. pendula 450
Hatiora 450, 774
H. salicornioides 451
Haworthia 451
H. attenuata 451
H. cymbiformis 451
H. margaritifera 451
H. marginata 451
H. pumila 451
H. tessellata 451
H. truncata 451
Hawthorn 283
Hazelnut 275, 451
'Aurea' 452
'Contorta' 452
'Purpurea' 452
Heath 97, 365
Heather 177
Hebe 452, 667, 920
H. albicans 452
H. andersonii 452
'Variegata' 452
H. buxifolia 452
H. colensoi 452
H. cupressoides 452
H. diosmifolia 452
H. elliptica 452, 453
H. franciscana
'Variegata' 453
H. hulkeana 453
H. macrantha 453
H. parviflora var.
angustifolia 453
H. pimeleoides var.
glaucocaerulea 453
H. salicifolia 453
H. speciosa 453
'Blue Gem' 453
'La Seduisante' 453
'Midsummer
Beauty' 453

H. vernicosa 453
Hedera 391, 453
H. canariensis 453, 454
'Gloire de Marengo'
454
H. helix 454
'Glacier' 454
'Luzii' 454
'Oro di Bogliasco'
454
'Parsley Crested' 454
Var. hibernica 454
Hedge nettle 847
Hedgehog cactus 350
Hedycarya 454
H. angustifolia 454
H. arborea 454
Hedychium 454
H. coccineum 455
H. coronarium 455
H. gardnerianum 455
Helenium 455
H. autumnale 455
'Wyndley' 455
H. bigelovii 455
Helianthemum 455
H. appenninum 456
H. nummularium 456
H. oelandicum subsp.
alpestre 456
Helianthus 456
H. annuus 456
H. decapetalus 456
H. x laetiflorus 456
H. tuberosus 456
Helianthus tuberosus 87
Helichrysum 146, 456
H. bellidioides 457
H. petiolare 457
H. sibthorpii 457
Heliconia 457

H. bihai 457
H. nutans 457
H. psittacorum 457
Heliopsis 457
H. helianthoides 458
'Patula' 458
Subsp. scabra 458
Heliotropium 458
H. arborescens 458
'Black Beauty' 458
'Iowa' 458
Helipterum 458, 775
Hellebore 458
Helleborus 458
H. argutifolius 459
H. foetidus 459
H. lividus 459
H. niger 459
H. orientalis 459
H. viridis 459
Helxine 835
Hemerocallis 459, 460
H. aurantiaca 460
H. citrina 460
H. fulva 460
'Flore Pleno' 460
H. middendorffi 460
H. minor 460
H. thunbergii 460
Hemiandra 460
H. pungens 460
Hemp agrimony 381
Hen and chickens 824
Hepatica 460
H. americana 461
H. x media 461
'Ballardi' 461
H. transsilvanica 461
Herald's trumpet 120
Hesper palm 147
Hesperis 461

H. matronalis 461
H. tristis 461
Heterocentron 461
H. elegans 461
Heuchera 462
H. americana 462
H. micrantha 462
H. sanguinea 462
Hibbertia 462
H. astrotricha 463
H. bracteata 463
H. dentata 463
H. montana 463
H. obtusifolia 463
H. procumbens 463
H. scandens 463
H. stellaris 463
H. stricta 463
Hibiscus 463
H. arnottianus 464
H. diversifolius 463, 464
H. heterophyllus 464
H. insularis 464
H. moscheutos 464
  'Southern Belle' 464
H. mutabilis 464
H. rosa-sinensis 463,
  464, 465
  'Ruth Wilcox' 464
H. sabdariffa 465
H. schizopetalus 465
H. syriacus 463, 464
H. tiliaceus 465
Hibiscus esculentus 644
Hibiscus sabdariffa 788
Hickory 199
Hicksbeachia 465
H. pinnatifolia 466
Himalayan fir 10
Hippeastrum 285, 446,
  466

H. aulicum 466
H. pratense 466
H. psittacinum 466
H. puniceum 466
H. reginae 466
H. reticulatum 466
H. striatum 466
Hoheria 466
H. angustifolia 467
H. lyallii 467
H. populnea 467
H. sexstylosa 467
Holly 482
Hollyhock 43
Holmskioldia 467
H. sanguinea 467
Homalocladium 467
H. platycladum 468
Honesty 562
Honey flower 522
Honey locust 426
Honey myrtle 595
Honeybush 598
Honeysuckle 557
Hop bush 336
Hops 472
Hornbeam 197
Horned poppy 425
Horse chestnut 32
Horseradish 468
Hosta 468
H. fortunei 469
H. lancifolia 469
H. plantaginea 469
H. plantaginea var.
  japonica 469
H. rectifolia 469
H. sieboldiana var.
  elegans 469
H. sieboldii 469
H. undulata var.

undulata 469
H. ventricosa 469
Hottentot fig 197
Hound's tongue 304
Houseleek 824
Hovea 469
H. acutifolia 470
H. elliptica 470
H. heterophylla 470
H. lanceolata 470
H. pungens 470
Hovenia 470
H. dulcis 470
Howea 470, 518
H. belmoreana 471
H. forsteriana 471
Hoya 471
H. australis 472
H. carnosa 471, 472
H. lanceolata subsp.
  bella 472
H. macgillivrayi 472
H. rubida 472
Humulus 472
H. japonicus 472
  'Variegatus' 472
H. lupulus 472
  'Aureus' 472
Hurricane palm 326
Hyacinth 473
Hyacinthoides 472
  Endymion hispanicus
  473
  Endymion non-scriptus
  473
H. hispanicus 473
  'Excelsior' 473
H. non-scripta 473
H. orientalis 474
Hyacinthus orientalis 473
Hydrangea 474, 818

H. anomala subsp.
  petiolaris 475
H. arborescens 475
  'Grandiflora' 475
H. aspera 475
  subspecies
  sargentiana 475
H. heteromalla 475
H. macrophylla 475
H. paniculata 475
  'Grandiflora' 475
H. quercifolia 475
Hortensias 475
Lacecaps 475
Hymenocallis 475
H. caribaea 476
H. x festalis 476
H. littoralis 476
H. x macrostephana
  476
H. narcissiflora 475,
  476
H. speciosa 476
Hymenosporum 476
H. flavum 476
Hyophorbe 476
H. lagenicaulis 476
H. verschaffeltii 476
Hypericum 477
H. calycinum 477
H. calycinum x *H.*
  patulum 477
H. forresti 477
H. x inodorum 477
H. monogynum 477
H. x moseranum 477
H. olympicum 477
H. patulum 477
H. patulum var. *forresti*
  477
H. perforatum 477

H. prolificum 478
Hypocalymma 478
  H. angustifolium 478
  H. cordifolium 478
  H. robustum 478
Hypoestes 473
  H. aristata 479
  H. phyllostachya 479
Hypoxis 479, 777
  H. hirsuta 479
  H. hygrometrica 479
  H. stellata 479
    Var. *elegans* 479
Hyssop 479
  H. officinalis 479

I

Iberis 482
  I. amara 482
  I. sempervirens 482
  I. umbellata 482
Ice plant 602
Ilex 482
  I. aquifolium 483
    'Argentea
      Marginata' 483
    'Ferox Argentea'
      483
    'Ferox Aurea' 483
    'Ferox' 483
    'Golden Queen' 483
    'J. C. van Tol' 483
    'Silver Queen' 483
  I. cornuta 483
  I. crenata 483
    'Compacta' 483
    'Helleri' 483
    'Hetzii' 483
    'Morris Dwarf' 483
Illicium 483, 850
  I. anisatum 484
  I. floridanum 484
  I. verum 484
Immortelle 456
Impatiens 484
  I. balsamina 484
  I. hawkeri 484
  I. mirabilis 484
  I. repens 484
  I. sodenii 485
  I. walleriana 484, 485
Incarvillea 485
  I. delavayi 485
  I. mairei var.
    grandiflora 485
  I. olgae 485
Incense cedar 177

Inch plant 172
Indian almond tree 853
Indian fig 738
Indigo 486
Indigofera 486
  I. amblyantha 486
  I. australis 486
  I. decora 486
  I. heterantha 486
  I. tinctoria 486
Indigofera tinctoria 112
Iochroma 486
  I. cyaneum 487
Ipheion 487
  I. uniflorum 487
Ipomoea 268, 487, 608
  I. acuminata 488
  I. alba 488
  I. horsfalliae 488
  I. indica 488
  I. pandurata 488
  I. purpurea 488
  I. tricolor 487
Ipomoea batatas 865
Iresine 488
  I. herbstii 489
    'Aureoreticulata'
      489
  I. lindenii 489
Iris 489, 490, 611
  I. ensata 489
  I. germanica 490
  I. kaempferi 489
  I. pallida 490
  I. sibirica 489
Iris xiphium hybrids 490
Ironwood 102
Ismene 475
Isopogon 491
  I. anemonifolius 491
  I. anethifolius 491

I. dubius 492
I. roseus 492
I. trilobus 492
Isotoma 492
  Isotoma axillaris 492
  Laurentia axillaris 492
Itea 492
  I. ilicifolia 493
  I. virginica 493
Ivory curl flower 154
Ivy 453
Ixia 493
  I. campanulata 493
  I. maculata 493
  I. patens 493
  I. viridiflora 493
Ixiolirion 493
  I. tataricum 494
Ixora 494
  I. chinensis 494
  I. coccinea 494

J

Jacaranda 495
  J. mimosifolia 495
Jackfruit 495
Jacobean lily 845
Jacobinia 501, 661
Jade vine 859
Jamaica sorrel 788
Japanese aralia 392
Japanese cedar 290
Japanese fir 10
Japanese laurel 101
Japanese raisin tree 478
Japanese umbrella pine
  819
Jasione 496
  J. humilis 496
  J. laevis 496
  J. montana 496
  J. perennis 496
Jasmine 496
Jasminum 496
  J. azoricum 496
  J. laurifolium f. *nitidum*
    496
  J. mesnyi 496
  J. nudiflorum 496
  J. officinale 497
  J. polyanthum 497
  J. rex 497
  J. sambac 497
  'Grand Duke of
    Tuscany' 497
Jewel vine 321
Jubaea 497
  J. chilensis 497
Juglans nigra 935
Juglans regia 935
Juncus 497
  J. effusus 498
  'Vittatus' 498

Juneberry 58
Juniper 498
Juniper berry 498
  J. communis 498
Juniperus 498
  J. bermudiana 499
  J. chinensis 499, 500
  'Aurea' 499
  'Kaizuka' 499
  'Keteleeri' 499
  'Stricta' 499
  'Torulosa' 499
  J. communis 499
  'Compressa' 500
  'Depressa Aurea' 500
  'Hibernica' 500
  J. conferta 500
  J. deppeana 500
  J. horizontalis 500
  'Bar Harbor' 500
  'Douglasii' 500
  'Gold Coast' 500
  'Kuriwao Gold' 500
  'Old Gold' 500
  'Pfitzeriana Aurea'
    500
  J. x *pfitzeriana* 500
  J. procumbens 500
  J. sabina 500
  'Tamariscifolia' 500
  J. scopulorum 500
  J. squamata 501
  'Meyeri' 501
  J. virginiana 500, 501
  'Gray Owl' 501
  'Hetzii' 501
  'Skyrocket' 500
Juniperus communis 498
Justicia 501
  Beloperone guttata 501

  Duvernoia
    adhatodoides 501
  J. adhatodoides 501
  J. brandegeana 501
  'Yellow Queen' 501
  J. carnea 501
  J. rizzinii 501

K

Kaempferia 504
  K. galanga 504
  K. pulchra 504
  K. rotunda 504
Kaempferia galanga 411
Kaffir lily 253
Kaffir plum 449
Kalanchoe 504
  K. beharensis 504
  K. blossfeldiana 504
  K. delagoensis 504
  K. fedtschenkoi 505
  K. manginii 505
  K. pinnata 505
  K. pumila 505
  K. tomentosa 505
  K. tubiflora 504
Kale 505
Kalmia 506
  K. angustifolia 506
  K. latifolia 506
  'Fresca' 506
  'Nipmuck' 506
  'Ostbo Red' 506
  'Silver Dollar' 506
Kangaroo paw 65
Kauri 35
Kauri pine 35
Kennedia 506
  K. coccinea 507
  K. macrophylla 507
  K. microphylla 507
  K. nigricans 507
  K. prostrata 507
  K. rubicunda 507
Kentia 470
Kerria 507
  K. japonica 507
  'Pleniflora' 507
Keteleeria 507

K. fortunei 507
Kigelia 508
  K. pinnata 508
King fern 62, 398
Kingia 508
  K. australis 509
Kiwi fruit 509
  'Chico' 510
  'Hayward' 510
  'Tomuri' 510
  'Vincent' 510
Knightia 510
  K. excelsa 510
Kniphofia 510
  K. caulescens 511
  K. foliosa 511
  K. northiae 511
  K. pumila 511
  K. uvaria 511
Knob celery 213
Koelreuteria 511
  K. bipinnata 512
  K. elegans 512
  K. paniculata 511
Kohl rabi 512
Kohleria 512
  K. eriantha 512
Kolkwitzia 513
  K. amabilis 513
Kopsia 513
  K. flavida 513
  K. fruticosa 513
Kowhai 837
Kreysigia 514
  K. multiflora 514
Kuma bamboo grass
  813
Kumquat 514
  F. japonica 515
  F. margarita 515
Kunzea 515

K. affinis 515
K. ambigua 515
K. baxteri 515
K. capitata 515
K. parvifolia 515
K. recurva 515
  Var. *montana* 515

L

Laburnum 518
  L. alpinum 518
  L. anagyroides 518
  'Pendulum' 518
  L. x watereri 518
  'Vossii' 518
Laccospadix 518
  L. australasica 519
Lacebark 143, 466
Lachenalia 519
  L. aloides 519
  'Nelsonii' 519
  Var. *aurea* 519
  Var. *conspicua* 519
  Var. *luteola* 519
  Var. *quadricolor* 519
  L. bulbifera 519
  L. liliiflora 519
  L. mutabilis 519
  L. orchioides 519
  Var. *glaucina* 519
Lactuca sativa 536
Lady palm 773
Lady's fingers 644
Lady's mantle 43
Lady's slipper 305
Lady's smock 192
Laelia 208, 519
  L. anceps 520
  L. autumnalis 520
  L. cinnabarina 520
  L. lundii 520
  L. tenebrosa 520
Lagarostrobus franklinii
  311
Lagenaria 520
  L. siceraria 520
  'Hercules' Club' 521
Lagerstroemia 521
  L. fauriei 521

L. floribunda 521
L. indica 521
  'Catawba' 521
  'Dallas Red' 521
  'Miami' 521
  'Petite' 521
  'Sioux' 521
  'White Dwarf' 521
L. speciosa 521
Lagunaria 521
  L. patersonii 522
Lambertia 522
  L. ericifolia 522
  L. formosa 522
  L. ilicifolia 523
  L. multiflora 523
Lamium 523
  L. galeobdolon 523
  L. maculatum 523
  'Aureum' 523
  'Beacon Silver' 523
  'White Nancy' 523
Lampranthus 523, 779,
  793
  L. amoenus 524
  L. aureus 524
  L. candidus 524
  L. coccineus 524
  L. purpureus 524
  L. roseus 524
  L. spectabilis 524
Lantana 524
  L. camara 524
  L. montevidensis 524
Lapageria 524
  L. rosea 525
  Var. *albiflora* 525
Lapeirousia laxa 67
Larch 525
Larix 525
  L. decidua 525

L. europaea 525
L. kaempferi 525
L. laricina 525
Larkspur 266
Lasiandra 895
Latan palm 525
Latania 525
  L. loddigesii 526
  L. lontaroides 526
  L. verschaffeltii 526
Lathyrus 526
  L. grandiflorus 526
  L. japonicus 526
  L. laetiflorus 526
  L. latifolius 526, 527
    'Albus' 527
  L. odoratus 526, 527
  L. splendens 527
Laurelia 527
  L. novae-zelandiae 527
  L. sempervirens 527
Laurentia 492
Laurus 527
  L. azorica 527, 528
  L. nobilis 527, 528
Laurus nobilis 117
Lavandula 528
  L. angustifolia 528
    'Hidcote' 528
    'Loddon Pink' 528
    'Munstead' 528
    'Nana Alba' 528
  L. dentata 528
  L. lanata 528
  L. spica 528
  L. stoechas 528
Lavatera 528
  L. 'Barnsley' 529
  L. 'Bredon Springs 529
  L. 'Burgundy Wine'
    529

L. arborea 529
L. assurgentiflora 529
L. rosea 529
L. trimestris 529
  'Loveliness' 529
  'Mont Blanc' 529
  'Pink Beauty' 529
  'Rosea' 529
  'Silver Cup' 529
Lavender 528
Lavender cotton 808
Leadwort 721
Leather fern 793
Leek 529
Lemon 530
  C. limon 530
    'Eureka' 530
    'Lisbon' 530
  C. sinensis 530
  C. x meyeri 'Meyer'
    530
Lemon balm 530
  M. officinalis 530
    'Aurea' 530
Lemon grass 531
  C. citratus 531
  C. exaltatus 531
  C. nardus 531
Lemon verbena 531
Lenten rose 458
Leonotis 532
  L. leonurus 532
Leontopodium 532
  L. alpinum 532
  L. haplophylloides 533
  L. japonicum 533
Leopard lily 124
Leopard's bane 338
Lepidium sativum 616
Lepidozamia 533
  L. hopei 533, 534

L. peroffskyana 534
Leptospermum 94, 534
  L. juniperinum 534
  L. laevigatum 534
  L. nitidum 535
    'Copper Sheen' 535
  L. petersonii 535
  L. scoparium 535
    'Chapmanii' 535
    'Nicholsii' 535
    Var. *rotundifolium*
    535
  L. squarrosum 535
Leschenaultia 535
  L. acutiloba 535
  L. biloba 535
    'Blue Flash' 535
  L. formosa 536
  L. macrantha 536
  L. tubiflora 536
Lettuce 536
Leucadendron 536, 539
  L. argenteum 537
  L. grandiflorum 537
  L. salignum 537
Leucanthemum 537
  L. x superbum 537
    'Esther Read' 538
    'Everest' 538
    'Horace Read' 538
    'Little Princess' 538
    'Mount Everest' 538
    'Silberprinzesschen'
    538
    'Wirral Supreme'
    538
Leucojum 411, 538
  L. aestivum 538
  L. autumnale 538
  L. vernum 538
Leucopogon 538

L. ericoides 539
L. fraseri 539
L. juniperinus 539
L. linifolius 539
L. milliganii 539
L. strictus 539
Leucospermum 539
  L. bolusi 539
  L. cordifolium 539
  L. reflexum 539
  L. tottum 539
Leucothoe 539
  L. davisiae 540
  L. fontanesiana 540
  L. grayana 540
  L. racemosa 540
Levisticum officinale 561
Lewisia 540
  L. brachycalyx 540
  L. columbiana 540
  L. cotyledon 540
  L. rediviva 541
  L. tweedyi 541
Leyland cypress 294
Liatris 541
  L. aspera 541
  L. pychnostachya 541
  L. spicata 541
Libocedrus 177, 541
  L. bidwillii 542
  L. plumosa 542
Licuala 542
  L. grandis 542
  L. ramsayi 542
  L. spinosa 542
Ligularia 543
  L. dentata 543
    'Desdemona' 543
    'Othello' 543
  L. hodgsonii 543
  L. japonica 543

L. przewalskii 543
Ligularia tussilaginea 391
Ligustrum 543
 L. japonicum 543
  'Rotundifolium' 544
 L. ovalifolium 544
  'Aureum' 544
 L. vulgare 544
Lilac 868
Lilium 544
 L. auratum 545
 L. candidum 44, 545
 L. henryi 545
 L. longiflorum 545
 L. regale 545
 L. rubellum 545
Lilly pilly 868
Lily of the Altai 493
Lily turf 550
Lily-of-the-valley 267
Lilyturf 648
Lime 546, 896
 'Bears' 546
 'Mexican' 546
Limonium 546
 L. latifolium 547
 L. macrophyllum 547
 L. perezii 547
 L. sinuatum 547
Linaria 547
 L. dalmatica 547
  'Canary Bird' 547
 L. maroccana 547
  'Diadem' 547
  'Excelsior' 547
  'Fairy Bouquet' 547
  'Northern Lights' 547
 L. reticulata 547
  'Aureopurpurea' 547

L. vulgaris 547
Linden 896
Ling 177
Linospadix 548
 L. minor 548
 L. monostachya 548
 L. palmerana 548
Linum 548
 L. flavum 549
  'Compactum' 549
 L. grandiflorum 549
 L. monogynum 549
 L. narbonense 549
  Heavenly Blue' 549
 L. perenne 549
 L. usitatissimum 548
Lipstick plant 32
Lipstick tree 133
Liquidambar 549
 L. formosana 550
 L. orientalis 550
 L. styraciflua 550
  'Burgundy' 550
Liriodendron 550, 748
 L. chinense 550
 L. tulipifera 550
  'Aureomarginatum' 550
Liriope 550
 L. exiliflora 550
 L. muscari 550
  'Variegata' 551
 L. spicata 551
Lithodora 551
 L. diffusa 551
  'Heavenly Blue' 551
 L. oleifolia 551
Lithops 551
 L. aucampiae 552
 L. divergens 552
 L. fulviceps 552

 L. julii 552
 L. karasmontana 552
 L. olivacea 552
 L. turbiniformis 552
Little club moss 823
Littonia 552
 L. modesta 552
Liverleaf 460
Living stone 551
Livingstone daisy 339
Livistona 553
 L *decipiens* 554
 L. alfredii 553, 554
 L. australis 553, 554
 L. benthamii 553
 L. chinensis 553
 L. mariae 554
 L. rotundifolia 554
  Var. *luzonensis* 554
llicium verum 850
Lobelia 554
 L. cardinalis 554
 L. erinus 555
  'Blue Cascade' 555
  'Cambridge Blue' 555
  'Crystal Palace' 555
  'Hamburgia' 555
  'Sapphire' 555
 L. inflata 555
 L. laxiflora 555
 L. siphilitica 555
 L. x speciosa 555
Lobivia 351
Lobster claw 457
Lobularia 555
 L. maritima 555
  'Carpet of Snow' 555
  'Little Gem' 555
  'Oriental Night' 555

  'Rosie O'Day' 555
  'Tetra Snowdrift' 555
  'Violet Queen' 555
Locust 784
Locust tree 219
Loganberry 555
Lomandra 556
 L. effusa 557
 L. filiformis 557
 L. gracilis 557
 L. leucocephala 557
 L. longifolia 556, 557
 L. multiflora 557
Lomatia 557
 L. fraxinifolia 557
 L. ilicifolia 557
 L. myricoides 557
 L. silaifolia 557
 L. tinctoria 557
Lonicera 557
 L. x brownii 558
 L. caerulea 558
 L. caprifolium 558
 L. flava 558
 L. fragrantissima 558
 L. x heckrottii 558
 L. hildebrandiana 558
 L. japonica 558
 L. nitida 558
 L. periclymenum 558
 L. sempervirens 558
Loofah 562
Loosestrife 568, 569
Lophomyrtus 558
 L. bullata 558
 L. x ralphii 558
Lophostemon 559
 L. confertus 559
  'Perth Gold' 559
  'Variegata' 559

Tristania conferta 559
Loquat 559
  'Champagne' 560
  'Gold Nugget' 560
  'MacBeth' 560
Loropetalum 560
  L. chinense 560
Lotus 560
  'Plenus' 561
  L. australis 561
  L. berthelotii 561
  L. corniculatus 561
  L. jacobaeus 561
Lovage 561
Love charm 254
Love-in-a-mist 632
Luculia 561
  L. grandifolia 562
  L. gratissima 562
Luffa 562
  L. acutangula 562
  L. cylindrica 562
Lunaria 562
  L. annua 563
  L. rediviva 563
Lungwort 753
Lupine 563
Lupinus 563
  L. albus 563
  L. arboreus 563, 564
  L. hartwegii 564
  L. luteus 564
  L. nootkatensis 564
  L. perennis 564
  L. polyphyllus 563, 564
  L. subcarnosus 564
  L. texensis 564
Lycaste 564
  L. aromatica 564
  L. deppei 564
  L. skinneri 564

Lychee 565
  'Brewster' 565
  'Groff' 565
  'Kwai Mi' 565
  'Mauritius' 565
Lychnis 565
  'Alba' 566
  L. chalcedonica 566
  L. coronaria 566
  L. flos-jovis 566
  L. viscaria 566
Lycopersicon esculentum 899
Lycopodium 566
  L. dalhousieanum 566
  L. phlegmaria 566
  L. squarrosum 566
Lycoris 566
  L. aurea 567
  L. radiata 567
  L. squamigera 567
Lygodium 567
  L. japonicum 568
  L. microphyllum 568
  L. scandens 568
Lysichiton 568
  L. americanus 568
  L. camtschatcense 568
Lysimachia 568
  L. atropurpurea 569
  L. clethroides 569
  L. nummularia 569
  'Aurea' 569
  L. punctata 569
  L. vulgaris 569
Lythrum 569
  L. alatum 569
  L. salicaria 569
  L. virgatum 569
  'Morden Gleam' 569

  'Morden Pink' 569
  'Morden Rose' 569
Lytocaryum 604

M

Macadamia 572
  M. integrifolia 572
  M. ternifolia 572
  M. tetraphylla 572
Macfadyena 572
  M. unguis-cati 573
Mackaya 573
  M. bella 573
Macleaya 573
  M. cordata 574
    'Kelway's Coral Plume' 574
  M. microcarpa 574
Maclura 574
  M. pomifera 574
Macropidia 574, 575
  M. fuliginosa 575
Macropiper 575
  M. excelsum 575
Macrozamia 575
  M. burrawang 576
  M. communis 576
  M. miquelii 576
  M. moorei 576
  M. pauli-guilielmi 576
Madagascar jasmine 853
Madagascar periwinkle 207
Madonna lily 841
Magnolia 576, 748
  M. campbellii 577
    Subspecies *mollicomata* 577
  M. delavayi 577
  M. denudata 577
  M. denudata x *liliiflora* 577
  M. grandiflora 577
  M. heptapeta 577

M. hypoleuca 577
M. kobus 577
M. kobus x M. stellata
   577
M. liliiflora 577
   'Nigra' 577
M. x loebneri 577
M. quinquepeta 577
M. sieboldii 577
M. x soulangeana 577
   'Alba' 577
   'Alexandrina' 577
   'Lennei' 578
   'Rustica Rubra' 578
M. stellata 577, 578
   'Rosea' 578
   'Waterlily' 578
Mahonia 578
M. aquifolium 578
M. japonica 578
M. lomariifolia 579
M. repens 579
   'Rotundifolia' 579
Maidenhair fern 27
Maidenhair tree 422
Malcolmia 579
M. maritima 579
Mallow 581
Malpighia 579
M. coccigera 580
M. glabra 580
Malus 580
M. x arnoldiana 580
M. baccata 580
   Var. mandschurica
      581
M. 'Dorothea' 581
M. floribunda 581
M. ioensis 581
   'Plena' 581
M. 'John Downie' 581

M. x magdeburgensis
   581
M. x purpurea 'Eleyi'
   581
M. spectabilis 581
   'Flore Pleno' 581
M. tschonoskii 581
M. yunnanensis 581
M. x zumi var.
   calocarpa 581
Malus domestica 70
Malus pumila 580
Malva 581, 582
M. alcea 581
M. moschata 581
M. sylvestris 581
Malvaviscus 582
M. arboreus 582
M. arboreus var.
   mexicanus 582
Mammillaria 582
M. bocasana 583
M. camptotricha 583
M. elongata 583
M. hahniana 583
M. longiflora 583
M. prolifera 583
M. senilis 583
Mandarin 583
   'Clementine' 583
   'Dancy' 583
   'Kara' 583
   'Kinnow' 583
   'Satsuma' 583
Mandevilla 583
   Dipladenia sanderi 584
M. x amabilis 584
M. x amabilis 'Alice
   du Pont' 584
M. laxa 584
M. sanderi 584

M. splendens 584
M. suaveolens 584
Mandioca 202
Manettia 584
M. bicolor 585
M. cordifolia 584
M. lute-orubra 585
Mangifera indica 585
Mango 585
Mangosteen 585
Manihot 586
M. arundinacea 586
M. dulcis 586
M. esculenta 586
Manihot esculenta 202
Manilkara zapota 809
Manioc 202
Maori honeysuckle 510
Maple 16
Maranta 586
M. arundinacea 587
   'Variegata' 587
M. bicolor 587
M. leuconeura 587
   Var. erythroneura 587
   Var. kerchoveana 587
Marattia 587
M. salicina 587, 588
Marguerite daisy 81
Marigold 872
Mariposa lily 178
Marjoram, sweet 588
Marmalade bush 858
Marrow 588
Marsh mallow 55
Marsh marigold 181
Marsilea 589
M. angustifolia 590
M. drummondii 590
M. mutica 590
Masdevallia 590

M. coccinea 590
M. trochilus 590
Mask flower 52
Masterwort 96
Mastic tree 713
Mat-rush 556
Matilija poppy 785
Matricaria 590
M. africana 591
M. aurea 591
M. matricarioides 591
M. recutita 591
M. suffruticosa 591
Oncosiphon africanum
   591
Oncosiphon
   suffruticosum 591
Matricaria recutita 229
Matthiola 591
M. incana 592
M. longipetala subsp.
   bicornis 592
Maurandya 592
   Asarina barclaiana 592
M. barclayana 592
May bush 844
Mazus 593
M. japonicus 593
M. pumilio 593
M. radicans 593
M. reptans 593
Meadow rue 886
Meadowsweet 399
Meconopsis 593
M. aculeata 593
M. betonicifolia 594
M. cambrica 594
   'Flore Pleno' 594
   Var. aurantiaca 594
M. delavayi 594
M. grandis 594

M. quintuplinervia 594
Medinilla 594
M. magnifica 594
Medlar 594
Megaskepasma 595
M. erythrochlamys 595
Melaleuca 119, 595
M. alternifolia 596
M. armillaris 596
M. bracteata 596
'Golden Gem' 596
'Revolution Green' 596
M. decussata 596
M. ericifolia 596
M. fulgens 596
M. hypericifolia 596
M. incana 596
M. laterita 597
M. linariifolia 596
M. nesophila 597
M. pulchella 597
M. squarrosa 596
M. steedmanii 597
M. styphelioides 597
Melastoma 597
M. denticulatum 597
M. malabathricum 597
M. polyanthum 597
Melia 597
M. azedarach 598
Var. *australasica* 598
'Umbraculiformis' 598
Melianthus 598
M. major 598
Melicytus 598, 599
M. lanceolatus 599
M. macrophyllus 599
M. ramiflorus 599
Melissa officinalis 530

Melocactus 599
M. bahiensis 599
M. communis 599
M. intortus 599
M. matanzanus 599
Melon 600
Citrullus lanatus 601
Var. *citroides* 601
Cucumis melo 600
Mentha species 609
Mertensia 601
M. ciliata 601
M. primuloides 601
M. pulmonarioides 601
Meryta 601
M. sinclairii 602
'Moonlight' 602
Mesembryanthemum 602, 793
M. crystallinum 602
M. nodiflorum 602
Mesembryanthenum 779
Mespilus germanica 594
Metasequoia 602, 603
M. glyptostroboides 603
Metrosideros 603
M. carmineus 603
M. excelsus 604
'Aureus' 604
M. excelus 603
M. fulgens 604
'Aurata' 604
M. kermadecensis 604
'Sunninghill' 604
'Variegatus' 604
Mexican orange blossom 239
Mexican sunflower 898
Michaelmas daisy 94
Michelia 604

M. champaca 604
M. doltsopa 604
M. figo 604
Mickey Mouse plant 642
Microcoelum 604
Lytocaryum weddellianum 604
M. weddellianum 604
Micromyrtus 605
M. ciliata 605
M. rosea 605
Microsorum 605
M. diversifolium 606
M. membranifolium 606
M. punctatum 606
M. scandens 606
Mignonette 771
Milfoil 17
Milkwort 726
Millettia 606
M. caffra 607
M. megasperma 606, 607
M. ovalifolia 607
Miltonia 607
M. phalaenopsis 607
M. regnellii 607
M. spectabilis 607
Miltoniopsis phalaenopsis 607
Mimosa 607
M. pudica 608
Mimulus 608
M. aurantiacus 608
M. cupreus 608
M. fremontii 608
M. guttatus 608
M. moschatus 608
M. ringens 608

M. x *hybridus* 608
Mina 608
Ipomoea lobata 609
M. lobata 609
Mint 609
M. x *piperita* 609
M. pulegium 609
M. spicata 610
M. suaveolens 610
Mint bush 740
Mirror plant 268
Miscanthus 610
M. sacchariflorus 610
'Aureus' 610
M. sinensis
'Variegatus' 610
'Gracillimus' 610
'Zebrinus' 610
Moccasin flower 305
Mock orange 692
Molten torch 56
Molucella 610
M. laevis 611
M. spinosa 611
Momordica charantia 132
Monarda didyma 127
Mondo grass 648
Monkey flower 608
Monkey nut 465
Monkey pod 804
Monkshood 20
Monstera 587, 611
M. acuminata 611
M. adansonii 611
M. deliciosa 611
Moraea 611
M. angusta 612
M. fugax 612
M. spathulata 612
M. villosa 612

Morning glor— 487

Morning, noon and
night 152

Morus 613

Moses in the basket
778

Moth orchid 91

Mother-in-law's tongue
807

Mountain ash 837

Mucuna 612
M. bennettii 612
M. pruriens 612

Muehlenbeckia 613
M. australis 613
M. axillaris 613
M. complexa 613

Mulberry 613
M. alba 613
M. nigra 614
'Black Beauty' 614
M. rubra 613, 614
Morus nigra 613

Mulla mulla 751

Mullein 918

Murraya 614
M. koenigii 614
M. paniculata 614
Murraya koenigi 297

Musa 614
M. acuminata 614
M. ornata 615
M. velutina 615
M. x paradisica 614

Muscari 615
M. armeniacum 615
M. azureum 615
'Album' 615
'Amphiboli' 615
M. comosum 615
'Plumosum' 615

M. macrocarpum 615
M. neglectum 615

Mushroom 615
Agaricus bisporus 615
Agaricus campestris 615
Lentinus edodes 615
Volvariella volvacea 615

Musk 608

Mussaenda 616
M. erythrophylla 616
M. frondosa 616

Mustard 616

Myoporum 617
M. debile 617
M. insulare 617
M. laetum 617
M. montanum 617
M. parvifolium 617
M. platycarpum 617

Myosotidium 617
M. hortensia 618

Myosotis 618
M. australis 618
M. azorica 618
Var. alba 618
M. palustris 618
M. scorpiodes 618
M. sylvatica 618

Myristica 637
Myristica fragrans 637

Myroxylon 619
M. balsamum 619

Myrrhis odorata 864

Myrtle 619

Myrtus 619
M. communis 619
'Variegata' 619

N

Nandina 622
N. domestica 622
'Harbor Dwarf' 622
'Moyer's Red' 622

Narcissus 622
N. bulbocodium 623
N. cantabricus 623
N. cyclamineus 623
N. poeticus 623
'Erlicheer' 623
'Grand Soleil d'Or'
623
'Paper White' 623
N. triandrus 623

Nardoo 589

Nasturtium 908

Native currant 538

Native flag 672

Native heath 358

Native iris 672

Native mulberry 454

Native poplar 647

Native tamarind 332

Nectarine 623

Needle bush 447

Nelumbo 623
N. lutea 624
N. nucifera 624

Nemesia 624
N. strumosa 625
'KLM' 625
'Mello Red and
White' 625
N. versicolor 625

Nemophila 625
N. menziesii 625

Neoporteria 625
N. curvispina 625
N. horrida 626
N. subgibbosa 626

N. umadeave 626

Neoregelia 626
N. ampullacea 626
N. carolinae 626
Var. tricolor 626
N. concentrica 626
N. fosteriana 626
N. marmorata 626
N. spectabilis 626

Nepenthes 626
N. ampullaria 627
N. x atrosanguinea 627
N. x balfouriana 627
N. mirabilis 627
N. rafflesiana 627
N. superba 627

Nepeta 627, 628
N. cataria 628
N. x faassenii 628
N. mussinii 628
N. racemosa 628

Nephelium lappaceum
764

Nephrolepis 628
N. cordifolia 628
N. exaltata 629
N. exaltata
'Bostoniensis' 629

Nerine 629
N. 'Fothergillii Major'
629
N. bowdenii 629
N. filifolia 629
N. flexuosa 629
'Alba' 629
N. masonorum 629
N. sarniensis 629

Nerium 629
N. oleander 630

Nerve plant 400

Net bush 180

Nettle tree 215
New Guinea creeper 612
New Zealand Christmas
  tree 603
New Zealand daisy 214
New Zealand flax 697
New Zealand rock lily
  86
Nicotiana 630
  N. 'Lime Green' 630
  N. affinis 630
  N. alata 630
  N. langsdorffii 630
  N. x sanderae 631
  N. suaveolens 631
  N. sylvestris 631
  N. tabacum 631
Nidularium 631
  N. billbergioides 631
  N. fulgens 631
  N. innocentii 631
    Var. lineatum 631
Nierembergia 631
  N. caerulea 631
    'Purple Robe' 631
  N. repens 631, 632
  N. scoparia 632
Nigella 632
  N. damascena 632
    'Miss Jekyll' 632
    'Oxford Blue' 632
  N. hispanica 632
    'Curiosity' 632
Nikau palm 780
Nikko fir 10
Ninebark 701
Nolina 632
  Beaucarnea recurvata
    633
  N. bigelowii 633
  N. recurvata 633

Nomocharis 633
  N. aptera 633
  N. farreri 633
  N. pardanthina 633
  N. saluenensis 633
Nopalxochia 634
  N. phyllanthoides 634
    'Deutsche Kaiserin'
    634
Norfolk Island hibiscus
  521
Normanbya 196, 634
  N. normanbyi 635
Nothofagus 635
  N. antarctica 635
  N. cunninghamii 635
  N. fusca 635
  N. gunnii 635
  N. moorei 635
Notholirion 636
  N. bulbiferum 636
  N. campanulatum 636
  N. thomsonianum 636
Notocactus 636, 668
  N. concinnus 636
  N. herteri 636
  N. leninghausii 636
  N. uebelmannianus
    637
Nutmeg 637
Nuytsia 637
  N. floribunda 638
Nymphaea 638
  N. alba 639
  N. caerulea 639
  N. capensis 639
  N. gigantea 639
  N. odorata 639
  N. tetragona 639
  Nymphaea alba 638
Nyssa 639

N. aquatica 639
N. sylvatica 639

O

Oak 761
Obedient plant 702
Ochna 642
  O. atropurpurea 642
  O. serrulata 642
Ochroma 642
  O. lagopus 642
  O. pyramidale 642
Ocimum basilicum 114
Ocotillo 402
Odontoglossum 643
  O. epterum 643
  O. cirrhosum 643
  O. grande 643
Odontonema 643
  O. barlerioides 643
  O. callistachyum 643
  O. schomburgkianum
    643
Oenothera 644
  O. acaulis 644
  O. biennis 644
  O. fruticosa 644
  O. fruticosa subsp.
    glauca 644
  O. macrocarpa 644
  O. perennis 644
  O. speciosa 644
Oil palm 354
Okra 644
Old man cactus 217
Olea 646
Olea europaea 646
Oleander 629
Olearia 645
  O. argophylla 645
  O. chathamica 645
  O. cheesemanii 645
  O. lirata 645
  O. phlogopappa 645

O. pimeloides 645
O. ramulosa 646
O. teretifolia 646
O. tomentosa 646
Olive 646
  Olea europaea
    subspecies *africana*
    646
Omalanthus 647
  O. populifolius 647
Oncidium 647
  O. cheirophorum 647
  O. flexuosum 647
  O. lanceanum 648
  O. sphacelatum 648
One-sided bottlebrush
  180
Onion 648
Ophiopogon 648
  O. jaburan 649
  O. japonicus 649
  O. planiscapus 649
Opuntia 649, 738
  O. aurantiaca 649
  O. basilaris 650
  O. bigelovii 650
  O. erinacea 650
    Var. *ursina* 650
  O. ficus-indica 650
  O. microdasys 650
  O. stricta 649
  O. tunicata 650
  O. vulgaris 649
  Opuntia ficus-indica
    649
Opuntia ficus-indica 738
Orange 650
  Citrus aurantium 650,
    651
  Citrus sinensis 651
Orange browallia 858

Orchid cactus 360
Orchid tree 58
Oregano 651
Oreocallis 47
Origanum vulgare 651
Ornithogalum 652
  O. arabicum 652
  O. balansae 652
  O. nutans 652
  O. pyrenaicum 652
  O. thyrsoides 652
Orthosiphon 652
  O. stramineus 653
Osbeckia 653
  O. stellata 653
Osmanthus 653
  O. americanus 653
  O. delavayi 653
  O. x fortunei 653
  O. fragrans 654
  O. heterophyllus 654
Osteospermum 654
  O. amplectans 654
  O. ecklonis 654
  O. fruticosum 654
  O. jucundum 654
Oswego tea 127
Owenia 654
  O. acidula 655
Oxalis 655
  O. adenophylla 656
  O. carnosa 656
  O. gigantea 656
  O. hirta 656
  O. lobata 656
  O. pes-caprae 656
  O. purpurea 656
  O. succulenta 656
Oxydendrum 656
  O. arboreum 656
Oxylobium 656

O. ellipticum 657
O. ilicifolium 657
O. lanceolatum 657
O. procumbens 657
O. robustum 657
O. scandens 657
Oxypetalum 657
  O. caeruleum 657
  Tweedia caerulea 657
Oyster plant 15

P

Pachyphytum 660
  P. compactum 660
  P. hookeri 660
  P. oviferum 660
Pachypodium 660
  P. lamerei 661
  P. namaquanum 661
  P. succulentum 661
Pachysandra 661
  P. procumbens 661
  P. terminalis 661
    'Variegata' 661
Pachystachys 661
  P. coccinea 662
  P. lutea 662
Paeonia 662
  P. delavayi 662
  P. emodi 662
  P. lactiflora 662
  P. lutea 663
  P. mlokosewitschii 663
  P. officinalis 663
    'Alba Plena' 663
    'Rosea Plena' 663
    'Rubra Plena', 663
    subspecies *humilis*
    663
  P. peregrina 663
  P. suffruticosa 662, 663
Paeony 662
Painted nettle 260
Pak-choi 136
Palmetto 798
Panax 423
Panax species 423
Pandanus 663
  P. cookii 664
  P. monticola 664
  P. pedunculatus 664
  P. tectorius 664

'Sanderi' 664
'Veitchii' 664
Pandorea 664, 724
P. doratoxylon 664
P. jasminoides 664
'Alba' 664
'Rosea' 664
P. pandorana 664
'Snowbells' 665
Pansy 926
Pansy orchid 607
Papaver 665
P. croceum 665
'Champagne Bubbles' 665
'Oregon Rainbows' 665
'Wonderland' 665
P. orientale 665
'Cedric Morris' 666
'Picotee' 666
P. rhoeas 666
P. somniferum 666
Papaya 674
Paper daisy 775
Paper flower 888
Paperbark 595
Paphiopedilum 666
P. bellatulum 666
P. concolor 666
P. insigne 666
P. niveum 666
P. parishii 666
P. philippinense 666
Paradisea 666
P. liliastrum 667
'Major' 667
P. lusitanicum 667
Parahebe 452, 667, 920
P. catarractae 667
P. linifolia 667

P. lyallii 667
P. perfoliata 667
Parlour palm 226
Parodia 636, 668
P. aureispina 668
P. chrysacanthion 668
P. maassii 668
P. nivosa 668
P. penicillata 668
Paronychia 668
P. argentea 668
P. argyrocoma 668
P. capitata 668
P. sessiliflora 669
P. virginica 669
Parrot beak 457
Parrot's beak 252
Parrot-pea 330
Parrotia 669
P. persica 669
Parsley 669
P. crispum var. tuberosum 670
Petroselinum crispum 670
Parsnip 670
Passiflora 671
P. x alatocaerulea 671
P. x allardii 671
P. antioquiensis 671
P. cinnabarina 671
P. coccinea 671
P. edulis 671
P. laurifolia 671
P. mixta 671
P. quadrangularis 671
P. racemosa 672
P. vitifolia 672
Passiflora mollissima 671
Passiflora edulis 672

Passiflora quadrangularis 433
Passion flower 433, 671
Passionfruit 672
P. mollissima 672
P. quadrangularis 672
Passiflora edulis 672
Pastinaca sativa 670
Patersonia 672
P. fragilis 673
P. glabrata 673
P. longiscapa 673
P. occidentalis 673
P. sericea 673
Paulownia 673
P. fortunei 674
P. tomentosa 674
Pavetta 674
P. borbonica 674
P. caffra 674
P. capensis 674
P. indica 674
P. natalensis 674
Pawpaw 674
C. papaya 675
Pea 675
Peace lily 841
Peach 623, 676
Prunus persica 676
Peacock flower 895
Peacock iris 611
Peanut 677
Pear 678, 757
Pyrus communis 678
'Anjou' 678
'Beurre Bosc' 678
'Clapp's Favorite' 678
'Doyenne du Comice' 679
'Seckle' 679

Pyrus pyrifolia 679
Pyrus ussuriensis 679
Pearl bush 387
Pebble plant 551
Pecan 679
Carya illinoinensis 679
Carya pecan 679
Pedilanthus 679
P. macrocarpus 680
P. tithymaloides 680
'Variegatus' 680
Pelargonium 680, 681
Pelargonium x domesticum 681
P. graveolens 681
P. x hortorum 681
P. odoratissimum 681
P. peltatum 681
P. tomentosum 681
Pellaea 681
P. falcata 682
P. paradoxa 682
P. rotundifolia 682
Peltophorum 682
P. dasyrachis 682
P. dubium 682
P. pterocarpum 682
Pennisetum 683
P. alopecuroides 683
P. clandestinum 683
P. latifolium 683
P. purpureum 683
P. setaceum 683
P. villosum 683
Penstemon 683, 699
P. azureus 684
P. barbatus 684
P. cobaea 684
P. fruticosus 684
P. heterophyllus 684
P. hirsutus 684

P. triphyllus 684
  'Apple Blossom' 684
  'Firebird' 684
  'Garnet' 684
  'Lady Hindley' 684
  'Sour Grapes' 684
Pentas 684
  P. bussei 684
  P. lanceolata 684
Peony 662
Peperomia 684
  P. argyreia 685
  P. bicolor 685
  P. caperata 'Emerald
    Ripple' 685
  P. dolabriformes 685
  P. glabella 685
  'Variegata' 685
  P. obtusifolia 685
  'Green and Gold'
    685
  'Variegata' 685
  P. scandens 685
  'Variegata' 685
Pepper 711
Pepper bush 877
Pepper tree 817
Perennial aster 94
Perennial wallflower
  368
Pericallis 686
Pericallis x *hybrida* 245,
  685
  P. x *hybrida* 686
  Senecio x *hybridus* 686
Periwinkle 925
Pernettya 686
  P. lanceolata 686
  P. macrostigma 686
  P. mucronata 686
  P. tasmanica 686

Persea americana 102
Persian ironwood 669
Persicaria 727
Persicaria odorata 924
Persimmon 686
  'Chocolate' 687
  'Fuyu' 687
  'Giant Fuyu' 687
  'Goshu' 687
  'Hachiya' 687
  'Tamopan' 687
Persoonia 687
  P. acerosa 688
  P. chamaepitys 688
  P. lanceolata 688
  P. levis 688
  P. pinifolia 688
  P. subvelutina 688
Peruvian lily 53
Petasites 688
  P. fragrans 688
  P. japonicus var.
    giganteus 688
Petrea 688
  P. arborea 689
  P. racemosa 689
  P. volubilis 689
  'Albiflora' 689
Petrophila 689
  P. acicularis 690
  P. biloba 690
  P. canescens 690
  P. linearis 690
  P. pedunculata 690
  P. pulchella 690
  P. sessilis 690
  P. teretifolia 690
Petroselinum crispum
  669
Petunia 690
  P. axillaris 690

  P. hybrida 690
  P. integrifolia 690
Phaius 691
  P. tankervilliae 691
Phalaenopsis 691
  P. amabilis 692
  P. amboinensis 692
  P. schillerana 692
  P. stuartiana 692
  P. violacea 692
Phaseolus lunatus 119
Phebalium 692
  P. ambiens 692
  P. dentatum 692
  P. nottii 692
  P. nudum 692
  P. squameum 692
Philadelphus 692, 693
  P. 'Manteau
    d'Hermine' 693
  P. 'Virginal' 693
  P. coronarius 693
    Aureus' 693
  P. delavayi 693
  P. x *lemoinei* 693
  P. mexicanus 693
  P. microphyllus 693
Philodendron 693
  P. bipinnatifidum 694
  P. crassinervium 694
  P. domesticum 694
  P. scandens 694
  P. selloum 694
Phlebodium 694
  P. aureum 694
  'Glaucum' 694
  var. *aureolatum* 694
Phlebodium aureum
  694
Phlomis 694, 695
  P. chrysophylla 695

  P. fruticosa 695
  P. russeliana 695
  P. samia 695
Phlox 695
  P. carolina 696
  P. divaricata 696
  P. douglasii 696
  P. drummondii 696
  P. paniculata 696
  'Blue Boy' 696
  'Brigadier' 696
  'Bright Eyes' 696
  'Mia Ruys' 696
  'Prince of Orange'
    696
  P. subulata 696
Phoenix 696
  P. canariensis 697
  P. dactylifera 697
  P. reclinata 697
  P. roebelenii 697
Phoenix dactylifera 315
Phormium 697
  P. colensoi 698
  P. cookianum 698
  P. tenax 698
  'Rubrum' 698
  'Variegatum' 698
  'Veitchianum' 698
Photinia 698
  P. x *fraseri* 'Robusta'
    698
  P. x *fraseri* 'Rubens'
    698
  P. serratifolia 698
Phygelius 699
  'African Queen' 699
  'Moonraker' 699
  P. aequalis 699
  'Yellow Trumpet'
    699

P. capensis 699
  'Coccineus' 699
Phyllodoce 699
  P. aleutica 700
  P. caerulea 700
  P. empetriformis 700
  P. nipponica 700
Phyllostachys 700
  P. aurea 700
  P. bambusoides 700
    Castillonis' 700
  P. nigra 700
    Var. *henonis* 701
Physalis 701
  P. alkekengi 701
    'Gigantea' 701
    'Pygmaea' 701
  P. ixocarpa 701
  P. peruviana 701
  P. pruinosa 701
Physalis peruviana 190
Physocarpus 701
  P. bracteatus 702
  P. capitatus 702
  P. malvaceus 702
  P. monogynus 702
  P. opulifolius 702
    'Luteus' 702
Physostegia 702
  P. virginiana 702
    'Alba' 702
    'Gigantea' 702
    'Vivid' 702
Phytolacca 702
  P. americana 703
  P. dioica 703
Picea 703
  P. abies 704
    'Clanbrassiliana'
      704
    'Globosa Nana' 704

'Nidiformis' 704
  P. glauca 704
    var. *albertiana*
      'Conica' 704
  P. omorika 704
  P. pungens 704
    'Glauca' 704
    'Koster' 704
  P. smithiana 704
Pickaback plant 899
Pieris 704
  P. formosa 705
  P. formosa var. *forrestii*
    705
  P. japonica 704, 705
    'Christmas Cheer'
      705
    'Flamingo' 705
    'Purity' 705
    'Valley Rose' 705
    'Valley Valentine'
      705
    'Variegatus' 705
    'White Cascade' 705
Pigeon wings 252
Pilea 705
  P. cadierei 705
  P. microphylla 705
  P. nummularifolia 705
Pimelea 706
  P. ferruginea 706
  P. ligustrina 706
  P. linifolia 706
  P. prostrata 706
  P. rosea 706
  P. spectabilis 706
  P. suaveolens 706
Pimenta dioica 48
Pincushion 447, 539
Pincushion cactuses 582
Pine 708

Pine nut 707
  P. cembra 707
  P. cembra ssp. *sibirica*
    707
Pineapple 706
  A. bracteatus var.
    tricolor 707
  A. c. var. *variegatus*
    707
  A. comosus 707
  Ananas nanus 707
Pineapple guava 392
Pineapple lily 378
Pinks 323
Pinus 708
  P. aristata 708
  P. bungeana 709
  P. canariensis 709, 711
  P. contorta 709
  P. coulteri 709
  P. densiflora 709
  P. elliottii 709, 710
  P. halepensis 709
  P. lambertiana 708,
    709, 710
  P. longifolia 711
  P. montezumae 709
  P. monticola 710
  P. mugo 710
    'Gnom' 710
  P. nigra 710
  P. palustris 710
  P. patula 710
  P. pinaster 710, 711
  P. pinea 711
  P. ponderosa 711
  P. radiata 709, 711
  P. roxburghii 711
  P. thunbergii 711
Pinus cembroides 707
Pinus pinea 'Fragilis' 707

Piper 711
  P. betle 712
  P. kadsura 712
  P. methysticum 712
  P. nigrum 711, 712
Piper species 191
Pisonia 712
  P. alba 712
  P. umbellifera 712
    'Variegata' 712
Pistachio 713
Pistacia 713
  P. chinensis 713
  P. lentiscus 714
  P. terebinthus 714
  P. vera 713, 714
Pistacia vera 713
Pisum sativum 675
Pitcairnia 714
  P. corallina 714
  P. flammea 714
  P. paniculata 714
Pitcher plant 812
Pithecellobium 714
  P. arboreum 715
  P. dulce 715
Pittosporum 715
  P. crassifolium 715
    'Variegatum' 715
  P. eugenioides 715
    'Variegatum' 715
  P. phillyreoides 716
  P. rhombifolium 716
  P. tenuifolium 716
  P. tobira 716
  P. undulatum 716
Planchonella 716
  P. australis 717
  P. laurifolia 717
  P. novo zelandica 716,
    717

Plane tree 717
Plantain lily 468
Platanus 717
 Platanus x hispanica 717
  P. occidentalis 717
  P. orientalis 717
Platycerium 717
  P. bifurcatum 718
  P. superbum 718
Platycodon 718
  P. grandiflorus 719
Platylobium 719
  P. alternifolium 719
  P. formosum 719
  P. triangulare 719
Plectranthus 719
  P. amboinicus 720
  P. argentatus 720
  P. australis 720
  P. oertendahlii 720
Pleioblastus pygmaeus 89
Pleione 720
  P. humilis 720
  P. limprichtii 720
  P. praecox 720
Plum 720
  P. insititia 721
  P. salicina 721
  Prunus domestica 721
Plum pine 723
Plum yew 723
Plum-yew 217
Plumbago 721
  P. auriculata 722
Plumeria 722
  P. rubra var. acutifolia 722
Podalyria 722
  P. calyptrata 722
  P. sericea 723

Podocarpus 723
  P. elatus 724
  P. ferrugineus 724
  P. macrophyllus 724
  P. salignus 723
  P. totara 724
  Prumnopitys ferruginea 724
Podranea 724
  P. ricasoliana 724
Pohutukawa 603
Poinciana 318
Polemonium 724
  P. caeruleum 725
  P. carneum 725
  P. elegans 725
  P. foliosissimum 725
  P. foliosissimum var. flavum 725
  P. reptans 725
Polianthes 725
  P. tuberosa 726
Polygala 726
  P. calcarea 726
  P. chamaebuxus 726
  P. x dalmaisiana 726
  P. myrtifolia 726
  P. paucifolia 726
  P. vayredae 726
Polygonatum 726, 727
  P. biflorum 726, 727
  P. multiflorum 727
  P. odoratum 726, 727
  'Variegatum' 727
Polygonum 727
  Fallopia baldschuanica 727
  P. baldschuanicum 727
  P. capitatum 727
  P. orientale 727
  Persicaria capitata 727

  Persicaria orientalis 727
Polygonum fagopyrum 155
Polypodium 605, 727
  P. cambricum 727, 728
  P. formosanum 728
  P. loriceum 728
  P. vulgare 728
Polyscias 728
  P. filicifolia 729
  P. guilfoylei 729
  'Victoriae' 729
Polystichum 729
  P. formosum 729
  P. proliferum 729
  P. setiferum 729
Pomaderris 729
  P. andromedifolia 730
  P. apetala 730
  P. ferruginea 730
  P. kumeraho 730
  P. lanigera 730
  P. pilifera 730
  P. rugosa 730
Pomegranate 730
Pomelo 731
  'Chandler' 731
  C. grandis 731
Poncirus 731
  P. trifoliata 732
Pony tail 119
Poor man's orchid 818
Popcorn 732
Poplar 732
Poppy 665
Populus 732
  P. alba 733
  P. balsamifera 733
  P. x canadensis 733
  P. deltoides 733

  P. nigra 733
  'Italica' 733
  P. tremula 733
  P. tremuloides 733
  P. yunnanensis 733
Portulaca 734
  P. grandiflora 734
  P. oleracea 734
Portulacaria 734
  P. afra 734, 735
  'Foliisvariegatus' 735
Posoqueria 735
  P. latifolia 735
Pot marigold 169
Potato 735
Potentilla 736
  P. atrosanguinea 737
  P. atrosanguinea var. argyrophylla 737
  P. fruticosa 737
  P. nepalensis 737
  'Miss Willmott' 737
  P. recta 737
Pouch flower 169
Poverty bush 363
Powder puff tree 170
Pratia 737
  P. angulata 738
  P. concolor 738
  P. macrodon 738
  P. nummularia 738
  P. pedunculata 738
  P. purpurascens 738
Prickly box 160
Prickly pear 738
Pride of Burma 58
Primula 738, 739
  P. auricula 739
  P. denticulata 739
  P. floribunda 739

P. x *kewensis* 739
P. malacoides 739
P. obconica 739
P. x *polyantha* 739
P. veris 739
P. verticillata 739
P. vulgaris 740
Princess palm 326
Privet 543
Prostanthera 740
  P. baxteri 741
  P. cuneata 741
    'Alpine Gold' 741
  P. incana 741
  P. incisa 741
  P. lasianthos 741
  P. nivea 741
    Var. *induta* 741
  P. ovalifolia 740, 741
  P. rotundifolia 741
Protea 742
  P. cynaroides 742
  P. eximia 742
  P. grandiceps 742
  P. latifolia 742
  P. mellifera 742
  P. neriifolia 742
  P. pulchella 742
  P. repens 742
Proteaceae 437
Prunella 743
  P. grandiflora 743
    'Alba' 743
    'Rosea' 743
    'Rubra' 743
  P. vulgaris 743
Prunus 743, 744, 745
  P. amygdalus 745
  P. armeniaca 744
    'Plena' 744
  P. avium 744

P. x *blireana* 745
P. campanulata 744, 745
P. cerasifera 745
  'Nigra' 745
P. cerasus 745
P. dulcis 745
  'Alba Plena' 745
  'Sinensis' 745
P. glandulosa 744, 745
P. laurocerasus 744, 745
P. lusitanica 744, 745
P. mume 744, 745
P. padus 745
P. persica 744, 745
  'Alba Plena' 745
  'Rosea Plena' 745
  'Versicolor' 745
P. serrulata 745
  'Amanogawa' 746
  'Cheal's Weeping Cherry' 746
  'Fugenzo' 746
  'Kanzan' 746
  'Kiku-shidare-zakura' 746
  'Kojima' 746
  'Mt Fuji' 746
  'Okumiyaku' 746
  'Shirofugen' 746
  'Shirotae' 746
  'Tai-Haku' 746
  'Ukon' 746
P. x *subhirtella*
  'Pendula' 746
P. x *subhirtella*
  'Pendula Rosea' 746
P. subhirtella 'Pendula' 744
P. x *yedoensis*

'Pendula' 744
  P. x *yedoensis* 746
Prunus amygdalus 48
Prunus armeniaca, 72
Prunus avium 233
Prunus cerasus 233
Prunus dulcis 48
Prunus persica 676
Pseuderanthemum 746
  P. atropurpureum 747
  P. reticulatum 747
Pseudobombax 747
  P. ellipticum 747
  P. grandiflorum 747
Pseudopanax 747
  P. chathamicus 747
  P. crassifolius 748
  P. ferox 748
  P. lessonii 748
Pseudosasa amabilis 700
Pseudotsuga 748
  P. menziesii 748
Pseudowintera 748
  P. axillaris 748
  P. colorata 749
Psidium species 440
Psoralea 749
  P. affinis 749
  P. pinnata 749
Pteris 749
  P. argyraea 750
  P. cretica 750
    'Albolineata' 750
  P. ensiformis 750
    'Evergemiensis' 750
    'Victoriae' 750
  P. tremula 750
  P. tripartita 750
  P. umbrosa 750
  P. vittata 750
Pterocarya 750

P. fraxinifolia 751
  P. stenoptera 751
Pterostylis 751
  P. grandiflora 751
Ptilotus 751
  P. exaltatus 752
  P. grandiflorus 752
  P. obovatus 752
  P. polystachyus 752
  P. spathulatus 752
Ptychosperma 196, 752
  P. elegans 753
  P. macarthurii 753
Pulmonaria 753
  P. angustifolia 753
  P. officinalis 753
Pultenaea 753, 754
  P. cunninghamii 754
  P. daphnoides 754
  P. flexilis 754
  P. juniperina 754
  P. microphylla 754
  P. pedunculata 754
  P. stipularis 754
  P. villosa 754
Pummelo 731
Pumpkin 754
  'Atlantic Giant' 755
  'Mammoth' 755
  C. moschata 755
  C. pepo 755
  C. pepo var. *pepo* 755
  Cucurbita maxima 755
Punica granatum 730
Purple granadilla 672
Purple pea 469
Purple wreath 688
Puya 755
  P. berteroniana 755
  P. spathacea 755
  P. venusta 756

Pyracantha 755
  P. 'Watereri' 756
  P. angustifolia 756
  P. coccinea 756
    'Lalandei' 756
  P. crenulata 756
Pyrostegia 756
  P. ignea 757
  P. venusta 757
Pyrus 757
  P. calleryana 757
  P. s. 'Pendula' 757
  P. salicifolia 757
  P. ussuriensis 757
Pyrus communis 678
Pyrus pyrifolia 678

Q

Quandong 760
Quassia 760
  Q. amara 761
Queen of the night 824
Queensland black palm
  634
Quercus 761
  P. palustris 761
  Q. canariensis 761
  Q. cerris 761
  Q. coccinea 761
  Q. ilex 761
  Q. robur 762
    'Concordia' 762
  Q. rubra 762
  Q. suber 762
  Q. virginiana 762
Quince 762
  'Apple' 762
  'Cooke's Jumbo' 762
  'Pineapple' 762
  'Smyrna' 762
Quisqualis 763
  Q. indica 763

R

Radicchio 763
Radish 764
  Raphanus sativus 764
    'Long Black
      Spanish' 764
    'White Chinese' 764
    Cherry Belle' 764
Rain flower 950
Rain lily 446
Rain tree 804
Rambutan 764
Randia 765
  R. benthamiana 765
  R. fitzalanii 765
  R. formosa 765
Rangoon creeper 763
Ranunculus 765
  R. acris 766
  R. asiaticus 766
  R. collinus 766
  R. lappaceus 766
  R. rivularis 766
Raoulia 767
  R. australis 767
  R. eximia 767
  R. glabra 767
  R. haastii 767
  R. mammillaris 767
  R. subsericea 767
  R. tenuicaulis 767
Raphanus sativus 764
Rasp fern 338
Raspberry 767
  Rubus idaeus 768
Rattle-box 288
Ravenala 768
  R. madagascariensis
    768
Rebutia 769
  R. albiflora 769

R. aureiflora 769
  R. kupperana 769
  R. minuscula 769
  R. senilis 769
    Var. kesselringiana
      769
Red alder 293
Red ash 52, 356
Red chicory 763
Red hot poker 510
Red pepper 191
Redwood 826
Reedmace 911
Regelia 769, 770
  R. ciliata 770
  R. grandiflora 770
  R. inops 770
  R. velutina 770
Rehmannia 770
  R. elata 770
  R. glutinosa 770
Reinwardtia 770
  R. indica 771
Reseda 771
  R. luteola 771
  R. odorata 771
Rewarewa 510
Rhagodia 772
  R. baccata 772
  R. nutans 772
  R. parabolica 772
Rhamnus 772
  R. alaternus 772
    'Argenteovariegata'
      773
  R. californica 773
  R. cathartica 772, 773
  R. frangula 772
  R. purshiana 773
Rhapis 773
  R. excelsa 773

R. humilis 773
Rheum x *cultorum* 780
Rhipsalidopsis 774
  Hatiora gaertneri 774
  Hatiora rosea 774
  R. gaertneri 774
  R. rosea 774
Rhipsalis 774
  R. cereuscula 775
  R. crispata 775
  R. dissimilis 775
  R. houlletiana 775
  R. paradoxa 775
Rhodanthe 775
  Acroclineum roseum 775
  Helipterum roseum 775
  R. anthemoides 775
  R. chlorocephala subsp. *rosea* 775
  R. floribunda 775
  R. manglesii 775
Rhododendron 775
  Broad-leaf rhododendrons 777
  Vireya rhododendrons 777
Rhodohypoxis 777
  R. baurii 777
Rhodoleia 778
  R. championii 778
Rhodophiala pratensis 466
Rhoeo 778
  R. spathacea 778
  'Vittata' 779
  Tradescantia spathacea 778
Rhoicissus 779
  R. capensis 779
Rhombophyllum 779

R. dolabriforme 779
R. neli 779
R. rhomboideum 780
Rhopalostylis 780
  R. baueri 780
  R. sapida 780
Rhubarb 780
  'Cherry' 781
  'Macdonald' 781
  'Strawberry' 781
  'Victoria' 781
Rhus 781, 782
  'Dissecta' 782
  R. glabra 782
  R. typhina 782
  R. verniciflua 782
  Rhus toxicodendron 781
  Toxicodendron radicans 781
Ribes 782
  'Brocklebankii' 782
  'King Edward VII' 782
  'Pulborough Scarlet' 782
  'White Icicle' 783
  R. americanum 782
  R. x *gordonianum* 782
  R. malvaceum 782
  R. odoratum 782
  R. sanguineum 782
  R. speciosum 783
  R. viburnifolium 783
Ribes species 297
Rice flower 706
Rice paper plant 884
Ricinocarpos 783
  R. bowmanii 783
  R. cyanescens 783
  R. glaucus 783
  R. pinifolius 783

R. speciosus 783
Ricinus 783
  R. communis 784
  'Carmencita' 784
  'Impala' 784
  'Red Spire' 784
  'Zanzibarensis' 784
Robinia 784
  R. x *ambigua* 784
  'Bella-rosea' 784
  R. hispida 784
  R. pseudoacacia 784
  'Frisia' 785
  R. viscosa 785
Rock bell 934
Rock cress 74, 100
Rock jasmine 60
Rock purslane 167
Rock rose 246, 455
Rocket 785
Romneya 785
  Romneya 785
  Var. *trichocalyx* 785
Romulea 786
  R. bulbocodium 786
  R. rosea 786
  R. sabulosa 786
Rondeletia 786
  R. amoena 787
  R. odorata 787
  R. strigosa 787
Root celery 213
Rosa 787
  Alba 788
  Bourbon 788
  Centifolia 788
  China 788
  Damask 788
  Gallica 788
  Hybrid Musk 788
  Hybrid Perpetual 788

  Moss 788
  Noisette 788
  Portland 788
  R. gallica var. *officinalis* 787
  R. rugosa 787
  Tea 788
Rose 787
Rose grass 777
Roselle 788
Rosemary 789
  R. officinalis 789, 790
  'Benenden Blue' 790
  'Tuscan Blue' 790
  Var. *albiflorus* 789
Rosmarinus species 789
Rossioglossum grande 643
Rosularia 790
  R. officinalis 790
  R. pallida 790
  R. paniculata 790
  R. platyphylla 790
  R. serrata 790
Rothmannia 790
  R. capensis 791
  R. globosa 791
  R. longiflora 791
Rowan 837
Royal palm 791
Roystonea 791
  R. regia 791
Rubus idaeus 767
Rubus Loganberry Group 555
Rubus ursinus 556
Rubus ursinus var. *loganobaccus* 143
Rudbeckia 791
  R. hirta 792

R. laciniata 792
  'Golden Glow' 792
  'Hortensia' 792
Ruellia 792
  R. elegans 792
  R. macrantha 793
  R. portellae 793
Rumex 838
Rumex scutatus 338
Rumohra 793
  R. adiantiformis 793
Ruschia 793
  R. acuminata 794
  R. dualis 794
  R. evoluta 794
  R. rubricaulis 794
Ruscus 794
  R. aculeatus 794
Rush 497
Rush broom 925
Russelia 794
  R. equisetiformis 795
  R. sarmentosa 795
Rusty pod 469
Ruta 795
  R. graveolens 795
  'Jackman's Blue' 795
  'Variegata' 795
Rutabaga 863

S

Sabal 798
  S. blackburniana 798
  S. minor 798
  S. palmetto 798
  S. umbraculifera 798
Sabal minor 828
Sacred bamboo 622
Saffron 799
Sage 799, 803
  Salvia officinalis 799
Sago cycad 300
Saguaro 195
Saintpaulia 800
  S. ionantha 800
Salix 800
  S. alba 801
  'Aurea' 801
  subsp. *vitellina* 801
  subsp. *vitellina*
    'Britzensis' 801
  S. alba 'Tristis' 801
  S. babylonica 801
  S. babylonica var.
    pekinensis 'Tortuosa'
    801
  S. caprea 801
    'Kilmarnock' 801
  S. cordata 801
  S. fragilis 801
  S. lanata 801
  S. purpurea 801
  S. x *sepulcralis* var.
    chrysocoma 801
Salpiglossis 802
  S. sinuata 802
Salsify 802
  Scorzonera hispanica
    802
  Tragopogon porrifoliu
    802

Saltbush 99
Salvia 803
  S. azurea 804
  S. elegans 'Scarlet
    Pineapple' 804
  S. farinacea 804
  S. guaranitica 804
  S. involucrata 804
  S. leucantha 803, 804
  S. microphylla 804
  S. officinalis 803, 804
  S. patens 804
  S. uliginosa 803, 804
Salvia officinalis 799
Saman 804
Samanea 804
  Albizia saman 804
  S. saman 804
Sambucus 805
  S. callicarpa 805
  S. canadensis 805
    'Aurea' 805
  S. nigra 805
    'Albovariegata' 805
    'Aurea' 805
    'Plumosa Aurea' 805
Sanchezia 805
  S. speciosa 806
Sandalwood 807
Sandersonia 806
  S. aurantiaca 806
Sanguinaria 806
  S. canadensis 806
    'Plena' 806
Sanguisorba minor 159
Sansevieria 807
  S. cylindrica 807
  S. trifasciata 807
    'Hahnii' 807
    'Laurentii' 807

Santalum 807
  S. acuminatum 808
  S. album 808
  S. freycinetianum 808
  S. lanceolatum 808
  S. spicatum 808
Santalum acuminatum
  760
Santolina 808
  R. virens 809
  S. chamaecyparissus
    808
  S. rosmarinifolia subsp.
    rosmarinifolia 809
Sapium 809
  S. sebiferum 809
Sapodilla 809
Saponaria 810
  S. caespitosa 810
  S. ocymoides 810
  S. officinalis 810
    'Alba Plena' 810
    'Rubra Plena' 810
Sapote, black 810
Saraca 811
  S. asoca 811
  S. indica 811
  S. thaipingensis 811
Sarcochilus 811
  S. ceciliae 812
  S. falcatus 812
  S. fitzgeraldii 812
  S. hartmannii 812
Sarcococca 812
  S. confusa 812
  S. hookeriana 812
  S. ruscifolia 812
Sarracenia 812
  S. flava 813
  S. leucophylla 813
  S. psittacina 813

S. purpurea 813
Sasa 813
  S. veitchii 813
Sassafras 340
Satin flower 247
Satureja species 813
Sausage tree 508
Savory 813
  S. hortensis 814
  S. montana 814
Saw palmetto 828
Saxifraga 814
  S. paniculata 814
  S. rosacea 815
  S. stolonifera 815
  S. umbrosa 815
Scabweed 767
Scadoxus 446, 815
  S. multiflorus 815
    subspecies
      katherinae 815
  S. puniceus 815
Scadoxus puniceus 446
Scaevola 815
  S. aemula 816
  S. albida 816
  S. calendulacea 816
  S. crassifolia 816
  S. frutescens 816
  S. ramosissima 816
  S. striata 816
Scallion 830
Scarlet jade vine 612
Scarlet wisteria 829
Scent myrtle 314
Schefflera 816
  S. actinophylla 817
  S. digitata, 817
  S. heptaphylla 816,
    817
Schinus 817

S. molle 817
S. terebinthifolius 817
Schizanthus 818
  S. pinnatus 818
  S. x wisetonensis 818
Schizophragma 818
  S. hydrangeoides 818
  S. integrifolium 818,
    819
Schlumbergera 819
  S. x buckleyi 819
  S. truncata 819
Sciadopitys 819
  S. verticillata 820
Scilla 820
  S. bifolia 820
  S. mischtschenkoana
    820
  S. peruviana 820
  S. siberica 820
  S. tubergeniana 820
Scleranthus 820
  S. biflorus 820, 821
  S. brockiei 821
  S. pungens 821
  S. uniflorus 821
Scorzonera hispanica 802
Screw pine 663
Scurfy pea 749
Scutellaria 821
  S. alpina 822
  S. costaricana 822
  S. indica 822
    Var. *parvifolia* 822
Sea holly 368
Sea lavender 546
Sea pink 84
Sea poppy 425
sea urchin 447
Sechium edule 238
Sedge 194

Sedum 822
  S. acre 822
  S. adolphii 822
  S. bellum 822
  S. morganianum 822
  S. multiceps 823
  S. nussbaumeranum
    822
  S. pachyphyllum 823
  S. rubrotinctum 823
    'Aurora' 823
  S. sieboldii 823
  S. spathulifolium 823
  S. spectabile 823
  S. stahlii 823
Selaginella 823
  S. braunii 823
  S. kraussiana 824
    'Aurea' 824
    'Brownii' 824
  S. pallescens 824
  S. uncinata 824
Selenicereus 824
  S. grandiflorus 824
  S. hamatus 824
  S. macdonaldiae 824
Self-heal 743
Sempervivum 824
  A. arachnoideum 825
  S. ciliosum 825
  S. marmoreum 825
  S. tectorum 825
Senecio 825
  Pericallis cruenta 825
  S. articulatus 825
  S. cruentus 825
  S. macroglossus 825,
    826
  S. petasitis 826
  S. rowleyanus 826
  S. serpens 826

Senecio x hybridus 685
Senna 202, 826
  S. artemisioides 826
  S. bicapsularis 826
  S. candolleana 826
  S. didymobotrya 826
  S. multijuga 826
Sentry palm 470
Sequoia 826, 827
  S. sempervirens 826,
    827
Sequoiadendron 827
  S. giganteum 828
  Wellingtonia gigantea
    828
*Sequoiadendron
  giganteum* 827
Serenoa 828
  S. repens 828
Serissa 828
  S. foetida 829
  S. j. rosea 829
  S. japonica 829
    'Variegata' 829
Sesbania 829
  S. drummondi 829
  S. emerus 829
  S. grandiflora 829
  S. tripetii 829
Setaria 829
  S. drummondii 829
  S. italica 829
  S. palmifolia 830
Shadbush 58
Shaddock 731
Shaggy pea 656
Shallot 830
Shasta daisy 537
She-oak 47, 205
Sheep's bit 496
Shell flower 231

Shield fern 72

Shooting star 36

Silene 830

S. dioica 831

'Rosea Plena' 831

S. laciniata 831

S. pendula 832

S. schafta 831

Silk cotton tree 137

Silk tassel bush 414

Silk tree 42

Silver beet 831

'Ruby Chard' 831

Beta vulgaris subsp. cicla 831

Silver spyridium 846

Silver torch cactus 248

Sinapis alba 61

Sinningia 831

S. canescens 832

S. cardinalis 832

S. leucotricha 832

S. regina 832

S. speciosa 832

Sinningia speciosa 429

Skullcap 821

Sky flower 343

Slipper flower 159, 679

Slipper orchid 656

Small-leaf eutaxia 385

Smithiantha 832

S. cinnabarina 833

S. multiflora 833

S. zebrina 833

'Orange King' 833

Smoke bush 265

Smoke tree 279

Snail flower 924

Snake bush 460

Snapdragon 69

Snowbell 861

Snowberry 866

Snowdrop 411

Snowdrop tree 448

Snowflake 538

Soap berry 44

Soapwort 810

Solandra 833

S. grandiflora 833

S. guttata 833

S. maxima 833

Solanum 833

S. aviculare 834

S. capsicastrum 834

S. jasminoides 834

S. lanceolatum 834

S. pseudocapsicum 834

S. rantonnetii 834

S. seaforthianum 834

S. wendlandii 834

S. wrightii 834

Solanum melongena 353, 873

Solanum tuberosum 735

Soldanella 834

S. hungarica 835

S. minima 835

S. montana 835

S. villosa 835

Soleirolia 835

S. soleirolii 835

Solenostemon 260

Solenostemon scutellarioides 260

Solidago 835

S. 'Goldenmosa' 836

S. canadensis 835, 836

S. virgaurea 836

Var. minuta 836

Sollya 836

S. heterophylla 836

Solomon's seal 726

Sophora 837

S. chrysophylla 837

S. japonica 837

'Pendula' 837

'Tortuosa' 837

S. microphylla 837

'Earlygold' 837

'Goldies Mantle' 837

'Goldilocks' 837

S. prostrata 837

S. tetraptera 837

S. tomentosa 837

Sophronitis 208, 519

Sorbus 837, 838

S. americana 838

S. aria 838

'Majestica' 838

S. aucuparia 838

'Fructu Luteo' 838

S. domestica 838

Sorrel 838

'Silver Shield' 839

Rumex scutatus 838

South African cabbage tree 298

Southern beech 635

Sowerbaea 839

S. juncea 839

S. laxiflora 839

Spanish broom 840

Spanish fir 10

Sparaxis 839

S. fragrans 840

S. pillansii 840

S. tricolor 840

Sparrmannia 840

S. africana 840

'Flore Pleno' 840

S. ricinicarpa 840

Spartium 840, 841

S. junceum 841

Spathiphyllum 841

S. 'Mauna Loa' 841

S. wallisii 842

Spathodea 842

S. campanulata 842

Spathoglottis 842

S. aurea 842

S. plicata 843

Speedwell 920

Spider lily 475, 566

Spider plant 250

Spinach 843

Spinach, New Zealand 843

Spinacia oleracea 843

Spindle tree 381

Spiraea 787, 844

S. cantoniensis 844

'Flore Pleno' 844

S. cantoniensis x S. trilobata 845

S. japonica 844

'Anthony Waterer' 844

'Bumalda' 844

'Goldflame' 844

'Snowmound' 844

S. nipponica 844

S. prunifolia 844

S. thunbergii 845

S. x vanhouttei 845

Spleenwort 92

Sprekelia 845

S. formosissima 845

Sprengelia 845

S. incarnata 846

S. monticola 846

S. sprengelioides 846

Spring onion 846

A. cepa 846

A. fistulosum 846
Spruce 703
Spyridium 846
　S. cinereum 847
　S. globulosum 847
　S. parvifolium 847
Squill 820
St John's bread 219
St John's wort 477
Stachys 847
　S. affinis 847
　S. byzantina 847
　　'Silver Carpet' 847
　S. lanata 847
　S. macrantha 847
　S. officinalis 847
Stachyurus 848
　S. chinensis 848
　S. praecox 848
Staff vine 212
Staghorn fern 717
Stanhopea 848
　S. oculata 849
　S. tigrina 849
　S. wardii 849
Stapelia 849
　S. gigantea 849
　S. hirsuta 849
Staphylea 849
　S. holocarpa 850
　　'Rosea' 850
　S. pinnata 850
Star anise 850
Star apple 850
Star cactus 98
Star flower 849
Star fruit 851
Star grass 479
Star jasmine 903
Star tulip 178
Starfish plant 849

Statice 546
Stenocarpus 852
　S. salignus 852
　S. sinuatus 852
Stephanandra 852
　S. incisa 853
　S. tanakae 853
Stephanotis 853
　S. floribunda 853
Sterculia 853
　S. foetida 854
　S. quadrifida 854
　S. rubiginosa 854
　S. villosa 854
Sternbergia 854
　S. colchiciflora 854
　S. lutea 854
Stewartia 854
　S. pseudocamellia 855
Sticherus 855
　S. flabellatus 855
　S. lobatus 855
　S. tener 855
Stigmaphyllon 856
　S. ciliatum 856
　S. lingulatum 856
　S. littorale 856
Stock 591
Stokes' aster 856
Stokesia 856
　S. laevis, 856
Stone-cress 33
Stonecrop 822
Stoneface 551
Storax 861
Stork's bill 367
Strawberry 857
　F. vesca 858
　F. virginiana 857
　Fragaria x *ananasa* 857

Fragaria vesca 857
Fragaria x *ananassa* 857
Strawberry tree 77
Strelitzia 858
　S. alba 858
　S. nicolai 858
　S. reginae 858
Streptosolen 858
　S. jamesonii 859
Strobilanthes 859
　Goldfussia anisophylla 859
　S. anisophyllus 859
　S. dyeranus 859
Strongylodon 859
　S. macrobotrys 860
Stylidium 860
　S. bulbiferum 860
　S. calceratum 860
　S. graminifolium 861
　S. laricifolium 861
Styphelia 861
　S. adscendens 861
　S. longifolia 861
　S. triflora 861
　S. tubiflora 861
　S. viridis 861
Styrax 861
　S. americanus 862
　S. japonicus 862
　S. officinalis 862
Sugar berry 215
Sumac 781
Summer squash 588
Sun orchid 886
Sun rose 455
Sundew 342
Sunflower 456
Swainsona formosa 252
Swainsonia 862

Clianthus formosus 862, 863
　S. formoa 863
　S. formosa 862
　S. galegifolia 863
　　'Albiflora' 863
　　'Splendens' 863
　　'Violacea' 863
　S. grayana 863
　S. procumbens 863
Swamp cypress 878
Swamp daisy 23
Swamp heath 845
Swede 863
Sweet Alison 555
Sweet alyssum 555
Sweet bay 527
Sweet box 812
Sweet bursaria 160
Sweet cicely 864
Sweet corn 864
　Zea mays var. *saccharata* 865
Sweet pepper 191
Sweet potato 865
Sweetgum 549
Swiss chard 831
Sword fern 628
Sycamore 717
Symphoricarpos 866
　S. albus 866
　S. x *chenaulti* 866
　S. microphyllus 866
　S. montanus 866
　S. orbiculatus 866
　　'Foliis Variegatis' 866
　S. racemosus 866
Symphytum officinale 263
Syncarpia 866

S. glomulifera 867
S. hillii 867
Syngonium 867
S. podophyllum 867
Syringa 868
S. x chinensis 868
'Alba' 868
'Saugeana' 868
S. x hyacinthiflora 868
S. pubescens subsp.
microphylla 868
S. pubescens subsp.
microphylla
'Superba' 858
S. x reflexa 868
S. reticulata 858
Var. *mandshurica*
868
S. vulgaris 864
Syzygium 380, 868
S. aromaticum 869
S. coolminianum 869
S. floribundum 869
S. francisii 869
S. jambos 869
S. luehmannii 869
S. oleosum 869
S. paniculatum 869
S. pycnanthum 869
S. wilsonii 869
Syzygium aromaticum
254

T

Tabernaemontana 872
Stemmadenia
grandiflora 872
T. divaricata 872
T. grandiflora 872
Tagetes 872
T. erecta 872
T. patula 873
T. tenuifolia 873
Tallow tree 809
Tamarillo 873
Tamarind 873
Tamarindus indica 873
Tamarisk 874
Tamarix 874
T. africana 874
T. aphylla 874
T. parviflora 875
T. pentandra 875
T. ramosissima 875
Tanacetum 875
T. balsamita 875
T. coccineum 875
T. parthenium 875
T. vulgare 875
Tanacetum balsamita
278, 279
Tangelo 875
'Minneola' 876
'Orlando' 876
'Sampson' 876
'Seminole' 876
Tangerine 583
Tansy 875
Tapioca 202
Taraxacum officinale 313
Taro 876
Tarragon 877
A. dracunculus
dracunculoides 877

Artemisia dracunculus
877
Tasmannia 877
T. insipida 878
T. lanceolata 878
T. purpurascens 878
T. stipitata 878
Tassel fern 566
Taxodium 878
T. distichum 878, 879
T. mucronatum 878,
879
Taxus 879
T. baccata 879
'Aurea' 879
'Fastigiata Aurea'
879
'Fastigiata
Aureomarginata'
879
'Fastigiata' 879
Var. *nana* 879
T. cuspidata 879
Tea-tree 534
Tecoma 879, 881
T. castaneifolia 880
T. garrocha 880
T. stans 880
Tecomaria 880
Tecomaria capensis 880
'Apricot' 881
'Aurea' 881
'Lutea' 881
Telopea 881
T. mongaensis 882
T. mongaensis x *T.*
speciosissima 882
T. oreades 882
T. oreades x *T.*
speciosissima 882
T. speciosissima 882

'Wirrimbirra White'
882
T. truncata 882
Templetonia 882
T. aculeata 882
T. retusa 882
T. sulcata 883
Terminalia 883
M. chebula 883
T. bellirica 883
T. catappa 883
Tetradenia 883
T. riparia 884
Tetragonia tetragonioides
843
Tetrapanax 884
T. papyrifer 884
'Variegata' 884
T. papyriferus 884
Tetratheca 884
T. ciliata 885
T. denticulata 885
T. ericifolia 885
T. juncea 885
T. pilosa 885
T. shiressii 885
T. thymifolia 885
Teucrium 885
T. chamaedrys 885
T. fruticans 885
T. marum 885
T. scorodonia 885
Thalictrum 886
T. aquilegifolium 886
T. chelidonii 886
T. dasycarpum 886
T. delavayi 886
'Album' 886
T. dipterocarpum 886
T. flavum 886
Thatch palm 889

Thelymitra 886
  T. ixioides 887
  T. pauciflora 887
  T. venosa 887
Theobroma 887
  T. cacao 887
Thevetia 887
  T. peruviana 888
Thomasia 888
  T. grandiflora 889
  T. macrocarpa 889
  T. petalocalyx 889
  T. sarotes 889
Thread palm 936
Thrift 84
Thrinax 889
  T. morrisii 889
  T. parviflora 889
  T. radiata 889
Thryptomene 889
  T. baeckeacea 890
  T. calycina 890
  T. ericaea 890
  T. saxicola 890
  'F.C. Payne' 890
  T. stenocalyx 890
  T. stenophylla 890
Thuja 177, 748, 890, 891
  T. occidentalis 891
    'Ellwangerana Aurea' 891
    'Ericoides' 891
    'Globosa' 891
    'Lutea' 891
    'Pyramidalis' 891
    'Rheingold' 891
  T. orientalis 891
    'Aurea Nana' 891
    'Beverleyensis' 891
    'Decussata' 891

    'Juniperoides' 891
    Rosedalis' 891
  T. plicata 891
    'Stoneham Gold' 891
    'Zebrina' 891
Thujopsis 177, 891
  T. dolabrata 892
    'Nana' 892
    'Variegata' 892
Thunbergia 892
  T. alata 892
    'Alba' 892
    'Aurantiaca' 892
    'Bakeri' 892
  T. erecta 892
  T. grandiflora 893
  T. mysorensis 893
Thyme 893
  T. x citriodorus 893
  T. herbabarona 893
  T. lanuginosus 893
  T. polytrichus 893
    Subsp. *britannicus* var. *albus* 893
  T. praecox 893
  T. pseudolanuginosus 893
  T. pulegioides x *T. vulgaris* 893
  T. serpyllum 893
  T. vulgaris 893
    'Argenteus' 893
Thymus 893
Thysanotus 894
  T. juncifolius 894
  T. multiflorus 894
  T. patersonii 894
  T. tuberosus 894
Tiarella 894
  T. cordifolia 895

  T. laciniata 895
  T. wherryi 895
Tibouchina 653, 895
  T. granulosa 895
  T. laxa 895
  T. mutabilis 895
  T. organensis 895
  T. urvilleana 895
Tickseed 270
Tiger flower 895
Tiger jaws 392
Tigridia 895
  T. pavonia 896
Tilia 896
  T. 'Petiolaris' 897
  T. americana 897
  T. cordata 897
  T. x europaea 897
  T. platyphyllos 897
    'Rubra' 897
  T. tomentosa 897
Tillandsia 897
  T. cyanea 898
  T. grandis 898
  T. ionantha 898
  T. lindenii 898
  T. streptophylla 898
  T. usneoides 897, 898
Tithonia 898
  T. diversifolia 898
  T. rotundifolia 898
Toad flower 849
Toadflax 547
Todea 898
  T. barbara 899
Tolmiea 899
  T. menziesii 899
Tomato 899
Toona 210, 900
  Cedrela sinensis 901
  T. australis 901

  T. ciliata 901
  T. sinensis 901
Torch ginger 372
Torenia 901
  T. hirsuta 902
  T. atropurpurea 901
  T. baillonii 901
  T. fournieri 901
Torreya 902
  T. californica 902
  T. nucifera 902
  T. taxifolia 902
Toxicodendron 902
  T. succedaneum 903
Trachelospermum 903
  T. asiaticum 903
  T. jasminoides 903
Trachycarpus 903
  T. fortunei 903, 904
  T. martianus 904
Trachymene 904
  T. coerulea 904
  T. cyanopetala 904
  T. incisa 904
Tradescantia 778, 904
  T. Andersoniana Group 904, 905
  T. fluminensis 904, 905
  T. virginiana 904, 905
Tragopogon porrifolius 802
Transvaal daisy 421
Traveller's joy 248
Traveller's palm 768
Tree anemone 196
Tree fern 299
Tree ivy 391
Tree tomato 873
Tree waratah 47
Trevesia 905

T. palmata 905
Trifolium 905
  T. incarnatum 906
  T. repens 906
  T. subterraneum 906
Trigger plant 860
Trillium 906
  T. erectum 905
  T. grandiflorum 906
  'Flore Pleno' 906
  'Roseum' 906
Tristania conferta 559
Tristaniopsis 906
  Tristania laurina 907
  Tristaniopsis laurina 907
Triteleia 150, 907
  Brodiaea ixioides 907
  Brodiaea laxa 907
  T. ixioides 907
  T. laxa 907
  'Koningin Fabiola' 907
  'Queen Fabiola' 907
Tritonia 907
  T. crocata 908
  T. disticha 908
Tropaeolum 908
  T. majus 908
  T. peregrinum 908, 909
  T. speciosum 909
  T. tuberosum 909
Tropical pitcher plant 626
Trout lily 370
Trumpet bush 879
Trumpet flower 120
Trumpet-creeper 187
Tuberose 725
Tulbaghia 909
  T. capensis 909

T. fragrans 909
T. simmleri 909
T. violacea 909
Tulip 909
Tulip tree 550
Tulipa 909, 911
  T. batalinii 911
  T. clusiana 911
  T. kaufmanniana 911
  T. tarda 911
Tung oil tree 919
Turk's cap 599
Turnip 911
Turnip-rooted celery 213
Turpentine tree 866
Turtlehead 231
Tussilago farfara 261
Tweedia 657
Typha 911
  T. angustifolia 911
  T. latifolia 912

U

Ulmus 912
  U. americana 912
  U. carpinifolia 913
  U. glabra 913
    'Lutescens' 913
    'Pendula' 913
  U. minor 913
    'Variegata' 913
  U. parvifolia 913
  U. procera 912, 913
    'Argenteovariegata' 913
    'Louis van Houtte' 913
  U. pumila 913
  Ulmus americana 912
Umbilicus 790
Umbrella fern 855

V

Vaccinium species 135
Vallota speciosa 306
Vanda 916
  V. coerulea 916
  V. Rothschildiana 916
  V. tessellata 916
  V. tricolor 916
Vanilla lily 839
Vase plant 131
Vegetable marrow 588
Vegetable oyster 802
Vegetable pear 238
Veitchia 916
  V. joannis 917
  V. merrillii 917
Veltheimia 917
  V. bracteata 917
  V. capensis 917
Venus's fly trap 330
Veratrum 917
  V. album 918
  V. californicum 918
  V. nigrum 918
  V. viride 918
Verbascum 918
  V. bombyciferum 918
  V. dumulosum 918
  V. olympicum 918
  V. phoeniceum 918
  V. thapsus 919
Verbena 919
  V. canadensis 919
  V. x hybrida 919
  V. peruviana 919
  V. rigida 919
    'Alba' 919
    'Lilacina' 919
Vernicia 920
  Aleurites fordii 920
  V. fordii 920

Veronica 452, 593, 667, 920
V. austriaca subsp. *teucrium* 921
V. chamaedrys 921
V. cinerea 921
V. gentianoides 921
'Variegata' 921
V. longifolia 921
'Alba' 921
V. pectinata 921
'Rosea' 921
V. prostrata 921
V. repens 921
V. spicata 921
Verticordia 921
V. acerosa 922
V. brownii 922
V. chrysantha 922
V. conferta 922
V. densiflora 922
V. grandis 922
V. mitchelliana 922
V. multiflora 922
V. nitens 922
V. plumosa 922
V. serrata 922
Vervain 919
Viburnum 922
V. x *bodnantense* 923
V. x *burkwoodii* 923
V. x *carlcephalum* 923
V. carlesii 923
V. carlesii x *V. macrocephalum* 923
V. carlesii x *V. utile* 923
V. japonicum 923
V. macrocephalum 923
V. odoratissimum 923
V. opulus 923

V. plicatum 'Mariesii' 924
V. plicatum forma tomentosum 923
V. rhytidophyllum 924
V. suspensum 924
V. tinus 924
Vicia faba 118
Victoria 924
V. amazonica 924
V. cruziana 924
V. regia 924
Vietnamese mint 924
Vigna 925
V. caracalla 925
V. radiata 926
V. unguiculata 926
subsp. *sesquipedalis* 926
Viminaria 926
V. juncea 926
Vinca 926
V. major 927
'Variegata' 927
V. minor 927
'Azurea Flore-pleno' 927
'La Grave' 927
Vine 930
Viola 927
V. altaica 928
V. betonicifolia 927
V. cornuta 927, 928
V. filicaulis 928
V. hederacea 928
V. lutea 928
V. odorata 928
'Alba Plena' 928
'Alba' 928
V. septentrionalis 928
V. tricolor 928

'Bowles' Black' 928
V. x *wittrockiana* 928
Violet 927
Viper's bugloss 352
Virgilia 929
V. capensis 929
V. divaricata 929
V. oroboides 929
Virgin's bower 248
Virginia stock 579
Vitex 929
V. agnus-castus 929, 930
V. lucens 930
V. trifolia 929, 930
Vitis 930
V. amurensis 930
V. coignetiae 930
V. labrusca 930
V. vinifera 930
Vitis species 434
Vitis vinifera 434
Vriesea 931
V. fenestralis 931
V. hieroglyphica 931
V. splendens 931

W

Wachendorfia 934
W. hirsuta 934
W. paniculata 934
W. thyrsiflora 934
Wahlenbergia 934
W. albomarginata 935
W. gloriosa 935
W. gracilis 935
W. stricta 935
Wake robin 906
Walking stick palm 548
Wallflower 231
Walnut 935
J. nigra 935
J. regia 935
'Concorde' 935
'Eureka' 935
'Franquette' 935
'Payne' 935
Juglans nigra 935
Wand flower 327
Waratah 881
Washingtonia 936
W. filifera 936
W. robusta 936
Washingtonia palm 936
Water chestnut 937
Water clover 589
Water fern 134
Water lily 638
Watsonia 937
W. borbonica 937
W. coccinea 937
W. marginata 938
W. meriana 938
W. pyramidata 937
Wattle 11
Wax flower 853
Waxflower 366

Wedding bush 783
Wedge pea 429
Weigela 938
  W. florida 938
    'Java Red' 938
    'Variegata' 938
  W. japonica 938
  W. praecox 938
Western Australian
  Christmas bush 637
Western rose 533
Westringia 938
  W. eremicola 938
  W. fruticosa 938
  W. glabra 938
  W. longifolia 939
  W. rigida 939
Whau 358
White alder 251
White beard heath 538
White paper daisy 59
Whitebeam 837
Whitey wood 51
Wild indigo 112
Wild pea 526
Wild plum 449
Wild pomegranate 159
Willow 800
Wind flower 950
Windmill palm 903
Window plant 394
Winged everlasting 59
Wingnut 750
Winter aconite 362
Winter cress 112
Winter hazel 275
Winter sweet 28, 235
Winter's bark 342
Wire plant 613
Wishbone plant 901
Wistaria 939

Wisteria 939
  W. brachybotrys 940
    'Murasaki Kapitan'
    940
    'Shiro Kapitan' 940
  W. floribunda 940
    'Alba' 940
    'Carnea' 940
    'Honbeni' 940
    'Kuchibeni' 940
    'Macrobotrys' 940
    'Rosea' 940
    'Shiro Noda' 940
    'Violacea Plena' 940
  W. frutescens 940
  W. japonica 940
  W. macrostachya 940
  W. sinensis 940
    'Alba' 940
Witch hazel 448
Wodyetia 940
  W. bifurcata 941
Wodyetia bifurcata 635
Wollemi pine 941
Wollemia 941
  W. nobilis 941
Woodruff 91
Woody pear 945
Wormwood 85
Woundwort 847

X

Xanthorrhoea 944
  X. arborea 944
  X. australis 944
  X. macronema 944
  X. media 944
  X. minor 944
  X. preissii 944
  X. resinosa 945
Xanthostemon 945
  X. chrysanthus 945
Xylomelum 945
  X. angustifolium 946
  X. occidentale 946
  X. pyriforme 946
Xylosma 946
  X. congestum 946

Y

Yam, white 946
  D. alata 947
Yarrow 17
Yellow flax 770
Yellow pea 430
Yellow-wood 723
Yesterday, today and
  tomorrow 152
Yew 879
Yucca 947
  Y. aloifolia 948
  Y. brevifolia 948
  Y. filamentosa 948
  Y. filifera 948
  Y. whipplei 948
Yucca brevifolia 823

Z

Zamia 948
  Z. furfuracea 949
Zamia palm 575
Zantedeschia 170, 949
  Z. aethiopica 949
    'Childsiana' 949
    'Green Goddess'
      949
  Z. albomaculata 949
  Z. elliottiana 949
  Z. rehmannii 949
Zauschneria 949
  Z. californica 950
Zea mays var. *praecox*
  732
Zea mays var. *saccharata*
  864
Zelkova 950
  Z. carpinifolia 950
  Z. serrata 950
  Z. sinica 950
Zephyr flower 950
Zephyranthes 950
  A. atamasco 951
  Z. candida 951
  Z. citrina 951
  Z. grandiflora 951
  Z. rosea 951
Zieria 951
  Z. arborescens 951
  Z. compacta 951
  Z. cytisoides 951
  Z. laevigata 951
  Z. smithii 951
Zig-zag plant 679
Zingiber officinale 422
Zinnia 952
  Z. elegans 952
    'Envy' 952
  Z. haageana 952

'Persian Carpet' 952
Zucchini 952
Zygocactus 819
Zygopetalum 953
  Z. mackaii 953

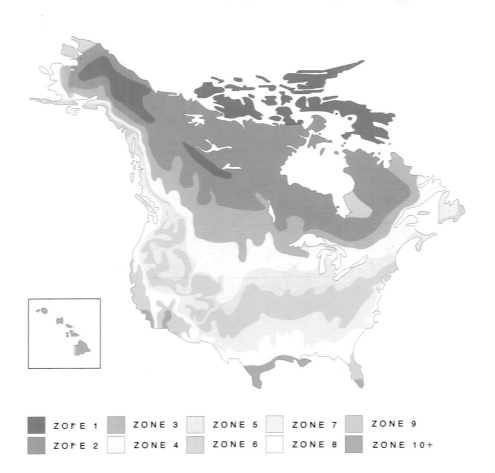

ZONE 1　ZONE 3　ZONE 5　ZONE 7　ZONE 9

ZONE 2　ZONE 4　ZONE 6　ZONE 8　ZONE 10+

Published by Bay Books, an imprint of
Murdoch Books Pty Limited.

Murdoch Books Pty Limited Australia
Pier 8/9
23 Hickson Road
Millers Point NSW 2000
Phone: + 61 (0) 2 8220 2000
Fax: + 61 (0) 2 8220 2558

Murdoch Books UK Limited
Erico House
6th Floor North
93-99 Upper Richmond Road
Putney, London SW15 2TG
Phone: + 44 (0) 20 8785 5995
Fax: + 44 (0) 20 8785 5985

Printed by Sing Cheong Printing Company
Printed in China